IMPORTANT INFORMATION ABOU

Summarizations and Modifications: Most of the statutes and court decisions referenced in this manual have been reduced, modified, and/or summarized for brevity and comprehension of the reader. Most statutes, particularly those enacted decades ago, are difficult to read and comprehend. This manual is designed to assist the reader by reducing and summarizing the content of the various relevant statutes. In the event of a conflict between information in this manual and the actual statute or court decision, obviously the statute or court decision should be followed.

Amendments: This manual is published annually. Court decisions are decided daily, and statutes are promulgated and amended regularly. This manual is intended to give the reader a solid foundation of the various aspects of the law relating to law enforcement. However, law enforcement personnel must keep themselves informed regarding important changes affecting their profession. The local district attorney's office, as well as the Municipal Police Training Committee, and similar entities are important resources toward this endeavor. We also recommend that you sign up for our periodic training bulletins.

Cops Teaching Cops

About the Author

This manual was created by Justin M. Hanrahan, Esq. Justin is a Massachusetts Police Lieutenant with more than twenty years of law enforcement experience. He has been instructing police officers and police supervisors in the areas of police management, critical incident management, and Statutory Law and Criminal Procedure for several years. Justin is also a practicing Massachusetts attorney. Justin lives with his wife and four daughters northwest of Boston.

The Legal Outline: Massachusetts Police Officer's Guide to Criminal Procedure, Statutory Law, Motor Vehicle Law & Juvenile Law.

ISBN 978-0-9861564-2-7

Hanrahan Consulting, LLC – 8 Calista Terrace, Westford, MA.

Dedicated to Daddy's Angels

Danielle, Lindsey, Emma, Avery & Charlotte
Thank you for putting up with all of the long hours

Pre-order the 2017 version now and SAVE!
Order now and pay only $99 and receive the 2017 MV Guide, and 2017 Legal Updates for Free!

Send in the below form and receive our 2017 Law Manual and MV guide for only $99. The law constantly changes, make sure that you use the latest reference to help you perform your duties.

You will receive the 2017 edition of the Law Manual and MV guide in early 2017.

ANNUAL RENEWAL REGISTRATION		
NAME		
ADDRESS		
CITY	STATE	ZIP
PHONE NUMBER		
METHOD OF PAYMENT: MASTER CARD □ VISA □ CHECK □ CASH □ DEPT. BILLING □ OTHER □		
ACCOUNT/PO # ______ EXPIRATION DATE		
E-MAIL ADDRESS		
HOW DID YOU HEAR ABOUT US?		

By completing the above registration you agree to receive Hanrahan Consulting, LLC's 2017 Law Manual at the reduced rate of $100 per year and receive the 2017 MV guide for free.

Fax form to: (978) 467-4257 or email to sales@masspromotions.us or mail to: Hanrahan Consulting, LLC 8 Calista Terrace, Westford, MA 01886.

For more information visit

www.HanrahanConsulting.com

(978) 692-2604

Keep Yourself Informed

FREE LEGAL UPDATES

Receive our regular legal updates all year; as Court Decisions are decided and the statutes are amended. Each decision and statute will be carefully broken down into an easy to understand format.

If you purchased from anywhere other than on-line or directly from Hanrahan Consulting, LLC. Send us an email including your name, agency, date and location of purchase and you will receive our legal updates for 2015 for FREE. This is for individuals only. Contact us for agency legal update rates.

Send an email to

law@hanrahanconsulting.com

to register your manual and receive FREE legal updates – be sure to include the above information.

SECTIONS

Section 1: **CRIMINAL PROCEDURE**...including motor vehicle and juvenile issues.

This section is based primarily on Court Decisions which dictate police actions and authority in a variety of circumstances, especially in the areas of search and seizure, custodial interrogation and arrestee rights.

Section 2: **STATUTORY LAW** (RELEVANT LAW ENFORCEMENT RELATED STATUTES)

This section covers the numerous legislative enacted laws which affect law enforcement. Some relevant court decisions, that interpret the various statutes, are referenced as needed to help you better understand the particular statute. This section provides the elements to hundreds of offenses as well as other important information.

Section 3: **JUVENILE LAW** (RELEVANT JUVENILE RELATED STATUTES)

This section covers the numerous legislative enacted laws which affect juveniles, from the school setting, to the protection of juveniles, to the juvenile delinquent. Some relevant court decisions, that interpret the various statutes, are referenced as needed to help you better understand the particular statute. For information on juvenile procedure (i.e. interrogation of a juvenile) see Section 1: Criminal Procedure..

Section 4: **MOTOR VEHICLE LAW** (RELEVANT MOTOR VEHICLE STATUTES)

This section covers the numerous legislative enacted laws which affect the operation of a motor vehicle. Some relevant court decisions, that interpret the various statutes, are referenced as needed to help you better understand the particular statute. For information on motor vehicle procedure (i.e. car searches, exit orders etc) see Section 1: Criminal Procedure.

CRIMINAL PROCEDURE

Section 1 OVERVIEW

Section 2 SEARCH & SEIZURE

Section 5 MOTOR VEHICLE ISSUES

Section 6 IDENTIFICATION PROCEDURES

SOME THINGS YOU SHOULD KNOW

The term **Criminal Law** generally refers to statutory law (i.e. laws enacted by the State Legislature…for instance Operating under the Influence of Alcohol, M. G. L. 90 § 24).

The term **Criminal Procedure** generally refers to Court decisions which dictate police procedure, such as *Miranda v. Arizona* or *Terry v. Ohio.* In Massachusetts, some law enforcement officials refer to criminal procedure as "con law" in reference to the Constitutional aspects of criminal procedure.

Common Law

Common law is the system of law originating in England, based on custom or court decisions rather than legislative action. It can be thought of as tradition that is legally enforceable. The law of the United States is based on the law the England, as the U.S. was once an English colony, and many of England's laws are still viable in the U.S. Part II, c. 6, art. 6, of the Massachusetts Constitution, carried into effect the common law of England, including common-law crimes, until altered or repealed by the Legislature or declared invalid by the court.[1]

Governing Laws

Massachusetts Police Officers are subject *both* to the U.S. Constitution and The Massachusetts Declaration of Rights, as well as statutory law.

The Massachusetts Declaration of Rights tends to be more restrictive as far as what the government (usually law enforcement) can do, particularly in the area of search and seizure.

Precedent

In regards to Court decisions, the term *precedent* refers to the rule or law that must be followed based on the decision of a high court (i.e. the issue in question has already been addressed and decided by a higher court). The court's ruling has the effect of law until or unless overturned by a higher court, meaning the lower courts must abide by the decision.

District/Superior Courts

Generally speaking District and Superior Court decisions do not have any *precedent*, meaning a decision from the district court does not have to be followed by other district courts. However, if you work in that particular jurisdiction you have little choice but to follow the decisions of that particular judge or court.

Massachusetts Appeals Court

A decision from the Appeals Court is binding on all Superior and District Courts in Massachusetts, unless and until it is overturned by the Massachusetts Supreme Judicial Court. Therefore, if an Appeals Court makes a decision regarding criminal procedure Massachusetts law enforcement officials must follow the decision unless or until it is overruled by a higher court.

[1] see, e.g., Commonwealth v. Chapman, 13 Met. 68 (1847).

Massachusetts Supreme Judicial Court (SJC)

The Supreme Judicial Court is the highest Court in Massachusetts and its decisions are binding on all other Massachusetts' Courts. Only a Federal District Court can overrule the SJC and only if the matter pertains to an issue pertaining to the US Constitution. This rarely occurs.

Federal Courts

There are times when an issue will be brought before a federal court because it involves a federal concern (e.g. the matter is argued on the basis of the Fourth Amendment). Decisions by Federal District Courts, and even Federal Appeals Courts, are not binding on state decisions, although they are persuasive. However a decision by the U.S. Supreme Court is binding on the state courts.

The **U.S. Supreme Court** is the highest Court in the land and usually will only hear a case if it is an issue affecting the rights provided to the people by the U.S. Constitution.

Often times, in Massachusetts, the SJC will decide their cases based on the Massachusetts Declaration of Rights and if the decision restricts actions by the police that would otherwise be permitted under the U.S. Constitution the prosecution cannot appeal the decision to the U.S. Supreme Court/Federal Court because the decision was based on the *state's constitution* and not the U.S. Constitution.

CRIMINAL PROCEDURE

GENERAL OVERVIEW

Criminal procedure relates to when law enforcement officer can search someone, seize someone, question someone, and similar issues. Essentially, criminal procedure refers to the rules that law enforcement must follow in their pursuit of criminal behavior. The foundation of criminal procedure begins with both the U.S. Constitution and the Massachusetts Declaration of Rights (Massachusetts own version of the Constitution). Criminal procedure is further defined by state and federal court decisions relating to police conduct and citizen rights. The Courts are daily deciding cases that further define, and in some cases change, the rules of criminal procedure. Additionally, some Massachusetts state statutes and rules further define what law enforcement in Massachusetts can and cannot do in terms of infringing on the rights of citizens and visitors. The key component to criminal procedure is the Exclusionary Rule. The Exclusionary Rule is the primary remedy utilized in order to deter law enforcement from violating "the rules."

Another important consideration for law enforcement in terms of criminal procedure is civil liability. If the proper procedure is not followed, not only can evidence be excluded but the violation may expose the officer and the agency to civil liability.

THE EXCLUSIONARY RULE

The **Exclusionary Rule is a court imposed deterrent on improper law enforcement tactics**. In many circumstances if the police fail to follow established law and rules of criminal procedure the court imposed remedy will be suppression (exclusion) of the evidence obtained. This is designed to deter *law enforcement officers* from infringing upon individuals' rights and freedoms and other improper law enforcement tactics.

The **Fruits of the Poisonous Tree doctrine** refers to the exclusion of all other evidence obtained as a result, or in connection, with the original improper tactic by the police.

For instance, if a police officer randomly stopped a car without lawful justification and discovered an illegal firearm in plain view, the firearm would be excluded at trial (i.e. the Exclusionary Rule). If a ballistics test revealed that this firearm was related to a series of murders, under the Fruits of the Poisonous Tree doctrine, not only would the firearm be excluded but the subsequent ballistic evidence linking the gun to the murders would also be excluded; and if the police used the ballistics information to obtain a warrant to search the defendant's home and uncovered more evidence all of that evidence would also most likely be excluded, and so on.

Department Policy/Procedures and the effect on the exclusion of evidence

A police officer's failure to follow department policy and/or procedure may result in the exclusion of evidence even though the actions may not have otherwise been unlawful. The foundational purpose of the exclusionary rule is to "deter unlawful police conduct." However, "since an administrative policy or "standards" or guidelines along do not have the force of law such a violation does not automatically require the application of the exclusionary rule and the suppression of evidence."[2]

[2] Commonwealth v. Brian Maingrette, Appeals Court (2014).

CRIMINAL PROCEDURE OVERVIEW

Exceptions to the Exclusionary Rule

There are some circumstances where despite improper tactics by the police the court will still permit the uncovered evidence into court. Despite this the police should never operate under the theory that a violation of Constitutional protections is justified because the evidence is likely to get in under one of the below listed exceptions:

a. **Inevitable Discovery Doctrine:** This typically occurs when the police can show that they would have uncovered the evidence any way by legal means. The inevitable discovery rule focuses first on the question of inevitability (whether the police would have found it any way by lawful means) and second on the character of the police misconduct.[3] Meaning inevitable discovery may still result in the loss of evidence if the police conduct was grossly improper.

   Under the inevitable discovery doctrine, if the Commonwealth can demonstrate by a preponderance standard that discovery of the evidence by lawful means was certain as a practical matter, the evidence may be admissible as long as the officers did not act in bad faith to accelerate the discovery of evidence, and the particular constitutional violation is not so severe as to require suppression."[4]

b. **Attenuation Doctrine***:* If the police action is far removed, particularly in regards to time, from the original wrongdoing the evidence may still be admissible. The discovery of the evidence is found to be too remote from the initial police wrongdoing.

   Hypothetical example of the attenuation doctrine: A police officer illegally enters a home and discovers cocaine. The homeowner is arrested and charged with unlawful possession of the drug. The homeowner is bailed and released. A week later the homeowner contacts the arresting officer and confesses to being the driver of a getaway car of a robbery that occurred months earlier, hoping that the confession will lead to leniency on the pending drug charge. The court is likely to find the subsequent confession too far removed from the illegal entry and discovery of the cocaine to apply the fruits of the poisonous tree and suppress the confession.

c. **Independent Source Doctrine**: Evidence initially obtained during an unlawful search or seizure may later be admissible if the evidence is later obtained through a constitutionally valid search or seizure that was untainted by the previous illegality.[5]

d. **Independent Action Doctrine:** The independent action doctrine relates to action taken by the defendant that is independent and often unrelated to the original law enforcement wrongdoing that may break the chain in the fruits of the poisonous tree. This exception, although rarely applied, often comes into fruition when the defendant assaults the detaining officer. Even though the stop may not have been based on reasonable suspicion or probable cause the fruits of the poisonous tree typically would not bar a prosecution when the suspect subsequently attacks the officers. However, this exception is not limited to assaults on police. This exception is tied to the independent source doctrine but instead of an independent source permitting the admissibility of the evidence; it is the independent action on the part of the defendant that will break the chain in the fruits of the poisonous tree doctrine.

e. **Civil Cases and Collateral matters**: the exclusionary rule will not apply in civil (i.e. non-criminal) cases. For instance, in care and protection of children cases evidence obtained in violation of the rules of criminal procedure will not be barred if the evidence is being used to remove the child from an unsafe environment.[6] Additionally, evidence that may not be admissible during a criminal trial generally is not barred from other proceedings, such as probable cause hearings, Grand Jury proceedings, and parole/probation hearings.

Good faith does not prevent the exclusionary rule when the police make the error

Under federal law, if the police violate the rules of search and seizure but they do it in good faith, meaning that they did not realize that what they were doing was unconstitutional, the court may still allow the evidence to be used at trial. However, in Massachusetts, even when the police make an error in good faith, meaning they honestly but wrongly believed what they were doing was lawful, the exclusionary rule will typically still apply.

[3] Commonwealth v. Perrot, *407 Mass. At 546-547.*
[4] Commonwealth v. Sbordone, 424 Mass. 802, 810 (1997).
[5] *Maryland v. Macon*. 472 U.S. 463 (1985).
[6] *The Care and Protection of Frank*, 409 Mass. 492 (1991).

Case example

In ***Commonwealth v. Censullo***, a police lieutenant was on patrol when he observed the defendant operating on what he believed was a one-way street in the wrong direction. The lieutenant initiated a motor vehicle stop and subsequently arrested the defendant for OUI. The lieutenant was in error, the portion of the road that the defendant was traveling on was not restricted to one-way travel. Despite the lieutenant's good faith belief that the defendant was committing a motor vehicle violation the stop was deemed invalid and the OUI evidence was suppressed under the exclusionary rule.[7]

Errors by Non-Law Enforcement Will Not Trigger the Exclusionary Rule

If the police reasonably rely on information provided by non-law enforcement personnel/entities, such as the court or the registry of motor vehicles, the Exclusionary Rule will generally not be applied.

Case example

Commonwealth v. Wilkerson, the Barnstable police arrested the defendant during a routine motor vehicle stop when the RMV check of the defendant's license status indicated that his license was revoked. During the subsequent inventory of his vehicle a rifle was discovered. It was later learned the RMV information was erroneous and the defendant had a valid license. Despite this error the evidence was not suppressed because it was not a law enforcement agency but an independent state agency.[8]

The Exclusionary Rule typically will not be applied when the police *reasonably* rely on information from an informant that later turns out to be wrong or false. The key is that the police *reasonably* relied on the information. Thus, it was not the mistake of the police but the mistake of the informant.

CIVIL LIABILITY

In addition to the Exclusionary Rule and the Fruits of the Poisonous Tree Doctrine there are other Court remedies that may be imposed for police misconduct and errors, specifically there is a potential for civil liability. Not only may the agency or municipality incur civil liability, in some cases the individual officer may be held personally liable.

Generally, law enforcement officers are protected from being held personally liable in civil cases for errors they make because they are granted what is called *Qualified Immunity*. The reason for qualified immunity is to encourage law enforcement officers to do their jobs without a constant worry of being successfully sued. If a police officer could be held personally liable for every error police officers would refrain from making arrests and conducting searches. Qualified immunity is designed to prevent that. However, qualified immunity is not absolute and police officers can still be held personally liable.

Qualified Immunity

Qualified immunity protects public officials from civil liability which occur during the course of their employment providing the act was in accordance with their course of employment and the officials acted reasonably. Qualified immunity serves two purposes:

1. the need to hold public officials accountable when they exercise power irresponsibly and
2. the need to shield officials from harassment, distraction, and liability when they perform their duties reasonably.

[7] *Commonwealth v. Censullo*, 40 Mass.App.Ct. 64 (1996).
[8] *Commonwealth v. Wilkerson*, 436 Mass. 137 (2002).

The court applies a two-prong analysis in determining questions of qualified immunity. These prongs, which may be resolved in any order, require that the court decide:

a. whether the facts alleged or shown by the plaintiff make out a violation of a constitutional right; and
b. if so, whether the right was 'clearly established' at the time of the defendant's alleged violation,"

The latter analysis of whether a right was "clearly established" further divides into two parts:

(i) 'the clarity of the law at the time of the alleged civil rights violation,' and

(ii) Whether, given the facts of the particular case, 'a reasonable defendant would have understood that his conduct violated the plaintiff's constitutional rights.'"

So, in order to determine if the officers are entitled to qualified immunity the plaintiff must have had a Constitutional Right violated and if such a right was violated the law that the police officers used to violate this right must have been clear to the point where a reasonable police officer in the defendants' shoes understood that their conduct violated a constitutional right.[9] The most common violation of Constitutional rights is an unlawful search and seizure, more specifically an unlawful arrest (e.g. an arrest without probable cause).

Arguable Probable Cause: even when it is determined probable cause to arrest does not exist; a police officer will still be entitled to qualified immunity if the officer can establish there was arguable probable cause to arrest. Arguable probable cause exists if either it was objectively reasonable for the officer to believe probable cause existed or if officers of reasonable competence could disagree on whether the probable cause test was met.[10]

Civil Liability Example(s)

In the 2014 case of ***Huff v. Reichert***, the 7th Circuit (Federal Court) affirmed the District Court's denial of the officer's qualified immunity. In this case, the officer stopped a vehicle for crossing the center line. After detaining the operator and his passenger for 16 minutes he issued the operator a written warning. He then detained the men for an additional **34 minutes** during which time the officer pat frisked both occupants and had a canine conduct an exterior and interior sniff of the car. No contraband was ever found. The officer told the men that they were free to leave but that they had to leave without the car. He also told them that if they chose to walk away they would be arrested for unlawfully walking on the highway. The Court found no justification for the detention and the officer was denied qualified immunity.

The 2011 case of ***Simon GLIK v. John Cunniffe*** is an excellent example of how law enforcement officials can open themselves up to civil liability.

Facts: Simon Glik was walking past the Boston Common on the evening of October 1, 2007, when he caught sight of three police officers -- the individual defendants here -- arresting a young man. Concerned that the officers were employing excessive force to effect the arrest, Glik stopped roughly ten feet away and began recording video footage of the arrest on his cell phone. After placing the suspect in handcuffs, one of the officers turned to Glik and said, "I think you have taken enough pictures." Glik replied, "I am recording this. I saw you punch him." An officer then approached Glik and asked if Glik's cell phone recorded audio. When Glik affirmed that he was recording audio, the officer placed him in handcuffs, arresting him for, unlawful audio recording in violation of Massachusetts's wiretap statute. Glik was taken to the South Boston police station. In the course of booking, the police confiscated Glik's cell phone and a computer flash drive and held them as evidence. Glik was also charged with disturbing the peace, and aiding in the escape of a prisoner.

G.L. c. 272 § 99 makes it a felony to *secretly* audio record another (see Invasion of Privacy section of this manual).The charges against Glik were later dropped for lack of probable cause.

Glik sued the City of Boston and three individual officers, as individuals, in Federal District Court for violations of his First and Fourth Amendments Rights, as well as state-law claims under the Massachusetts Civil Rights Act and for

[9] Glik v. Cunniffe et. Al (2011).
[10] *Zalaski v. City of Hartford*, 2013 U.S. App. LEXIS 14898 (2d Cir. Conn. July 23, 2013).

malicious prosecution. The officers filed a motion to dismiss the claims against them claiming that they were entitled to qualified immunity. The District Court denied the motion and the matter was appealed.

Was Glik's First Amendment Right Violated?

The Court ruled that the law is clear that the First Amendment protects freedom of speech and freedom of the press (including gathering of information from the general public, not just the professional media). The Court decided that the filming of government officials performing their duties in a public place is clearly protected by the First Amendment.

Was the Right to Film Clearly Established?

The Court wrote: "though not unqualified (meaning there are some situations where it may not be permitted), a citizen's right to film government officials, including law enforcement officers, in the discharge of their duties in a public space is a basic, vital, and well-established liberty safeguarded by the First Amendment."

Was Glik's Fourth Amendment Right Violated?

The Fourth Amendment requires that an arrest be made on probable cause. In order to determine if probable cause existed the court looks to Massachusetts General Law, specifically the wiretap statute (c. 272 §99). Chapter 272 § 99 prohibits secret interception. Established case law indicates that openly recording (i.e. pointing a camera at someone) is not secret. The Court found in this case that the officers admitted that they were aware of the recordings (i.e. "I think you've taken enough pictures"). Although the officers argued that they believed that Glik was only taking pictures and not recording audio, the court found this argument unpersuasive, ruling that it is commonly known that today cell phones commonly have the ability to record video (including audio).

The recording was not secret and therefore the officers lacked probable cause.

Conclusion

The officers are entitled to qualified immunity "so long as the presence of probable cause is at least arguable." The presence of probable cause was not even arguable here, according to the Court.

The Court ruled "for the reasons set forth above, we affirm the district court's order denying appellants' (the officers) claim of qualified immunity."

Attorney Hanrahan's Note: This is a civil case and the basis of the case is whether or not the officers can be immune from personal civil liability (leaving the City solely liable). Because they made an arrest without probable, and the court determined that a reasonable officer would have known that probable cause did not exist, the officers were denied qualified immunity (meaning they can be found personally liable for the plaintiff's damages).

This case stresses the importance of proper legal training for police officers. It is quite possible that these officers believed that they were making a valid arrest. *Com. v. Manzelli* which was decided a few months before this incident occurred, wherein the defendant was convicted of the wiretap statute for *secretly* recording an officer (in the Manzelli case the defendant was convicted for secretly recording an MBTA police officer during a political rally). This may have lead to their belief that what Glik was doing was violating the statute. As a result the officers were at risk of being held **personally liable.**

Secretly recording someone, even a police officer in public, is still a violation of c. 272 § 99. In fact, the SJC and the Massachusetts Appellate Court have upheld convictions for this very conduct. The problem is police officers often do not fully understand the law (as a result of inadequate training or as a result of not paying full attention while being trained).

SEARCH & SEIZURE

OVERVIEW

Most criminal procedure issues stem from the Fourth Amendment of the U.S. Constitution which protects citizens from unreasonable searches (invasion of privacy) and seizures (arrests and detentions) by the government, mainly law enforcement. In Massachusetts, law enforcement officers must also comply with Article 14 of the Massachusetts Declaration of Rights which is the Massachusetts equivalent of the Fourth Amendment. In order to understand the Fourth Amendment's requirements it is important to understand the history of the United States. The United States of America (U.S.) was once a colony of Great Britain and as a colony the people of the U.S. were often subject to searches and seizures by the British government with little to no justification. When the U.S. colonists broke away and formed their own government they created the U.S. Constitution. This Constitution was designed to provide the citizens with certain protections from the government. In a law enforcement context the Fourth Amendment is the most important of those protections.

The Fourth Amendment requires that all searches and seizures must be reasonable. For Fourth Amendment searches and seizures to be deemed "reasonable" they generally must be **conducted with both probable cause and a warrant**. However, there are many exceptions to the warrant requirement, with fewer exceptions to the probable cause requirement. To truly understand criminal procedure a police officer must understand these baseline requirements and also understand that all other searches and seizures are exceptions to the warrant requirement.

PROBABLE CAUSE

In most Criminal Procedure circumstances, particularly in the search and seizure context, law enforcement officials need probable cause to act.

WHAT IS PROBABLE CAUSE?

Probable cause exists, where the facts and circumstances within the knowledge of the police are enough to warrant a prudent person in believing that the individual has committed or was committing an offense, or in the event of a search, where the facts and circumstances within the knowledge of the police are enough to warrant a prudent person in believing that evidence or contraband is present.

Attorney Hanrahan's note: in layman's terms probable cause exists when the facts indicate that it is more likely than not that the suspect committed the crime, or as it pertains to a search, facts indicate that it is more likely than not that evidence or criminal contraband will be found in the suspected location.

The Court has stated "in dealing with probable cause…we deal with probabilities. These are not technical; they are the factual and practical considerations of everyday life on which reasonable and prudent persons, not legal technicians, act".[11]

[11] *Commonwealth v. Hason*, 387 Mass. 169/ 174 (1982), quoting from Brinegar v. United States, 338 U.S. 160, 175 (1949).

COMMON SOURCES OF INFORMATION FOR PROBABLE CAUSE

The sources of information which provide an officer with probable cause to arrest may be many and varied. Probable cause can be supported by a combination of personal observations, first-hand knowledge and reliable information from others. The following list contains some common examples, but the establishment of probable cause is not limited to these factors alone.

Note: Generally, a **combination** of these factors must be present in order for probable cause to be present. Rarely will one factor alone be enough. However, the first four listed below often times will be enough to establish probable cause, even without any other factors.

1. Officer's Personal Observations (see detailed explanation below).
2. Information from witnesses, victims & informants (see Information from Witness, Victims and Informants section).
3. Admissions (e.g. "Yes, I was at my girlfriend's house last night") & Confessions (ex. "Yes, I killed my girlfriend at her house last night").
4. Reliable Databases: Government Databases, such as CJIS, NCIC and the RMV, indicating that the suspect is wanted or has a suspended/revoked license/registration can be relied upon to establish probable cause/reasonable suspicion absent any information to the contrary.

Rarely, if ever, will one of the below sources by itself be enough to establish reasonable suspicion or probable cause (see the Temporary Detentions section of this manual for more on reasonable suspicion).

5. Nature of the area (i.e. high crime area)
6. Proximity to a recent crime
7. Running from the sight of the police
8. Matching the description of the suspect
9. Criminal history and associates
10. Evasive/implausible answers
11. Furtive movements
12. Time of day or night
13. Nervousness
14. Unable to produce documents (during a MV stop)
15. And a variety of other, less common, factors.

Note: these topics are covered in more detail in the Temporary Detention section of this manual.

OFFICER'S OWN OBSERVATION OF CRIMINAL ACTIVITY

Since the majority of probable cause establishment issues deal with the officer's own observations a more detailed explanation is needed. Obviously when a police officer observes criminal behavior his/her observations may be used to establish probable cause. An officer may establish probable cause by his/her own senses, an officer's sight being the most common (i.e. an officer who observes someone breaking into a building). However, an officer's sense of touch (ex. feeling a weapon during a pat frisk), sense of smell (ex. detecting the odor of alcohol during an OUI investigation) and even sense of taste in very rare circumstances, can be used.

In addition, the training and experience of the officer may also help elevate the officer's observations to probable cause. For instance, a seasoned drug detective may observe suspicious activity and be able to form the reasonable opinion of criminal activity. A rookie officer observing the same activity may not be able to reasonably form the needed probable cause because of the officer's lack of training and experience.

SPECIAL FOCUS: Probable Cause for Drug Transactions

Observing "Drug Activity"

What actually constitutes criminal behavior is not always clear. The courts will look at the entire "silent movie," particularly with observed drug transactions.[12] What constitutes probable cause is based on a case by case basis; the Court will look at the "big picture" or the totality of the circumstances when determining whether or not probable cause existed when analyzing a case.

While the appearance of a single factor suggesting illicit activity would be insufficient to establish probable cause, the presence of multiple factors "tends to establish that the defendant was currently committing a crime when he was observed." Among the factors the court will consider are:

a. the unusual nature of the transaction
b. the furtive actions of the participants
c. whether the encounter occurs in a place known to the police as a place of high incidence of drug traffic; and
d. whether an experienced officer on the scene, who had made numerous drug arrests in the neighborhood, considered the event as revealing a drug sale accomplished by the defendant. [13]

Must an actual object exchange be observed during a drug transaction? The Court has stated "While 'whether the officer sees an object exchanged is an important piece of evidence that supports probable cause, and its absence weakens the Commonwealth's probable cause showing,' it 'would critically handicap law enforcement to require in every circumstance that an officer not only witness an apparent exchange, but also see what object was exchanged, before making a search incident to an arrest.'" [14] It is not possible to develop a bright line rule of what type of observed activity will amount to probable cause as each incident is unique.

Case Examples

In the 2015 case of ***Commonwealth v. Freeman***, the Appeals Court ruled that the observation of an exchange between two men in the street made by an experienced narcotics investigator may be enough to establish probable cause that an illegal transaction has taken place.

In the 2009 case of ***Commonwealth v. Rodriguez***, the Court ruled that the swallowing an item in response to police presence indicates the illegal nature of the substance.[15]

THE COLLECTIVE KNOWLEDGE DOCTRINE

Normally, the police officer who makes the arrest (or search) must have personal knowledge sufficient to constitute probable cause. That is, his or her own observations, facts of which he or she has first-hand knowledge, and reliable information of which he or she is personally aware, may be combined to form the basis for probable cause. However, the knowledge of one police officer ... is the knowledge of all" this is referred to as the Collective Knowledge Doctrine.[16] Even if the facts known by one officer may not rise to probable cause (or reasonable suspicion) by itself, when this information is taken into consideration with facts known by another officer (working in conjunction with one another) the two sources of information may be combined to formulate probable cause (or reasonable suspicion).

Note: Even knowledge <u>not yet shared</u> between officers, if taken as a whole amounts to probable cause, it will fall within the collective knowledge doctrine.

---

[12] *Commonwealth v. Santaliz,* 413 Mass. at 242
[13] *Commonwealth v. Gant,*51 Mass.App.Ct. 314, 318 (2001) ("[I]t is settled by numerous decisions that a concurrence of [multiple] factors ... readily cumulate to provide probable cause"), quoting from *Commonwealth v. Rivera,* 27 Mass.App.Ct. 41, 43 (1989)
[14] *Commonwealth v. Kennedy,* 426 Mass. at 711. Accord *Commonwealth v. Coronel,*70 Mass.App.Ct. 906, 907 (2007).
[15] *Comm. v. Rodriguez,* 75 Mass. App. Ct. 235 (2009)
[16] *Commonwealth v. Zirpolo,*37 Mass.App.Ct. 307, 311, 639 N.E.2d 1083 (1994), quoting from *Commonwealth v. Lanoue,* 356 Mass. 337, 340, 251 N.E.2d 894 (1969).

Case Example

In ***Com. v. Quinn***, officers responded to a report of a B&E to a gas station at 1:45 A.M. The officers on scene found footprints and fresh tire marks in the snow. The tire marks indicated that the vehicle headed toward route 18. Another officer, who had not received the information about the tire tracks and direction of travel, stopped the only motor vehicle in sight which was traveling on Route 18; evidence from the break in was seen in plain view during the stop. Even though the officer who stopped the vehicle did not have reasonable suspicion based on his own observations, the court ruled that the collective knowledge of all of the officers involved in the joint effort amounted to reasonable suspicion.[i]

DURATION OF PROBABLE CAUSE

Probable cause to search is fleeting; that is it dissipates over time. An officer may have probable cause that a suspect has contraband in his car today, however if he locates the vehicle a week later the probable cause will likely no longer exist because the item was likely removed. But unlike probable cause to search, probable cause to arrest, once formed, will continue to exist for an indefinite future, unless and until intervening facts come to light that negates the probable cause.[17]

- In the 2007 case of ***Commonwealth v. Suggs***, a Lynn police officer stopped the defendant for a motor vehicle violation and discovered that the defendant's license was suspended and the vehicle's insurance was revoked. Instead of arresting the defendant the officer issued him a citation. While waiting for the tow truck to arrive another officer who arrived on scene recognized the defendant's passenger and knew of his reputation for carrying handguns. The officer then changed his mind and decided to arrest the defendant instead of issuing the citation. During the arrest a handgun was discovered. The Appeals Court upheld the arrest reasoning that the probable cause had not dissipated simply because a citation was issued.[18]

SEARCH & SEIZURE OVERVIEW

[17] *Commonwealth v. Walker*, 370 Mass. 548, 560 (1976).
[18] *Commonwealth v. Suggs*, 70 Mass.App.Ct. 1104, 874 N.E.2d 506, (2007).

SEARCH & SEIZURE

SEIZURES

A Constitutional seizure occurs when someone (or something in terms of an object) is detained by a government agent, more specifically a law enforcement official, even if only for a brief period. The most common type of seizure by law enforcement is an arrest, but it is not the only form of Constitutional seizure.

ARRESTS

Generally, police need an arrest warrant in order to affect an arrest. However, there are four exceptions to the arrest warrant requirement in order to affect an arrest (see the Arrest Powers section for more).

TEMPORARY DETENTIONS

One of the most important exceptions to the warrant requirement, in regards to seizures, is the Temporary Detention exception. Not only is it an exception to the warrant requirement it is also an exception to the probable cause requirement. It is a unique and powerful tool for law enforcement when investigating criminal activity.

Authority to Conduct a Threshold Inquiry

In the 1968 case of *Terry v. Ohio*, the US Supreme Court ruled that police officers could detain someone on less than probable cause without violating the Fourth Amendment protection against unreasonable search and seizure. The Court ruled that the police may conduct brief detentions providing that the police have at least **reasonable suspicion**.

Terry v. Ohio

In ***Terry v. Ohio*** a police officer observed three suspects apparently casing a store for an anticipated robbery. Even though the level of suspicion had not risen to the level of probable cause the police officer approached the suspect to inquire and during the inquiry uncovered a weapon during a pat frisk. The U.S. Supreme court upheld the detention and pat frisk of the suspects carving out an exception to the requirement that police must have probable cause in order to conduct a Constitutional seizure.

Additional Authority in Massachusetts

Additionally, Massachusetts has a general law, M.G.L. c. 41 § 98, which permits police to detain and investigate suspicions persons.

Terminology

The term *Terry Stop* originates from the case of *Terry v. Ohio*. However, police officers, and the courts, often use other terms such as *temporary detentions, investigative detentions* and *threshold inquiries* to also describe a temporary detention of a person by a police officer. There are many different terms but they all mean the same thing, a police officer temporarily stops a person suspected of criminal activity.

Purpose

The purpose of an investigative detention is for the officer to either confirm his/her suspicion and take appropriate legal action or dispel his/her suspicion and let the person continue about their business. If the officer confirms his/her suspicion the person can be arrested (if an arrestable offense exists), summoned to court for the criminal behavior, or some other alternative. If the officer determines that the person is not involved in criminal activity the person must be released.

Attorney Hanrahan's note: often a police officer may still be suspicious that the person is involved in criminal activity but he/she has exhausted all leads and lacks probable cause to execute an arrest. In these situations, it is recommended that the officer document the incident (often in the form of a Field Interrogation Observation Report) in the event further evidence is discovered at a later time the suspect can be linked to the crime.

Reasonable Person Standard

A seizure occurs when a reasonable person would not feel free to leave the presence of the officer. Obviously if the police officer physically detains a person the person would not feel free to walk away. But physical restraint is not required for a seizure to take place. The officer's words, actions, tone of voice and similar factors are often important factors; this is often based on the officer's show of authority. For more on the Show of Authority see the Encounter section later in this section.

The courts have even declared that interfering with someone's ability to enter or leave their own home could create a seizure of the person.

- In ***Commonwealth v. Ramos***, photographs taken by the State Police of a defendant were suppressed where the Troopers congregated outside her apartment and notified her that they would not leave until she came out of the apartment and that, if she continued to refuse, they would have the fire department break down the door.[19] The SJC ruled that a person is seized, for the purposes of the Massachusetts Declaration of Rights, when the police, without reasonable suspicion or probable cause, deprive an individual of the ability either to remain in or leave a residence without police interference.[20]

Justification to Conduct a Threshold Inquiry is Reasonable Suspicion of Criminal Activity

''A police officer may stop an individual and conduct a threshold inquiry if the officer reasonably suspects that the individual has committed, is committing, or is about to commit a crime. To qualify as 'reasonable,' the officer's suspicion 'must be based on **specific, articulable facts and reasonable inferences** drawn therefrom.' Specific and articulable facts means that the officer can point to specific describable pieces of information that would indicate that the person detained is involved in criminal activity. A "gut feeling" or other generic statements will not hold up in court.

The standard is objective: would the facts available to the officer at the moment of the seizure or the search warrant a person of reasonable caution in the belief that the action taken was appropriate?

FACTORS THAT OFTEN CONTRIBUTE TO REASONABLE SUSPICION (AND PROBABLE CAUSE) OF CRIMINAL WRONGDOING

Reasonable suspicion is like probable cause but to a lesser degree. The same factors which contribute to probable cause (see Criminal Procedure section of this manual) can also establish reasonable suspicion and vice versa. Below is a list of some of the more common factors that relate to investigative detentions.

Note: Generally, a combination of these factors must be present in order for reasonable suspicion to be present. Rarely, if ever, will one factor alone be enough. Additionally, the SJC has stated that even factors that are each seemingly innocent of themselves may, when taken together, amount to a reasonable belief of criminal activity.[21]

a) ***Unprovoked Flight***: this is a factor, but flight alone is not enough to amount reasonable suspicion of criminal activity. The Court has stated that there could be many non-criminal reasons why someone would flee upon seeing the police. So **flight by itself would not be enough**. However, flight coupled with other factors may justify a detention. The SJC has stated "flight is perhaps the classic evidence of consciousness of guilt".[22]

   In ***Commonwealth v. Sanchez,*** the police conducted an encounter based on the suspect's appearance and behavior upon exiting a plane. After consenting to a search the suspect fled. The SJC ruled that once the suspect fled, after consenting to a search, reasonable suspicion of criminal activity was present.

   Note: for more on *unprovoked flight* see the **Encounter section** later in this section.

b) ***Furtive Conduct***: (i.e. attempting to hide something) along with other factors can give rise to reasonable suspicion. However, furtive conduct alone typically will not justify a detention.

   In ***Commonwealth v. Wooden,*** the suspect's stuffing an object into his jacket, with nothing more, did not amount to reasonable suspicion.

---

[19] Commonwealth v. Ramos, 430 Mass. 545, 721 N.E. 2d 923 (2000).

[21] *Commonwealth v. Fraser*, 410 Mass. 541, 545 (1991).
[22] See *Commonwealth v. Carrion*, 407 Mass. 263, 277 (1990); referenced in the 2014 case of *Com. v. Thomas Woods* SJC

In ***Commonwealth v. Bacon,*** when the suspect tried to conceal his face upon the approach of the police, with nothing more. The Court ruled that it did not amount to reasonable suspicion.

c) ***Criminal History:*** this alone is never enough, but may be considered with other factors. A suspect's criminal record can be used as a factor in establishing reasonable suspicion/probable cause, particularly if the crime that the officer is investigating is consistent with the suspect's criminal history, despite the fact that the suspect's criminal record generally cannot be introduced during a criminal trial.[23]

d) ***Nervousness:*** the fact that the suspect is nervous can be a factor to consider but alone is not enough. However, when nervousness is coupled with other indicators it is a factor that the officer can take into consideration.

e) ***Evasive answers:*** (e.g. lies) can be a contributing factor, but generally evasive answers alone are not enough. The SJC held that intentionally false and misleading statements by a defendant could be found to indicate consciousness of guilt.[24]

f) ***Nature of the Area:*** a high crime rate in the particular area is a consideration, but this alone does not amount to reasonable suspicion or probable cause of criminal activity. The police cannot detain people merely because they are present or residing in a high crime area. But the nature of the area is a factor that can be considered. For instance, a rash of burglaries in the area would be a factor to consider when investigating a person lurking around a building late at night.

g) ***Wanted posters and BOLOS:*** these may be utilized to establish reasonable suspicion however the agency that issued the BOLO must have had reasonable suspicion to justify the BOLO, otherwise the stop will be deemed unlawful.

h) ***Training and Experience***: the training, knowledge and experience or expertise of the police officer may be considered in establishing reasonable suspicion/probable cause. For instance, a seasoned drug investigator is more likely to be able to justify a detention based an observed hand-to-hand drug transaction more so than the same transaction observed by a rookie police officer with little to no experience investigating street level drug transactions.

i) ***Descriptions***: Provided the source of the suspect description is legally valid (see the two-pronged test) a person who matches the description of a suspect may be a basis for establishing reasonable suspicion and/or probable cause. Obviously, the more detailed the description the more likely the court will find reasonable suspicion/probable cause. If the description is vague and could match numerous people in the area reasonable suspicion to stop a particular individual will most likely be lacking.

Case example

In ***Commonwealth v Cheek,*** the victim was stabbed in the Roxbury section of Boston. The victim was conscious and alert when the police and EMT's arrived. He described the suspect as a black male with a ¾ length goose down jacket. A BOLO was broadcasted and the defendant was stopped by police a short distance away. A firearm was located on the defendant during a pat frisk. The SJC ruled that race coupled with a particular type of jacket was not enough to justify the seizure. The SJC reasoned that this description would have matched the description of numerous people in the area, a predominately black part of the city, and that wearing a goose down jacket (a common garment at the time, on a cold fall night was not unique.

Attorney Hanrahan's note: If all you have to go on is a vague description it does not mean that you need to ignore someone who matches the vague description provided. In the *Cheek* case above, had the police *encountered* the suspect there would not have been a seizure. See the **Encounter** section later in this manual.

j) ***Proximity to the crime scene*:** the suspect's proximity to the crime scene, coupled with other factors, is a factor that can establish of reasonable suspicion of criminal activity. For instance, a person who is in close proximity to the crime scene and matches the general description of a suspect who just fled the scene on foot is more likely to be the suspect than someone located a great distance from the scene who also matches the general description.

k) ***Race*:** it is unconstitutional for police officers to stop someone based solely on race or ethnicity *alone*. However, the race of a particular suspect can be used as a factor in narrowing the range of possible suspects who are in the particular vicinity of a crime.

[23] Commonwealth v. Wright, Appeals Court (2014).
[24] *Commonwealth v. Porter*, 384 Mass. 647, 653 (1981) quotedin the 2014 case of Com. v. Woods (SJC)

Note: in ***Commonwealth v. Lora***, the SJC concluded that by expanding the scope of the exclusionary rule it could deter racial profiling, meaning if the Court finds evidence of racial profiling the evidence uncovered will most likely be suppressed.

l) ***Unusual Conditions/lack or people in the area***: Although vague descriptions, alone, typically will not amount to reasonable suspicion or probable cause, the lack of people in a particular area, such as in the case of extreme weather conditions, may be factor in justifying a detention. For instance, in the 2013 case of ***Commonwealth v. McKoy***, the Appeals Court upheld the detention of two men walking down the street when they attempted to conceal their faces, in a high crime area, after the police received a radio call of shots fired in the area. At the time, it was late at night during an extreme snow storm and the streets were otherwise void of pedestrians. The fact that the two suspects were the only people out in such conditions was a factor that justified the detention, despite the fact that the police had not received a description of any suspects.

m) ***Tips and Witness Reports***: an eyewitness report of criminal activity from an identified person concerning a particular suspect is generally enough to establish reasonable suspicion of criminal activity providing the tipster meets the two-prong test. **See Victims, Witnesses and Informants section of this manual for more on the two-prong test.**

n) ***Drug Courier Profile:*** the SJC has affirmed the use of drug Courier profiling. Factors that should be considered are:

- The length of stay
- the use of hard sided luggage
- certain targeted states which are close to Mexico
- the use of public or cell phones in lieu of the hotel phone
- erratic behavior
- and other factors

The Drug Carrier profile is typically limited to Airports, Train stations and similar travel entities.

o) ***Reports of a Firearm*:** the report of a firearm alone is not indicative of criminal behavior because people can lawfully carry a firearm (e.g. they are properly licensed). The carrying of a firearm by a properly licensed person is not a criminal offense. In order for the police to stop someone based on the report of the person carrying a firearm the police must have **reasonable suspicion of criminal behavior** or **reasonable belief** that the person is armed and dangerous. However, a report of a gun always warrants an investigation; it is a matter of how you conduct the investigation.[25]

Attorney Hanrahan's Note: an officer can always "encounter" someone believed to be armed and engage in conversation regarding the possession of a firearm. M.G. L. chapter 140 § 129C, requires the holder of a License to Carry (LTC) to present his license upon the "demand" of a police officer. Failing to present a license is a legal presumption that the person is unlicensed. The burden is on the licensee to prove that they are properly licensed. Even though the statute uses the language "demand" if the officer lacks reasonable suspicion the presentation of a license should be requested. A demand will most certainly be deemed a show of authority creating a seizure. In any event, officer safety should always be the priority.

Although a report of someone with a firearm is not in and of itself indicative of criminal behavior there are other factors that may be indicative of being unlawfully armed or otherwise armed and dangerous.

Indications of being unlawfully armed:

There are many ways that a report of a firearm could raise suspicion of criminal activity. The behavior and/or demeanor of the person reported to be in possession of a firearm is often a factor. The Court has indicated that there are various "collective factors" which can be used in the aggregate to develop reasonable suspicion that a person is unlawfully armed. In some situations it is unlawful to possess certain weapons altogether. Below are some examples:

TEMPORARY DETENTIONS

[25] See Commonwealth v. Johnson, 36 Mass.App.Ct. 336 (1994).

- **Straight Arm Method**: the SJC has ruled that walking with a stiff arm pressed against the side is an indication, when coupled with other factors (i.e. high crime area, nervous, etc), that the person is unlawfully armed (see *Com v. DePeiza*).
- **Youthfulness**: you must be 21 years of age in order to lawfully possess an LTC in Massachusetts. A person under 21 who possess a firearm is doing so unlawfully.[26]
- **Shots fired**: fleeing from an area immediately after shots have been fired, coupled with a witness indicating that the suspect was carrying a firearm, is an indication that person is unlawfully armed or at least involved in criminal behavior.
- **Inherently Dangerous Weapon**: Although carrying a firearm alone is not indicative of criminal behavior, there are some weapons that are inherently dangerous and thus it is a crime just to possess them even with an LTC, such as a sawed-off shotgun. Other weapons, such as machine guns, assault weapons, disguised firearms, stun guns, large capacity weapons, silencers and prohibited weapons, such as brass knuckles, would likely fall into this category because they are unlawful to possess by nearly all classes of citizens, even by those licensed, with few exceptions (i.e. a police officer may carry some of these items).
- **Intoxication**: it is a criminal offense to carry a firearm while intoxicated, even if properly licensed.[27]
- **Brandishing a weapon in public**: Carrying a weapon, in and of itself, is not indicative of criminal behavior but brandishing a weapon in public, without an obvious justification, would most likely create reasonable suspicion of criminal behavior.[28]
- **Publicly loading a weapon**: In *Commonwealth v. Haskell* (2003), the Appeals Court stated that "the act of public loading a handgun is an event that creates reasonable suspicion that a crime may be about to take place."

THE SCOPE OF THE TEMPORARY DETENTION

Typically the scope of the temporary detention must be limited to determining whether or not the person detained is involved in criminal activity. If the officer's suspicion is dispelled the officer must end the detention. Generally, a verbal inquiry is enough to make this determination. However the courts have permitted more intrusive methods in some circumstances:

***Show Ups/Bring Backs*:** A suspect, when located, may be detained where he or she was found so that an eyewitness can be taken to the location to make an in-person identification. Likewise, police may take the suspect back to the crime scene to see if a witness can identify him or her. However, it is often best to bring the witness to the suspect whenever possible because it is less intrusive and the Court will be less likely to deem the level of detention to have risen to an arrest requiring probable cause. **See Identification section for more on show-ups and bring backs.**

***Identification Methods*:** The United States Supreme Court has upheld the taking of photographs and fingerprints during a Terry stop, and some federal courts have indicated that the police may take voice exemplars and writing samples and even foot sole impressions during a Terry stop. The methods are wide and varied as long as they are reasonable under the circumstances. However, the tactics are not without limits. In one case the Court ruled that requesting that the suspect remove his shoes was tantamount to arrest and beyond the scope of a temporary detention, at least for the facts of this particular case. See the Identification section of this manual for more.

Detaining Property: Although the vast majority of temporary detentions involve the detention of a person it is possible to temporarily detain property on reasonable suspicion. For instance, a police officer may lawfully detain a motor vehicle on reasonable suspicion so that the vehicle could be identified by an eye witness, provided it was reasonable under the circumstances.[29]

[26] Chapter 140 § 129C
[27] See c. 269 § 10H and *Commonwealth v. McCauley*, 11Mass.App.Ct. 780 (1981).
[28] See Commonwealth v. Fitzgibbons, 23 Mass.App.Ct. 301 (1986).
[29] U.S. v. Place, 462 U.S. 696 (1983).

The Length of the Detention

The SJC has never definitively set a time limit on the length of the detention. However, the length of the detention must be consistent with the need for furthering the investigation.[30] In deciding the permissible duration of a Temporary Detention, the court will look to the following issues:

a. The diligence with which the police pursue the investigation.

b. Whether the police investigation confirms or dispels the suspicion.

c. To what extent the suspect's actions contribute to the length of detention.

Case examples regarding the length of detention

- ***Commonwealth v. Sanderson***, the court ruled that detaining a suspect for 40 minutes while awaiting the arrival of a drug sniffing dog was unreasonable under the specific circumstances of this case.

- ***Commonwealth v. Carrington***, the court ruled that the police exceeded the bounds of a threshold inquiry when they transported the suspect to the police station to conduct an identification one hour after the arrival to the station.

The above cases only serve as brief examples and are limited to the facts of the particular cases. Similar conduct, under different circumstances, may not necessarily be deemed unlawful. Each case is based on the facts and circumstances of the particular situation.

PROPORTIONALITY

If the police response is disproportionate to the purpose of the stop the Court may find that the suspect was "under arrest" and absent *probable cause* the stop will be deemed invalid, even if the officers had reasonable suspicion. A way to understand this confusing concept is to think of it as a Court imposed penalty for excessive force. Below is a list of common factors that the Court considers when deciding whether or not the stop was proportionate to the circumstances of the incident:

1. The degree to which a suspect's movement is restrained,
2. The degree of force used by the police,
3. The length of the encounter,
4. The number of officers compared to the number of suspects
5. The nature of the inquiry,
6. The possibility of flight, and,
7. Most important, the danger to the safety of the officer(s) or public or both.

Important factors regarding Proportionality

- Handcuffing the suspect does *not automatically* transform a Terry stop into an arrest as long as it is justified based on the circumstances, but suspects stopped based on reasonable suspicion cannot be handcuffed as a matter of course.[31] There must be justification under the circumstances.
- Demanding that a suspect lie on the ground does *not automatically* transform a Terry stop into an arrest, providing it is justified under the circumstances.
- Placing the suspect in the rear of a cruiser does *not automatically* transform a Terry stop into arrest.

PAT FRISK (sometimes referred to as a *protective frisk*)

A pat frisk is a brief cursory search of the suspect's outer clothing to ensure that the suspect does not possess a **weapon** which could be used to assault the officer. The police can only do what is minimally necessary to determine whether or not a weapon is present. Police officers cannot lawfully pat frisk everyone that they detain. They must have a reasonable fear for their safety. The pat frisk is limited to the outer clothing. However, if an

TEMPORARY DETENTIONS

30 *U.S. v. Sharpe* 407 U.S. 675 (1985)
31 Commonwealth v. Pandolfino, 33 Mass. App. Ct. 96 (1992)

officer is conducting a lawful pat frisk and **inadvertently uncovers evidence of criminal activity in the process the evidence will be admissible against the suspect**.

Fear for Safety

The fear for safety that is required in order to justify a pat frisk generally stems from one or two sources: the underlying offense and/or the behavior of the suspect.

Suspect's Behavior

Frequently the suspect's actions alone during a threshold inquiry will give rise to the officer's concern for his or her safety. Behaviors such as a refusal to comply with requests to remove hands from pockets or to otherwise show hands, and other furtive movements are common factors that raise officer concern. However, the circumstances and actions that may cause a reasonable fear for safety are broad and varied.

Case example

In the 2013 case of ***Commonwealth v. Jones***, the officer conducting the threshold inquiry asked the suspect if he had anything on him that "might harm, poke or prick" the officer and the suspect replied "yes" or "yeah." The Appeals Court stated that "once Jones admitted that he was carrying an object potentially harmful to the inquiring officer, Jones created an objective basis for the pat frisk."

Nature of the offense

Often times the nature of the underlying offense may alone justify a pat frisk (e.g. the detainee was suspected of being involved in a recent armed robbery; this alone would justify a pat frisk even without any additional concerning behavior on the part of the suspect).

However, what the officer believes to be a crime involving a fear for safety and what the Court will deem a crime indicative of being armed and dangerous are not always in agreement. Recently the SJC decided that street level drug dealing, by itself, does not automatically justify a pat frisk (as it once did). The police will now need some other indication that the person is armed and dangerous (or unlawfully armed) in order to justify a pat frisk for weapons.

In the 2009 case of ***Commonwealth v. Gomes***, the SJC ruled that street level drug dealing does not, by itself, justify a pat frisk for weapons. An important factor in this case was that the officers were familiar with the defendant and never knew him to carry weapons.

Other factors

Although the *suspect's behavior* and the *nature of the offense* are generally the main factors in creating a concern for safety, these are not the only factors. The causes are essentially limitless as each circumstance is unique.

In the 2014 case of ***Commonwealth v. Whitehead***, when an officer suspected that a student of Cape Cod Community College may have possessed a weapon the Court ruled that the officer was justified in pat frisking the student. The SJC stated "in the wake of school shootings such as occurred in Columbine, Colorado; Santee, California; and Newtown, Connecticut, we take judicial notice of the actual and potential violence in…schools."

Pat Frisk during an Encounter

The SJC has stated that police officers may not escalate a consensual encounter into a protective frisk absent a reasonable suspicion that an individual has committed, is committing, or is about to commit a criminal offense *and* is armed and dangerous. [32]

The Pat Frisk Method

The officer should use his/her hands to *feel* for a weapon. In ***Commonwealth v. Flemming*** the court ruled that the preferred method of pat frisk is to pat frisk the outer-clothing, not to lift or remove clothing, absent other circumstances justifying it. If a pat frisk reveals a suspicious item a further inquiry may be conducted.[33]

[32] *Commonwealth v. Narcisse*, SJC May 27, 2010
33Com .v. Flemming, 76 Mass.App.Ct. 632 (2010)

Pat Frisk Must be Reasonably Designed to Uncover Weapons

Police must not exceed the scope of a valid pat frisk and it must be "reasonably designed" to uncover threatening weapons. In ***Commonwealth v. Cruz-Rivera*** (2009), the officers inspected the interior of a motor vehicle during a routine traffic stop after the operator was seen making furtive movements. The officers did not locate any weapons but they did locate a small pill bottle. The officers opened the pill bottle and discovered illegal drugs. The officers testified that a small weapon could have fit in the pill bottle. The Court found it unreasonable that an operator who was about to be released would attack two armed police officers with a miniature weapon.

Pat Frisking Companions

It is unlawful to automatically pat frisk companions of criminal suspects absent a reasonable fear that the companion may be armed and dangerous.

Pat Frisking Containers/Bags

Generally, the police may pat frisk containers carried by a suspect as long as the police were justified in conducting the pat frisk and the container could reasonably contain a weapon. If the nature of the container does not avail itself to a pat frisk the officer may be justified in opening it to inspect the contents for weapons.

Nature of the Container is Vital

Since containers come in an infinite variety of sizes, shapes, and materials, courts decline to impose a rule that would automatically require a preliminary pat frisk of any and all containers prior to searching them for weapons during a Terry stop. There are times when a pat frisk of a container will provide no useful information as to its contents, and will therefore do nothing either to confirm or to dispel an officer 's suspicion that there is a weapon inside.

An obvious example would be a container with a hard exterior — it would be pointless to pat frisk a cardboard box, or a hard-sided suitcase.

> In ***United States v. McClinnhan***[34], an officer was permitted to open a briefcase without a preliminary frisk since the pat frisk would have been futile.

At the opposite extreme is a pat frisk of a small container made of soft material, as a pat frisk of such a container would unquestionably suffice to uncover the presence of any weapon or hard object or to confirm that no potential weapon is inside.

> In ***People v. Corpany***,[35] a pat-down of ''fanny pack'' indicated that it did not contain any weapon, the further search of the fanny pack was not justified as protective search.

Pat frisk Prior to Inspecting Contents

Where a pat frisk would likely reveal whether or not a weapon is present, the courts have required a preliminary pat frisk of the container in question before opening it to inspect further. This rule was recently reiterated in the 2014 Appeals Court case of Commonwealth *v. Rutledge.*

> In ***State v. Coons***,[36] where an officer emptied and searched an eight-inch by nine-inch drawstring bag without first frisking it, the search was deemed unreasonable because it was not confined ''to what was minimally necessary to discover the presence of a weapon ''.

Some Soft Containers will Still Need to be Inspected

The mere fact that a particular container is made of soft or pliable material does not necessarily mean that a pat frisk will provide useful or reliable information as to the presence or absence of weapons inside.

[34] *United States v. McClinnhan,* 660 F.2d 500, 504 (D.C. Cir. 1981).
[35] See *People v. Corpany*, 859 P.2d 865, 871 (Colo.1993).
[36] *State v. Coons*, 137 N.H. 365,367 – 368, 627 A.2d 1064 (1993).

A pat frisk of a full duffel bag can discern a weapon if that weapon is located near the bag's outer surface, but even the most thorough palpation of such a bag could not detect a weapon or hard object packed deeper in the middle. If a pat frisk reveals a hard object near the surface, the bag will have to be opened to retrieve it, or, if the pat frisk uncovers no hard object, the bag will still have to be opened to determine whether a weapon is hidden deeper inside. In other words, while a pat frisk may provide added justification for opening the bag, it will not suffice to avoid opening such a bag.

Case examples

In ***Worthey v. State***,[39] the pat frisk of a purse was inconclusive and therefore the officer acted reasonably in opening the purse to check for weapons inside.

The container in question in the 2003 case of ***Com. v. Pagan***, although constructed of pliable material, was full of heavy, hard objects. Simply from looking at it and lifting it (which the officers had done), it was evident that a pat frisk could not possibly suffice to dispel the suspicion that burglarious implements (which could be used as weapons) or other potential weapons were inside.[40]

The Plain Feel Doctrine

If during a pat frisk for weapons the officer, based on his training and experience, detects evidence of a crime or contraband and it is **immediately apparent** as to the nature of the item, the item may be seized under the plain feel doctrine, even though the item is not a weapon. In practice, this is rarely accepted by the court.

Note: if an officer simultaneously discovers contraband while frisking for a weapon the contraband will be admissible. For instance in ***Commonwealth v. Johnson*** at the completion of a high-speed chase the officer witnessed the suspect immediately stick something down the front of his pants the officer immediately reached in and removed the item discovering a bag of cocaine. The court upheld the discovery as the officer had to take swift measures to discover the true facts in nature of the item hidden.

ENCOUNTERS

Not every interaction between a law enforcement official and a member of the public constitutes an intrusion of constitutional dimensions. A police officer does not seize an individual on the street merely by approaching him and speaking, or even questioning, him. Only when the officer, by means of physical force or show of authority, has in some way restrained the liberty of a citizen will the court conclude that a 'seizure' has occurred.

Case example

In the 2012 case of ***Commonwealth v. Damelio***, the Appeals Court ruled that when a plainclothes officer approaches a person and displays his badge and identifies himself it does not automatically amount to a Constitutional seizure absent some type of restraint on the person's liberty by physical means or by a show of authority.

Police have seized a person in the constitutional sense "only if, in view of all the circumstances surrounding the incident, a reasonable person would have believed that he was not free to leave." Citizens have no legal duty to cooperate with police inquiries; if approached by police officers, a person need not answer any questions posed to him and, in fact, may decline to listen to the questions at all and go on his way.[41]

The "Show of Authority Test"

A key determination on whether or not an encounter rises to the level of a detention is whether or not the police officer imposes or shows his/her authority. A show of authority occurs when the officer, either through his actions or words,

[39] See, e.g., *Worthey v. State*, 805 S.W.2d 435, 438 (Tex.Crim.App.1991).
[40] *Com. v. Pagan*, 440 Mass. 62, 793 N.E.2d 1236 (2003).
[41] Florida v. Royer, 460 U.S. 491, 497-501 (1983).

indicates to the person, that he is not able to walk away or otherwise must give in to the command of the officer. This is referred to as the **Show of Authority Test.**

Whether the person is free to leave is based on a reasonable person standard, and not on the subjective state of mind of the officers.[42] The subjective intention of the officer to detain the suspect, had he attempted to leave, is irrelevant except insofar as it may have been conveyed to the defendant. [43]

Fleeing Suspect

The SJC has ruled that just because a person flees (on foot) from the sight of the police does not mean that the person has committed a crime. Therefore simply fleeing alone does not rise to the level of reasonable suspicion of criminal activity. Thus, seizing someone for merely running away from the police, with nothing more, would be unconstitutional.

Pursuit of Suspect

If the police pursue a suspect and "display their authority," such as order the suspect to stop; the chase will be deemed a seizure requiring at least reasonable suspicion, even if the suspect is never captured. However, following a suspect, without a show of authority, will most likely not be deemed a seizure requiring reasonable suspicion or probable cause.

This is important because if the police "show their authority" and command someone to stop, or pursue them in a manner where the person pursued would be aware that they were being commanded to stop, and the police lacked reasonable suspicion, the stop would be deemed unlawful and any evidence uncovered during or after the chase would be suppressed as a result of an unlawful seizure (exclusionary rule). It is not uncommon for criminal suspects to discard evidence during their flight. If the court finds that the officer conducted a seizure (by way of a chase while showing authority) the otherwise admissible discarded evidence will most likely be suppressed.

Significant cases

In ***Commonwealth v. Stout*** (1996), the SJC ruled that for purposes of art. 14 of the Declaration of Rights of the Massachusetts Constitution, a person is "seized" when a police officer initiates a pursuit **with the obvious intent of requiring the person to submit to questioning,** that is, when a person's personal liberty has been significantly restrained by the police. **Attorney Hanrahan's note:** under federal law (i.e. the Fourth Amendment) a person is not seized until he is either captured or he submits [see *California v. Hodari D.* 499 US 621 (1991)].

The defendant in the 2004 case of ***Commonwealth v. Perry*** was *not seized* in the constitutional sense when a police officer began running after him after he started to run. The officer made no show of authority or attempt to stop or restrain the defendant's movement. The officer did not speak to the defendant, and the record did not indicate that the defendant was even aware that the officer was running behind him.[44] **Attorney Hanrahan's note:** thus, merely surveilling someone's movements, even at a fast pace, is not a seizure absent some indication to the person surveilled that they must stop.

In the 2007 case of ***Commonwealth v. Sykes***, the court deemed a seizure had not taken place where a plain clothes officer in an unmarked cruiser followed the defendant on his bicycle and asked the defendant if he could talk with him. However, a seizure did take place when the defendant got off of his bike and began running with the officer chasing behind him. But the court decided that the chase was justified by way of reasonable suspicion based the defendant's flight, abandonment of the bicycle and the high crime area location.[45]

TEMPORARY DETENTIONS

[42] Whren v. United States, 517 U.S. 806, 812-813 (1996); Commonwealth v. Smigliano, 427 Mass. 490, 493 (1998).
[43] Commonwealth v. Barros, 435 Mass. 171, 173-174 (2001),
[44] *Commonwealth v. Perry*, 62 Mass. Appt.Ct.500, 818 N.E.2d186 (2004).
[45] *Com. v. Sykes*, 449 Mass. 308 (2007)

Taking possession of identification or other property

Taking a person's identification and holding onto the identification during an encounter will transform the encounter into a seizure requiring at least reasonable suspicion.

Significant case

In the 2009 SJC case of ***Commonwealth v. Lyles***, Boston Housing Authority police Officers O'Connor and Saunders, who were on patrol and wearing plain clothes, observed the defendant in the area around a community housing development, with respect to which the police had received complaints about drug activity. The defendant was alone, and he was not known to either officer. Based only on their observation of the defendant as he walked along a public sidewalk, the officers got out of their vehicle, approached the defendant, displayed their badges, identified themselves, inquired as to the defendant's name, and asked him for identification. The defendant provided some form of identification to the officers. While they were still standing on the sidewalk, Officer O'Connor proceeded to radio for a check of outstanding warrants, and, when he discovered that there was one; he placed the defendant under arrest. During the subsequent booking procedure, the officers found nineteen plastic bags of heroin and $263 in cash on the defendant's person. **The SJC deemed that a reasonable person would not feel that they were free to walk away while the police held his/her identification.**[46]

Returning ID: In the 2010 case of ***Com. v. Mathis,*** the SJC ruled that "where the retention of documents serves as an inferred command to remain on the scene during a warrant check, their return may be viewed as a positive act that removes the command." Simply put, any implied command dependent on the retention of documents is no longer in effect once the documents are returned.

Volunteering ID: In 2010, the SJC ruled that a seizure did not occur when the defendant voluntarily handed the officer his driver's license during an encounter. The officer held it briefly and returned it.[47]

Attorney Hanrahan's Note: I recommend that you do not take the ID in-hand unless it is absolutely necessary to avoid a challenge later on. It may be a better practice to have the person encountered hold the ID and display it to you while it remains in their possession. Remember, if you have reasonable suspicion taking the ID is not an issue because you have justification to temporarily seize the suspect.

Activating Blue Lights: Activating Blue Overhead cruiser lights signals to the person that they are not free to leave and will transform an encounter into a seizure, unless the interaction takes place in a break down lane and the lights are used to warn on-coming traffic, this would be permissible under the Community Caretaking Doctrine.[48]

White Take-Down Lights: The use of the white takedown lights will not, without more, create a seizure.[49]

Loudspeaker: The use of the Loudspeaker does not automatically turn an encounter into a seizure.[50]

Restricting freedom of movement: Generally, if an officer restricts a person's movement during an encounter the Courts will find that the encounter was actually a seizure. Handuffing, blocking in a vehicle, and similar actions will generally be deemed a seizure.

Examples of Situations wherein the Courts have found police action did not transform an Encounter into a Seizure (Investigative Detention):

- Asking a suspect for a cigarette (the brand of which was later used against him in a rape conviction).
- Running the person for warrants (remember don't hold ID).
- Approaching a person and asking basic questions.

However, ordering a person to spit or remove his/her shoes during an encounter has been deemed to be a seizure. Again, remember, the "show of authority" test.

[46] *Commonwealth v. Lyles*, 453 Mass. 811 (2009).
[47] *Comm. v. DePeiza*, 449 Mass. 367 (2007).
[48] Com. v. Smigliano, 427 Mass. 490 (1998) and Com. v. Evans, 436 Mass. 369 (2002).
[49] Com. v. Barbosa, 49 Mass.App.Ct. 344 (2000).
[50] Com.v. Scott, 57 Mass.App.Ct. 36 (2003)

COMMUNITY CARETAKING/EMERGENCY SITUATIONS AND BRIEF DETENTIONS

There are certain interactions between police officers and citizens that do not require judicial justification, as local police officers are charged with community caretaking functions, totally divorced from the detection, investigation, or acquisition of evidence relating to violation of any criminal statute.

This exception also applies to searches (see Warrantless Searches section for more on this topic)

No reasonable suspicion requirement but must be *reasonable*

Under the "community caretaking doctrine," police officers are allowed, without reasonable suspicion of any criminal activity, to approach and detain citizens for community caretaking purposes. The justification is not to investigate a crime but to ensure the safety and wellbeing of others.

Significant cases:

In ***Com. v. Hurd***, the police received information from an anonymous caller that a man who appeared to be drunk was getting into a blue automobile with New Hampshire license plates in front of a package store. There were three small children in the automobile. The police responded to the call and, when they arrived at the location, they saw the automobile approaching the entrance to Route 128, a high speed highway. The court relaxed the basis of knowledge and reliability test because of the emergency presented.[51]

In ***Com. v. Lubiejewski,*** where a trooper arrested a motorist for operating under the influence and operating a motor vehicle negligently so as to endanger, the Appeals Court ruled that the community caretaking doctrine did not apply.[52] There the basis for the charge was an anonymous motorist's report that a truck was operating on the wrong side of Route 195. The trooper used the reported plate registration number and proceeded to the operator's residence. He observed the truck driving away but not improperly. He stopped the vehicle, had the operator perform a field sobriety test and concluded he had been operating under the influence. Because the reasonable inference was that the trooper was engaged in "the detection, investigation, or acquisition of evidence relating to the violation of a criminal statute,"[53] the court ruled that the community caretaking function could not be used to justify the stop.[54]

Attorney Hanrahan's Note: In 2015, the SJC decided *Commonwealth v. DePiero. DePiero* had a very similar fact pattern to *Lubiejewski*. After receiving an anonymous report of a drunk driver a state trooper responded to the home of the registered owner and stopped the operator as he pulled into his driveway approximately a minute after the trooper's arrival. A key difference in these two cases was that in *DePiero* the registered owner was on probation for OUI. A suspect's criminal history, which is consistent with the crime reported by the tipster, can positively impact the veracity of the anonymous report.

In ***Commonwealth v. McCauley***, an anonymous caller reported that an intoxicated man at a particular bar repeatedly dropped a firearm on the floor. The Court ruled that this presented an emergency situation requiring police action.

Disabled or stranded motorists

- **Breakdown lane:** A police officer can check on vehicles stopped in the breakdown lane to ensure no one is in need of assistance.
- **Rest Area**: In ***Commonwealth v. Murdough,*** the Court ruled that officers may check on motorists parked in rest areas, especially in winter to ensure the occupants are not in need of assistance.

TEMPORARY DETENTIONS

[51] *Com. v. Hurd,* 29 Mass.App.Ct. 929 (1990).
[52] *Com. v. Lubiejewski*, 49 Mass.App.Ct. 212 (2000).
[53] *Cady v. Dombrowski*, supra.
[54] *Com. v. Sondrini*, 48 Mass. App. Ct. 704, 724 N.E. 2d 748 (2000).

MOTOR VEHICLE STOPS

Stopping a motor vehicle and detaining its occupants is a "seizure" for Fourth Amendment purposes, therefore the police must have (at least) **reasonable suspicion that criminal activity is occurring** or **that a motor vehicle violation exists**, or has occurred, before they may stop a motor vehicle.[55]

Criminal Activity

If a police officer has reasonable suspicion or probable cause that an occupant of a motor vehicle has committed (or is about to commit) a crime the officer may initiate a stop, just as if the suspect was walking on foot.

Traffic Violations

Chapter 90C § 2 and 3(A), authorize police to issue citations for motor vehicle *traffic* violations, including civil infractions.[56] Chapter 94C requires that a police officer issue a citation in-hand at the time of the violation (with few exceptions) this implies that police has the authority to stop the vehicle in order to comply with this requirement.

In ***Commonwealth v. Rodriguez*** (2015) the SJC stated "many of our traffic violation statutes regulate moving cars and relate directly to the promotion of public safety; even those laws that have to do with maintaining a vehicle's equipment in accordance with certain standards may also be safety-related. Permitting stops based on reasonable suspicion or probable cause that these laws may have been violated gives police the ability to immediately address potential safety hazards on the road. Thus, although a vehicle stop does represent a significant intrusion into an individual's privacy, the governmental interest in allowing such stops for the purpose of promoting compliance with our automobile laws is clear and compelling."

Attorney Hanrahan's note: In *Rodriguez*, the SJC stated that police do not have the authority to stop a motor vehicle to issue a citation for non-criminal amounts of marijuana because this is regulated by c. 94C and not 90C. See the Motor Vehicle Stops section of this manual for more on motor vehicle stops.

ROAD BLOCKS

Despite the lack of individualized suspicion (suspicion involving the particular person/car stopped), there are some rare circumstances wherein the police may lawfully conduct road blocks and conduct a brief detention of all vehicles/people passing through the road block.

Sobriety Roadblocks

The U.S. Supreme Court has upheld the constitutionality of sobriety roadblocks.[57] The Court ruled that the brief intrusion is superseded by the grave danger to public safety posed by intoxicated drivers. However, there are limits and specific requirements that must be followed in order for a sobriety road block to be deemed lawful. For a full analysis of Sobriety Road Blocks see the Motor Vehicle Stop Section in the Criminal Procedure part of this manual. This is closely tied to the Community Caretaking/Public Safety exception to the Fourth Amendment and Article 14.

Drug Interdiction Road Blocks are Unlawful in Massachusetts

Generally, drug interdiction road blocks are illegal because, unlike sobriety check points, although drugs are dangerous they do not necessarily pose an immediate threat to the public. The U.S. Supreme Court has indicated that drug interdiction road blocks are permissible within a certain distance of the U.S. border.

Roadblocks Permissible for Apprehension of Dangerous Person

Following a shooting, or in situations involving other violent crimes where the police are attempting to apprehend fleeing, dangerous persons they may set up a roadblock along routes likely to be taken by such suspects. The usual rules requiring particularized suspicion before stopping a motor vehicle will not apply in such cases. The need to quickly

---

[55] *Delaware v. Prouse*, 440 U.S. 648, 99 S.Ct. 1391 (1979).
[56] *Commonwealth v. Rodriguez*, SJC 2015
[57] See, *Michigan Department of State Police v. Sitz*, 496 U.S. 444, 110 S.Ct. 2481 (1990).

apprehend a dangerous person who is likely to harm others outweighs the brief intrusion. This is also closely tied to the Community Caretaking/Public Safety exception to the Fourth Amendment and Article 14.

ADMINISTRATIVE SEIZURES

A police officer may lawfully detain someone who is located within a secure area provided that some type of advanced notice is provided. For instance, a police officer may temporarily detain a person located in a secure area of an airport providing the airport has signs warning that you may be subject to detention. In all cases the detention must be reasonable.

TRUCK TEAM STOPS

The Appeals Court has upheld random administrative stops by trained "truck team" police officers of commercial vehicles for the enforcement of commercial motor vehicle safety standards. The court noted that these stops are reasonable since they are conducted for a legitimate safety purpose, are narrow in scope, and are done pursuant to an established statutory directive (federal law).[58]

These stops are similar to administrative inspections of closely regulated business – see the Search section of this manual for more on administrative searches.

[58] *Commonwealth v. Leboeuf*, 78 Mass. App. Ct. 45 (2010).

INFORMATION FROM VICTIMS, WITNESSES, & INFORMANTS

The concepts in this section (information from victims, witnesses and informants) apply not just in conducting temporary detentions; the same concepts apply when establishing probable cause in all contexts, including search warrants. However, the most common scenario where these concepts become important is in relation to temporary detentions and arrests therefore these concepts are addressed in this section. For more on informants, in relation to search warrants see the Search Warrant section of this manual.

In order for information supplied to the police by a third party to rise to the level of probable cause/reasonable suspicion the information must meet the two-pronged *Aguilar-Spinelli* test. This test means that **the third party must:**

1. Have a **Basis of Knowledge,** and

2. There must be a reduced risk that the person is not being dishonest. This is often referred to as **"veracity."**

The reason for this two-pronged test requirement is to eliminate, or at least reduce, false reports of criminal activity resulting in law enforcement intruding on the rights of innocent citizens. The law is designed to protect citizens from government intrusion based on rumor or innuendo.

Significant case

In ***Commonwealth v. Lyons,*** the State police received an anonymous telephone call at approximately 1:15 A.M. stating that two white males, one of whom was named Wayne, had just purchased narcotics in Chelsea and would be heading for Bridgton, Maine. The caller stated that they would be driving in a silver Hyundai automobile with Maine registration 440-44T. The troopers then set up surveillance. At approximately 2:00 A.M. the police observed the Hyundai which contained two white males and matching registration. The police stopped the vehicle. The operator was identified as Wayne Lyons of Bridgton, Maine. During the stop the police observed cocaine in plain view and both of the occupants were subsequently arrested. The SJC held that the investigating troopers did not have reasonable suspicion to support the stop.

The SJC reasoned that the police did not have sufficient articulable facts for the investigatory stop. The tip provided no information regarding either the basis of the informant's knowledge or his reliability. Furthermore, the quantity and quality of the details corroborated by the police were simply insufficient to establish any degree of suspicion that could be deemed reasonable. The trooper was able to verify only the description of the automobile, the direction in which it was headed, and the race and gender of the occupants before making the stop. These details do not reveal any special familiarity with the defendants' affairs that might substitute for explicit information about the basis of the caller's knowledge. Indeed, another driver equipped with a car telephone could have provided the same details. Likewise, the informant's reliability was only slightly enhanced by this corroboration because the police verified no predictive details that were not easily obtainable by an uninformed bystander. The corroboration went only to obvious details, not nonobvious details.

If the police act on information that is deemed to have not met the two-pronged test of *Aguilar-Spinelli,* in most cases any evidence uncovered will be excluded via the Exclusionary Rule.

Note: Federal law uses the Totality of the Circumstances Test, meaning the court will look at the "big picture" to determine if probable cause/reasonable suspicion existed. Massachusetts continues to require the more stringent two-pronged test.

THE BASIS OF KNOWLEDGE PRONG

HOW DO YOU ESTABLISH THE BASIS OF KNOWLEDGE?

The basis of knowledge prong requires that the reporting person explain *how they know* what they are reporting. It generally must be from first hand information. Of the two tests this is by far the simplest and often easiest to meet. Often times the person will automatically offer how they know, e.g. "I just saw two men breaking into my neighbor's house." If the caller does not automatically offer his/her basis of knowledge it can easily be established by asking "how do you know this", or something similar.

THE VERACITY PRONG

The term veracity essentially means truthful and reliable. There must be a reduced risk that the report is false. Before law enforcement detains someone (i.e. intrudes on the citizen's Constitutional protections) based on a report from a third part the police must verify the reporting party's veracity, absent some type of exigency.

HOW DO YOU ESTABLISH IF SOMEONE IS TRUTHFUL/RELIABLE?

Identified Individuals

Satisfying the veracity prong is obviously much more difficult than establishing the reporting party's basis of knowledge. However, the easiest, and most common, method of verifying someone's truthfulness (at least for the purposes of the "two-pronged test") is to properly identify the person. Named/known persons are generally deemed truthful because it is believed that people who can face consequences for supplying false information will provide truthful information. The possibility of legal repercussions (i.e. false report of criminal activity) lessens the likelihood that someone will fabricate criminal activity. If the person is not completely identified he/she may still be deemed reliable if the person places his/her anonymity at risk.

Information from Victims

Information received from a **victim** of a crime is generally deemed to be reliable, absent some indication that the victim if not being truthful or is otherwise unreliable. However, the victim must still meet the two-pronged test. Just because someone calls the police and reports being a victim of a crime this would not automatically make the person reliable, particularly if the victim was anonymous.

Information from Informants

Unlike a witness or a victim, informants are often motivated by their own self-interest (such as reducing criminal charges against themselves) and therefore their information is often questionable even if they are properly identified. Establishing probable cause with the use of informants is discussed in more detail later in this section.

Identifiable Individuals

Placing anonymity at risk: It is believed that if the police have the ability to take action against the reporter for providing false information that a provider of information is less likely to provide false information. Therefore, when a person identifies himself, or at least places his/her anonymity at risk, the person is typically deemed to be reliable. Placing identity at risk generally occurs when the person provides information, or otherwise exposes a clue to their identity, that would make it possible for the police to track the person down if needed.

- **Providing Name and other Verifying Information**: Obviously, when a person provides his/her name along with other verifiable information, such as address and telephone number, it can be assumed that the information provided is truthful. However, because "informants" (as opposed to an uninvolved witness) may have ulterior motives (e.g. eliminate competition or escape prosecution) so-called informants are treated differently. See the informant section for more.
- **Face to Face reports**: face to face reports are generally deemed reliable because the reporting person placed their anonymity at risk. The courts presume that if the report was false the officer would be able to track down the reporting person based on their physical appearance.
- **Caller ID & similar technology:** in at least one decision the SJC upheld a police detention as a result of an anonymous caller whose cell phone number came up on the department's caller ID system. The caller confirmed that the number on the agencies caller ID display was that of her cellular telephone. The court reasoned that the caller was presumed reliable because the caller could have been tracked down by the police via the caller's cell phone if the report had been false.

Significant case

In the 2007 case of ***Commonwealth v. Costa***[59], a cell phone caller was found to be reliable when reporting a teen with a gun near a park. The reporting person put her anonymity at risk by using her cell phone to make the call. The caller was informed by the dispatcher that the call was being recorded and her phone number was repeated back to her after it was displayed on the department's caller ID system. The Court found that, if necessary, the identity of the caller could have been traced through the phone number.

Attorney Hanrahan's Note: Technology has changed since 2007 when the *Costa* case was decided. So-called "throw-away phones" are common as well as software and "apps" which allow the caller to alter the caller ID display. It is not recommended that you rely solely on the caller's caller ID display. You should always try to properly identify anyone reporting criminal activity.

In 2014, the U.S. Supreme Court ruled that in ***Navarette v. California***,[60] in which the US Supreme Court held that the use of the 911 emergency system itself is an "indicator of veracity." In *Navarette*, the US Supreme Court reasoned that technological advances would lead the caller to believe that they could be easily identified and subject to prosecution making the caller less likely to fabricate a report. However, the SJC rejected to adopt this logic here in Massachusetts. The SJC reasoned "even if the police are able to recover the telephone number and identity of 911 callers, 'it proves absolutely nothing . . . unless the anonymous caller was aware of that fact. It is the tipster's belief in anonymity, not its reality, that will control his behavior'" (quoting from the dissenting opinion in *Navarette*). The key is that the reporting person's knowledge that his/her anonymity has been exposed.

Excited Utterances

In a 2010 decision, the Court ruled that excited utterances are deemed reliable; meaning if someone reports witnessing a shocking crime while still under the stress of the event the reporting party would not fabricate the report.

Significant Case

In the 2010 case of ***Commonwealth v. Depina,*** the defendant was detained by officers after a broadcast was put out over the radio regarding a recent shooting and a fleeing suspect. The information regarding the person fleeing the scene came from an anonymous caller to an emergency 911 line. She told police that she was "on Middle Street" and had heard two to three shots on Chancery Street, in her "back yard." She had not seen the shooting, but she had seen a person running toward Kempton Street after the shooting. She described the fleeing person as a "tan" colored "kid"; she said he was wearing a white shirt, blue "jean" shorts, and a hat. It was determined that the caller met the basis of knowledge test as she personally observed the event but she hung up the phone before identifying herself. The SJC ruled that corroboration is not the only way the Commonwealth can establish the reliability of an anonymous caller. Under our common law of evidence, we have recognized that a statement may be sufficiently reliable to be admitted in evidence as an exception to the hearsay rule where it is made in reaction to a startling or shocking event if its utterance was "spontaneous to a degree which reasonably negated premeditation or possible fabrication and if it tends to qualify, characterize and explain the underlying event."[61]

Attorney Hanrahan's note: although the excited utterance may help with the veracity of the anonymous caller it is not recommended that you solely rely on this to satisfy the veracity prong. This is often a difficult burden to meet. In fact, in 2015 the SJC rejected an Appeals Court decision ruling that the excited utterance satisfied the veracity prong (see *Commonwealth v. DePiero*) indicating that the excited utterance alone may not be enough to satisfy the veracity prong in many situations.

[59] *Commonwealth v. Costa*, 448 Mass. 510, 862 N.E. 2d 510 (2007).
[60] ***Navarette v. California***, 134 S.Ct. 1683 (2014)
[61] *Commonwealth v. Depina*, SJC (2010)

Exceptions/Deviations from the strict adherence to the Two-Prong Test Requirement

Although Massachusetts courts have not adopted the Totality of the Circumstances test (like the federal courts) the Massachusetts Courts have granted, in some cases, some leeway to the veracity prong when the reporting party has failed to be identified or otherwise placed his/her anonymity at risk. The following are some factors that may add to the tipster's veracity:

Lack of Specificity can add to Reliability: In the 2010 case of ***Commonwealth v. DePina***, the SJC stated that the veracity of a 911 caller was enhanced *by her lack of specificity*: "If the caller had intended for some malicious purpose to point the police in the direction of an innocent person, it seems likely she would have provided a more detailed description of the person fleeing and claimed to have seen a firearm in his hand."

Suspect's Criminal History: In the 1985 case of ***Commonwealth v. Germain***, the SJC ruled that the defendant's record of recent convictions for similar crimes indicate reliability of anonymous tip under Aguilar-Spinelli analysis. This was reiterated on the 2015 case of case of ***Commonwealth v. DePiero***. In *DePiero*, an anonymous caller reported an OUI operator on Memorial Drive in Cambridge. Dispatch broadcasted that the vehicle's registered owner was on probation for OUI (discovered from a DCJIS inquiry). This was a significant factor that lead to the SJC's decision to uphold the subsequent stop of the suspect as he pulled into his driveway.

SPECIAL CIRCUMSTANCES

"Totem Pole" Hearsay

If the reporter of information reports that he or she "heard from a someone else," this will not satisfy the basis of knowledge or the veracity test. When dealing with a chain of hearsay *each link* must be tested and found reliable under *Aguilar- Spinelli*.[62] The test must be satisfied based on information from the reporter of the facts.

In the 2012 case of ***Commonwealth v. Arias***, the Transit Police received a tip from an MBTA maintenance supervisor that one of the cleaning contractor employees was known to carry a gun. The maintenance supervisor reported that he "received information" from an unnamed source. Based on this tip the officers conducted a threshold inquiry and later discovered a firearm. The SJC ruled that the stop was unlawful because the "unnamed source" did not meet the two-pronged test.

Radio Broadcasts and Police Bulletins

If police officers act on information supplied by police radio broadcasts and/or police bulletins the source of information must meet the same standards in order for it to amount to reasonable suspicion or probable cause.

When police officers on the street stop a defendant in reliance on a police dispatch, the stop is lawful only if:

(1) The information on which the dispatch was based had sufficient indicia of reliability, and

(2) The description of the suspect conveyed by the dispatch had sufficient particularity that it was reasonable for the police to suspect a person matching that description. [63]

POLICE CORROBORATION

In many cases, even if the reporting party did not meet the *Aguilar-Spinelli* two-pronged test, the police can make up a deficiency in one, or both, of the prongs by corroborating (verifying by their own observation) the information provided.

In the 2012 case of ***Commonwealth v. Andersen***, the SJC stated "where the caller is anonymous, there are *at least* two ways to establish the caller's reliability.[64] The first is through independent corroboration by police observation or investigation of the details of the information provided by the caller. A second way to establish the caller's reliability is by demonstrating that the caller had just witnessed a startling or shocking event, that the caller described the event, and that the description of the event was made so quickly in reaction to the event as

[62] See *Peterson, supra*. See generally Smith, Criminal Practice and Procedure § 208 (2d ed.1983 & Supp.2005); see also *Commonwealth v. Zorn*, 66 Mass.App.Ct. 228, 846 N.E.2d 423 (2006).
[63] See *Commonwealth v. Depina, supra* at 243; *Commonwealth v. Lopes*, 455 Mass. 147, 155 (2009). See also *Commonwealth v. Riggieri*, 438 Mass. 613, 615-616 (2003); *Commonwealth v. Mercado*, 422 Mass. 367, 371-372 (1996).
[64] Commonwelath v. Eric Anserson, SJC (2012)

VICTIMS, WITNESSES & INFORMANTS

reasonably to negate the possibility that the caller was falsifying the description or was carrying out a plan falsely to accuse another."

Thus anytime criminal or suspicious activity is reported the can, and in most cases should, conduct an investigation. Even if the tip did not meet the two-prong test in most cases the police can corroborate, or at least attempt to corroborate, the information and take action as appropriate and warranted.

Attorney Hanrahan's Important Note: The police have a duty to investigate reports of criminal activity. Even if the reporting person does not meet the two-pronged test or the description is not sufficiently detailed the police should still respond and conduct a cursory investigation, such as conducting surveillance, to investigate the report and see if they can establish reasonable suspicion or probable cause without the need of the reporting party.

ESTABLISHING PROBABLE CAUSE WITH THE USE OF INFORMANTS

When utilizing an informant to obtain a search warrant the affidavit must set forth (1) facts sufficiently detailing the manner in which the information in the affidavit was obtained, so as to assure the magistrate that the allegations are derived, not from casual rumor, but rather from first-hand knowledge (the "basis of knowledge" prong); and (2) facts sufficiently establishing the inherent credibility of the informant, or the reliability of his information on this occasion (the "veracity" prong). [65]

Like with other third parties, independent police corroboration of detailed information supplied by the informant can compensate for deficiencies in either or both prongs of the *Aguilar-Spinelli* test."

Note: See the Search Warrant section of this manual and/or Hanrahan Consulting, LLC's Legal Guide to Drug Investigations for a detailed analysis of utilizing informants.

Specific Details May Make Up For a Deficiency in the Two-Prong Test

Detailed information: often times if the reporting party provided a **specific detailed** description and the police are able to corroborate the detailed description this corroboration will make up for a deficiency because it can be assumed that reporting person personally observed the suspect/incident based on the specific detail.

Commonwealth v. Eric Anderson (2012): Approximately two minutes after the clerk was robbed at 4:58 P.M., Boston police Officer Matthew Fogarty responded to the scene. Shortly thereafter, he spoke with Thanh Nguyen, the store clerk, who told him that two "skinny" black males had entered the market, each wearing a bandana over his face. One of the robbers displayed a handgun. Nguyen did not see them enter a vehicle but he suspected that is how they got away. Approximately eight minutes after the robbery, an anonymous caller telephoned the community service line at the police station. The police dispatcher reported that the caller had seen two black males "hop into" a silver or gold Toyota Camry automobile, with Massachusetts registration number 22CO77, and "they headed up Parkman Street towards Dorchester Avenue minutes ago after that robbery." The dispatcher also reported that the caller had said the vehicle was driven by a woman. The police were able to track down the suspect vehicle with this information and the occupants were ordered out. A firearm and other evidence were discovered. Since the caller stated that she had witnessed the suspects her basis of knowledge was established. In regards to the veracity prong, the court explained the following:

Corroboration: There was some corroboration of the information provided by the anonymous caller. The Court stated "we can infer the caller recognized that the suspects appeared to have just committed a crime and were making their getaway; otherwise it would have made no sense to contact the police and provide the registration plate number of a departing vehicle. In fact, there had been a robbery of a market one block away from Parkman Street eight minutes earlier that had been committed by two masked black men. There was also corroboration for the caller's report that the robbers had escaped in a vehicle, because Nguyen followed them on foot after they left the store but lost sight of them, which suggests that they had entered a waiting getaway car. There was corroboration of the caller's observation of the registration plate and the female driver because, once the police substituted a "D" for a "O," they learned that such a registration plate was assigned to a silver or gold Camry automobile that was owned by a woman in Dorchester. There was further corroboration in that this same vehicle was spotted within forty minutes of the robbery in a location that was approximately one and one-half miles from the market."

[65] *Commonwealth v. Reyes*, 423 Mass. 568, 571 (1996).

Startling event: The Court stated "For purposes of evaluating the reliability of an anonymous caller in determining whether the police had reasonable suspicion to make an investigative stop, the anonymous call here may be comparable to an excited utterance. If a person wants to harass an enemy by providing false information to the police that would trigger an investigative stop, the person is unlikely to wait until the caller has just seen someone flee a crime scene."

The Court concluded that the anonymous caller passed the veracity test needed for reasonable suspicion where there was independent corroboration of the information furnished by the caller and where the call was made immediately after the startling event of observing two men who appeared to have just committed a crime make their getaway. In these circumstances, the police would have been remiss had they not conducted an investigative stop of this vehicle.

Predicted Information: if the reporting person is able to provide **predicted information** and the police can corroborate this predicted information this may make up for deficiencies in either prong. It can be presumed that the reporting person had more information than a passerby would have because they were able to predict the future acts of the suspect.

PROTECTING CONFIDENTIALITY

Witness/Reporters of Criminal Activity Protection

The Massachusetts Public Record law provides an exemption for the names of reporters of crime from public disclosure. Exemption F of the public records law provides that information may be withheld to provide an assurance of confidentiality to private citizens so that they will speak openly about matters under investigation. Accordingly, any details in witness statements, which if released create a grave risk of directly or indirectly identifying a private citizen who volunteers as a witness are indefinitely exempt. When a reporter of criminal activity is hesitant to identify himself/herself the law enforcement official may reassure the reporter that his/her name can be withheld from public record. However, the law enforcement official should ensure that his/her agency has safeguards in place to ensure that the reporter's information is not released as a public record.

Although the name of the reporter may be withheld from the public record, the defendant may still be able to obtain the information through the discovery process. This topic is covered in more detail in the Search Warrant section of this manual.

Witness Protection

501 CMR 10 provides witness protection services to those who are considered "critical witnesses." Part of these protections includes non-disclosure of the witness's identity and whereabouts.

EMERGENCY SITUATIONS/COMMUNITY CARETAKING

Emergency Situations: An officer's community caretaking or emergency exception function may come into play when the police receive a report of a dangerous situation jeopardizing public safety. If the situation is deemed to be an emergency the reliability and basis of knowledge requirement of the reporting person normally required to establish reasonable suspicion to stop a motor vehicle may not be needed. The standard in this situation would be **mere reasonableness**.

See the Community Caretaking topic in the Temporary Detention section of this manual.

SUFFICIENCY OF THE DESCRIPTION

Even when the caller meets the two-pronged test, if the description is not detailed enough to narrow down the suspect the subsequent stop by the police will most likely be deemed unlawful resulting in the suppression of all uncovered evidence. This legal requirement is designed to protect the public from random detainments from the police. It is imperative that the call-taker obtain as much detailed information as possible.

Significant Case Examples:

In ***Commonwealth v. Cheek***, police officers were on routine patrol in the Grove Hall neighborhood in the Roxbury section of Boston on November 12, 1990, when, at approximately 11:20 P.M., they received a report that a victim had been stabbed in the back, but was conscious. The suspect in the stabbing was described as a "black male with a black 3/4 length goose down jacket." The officers began to search the Grove Hall area for a suspect, and "[s]subsequently ... observed a black male ([Cheek]) walking on a street approximately one-half mile from the scene of the reported stabbing [,] ... wearing a dark-colored three-quarter length goose-down jacket." When the police approached Cheek and asked him his name, his response was not clear to the officers and his hands were in his coat pocket. The police conducted a pat frisk of Cheek and recovered a .38 caliber handgun from his coat pocket. Cheek was arrested, and a subsequent booking search of him revealed seventeen plastic bags of marijuana.

Cheek filed a motion to suppress the evidence obtained as a result of the police searches. The Supreme Judicial Court reversed the defendant's conviction, concluding that the description could not have provided the police with reasonable suspicion that the defendant was the perpetrator of the reported stabbing. It wrote, "[s]significantly, the description of the suspect as a 'black male with a black 3/4 length goose' could have fit a large number of men who reside in the Grove Hall section of Roxbury, a predominantly black neighborhood of the city. The officers possessed no additional physical description of the suspect that would have distinguished the defendant from any other black male in the area.... Moreover the Commonwealth presented no evidence to establish that a '3/4 length goose' jacket, the sole distinctive physical characteristic of the garment, was somehow unusual or, at least, uncommon as an outer garment worn on a cold fall night."

Commonwealth v. Lopes – October 2009
Facts

At approximately 9:50 A.M., officers of the Boston PD, responding to a 911 call of a shooting, arrived at 47 Clarence Street. The victim's minivan was stopped in the middle of the street with the engine still running. The victim was seated in the driver's seat, slumped toward the middle of the vehicle, with a gunshot wound behind his left ear. The victim was transported by ambulance to a Boston hospital where he was pronounced dead a few hours later.

The police spoke with an eyewitness, Antonio Fidalgo (a cousin of the victim), who had discovered the victim. Minutes before the shooting, Fidalgo had seen a long brown van with tinted windows and a Cape Verdean flag hanging from the inside rear view mirror parked in front of 47 Clarence Street. He saw at least two men inside, one in the driver's seat wearing what he described as a round "Jamaican hat," and another man moving around in the back seat area. The van was gone when he returned to the street and found the victim.

At approximately 11 A.M., a report was broadcast over the Brockton police radio asking police to be on the lookout for a **brown van with tinted windows and a Cape Verdean flag** in the rear with respect to a Boston homicide. After hearing the police broadcast, a Brockton school police officer working a construction detail on Warren Avenue in Brockton observed a van that he thought matched the broadcast description stopped next to him in traffic. He radioed for assistance and, within minutes, Brockton police officers arrived at the scene. One officer, with his gun drawn, approached the driver's side of the van (which was still stopped in the middle lane of Warren Avenue) and asked the driver (the defendant) whether he had just come from Boston. The defendant replied "yes." The defendant and his passenger then were ordered out of the van, handcuffed, and pat frisked for weapons (none was found).

Boston police officers applied for and obtained a warrant to search the impounded van, and the search was executed on April 24. In the van, police officers discovered $2,006 in cash and brown paper "counting bands" among other evidence.

This evidence was used to charge the suspects with the murder/robbery. One of the suspects later confessed to the crimes.

The Court stated: the two-pronged test was satisfied. The source of the information was Fidalgo, who had identified himself to the police and had seen the van in front of Davey's Market minutes before, but not minutes after, his cousin was shot. Because the basis of his knowledge was his own personal observation, he gave his true name to the police, and he was a cousin of the victim, Fidalgo's information more than satisfied both the basis of knowledge test and the veracity test.

The description need not be as singular as a registration plate number, but it must not be so broad as to fit a large number of motor vehicles in the area where the stop occurred. Here, significant details given by Fidalgo--**the van's make, the two occupants, the description of the driver, the time of the homicide**--were not transmitted to Brockton police. Officer Robert Smith had to determine whether there was reasonable suspicion that the van stopped near him was the van involved in the homicide based **only on its color, its tinted windows, and the Cape Verdean flag** hanging from the inside rear view mirror. We conclude that the probability that a reddish brown van with tinted windows and a Cape Verdean flag was the van involved in the homicide was sufficiently high that Officer Robert Smith was justified in stopping the van.

Attorney Hanrahan's Note: Always make sure that you obtain a detailed description when taking a report from a witness. A "white male, with blue jeans" is not going to be a sufficient description, in most circumstances, to justify a temporary detention. The more detail the more likely the stop will be upheld. Reasonable suspicion that a crime occurred is not enough to justify a stop; you must have reasonable suspicion that the particular person that you are detaining committed a crime. This is sometimes referred to as **"individualized" reasonable suspicion.**

TIME OF DAY, LOCATION, and OTHER CONDITIONS

Although it is true that the more detailed a description the less likely a subsequent detention will be suppressed due to lack of specificity an otherwise vague description may suffice depending on other circumstances. For instance, if a witness provided only a vague description of a "white male in his twenties with blue jeans" it would most likely be deemed insufficient if the suspect was stopped in the middle of the day in a bustling part of the city with numerous people in the area. However, the same description may be sufficient if the suspect was stopped in the middle of the night, during a blizzard, where very few people were out in public – see 2013 Appeals Court decision in *Commonwealth v. McKoy*.

ARREST POWERS

There are basically five categories of arrest powers for Massachusetts Police Officers (listed below). It is important that police officers know which of the below categories the various offenses fall into as it affects their arrest powers.

(1) ARREST WARRANT: The preferred method of making arrest an arrest is via an arrest warrant. The Fourth Amendment indicates that all warrantless seizures are presumed unreasonable. However, the courts, and the legislature, have carved out exceptions to the arrest warrant requirement (see below).

Exceptions to the Constitutional warrant requirement for arrests:

(2) FELONY OFFENSE: Felonies are serious crimes and because of this as far back as 1911 the Court carved out an exception to the warrant requirement in the case of a felony offense so that the police can quickly take these offenders into custody and prevent further harm. If the crime is a felony the officer may make a warrantless arrest provided the officer has probable cause that the suspect committed the crime. This is so even if the crime was not committed in the officer's presence.[66]

Note: a felony is any crime punishable by incarceration in a state prison.

MISDEMEANORS: Generally speaking, misdemeanors are not arrestable without a warrant. However, there are **three exceptions** to this general rule:

Statutory Authority:

(3) Misdemeanors with Statutory Powers of Arrests for Offenses Committed in the Officer's Presence: In some statutes (i.e. laws/crimes) the legislature granted police officers the power to arrest for the misdemeanor crime but only if the crime was committed in the officer's presence even if a breach of the peace was not involved.

(4) Misdemeanors with Statutory Powers of Arrest for Offenses where Probable Cause exists, even if not committed in the officer's presence: In some cases the legislature has granted police officers the power to arrest for certain misdemeanors providing the officer has probable cause, similar to the power of arrest for a felony. This is considered a statutory exception to the warrant requirement.

Last Resort: a police officer may effect an arrest for a misdemeanor offense involving a breach of the peace committed in his/her presence without a warrant even if the Legislature did not provide statutory power:

(5) Misdemeanor involving a Breach of the Peace and in the Presence of an Officer: The SJC, in *Commonwealth v. Gorman*, ruled that an arrest may be executed if the misdemeanor is committed in the officer's presence and the crime has created an actual, or potential, breach of the peace.

"At common law, 'a peace officer, in the absence of statute ... may arrest without a warrant for a misdemeanor which (1) involves a breach of the peace, (2) is committed in the presence or view of the officer ... and (3) is still continuing at the time of the arrest or only interrupted, so that the offence and the arrest form parts of one transaction' [67]

Most crimes committed in a public place create a breach of the peace. A breach of the peace may be defined as a "violation of public order or decorum which disturbs the public peace and tranquility; or any act of disorderly conduct which disrupts the public peace." It is generally considered a *condition.*

Attorney Hanrahan's Note: "In presence" is commonly interpreted to refer to having personal knowledge that the offense in question has been committed, made known to the officer through any of the officer's five senses. *Personal knowledge* means the information was not provided by someone else.[68]

Probable cause to arrest: All that is required is "reasonably trustworthy information…sufficient to warrant a prudent man in believing that the defendant had committed…an offense."[69] In the 2012 case of *Commonwealth v. Bell*, the Appeals Court stated "the requirement of sufficient evidence to establish the identity of the accused and probable cause to arrest him is considerably less exacting (i.e. rigorous) than the requirement that a judge must apply at trial or at a probable cause hearing…" Additionally, there is no requirement that the police effect an arrest as soon as probable cause becomes apparent.[70]

---

[66] *Comm. vs. Phelps, Mass. 396, 95 N.E. 868. (1911)*
[67] *Commonwealth v. Howe*, **405 Mass. 332**, 334, **540 N.E.2d 677** (1989), quoting *Commonwealth v. Gorman*, **288 Mass. 294**, 297, 192 N.E. 618 (1934).
[68] See People v. Burgess (1947) 79 Cal.App.2nd 174, 176
[69] Com. v. Bell (2012) quoting from Commonwealth v. O'Dell, 392 Mass. 445 (1984).
[70] *Commonwealth v. Suggs* (2007) quoting *Commonwealth v. Labitue*, 49 Mass.App.Ct. 913, 914-915 (2000).

For more on probable cause see the Probable Cause section in the Criminal Procedure Overview section of this manual.

SUMMONS

An arrest is not required to bring charges against someone for committing a criminal act. In most cases the defendant can/is "summoned" for the offense. A criminal complaint is taken out at the court and the defendant is summoned into court to answer for the charges.

Chapter 276 § 25 states "A summons shall require the defendant to appear before the court at a stated time and place on the return day and shall be served by an officer authorized to serve criminal process by giving to the defendant in hand or by leaving at his dwelling house or last and usual place of abode with some person of suitable age and discretion then residing therein an attested copy not less than twenty-four hours before the return day, or by mailing an attested copy to the defendant's last known address."

SOME COMMON FELONIES

Below is a list of some of the more common felonies. See the Statutory Law section of this manual for a detailed analysis of the various elements for each offense.

CRIMES AGAINST THE PERSON

- Murder and attempted murder (c. 265 § 1)
- Felony A&B – against a person with an intellectual disability, to collect loan, on an elder (60 or over), causing serious bodily injury (a permanent disfigurement, loss or impairment of a bodily function, limb or organ, or a substantial risk of death.), defendant on the plaintiff of an RO, on a pregnant person.
- A&B dangerous weapon (inherently dangerous or item as used) (c. 265 § 15A)
- Assault (no actual contact) – dangerous weapon (c. 256 § 15B)
- Stalking (c. 265 § 43)
- Strangulation/suffocation (c. 265 § 15D)
- Human/Sex trafficking (c. 265 § 49, § 50)

CRIMES AGAINST PROPERTY

- Arson and attempted Arson (c. 266)
- B&E and Burglary offenses (except B&E with intent to commit a misdemeanor)
- Credit card violations with value obtained over $250 (c. 266 § 37A-C)
- Defacement/Damage of Property (c. 266 § 126A)
- Destruction of Property – damage value over $250 (c. 266 § 127)
- Larceny from a Building (any value) (c. 266 § 20)
- Larceny from a Person (any value) (c. 266 § 25)
- Larceny over $250; or Firearm or Trade Secret (but not attempted) (c. 266 § 30)
- Receiving Stolen Property (over $250) (c. 266 § 60)
- Robbery (c. 265 § 19)
- Possession of Burglarious tools (c. 266 § 49)
- Forgery/theft of registry document (c. 90 § 24B)

SEX RELATED CRIMES

- Child pornography – possessing, creating, and distributing (child under 18 years of age) (c. 272 § 29, A, B, & C)
- Enticement of a Child (child under 16) (c. 265 § 26C)
- Incest (c. 272 § 17)
- Open & Gross lewdness (publicly and causing person to be shocked and alarmed) (c. 272 § 16)
- Sex Offender Fails to Register (non-homeless)
- Rape (c. 265)

PUBLIC JUSTICE CRIMES

- Bribery/Accepting a bribe (c. 268A § 2)
- Firearm: unlawful possession/carry outside of home or business (c. 269 § 10)
- Forgery (c. 267 § 1)
- Forgery/theft of registry document (c. 90 § 24B)
- Intimidation of a witness/misleading police (c. 268 § 13B)
- Uttering: the passing of a forged document (c. 267 § 5)
- A&B on a police officer and attempting to disarm (c. 265 § 13D)

MISCELLANEOUS CRIMES

- Cruelty to Animals offense (c. 272 § 77)
- Exhibition/Possession of fighting animals (c. 272 § 94)
- Kidnapping (c. 265 § 26)
- Parental Kidnapping and child taken out of Massachusetts or exposed to danger (c. 265 § 26A)
- Unlawful carrying of a dangerous weapon: firearm, brass knuckles, slung shot, nunchaku, switch knives, double-edged knives and so on [269 § 10(b)]

And many others – see statutory law section for more information.

Some common misdemeanors with statutory power of arrest

Misdemeanor: Statutory Right with probable cause (whether or not it was committed in the Officer's presence)

- Assault & Battery on a Public Transportation Operator (c. 265 § 13D)
- Carrying a firearm on school grounds [c. 269 § 10(j)]
- Domestic A&B (c. 209A & c. 265 § 13M)
- Harassment Prevention Order violations (c.258E)
- Homeless Sex offender - fail to register (c. 6 § 178)
- Identity Fraud (c. 266 § 37E)
- Knowingly being present where heroin is kept (includes in the company of person known to possess heroin) (c. 94C § 35)
- Library offenses – most (266 § 99A)
- Nearly all Drug offenses (exception: marijuana possession – ounce or less - and hypodermic needle possession no longer criminal) (c. 94C § 34)
- OUI (c.90 § 24)
- Possession of Motor Vehicle with altered VIN [c. 266 § 139(c)]
- RO/Vacate order violations (**mandatory arrest**) (c. 209A § 6)
- Sex Offender engaged in Ice Cream Truck Vending (c. 265 § 48)
- Shoplifting (c. 266 §30A)
- Surreptitious Video recording of nude/partially nude person (c. 272 § 104)
- "Upskirting law" (c. 272 § 105)
- Tagging (c. 266 § 126A & B)
- Tampering with Fire Alarm or Police Signal Box (c. 268 § 32)
- Theft of Registration Plate (c. 266 § 139)
- Unlawful possession of a Stun Gun (c. 140 § 131J)
- Unlawful possession, ownership, or transfer of ammunition, firearms, rifles & shotguns [c. 269 § 10(h)(1)]

Misdemeanor: Statutory Right: committed the **in Officer's Presence only.**

- Absent without Leave from the Military (c. 33 § 61C)
- Bathing/Fouling Water Supply (c. 111 § 173 § 171)
- Boating violations (various) (c. 90B § 13)
- City Ordinance violations (c. 272 § 59)
- Credit card violations (any value) (c. 266 § 37)
- Disorderly conduct (c. 272 § 53, 54)
- DYS escapee (c. 120 § 13)
- Failing to Stop for a Police Officer (c. 90 § 25)
- Fish & Game violations (c. 131 § 87)
- Fugitive from Justice (crime in other state punishable by death or term exceeding 1 year) (276 § 20B)
- Gambling offenses (c. 272 § 10A & 271 § 2)
- Hawker & Peddler Violations (c. 101 § 32)
- Indecent Exposure in public (c. 272 § 53, 54)
- Inhaling Vapors for Effect (c.270 §18)
- Larceny (any value) (c. 276 § 28)
- Leaving the scene of a Motor vehicle accident WITH injury (c. 90 § 21, also see c. 90 § 24)
- Lewd & lascivious (c. 272 § 53, 54)
- License not in Possession (Out of State Operator) (c. 90 § 21)
- Liquor violations (SEEKMIST) (c. 138 § 34)
- Littering (refusal to give name) (c. 272 §60)
- Obstructing a Medical or Reproductive Facility (c. 266 § 120E½)
- Operating after suspension/revocation (c. 90 § 23 via § 21)
- Operating without a license (c. 90 § 10)
- Peeping Tom in public (c. 272 § 53, 54)
- Prostitution offenses (c. 272 § 53) – note some are felonies.
- Railroad violations (trespassing, throwing missiles)
- Sale of Fireworks or Possession with intent to sell (c. 148 § 39)
- Spitting (expectorating) on sidewalk (unknown to officer) (c. 270 § 14)
- Trespass (c. 266 § 120)
- Unlawful possession of explosives (c. 143 § 35)
- Unlawful possession/transportation of alcohol by a minor (c. 138 § 34C)
- Untaxed Cigarette Violations/Transportation (c. 64C § 35, also see § 8)
- Using Without Authority (c. 90 § 21)
- Violation of Election laws
- Waterways - any misdemeanor in presence committed in or upon any of the rivers, harbors, bays or sounds within the Commonwealth (c.91 § 58)

Below is a list of some unique arrest powers which are not covered elsewhere in this manual.

C. 272 § 59. CITY ORDINANCE VIOLATIONS

This statute authorizes a Police Officer to arrest a person found in public violating a city ordinance as delineated below:

REMAINING IN PUBLIC IN VIOLATION OF TOWN/CITY ORDINANCE/BYLAW

Whoever *remains* in a street or elsewhere in a town in willful violation of

- an ordinance or by-law of such town
  or
- any rule or regulation for the government or use of any public reservation, parkway or boulevard made under authority of law by any department, officer or board in charge thereof.

Arrest: The offender may be arrested without a warrant by an officer authorized to serve criminal process in the place where the offence is committed and kept in custody until he can be taken before a c1ourt having jurisdiction of the offence.

Attorney Hanrahan's Comment: The legislature specifically included the term *remains* is this law. Although they do not define what they intended by the term *remains*, I recommend that you only arrest for a non-public drinking city/town violation (see below) when the violator refuses to cease whatever conduct is prohibited after being so warned, and then only when the violator is in a public place.

VIOLATION OF A PUBLIC DRINKING ORDINANCE

- Whoever is in a street or elsewhere in a town
- in willful violation of an ordinance or by-law of such town or of any rule or regulation for the government or use of any public reservation, parkway or boulevard made under authority of law by any department, officer or board in charge thereof,
- the substance of which is the drinking or possession of alcoholic beverage,

Arrest: The offender may be arrested without a warrant by an officer authorized to serve criminal process in the place where the offence is committed and kept in custody until he can be taken before a court having jurisdiction of the offence.

ACCOSTING ANOTHER IN VIOLATION OF A TOWN/CITY ORDINANCE/BY-LAW

Whoever in a street or other public place accosts or addresses another person with profane or obscene language, in willful violation of an ordinance or by-law of such town,

Arrest: The offender may be arrested without a warrant by an officer authorized to serve criminal process in the place where the offence is committed and kept in custody until he can be taken before a court having jurisdiction of the offence.

Note: Chapter 40 sec. 21D states that the paying of a City Ordinance fine shall not be deemed a criminal violation.

C. 276 § 20B. FUGITIVE FROM JUSTICE ARREST **WITHOUT** WARRANT

The arrest of a person may be lawfully made by any officer authorized to serve warrants in criminal cases, without a warrant, upon **reasonable information** that the accused stands **charged in another state with** a crime punishable **by death or by imprisonment for a term exceeding one year**.

But when so arrested the accused shall be taken with all practicable speed before a court or justice authorized to issue warrants in criminal cases and complaint shall be made against him under oath setting forth the ground for the arrest as in the preceding section; and thereafter his answer shall be heard as if he had been arrested on a warrant.

Note: Chapter 276 § 20A permits the arrest of a person wanted out of state for a crime wherein the punishment is 1 year or less but a Massachusetts arrest warrant must be sought in this case, a warrantless arrest would not be permissible.

C. 276 § 28. *ARREST WITHOUT WARRANT FOR CERTAIN OFFENSES*

STEALING: Any officer authorized to serve criminal process may arrest, without a warrant, and detain a person found **in the act of stealing property in the presence of the officer regardless of the value of the property stolen and may arrest, without a warrant,**

RO VIOLATION: Any officer authorized to serve criminal process may detain a person whom the officer has probable cause to believe has committed a misdemeanor by violating a temporary or permanent vacate, restraining, suspension and surrender.

DOMESTIC ABUSE: Any officer authorized to serve criminal process may arrest, without a warrant, and detain a person whom the officer has probable cause to believe has committed a misdemeanor involving abuse as defined in c. 209A § 1 or has committed an assault and battery in violation of c. 265 § 13A against a family or household member as defined in c.209A § 1.

KNOWLEDGE OF WARRANT: Any officer authorized to serve criminal process may arrest and detain a person charged with a misdemeanor, without having a warrant for such arrest in his possession, if the officer making such arrest and detention shall have actual knowledge that a warrant then in full force and effect for the arrest of such person has in fact issued.

C. 90 § 21. *ARREST WITHOUT WARRANT FOR CERTAIN MV OFFENSES*

Attorney Hanrahan's Note: This chapter grants authority to arrest for a variety of motor vehicle violations where the actual statute dealing with the particular offense may not specifically grant authority to arrest.

ARREST FOR OPERATING WITHOUT A LICENSE: Any officer authorized to make arrests may arrest without a warrant and keep in custody for not more than twenty-four hours, unless a Saturday, Sunday or a legal holiday intervenes, any person who, while operating a motor vehicle on any way, as defined in section one, violates the provisions of the first paragraph of chapter 90§ 10. Any arrest made pursuant to this paragraph shall be deemed an arrest for the criminal offense or offenses involved and not for any civil motor vehicle infraction arising out of the same incident.

ARREST FOR LICENSE SUSPENSION/REVOCATION: Any officer authorized to make arrests, provided such officer is in uniform or conspicuously displaying his badge of office, may arrest without a warrant and keep in custody for not more than twenty-four hours, unless Saturday, Sunday or legal holiday intervenes, any person, regardless of whether or not such person has in his possession a license to operate motor vehicles issued by the registrar, if such person upon any way or in any place to which the public has the right of access, or upon any way or in any place to which members of the public have access as invitees, operates a motor vehicle after his license or right to operate motor vehicles in this state has been suspended or revoked by the registrar.

ARREST FOR OUI: whoever upon any way or place to which the public has the right of access, or upon any way or in any place to which members of the public have access as invitees, or who the officer has probable cause to believe has operated or is operating a motor vehicle while under the influence of intoxicating liquor, marihuana or narcotic drugs, or depressant or stimulant substances, all as defined in section one of c. ninety-four C, or under the influence of the vapors of glue, carbon tetrachloride, acetone, ethylene, dichloride, toluene, chloroform, xylene or any combination thereof,

ARREST FOR USING WITHOUT AUTHORITY: whoever uses a motor vehicle without authority knowing that such use is unauthorized.

ARREST FOR REFUSING TO STOP/ID SELF TO POLICE: any person who, while operating or in charge of a motor vehicle, violates the provisions of C. 90 § 25.

ARREST FOR LEAVING THE SCENE WITH PERSONAL INJURY: whoever operates a motor vehicle upon any way or in any place to which members of the public have a right of access as invitees or licensees and without stopping and making known his name, residence and the register number of his motor vehicle goes away after knowingly colliding with or otherwise causing injury to any person.

ARREST FOR RECKLESS/NEGLIGENT OPERATION CAUSING SERIOUS BODILY INJURY: whoever operates a motor vehicle recklessly or negligently so that the lives or safety of the public might be endangered in violation of paragraph (a) of subdivision (2) of section 24 and by such operation causes another person serious bodily injury as defined in section 24L, or

ARREST FOR MV HOMICIDE: whoever commits motor vehicle homicide in violation of subsection (a) or (b) of section 24G.

Any person who is arrested pursuant to this section shall, at or before the expiration of the time period prescribed, be brought before the appropriate district court and proceeded against according to the law in criminal or juvenile cases, as the case may be, provided, however, that any violation otherwise cognizable as a civil infraction shall retain its character as, and be treated as, a civil infraction notwithstanding that the violator is arrested pursuant to this section for a criminal offense in conjunction with said civil infraction.

An investigator or examiner appointed under section twenty-nine may arrest without a warrant, keep in custody for a like period, bring before a magistrate and proceed against in like manner, any person operating a motor vehicle while under the influence of intoxicating liquor or marihuana, narcotic drugs, depressants or stimulant substances, all as defined in section one of c. ninety-four C, irrespective of his possession of a license to operate motor vehicles issued by the registrar.

C. 101 § 32. *ARREST OF HAWKERS, PEDDLERS AND DOOR-TO-DOOR SALESPERSONS; PROSECUTION*

The deputy director, inspectors of standards and, within their respective jurisdictions, sealers or deputy sealers of weights and measures, constables **and police officers shall arrest** and prosecute **every hawker and peddler, and transient vendor**, who they may have reason to believe is violating any provision of chapter 101 (Transient Vendor Laws).

ARREST POWERS: The chief of police**, a police officer**, or other official designated by a city council of a city or a board of selectmen of a town, **may arrest and prosecute a person who engages in the sale of goods door-to-door for future delivery who such official has reason to believe is violating the provisions of section thirty-four** (laws regarding hawkers and peddlers).

C. 91 § 58. *Waterway Violations: ARREST WITHOUT WARRANT*

Any officer qualified to serve criminal process may, within his jurisdiction, **arrest without a warrant** any person found in the act of committing a misdemeanor in or upon any of the **rivers, harbors, bays or sounds** within the commonwealth.

ARRESTS WITH A WARRANT and ARREST EXECUTION

ARREST WARRANTS PREFERRED METHOD OF ARREST

Both the United States Supreme Court and the Massachusetts Supreme Judicial Court have repeatedly stated that arrests, whenever possible, must be made pursuant to an arrest warrant. To encourage the seeking of arrest warrants, the courts have expressed the view that, where probable cause to arrest is marginal, they will sustain an arrest made pursuant to a warrant although a warrantless arrest might have been held invalid.

ARREST WARRANT CRITERIA

An arrest warrant is an order in writing, issued by an authorized court official, directed to officers authorized to serve criminal process and commanding them to arrest the person named or described therein and to bring such person before the court to answer to a criminal charge.

Important factors regarding arrest warrants

- The magistrate who issues an arrest warrant must have probable cause at the moment the warrant is issued. Information obtained later cannot be used to formulate probable cause[71]
- An application for a warrant may be based entirely on hearsay that would not be admissible at trial.[72]
- When executing an arrest warrant, a police officer's powers are state-wide.[73]
- The District Court may authorize the issuance of an arrest warrant in any case except where the accused is a juvenile less than 12 years of age, in which case the use of a summons should be used first, if the child does not appear a warrant may be issued.[74]

CONTENT OF ARREST WARRANT

Description of Person to be Arrested

- An arrest warrant must particularly describe the person to be seized.[75] Normally, reciting the person's name is sufficient.[76] Of course, additional identifying information - which will make locating and identifying the person to be arrested easier for the arresting officer - should also be included. Such things might include the person's residence, occupation and place of employment, identifying physical characteristics and other similar information.
- If the name of the person to be arrested is not known, whatever nickname or alias by which he or she is known should be recited in the arrest warrant.
- The warrant should also include the best physical description and any other information which would make it as easy as possible to locate and identify that person.

John Doe Warrants

- A so-called "John Doe" warrant, ***without*** **a further satisfactory and sufficient description**, is illegal and void.[77]

Offenses

- The warrant shall recite the substance of the offense charged and it shall command that the defendant be arrested and brought before the court.

Oath or Affirmation

- An arrest warrant issued pursuant to a complaint must be founded upon probable cause supported by oath or affirmation.[78]
- An arrest warrant shall be signed by the authorized court official issuing it.
- An officer applying for an arrest warrant may do so orally (along with any other supporting witnesses) to the person who is authorized to issue such warrant. Note: Search Warrant affidavits must be in writing.

---

[71] *Commonwealth v. Fielding*, 371 Mass. 97, 353 N.E.2d 719 (1977).
[72] *Commonwealth v. Stoico*, 45 Mass. App. Ct. 559, 669 N.E. 2d 1249 (1988).
[73] *Commonwealth v. Martin*, 98 Mass. 4 (1867); *Commonwealth v. Kerr*, 409 Mass. 284, 565 N.E.2d 1201 (1991).*See, generally, Commonwealth v. Wing Ng*, 37 Mass. App. Ct. 283, 639 N.E.2d 398 (1994).
[74] M.G.L. c. 119, § 54.
[75] *Won Sun v. U.S.*, 371 U.S. 471, 83 S.Ct. 407 (1963).
[76] Mass. R. Crim. P. 6(b)(1).
[77] *Commonwealth v. Crotty*, 92 Mass. 403 (1865).
[78] *Commonwealth v. Baldassini*, 357 Mass. 670, 260 N.E.2d 150 (1970).*See, Commonwealth v. Grzembski*, 393 Mass. 516, 471 N.E.2d 1308, 1311, note 7 (1984).

OBTAINING AN ARREST WARRANT

Obtaining an arrest warrant requires that the police establish to the satisfaction of an impartial judge (Supreme Judicial, Superior or District Courts),[79] or clerk/magistrate of the District Court (or their assistants),[80] that a crime has been committed and that there is probable cause to arrest the person named or described by the officer.[81]

ARREST WARRANT JURISDICTION

- Arrest warrants from a District Court may be issued for the arrest of an individual accused of committing a crime in the court's county or for such individual who is found in its county.
- A Massachusetts police officer may arrest an individual in any county in Massachusetts if the arrest is based on a valid arrest warrant, even if the police officer is a police officer in a municipality of another county.[82]
- A prisoner arrested out of the county where the warrant is returnable for a misdemeanor, if such person so requests, must be taken before a court in the county where the arrest was made to be admitted to bail.[83]
- If the crime charged is a felony, the officer who makes an arrest in another county shall convey the prisoner to the county where the warrant was issued.[84] (**Note:** In practice, generally the department holding a warrant will dispatch officers to return a felon arrested by another department).

EXECUTING AN ARREST WARRANT

Possession of the Arrest Warrant

The officer need not have the warrant in his or her possession at the time of arrest.[85] But, upon request, he or she must show the warrant to the defendant as soon as possible. According to the Massachusetts Rules of Criminal Procedure, if the officer does not have the warrant in his or her possession at the time of arrest, he or she shall then inform the defendant that a warrant has been issued and of the offense charged, but if the officer does not then know of the offense charged, he or she must inform the defendant thereof within a reasonable time after the arrest.[86]

Delay in the Execution

By statute, an officer who willfully delays service of a warrant is subject to a statutory fine of not more than fifty dollars ($50.00).[87] In addition, an *unreasonable* delay by the police in making an arrest after a warrant has been issued could result in the charges being dismissed. In *Com. v. Jones*, the SJC reasoned that an unreasonable delay could affect the defendant's ability to recall the events and jeopardize his defense.[88]

Return of the Arrest Warrant

The officer executing a warrant shall make a return thereof to the issuing court.[89] A defendant who has been arrested shall be brought before the court if it is in session and, if not, at its next session.

Arrest of Juveniles

Upon the arrest of a juvenile, the officer in charge of the police station shall notify the parent or guardian of the juvenile and the Probation Officer.[90] This is to permit the prompt release of a juvenile consistent with M.G.L. c. 119, § 66, which discourages the detention of juvenile offenders unless, in the opinion of the arresting officer or the Probation Department, cause exists to hold such juvenile. **See Juvenile Section of this manual for more.**

---

[79] M.G.L. c. 276, § 21.
[80] M.G.L. c. 318, § 32.
[81] *Coolidge v.New Hampshire*, 403 U.S. 443, 91 S.Ct. 2022 (1971).
[82] See M.G.L. c.276 § 23; M.G.L. c. 218 § 37.
[83] M.G.L. c. 276, § 29.
[84] M.G.L. c. 276, § 32.
[85] M.G.L. c. 276, § 28; *Commonwealth v. Walker*, 370 Mass. 548, 350 N.E.2d 678 (1976).
[86] Mass. Rules of Criminal Procedure 6(c)(3).
[87] M.G.L. c. 268, § 22.M.G.L. c. 268, § 22.
[88] *Commonwealth v. Jones*, 360 Mass. 498, 275 N.E.2d 143 (1971); *Commonwealth v. Horan*, 360 Mass. 793, 277 N.E.2d 491 (1972).
[89] *Id.* at 6(c)(4).
[90] M.G.L. c. 119, § 67.

ARRESTS IN A DWELLING

The law recognizes special protections in the home. In order to arrest someone in their home the police need a warrant (either an arrest warrant or a search warrant), consent to enter, or exigent or emergency circumstances. This is sometimes referred to as the *Payton Rule*.

AN ARREST WARRANT REQUIRED

- An arrest warrant "encompasses the power to enter a [suspect's] residence for the purpose of executing the warrant."[91] A separate search warrant is not required.[92]
- In addition to authorizing the arrest of a person in his or her home or dwelling where the police have reason to believe the suspect is, the police may enter and arrest an individual in a **hotel room** registered in his name.[93]

A "Reasonable Belief" standard

The police with a valid arrest warrant are only required to have a ***reasonable belief* that the location to be searched is the arrestee's residence,** and a ***reasonable belief* that the arrestee is in his or her residence** at the time the arrest warrant is executed.

> In ***Commonwealth v. Silva,*** police had a reasonable belief that the apartment was the suspect's dwelling and that the suspect was within that dwelling at the time the police sought to execute the arrest warrant, and thus the police entry and subsequent arrest of the defendant was lawful even though the suspect was not at home, where the building manager informed the police that the suspect was the sole lessee actively paying rent, the apartment door was ajar, the police looked through the hole and observed activity in the apartment, and the police made a tentative identification of the suspect before entering the apartment, although the person turned out to be the defendant, not the person for whom they had an arrest warrant.[94]

In the 2014 case of ***Commonwealth v. Gentile***, the SJC ruled that a law enforcement official's belief must be supported by "**specific articulable facts**" that, based on the totality of circumstances, permit a reasonable inference that, at the time of entry, the defendant is in the premises.

The time of day may be a factor

In ***Commonwealth v. DiBenedetto***, the "early morning entry" [between 5 a.m. and 6 a.m.] provided "reason to believe" defendant was home.[95]

In the ***United States v. Bervaldi,*** the court ruled that it was reasonable to believe, in the absence of contrary evidence, that the suspect would be at his residence at 6:00 in the morning.

Police Cannot Enter and Wait for Suspect to Return

When serving an arrest warrant the police cannot enter the suspect's home and wait for the suspect to return home, even if they have a reason to believe that the suspect will return to his home in a short period of time. Similarly, if the police enter a dwelling with a reasonable belief that the defendant is home they cannot remain in the home and wait for the defendant to return home.[96]

> In the 2009 case of ***Commonwealth v. Webster***, the Boston police had an arrest warrant for the defendant, Webster. They received information that Webster would be returning to his home within a short period of time. The officers went to Webster's apartment and instructed Webster's mother's fiancée to allow them in and waited for Webster to arrive. Eventually Webster returned and was placed under arrest. A firearm was discovered in his waistband. The Court stated "either because they had no right to enter, or because they had no right to stay, or both, the officers had no right to be inside the apartment when the defendant arrived…The

[91] *Commonwealth v. Nova*, 50 Mass.App.Ct. 633, 634-635, 740 N.E.2d 1021 (2000). See *Commonwealth v. Pietrass*, 392 Mass. 892, 897, 467 N.E.2d 1368 (1984) (arrest warrant allows police to enter dwelling).
[92] *Commonwealth v. Acosta*, 416 Mass. 279, 281, 627 N.E.2d 466 (1993). See *Commonwealth v. Allen*, 28 Mass.App.Ct. 589, 592, 554 N.E.2d 854 (1990) ("A person's home is not a castle against execution of a lawful arrest warrant directed against that person"). *Steagald v. United States*, 451 U.S. 204, 213, 101 S.Ct. 1642, 68 L.Ed.2d 38 (1981) (separate search warrant required to enter third party's residence to execute arrest warrant); *Commonwealth v. Silva*, 802 N.E.2d 535, 440 Mass. 772 (2004).
[93] *Commonwealth v. Brown*, 32 Mass. App. Ct. 669, 593 N.E.2d 245 (1992).
[94] *Commonwealth v. Silva*, , 802 N.E.2d 535 (2004).
[95] ***Commonwealth v. DiBenedetto***, 427 Mass. 414, 417–418, 693 N.E.2d 1007 (1998)
[96] *Commonwealth v. Webster*, MA App. Ct. (2009)

officers exploited their unlawful entry and their continued presence in the defendant's home to effectuate his arrest. Their behavior exemplified an 'unconstitutional shortcut'." The evidence was suppressed.[97]

Civil Liability

Like all violations of Constitutional rights, arresting someone in their home without a warrant (or one of the few exceptions to the warrant requirement) may leave the officer, the agency, and the municipality susceptible to civil liability. Recently, the Federal Appeals Court (8th circuit) denied qualified immunity to an officer who entered the home of a man who violated a Town ordinance to place him under arrest without a warrant.[98] See the Civil Liability section in the Overview section of this manual for more on civil liability and qualified immunity.

Third Party Dwelling

If a police officer seeks to arrest a suspect in a third party's dwelling, he or she must first obtain an arrest warrant authorizing the arrest *and* a search warrant authorizing the search of the third party's dwelling, unless exigent circumstances are present [99] or lawful consent to enter and search is obtained.[100]

However, the privacy interest is with *the resident* not the person wanted on the warrant.[101] When an arrestee is present in a third party's home rather than his own, the arrestee has the same right under the Fourth Amendment and Art. 14 to require that the police have a *reasonable basis to believe he will be present* when they enter the home in search of him, **but no more** – meaning if the police enter the third party home with only an arrest warrant the arrestee has no right to object to the entry of the third party's home as long as the police had a reason to believe he was there. The SJC stated that to do this would grant the defendant greater protections in the home of a friend than in his own home.[102] However, absent consent or an exigent situation, this would still be an unlawful entry, and any evidence located in the home connected to the resident would be subject to suppression, and the resident would have grounds for a violation of Constitutional rights in a civil proceeding.

Out of State Warrant

Executing an arrest on an out-of-state arrest warrant is considered a warrantless arrest when made under the authority of c. 276 § 20B (fugitive from justice law), therefore Massachusetts police officers need to apply for either a search warrant or an arrest warrant in order to make an arrest in a home if one of the exceptions to the warrant requirement are not present.

In ***Commonwealth v. Derosia***, the Keene Police (in New Hampshire) contacted the Gardner Police (in Massachusetts) and informed the Gardner Police that the defendant was staying with his mother in Gardner and that there was an outstanding New Hampshire arrest warrant for firearm possession. The Gardner Police went to the home and when the defendant answered the door the police entered and frisked the defendant finding a firearm. The SJC ruled that there were no exigent circumstances present and the police did not have a warrant therefore the entry was unlawful.[103]

Knock and Announce Rule

- To serve an arrest warrant on private property, police officers must first announce their authority and purpose and wait a reasonable period to be admitted.[104] Once a reasonable time has passed and they have not been admitted voluntarily, they may use whatever force is reasonably necessary to gain entrance.[105] The least amount of force that will accomplish an entrance should always be used. Aggressive knocking (even kicking) is allowed since they do not constitute forcible entry.[106]
- The Knock and Announce Rule is applicable only to forcible entries.[107] See the Search Warrant section of this manual for more on the knock and announce rule.

[97] *Commonwealth v. Webster*, MA App. Ct. (2009)
[98] Mitchell v. Shearrer, 2013 U.S. App. LEXUS 18756.
[99] *Warden v. Hayden*, 387 U.S. 294, 87 S.Ct. 1642 (1967); *U.S. v. Santana*, 427 U.S. 38, 96 S.Ct. 2406 (1976).
[100] *Commonwealth v. DeRosia*, 402 Mass. 284, 522 N.E.2d 408 (1988).
[101] *Steagald v. United States*, 451 U.S. 204 (1981).
[102] *Commonwealth v. Tatum*, SJC (2013).
[103] *Commonwealth v. DeRosia*, 402 Mass. 284, 522 N.E.2d 408 (1988).
[104] *Commonwealth v. Antwine*, 417 Mass. 637, 632 N.E.2d 818 (1994).
[105] *Commonwealth v. Reynolds*, 120 Mass. 190 (1876) (invalidated in part by *Steagald v. U.S.*, cited above).
[106] *Commonwealth v. Rivera*, 429 Mass. 620, 710 N.E. 2d 950 (1999).
[107] *Commonwealth v. Sepulveda*, 406 Mass. 180, 546 N.E.2d 879 (1989).

Exception to the Knock and Announce Rule

- The requirement that the police knock, identify themselves, and announce their purpose "[b]before attempting forcibly to enter a private dwelling to execute a warrant,"[108] may be suspended where necessary to "avoid the potential destruction of evidence."
- To justify the unannounced entry, the Commonwealth must show that there is probable cause to believe that the evidence will be destroyed if the knock and announce rule is observed.
- This showing must be made in advance in an affidavit submitted to the magistrate together with the warrant application.[109]
- The showing may also be made after the fact, "if exigent circumstances arise at the threshold of the search [or arrest] justifying both the unannounced entry and the failure to obtain prior judicial authorization."
- In deciding whether enough facts were present to amount to probable cause to believe that the evidence would be destroyed, a court "will not examine each fact in isolation, but rather examine all of the facts together."[110] Even several factors, "innocent of themselves," when combined, may amount to probable cause.[111] The police officers' expertise and experience may be considered as a factor in the probable cause determination.[112]

On-site Reassessment or doorway reappraisal - No Knock Warrant

Even where the police have a "no knock" warrant, they must still review the circumstances at the scene and not enter unannounced if the facts justifying such a procedure are no longer present.[113] The police may attempt to deceive the suspect into voluntarily opening the door, or gain entrance by a ruse, if this will result in a safe and successful apprehension with less destruction of property or risk of harm to persons.[114] What this means is that if a police officer unlawfully enters the home of a third party to arrest a visitor in a warrant the arrestee will have no right to object to the entry (i.e. any evidence found implicating the arrestee will not be suppressed). However, the officer would still be violating the rights of the resident, and any evidence uncovered against the resident will likely be suppressed. Additionally, the resident may have cause to bring a civil action against the officer.

For a detailed explanation of the Knock and Announce Rule see the Search Warrant section of this manual.

ARREST WARRANTS & EXECUTION

108 *Commonwealth v. Antwine,* 417 Mass. 637, 638, 632 N.E.2d 818 (1994)
109 *Commonwealth v. Jimenez,*
110 *Commonwealth v. West,*55 Mass.App.Ct. 467, 470, 771 N.E.2d 815 (2002).
111 *Commonwealth v. Fisher,*54 Mass.App.Ct. 41, 44, 763 N.E.2d 1106 (2002).
112 *Commonwealth v. West, supra.* See *Commonwealth v. Feijoo,* 419 Mass. 486, 498, 646 N.E.2d 118 (1995) (officer's experience in investigating child abuse is factor supporting probable cause).
113 *Commonwealth v. Antwine*, 417 Mass. 637, 632 N.E.2d 818 (1994).
114 *Commonwealth v. Cundriff*, 382 Mass. 137, 415 N.E.2d 172 (1980).

WARRANTLESS ARRESTS IN A DWELLING

ENTERING PRIVATE PROPERTY TO MAKE A WARRANTLESS ARREST

Not all arrests require a warrant. The courts, and in rare cases the legislature, have created a number of exceptions to the warrant requirement established by the Fourth Amendment, even when an arrest is made in a home.

CONSENT

Police officers may enter private property to make a warrantless arrest when they have been granted permission by someone with authority, or in some cases *apparent authority*, over the premises. See the Consent section in the Warrantless Search section of this manual for more.

EXIGENT CIRCUMSTANCES TO ARREST IN A DWELLING

The police may enter a premises or a private dwelling to make an arrest without a warrant where exigent circumstances are present. However, for the purposes of making an arrest the criteria is not exactly the same as the criteria to enter in order to seize evidence. In the leading case of ***Commonwealth v. Forde,***[115] the Supreme Judicial Court declared that police must be able to show that it was impractical to obtain an arrest warrant and that an immediate arrest was necessary. Some of the factors which support a finding of exigent or emergency conditions to enter a home an arrest were delineated in *Commonwealth v. Forde* and include the following:

a. The crime was one of violence and the suspect was known or believed to be armed;

b. The suspect was known or reasonably believed to be in the building;

c. There was a likelihood that the suspect would or might escape if not apprehended immediately;

d. Whether entry would require force or could be accomplished in a peaceable manner;

e. Whether entry would have to be made at night or could be made during the daytime (when court magistrates authorized to issue warrants are more available); and,

f. The length of time it would take to obtain a warrant.[116]

> In its 1999 decision of ***Commonwealth v. Morrison,*** the SJC found that exigent circumstances existed, justifying the warrantless entry of an apartment to arrest an overnight guest of the woman that had a restraining order against the defendant.[117] The court found that exigent circumstances were present since a witness reported that the pregnant woman was engaged in a furious argument with a man whom the police were justified in concluding was probably the defendant (and the subject of a restraining order). Even though the woman said she did not want protection, and that she would ask the court in the morning to vacate the order, this made no difference. The SJC noted that domestic violence victims often tend to minimize and deny the severity and extent of abuse.

Case Examples of circumstances that the court determined were <u>not</u> exigent

- In ***Commonwealth v. Midi,*** exigent circumstances were not found where the police entered a domestic violence suspect's apartment to make a warrantless felony arrest.[118] There the court found no evidence that the suspect was considered dangerous, that he had made any threats, that the victim had expressed fear that he would do her harm, that another crime would be committed, or that evidence would disappear.[119]
- In ***Commonwealth v. DiGeronimo***, the court held that the preservation of intoxication evidence was not a sufficiently important exigency (in a misdemeanor OUI case) to justify a warrantless entry into the suspect's house to effect an arrest. The possibility of alcohol evidence dissipating did not reach the level of exigency required for a warrantless entry.[120]

Note: the police cannot knowingly create an exigency in order to circumvent the warrant requirement. See the warrantless search section of this manual for more on this topic.

---

[115] *Commonwealth v. Forde*, 367 Mass. 798, 329 N.E.2d 717 (1975).
[116] *See, Commonwealth v. Hoffman*, 385 Mass. 122, 430 N.E.2d 1190 (1982); *Commonwealth v. Pietrass*, 392 Mass. 892, 467 N.E.2d 1368, 1372 (1984); *Commonwealth v. Jeffers*, 27 Mass. App. Ct. 1162, 539 N.E.2d 1040 (1989); *Commonwealth v. Viriyahiranpaiboon*, 412 Mass. 2234, 588 N.E.2d 643 (1992).
[117] *Commonwealth v. Morrison*, 429 Mass. 511, 710 N.E. 2d 584 (1999).
[118] *Commonwealth v. Midi*, 46 Mass. App. Ct. 591, 708 N.E. 2d 124 (1999).
[119] *Commonwealth v. Midi*, 46 Mass. App. Ct. 591, 708 N.E. 2d 124 (1999).
[120] *Commonwealth v. DiGeronimo*, 38 Mass. App. Ct. 714, 652 N.E.2d 148 (1995).

Entering a premise to quell a breach of the peace

The courts have permitted, in rare circumstances, the police to enter private property, including dwellings, in order to quell an ongoing breach of the peace.

- In ***Commonwealth v. Mullins***, the police were authorized to enter an apartment and arrest the occupant for the loud playing of a radio which disturbed the neighbors, when such conduct was continuing when the police arrived.[121] The police had also repeatedly responded and asked the occupant to lower the radio and it was subsequently turned back up each time.

Compare with:

- In ***Commonwealth v. Kiser***, police officers who had allegedly been assaulted by the occupant of an apartment when the occupant attempted to prevent the police entry as they investigated a report of a loud party lacked exigent circumstances justifying the entry into the premises to effect a warrantless arrest of the occupant.[122] In this case the occupant agreed to turn down the music after being asked to do so by the police. The occupant's conduct could not be termed violent, since even the police officer testified that the occupant was attempting to keep the officer from looking in the apartment, not to attack him, and the police knew where the occupant lived and could easily obtain a warrant.

Fresh and Continues Pursuit

A police officer who is in pursuit of a fleeing felon may pursue the felon (or jailable misdemeanor) from a public place into a private home or a private building. **See the Warrantless Search section of this manual for more on this topic.**

Arrests on the Threshold

Generally, a warrantless arrest on a threshold of a dwelling is valid as occurring in a public place.[123] Should a suspect thereafter flee from the threshold inside a building, the police may pursue him or her if they believe that a failure to do so would result in the loss or destruction of evidence, or if *exigent circumstances* are present which otherwise justify the warrantless entry of a dwelling.

However, in Massachusetts, the SJC has indicated that it does not want to create a situation where the Courts are bogged down with arguments over whether or not the arrest was executed on the threshold or inside the home. For this reason, if the police approach the defendant's home with probable cause to make an arrest of a known suspect, they must have a valid warrant or exigent circumstances in order to make an arrest. The SJC, in ***Commonwealth v. Marquez***, ruled the arrest of a suspect on the threshold of his residence is impermissible because it may encourage police officers to forego the arrest warrant requirement.[124] However, if probable cause to arrest did not develop until after the police were at the residence, with the suspect at the threshold, a warrantless arrest at the threshold would be permissible.

COMMUNITY CARETAKER/EMERGENCY CIRCUMSTANCES

Where the police — in their role as a *community caretaker* — find themselves compelled to enter a private dwelling "to protect or preserve life or avoid serious injury", (e.g., neighbor reports cries of pain coming from inside dwelling), they may do so even in the absence of a criminal exigency.[125] Once lawfully inside, they may effect an arrest if other previously mentioned legal requirements are met.

PRIVATE BUSINESS

Business premises, where their occupants have a legitimate expectation of privacy, are entitled to constitutional protections (although not to the same degree as dwelling places).[126] In the absence of exigent circumstances or consent, the police must obtain a warrant before entering private business or commercial premises to make an arrest.[127]

---

[121] *Commonwealth v. Mullins*, 31 Mass. App. Ct. 954, 582 N.E.2d 562 (1991).
[122] *Commonwealth v. Kiser*, 48 Mass. App. Ct. 647, 724 N.E. 2d 348 (2000).
[123] *U.S. v. Santana*, 427 U.S. 38, 96 S.Ct. 2406 (1976); *Commonwealth v. Boswell*, 374 Mass. 263, 372 N.E.2d 237 (1978).*U.S. v. Santana*, 427 U.S. 38, 96 S.Ct. 2406 (1976); *Commonwealth v. Boswell*, 374 Mass. 263, 372 N.E.2d 237 (1978).
[124] *Commonwealth v. Marquez*, 434 Mass. 370, 749 N.E.2d 673Mass. (2001).
[125] *Commonwealth v. Bates*, 28 Mass. App. Ct. 217, 548 N.E.2d 889 (1990); *Mincey v. Arizona*, 437 U.S. 385, 98 S.Ct. 2408 (1978).
[126] *Marshall v. Barlow's, Inc.*, 436 U.S. 307, 98 S.Ct. 1816 (1978).
[127] *Commonwealth v. Olivares*, 30 Mass. App. Ct. 596, 571 N.E.2d 416 (1991).

ARREST PROCEDURES AND ARRESTEE RIGHTS

USE OF FORCE IN MAKING ARREST

In making an arrest, police are authorized to use that amount of force which is reasonably necessary to accomplish the arrest and detain and secure the arrestee.[128]

The nature and severity of the force which would be reasonably necessary depends on all the circumstances, including such factors as:

- The seriousness of the offense - especially the degree of violence or harm involved or threatened,
- The physical characteristics and ability of the offender and the arresting officer,
- The presence of weapons,
- The proximity of other persons who might be in danger or who might interfere with the arrest,
- The number of offenders in relation to the number of police,
- The offender's known reputation for resorting to violence,
- And many other factors.

NO RIGHT TO RESIST ARREST

In the absence of excessive or unnecessary force by an arresting officer, an arrestee has no right to resist a lawful or even an unlawful arrest.[129] M.G.L. c.268, §32b criminalizes the action of resisting arrest.[130] An officer may use whatever force is reasonably necessary to overcome the arrestee's resistance, but may not use excessive force.

See the Public Justice section of this manual for more on Resisting arrest.

ARRESTEE/DETAINEE RIGHTS

PROTECTIVE CUSTODY

The protective custody (PC) laws are designed to protect intoxicated persons from being harmed and/or harming others. When a person is taken into protective custody he/she is not considered "under arrest." A person who is incapacitated may be assisted by a police officer with or without consent to:

1. his residence
2. to a facility, or
3. to a police station.

Breathalyzer: A PC who has been taken to the police station has a right to a breathalyzer test (they should be informed in writing).

Breath results:
BAC of .00 - .05: Immediate release
BAC of .051 - .099: police can use coordination tests
BAC of .10 or above: held in protective custody

Duration: The PC may be held until no longer **incapacitated** but no longer than 12 hours.

[128] *Commonwealth v. Klein*, 372 Mass. 823, 363 N.E.2d 1313 (1977).
[129] *Commonwealth v. Moreira*, 388 Mass. 596, 447 N.E.2d 1224 (1983); *Commonwealth v. Francis*, 24 Mass. App. Ct. 526 (1987).
[130] See *Commonwealth v. Katykhin*, 59 Mass.App.Ct. 261, 794 N.E.2d 1291 (2003).

Incapacitated: the condition of an intoxicated person who, by reason of the consumption of intoxicating liquor is (1) unconscious, (2) in need of medical attention, (3) likely to suffer or cause physical harm or damage property, or (4) disorderly.

Drugs: The PC law does not include those who are intoxicated by drugs.

Phone call right applies "upon presumption."

See the Alcohol section under the Statutory Law Section for more on Protective Custody.

RIGHT TO INDEPENDENT MEDICAL EXAM

A person who has been arrested for OUI has the right to have an independent medical exam at his expense and at his request. The person arrested shall be given a copy of M.G.L. c. 263, § 5A, unless a copy is conspicuously posted in the station or place of detention.

Invoking right to medical exam: The police are not required to transport the arrestee to the hospital if he/she requests an independent medical exam. Basically, the only requirement is that the police arrange to have the person promptly bailed.

No right to breathe test: Technically, a person arrested for OUI does not have a legal right to a breathalyzer test, although it is strongly advised to offer one.

See the Motor Vehicle law section of this manual for full coverage of OUI related laws & requirements.

RIGHT TO TELEPHONE CALL

A person arrested has a legal right to make a telephone call within one hour of being booked and they should be notified of this right upon arrival or "upon being booked."

Chapter 276 § 33A states "the police official in charge of the station or other place of detention having a telephone wherein a person is held in custody, shall permit the use of the telephone, at the expense of the arrested person, for the purpose of allowing the arrested person to communicate with his family or friends, or to arrange for release on bail, or to engage the services of an attorney. Any such person **shall be informed forthwith upon his arrival at such station** or place of detention, of his right to so use the telephone, and such use shall be permitted within one hour thereafter."

The right to a phone call begins at the time of formal arrest (i.e. booking) and not when custody begins.[131]

Failure to allow phone call: If the police intentionally neglect to allow the arrestee to make a phone call the exclusionary rule may be utilized but if the error is an oversight the exclusionary rule is not automatic. Generally, if the police mistakenly neglect to allow a phone call the exclusionary rule will not be imposed.

RIGHT TO KNOW REASON FOR THE ARREST

A person arrested has a legal right to know why he/she were arrested. Chapter 263 § 1 imposes a criminal penalty for failing to provide the true reason for the arrest, which includes refusing to answer questions related to why the arrest was made and also providing false reasons. **Note:** the charge can be changed at the complaint, booking, or indictment stage.

RIGHT TO PROMPT PRESENTMENT

A person arrested has a legal right to be brought to court in a timely fashion. As a result of this right the Courts have created was is referred to as the Safe Harbor Rule. The **Safe Harbor Rule** (sometimes referred to as the **Rosario Rule**) limits police questioning to a maximum of 6 hours from the time of the arrest. Sometimes call "the Rosario Rule." **See the Interview & Interrogation section of this manual for more.**

[131] Commonwealth v. Rivera 441 Mass. 358 (2004)

RIGHT TO AN INDEPENDENT DETERMINATION OF PROBABLE CAUSE

Jenkins Hearing: If an arrested individual is not released on bail, the Massachusetts Constitution (Part 1, Art. 14) requires that a probable cause determination must be made within 24 hours of the arrest.[132] The department should contact a court official and have them evaluate and approve the probable cause used to make the arrest.

Warrant Arrest: Someone arrested on a warrant and being held beyond 24 hours does not have a right to a Jenkins Hearing, as probable cause has already been established by the issuing of the warrant.

FOREIGN NATIONALS – CONSULAR NOTIFICATION

The SJC ruled that foreign nationals arrested or detained have the right to have their consulate notified, pursuant to Article 6 of the Vienna Convention. If these rights are not followed the defendant may challenge his/her conviction.[133] The defendant must show that the outcome of the case would have been different had the consulate been notified. When a non-US resident is placed under arrest, from a nation covered under Article 6 of the Vienna Convention (includes most modern nations) the arresting agency should notify the appropriate US consulate of the arrest.

Pursuant to the Vienna Convention, police officers must:[134]

(1) Notify <u>all</u> foreign nationals who are arrested or detained "without delay" that they have a right to have their consulate notified of their detention. If a foreign national requests consular notification, the police shall inform the consulate "without delay."

(2) Notify a foreign national's consulate, regardless of whether the detainee requests that you do so (and even if they request that you do not do so), if the detainee is from any of the 57 "mandatory notification: countries which require that their consular officials be notified (see appendix for list of mandatory notification countries).

Note: See the end of this section for a list of countries covered.

HEARING IMPAIRED ARRESTEE

A police officer who arrests a hearing impaired or deaf person must obtain (and according to the statute the arresting officer must pay for) a qualified interpreter to assist the person concerning any interrogation, warning, notice of rights or the taking of any statement.[3] Failure to do so may make invalid any notice given with respect to his or right to an independent medical examination under M.G.L. c. 263, § 5A. In fact, any statement or expression not obtained through an interpreter will be inadmissible in evidence.

RIGHT NOT TO BE UNLAWFULLY ARRESTED

A police officer may face criminal penalties for making a false arrest. See below statutes:

> G.L. chapter 263 § 2 states "an officer who arrests or takes into or detains in custody a person, pretending to have a process (i.e. warrant) if he has none, or pretending to have a different process from that which he has, shall be punished by a fine of not more than $1,000 or by imprisonment for not more than one year."

Although, a police officer may face criminal charges for making a false arrest, the arrestee has no right to resist (even if the arrest is false). The only time an arrestee may lawful resist arrest is when an officer is using excessive force to make the arrest. See Chapter 263 § 3 below immunity for assisting officers:

> G.L. chapter 263 § 3 states "No action, except for use of excessive force, shall lie against any officer other than the arresting officer, by reason of the fact that, in good faith and in the performance of his duties, he participates in the arrest or imprisonment of any person believed to be guilty of a crime unless it can be shown that such other officer in the performance of his duties took an active part in the arrest or imprisonment as aforesaid, either by ordering or directing that said arrest or imprisonment take place or be made, or by actually initiating the making and carrying out of said arrest and imprisonment. No action, except for use of excessive force, shall lie against any bystander assisting an officer in making an arrest, at the request of the officer.

RIGHT TO MEDICAL TREATMENT

Arrested persons should be inspection for illnesses and injuries and offered medical necessary medical treatment. Chapter 276 § 33 states " Whenever a person is arrested for a crime and is taken to or confined in a jail, police station or

[132] *Jenkins v. Chief Justice of Dist. Court Dept.*, 416 Mass. 221, 619 N.E.2d 324 (1993).
[133] *Com. v. Gautreaux*, 458 Mass. 741 (2011)
[134] Middlesex DA's Caselaw Update – Chiefs quarterly Meeting 6/7/2011

lockup, **the officer in charge** thereof shall **immediately examine the prisoner**, and if he finds any **bruises, cuts or other injuries** shall **forthwith make a written report thereof to the chief of police** of the town concerned, or in Boston to the police commissioner, and in towns where there is no chief of police to the selectmen. The requirement that the prisoner be examined shall not be deemed to compel the removal of clothing. When a person is transferred from one place of confinement to another prior to his arraignment in court or to his release, the requirement that he shall be examined shall apply only to the place to which he is first taken after his arrest. The law states that "whoever violates this section shall be punished by a fine of not more than $10."

Civil Liability

Police officers can also be found civilly liable when they are purposefully indifferent to the medical needs of an arrestee. If a prisoner requires medical attention it must not be delayed.[135]

RIGHT TO BAIL

An arrestee has a Constitutional right to bail. However, A person arrested on a **default warrant** for a felony or a misdemeanor punishable by imprisonment for more than 100 days may be released on bail or recognizance **only by a justice of the court having jurisdiction over the place where the person was arrested or is being held, or by a justice of the court that issued the warrant.**

Chapter 262 § 24 states that the maximum fee to be charged by any person authorized to take bail or release on **personal recognizance** in the case of a person arrested for any misdemeanor or felony **shall be $40**. If, in addition to recognizing for a court within the territorial jurisdiction of the magistrate authorizing the release, the arrested person is being required to recognize for a court outside of such territorial jurisdiction, the person, so authorized, may charge an **additional $5** for each such extraterritorial recognizance, but in **no event shall the total fee for any release exceed $50**

Note: before a court official releases someone on bail the court official is suppose to check the warrant management system to ensure there are no other outstanding warrants.

Arrestee Must Comply with Booking

In the 1994 case of *Commonwealth v. Whitcomb*, the Appeals Court ruled that "until the booking procedures were completed, we hold that the defendant was not entitled to a bail hearing."[136]

ARREST PROCEDURES & ARRESTEE RIGHTS

[135] Johnson v. Summers, 411 Mass. 82 (1991)
[136] Commonwealth v. Whitcomb, 37 Mass.App.Ct. 929 (1994)

STATUTORY LOCK-UP REQUIREMENTS

POLICE LOCK-UP REQUIREMENTS	
Town; erection and maintenance of lockup **c. 40 § 34**	Summarized: Each town containing more than 5,000 inhabitants shall, maintain a secure and convenient lockup to which persons arrested without a warrant may be held **Penalty:** If a town neglects to provide and maintain a lockup as herein required, it shall forfeit $10.00 for each month during which such neglect continues. **Note:** This statute permits a magistrate to order a municipal lock-up (i.e. police department) to hold a bailable arrestee who was arrested in the Town, or in a Town where the court is located. **Definition**: for the purposes of this section, the word "maintain" shall include the provision of any prescribed medication and nutritionally adequate meals to a person committed to such lockup
Bar Coverings **c. 40 § 36B**	Each Police holding cell **shall have a protective covering of high-impact, transparent wall facing**. Such protective covering shall cover all bar structures accessible to such detained persons. Adequate ventilation shall be provided to persons detained in the cell.
Audio Monitoring **c. 40 § 36B**	At **least one** cell within the lockup facility shall have installed within it an electronic audio system whereby a police officer or other lockup personnel at the duty desk within the lockup facility is able to audibly monitor the cell. **Exception:** an audible device is not required if at least one of the cells within lockup facility is within audible range of the duty desk without electronic assistance.
Cell Checks **c. 40 § 36B**	Each occupied cell should be **physically or visibly** checked by a law enforcement officer or other lockup personnel as often as is required by a reasonable standard of care of detainees. Every lockup facility **shall have** installed within the cell area an **electronic security device** which w**ill record the date and time of day of each cell check** made by a law enforcement officer or other lockup personnel. All checks made shall be recorded on such electronic security device.
Suicide/Death in a Lock-up	Whenever a person is in police custody, and commits suicide or dies at a lockup facility (or inflicts self-injury which subsequently results in his death), the OIC shall make a report of the incident, identifying the deceased and describing the circumstances of the death. **Report Requirements:** One copy of the report shall be sent, within 7 days of the death (including related documents) to the medical examiner's office, and one copy of the report shall be retained in the lockup files. **Next of Kin Rights:** The medical examiner may send a copy, along with other related documents, upon request (within 14 days), to the next of kin. If an autopsy is performed the next of kin have **48 hours** to have a physician of their choice to perform their own autopsy.
Threat/Attempt OIC requirement **c. 40 § 36A**	Whenever a person in police custody attempts or threatens suicide at a lockup facility, the OIC shall, **within 24 hours**, record in the criminal history systems board computer the name, address, and the age of the person, the charge or reason for the detention and the nature and date of the attempt or threat. Note: this information shall be made part of the criminal offender record information system. It shall be disseminated only to those agencies and offices authorized under section one hundred and seventy-two of c. six. **Notify Receiving Agency** Whenever a person in police custody attempts or threatens suicide at a lockup facility and the person is transferred to another lockup facility, the OIC shall notify **in writing** the receiving lockup facility of the exact nature of the attempt or threat.
Accessibility of lockup to police **c. 40 § 37**	Police lockups shall at all reasonable hours be accessible to the state police, sheriffs, constables and police officers for any legal and proper use; and a keeper thereof neglecting to keep it so accessible, or refusing to said officers the use of the same, shall be punished by a fine of not less than $5.00 nor more than $20.00.
Separation f Sexes **c.276 § 53**	An officer who, having the custody or control of prisoners, causes or permits male and female prisoners to be transported together to or from a court in a vehicle, in a city of more than 30,000 inhabitants according to the latest census, shall be punished by a fine of not more than $20.

COMPELLING EVIDENCE FROM DETAINED OR ARRESTED PERSONS

Under certain circumstances, the police may force a suspect to provide physical evidence without violating his or her Fourth Amendment protection against unreasonable searches and seizures. Courts generally only allow the compelled seizure of physical evidence from arrestees. The Supreme Court has held that police may require an arrested suspect to provide physical evidence, such as hair, voice or handwriting samples, as well as fingerprints and DNA.

Two bases for permitting police to compel arrestee to submit physical evidence

There are two bases for permitting the police to compel arrestee to submit physical evidence. First, the seizure of the physical evidence is justified because it is not an "unreasonable" search since the police did have probable cause to make the arrest. Second, arrestees are found to have a lower expectation of privacy of what is an acceptable intrusion of their person by virtue of their arrest.

Exclusionary rule and fruits of the poisonous tree applies

The tangible or physical evidence may be excluded at trial if it was obtained during an unlawful arrest or detention, since that constitutes a search which was not supported by probable cause.[137] The physical evidence taken from the suspect may also be excluded if a severe intrusion of the body was made to obtain it (e.g., stomach pumping.)[138]

TYPES OF EVIDENCE THAT MAY BE TAKEN FROM AN ARRESTEE

In regards to the Fifth Amendment, courts have consistently held that the right against self-incrimination only applies to testimonial evidence. Although the Fifth Amendment to the United States Constitution dictates that no person "shall be compelled in any criminal case to be a witness against himself . . .," that Amendment is not violated when tangible or physical evidence is taken from a suspect, against his or her will, where the evidence is not testimonial in nature.[139]

When a suspect is arrested and evidence related to the crime is found on the arrestee's person it may be seized as a **search incident to arrest**. Similarly, the following evidence or identifying information *may* be taken from an arrestee providing *it is relevant* to the case:

Fingerprints

Fingerprints may be taken of arrested persons.[140] M.G.L. c. 263, § 1A provides that, "Whoever is arrested by virtue of process, or is taken into custody by an officer, and charged with the commission of a felony shall be fingerprinted . . ."[141] Although the statute specifically states "felony" it is generally accepted that fingerprints are permissible on misdemeanor arrests as well. Generally, the purpose of taking the arrestee's fingerprints is for identification purposes but they may also be taken for evidentiary purposes.

Photographs

Photographs of a suspect may be taken in public.[142]. Also, M.G.L. c. 263, § 1A declares that persons arrested or taken into custody and charged with a felony "may be photographed". Although the statute specifically states "felony" it is generally accepted that fingerprints are permissible on misdemeanor arrests as well. Generally, the purpose of taking the arrestee's photograph is for identification purposes but they may also be taken for evidentiary purposes.

ARREST PROCEDURES & ARRESTEE RIGHTS

---

[137] *Davis v. Mississippi*, 394 U.S. 721, 89 S.Ct. 1394 (1969) (fingerprint evidence taken from defendant who was arrested without probable cause and unlawfully detained was excluded)
[138] *Rochin v. California*, 342 U.S. 165, 72 S.Ct. 205 (1952) (police tried to pry pills out of the suspect's mouth as he tried to swallow them; failing, police took him to a hospital where an emetic solution and stomach pump were used to retrieve the pills; the Court held those police practices to be "conduct that shocks the conscience" and violative of due process). *See, Matter of Lavigne*, 418 Mass. 831, 641 N.E.2d 1328 (1994) (court held that the compelled extraction of a person's blood is intrusive and requires that the suspect be afforded notice and opportunity to be heard before compelling his compliance). *But see, Commonwealth v. Miles*, 420 Mass. 67, 648 N.E.2d 719 (1995) (court held that physical exam to check suspect for poison ivy is considerably less intrusive and condition is temporary, thereby justifying compelled submission without a prior hearing.)
[139] *U.S. v. Dionisio*, 410 U.S. 1, 93 S.Ct. 764 (1973) (Court upheld grand jury subpoena requiring defendant to provide a voice sample).
[140] *Napolitano v. U.S.*, 340 F.2d 313 (1st Cir. 1965).
[141] *See,Davis v. Mississippi* (cited above) for a decision in which fingerprint evidence was excluded because the defendant had been illegally taken into custody.
[142] *U.S. v. Crews*, 445, U.S. 463, 100 S.Ct. 1244 (1980); *Commonwealth v. Haas*, 373 Mass. 545, 369 N.E.2d 692 (1977).

Handwriting samples may be taken if related to the case.[143]

Clothing and Footwear may be seized without a warrant if it is relevant evidence, for instance a person who is being charged with assault & batter by means of a shod foot should have his/her footwear seized as evidence. The jury needs to decide whether or not the footwear was capable of inflicting serious bodily injury and generally the actual item needs to be presented.

Further analysis permissible

In the 2015 case of ***Commonwealth v. Arzola***, the SJC ruled that a search warrant was not required to analyze a blood stain on a lawfully seized article of clothing that was seized subsequent to the defendant's arrest for a robbery involving a stabbing. The Court "A defendant generally has a reasonable expectation of privacy in the short he or she is wearing, but where, as here, the shirt was lawfully seized, a defendant has no reasonable expectation of privacy that would prevent the analysis of that shirt to determine whether blood found on it belonged to the victim or the defendant."

Voice samples

Voice samples may be taken if relevant to the case.[144] Voice samples do not require Miranda warnings as long as the intent is strictly to identify the voice of the suspect and not illicit an incriminating statement.

Fingernail scrapings and clippings may be taken without a warrant if relevant to the case/investigation.[145]

Blood samples for OUI

Blood samples for alcohol content analysis may be taken using standard medical procedures by qualified medical authorities.[146] **Note:** See the OUI section of this manual for more on this topic.

Breathalyzer Tests

A person arrested for operating under the influence of alcohol may face sanctions, in the form of license and right to operate suspensions, for not submitting to a breath or blood test to determine their blood alcohol content. However, a person arrested for OUI does not have a "right" to a Breathalyzer test. A person taken into protective custody does have a right to a Breathalyzer test. **Note**: See OUI section of this manual for more on this topic.

Hair samples

Hair samples from the suspect's head, chest and pubic area may be taken without a warrant if relevant to the investigation.[147] Attorney Hanrahan's note: in regards to taking pubic hair samples, in most cases this type of evidence seizure will involve a "strip" search. Be sure to comply with strip search procedures discussed later in this section.

Benzidine test

Benzidine test (to detect blood) may be administered without a warrant to an arrestee's body or clothing if relevant to the investigation.[148]

Videotapes

Courts find that videotapes are a reliable evidentiary resource.[149] Videotapes are admissible as evidence provided they are relevant, they provide a fair representation of that which they purport to depict, and they are not otherwise barred by an exclusionary rule.[150]

---

[143] *U.S. v. Mara*, 410 U.S. 19, 93 S.Ct. 744 (1973) (grand jury witness compelled by subpoena to provide handwriting samples).
[144] *U.S. v. Dionisio*, 410 U.S. 1, 93 S.Ct. 764 (1973) (suspect of grand-jury probe compelled by subpoena to provide voice exemplar).
[145] *Commonwealth v. Murphy*, 412 U.S. 291, 93 S.Ct. 2000 (1973) (suspect, not under arrest and who voluntarily came to police station, could have scrapings removed from under his fingernails where police had probable cause to suspect him of the strangulation death of his wife). *Commonwealth v. Appleby*, 358 Mass. 407, 265 N.E.2d 485 (1970) (fingernail clippings taken as part of search incident to arrest).
[146] *Schmerber v. California*, 384 U.S. 757, 86 S.Ct. 1826 (1966) (the defendant was under arrest).
[147] *Commonwealth v. Taryer*, 369 Mass. 302, 345 N.E.2d 671 (1975) (the defendant was under arrest). See *Commonwealth v. Downey*, *Supra*, (A grand jury has the power to order a defendant to provide hair samples).
[148] *Commonwealth v. Appleby*, 358 Mass. 407, 265 N.E.2d 485 (1970) (upheld as part of a search incident to arrest).

Gun Powder Residue Tests: gun powder residue tests may be taken if relevant to the investigation.

Field Sobriety Tests

Although this generally occurs prior to an arrest, a motorist that is lawfully detained or arrested may be ordered to perform standard field sobriety tests to help determine whether he or she was operating under the influence.[151]

DNA Testing

In 2013, the U.S. Supreme Court ruled (in a 5-4 decision) that police can take a cheek swab of a person arrested for a serious offense without violating the Fourth Amendment. The Court held that "taking and analyzing a cheek swab of an arrestee's DNA is, like fingerprinting and photographing, a legitimate police booking procedure." The Court also stated that this type of testing "involves minimal intrusion."[152] However, the SJC tends to be more restrictive when it comes to the Massachusetts Constitution, specifically Article 14. Whether or not a DNA sample may be taken from an arrestee here in Massachusetts has yet to be decided. However, a search warrant may be sought to obtain this type of evidence.

However, in 1999 the SJC upheld the constitutionality of the state's law that required the involuntary collection of blood samples from all persons *convicted* of one of 33 listed statutes (DNA samples).[153] This law now provides for DNA collection from all *convicted* felons.[154] The law relates to the submission of samples *upon conviction*. See information on the state DNA registry below:

State DNA Registry

C. 22E § 3. SUBMISSION OF DNA SAMPLE

Any person who is convicted of an offense that is punishable by **imprisonment in the state prison (F) (i.e. felony)**
and any person adjudicated a youthful offender by reason of an offense that would be punishable by imprisonment in the **state prison (F)** if committed by an adult **shall submit a DNA sample to the department within 1 year of such conviction** or adjudication or if incarcerated, before release from custody

The results of such sample shall become part of the state DNA database.

C. 22E § 4. COLLECTION OF DNA SAMPLES

Only the following people can collect DNA samples from a felon:

- a physician,
- a registered professional nurse,
- a licensed practical nurse,
- a phlebotomist,
- a health care worker with phlebotomist training, or
- a person licensed and trained by the director

None of the above shall be subject to civil liability for the act of withdrawing blood, or any other act directly related to the taking of a DNA sample; provided, however, that they shall employ recognized medical procedures and comply with all regulations or procedures promulgated by the director for the collection of DNA samples.

Use of Force to Collect:

Duly authorized law enforcement and correction personnel **may employ reasonable force to assist in collecting DNA samples** in cases where an individual refuses to submit to such collection as required under this chapter;

[149] *See, Commonwealth v. Harvey*, 397 Mass. 351, 491 N.E.2d 607 (1986)
[150] *Commonwealth v. Vitello*, 376 Mass. 426, 381 N.E.2d 582 (1978).
[151] *Commonwealth v. Blais*, 428 Mass. 294, 701 N.E. 2d 314 (1998).
[152] *Maryland v. King*, United States Supreme Court (2013).
[153] *Lundry v. Attorney General*, 429 Mass. 336, 709 N.E. 2d 1085 (1999).
[154] M.G.L. c.22E, §1.

provided, further, that such law enforcement and correction personnel shall not be subject to criminal prosecution or civil liability for the use of such reasonable force.

REFUSAL EVIDENCE

Although physical evidence can be compelled from an arrestee, evidence from an arrested individual indicating that they refused to perform certain tests cannot be used against the arrested person. The SJC has equated refusal to perform or to submit to tests equivalent to testimonial evidence protected by Article 12 of the Massachusetts Declaration of Rights. This typically arises in O.U.I. cases.

This protection also extends to the refusal to take field sobriety tests.[155]However, this protection is limited to state action. Refusals made to medical personnel, which are not directed by law enforcement or other state actors, are not protected.

In the 2008 case of ***Commonwealth v. Arruda,*** officers investigated a motor vehicle accident with injuries and the defendant was arrested for O.U.I. The defendant was transported to the hospital with chest pains. The arresting officer asked the defendant to submit to a blood alcohol test and the defendant refused. The officer remained with the defendant during treatment because he was under arrest. During treatment the medical personnel repeatedly asked the defendant to submit to a blood test to ensure he was not suffering from a cardiac contusion. The requests were prompted by medical treatment and not by the police. The defendant repeatedly refused. The Appeals Court permitted evidence of the refusal in the defendant's trial reasoning that Article 12 protects against state action and not refusals made to private individuals.[156]

Also, the Courts recently ruled that although refusing to submit to tests is not admissible, once an arrestee consents to take a test (in this case a breathalyzer) and then intentionally tries to sabotage the test (i.e. failing to properly blow into the machine) his actions will be admissible.[157]

DETAINEE SEARCHES

BOOKING INVENTORY SEARCHES

Once the police take someone into custody they can account for the belongings of the detained person by way of an inventory. If evidence is uncovered during the inventory it may be seized under the plain view doctrine (see the Search section of this manual for more on the Plain View Doctrine). However, in order for the inventory to be lawful it must be guided by a written department policy.

Intent is to Safeguard Property and to Maintain a Safe Environment Not to Uncover Evidence

The intent of the inventory of a detainee's property is to safeguard the detainee's property and to maintain a safe environment within the holding facility; it is not to gather evidence. If evidence or contraband is uncovered while conducting an inventory inspection the evidence or contraband will be admissible under the plain view doctrine provided it is within the written procedures and the procedures are reasonable. If the inventory goes beyond the intent to safeguard property or to maintain safety any evidence or contraband discovered will likely be suppressed.

Case examples

In ***Commonwealth v. Solo,*** the defendant was arrested for a motor vehicle violation and during the inventory inspection the officer perused through a business card holder containing numerous business cards and other papers. The officer discovered writings which implicated the defendant in gaming violations. The court ruled that the discovery of the gaming violations were beyond the scope of a booking inventory and suppressed the evidence.[158]

In the 2014 case of ***Commonwealth v. White***, the SJC ruled that police exceeded the intent of an inventory when the police located pills during the inventory of the arrestee's vehicle and utilized the Internet to discover what type of pills they were. The plain view doctrine also did not apply because the incriminating nature was not immediately apparent.

[155] *Commonwealth v. Healy*, 451 Mass. 1101 (2008)
[156] *Commonwealth v. Arruda*, 422 Mass. 1501 (2008).
[157] *Commonwealth v. Curley*, October 25, 2010
[158] *Commonwealth v. Sullo*, 26 Mass. App.Ct. 766 (1989).

Locked Containers Cannot be Broken Open/Damaged

As previously mentioned, one of the reasons the Court permits law enforcement personnel to conduct inventory "searches" is to safeguard property. If the property that is being safeguarded needs to be damaged (i.e. broken open) it defeats one of the primary intents of the inventory search. Therefore, officers cannot force or break open containers for the purpose of inventorying the contents.[159]

Case example

In the 2009 case of ***Commonwealth v. Vanya V., a juvenile***, Officer Gallo of the Marblehead Police Department arrested the defendant. The defendant was carrying a locked bank bag... At booking, the Marblehead police cut open the canvas bank bag in order to inventory the contents of the bag. During the inventory a digital scale, plastic baggies, marijuana and cash were discovered. The defendant was charged with distribution of drugs among other charges. The Court ruled that "permitting an officer to destroy or break into a locked container runs counter to the very purpose of the inventory exception."

Scope of the Inventory Inspection

The scope of the inventory inspection is guided by the scope of the written guidelines. If the agency wants to have its officers inspect closed containers, handbags and the like the written guidelines must specify the scope.

STRIP AND VISUAL BODY CAVITY SEARCHES

A strip search is generally regarded as the inspection of a naked individual particularly the genitalia, female breasts, or buttocks. The SJC has indicated that strip searches are demeaning and should not be conducted as a matter of routine practice.[160] Visual body cavity searches generally extend to a visual inspection of the anal and genital areas and often include some action by the detainee, such as having the detainee squat.

The SJC has declared that in order to conduct a strip search or a visual body cavity search at a police facility the police must have *probable cause* that the detainee has evidence, weapons, or contraband hidden on their person.[161]

STRIP SEARCHES

The SJC has ruled that probable cause is required in order to conduct a strip search; and in *Commonwealth v. Prophete,* the SJC ruled that a strip search refers to the removal of the last layer of clothing (i.e. removal of the underwear). However, in the 2012 case of ***Commonwealth v. Morales***, the SJC stated "a strip search also may occur when a detainee remains partially clothed, but in circumstances during which a last layer of clothing is *moved* (and not necessarily *re*moved) in such a manner whereby an intimate area of the detainee is viewed, exposed, or displayed."

Search Incident to an Arrest

Although probable cause is typically not required to conduct a search incident to an arrest; searches incident to an arrest "may be unconstitutional notwithstanding the lawful arrest, because they involve inspections of such a highly personal nature, or are conducted in such a manner, as to constitute an unreasonable intrusion on an individual's privacy." A search of a defendant "lawfully could progressively extend into a strip (or a visual body cavity) search **only if such a search was justified by probable cause** to believe that the defendant had concealed drugs on his person or his clothing that would not otherwise be discovered by the usual search incident to arrest."

[160] *Commonwealth v. Thomas,* 429 Mass. 403 (1999).
[161] *Commonwealth v. Thomas,* 429 Mass. 403 (1999).

Strip Search in Public

In the 2012 case of ***Commonwealth v. Morales,*** the SJC ruled that strip searches in public places, absent some exigency, are unconstitutional. In *Morales*, the defendant was hiding drugs between his buttocks when he was arrested. During his attempt to escape the arrest his pants were lowered exposing his buttocks and the officer retrieved the drugs. The officers eventually handcuffed him and left him lying face down in the street, with his buttocks exposed, for an extended period of time. The SJC stated "with no exigency existing, the defendant should have been transported to a private space or location. Doing so would have avoided what followed, namely, the public exposure of his buttocks, an embarrassing and humiliating intrusion of the defendant's privacy. Indeed, the policy of the Lowell police department prohibits strip searches outside the confines of a police station. In the circumstances, the location of this search was inappropriate." The evidence was suppressed.

How a search is conducted is of the utmost importance and at all times the potential harm to the detainee's health and dignity should be taken into account. Whether a person of the same gender conducts the search should also be given consideration.[162]

BODY CAVITY SEARCH

A Warrant is required in order to conduct an intrusive Body Cavity Search

In order to conduct an intrusive body cavity search the police must obtain a search warrant, issued by a judge, and the search must be conducted by a ***medical professional***. The Court has also indicated that this type of search requires a "high degree of probable cause." A body cavity search involves the inspection of a body cavity (e.g. rectum, vagina, etc.)

[162] Commonwealth v. Morales (2012) SJC

CONSULAR MANDATORY NOTIFICATION COUNTRIES

The following countries and jurisdictions *require* consular notification:

Albania
Algeria
Antigua and Barbuda
Armenia
Azerbaijan
Bahamas
Barbados
Belarus
Belize
Brunei
Bulgaria
China (including Macao and Hong Kong)[1]
Costa Rica
Cyprus
Czech Republic
Dominica
Fiji
Gambia
Georgia
Ghana
Grenada
Guyana
Hungary
Jamaica
Kazakhstan
Kiribati
Kuwait
Kyrgyzstan
Malaysia
Malta
Mauritius
Moldova
Mongolia
Nigeria
Philippines
Poland[2]
Romania
Russia
Saint Kitts and Nevis
Saint Lucia
Saint Vincent and the Grenadines
Seychelles
Sierra Leone
Singapore
Slovakia
Tajikistan
Tanzania
Tonga
Trinidad and Tobago
Tunisia
Turkmenistan
Tuvalu
Ukraine
United Kingdom[3]
Uzbekistan
Zambia
Zimbabwe

[1]Notification is not mandatory in the case of persons who carry "Republic of China" passports issued by Taiwan. Such persons should be informed without delay that the nearest office of the Taipei Economic and Cultural Representative Office ("TECRO"), the unofficial entity representing Taiwan's interests in the United States, can be notified at their request.

[2]Mandatory only for foreign nationals who are not lawful permanent residents in the United States (i.e., "green card" holders). Otherwise, upon the national's request.

[3]The bilateral consular convention between the United States and the United Kingdom applies to British nationals from Great Britain (England, Wales, and Scotland); Northern Ireland; the Crown Dependencies of Jersey, Guernsey, and the Isle of Man; and the British Overseas Territories, including Anguilla, Bermuda, the British Virgin Islands, the Cayman Islands, Gibraltar, Montserrat, and the Turks and Caicos Islands, along with other island territories. Residents of the Overseas Territories may be traveling on a passport issued by the territory with no indication that the territory is British. Nevertheless, for them and all others from a British possession listed above, consular notification and access should be provided to the nearest U.K. consulate.

Source: http://travel.state.gov/content/travel/english/consularnotification/countries-and-jurisdictions-with-mandatory-notifications.html - **Check for updates as this list may change**.

JURISDICTION

OVERVIEW

A police officer can generally investigate criminal activity (i.e. interview suspects and witnesses, gather evidence, conduct surveillance, etc.) anywhere. However, a police officer's authority to enforce the law (i.e. execute arrests, initiate criminal charges and issue citations) is generally restricted to within the jurisdictional boundaries of his/her employer. A valid arrest requires that the officer have lawful authority to execute the arrest. For example, under normal circumstances, a municipal police officer does not have authority to arrest outside the jurisdictional limits of the city or town which employs him or her. [163] Although all other elements of an arrest may be present, the arrest is invalid if the officer attempts an arrest under circumstances where he or she lacks lawful authority to arrest. However, there are many exceptions to this jurisdictional limitation. For these reasons it is important that police officers understand their jurisdictional authority and the exceptions that exist.

Massachusetts State Police

The Massachusetts State Police have law enforcement authority within the boundaries of the Commonwealth of Massachusetts.[164] However, in practice, their enforcement activities are primarily executed on state highways, state owned/controlled property and in municipalities that do not have full-time law enforcement.

The Massachusetts Environmental Police

The Massachusetts Environmental Police have law enforcement authority within the boundaries of the Commonwealth of Massachusetts. However, in practice their enforcement activity is generally limited to the protection of wild life and conservation land.[165]

The Massachusetts Bay Transit Authority Police (Transit Police)

Chapter 664 of the Acts of 1968 (amended by Chapter 829 of the Acts of 1970 and Chapter 329 of the Acts of 1993) authorizes the establishment of a police department by the MBTA. Section 1 of c. 664 states that "such police officers shall have, within the territorial limits of the authority, the powers and duties conferred or imposed upon police officers of cities and towns" under G. L. c. 41, Section 98, and "shall have the powers and duties which are conferred or imposed upon police officers" of railroads, street railways and steamboats under G. L. c. 159, Section 93. Prior to Chapter 664 of the Acts of 1968 the authority of the transit police was limited to the railroads, street railways and steamboats. However, Chapter 664 of the Acts of 1968 expanded the Transit Police authority to the same "duties and powers" of the police officers in cities and towns "within the territorial limits of the authority."[166]

In short, Transit police have jurisdictional authority in every city and town that the MBTA transit system reaches. At the time of the printing of this manual the MBTA system is present in 178 cities and towns (more than half of the state). However, in practice, Transit Police enforcement is generally limited to the MBTA transit system and the property of the MBTA.

The Massachusetts Port Authority Police ("MassPort Police")

The MassPort Police have limited jurisdiction over MassPort property (seaports and maritime facilities). They do not have the authority to enforce motor vehicle regulations (i.e. "chapter 90") but they can execute arrests. There is essentially no precedent on the jurisdictional authority of the MassPort Police.

Massachusetts Department of Mental Health (DMH) and Department of Developmental Services (DDS) Police

DMH and DDS Police have authority under M.G. L. 22C § 59. They can enforce the law, including the issuance of civil citations on public ways within properties controlled by those agencies.

[163] *Commonwealth v. Zirpolo*, 37 Mass.App. Ct. 307, 639 N.E.2d 1083 (1994).
[164] M.G.L. chapter 22C § 10.
[165] M.G.L. chapter 21A § 10A.
[166] See *Commonwealth v. Mottola*, 10 Mass.App.Ct. 775 (1980)

County Sheriff Deputies

Under chapter 37 § 11 the deputy sheriffs of the 13 counties of Massachusetts have law enforcement authority in their respective counties. However, in practice, the duties of the County Sheriff Deputies are generally limited to the operation of their respective county's house of correction.

Note: Sheriff Deputies can issue citations for civil motor vehicle violations but they cannot arrest powers for non-criminal motor vehicle violations under chapter 90 § 21.

MSPCA Police

The MSPCA Police are a full-time law enforcement agency that investigates animal cruelty complaints. They are commissioned as special state police officers and their jurisdiction is statewide yet it is limited to animal cruelty.

Municipal Police

The authority of police officers of the 351 cities and towns in Massachusetts is generally limited to the jurisdictional boundaries of the city or town of which the police officer is employed.

Case example

In ***Commonwealth v. Grise***, two Ludlow police officers, while traveling through the city of Springfield, observed a vehicle ignore a red light and weave back and forth between lanes. "Believing that the defendant may have been operating under the influence of intoxicating liquor, one of the Ludlow officers put on the overhead blue lights of the police cruiser and stopped the defendant's car within the Springfield city limits. Based upon his observations of the defendant, the officer arrested him for operating under the influence of intoxicating liquor. He placed the defendant in the Ludlow police cruiser, and called the Springfield police for assistance. Springfield police officers transported the defendant to the Springfield police department. The SJC concluded that the arrest was unlawful because it occurred outside the arresting officer's jurisdiction, and that evidence which would not have been obtained but for the arrest should be suppressed.[167]

Campus ("special") Police

An employee of a college, university, other educational institution, or hospital, who is appointed and sworn in as a special State police officer, has "the same power to make arrests as regular police officers for any **criminal offense** committed in or upon lands or structures ***owned, used or occupied*** by" their employing institution.[168] For instance, a campus police officer may make an arrest for a criminal offense on the main street in front of the campus, even though it is a public street, as long as the street is *used* by the college.

The SJC has stated that the authority to make an arrest may extend "to the environs surrounding the campus when the 'special vigilance of an officer might be required to keep the peace and preserve order amongst those frequenting [the campus and] those carrying persons to and from it' " as long as the initial offense was committed in or upon lands or structures *owned, used or occupied* by "their employing institution." [169]

Many college campus police are also sworn in as county deputy sheriffs which can expand the authority granted by chapter 22C § 63.

Motor Vehicle Citation Authority for Campus Police

Chapter 90C § 2A permits campus police officers of Commonwealth run colleges and universities to issue citations for civil motor vehicle infractions "limited to the issuance of citations for violations occurring on the property of state universities and community colleges". However, campus officers of private universities (with power originating from G.L. c. 22C § 63) do not have authority to issue citations for civil motor vehicle infractions.

[167] *Commonwealth v. Grise*, 398 Mass. 247 (1986).
[168] G.L. c. 22C § 63.
[169] *Commonwealth v. Smeaton*, SJC (2013).

EXCEPTIONS TO THE JURISDICTIONAL LIMITATION OT ARREST

ARREST WARRANTS - Statewide Jurisdiction

Warrants and other processes issued for the apprehension of persons charged with crime and child support warrants (issued pursuant to c. 215 § 34A) may be served in **any part of the Commonwealth** by an officer authorized to serve criminal process in any county. The officer may also command aid and exercise the same authority as if in his own county. [170] In short, a police officer may make an arrest, under the authority of an arrest warrant, anywhere in Massachusetts, even outside of his/her local jurisdiction.

TRANSFERRED AUTHORITY: M.G.L. c. 37 § 13 and c. 268 § 24

The SJC stated that under c. 37 § 13, a sheriff "may require suitable aid in the execution of their office in a criminal case, in the preservation of the peace, [or] in the apprehending or securing of a person for a breach of the peace."[171] Although c. 37 § 13 utilizes the tem sheriff it applies to constables by virtue of G. L. c. 41 § 94 (1994 ed.), which provides that constables "shall have the powers of sheriffs to require aid in the execution of their duties," and to police officers by virtue of G. L. c. 41, Section 98, which provides that "police officers of all cities and towns shall have all the powers and duties of constables except serving and executing civil process."[172]

Thus, a police officer may request the help of citizen, even one who happens to be a police officer in another jurisdiction, to assist him making an arrest or maintaining public order.

In fact, private citizens have a legal duty to come to the aid of a police officer when requested to do so; M.G.L. c. 268 § 24 states "whoever, being required in the name of the Commonwealth by a sheriff, deputy sheriff, constable, police officer or watchman, neglects or refuses to assist him in the execution of his office in a criminal case, in the preservation of the peace or in the apprehension or securing of a person for a breach of the peace...shall be punished by a fine...or by imprisonment for not more than one month."

In ***Commonwealth v. Twombly***[173], the SJC delineated how a police officer can request aid pursuant C. 37 § 13. The statute sets forth ***four situations*** in which police officers may require suitable aid in:

- the execution of their office in a criminal case
- the preservation of the peace
- the apprehending or securing of a person for a breach of the peace and
- cases of escape or rescue of persons arrested upon civil process

Case example

In ***Commonwealth v. Morrissey***, A Sterling police officer was in the neighboring town of West Boylston when he observed an automobile run a stop sign and operating erratically. The Sterling officer reported his observations to a West Boylston officer, who then asked the Sterling officer to stop the vehicle. The Sterling officer did so within the West Boylston town limits. When the West Boylston officer arrived on scene the operator was placed under arrest for OUI. The defendant argued that the Sterling officer had no legal police authority to conduct a stop in West Boylston for a misdemeanor. The SJC held that the stop was lawfully based on properly transferred authority.[174]

[170] C. 276 § 23
[171] *Commonwealth v. Morrissey*, 422 Mass. 1 (1996)
[172] *Commonwealth v. Morrissey*, 422 Mass. 1 (1996)
[173] *Commonwealth v. Twombly*, 435 Mass.440 (2001).
[174] *Commonwealth v. Morrissey*, 422 Mass. 1 (1996)

MUTUAL AID PROVISIONS

If an officer is acting pursuant to a mutual aid agreement or a request for mutual aid, the officer may have the authority to effect an arrest outside his or her jurisdiction.

M.G.L. c. 41 § 99: *Request for Help*

Chapter 41 § 99 authorizes the commanding officer (or mayor or selectmen) of one jurisdiction to request assistance from the commanding officer of another jurisdiction to provide police officers for assistance. The statute states the police officers shall have the "authority of police officers" in the requesting community's jurisdiction. However, the statute specifically denies authority to serve "civil process." This provision is generally used on a temporary emergency type basis. However, this statute can also be utilized to swear in neighboring police officers as special police officers. For long term agreements c. 40 § 8G should be used.

M.G.L. c. 40 § 8G: *Longstanding Mutual Aid Agreements*

Chapter 40 § 8G states "A city or town which accepts this section may enter into an agreement with another city or town, or other cities and towns including cities and towns in states contiguous to the commonwealth, to provide mutual aid programs for police departments to increase the capability of such departments to protect the lives, safety, and property of the people in the area designated in the agreement. Said agreement may include the furnishing of personal services, supplies, materials, contractual services, and equipment when the resources normally available to any municipality in the agreement are not sufficient to cope with a situation which requires police action." This statute is generally used for long term mutual aid agreements.

In the 2013 case of ***Commonwealth v. Bartlett***, the SJC upheld the stop and subsequent arrest of a drunk driver by a Merrimac police officer while in the Town of Amesbury because the two agencies had a mutual aid agreement in effect.

Attorney Hanrahan's Note: These types of mutual aid agreements are becoming more common place. In fact, in 2013, the Middlesex County Chiefs of Police Association drafted a county-wide mutual aid agreement wherein the police officers employed by the communities who have signed onto the agreement (signatory communities) will have full police powers in the other signatory communities. The intent is to establish a county-wide jurisdiction for municipal police in Middlesex County. However, there are limitations; for instance, the current version of the agreement indicates that the jurisdictional authority only applies to officers who are *on-duty*. At the time of the printing of this manual most of the municipalities in Middlesex County have signed the agreement. If your community is covered under this agreement be sure to review the actual agreement before taking any legal action outside of your jurisdiction.

SPECIFIC LEGISLATION

In some very rare situations specific legislation has been enacted expanding the authority of police officers from one municipality into certain parts of neighboring cities/towns. Chapter 22 of the Acts of 1988 grants jurisdictional authority of Boston, Brookline and Newton police officers 500 yards into the other two mentioned communities.

FELONY OFFENSE

Citizen's Arrest

In Massachusetts, a private citizen has the power to arrest a person who has *in fact committed* a **felony**. Therefore, unless the arrested person is actually found guilty, a false arrest suit may be brought against such private person.

On the other hand, a police officer may make a citizen's arrest in another community if he or she has *probable cause* to believe that a felony has been committed and that the person arrested has committed it.[175]

[175] *Commonwealth v. Harris*, 11 Mass. App. Ct. 165, 415 N.E.2d 216 (1981); *Commonwealth v. Gullick*, 386 Mass. 278, 435 N.E.2d 348 (1982); *Commonwealth v. Dise*, 31 Mass. App. Ct. 701, 583 N.E.2d 271 (1991).

Case example

In ***Commonwealth v. Clairborne,*** Brookline and Newton detectives were investigating a string of armed robberies in their cities. Shortly after the fifth robbery took place, Brookline detectives, while in the City of Boston, observed the suspect vehicle. They stopped the suspect in Boston and uncovered a weapon and other evidence. The SJC ruled that the stop was permissible because the Brookline detectives had *probable cause* (based on the detailed description and vicinity of the crime). Even though the detectives only intended to conduct a threshold inquiry this did not negate the fact that they actually had probable cause for the felony, the stop, and subsequent arrest was permissible as a citizen's arrest.[176]

Attorney Hanrahan's Note: A citizen is not limited to the jurisdiction of his/her employer. Therefore, a "citizen's arrest" is not limited to a particular jurisdiction as long as the arrest takes place in Massachusetts (citizen arrest laws in other states may be not be consistent with Massachusetts).

FRESH AND CONTINUED ("HOT") PURSUIT

When in fresh and continued pursuit, officers may (under limited circumstances) cross municipal or state borders and make an arrest.[177]

In specific circumstances, an officer may make a warrantless arrest in a jurisdiction in Massachusetts other than his or her own city or town. In other circumstances, the officer may make a warrantless arrest in a state other than Massachusetts. These statutory powers of arrest are discussed below:

<u>Within Massachusetts</u>

Under M.G.L. c. 41, § 98A, where a crime for which an officer could make a warrantless arrest (be it felony or misdemeanor) in his or her own jurisdiction (generally city or town) is committed in his or her presence and in the officer's own jurisdiction, he or she may "on fresh and continued pursuit" arrest the offender in any other city or town in Massachusetts and return that person to the jurisdiction where the offense was committed.[178]

While an officer need not yet have probable cause to arrest an individual before pursing him or her across municipal boundaries, the officer must have *some reason to believe* that the suspect committed an arrestable offense before pursuing that individual into another municipality.[179]

It would be possible, for example, to follow an erratic driver across municipal boundaries, stop and administer field sobriety tests and arrest him or her for driving under the influence.[180] Provided the officer had reasonable suspicion that the operator was committing an arrestable offense (i.e. OUI) while operating within his/her jurisdiction.

The fresh and continued pursuit statute has three requirements:

1. That the offense is one for which a warrantless arrest is authorized;
2. That the offense was committed in the officer's presence; and,
3. That the offense was committed within the officer's jurisdiction.

If all three conditions are met, the officer may engage in fresh and continued pursuit of the offender and arrest him or her in any city or town in Massachusetts. [181]

Attorney Hanrahan's note: Many police officers mistakenly believe that this exception to the jurisdictional limitation is limited to "car chases." This is not the case. Although a vehicular pursuit is a common scenario wherein this exception is utilized, the "pursuit" does not have to be a suspect fleeing. In fact, it doesn't even have to involve a vehicle at all. It should be thought of as a continuous following.

[176] *Commonwealth v. Clairborne*, 423 Mass. 275 (1996).
[177] MGL c. 40, s. 8G and c. 41, s. 99.
[178] *Commonwealth v. Dise*, 31 Mass. App. Ct. 701, 583 N.E.2d 271 (1991).
[179] *Commonwealth v. Trudel*, 42 Mass. App. Ct. 903, 674 N.E.2d 262 (1997).
[180] *Commonwealth v. O'Hara*, 30 Mass. App. Ct. 608, 571 N.E.2d 51 (1991).

[181] *Commonwealth v. LeBlanc*, 407 Mass. 70, 551 N.E.2d 906 (1990); *Commonwealth v. Owens*, 414 Mass. 595, 609 N.E.2d 1208 (1993).

Case examples

- In ***Commonwealth v. LeBlanc***, the officer pursued the defendant across town lines because he observed the defendant commit a nonarrestable traffic violation, going through a red light. After stopping the defendant, the officer noticed a strong odor of alcohol. When the defendant failed two field sobriety tests, the officer arrested him for operating a motor vehicle while under the influence of liquor. The court noted that "the Legislature, through G. L. chapter 41, Section 98A . . ., permitted extraterritorial `fresh pursuit' arrests for any *arrestable offense*, whether it be a felony or misdemeanor, initially committed in the arresting officer's presence and within his jurisdiction." The court ruled that "the officer must have *some reason to believe* that the suspect has committed an arrestable offense before he can pursue and arrest an individual pursuant to Section 98A." Because the offense for which the officer pursued the motorist in LeBlanc was a nonarrestable offense, the Court ruled that the officer did not have any authority to make a warrantless arrest outside his jurisdiction.[182]

- In ***Commonwealth v. O'Hara,*** "On April 30, 1987 at 3:15 A.M., Officer Tucker of the West Bridgewater Police was operating a stationary radar unit near the Brockton line. He observed a motor vehicle traveling northerly at speeds varying between 10 and 37 (posted 40) miles per hour. It crossed the center line on a couple of occasions. He did not observe any other vehicle. The officer followed the car because he felt the operator was drunk due to the observation he had made of the operation of the motor vehicle. He followed the motor vehicle some 300 to 400 feet into Brockton. After following the defendant for a distance in excess of one-quarter mile, the officer noticed the defendant make a slow right-hand turn. The officer thereupon stopped the defendant, made additional observations and arrested the defendant for operating under the influence of alcohol." The Court ruled that the West Bridgewater police officer at 3:15 A.M. observed the defendant's vehicle traveling in that town at speeds varying from 10 to 37 miles per hour. There were no other vehicles on the road. The vehicle crossed over the center line of the roadway on two occasions. Based on those facts the officer clearly had "some reason to believe" that the defendant was operating a motor vehicle either while under the influence of an intoxicating substance or, negligently so as to endanger, both arrestable offenses. Therefore, the arrest in Brockton was lawful.

- In ***Commonwealth v. Head,*** a police officer who had observed a motorist driving through a red light without stopping, after which the motorist failed to stop when the officer activated his lights and siren and directed the operator to pull over, was authorized to commence a fresh pursuit of the motorist, and to stop the motorist after he drove outside of the officer's jurisdictional authority.[183]

- In ***Commonwealth v. Magazu,*** an officer who was outside of his jurisdiction, when he observed someone driving under the influence, and then followed the vehicle as it drove into his jurisdiction for a brief period, had authority to arrest the driver a short way into a third jurisdiction.[184]

- In ***Commonwealth v. Gray***, when Det. Joseph Deignan displayed his badge against the window of his unmarked car indicating the suspect to pull over, the suspect committed the arrestable offense of failing to stop for a police officer and Det. Deignan was authorized to pursue him across municipal boundaries.

For the purposes of the "in the officer's presence" requirement, it is only required that *an officer* witness the offense not necessarily the same officer who pursues and arrests the suspect across jurisdictional boundaries.

- In ***Commonwealth v. Zirpolo***, a Framingham police officer who observed an intoxicated operator leave a nightclub where he was working a detail, strike a parked car and flee the scene, radioed the information to other officers. A different Framingham officer observed the vehicle operating in Framingham, but he did not observe the operator commit any violations. This second officer then activated his blue lights. The vehicle stopped just over the line in Natick. The operator was found to be intoxicated and was subsequently arrested. The stop was deemed valid even though the pursuing officer did not personally see the arrestable offense. The fact that the arrestable offense was not committed in the arresting officer's immediate presence is immaterial considering that the offense was committed in a brother officer's presence. Both Framingham police officers were acting in a joint effort to apprehend the defendant for an arrestable offense on the night in question. Under the collective knowledge doctrine as it relates to probable cause to arrest (an issue not before

JURISDICTIONAL AUTHORITY

[182] *Commonwealth v. LeBlanc*, 407 Mass. 70 , 71 (1990).
[183] *Commonwealth v. Head*, 49 Mass. App. Ct. 492, 730 N.E.2d 891 (2000). (The evidence also established that the defendant committed the arrestable offense of driving to endanger in the officer's home community.)
[184] *Commonwealth v. Magazu*, 48 Mass. App. Ct. 466, 722 N.E. 2d 488 (2000).

us), "it is unnecessary for the detaining officer to know all the information pertaining to the incident . . . .' [T]he knowledge of one [police officer] . . . [is] the knowledge of all.'" [185]

Out of State

Under M.G.L. c. 276, §§ 10A-10D, if another state has equivalent statutory provisions, a law enforcement officer from that state who enters Massachusetts on fresh pursuit of a person who committed a felony in the officer's own state may continue such fresh pursuit in Massachusetts and arrest the offender here.

- In ***Commonwealth v. Savage,*** *a*n out-of-state trooper lacked statutory authority to stop a defendant's motor vehicle in Massachusetts based on the suspicion that the defendant operated a vehicle while under the influence of liquor.[186] The court noted that the statute authorizing out-of-state officers to make arrests in Massachusetts applied only to *felonies*. There the initial offense of OUI was a misdemeanor, and the trooper was not in "fresh pursuit" of the defendant's motor vehicle at the moment he crossed the state line as required by statute.[187]

Chapter 276 § 10B requires that the out-of-state officer immediately take the person arrested to court in the county in which the arrest was made. The Court shall conduct a hearing for the purpose of determining the lawfulness of the arrest. If the court determines that the arrest was lawful the person arrested must wait a reasonable time the issuance of a rendition warrant by the governor of the state from which he fled. If such justice, associate justice or special justice determines that the arrest was unlawful he shall discharge the person arrested.

Conversely, since that other state has equivalent statutory provisions, a Massachusetts police officer, if on fresh pursuit of a person who committed a felony in Massachusetts, may continue such fresh pursuit into that other state and make an arrest there.

Subsequent to making such an arrest in another state, the Massachusetts police officer must follow the custody, bail, court and rendition procedures of the state in which the arrest is made. At least forty-one (41) states, including New York, and the five (5) other New England states have adopted reciprocal felony fresh pursuit statutes.[188]

JURISDICTIONAL BORDERS

Although a police officer's authority generally is limited within the territorial limits of the officer's jurisdiction, the courts consider the good faith of the officer concerning action along the jurisdictional border.

In ***Commonwealth v. Coburn,*** a Concord police officer patrolling Route 2 observed the defendant's speeding vehicle traveling east at about 4:00 A.M. The officer pulled the defendant over just before an "Entering Lincoln" sign. The defendant was arrested for O.U.I. The defendant later realized that the "Entering Lincoln" sign was actually 30 feet into the Town of Lincoln, thus the actual stop occurred in the Town of Lincoln. The defendant appealed his conviction claiming the Concord officer did not have jurisdictional authority to make the arrest. The court upheld the conviction stating that "the officer's lack of knowledge of the precise location of the imaginary line between Concord and Lincoln cannot be viewed as unreasonable or based on misconduct attributable to the police."[189]

---

[185] Commonwealth v. Lanoue, 356 Mass. 337 , 340 (1969), quoting from Commonwealth v. McDermott, 347 Mass. 246 , 249 (1964). See also Commonwealth v. Gullick, 386 Mass. 278 , 283-284 (1982).
[186] *Commonwealth v. Savage*, 430 Mass. 341, 719 N.E. 2d 473 (1999).
[187] (M.G.L. c.276§10A).*Id.*
[188] *See,Commonwealth v. Gullick*, 386 Mass. 278, 435 N.E.2d 348 (1982), where M.G.L. c. 276, §§10A-10D did not apply, but citizen's arrest power was utilized.
[189] *Commonwealth v. Coburn,*62 Mass.App.Ct. 314, 816 N.E.2d 177 (2004).

SPECIAL STATUTORY POWERS FOR DOMESTIC VIOLENCE RELATED OFFENSES

Generally, a municipal police officer would not have the authority to arrest a suspect who is wanted in another Massachusetts jurisdiction without an arrest warrant. However, the legislature carved out a specific exemption when it comes to misdemeanor domestic violence offenses.

M.G.L. c. 276 § 28 states in part...Any officer authorized to serve criminal process may arrest, without a warrant, and detain a person:

a. whom the officer has probable cause to believe has committed a misdemeanor by violating a (Massachusetts issued) temporary or permanent vacate, restraining, suspension and surrender, or no-contact order.

b. whom the officer has probable cause to believe has committed a misdemeanor involving abuse as defined 209A or has committed an assault and battery against a family or household member

Note: Although there is no Court decision directly on point, it is interpreted by most that this statute grants officers the authority to execute an arrest for one of the above offenses even if the offense was committed outside of the officer's jurisdiction. However, this does **not** grant police officers authority to **make arrests outside their jurisdiction**. For instance, a Cambridge police officer arrest a suspect, located in Cambridge, who committed a domestic violence offense in the City of Boston, but the statute does not grant a Boston Police Officer to enter Cambridge and arrest a domestic violence suspect for a domestic violence offense that occurred in Boston, without a warrant.

CITIZEN DETENTIONS

In a 2011 decision, the SJC seemed to deviate somewhat from its previous position on municipal police officers acting outside of their jurisdiction. See the case example below:

Com. v. Limone: On the afternoon of August 4, 2006, Officer Robert Kelleher of the Somerville police department was returning to his home in Woburn, northbound on Interstate Route 93 north, after work. Kelleher was still in uniform, but was driving his private vehicle. As he approached the Medford exit, he saw a red Oldsmobile operating unusually (making several lane changes etc.). Kelleher took the Montvale Avenue exit, and came to a stop at a red light. While stopped, his vehicle was struck in the rear by the red Oldsmobile.

Kelleher got out of his car and approached the Oldsmobile, which was being operated by Joshua LIMONE. He told LIMONE that he had struck his car, for which LIMONE apologized repeatedly. At this point, Kelleher formed the opinion that LIMONE was under the influence of alcohol, and told LIMONE to step out of the car. LIMONE did so. Concerned that LIMONE would leave the scene and cause injury to another person, Kelleher then reached into the Oldsmobile and took the keys from the ignition. He did not ask LIMONE for his license and registration, did not attempt to investigate or collect evidence, nor did he ask LIMONE to perform field sobriety tests. Rather, Kelleher told LIMONE to get back into his car, and then Kelleher returned to his own car and called the Woburn police on his cellular telephone. The two waited in their separate cars for the Woburn police to arrive.

Officer David Simonds of the Woburn police department arrived at the scene. LIMONE was later arrested for OUI (seventh offense) and operating after revocation.

The SJC stated the following: Kelleher's actions in this case did not amount to an arrest. Kelleher's actions in telling the defendant to step out of the car, removing and retaining his keys from the ignition, and telling him to sit and wait in his car, fell short of an "arrest" sufficient to trigger the citizen's arrest rule. Instead, Kelleher's actions were more akin to an investigatory "stop," short of an arrest.

The SJC Ruled "*in the circumstances of this case,* it was reasonable for Kelleher--as it would be for a private citizen--to prolong the "stop" until the Woburn police arrived, in order to ensure the safety of the public and of the defendant himself."The court stated "Kelleher's actions are more consistent with an intent to stop for questioning than an intent to arrest... his actions were only minimally intrusive, given his purpose of ensuring the safety of the public and of the defendant himself."

In addition the Court stated "We decline,...to create a "Superman" rule of law that would require out-of-jurisdiction, off-duty police officers to change into civilian clothing before interacting with private citizens following traffic accidents. *So long as the officer does not use the indicia of his authority to collect evidence that a private citizen would be unable to gather*, and the officer takes only reasonable preventive measures falling short of an actual arrest, the happenstance of the officer's being in uniform alone will not convert the interaction into an arrest.

The Court concluded that "Kelleher did not 'arrest' the defendant for the purposes of triggering the common-law rule against performing a citizen's arrest for a misdemeanor, and that his actions were reasonable preventive measures to ensure public safety, we agree ... that there is no need to exclude the evidence."

Attorney Hanrahan's Note: This decision seems somewhat contrary to previous decisions by the SJC in that it implies that a police officer could conduct a threshold inquiry outside of his/her jurisdiction as long as it does not amount to an arrest. However, the court does not state this directly and in this case the defendant stopped on his own (i.e. the officer did not indicate for him to pull over). We will have to wait and see how this will evolve in decisions to come. It would seem that the focus on the incredibly low conviction rate of drunk drivers in Massachusetts played a role in this case (at the time of this decision the SJC was in the process of conducting an investigation as to why the drunk driving conviction rates are so low in Massachusetts). In fact, the SJC, in the footnotes of the decision, acknowledged receiving an amicus brief submitted by Mothers Against Drunk Driving and the Massachusetts Chiefs of Police Association.

INEVITABLE DISCOVERY

The inevitable discovery exception to the exclusionary rule may be applied to a seizure made by a police officer acting outside his jurisdictional authority.

Case example:

Commonwealth v. Lahey (2011): On the evening of December 25, 2007, Norton police Officer Zaccardi escorted an ambulance to the hospital in the neighboring town of Attleboro. After the arrival of the ambulance, Zaccardi drove his marked patrol car back toward Norton on Route 123, a two-lane east-to-west highway. As he traveled in the eastbound lane and still in Attleboro, he saw the defendant's car coming westward in the eastbound lane. It was moving at an excessive speed, and passing vehicles erratically. Zaccardi swerved off the roadway to avoid a head-on collision.

Zaccardi then reversed direction, turned on his patrol car's light bar and siren, and began pursuit of the defendant's car. Simultaneously he radioed his Norton police dispatcher and directed him to notify the Attleboro police dispatcher to send assistance to the pursuit. Zaccardi saw the defendant attempt unsuccessfully to pass vehicles; oncoming traffic blocked that maneuver. He overtook the defendant after one-half mile and forced him to the side of the road.

Zaccardi walked to the defendant's car, requested and received his keys and driver's license, and instructed him and a passenger to place their hands on the dashboard. At that time, he could hear the siren of an approaching Attleboro cruiser. It arrived within approximately 20 to 30 seconds of Zaccardi's receipt of the keys and license. Two Attleboro officers then conducted an investigation. Zaccardi briefed them and left within a few minutes. An Attleboro officer testified that their cruiser had reached the location of the stop in "less than one minute" after receipt of dispatch.

The defendant argued that the Norton officer conducted an unlawful stop because he did not have jurisdictional authority in the Town of Attleboro. The Commonwealth did not argue that Officer Zaccardi had authority to make the stop. Their argument was inevitable discovery, arguing that the Attleboro officers were on their way to the scene and that they arrived within a minute, thus they would have intercepted the defendant even if Zaccardi had not made the stop.

Court's Analysis: Even though an unauthorized extraterritorial stop is a statutory violation, and inevitable discovery is an issue applied to constitutional law, there is nothing that prevents these issues from being applied to the same case. In

this case, the Attleboro officers arrived within a minute of the Norton officer's unlawful stop. The motion judge found that because of this the inevitable discovery doctrine applied because even if Zaccardi had not made the stop the Attleboro officers would have intercepted the defendant and made the same discovery.
The evidence is admissible under the inevitable discovery doctrine.

Attorney Hanrahan's Recommendation: As previously mentioned, G.L. c. 37 § 13 permits a police officer to transfer his/her authority to another person (even someone who happens to be a police officer in another jurisdiction) in order to quell a breach or the peace or to make an arrest. When officers are faced with a similar situation as presented here the safest course of action would be for the officer out of his/her jurisdiction to radio the department with jurisdiction. A police officer from the agency with jurisdiction can then transfer his/her authority to the out-of-town officer (i.e. "stop that car for me.") and the out-of-town officer would then have legal authority to take action. This could all occur within seconds via the radio.

Massachusetts Municipal and State Police Authority to Enforce Federal Law

In the 2014 case of ***Commonwealth v. Craan***, the SJC reiterated that the "general rule is that local police are not precluded from enforcing federal statutes," however "their authority to do so derives from state law." Where state police officers make an arrest for a violation of federal law, "the lawfulness of the arrest without a warrant is to be determined by reference to state law."

Attorney Hanrahan's Comment: Generally, State and Municipal officers only enforce federal law when working in conjunction with federal law enforcement agencies (e.g. drug task force). It is possible for state and local officers to make an arrest for a violation of federal but there must be some connection to a state law.

SEARCH OVERVIEW

Fourth Amendment and Article 14 Protects Against Government Intrusion

The Fourth Amendment and Article 14 protect citizens from unreasonable government (primarily law enforcement) searches (and seizures). A search takes place when a government official invades the privacy of another. However, the expectation of privacy must be reasonable. **If the expectation of privacy is not reasonable there is no "search."**

REASONABLE EXPECTATION OF PRIVACY IS THE CRITICAL COMPONENT

If there is no reasonable expectation of privacy than no search actually takes place. The standard is based on what society deems reasonable not just the defendant's perspective. A person must show that he subjectively believed that he had a privacy interest in the thing searched *and* that this expectation is one which society is prepared to recognize as reasonable, in order for federal or state constitutional privacy protections to be implicated.

Case examples

- In ***Commonwealth v. Cabral***, a defendant who spit on the sidewalk did not have an expectation of privacy in his saliva or from his DNA extracted from the saliva.[190]
- In ***Commonwealth v. Bly***, the defendant had no expectation of privacy regarding the DNA extracted from a cigarette butt left behind during a police interview.[191]
- In the 2008 case of ***Commonwealth v. Porter P***., *a juvenile*, the SJC ruled that the defendant did have a reasonable expectation of privacy in his locked bedroom located in a Boston homeless shelter where the defendant resided with his mother. Despite shelter policy which subjects residents to searches of the living areas.
- In the 2012 case of ***Commonwealth v. Carnes***, a murder suspect hid a backpack in the backyard of a friend while trying to flee capture. The police located the backpack and searched it uncovering the murder weapon. The defendant argued that he had a subjective expectation of privacy. However, the court upheld the search stating that it was not an expectation that society would recognize.

In determining the reasonableness of one's expectation of privacy in a place or thing searched, the court will consider:

1) the character of the place where the government activity occurs,
2) whether the defendant owned the place involved,
3) whether he controlled access to the place,
4) whether the defendant had a possessory interest in the item taken or inspected, and
5) whether the defendant had taken normal precautions to protect his privacy.

Guests in a home

Generally, if the police conduct an illegal search of a home it would be the resident(s), those who reside in the home, who have a reasonable expectation of privacy, not someone who was just stopping by for a brief visit. However, an overnight guest would have a reasonable expectation of privacy even in a home that they do not live in.

Overnight Guest: The U.S. Supreme Court held that an overnight guest (as opposed to a *mere visitor*) has a reasonable expectation of privacy in the home in which he or she is staying.[192] However, there are exceptions.

- In ***Commonwealth v. Morrison***, the SJC ruled that an overnight guest who is forbidden from entering the property because of a restraining order may not object to the police entrance.[193]
- In the 2002 Appeals Court case of ***Commonwealth v. Mallory***,[194] the Court ruled that a defendant did not have a reasonable expectation of privacy in a bedroom that was searched by the police without a warrant pursuant to a rape investigation; the defendant did not own or rent the room, but was a guest who provided some food money; the host routinely entered the room, and **the host/guest relationship was destroyed when the defendant raped the host's daughter and then fled**.

---

[190] *Commonwealth v. Cabral*, 69 Mass. App.Ct. 68 (2007)
[191] *Commonwealth v. Bly*, 448 Mass. 473, 862 N.E.2d 341 (2007)
[192] *Minnesota v. Olson*, 495 U.S. 91, 110 S.Ct. 1684 (1990); *Commonwealth v. Acosta*, 416 Mass. 279, 534 N.E.2d 1167 (1993); *Commonwealth v. Allen*, 28 Mass. App. Ct. 589, 554 N.E.2d 854 (1990).*Minnesota v. Olson*, 495 U.S. 91, 110 S.Ct. 1684 (1990); *Commonwealth v. Acosta*, 416 Mass. 279, 534 N.E.2d 1167 (1993); *Commonwealth v. Allen*, 28 Mass. App. Ct. 589, 554 N.E.2d 854 (1990).
[193] *Commonwealth v. Morrison*, 429 Mass. 511, 710 N.E. 2d 584 (1999).
[194] *Commonwealth v. Mallory*, 56 Mass. App. Ct. 153, 775 N.E.2d 764 (2002)

- In the 2014 case of ***Commonwealth v. Copney***, the SJC ruled that an extended stay house guest, wherein the resident is forbidden from having extended visitors, cannot claim a reasonable expectation of privacy in the dwelling. In *Copney*, the defendant was living with his girlfriend, Brittany Smith, in her dorm room at Harvard University. Harvard's dormitory policy prohibited Smith from allowing Copney to stay in her dorm room for more than a "brief stay." Because Copney was forbidden from living in the dorm room he could not claim that he had a reasonable expectation of privacy.

Physical Intrusion by Police not Necessary

It is also important to note that the intrusion (i.e. invasion of privacy) need not be physical and need not constitute a trespass onto the private property of the person who is the subject of the search.[195]

- In ***Katz v. U.S.***,[196] the U.S. Supreme Court held unconstitutional the warrantless use of an electronic hearing device to record a private conversation from a public pay telephone even though the electronic listening device was on the outside of the telephone booth and did not physically intrude into the booth, nor did it intrude upon any private property of the caller. Nonetheless, the Court held that the caller had a reasonable expectation of privacy — freedom from both visual and auditory intrusion — in using the telephone in the booth.

Attorney Hanrahan's Comment: The telephone aspect is not the crux of this decision. The point is that a government intrusion need not be physical (e.g. a police officer could invade someone's privacy by using a high powered listening device from a public location to listen to a conversation of a person who is in a private home). Telephone conversations actually have no expectation of privacy because a user never can really be certain who else may be listening (see below).

NON-SEARCH SITUATIONS

The following are situations wherein evidence may be viewed (and in most cases even seized); however no actual search takes place because the person does not have a reasonable expectation of privacy.

PLAIN VIEW

A person cannot have a reasonable expectation of privacy in something that is in "plain view". When a person fails to take precautions from exposing, what they would otherwise deem private, from the view of the public, or significant numbers of other persons, there can be no reasonable expectation of privacy. It has long been settled that objects falling in the plain view of an officer who has a right to be in a position to have that view may be introduced into evidence. Therefore, if an item is in "plain view" the police did not "search" for that item; rather it was out for people to see. If there was no "search" than the constitutional protections do not apply.[197]

No search if open to public view

What a person knowingly exposes to the public ... is not a subject of Fourth Amendment protection."[198]

Courts, in various decisions, have determined that defendants have no reasonable expectation of privacy in the following examples:

- Public shopping area of a supermarket (as opposed to the basement which is designated "Employees Only").[199]
- Private clubs, which do not regulate admission to members and guests, do not have a reasonable expectation of privacy.[200] Where club owners fail to check patrons' identities and admit non-members (including an undercover officer), the reasonable expectation of privacy is lost.[201] Also, public areas of private clubs (as opposed to areas reserved for members only or marked for "authorized personnel") are not protected.[202]
- A prison cell, regardless of whether observations are made of objects in plain view,[203] or result from a reasonable, non-obtrusive strip search.[204]

---

[195] *See, e.g., Commonwealth v. Adams*, 22 MLW 2049 (Superior Court 1994) (court held that an infrared scan of a defendant's house did violate the resident's reasonable expectation of privacy).
[196] *Katz v. U.S.*, 389 U.S. 347, 88 S.Ct. 507 (1967.
[197] *Commonwealth v. Carter*, 424 Mass. 400, 676 N.E.2d 841 (1997) (no expectation of privacy in items left on porch).
[198] *Katz v. United States*, 389 U.S. 347, 351, 88 S.Ct. 507, 19 L.Ed.2d 576 (1967).
[199] *Commonwealth v. Lee*, 32 Mass. App. Ct. 85, 585 N.E.2d 759 (1992).
[200] *Commonwealth v. Cadoret* 388 Mass. 148 (1983.
[201] *Commonwealth v. D'Onofrio*, 396 Mass. 711, 488 N.E.2d 410 (1986).
[202] *Commonwealth v. Cadoret*, 388 Mass. 148, 445 N.E.2d 1050 (1983).

SEARCH OVERVIEW

- Urinal area of public restrooms, when observed by police looking through a ventilation duct (as opposed to the closed door stalls).[205]
- Conversations heard without using electronic listening device.[206]
- Odors in a public place.[207]
- Activities or things observed in *public* through use of binoculars or similar devices.[208]
- Activities or things observed by the use of aircraft, even if low-flying so long as in public airspace, without the use of high-powered cameras (or perhaps night vision devices), and not interfering with a defendant's use of his property.[209]

Seizing Evidence via Plain View

Just because the item may be visible in plain view does not mean that a police officer can necessarily seize it. The plain view seizure exception allows police to seize an object without a warrant if the following criteria are met:

- The Police "are **lawfully in a position** from which they **view an object**,
- Its incriminating character is **immediately apparent**, and
- The police have a **lawful right of access** to the object." [210]
- The officer came across the object inadvertently.

Each of these criteria is explained below:

Police must be in a lawful Position to View: This simply means that if the police make an unlawful entry, unlawful stop, or trespass their discovery will not be in "plain view." At the time the officer views the object his/her positioning must be lawful.

Incriminating nature must be immediately apparent or in the case of *mere evidence* "plausibly related:" this means that if the police need to inspect the item to determine its nature it is not a plain view discovery because it was not immediately apparent. The Court stated with respect to "contraband, weapons, or other items illegally possessed, where the incriminating character of the object is **immediately apparent**" or, with respect to "other types of evidence ('mere evidence'), where the particular evidence is **plausibly related** to criminal activity of which the police are already aware." [211]

For instance, if during a routine motor vehicle stop the police officer observes a stereo system in the back seat and the officer on a whim decides to remove the system and run the serial numbers to see if it is stolen this would not be considered plain view, even if the serial numbers came back as a stolen system, because the incriminating nature was not immediately apparent – it had to be inspected. However, if the police are investing a recent B&E and stop a car fitting the description of a witness and observe a stereo system in the back seat which is the same type as the one stolen during the B&E the incriminating nature would be immediately apparent and thus would be a plain view discovery.

- In the 2008 case of ***Commonwealth v. Pierre***, the plain view seizure exception applied to compact discs that were discovered in the defendant's possession during execution of valid search warrant. The Cambridge police were executing a search warrant for narcotics when they came across a storage locker and boxes containing hundreds of CD's that looked like generic unlabeled CD-Rs, contained in cases with photocopied covers and grouped in similar units of five to fifteen with some covered in plastic. The officers were lawfully present in relation to the storage locker and the cardboard boxes that contained them. The officers had probable cause to seize the discs, because the organization and physical appearance of discs were sufficient for the officer to reasonably infer that they were counterfeit copies intended for sale. [212]

---

[203] *Commonwealth v. McCollins*, 23 Mass. App. Ct. 436, 506 N.E.2d 146 (1987).
[204] *Lanston v. Commissioner of Corrections*, 404 Mass. 165, 533 N.E.2d 1375 (1987).
[205] *Commonwealth v. Bloom*, 18 Mass. App. Ct. 951, 468 N.E.2d 667 (1984).
[206] *Commonwealth v. Ling*, 370 Mass. 239, 346 N.E.2d 703 (1976).
[207] *U.S. v. Ventresca*, 380 U.S. 102, 85 S.Ct. 741 (1965).
[208] *Commonwealth v. Ortiz*, 376 Mass. 349, 380 N.E.2d 669 (1978).
[209] *California v. Ciraolo*, 476 U.S. 207, 106 S.Ct. 1809 (1986); *Dow Chemical Company v. United States*, 476 U.S. 227, 106 S.Ct. 1819 (1986).;*See also, Commonwealth v. Ling*, 370 Mass. 238, 346 N.E.2d 703 (1976) (flashlight); *State v. Vogel*, 428 N.W.2d 272 (S.D. 1988) (zoom lens).
[210] *Commonwealth v. Santana,* 420 Mass. 205, 211, 649 N.E.2d 717 (1995).
[211] Commonwealth v. William WHITE, Jr. SJC (2014)
[212] *Commonwealth v. Pierre*, 71 Mass. App. Ct. 58 (2008)

Lawful right of Access: this means that the police must be able to lawfully enter the area where the item is located.

- In ***Commonwealth v. Nielsen*,** the defendant was a student living in a dormitory at Fitchburg State College. College officials were conducting a door to door health and safety check after receiving information that a cat was being housed in one of the dormitories. When they inspected the defendant's room they discovered two four-foot tall marijuana plants, along with lights, fertilizer, and numerous other materials for marijuana cultivation and use. The officials stopped their investigation at that point, and requested the assistance of the Fitchburg State College campus police. The police arrived at the suite**, entered the bedroom** (without a warrant, consent or exigent circumstances), and observed the marijuana plants and other apparatus. All of the evidence was seized. The Commonwealth argued, among other things, that the discovery was permissible under the plain view doctrine. The Court ruled that discovery was not within the plain view doctrine because the officers were not lawfully present when they viewed the object inside the room.[213]

Discovery must be inadvertent

In Massachusetts, in order for the plain view doctrine to apply the police must come across the seized item *inadvertently.* There is a legal preference for a warrant, and if a police officer has probable cause in advance the Court expects that the police officer will seek a warrant and not try to utilize the plain view exception as a way of circumventing the search warrant requirement. Under federal law, the inadvertence requirement to the plain view seizure is not required.

The requirement in Massachusetts that the discovery of evidence in question be "inadvertent," for purposes of applying the plain view exception is applied most commonly in the context of a search warrant, **meaning only that the police must have lacked probable cause to believe**, prior to the search, that the specific items would be discovered during the search.[214] If they had probable cause prior to the execution of the warrant they should have spelled it out in their affidavit.

The rationale behind the requirement that discovery of evidence in question occur inadvertently, for the purposes of applying the plain view exception to search warrant requirement, is that the courts will not excuse officers from the general requirement of a warrant to seize if the officers know the location of evidence, have probable cause to seize it, intend to seize it, and yet do not bother to obtain a warrant particularly describing that evidence.

Police must also have *probable cause* to believe evidence related to a crime

In order to seize items which come into plain view during a lawful search (with or without a warrant), which items were not the object of the initial search, which are not weapons or contraband but simply potential evidence, officers must have probable cause to believe that such items are related to some crime.

- In ***Commonwealth v. Hawkins***, without knowing certain bonds were stolen, officers could not seize them even though the names on the bonds did not match those on the apartment the police were searching for drugs.[215]
- In ***Commonwealth v. Moynihan***, officers lawfully seized clothing in plain view from the suspect's automobile which had been towed in connection with another arrest since the jacket and coat matched the victim's description and were in plain view on the back seat and probable cause existed that the clothing was evidence.[216]
- In ***Commonwealth v. Rodriguez***, a mere hunch about clothing seized during warrant search in connection with rape investigation was not sufficient.[217]

Closed Containers and the Plain View Doctrine:

The SJC in the 2012 case of ***Commonwealth v. Magri***, quoting from ***Commonwealth v. Straw***, stated "in cases involving closed containers ... the plain view doctrine may support the warrantless *seizure* of a container believed to contain contraband but any subsequent *search* of the concealed contents of the container must be accompanied by a warrant or justified by one of the exceptions to the warrant requirement".

[213] *Commonwealth v. Neilson*, 423 Mass. 75 (1996).
[214] *Commonwealth v. Balicki*, 436 Mass. 1, 762 N.E.2d 290 (2002).
[215] *Commonwealth v. Hawkins*, 361 Mass. 384, 280 N.E.2d 665 (1972).
[216] *Commonwealth v. Moynihan*, 376 Mass. 468, 381 N.E.2d 575 (1978).
[217] *Commonwealth v. Rodriguez*, 378 Mass. 296, 391 N.E.2d 889 (1979).

SEARCH OVERVIEW

PLAIN SMELL

The odor of freshly burnt (or even raw) marijuana, coupled with an officer's training and experience, amounts to probable cause that marijuana is present (but not criminal amounts). The most common situation when the Plain Smell Doctrine is utilized is during a motor vehicle stop. But the plain smell doctrine has also been used to establish probable cause in homes and even on the body of a suspect.

- In ***Commonwealth v. Skea,*** after detecting a "pretty heavy" odor of burnt marijuana, police officers had probable cause to believe that marijuana had recently been smoked in the vehicle and that evidence of marijuana use and possession would be found within it.[218]

However, since the possession of an ounce or less of marijuana is no longer criminal a search under the plain smell doctrine will no longer permit a search unless the officer has probable cause to believe that more than an ounce is present, thus making possession criminal, or some other crime is involved (i.e. OUI drugs, distribution and so on).

Raw Marijuana

In the 2014 Appeals Court case of ***Commonwealth v. Fontaine***, the Court stated that the mere odor of raw marijuana *alone* does <u>not</u> amount to reasonable suspicion. However, when the odor of raw marijuana is detected by an ***experienced*** officer, the odor is ***overwhelming*** and ***pervasive*** (i.e. detected throughout the vehicle) there is **reasonable suspicion** that more than an ounce of marijuana is present.

Also, in the 2014 SJC case of ***Commonwealth v. Overmeyer***, the Court ruled that the odor of unburnt marijuana does not amount to probable cause to believe that criminal amounts of marijuana or evidence is present.

Note: See the Motor Vehicle Search section for a full analysis of this issue.

Non-Marijuana: Although the vast of majority of plain smell issues have dealt with burnt (and raw) marijuana the concept of plain smell still applies. For instance, if you were investigating a recent arson incident and you came across a potential suspect and detected the odor of gasoline coming from his person that most certainly would be a contributor in the establishment of probable cause (and subsequent trial). Only the odor of marijuana was affected by this change in the law not the legal concept.

OPEN FIELDS

An "open field" is that portion of the privately owned land surrounding a person's dwelling house that is too remote or removed from the physical dwelling to be considered part of the "house" to be protected by the Fourth Amendment.[219]

- In ***Hester v. U.S.***,[220] the U.S. Supreme Court stated that open fields, although privately owned, are not protected by the Fourth Amendment. Police do not need a warrant or even probable cause to make observations of activities or make searches of property located in open fields that are removed from a house and curtilage.

Since activities or property located in open fields is voluntarily exposed to public view, no reasonable expectation of privacy arises.

- In ***Oliver v. United States***,[221] the Supreme Court held that, even if fields are fenced and posted with "no trespassing" signs, there was no reasonable expectation of privacy if they were beyond the curtilage of the residence or building.

Aerial Observations (may need reasonable suspicion)

In ***Commonwealth v. One 1985 Ford Thunderbird,*** 416 Mass. 603 (1994), the SJC held that a helicopter surveillance of the defendant's back yard was not an "illegal search" where the police had a ***reasonable suspicion*** that illegal activity was taking place. In this case**,** the State police helicopter flew over the defendant's back yard from approximately 700 feet. Various photographs were taken showing a considerable amount of marijuana being grown in the defendant's

[218] See *Commonwealthv. Skea*, 18 Mass.App.Ct. 685, 695, 470 N.E.2d 385 (1984).
[219] *Hester v. U.S.* , 265, U.S. 57, 44 S.Ct. 445 (1924); *Commonwealth v. John G. Grant & Sons, Inc.*, 403 Mass. 151, 512 N.E.2d 522 (1988).
[220] 265 U.S. 57, 44, S.Ct. 445 (1924).
[221] *Oliver v. United States*, 466 U.S. 170, 104 S.Ct. 1735 (1984).

swimming pool. Since the police had received a tip from an informant, they had reasonable suspicion. The Court did not state whether or not that this type of aerial surveillance can take place without reasonable suspicion.[222]

The SJC indicated that had the helicopter interfered with the defendant's normal use of the yard it would have been unreasonable search. The Court referred to the following two out-of-state court decisions:

- ***People v. Sneed***, (1973), where there was helicopter surveillance from an altitude of twenty to twenty-five feet, it was "unreasonable and probably illegal."
- ***Commonwealth v. Oglialoro***, (1990), where helicopter surveillance from an altitude of fifty feet caused a substantial hazard within the curtilage and constituted an unreasonable search.

ABANDONED PROPERTY AND DENIAL OF OWNERSHIP

When a person abandons property, he or she forfeits his right of privacy regarding that property. Similarly, when a person denies the property belongs to him/her the person generally loses any expectation of privacy.

Generally, items left unattended on a public way, or in some cases even private property (see *Com. v. Nattoo* below) have been abandoned and thus are not protected by the Fourth Amendment, even if the owner intends to come back and retrieve it at some other time. Abandoned or discarded property may be searched by police and seized in most circumstances. Such a search and seizure is not governed by the Fourth Amendment because no one has a reasonable expectation of privacy in such property.

- In the 2009 case of ***Commonwealth v. Nattoo,*** the defendant was staying in a mobile home that had recently been sold. When the new owner arrived to occupy the mobile home he called the police because the defendant was found inside. The defendant removed his belongings (several trash bags and a television) to the driveway and called his girlfriend to pick up his belongings. While on scene the police discovered a warrant for the defendant and placed him under arrest. The defendant did not ask to take his belongings with him. After leaving the scene the new owner called the police again because the bags and television were left behind. The police returned to retrieve the belongings and inspected the bags before placing them in his cruiser. A loaded gun was discovered. The court ruled that the defendant did not have a reasonable expectation of privacy in his belongings even though he was involuntarily removed from the scene. [223]

Denial of Ownership

Generally if a person denies ownership of an item they forfeit their right to privacy, unless the item is in the person's home or some other area where the person has an expectation of privacy.[224] A key factor is whether the person **actually intended to abandon the item**.

- In the 2008 case of ***Commonwealth v. Augello,*** the police were investigating a recent break-in where the defendant was seen in the area carrying a black suitcase. The police went to the defendant's home and were invited in by a roommate. Once inside they observed a black suitcase. Both the defendant and his roommate denied ownership of the suitcase. The police opened the suitcase instead of obtaining a warrant reasoning it was abandoned property. Evidence was discovered inside the suitcase. The court ruled that in order for an item to be considered abandoned the owner **must have had the intent to abandon the item**. The court explained that simply verbally denying ownership is not enough to establish abandonment. The fact that item was in the defendant's home is strong indication that the property was not abandoned. [225]

Attorney Hanrahan's Comment: whether or not something is abandoned largely depends on the intent of the possessor. If someone continues to store an item in their home it could be inferred that the person did not intend to abandon the item.

[222] *Commonwealth v.One 1985 Ford Thunderbird*, 416 Mass. 603 (1994).
[223] *Commonwealth Nattoo*, 42 Mass. 826 (2009)
[224] *Commonwealth v. Augello*, 452 Mass. 1021 (2008)
[225] *Commonwealth v. Augello*, 451 Mass. 1101 (2008)

Discarded items

Generally, if a person discards his property he has forfeited his expectation of privacy.

- In ***Commonwealth v. Nutile***, the Court ruled that if a motorist, while being chased by a police cruiser, throws articles out of the car window, that person has abandoned them and they may be seized and searched by the police without probable cause or a warrant because no one has a privacy interest in those articles once they are discarded.[226]
- In ***Commonwealth v. Straw***, the police were executing a default warrant at the defendant's house. One officer went to the rear of the house in case the defendant tried to flee. Another officer went to the front door and spoke with the defendant's mother. The officer at the rear of the house observed a suitcase get thrown from a window by the defendant. The suitcase landed between the house and the fence (within the curtilage). The police seized the suitcase and discovered drugs. The SJC suppressed the evidence stating that the police needed a warrant to open the suitcase. The fact that the defendant placed the items in a locked suitcase and the suitcase remained within the curtilage were significant factors which the Court felt were enough to show the defendant did not have the intent to abandon the suitcase or its contents.[227]

Attorney Hanrahan's Note: a key distinction between these two cases is the fact that, in *Straw*, the discarded item remained on the defendant's property.

Trash: As long as the trash is left on the public curbside (not within the curtilage) for pick up the expectation of privacy will be lost.[228]

Airline baggage: In ***Commonwealth v. Small***, the Court ruled that keeping an airline baggage tag in one's possession means a passenger has not abandoned his or her luggage, even after leaving it unclaimed for three hours at the airport.[229]

In a Vehicle: In the 2013 case of ***Commonwealth v. Perkins***, the SJC ruled that passengers of a motor vehicle who flee during a motor vehicle stop (for a civil infraction) do not automatically abandon items that they leave behind in a motor vehicle. The Court stated, "there is no evidence that (the defendants), by leaving items in a *closed car*, intended to permanently relinquish control of those items."

Abandoned Apartments and Hotel Rooms

a. **Apartments:** When a person vacates an apartment, he or she abandons any interest in that apartment and items left behind. With the permission of the landlord, police may enter the vacated apartment and seize any or all items discarded by the former tenant.[230]

b. **Hotel Room:** A guest also loses his/her expectation of privacy in a hotel room when:

    a. He/she abandons the room , or

    b. Once his/her rental period expires, or[231]

    c. He/she is evicted by the hotel.[232]

Case examples

In ***Commonwealth v. Paszko***, items (coat and drug paraphernalia) left abandoned in hotel room, even though defendant paid for additional days and kept the key to the room were deemed abandoned.[233] Abandonment in this case was proven by (1) registration at another hotel; (2) removing all other personal property; (3) spending the next night out of state; and (4) traveling in an easterly directly in New York when arrested, far from the hotel room in Michigan.[234]

[226] *Stack v. U.S.*, 368 F.2d 78 (1st Cir. 1966); *Commonwealth v. Nutile*, 31 Mass. App. Ct. 614, 582 N.E.2d 547 (1991).
[227] *Commonwealth v. Straw*, 422 Mass. 756 (1996)
[228] *Commonwealth v. Pratt*, 407 Mass. 647, 555 N.E.2d 559 (1990).
[229] *Commonwealth v. Small*, 28 Mass. App. Ct. 533, 552 N.E.2d 599 (1990).
[230] *Abel v. U.S.*, 362 U.S. 217, 80 S.Ct. 683 (1960); *See also,Commonwealth v. Lanigan*, 12 Mass. App. Ct. 913, 423 N.E.2d 800, *cert. den.*488 U.S. 1007, 109 S.Ct. 788 (1981); *Commonwealth v. Pina*, 406 Mass. 540, 549 N.E.2d 106 (1990).
[231] *Commonwealth v. Netto,* 438 Mass. 686, 698 (2003) and *Commonwealth v. Paszko,* 391 Mass. 164, 184-185 (1984).
[232] *Commonwealth v. Molina* (2011).
[233] *Commonwealth v. Paszko*, 391 Mass. 194, 461 N.E.2d 222 (1984).
[234] *Commonwealth v. Paszko*, 391 Mass. 194, 461 N.E.2d 222 (1984).

In the 2011 case of ***Com. v. Molina***, the defendant rented a hotel on-line for three nights. At check-in he signed an agreement to obey the hotel rules or face eviction. The defendant immediately began having unruly visitors and at one point he was informed by the hotel manager that he was "gone" of the hotel received one more complaint. Soon thereafter the hotel began receiving complaints about marijuana emanating from the defendant's room. While the defendant was not present the hotel manager, along with security, entered the room to evict the defendant. After receiving no response they entered and found evidence of drug use. The manager double-locked the door with the intention of denying him reentry. The Boston Police were contacted and the manager granted them access to the room. Once inside they discovered more than $10,000 in cash, a firearm and significant amounts of cocaine, mescaline and marijuana. The SJC ruled that under the circumstances the defendant did not possess a reasonable expectation of privacy because he was lawfully evicted.

TELEPHONE CONVERSATIONS

In ***Commonwealth v. Eason***,[235] the SJC held that there is no expectation of privacy in a telephone conversation, the popularity of cordless and cellular telephones have made it unreasonable to expect privacy in a telephone conversation.

In ***Commonwealth v. Cote***, the SJC held that a person has no reasonable expectation of privacy in telephone message records maintained by a paid operator staffed telephone answering service.[236]

Attorney Hanrahan's Comment: Although there is no expectation of privacy, you still must be cognizant of M.G.L. chapter 272 § 99, the wiretap statute. A violation of the wiretap statute will not only lead to the suppression of evidence but may also be a criminal violation. Also, although there may be no expectation of privacy in a telephone conversation, there is an expectation of privacy of a cellular telephone's content. See the Surveillance section of this manual for more on this topic.

STATE ACTION

The Fourth Amendment applies only to searches and seizures conducted by officials, employees, or agents of a federal, state or local government. This commonly referred to as *state action.* Searches conducted by private citizens, who are not encouraged by law enforcement, typically are not governed by the Fourth Amendment.

NON-GOVERNMENT ACTORS

Property turned over to the police by "concerned citizens," acting on their own, may serve as a basis for an arrest or search warrant (if reasonably authenticated) even if the suspect had a reasonable expectation of privacy. For example, drugs found in a person's bedroom by a parent, friend or cleaning person could be used as evidence against the defendant even though the defendant may have had an expectation of privacy.

Case example

- In the 2003 case of ***Commonwealth v. White***[237], the Appeals Court ruled that threatening letters sent to the victim by the defendant should not be suppressed. The letters were turned over to the Commonwealth by the victim's mother, who was checking the victim's mail in the victim's absence from the home. The mother turned the letters over to the authorities on her own initiative. (Thereafter, the victim also voluntarily turned over to the Commonwealth other letters that she had received from the defendant.) The motion judge found that no government agent participated in, or instigated, the retrieval or production of the letters. Under settled principles of law, the Court explained that there can be no constitutionally-based violation absent governmental action.[238] Hence, the Court ruled that this private conduct did not warrant suppression.

SEARCH OVERVIEW

[235] *Commonwealth v. Eason*, 427 Mass. 595 (1998).
[236] *Commonwealth v. Cote*, 407 Mass. 827 (1990).
[237] *Commonwealth v. White,* 60 Mass.App.Ct. 193, 800 N.E.2d 712 (2003).
[238] See *Commonwealth v. Jung,* 420 Mass. 675, 686, 651 N.E.2d 1211 (1995). See also *Commonwealth v. Leone,* 386 Mass. 329, 333, 435 N.E.2d 1036 (1982).

QUASI-GOVERNMENT ACTORS

Although the Fourth Amendment and Article 14 protect citizens against searches conducted by state actors, the courts have often lessened those protections when the government employee conducting the search is not a law enforcement officer nor working at the direction of a law enforcement officer.

Searches by Public School Officials

The 2003 SJC case of ***Commonwealth v. Lawrence L.***, confirmed that the Fourth Amendment's prohibition on unreasonable searches and seizures applies to searches conducted by public school officials, although not to the same extent as to law enforcement officials.[239]

Search Warrant not required for School Officials

In the school environment, the SJC explained that the typical requirements of search warrant and probable cause to search are relaxed when a school official conducts a search of a student. The warrant requirement, in particular, is unsuited to the school environment: requiring a teacher to obtain a warrant before searching a child suspected of an infraction of school rules (or of the criminal law) would unduly interfere with the maintenance of the swift and informal disciplinary procedures needed in the schools.[240]

Attorney Hanrahan's Note: School Resource Officers are held to the same standard as other officers and may not operate on the relaxed standard granted to school officials.

Working in conjunction or at the direction of Law Enforcement

The relaxation of the warrant and probable cause requirements are only applicable to school officials who are not acting in conjunction with or at the request of law enforcement agencies and officials.

Memorandum to cooperate with Police does not trigger state action

The Court in *Lawrence L.* also ruled that a memorandum between the police and the school that contains guidelines for school officials to report detected criminal behavior to the police does not result in school officials becoming agents of the police, and thus in *Lawrence L.* the vice-principal who searched the juvenile defendant for marijuana was not acting as an agent of law enforcement. The Court ruled that the memorandum between school officials and police did nothing more than provide guidelines for school officials to contact law enforcement in the event that students are found illegally to possess controlled substances.[241]

Search by School Staff must still be reasonable

The U.S. Supreme Court, in ***New Jersey v. T.L.O.*** ruled that school officials and teachers may search the person of a student (including purses) if, under all of the circumstances, "there are reasonable grounds for suspecting that the search will turn up evidence that the student has violated or is violating either the law or the rules of the school."[242]

- In ***Commonwealth v. Lawrence L***, the school vice-principal had probable cause to search the juvenile defendant for drugs. The vice-principal testified that the juvenile "reeked" of marijuana when he spoke to the juvenile early in the afternoon, the vice-principal had knowledge of a previous incident that had occurred just one month earlier where marijuana had been found on the juvenile, and when the vice-principal asked the juvenile if he had been smoking marijuana, the juvenile's response that he did not do such "here" anymore, was ambiguous.[243]
- In ***Commonwealth v. Smith***, the school assistant headmaster had reasonable grounds for searching the student defendant, and thus, the search was reasonable at its inception, for the purposes of determining whether the search was reasonable under the totality of the circumstances; the headmaster was aware that the defendant had not entered the building through the single entrance with metal detectors as required by the school rules, the defendant had avoided leaving his bag in the headmaster's office, which was the usual practice, the defendant had been told on the day before the search not to return without a parent, and the defendant had been in an unauthorized area of the school during class, in violation of the school rules.[244]

Attorney Hanrahan's Note: School Officials are not required to read Miranda warnings before questioning a juvenile.

---

[239] *Commonwealth v. Lawrence L*, 439 Mass. 817, 792 N.E.2d 109 (2003).
[240] *Commonwealth v. Smith*, 72 Mass. App.Ct. 175, 889 N.E.2d 439 (2008)
[241] *Commonwealth v. Lawrence L*, 439 Mass. 817, 792 N.E.2d 109 (2003).
[242] *New Jersey v. T.L.O.*, 469 U.S. 325, 105 S.Ct. 733 (1985).
[243] *New Jersey v. T.L.O.*, 469 U.S. 325, 105 S.Ct. 733 (1985).
[244] *Commonwealth v. Smith*, 452 Mass. 1104, 893 N.E.2d 1237 (2008)

Searches by "Special" Police Officers

When a special police officer employed by a private entity takes action in order to protect the property of his employer, and not necessarily to further a criminal investigation, the state action which triggers Constitutional protections will most likely be absent.

In the 2009 case of ***Commonwealth v. Carr***, the Boston College (private school) campus police entered the defendant's dorm room after receiving information that the defendant possessed knives, and possibly a gun, in violation of school rules and policy. The officers entered with the intention of enforcing school rules, i.e. the possession of unauthorized weapons that may not necessarily be unlawful to possess, and not to conduct a criminal investigation. Once inside the officers uncovered knives and a toy handgun (toy guns were also prohibited at the college). The officers asked for further consent to search for more unauthorized items and were granted permission. They subsequently uncovered drugs. The Appeals Court upheld the entry because the officers where serving as agents of the private school, enforcing the school rules, and not as state actors conducting a criminal investigation. [245]

However, in a seemingly similar case the SJC came to a different conclusion:

In ***Commonwealth v. Neilsen***, officials of Fitchburg State College, a public entity, entered a dormitory room to investigate the prohibited keeping of a pet. The college had expressly reserved the right to inspect dormitory rooms. In the course of the investigation, the officials inadvertently discovered marijuana being cultivated. Rather than seizing the marijuana and turning it over to the police, or providing information to the police with which a search warrant could be obtained, the officials invited the police to enter. The Court in *Neilson* concluded that the constitutional violation occurred not when the college officials entered to enforce the college's health and safety regulations, but when the police entered the room, searched, and seized evidence without a search warrant, consent, or exigent circumstances. As observed in Neilson, the defendant's consent was given not to the police, but to the college officials, who "had no authority to consent to or join in a police search for evidence of crime." [246]

Attorney Hanrahan's Note: In contrast to *Neilson*, the police in the *Carr* case entered to enforce a residency condition relating to the health and safety of all the dormitory occupants, not in furtherance of a criminal investigation.

Searches by Fire Officials

In ***Commonwealth v. Jung***, fire fighters responded to a house fire at 11:23 PM and the fire was extinguished by 2:00 AM. Fire officials arrived the next day to further investigate the cause of the fire. During their investigation they observed evidence linking the owners of the property to arson. The SJC ruled that the fire officials did not need a warrant to enter the fire damaged home to investigate the origin and cause of the fire within a reasonable time after the fire was extinguished.[247] Also, by allowing a private insurance investigator to use the ladder truck to take an aerial photo did not create a state action situation.

STANDING TO CHALLENGE SEARCHES

The term "standing" refers to whether or not a defendant can contest the search of a given area. Obviously, if the search took place in the defendant's home, automobile or on his person the defendant would have "standing" to challenge the search because clearly he would have an expectation of privacy. However, if the search was conducted of an automobile, home or other location which the accused did not himself have a reasonable expectation of privacy in standing to object is not always so clear. If the defendant has standing and the evidence is unlawfully obtained the evidence will be subject to suppression under the Exclusionary Rule.

The Federal Rule

The Fourth Amendment protects persons against unreasonable searches of "their persons [and] houses," and thus is a personal right that must be invoked by an individual. But the extent to which the Amendment protects people may depend upon where those people are. While an overnight guest may have a legitimate expectation of privacy

[245] *Commonwealth v. Carr*, Mass.App.Ct. (2009)
[246] *Commonwealth v. Neilson*, 423 Mass. 75 (1996)
[247] *Commonwealth v. Jung*, 420 Mass. 675, 651 N.E.2d 1211 (1995)

in someone else's home,[248] one who is merely present with the consent of the house holder may not.[249] And an expectation of privacy in commercial property is different from, and less than, a similar expectation in a home.[250]

In the 1998 Supreme Court case of ***Minnesota v. Cartera,*** a police officer arrested two persons seen through an apartment window bagging cocaine.[251] The U.S. Supreme Court ruled that the purely commercial nature of the transaction, the relatively short period of time that the defendants were on the premises, and the lack of any previous connection between them and the householder all led to the conclusion that their situation is closer to that of one simply permitted on the premises. They, therefore, lacked standing to challenge the legality of the officer's observations, which the Supreme Court held was not a search.

In short, the federal rule is that the defendant must show that he or she had a reasonable expectation of privacy in the searched premises.[252]

The Massachusetts Rule

Massachusetts has adopted an *automatic standing rule* except for those instances in which an arrest warrant is issued, meaning that a person who is facing incriminating evidence based on a search by law enforcement officials will be able to automatically object to the search even if the defendant's expectation of privacy wasn't affected. [253] But the court later set limitations; in ***Commonwealth v. Frazier***,[254] the court limited the automatic standing rule to seizures from *residences and automobiles* where *possession* is an essential element.

The automatic standing applies even when:

a. The defendant did not have possession at the time of the seizure,
b. The defendant was not present when the search took place,
c. The dwelling or vehicle was not the defendant's.

In ***Commonwealth v. Frazier***, where the police seized a woman's purse which contained cocaine and charged the defendant with both trafficking and conspiracy (alleging the defendant to be the woman's distribution partner), the defendant had standing to challenge the search in only the trafficking case. Possession was not an element of the conspiracy charge.[255]

Hotel Rooms

In Federal cases, a guest in another's hotel room has no standing to challenge a search even where seized evidence is to be used against him.[256] A similar result was reached in the Massachusetts case of ***Commonwealth v. Price***[257] where the defendant lacked standing to challenge the action of the State Police who, pursuant to a warrant, videotaped Price negotiating a drug deal in a hotel room. The court decided that the defendant had no expectation of privacy in the room which was not registered in his name (but that of a stranger), where the deal involved people he had just met, and when the arm's-length deal was conducted with manifestations of suspicion/ distrust.

Overnight Guest: An overnight guest of a lawful occupant has standing to raise privacy claims in respect to a search of that occupant's premises.

Protective Order

However, in ***Commonwealth v. Morrison***, the subject of a protective order barring him from the premises lacked standing to an object to a search of the premises.[258]

Standing in the workplace

With advancements in technology come more complex issues involving standing. In ***Commonwealth v. Bryant***,[259] the Massachusetts' SJC held an employee did not have standing to challenge a search warrant targeting computer files at his place of employment. The court reasoned that the defendant did not establish an expectation of privacy in the documents sought. The defendant did not own the place involved, he did not control access to the area and the files in question were accessible to any employee.

---

[248] *Minnesota v. Olson*, 495 U.S. 91, 110 S.Ct. 1684, 109 L.Ed.2 85 (1990).
[249] *Jones v. U.S.*, 362 U.S. 257, 80 St. Ct. 725, 4 L.Ed.2 697 (1960).
[250] *New York v. Burger*, 482 U.S. 691, 107 S. Ct. 2636, 96 L.Ed.2d.601 (1987).
[251] *Minnesota v. Carter*, 525 U.S. 83, 119 S.Ct. 469, 142 L.Ed.2d 373 (1998).
[252] *U.S. v. Silvucci*, 448 U.S. 83, 100 S.Ct. 2547 (1980) and *Rawlings v. Kentucky*, 448 U.S. 98, 100 S.Ct. 2556 (1980).
[253] *Commonwealth v. Amendola*, 406 Mass. 592, 601, 550 N.E.2d 121 (1990).
[254] *Commonwealth v. Frazier*, 410 Mass. 235, 571 N.E.2d 1356 (1991).
[255] *Commonwealth v. Frazier*, 410 Mass. 235, 571 N.E.2d 1356 (1991).
[256] *U.S. v. Adamo*, 742 F.2d 927 (6th Cir. 1984); *U.S. v. Grandstaff*, 813 F.2d 1353 (9th Cir. 1987)
[257] *Commonwealth v. Price*, 408 Mass. 668, 562 N.E.2d 1355 (1990).
[258] *Commonwealth v. Morrison*, 429 Mass. 511, 710 N.E. 2d 584 (1999).
[259] *Commonwealth v. Bryant*, 447 Mass. 494, 852 N.E.2d 1072 (2006).

Attorney Hanrahan's note: a police officer should not conduct an unlawful search with the mindset that it is permissible because the subject of the search has not standing to object. Standing is usually an issue for trial. It was included in this manual for informational purposes.

SPECIAL PRECAUTIONS FOR THE HOME

Although the Fourth Amendment protects against *all* unreasonable searches there is greater protection provided to dwellings under both the Federal and State Constitutions.[260] The U.S. Supreme Court has stated that the "physical entry of the home is the chief evil against which the wording of the Fourth Amendment is directed."[261] The SJC has declared that "the right of police officers to enter into a home, for whatever purpose, represents a serious governmental intrusion into one's privacy." In general, art. 14 of the Massachusetts Declaration of Rights allows the police to *enter* a home in four circumstances: [262]

1. A judicial **warrant** supported by probable cause.
    a. Search Warrant (see Search Warrant section)
    b. Arrest Warrant: an arrest warrant may grant a police officer access to the arrestee's home (see Arrest Warrant section of this manual for more).
2. Probable cause plus **exigency.** There are essentially two types of exigency:
    a. Exigency to preserve evidence wherein the evidence will otherwise be destroyed.
    b. Exigency to arrest a dangerous person (see the Forde Factors in the Arrest Section of this manual).
3. Under the "**emergency aid**" doctrine, where the police have "an objectively reasonable basis to believe that there may be someone inside who is injured or in imminent danger of physical harm." **NOTE**: courts have extended this to include the prevention of property destruction and damage in addition to human harm and injury.
4. The voluntary **consent** of a person with common authority over the home.

Each of these topics are fully covered in other areas of this manual.

What Constitutes a Home?

The law frequently refers to what a layperson calls a home, a dwelling. A dwelling is where someone resides. For instance, a residential house may not be legally deemed a dwelling if it has been abandoned and vacant for a prolonged period of time. However, a hotel room may be deemed a dwelling if someone resides there for a prolonged period of time. The home, or dwelling, does not just entail the main structure. It also may extend to the so-called curtilage.

Curtilage

The curtilage, although on the exterior of the dwelling structure, is generally provided the same protections as the interior of the home.
"The curtilage concept originated at common law to extend to the area immediately surrounding a dwelling house the same protection under the law of burglary as was afforded the house itself."[263] Today, the curtilage concept arises more commonly in the context of the Fourth Amendment and defines both the area to which Fourth Amendment protections extend and the area where police may search pursuant to a warrant. A warrant that authorizes the search of a particular dwelling also authorizes the search of areas within the curtilage of that dwelling. For curtilage issues as it applies to search warrants see the search warrant section of this manual for more. This section focuses on the privacy protections of curtilage.

As mentioned above, the word "curtilage" is used to refer to that area surrounding a house which is constitutionally protected under the Fourth Amendment.264 If the area is found to be within the "curtilage" of the dwelling house, the court will always find that the person did have a reasonable expectation of privacy in such area

SEARCH OVERVIEW

[260] See, e.g., *Georgia* v. *Randolph*, 547 U.S. 103, 115 (2006); *Minnesota* v. *Carter*, 525 U.S. 83, 99 (1998) (Kennedy, J., concurring) ("it is beyond dispute that the home is entitled to special protection as the center of the private lives of our people"); *Commonwealth* v. *Blake*, 413 Mass. 823, 829 n.8 (1992).
[261] Commonwealth v. Lopez, 458 Mass. 383, 389–390, 937 N.E.2d 949 (2010), quoting United States v. United States Dist. Court for the E. Dist. of Mich., 407 U.S. 297, 313, 92 S.Ct. 2125, 32 L.Ed.2d 752 (1972)
[262] *Com. v. Porter P.*, a juvenile, SJC 2010
[263] *Commonwealth* v. *McCarthy*, 428 Mass. 871, 873 (1999), quoting *United States* v. *Dunn*, 480 U.S. 294, 300 (1987).
[264] *Rozencrantz v. U.S.*, 356 F.2d 310 (1st Cir. 1969)

The Supreme Court in ***U.S. v. Dunn,*** listed four criteria for deciding whether an area falls within the curtilage of a residence.[265] They include:

- proximity to home;
- surrounded by an enclosure (fence);
- use made of area (e.g., domestic); and
- actions the resident took to shelter the area from view of a passerby.

Case example

In the 2008 case of ***Commonwealth v. Kirschner***, officers responded to a loud party complaint which included the use of fireworks. The defendant explained to the officers that the people who set off the fireworks were not welcomed guests and had left prior to the arrival of the police. The officers then entered the back yard, without the consent of the defendant, to see if the unwanted guests had left. While in the back yard the officers observed marijuana on the rear deck of the house. The court suppressed the marijuana because the offices were without justification to enter the curtilage of the defendant's dwelling. [266]

Walkways and Access ways

Whether or not a walkway or access way falls within the protective part of the curtilage largely depends on whether or not a visitor or member of the public would be expected to pass through the area in order to contact the occupants. For instance, if a delivery person must pass through the area to contact the resident it is likely the court would deem the area outside of the protective part of the curtilage. Like with any other search topic it always hinges on the expectation of privacy.

- In ***Commonwealth v. Butterfield***, the walkway leading from the driveway of a home to its back door was not part of the curtilage of the home entitled to Fourth Amendment protection; the walkway was the one which a visitor would naturally use to reach the back door and lacked characteristics creating an inference of privacy.[267]

- Similarly, in ***Commonwealth v. Pietrass***, the SJC ruled where a house has a screened front porch through which one must pass to reach the true "front door", this area will not constitute part of the (protected) curtilage.[268]

Apartment Complexes/Multi-unit Homes

Apartment dwellers have little, if any, claim for curtilage. Common areas, a common cellar, and a common hallway (or the ceiling above it) generally do not constitute an apartment's curtilage.[269] However, in rare cases such as a locked storage area in a common basement may be within the curtilage of an apartment. Again, like with any search, it all depends on the reasonable expectation of privacy.

Attorney Hanrahan's Comment: Police officers often get confused with the concept of curtilage because some cases will indicate that a walkway is not a protected part of the curtilage but other cases will indicate that a car parked in a nearby lot is part of the curtilage. The confusion stems from the fact that there are two competing aspects of curtilage – **warrantless searches** and **search warrant execution**. When conducting a *warrantless search* the police may argue that an area around the home was not within the curtilage because the area is accessible to visitors, thus justifying the warrantless inspection of that part of the home's exterior. However, when executing a **search warrant** the warrant typically allows a search of the entire home – including the curtilage. In this case the police will argue that the area searched, exterior of the main structure or apartment, was within the curtilage and thus authorized under the search warrant.

Case examples

- In ***Commonwealth v. McCarthy,*** a visitor's parking space at an apartment complex was not within the curtilage of the apartment, and thus a search warrant issued for the apartment did not encompass that parking space.[270]

- In ***Commonwealth v. Lodge,*** the area within the walls behind a refrigerator was within the curtilage of the apartment.[271] There the police had a warrant to search for a weapon in the defendant's apartment. He hid the murder weapon (a handgun) in the kitchen wall space behind the refrigerator.

---

[265] *U.S. v. Dunn*, 480 U.S. 294, 107 S.Ct. 1134 (1987).
[266] *Commonwealth v. Kirschner*, 67 Mass.App.Ct. 836 (2006)
[267] *Commonwealth v. Butterfield*, 44 Mass. App. Ct. 926, 691 N.E. 2d 975 (1998)
[268] *Commonwealth v. Pietrass*, 392 Mass. 892, 467 N.E.2d 1368 (1984).
[269] *Commonwealth v. Montanez*, 410 Mass. 290, 571 N.E.2d 1372 (1991); *Commonwealth v. Pacheco*, 21 Mass. App. Ct. 565, 488 N.E.2d 42 (1986); *Commonwealth v. Thomas*, 358 Mass. 771, 267 N.E.2d 489 (1971)
[270] *Commonwealth v. McCarthy*, 428 Mass. 871, 705 N.E. 2d 1110 (1999).
[271] *Commonwealth v. Lodge*, 431 Mass. 461, 727 N.E. 2d 1194 (2000).

- In the 2008 case of ***Commonwealth v. Pierre***, the basement of defendant's building, containing storage lockers, was located within curtilage of the defendant's apartment, and thus, the search warrant authorized the search of the basement as an area appurtenant and within curtilage; the stairs in defendant's kitchen that linked the apartment to the basement suggested that the basement was sufficiently proximate to the apartment, despite the fact that two floors separated the apartment and the basement, curtilage of the apartment could still cover the basement with respect to separate areas subject to the tenant's exclusive control, and each storage locker in the basement corresponded to one apartment.[272]

COMPUTER & TECHNOLOGY RELATED SEARCHES

With the rapid advancement of technology police officers are often dealing with more and more crime incidents that take place in a digital or virtual location. The Courts have typically applied intrusions into these digital or virtual locations the same as physical locations. Like all Fourth Amendment Search and Seizure issues it all comes down to the expectation of privacy. In a computer sense, the question is *did the defendant have an expectation of privacy in the computer files, email, text message, etc.*? If an expectation of privacy did exist *was there an exception to the search warrant requirement present* (e.g. exigent circumstances, consent, etc.)?

Although the law often advances much slower than technology, the cases involving computers and similar technology typically are consistent with general searches. If you apply the same concepts to the search of a computer and its contents it will be applicable to the search of a home or other protected location.

Cellular Telephone Searches

In the 2014 U.S. Supreme Court case of ***Riley v. California***, the Court ruled that contents of a cell phone are unique and expansive, unlike other everyday items carried by people (e.g. wallet, purse, etc.), thus absent an exception to the search warrant requirement the police would need a search warrant to search the contents of a cellular telephone. See the Surveillance section of this manual for information on obtaining location data from a cell phone and see the Search Incident to Arrest later in this section for more on *Riley v. California*.

Searching a Computer

Generally, the contents of a computer (files, images, Internet history, etc.) will have a Fourth Amendment protected expectation of privacy. However, if the computer's files are accessible to multiple users or even to the public the reasonable expectation of privacy, and thus the Fourth Amendment protections, will likely be lost.

Seizing the computer pending a search warrant

The SJC has indicated that seizing a computer, without searching its contents, while officers apply for a search warrant is permissible providing that the impoundment is reasonable considering the circumstances.[273] This can be equated to freezing the scene at a traditional crime scene.

- In ***Commonwealth v. Hinds***, the SJC stated that it was reasonable for the police to seize the defendant's computer because files easily could be destroyed and posting an officer in the defendant's home would be more intrusive than securing the hard drive and keyboard.[274]

Also, in *Hinds,* the SJC ruled that while searching the hard drive for emails with the consent of the owner, the officer was justified in opening a JPEG file under the plain view doctrine, when the officer recognized the name as a familiar child pornography file.

The Effects of M.G.L. 276 § 3A

M.G.L. 276 § 3A requires that once a search warrant is executed a return must be filed within 7 days. Due to the vast amount of data stored on a computer's hard drive, coupled with the technological complexities involved, often makes it impractical to complete the entire search within 7 days. The SJC has indicated that a return filed within 7 days indicating which devices will be searched is sufficient to satisfy 276 § 3A.[275]

[272] *Commonwealth v. Pierre*, 71 Mass.App.Ct. 58, 879 N.E.2d 131 (2008)
[273] *Commonwealth v. Kaupp*, 453 Mass. 102 (2009)
[274] *Commonwealth v. Hinds*, 437 Mass. 54, 62 (2002)
[275] *Commonwealth v. Kaupp*, 453 Mass. 102 (2009)

In the 2009 case of ***Commonwealth v. Kaupp***, School officials of Northeast Metropolitan Vocational High School (high school) in Wakefield discovered an unauthorized open share network on the school's computer network. An investigation eventually led to the discovery of child pornography and to the defendant, a teacher at the school. Detective James, of the Medford Police (who was assisting Wakefield), seized the computer to prevent any evidence from being destroyed and applied for a search warrant. The search warrant was executed and a return was filed with the court within 7 days. However, the search of a mirror image of the computer's hard drive continued long after the initial return was filed. The defendant made a number of arguments including that the that search continued beyond 7 days in violation of G.L. c. 276, § 3A. In regards to the 7 day search warrant return requirement, the Court stated "(the) required warrant return procedures are ministerial, and failure to comply therewith is not ground for voiding an otherwise valid search… In this case, the critical question is whether the search warrant was executed within seven days of its issuance. Under similar provisions and rules in other jurisdictions, courts have held that the police do not need to complete forensic analysis of a seized computer and other electronic data storage devices within the prescribed period for executing a search warrant. Because a written return listing the devices to be examined was filed seven days after the search warrant issued, there was no violation of G.L. c. 276, § 3A."[276]

PLAIN VIEW AND TECHNOLOGY

In ***Commonwealth v. Tarjik*** (2015), the court ruled that during the execution of a search warrant for digital images on a computer, cellular phone and video camera, the police were justified in seizing memory cards found in plain view even though the memory cards were not specifically listed on the warrant. The police were investigating the defendant after the defendant's step-daughter reported that she was raped by her step-father and that he photographed and videotaped some of the assaults on his cellular phone and digital camera. The Court ruled that although the original warrant did not include memory cards, the cards were "plausibly related to criminal activity." See Plain View depicted earlier in this section.

[276] *Commonwealth v. Kaupp*, 453 Mass. 102 (2009)

WARRANTLESS SEARCHES

OVERVIEW

Generally, in order to conduct a lawful search the police need both (1) probable cause and (2) a search warrant. However, there are many exceptions to both the probable cause and the warrant requirement. The most common exceptions to the search warrant include: (1) consent, (2) officer safety searches, including pat frisks and protective sweeps, (3) exigent circumstances, (4) community caretaking, (5) the automobile exception and (6) search incident to arrests.

There are essentially ten recognized exceptions to the Search warrant requirement. If an expectation of privacy exists and the police conduct a search without a warrant the police must be able to point to one of the below listed exceptions otherwise the search is unlawful.

1. WARRANTLESS *EXIGENT* ENTRY FOR *CRIMINAL CONDUCT*

There are times when the police must act quickly and the time needed to obtain a warrant is not possible; the situation is exigent. In order to use the exigent exception to the **search warrant** requirement, the Commonwealth must demonstrate that it was **impractical to get a warrant**, the police had **probable cause** and they were faced with **exigent circumstances** such as:

1. danger to the officers lives, or
2. danger to the lives of others, or
3. the destruction of evidence,

There are Two Different Types of Exigency

There are essentially two types of exigent circumstances in regards to criminal conduct: exigent circumstances regarding the **destruction of evidence** and exigent circumstances regarding the **apprehension of a criminal suspect**. The exigencies which would excuse the lack of an arrest warrant may differ from those supplying the excuse for the lack of a search warrant.[277]

EXIGENCY TO MAKE A WARRANTLESS *ARREST* IN A DWELLING/BUILDING

In order to enter a home to execute a warrantless arrest under an exigent exception there must be some valid concern that the suspect is a threat to the safety of others and that an immediate arrest is critical. In the 1975 case of ***Commonwealth v. Forde,*** the SJC indicated the following factors as considerations on whether or not it is impractical to obtain an arrest warrant before entering a premise to execute an arrest:[278]

a. The crime was one of violence and the suspect was known or believed to be armed;
b. The suspect was known or reasonably believed to be in the building;
c. There was a likelihood that the suspect would or might escape if not apprehended immediately;
d. Whether entry would require force or could be accomplished in a peaceable manner;
e. Whether entry would have to be made at night or could be made during the daytime (when court magistrates authorized to issue warrants are more available); and,
f. The length of time it would take to obtain a warrant.[279]

WARRANTLESS SEARCHES

[277] Commonwealth v. Forde, 367 Mass. 798 (1975).
[278] Commonwealth v. Forde, 367 Mass. 798 (1975)
[279] *See, Commonwealth v. Hoffman*, 385 Mass. 122, 430 N.E.2d 1190 (1982); *Commonwealth v. Pietrass*, 392 Mass. 892, 467 N.E.2d 1368, 1372 (1984); *Commonwealth v. Jeffers*, 27 Mass. App. Ct. 1162, 539 N.E.2d 1040 (1989); *Commonwealth v. Viriyahiranpaiboon*, 412 Mass. 2234, 588 N.E.2d 643 (1992).

Specialized Exigent Warrantless Entry Arrests

Below are some specialized situations wherein the Courts have upheld the warrantless entry of a home to execute an arrest:

Quell an Ongoing Breach of the Peace

Under very rare circumstances the police may make a warrantless entry in order to quell an ongoing breach of the peace, including one that results in the arrest of an occupant. Although it is not your typical Forde Factor entry it would otherwise be lawful to quell an ongoing breach of the peace.

Significant Cases

In ***Com. v. Mullins,*** the police were authorized to enter an apartment and arrest the occupant for the loud playing of a radio which disturbed the neighbors, when such conduct was continuing when the police arrived.[280] The police had also repeatedly responded and asked the occupant to lower the radio and it was subsequently turned back up each time.

Compare with:

In ***Com. v. Kiser***, police officers who had allegedly been assaulted by the occupant of an apartment when the occupant attempted to prevent the police entry as they investigated a report of a loud party lacked exigent circumstances justifying the entry into the premises to effect a warrantless arrest of the occupant.[281] In this case the occupant agreed to turn down the music after being asked to do so by the police. The occupant's conduct could not be termed violent, since even the police officer testified that the occupant was attempting to keep the officer from looking in the apartment, not to attack him, and the police knew where the occupant lived and could easily obtain a warrant.

Pursuit and fleeing suspects

Where the police are in hot pursuit of a person suspected of an arrestable offense, they may make reasonable warrantless entries and warrantless searches to apprehend the suspect, seize weapons and secure evidence of the crime. The fact that the person is actively fleeing contributes to the exigency of the situation. However, at the time of the warrantless entry the exigent situation must still exist.

In the leading case in this area, ***Warden v. Hayden***,[282] the United States Supreme Court held that warrantless searches were justified because "the exigencies of the situation made that course imperative." The Court emphasized that the Fourth Amendment does not require police to delay in an investigation of a crime where to do so would endanger their lives or the lives of others. The crime was armed robbery. The police knew that eyewitnesses had seen the suspect flee into the building only minutes before they arrived. A full search of the premises was required to seize any and all weapons that might be on the premises and to determine what persons were present (both to secure the premises and determine who to arrest).

Although the "hot pursuit" type of exigent circumstance involves a chase of some sort, the chase need not be extended.

- In ***U.S. v. Santana***, where the police encountered a suspect on the doorstep to her apartment and she stepped back into the apartment where she could readily destroy or conceal the evidence (narcotics), the police were justified in making an immediate warrantless entry into the apartment and seizing the evidence.[283]

Once the original "hot pursuit" has ended and the suspect has been captured and the premises are secured, all other searching must stop until a warrant can be obtained.[284]

Jailable Misdemeanors: In 2015, in the case of ***Commonwealth v. Jewett***, the SJC ruled that the hot pursuit of a suspect who flees into a private home while being pursued by an officer who has probable cause to believe that the suspect has committed a ***jailable*** misdemeanor offense creates a sufficient exigency to justify a warrantless entry into the home.

---

[280] *Com. v. Mullins*, 31 Mass. App. Ct. 954, 582 N.E.2d 562 (1991).
[281] *Com. v. Kiser*, 48 Mass. App. Ct. 647, 724 N.E. 2d 348 (2000).
[282] *Warden v. Hayden*, 387 U.S. 294, 87 S.Ct. 1642 (1967).
[283] *U.S. v. Santana*, 427 U.S. 38, 96 S.Ct. 2406 (1976); *See, Welsh v. Wisconsin*, 466 U.S. 740, 140 S.Ct. 2091 (1984).
[284] *See, Mincey v. Arizona*, 437 U.S. 385, 98 S.Ct. 2408 (1978); *Commonwealth v. Hall*, 366 Mass. 790, 323 N.E.2d 319 (1975).

Statutory Empowered Exigency

In very rare circumstances, the legislation has created situations wherein the police are permitted to make warrantless entries. Chapter 272 § 89 below is one such piece of legislation.

Exhibition Place of Fighting Animals (Chapter 272 § 89)

This statute states that "any officer authorized to serve criminal process, or any special police officer duly appointed by the colonel of the state police at the request of the Massachusetts Society for the Prevention of Cruelty to Animals, or any municipal officer involved with animal control

- may, **without a warrant**, enter any place or building
- in which there is an exhibition of any fighting birds, dogs or other animals, preparations are being made for such an exhibition, or birds, dogs or other animals are owned, possessed, kept, trained, bred, loaned, sold, exported or otherwise transferred in violation of Chapter 272 section 94.
- Any such officer may **arrest all persons there present** and take possession of and remove from the place of seizure such animals there found in violation of said section 94, and hold the same in custody subject to the order of court as hereinafter provided. "

Attorney Hanrahan's Note: Laws that permit law enforcement officers to conduct warrantless searches are very rare (chapter 130 § 9 permits law enforcement officials to board boats and search for violations of fishing laws without a warrant and only on reasonable suspicion). These laws may even be unconstitutional in some circumstances, as the legislature cannot overrule the Fourth Amendment.

EXIGENT CIRCUMSTANCES FOR THE *PRESERVATION OF EVIDENCE*

Exigency created by the potential, imminent disappearance of evidence is a well-established exception to the warrant requirement. If the police officer has probable cause that evidence to a crime will be destroyed or otherwise lost and there is not time to obtain a warrant, the officer may enter the premises without a warrant to preserve the evidence.

- In ***Commonwealth v. Rotolo***, where officers overheard a defendant, who had been taken into custody on suspicion of bank robbery, telephoning his father to ask him to remove clothing and other items from the defendant's room before the police arrived, exigent circumstances were found.[285]
- In ***Commonwealth v. Lee***, the police were justified in making a warrantless entry into the basement of a Supermarket to retrieve marked bills related to drug distribution. Given the nature of the business, the money could have been easily laundered.

Total destruction of the evidence is not required. In the 2015 case of ***Commonwealth v. Ramos***, Officer Avery of the Lynn Police Department tracked a LoJack signal to a suspected chop shop location (a garage adjacent to a private home). After knocking on the door Off. Avery heard tools dropping and people running . After securing the suspect's who fled he then entered the garage and observed the stolen vehicle inside. The SJC upheld the entry under the exigent circumstances exception. Although it was unlikely, or even impossible, that the evidence may have been totally destroyed (e.g. flushed down the toilet) it was possible that some evidence may have been lost if an immediate entry was not made (i.e. the VIN numbers could have been removed or obliterated).

Drugs

Although the easily disposable nature of drugs is a factor, the mere presence of drugs alone is not enough to meet the exigency requirement for a warrantless search.

- In ***Commonwealth v. Huffman***, the police were not justified in making a warrantless entry into an apartment, even where they can see through an open door and a window that the occupants are putting marijuana in bags. There was time to get a warrant and the occupants were unaware of the police presence.[286]

WARRANTLESS SEARCHES

[285] *Commonwealth v. Rotolo*, 45 Mass. App. Ct. 927, 701 N.E. 2d 366 (1998).
[286] *Commonwealth v. Huffman*, 385 Mass. 122, 430 N.E.2d 1190 (1982).

Alcohol and Intoxication

While destruction of evidence has been found to support an exigency finding for purposes of warrantless searches, the court does not consider the destruction of internal intoxication evidence — e.g., sobering up — as amounting to an exigency.[287]

- In ***Commonwealth v. DiGeronimo***, the police were investigating a hit and run accident wherein the suspect was believed to be intoxicated. The police went to the suspect's home within minutes of the accident. Although they could observe the suspect through the window, the suspect would not answer the door. The police forced entry in order to protect the evidence of intoxication from dissipating. The court ruled that the forced, warrantless entry was not justified by the need to preserve evidence of intoxication.[288]

Attorney Hanrahan's Note: there is no guarantee that the suspect would have submitted to any testing, taking this fact into consideration arguably there was no evidence to preserve.

- In ***Commonwealth v. Marshall,*** the Appeals Court upheld an arrest for OUI where the defendant was encountered on his porch (no expectation of privacy) and brought into his apartment because of his instability.

Although the courts have held that intoxication evidence does not pose an exigency, the possibility of destroying evidence related to underage drinking was considered an exigent situation justifying the warrantless entry into a home.

- In the 2008 case of ***Commonwealth v. Sueiras***, the defendant, a school teacher, was suspected of frequently hosting under-age drinking parties at her home. A juvenile probation officer, who received many complaints about the defendant's behavior, set up surveillance of the defendant's home. One evening, the probation officer observed many juveniles enter the defendant's home empty handed. Some juveniles were later seen leaving carrying alcohol. They were stopped and the probation officer detected alcohol on their breath. The juveniles admitted that the alcohol was provided by the defendant. The probation officer then called the police. When the police arrived they observed, through a window, many youths in the home along with numerous cans and bottles of alcohol located near the juveniles. The police officer knocked on the door and was greeted by the defendant. The defendant claimed no knowledge of what was taking place, claiming to have been upstairs while the guests were downstairs. The officer asked for permission to enter, the defendant was hesitant. The officer entered and found juveniles in the possession of alcohol. This case was decided on whether or not the police officer had exigent circumstances to enter the defendant's home without a warrant or consent (as consent was not clearly given). The SJC stated "we conclude that the warrantless entry and search of the defendant's home **did not** violate her rights under the Fourth Amendment to the United States Constitution or art. 14 of the Declaration of Rights of the Massachusetts Constitution because the probable cause and exigent circumstances exception was satisfied. There was probable cause to believe that a crime was being committed inside the defendant's residence. Immediate entry into the defendant's residence was necessitated in that any delay caused by securing a warrant would have likely resulted in the imminent destruction or loss of evidence. "

Exigent Circumstances to Search a *Person* for Evidence

A search of a person under the theory of exigent circumstances is very rare.[289] The vast majority of searches of this nature are ultimately justified on a search incident to arrest theory (see Search Incident to Arrest later in this section). "The likely reason…is that in the great majority of cases the police either find nothing or effect an arrest."[290] A search incident to an arrest may be conducted before the formal arrest.

A search incident to an arrest is more legally prudent (see Search Incident to an Arrest later in this section). When a search of a person is based on exigency the burden shifts to the police to prove that a warrant was impractical, this burden does not exist under a search incident to an arrest. Additionally, when a search of this nature is made under exigent circumstances the search "must be limited to the scope of those areas of the person or his clothing which could reasonably be thought to contain the items."[291] In contrast, a search incident to an arrest "justifies a full body search even

---

[287] *See, Commonwealth v. DiGeronimo*, 38 Mass. App. Ct. 714, 652 N.E.2d 148 (1995) (police were not justified in entering suspect's home to preserve intoxication evidence); *Commonwealth v. Lopez*, 38 Mass. App. Ct. 748, 652 N.E.2d 619 (1995).
[288] *Commonwealth v. DiGeronimo*, 38 Mass. App. Ct. 714, 652 N.E.2d 148 (1995)
[289] Commonwealth v. Skea, 470 Mass.App.Ct. 685 (1984).
[290] Commonwealth v. Skea, 470 Mass.App.Ct. 685 (1984).
[291] Chimel v. California

in the absence of probable cause to think [evidence] will be located."[292] Also, in many circumstances where the police would have prior probable cause that a specific suspect will have contraband on their person (i.e. a known drug dealer) the police may be required to obtain an anticipatory warrant.

There are some very rare situations where an exigent circumstance search of a person would be permissible but a search incident to arrest search would not be permitted. For instance, a jewel thief is spooked by the presence of the police and slips the stolen jewels into the pocket of an unsuspecting bystander. There would be probable cause to search the bystander under an exigency theory if the bystander did not consent but there would not probable cause to arrest (because the bystander was not aware that he possessed stolen items and thus committed no crime). There are very few cases on record where the police uncover evidence on a person wherein there would not be authority to arrest. For these reasons, a search incident to arrest justification would be a better mechanism to conduct a search of person in most circumstances.

Plain View note: once police enter under an exigent circumstance any criminal contraband or evidence will fall under the Plain View. See the plain view discussion in the Search Overview section of this manual.

THE POLICE CANNOT CREATE THE EXIGENCY (if they have probable cause)

The police cannot use the exigent circumstance exception to the warrant requirement to circumvent obtaining a warrant if the police knowingly create the exigency, and they have probable cause to obtain a warrant prior to the exigency creation, the exception may not apply.

In ***Commonwealth v. Hamilton,*** the police received an anonymous tip that drugs were being sold out of a hotel room in Malden. Malden officers set up surveillance. The officers soon observed a man exit the room who appeared under the influence of drugs. They also observed fresh puncture marks on his arm consistent with the use of illegal narcotics. The police then knocked on the door and when the door was opened the observed evidence of drug distribution from the doorway. The officers entered and seized the evidence. The court suppressed the entry and seizure of the evidence, reasoning that there was no indication that the occupant was aware of the police nor was there a lack of time to get a warrant. Exigent circumstances might have existed when the defendant opened the door but the exigency was created by the police.[293]

This area of the law is evolving. In the 2011 U.S. Supreme Court case of ***Kentucky v. King***, the Court stated "where… the police did not create the exigency **by engaging or threatening to engage in conduct that violates the Fourth Amendment**, warrantless entry to prevent the destruction of evidence is reasonable and thus allowed." Whereas earlier Massachusetts cases have held that *any* police created exigency would negate the exigent circumstances exception to the warrant requirement, the U.S. Supreme Court has indicated that only police created exigency that *violates the Fourth Amendment* would negate the exigent circumstances exception. For instance, a police officer walks by a street level apartment and observes the homeowner, through an unobstructed window, packaging drugs. The homeowner does not notice the officer thus no exigency exists. However, now the officer knocks on the door, reports his observations, and requests consent to search (a request for consent does not violate the Fourth Amendment). The homeowner refuses to consent, however now the homeowner is aware that the police know about his drug activity and exigent circumstances have developed. Under existing Massachusetts case law (e.g. *Hamilton* above) the exigency was wrongly created by the officer, but under the U.S. Supreme Court case (*Kentucky v. King*) the police request for consent does not negate the exigency. Because Massachusetts Courts often interpret Article 14 of the Massachusetts Declaration of Rights more stringently that the U.S. Supreme Court interprets the Fourth Amendment it is possible that the Massachusetts Courts will continue to hold that all knowingly police created exigency (with probable cause) will negate the exigent circumstances exception. We will have to wait and see how the Massachusetts Courts rule on this matter.

Attorney Hanrahan's Note: to clarify what I mean by knowingly create the exigency *with probable cause*, I offer this example: A police officer responds to a loud party complaint. He knocks on the door and an occupant answers the door. Once the door is open the police officer can observe illicit drug activity taking place within. Exigent circumstances have developed and it was created by the officer knocking on the door. However, the officer did not have probable cause that drugs would be located within the home thus, even under existing

[292] US v. Robinson
[293] *Commonwealth v. Hamilton*, 24 Mass. App. Ct. 290, 508 N.E.2d 870 (1987).

WARRANTLESS SEARCHES

Massachusetts case law regarding police created exigency, this would not negate the exigent circumstances exception because the officer did not have the ability to obtain a warrant prior to creating the exigency (because there was no probable cause prior to the exigency being created).

2. WARRANTLESS EMERGENCY ENTRY UNDER *COMMUNITY CARETAKING* *(often called the Emergency Circumstances Exception)*

Police have a dual role; they must serve as law enforcement officers wherein they make arrests and search for evidence but they also serve as community caretakers wherein they ensure the community's safety, help people in danger, mitigate property damage, regulate traffic, administer first aid and so on. When the police are acting as community caretakers their actions are judged on the basis of *reasonableness* and not reasonable suspicion or probable cause. To this end, the police may make a warrantless search/entry if they have a reason to believe someone is in danger, or that property is being destroyed, or even that an animal is in peril. However, once the emergency is over the police must obtain a warrant to continue to search once the premises are secured. [294]

PERSON REQUIRING IMMEDIATE HELP

Sometimes under the community caretaking function, the police may conduct a warrantless search if they encounter a person in need of immediate care, even if no criminal conduct is thought to be involved.[295]

- In ***Commonwealth v. McCarthy***, an officer responding to report of "an unconscious woman" and discovered the woman having an apparent seizure. The officer had reasonable grounds to believe that an emergency existed, and he was permitted to conduct a warrantless search of the woman's handbag under emergency exception to warrant requirement, where emergency medical technicians (EMTs) who responded to the officer's call for assistance stated that the woman appeared to be suffering from a drug overdose, and they asked the officer what drugs, if any, she might have taken. The officer looked into the woman's purse and found illicit drugs. The search was deemed lawful.[296] **Attorney Hanrahan's Note**: today under the new so-called "Good Samaritan Law" the suspect, under similar circumstances, could not be prosecuted.

- In ***Commonwealth v. Lindsey***, the Chelsea Police Department received a 911 call about an elderly woman trembling outside her house asking for help. When the police arrived the woman was no longer outside of her house. No one answered the door so the police, with the help of the fire department, forced entry into the home fearful that the woman may be in need of medical assistance. While searching for the woman, the officers entered an unlocked second-floor bedroom where they saw in plain view two handguns on top of a dresser, at least one of which had a silencer on it. Other firearms, gun parts, and ammunition were strewn about the second floor and in plain view. The discovery was deemed lawful under the emergency exception.[297]

- In ***Commonwealth v. Allen***, the evidence did not support a finding that the occupant, whom the officer knew to be disabled and incapable of caring for himself, was in a life-threatening situation while at the defendant's apartment requiring an immediate, warrantless entry into apartment under emergency exception to warrant requirement.[298] The officer observed the occupant sitting in a chair watching television, the officer made no attempt to communicate with the occupant to see if he had been left alone, and the officer took no other steps to ascertain if the occupant had in fact been left alone.[299]

- In the 2009 case of ***Commonwealth v. Erickson***, a barking dog complaint which lead to the discovery of sickly and dying animals viewed through a window, strong odors emanating from the apartment, coupled with a report from a neighbor that the tenant had not been seen in some time justified an emergency entrance into the apartment. The Court stated "it is clear that the officer was justified in his belief that the tenant could be inside the apartment and was injured, dying, or dead."[300]

---

[294] *See,Mincey v. Arizona*, 437 U.S. 385, 98 S.Ct. 2408 (1978); *See also, Thompson v. Louisiana*, 469 U.S. 17, 105 S.Ct. 409 (1984); *Commonwealth v. Lewin*, 407 Mass. 617, 555 N.E.2d 551 (1990).
[295] *Mincey v.Arizona*, 437 U.S. 385, 98 S.Ct. 2408 (1978); *Commonwealth v. Rexach*, 20 Mass. App. Ct. 919, 478 N.E.2d 744 (1985), *rev. den.*482 N.E.2d 328 (1985).
[296] *Commonwealth v. McCarthy,*71 Mass.App.Ct. 591, 884 N.E.2d 991 (2008)
[297] *Commonwealth v. Lindsey*, 72 Mass. App. Ct. 485 (2008).
[298] *Commonwealth v. Allen*, 54 Mass. App. Ct. 719, 767 N.E.2d 1086 (2002).
[299] *Commonwealth v. Allen*, 54 Mass. App. Ct. 719, 767 N.E.2d 1086 (2002).
[300] *Commonwealth v. Erickson*, 72 Mass.App.Ct. 172 (200)

- In ***U.S. v. Barone,*** where the police heard loud and repeated screams and were able to determine the premises from which the screams came, they were justified in making an immediate warrantless entry and search of the premises sufficient to secure the scene or determine that no danger to public peace or public safety exists.[301]

- In ***Commonwealth v. Cunningham***, (Superior Court case) the court upheld the warrantless entry to take custody of a child at the direction of DCYF.

- In a civil case, regarding a warrantless entry to take custody of a mentally ill person, under a section 12 ("pink slip"). The 1st Circuit upheld the entry as a **"special needs" entry**.[302]

Recent Violent Crime within Premises

Several court decisions have upheld warrantless entries where a recent violent crime has ***recently*** taken place. Although these entries involve criminal conduct the Courts have allowed entries not to preserve or seize evidence but to assist someone who may be in danger (i.e. Community Caretaking Function).

- In ***Commonwealth v Lanigan***, a Brutal stabbing and kidnapping which occurred at the suspect's home justified a warrantless entry shortly after the attack.

- In ***Commonwealth v. Young,*** the SJC upheld an entry into a building as the police followed a blood trail. They were also authorized to make plain view discoveries while inside.

- In ***Commonwealth v. Jeffers***, the police were justified in making a warrantless entry into a dwelling shortly after a victim had been robbed at gun point inside the dwelling. The victim also reported to police that two small children were present inside at the time of the robbery.[303]

- In ***Commonwealth v. Freiberg***, the police discovered a living victim who had been buried alive in the backyard of the suspect's home. The police were justified in entering the home without a warrant to ensure there were no other victims in immediate danger.

- In ***Commonwealth v. Paniaqua***, exigent circumstances existed authorizing a police officer's warrantless entry into an apartment in a building from which shots had been fired just a few minutes earlier.[304]

- In ***Commonwealth v. Donoghue***, at night, following a very brutal crime, the police had probable cause to believe that an armed and dangerous suspect was in his apartment. They were concerned he might have someone else with him or that he might hide or destroy evidence and thus the warrantless exigent entry was justified.[305]

Emergency May Still Exist Even After Passage of Time

In the 2008 case of ***Commonwealth v. Townsend,*** after two unsuccessful well-being checks which occurred over a period of two days, the Pittsfield Police conducted a warrantless forced entry into an apartment after the victim had been missing for more than two days. The victim was found dead on the living room floor partially covered by a sheet. Evidence linking the defendant was also discovered. The defendant claimed that because the police allowed some time to pass before making an entry that the emergency exception did not apply. The SJC ruled that "allowing some time to pass does not automatically negate the emergency exception."[306]

WARRANTLESS SEARCHES

[301] *See, U.S. v. Barone*, 330 F.2d 547 (2d Cir. 1964).
[302] *McCabe v. Life-Line ambulance Service*, 77 F.3d 540
[303] *Commonwealth v. Jeffers*, 27 Mass. App. Ct. 1162, 539 N.E.2d 1040 (1989).
[304] *Commonwealth v. Paniaqua*, 413 Mass. 796, 604 N.E.2d 1278 (1992).
[305] *Commonwealth v. Donoghue*, 23 Mass. App. Ct. 103, 499 N.E.2d 832 (1986).
[306] *Commonwealth v. Townsend*, 453 Mass. 413 (2008).

PROPERTY DAMAGE: BURNING BUILDING, EMERGENCIES, DISASTERS & PROPERTY DESTRUCTION

As Community Caretakers police also have a duty to preserve property, as well as life. If the police have a reasonable concern that property is in danger of being lost/destroyed the police may make an emergency entry/search in order to preserve property.

A burning building presents an emergency situation and may be entered immediately and without a warrant to save lives and property. Once police (or fire officials) enter such a building, they may seize evidence found in plain view and may remain there a reasonable length of time to investigate the cause of the fire.[307]

- In the 2013 case of ***Commonwealth v. Cantelli***, the Appeals Court upheld the police entry into a home in order to assist building management and a constable enforce an civil injunction ordering the removal of the resident's gas oven. The previous day the resident had filled the building with explosive levels of gas. The Court ruled that whether the defendant had turned the gas on intentionally or accidentally, the risk of created by the defendant's proximity to the gas stove was identical.
- In ***Commonwealth v. Ringgard***, the officers' warrantless entry into a residence was reasonable in light of the dangerous situation threatening life and safety of any occupants. The officers received a call from the dispatcher indicating a possible break-in and fire, upon arrival they observed black smoke billowing from a broken front window, they looked through the window, and saw a hallway filled with smoke and an inner door that was ajar, through which they saw a kitchen with flames coming out from around a stove and a man standing several feet from flames. Their subsequent entry and seizure of a firearm found in plain view was lawful.[308]

ANIMALS IN PERIL

In the 2014 case of ***Commonwealth v. Duncan***, the SJC ruled that the Emergency Aid exception encompasses warrantless searches to protect non-human life. In *Duncan*, the police responded to a citizen's call about a neighbor's dog making unusual sounds. It was a cold wintery day. The officers responded and climbed on a snow bank in the driveway to see over the fence into the back yard. They observed two deceased dogs, seemingly frozen to death, and another dog near death. The officers entered the curtilage to save the dog. The evidence observed was used against the homeowner on animal cruelty charges. The Court upheld the entry into the curtilage.

The SJC did seem to set some limitations on this type of entry. The SJC stated "when there is an objectively reasonable belief that an emergency exists involving human life, i.e., that a person is injured or in imminent danger of physical harm, nothing further ordinarily is necessary to justify a warrantless police entry. In contrast, where nonhuman animal life is similarly imperiled, **other factors** appropriately enter the calculus in determining whether such entry is justified."

The other factors mentioned include:

1. Whether or not the animal's condition was caused by human abuse or neglect. The SJC stated "although true emergencies that do not arise as a result of any human action may befall animals, the threshold for police entry in such situations will be considerably higher."
2. The species of the animal in need is an important consideration.
3. The nature of the privacy interest at issue.
4. Whether any efforts were made to obtain the consent of the property owner prior to making entry onto the property.
5. The extent of the intrusion, including any damage done to the property.

The SJC concluded by stating "inevitably, of course, there will be countless and varied iterations of emergency aid scenarios involving animals, and these factors do not purport to be exhaustive. The reasonableness of the search must be determined on a case-by-case basis upon consideration of the totality of the circumstances."

[307] *Commonwealth v. Ploude*, 44 Mass. App. Ct. 137, 688 N.E. 2d 1028 (1998).
[308] *Commonwealth v. Ringgard*, 71 Mass.App.Ct. 197, 880 N.E.2d 814 (2008)

FREEZING THE SCENE

If the police enter a private area due to exigent or emergency circumstances and the scene has been stabilized the police will not be justified in conducting a further search without a warrant or an exception to the warrant requirement. Generally, the police will have to secure the scene until a search warrant can be obtained.

- In ***Mincey v. Arizona***,[309] police conducted a raid of the defendant's apartment. They arrested several persons, removed all others from the scene and posted a police guard. The extensive searches conducted after that point were unconstitutional in the absence of a warrant.

The U.S. Supreme Court noted the following factors as indications that the scene has become secure enough to require a warrant before further searches may be conducted:

a. The only person present, the suspect, has been arrested or otherwise removed from the premises;
b. All occupants of the premises have been removed and the police have or could have posted a guard to prevent others from entering until a warrant could be obtained;
c. A search warrant could have been obtained without significant delay; and,
d. There is no showing that evidence could have been destroyed or removed from the scene in the time it would have taken to obtain a search warrant.

Post a guard

Once the crime scene or premises has been secured, if it is feasible to do so, police must, before conducting further searches, post a guard until a search warrant can be obtained. When securing a residence while applying for a search warrant it must be secured from the outside absent some indication that someone is inside who may destroy evidence.

In the 2013 case of ***Commonwealth v. Gray***, the SJC stated "there is a fundamental difference between securing or controlling the perimeter of a dwelling from the outside and the entry and physical surveillance of a dwelling from the inside." Because "any evidence located within an unoccupied dwelling can be fully protected by controlling access to that dwelling from the outside, there can be no justification for a warrantless entry absent at least an objectively reasonable belief that someone is inside."

- In ***Commonwealth v. Hall***,[310] police had conducted a warrant search of a second floor apartment. They arrested the defendant, his wife and the only two other persons present. The police found papers indicating that the defendant owned the building. An officer learned that large quantities of drugs were in a vacant third floor apartment. Because the warrant only authorized a search of the second floor apartment, the police tried to contact court officials to obtain a warrant to search the third floor apartment. They were unsuccessful (it was close to midnight). The police then conducted a warrantless search of the third floor. The court held that search violated the Fourth Amendment, observing that "(a) number of police officers were on hand; they could readily have maintained a presence to prevent suspicious access to the premises until a warrant could be obtained." The Court added that the person present in the second floor apartment had been arrested and "there was no showing that the police feared the appearance . . . of confederates bent on preventing seizure of a possible cache in the third floor apartment or threatening or attacking the police; had any associates of the (defendant's) appeared, they could have been denied entrance."[311]

- In ***Commonwealth v. Lanigan***,[312] the Appeals Court upheld the padlocking of the defendant's apartment in order to preserve any evidence that might be located in it pending the police obtaining a warrant.

Once the owners and occupants of the premises have been removed and a guard posted , the police have authority to deny third parties from entering the scene or premises in order to prevent the destruction or removal of evidence.

WARRANTLESS SEARCHES

[309] *Mincey v. Arizona,* 437 U.S. 385, 98 S.Ct. 2408 (1978).
[310] *Commonwealth v. Hall*, 366 Mass. 790, 323 N.E.2d 319 (1975).
[311] *See also,Commonwealth v. Lanigan*, 12 Mass. App. Ct. 913, 423 N.E.2d 800, *cert. den.*488 U.S. 106, 109 S.Ct. 788 (1981).
[312] *Commonwealth v. Lanigan,* 12 Mass. App. Ct. 913, 423 N.E.2d 800, *cert. den.*458 U.S. 1006, 109 S.Ct. 788 (1981).

Location must be secured from the exterior absent reasonable suspicion

In the 2013 case of ***Commonwealth v. Gray***, the SJC ruled that once the exigency has ended the premises must be secured from the exterior while the police apply for a warrant, absent reasonable suspicion that evidence may be destroyed from within if a police officer is not positioned inside.

Unlawful to Freeze the Scene absent Exigent Circumstances

In the 2015 case of ***Commonwealth v. Komenus***, the police had probable cause that the defendant was selling drugs from his home. They lured him out of his home under the guise his parked vehicle was struck by another vehicle. Once outside they advised him that they were aware of his drugs sales and where going to enter the apartment. The officers then entered the apartment to secure the scene while they applied for a search warrant. The Court stated "before Officer DeNuccio knocked on the defendant's door, no exigent circumstances justified the officers' entry into the defendant's apartment. There was no evidence of a 'specific threat that drugs inside the apartment were in imminent danger of being destroyed or that a police presence outside the apartment until a warrant could be obtained would not have prevented any such destruction.' Moreover, even after the initial interaction by police with the defendant, but prior to their entry into his apartment, there was no apparent threat that the defendant would destroy evidence within the apartment; the defendant was outside the apartment and, in any event, the police had probable cause to arrest him based on the information provided by his arrested customer regarding a recent purchase of drugs from him. There was likewise no evidence to support an objectively reasonable belief that anyone other than the defendant was in the apartment." The entry was unlawful.

3. SEARCHES MADE WITH CONSENT

As with other constitutional rights, the right to be free from search except one conducted pursuant to a duly authorized search warrant can be "waived" by the person to be searched or by the person who owns or controls the property to be searched. This "waiver" takes the form of consent. If a person consents to a search by law enforcement officers, a search warrant is not necessary, nor is probable cause. Where a person consents to a search he or she has effectively given up his or her expectation of privacy, therefore, in a sense no "search" has taken place. However, this waiver of rights must be provided freely and voluntarily.

CONSENT MUST BE FREELY/VOLUNTARILY GIVEN

The voluntariness of an individual's consent to a warrantless entry is an issue of fact, and must be examined in light of the **totality of the circumstances** of the case.[313]

The right to refuse need not be communicated but it will be considered when weighing the voluntariness: Although a police officer is not legally required to inform the person that he or she has the right to refuse consent, the court will weigh the fact of whether the person knew he or she could refuse consent in determining whether consent was given freely and voluntarily.[314]

Written consent not required: Although written consent is not required, it does help prove that it was voluntarily given[315] and it should be sought whenever possible to counter any later claims by the defendant that he did not know that he had the right to refuse.

Consent Must Be Free of Coercion by the Police

Consent must be free of coercion, force, duress, stealth or duplicity. The person must not be forced or tricked into giving consent. Courts look to the words and actions of the police as well as the experience and circumstances of the person giving consent to determine whether consent was obtained freely and voluntarily.[316]

The age, maturity, education and degree of intoxication will all be examined in determining voluntariness. With younger suspects or suspects of limited intelligence it would be best to carefully explain the right to refuse and to be careful not to be overbearing as the Court may later find the consent was coerced.

[313] See *Schneckloth v. Bustamonte, supra* at 248-249, 93 S.Ct. 2041; *Commonwealth v. Sanna, supra* at 97, 674 N.E.2d 1067.
[314] *Commonwealth v. Sanna*, 424 Mass. 92, 674 N.E.2d 1067 (1997) (notice of right to refuse will be considered, but is not determinative); *Schneckloth v. Bustamonte,* 421 U.S. 218, 93 S.Ct. 2041 (1973); *Commonwealth v. Cantalupo*, 380 Mass. 173, 402 N.E.2d 1040 (1980).
[315] *Commonwealth v. Reed*, 417 Mass. 558, 631 N.E.2d 552 (1994).
[316] *U.S. v. Cepulonis*, 530 F.2d (1st Cir. 1976); *U.S. v. Mendenhall*, 446 U.S. 544, 100 S.Ct. 1870 (1980).*See,Schneckloth v. Bustamonte*, 412 U.S. 218, 93 S.Ct. 2041 (1973) for a discussion of "voluntariness."

The police cannot order or compel a person to consent to a search. The police must make it clear that they are requesting *permission* to search. When given in reply to a demand by armed police officers, consent *may* be deemed involuntary.[317] With this in mind, when officers are in uniform or have weapons showing, care should be taken to minimize the appearance of coercion.[318]

Threats to obtain a warrant and actual possession of a warrant

Where the police *have probable cause* to obtain a search warrant, the police may inform the person that, if he or she does not consent to a search, they will seek a warrant. Doing so does not make the consent, if it is obtained, coerced.[319]However, the police must actually have probable cause. If probable cause does not exist and the police threaten to obtain a warrant if consent is not granted the consent will most likely be deemed invalid.

By contrast, if the police have a search warrant, they cannot inform the person of that fact and then seek consent to search. A warrant means that the person has no right to refuse or object to the search. A warrant is, in effect, legal coercion to conduct a search.[320]

Consent while under arrest

The U.S. Supreme Court stated in ***U.S. v. Watson***,[321] "the fact of custody alone has never been enough in itself to demonstrate a coerced confession or consent to search."[322]

Once a suspect has been arrested, the voluntariness of any consent will **at least be suspect**.[323] In any custody situation there exists a degree of duress. The question is whether the officers used coercive tactics or took unlawful advantage of the custody situation to obtain the consent.[324] The best practice would be to inform the arrestee that he has a right to refuse.

Case example

- In ***Commonwealth v. Beasley***, where an arrested individual was guarded by troopers (who had his car keys) at night on the side of the road, the consent to search his truck was not found to be voluntary. The troopers had found marijuana in the passenger compartment and had not informed the defendant of his right to refuse to consent to the search of the vehicle's trunk.[325]

Consent to enter by Trickery

Should the police gain entry to the defendant's premises by trickery (such as posing as repairmen searching for a gas leak), in the absence of a warrant such entry will be unlawful and any evidence seized will be suppressed.[326] This restriction against trickery or deceit would not apply where police undercover officers are invited onto a person's premises (or home) to purchase drugs.[327] However, if the police were equipped with a warrant a rouse may be used to obtain a peaceful entry.

Must be "unequivocal" however non-verbal consent is permissible

The "waiver of constitutional rights must be unequivocal and specific."[328]There must be little or no doubt that consent was given and there must be specificity as to the nature and extent of the search to which consent was given. Unequivocal means undeniable or clear-cut. However, courts have permitted non-verbal and even implied acts and gestures to indicate consent in some cases.

- In ***Commonwealth v. Costa***, Detective Jose responded to the suspect's home during his investigation of a statutory rape incident. The suspect's mother answered the door. Det. Jose asked her if the defendant was home. In response, the defendant's mother pointed down the hall. When Jose asked the defendant's mother if the victim was also present in the home, she nodded and pointed again down the hall. At that point, Jose asked her if he could "go and see [the defendant]." In response, the defendant's mother walked further into the house and "pointed into a bedroom." The court deemed the mother consented to the detective's entry.[329]

[317] *U.S. v. Smith*, 308 F.2d 657 (2nd Cir. 1962).
[318] *U.S. v. Mayer*, 552 F.2d 729 (6th Cir. 1977).
[319] *Commonwealth v. Harmond*, 376 Mass. 557, 382 N.E.2d 203 (1978).
[320] *Bumpers v. North Carolina*, 391 U.S. 543, 88 S.Ct. 1788 (1968).
[321] *U.S. v. Watson*, 423 U.S. 411, 96 S.Ct. 820, 46 L.Ed.2d 598 (1976).
[322] See also, *U.S. v. Cepulonis*, 530 F.2d 238 (1st Cir.), *cert. denied* 426 U.S. 908, 96 S.Ct. 2231, 48 L.Ed.2d 834 (1976), and *U.S. v. Rodriguez Perez*, 625 F.2d 1021 (1st Cir. 1980).
[323] *U.S. v. Watson*, 423 U.S. 411, 96 S.Ct. 820 (1976); *Commonwealth v. Aguiar*, 370 Mass. 490, 350 N.E.2d 436 (1976)
[324] *U.S. v. Jones*, 475 F.2d 723 (5th Cir.), *cert. denied*, 414 U.S. 841, 94 S.Ct. 96, 38 L.Ed.2d 77 (1973); See also *U.S. v. Vendrell-Pena*, 700 F.Supp. 1174 (D. Puerto Rico 1988).
[325] *Commonwealth v. Beasley*, 13 Mass. App. Ct. 62, 430 N.E.2d 437 (1982).
[326] *People v. Jefferson*, 350 N.Y.S. 2d 3, (1973).
[327] *Lewis v. U.S.*, 385 U.S. 206, 87 S.Ct. 424 (1966); *Commonwealth v. Miller*, 361 Mass. 644, 282 N.E.2d 394 (1972).
[328] *Commonwealth v. McGrath*, 365 Mass. 631, 310 N.E.2d 601 (1974).
[329] *Commonwealth v. Costa*, 69 Mass.App.Ct. 823, 872 N.E.2d 750, (2007)

WARRANTLESS SEARCHES

- In ***Commonwealth v. Voisine***, police had consent of the apartment lessee to enter the apartment so as to allow for their warrantless arrest of the defendant at the apartment and seize from the apartment items which belonged to the first-degree murder victim, despite the fact that the lessee communicated her consent by pointing to bedroom in which defendant was hiding rather than by speaking (at trial she admitted that she granted consent).[330] The defendant was an overnight guest in the apartment and the lessee knew that she did not have to let police into apartment.

The Prosecution has the burden

Because the right to be free from search except one pursuant to a search warrant is so important, consent to a warrantless search must be shown by **clear and convincing evidence**.[331]

SCOPE OF CONSENT

Once consent to search is given it will be limited in scope to the consent given. For instance, if a police officer requested, and was granted, consent to search for a large screen television inspection of a nightstand drawer would be beyond the scope of the consent granted, absent additional consent to search the drawer. But in some cases consent automatically extends based on the character of the area.

> In ***Florida v. Jimeno,*** the U.S. Supreme Court ruled that assuming consent is obtained voluntarily to search the interior of a motor vehicle, this consent extends to the contents of closed containers discovered inside the vehicle capable of holding the object for which the police were conducting the search, without having to ask the suspect for permission to open each container (unless he or she limited or revokes his or her consent, of course).[332]

Since the police are engaging in a search pursuant to a person's consent, the nature, extent and scope of that search depends on the nature, extent and scope of the consent. The time and place where consent is given and the exact areas and items included in the consent determine when the police may search, where they may search and for what they may search.[333]

Consent to enter and Consent to Search

There is an important difference between receiving consent to *enter* an area or premises and receiving consent to *search* that area or premises. Specific consent to search must be given. If an officer receives permission to enter a building, apartment, room or area, that does not necessarily mean he or she may conduct a search. Once an officer is in the area or on the premises by lawful authority or consent, he or she may seize evidence or contraband found in plain view.[334]

TIMING OF CONSENT

Consent Must Be Obtained before the Search is Commenced

The search must be conducted contemporaneously with the consent or at least without undue delay after consent has been obtained. For instance, consent granted to search a vehicle today would not still be valid three weeks later. The search would have to take place at, or at least close to, the time the consent was granted.

WITHDRAWN CONSENT

Once consent is given, it may be revoked at any time. Once consent is revoked, the search by police must stop unless it is justified for some independent reason.

COMPROMISED CONSENT

Consent to search obtained through exploitation of a prior illegality (unlawful police action), particularly very close in time following the prior illegality, is not regarded as freely given, unless the taint of the illegality has been attenuated.[335]

---

[330] *Commonwealth v. Voisine*, 414 Mass. 772, 783, 610 N.E.2d 926 (1993)
[331] *See,Drumond v. U.S.*, 350 F. 2d 983 (8th Cir. 1965).
[332] *Florida v. Jimeno*, 111 S.Ct. 1801 (1991); *Commonwealth v. Lantigua*, 38 Mass. App. Ct. 526, 649 N.E.2d 1129 (1995).
[333] *Commonwealth v. Cantaluvo*, 389 Mass. 173, 402 N.E.2d 1040 (1980).
[334] *Robbins v. Mackenzie*, 364 F.2d 45 (1st Cir. 1966); *Commonwealth v. Walker*, 370 Mass. 548, 350 N.E.2d 678 (1976), *cert. den.*429 U.S. 943, 97 S.Ct. 362 (1976).
[335] *Commonwealth v. Allen*, 54 Mass. 719, 767 N.E.2d 1086 (2002).

In other words, an illegal search or some other unlawful action on the part of the police will tarnish any subsequent grant of consent. It is the burden of the Commonwealth to prove that the taint created by an illegal action has been sufficiently attenuated to allow the admission of the evidence derived from the prior illegality.

- In ***Commonwealth v. Hurd***, a defendant's consent to the animal control officer and a police officer to remove dogs that were dead or dying from his premises was not voluntary, for purposes of determining the validity of that seizure in a prosecution for cruelty to animals, where consent was obtained through exploitation of a prior illegal entry – the previous unlawful entry of the back yard.[336] The police had previously entered the yard without a warrant and discovered the dying animals after confronting the suspect with this fact they requested consent from the defendant. This tainted the subsequent consent. The Court ruled that the entry was not valid under exigent circumstances.

Attenuation: Connection between a prior illegality and a subsequent search can be attenuated by reason of lapse in time, intervening circumstances, or a disconnection between the prior illegality and the person giving consent to search, such that compromised consent is cleansed of the taint of the prior illegality. In other words, the passage of time or a change of circumstances may erase the prior illegality and the consent may be properly received.

AUTHORITY TO GRANT CONSENT

If the person (i.e. the body) of the suspect is to be searched, only he or she can give consent to a search. If the premises or property to be searched is owned and used *exclusively* by the suspect, only he or she can consent to a search of the premises or property.

Actual authority to grant consent

Obviously the exclusive owner of property may grant consent to search, however, there are times when someone other than the actual owner/custodian of the property searched has so-called "actual" authority to grant consent to search the property.

A third party with actual authority to consent must possess "common authority over or other sufficient relationship to the premises or effects sought to be inspected."[337]

In the 2010 case of ***Com. v. Porter P***., the SJC ruled that a person may have actual authority to consent to a warrantless search of a home by the police **only if:**

- the person is a co inhabitant with a shared right of access to the home, that is, the person lives in the home, either as a member of the family, a roommate, or a houseguest whose stay is of substantial duration and who is given full access to the home; or
- the person, generally a landlord, shows the police a written contract entitling that person to allow the police to enter the home to search for and seize contraband or evidence. No such entitlement may reasonably be presumed by custom or oral agreement.

Apparent authority to consent

In ***Illinois v. Rodriguez,*** the United States Supreme Court held that the Fourth Amendment's prohibition of "unreasonable searches and seizures" is not violated when a warrantless entry of a home is based on the consent of a third party who the police, at the time of entry, reasonably, but mistakenly, believed had common authority over the premises.

The mistake must be one of fact and not of law. For example, mistakenly believing that the person who answered the door and claimed to be a resident was an actual resident (but was not) would be a mistake of fact. Mistakenly believing that a landlord could grant consent to search his tenant's home would be a mistake of law, not a mistake of fact.

If the police officer has the voluntary consent of an individual with the *apparent authority* to give consent, the entry and search will **only be lawful if the (reasonable) mistake of fact occurs <u>despite diligent inquiry</u>** by the police as to the consenting individual's common authority over the home. In other words, the entry and/or search

[336] *Commonwealth v. Hurd*, 51 Mass. App. Ct. 12, 743 N.E.2d 841 (2001).
[337] *U.S. v. Matlock*, 415 U.S. 164, 94 S.Ct. 988 (1973).

WARRANTLESS SEARCHES

by police may be based on the authority given by someone who appeared to have authority (but actually did not) as long as the police ask the person if he/she has the authority to permit entry or an inspection. Even if the person lies, or is otherwise mistaken, the entry/inspection will still be valid because the police inquired first.

Police Inquiry Generally Required for Apparent Authority to be upheld

To conduct a diligent inquiry, a police officer must take two basic steps:

1. The police officer must base his conclusion of actual authority on facts, not assumptions or impressions.
2. He must continue his inquiry until he has reliable information on which to base a finding of actual authority to consent.

Even when the consenting individual explicitly asserts that he lives there, if "the surrounding circumstances could conceivably be such that a reasonable person would doubt its truth, the police officer must make further inquiry to resolve the ambiguity." Police must not only thoroughly question the individual consenting to the search with respect to his or her actual authority, but also pay close attention to whether the surrounding circumstances indicate that the consenting individual is truthful and accurate in asserting common authority over the premises. [338]

However, in the 2013 case of ***Commonwealth v. Santos***, the SJC stated "we take this opportunity to clarify the two-step inquiry required when police enter a home, without a warrant and absent exigent circumstances, after they gain consent from someone they believe to have actual authority over the premises. We conclude that… police need not conduct a "further inquiry," the second part of the due diligence analysis, *where they possess sufficient facts to form the basis for a reasonable conclusion that a third party has authority to give consent to enter a defendant's home.*

In other words, "police have a duty of further inquiry" when faced with "contrary facts tending to suggest that the person consenting to the search lacks actual authority." Absent those contrary facts or "surrounding circumstances that could conceivably be such that a reasonable person would doubt its truth," an officer's conclusion that he has consent to enter a premises, if based on "facts, not assumptions or impressions," may satisfy the first of the two-part inquiry of due diligence.

The SJC stated that "while it is best practice for police, prior to entry, simply ask who is the resident of the home…in this situation (i.e. "an ongoing emergency, public and perhaps medical") the officers did not make a further inquiry because the facts where unambiguous (meaning the facts where clear) to conclude that they had consent to enter."

Joint-owner or joint-user

If the suspect does not own the premises or property exclusively, that is, if he or she owns them jointly with another person or if another person has a right of access to or authority over the premises or property, that other person may consent to a search of the premises or property even though the suspect or defendant does not know the other person has given consent.

- In ***Commonwealth v. Moore***, the court upheld the consent of a victim who was an occupant of the defendant's apartment who consented to police entry and search of the apartment.[339] The victim was a 14 year old girl who was taken in by the defendant pimp. After being abused by the defendant, including branded on the face with a hot knife, the victim reported the incident to the police and brought them back to the apartment where she turned over the knife and other household items used to burn her.

- In ***Commonwealth v. Rodriguez***, the court ruled that a co-defendant, who jointly occupies an apartment with another co-defendant, may consent to the search of the common areas of the apartment.[340]

- In ***Commonwealth v. Connolly***, the court ruled that any tenant of an apartment building may consent to a police search of areas common to all tenants such as a stairway or basement.[341]

- In ***Frazier v. Cupp***, the U.S. Supreme Court held where two persons jointly own a duffel bag; either may consent to a police search of the duffel bag.[342]

Closed Container in the Common Areas: In 2012 the SJC ruled that a housemate may not grant consent to search a closed container belonging to another housemate even if the container is located in the common area. The SJC stated "even if a co inhabitant (housemate) of a home has actual authority to consent to a search of the home, the consent would

[338] Com. v. Porter P., a juvenile, SJC (2010)
[339] *Commonwealth v. Moore*, 359 Mass. 509, 269 N.E.2d 636 (1971); *Commonwealth v. Maloney*, 399 Mass. 785, 506 N.E.2d 1147 (1987).
[340] *Commonwealth v. Rodriguez*, 364 Mass. 87, 300 N.E.2d 192 (1973).
[341] *Commonwealth v. Connolly*, 356 Mass. 617, 255 N.E.2d 191 (1970).
[342] *Frazier v. Cupp*, 394 U.S. 731, 89 S.Ct. 1420 (1969).

not extend to a closed suitcase, overnight bag, or gym bag located inside the home that did not belong to the co inhabitant (housemate)" unless the housemate has an interest in the container as well."[343]

Presence of Additional Co-inhabitants: The voluntary consent of any joint-owner or joint-user of a premises or property is valid, unless objected to by another joint-owner who is present.

- In ***Georgia v. Randolph***, after a domestic dispute the defendant's wife summoned the police. When the police arrived the wife informed the police of her husband's drug use. The police asked for consent to search to which the husband objected but the wife consented. The U.S. Supreme court stated that a consent search cannot be justified over the express refusal by a physically present resident. The court also stated that the police could not remove the resident who refused to grant consent in order to conduct a search through the grant of consent from another resident.[344]
- In the 2008 case of ***Commonwealth v. Occasion***, the Appeals Court upheld a consent search granted by the defendant's mother of the adult defendant, where the two shared an apartment, even though the defendant was present. However, the defendant did not object to the search. [345]

Spouses

One spouse may consent to the search of premises or property jointly owned, occupied or used with the other spouse.[346] This can be done without the knowledge or consent of the other spouse.[347] Thus, consent of one spouse to search a house is valid where the spouse who gives consent is present and living in the house.[348] However, the consent of one spouse is invalid if the other is present and objects to the search.

- In ***Com .v Podgurski***, even though the defendant's wife temporarily resided in a shelter, she may consent to a search of the house in which they resided.[349] (The wife in this case had obtained an emergency abuse prevention order.)

Parent-child, family members and friends

Family members who live in a home together may validly consent to a search of that home just like any other roommate situation.[350] However, age is a factor that should be considered.

Generally, a parent may consent to the search of premises or property under the parent's control, although it involves searching areas or property used by the child.[351] This is true whether the child is a minor or an adult. However, an older child or an adult child may have exclusive access (often locked) to certain areas or property. Where that is true, the parent's consent may not be effective. On the other hand, where a child (minor or adult) lives with a parent and the parent has general access to the child's room, the parent may give consent to a police search of the child's room.[352]

Generally, a child cannot give consent to a police search of premises or property owned by the child's parents.

Property voluntarily surrendered to the police through the family or friends of the defendant may be searched.

- In ***Commonwealth v. Lopes***, for example, where the police requested specific clothing of the defendant and that clothing was handed over to the police by the defendant's girlfriend who had received the clothing from the defendant's mother (with whom he lived), the police could properly search the clothing.[353]
- In ***Commonwealth v. Hinds***, a defendant's brother gave valid consent to police officers to enter their house to search for computer files, and thus a subsequent search of the brother's computer, which led to a computer file on which the defendant had stored child pornography. The police were looking for computer evidence regarding two homicides committed by another family member, and the brother stated that he consented to the police officer's entrance and search of his computer.[354] The police officer did not exceed the scope of consent to search, given to the officer by the defendant's brother, when the officer entered the defendant's computer directory from the brother's computer through the brother's network connection and discovered that

[343] Commonwealth v. Magri, 462 Mass. 360 (2012)
[344] *Georgia . Randolh*, 547 U.S. 103, 126 S.Ct. 1515 (2006)
[345] *Commonwealth v. Ocasio*, 71 Mass. App. Ct. 304 (2008).
[346] *Commonwealth v. Martin*, 358 Mass. 282, 264 N.E.2d 366 (1970).
[347] *Commonwealth v. Dearan*, 364 Mass. 193, 302 N.E.2d 912 (1973).
[348] *Commonwealth v. Rooney*, 365 Mass. 484, 313 N.E.2d 105 (1974); *Commonwealth v. Rexach*, 20 Mass. App. Ct. 919, 478 N.E.2d 744 (1985) ,*rev. den.*482 N.E.2d 328 (1985).
[349] *Commonwealth v. Podgurski*, 44 Mass. App. Ct. 1105, 691 N.E. 2d 980 (1998), *rev. den.*427 Mass. 1105, 695 N.E. 2d 698 (1998).
[350] *Commonwealth v. Podgurski*, 44 Mass. App. Ct. 1105, 691 N.E. 2d 980 (1998).
[351] *Commonwealth v. Ortiz*, 422 Mass. 64, 661 N.E.2d 926 (1996); *Commonwealth v. Mendes*, 361 Mass. 507, 281 N.E.2d 243 (1972) (Sister could consent to police search of closet in sister's house which was also used by her brother.)
[352] *U.S. v. DiPrima*, 472 F.2d 550 (1st Cir. 1973).
[353] *Commonwealth v. Lopes*, 362 Mass. 448, 287 N.E.2d 118 (1972); *See alsoNelson v. Moore*, 470 F.2d 1192 (1st Cir. 1972). (Pipe allegedly used by defendant in assault and battery was turned over to police by neighbor who had borrowed it from defendant).
[354] *Commonwealth v. Hinds*, 437 Mass. 54, 768 N.E.2d 1067 (2002).

the defendant had stored child pornography in that file; the defendant had consented to a search of his own computer for electronic mail prior to the discovery of the pornography files. Similarly, the police officer did not exceed scope of the consent, given to the officer by the defendant, to search his computer for electronic mail, which led to the discovery of child pornography stored on the defendant's computer; the defendant did not tell the officer that his consent applied only to certain directories.

Landlord-tenant

Generally, a landlord has no authority to consent to a police search of a tenant's premises or property. However, if the true tenant disavows that he rents the premises or if the tenant abandons the premises, then the landlord may consent to a police search of the premises.[355]In addition, in a multi-unit building, the landlord or any tenant, would, in most circumstances, be able to grant consent to search the common areas of the building.

Hotel-patron

A hotel manager or other employee cannot give consent to a police search of a guest's room or property. [356] However, once the guest has left their expectation of privacy goes with them (see the abandoned property section in the Search chapter of this manual for more).

Host-guest

Generally, persons who invite another person to visit or stay on their premises can give consent to a police search of the premises without the guest's knowledge or consent.

However, if the guest has exclusive use of certain areas or property or otherwise has a reasonable expectation of privacy regarding certain areas or property, the host cannot consent to a police search of those areas or property. These are usually rooms (such as the guest's bedroom) and areas or property (such as a suitcase or dresser drawer) which the guest reasonably believes the host would not intrude upon and, therefore, would not allow others to intrude upon.

Employer-employee

Generally, an employer may consent to a police search of areas or property on the employer's premises even though they may be used or occupied by an employee. However, if an employee is given exclusive use or occupancy of an area or property (such as a desk, filing cabinet or locker) and the employer respects the employee's privacy regarding that area or property, the employer cannot give consent to a police search).[357]

Employee-employer

Generally, an employee cannot consent to a police search of his employer's premises or property unless that employee has been given authority, either expressly or impliedly, to have charge of the premises or property.

An employee with very restricted authority, such as a machinist or office worker, generally would not have authority to consent to a police search. Other employees, however, may have, expressly or impliedly, such control over the employer's premises or property that they have authority to consent to a police search. This would include, under proper circumstances, a custodian in charge of the premises, the clerk or manager in charge of the store or premises, or a security guard.

- In ***Com v. Wahlstrom***, a clerk left in sole charge of a small store was found to have authority, at least apparent authority, to consent to a police search of all areas and property under his control and supervision.[358]

School authorities-student

School authorities may have authority to consent to a police search of student property stored in a locker or other area if the school authorities retain the right of access to that locker or area (for example, by retaining a separate set of keys to the locker) **and have notified students that lockers are subject to being searched**.[359] However, this largely depends on the school policy and the students' reasonable expectation of privacy. Since the consent of school officials may not be sufficient to allow a police search, officers should limit their searches to situations involving probable cause and a warrant, unless an exception to the warrant requirement applies.

[355] *See,Commonwealth v. Sandler*, 368 Mass. 729, 335 N.E.2d 903 (1975); *Abel v. U.S.*, 362 U.S. 217, 80 S.Ct. 683 (1980); *Commonwealth v. Lanigan*, 12 Mass. App. Ct. 913, 423 N.E.2d 800 (1981).
[356] *Stoner v. California*, 376 U.S. 483, 84 S.Ct. 889 (1964).
[357] *U.S. v. Blok*, 188 F.2d 1019 (D.C. Cir. 1951).
[358] *Commonwealth v. Wahlstrom*, 375 Mass. 115, 375 N.E.2d 706 (1978).
[359] *Commonwealth v. Snyder*, 413 Mass. 521, 597 N.E.2d 1363 (1992); *See,New Jersey v. T.L.O.*, 469 U.S. 325 (1985).

If, on the other hand, the student has exclusive access to the locker or other area and reasonably believes that the school authorities will respect his or her privacy regarding the locker or other area, the school authorities probably do not have authority to consent to a police search.

Also, school officials generally do not have authority to give consent to a police search of a student's dormitory room or other area where the student lives and has a reasonable expectation of privacy.[360]

Attorney-client

An attorney, when duly authorized by his client to do so, may validly give consent to a police search of premises or property owned by or used by his client.

Bailee-bailor

A bailee is a person to whom another person has entrusted property (the borrower). The person who owns the property is called the bailor (the lender).

If the bailor has entrusted property to a bailee, for example, by loaning his automobile to a relative or friend, the bailee may consent to a police search of the property while the property is in his or her possession and control.[361] This can be done without the knowledge or permission of the bailor who owns the property.[362] Evidence found in the car which incriminates the owner (the bailor) may be used against him or her in court.[363]

However, if the bailee has only limited custody of the entrusted property, he or she may not have authority to consent to a police search. For example, if a person entrusts property to a second person, not to be used by the second person, but only to be shipped or stored by the second person, the second person (the bailee) probably does not have authority to consent to a police search.[364]

4. SEARCH INCIDENT TO LAWFUL ARREST

Both U.S. Supreme Court case law and Massachusetts General Laws permit the search of an individual and his immediate area as a result of lawful arrest.

The search-incident-to-arrest exception, under the Fourth Amendment "has traditionally been justified by the reasonableness of searching for weapons, instruments of escape, and evidence of crime when a person is taken into official custody and lawfully detained."[365]
The SJC has explained that the purpose of a search incident to an arrest is:

1. To prevent an individual from destroying or concealing evidence of the crime for which the police have probable cause to arrest, or
2. To prevent an individual from acquiring a weapon to resist arrest or to facilitate an escape.[366]

A search incident to arrest, similar to the search of a person pursuant to a warrant, generally is limited to the body of the person arrested and the area and items within his or her immediate possession and control at the time. However, there are limits to the scope of this type of search. Massachusetts police officers are governed by the more stringent chapter 276 § 1.

Massachusetts standard (chapter 276 § 1)

M.G.L. c. 276, § 1 "authorizes a search to be made incident to an arrest only (1) for the purpose of seizing evidence of the crime for which the arrest has been made in order to prevent its destruction or concealment or (2) for the purpose of removing any weapon the person arrested might use to resist arrest or to escape."[367]

- In ***Commonwealth v. Toole,*** the search of a truck cab following a defendant's arrest on an outstanding warrant for assault and battery, while reasonable for Fourth Amendment purposes, was held to violate M.G.L. c. 276, §1 because the search was not made for evidence of the crime for which the defendant was arrested nor for

[360] *Piazzola v. Watkins*, 42 F.2d 284 (5th Cir. 1971).
[361] *Commonwealth v. Campbell*, 352 Mass. 387, 226 N.E.2d 211 (1967).
[362] *Frazier v. Cupp*, 394 U.S. 731, 89 S.Ct. 1420 (1969).
[363] *See also,Nelson v. Moore*, 470 F.2d 1192 (1st Cir. 1972). (Pipe allegedly used by the defendant in assault and battery was handed over to police by a neighbor who had borrowed it from the defendant.)
[364] *Corngold v. U.S.*, 367 F.2d 1 (9th Cir. 1966).
[365] United States v. Edwards, 415 U.S. 800, 802-803 (1974). See United States v. Robinson, 414 U.S. at 230-234; Chimel v. California, 395 U.S. 752, 762-763 (1969).
[366] *Commonwealth v. Perkins*, SJC (2013).
[367] *Commonwealth v. Wilson*, 389 Mass. 115, 118, 448 N.E.2d 1130 (1983).

weapons which the defendant might use to resist arrest or escape. Therefore, the Court allowed the defendant's motion to suppress the gun as evidence.[368]

- In ***Commonwealth v. Cassidy***, after placing a driver under arrest for kidnapping the eleven year old boy found in his vehicle, and placing the individual in the cruiser in handcuffs, a search of the passenger compartment was not justified and the marijuana found was suppressed. In this case the officer had no information from which he might conclude that a weapon had been used in the crime, so no search for evidence of the crime was proper.[369]

Arrest must be valid

There must be a valid arrest based on probable cause. If the arrest is unlawful, any weapons seized or any evidence or other items obtained during a search incident to that unlawful arrest will be inadmissible at trial.[370]

If, however, an officer conducts a search incident to an outstanding arrest warrant, which he or she believed was lawful, the seized evidence need not be suppressed if the erroneous standing warrant resulted from clerical errors of court employees.[371] See the Criminal Procedure Overview at the beginning of this manual for more on this topic.

Search for weapons no justification needed

A search for weapons made incident to an arrest may be conducted, no matter what the crime for which the arrest was made. Once a custodial arrest occurs, no additional justification is required for a search of a person for weapons that otherwise might be used to resist arrest or to escape, or to discover evidence of the crime for which the arrest was made.[372]

Evidence encountered during search for weapons

Should an officer, while conducting a search for weapons or evidence of the crime for which a person is being arrested, and limiting his or her search to areas where such evidence might be found, discover evidence of other crimes (effectively in *plain view*), such evidence will be admissible into evidence.[373]

The search is not without limitations and must be legitimate

Just because there is a remote possibility that evidence for which the arrest was made might be found does not grant the officer free reign to search for anything incriminating. The search must be legitimately made toward the purpose of locating evidence for which the arrest was made or for locating weapons.

- In ***Commonwealth v. Rose***, when a trooper arrested a motorist for operating a motor vehicle under the influence of alcohol and placed him in handcuffs in the cruiser, any further search of the vehicle for evidence of the crime required both legitimate objective and subjective purposes. Opening a nylon bag and a suitcase found under the driver's seat was viewed by the Court as a general search for whatever the trooper could find. It therefore suppressed the drug paraphernalia and scale, even though those containers theoretically could have held evidence related to the OUI (alcohol) arrest (e.g., cans or bottles).[374]

Timing of the search and proximity to the arrest

When it is practical to do so, the search should be conducted at the time of the arrest and in the immediate vicinity of the arrest.[375] However, a partial or hasty search at the scene of the arrest may be followed up by a thorough search at the police station or at another location where a search may be conducted safely.[376]

- In ***Commonwealth v. Pierre***, Lynn and Cambridge Police Officers were serving an arrest warrant in the City of Lynn. During the arrest of the subject of the warrant, companions of the arrestee were detained. One of the companions, Pierre, dropped a plastic bag that he was carrying just before he entered a nearby vehicle. Pierre was subsequently arrested when a gun was discovered in the vehicle. The bag that Pierre had dropped was placed in the vehicle and the vehicle was towed to the police station where the bag was later searched and another gun was located. The Commonwealth justified the search of the bag as a search incident to an arrest. The court denied this reasoning because the search had occurred approximately one hour after the arrest and the suspects had been arrested

[368] *Commonwealth v. Toole*, 389 Mass. 159, 448 N.E.2d 1264 (1983).
[369] *Commonwealth v. Cassidy*, 32 Mass. 160, 587 N.E.2d 235 (1990).
[370] *Commonwealth v. Haas*, 373 Mass. 545, 369 N.E.2d 692 (1977).
[371] *Arizona v. Evans*, 115 S.Ct. 1185 (1985).
[372] *Commonwealth v. Prophete*, 443 Mass. 548, 823 N.E.2d. 343 (2005).
[373] *Commonwealth v. Beasley*, 13 Mass. App. Ct. 62, 430 N.E.2d 437 (1982).
[374] *Commonwealth v. Rose*, 25 Mass. App. Ct. 905, 514 N.E.2d 683 (1987).
[375] *Stoner v. California*, 376 U.S. 483, 84 S.Ct. 889 (1964); *Shirley v. California*, 395 U.S. 818, 89 S.Ct. 2503 (1969).
[376] *U.S. v. Deleo*, 422 F.2d 487 (1st Cir. 1970).

and removed from the area. The court stated that had the "police searched the bag when the defendant was arrested, it would have been a lawful search incident to an arrest."[377]

.Justification for delay

Should there be a good reason to delay seizing items of evidence on an arrested person — such as waiting until the next day to take the arrestee's clothing where there was no substitute clothing available when he was placed in the cell — this will still qualify as a search (and seizure) incident to an arrest.[378]

Search incident to an arrest before the arrest

A search incident to arrest may precede formal arrest, provided that probable cause to arrest exists at the time the search is made, independent of the results of the search.[379] Where the police have probable cause to arrest, they may detain a person - without placing him or her under arrest - and conduct a limited search incident to detention - to preserve destructible evidence.[380]

However the court will not permit a search incident to arrest where the suspect is not arrested until much later, or is never arrested.[381] The SJC has stated "to permit a search incident to arrest where the suspect is not arrested until much later, or is never arrested, would sever this exception completely from its justifications. It would, in effect, create a wholly new exception for a "search incident to probable cause to arrest. This we decline to do." [382]

- In ***Commonwealth v. Brillante***, even though the state police had probable cause to arrest a driver for cocaine possession, their delay in making a formal arrest until after searching the passenger compartment (where they found more evidence) and the driver himself for drugs were permissible.[383] The Court stated that where a formal arrest followed quickly a challenged search, it was not particularly important that the search preceded the arrest.[384]

Within the arrestee's immediate control

The area or premises within the arrestee's immediate control may be searched, that is, the area from within which he or she might gain possession of a weapon or destructible evidence may also be searched thoroughly so that the police may uncover and remove weapons, fruits, instrumentalities, contraband and evidence.[385] It is generally limited to the lunging, reaching, and grabbing, area of the arrestee.

There is no determinative rule limiting the physical scope of a search incident to arrest to a particular number of feet.[386] Rather, the scope of the search must be judged looking at the facts and circumstances of the arrest.[387] In evaluating whether a search incident to arrest exceeded the area within the defendant's immediate control the Court stated "we note that a police officer's decision how and where to conduct the search is "a quick ad hoc judgment." A search incident to arrest "may be valid even though a court, operating with the benefit of hindsight in an environment well removed from the scene of the arrest doubts that the defendant could have reached the items seized during the search." [388]

- In ***Commonwealth v. Garcia***, a warrantless search of a locked mailbox and a magnetic key inside the mailbox was not justified by an exception to the warrant requirement for searches incident to arrest, regardless of whether the suspect was standing in a hallway containing mailboxes.[389] The mailbox was not within the defendant's immediate control following his arrest. Since he could not have gained access to the locked mailbox and the key inside, he did not pose any threat that evidence might have been destroyed, nor could he have reached for a weapon.

WARRANTLESS SEARCHES

---

[377] *Commonwealth .v Pierre*, 72 453 Mass. 1010 (2009).
[378] *Commonwealth v. Ross*, 361 Mass. 663, 296 N.E.2d 810 (1972).
[379] *Commonwealth v. Johnson*, 413 Mass. 598, 602 N.E.2d 555 (1992); *Commonwealth v. Ciaramitaro*, 51 Mass. App. Ct. 638, 747 N.E.2d 1253 (2001); *Commonwealth v. Kotlyarevskiy*, 59 Mass.App.Ct.240, 794 N.E.2 1276 (2003).
[380] *U.S. v. Murphy*, 412 U.S. 291, 93 S.Ct. 2000 (1973). (Husband, whom police had probable cause to arrest for murder of his strangled wife, came voluntarily to police station. However, he refused consent to let police take samples of a dried, blood-like material under his fingernails. Without arresting him, police forcibly took samples from under his fingernails. The Court upheld that limited search incident to detention, since probable cause to arrest existed, although it was not exercised at the time.) *See also,Howlings v. Kentucky*, 444 U.S. 98,100 S.Ct. 338 (1980).
[381] *Commonwealth v. Washington*, 449 Mass. 476, 869 N.E.2d 605 (2007)
[382] *Commonwealth v. Alvarado*, 420 Mass. 542, 554 (1995)
[383] *Commonwealth v. Brillante*, 399 Mass. 152, 503 N.E.2d 459 (1987).
[384] *Commonwealth v. Rivera*, 27 Mass. App. Ct. 41, 534 N.E.2d 24 (1989), *rev. den.*404 Mass. 1103, 537 N.E.2d 157 (1989).
[385] *Chimel v. California*, 376 U.S. 483, 845 S.Ct. 889 (1964).
[386] Commonwealth v. Elizono quoting People v. Williams, 57 Ill. 2d 239, 246, cert. denied, 419 U.S. 1026 (1974).
[387] See Com. v. Elizondo (1998) also United States v. Lucas, 898 F.2d 606, 608 (8th Cir.), cert. denied, 498 U.S. 838 (1990).
[388] See Commonwealth v. Elizono (1998)
[389] *Commonwealth v. Garcia*, 34 Mass. App. Ct. 386, 612 N.E.2d 674 (1993)

- In ***Commonwealth v. Elizondo***, where a search of the defendant's bathroom was valid, even though he was handcuffed, since, during the course of a controlled drug transaction, the defendant entered the bathroom – even though for less than 10 seconds – and returned with cocaine.[390] In this case the defendant was arrested, handcuffed, and secured within four or five feet of the bathroom, and the bathroom door was open.

No Search Incident to an Arrest once the Arrestee is Secured

In 2009 the US Supreme Court decided ***Arizona v. Gant.*** The Supreme Court decided once an individual is arrested, handcuffed, and placed in a cruiser, or otherwise secured, a search of the areas within the immediate control of the arrestee's location at the time of the arrest would not be permissible, under a search incident to an arrest theory, as the arrestee is not in a position to destroy or conceal evidence.[391]

This has long been the case in Massachusetts, however in *Arizona v. Gant* where the Court changed its previous position, allowing a search for *any* evidence, weapons, or contraband, even after the arrestee had been secured, to now only permitting the search for evidence if the police "reasonably believe" the area contains evidence related to the crime for which the arrest was made. [392]

Attorney Hanrahan's Note: In the vast majority of situations a police officer is going to handcuff and secure an arrestee for safety purposes and thus take away the justification to search the area around the arrestee. Given safety concerns this would be the most prudent action. However, there are times when a police officer may leave an arrestee unsecured. *Commonwealth v. Quilter* is a good example (and a common scenario).

- In the 2012 case of ***Commonwealth v. Quilter***, the Boston Police went to Quilter's home to execute an arrest warrant for trespassing. . Quilter, dressed only in underclothes, answered the front door. When notified that the officers were there to execute a warrant for his arrest, he asked if he could get dressed. The officers escorted QUILTER to his bedroom. While in the bedroom one of the officers noticed that Quilter sat on the bed, not close to the closet where his clothes were, but on the far end of the bed, away from the closet. One of the officers had Quilter stand up and he lifted Quilter's mattress discovering a firearm. The Appeals Court stated "in executing the arrest warrant, the police had the power to enter the defendant's home. They were authorized to accompany him to his room and had the right 'to remain ... at [his] elbow at all times,' even in the absence of any indication that he might have a weapon available or might attempt to escape." The Court went on to say "whether the defendant was seated on the bed or standing next to it, the firearm was within 'the one lunge zone"' and thus the search was justified as a search incident to the arrest.

Even if Arrestee is secured a Search Incident to an Arrest may be permissible if cohorts are in the area and may destroy/conceal evidence on the arrestee's behalf

In 2012, the SJC has indicated that although the arrestee's ability to access weapons and evidence in the area around the location of the arrest, once the arrestee is handcuffed and secured, is not generally not permissible as a search incident to arrest, if the arrestee was accompanied by others who are still present the search may still be justified. See *Commonwealth v. Young* below:

- In the 2012 case of ***Commonwealth v. Young***, the SJC ruled that the police were justified in ordering passengers out of a vehicle to facilitate a *search incident-to-an-arrest* of an occupant who was observed with drugs in his shirt pocket during a routine traffic stop, even after the arrestee has been handcuffed and removed. The SJC distinguished this case from *Gant* because although the arrestee was removed and secured, other passengers remained in the vehicle and could have concealed or destroyed evidence on behalf of the arrestee. [393]

Searching companions

There is no automatic right to search the companion of a person validly arrested.[394] A person who is merely present in a suspected car does not lose the immunities from a search of his or her person to which he or she would otherwise be entitled. The officer must have some additional justification and an exception to the search warrant requirement.

[390] *Commonwealth v. Elizondo*, 428 Mass. 322, 701 N.E. 2d 325 (1998).
[391] *Commonwealth v. Bongarzone*, 390 Mass. 326, 455 N.E.2d 1183 (1983); *Commonwealth v. Brillante*, 399 Mass. 152, 503 N.E.2d 459 (1987); *Commonwealth v. Borden*, 403 Mass. 1008, 530 N.E.2d 1242 (1988).
[392] *Arizona v. Gant,* 540 U.S. 963 (2009).
[393] Commonwealth v. Young, SJC January 2012
[394] *Commonwealth v. Prevost*, 44 Mass. App. Ct. 398, 691 N.E. 2d 592 (1998), *rev. den.*427 Mass. 1104, 695 N.E. 2d 667.

Search of baggage/containers

Once the arrestee has been secured the police may still search articles or containers which the arrestee was holding or carrying at the time of the arrest such as a suitcase, briefcase, handbag, pocketbook or carton, providing *the police have probable cause the item contains evidence or contraband.*[395]

Containers or property that are securely within the exclusive control of the police may be searched without a warrant **only** if it is reasonably believed that they contain explosives, other imminently dangerous material or evidence that will decompose or otherwise be lost in a short period of time **or, if the police have probable cause to search the container.**[396]

No need to secure baggage and obtain a warrant when probable cause exists: this is sometimes referred to as a "Madera search" after the case of ***Commonwealth v. Madera.***

In ***Commonwealth v. Madera***, even in the absence of exigent circumstances, the court stated that police are allowed to search a bag carried by the arrested individual **where the police have probable cause** to believe the bag contains evidence of the crime for which the person was arrested, or even just probable cause that the bag of the arrested person contains unrelated evidence or contraband.

- In ***Commonwealth v. Madera,*** Springfield police received information from an informant that the defendant was on his way back via bus from New York after purchasing large quantities of heroin. Seven plainclothes police officers arrested the defendant as he exited the bus carrying a gym bag. The police searched the gym bag and discovered large quantities of controlled substances. The defendant claimed that the search of the gym back was unlawful. The court stated there was no justification for the warrantless search in this case on the ground that the police were concerned for their safety and searched for a weapon to which the defendant might seek access. Nor is this a case in which the search of the seized container was justified because there was a risk the defendant might destroy the evidence. These concerns may be good reasons in some circumstances for a warrantless search of a container following an arrest on probable cause, but here the police presence was substantial and the risk of the defendant successfully repossessing the bag was minimal. The proper question, in our view, is whether art. 14 requires the suppression of a controlled substance found during a warrantless, contemporaneous, but not exigent search of a closed container carried by a person whom the police lawfully arrested in the belief, founded on probable cause, that he was unlawfully carrying a controlled substance. The defendant's arrest and the seizure of the bag were constitutionally proper. There was probable cause to search the bag. **To require a search warrant in such a case would afford insignificant protection to a defendant and would unnecessarily burden the criminal justice system.**[397]

The court noted that once the bag was seized by the police there was no reason to fear that the suspect would gain access to any weapon inside or destroy any evidence contained in the bag. However, the court recognized the burden it would be placing on the court and police to require a warrant in such case and it felt the extra protection was insignificant.

Search of baggage must be contemporaneous and in proximity with the arrest: a warrantless search of luggage or other containers or personal property seized at the time and place of the arrest cannot be justified as a search incident to the arrest if the search is remote in time and place from the arrest or if the container or property is securely in police custody and there is no reason to fail to obtain a search warrant.[398]

Attorney Hanrahan's Note: Although the search of a container, bag etc. carried by a person under arrest requires probable cause to search, once the arrestee is secured, these items are lawfully inspected under a booking inventory search (provided the agency has a booking inventory policy).

Circumstances Surrounding the Container may Amount to Probable Cause

As noted above (*Madera Search*), if the police have probable cause that a container being carried by an arrestee contains evidence or criminal contraband the police may search it without a warrant. In *Commonwealth v. Clermy*, the arrestee was found to have a small pill bottle secreted in his underwear when he was being searched subsequent to his arrest. The police were justified in opening the pill bottle and inspecting its contents because

[395] *See, Pira v. U.S.*, 387 F.2d 609 (1st Cir. 1967); *U.S. v. Ross*, 456 U.S. 798, 102 S.Ct. 2157 (1982); *Commonwealth v. Madera*, 402 Mass. 156, 521 N.E.2d 738 (1988).
[396] *California v. Acevedo*, 111 S.Ct. 1982 (1991).
[397] *Commonwealth v. Madera*, 402 Mass. 156 (1988).
[398] *U.S. v. Chadwick*, 433 U.S. 1, 97 S.Ct. 2476 (1977).

WARRANTLESS SEARCHES

the very nature of the circumstances created probable cause that the bottle contained criminal contraband or evidence as most people do not carry prescription medication in their underwear.

Attorney Hanrahan's Note: The law surrounding *search-incident-to-arrest* is typically a moot point because many of these discovered items are uncovered by other lawful means (i.e. inventory searches, or automobile exception searches, etc.). Despite this there are times when the search-incident-to-arrest exception to the warrant requirement can be very important. In any case, as enforcers of the law it is important to understand this concept.

Warrant Arrest

In the 2014 case of ***Commonwealth v. White, Jr.***, the SJC ruled that when someone is arrested on a warrant the search incident to arrest exception will be limited to weapons unless the crime was recently committed and/or the officer has reason to believe related evidence to the crime is in the arrestee's possession.

Attorney Hanrahan's note: remember one of the reasons for permitting a search incident to arrest is to uncover any evidence, connected to the arrestable offense, that may have been discarded/hidden by the arrestee. When arresting someone on a warrant this dynamic changes as the warrant arrest may take place long after the initial crime and thus any evidence connected to the crime is likely long gone.

Search of Arrestee's Cell Phone as a Search Incident to Arrest

In the 2014 U.S. Supreme Court case of ***Riley v. California***, the U.S. Supreme Court ruled that the police generally may not, without a warrant, search digital information on a cell phone seized from an individual who has been arrested. The Court reasoned:

Digital evidence stored on a cell phone cannot be used to harm the officer thus the safety exception does not apply (although the physical features of the phone may be inspected to ensure it does not pose a danger).

In relation to the destruction of evidence, the possibility of some type of remote data wipe is different from an arrestee reaching for physical evidence. Additionally, the intrusion into a cell phone is considerably more intrusive than the physical items carried by the arrestee. The data stored on cell phones is massive and can go back decades. Cell phones can also be connected to remote servers and thus the search may extend well beyond what is within the immediate control of the arrestee.

Attorney Hanrahan's note: Typically, the SJC is much more restrictive in regards to police searches and seizures compared to the U.S. Supreme Court. However, in a rare situation *Riley v. California* essentially overturned SJC case law from 2013 permitting the search of a cell phone, in limited circumstances, as a search incident to arrest. Additionally, although Court ruled that the police cannot generally search a cell phone as a search incident to arrest it does not preclude the police from searching cell phones under other exceptions to the search warrant. For example, if the police had probable cause to believe that the contents of a cell phone contained evidence and that the evidence was about to be wiped the police would be justified in searching the cell phone contents if they were unable to otherwise preserve the contents (i.e. secure the scene) , or if police had a reasonable belief that the owner of the cell phone was abducted and in danger the police may be permitted to search the contents of the cell phone, under the emergency exception, to try to locate and rescue the victim.

5. PAT FRISKS

A pat frisk is a limited search of the outer clothing in order to determine whether or not a person is armed. It is strictly limited to a search for weapons. The officer must have a reasonable fear for his safety or the safety of the public. Because Pat Frisk searches are only permissible in relation to a Temporary Detention this aspect of warrantless search is covered in the Temporary Detention section of this manual. Additionally, in regards to a motor vehicle, police officers may extend a pat frisk into a motor vehicle, under some circumstances; this concept is covered in the Motor Vehicle Search section of this manual.

6. PROTECTIVE SWEEP

The term *protective sweep* has been used by the courts in at least three different contexts. The traditional, or unique, use of the term refers to the authority of police to check other rooms and hiding spaces of a home when executing an arrest inside the home when they have reason to believe someone may interfere. The other two uses of the terms are really just extension of other search warrant exceptions.

DURING AN ARREST

While executing an arrest in a dwelling or building the police may search other rooms (and other locations where someone may be hiding) in the house or building or apartment if they suspect that other people may be present who might be accomplices of the arrestee or who might come to his or her aid.[399]

- In ***Commonwealth v. Flowers***, where police entered an apartment in which a kidnap and assault victim was being held and, after seizing four men present, learned from the victim that five men, all armed, were involved, "The police officers were justified in believing that it was imperative to their safety that the entire apartment be searched for this fifth man." Guns, ammunition and holsters found in plain view during the protective sweep search for the fifth man were admissible.[400]

Scope of the protective sweep

The police may conduct such a *protective sweep* only as long as necessary to assure that no accomplices are present. The sweep is limited to a quick visual inspection (not full search) of areas in which an accomplice might be hiding.[401] Once the arrest is completed, the police must depart.

- In ***Commonwealth v. Mejia,*** during the course of protective sweep, the court upheld the officer's action of ripping a mattress from the bed to make certain that no one was hiding beneath bed, rather than conducting tidy and methodical protective sweep and exposing himself to grave danger by first looking beneath bed. The court ruled this did not exceed scope of permissible protective sweep of the apartment, and thus, the loaded handgun which officer found beneath mattress was discovered within course of permissible protective sweep. The police had entered the apartment under chaotic and dangerous circumstances and without the knowledge of layout of interior or opportunity for any meaningful deliberation, and the police did not know whether others remained hidden in the apartment.[402]

Reasonable belief required for Protective Sweep

In order for officers to perform a limited search incident to arrest they must possess a *reasonable belief*, based on **specific and articulable facts** that, taken together with rational inferences drawn from those facts, reasonably warrant the officers to believe that the area to be swept harbors an individual who poses a danger to the officer or others,[403] or in certain circumstances, a potentially instrumentality.[404]
The mere presence of an individual, without a reasonable basis for suspecting that such person poses a danger to the police or others, is not sufficient to justify a protective sweep of the premises incident to an arrest.

The articulable facts justifying such a sweep can arise from the violence implicit in an arrestee's criminal history.[405]

The articulable facts can also arise from the arrestee's conduct prior to the arrest, such as a violent flight. [406]

COMMUNITY CARETAKING OR EMERGENCY AID PROTECTIVE SWEEPS

The police may also make a so-called protective sweep to locate and protect any injured person who may be on the premises. The intent is not to locate evidence or arrest a suspect but to render emergency aid. The police must have an "objectively reasonable basis" to believe that there may be someone who is injured or in imminent danger of physical ham. [407] This is actually a type of emergency exception however the courts often use the term protective sweep in this context as well.

- In ***Mincey v. Arizona,***[408] a police narcotics raid suddenly erupted into a volley of gun shots. One officer was shot and collapsed. His assailant was found wounded. Police then conducted a quick search of the entire apartment to determine if other persons might have been injured. The U.S. Supreme Court upheld that protective sweep to locate and protect injured persons or other victims.

[399] *Maryland v. Buie*, 494 U.S. 325, 110 S.Ct. 1093 (1990).
[400] *Commonwealth v. Flowers*, 1 Mass. App. Ct. 415, 298 N.E.2d 989 (1973).
[401] *Commonwealth v. Bowden*, 379 Mass. 472, 399 N.E.2d 482 (1980).
[402] *Commonwealth v. Mejia*, 64 Mass.App.Ct. 238, 832 N.E.2d 693 (2005).
[403] *Commonwealth v. Dubois*, 44 Mass. App. Ct. 294, 690 N.E. 2d 466 (1998).
[404] *Com. v. McCollum*, App. Ct. (April 2011).
[405] *Com .v .DeJesus*, 70 Mass.App.Ct. 114, 119-120 (2007)
[406] *Com. v. McCollum*, App. Ct. (April 2011).
[407] *Commonwealth v. Peters*, 453 Mass. 818 (2009).
[408] *Mincey v. Arizona*, 437 U.S. 385, 98 S.Ct. 2408 (1978).

Multiple Sweeps

In some circumstances, police may be permitted to conduct a second sweep but only when, having considered the information learned from the first sweep, there continues to be an objectively reasonable basis to believe that an injured victim may still be inside.

- In the 2009 case of ***Commonwealth v. Peters***, the Falmouth PD responded to a reported disturbance. The officers discovered that bullet entered a home and appeared to come from the neighbor's (the defendant's) home. After conducting an initial protective sweep, the officer later conducted a second protective sweep, this time discovering handguns and drugs. The SJC stated that "during the roughly fifteen to twenty minutes that the officers had been in the three-bedroom home, they saw and heard nothing to indicate imminent danger. There was no sign of a struggle, no blood, and, apart from barking dogs, no unusual sounds." The Court determined that an objectively reasonable basis to believe that an injured victim may still be inside was not present in this case.[409]

The SJC did indicate that there "undoubtedly are circumstances in which two warrantless protective sweeps of a home in quick succession, one rapid without attention to detail to locate a potential assailant or assailants, and the second more deliberate in search of persons who may be injured, would both fall within the permissible scope of the emergency aid exception. **We do not declare a "one sweep rule" through this decision.** A second warrantless protective sweep may be lawfully conducted but only when, in light of all the circumstances known to the officers at the time, there continues to be an objectively reasonable basis to believe that there is someone in the home in need of assistance." [410]

- In the 2012 case of ***Commonwealth v. Entwistle***, the SJC again upheld a second protective sweep even after the first did not reveal anyone in danger. In this case the Court analyzed the justification for each entry on its individual merits.

VEHICLE PROTECTIVE SWEEPS

During a motor vehicle stop wherein the officer has a fear for his/her safety, the officer may be justified in ordering the occupants out of a motor vehicle. Prior to allowing the occupants back into the vehicle the officer may be justified in conducting a "protective sweep" of vehicle's interior for weapons. Although the same term is used this is actually a form of a pat frisk. This is covered in more detail in the Motor Vehicle Stop section of this manual.

ADMISSIBILITY OF EVIDENCE OBSERVED IN PLAIN VIEW DURING A PROTECTIVE SWEEP

Provided the protective sweep is lawful, any evidence or contraband discovered in plain view while conducting the protective sweep may be lawfully seized.

Only evidence and contraband that is discovered within the scope of the protective sweep will be admissible.[411] For instance, while conducting a protective sweep for cohorts who may aid in the escape of the arrestee the officer opens up a nightstand drawer and finds drugs; the discovery will most likely be suppressed because a cohort could not hide in a typical nightstand drawer.

7. INVENTORY SEARCHES

Inventory "searches" do not require a warrant. They are <u>not</u> intended to uncover evidence; they are primarily intended to account for the belonging/valuables of the owner. However, an invasion of privacy often takes place thus they are an exception to the search warrant requirement. Booking Inventory searches are discussed in the **Arrest Procedures section** of this manual and motor vehicle inventories are discussed in the **Motor Vehicle Search section** of this manual.

8. MOTOR VEHICLE EXCEPTION

If police have probable cause that criminal contraband or evidence is located within a vehicle that is located on a way the police can search the vehicle without a warrant. This topic is thoroughly covered in the **Motor Vehicle Search section** of this manual.

---

[409] *Commonwealth v. Peters*, 453 Mass. 818 (2009).
[410] *Commonwealth v. Peters*, 453 Mass. 818 (2009).
[411] *Commonwealth v. Lewin*, 407 Mass. 617, 555 N.E.2d 551 (1990).

9. ADMINISTRATIVE SCREENING SEARCHES

The Courts generally permit administrative searches at airports, court houses, schools and other government buildings to ensure the safety of the people entering the building. There typically has to be some type of *advanced notice* so that the person can elect not to subject themselves to a search. In a sense these searches are somewhat consensual. The inspections (or searches) are permissible because the minimal amount of intrusion is outweighed by the need for public safety; thus they are reasonable despite the lack of a warrant.

10. PROBATIONERS AND PAROLEES

The United States Supreme Court has, in a series of cases, established that, under the Fourth Amendment, *probationers* and *parolees* **have a significantly diminished expectation of privacy**.

In ***Griffin v. United States***, the U.S. Supreme Court held, that a warrantless search of a probationer's home, pursuant to a State regulation requiring reasonable grounds and approval of the probationer's supervisor for such a search, did not violate the probationer's privacy rights under the Fourth Amendment.[412]

Years later, in ***United States v. Knights***, the Court indicated that a warrantless search based on **reasonable suspicion** that a probationer (who was subject, as a condition of his probation, to warrantless searches) was engaged in criminal activity was not intrusive because of the "probationer's significantly diminished privacy interests."[413]

Most recently, the U.S. Supreme Court found that a parolee's expectation of privacy is diminished *even beyond that of a probationer.*[414]

Massachusetts is more stringent but recognizes a reduced expectation of privacy

Massachusetts Courts have also recognized a diminished expectation of privacy for probations and parolees but not to the extent as federal courts.

Probationers

Under art. 14 (of the Massachusetts Declaration of rights), the SJC has established that a *probationer* has a diminished expectation of privacy. However, the SJC has maintained that art. 14 affords greater protections for probationers than does the Fourth Amendment. The Massachusetts standard is that a search of a probationer is permissible on reasonable suspicion however *a warrant is still required absent a recognized exception to the warrant* requirement. A warrant for a probationer can be issued on reasonable suspicion (probable cause not required).

Parolees

In the 2016 case of ***Commonwealth v. Moore***, the SJC stated "we now conclude that art. 14 provides to a parolee an expectation of privacy that is less than even the already diminished expectation afforded to a probationer."

The SJC stated "we conclude that, with regard to parolees, imposing a warrant requirement would hinder the Commonwealth in addressing its significant supervisory interests." Thus, in order for a *parole officer* to search a parolee the parole officer only needs reasonable suspicion. A warrant is not required.

Attorney Hanrahan's Note: In order to conduct a search of a probationer or parolee, under the lesser standard of reasonable suspicion as described above, the search should be initiated by the suspect's probation or parole officer. However, it can often be a strategic tactic to coordinate with a probation and parole when you are investigating a suspect on probation or parole.

WARRANTLESS SEARCHES

[412] Griffin v. United States, 483 U.S. 868, 875-876 (1987)
[413] United States v. Knights, 534 U.S. 112, 121 (2001)
[414] See Samson, 547 U.S. at 850, 852 (allowing suspicionless and warrantless searches of parolees based purely on status as parolees).

11.STATUTORY ADMINISTRATIVE INSPECTIONS

Several statutes related to highly regulated businesses require the premises or the books and records kept there to be open for inspection by police and other licensing and enforcement personnel. **These are not intended for criminal investigations** but for compliance with licensing requirements. The Supreme Court has held that administrative searches are not beyond the scope of the Fourth Amendment, however. Therefore, inspections made pursuant to the statutes must, nevertheless, be made with the consent of an appropriate person (absent a warrant). Several statutes provide penalties in the event a premises owner fails to permit the inspections. If, in spite of the penalty, an owner refuses to permit an inspection, the police may not make a forcible entry without a warrant unless exigent circumstances and probable cause exist.[415]

Administrative Inspection Warrants

Some highly regulated businesses are required permit the police and other inspecting agents to inspect their premises and records without any court involvement. However, some inspections require a so-called "administrative inspection warrant." These "warrants" are designed to uncover criminal evidence they are intended to ensure compliance with the regulations of the industry.

Probable cause for an administrative inspection is less stringent than for a criminal investigation.

In ***Commonwealth v. Frodyma***, 386 Mass. 434 (1982), [416] the SJC offered the following situations establishing probable cause for the issuance of an administrative inspection warrant for a pharmacy by:

- a showing that the premises had never been previously been inspected
- presenting specific evidence of an existing violation of the regulatory scheme
- a complaint received by the regulatory agency, or
- where a pharmacist or physician had recently made unusually large purchases of controlled substances

Some of the statutes which provide authority for administrative inspections of closely regulated businesses by police include:

- M.G.L. c. 138, § 29 - Inspection of druggists' books listing sales of alcoholic beverages (penalty § 62).
- M.G.L. c. 138, § 63 - entry of licensed liquor premises; taking of samples. (penalty § 63A)
- M.G.L. c. 140, § 25 - police may inspect lodging house at request of licensing authority.
- M.G.L. c. 140, § 27 - register of every inn, lodging house, camp, motel, and mobile home park open to inspection by police. (Penalty provided). **SEE IMPORTANT NOTE AT THE END OF THIS SECTION.**
- M.G.L. c. 140, § 32I - register of mobile home park to be open to police inspection (penalty provided).
- M.G.L. c. 140, § 37 - register of public lodging house to be open to police inspection (penalty § 40).
- M.G.L. c. 140, § 38 - police given free access to every public lodging house (penalty § 40)
- M.G.L. c. 140, § 52 - police may enter and inspect massage and vapor bath premises (penalty § 53)
- M.G.L. c. 140, § 66 - police officer authorized by selectmen (or police chief in a city) may enter used car or used auto parts dealership to ascertain how he conducts his business and to examine all second hand vehicles and parts thereof, and all books, papers and inventories relating thereto. (penalty § 67)
- M.G.L. c. 140, § 73 - police officers authorized by chief may inspect pawn shops and examine all articles, books and inventories related thereto (penalty § 74)
- M.G.L. c. 140, § 81 - any officer authorized in writing by the mayor, the board of police, the superintendent of police, a deputy superintendent or the chief inspector of police or any officer of the state police, may inspect the record book relative to loans made by a pawnbroker (penalty § 82).
- M.G.L. c. 140, § 123 - firearms dealers must keep their sales record books available for police inspection (penalty § 128).
- MGL. c. 140, § 201 - a police officer may at any time enter a billiard, pool or sippio room, bowling alley, skating rink, the licensed premises of a common victualler or room connected therewith, or a grove required to be licensed under section 188 or any building therein, for the purpose of enforcing any law (penalty provided for obstruction, or hindering entrance of officer).

---

[415] *Commonwealth v. Cadoret,* 15 Mass. App. 654, 447 N.E.2d 685 (1983); *See also,Commonwealth v. Baldwin*, 11 Mass. App. Ct. 386, 416 N.E.2d 544 (1981) (suggesting that denial of permission must necessarily be clear and unequivocal or it may be presumed that there is consent to inspect without a warrant.)
[416] *Commonwealth v. Frodyma*, 386 Mass. 434 (1982).

See below statutes for more on Administrative Inspections and similar Record Keeping Inspection Laws:

C. 266 § 142. RECORD OF PURCHASES BY DEALERS IN SCRAP COPPER WIRE

- Whoever is in the business of purchasing copper line wire or scrap copper wire shall
- enter in a book kept for that purpose a description of the same,
- the quantity purchased, the purchase price and a name and address of the seller.

Said book shall at all times be open to the inspection of the chief of police of a city or town or any other officer having similar duties or any officer authorized by either of them, or a state police officer.

Penalty: Whoever violates any provision of this section shall be punished by a fine of not more than fifty dollars.

ARREST POWERS: **Misdemeanor** – there is no statutory authority granting powers of arrest for this offense.

C. 266 § 142A. GOLD, SILVER AND PLATINUM DEALERS RECORD KEEPING/INSPECTION

- Whoever is in the business of purchasing gold, silver or platinum
- shall enter in a book kept for that purpose
- a description of the item, quantity purchased, the purchase price and the name and address of the seller;
- provided that the purchase price of such item is at least fifty dollars.

Note: Any person who sells gold, silver or platinum shall be required to show to the buyer prior to said sale identification which includes a photograph of said seller.

Inspection: Said book shall at all times be open to the inspection of the chief of police of a city or town or of any other officer having similar duties or any officer authorized by either of them, or a state police officer.

Penalty: Whoever violates any provision of this section shall be punished by a fine of not more than $1,000 dollars or imprisonment of not more than one year, or both such fine and imprisonment.

ARREST POWERS: **Misdemeanor** – there is no statutory authority granting powers of arrest for this offense.

THE VALIDITY OF SOME OF THE REQUIREMENTS ARE IN QUESTION

In 2015 the US Supreme Court, in the case of ***City of Los Angeles v. Patel***, ruled that a Los Angeles municipal code that required hotel operators to allow police to inspect the register without a warrant was unconstitutional. Although the decision was based specifically on the Los Angeles code much of the reasoning would apply to Massachusetts' hotel register law (and similar laws). The Supreme Court stated "contrary to liquor sales, firearms dealing, mining or running an automobile junkyard, the majority did not find that hotel industry is intrinsically dangerous and therefore should not be subject to government oversight."

Attorney Hanrahan's Note: There are many in Massachusetts that do not believe that the US Supreme Court decision impacts the Massachusetts hotel registry inspection law because the Los Angeles code and the MA law are somewhat different. We will have to wait for the Massachusetts Court to hear and decide on the matter before we know for sure but I recommend that your request consent to search these types of records first before you demand. If the records are handed over voluntarily there is constitutional objection to argue.

SEARCH WARRANTS

OVERVIEW

Search warrant definition and purpose

A search warrant is an order, in writing, issued by a judge, clerk/magistrate or other authorized court official directed to officers authorized to serve search warrants ordering them to search, in the daytime and/or nighttime, designated premises or persons for particularly described articles and to bring those described articles, when found, and the persons in whose possession they are found, before the court.[417]

Authority to issue search warrants

Search warrants may be issued by a Justice/Judge of the Supreme Judicial Court, Superior Court or District Court. They may also be issued by the Clerk/Magistrate, Assistant Clerk/Magistrate, Temporary Clerk/Magistrate and Temporary Assistant Clerk/Magistrate of the District (but not Superior) courts.

The purpose of a search warrant

The purpose of requiring the police to apply for a search warrant is to enable an impartial judicial official to review the probable cause and reasonableness of a search and the particularity with which the place or persons to be searched and the articles to be seized are described.[418] Searches and seizures conducted outside of the scope of a valid warrant are presumed to be unreasonable.[419]

Judicial preference for search warrants

In order to encourage the police to use the search warrant procedure, courts show a certain leeway or leniency in the after-the-fact review of the sufficiency of applications for search warrants.[420] In the case of ***Commonwealth v. Blye***,[421] the Appeals Court declared that "although it may not be easy to determine when an affidavit accompanying an application for a search warrant demonstrates the existence of probable cause in a particular case, the resolution of doubtful or marginal cases should be determined largely by the preference to be accorded to search warrants."

C. 276 § 2A. FORM OF WARRANT

The warrant shall be in substantially the following form:

THE COMMONWEALTH OF MASSACHUSETTS

(COUNTY), ss. (NAME) COURT.

To the Sheriffs of our several counties, or their deputies, any State Police Officer, or any Constable or Police Officer of any city or town, within our said Commonwealth.

Proof by affidavit having been made this day before (name of person authorized to issue warrant) by (names of person or persons whose affidavits have been taken) that there is probable cause for believing that (certain property has been stolen, embezzled, or obtained by false pretenses; certain property is intended for use or has been used as the means of committing a crime; certain property has been concealed to prevent a crime from being discovered; certain property is unlawfully possessed or kept or concealed for an unlawful purpose).

We therefore command you in the daytime (or at any time of the day or night) to make an immediate search of (identify premises) (occupied by A.B.) and (of the person of A.B.) and of any person present who may be found to have such property in his possession or under his control or to whom such property may have been delivered, for the following property:

(description of property)

and if you find any such property or any part thereof to bring it and the persons in whose possession it is found before (court having jurisdiction) at (name of court and location).

Dated at (city or town) this _________ day of _________, (insert year).

Clerk.

---

[417] M.G.L. c. 276, § 2.
[418] *The Matter of Lavigne*, 418 Mass. 831, 641 N.E.2d 1328 (1994).
[419] *Commonwealth v. Balicki*, 436 Mass. 1, 762 N.E.2d 290 (2002).
[420] *Commonwealth v. Corradino*, 368 Mass. 411, 332 N.E.2d 907 (1975).
[421] *Commonwealth v. Blye*, 5 Mass. App. Ct. 817, 362 N.E.2d 240 (1977).

THE AFFIDAVIT AND WARRANT REQUIREMENTS

The affidavit can be thought of as an application for the search warrant. When police officers have probable cause to search, before they will be issued a search warrant by the court, they must complete an affidavit detailing the information within the officer's knowledge.

C. 276 § 2B. AFFIDAVIT IN SUPPORT OF APPLICATION FOR WARRANT; CONTENTS AND FORM

A person seeking a search warrant shall appear personally before a court or justice authorized to issue search warrants in criminal cases and shall give an affidavit in substantially the form hereinafter prescribed. Such affidavit shall contain the facts, information, and circumstances upon which such person relies to establish sufficient grounds for the issuance of the warrant. The person issuing the warrant shall retain the affidavit and shall deliver it within three days after the issuance of the warrant to the court to which the warrant is returnable. Upon the return of said warrant, the affidavit shall be attached to it and shall be filed therewith, and it shall not be a public document until the warrant is returned.

The affidavit in support of the application for a search warrant shall be in substantially the following form:

THE COMMONWEALTH OF MASSACHUSETTS.

(COUNTY), ss. (NAME) COURT. ...., (insert year).

I, (name of applicant) being duly sworn, depose and say:

1. I am (describe position, assignment, office, etc.)

2. I have information, based upon (describe source, facts indicating reliability of source and nature of information; if based on personal knowledge and belief, so state).

3. Based upon the foregoing reliable information (and upon my personal knowledge) there is probable cause to believe that the property hereinafter described (has been stolen, or is being concealed, etc.) and may be found (in the possession of A.B. or any other person) at premises (identify).

4. The property for which I seek the issuance of a search warrant is the following: (here describe the property as particularly as possible).

Wherefore, I respectfully request that the court issue a warrant and order of seizure, authorizing the search of (identify premises and the persons to be searched) and directing that if such property or evidence or any part thereof be found that it be seized and brought before the court; together with such other and further relief that the court may deem proper.

...................Name.

Then personally appeared the above named __________________ and made oath that the foregoing affidavit by him subscribed is true.

Before me this __________ day of __________, (insert year).

Justice or Special Justice, Clerk or Assistant Clerk of the ________ Court.

Affidavit requirements

Under the provisions of M.G.L. c. 276, § 2B, a **police officer seeking a search warrant must appear personally** before a judge or other court official authorized to issue search warrants in criminal cases and present an affidavit. However, in the 2012 case of ***Commonwealth v. Nelson***, the SJC upheld the validity of a search warrant issued over the phone and by fax when the officer exhausted all efforts to locate a judge and was only able to get a hold of a judge who was out of state on vacation. This was a rare exception and generally affidavits must be presented in person.

The affidavit must establish probable cause. That is, it must contain the facts, information and underlying circumstances which have led a police officer reasonably to believe that a particular crime has been, is being, or is about to be committed, and that seizable property connected with that crime is likely to be found in the place or upon the person to be searched. The affidavit may not be buttressed (i.e. be supplemented/backed up) by oral testimony. All facts and circumstances must be within "the four corners" of the affidavit, meaning it must be in writing on the affidavit.

In preparing an affidavit, it is incumbent upon an officer to make a full presentation of the facts in the affidavit itself. It is the duty of the judge or magistrate engaged in issuing warrants to make a real scrutiny of such affidavit and to insist upon a sufficient statement of the basis of the officer's knowledge and to refuse to issue a warrant when an affidavit does not make a full presentation sufficient to establish probable cause.[422]

See more on Probable Cause Requirements later in this section.

Premises must be particularly described

The description of the place to be searched must sufficiently describe the location to be searched. Generally, the address and a physical description will suffice. However, the actual street address is not required if the premises is described in enough detail to differentiate it from other homes and buildings, "it must be sufficiently particular for an officer to identify the place intended with reasonable effort."[423]

Items to be seized must be particularly described

The Fourth Amendment to the United States Constitution, Article 14 of the Massachusetts Declaration of Rights and chapter 276 § 2, mandate that a search warrant must describe with *sufficient particularity*, the articles or things to be seized. The requirement prevents law enforcement from conducting an unguided search for anything they can find incriminating against the defendant. [424]

- In ***Commonwealth v. Taylor***, a search warrant that issued for simply "antique jewelry" was deemed invalid for lack of particularity.[425]

The effect of defective affidavits

Deliberate misrepresentations will render a search warrant invalid,[426] as will intentional, nontrivial misstatements.[427] However, inaccuracies which do not affect the integrity of an affidavit do not destroy probable cause for a search warrant.[428]

Also, information obtained in violation of other legal requirements used to obtain probable cause for the issuance of the search warrant will likely render the search warrant invalid.

- In ***Com v. Ford,*** where an affidavit was based **solely** on information acquired during an invalid warrantless search, the seizure of evidence under that warrant was held illegal and was suppressed.[429]
- In ***Com. v. Manning***, the SJC upheld the issuance of a search warrant that was based, **in part**, on information supplied by someone who was unlawfully arrested without probable cause.[430]
- In ***Mass. v. White***, where an affidavit was based solely on information acquired in violation of *Miranda*, the seizure of evidence under that warrant was held illegal and suppressed.[431]
- In ***Com. v. Lima***, the Appeals Court ruled that a search warrant issued for the search of multiple items that was later deemed to have lacked probable cause for one of the particular items did not invalidate the lawfulness of the search for the other items.

---

[422] *Commonwealth v. Causey*, 356 Mass. 125, 248 N.E.2d 249 (1969).
[423] Commonwealth v. Demogenes, 14 Mass. App. Ct. 577 (1982).
[424] *United States v. Diamond*, 808 F.2d 922 (1st Cir. 1987).
[425] *Commonwealth v. Taylor*, 383 Mass. 272 (1981).
[426] *Commonwealth v. Murray*, 359 Mass. 541, 269 N.E.2d 641 (1971).
[427] *U.S. v. Belculfine*, 508 F.2d 58 (1st Cir. 1974).
[428] *Commonwealth v. Rugaber*, 369 Mass. 765, 343 N.E.2d 865 (1976).
[429] *Commonwealth v. Forde*, 367 Mass. 798, 329 N.E.2d 717 (1975).
[430] *Commonwealth v. Manning406 Mass. 421 (1990).,*
[431] *Mass. v. White*, 374 Mass. 132, 371 N.E.2d 777 (1977), *affirmed*, 439 U.S. 280 (1979).

Intent of the Police Officer is Significant in Regards to Errors

In ***Commonwealth v. Nine Hundred and Ninety-Two Dollars***,[432] the Supreme Judicial Court held that where there was a showing of only negligence in making false statements in an affidavit, this alone would not require suppression of the fruits of the resulting search.

The Court observed that the bad faith or good faith of the police affiant is a major consideration in determining whether the false statements in the affidavit were made knowingly and intentionally or with reckless disregard for the truth, or only negligently. Intentional falsehoods and those made with reckless disregard for the truth "bespeak of bad faith" and should be penalized, whereas "good faith but negligent conduct" should not.

Ambiguity in the Affidavit

Ambiguity in the description of the premises to be searched may be overcome by the executing officer's familiarity with the target location.[433] Especially, where an officer has acquired such trustworthy information that there is no probability or reasonable possibility that the wrong residence could be searched.

- In ***Commonwealth v. Toledo***, an officer applied for a search warrant but had mistakenly put the wrong street name in his application as the location to be searched. The Appeals Court held that the defect in the warrant was not a lack of particularity but rather an ambiguity that was overcome by amount of information supplied in the officer's affidavit.[434] In his affidavit the officer used such investigatory techniques as a reverse phone directory, a motor vehicle license search, a board of probation check and postal information all in an effort to confirm the correct address to be searched.

Technical Errors

A search warrant will still be valid despite technical errors or ministerial defects such as:

a. Failure to insert the name of the affiant and date in the acknowledgment section of the affidavit.[435]
b. Police officer's failure to sign the affidavit.[436]
c. The incorrect chapter and section listed on the warrant did not invalid the warrant.[437]
d. Accidentally deleting the words "there is probable cause" from a warrant.[438]
e. Not placing the affiant's name in the correct space on his affidavit beneath his signature.[439]
f. Judge accidentally fails to sign an otherwise valid warrant he intended to issue.[440]

CHALLENGING THE VALIDITY OF THE AFFIDAVIT

In ***Franks v. Delaware***, the US Supreme Court prescribed a process by which a defendant could challenge the validity of an affidavit supporting a search warrant. This sometimes referred to as a **Franks Hearing**.

The defendant must make a substantial preliminary showing that the affidavit contained one or more false statements made *intentionally or with reckless disregard for the truth* and providing information necessary to the finding of probable cause. That initial showing, by papers or otherwise, entitles the defendant to an evidentiary hearing.

If, at the evidentiary hearing, the defendant proves by a *preponderance of the evidence* that the intentionally or recklessly false statements proved necessary to the finding of probable cause and the issuance of the warrant, the warrant becomes void and the products of the search excluded from trial as violative of the Fourth and Fourteenth Amendments to the United States Constitution. [441]

Massachusetts decisions applying the *Franks* doctrine have subsequently relaxed the initial requirement so as to authorize a judge, as a matter of sound discretion, to order an evidentiary hearing upon the mere demonstration that an affidavit contained misstatements. [442]

[432] Commonwealth v. Nine Hundred and Ninety-Two Dollars, 383 Mass. 764, 422 N.E.2d 767 (1981).
[433] *Commonwealth v. Toledo*, 66 Mass. App. Ct. 688 (2006).
[434] *Commonwealth v. Toledo*, 66 Mass. App. Ct. 688 (2006).
[435] *Commonwealth v Hanscom*, 2 Mass. App. Ct. 840, 410 N.E.2d 732 (1974).
[436] *Commonwealth v. Young*, 6 Mass. App. Ct. 953, 383 N.E.2d 515 (1978).
[437] *Commonwealth v. Burt,* 393 Mass. 703 (1985).
[438] *Commonwealth v. Truax*, 397 Mass. 174, 490 N.E.2d 425 (1986).
[439] *Commonwealth v. Chamberlin*, 22 Mass. App. Ct. 946, 494 N.E.2d 63 (1986).
[440] *Commonwealth v. Pellegrini*, 405 Mass. 86, 539 N.E.2d 514 (1989).
[441] *Franks v. Delaware,* 438 U.S. 154, 155-156, 171-172 (1978).

[442] *Commonwealth v. Douzanis,* 384 Mass. 434, 439 (1981).*Commonwealth v. Signorine,* 404 Mass. 400, 406 (1989).*Commonwealth v. Alcantara,*53 Mass.App.Ct. 591, 594 (2002).

Challenging a Search Warrant involving a Confidential Informant

There is a two-step process by which a defendant can challenge the veracity of statements in a search warrant affidavit.[443] The first step involves the holding of a threshold Amaral hearing, the purpose of which is to determine whether the defendant is constitutionally entitled to the second step, a Franks hearing.

If, the warrant was issued, at least, in part from information from a confidential informant, and the defendant can assert through an affidavit facts that cast doubt on the information provided by a confidential informant, the judge can hold "in camera" (judge only) hearing on the matter (this is sometimes referred to as an **Amaral Hearing**). It must be based on more than just suspicion but persuasive facts.

SEIZABLE ITEMS

Under M.G.L. c. 276, § 1, property or articles that may be seized under a search warrant are as follows:

a. Property or articles stolen, embezzled, obtained by false pretenses, or otherwise obtained in the commission of a crime;
b. Property or articles which are intended for use, or which are or have been used, as a means or instrumentality of committing a crime, including, but not in limitation of the foregoing, any property or article worn, carried, or otherwise used, changed or marked in the preparation for or perpetration of or concealment of a crime;
c. Property or articles, the possession or control of which is unlawful, or which are possessed or controlled for an unlawful purpose; except property subject to search and seizure under M.G.L. c. 138, §§ 42 through 56, inclusive;
d. The dead body of a human being; and
e. The body of a living person for whom a current arrest warrant is outstanding.

As used in this statute, the word "property" includes books, papers, documents, records and any other tangible objects.

Case Law Note

- In the case of ***Warden v. Hayden***,[444] the Supreme Court stated that a search warrant may also be issued to search for and seize evidentiary items outside of the general category of seizable property provided it can be established that there is a logical connection between the evidentiary item seized and the particular crime committed. Additionally, before an item may be seized, the government must show that there exists a nexus between the item to be seized and criminal behavior.[445]

  a. Other statutes specify items which are subject to seizure with a warrant, such as:
  b. A bird, dog or other animal kept or trained for fighting in violation of M.G.L. c. 272, § 89;
     An animal treated cruelly in violation of M.G.L. c. 272, §§ 77-81;
  c. Hazardous waste and their conveyances and containers used in violation of M.G.L. c. 21C and all books and records containing evidence of such violations; and
  d. Premises containing evidence of violations of orders issued by the Commissioner of Public Health when an air pollution emergency is declared with the approval of the Governor pursuant to M.G.L. c. 111, § 2B.

Special Provisions for Alcohol

Search Warrant requirements for non-dwelling:

Chapter 138 § 42 states "If two persons of full age (18 or older) make complaint to a district court or justice of the peace authorized to issue warrants in criminal cases that they have reason to believe and do believe that alcoholic beverages, described in the complaint, are kept or deposited by a person named therein in a store, shop, warehouse, building, vehicle, steamboat, vessel or place, and are intended for sale contrary to law, such court or justice, if it appears that there is probable cause to believe said complaint to be true, shall issue a search warrant."[446]

Limitations on searching a dwelling for alcohol

While M.G.L. c. 138 provides for the seizure by warrant of illegally kept alcoholic beverages, their vessels and implements of sale and furniture used in the illegal sale or keeping of such beverages, special rules apply to alcoholic

[443] Commonwealth v. Davis (2013) quoting from Franks v. Delaware, 438 U.S. at 155-156; Commonwealth v. Amral, 407 Mass. 511, 522-525 (1990).
[444] *Warden v. Hayden*, 387 U.S. 294, 87 S.Ct. 1642 (1967).
[445] *Matter of Lavigne*, 418 Mass. 831, 641 N.E.2d 1328 (1994).
[446] M.G.L. c. 138 § 42

beverages illegally kept in a *dwelling*. A dwelling may not be searched without a warrant, upon penalty of a $100 fine.[447] A warrant may authorize a search of a dwelling for alcohol[448] only if:

The dwelling is used for an inn, tavern, store, grocery, eating house or place of common resort[449]; or

There is evidence that alcoholic beverages have been sold therein illegally within the month before an application is made for a warrant, and that the alcohol is still being kept there.

Non-Seizable Items

Special protection is afforded to documents in the possession of **lawyers, clergy and psychotherapists**,[450] where it is known or reasonably assumed that a confidential relationship exists with any person and such relationship is protected by testimonial privilege.

Two exceptions exist to such prohibition:

1. A judge may issue a warrant if probable cause is shown that the documentary evidence will be destroyed, secreted or lost unless the warrant is issued; or
2. Where there is probable cause to believe that the lawyer, clergy or psychotherapist is committing or is about to commit a crime, the police may either make a warrantless search, if otherwise justified, or obtain a warrant.

PROBABLE CAUSE AND SEARCH WARRANTS

A valid search warrant must be based on a finding of probable cause. [451] To establish probable cause, an affidavit must contain sufficient information to support a disinterested magistrate's determination that the items related to the criminal activity being investigated reasonably may be expected to be found in the place to be searched at the time the warrant issues.[452]

Probable Cause Must Be Established Within the Affidavit

Only facts known before search are considered: In determining whether there was probable cause for a search warrant to issue, the reviewing court does not examine the facts subsequently revealed; instead "our inquiry as to the sufficiency of the search warrant application always begins and ends with the 'four corners of the affidavit.' "[453]

Any fact that is not set out in the affidavit cannot be inserted or used later for the purpose of establishing probable cause.

- In ***Commonwealth v. Penta***,[454] the Court declared that the contents of an affidavit supporting a search warrant *cannot be buttressed by oral testimony* as to what may have been stated to the magistrate at the time the search warrant was issued. While it has been held in a number of cases that affidavits for search warrants must be tested and interpreted by magistrates in a common sense and realistic fashion without technical requirements or elaborate specificity, it should be understood clearly that "if an application for a search warrant lacks underlying facts and information and an indication as to the source of the officer's information or personal knowledge, such warrant will be invalid."[455]

Probable cause determined by reading affidavit as a whole

Search warrant affidavits should be interpreted "in a commonsense and realistic fashion,"[456] and "read as a whole, not parsed, severed, and subjected to hypercritical analysis."[457] All reasonable inferences which may be drawn from the information in the affidavit may also be considered as to whether probable cause has been established.

Deference given to Magistrate's Determination

Courts give considerable deference to the magistrate's determination,[458] and even "the resolution of doubtful or marginal cases … should be largely determined by the preference to be accorded to warrants".[459]

[447] M.G.L. c. 138, § 46.
[448] M.G.L. c. 138, § 43.
[449] M.G.L. c. 138, § 43.
[450] M.G.L. c. 276, § 1.
[451] *Commonwealth v. Upton*, 394 Mass. 363, 368, 476 N.E.2d 548 (1985).
[452] See *Commonwealth v. Cinelli*, 389 Mass. 197, 213, 449 N.E.2d 1207, cert. denied, 464 U.S. 860, 104 S.Ct. 186, 78 L.Ed.2d 165 (1983).
[453] *Commonwealth v. O'Day*, 400 Mass. 296, 297, 798 N. E.2d 275 (2003), quoting from *Commonwealth v. Hardy*, 63 Mass.App.Ct. 210, 211, 824 N.E.2d 883 (2005).
[454] *Commonwealth v. Penta*, 352 Mass. 271, 225 N.E.2d 58, 60 (1967).
[455] *Commonwealth v. Von Utter*, 355 Mass. 597, 246 N.E.2d 806 (1969).
[456] *Commonwealth v. Donahue*, 430 Mass. 710, 712, 723 N.E.2d 25 (2000), quoting from *United States v. Ventresea, supra* at 108, 85 S.Ct. 741 (1965).
[457] *Commonwealth v. Blake*, 413 Mass. 823, 827, 604 N.E.2d 1289 (1992).

SEARCH WARRANTS

Information must not be stale

Probable cause to justify the issuance of a search warrant must exist at the time the warrant issues. If the information specified in the affidavit is "stale", it may prevent a finding of probable cause to conduct a search. For instance, if the police have information that a suspect has drugs in his house they cannot wait several days to obtain a warrant because the probable cause will become stale, unless there is indication that the possession is ongoing and continuing.

If the items to be seized are disposable or easily moved they are much more likely to quickly become stale, as opposed to durable items.

If the criminal activity is continuous and ongoing it is less likely to become stale overtime.

- In ***Commonwealth v. Higginbotham,*** 12 days passed between the initial arrest and the search for an armed robbery for evidence of stolen cash and information from codefendant revealed that the money was hidden inside a furnace. Despite this the Court held that there was a substantial basis upon which to find probable cause to issue the search warrant.[460]

NEXUS MUST BE ESTABLISHED

A Nexus must exist between the criminal activity and the location to be searched

The establishment of probable cause to believe that a person is guilty of a crime does not necessarily constitute the probable cause to search the person's residence.[461] There must be a connection (nexus) between the place to be searched and the crime, aside from the fact that the suspect lives there.

To satisfy this "nexus" requirement the affidavit "must provide a substantial basis for concluding that evidence connected to the crime will be found on the specified premises."

The connection between items to be seized and the place to be searched may be found by looking at:

a. the type of crime,
b. nature of the items,
c. the suspect's opportunity to conceal items, and
d. inferences as to where the items are likely to be hidden.[462]

The nexus between the items to be seized and the place to be searched need not be based on direct observation".[463]

The police must provide "particularized information based on police surveillance or otherwise, that would permit a reasonable inference that the defendant likely kept a supply of drugs" in the home.[464]

Police may rely on a variety of investigatory sources in making the necessary showing, including police surveillance and statements from credible informants. [465]

This issue frequently comes up with illicit drug sale investigations. However, the nexus requirement is not limited to drug distribution cases; it applies to all search warrants. When the target of the search is a residence where drug-selling activity is reported, the affidavit must present "a sufficient nexus between the defendant's drug-selling activity and his residence to establish probable cause to search the residence." [466] Typically, a pattern of repeated activity giving rise to a reasonable inference that a dealer's residence is being used as a base for his drug operation[467] will help establish a sufficient nexus.

Where police do rely on a single observation of a suspected drug dealer leaving his residence and proceeding to the location of a drug sale, the suspect's location immediately prior to the sale *is of greater significance to the nexus determination than are his activities after the sale*. Before a sale, the drug dealer either is in possession of drugs, or must proceed to a location to obtain the drugs. The inference that drugs will be found in the house is less strong if based solely on police observations of a suspected dealer returning home after a sale.[468]

---

[458] *Commonwealth v. Germain*, 396 Mass. 246, 249, 780 N.E.2d 26 (2002).
[459] *Commonwealth v. Germain*, 396 Mass. 413, 418, 486 N.E.2d 693 (1985), quoting from *United States v. Ventresea*, 380 U.S. 102, 108-109, 85 S.Ct. 741, 13 L.Ed2d (1965). *Commonwealth v. Querubin*, 60 Mass.App.Ct. 695, 698, 805 N.E.2d 84 (2004).
460*Commonwealth v. Higginbotham,* 11 Mass. App. Ct. 912 (1981).
461*Commonwealth v. Pina,* 453 Mass. 438 (2009).
462*Commonwealth v. Pina,* 453 Mass. 438 (2009).
463*Commonwealth v. Donahue*, 430 Mass. At 712, 723 N.E.2d 25, quoting from *Commonwealth v. Cinelli*, 389 Mass. At 213, 449 N.E.2d 1207463.
464 *Commonwealth* v. *Pina,* 453 Mass. 438 (2009)
465 *Commonwealth* v. *O'Day,* 440 Mass. 296, 298 (2003).
[466] *Com. v. O' Day*, 440 Mass. 296, 301 (2003)
[467467] *Com. v. Escalera*, 2011
468 *Commonwealth v. Jose Escalera*, 462 Mass. 636 (2012).

Case examples involving a nexus to search

- In ***Commonwealth v. O'Day***, observations by the police of a suspect on multiple occasions leaving his residence and proceeding directly to a prearranged location to sell drugs can support a reasonable inference that the suspect is a drug dealer who stores drugs or packages drugs for resale in his residence. [469]
- In ***Commonwealth* v. *Cruz,*** the defendant engaged in six controlled sales, all occurring in parking lot of his apartment building. This was sufficient to establish a nexus.[470]
- In ***Commonwealth* v. *Hardy***, the defendant left from his apartment for two controlled sales; and an informant stated that the defendant stored drugs in the defendant's apartment. This was sufficient to establish a nexus.[471]
- A single observation of a suspect leaving his home for a drug deal may also support an inference that drugs will be found in the home where it is coupled with other information, such as statements from credible informants. In ***Commonwealth* v. *Young,*** a single controlled purchase coupled along with an informant's statements that the defendant "always" selected sale locations within walking distance of his apartment was sufficient to establish a. nexus.[472]
- In the 2012 case of ***Commonwealth v. Tapia***, the SJC ruled that three controlled buys, with one of which the defendant was seen leaving her apartment, coupled with other factors such as the phone number in which the confidential informant used to arrange the purchases was tied to the defendant's apartment, established a sufficient nexus between her drug dealing activity and her apartment to issue a search warrant for the search of her apartment.
- In ***Commonwealth* v. *Luthy,*** in two controlled purchases, police observed the defendant driving from and returning to his residence only once; an informant provided information that the defendant was selling large quantities of drugs on a steady basis, and the usual mode of operation was to deliver drugs away from his residence.[473]
- In ***Commonwealth* v. *Olivares,*** a nexus was not established where the police observed the defendant leaving his residence for a single controlled sale and there was no other information connecting his residence to the drug activity.[474]
- In the 2009 SJC case of ***Commonwealth v. Pina***, Det. Safioleas of the New Bedford Police Department had received information from a confidential informant regarding a cocaine delivery service being conducted in New Bedford. The informant told Det. Safioleas that he frequently purchased cocaine from Robert Pina, who resided in an apartment at 984 Sharon Street. The informant explained that in order to purchase cocaine he would call a telephone number that had been provided by the defendant. Pina would then instruct the informant to meet him at a certain location and at a certain time, at which place and time the drug purchase ultimately would be completed. The transactions did not take place at Pina's apartment. Det. Safioleas orchestrated a controlled purchase of cocaine from Pina. The informant placed a telephone call to Pina to arrange for the purchase. A second New Bedford police detective observed the defendant leave his apartment and drive directly to the location where the informant had been instructed to proceed. Det. Safioleas observed the defendant and the informant meet briefly and then separate. Three days later Det. Safioleas applied for a search warrant for an apartment at 984 Sharon Street in New Bedford. A magistrate issued the warrant that same day, and the search of the apartment was executed three days later. The SJC ruled that "the only particularized information contained in the affidavit connecting the defendant's observed drug activity with the apartment in which he lived was a single observation of the defendant driving from the apartment to a location where he sold an unspecified quantity of cocaine to the informant. The lapse of time between that observation and the application for the search warrant (three days) raises further concerns."[475]
- In the 2009 case of ***Commonwealth v. Takvorian***, on the evening of January 16, 2006, Sergeant Cook of the Peabody police department stopped an automobile driven by the defendant with an expired license plate. While speaking to the defendant, Sgt. Cook observed two large plastic tote containers sitting on the back seat of the vehicle. Cook observed, in plain view, vials and vial tops inside the top container. Evidence of steroids and other drugs were discovered in the containers. One of the containers also contained a piece of mail addressed to 12 America Drive, in Peabody. On the basis of the foregoing information, Detective Richards drafted an affidavit which stated that "there is probable cause to believe that Oxycontin, steroids, various chemicals used in the production and manufacturing of steroids and other performance enhancing drugs as

469 *Commonwealth* v. *O'Day*, 440 Mass. 296, 298 (2003).
470 *Commonwealth* v. *Cruz*, 430 Mass. 838, 841 (2000)
471 *Commonwealth* v. *Hardy*, 63 Mass. App. Ct. 210, 211-212 (2005)
472 *Commonwealth* v. *Young*, 77 Mass. App. Ct. 381, 383-384, 388 (2010)
473 *Commonwealth* v. *Luthy*, 69 Mass. App. Ct. 102, 103-106 (2007)
474 *Commonwealth* v. *Olivares*, 30 Mass. App. Ct. 596, 597-598, 600-601 (1991)
475 *Commonwealth v. Pina*, 453 Mass. 438 (2009).

well as associated paraphernalia, equipment and implements can be found in or around the residence located # 12 America Drive, Peabody, MA." A search warrant was issued.[476]

- In the 2011 case of ***Commonwealth v. Escalera***, the defendant was seen leaving and returning to his residence multiple times to what were either known drug sales or to encounters that could readily be inferred to be drug transactions. The Appeals Court ruled that "a pattern of activity such as this, in our view, provides sufficient nexus to a dealer's residence to satisfy probable cause to search it. In addition, the defendant's use of multiple cars makes it more likely that he stored drugs in his residence, rather than in his vehicles."
- In the 2011 case of ***Commonwealth v. Monteiro***, an illegal drug delivery service wherein the suspect repeatedly left his home to deliver drugs then immediately returned to his home after the delivery established a sufficient nexus between the drug dealing and the suspect's home to justify the issuance of a search warrant to search the suspect's home.

SPECIAL PRECAUTION FOR MARIJUANA SEARCH WARRANTS

In the 2015 case of ***Commonwealth v. Canning***, the SJC ruled that if police seek a warrant to search property for evidence of illegal marijuana possession or cultivation, they must offer information sufficient to provide probable cause to believe the individual is not properly registered under the Medical Marijuana act to possess or cultivate the suspected substance. Under the act, cultivation of marijuana is expressly permitted if a person or entity is properly registered to do so, and the cultivation does not exceed the amount necessary to yield a 60 day supply of medical marijuana.

Attorney Hanrahan's Note: The marijuana laws are very fluid at the current moment and are likely to continue to get cloudier. The passage of Question 2 (decriminalization of an ounce or less) and the Medical Marijuana law have changed the way police react to marijuana situations and it is likely to continue to change. There is currently an effort to decriminalize all amounts of marijuana in Massachusetts and it is gaining some steam.

This case begs the question - in order to execute a search or an arrest for the *unlawful distribution* (as opposed to cultivation) of marijuana must the police first show that the suspect does not have a license to dispense? Take it a step further, must the police show evidence of someone distributing oxycodone, for instance, is not a duly licensed pharmacist?

Whether or not someone is licensed for marijuana use/dispensing is now accessible via a CJIS search (MMJ query). However, it currently *requires* the CJIS operator to enter the user's mother's maiden name which creates an obvious hurdle.

On a positive note, the SJC did indicate in the footnotes of the case "this is not to say that such an affidavit always must contain facts directly establishing that the person whose property the police seek to search for evidence of unlawful marijuana cultivation is or is probably not registered to do so; reasonable inferences may be drawn that a suspected marijuana cultivation operation is unlawful from other facts. For example, except for registered medical marijuana treatment centers, it remains unlawful to cultivate marijuana for sale. Facts indicating that a confidential informant recently purchased marijuana from the owner of the property where the cultivation operation is suspected to be taking place would likely supply the requisite probable cause to search that property for evidence of unlawful cultivation, as would information that police recently had observed marijuana plants growing on the property and that, in the opinion of a properly qualified affiant, the number of plants exceeded the quantity necessary to grow a sixty-day supply of ten ounces"

INFORMATION FROM THIRD PARTIES

Generally, in order for information to rise to the level of probable cause the person providing information must meet the two-pronged *Auguilar-Spinelli* Test. In other words the police must obtain the person's basis of knowledge and veracity. For a detailed discussion on the two-pronged test see the Temporary Detention section of this manual. This section of the manual focuses on so-called informants because this type of provider of information is often associated with search warrants.

Not all third-party providers of information are treated equally.

---

[476] *Commonwealth v. Takvorian*, Mass.App.Ct. (2009).

Police Officers

Police officers and other government officials involved in an investigation are presumed to be reliable and their information credible.[477] Thus, information provided by an identified police officer can be relied upon in an affidavit. Obviously, the officer's basis of knowledge must be established.

Identified Victims

Identified victims are generally deemed to be reliable absent information to the contrary. Thus victim information may be used to establish probable.

Identified Witnesses

Witnesses who place their anononymity at risk are generally deemed to be reliable. See the Temporary Detention section of this manual for more on this topic.

Anonymous Witnesses and Crime Reporters

Information provided by anonymous persons typically will not amount to probable cause absent some independent police corroboration. See the Temporary Detention section of this manual for more on this topic.

Police Informants

Because the motivation of a typical police informant (as opposed to an uninvolved citizen witness) is often questionable (e.g. they are often motivated to avoid criminal prosecution), the courts will highly scrutinize police informants, particularly confidential informants. For this reason it is critical that when an affidavit is based, even in part, on information from a police informant that the basis of knowledge and particularly the veracity of the informant be shored up.

Confidential Informants

A confidential informant is known to the police but his/her identity is concealed from the defendant and the Court. Their identity is often kept confidential in order to protect them from retribution by the defendant and others or to be able to continue to use the informant in additional operations, or both. Because confidential informants are frequently motivated by their own self-interest (e.g. to escape criminal charges) the Court will scrutinize information provided by these types of information givers much more so than other persons who provide information.

When a supporting affidavit relies on information gleaned from confidential informants, the Court will apply the two-prong *Aguilar-Spinelli* standard.[478] The *Aguilar-Spinelli* standard requires that the magistrate "be informed of (1) some of the underlying circumstances from which the informant concluded that the contraband (or evidence) was where he claimed it was (the basis of knowledge test), and (2) some of the underlying circumstances from which the affiant concluded that the informant was 'credible' or his information 'reliable' (the veracity test)."[479]

Shoring up deficiencies in the Two-Prong test when it comes to informants

Basis of Knowledge

A high level of detail in descriptions, consistent with the kind of firsthand knowledge through personal observation can be held to satisfy the basis of knowledge prong.[480] This is because the highly detailed information can show that the person had first-hand knowledge of the matter.

Veracity (credibility/reliability)

As previously mentioned, an identified person is generally deemed reliable. When it comes to a confidential informant it is helpful if, at least, the police know the identity of the informant, even if the informant's name will not be revealed in court, opposed to an informant who is anonymous to the police as well (e.g. anonymous phone tip). In *Commonwealth v. Welch,* the SJC indicated that the informants' credibility can be bolstered by police knowledge of the defendant's identity and residence.[481]

[477] See *United States v. Ventresca,* 380 U.S. at 111, 85 S.Ct. 741; Grasso & McEvoy, *supra* at §10-5(a)(1). See also *Commonwealth v. Cruz,* 373 Mass. at 684, 369 N.E.2d 996; see also, *Commonwealth v. Zorn,* 66 Mass.App.Ct. 228, 846 N.E.2d 423 (2006).
[478] See *Spinelli v. United States,* 393 U.S. 410, 415 (1969); *Aguilar v. Texas,* 378 U.S. 108, 114 (1964).
[479] *Commonwealth v. Upton,* 394 Mass. 363, 375 (1985), quoting *Aguilar v. Texas,* 378 U.S. 108, 114 (1964). See *Spinelli v. United States,* 393 U.S. 410, 415 (1969).
[480] See, e.g., *Commonwealth v. Mubdi,* 456 Mass. 385, 396 (2010); *Commonwealth v. Alfonso A.,* 438 Mass. 372, 374 (2003).
[481] See *Commonwealth v. Welch,* 420 Mass. 646, 651 (1995).

Track Record

An informant who has a track record of providing credible and reliable information will have more credibility than one who has not. The SJC has indicated that reliability can be established through previous instances where the informant's information led to the confiscation of illegal narcotics [482] and even arrests leading to indictments.[483] The more details and examples that can be shown of the informant's previous reliable information, especially information that has been later vetted by a court (i.e. indictment, conviction, etc.) the more likely the court will find the subsequent information reliable.

If an informant has previously provided unreliable information, this too must be disclosed and it will make it much more difficult convincing the court of the informant's reliability in subsequent matters.[484]

Admissions of Guilt

An informant who admits guilt and/or criminal liability in a criminal event may help shore up his/her credibility. But there must be some reasonable fear of prosecution.[485] This is often referred to as *declarations of penal interest.* The thought is that if someone admits to criminal conduct, wherein they could be prosecuted, they would not be dishonest about it.

Police Corroboration

Police corroboration is always beneficial even with a named informant or witness, but it is particularly helpful with a confidential informant. Corroboration occurs when the police are able to verify the details, or at least partial details, by their own observation or other source. This corroboration can shore up any deficiency in the veracity (or basis of knowledge) of the informant. [486]

For instance, the police receive a tip that the resident of 25 Chapman Street is selling drugs from his home. The informant has no track record and offers no declaration of penal interest. Based on this tip alone the police would not be able to obtain a warrant. However, if the police begin to conduct surveillance of 25 Chapman Street and subsequently observe signs of drug distribution they may be able to develop probable cause based on these observations. This corroboration will make up for the deficiencies in the informant's tip.

Additionally, the Court has indicated "controlled buys" can be used to corroborate an informant's description of the defendant's drug business.[487]

Compensating Informants

The Court has indicated that compensating informants is a reasonable investigative technique. However, the payment cannot be based on a contingent basis (e.g. fee paid only upon a conviction).[488]

Attorney Hanrahan's note: it should be noted that paying informants may be a used by the defense to sway the jury into questioning the validity of the information (e.g. he made it up to get paid). Independent police corroboration can help counter this in many cases.

Non-Disclosure of Informant to the Defendant

Ordinarily, the Commonwealth may withhold from a criminal defendant the identity of a confidential informant.[489] The Court has long recognized the Commonwealth's privilege not to disclose the identity of a confidential informant. [490] This privilege assists the police in obtaining evidence of criminal activity. More importantly for present purposes, keeping an informant's identity confidential also protects his well-being; disclosing an informant's identity might jeopardize his safety and even his life.[491]

However, a limitation on the privilege "arises from the fundamental requirements of fairness. Where the disclosure of an informant's identity... is relevant and helpful to the defense of an accused, or is essential to the fair determination of a cause, the privilege must give way." [492]

There is "no fixed rule" to determine when disclosure is required. Rather, "the problem is one that calls for balancing the public interest in protecting the flow of information against the individual's right to prepare his defense." Relevant factors

[482] See *Commonwealth v. Perez-Baez,* 410 Mass. 43, 45-46 (1991).
[483] *Commonwealth v. Soto*, 35 Mass.App.Ct. 340 (1993).
[484] *United States v. Vigeant,* 176 F.2d 565 (1999).
[485] Commonwealth v. Melendez, 407 Mass. 53 (1990).
[486] *Spinelli v. United States*
[487] See *Commonwealth v. O'Day, supra* at 301-302
[488] Commonwealth v. Grateaux, 49 Mass.App.ct. 1 (2000).
[489] *Commonwealth v. Dias,* **451 Mass. 463**, 468 (2008), and cases cited. *See, e.g., Commonwealth v. Elias,* **463 Mass. 1015**, 1016 (2012).
[490] *Commonwealth v. Madigan,* 449 Mass. 702, 705-706 (2007).
[491] *Commonwealth v. Madigan,* **449 Mass. 702**, 706 (2007), quoting *Commonwealth v. Douzanis,* **384 Mass. 434**, 441 (1981).
[492] *Roviaro v. United States,* **353 U.S. 53**, 60-61 (1957).

include, but are not limited to, "the crime charged, the possible defenses, [and] the possible significance of the informer's testimony."[493]

- In ***Commonwealth v. Lugo,*** the SJC reframed this inquiry and asked simply "whether disclosure would have provided material evidence needed by the defendant for a fair presentation of his case to the jury."[494] The Court may hold what is referred to as an *Amaral hearing* to determine whether or not the informant's identity must be revealed to the defendant.

Non-disclosure to Public

Additionally, the Massachusetts Public Records law provides an exemption of the names of reporters of crime from public disclosure. Exemption F of the public records laws provides that information may be withheld to provide an assurance of confidentiality to private citizens so that they will speak openly about matters under investigation. Accordingly, any details in witness statements, which if released create a grave risk of directly or indirectly identifying a private citizen who volunteers as a witness are indefinitely exempt.

Witness Protection

501 CMR 10 provides witness protection services to those who are considered "critical witnesses." Part of these protections include non-disclosure of the witness's identity and whereabouts.

ANTICIPATORY SEARCH WARRANTS

In some circumstances search warrants may be issued to search a particular place even though the item(s) to be seized has yet to arrive at the location to be searched.

Anticipatory search warrants typically relate to contraband in transit, where a specific described item is known to be on route to a specific person, often at a specified place, and the warrant is issued before the item reaches that person's hands or the premises to be searched. [495]

- In ***Commonwealth v. Rodriguez,*** Customs agents discovered cocaine secreted in the frame of a bicycle which was to be delivered to the home of a Springfield resident. The police obtained an anticipatory search warrant to search the residence in anticipation that the item would be delivered. An officer then posed as a delivery person, delivered the package and the served the search warrant for the home which was issued in anticipation for the delivery.[496]

Note: the Appellate Court has indicated that an anticipatory search warrant executed beyond 7 days would be invalid.[497] Also, a controlled delivery, as in *Rodriguez* above, is not mandatory in order to obtain an anticipatory search warrant.[498]

EXECUTING A SEARCH WARRANT

GENERAL REQUIREMENTS

Warrant must be on scene

The warrant must be brought to the scene with the police and presented, on demand, to the owner or occupant of the premises. It is a preferred practice to bring a copy of the affidavit as well. Especially where the exact description of the items to be seized is contained in the affidavit, having a copy present will help assure a proper search and avoid a general sweep of the premises. If the police fail to bring the affidavit which describes the object of the search in detail, and the warrant itself is worded vaguely, items seized may be suppressed.[499]

- In 2007 SJC case of ***Commonwealth v. Valerio,*** although the search warrant failed to include the specific items to be seized the search was still valid because the items were described in the affidavit and the affidavit was attached to the warrant and on scene at the time of the search.[500]

[493] *Roviaro v. United States,* **353 U.S. 53**, 60-61 (1957).
[494] ***Commonwealth v. Lugo***, **406 Mass. 565**, 574 (1990),
[495] *Commonwealth v. Douglas,* 399 Mass. 141, 144 (1987)..
[496] *Commonwealth v. Rodriguez,* 450 Mass. 302, 877 N.E.2d 1274 (2007)
[497] *Commonwealth v. Weeks,* 13 Mass.App.Ct. 194 (1982).
[498] *Commonwealth v. Rosa,* 17 Mass.App.Ct. 495 (1984).
[499] *Commonwealth v. Taylor,* 383 Mass. 272, 418 N.E.2d 1226 (1981).

SEARCH WARRANTS

Timing

Upon the issuance of a search warrant, the police should make an effort to execute it promptly. Although M.G.L. chapter 276 § 2A requires that a search warrant be executed *immediately*, the courts construe that to mean within a reasonable time after it is issued.

A criminal search warrant must be returned to the court as soon as it has been served but no more than 7 days after its issuance.[501] Thus, no search warrant may be validly executed more than seven days after it was issued. The 7 days begin to run after the day the warrant was issued.

Courts will look at a variety of factors in determining the reasonableness of the timing of the execution of a warrant by the police. These include the safety of the officers, the distance, traffic conditions, weather, and the inability of the police to locate the person or premises to be searched. Where a defendant proves that he or she was prejudiced by an unreasonable delay in the execution of a warrant, evidence seized may be suppressed.[502]

Night time searches

A search which takes place between 10:00 p.m. and 6:00 a.m. is a nighttime search.[503] Such searches are authorized under M.G.L. c. 276, § 2. There is no particular statutory requirement applicable to an application for a nighttime search warrant and no requirement that the magistrate state or identify the cause for issuing such a warrant. If the magistrate issues a search warrant which can be executed in the nighttime, he or she is presumed to have had cause for doing so.[504]

However, courts recommend that police insert in an affidavit the reasons justifying a nighttime search, although, currently, this is not legally required.[505] The Massachusetts Courts may find a stricter reasonableness standard in Article 14 of this state's constitution and require police to justify nighttime searches, especially of residences.

- In ***Commonwealth v. Yazbek***, where officers sledge hammered the door of a single family residence at 11:00 p.m., with the occupants in their pajamas, the Appeals Court narrowly upheld the search and did so only because there were recent drug sales at 11:00 p.m. there and retail narcotics were found during the search.[506]

SCOPE OF SEARCH

A search may only extend to those areas where the objects authorized by the warrant reasonably could be found.[507] For instance, a search for a stolen big screen television set normally would not justify opening and examining the contents of a small desk drawer, whereas a search for narcotics, stolen checks, or currency would.

Once all of the items listed in a warrant have been found, the search must cease.

Unusual locations

The police are not limited to likely areas where the subject of the search may be. Particularly with narcotics, offenders find creative locations to secrete contraband and criminal evidence.

In ***Commonwealth v. Wills,*** the police were justified in searching a photo album when searching for a weapon since a photo album could have been hollowed out; it was permissible to search it for a knife or similar small weapon.[508]

Curtilage

A warrant that authorizes the search of a particular dwelling also authorizes the search of areas within the curtilage of that dwelling.[509]

Generally, a search warrant extends to vehicles within the curtilage of the premises being searched as well.

Although parking lots of multi-unit buildings typically are not within the curtilage, the SJC recently ruled that the driveway of a three-family home was within the curtilage. [510]

For more on curtilage see the Searches in General section of this manual.

[500] *Commonwealth v. Valerio*, 449 Mass. 562, 870 N.E.2d 46 (2007)
[501] *Commonwealth v. Cromer*, 365 Mass. 519, 313 N.E.2d 557 (1974); M.G.L. c. 276, § 3A.
[502] *Commonwealth v. Cromer*, (cited above).
[503] *Commonwealth v. Grimshaw*, 413 Mass. 73, 595 N.E.2d 302 (1992).
[504] *Commonwealth v. Siano*, 52 Mass.App.Ct. 912, 755 N.E.2d 324 (2001).
[505] *Commonwealth v. DiStephano*, 22 Mass. App. Ct. 535, 450 N.E.2d 637 (1986).
[506] *Commonwealth v. Yazbek*, 31 Mass. App. Ct. 769, 583 N.E.2d 901, *rev. den.*587 N.E.2d 790 (1992).
[507] *Kreman v. U.S.*, 353 U.S. 346, 77 S.Ct. 828 (1957).
[508] *Commonwealth v. Wills*, 398 Mass. 768, 500 N.E.2d 1341 (1986).
[509] *Commonwealth* v. *McCarthy*, 428 Mass. 871, 873 (1999), quoting *United States* v. *Dunn*, 480 U.S. 294, 300 (1987).
[510] *Commonwealth v. Fernandez*, SJC October 4, 2010.

Attic

In ***Commonwealth v. Wallace***, the attic in a two and one-half story house was a part of the second-floor apartment, and thus the search warrant authorizing a search of the second-floor apartment could be read to extend to the attic space, and the police officers were not required to apply for a second warrant once the fact that attic was part of the apartment was discovered. The only entrance to the attic was immediately adjacent to the second-floor apartment rear door, which was ajar when police executed the search, and both the rear door of the apartment and the attic entrance opened up to a landing in a hallway that led directly down to a locked door at the street.[511]

Basement

In ***Commonwealth v. Pacheco***, the Mass. Appellate Court ruled that a search may extend to that portion of the cellar used by an apartment occupant so long as the police have probable cause to search the apartment itself.[512]

Note: In ***Commonwealth v. Rodriguez***, the court upheld the search of a basement even though you would have to travel through a different apartment than the one listed on the warrant. This was permitted because the defendant utilized the basement for storage.

KNOCK AND ANNOUNCE RULE

A police officer usually must (1) knock, (2) identify himself or herself as a police officer, and (3) state his or her purpose before entering a dwelling.[513] Failure to do so may result in the entry being declared illegal and any seized evidence being suppressed.[514]

The purposes of the "knock and announce" rule are threefold: (1) to protect the privacy interests of individuals; (2) to minimize the likelihood of property damage; and (3) to reduce the possibility of violence after an unannounced entry.[515]

Wait Period

The police do not have to wait inordinate amount of time after knocking and announcing their presence. Once a reasonable time has passed and they have not been admitted voluntarily, they may use whatever force is reasonably necessary to gain entrance.[516]

- In ***Commonwealth v. Bush,*** a five-second delay between the time the police knocked on the defendant's door, announcing their presence and intention to execute search warrant, and their forced entry into the apartment was reasonable and satisfied the knock and announce requirement; given the darkened hallway, the "scurrying" sounds without a verbal response, and the officers' awareness that there might be a firearm in apartment, it was reasonable for police to fear a threat to their safety within five seconds, and occupants of apartment had plenty of time to respond to continued announcing while detective was ramming door, and could have stopped forcible entry had they done so. [517]
- In ***Commonwealth v. Sepulveda***, officers were authorized to rush into the apartment as soon as the occupants opened the door.[518]

Knock and trickery entry

Police officers in possession of a warrant may knock on the door and gain compliance by trickery.

- In ***Commonwealth v. Goggin***, officers were justified in knocking and claiming to be collecting for "Pop Warner Football". When the occupant opened the door and saw the officers with badges displayed, he attempted to slam the door shut. The police were authorized to block the door, to announce their reason for entry, and to use reasonable force to gain entry.[519]

Note: The key here is that the police identified themselves and their purpose before crossing the threshold.

---

[511] *Commonwealth v. Wallace*, 67 Mass.App.Ct. 901, 852 N.E.2d 1117 (2006)
[512] *Commonwealth v. Pacheco*, 21 Mass. App. Ct. 565, 488 N.E.2d 42 (1986).
[513] *Richards v. Wisconsin*, 117 S.Ct. 1416 (1997); *Wilson v. Arkansas*, 105 S. Ct. 1914 (1995); *Commonwealth v. Gondola*, 28 Mass. App. Ct. 286, 550 N.E.2d 880 (1990).
[514] *Commonwealth v. Scalise*, 387 Mass. 413, 439 N.E.2d 818 (1982).
[515] Richards **v.** Wisconsin, 520 U.S. 385, 393 n. 5 (1997).
[516] *Commonwealth v. Reynolds*, 120 Mass. 190 (1876) (invalidated in part by *Steagald v. U.S.*, cited above).
[517] *Commonwealth v. Bush*, 71 Mass.App.Ct. 130, 879 N.E.2d 1247 (2008)
[518] *Commonwealth v. Sepulveda*, 406 Mass. 180, 546 N.E.2d 879 (1989).
[519] *Commonwealth v. Goggin*, 412 Mass. 200, 587 N.E.2d 775 (1992).

SEARCH WARRANTS

Suppression of evidence

The US Supreme Court case of ***Hudson v. Michigan***, decided June 15th, 2006 ruled that the 4th Amendment's so-called "knock and announce" rule does not require suppression of evidence found in a search.[520] This, however, does not change the standard the Massachusetts courts will apply. Our SJC has ruled that in this state, evidence seized in violation of the common law knock and announce rule will be suppressed.[521]

Ordinarily, the police will be held to a very high standard of technical compliance. Suppression of evidence gathered during an unauthorized no-knock search generally will be the result.[522] However, the court will consider the degree to which the improper entry undermined the principles behind the law as well as the extent to which exclusion will tend to deter future violation.[523]

- In ***Commonwealth v. Lopez,*** the court found no need to suppress evidence seized where the police entered the suspect's apartment peacefully via an open door with due regard for his privacy, despite a wrongfully issued no-knock warrant.[524]
- In the 2001 case of ***Com v. Siano,***[525]the Appeals Court ruled that the terms of a search warrant were satisfied, despite technical violation of the knock and announce rule when police entered an unlocked, enclosed porch used as a family room before knocking on the kitchen door, as policies underlying the rule were not violated and the rule's objectives were substantially achieved, in that there was no forced entry, no invasion of privacy since the police knew the defendant and he invited them in, and no property damage.

The courts have ruled the following entries illegal and suppressed the evidence seized:

- In ***Commonwealth v. Manni***, a police officer knocked on the door and *simultaneously* turned the knob and opened the unlocked door, and announced his identity and purpose as soon as he got into the room.[526]

- In ***Commonwealth v. Gondola***, the officer knocked on the apartment door, no one answered, and he entered through the unlocked door and announced his identity **after** he crossed the doorway.[527]

NO KNOCK ENTRY

There are certain exceptions to the general rule that the police must knock and announce their presence when serving a search warrant. This requirement may be suspended provided the police have probable cause to believe that such announcement will:

a. Jeopardize the safety of the officers or occupants; or
b. Result in the escape of a person sought; or
c. Lead to the destruction of evidence.[528]

Standard of belief

The common-law standard in Massachusetts has been and remains *probable cause* that evidence will be destroyed if the police follow the usual course of knocking and announcing, even though the U.S. Supreme Court held in ***Richards v. Wisconsin***,[529] that reasonable suspicion suffices for Fourth Amendment purposes. In ***Commonwealth v. Macias,*** the SJC could see no reason to depart from the rule that probable cause is the standard[530].

Pre-authorization by court

The decision whether to dispense with the requirement of announcement when serving a search warrant should be left to judicial officers, whenever police have sufficient information at the time of application for a warrant to justify such a request. The affidavit submitted in support of a request for a no-knock search warrant must contain sufficient information to allow the judge or clerk/magistrate to determine whether it is appropriate to issue a no-knock warrant.[531]

---

[520] *Hudson v. Michigan*, U.S.Mich., 126 S.Ct. 2159 (2006).
[521] *Commonwealth v. Macias*, 429 Mass. 698, 711, N. E. 2d 130 (1999).
[522] *Commonwealth v. Manni*, 398 Mass. 741, 500 N.E.2d 807 (1986).
[523] *Commonwealth v. Gomes*, 408 Mass. 432, 556 N.E.2d 100 (1990).
[524] *Commonwealth v. Lopez*, 31 Mass. App. Ct. 547, 581 N.E.2d 865 (1991).
[525] *Com v. Siano*, 52 Mass.App.Ct. 912, 755 N.E.2d 324 (2001).
[526] *Commonwealth v. Manni*, 398 Mass. 741, 500 N.E.2d 807 (1986).
[527] *Commonwealth v. Gondola*, 28 Mass. App. Ct. 286, 550 N.E.2d 880 (1990).
[528] *Commonwealth v. Scalise*, 387 Mass. 413, 439 N.E.2d 818 (1982).
[529] *Richards v. Wisconsin*, 520 U.S. 385, 61 CrL 2057 (1977).
[530] *Commonwealth v. Macias*, 429 Mass. 698, 711, N. E. 2d 130 (1999).
[531] *Wilson v. Arkansas*, 105 S.Ct. 1915 (1995); *Commonwealth v. Scalise*, 387 Mass. 413, 439 N.E.2d 818 (1982).

Case examples where no knock warrant was authorized

- In ***Commonwealth v. Benlien***, where there were small quantities of drugs which could readily be destroyed, the premises allowed occupants to observe the approaching police, there were large dead bolts on the locked doors, and occupants had an internal avenue of escape through the cellar, a no-knock warrant was properly issued.[532]

- In the 2008 case of ***Commonwealth v. Santiago,*** based on information from a robbery suspect, a Wilbraham police officer sought a warrant to search the Springfield residence of the defendant, Luis Santiago, for stolen goods and the weapon (a BB pistol) used in an armed home invasion. The affidavit in support of the warrant application described Santiago as an active drug dealer with a lengthy criminal history including twenty-five "arraignments" for "narcotics offenses," four "arraignments for firearms violations," and arraignments "for an assault and battery and violation of an abuse prevention order." The affidavit also included information that Santiago owned two dogs, one being a "pit bull," that he kept on the premises. The SJC noted that the presence of a dangerous breed of dog alone would not be enough to justify a no knock warrant this factor coupled with other factors such as the history of narcotics sales, possession of a weapon and the suspect's history of carrying other weapons justified the no knock warrant.[533]

Drug cases alone not enough

Although most no knock warrants involve the possession and distribution of drug offenses, the mere fact that drugs are involved and that they are, by their nature, readily disposable or destructible, is insufficient to provide the necessary showing of probable cause sufficient so that police officer need not knock and announce their presence at the time they execute a search warrant.[534] A judge or clerk /magistrate may, however, take into account, along with other factors, the fact that drugs are readily disposable, in deciding whether a no-knock warrant should be issued.[535]

Doorway/threshold reappraisal

Even an authorized no-knock entry upon execution of a search warrant may turn out to be unlawful if the situation actually encountered by the police is less exigent than what was anticipated. If the circumstances justifying the no-knock warrant have changed the police officers must knock and announce their purpose.[536]

Police who execute a search warrant must make a *threshold reappraisal* of the actual circumstances which they face upon execution of the warrant, since changed circumstances may render a previously obtained no-knock authorization no longer effective.[537]

The Commonwealth has the burden of showing that both a no-knock entry at the time of execution of a search warrant was properly authorized initially and that such entry was justified at the time of the warrant's execution.[538]

- In the 2002 SJC case of ***Commonwealth v. Jiminez,*** the Court ruled that a search warrant affidavit for an apartment allegedly involved in drug activity was inadequate to establish probable cause that the officers' safety would be jeopardized, and thus the search warrant with a no-knock provision was not properly issued.[539] While the affidavit contained a great deal of detail about the defendant's drug operation, it contained no particular facts and circumstances suggesting that there might have been weapons on the premises, that the defendant or the codefendant might have carried or possessed weapons, or that either had a history of weapons possession or violence. When the police arrived at the threshold of the apartment to be searched, there was no basis to believe that the occupants might have had notice of their presence and to destroy evidence, as most relevant concerns set forth in the affidavit, such as the likelihood of being observed approaching the building and the delay likely to be encountered in breaking through the locked door on the first floor, proved not to be present at the time of the execution of the warrant.

SEARCH WARRANTS

[532] *Commonwealth v. Benlien*, 27 Mass. App. Ct. 834, 544 N.E.2d 865 (1989).
[533] *Commonwealth v. Santiago,* (2008)
[534] *Richards v.* Wisconsin, 117 S.Ct. 1416 (1997) (Supreme Court struck down state's blanket exception to the knock and announce rule for drug cases); *Commonwealth v. Macias*, 429 Mass. 698, 711 N.E. 2d 130 (1999); *Commonwealth v. Chausse*, 30 Mass. A 956, 571 N.E.2d 425 (1991); *Commonwealth v. Jimenez*, 53 Mass. 902, 753 N.E.2d 635 (2001).
[535] *Commonwealth v. Mendez,* 32 Mass. App. Ct. 928, 587 N.E.2d 248 (1992).
[536] *Commonwealth v. Scalise*, 387 Mass. 413, 439 N.E.2d 818 (1982); *Commonwealth v. Macias*, 429 Mass. 698, 711 N.E. 2d 130 (1999).
[537] *Commonwealth v. Jimenez*, 53 Mass. 902, 753 N.E.2d 635 (2001).*Commonwealth v. Scalise*,.at 421, 439 N.E.2d 818; *Commonwealth v. Macias, supra* at 704, 711 N.E.2d 130; *Commonwealth v. Benlien, supra* at 837, 544 N.E.2d 865. Cf.; *Richards v. Wisconsin, supra* at 395, 117 S.Ct. 1416 ("reasonableness of the officers' decision [to enter without knocking and announcing] must be evaluated as of the time they entered the [premises]").
[538] *Commonwealth v. Jimenez*, 53 Mass. 902, 753 N.E.2d 635 (2001).
[539] *Commonwealth v. Jimenez*, 438 Mass. 213, 780 N.E.2d 2, (2002).

NO-KNOCK WITHOUT ADVANCE APPROVAL

Where circumstances at a premise justify an unannounced entry, the police may dispense with the knock and announce requirement provided the Commonwealth can show that this is necessary to prevent violence or the destruction of evidence.[540]Such a showing can also be made after the fact, **even if the warrant did not authorize a no-knock entry**, if exigent circumstances arise at the threshold of the search justifying both the unannounced entry and the failure to obtain prior judicial authorization.[541]

- In ***Commonwealth v. Osorno***, such a no-knock entry was upheld where the police spotted an occupant running towards the bathroom carrying a plastic bag.[542]

Useless gesture exception

In circumstances where the occupant(s) knows of the police presence and purpose the knock and announce rule may not be required as it would be deemed a *useless gesture.* Similarly, in situations where the occupants would not be able to hear the knock and announce (e.g. the occupants are playing excessively loud music and would not be able to hear the announcement) the court may also find full compliance with the knock and announce requirement unnecessary as it would be deemed a useless gesture.

- In ***Commonwealth v. Antwine***[543], the SJC indicated that adherence to the knock and announce rule would be a "useless gesture" in cases where the defendant would know why the police were present (i.e. knowledge of an outstanding arrest warrant) or where the occupants were asleep and would not have heard the announcement. This *applies only to announcing the purpose of the entry*, the police would still need to knock and announce their presence prior to entry.

- In ***Commonwealth v. Herring***, the court concluded that the occupants of the apartment did not hear the police knocking or announcing their presence prior to their entry. Therefore, an announcement of purpose by the police would have been a useless gesture.[544] The officer in charge knocked three times on the outer door, then "in a clear loud voice," announced "police." After a five to ten second wait, there being no response from within the apartment, an officer signaled one of his men to force the door with a battering ram. The assembled officers then moved into the apartment and yelled, "police." In a matter of seconds, they went down a hallway and saw three men seated on a couch in the living room. The occupants could not hear the police announce their presence at the outer door. They certainly would not have heard the officers announce their purpose at that point either. Therefore, in the circumstances of the *Herring* case, the Appeals Court concluded that the "useless gesture" exception to the rule discussed in *Commonwealth v. Antwine*[545], applied.

THIRD PARTY SEARCHES WHILE EXECUTING A SEARCH WARRANT

A third party is someone who is not suspected of criminal activity. If probable cause exists to believe that a crime has been committed, a warrant may issue for the search of any property which the magistrate believes may be the place of concealment even if the place to be searched and the property to be seized belongs to a third party who is not suspected of criminal activity.[546]

[540] *Commonwealth v. Gomes,* 408 Mass. 43, 556 N.E.2d 100 (1990); See*Commonwealth v. Macias, supra* at 701, 711 N.E.2d 130; *Commonwealth v. Antwine, supra* at 639, 632 N.E.2d 818; *Commonwealth v. Scalise, supra* at 418, 439 N.E.2d 818; *Commonwealth v. Cundriff, supra* at 147 n. 15, 415 N.E.2d 172. See also *Wilson v. Arkansas, supra* at 936, 115 S.Ct. 1914.
[541] *Commonwealth v. Scalise, supra* at 422 n. 8, 439 N.E.2d 818.
[542] *Commonwealth v. Osorno*, 30 Mass. App. Ct. 327, 568 N.E.2d 627 (1991).
[543] *Commonwealth v. Antwine*, 417 Mass. 637, 632 N.E.2d 818 (1994).
[544] *Commonwealth v. Herring*, 66 Mass. App. Ct. 360 (2006).
[545] *Commonwealth v. Antwine*, 417 Mass. 637, 639-640, 632 N.E.2d 818 (1994).
[546] *Zurcher v. Stanford Daily*, 436 U.S. 547, 98 S.Ct. 1970 (1978).

MULTIPLE-OCCUPANCY BUILDING SEARCHES

''A warrant which directs the search of an entire multiple-occupancy building, when probable cause exists to search only one or more separate dwelling units within the building, is void because of the likelihood that all units within the dwelling will be subjected to unjustified and indiscriminate search.''[547]

Three Exceptions to Restriction on Entire Building Search

There are, however, three exceptions to this general rule.

1. First, ''where probable cause exists to search the whole building'';
2. Second, where the defendant has the ''run of'' the building, i.e., ''where it is shown that general access to, and control over, all of the building's subunits are available to building occupants''; and,
3. Third, ''where the officers who applied for, and executed, the warrant did not know or have reason to know prior to the actual search that the building was not a one-family dwelling.''[548]

Case examples

- In ***Commonwealth v. LaPlante,***[549] ''the judge found that the premises had one mailbox with one number on it, one electric meter, and one central doorway. The judge determined that the police spoke with the town clerk and learned from the clerk that one family lived at that address. The judge noted that, although there were two gas meters on the structure, all other indicators of occupancy pointed to a single-family house.'' The court affirmed the denial of the defendant's motion to suppress evidence. ''If the police, after reasonable investigation, did not know and reasonably could not have known of the multi-unit character of the premises at the time of the warrant's issuance, a warrant to search the entire premises is valid.''[550]
- In the 2005 SJC case of ***Commonwealth v. Dew***, the Court held that the evidence supported the conclusion that the murder defendant had access to and use of all units in a multi-family home in which he resided, and thus a search warrant encompassing a search of the entire home was appropriate.[551]

Burden is on the Defendant

Ultimately, the issue comes down to a question of fact as to the reasonableness of the efforts by the police. ''The burden is on the defendant, in challenging the seizure of evidence pursuant to a search warrant, to show that the police reasonably should have known that there were two separate apartments in what appeared to be a single-family house.''[552]

POLICE CONDUCT DURING THE SEARCH

Videotaping During Execution of Search Warrant without Judicial Approval

- In ***Commonwealth v. Balicki***, the court suppressed evidence related to the *extensive* videotaping and photographing of the dwelling's interior where the search warrant did not authorize it. The Court stated that simply taking photos of items that the police have a right to seize at the time is most likely not unconstitutional. [553] However, in this case the Court found the videotaping and photographing too extensive, particularly without a warrant.

Bringing Civilians along

In ***Commonwealth v. Sbordone***, 424 Mass. 802 (1997), the SJC held that police may utilize civilians in some situations where their assistance is necessary or will materially assist the police in executing the warrant. Such as locating and identifying items to be seized, and in cases involving certain expertise, such as computer searches, or in cases involving body cavity searches where a physician is needed.[554]

[547] *Commonwealth v. Erickson,* 14 Mass.App.Ct. 501, 504, 440 N.E.2d 1190 (1982).
[548] *Commonwealth v. Luna,* 410 Mass. 131, 136, 571 N.E.2d 603 (1991).
[549] *Commonwealth v. LaPlante,* 416 Mass. 433, 438, 622 N.E.2d 1357 (1993).
[550] *Id.* at 439, 622 N.E.2d 1357.
[551] *Commonwealth v. Dew,* 443 Mass. 620, 823 N.E.2d 771 (2005).
[552] *Luna, supra* at 137, 571 N.E.2d 603.
[553] *Commonwealth v. Balicki*, 436 Mass. 1 (2002).
[554] *Commonwealth v. Sbordone*, 424 Mass. 802 (199.)

DEALING WITH OCCUPANTS

The U.S. Supreme Court held in ***Michigan v. Summers***[555], that, "for Fourth Amendment purposes ... a warrant to search for contraband founded on probable cause implicitly carries with it the limited authority to detain the occupants of the premises while a proper search is conducted."

- In ***Michigan v. Summers,*** the police officers who were about to execute a warrant to search the defendant's home for narcotics encountered the defendant going down his front steps. They asked him to let them in, and detained him while they searched the home. On discovering drugs in the basement, the police arrested the defendant and searched him, finding an envelope containing heroin in his pocket. The Court reasoned that "limited intrusions" on personal liberty incident to a search may be justified under the Fourth Amendment on less than probable cause by "substantial law enforcement interests ... so long as police have an articulable basis for suspecting criminal activity."[556]

Three interests justifying detention of occupants without probable cause

The Court identified three law enforcement interests that justify a detention on less than probable cause when officers execute a search warrant.

1. The first is **"preventing flight in the event that incriminating evidence is found**."[557]
2. The second interest is "**minimizing the risk of harm to the officers**. Although no special danger to the police [need be shown], the execution of a warrant to search for narcotics is the kind of transaction that may give rise to sudden violence or frantic efforts to conceal or destroy evidence. The risk of harm to both the police and the occupants is minimized if the officers routinely exercise unquestioned command of the situation."[558]
3. The third law enforcement interest involves "**the orderly completion of the search** [that] may be facilitated if the occupants of the premises are present. Their self-interest may induce them to open locked doors or locked containers to avoid the use of force that is not only damaging to property but may also delay the completion of the task at hand."[559]

Attorney Hanrahan's Note: in most cases if probable cause exists to search probable cause most likely exists to arrest most, if not all, of the occupants that are connected to the criminal activity.

Searching/Frisking the Occupants

A warrant which does not specifically name or authorize the search of "all persons present" will not authorize the search of someone who is present during the search.[560]

If officers have an articulable suspicion that an occupant is armed, a *Terry* type frisk is allowed. The standard during a search warrant in regards to a pat frisk is the same as a pat frisk during a temporary detention; the officer must be able to point to specific and articulable facts that would cause him/her to fear for his/her safety. Obviously the nature of the crime justifying the warrant will likely play a role in the officer's fear for safety.

All Persons Present Search Warrants

The Supreme Judicial Court has declared that "all persons present" or "any persons present" warrants will be scrutinized strictly and will be upheld only in special circumstances.[561]

In ***Commonwealth v. Smith*** the SJC concluded that an application for an all persons present warrant must:

a. "carefully delineate the character of the premises, for example, its location, size, the particular area to be searched, means of access, neighborhood, its public or private character and any other relevant fact"; and
b. "specifically describe the nature of the illegal activity ... [alleged] at the location, the number and behavior of persons observed ... during the times of day or night [for which] the warrant is sought," and "whether any person apparently unconnected with the illegal activity has been seen at the premises."

Further, "the warrant itself must limit the location of the search to the area in which the criminal activity is believed to occur and, according to the circumstances, may also specify the time for the search.[562]

[555] *Michigan v. Summers, supra* at 705, 101 S.Ct. 2587 (1981).
[556] *Id.* at 699, 101 S.Ct. 2587.
[557] *Id.* at 702, 101 S.Ct. 2587.
[558] *Id.* at 702-703, 101 S.Ct. 2587.
[559] *Id.* at 703, 101 S.Ct. 2587.
[560] *Ybarra v. Illinois*, 444 U.S. 85, 100 S.Ct. 338 (1979).
[561] *Commonwealth of Souza*, 42 Mass. App. Ct. 186, 675 N.E.2d 432 (1997); *Commonwealth v. Smith*, 370 Mass. 335, 348 N.E.2d 101 *cert. den.*429 U.S. 944, 97 S.Ct. 520 (1976).
[562] *Commonwealth v. Souza*, 42 Mass.App.Ct. 186

Note: When executing an all persons present warrant the police should take precautions from allowing others to enter once the search has commenced. The "all persons present" warrant provision generally will not extend to those who arrive after the search has begun.[563]

All Persons Present Warrant for a Business Open to the Public Is May Not Be Valid

In ***Commonwealth v. Baharoian***, the court suppressed an "all persons present" clause in a warrant to search a small variety store for evidence of gambling. The warrant also contained the names of three suspects who were found on the premises and in possession of gambling evidence. The evidence seized in relation to the three names suspects was admissible but the evidence found against those not names were suppressed. The Court stated that, "much turns...on whether the premises to be searched are small, confined and private, or relatively public."[564]

Searching Persons Present But Not Named or Referred To In the Warrant

If, when the police conduct a search, persons not named in or referred to in the warrant are present, they may *not* search those persons unless probable cause exists in regard to the particular person to be searched, or the police have a reasonable suspicion that the person is armed. The fact that the person is present where criminal activity is believed or *known* to have occurred is not, in and of itself, enough to constitute probable cause particularized to that individual.[565]

Detaining Persons outside the Vicinity of the Premise

In the 2004 SJC case of ***Commonwealth v. Catanzaro***, the court ruled that for purposes of Article 14, like the Fourth Amendment, "it is constitutionally reasonable to require a citizen to remain while officers of the law execute a valid warrant to search his home."[566]

- In ***Catanzaro***, the defendant and his girlfriend had walked fifty to seventy feet down the driveway when the police stopped them, "as soon as practicable" after they had left the apartment.[567] The detention of the defendant's girlfriend just outside her apartment comported with the requirements of the Fourth Amendment. The SJC explained that a warrant to search for contraband founded on probable cause implicitly carries with it the limited authority to detain the occupants of the premises while a proper search is conducted.[568]The detention of the defendant's girlfriend that occurred when police officers stopped her and the defendant in the driveway outside the apartment to execute a search warrant for the apartment and "any person present" was justified under the Fourth Amendment, and, once the defendant's girlfriend blurted out that the apartment was hers, the police had sufficient basis to bring her back to the apartment while they searched it.

The Court ruled that under art. 14, the police needed reasonable suspicion that the girlfriend was committing, had committed, or was about to commit a crime, to justify detaining her and bringing her back to the apartment.[569] Her spontaneous acknowledgment that it was her apartment provided such a basis, because a neutral, detached magistrate had already determined there was probable cause to believe narcotics were being sold there.[570]

Detaining an Occupant a Significant Distance Away

In the 2005 case of ***Commonwealth v. Charros***, the SJC ruled that an officer's detention of the defendants, after the defendants had left their home in a van and traveled **approximately one mile**, was not justified in connection with the execution of a warrant to search the defendants' home for drugs since there was no connection between the place of seizure and the premises to be searched, and no exigencies necessitated the officers' plan to stop the defendants away from their home and take them back to perform the search.[571]

SEARCH WARRANTS

[563] Commonwealth v. Souza, 42 Mass. App. C.t 186 (1997).
[564] *Commonwealth v. Baharoian*, 25 Mass.App.Ct. 35 (1987).
[565] *Ybarra v. Illinois*, 444 U.S. 85, 100 S.Ct. 338 (1979); *See also, Commonwealth v. Fennell*, 13 Mass. App. 901, 429 N.E.2d 1046 (1982).
[566] *Commonwealth v. Catanzaro*, 441 Mass. 46, 803 N.E.2d 287 (2004).
[567] *Commonwealth v. Catanzaro*, 441 Mass. 46, 803 N.E.2d 287 (2004).
[568] See also, *United States v. Cochran*, 939 F.2d 337, 339 (6th Cir.1991), cert. denied, 502 U.S. 1093, 112 S.Ct. 1166, 117 L.Ed.2d 413 (1992). Contrast *United States v. Boyd*, 696 F.2d 63, 65 n. 2 (8th Cir.1982), cert. denied, 460 U.S. 1093, 103 S.Ct. 1794, 76 L.Ed.2d 360 (1983) (holding *Summers* unavailing when police stopped resident several blocks from his home to effect search warrant).
[569] See, e.g. *Commonwealth v. Eckert*, 431 Mass. 591, 599, 728 N.E.2d 312 (2000). See also J.A. Grasso & C.M. McEvoy, Suppression Matters Under Massachusetts Law § 4-2(e) (2003).
[570] See *Michigan v. Summers, supra* at 703, 101 S.Ct. 2587.
[571] *Commonwealth v. Charros*, 443 Mass. 752, 824 N.E.2d.809 (2005

POST SEARCH REQUIREMENTS

Filing the Return

An inventory of goods seized pursuant to a warrant must be prepared by the police. This is to preserve a so-called *chain of custody.* A means of ensuring that the evidence was fully accounted for preventing the likelihood that someone tampered with the evidence. A *chain of custody* issue may arise where officers are unable to state where or when during the course of a search or how certain items were seized, thus resulting in suppression of such evidence.[572]

Property seized in plain view that is not mentioned in the warrant and any other property seized that is not mentioned in the warrant should be particularly described in a **separate list** attached to the return of the warrant. Whether failure to list seized items will result in suppression has not been decided by the Supreme Judicial Court.[573] The Appeals Court, however, hinted that omitted items *may* end up being suppressed.[574]

A search warrant must be returned to the court as soon as it has been served but no more than 7 days after its issuance.[575] Note: the 7 days begins to run the day after the issuance of the warrant.[576] Failure to return the warrant within the 7 days will not automatically invalidate an otherwise lawful search.[577]

Once the warrant has been returned the affidavit becomes a public record. However, the court may impound for safety reasons or for sex abuse.

The fact that the return is made by a different officer than the one who executed the warrant, although in technical violation of M.G.L. c. 276, § 3A, will not invalidate the warrant. As the duties are ministerial and the defendant's substantive rights are not adversely affected.[578]

Lost Paperwork: In ***Commonwealth v. Occasion***, the SJC held that suppression is not mandatory where the contents of the search warrant can be demonstrated by secondary evidence. There are essentially two purposes of the return and inventory requirements of C. 276 § 3A:[579]

1. it provides defense counsel with access to related documents supporting the issuance of the warrant
2. it protects the searched party from having his seized property stolen or misplaced by the police

Preserving Evidence

Property and articles seized must be kept in a safe manner for use as evidence under the direction of the court. Depending on how exculpatory (favorable to the defendant) the evidence was and how culpable the police were, a court may dismiss a case or fashion some other appropriate remedy where seized evidence is lost or not preserved until trial.[580]

In Massachusetts, a defendant in a case where evidence is lost or destroyed by the prosecution does not have to show bad faith in order to have an indictment dismissed. [581]

Returning Seized Property

The returning or disposing of seized property is governed by M.G.L. c 276, §§ 3-8. With the exception of contraband, a defendant is generally entitled to the return of seized evidence which has been suppressed by a court. In fact, should a department lose property that a court ordered be returned to a defendant, the department may be civilly liable for the value of such property.[582]

In some cases the court may rule that "public interest" precludes the return of certain property to a defendant. In ***Commonwealth v. Beldotti***, the defendant was convicted of a brutal rape, torture, and murder of a young female. The defendant was serving a life sentence without the possibility of parole. He sent a letter to the DA's office requesting numerous items seized during a search warrant be turned over to a family member. The court declined to order the return of dildos and other sexually explicit material, even though otherwise lawful to possess, as it would spark public outrage and undermine confidence in the criminal justice system. [583]

[572] *Commonwealth v. Lewin*, 408 Mass. 147, 557 N.E.2d 721 (1990).
[573] *Commonwealth v. DeMasi*, 362 Mass. 52, 283 N.E.2d 845 (1972)
[574] *Commonwealth v. Aldrich*, 23 Mass. App. Ct. 157, 499 N.E.2d 856 (1986).
[575] *Commonwealth v. Cromer*, 365 Mass. 519, 313 N.E.2d 557 (1974); M.G.L. c. 276, § 3A.
[576] *Commonwealth v. Cromer*, 365 Mass. 519 (1974)
[577] *Commonwealth v. Vitrello*, 367 Mass. 224 (1975).
[578] *Commonwealth v. Chandler*, 29 Mass. App. Ct. 571, 563 N.E.2d 235 (1990).
[579] *Commonwealth v. Ocasio*, 434 Mass.1 (2001).
[580] *Commonwealth v. Willie*, 400 Mass. 427, 510 N.E.2d 258 (1987).
[581] See*Commonwealth v Henderson*, 411 Mass. 309, 582 N.E.2d 496 (1991)
[582] *Commonwealth v. Sacco*, 401 Mass. 204, 515 N.E.2d 1185 (1987).
[583] *Commonwealth v. Beldotti*, 41 Mass.App.Ct, 185 (1996)

STATUTES RELATED TO SEARCH WARRANTS

C. 276 § 1. COMPLAINT; WARRANT FOR DESIGNATED PROPERTY OR ARTICLES; SEARCH INCIDENT TO ARREST; DOCUMENTARY EVIDENCE SUBJECT TO PRIVILEGE

Section 1. A court or justice authorized to issue warrants in criminal cases may, upon complaint on oath that the complainant believes that any of the property or articles hereinafter named are concealed in a house, place, vessel or vehicle or in the possession of a person anywhere within the commonwealth and territorial waters thereof, if satisfied that there is probable cause for such belief, issue a warrant identifying the property and naming or describing the person or place to be searched and commanding the person seeking such warrant to search for the following property or articles:

1. First, property or articles stolen, embezzled or obtained by false pretenses, or otherwise obtained in the commission of a crime;
2. Second, property or articles which are intended for use, or which are or have been used, as a means or instrumentality of committing a crime, including, but not in limitation of the foregoing, any property or article worn, carried or otherwise used, changed or marked in the preparation for or perpetration of or concealment of a crime;
3. Third, property or articles the possession or control of which is unlawful, or which are possessed or controlled for an unlawful purpose; except property subject to search and seizure under sections forty-two through fifty-six, inclusive, of c. one hundred and thirty-eight;
4. Fourth, the dead body of a human being.
5. Fifth, the body of a living person for whom a current arrest warrant is outstanding.

A search conducted incident to an arrest may be made only for the purposes of seizing fruits, instrumentalities, contraband and other evidence of the crime for which the arrest has been made, in order to prevent its destruction or concealment; and removing any weapons that the arrestee might use to resist arrest or effect his escape. Property seized as a result of a search in violation of the provisions of this paragraph shall not be admissible in evidence in criminal proceedings.

The word “property”, as used in this section shall include books, papers, documents, records and any other tangible objects.

Nothing in this section shall be construed to abrogate, impair or limit powers of search and seizure granted under other provisions of the General Laws or under the common law.

Notwithstanding the foregoing provisions of this section, no search and seizure without a warrant shall be conducted, and no search warrant shall issue for any documentary evidence in the possession of a lawyer, psychotherapist, or a clergyman, including an accredited Christian Science practitioner, who is known or may reasonably be assumed to have a relationship with any other person which relationship is the subject of a testimonial privilege, unless, in addition to the other requirements of this section, a justice is satisfied that there is probable cause to believe that the documentary evidence will be destroyed, secreted, or lost in the event a search warrant does not issue. Nothing in this paragraph shall impair or affect the ability, pursuant to otherwise applicable law, to search or seize without a warrant or to issue a warrant for the search or seizure of any documentary evidence where there is probable cause to believe that the lawyer, psychotherapist, or clergyman in possession of such documentary evidence has committed, is committing, or is about to commit a crime. For purposes of this paragraph, “documentary evidence” includes, but is not limited to, writings, documents, blueprints, drawings, photographs, computer printouts, microfilms, X-rays, files, diagrams, ledgers, books, tapes, audio and video recordings, films or papers of any type or description.

C. 276 § 2. REQUISITES OF WARRANT

Search warrants shall designate and describe the building, house, place, vessel or vehicle to be searched and shall particularly describe the property or articles to be searched for. They shall be substantially in the form prescribed in section two A of this chapter and shall be directed to the sheriff or his deputy or to a constable or police officer, commanding him to search in the daytime, or if the warrant so directs, in the nighttime, the building, house, place, vessel or vehicle where the property or articles for which he is required to search are believed to be concealed, and to bring such property or articles when found, and the persons in whose possession they are found, before a court having jurisdiction.

C. 276 § 3. SEIZURE, CUSTODY AND DISPOSITION OF ARTICLES; EXCEPTIONS

If an officer in the execution of a search warrant finds property or articles therein described, he shall seize and safely keep them, under the direction of the court or justice, so long as necessary to permit them to be produced or used as evidence in any trial. As soon as may be, thereafter, all property seized under clause First of section one shall be restored to the owners thereof; and all other property seized in execution of a search warrant shall be disposed of as the court or justice orders and may be forfeited and either sold or destroyed, as the public interest requires, in the discretion of the court or justice, except:

(a) Diseased animals or carcasses thereof, or any tainted, diseased, corrupt, decayed or unwholesome meat, fish, vegetables, produce, fruit or provisions of any kind, or the meat of any calf killed when less than two weeks old, or any product thereof kept or concealed with intent to kill, sell or offer the same for sale for food, shall be destroyed or disposed of in accordance with section one hundred and forty-six of c. ninety-four by the board of health or by an officer designated by the court or justice; and diseased animals found to have been kept or concealed in a particular building, place or enclosure shall be destroyed or disposed of by the division of animal health and department of food and agriculture without compensation to the owners thereof.

(b) Rifles, shotguns, pistols, knives or other dangerous weapons which have been found to have been kept, concealed or used unlawfully or for an unlawful purpose shall be forfeited to the commonwealth and delivered forthwith to the colonel of the state police for destruction or preservation in the discretion of the colonel of the state police.

(c) Money seized under clause Third of section one shall be forfeited and paid over to the state treasurer.

(d) Any property, including money seized under section one, the forfeiture and disposition of which is specified in any general or special law shall be disposed of in accordance therewith.

C. 276 § 3A. TIME FOR RETURN OF WARRANT

Every officer to whom a warrant to search is issued shall return the same to the court by which it was issued as soon as it has been served and in any event not later than seven days from the date of issuance thereof, with a return of his doings thereon; provided, however, that a justice of the superior court may at any time receive complaints and issue search warrants returnable in seven days before a district court named in such warrant and in that event the officer shall make his return to such district court as directed.

K9 SEARCH and SEIZURE ISSUES

DOG SNIFF and PROBABLE CAUSE

Probable Cause: A positive indication by a *properly trained* dog is sufficient to establish probable for the presence of a controlled substance.[584] However, it is best to indicate other factors, in addition to the dog's alert, to sure up probable cause.

Training Records and Performance: The introduction of the dog's training records and certification is sufficient to prove that a drug detection dog is reliable. The introduction of field records is not required.[585]

Case Example:

- In ***Florida v. Harris***, the police pulled over the defendant on a routine traffic stop. The defendant, Harris, was nervous and they observed an open beer can so they asked for consent to search the vehicle. Harris refused to grant consent. The officers deployed a drug sniffing dog. The dog alerted that the vehicle contained drugs. A subsequent search of the car uncovered methamphetamine making ingredients. The defendant was arrested and charged. While out on bail Harris was stopped by police for another motor vehicle infraction. The same drug dog was deployed again and again he hit on the car. This time nothing was found. Harris filed a motion to suppress the dog's initial hit as unreliable. The Florida Supreme Court upheld Harris' motion ruling that a dog's performance history was required in order to prove the dog's indication of the presence of drugs to rise to the level probable cause. The U.S. Supreme Court overruled the Florida Supreme Court stating that field performance records are not required, the dog's training and certification was sufficient.

However, exaggerating the dog's ability and experience and even omitting mitigating information, can negatively affect the establishment of probable cause.

Case Example:

- In ***Commonwealth v. Ramos*** (2008), Det. Noone of the Lowell PD submitted an affidavit to search a self-storage unit related to the distribution of narcotics. The affidavit was based largely on a hit by a drug-sniffing dog. The affidavit indicated that the dog had extensive training and more than 150 documented finds which have led to the seizure of narcotics. It was later learned that the dog only detected drugs on five or six occasions in the field and the other finds were during training exercises. The affidavit also omitted that the dog had made two false positive reactions in the past 6 months, one only 10 days prior to the alert on the storage unit. The K9 handler, Off. Levasseur, later testified that drug sniffing dogs sometimes alert falsely out of a desire to please their handler or that they may falsely alert when detecting stale remnants or only traces of drugs. There is a technique referred to as "extinction training" which can prevent this false positive but this particular dog was not so trained. The Court ruled that the misstatement of the dogs seizures, coupled with the omission of the dogs false alerts, resulted in a lack of probable cause to issue the search warrant.

K9 SEARCH & SEIZURE

[584] U.S. v. Diaz, 25 F. 3d. 392 (1994)
[585] Florida v. Harris (2013)

OPEN AIR SNIFFS

Open Air Sniff of Items in Public

Typically, what a person exposes to the public does not carry with it a reasonable expectation privacy. Therefore what is exposed to the public is not protected by the Fourth Amendment and thus observation of that object is not a search in the constitutional sense.

When odors are emitting from a vehicle located in public the owner or custodian of that vehicle does not have an expectation of privacy in those odors, even if the odors are only detectable by a trained drug sniffing dog.[586] Although odors that may not be detectable by a human can be detected by a dog, the sniff by the dog only detects the presence of illegal items and not lawfully possessed items and thus the sniff by a trained dog is unique to other more intrusive types of searches by law enforcement.

Other Implications and Considerations

Although an open air sniff of an object (e.g. a car) is generally not considered a search the actions surrounding the search may implicate other Fourth Amendment protections.

Marijuana: the increasing trend of decriminalizing marijuana may pose a problem when utilizing K9's to detect drugs. For instance, can your K9 decipher the quantity of marijuana present (i.e. more than an ounce)? Can your K9 distinguish between medical marijuana and illicit marijuana? Can your K9 communicate to you whether or not he detects marijuana as opposed to some other illicit drug? These are questions likely to be posed by defense attorneys as the decriminalization of marijuana continues.

OPEN AIR SNIFF OF A PERSON

In ***Commonwealth v. Feyernold,*** the Appeals Court alluded that the open air sniff of a person in public raises issues different from a reasonable expectation of privacy concern because the very act of sniffing a person, and the touching that may accompany that sniffing, may be degradingly intrusive.

TERRY STOPS & SEIZURE OF OBJECTS

If the person in possession of the object sniffed is detained the principles of *Terry v. Ohio* will. The police must have reasonable suspicion that the person is involved in criminal activity. Additionally, if the object is seized by the police the same principles of *Terry v. Ohio* will apply to the seizure of the object; meaning the scope and length of the detention must be reasonable and the police must diligently pursue their investigation.

Case Example

- In ***US v. Place*** (1983), DEA agents suspected that the defendant, Raymond PLACE, was transporting drugs from Miami to New York by way of air travel. The agents had reasonable suspicion to temporarily detain PLACE based on their observations. The agents approached PLACE in the airport and asked for consent to search his luggage. PLACE declined. The agents then seized his luggage and reported that they were taking them to a judge to apply for a search warrant; 90 minutes later the agents subjected the bags to a sniff by a trained drug detecting canine. The dog alerted that one of the two bags contained drugs. Because it was late Friday afternoon the agents retained the baggage until Monday morning when they applied for a warrant. Upon opening the bag, the agents discovered 1,125 grams of cocaine. The U.S. Supreme Court ruled that the seizure of an item lawful based on reasonable suspicion. The Court, in its decision, permitted the seizure of luggage suspected of containing narcotics on the same principles of *Terry v. Ohio*. The detention must be based on an effort to confirm or dispel their suspicion. Although the Court

[586] *Commonwealth v. Feyenord*, 62 Mass.App.Ct. 200 (2003)

upheld the initial detention of the luggage on reasonable suspicion the Court held that the detention of the luggage for 90 minutes (based only on reasonable suspicion at that time) was unreasonable, particularly given the fact that the agents knew when PLACE would be landing and could have arranged for the drug sniffing dog to be present when he landed.

MOTOR VEHICLE STOPS

Although an open air sniff of a vehicle located in public is not "search" if the length of the detention is unreasonable under the circumstances the stop will be deemed unlawful.

Civil infractions

The police are allowed to stop (i.e. seize) the operator of a motor vehicle for a non-criminal, civil motor vehicle infraction because it is necessary in order to regulate the safe flow of traffic. The nature of the stop should be brief and limited to the nature of the violation, absent some indication of criminal activity. Any detention that takes place that is longer than is reasonably necessary to address the civil infraction, absent indication of criminal activity, will make the prolonged detention unlawful. Therefore, taking additional time to have a K9 inspect the exterior of the vehicle will make the length of the detention unreasonable and thus unlawful.

In ***Illinois v. Caballes*** (2005), the U.S. Supreme Court stated "a seizure that is justified solely on the interest in issuing a warning ticket to the driver may become unlawful if it is prolonged beyond the time reasonably required to complete that mission."

What if the civil motor vehicle stop is not prolonged?

In ***Illinois v. Caballes*** (2005), the U.S. Supreme Court upheld the dog sniff of a motor vehicle stopped for a civil motor vehicle infraction. In this case the back-up officer, a K9 officer, walked his dog around the stopped vehicle while the primary officer wrote out a warning. The stop was not prolonged in any way by the dog sniff. The U.S. Supreme Court held that the exterior sniff of the vehicle was not a violation of the Fourth Amendment because as previously decided a sniff of a vehicle in public is not a search and in this case the vehicle detention was not prolonged in order to conduct the sniff.

However, Massachusetts Courts tend to be more restrictive when it comes to search and seizure matters often deciding search cases on Article 14 of the Massachusetts Declaration of Rights. It is likely that a Massachusetts court will rule differently if similar facts were presented. Careful documentation that the stop was in no way prolonged in an effort to conduct a dog sniff is vital.

Criminal Activity

If the police stop a vehicle that is based on reasonable suspicion of criminal activity, or the vehicle is stopped for a civil motor vehicle infraction and the police subsequently develop reasonable suspicion of criminal activity, the length of detention may be prolonged for as long as it is reasonable under the circumstances with purpose of furthering the investigation.

If the circumstances warrant, the length of detention can extend for the time needed for a trained K9 to respond. There is no set time limit; it all comes down to what is reasonable under the circumstances. For instance, a person who is being detained under the suspicion of being involved in a B&E most likely would not justify a prolonged detention awaiting for the arrival of a drug sniffing K9. However, if the detainee was suspected of drug trafficking the prolonged detention while awaiting the arrival of a drug sniffing canine may be permissible if it is reasonable under the circumstances. The length of detention will likely be weighed against the level of reasonable suspicion present.

Additionally, if the person is under arrest the length of detention while awaiting a drug sniffing canine typically will not be an issue since the person is under arrest and not being *temporarily detained* as in the case of a threshold inquiry.[587]

Case example

In the 2005 case of ***Commonwealth v. Feyenord***, the SJC ruled that even assuming the defendant had an expectation of privacy regarding the odors emanating from his car, a police drug dog's sniffing of the car exterior did not amount to a search.[588] In ***Feyenord***, during a stop for a motor vehicle infraction the police developed reasonable suspicion of criminal activity. The defendant was held for 30 minutes while a canine, which arrived within 15-20 minutes of being called, sniffed the vehicle's exterior. The SJC found this reasonable and that it did not constitute a search.

Stationary Vehicle in Public

If a vehicle is stopped in public and the vehicle owner is not being detained by police there is typically no Fourth Amendment concerns when it comes to the exterior sniff of a vehicle.

Case example

- In ***Commonwealth v. Mateo-German***, the defendant's vehicle had run out of gas on route 140. A trooper (who happened to be a K9 officer) stopped behind the defendant's vehicle to check on his wellbeing. The defendant advised the trooper that he had run out of gas and he used the trooper's phone to call a friend to bring him some gasoline. While the men waited for the friend to deliver gasoline the two men engaged in casual conversation. The defendant seemed exceptionally nervous and some of his statements were inconsistent. The trooper asked the defendant if he would mind if his dog conducted a sniff of the exterior of the vehicle. The defendant agreed indicating that he had nothing to hide. The dog alerted to the driver's side of the vehicle. The defendant then consented to the dog sniff of the interior. The trooper discovered a hidden compartment cut into the vehicle's gasoline tank which contained large amounts of heroin and cocaine. The SJC ruled that the trooper did not need the defendant's consent to sniff the exterior of the vehicle since it is not a search and the defendant was not seized by the trooper. The SJC also ruled that consent was not needed to enter the vehicle because the dog's alert, coupled with the defendant's nervousness and inconsistent statements, amounted to probable cause.

SNIFF OF A HOME

The home has routinely been granted the most stringent Constitutional protections when it comes to the Fourth Amendment protections. These protections extend to the area immediately surrounding the home, commonly referred to as the curtilage. The curtilage offers the same Fourth Amendment protections as does the interior of the home; and although in some cases the police may lawfully enter the curtilage under a legal license theory (e.g. to ring the doorbell) this license does not extend to bringing a drug sniffing dog onto the property.

Case example

- In ***Florida v. Jardines***, the police received an anonymous, unconfirmed, tip that the defendant, Joelis JARDINES, was trafficking in illegal drugs. The police took a drug sniffing dog to JARDINES front porch and the dog altered under JARDINES' front door. The police then used this information to obtain a search warrant. JARDINE claimed that his Fourth Amendment rights were violated. The U.S. Supreme Court agreed with JARDINES. The Court stated:

The right to be free from government intrusion in the home "would be of little practical value if the State's agents could stand in a home's porch or side garden and trawl for evidence with impunity; the right to retreat would be significantly

[587] Most of these issues are analyzed in *Commonwealth v. Feyernold*
[588] *Commonwealth v. Feyenord*, 445 Mass. 72, 833 N.E.2d 590 (2005).

diminished if the police could enter a man's property to observe his repose from just outside the front window. We therefore regard the area "immediately surrounding and associated with the home" — what our cases call the curtilage — as "part of the home itself for Fourth Amendment purposes."

The Court went on to acknowledge that although the curtilage is protected the police may travel onto the curtilage in some circumstances, just as a normal visitor may enter the porch to knock on the door so can a police officer. The Court referred to this as an "implicit license." The Court stated:

This implicit license typically permits the visitor to approach the home by the front path, knock promptly, wait briefly to be received, and then (absent invitation to linger longer) leave. Complying with the terms of that traditional invitation does not require fine-grained legal knowledge; it is generally managed without incident by the Nation's Girl Scouts and trick-or-treaters. Thus, a police officer not armed with a warrant may approach a home and knock, precisely because that is "no more than any private citizen might do."

However the court went on to say "but introducing a trained police dog to explore the area around the home in hopes of discovering incriminating evidence is something else. There is no customary invitation to do that. An invitation to engage in canine forensic investigation assuredly does not inhere in the very act of hanging a knocker. To find a visitor knocking on the door is routine (even if sometimes unwelcome); to spot that same visitor exploring the front path with a metal detector, or marching his bloodhound into the garden before saying hello and asking permission, would inspire most of us to — well, call the police."

Relevant statutes:

Chapter 140 § 55A: If an action is brought against a law enforcement officer because of damage caused by a dog which said officer was caring for or maintaining in connection with his official duties, the commonwealth or the political subdivision employing said officer shall indemnify him for expenses or damages incurred in the settlement or defense of such action; provided that in the case of an officer employed by the commonwealth the settlement or defense of such case shall have been made by the attorney general, and that in the case of an officer employed by a city or town such settlement or defense shall have been made by the city solicitor or town counsel or by an attorney legally employed for the purpose by a city or town.

Chapter 41 § 100H. If an action is brought against a law enforcement officer because of damage caused by a dog which said officer was caring for or maintaining in connection with his official duties, the political subdivision employing said officer shall indemnify him for expenses or damages incurred in the settlement or defense of such action; provided that in the case of an officer employed by a city or town such settlement or defense shall have been made by the city solicitor or town counsel or by an attorney legally employed for the purpose by a city or town.

SURVEILLANCE AND INTERCEPTING COMMUNICATIONS

SURVEILLANCE

Police may make a visual investigation of activities going on in plain view in public areas. Public areas include areas inside buildings that are open to or accessible to the public, including landings and stairwells to apartments, hotels, and inns.[589]

Mechanical or electronic surveillance

Police often use mechanical or electronic devices to observe or detect criminal activity. This section reviews the legality of devices which do not intercept communications but which enable the police to make observations or monitor activity. Because of the complex legal issues involved in mechanical and electronic surveillance, the police should review their practices with the local district attorney's office.

Flashlight: Police officers may use a flashlight to illuminate areas which they have the lawful right to view or search.[590]

Searchlight: Police officers may use a searchlight to illuminate areas which they have the lawful right to view or search.[591]

White Takedown Lights: Police may use their white takedown lights to illuminate a motor vehicle in a public area.[592]

Binoculars: Police officers may use binoculars to observe persons in public areas.[593] However, devices, such as binoculars and telescopes, which enhance a police officer's natural powers of observation, may be impermissible when used to spy into private premises.

Night Vision: Night vision use would not be a violation of the Fourth Amendment provided the observed activity occurred in a public location.

Ultraviolet light: Police officers may dust a package with fluorescent powder then, without arresting the recipient of the package, examine his hands with an ultraviolet light to detect traces of the fluorescent powder.[594]

Pen register or cross frame unit trap

A **pen register** is an electronic device that records the numbers dialed from a particular telephone line.[595]

A **cross frame unit trap** is placed on a particular telephone line in order to record the telephone numbers of incoming calls to the telephone line under surveillance,

Since a pen register or cross frame unit trap reveals information concerning the identity of parties to a wire communication (by noting their telephone numbers) and because those devices also reveal information concerning the existence of a wire communication, a pen register or cross frame unit trap must be installed in accordance with M.G.L. c. 272, § 99.[596]

In 1986, the federal government passed the Electronic Communications Privacy Act.[597] Under the Act, it is unlawful for anyone to use pen registers or similar trap and trace mechanisms without a court order. There are a few limited exceptions to this general rule, the most pertinent of which is the allowance of telecommunication services to do so if the telephone user has consented.

As a result of this act, law enforcement agencies in Massachusetts must receive a court order before they may implement a pen register trace, as well as comply with the requirement of M.G.L. c. 272, § 99.

The federal statute further indicates that the court order may be issued by "any court of competent jurisdiction". Coupling that provision with the general provisions of M.G.L. c. 272, § 99B, **the Superior Court is the only Massachusetts state court that is "competent"**.

[589] *Commonwealth v. Panetti*, 406 Mass. 230, 547 N.E.2d 46 (1989); *Commonwealth v. Serbagi*, 23 Mass. App. Ct. 57, 498 N.E.2d 1363 (1986).*But see,Commonwealth v. Montanez*, 410 Mass. 290, 571 N.E.2d 1372 (1991) (there may exist situations where tenant has reasonable expectation of privacy in normally "public" area).
[590] *Commonwealth v. Cavanaugh*, 366 Mass. 277, 317 N.E.2d 480 (1974) (flashlight used to observe interior of car parked on public street). *Commonwealth v. Haefeli*, 361 Mass. 271, 279 N.E.2d 915 (1972) (flashlight used to observe interior of automobile being searched incident to an arrest); *Commonwealth v. Oreto*, 20 Mass. App. Ct. 581, 482 N.E.2d 329 (1985).
[591] *See, U.S. v. Lee*, 274 U.S. 559, 47 S.Ct. 746 (1927) (searchlight used to observe contraband on boat deck).
[592] *Commonwealth v. Briand,*71 Mass.App.Ct. 160 (2008),
[593] *Commonwealth v. Oritz,* 376 Mass. 349, 380 N.E.2d 669 (1978) (binoculars used by police officer standing on public street to observe defendant in a public park.).*See also,U.S. v. Lee,* 274 U.S. 559, 47 S.Ct. 746 (1927) (use of field glasses; dicta)

[595] Smith v. Maryland, 442 U.S. 735, 737, 742 (1972).
[596] *Dist.Atty. v. New England Tel. & Tel. Co.*, 379 Mass. 586, 399 N.E.2d 866 (1980) (held that installation of pen register or cross frame unit trap requires compliance with M.G.L. c. 272, § 99 and that Superior Court can order telephone company to provide law enforcement officials with necessary technical assistance for such installation). *See also,Smith v. Maryland*, 442 U.S. 735, 99 S.Ct. 2577 (1979) (register did not violate Federal Fourth Amendment).
[597] Electronic Communications Privacy Act., 18 U.S.C.A. 201 et. seq.

Any court orders issued must contain: the identity of the person who has leased the phone line to be involved; the name of the subject under criminal investigation; the number of device units to be used; the geographic scope and limits of the device; and a brief statement indicating what information the police hope to obtain from using the pen register.

GPS TRACKING/MONITORING

The SJC has determined that utilizing a GPS tracking device on a suspect's vehicle constitutes a seizure under art. 14 of the Massachusetts Declaration of Rights and in 2012 in *US v. Jones* the US Supreme Court also ruled that the utilization of a GPS unit to track the movements of a motor vehicle constitutes a search under the Fourth Amendment.

The SJC declared "when an electronic surveillance device is installed in a motor vehicle, be it a beeper, radio transmitter, or GPS device, the government's control and use of the defendant's vehicle to track its movements interferes with the defendant's interest in the vehicle notwithstanding that he maintains possession of it. The owner of property has a right to exclude it from "all the world," and the police use "infringes that exclusionary right."[598] Therefore, use of a GPS device requires a warrant, absent an exception to the warrant requirement (i.e. exigency).

Criteria

The Commonwealth must establish, before a magistrate, probable cause to believe that a particularly described offense has been, is being, or is about to be committed, and that GPS monitoring of the vehicle will produce evidence of such offense or will aid in the apprehension of a person who the applicant has probable cause to believe has committed, is committing, or is about to commit such offense.[599]

Duration

The monitoring period must be no longer than fifteen days from the date of the warrant's issuance. The SJC stated "in concluding that a 15-day period is appropriate, we are guided by the Legislature's determination that a maximum period of fifteen days for electronic surveillance of wire communications is reasonable, G.L. c. 272, § 99 I 2. The return should indicate the date that the GPS device was installed."[600]

CELL PHONE TRACKING/DATA

According to the Pew Research Center more than 90% of American adults carry a cell phone regularly. Cell phone technology allows for the location tracking of the cell phone's location with great accuracy and ease. This tracking mechanism can be a very effective investigative tool.

The Federal Stored Communications Act (SCA)

The Federal Stored Communications Act directs how government entities may obtain communication records from third-party providers of electronic communication services.

The federal law states that "a court order for disclosure…may be issued by any court of competent jurisdiction and shall issue only if the governmental entity offers **specific and articulable facts** showing that there are reasonable grounds to believe that the…records or other information sought, are relevant and material to an ongoing criminal investigation." The standard for the federal law is less than probable cause.

Telephone Billing Records

In ***Commonwealth v. Vinnie***, the Court ruled that there is no reasonable expectation of privacy under article 14 in telephone billing records and therefore a search warrant is not required; records may be obtained under G.L. 271 § 17B, by administrative subpoena on "reasonable grounds for belief" of the telephone's use for "unlawful purpose."

Cell Phone Location Information (CSLI) requires a warrant in Massachusetts

In the 2014 case of ***Commonwealth v. Augustine***, the SJC ruled that obtaining cell site location information (CSLI) is a search for the purposes of Article 14 of the Massachusetts Declaration of Rights and absent an exception to the warrant requirement a search warrant must be obtained in order to obtain this information. The

---

[598] *Commonwealth v. Connolly*, SJC (Sept. 2009)
[599] *Commonwealth v. Connolly*, SJC (Sept. 2009)
[600] *Commonwealth v. Connolly*, SJC (Sept. 2009)

SURVEILLANCE & INTERCEPTING

Court explained that the "digital age has dramatically altered the societal landscape…the cellular telephone has become an indispensable part of modern American life. Cellular telephones physically accompany their users everywhere – almost permanent attachments to their bodies." Because of this the Court ruled that clearly tracking a person's movements impacts a person's reasonable expectation of privacy.

Attorney Hanrahan's note on warrant exceptions: Like with any other setting wherein a warrant is required if an exception to the warrant requirement exists the police can forego the search warrant. For instance, if the police are looking for someone who they have a reason to believe is missing and in danger they may request the location information from the carrier without a warrant under the **Emergency Exception** to the warrant requirement.

Cell Phone "Repoll" records do not require a search warrant

In the 2014 case of ***Commonwealth v. Collins***, the SJC ruled that where telephone records reveal "repoll" numbers (general cell tower area information) rather than CSLI information, a search warrant is not required. Repoll information can identify a general location of the cell phone, perhaps as large as 100 miles, whereas CSLI information can pinpoint the cell phone's location with precision.

Although a search warrant is not required a court order would still be required pursuant to 18 U.S.C. § 2703(d), which requires "specific and articulable facts showing that there are reasonable grounds to believe that the contents of…the records…sought, are relevant and material to an ongoing criminal investigation."

How to obtain Cell Phone Location Data

As mentioned earlier, in order to obtain CSLI information a search warrant must be obtained and a court order would be required obtain other cell phone records. However, in an emergency, the police can contact the user's cellular provider. The provider will typically require a form to be completed and faxed back before releasing the information. If you are unsure of the provider service you can typically call any of the major providers and they can usually let you know which provider carries the service by the phone number.

INTERCEPTING COMMUNICATIONS

M.G.L. c. 272, § 99 makes it a crime (a felony) to intercept secretly a wire or oral communication. "Intercepting" is defined as *secretly* hearing, transmitting or recording any oral or wire communication (except those broadcast on public airwaves) by means of an "intercepting device."

An "intercepting device" is any device or apparatus capable of transmitting, receiving, amplifying or recording wire or oral communications, other than a hearing aid, telephone or telegraph or similar instrument. The unaided, naked ear is not an intercepting device. Thus, overhearing a conversation or communication, even secretly, by use of the unaided, naked ear is not a violation of M.G.L. c. 272, § 99.

Police should also be aware that Title III of the Omnibus Crime Control and Safe Streets Act of 1968 (18 U.S. Code, Section 2511 and following) and the 1986 Electrical Communications Privacy Act are the major federal statutes governing the interception, transmitting and recording of oral or wire communications. However, the state statute, M.G.L. c. 272, § 99, is more narrowly written than the federal statutes; compliance with the state statute would normally be sufficient to comply with the federal statutes. This may not be so for non-law enforcement however, see interception by private parties later in this section.

There are essentially two ways that law enforcement can secretly record oral or wire communications without violating c. 272 § 99. The police must either have a warrant issued pursuant to c. 272 § 99 or there must be a one party consent. In either event, the crime the police are investigating must be related to a designated offense.

Wiretap Warrants under c. 272 § 99

In order for the police to obtain a warrant to intercept a private communication the police must demonstrate that there is probable cause that the crime being investigated involves a "designated offense". The police must also show that normal investigative procedures have been tried and have been unsuccessful.

By statute, "the attorney general, any assistant attorney general specially designated by the attorney general, any district attorney, or any assistant district attorney specially designated by the district attorney may apply" for a warrant pursuant to 272 § 99. Officers wishing to utilize this tool need to coordinate with either the DA's office or the Attorney General's Office.

Applications for a c. 272 § 99 must be made to a judge of competent jurisdiction in the county where the interception is to occur, or the county where the office of the applicant is located, or in the event that there is no judge of competent jurisdiction sitting in said county at such time, to a judge of competent jurisdiction sitting in Suffolk County; except that for these purposes, the office of the attorney general shall be deemed to be located in Suffolk County.

Designated Offenses

The term "designated offense" shall include the following offenses in connection with **organized crime**: arson, assault and battery with a dangerous weapon, extortion, bribery, burglary, embezzlement, forgery, gaming in violation of Chapter 271 § 17, intimidation of a witness or juror, kidnapping, larceny, lending of money or things of value in violation of the general laws, mayhem, murder, any offense involving the possession or sale of a narcotic or harmful drug, perjury, prostitution, robbery, subornation of perjury, any violation of this section, being an accessory to any of the foregoing offenses and conspiracy or attempt or solicitation to commit any of the foregoing offenses.

Organized Crime

Organized crime consists of a continuing conspiracy among highly organized and disciplined groups to engage in supplying illegal goods and services. Organized crime must be demonstrated by some evidence of an *ongoing* illegal business operation.[601]

- In ***Commonwealth v. Jarabek,*** a scheme between two municipal officials to extort kickback from a single contractor **did not** constitute organized crime.[602]
- In ***Commonwealth v. Thorpe***, the organized crime element was satisfied where the defendant was engaged in selling advanced copies of police promotional examinations. The defendant was part of a tightly knit group with considerable security and discipline.[603]
- In the 2011 case of ***Commonwealth v. Tavares***, the SJC suppressed evidence related to a one-party consent interception involving a drive-by shooting which resulted in death. The shooting was motivated by a grudge related to stolen firearm and involved a group of men who were involved in many violent crimes. The SJC ruled that although murder is a designated offense there was no evidence that the group was engaged in "supplying illegal goods and services" as required by the statute.
- In ***Commonwealth v. Zuluaga***, the trooper in his affidavit stated "It is my experience that persons involved in the distribution of kilogram and multi-kilogram quantities of cocaine necessarily conduct their activities in concert with others." This affirmation, the Zuluaga court reasoned, in the factual context of the case, was sufficient to demonstrate a connection to organized crime.[604]
- In the 2014 case of ***Commonwealth v. Burgos***, the SJC ruled that a retaliatory killing alone, without a clear link to the goals of a criminal enterprise, does not amount to a connection to organized crime justifying the use of an interception device.

Duration

The warrant is valid for only 15 days of consecutive interception. The clock does not begin to run until the actual interception begins, however the interception may not exceed 30 days from the day the warrant was executed (i.e. the was device installed).[605]

Warrant permissible for Cell Phones and Text Messages

In the 2013 case of ***Commonwealth v, Moody,*** the SJC held that "a Superior Court judge possesses the authority under the Massachusetts wiretap statute to issue warrants permitting the interception of cellular telephone calls and text messages" despite the fact that the legislature did not specifically mention these devices in the statute.

Warrantless interception – one party consent

The police may intercept communications without a warrant if they have *reasonable suspicion* that the crime involves *organized crime* (i.e. connected to a designated offense) and the *police themselves or an agent of the police* (i.e. an informant) who *consents* to the interception (i.e. an informant) are a party to the communication.

[601] *Commonwealth v. Thorpe*, 384 Mass. 271, 277 (1981).
[602] *Commonwealth v. Jarabek*, 384 Mass. 293, 296 (1981).
[603] *Commonwealth v. Thorpe*, 384 Mass. 271 (1981)
[604] Commonwealth v. John Davis, Appeals Court (2013) quoting Com. v. Zuluaga, 43 Mass.App.Ct. 629 (1997).
[605] M.G.L.A. c. 272, § 99

SURVEILLANCE & INTERCEPTING

- In ***Commonwealth v. Abdul-Kareem***, the Massachusetts Appeals Court ruled a wiretap recording of a meeting between the defendant and a police informer, entered as evidence in the defendant's trial for conspiracy to commit mayhem and conspiracy to commit assault and battery by means of a dangerous weapon, was admissible under the one-party consent exception to the general ban on surreptitious recording, which permitted wiretap consented to by one party to a conversation if the investigation involved a statutorily "designated offense" occurring in connection with organized crime, where assault and battery with a dangerous weapon was a "designated offense," and the connection with organized crime was adequately suggested by a description of the proposition put to the informer by the defendant.[606]

Even with one-party consent if the interception does not involve a "designated offense" a warrant would be required in order to intercept.

- In the 2014 case of ***Commonwealth v. Mitchell***, the SJC ruled that when law enforcement, acting in good faith, instructs a cooperating witness to attempt to elicit information regarding a "designated offense" the recorded conversation does not require a warrant under chapter 272 § 99 even if the cooperating witness ultimately discusses something other than a designated offense.

Warrant required in dwelling – even with one-party consent

The law grants greater protections to communications taking place within a private dwelling. If the communication takes place within a dwelling, even with one-party consent, the police must have a warrant absent exigent circumstances.[607] This warrant is commonly referred to as a *Blood* warrant, from the landmark case of ***Commonwealth v. Blood***.

Live testimony still permissible

Although the recordings of improperly or unlawfully intercepted communications will be suppressed the live testimony of someone who was involved in the communication may not be.

- In ***Commonwealth v. Jarabek***, the SJC ruled that live testimony of a participant about conversations that had been unlawfully recorded was admissible, even though the recordings of the conversations were subject to suppression under the Massachusetts Interception statute.[608]

M.G.L. c. 272 § 99 and exigent circumstances

Similar to other searches, if exigent circumstances arise and a warrant cannot be obtained the recording of intercepted communications may still be admissible.

- In ***Commonwealth v. Rodriguez***, Customs agents discovered cocaine secreted in the frame of a bicycle which was to be delivered to a Springfield resident. The police obtained an anticipatory search warrant and delivered the item to the address. The resident claimed that a friend arranged delivery and that he was unaware of the contents. The police doubted the story and the resident phoned his friend, the defendant. The defendant stated that he was on his way to the house to pick up the item. The police put a wire on the resident to monitor the conversation. The court ruled that the defendant had an expectation of privacy in the dwelling which would have required a so-called Blood warrant. However, the police could not have anticipated the events and did not have time to obtain a warrant to conduct the interception. Therefore, the SJC upheld the intercept under an exigency theory. [609]

If not secretly recorded there is no violation of M.G.L. c. 272 § 99

There is no "interception" (the statute is not violated) if the wire or oral communication is not **secretly** heard, transmitted or recorded. If all parties to the wire or oral communication know or ought to know that the communication is being overheard, transmitted or recorded, the statute is not violated.

- In ***Commonwealth v. Jackson***,[610] a kidnapper stated twice during nine telephone calls to the victim's brother that he knew or expected that the telephone calls were being tape recorded. The Supreme Judicial Court held that the kidnapper had "actual knowledge" that the telephone conversations were being recorded (by the victim's brother). Therefore, they were not recorded "secretly" and did not come within the prohibition of M.G.L. c. 272, § 99.

[606] Commonwealth v. Abdul-Kareem, 56 Mass. App. Ct. 78, 775 N.E.2d 454 (2002).
[607] ***Commonwealth v. Blood*** ,400 Mass. 61, 507 N.E.2d 1029 (1987).
[608] *Commonwealth v. Jarabek*, 384 Mass. 293 (1981).
[609] *Commonwealth v. Rodriguez,* 450 Mass. 302, 877 N.E.2d 1274 (2007)
[610] *Commonwealth v. Jackson*, 370 Mass. 502, 349 N.E.2d 337 (1976).

Warning or notice of recording

If the parties to a wire or oral communication are told that it is being recorded or a periodic "beeper" is used, the court is likely to conclude that the conversation was not recorded "secretly."

Prior authorization

There is no "interception" if the person hearing, transmitting or recording the wire or oral communication was given "prior authority by all parties to such communication . . . " Of course, if all parties have given such prior authorization to hear, transmit or record the wire or oral communication, it is not being intercepted "secretly."

Overhearing via an intercom device and cell monitoring

There is no violation of the statute if the communication is overheard by means of an office intercom used in the *ordinary course of business.*[611]

- In the 1980 case of ***Commonwealth v. Look,*** the SJC held that a police department's intercom system fell within the writings of the statute's exception (ordinary course of business).[612]Intercom interception by desk officers of conversation between defendant and police officer was not illegal under federal eavesdropping statute, because defendant's statements did not fall within definition of "oral communications" of such statute, and thus was not subject thereto, where such statute required that speaker had a justifiable expectation of privacy with regard to "oral communications," but defendant, who was talking to officer after being told that anything he said may be used against him in court, could not justifiably claim to have expectation of privacy as to any statements he made.

The 2006 Appeals Court case of ***Commonwealth v. Pierce*** ruled that the police station's intercom system over which an officer heard an incriminating statement from an individual in a jail cell, was an office intercommunication system used in the ordinary course of business.[613] The Court found that this fell within one of the wiretap statute's specified exceptions from the general prohibition on the secret interception of oral communications. At the motion hearing, an officer testified that the intercom system, which included a camera overlooking the jail cell, was a safety device that allowed the police to ensure that prisoners did not harm themselves. It also helped detect if they were planning to harm an officer. The Court concluded, therefore, that maintaining safety was a legitimate business practice of a municipal police department.

NOTE: M.G.L. c.40, §36B requires an electronic monitoring system in cells unless at least one cell is "within audible range of the duty desk without electronic assistance."

Police Interrogations

In the 2012 case of ***Commonwealth v. Ashley***, the SJC ruled that recording an interrogation without informing the suspect of the recording is not necessarily a violation of the wiretap statute (G.L. c. 272 § 99). The Court stated the recording of an interrogation is not "surreptitious eavesdropping," when the defendant was fully aware that he was engaged in an interrogation with police who repeatedly expressed their intention to get it "down on paper" and memorialize the interview. Because it is obvious that, during this particular interrogation, the defendant did not intend to keep his statements private, the Court ruled that the recording of the interrogation did not amount to surreptitious eavesdropping; even if a literal application of the statute might imply a violation. The Court stated "we do not view the statute as intended to apply in these circumstances."

Interception by Private Parties; Admissibility

In the event that private parties, other than the police, unlawfully intercept communications, such communications may or may not be admissible at trial, depending on the discretion of the trial judge.[614]

The Massachusetts wiretap statute, which prohibits secret electronic recording by a private individual of any oral communication, does not mandate that all unlawfully intercepted communications should be suppressed.

- In the 2002 case of ***Commonwealth v. Barboza,*** the secret recording by a father, in his own home, of his minor son talking on the telephone with the defendant, motivated by concerns that his son was being sexually

[611] *See,* § 99(D)(1)(b) and *Commonwealth v. Look*, 379 Mass. 893, 402 N.E.2d 470 *cert. den.*449 U.S. 827, 101 S.Ct. 92 (1980).
[612] *Commonwealth v. Look*, 379 Mass. 893, 402 N.E.2d 470 (1980), *cert. den.*449 U.S. 827, 379 Mass. 893, 402 N.E.2d 470 (1980), *cert. den.*449 U.S. 827.
[613] *Commonwealth v. Pierce,* 66 Mass.App.Ct. 283, 846 N.E.2d 1189 (2006).
[614] *Commonwealth v. Santaro, Jr.*, 406 Mass. 421, 568 N.E.2d 862 (1990).

exploited by the defendant, without police knowledge, did not violate the federal wiretap statute. The Appeals Court held that the defendant was not entitled to suppression of two telephone conversations between the defendant and the alleged victim that were secretly recorded by the victim's father, without the knowledge of police, despite the fact that the recordings violated the wiretap statute, in a prosecution for sex offenses. The Court pointed out that the deterrent purpose of the exclusionary rule, which was to deter future police misconduct, would not be served by suppressing such conversations, and there was no reason why the rule should protect the defendant from the consequences of the unlawful interception by a father, a private citizen, acting in the privacy of his own home, without any government involvement, to protect a victim from sexual exploitation by the defendant.[615]

The Federal Law Impact on Intercepting by Private Citizens

The Federal wiretap statute "makes it a crime, except in limited circumstances, to intentionally intercept [an oral communication] or to intentionally disclose the contents of such a communication."[616]

In addition to providing criminal penalties for violations of the statute, the statute contains an exclusionary rule provision, "prohibiting the admission in evidence of unlawfully intercepted 'wire' or 'oral' communications, and evidence derived therefrom."[617] Unlike the Massachusetts statute, this exclusionary provision applies to all interceptions, even by private citizens, not just law enforcement.

However, there is an exception to this rule when one party consents to the interception; "conversations intercepted with the consent of either of the parties are explicitly exempted from Title III liability."[618] Under the so-called "consent exception".

The consent provision of the Federal wiretap statute has been interpreted to allow a parent or guardian, acting to protect the welfare of his or her child or children, to vicariously consent to the recording of the child's conversations with another.[619]

In the 2013 case of ***Commonwealth v. FW***, the SJC ruled that the vicarious consent provision may apply to someone other than a parent or guardian. In this case the older sister of the victim, who was Autistic and non-verbal, suspected that her little sister was being sexually abused by her grandfather (as she was when she was young). In order to prove her suspicion she set up a hidden surveillance camera. The video showed the grandfather pushing the child's head toward his groin and stating "put it in your mouth." The SJC held that evidence was admissible.

Criminal Secret Recording

Chapter 272 § 99 makes a felony offense to secretly intercept communications without either a warrant or one of the specifically enumerated exceptions (i.e. one-party consent). See the Invasion of Privacy section of this manual for more on the criminal aspect of 272 § 99.

NAKED EAR EAVESDROPPING

For criminal law, eavesdropping generally refers to overhearing conversations by means of the naked ear unaided by electronic or mechanical devices. Overhearing a conversation by means of the unaided ear is not governed by M.G.L. c. 272 § 99 and typically as long as the law enforcement officer was not trespassing at the time the information is admissible at trial.

Eavesdropping in private dwelling

The U.S. Supreme Court has stated that, "What a person knowingly exposes to the public, even in his own home or office, is not a subject of Fourth Amendment protection."[620]Similar decisions in Massachusetts have echoed the Supreme Court's position.

- In ***Commonwealth v. Dinall***, the Supreme Judicial Court has held that it was proper for police officers to overhear a conversation coming from a second floor apartment where the police officers were standing in the hallway outside that apartment.[621] The hallway outside the apartment was "an area which could be freely entered by anyone" and the

[615]M.G.L.A. c.272, §99.
[616] *Commonwealth v. Damiano*, 444 Mass. 444, 447 (2005), quoting 18 U.S.C. § 2511.
[617] *Commonwealth v. Damiano*, *supra* at 447-448. See 18 U.S.C. § 2515 (2006).
[618] Pollock v. Pollock, 154 F.3d 601, 606 (6th Cir.1998).
[619] See Thompson v. Dulaney, 838 F.Supp. 1535, 1543-1544 (D.Utah 1993).
[620]*Katz v. U.S.*, 389 U.S. 347, 88 S.Ct. 507 (1967).
[621]*Commonwealth v. Dinnall*, 366 Mass. 165, 314 N.E.2d 903 (1974).

police did not use electronic devices nor did they put their ears against a door or wall. The overheard conversation could be used to establish probable cause for a search warrant.

Note: Residents of apartment buildings with a system to exclude non-residents from the common areas, particularly in a building with only a few units (i.e. two family dwelling), are likely to have a reasonable expectation of privacy in their conversations overheard by police outside their door.[622]

- Similarly, in ***Commonwealth v. Anderson***, when a police officer was standing outside an apartment that was under surveillance and overheard an argument emanating from inside the apartment about the quality of cocaine that was being sold therein, that conversation could be recited in a search warrant affidavit as a basis for probable cause.[623]

However, the legality of such eavesdropping depends on whether the person(s) inside the apartment or other private dwelling had a reasonable expectation that their conversation would not be overheard. In the above two cases, the apartments were located in multiple apartment buildings most of which were occupied. In those circumstances, the courts have consistently held that a person cannot complain if outsiders (including police) overhear conversations which are so loud that they can be heard outside the doors and walls of the apartment or other dwelling.[624] A different conclusion was reached in the SJC case of *Commonwealth v. Hall.*[625] In that case, although a three-story building was involved, the defendant was the sole occupant (living in the second floor apartment). Also, he was the landlord and, as such, had control over and a privacy interest in the entire building. Furthermore, the front door through which the police gained surreptitious entry had a lock and buzzer system which the Court noted "was designed to exclude members of the public and to admit none but the defendant's own guest and invitees." The Court also observed that, "police do not have carte blanche to pass through doors that are unlocked or even ajar if the area beyond has a private character." The overheard conversation could not be used in a search warrant affidavit because it violated the defendant's reasonable expectation of privacy.[626]

- In ***Commonwealth v. Panetti***, 406 Mass. 230 (1989), [627]a police eavesdropper climbed into a crawl space immediately under the defendant's apartment and listened to various incriminating statements. The police officer had permission from the landlord. The Court stated that, "[w]hile a person has no reasonable expectation of privacy in conversations that can be overheard by the unaided ear of an eavesdropper lawfully in a contiguous apartment, whether above, beside, or below that person's apartment, a person does have a reasonable expectation of privacy against being overheard by a police eavesdropper who has slipped into a crawl space used for access to pipes and wiring under the defendant's first floor apartment." Since a reasonable expectation of privacy existed, police must have been acting under a warrant, consent, or exigency circumstances. Since they were not, the overheard evidence could not be used.

Custodial eavesdropping

The Supreme Judicial Court has noted that a person in a jail cell or other place of confinement "may expect to be observed and overheard" because of the open front of the cell, blocked only by bars.[628] The court also noted that "evidence is admissible which is obtained by surreptitiously listening to conversations in a place of confinement after arrest."[629] However, if law enforcement informs the detainee that he/she is not being listened to (i.e. the person develops an expectation of privacy) than the communication will likely be protected.

- In the 1965 SJC case of ***Commonwealth v. Guerro,***[630] two police officers positioned themselves near the defendant's cell at the police station on the evening he was incarcerated. The police were able to overhear conversations between the defendant and his family in which he made incriminating statements. The supreme judicial court upheld the admissibility of the police officers' testimony as to what they overheard. The court emphasized that there was no arrangement between the police and the defendant's family to elicit incriminating remarks.

SURVEILLANCE & INTERCEPTING

[622]*Commonwealth v. Hall,* 366 Mass. 790 (1975).
[623]*Commonwealth v. Anderson*, 362 Mass. 74, 284 N.E.2d 219 (1972).
[624]See *Commonwealth v. Boswell*, 374 Mass. 263, 269, 372 N.E.2d 237 (1978). In a common hallway, eavesdropping is not a search in the constitutional sense. *Commonwealth v. Collins*, 11 Mass. App. Ct. 26, 414 N.E.2d 1008 (1981); eavesdropping through a common door between two hotel or motel rooms is permissible.
[625]*Commonwealth v. Hall*, 366 Mass. 790, 323 N.E.2d 319 (1975).
[626]*See alsoCommonwealth v. Panetti*, 406 Mass. 230, 547 N.E.2d 46 (1989); (eavesdropping from a crawl space held invalid).
[627]*Commonwealth v. Panetti*, 406 Mass. 230 (1989),
[628]*Commonwealth v. Wakelin*, 230 Mass. 567, 574, 120 N.E. 209 (1918)[dictograph]; *Commonwealth v. Sacco*, 259 Mass. 128, 141, 156 N.E. 57 (1927).
[629]*Commonwealth v. Dougherty*, 343 Mass. 299, 178 N.E.2d 584 (1961).
[630]*Commonwealth v. Guerro*, 349 Mass. 277, 207 N.E.2d 887 (1965).

- In ***Commonwealth v. Kelley,***[631] the Appeals Court upheld the admissibility of a police officer's testimony as to a conversation inadvertently overheard by the officer between the defendant and an accomplice while in adjoining cells.

Attorney Hanrahan's Note: When an attorney visits a detainee and requests privacy, and privacy is granted, it generally would not be permissible to listen in on the conversation. However, there is no requirement (currently) that requires the police to allow a private conversation between an attorney and an arrestee. Therefore as long as the detainee and the attorney are advised that their conversation is being recorded or monitored there should be no expectation of privacy concerns.

[631] *Commonwealth v. Kelley*, 10 Mass. App. Ct. 847, 406 N.E.2d 1327 (1980).

INTERVIEW & INTERROGATION

In order for a statement made by a person who was subject to custodial interrogation at the time of the statement to be admissible (1) the police must have adhered to the Miranda requirements (see below), (2) the defendant must have knowingly, intelligently and voluntarily waived his rights, and (3) the defendant must have made the statements freely and voluntarily (i.e. free of coercion).[632]

Fifth Amendment - Privilege against Self-Incrimination

The Fifth Amendment to the U.S. Constitution declares that no person "shall be compelled in any criminal case to be a witness against himself. " The Miranda warnings seek to protect that right by requiring the police to inform a person, before custodial interrogation may begin, that, first, he or she has the right to remain silent and, second, that anything he or she does say can and will be used against him or her in court.[633]

Fourteenth Amendment - Due Process

The Fourteenth Amendment to the U.S. Constitution declares that no state shall "deprive any person of life, liberty or property without due process of law." Police interrogation, therefore, must comply with *due process of law*. Additionally, Article 12 of the Massachusetts Constitution likewise requires that interrogation statements be given voluntarily.

Illegally obtained confessions are not admissible: An involuntary or coerced admission or confession is inherently repugnant to due process and cannot be cured by giving the Miranda warnings. Because a coerced admission or confession is unconstitutional, it cannot be used in court, for any reason, against the defendant, whether it was obtained while the defendant was in police custody or otherwise. The test is whether the will of the suspect was so overborne that the statement obtained was not that person's free and voluntary act.[634]

The Commonwealth bears the Burden to prove Statements were Voluntarily, Knowingly & Intelligently Given

If a statement made by a defendant while in custody and being questioned is going to be used against him/her the Commonwealth bears the burden of establishing that a defendant's right to remain silent was " 'voluntarily, knowingly and intelligently' waived."[635] The standard of proof in Massachusetts is "beyond a reasonable doubt."

In determining whether an incriminating statement was made voluntarily, and in compliance with due process of law, a court examines whether, in light of the *totality of the circumstances* surrounding the making of the statement, the will of the defendant was overborne to the extent that the statement was not the result of his or her free and voluntary act.[636] The court considers all of the relevant circumstances surrounding the interrogation and the individual characteristics and conduct of the defendant.[637] Age and inexperience are two factors among many for a judge to consider.[638]

MIRANDA OVERVIEW

The landmark 1966 case of ***Miranda v. Arizona*** created the rule that the police must inform a person who is in custody and being interrogated that they have certain rights (right to an attorney and right not to speak). This is the origin of what is known today as **the Miranda Warnings**. If the police fail to inform the suspect of these rights/warnings, in most cases the statements, and evidence derived from these statements, will be suppressed at trial.

Custody and Interrogation: Anytime a citizen is in custody and he/she is being interrogated the police must advise the person of his/her Miranda rights or the statements will most likely be excluded.

CUSTODY

A suspect is in custody when his or her freedom "is curtailed to a 'degree associated with formal arrest'"[639] or otherwise deprived of his or her freedom of action in a significant way.

INTERVIEW & INTERROGATION

[632] Commonwealth v. Gracia, 379 Mass. 428 (1980).
[633] *See also*, Art. 12, Massachusetts Constitution, for a corresponding state right against self-incrimination.
[634] *Commonwealth v. Cruz*, 373 Mass. 676, 369 N.E.2d 996 (1975).
[635] *Commonwealth v. Hooks*, 375 Mass. 284, 288, 376 N.E.2d 857 (1978), quoting *Miranda v. Arizona*, 384 U.S. 436, 444, 86 S.Ct. 1602, 16 L.Ed.2d 694 (166). See *Commonwealth v. Edwards*, 420 Mass. 666, 669-670, 651 N.E.2d 398 (1995
[636] *Commonwealth v. Magee*, 423 Mass. 381, 668 N.E.2d 339 (1996); see also, *Commonwealth v. Leahy*, 445 Mass. 481, 838 N.E.2d 1220 (2005).
[637] *Commonwealth v. James*, 427 Mass. 312, 693 N.E. 2d 148 (1998).
[638] *Id.*
[639] *Com. v. Morse*, 427 Mass. 117, 123, 691 N.E.2d 566 (1998), quoting *Berkemer v. McCarty*, 468 U.S. 420, 440, 104 S.Ct. 3138, 82 L.Ed.2d 317 (1984).

Based on a reasonable person standard

The critical question in making the custody determination is "whether, considering all the circumstances, a reasonable person in the defendant's position would have believed that he was in custody."[640]

Officer's Subjective Belief is Not Ruling

According to the 2000 Appeals Court case of ***Commonwealth v. Coleman,***[641] the officer's subjective view that an individual under questioning is a suspect, if undisclosed, does not bear on the question of whether the person is in custody for *Miranda* purposes, except where such suspicions are communicated or otherwise manifested to the person being questioned.

Attorney Hanrahan's Note: In other words even if the police officer has no intention to let the suspect walk away this will have no impact on the Miranda requirements unless that intention is communicated to the suspect. It is based on whether a reasonable person would feel that they were in custody under the circumstances, not what was in the officer's head at the time.

Four Indicia of Custody – *The Groome Factors*:[642] The SJC has indicated that four criteria are considered when determining whether or not a person was in custody:

1. **The place of the interrogation**: The location of the interrogation will play a role in whether or not the suspect was "in custody" at the time of the interrogation. The fact that an interrogation takes place at a police station, however, does not *automatically* render it custodial. The test is whether a reasonable person in the suspect's situation would understand that he is free to leave at any time.[643]
    - In ***Commonwealth v. Lopes***, once the handcuffs were removed and the suspect was told that he was not under arrest and that he was free to leave the station, the suspect was no longer in custody and police were free to resume questioning without the need for Miranda despite the fact that the interrogation took place at the station.[644]
    - In ***Commonwealth v. Almonte,*** the SJC ruled that the interrogation was not custodial where defendant spontaneously walked into police station and requested to talk to police).[645]
    - In ***Commonwealth v. Brum***, the SJC ruled that the interrogation was not custodial even though it took place at the police station because it was at the time and place of the defendant's choosing, and the defendant was expressly told that he was free to leave, and the defendant was released after questioning.[646]
    - Even someone incarcerated may not be in custody for the purposes of Miranda if the person has the ability to end the questioning and leave the area. In the 2010 case of ***Commonwealth v. Smith***, the SJC ruled that the defendant who was in prison not to be in custody for purposes of Miranda where he was interviewed in a common area room outside of his cell block. The interview was cordial and not aggressive, and the defendant was the one who controlled when the interview ended.
2. **Whether the police advised the person that he is a suspect**: if a suspect is aware that he is the focus of the investigation this will impact his belief as to whether or not he is free to leave. However, a police officer's undisclosed belief that the person being questioned is a suspect does not bear upon the question of whether he is in custody for Miranda purposes.[647]
3. **The nature of the interrogation:** (e.g. aggressive questioning), a person questioned in a threatening or aggressive manner may reasonably conclude that he is in custody. To the contrary, a conversation that is casual in nature will be less likely to lead a person to believe that they are in custody.
4. **Free to Leave at the Conclusion:** Whether the suspect was free to leave at the end or whether the person was arrested at the completion of the questioning is a strong indicator that the person was not free to leave.

[640] *Commonwealth v. Brumm,* 438 Mass. 103, 111, 777 N.E.2d 1238 (2002), quoting *Commonwealth v. Damiano,* 422 Mass. 10, 13, 660 N.E.2d 660 (1996).
[641] *Commonwealth v. Coleman*, 49 Mass. App. Ct. 150, 727 N.E. 2d 103 (2000).
[642] *Com. v. Groome*, 435 Mass. 201, 211-212 (2001)
[643] *California v. Beheler*, 463 U.S. 1121-25 (1983).
[644] *Commonwealth v. Lopes*, 455 Mass. 147, 163 (2009)
[645] *Commonwealth v. Almonte,* 444 Mass. 511, 517-18 (2005)
[646] *Commonwealth v. Brum*, 438 Mass. 103, 111-12 (2002)
[647] *Commonwealth v. Groome*, 435 Mass. 201, 212 n.13 (2001)

There is no specific formula for weighing the relevant factors of custody,[648] but "rarely is any single factor conclusive."[649]

Attorney Hanrahan's Note: As you can see there is no bright line rule on determining when someone is in custody for the purposes of Miranda, each circumstance is slightly different. For this reason, it is often legally prudent to advise the suspect of this/her Miranda rights if there is any possibility that the court may later find the person was in custody. Otherwise the statements may be lost.

INTERROGATION

Basically if the questions are accusatory or designed to elicit an incriminating response the questioning will be considered interrogation. However, interrogation is not limited to typical questioning. In fact, an interrogation can take place without any words at all. There are two types of interrogation:

Express Questioning

Express questioning simply means verbal or written questions intended to elicit a response from the suspect. This is the most common type of interrogation. For example, a police officer asks a suspect "Did you kill your wife?" This would be a clear example of express questioning as it is clearly designed to elicit an incriminating response.

The Functional Equivalent

The term *functional equivalent* encompasses "any words or actions on the part of the police (other than those normally attendant to arrest and custody) that the police should know are reasonably likely to elicit an incriminating response from the suspect."[650]

- In ***Brewer v. Williams***, a deeply religious defendant was charged with the murder of a ten year old female. The body of the girl could not be found. The defendant was being transported by the police in a cruiser. Although the police officers did not question the defendant, an officer, aware of the defendant's religious convictions, commented to another officer, "this little girl should be entitled to a Christian burial." As a result, the defendant made various incriminating statements and agreed to take the detectives to find the body. The Court suppressed the incriminating statements because the conduct of the police was intended and likely to illicit an incriminating response,[651]

At times, an interrogation could take place merely by the actions of the police. For instance, walking an accomplice by the detained defendant, with the hopes that it would elicit an incriminating response, could be considered an interrogation for the purposes of Miranda.

STATE ACTION

Generally, Constitutional protections protect people from the government, in particular the law enforcement. When the government is involved the term often used is "state action."

Non-Government Actors

Private citizens

Typically, actions by private citizens do not protect the defendant from uncovered evidence that would otherwise be suppressed if the same action was taken by a state actor. However, if the private citizen is working on behalf of the police (or the government) the person will be deemed to be an *agent* of the police and state action will most likely be found.

If a private citizen initiates the conduct on his or her own, agent status will not be found. This is true even if the police (1) reward the citizen for his or her cooperation and/or (2) knew about his or her intended conduct in advance.[652] For example, a department store security guard is not required to provide Miranda warning before questioning a shoplifter.

Statements elicited by a private citizen who is acting on behalf of the police are inadmissible if the Miranda warnings were not given and a custodial setting existed.[653]

[648] See *Commonwealth v. Haas,* 373 Mass. 545, 552, 369 N.E.2d 692 (1977), *S.C.,* 398 Mass. 806, 501 N.E.2d 1154 (1986).
[649] *Commonwealth v. Bryant,* 390 Mass. 729, 737, 459 N.E.2d 792 (1984).
[650] *Commonwealth v. Rubio,*27 Mass.App.Ct. 506, 512, 540 N.E.2d 189 (1989), quoting from *Rhode Island v. Innis,* 446 U.S. at 301, 100 S.Ct. 1682. See *Commonwealth v. Morse,* 427 Mass. 117, 123, 691 N.E.2d 566 (1998).
[651] *Brewer v. Williams*, 430 U.S. 387 (1977)
[652] *Commonwealth v. Harmon*, 410 Mass. 425 (1991); *Commonwealth v. Rancourt*, 399 Mass. 269, 503 N.E.2d 960 (1987); *Commonwealth v. Paradiso*, 24 Mass. App. Ct. 142, 507 N.E.2d 258 (1987).

For a private citizen to constitute an "agent", the police must initiate the citizen's help. The police must take the first step.[654] That is the police must initiate, or otherwise direct, the citizen to take action.

Quasi-Government Actors

Public School Officials

Questioning by public school officials, who are not acting on behalf of the police, are not required to give Miranda warnings prior to questioning a student[655].

DCF workers

Typically questioning by DCF workers do not require Miranda warning absent some coordination or prompting by the police. Although DCF has its own warnings that it requires its case workers to advise to parents and guardians of children under certain circumstances.

Private Individuals and the Fourteenth Amendment

As previously mentioned, custodial interrogation does not apply to a private citizen who is not acting in conjunction with police.[656] However, although *Miranda* does not apply to questioning by non-law enforcement officers, the Fourteenth Amendment does.

Coercion

Courts will not admit incriminating statements if they were made involuntarily as the result of coercion - no matter who elicited them.[657] This is the case whether the statements are the products of physical or mental coercion.[658]

The SJC has declared that coercion applied by a private party may render a defendant's confession to that private party involuntary, requiring that the confession be suppressed as violative of due process.[659]

The Commonwealth has the burden of proving to the judge that the statements were voluntarily made.[660]

NON-MIRANDA SITUATIONS & EXCEPTIONS

It is useful to distinguish specific circumstances which do not require the Miranda warnings because interrogation is not involved, or because, although there is questioning by the police, the person being questioned is not in custody, the questioning was not conducted by the police or there is a rare exception to the rule.[661]

Volunteered, Spontaneous Statements

Statements which are spontaneous, unprovoked and volunteered by a defendant are not the product of a custodial interrogation conducted in violation of rights which *Miranda* warnings were designed to protect.

- In ***Commonwealth v. Duguay***, a statement made by the defendant as he rode in a police cruiser after agreeing to accompany the police officer to the station, that "if I tell you what happened, you'll put me in jail for the rest of my life," was voluntary, where the defendant blurted out the statement without prompting. The police officer's comments in that case as the defendant rode in the police cruiser to the police station, "just tell them what happened," was not tantamount to questioning, for the purposes of determining the admissibility of the statements that followed. The officer did not initiate the conversation, but merely answered the defendant's question about what the police wanted to know.[662]

- In ***Commonwealth v. Mitchell,*** a statement by the defendant under arrest for drug distribution that "I was just trying to make some money for Christmas. I got no job" in response to an officer's statement "tough luck getting locked up so close to Christmas" was deemed to be a spontaneous statement.[663]

[653] *Maine v. Moulton*, 474 U.S. 159, 106 S.Ct. 496 (1985).
[654] *Massiah v. U.S.*, 377 U.S. 201, 84 S.Ct. 1199 (1964) (agent status was found where government pre-arranged to provide benefits to inmate in return for obtaining statements from co-conspirator).
[655] *Com. v. Snyder*, 413 Mass. 521 (1992)
[656] *Commonwealth v. Tynes*, 400 Mass. 369, 510 N.E.2d 244 (1987); *Commonwealth v. Smallwood*, 379 Mass. 878, 401 N.E.2d 802 (1980).
[657] *Commonwealth v. Benoit*, 410 Mass. 506, 410 N.E.2d 506 (1991); *Commonwealth v. Blanchette*, 409 Mass. 99 (1991); *Commonwealth v. Libran*, 405 Mass. 634, 543 N.E.2d 5 (1989).
[658] *Commonwealth v. Mahnke*, 368 Mass. 662, 672, 335 N.E.2d 660 (1975), *cert. den.* in 425 U.S. 959, 96 S.Ct. 1739 (1976).
[659] *Commonwealth v. Brandwein*, 435 Mass. 623, 760 N.E.2d 724 (2002).
[660] Commonwealth v. Allen, 395 Mass. 448 (1985).
[661] *E.g., Commonwealth v. Wood*, 36 Mass. App. Ct. 3504, 631 N.E.2d 1075 (1994) (routine booking questions are not generally interrogation questions because they are not intended or likely to prompt an incriminating response); See *Pennsylvania v. Muniz*, 496 U.S. 582, 110 S.Ct. 2638, 110 L.Ed.2d 528 (1990).
[662] *Commonwealth v. Duguay*, 430 Mass. 397, 720 N.E. 2d 458 (1999); *Commonwealth v. Ferrer*, 68 Mass. App. Ct. 544, *** (2007) (officer's response to a spontaneous statement was not the functional equivalent to an interrogation but rather a "natural reflex invited by the defendant's comment"); *Commonwealth v. Gittens*, 55 Mass. App. Ct. 14, 150 *** (2002).
[663] *Commonwealth v. Mitchell* 47 Mass. App. Ct. 178, 180-81 (1999)

The Presence of an Attorney

In ***Commonwealth v. Simon***, the SJC ruled that Miranda warnings were not required when the suspect was questioned by police in a custodial setting when the suspect's attorney was present during questioning and the suspect had an opportunity to consult with his attorney prior to questioning.[664]

Attorney Hanrahan's Note: Despite the holding in *Simon* I strongly recommend that you continue to advise Miranda warnings when otherwise required even if the defendant's attorney may be present. A different set of circumstances may result in a different result than the one in *Simon.*

The Roadside Questioning Exception

In the 1997 SJC case of ***Vanhouton v. Commonwealth***,[665] the court reiterated the general rule that routine traffic stops, including O.U.I. stops, are non-custodial and do not require the officer to give Miranda warnings before asking the operator questions about his or her possible intoxication. Moreover, the *Vanhouton* decision went on to state that alphabet tests, which are routinely part of field sobriety tests, do not constitute "interrogation for *Miranda* purposes."[666]

The questioning of a suspect who otherwise happens to be in a vehicle does not meet the roadside questioning exception. The roadside questioning exception applies only to routine motor vehicle stops. For instance, if a police officer stopped a vehicle because the operator was a suspect in a recent breaking and entering offense Miranda warnings would be most likely be required in order to question the suspect about the crime. The exception only applies to routine motor vehicle stops.

The Public Safety Exception

The Supreme Court has recognized a limited exception to the Miranda requirements where police are confronted by a situation which requires a few limited questions to ensure the safety of the police officers or other persons and the urgency of the situation makes it unreasonable for police to hesitate in their questioning long enough to give the Miranda warnings.

- In ***New York v. Quarles***,[667] police pursued an armed rape suspect into a grocery store. When he was arrested, he had no weapon but did have an empty holster. Police asked "where's the gun?" before advising the suspect of his Miranda rights. The Supreme Court allowed the suspect's response and the gun into evidence. An unattended gun in public poses a serious public safety danger.

Attorney Hanrahan's Note: The *public* safety exception is not limited to public locations. For instance, if a similar event occurred in a private dwelling the officer would not have provide Miranda warnings before asking where the weapon was located.

Undercover law enforcement personnel exception

The Supreme Court has held that undercover law enforcement personnel need not provide Miranda warnings to suspects.[668]

Routine booking questions

As the U.S. Supreme Court case of ***Rhode Island v. Innis*** indicates, questions which are normally attendant to arrest and custody — e.g., booking questions — are not interrogating questions because they are not likely to elicit incriminating responses.[669]

- In ***Com. v. Ramirez***[670], the defendant gave a false name during booking. This was later used against him even though he made the statement without being advised of his Miranda warnings. The court upheld the admissibility of the statements under the routine booking question exception.

The Massachusetts Appeals Court, however, has said that booking questions may, in rare instances, constitute interrogating questions.[671]

---

[664] *Comm. v. Simon,* 456 Mass. 280 (2010).
[665] *Vanhouton v. Commonwealth*, 424 Mass. 327, 676 N.E.2d 460 (1997).
[666] See also, *Commonwealth v. Wholley*, 429 Mass. 1010, 709 N.E. 2d 1117 (1999).
[667] *New York v. Quarles*, 467 U.S. 81, 104 S.Ct. 2626 (1984).
[668] *See,Illinois v. Perkins*, 110 S.Ct. 2394 (1990).
[669] *Rhode Island v. Innis,* 446 U.S. 291, 100 S.Ct. 1682 (1980).
[670] *Com. v. Ramirez,*55 Mass.App.Ct. 224 (2004).
[671] *Commonwealth v. Woods*, 36 Mass. App. Ct. 950, 631 N.E.2d 1025, *rev. granted* 418 Mass. 1104, 638 N.E.2d 913 (1994) (held asking unemployed arrestee where he worked was incriminating since he was arrested while processing a large amount of cash).

Caution should be used when asking "booking" questions related to employment and occupation if there is a chance that these types of statements may be used against the defendant (i.e. drug dealing). In situations like this it is best to provide Miranda warnings prior to asking booking questions.

- In the 2011 case of ***Com. v. Dixon***, the Appeals Court suppressed statements made by the defendant when he responded to a question "was a weapon used" made by the booking officer to the arresting officer. The question was prompted by the booking software which required an answer. The arresting officer was standing beside the defendant at the time and the defendant believed that the question was directed at him and subsequently made an incriminating response. The Court ruled that the deciding factor is whether a reasonable person in the defendant's position would have perceived the question to be interrogation. The court ruled under these circumstances a reasonable person would have.

Attorney Hanrahan's Note: I recommend that you provide Miranda warnings before asking routine booking questions to avoid the possibility of a legal challenge later.

General Investigative Questioning

Non-custodial preliminary or investigative questioning need not be preceded by the Miranda warnings.[672] The U.S. Supreme Court stated in the *Miranda* decision, "General on-the-scene questioning as to facts surrounding a crime or other general questioning of citizens in the fact-finding process is not affected by the Miranda decision."[673] Thus, there is no requirement that warnings be given prior to general on-the-scene questioning as to the facts surrounding a crime or other general questioning of citizens in the fact-finding process.[674]

Questioning during Temporary Detentions

The police are permitted to temporarily detain a person if they have reasonable suspicion that the person has, is, or about to commit a crime (see Temporary Detention section for more). The intent of permitting this type of brief detention is to permit the police to conduct a brief inquiry to determine whether or not criminal activity is actually involved. If not, the person should be promptly released.

In ***Berkemer v. McCarty,*** the US Supreme Court ruled that in Terry-type situations, although the suspect is not free to leave, this type of detention is not the type of intrusion needed to amount to "custody" which would trigger Miranda. This was confirmed under Massachusetts law in the 1986 case of ***Com. v. Shine***.

However, in the 2005 case of ***Com. v. Hilton***, the SJC stated "we have encouraged police to give Miranda warnings prior to the point at which an encounter becomes custodial rather than wait until the exact moment when the warnings are constitutionally required".[675]

- In the 1996 case of ***Commonwealth v. Damiano***[676], the SJC ruled that Miranda warnings were required when at the scene of a homicide, before the suspect was placed under arrest, the suspect was handcuffed and placed in the back of a police cruiser and questioned about the incident. The SJC ruled no reasonable person would have felt that they were free to leave under the circumstances.

If Miranda warnings are offered when they may not be constitutionally necessary they must still be adhered to nonetheless if the suspect invokes his rights. In the 2012 case of ***Commonwealth v. Baye***, the SJC referred to a Federal District Court case wherein the Court stated "where the police provide precustodial warnings but then ignore the defendant's attempts to avail himself of those rights, the "coercive effect of continued interrogation [is] greatly increased because the suspect [could] believe that the police `promises' to provide the suspect's constitutional rights were untrustworthy, and that the police would continue to" ignore subsequent invocations, rendering such invocations futile.[677]

Attorney Hanrahan's Recommendation: In practice this is a very grey area of the law. Many statements have been lost in what would seem like a Terry-type situation because Miranda warnings were not imparted. In practice, it is often best to give the Miranda warnings anytime a person is not free to leave and is being asked questions that are designed, or may be interpreted as being designed, to elicit an incriminating response. Particularly in a serious case where the statements may be vital to the prosecution. If the person then invokes those rights you must honor their invocation of

[672] *See,Commonwealth v. Podlaski*, 377 Mass. 339, 385 N.E.2d 1379 (1979) and *Commonwealth v. Borodine*, 371 Mass. 1, 353 N.E.2d 649 (1976), U.S. *cert. den.*in 429 U.S. 1049 (1976); *Commonwealth v. Doyle*, 12 Mass. App. Ct. 786, 429 N.E.2d 346 (1981); *Commonwealth v. Callahan*, 401 Mass. 627, 519 N.E.2d 245 (1988).
[673] *Commonwealth v. Smallwood*, 379 Mass. 878, 401 N.E.2d 802 (1980).
[674] *Com. v. Merritt*, 14 Mass.app.Ct. 601, 604 (1982), quoting from *Miranda v. Arizona*
[675] *Commonwealth v. Hilton*, 443 Mass. 597, 610 n.7 (2005)
[676] *Com. v. Damiano*, 422 Mass. 10 (1996).
[677] Tukes v. Dugger, 911 F.2d 508, 516 n.11 (11th Cir. 1990), cert. denied sub nom. Singletary v. Tukes, 502 U.S. 898 (1991).

rights and cease questioning or face the possibility of losing the statements, even if the Miranda warning were not otherwise required. Each case is different and it is the astute investigator who can carefully navigate this grey area.

PROVIDING THE MIRANDA WARNINGS

The Actual Miranda Warnings

Prior to custodial interrogation by police, the person must be advised that:

1. You have the right to remain silent.
2. Anything you say can and will be used against you in a court of law.
3. You have the right to consult with an attorney before answering questions and to have an attorney present during any questioning.
4. If you cannot afford an attorney one will be appointed to you by the Commonwealth.
5. If you decide to answer questions you may stop at anytime (this fifth warning is not legally required but recommended by Massachusetts Courts).

Each of the four required Miranda provisions must be given *in substance* (but not necessarily word for word) to be valid.[678] If the warnings are only partially provided the subsequent statements will most likely be deemed invalid.

Important note: ensure that your Miranda warning forms and cards are not too narrowly defined. In the 2014 case of ***Commonwealth v. Wadlington***, the Miranda warnings provided included the non-required fifth warning and indicated that the suspect "may stop at anytime **to talk with a lawyer**." The SJC indicated that this was misleading because a suspect can stop at anytime for any reason not to just speak with a lawyer.

Timing of the Miranda warnings

The warnings should be provided prior to the commencement of questioning. Once a statement is obtained in violation of Miranda a subsequent advisement of rights will not cure the violation and the statements will be subject to suppression.

Break in the stream of questioning

Where a suspect has begun to speak before being read his or her Miranda rights, and the police wish to give those rights, they must first "break the stream of the questioning" before reading the warning and continuing the interrogation.[679] This typically can be accomplished, if at all, by letting a substantial amount of time pass before proceeding with questioning. Miranda warnings should also be provided before resuming, even if the warnings were previously provided.

Notice in writing is preferred but not required

Although not legally required, the better practice of providing a suspect of his/her Miranda rights would be to utilize a Miranda Rights form (see for sample form on next page). This will help rebut any claim that the suspect was not advised of his/her rights.

- In the 2002 case of ***Commonwealth v. Ortiz,*** the SJC ruled that the defendant made knowing, voluntary, and intelligent waiver of *Miranda* rights, though he refused to sign the Miranda waiver, where the defendant gave no indication that he did not want to be questioned further and continued talking despite his understanding that he had a right to remain silent. [680]

Given the potential for one's statements being found involuntary and inadmissible, it is advisable that a written waiver be signed by the suspect, if possible.[681] If he refuses, a waiver may, nonetheless, be indicated by a person's actions and words even if he or she refuses to sign a written waiver.[682]

[678] *Commonwealth v. Woods*, 419 Mass. 366, 645 N.E.2d 1153 (1995); *Commonwealth v. Miranda*, 37 Mass. App. Ct. 939, 641 N.E.2d 139 (1994); *Commonwealth v. Osachuk*, 418 Mass. 229, 635 N.E.2d 1182 (1994); *Commonwealth v. Adams*, 389 Mass. 265, 450 N.E.2d 149 (1983).
[679] *Commonwealth v. Smith*, 412 Mass. 823, 593 N.E.2d 1288 (1992).
[680] *Commonwealth v. Ortiz,* 435 Mass. 569, 760 N.E.2d 282 (2002).
[681] *Commonwealth v. Reed*, 417 Mass. 558, 631 N.E.2d 552 (1994).
[682] *North Carolina v. Butler*, 441 U.S. 369, 99 S.Ct. 1755 (1979).

Reading from a Card

In ***Tague v. Louisiana***,[683] the U.S. Supreme Court found no evidence of a knowing, voluntary and intelligent waiver. This was due largely to the police officer's failure to prove that he gave the warnings properly and that the person understood them and knowingly waived them. The officer testified that he read the suspect the Miranda warnings from a card but <u>he could not produce the card at court nor could he recall the warnings from memory</u>. Moreover, the officer did not ask the suspect if he understood the rights of which he was advised.

The Supreme Judicial Court, since 1978, has recommended that the police *read* Miranda warnings from a card, rather than providing the same from memory.[684]

Police should carry Miranda cards with them, use them to advise a person of the warnings and have the same or an identical card available to be admitted into evidence at trial.

In the 2006 of ***Commonwealth v. Dagraca,*** *the* Supreme Judicial Court ruled that the Miranda warnings were incomplete and that accordingly the statements should not be admitted where the statements were recited from memory and not from a card.[685]

Errors by police not always fatal

Due to the enormous weight of a confession and the strict legal requirements surrounding their introduction at trial officers should use extreme caution to ensure that the rules and laws surrounding interrogations are properly followed. Although, minor technicalities and errors by the police will not always result in a confession or incriminating statements being suppressed, particularly when the defendant had been advised of his rights on more than one occasion.

- In ***Commonwealth v. Gaboriault***, a police detective's use of term "formality" in describing a second recitation of Miranda warnings given to a murder defendant did not render the warnings inadequate. The defendant was read Miranda warnings three times, and after all three readings, indicated a willingness to speak with officers, he signed a Miranda card acknowledging rights he was given, prior to his statement, he never asked for an attorney or whether he could make a telephone call, and he was given more time to reflect on his waiver because of malfunctioning video equipment in the first interrogation room, which required him to wait until another room was prepared.[686] Despite this decision minimizing the Miranda rights may lead to suppression and is not recommended.

  Note: Avoid statements such as "this is just a formality" or similar statements which minimize the importance of the suspect's rights as these types of statements may be a negative factor when weighing the validity of a waiver.

- In ***Commonwealth v. Scott,*** an alleged failure of an officer who gave the first *Miranda* warnings to the defendant to recite the warnings in their entirety did not require suppression of the defendant's subsequent statements, where other officers on two separate occasions advised the defendant of the full *Miranda* warnings before he made his statement, and the defendant read and signed the card that had the warnings printed on it before he gave his statement.[687]

Duration of the Miranda warnings

According to the SJC, *"Miranda* warnings, once given, are not to be accorded unlimited efficacy or perpetuity."[688] Despite this "there is no requirement that an accused be continually reminded of his rights once he has waived them."[689] However, where there has been a significant lapse of time between initial Miranda warnings and inculpatory statements, "the ultimate question is: Did the defendant, with a full knowledge of his legal rights, knowingly relinquish them?"[690]

It is good practice to re-advise a detained suspect of his/her Miranda rights after a break in questioning, or even during a prolonged interrogation. However, from a strategic standpoint continually advising the suspect of his/her Miranda rights may prompt the suspect to stop talking.

If a suspect is transferred from one agency to another the better practice would be to re-advise the suspect of the Miranda warnings once the custody has been transferred.

---

[683] *Tague v. Louisiana*, 444 U.S. 469, 100 S.Ct. 652 (1980).
[684] *See, Commonwealth v. Lewis*, 372 Mass. 203, 205 (1978): *Commonwealth v. Ayala*, 29 Mass. App. Ct. 592, 563 N.E.2d 249 (1990).
[685] *Commonwealth v. Dagraca*, 447 Mass. 546, 854 N.E.2nd 1249 (2006).
[686] *Commonwealth v. Gaboriault*, 439 Mass. 84, 785 N.E.2d 691 (2003).
[687] *Commonwealth v.* Scott, 430 Mass. 351, 718 N.E. 2d 1248 (1999).
[688] *Commonwealth v. Cruz* 373Mass. 676, 687, 369 N.E.2d. 996 (1977). Quoting *United States v. Hopkins,* 433 F2d. 1041, 1045 (5th Cir.1970).
[689] *Commonwealth v. Mello,* 420 Mass. 375, 385-386, 649 N.E.2d. 1106 (1995), quoting *Biddy v. Diamond,* 516 F2d. 118, 122 (5th Cir. 1975), cert. denied, 425 U.S. 950, 96 S.Ct. 1724, 48 L.Ed.2d. 194 (1976).
[690] *Commonwealth v. Silanskas, supra* at 687, 369 N.E.2.d. 996.*Commonwealth v. Sirios* 437 Mass. 845, 777 N.E.2d. 125 (2002).

MIRANDA RIGHTS & RECORDING FORM
MIRANDA ADVISEMENTS

Before asking you any questions, it is my duty to advise you of your rights.

1. You have the right to remain silent.
2. If you choose to speak, anything you say can and will be used against you in a court of law.
3. You have the right to consult with a lawyer before answering any questions, and you may have a lawyer with you during questioning.
4. If you cannot afford a lawyer and want one, a lawyer will be provided for you at no cost before any questioning.
5. If you decide to answer questions, you may stop at any time.

Do you understand each of the rights I have just read to you?

□ Yes □ No ______ Initials

6. Having these rights in mind, do you wish to speak with me now?

□ Yes □ No ______ Initials

Signature____

Officer Witness ____

Date: ________________ Time ______ Location: ________________________

TAPE RECORDING

If recording not offered state reason why:
____

It is the policy of this department to record all interviews so that there is a record of our discussion. Do we have your permission to tape record our discussion?
□ Yes, I agree to have our discussion recorded. ______ Initials
□ No, I do not want our discussion recorded. ______ Initials

Be advised that you may change your decision at any time during this interview.

Signature ____

Officer witnessing ID ____

Date: ________________ Time ________ Location: ________________________
□ Having at first decided not to be recorded, I now choose to have the rest of my interview recorded.
Current Time: ____________ ______Initials
□ Having at first agreed to be recorded, I now choose to have the remainder of my interview not recorded.
Current Time: ____________ ______Initials

Signature ______________________________Date: ________________ Time ______

INTERVIEW & INTERROGATION

WAIVING MIRANDA RIGHTS

Once a person has been given the Miranda warnings, he or she may waive any or all of the rights contained therein, but he or she must do so in a knowing, voluntary and intelligent manner.[691] The state bears the burden of proving beyond a reasonable doubt that the defendant's waiver of his or her Miranda rights was valid.[692]

The preferred method of waiving rights is by way of a written waiver signed by the suspect. However, a signed waiver is not legally required. In fact, even when presented with a written waiver the suspect may refuse to sign it yet still waive his or her rights in other ways. A suspect may waive his or her rights by verbally agreeing to answer questions or a waiver may be implied by the suspect's words or actions.[693] For instance, after being advised of his Miranda rights the suspect begins to discuss the circumstances of the incident for which he was detained.

What if the Suspect Claims that he/she does not understand?

If the suspect claims that he or she does not understand the rights they should be repeated in their entirety.

Totality of the circumstances

In making the determination as to whether the suspect waived his/her rights, courts examine factors such as "promises or other inducements, conduct of the defendant, the defendant's age, education, intelligence and emotional stability, experience with and in the criminal justice system, physical and mental condition, the initiator of the discussion of a deal or leniency ... and the details of the interrogation, including the recitation of Miranda warnings."[694]

Testing the validity of incriminating statements made by a defendant who is in custody involves a two-fold inquiry:

1. whether there has been a knowing and intelligent waiver of *Miranda* rights, and
2. whether the statements were voluntary and not the result of coercion or intimidation.[695]

Both inquiries are determined in light of the totality of the circumstances and share many of the same relevant factors.[696]

To be valid the waiver must be made voluntarily, knowingly, and intelligently."[697] Relevant factors to consider when determining the validity of a defendant's *Miranda* waiver and voluntariness of the statement include, but are not limited to:[698]

a. Physical and mental condition of the defendant,
b. Promises or other inducements made by law enforcement,
c. Conduct of the defendant,
d. The defendant's age, education, intelligence, and emotional stability,
e. Experience with and in the criminal justice system,
f. The discussion of a deal or leniency, and
g. The details of the interrogation, including the recitation of *Miranda* warnings.

FACTORS THAT MAY INFLUENCE THE ADMISSIBILITY OF STATEMENTS/WAIVER OF RIGHTS

The presence of one or more factors suggesting a statement may have been made involuntarily is not always sufficient to render a statement involuntary.[699] The Court will look at the ***totality of the circumstances***. However, certain conditions or actions are more likely than others to cause the court to rule the statement inadmissible. The following are conditions that the investigators should be familiar with:

[691] *Miranda v. Arizona*, (cited above); *Commonwealth v. Magee*, 423 Mass. 381, 668 N.E.2d 339 (1996).
[692] *Commonwealth v. Edwards,* 420 Mass. 666, 651 N.E.2d 398 (1995); *Commonwealth v. Rodriguez*, 425 Mass. 361, 682 N.E. 2d 591 (1997).
[693] *Com. v. Aarhus*, 387 Mass. 735 (1982).
[694] Commonwealth v. Tolan, 453 Mass. 634, 642 (2009), quoting Commonwealth v. Mandile, 397 Mass. 410, 413 (1986)
[695] *Commonwealth v. LeBlanc*, 433 Mass. 549, 744 N.E.2d 33,(2001).
[696] *Commonwealth v. Hunter*, 426 Mass. 715, 690 N.E. 2d 815 (1998); *Commonwealth v. Hunter*, 426 Mass. 715, 690 N.E. 2d 815 (1998).
[697] *Commonwealth v. Pucillo*, 427 Mass. 108, 692 N.E. 2d 15 (1998).*Commonwealth v.* Scott, 430 Mass. 351, 718 N.E. 2d 1248 (1999); *Commonwealth v. Edwards,* 420 Mass. 666, 669-670, 651 N.E.2d 398 (1995), citing *Miranda v. Arizona*, 384 U.S. 436, 86 S.Ct. 1602, 16 L.Ed.2d 694 (1966).
[698] *Commonwealth* v. *Tolan*, 453 Mass. 634, 642 (2009), quoting *Commonwealth* v. *Mandile,* 397 Mass. 410, 413 (1986)
[699] *Commonwealth v. Pucillo*, 427 Mass. 108, 692 N.E. 2d 15 (1998).*Commonwealth v.* Scott, 430 Mass. 351, 718 N.E. 2d 1248 (1999); *Commonwealth v. Edwards,* 420 Mass. 666, 669-670, 651 N.E.2d 398 (1995), citing *Miranda v. Arizona*, 384 U.S. 436, 86 S.Ct. 1602, 16 L.Ed.2d 694 (1966).

DEFENDANT'S CONDITION MAY EFFECT WAIVER OF RIGHTS AND VOLUNTARINESS OF STATEMENTS

Drugs and intoxication

In deciding whether one's statements were *knowingly* and *voluntarily* made, the court will also consider whether the suspect was under the influence of intoxicating liquor or drugs (prescription or illicit) at the time the statements were made. If it is determined that the suspect was incapable of withholding the information, it cannot be admitted against him or her.[700] However, just because someone was under the influence at the time of the waiver it does not automatically invalidate that waiver.

The court will consider a person's statements involuntary if it concludes that the statements stem from drug abuse, withdrawal or a concussion.[701] While there is no per se rule excluding as involuntary statements made during drug withdrawal, the prosecution bears a "heavy burden" to show that the defendant's waiver of his Miranda rights, and his subsequent confession, were voluntary.[702]

- In the 2004 case of ***Commonwealth v. Ringuette,***[703] the Court's consideration of "the totality of relevant circumstances,"[704] led it to conclude that the defendant's statements were properly admitted. In *Ringuette,* the defendant's confession was voluntary though he was suffering post-ingestion effects from using cocaine.[705] The defendant appeared to officers to be sober, coherent, responsive, and in control of his faculties. He responded appropriately to general questions about his background and openly discussed his addiction to crack cocaine, and after the defendant's statement regarding the purse snatchings had been reduced to writing, he read the statement and asked officers to remove his alleged accomplice's name.[706]
- In the 2007 case of ***Commonwealth v. LeClair***, the waiver was still valid despite the defendant's admission of drug ingestion just prior to the questioning where the defendant appeared lucid and cooperative, despite crying at one point and appearing nervous. [707]

Police not required to Administer Sobriety Tests before Questioning

In *Commonwealth v. Pina*, the police observed the defendant over several hours and believed, based on his conduct and their prior experiences with him, that he was not intoxicated, despite their recognition of indications that he had consumed alcohol. The failure of the police to test a defendant's sobriety before interrogating him did not require the suppression of his statements.[708]

Attorney Hanrahan's recommendation: if a suspect who is being questioned has consumed alcohol and/or drugs prior to the interrogation it is a good practice to ask general knowledge questions, such as "what month is it?", "who is the President of the United State?" and similar general knowledge questions. These types of questions may reveal whether or not the person is so impaired as to understand what is occurring. Additionally, the fact that the defendant was able to answer these types of questions may be used later to counter claims by the defense that the defendant was so impaired that he/she was incoherent and incapable of waiving rights.

Mental condition and mental state

The suspect's mental capacity and his mental state may affect his ability to waive his Miranda rights or to otherwise voluntarily make a statement[709] but even those with mental deficiencies may still waive Miranda rights.

- In ***Commonwealth v. Davis,*** the investigator questioned a murder suspect in the third-person. The suspect was diagnosed with border-line personality disorder (which was unknown to the officer at the time) and at times went by the nickname of "skipper." The investigator asked the suspect about the actions of "skipper" as if skipper was a different person. The subsequent confession was admissible. The court will not necessarily find that a statement is involuntary simply because it was given by a suspect's alter-ego.[710]
- In ***Commonwealth v. LeBeau,*** a murder defendant was not suffering from sleep deprivation at time of his inculpatory statement to police, despite fact that defendant was at police barracks from approximately

[700] *Commonwealth v. Waters*, 420 Mass. 276, 649 N.E.2d 724 (1995); *Commonwealth v. Benoit*, 410 Mass. 506, 574 N.E.2d 347 (1991); *Commonwealth v. Libran*, 4056 Mass. 634 (1989).
[701] *Commonwealth v. Allen*, 395 Mass. 448, 480 N.E.2d 630 (1985).
[702] *Commonwealth v. Paszko*, 391 Mass. 164, 175-176, 461 N.E.2d 222 (1984) (citations omitted).
[703] *Commonwealth v. Ringuette,* 80 Mass.App.Ct. 351, 801 N.E.2d 813 (2004).
[704] *Commonwealth v. Mahnke,* 368 Mass. 662, 680, 335 N.E.2d 660 (1975).
[705] *Commonwealth v. Ringuette*, 801 N.E.2d 813, 60 Mass.App.Ct. 351 (2003).
[706] *See id.*;*Commonwealth v. LeClair,* 68 Mass. App. Ct. 482, *** (2007) (numerous factors demonstrated that the defendant's ingestion of narcotics did not hinder his ability to waive his Miranda rights).
[707] *Commonwealth v. LeClair*, 68 Mass. App. Ct. 482 (2007)
[708] *Commonwealth v. Pina*, 430 Mass. 66, 713 N.E. 2d 944 (1999).
[709] *See, e.g.,Commonwealth v. Hooks*, 38 Mass. App. Ct. 301, 647 N.E.2d 440 (1995) (ninety minute delay between giving Miranda and initiating questioning did not nullify suspect's voluntary willingness). *Commonwealth v. Mello*, 420 Mass. 375, 635 N.E.2d 5 (1995) (six hour break between original waiver and subsequent confession which was admissible).
[710] *Commonwealth v. Davis*, 403 Mass. 575, 531 N.E.2d 577 (1988).

INTERVIEW & INTERROGATION

midnight to 7:15 in the morning with no sleep prior to giving statement at issue; the defendant never indicated that he was tired or otherwise physically uncomfortable, nor did he ask the officers to take break so that he could sleep or return home, and the officers testified that they did not observe any signs of intoxication or other mental incapacity.[711]

Mental capacity and intelligence

While illiteracy and low intelligence are factors in examining the totality of the circumstances, a mentally deficient adult may make an effective waiver.[712] People with low intelligence can waive their *Miranda* rights. However, circumstances and techniques of custodial interrogation which pass constitutional muster when applied to an adult of normal intelligence may not be constitutionally tolerable when applied to one who is mentally deficient.

- According to the 1997 SJC case of ***Commonwealth v. Hartford,*** the police, and ultimately judges, must give special attention to whether a person of low intelligence properly waived their Miranda rights and voluntarily and knowingly made a statement to the police.[713] In *Hartford* the Court found that a person with an IQ of 73 had properly waived his Miranda rights. It also noted that a person with limited reasoning ability does not have to be afforded the same protections concerning the waiver of rights as are extended to juveniles.
- This position was just recently reiterated in the 2012 case of ***Commonwealth v. Delacruz***, although the defendant had some intellectual disabilities ("borderline mentally retarded") this fact did not automatically make his statements inadmissible.

Physical Condition of the Suspect

The physical condition of the suspect may also play a role into whether or not the suspect was able to waive his/her rights.

- In ***Mincey v. Arizona*** (1978) the suspect was hospitalized in intensive care and was slipping in and out of consciousness. The Court ruled the statement was involuntarily made as the suspect was clearly confused and unable to think about the events in question.

Language barriers

The fact that Miranda warnings are given in a language other than a defendant's primary language do not render a waiver invalid if it is shown that the waiver was made knowingly, intelligently and, in all respects, voluntarily. When dealing with someone who does not speak English at all or speaks only very limited English an interpreter should be sought. The law does not require a qualified interpreter, a police officer, or other reliable person, fluent in the suspect's language may be utilized. However, if the warnings are translated into the suspect's language they must be accurate. Any inaccuracy in the warnings may render the subsequent waiver invalid.

- In the 1997 SJC case of ***Commonwealth v. Rodriguez,*** a defendant was found to have waived voluntarily his Miranda rights where he received the warning in Spanish.[714] In *Rodriguez*, the defendant acknowledged to the police that he understood that he was waiving his rights, and he neither invoked his right to remain silent nor requested an attorney. He had been informed that he was under arrest for homicide, and the police did not offer any deals or leniency in exchange for his confession during questioning that lasted only about two hours.

Hearing Impaired

A qualified interpreter must be obtained when dealing with a person who is deaf or hearing impaired to assist the person concerning any interrogation, warning, notice of rights or the taking of any statement.[3] Failure to do so will invalidate any statement or expression not obtained through an interpreter will be inadmissible in evidence. Even providing rights in writing will not suffice[715]

Attorney's offer of assistance

A suspect cannot make an informed waiver of his Miranda rights if he is kept ignorant by police of an attorney's attempts to provide him with assistance and advice. If the waiver is not informed, it is not valid. Any attempt to contact a suspect who is being questioned must be relayed to the suspect immediately; otherwise all statements will likely be suppressed. **See Attorney Contact section below for more.**

---

[711] *Commonwealth v. LeBeau*, 451 Mass. 244, 884 N.E2d 956 (2008)
[712] *Commonwealth v. Garcia*, 443 Mass. 824, 824 N.E.2d 864 (2005).
[713] *Commonwealth v. Hartford*, 425 Mass. 378, 681 N.E. 2d 278 (1997).
[714] *Commonwealth v. Rodriguez*, 425 Mass. 361, 682 N.E. 2d 591 (1997).
[715] *Com. v. Kelley*, 404 Mass. 459 (1989).

POLICE CONDUCT MAY EFFECT WAIVER OF RIGHTS AND VOLUNTARINESS OF STATEMENTS

Conduct by the police can, and often does, effect the admissibility of an interrogation. Officers must be careful not to push the envelope during an interrogation as it can result in an opposite outcome of what it is intended to accomplish.

In the 2013 case of ***Commonwealth v. Ortiz***, the Appeals Court that the nineteen year old defendant's will was overborne by improper police interrogation tactics. Those tactics included misrepresenting statements given by witnesses; informing the defendant that the interview was his "last chance" to tell his story; and assuring the defendant, who had been steadfast in denying that he had given the suspected shooter a gun, that he would not be culpable if the defendant had given the shooter the gun for a purpose other than to rob or kill the victim and that the shooter had acted like a "cowboy."

Coercive conduct runs the gamut from the most blatant and clearly improper physical abuse to promises or misrepresentations. Regardless, they are all improper and will constitute coercion.

Physical Force: It is coercive for the police to extract statements by physical force.[716]

Threats of Abuse: Coercion is also present where there is no actual physical abuse, but merely the threat of possible violence.[717] Statements elicited by an implied threat are inadmissible.[718]

Deprivation of water, food, sleep, clothing and bathroom use may make an otherwise voluntary statement involuntary. It is wise to take occasional breaks, offer food and water and comply with reasonable requests by the suspect. This may be used to counter later claims of coercion and mistreatment.

Acknowledgement of Suspicion: the police are not required to inform the person being interrogated or questioned that they are a suspect in the crime. However, if the person is under arrest statutory law requires the police to inform the arrestee the true reason for the arrest.

Misrepresentations or Trickery: While the use of false statements during an interrogation is a relevant factor on both the waiver and voluntariness, such trickery does *not necessarily require suppression of the statement.* Rather, the interrogator's use of trickery is to be considered as part of the ***totality of the circumstances*,** the test that is used to determine the validity of a waiver and the voluntariness of any statement. Close analysis of case law related to trickery suggests that where the use of a false statement is the *only* factor pointing in the direction of involuntariness, it not will ordinarily result in suppression.[719] However, the courts seem much more tolerant of trickery after the defendant has agreed to speak and has already waived his rights.

Pre-waiver: In ***Commonwealth v. Jackson*,** the Worcester police were separately interrogating both the defendant and his girlfriend regarding a murder. The defendant twice expressed his wish to remain silent, however the police continued to make statements that they knew he was the killer. The police then informed the defendant that his girlfriend gave a statement implicating him in the murder. She had not made such a statement. The defendant then agreed to make a statement implicating himself in the crime. The SJC ruled that the waiver was not knowingly, intelligently and voluntarily waived because he was tricked into waiving his rights.[720]

However, once validly waived the police are more likely to successfully use a rouse to obtain information from the suspect. But, the use of trickery to help induce a defendant's statements is one of the factors a jury may consider in deciding whether a defendant's statement or confession was voluntary[721] and *material* misrepresentation or tricks make subsequent statements inadmissible.[722] The court will look at the totality of the circumstances to determine whether or not the statements were improperly induced.

Post Waiver: In ***Commonwealth v. Selby***, the court upheld a suspect's confession which had been prompted by the officer's knowingly-false statement that the suspect's fingerprints were found inside victim's house.[723]

- In the 2009 case of ***Commonwealth v. Jones***, the offense in question occurred on or about July 2, 1975. The victim was initially believed to have died from natural causes. In 1997, the victim's body was exhumed and a

[716] *Commonwealth v. Collins*, 11 Mass. App. Ct. 126, 414 N.E.2d 1008 (1981) (defendant was interrogated at gun point while lying naked on bathroom floor); *Beecher v. Alabama*, 389 U.S. 35 (1967) (confession came at gun point); *Brown v. Mississippi*, 297 U.S. 278, 56 S.Ct. 461 (1936) (defendant was tortured during interrogation); *Mincey v. Arizona*, 437 U.S. 385, 98 S.Ct. 2408 (1978).
[717] *Commonwealth v. Harris*, 371 Mass. 462, 358 N.E.2d 982 (1976).
[718] *Beecher v. Alabama*, 389 U.S. 35, 88 S.Ct. 189 (1967); *Lynumn v. Illinois*, 372 U.S. 528, 83 S.Ct. 917 (1963)
[719] *Commonwealth v. Holley,* Mass.App.Ct.(2011) quoting from *Com. v. DiGiambattista.*
[720] *Commonwealth v. Jackson*, 377 Mass. 319, 386 N.E.2d 15 (1979).
[721] *Commonwealth v. Selby*, 426 Mass. 168, 686 N.E. 2d 1316 (1997).
[722] *Commonwealth v. Berry*, 37 Mass. App. Ct. 200, 638 N.E.2d 1367 (1994); *Commonwealth v. Jackson*, 377 Mass. 319, 386 N.E.2d 15 (1979) (officers told suspect that his girlfriend had already confessed); *Commonwealth v. Meehan*, 377 Mass. 522, 387 N.E.2d 527 (1979) (officers misrepresented the strength and amount of incriminating evidence it had against the suspect); *Arizona v. Fulminante*, 111 S.Ct. 1246 (1991).
[723] *Commonwealth v. Selby*, 420 Mass. 656, 651 N.E.2d 843 (1995).

INTERVIEW & INTERROGATION

new autopsy was conducted this new autopsy indicated that the victim had died from "asphyxia by compression of the neck" and that "it [was] very likely that there's an element of chest compression and likely smothering along with the neck compression." The defendant was interviewed by police in 1997. He initially denied any memory of the victim or her family, but then acknowledged he had been with her on the night in question. He said they had been kissing and rolling around on the golf course, where her body was found the next morning, but that they had parted company on good terms and separately walked home. The interview took place in an employee lounge of an office building. Approximately eight feet from the head of the table, the police placed a clear plastic bag containing a white bra and another clear plastic bag containing a white sweater. Several manila file folders that contained crime scene photographs and an aerial photograph of the golf course were placed with the clothing. One file had the letters DNA written on its front. The police had recovered no DNA evidence and the clothes had no evidentiary connection to the case. Although these items were clearly visible during the interview, the police never referred to them. The Appeals Court ruled that the statements were still voluntary despite the fabricated evidence. The voluntariness was demonstrated by the defendant's "steadfast denial of wrongdoing."[724]

- In 2011 case of ***Com. v. Tremblay***, the SJC did not suppress statements made by the defendant even though the officer "agreed to go off the record." The "off the record" statements were later used against him. Under the particular circumstances of this case the court found that the agreement to go off the record was not so manipulative or coercive as to render the statements involuntary.

Even if the misrepresentation or trickery was used after the waiver of rights there is still the likelihood that the court will deem the conduct impermissible, particularly when weighed with other circumstances surrounding the interrogation. In general, the courts disfavor trickery or ruses when it comes to interrogation. Although these strategies are often very effective in eliciting a confession or admission they should be used with great caution. There is a risk that the courts will find that the confession or admission was not made voluntarily, knowingly and intelligently; and in instances of particularly egregious misrepresentations, even after a valid waiver, the court will most certainly deem the technique impermissible (see example below):

- In ***Com. v. Novo***[725], the police interrogator informed the suspect that if he did not first tell the police his side of the story he would not be permitted to tell his side later to the jury during trial. The SJC ruled that such a "now-or-never" technique of misrepresenting the suspect's right to defend himself at trial was particularly egregious and cast substantial doubt as to the voluntariness of the confession.

Offering Leniency/Suggesting Truthfulness

Any offer of leniency in exchange for a confession or statement will result in suppression of statements. However, as long as no promises are made, the police may indicate that the suspect's cooperation will be brought to the attention of the district attorney. The police should also stress that only the district attorney has the authority to reduce or drop the charges.

An officer may suggest *broadly* that it would be better for a suspect to tell the truth, as long as there is no assurance, express or implied, that it will aid the defense or result in a lesser sentence.[726]The touchstone is whether the police "assured" the defendant that his or her confession would aid their defense or result in a lesser sentence.[727]

- In the 2009 case of ***Commonwealth v. Tolan***, the defendant was suspected of killing her husband in what appeared to be a phony suicide scene. The defendant voluntarily agreed to accompany the police to the station and discuss the incident. The questioning began at 11:20 A.M. The room was comfortable and adequately ventilated. During the interrogation, the police repeatedly offered the defendant food, drinks, and the opportunity to use the restroom. The police secured the defendant's waiver of her Miranda rights at several points during the interrogation, though they also informed her that she was not under arrest. During the 11 hour interview the defendant made some inconsistent and incriminating statements. The officers made the following four statements during the interrogation that the defendant claims made her statements involuntary: "You can do yourself a lot of good if you tell us what happened"; "We'll help you because that's why we're here, to find the truth"; "Now it's time to help yourself out"; and, "You need to help yourself by telling the truth." The SJC ruled that "none of the statements made by the officers provides the type of "assurance" forbidden by *case law;* all are more similar to the broad suggestion that it would be "better" to

[724] *Commonwealth v. Jones*, Mass.App.Ct. (2009).
[725] *Com. v. Novor*, 442 Mass. 262 (2004)
[726] *Commonwealth v. Brandwein,* 435 Mass. 623, 760 N.E.2d 724 (2002); Compare *Commonwealth v. Mandile,* 397 Mass. 410, 414-415, 492 N.E.2d 74 (1986) (police statements that cooperation would be brought to attention of district attorney did not render confession involuntary), and *Commonwealth v. Williams,* 388 Mass. 846, 855, 448 N.E.2d 1114 (1983) (same), with *Commonwealth v. Meehan,* 377 Mass. 552, 564-565, 387 N.E.2d 527 (1979), cert. dismissed, 445 U.S. 39, 100 S.Ct. 1092, 63 L.Ed.2d 185 (1980) (confession involuntary where induced by police statements that confession would "help" defense, and that "truth" was going to be "good defense").
[727] *Id.* at 564, 387 N.E.2d 527.

tell the truth. The officers "did not overstep the permissible line" by offering leniency or promising that a confession would assist in the defense."

- In ***Commonwealth v. Burgess***, a police officer's encouragement to a defendant to "get it off his chest", after the defendant stated he had killed the victim and then stated he did not think he could continue, was not improper and did not render subsequent statements involuntary under a theory of coercion, where no officer gave any hint or assurance that, by confessing, the defendant could anticipate or would receive any favorable treatment from the Commonwealth.[728]
- In ***Commonwealth v. Souza,*** the interrogating officers in a murder case advised the defendant that it was in his "best interest to deal with them at this point, to set the record straight in regards to what happened." The SJC ruled that this statement did not make the confession involuntary. [729]

However, police statements can render an otherwise voluntary confession inadmissible:

- In the 1989 SJC case of ***Commonwealth v. Lahti,***[730] the Court found the police promise of leniency and threat of failure to confess leading to harsher treatment required suppression. Direct or implied promises to a suspect regarding what will or will not happen if he or she makes various statements are improper. Any statements made in reliance of such promises will be inadmissible.[731]

The Promise for Help

While the promise of psychiatric help standing alone will not invalidate a defendant's statement on the ground that it was not given voluntarily, it may if the help is offered as a quid pro quo for the statement, or if, in the totality of the circumstances, the police overbore the defendant's free will, inducing in him or her a belief that help, rather than punishment, would be forthcoming.[732]

In ***Com. v. DiGiambattista***, the SJC found that repeated suggestions by the police that the suspect needed counseling for his alcoholism, along with minimizing the suspect's burning of the apartment building as understandable given the poor conditions created by the landlord, created an implied promise of leniency and resulted in the confession to be deemed involuntary.

In ***Com. v. Magee***[733], the promise for medical treatment in exchange for a statement rendered the statement involuntary.

Threatening to impact family member

In the 2015 case of ***Commonwealth v. Monroe***, the SJC ruled that aggressive questioning, *particularly threats concerning a person's loved one*, may impinge on the voluntariness of a defendant's confession. In this case, threatening the defendant that his child would be taken away from the child's mother (the defendant's girlfriend) and raised by strangers resulted in coercion and made the statements involuntary.

If the police make statements indicating that they will arrest and charge a family member if the suspect does not cooperate the statements will most likely be suppressed particularly if the police did not actually have probable cause to arrest the family member.[734]

- In ***Com. v. Hunt***[735], both the defendant and his wife were arrested in relation to a shooting at a night club. The defendant was told that if he confessed to the crime his wife would be released. The wife's arrest lacked probable cause. The defendant subsequently confessed. The Court ruled that the confession was involuntary as the concern for one's family member may be a significant factor in inducing an involuntary confession.

However, if the police actually have probable cause to arrest the family member advising the suspect of that fact will not automatically have an impact of the validity of the statements.[736]

- In ***Com. v. Berg***[737], during the execution of a search warrant of a home for drugs the police warned the defendant that if they could not ascertain the owner of the drugs discovered both the defendant and his mother (who also lived in the house) would be arrested. The defendant subsequently confessed (he had previously

[728] *Commonwealth v. Burgess*, 434 Mass. 307, 749 N.E.2d 112 (2001).
[729] *Commonwealth v. Souza*, 428 Mass. 478, 481-482 n.3 (1998).
[730] *Commonwealth v. Lahti*, 398 Mass. 289, 401 N.E.2d 511 (1989).
[731] *Commonwealth v. Carey*, 407 Mass. 528, 554 N.E.2d 1199 (1991); *Commonwealth v. Shine*, 398 Mass. 641, 500 N.E.2d 1299 (1986); *Commonwealth v. Silva*, 21 Mass. App. Ct. 536, 488 N.E.2d 34 (1986).
[732] *Commonwealth v. Felice*, 44 Mass. App. Ct. 709, 693 N.E. 2d 713 (1998), *rev. den.* 427 Mass. 1107, 700 N.E. 2d 268 (1998).
[733] *Com. v. Magee*, 423 Mass. 381 (1996).
[734] *C ommonwealth v. Hunt*, 12 Mass.App.Ct.841 (1981).
[735] *Com. v. Hunt*, 12 Mass.App.Ct. 841 (1981)
[736] *Commonwealthv. Berg*, 37 Mass.App.Ct. 200 (1994).
[737] *Com. v. Berg*, 37 Mass.App. Ct. 200 (1994)

been provided his Miranda rights and waived them). The Court held that the statement was voluntarily made. When the search was executed the mother was found in the same room as the drugs.

Defendant's Words and Actions May have an Effect

In ***Commonwealth v. Wallen,*** the defendant's efforts to exculpate himself support a finding of capacity to understand and waive Miranda rights.[738]

No Single Factor is usually Dispositive

In deciding whether the statement was coerced, no single factor is usually dispositive. Instead, the court generally relies on the existence of several factors present in the surrounding circumstances. It considers the "totality of the circumstances."[739]

INVOCATION OF RIGHTS

There are two essential, yet distinct, rights in relation to a custodial interrogation: the right not to be compelled to incriminate oneself and the right to legal counsel. How these rights are applied and analyzed are also distinct.

INVOCATION OF RIGHT TO REMAIN SILENT

An individual may assert his or her right to remain silent and terminate police questioning at any time prior to or during an interview, even after waiving that right. Once the right to remain silent has been asserted, it must be *scrupulously honored.* However, it is possible to reinitiate questioning once the right to remain silent has been invoked (under limited circumstances – see section below on Further Questioning after Invocation of Rights).

Typically, the right to remain silent is typically invoked verbally or by indication on a standardized form. However, the invocation of the right to remain silent is not limited to verbal or written methods.

- In the 2012 case of ***Com. v. Clarke***, when the defendant was asked if he wished to discuss the incident he shook his head in the negative. The SJC ruled that this was an invocation of the right to remain silent and the subsequent statements were suppressed. The police had later resumed questioning and the court found that the defendant's right was not scrupulously honored even though he later agreed to talk (after being re-questioned).

Attorney Hanrahan's Recommendation: In practice, if there is ever any doubt as to whether or not the suspect has invoked his/her right to remain silent the best practice would be to ask for a clarification, such as "do you want to talk about this, yes or no?" If the suspect replies "no" all questioning must cease, if he says "yes" questioning can move forward.

Police must scrupulously Honor the Invocation of the Right to Remain Silent

When a suspect invokes his or her right to remain silent under *Miranda v. Arizona,* and is subsequently re-approached for interrogation, the inquiry is: "whether the person's right to be free from interrogation, once exercised, was 'scrupulously honored' before questioning resumed."

The US Supreme Court in ***Michigan v. Mosley*** identified the following factors (sometimes referred to as the Mosely Factors) to be considered as to whether or not the defendant's invocation of his/her rights was scrupulously honored:

1. Whether a significant amount of time elapsed between the suspect's invocation of the right to remain silent and further questioning;
2. Whether the same officer conducted both the interrogation where the suspect invoked the right and the subsequent interrogation, and whether the venues differed;
3. Whether the suspect was given a fresh set of Miranda warnings before the subsequent interrogation;
4. Whether the subsequent interrogation concerned the same crime as the interrogation previously cut off by the suspect; and
5. The persistence of the police in wearing down the suspect's resistance in order to change his mind.

No one factor is determinative, nor should these be understood as setting forth an exhaustive set of criteria. Typically one factor will not determine the admissibility of the statements. **The courts will look at the totality of the circumstances**. The Mosley factors were specific to the Mosley case and are not a set of rules that must be followed. However, they can be a helpful guide in similar situations.

---

[738] *Commonwealth v. Wallen,* 35 Mass. App. Ct. 915, 917 (1993)

[739] *See generally,Illinoisv. Gates*, 462 U.S. 213, 103 S.Ct. 2317 (1983) (in deciding the validity of a search and seizure case, court held validity is decided by looking at the totality of circumstances); *Commonwealth v. Selby*, 420 Mass. 656, 651 N.E. 2d 843 (1995); *Commonwealth v. Selby*, 426 Mass. 168, 686 N.E. 2d 1313 (1997); *Commonwealth v. James*, 427 Mass. 312, 693 N.E. 2d 148 (1998).

Attorney Hanrahan's Recommendation: Once a defendant has invoked his right to remain silent it is very rare for the Courts to find any subsequent non-spontaneous statements admissible (unless the defendant is the one who reinitiates questioning). It may be wise in many cases with otherwise strong evidence to forgo any attempt to resume the interrogation as this could potentially jeopardize the entire case. If a subsequent interrogation is necessary, it is very important to carefully follow the *Mosley* factor guidelines as much as possible, such as letting a few hours pass, changing the venue of the interrogation, have the interrogation conducted by a different investigator, re-advising the Miranda rights and so on – before resuming any questioning. Another option is to release the suspect (if appropriate) and then attempt to resume questioning – see Invocation Ends when Custody ends later in this section.

Once waived (i.e. agrees to speak) the suspect must clearly indicate later invocation of the right to remain silent

If a defendant who has initially waived his or her right to remain silent wishes later to cut off questioning, he or she must indicate in some manner that he or she is invoking the right they previously waived; there must be either an expressed unwillingness to continue or an affirmative request for an attorney.

- In ***Commonwealth v. Sicari,*** a defendant's 30 to 40 minute period of silence, in the middle of a lengthy interview, and after two written waivers of his *Miranda* rights, was neither an "expressed unwillingness" to continue the questioning nor an unambiguous request limiting further police questioning to clarify defendant's intention. The defendant did not invoke his right to terminate police questioning by remaining silent for an interval of 30 to 40 minutes after being confronted with evidence inconsistent with his prior statements to police; the defendant, who had waived his *Miranda* rights, had engaged in a day-long series of voluntary interactions with the police to misdirect the investigation away from himself. The questioning suggested that the defendant was increasingly aware that an attempt to shield himself from blame was unraveling and that he needed to reevaluate his strategy and the defendant broke his silence, having formulated a narrative that pointed blame at a codefendant and minimized his role in the child's kidnapping and murder.[740]
- In ***Commonwealth v. Robidoux***, the defendant was on trial for murder of his ten month old son after receiving a purported revelation from God to withhold food. While being interrogated by police the defendant would answer many questions but when asked about his wife and deceased son he either remained silent or stated he would not speak about his family. The SJC ruled that a refusal to answer certain questions did not require the police to ask the defendant whether he would like to reassert his right to silence. The SJC ruled that the defendant must make an express reassertion himself.[741]

INVOCATION OF RIGHT TO COUNSEL

When a suspect in custody makes an unequivocal and unambiguous (in other words clear and obvious) request for counsel, all questioning must cease.[742] If the request for counsel if not clear the interrogating officers should cease the interrogation and ask for clarification.

Statements obtained following an invocation of the right to counsel are presumed involuntary unless the Commonwealth proves beyond a reasonable doubt that the defendant "initiated further communication, exchanges, or conversations with the police,"[743] and thereby voluntarily, knowingly, and intelligently waived his right to counsel.[744] This is sometimes referred to as the ***Edwards Rule.*** This bar on continued questioning includes questioning on different and distinct offenses. *All* questioning must cease. However, the suspect may re-initiate questioning (see section on Further Questioning after Invocation of Rights). The so-called *Mosley Factors* do not apply when a suspect invokes his/her right to an attorney.

This restriction applies even after a prolonged delay. In ***Commonwealth v. Perez***[745], Perez was a defendant in a murder case. He was apprehended in Puerto Rico and he invoked his right to counsel. Six months later he was extradited to Lowell. While at the Lowell PD he was advised of his Miranda rights and subsequently made some incriminating statements. The Appeals Court ruled that the statements violated the Edwards Rule.

[740] *Commonwealth v. Sicari,* 434 Mass. 732, 752 N.E.2d 684 (2001).
[741] *Commonwealth v. Robidoux* 450 Mass. 144, 877 N.E.2d 232 (2007)
[742] See *Edwards v. Arizona,* 451 U.S. 477, 484-485, 101 S.Ct. 1880, 68 L.Ed.2d 378 (1981); *Commonwealth v. Brant*, 380 Mass. 876, 882, 406 N.E.2d 1021, cert. denied, 449 U.S. 1004, 101 S.Ct. 545, 66 L.Ed.2d 301 (1980).
[743] *Edwards v. Arizona, supra.*
[744] *Commonwealth v. Rankins*, 429 Mass. 470, 473, 709 N.E.2d 405 (1999); *Commonwealth v. Judge*, *supra* at 448, 650, N.E. 2d 1242.
[745] *Com. v. Perez,* 411 Mass.App.Ct. (1991)

However, if there is a break in custody the Edwards Rule will not apply. In ***Com. v. Galford***[746], the SJC ruled that a break in custody will end the previous invocation of the right to counsel. In this case the defendant was arrested on a drug charge; he invoked his right to counsel and was subsequently released on bail. A few days later he was again arrested on a murder charge. During the second arrest he waived his Miranda rights and made some incriminating statements. These statements were admissible despite his invocation of rights during the previous arrest.

Ambiguous Request (i.e. unclear request for counsel)**:**

Prior to the SJC's 2012 decision in ***Commonwealth v. Santos***, the police were encouraged to request clarification if during the interrogation the defendant made an unclear request for an attorney. However, in *Santos* the SJC created a new bright-line rule; when the circumstances indicate an uncertain request for an attorney; the interrogating officer must cease the interrogation, <u>but is entitled to ask a question to clarify the defendant's intent</u>. The question-- for example, in a form such as, "I just want to be sure--do you want an attorney?"--should be brief, worded only to elicit an affirmative or negative response concerning whether the suspect wants an attorney, and should not be designed to keep the suspect talking. After such an inquiry to clarify whether a suspect has indeed requested an attorney, nothing further should be asked unless the suspect responds to the question in the negative.

Attorney Hanrahan's note: Although this decision was based solely on the request for counsel it would probably be wise to follow the same rule if the suspect makes unclear request to remain silent.

Refusing to Sign Waiver without Presence of an Attorney

A defendant's *refusal to sign* without the presence of an attorney does not preclude the police from conducting the interrogation provided the defendant *agrees to answer questions* without an attorney.[747]

DEFENDANT MAY REINITIATE QUESTIONING

Whether the defendant invoked his right to remain silent or his right to an attorney, or both, the defendant can re-initiate further questioning and any further questioning would not violate his/her rights. If the suspect does reinitiate questioning the police should re-advise him or her of his rights and obtain a valid waiver.

INVOCATION ENDS WHEN CUSTODY ENDS

If the suspect invokes his right to remain silent or his right to an attorney this invocation will end when the suspect is no longer in custody.

- In the 2011 case of ***Com. v. Lopes,*** the defendant was arrested by Brockton police following a BOLO issued by the Boston PD regarding a recent homicide. The Brockton PD arrested the defendant, advised him of his Miranda rights and he refused to talk. Boston homicide detectives who were on their way to Brockton advised Brockton PD un-arrest the defendant but to ask him if he was willing to wait and speak with Boston detectives. The defendant agreed to wait. Boston PD then re-advised the defendant of his Miranda rights and the defendant agreed to speak (by signing a waiver). The SJC ruled that "once the defendant was no longer in custody and was free to leave, the obligations of the police arising from Miranda, including the obligation to refrain from further questioning for a significant period of time after an invocation of silence, no longer applied."

Attorney Hanrahan's Note: This can be used very effectively strategy to use when a suspect invokes his/her rights but a statement is otherwise vital to the investigation. Attempting to reinitiate questioning after the suspect has been bailed is often a viable option.

INVOCATION CANNOT BE USED AGAINST THE DEFENDANT

If a defendant chooses to invoke his right to remain silent this invocation cannot be used against the defendant, even if the defendant was not under arrest at the time of the invocation. [748]

- In ***Commonwealth v. Chase***, the defendant was suspected of committing arson. The defendant was questioned in a non-custodial setting and prior to the establishment of probable cause. Despite the lack of probable cause and the non-custodial setting the trooper read the defendant his Miranda warnings. The defendant's subsequent invocation

[746] *Com. v. Galford*, 413 Mass. 364 (1992).
[747] Commonwealth v. Santana, SJC (2013).
[748] *Commonwealth v. Chase,* 70 Mass.App.Ct. 862 (2007)

was not admissible in court, and even a subsequent invocation during the execution of a search warrant at the defendant's residence, four days after the Miranda warnings were given was also excluded from trial.[749]

INVOCATION OF RIGHTS WILL NOT PREVENT SUBSEQUENT CONSENT

Despite the fact that a suspect invokes his Miranda rights this alone will not prevent the police from obtaining consent o search from the suspect.

In the 2013 case of ***Commonwealth v. Leftkowski***, the Appeals Court ruled that the defendant's consent to a DNA swab was lawful despite the fact that they defendant had invoked his Miranda rights.

RIGHT TO BE NOTIFIED OF AVAILABLE LEGAL ASSISTANCE

According to the SJC's 2000 decision in ***Commonwealth v. Mavredakis,*** the Massachusetts Constitutional privilege against self-incrimination is more expansive than its federal counterpart, and includes the right to be informed of an attorney's efforts to render assistance.[750]

If an attorney identifies himself or herself to the police, **in person or by phone**, as counsel acting on a suspect's behalf, the police must **immediately** stop any questioning and inform the suspect of the attorney's availability, permitting the suspect to choose whether to speak with the attorney or to decline the offer of assistance.[751] If the police fail to inform a suspect that an attorney has offered legal assistance, any waiver of rights by the defendant becomes inoperative for further admissions.[752]

- In the 2010 case of ***Commonwealth v. McNulty,*** the SJC added that the police must also relay any message (that is related to the suspect's right to counsel) to the suspect sent by the attorney, even if the attorney communicates to the police that he does not want his client to speak with the police, the police must notify the suspect of the attorney's recommendation that he/she not speak. If the police neglect or refuse to relay the message any subsequent statements will most certainly be suppressed.
- In the 2013 case of ***Commonwealth v. Rivera***, the SJC ruled that although the police must relay messages from the attorney to the client, the police are not required to advise the suspect that his/her attorney instructed the police not to talk with the suspect.

Bright line rule

Mavredakis established a "bright-line rule, providing that police must stop questioning and inform a suspect immediately of attempts of an attorney identifying himself or herself as counsel acting on the suspect's behalf to contact the suspect."[753]

"The consequence of the failure so to inform a suspect is that any waiver of rights that has been given becomes 'inoperative' for further admissions." In other words, any statements made after the attorney makes an attempt to contact will be deemed in admissible, under the theory of an invalid waiver, until the attempt to contact is passed on to the person being interrogated.

In essence, a suspect cannot make an informed waiver of his Miranda rights if he is kept ignorant by police of an attorney's attempts to provide him with assistance and advice. If the waiver is not informed, it is not valid.

Once informed of his or her attorney's offer for assistance the suspect must be given the opportunity to choose whether or not to continue the interrogation. At this time, the police should re-advise the suspect of his or her Miranda rights.

Third party's offer – no obligation

A promise made by a third party, however, is not the "concrete offer of assistance" by an attorney envisioned by *Mavredakis.* The police, therefore, have no obligation to inform a suspect that a third party intends to retain legal counsel for the suspect because this is not a concrete offer of assistance.[754]

[749] *Commonwealth v. Chase,* 70 Mass.App.Ct. 862 (2007)
[750] *Commonwealth v. Mavredakis*, 430 Mass. 848, 725 N.E. 2d 169 (2000).
[751] *Commonwealth v. Mavredakis*, 430 Mass. 848, 725 N.E. 2d 169 (2000).
[752] *Commonwealth v. Mavredakis*, 430 Mass. 848, 725 N.E. 2d 169 (2000).
[753] *Commonwealth v. Beland, 436 Mass. 273, 287, 764 N.E.2d 324 (2002). Mavredakis, supra at 861, 725 N.E.2d 169 ("duty to inform applies whether the attorney telephones or arrives at the station").*
[754] *Commonwealth v. Nelson*, 55 Mass. App. Ct. 911, 774 N.E.2d 634 (2002).

Police Agencies should develop a policy for confirming that a person claiming to be an attorney representing a suspect is an actual attorney

In *Mavredakis,* the SJC suggested that police agencies should develop a procedure on how to confirm that a person claiming to be an attorney representing a suspect is an actual attorney.

The Massachusetts Board of Bar Overseers (BBO) is the organization charged with licensing and overseeing attorneys in Massachusetts. The status of any Massachusetts attorney can be confirmed by visiting http://massbbo.org/bbolookup.php and entering the attorney's first and last name.

In addition, all attorneys in Massachusetts are issued a BBO card with a distinct 6 digit BBO identification number. An attorney should be able to provide you with this card to verify his or her status or at the very least recite his or her 6 digit BBO number.

Inevitable Discovery Exception

In the 2012 case of ***Commonwealth v. Morales***, the SJC applied the inevitable discovery doctrine to a violation of the defendant's right to be notified of his attorney's message. In this case the defendant had already made a full confession and then agreed to take the police to the scene of the crime. While the police and the defendant were in a remote area the police were able to receive the message regarding the attorney's presence but they neglected to pass on the attorney's instruction not to answer questions. Shortly thereafter the victim's body was found. The SJC upheld the discovery of the victim's body despite the failure to relay the message. The defendant had already confessed and provided the police with enough details that they would have discovered the victim's body with the defendant's further cooperation.

ATTORNEY INSTRUCTION PRE-INTERROGATION

If an attorney, who represents the suspect, advises the investigator that he/she wishes to be present during a forthcoming interrogation of the suspect the police must inform the suspect of the availability of the attorney before a Miranda waiver will be deemed valid.[755]

- In ***Commonwealth v. Sherman***, Trooper Manning received information that the defendant might have been involved in housebreaks. On August 14, he encountered the defendant on a public street. He asked the defendant to meet him at the North Adams police station. The defendant drove to the station. At the station, the defendant was taken to an interrogation room, told that he was a suspect, and given his Miranda rights. He did not request an attorney. In response to Trooper Manning's questions, the defendant made a statement implicating himself in two housebreaks. Earlier on that morning, Trooper Manning had seen Ms. Rita Scales in North Adams District Court. Ms. Scales was a trial attorney on the staff of the Massachusetts Defenders Committee. She was representing the defendant on a pending case involving a charge of breaking and entering in Florida, Massachusetts. Officer Manning approached her and told her that he intended to question the defendant about the Savoy, Massachusetts, housebreaks. She asked him to tell her when and where he was going to question the defendant, and stated that she wanted to be present when the questioning took place. He did not respond. Trooper Manning spoke to Ms. Scales because he knew that she was either representing the defendant at the time or had represented him in the past. Trooper Manning did not inform Ms. Scales nor did he inform the defendant of her interest in being present. The SJC deemed the statements made by the defendant to be invalid as a result of an invalid waiver of his Miranda rights because the police failed to notify him of his attorney's availability.[756]

Police have no duty to contact attorney for defendant

In the 2003 case of ***Commonwealth v. Collins***, the SJC ruled that the police have no inherent constitutional duty to inform a defendant's (already retained) attorney that the defendant has been arrested or even that the defendant, already arrested, will be interrogated. [757] While our law requires the police to facilitate the attempts of those in custody to contact their attorneys, the police need not make the telephone calls themselves. [758]

[755] *Commonwealth v. Sherman,* 389 Mass. 287 (1983).
[756] *Commonwealth v. Sherman,* 389 Mass. 287 (1983).
[757] *Commonwealth v. Sherman,* 389 Mass. 287, 291, 450 N.E.2d 566 (1983); *Commonwealth v. Santo,* 375 Mass. 299, 305, 376 N.E.2d 866 (1978); *Commonwealth v. Andujar,* 7 Mass.App.Ct. 777, 783, 390 N.E.2d 276 (1979). See also *Commonwealth v. Mandeville,* 386 Mass. 393, 401, 436 N.E.2d 912 (1982).
[758] M. G.L. c. 276, § 33A

THE SAFE HARBOR RULE

Right to prompt presentment

A person arrested has a Constitutional right to be brought to court in a timely fashion. As a result of this right the Courts have created was is referred to as the Safe Harbor Rule. The Safe Harbor Rule limits police questioning to a **maximum of 6 hours** from the time of the *arrest*. Sometimes call "**the Rosario Rule**" after the 1996 SJC case of Commonwealth v. Rosario.

The right can be waived: The arrested person can waive his/her right to prompt presentment and be questioned beyond six hours. The police must advise the arrestee of his/her right to prompt present (preferably in writing and have the person sign the waiver – see example on next page, or the waiver should be recorded). It is also good practice to re-advise the arrestee of his/her rights under Miranda and offer another telephone call.

Note: Additionally, the right can be waived even if the questioning did not begin until more than six hours after the arrest.[759]

Does not Apply to Out-of-State Arrests: Persons wanted in Massachusetts but arrested out of state are not protected by the six hour rule. The danger that triggered the need for the rule--that police officers would delay a defendant's arraignment in order to procure a confession from an unrepresented defendant--does not arise when the defendant must await a rendition hearing before being transported to Massachusetts for arraignment.[760]

In the 2012 case of ***Commonwealth v. Van Tran***, the suspect was arrested in China and had to be transported back to the U.S. The SJC stated that international travel is the type of unusual circumstance that would permit a delay in the 6 hour rule.

However, in the 2012 case of ***Commonwealth v. Delacruz***, the SJC stated "although we have recently stated that the safe harbor rule 'applies by its terms only to persons arrested in Massachusetts,' we nevertheless may consider whether the circumstances of a particular interrogation 'violated the spirit of the rule.'"

Rule may not be limited to Interrogation: In the 2013 case of ***Commonwealth v. Fortunato***, the SJC alluded that the 6 hour rule may apply to all statements not just statements made during interrogations (i.e. it may apply to spontaneous statements). The SJC did not decide the case on this issue because they found that the defendant was in custody, however, the court alluded that it may apply to non-interrogation scenarios.

Issues that Stop the Clock: In *Rosario*, the SJC stated that there may be some exceptional circumstances which would stop the six hour clock because it would be impractical to question the suspect, such as a natural disaster, emergency, or self-induced intoxication by the suspect.

INTERVIEW & INTERROGATION

[759] *Com. v. Morgan*, SJC 2011
[760] *Com. v. Morganti*, SJC 2009

RIGHT TO PROMPT PRESENT
WAIVER FORM

I, ______________________, have been informed that I have the right to be brought to court within a reasonable period of time when the court is open, to be arraigned on the charges on which I have been arrested.

I have been informed that the _______________ District Court is open Monday through Friday, 8:30 A.M. to 4:30 P.M., except legal holidays.

I have also been informed that the police may not question me if more than six (6) hours have passed since the time of my arrest, unless I give them permission to do so. I understand that if I am disabled from drug or alcohol intoxication at the time of my arrest, the six (6) hour time period for questioning does not begin until my disability ends.

Having these rights in mind, I wish to continue speaking with police.

Signature____

Officer Witness ____

Date: _____________ Time______ Location: ______________________

RECORDING REQUIREMENTS

Police officers must record electronically **all** interrogations that are conducted at a place of detention, and other *custodial interrogations* (no matter where they take place) whenever practicable, or face a cautionary jury instruction, pursuant to a rule promulgated by the SJC in the 2004 case of *Commonwealth v. DiGiambattista.*[761]

Remedy for Violation of Requirement: Cautionary Jury Instruction

When the prosecution introduces evidence of a defendant's statement or confession that results from either an questioning conducted at a place of detention (e.g., a police station), or as a result of a *custodial interrogation*, and there is not at least an audiotape recording of the complete interrogation, the defendant is entitled to a jury instruction advising that this state's highest court has expressed a preference that such interrogations be recorded whenever practical, and cautioning the jury that, because of the absence of any recording of the interrogation in the case before them, they should weigh evidence of the defendant's alleged statement with great caution and care.

In the 2007 case of ***Commonwealth v. Burton***, the SJC *declined to impose the exclusionary rule* when the police made no effort to record an interview with the defendant who was convicted of murder. The cautionary jury instruction remains the remedy.[762]

The entire interrogation must be recorded

The entire interrogation must be recorded in order to avoid the cautionary jury instruction. If the defendant alleges that any portion was not recorded, at least if the judge finds any basis for such claim, a cautionary jury instruction will most likely be given. However, there is no requirement that a prosecutor introduce the entire recording at trial, so long as it is available to the defense.

Must the suspect be aware of the recording?

In the 2012 case of ***Commonwealth v. Ashley***, the Appeals Court ruled that failure to advise the suspect, who was in custody and being interrogated, of the recording was not a violation of the wiretap statute (c. 272 § 99). The Court stated "the recording of an interrogation is not 'surreptitious eavesdropping,' when the defendant was fully aware that he was engaged in an interrogation with police who repeatedly expressed their intention to get it "down on paper" and memorialize the interview. Because it is obvious that, during this interrogation, Ashley did not intend to keep his statements private, recording of the interrogation does not amount to surreptitious eavesdropping; even if a literal

[761] ***Commonwealth v. DiGiambattista*, 442 Mass. 423, 813 N.E.2d 516 (2004).**
[762] *Commonwealth v. Burton*, 450 Mass. 55, 876 N.E.2d 411 (2007)

application of the statute might imply a violation. The Court stated "we do not view the statute as intended to apply in these circumstances."

Attorney Hanrahan's Note: Despite this decision it is probably best to advise the suspect of the recording to avoid any challenges later. With slightly different circumstances the outcome may be different.

Technically there is No "right" to refuse recording

If the suspect refuses to speak unless the recording devise is turned off, officers must make a decision on how to proceed. While the individual has no "right" to order the recording stopped, he or she does have the right to refuse to speak or to answer questions. This would effectively bring any interrogation to a halt. In most cases, it is best to comply with the defendant's request; a statement with a cautionary jury instruction is often better than no statement at all.

- In the 2011 case of ***Commonwealth v. Tavares***, the Appeals Court ruled that a cautionary jury instruction must be provided upon request of the defendant even if the defendant requested that the interrogation not be recorded.

Prosecution may offer explanation

The Court recognized that there may be circumstances where the prosecution may want to explain why all or a portion of an interrogation was not recorded. This may be done and the jury will be allowed to assess what weight it gives to the lack of a recording. This will also apply where a recording device malfunctions or is unavailable.

Similarly, if the defendant refused to speak unless the recorder was turned off, the prosecution may explain this to the jury. It will not, however, avoid the cautionary instruction. As the SJC pointed out in *DiGiambattista*, "The mere presence of such reasons or justifications, however, does not obviate the need for the cautionary instruction."

INTERVIEW RECORDING FORM

It is the policy of this department to record all interviews at the police station so that there is a record of our discussion. Do we have your permission to tape record our discussion?

□ Yes, I agree to have our discussion recorded. ______ Initials
□ No, I do not want our discussion recorded. ______ Initials

Be advised that you may change your decision at any time during this interview.

Signature ____

Officer witnessing ID ____

Date: ______________ Time ________ Location: ____________________

□ Having at first decided not to be recorded, I now choose to have the rest of my interview recorded.

Current Time: ____________ ______Initials

□ Having at first agreed to be recorded, I now choose to have the remainder of my interview not recorded.

Current Time: ____________ ______Initials

Signature ____

Officer witnessing ID ____

Date: ______________ Time ________ Location: ____________________

INTERVIEW & INTERROGATION

At least Audio Recordings

The SJC set a minimum standard for recordings. An audio recording is the least that is required.

Only applies to Criminal Suspects

The recording requirement of interrogations (or interviews) conducted at a place of detention does not apply when the police are not even aware that a crime has occurred and before the police have identified a suspect.[763] In other words, the requirement does not apply to non-criminal suspects being interviewed at the police station.

MIRANDA VIOLATIONS AND THE EFFECT ON EVIDENCE

The law indicates that statements made by a defendant in police custody in response to interrogation must be suppressed when the *Miranda* warnings are deficient.[764] Similarly, statements obtained in violation of *Miranda* cannot be used to support a search warrant [765] or to obtain physical evidence, with few and rare exceptions.

VIOLATION OF MIRANDA AND SUPPRESSION OF PHYSICAL EVIDENCE

Federal Rule

In *Patane*[766], the Supreme Court, in a five-to-four decision, held that, while "unwarned statements may not be used in evidence in the prosecution's case in chief," "the Self-Incrimination Clause ... is not implicated by the introduction at trial of physical evidence resulting" from such statements so long as they were not the product of improper coercion (i.e., were "voluntary").[767] Consequently, the Court concluded that the exclusion of physical evidence obtained in violation of Miranda principles is not required by the Fifth Amendment to the United States Constitution.

Massachusetts Rule

The question presented in the 2005 SJC case of ***Commonwealth v. Martin*** was whether the failure to give Miranda warnings to a suspect in custody will continue to require suppression of physical evidence derived from an unwarned statement he made in response to police interrogation.

- In ***Commonwealth v. Martin***, the SJC concluded that the U.S. Supreme Court's construction of the Miranda rule, which was intended to secure the privilege against compelled incrimination in the context of inherently coercive custodial interrogations, was no longer adequate to safeguard the parallel but broader protections afforded Massachusetts citizens by art. 12. The SJC adopted a common-law rule governing the admissibility of physical evidence obtained in these circumstances. Such evidence, if derived from unwarned statements where Miranda warnings would have been required by Federal law in order for them to be admissible, is presumptively excludable from evidence at trial as "fruit" of the improper failure to provide such warnings.[768]

In short, in Massachusetts, physical evidence obtained as a result of an interrogation which violated the Miranda rule will be suppressed.

VIOLATION OF MIRANDA AND SUBSEQUENT STATEMENTS

In Massachusetts, the taint of an illegally obtained statement is presumed to remain with subsequent statements, as Massachusetts does not follow the Federal rule where the subsequent administration of Miranda warnings automatically removes remaining taint. Even so, "[i]t has never been the law that once the police fail in their obligations under *Miranda* all subsequent uncounseled statements by an accused must be excluded.

[763] *Commonwealth v. Issa*, SJC (2013).
[764] *Commonwealth v. Duguay*, 430 Mass. 397, 720 N.E. 2d 458 (1999). (Detective failed to inform the defendant that if he could not afford an attorney, he had the right to court-appointed counsel.)
[765] *Mass. v. White*, 374 Mass 132, 371 N.E.2d 777 (1977), *affirmed* 439 U.S. 280, 99 S.Ct. 712 (1979); *Commonwealth v. Benoit*, 382 Mass. 210, 415 N.E.2d 818 (1961). Nor can they be used to support probable cause to arrest; *Commonwealth v. Haas*, 373 Mass. 545, 369 N.E.2d 692 (1977).
[766] *Patane, supra* at 2628, quoting *Dickerson v. United States*, 530 U.S. 428, 443-444, 120 S.Ct. 2326, 147 L.Ed.2d 405 (2000).
[767] *United States v. Patane*, 542 U.S. 630, 124 S.Ct. 2620, 159 L.Ed.2d 667 (2004).
[768] ***Commonwealth v. Martin***444 Mass. 213, 827 N.E.2d 198 (2005).See *Commonwealth v. DiMarzio*, 436 Mass. 1012, 1013, 767 N.E.2d 1059 (2002) (marijuana located as result of unwarned statement made after defendant placed in custody properly suppressed as "fruit of the poisonous tree"); *Commonwealth v. Barros*, 56 Mass.App.Ct. 675, 678-679, 779 N.E.2d 693 (2002) (evidence found in defendant's bedroom as result of unwarned custodial questioning suppressed).

The taint of a Miranda violation is "not ineradicable."[769] "According to Massachusetts cases, the taint of an earlier Miranda violation may be removed if either:

1. Sufficient time has elapsed and there has been a sufficient break in the course of events to allow the conclusion that the taint has been dissipated,
   or
2. The pre-Miranda interview led to no inculpatory statement." [770]

- In the 2003 SJC case of ***Commonwealth v. Jordan***, the court ruled that a defendant's second and third incriminating statements about the murder, which were preceded by "Miranda" waivers and were given three and four months, respectively, after the initial incriminating statement that the defendant claimed was induced by a false impression of immunity would have been admissible under the "cat out of the bag" and "break in the stream" tests, even if earlier statement had been involuntary.[771]

EFFECT OF UNLAWFUL ARREST OR SEARCH ON STATEMENTS

Scrutinized by the Courts

Where a person has been arrested unlawfully and subjected to custodial interrogation, the courts will scrutinize the circumstances to determine whether statements made should be excluded as the result of exploiting the illegal arrest - even if Miranda warnings were given. The court will look to the amount of time which transpired between the arrest and the interrogation, the presence of intervening factors and the purpose and flagrancy of police misconduct in making an unlawful arrest.[772]

More likely to be admissible if probable cause existed

Despite a defendant's unlawful warrantless arrest in his apartment, his post arrest statements at the police station were admissible in an armed robbery prosecution, where the police had probable cause to arrest him and his post arrest statements were not made at his home.

Where the police have probable cause to arrest a suspect, the Fourth Amendment's exclusionary rule does not bar the admission of a statement made by the defendant outside of his home, even though the statement is taken after an arrest made in the home in violation of his rights.

- In ***Commonwealth v. Molina***, the officers' observations and the defendant's statements made inside the defendant's apartment were inadmissible in evidence at trial, where the officers' presence in the apartment was due to their unlawful entry to execute the warrantless arrest of the defendant.[773] However, the defendant's statements to officers at the police station, subsequent to the officers' unlawful warrantless arrest of the defendant in his dwelling, were admissible at trial, where the arrest was supported by probable cause.

Statements obtained prior to the unlawful arrest may still be admissible

Statements made prior to an unlawful arrest will not necessarily be excluded because of the subsequent unlawful arrest.

In ***Commonwealth .v Marquez***, suppression of statements that a defendant made at his apartment before his unlawful arrest, including his admission regarding his identity and his statement that the mountain bike in his apartment was not his, and the officer's observation of the bike, was not required, where the statements and observation preceded the illegal police conduct of arresting defendant in his apartment without a warrant.[774]

[769] *Commonwealth v. Larkin,*429 Mass. 426, 436-437 (1999).
[770] *Commonwealth v. Harris*, Mass.App.Ct. (2009).
[771] *Commonwealth v. Jordan*, 439 Mass. 47, 785 N.E.2d 368 (2003).
[772] *Dunaway v.New York*, 442 U.S. 200, 99 S.Ct. 2248 (1979); *Commonwealth v. Hooks*, 38 Mass. App. Ct. 301, 647 N.E.2d 440 (1995); *Commonwealth v. Reyes*, 38 Mass. App. Ct. 483, 649 N.E.2d 166 (1995).
[773] *Commonwealth v. Molina*, 439 Mass. 206, 786 N.E.2d 1191 (2003).
[774] *Commonwealth v. Marquez,*749 N.E.2d 673, 434 Mass. 370.

JUVENILES AND INTERROGATION

Because juveniles are more susceptible than adults to coercion and intimidation the courts will consider whether a reasonable person in the juvenile's position would have understood his situation.[775] Additionally, a juvenile is more likely to be determined *in custody* or *subject to interrogation* than an adult may be under similar circumstances because of their age. For these reasons the Courts require special precautions when a juvenile is being interrogated.

SPECIAL PRECAUTION

Due to the fact that juveniles are easily intimidated and coerced special precautions should be taken, such as limiting the number of officers present during the custodial interrogation, the tone and manner of speech should be appropriate and an adult who has an interest in the child's wellbeing must be present (with few exceptions).

The **general rule** is that if a child is age 17 years or younger an **interested adult** must be present during any custodial interrogation. The purpose of the interested adult rule is to put the juvenile on a roughly even footing with an adult defendant in terms of understanding and making a meaningful decision to waive or invoke the Miranda rights.[776]

There is a very rare exception to this rule when the child is age 14 years or older and the child is highly intelligent, sophisticated, and knowledgeable. However, this is an *exception* and it is generally a poor strategy in regards to an interrogation (see below).

Child under 14 – an interested adult must be present and have *actual opportunity* to consult

For the Commonwealth to successfully demonstrate a knowing and intelligent waiver by a juvenile who is **under the age of fourteen**, it ***must*** show that:

a. a parent or other interested adult was present during the questioning,

b. the adult understood the warnings, and

c. the adult had the *opportunity* to explain the juvenile's rights to him so that the juvenile understood the significance of waiver of those rights.[777]

The warnings should be provided to both the adult and the child. The court has also indicated that the Commonwealth must show that the interested adult understood the Miranda warnings. [778]

The Commonwealth need not prove ''that the juvenile, and the adult assisting him, made full use of the opportunity provided to them actually to discuss the juvenile's rights and the possible consequences of a waiver."[779] However, the SJC has emphasized that an "***actual opportunity*** to discuss the juvenile's rights" is required.

There is no requirement that the police inform the juvenile and the adult of the right to consult. However, the Supreme Judicial Court has suggested that the **better practice** ''with any juvenile is for the investigating officials explicitly to inform the juvenile's parent, or other interested adult, that an opportunity is being furnished for the two to confer about the juvenile's rights,''[780] before questioning begins.[781]

The best practice therefore would be for the officer to **encourage the juvenile and the adult to discuss the rights and provide them with some privacy in order to discuss the rights**, followed by an acknowledgement that the rights are understood, before proceeding with the interrogation..

When the Child Ages 14, 15, 16 and 17 – interested adult required but exception possible

When juveniles age 14 or over are involved there is an rare alternative to the interested adult and opportunity to consult rule. If the juvenile has a high degree of intelligence, experience, knowledge or sophistication the juvenile *may* be capable of waiving his or her rights without the help of an interested adult. [782] **However, in practice this is difficult to prove and is rarely accepted by the Court.** It would be unwise to interrogate a youth with the plan to later convince the court that the child was "sophisticated." This exception is usually argued after the police mistakenly interrogate a juvenile without the presence of an interested adult and then make efforts not have the statements suppressed.

---

[775] *Commonwealth v. Ira*, 439 Mass. 805, 791 N.E.2d 894 (2003)
[776] *Commonwealth v. Pacheco*, Appeals Court 2015
[777] See *Commonwealth v. A Juvenile, supra* at 134, 449 N.E.2d 654.
[778] *Commonwealth v. Philip S.*, 414 Mass. 804, 611 N.E.2d 226
[779] *Commonwealth v. Philip S.*, 414 Mass. 804, 811, 611 N.E.2d 226 (1993).
[780] *Commonwealth v. Philip S., supra* at 811 n.5,611 N.E.2d 226
[781] Commonwealth v. Philip S., 414 Mass. At 811 n.5 (1993)
[782] *Commonwealth v. A Juvenile*, 389 Mass. at 134, 449 N.E.2d 654 (1983)

In ***Commonwealth v. McCra***, the SJC ruled that in general, when police interrogation involves a juvenile over the age of 14 the juvenile "may properly waive his constitutional rights if, after having been advised of those rights, he was afforded an opportunity to consult with an interested adult who was informed of and understood those rights."[783] Whether juvenile had a "realistic opportunity" to consult is the **critical question**, not whether he actually availed himself of the opportunity. The Commonwealth is not required to establish that the adult and juvenile actually had a private consultation.[784]

Despite these exceptions, when dealing with a child age 14, 15, 16 or 17 the safest and more prudent route would be to have an interested adult present, advise both the adult and juvenile the Miranda warnings, and provide them a so-called *meaningful opportunity* prior to questioning the juvenile.

Consultation after Questioning has Begun

In the 2015 case of ***Commonwealth v. Pacheco***, the Appeals Court ruled that the police cannot deny a juvenile, who is the subject of custodial interrogation, the opportunity to consult with an adult, regarding his/her Miranda rights, in the midst of an interrogation, even though they had already been provided the opportunity to consult prior to the commencement of the interrogation.

Private Consultation not Required unless Requested

The Supreme Judicial Court has specifically declined to impose a requirement that the police allow the juvenile and adult to consult in private.[785] However, this does not preclude the police from allowing a private consultation if one is requested. If private consultation is requested it should be honored.[786]

Interrogations of suspects 18 years of age or older do not require an interested adult.

In ***Commonwealth v. Trombley***, the defendant who was 17 years old (see note below) was not entitled to have mother present during interview with police regarding a housebreak investigation.[787]

Attorney Hanrahan's note: In 2013, the Legislature changed the age of an adult for the purposes of criminal prosecution from 17 to 18 years. In 2015, the SJC, in *Commonwealth v. Rashidi Smith*, ruled that the 2013 legislative change should apply to interrogations as well for "considerations of consistency" even though the interested adult rule is a common law rule and not a legislative mandate.

RIGHTS BELONG TO THE CHILD

Although an interested adult is present the rights ultimately belong to the child. If a child invokes his/her rights (e.g. I'd like a lawyer) the parent cannot overrule the child's invocation of rights.

THE INTERESTED ADULT

Interested adult only required for custodial interrogations

The interested adult requirement only applies with Custodial Interrogations (i.e. Miranda situations). However, it would be prudent in most cases to have an interested adult present anytime a child is questioned about a crime, even if the child is not in custody. In ***Commonwealth v. Ira***, the SJC stated "the interested adult rule is inapplicable when the interrogation is not custodial, because there is no obligation to inform a juvenile of Miranda rights." [788]

Who qualifies as an interested adult?

A consulting adult need not be the parent of the juvenile,[789] nor even be completely free of conflicting loyalties or tensions. [790] However, if a parent is available it would, in most cases, be best to have a parent present during the interrogation. Conversely, one is not an interested adult if he or she is "actually antagonistic" toward the juvenile, [791] or if there is a lack of relationship between the child and the adult, [792] or if a substantial conflict exists.[793]

---

[783] ***Commonwealth v. McCra***, 427 Mass. 564, 567 (1998).
[784] Commonwealth v. Pacheco, Appeals Court (2015) quoting Commonwealth v. MacNeil, 399 Mass. 71, 74 (1987) and Commonwealth v. Philip S., 414 Mass. 804, 811-812 (1993).
[785] *Commonwealth v. Pacheco*, Appeals Court 2015 quoting from *Commonwealth v. Ward*, 412 Mass. 395, 397 (1992).
[786] See *Commonwealth v. Ward*, 412 Mass. 395 (1992).
[787] *Commonwealth v. Trombley*, 72 Mass.App.Ct. 183, 889 N.E.2d 446 (2008)
[788] *Commonwealth v. Ira I.*, 439 Mass. 805, 815 n. 11 (2003)
[789] *Commonwealth v. Alfonso A.*, 438 Mass. 372, 383, 780 N.E.2d 1244 (2003)
[790] *Commonwealth v. Berry*, 410 Mass. 31, 35-36, 570 N.E.2d 1004 (1991)
[791] *Commonwealth v. Philip S.*, 414 Mass. 804, 809, 611 N.E.2d 226 (1993)
[792] *Commonwealth v. Alfonso A.*, 438 Mass. at 383-384, 780 N.E.2d 1244
[793] *Commonwealth v. A Juvenile*, 402 Mass. 275, 279-280, 521 N.E.2d 1368 (1988)

Case examples

- In ***Commonwealth v. Berry***, the fact that defendant's aunt was also the sister of victim did not preclude her from acting as interested adult.[794]
- In ***Commonwealth v. McCra,*** the court ruled that a father could[795] serve as interested adult despite prior night's violent confrontation with juvenile.
- In ***Commonwealth v. A Juvenile,*** an employee of a private organization under contract with **Department of Youth Services (DYS)** to run home for troubled adolescents, to which defendant had been committed, **could *not* serve as interested adult.**[796]
- In the 2007 case of ***Commonwealth v. Escalera,*** a juvenile's foster parent was qualified to act as an interested adult for *Miranda* purposes so as to render juvenile's statements to police, given in the presence of foster parent, admissible at trial; juvenile's foster mother was present, understood the nature of the *Miranda* rights, and had an opportunity to discuss those rights with the juvenile, and, although foster parent had a contractual relationship with the state, any resulting conflict was resolved in deference to foster parent's rights and privileges as a parent or guardian who provided care to juvenile.[797]

Note: Just because an adult advises the child to tell the truth does not make the adult "uninterested,"

Adult must be 18 years of older

- In ***Commonwealth v. Guyton***, a sister who was 13 days shy of her 18th birthday was not an adult for the purposes of "an interested adult." [798]

The advise does not have to be sound legal advise

Although it is required that the interested adult be present during the interrogation to assist the child, there is no requirement that the interested adult's advise be sound legal advice. The key is that "it must be reasonably apparent to the police questioning the juvenile that the adult who is present has the capacity to appreciate the juvenile's situation and is not antagonistic towards the juvenile and is able to give advice".[799]

- In the 2013 case of ***Commonwealth v. Quint, a juvenile***, the SJC upheld the confession by the juvenile suspect despite the fact that the suspect's mother, who was serving as his interested adult, repeatedly pressured him to tell the truth. It was evident that there was no animosity between the mother and son, her motivation was to convince her son to own up to his wrongdoing and to +turn around his life.

Interested Adult and Miranda requirement may be waived in emergency situations

- In ***Commonwealth v. Alan A***., police officers, who located a juvenile who had run away from home after stealing his father's loaded gun in the home of the juvenile's girlfriend, reasonably feared that they and others were in danger unless the gun was found, so that the public safety exception to the warning requirement under *Miranda* allowed officers to question the juvenile regarding the location of the gun without first giving him the *Miranda* warnings, or giving the juvenile the opportunity to speak with his parents or an interested adult; the police did not know where gun was, and the questions were not asked to obtain testimonial evidence against the juvenile.[800]

This rule also applies to children under 14 even with parent present. In ***Commonwealth v. Dillon D***. 13 year old child came to school with bag containing 50 bullets. Police read Miranda without mom there. Mom showed up 25 minutes later and she was not advised of Miranda warnings. The child then told the officer where gun was hidden. Court ruled it was an emergency situation.

[794] *Commonwealth v. Berry*, 410 Mass. 31, 35-36, 570 N.E.2d 1004 (1991)
[795] *Commonwealth v. McCra*, 427 Mass. 564, 568-569, 694 N.E.2d 849 (1998)
[796] *Commonwealth v. A Juvenile*, 402 Mass. 275, 279-280, 521 N.E.2d 1368 (1988)
[797] **Commonwealth v. Escalera,** 70 Mass. 729 (2007).
[798] *Commonwealth v. Guyton*, 405 Mass. 497 (1989)
[799] *Commonwealth v. Berry*, 410 Mass. 31 (1991).
[800] *Commonwealth v. Alan A*,47 Mass.App.Ct. 271, 712 N.E.2d 1157 (1999)

JUVENILE MIRANDA RIGHTS & RECORDING FORM
MIRANDA ADVISEMENTS

Name of Adult: ____________________ Relationship to Child: _______________ Age of Child: _______

Before asking you any questions, it is my duty to advise both of you of the juvenile's rights.

1. You have the right to remain silent.
2. If you choose to speak, anything you say can and will be used against you in a court of law.
3. You have the right to consult with a lawyer before answering any questions, and you may have a lawyer with you during questioning.
4. If you cannot afford a lawyer and want one, a lawyer will be provided for you at no cost before any questioning.
5. If you decide to answer questions, you may stop at any time.
6. Both of you have the right to discuss these rights before deciding whether or not to speak.

Do you understand each of the rights I have just read to you?

Adult: □ Yes □ No _____ Initials **Juvenile:** □ Yes □ No _____ Initials

To Adult: Do you understand that your role is to advise the juvenile about whether or not to waive these rights?
□ Yes □ No _____ Initials

You will now be provided an opportunity to discuss these rights.
Start Time of Consultation _____ AM/PM End Time of Consultation: _____ AM/PM □ chose not to consult

To Juvenile: With these rights in mind, do you wish to speak to now? □ Yes □ No

Signature of Juvenile ____
Signature of Adult ____
Officer Witness ____

Date: ________________ Time ______ Location: __________________________

TAPE RECORDING

If recording not offered state reason why: ____

It is the policy of this department to record all interviews so that there is a record of our discussion. Do we have your permission to tape record our discussion?

□ Yes, I agree to have our discussion recorded. ______ Juvenile's Initials ______ Adult's Initials
□ No, I do not want our discussion recorded. ______ Juvenile's Initials ______ Adult's Initials

Be advised that you may change your decision at any time during this interview.

Signature of Juvenile____
Signature of Adult ____
Signature of Officer Witness: ____

Date: ________________ Time ________ Location: __________________________
□ Having at first decided not to be recorded, I now choose to have the rest of my interview recorded.
Current Time: _____________ ______ Juvenile's Initials ______ Adult's Initials

JUVENILE INTERROGATION

POST ARRAIGNMENT QUESTIONNING - 6TH AMENDMENT RIGHTS

The definitions of "interrogation" under the Fifth and Sixth Amendments are not necessarily interchangeable since the policies underlying the two constitutional protections are quite distinct.[801]

Once a defendant has been formally charged they have a Constitutional Right to be represented by counsel. **This right applies even if the suspect is not in custody**. The 6th Amendment protection is more expansive than the 5th Amendment protections in that it is not limited to custodial interrogation. It protects the defendant from all attempts by law enforcement to obtain incriminating statements, about the pending offense, without the assistance of counsel. However, this right is charge specific, meaning law enforcement is able to question the defendant on an unrelated charge.[802]

The Sixth Amendment guarantees an accused the right to counsel upon the commencement of formal adversary proceedings.[803] Thereafter, government agents may not deliberately elicit statements from a defendant outside the presence of counsel.[804] Any evidence obtained in violation of this rule must be suppressed.[805]

In the 2015 case of ***Commonwealth v. Foxworth***, the SJC reiterated that "Article 12 provides at least as much protection in (these cases) as does the Sixth Amendment. This rule applies not only to overt interrogation by government officers, but also to "indirect and surreptitious" interrogation by persons acting as government agents.[806]

Questioning Not Permitted

Right to counsel attaches and questioning is prohibited once the defendant has been formally charged and either requests counsel or counsel has been appointed.

Defendant May Waive Protections

Nothing in the Sixth Amendment prevents a suspect charged with a crime and represented by counsel from voluntarily choosing, on his own, to speak with police in the absence of an attorney.[807]

- In ***Commonwealth v. Anderson,*** the defendant was incarcerated in the Maine State Prison when he learned that he had been indicted for murder in Massachusetts. He had already been appointed counsel and his attorney sent written notice to the prosecution not to contact the defendant without the attorney's knowledge. The defendant notified the director of security at the prison that he wanted to confess to the murder. The director contacted the investigating officers. The investigating officers went to Maine to speak with the defendant. The officers advised the defendant of his right to an attorney and the fact that his attorney requested that he not be interviewed. The defendant decided to speak anyway. The SJC ruled that the defendant initiated the conversation and waived his rights.[808]

If the defendant chooses to waive his 6th Amendment right to counsel and speak with law enforcement without the assistance of his attorney the police must advise the defendant that he has a right to have his attorney present. In addition, if the attorney had indicated to the police that he or she does not want the police to speak with his client the police must advise the defendant of this fact in order for the waiver to be valid. These rights and information must be provided to the defendant even if he or she is not in custody.

MONTEJO v. LOUISIANA AND THE EFFECTS ON MASSACHUSETTS LAW

In May of 2009 the U.S. Supreme Court decided *Montejo v. Louisiana,* and in this decision the Supreme Court overturned their previous 1986 decision in *Michigan v. Jackson* stating that it is not enough just to have been formally charged, the defendant *must accept the appointment of an attorney*.

However, Massachusetts Courts are likely to continue to prohibit law enforcement from questioning defendants once they have been formally charged even if they have not formally accepted the representation. The SJC has interpreted the art. 12 right to counsel more expansively than the Sixth Amendment in previous decisions.[809] It is recommended that Massachusetts officers continue to follow the requirement of counsel under the Sixth Amendment (and Article 12) even under circumstances where the defendant may not have officially accepted counsel appointed to him/her.

---

[801] *Rhode Island v. Innis*, 446 U.S. 291, (1980)
[802] *Commonwealth v. Rainwater*, 425 Mass. 540, 681 N.E.2d 1218 (1997)
[803] *Brewer v. Williams,* 430 U.S. 387, 401 (1977).
[804] Massiah v. United States, 377 U.S. 201, 206 (1964).
[805] *Maine v. Moulton*, 474 U.S. 159, 172-176 (1985).
[806] See *Commonwealth v. Harmon*, 410 Mass. 425, 428 (1991) , quoting *Massiah*, supra.
[807] *Commonwealth v. Anderson*, 448 Mass. 548, 862 N.E.2d 749 (2007)
[808] *Commonwealth v. Anderson*, 448 Mass. 548, 862 N.E.2d 749 (2007)
[809] *Commonwealth v. Rainwater*, 425 Mass. 540, 553 (1997), cert. denied, 522 U.S. 1095 (1998).

FORMAL ADVERSARIAL CRIMINAL PROCEEDINGS

The Sixth Amendment right to counsel triggers when the accused is *formally charged*. The U.S. Supreme Court has stated that the right to counsel attaches at or after initiation of adversary judicial criminal proceedings, whether by way of formal charge, preliminary hearing, indictment, information or arraignment, "for only then has the government committed itself to prosecute."[810]

The issuance of an arrest warrant or a complaint does not rise to the level of a formal charge. [811] This rule of law was recently reiterated by the SJC in ***Commonwealth v. Holliday***, "Criminal complaints do not trigger Sixth Amendment rights where they function primarily as prerequisites to arrest warrants."[812]

Rendition Hearings do not trigger Sixth Amendment Protections.[813]

Typically in Massachusetts, a suspect has been *formally* charged when he or she has been arraigned, indicted or has appeared before a probable cause hearing[814] but rendition hearings are typically not considered *formally* charged.

CHARGE SPECIFIC

The prohibition of questioning a defendant after being formally charged is limited to further questioning of the crime for which the defendant has been charged.[815]

- In ***Commonwealth v. St. Peter,*** a manslaughter defendant was not entitled, pursuant to Sixth Amendment, to have counsel (appointed to represent him on unrelated charge of operating while under the influence) present during interrogation with respect to victim's death, especially where prior to interrogation the defendant was read his Miranda rights, indicated that he understood them and wished to speak with police, and signed a waiver form.[816]

PRIVATE INDIVIDUALS WORKING AS GOVERNMENT AGENTS

Statements elicited by a private citizen who is acting on behalf of the police will likely violate the Sixth Amendment right to counsel if the defendant has been formally charged. For a private citizen to constitute an "agent", the police must initiate the citizen's help. They must take the first step. This is sometimes referred to as the *Massiah* Rule, after the US Supreme Court case by the same name[817] If a private citizen initiates the conduct on his or her own, agent status will not be found. This is true even if the police (1) reward the citizen for his or her cooperation and/or (2) knew about his or her intended conduct in advance. The key is for the police to promise nothing in return for his or her actions.[818]

- In ***Commonwealth v. Gajka,*** where a cellmate initiated questioning about a homicide, hoping he would use the information to receive a lighter sentence. The defendant's statements were admissible since the cellmate was not the "agent" of the police who neither encouraged nor sought his assistance.[819]
- In the 2009 case of ***Commonwealth v. Young,*** the defendant was in jail awaiting trial on a murder charge when he made incriminating statements to a fellow inmate, Williams, who was also awaiting trial on a murder charge. Williams had previously signed an agreement with the Commonwealth agreeing to testify "completely and truthfully" in the defendant's trial in exchange for a plea of second degree murder. The defendant claimed that the statements should be suppressed as they violated his Sixth Amendment rights. The Court ruled that Williams was not an agent of the police, and even if he was there was no evidence that the Commonwealth intentionally placed the two men together to elicit statements, and there was no questioning or interrogation.[820]

However, if the government has a prearranged long term agreement with an inmate to obtain information in exchange for leniency the court may deem this a violation of the 6th Amendment.

[810] ***Commonwealth v. Simmonds***, 386 Mass. 234, 434 N.E.2d 1270 (1982) quoting from *Kirby v. Illinois*, 406 U.S. 682, 92 S.Ct. 1877, 32 L.Ed.2d 411 (1972).
[811] *Commonwealth v. Smallwood*, 379 Mass. 878 (1980)
[812] *Commonwealth v. Holliday*, 450 Mass. 794, 882 N.E.2d 309, (2008)
[813] *Judd v. Vose*, 813 F.2d 494 (1st Cir. 1987).
[814] Middlesex DA's 2011 Police Training Manual page 187
[815] *Maine v. Moulton*, 106 S.Ct. 477 (1985)
[816] Commonwealth v. St. Peter, 722 N.E.2d 1002 (2000)
[817] *Massiah v. U.S.*, 377 U.S. 201, 84 S.Ct. 1199 (1964) (agent status was found where government pre-arranged to provide benefits to inmate in return for obtaining statements from co-conspirator).
[818] *Commonwealth v. Harmon*, 410 Mass. 425 (1991); *Commonwealth v. Rancourt*, 399 Mass. 269, 503 N.E.2d 960 (1987); *Commonwealth v. Paradiso*, 24 Mass. App. Ct. 142, 507 N.E.2d 258 (1987).
[819] *Commonwealth v. Gajka*, 425 Mass. 751, 682 N.E. 2d 1345 (1997).
[820] *Commonwealth v. Young*, 73 Mass. App. Ct. 479, (2009).

- In ***Commonwealth v. Murphy***, a jailhouse informant had an agreement with the United States Attorney's Office to provide information in exchange for a more lenient sentence. The SJC deemed the informant to be a government agent even though the defendant was not a specific target of the agreement. [821]

Note: A confession made during a court-ordered psychiatric exam is not admissible in evidence.[822]

OTHER GOVERNMENT OFFICIALS

Social Workers

An investigator for Social Services was an agent of law enforcement, and thus, an interview with the defendant after he was arrested and charged with rape regarding the circumstances of rape constituted "police interrogation," for purposes of the Sixth Amendment right to counsel, even though the investigator's responsibilities were for the care and protection of child victim, where the investigator would have been required to turn any incriminating responses over to the police and the prosecutor.[823]

Court Officers

Court officers, while not police officers, are authorized to perform police duties, see G.L. c. 221, § 70A, wear a uniform and a badge, and may be required to report observations of criminal activity to a supervisor or the police. Therefore, court officers are agents of law enforcement authorities for Sixth Amendment purposes.[824] Leaving the law enforcement analysis aside, court officers are required, as part of their usual employment duties, to interact with defendants without counsel present, and "by virtue of their presence in the court room during ongoing proceedings, court officers regularly become aware ··· of the nature of the pending charges and the specific evidence against a defendant. The right to the assistance of counsel would be seriously 'dilute[d],' if court officers could, on their own initiative, question defendants about their pending cases and then turn a defendant's incriminating responses over to the police and prosecutor."[825]

[821] *Commonwealth v. Murphy*, 448 Mass. 452, 862 N.E.2d 30 (2007)
[822] M.G.L. c.123, §15(b); c.233, §20B(b); *Commonwealth v. Buck,* 64 Mass.App.Ct. 760, 835 N.E.2d 623 (2005).
[823] *Commonwealth v. Howard,* 446 Mass. 563, 845 N.E.2d 368 (2006).
[824] Commonwealth v. Hilton, 443 Mass. 597, 823 N.E.2d 383 (2005).
[825] *See Id.*

Section 5 TRIAL ISSUES

OVERVIEW

Although trial matters are typically concerns of the DA's office and not the police officer there are some trial issues that police officers should be familiar with. This section will covers some of those issues.

EVIDENCE ISSUES

REFUSAL EVIDENCE

Police Officers cannot testify to the fact that the defendant refused to take either Field Sobriety Tests or police prompted BAC testing. If this testimony is inadvertently revealed a mistrial is the most likely outcome.

In ***Commonwealth v. McGrail***, the SJC stated "a prosecutor wants to admit evidence that the defendant refused to take a field sobriety test so that the jury may infer that it is the equivalent of his statement, "I have had so much to drink that I know or at least suspect that I am unable to pass the test." Such refusal evidence, therefore, would be relevant to show that the defendant believed that the test results would tend to incriminate him. Because the refusal, in essence, constitutes testimony concerning the defendant's belief on a central issue to the case, we conclude that the evidence of the defendant's refusal to submit to a field sobriety test constitutes testimonial or communicative evidence."

The SJC went on to say "allowing such refusal evidence to be admissible at trial would compel defendants to choose between two equally unattractive alternatives: 'take the test and perhaps produce potentially incriminating real evidence; refuse and have adverse testimonial evidence used against him at trial.'"[826]

For more on refusal evidence see the Arrest Processing and Arrestee Rights and the OUI sections of this manual.

Refusal to answer Questions

A suspect's refusal to answer questions because he/she invokes his/her 5th Amendment protections cannot be used against them at trial.

FINGERPRINTS

In the 2015 case of *Commonwealth v. French*, the Appeals Court ruled that a fingerprint alone may not serve as the sole basis of a conviction (or a prosecution). But the fingerprint evidence coupled with no other plausible excuse for its presence may suffice.

COMPELLING EVIDENCE FROM NON-SUSPECT THIRD PARTY

In the 2006 case of ***Commonwealth v. Draheim***, the SJC ruled that evidence may be compelled from third parties when the Commonwealth has probable cause to believe that a crime was committed, and that the sample will provide evidence relevant to the question of the defendant's guilt. Additional factors concerning the seriousness of the crime, the importance of the evidence, and the unavailability of less intrusive means of obtaining it.

Case example

In the 2014 case of ***Commonwealth v. Kostka***, Timothy Kostka was charged murder and related crimes after the elderly victim was found deceased from multiple stab wounds. DNA evidence was recovered from the victim's fingernails. Timothy has a twin brother, Christopher. The Commonwealth obtained a court order ordering Christopher to submit to a DNA swab to rule out that Christopher and Timothy were identical twins. It was believed that they were fraternal twins. Identical twins have the same DNA, fraternal twins do not. The Commonwealth wanted to counter a potential defense that the DNA could have belonged to Christopher; however he was not a suspect. The SJC approved the order compelling DNA evidence from Christopher.

TRIAL ISSUES

[826] Com.v.. McGrail, 419 Mass. 774 (1995).

THE CONFRONTATION CLAUSE & HEARSAY

The Sixth Amendment's confrontation clause provides that "[i]n all criminal prosecutions, the accused shall enjoy the right…to be confronted with the witnesses against him…."

Most of the issues surrounding the Confrontation Clause are issues for the prosecution to deal with at trial. The important issue for police officers investigating criminal offenses is to ensure that you take proper notes and document victim, witness and suspect statements. However, in this section we will provide you with a broad overview of these issues to help you understand these concepts and perform your duties to the best of your ability.

Bar on out-of-court statements

Typically, statements made outside of court which relate to the guilt of the defendant are not admissible unless the person who actually made the statement testifies to his/her statement made. For instance, if a witness reports her observations to a police officer, the police officer typically cannot testify to what the witness told him (with some rare exceptions); the witness herself must testify to what she saw, so that the defendant "can face his accuser."

These out-of-court statements cannot be admitted into court unless they pass two tests.

1. First, the statement must be admissible under the common-law **rules of evidence** as an **exception to the hearsay rule**.
2. Second, the statement must be **nontestimonial** for purposes of the confrontation clause of the Sixth Amendment. [827]

Rule of Hearsay Evidence

Generally, so-called hearsay is excluded from a criminal trial. This is a rule of a Court and not a Constitutional Matter. Basically, hearsay is a statement made outside of court which is used to prove the defendant committed the offense for which he is on trial. Because these types of statements are not made under oath and are made without the defendant's ability to cross examine the person making the statement these statements are generally prohibited from trial, with few exceptions.

Typically, in order for an out-of-court statement to be used as evidence against a defendant the person who made that statement (the declarant) must testify in court. This permits the accused to confront the accuser and test the validity of the information.

There are some rare circumstances wherein the Court will permit hearsay statements because the nature of the statements makes them otherwise reliable. Below are some of the most common exceptions that police officers may be involved with:

Excited Utterance

An excited utterance is one of the exceptions to the common-law rule of evidence prohibiting hearsay statements. A statement will be considered a spontaneous [or excited] utterance if:

a. there is an occurrence or event "sufficiently startling to render inoperative the normal reflective thought processes of the observer," and
b. if the statement was "a spontaneous reaction to the occurrence or event and not the result of reflective thought."[828]

Attorney Hanrahan's Note: In short, the statement was made under the stress of the event and not in a situation wherein someone would likely be fabricating a lie and if the statement was not made to provide evidence it will not violate the 6th Amendment.

Dying Declarations

There are times when a statement is made by a victim who is facing certain and rapidly approaching death. Often these statements related to cause of the injury leading to the impending death (e.g. "Johnny stabbed me.") Because it is believed that someone who is facing certain death would not lie about who caused their death the courts have carved out an exception to the hearsay prohibition.

In homicide prosecutions in Massachusetts, a victim's out-of-court statement may qualify as a dying declaration if the "statement is made ... under the belief of imminent death and [the person who made the statement] died shortly after

[827] *Com. v. Beatrice*, SJC July 2011
[828] *Com. v. Beatrice*, SJC July 2011

making the statement, concerning the cause or circumstances of what [dying person] believed to be his own impending death or that of a co-victim."[829]

Attorney Hanrahan's Note: Obviously if the declarant dies he/she cannot be presented at trial to comply with the Confrontation Clause of the Constitution. However, the SJC ruled that the admission of a dying declaration does not implicate the defendant's constitutional right to confrontation.[830] The constitutional right "is most naturally read as a reference to the right of confrontation at common law," and the dying declaration was recognized at common law as an exception to the right of confrontation when the Sixth Amendment to the United States Constitution was adopted. For more on the Confrontation Clause see the ***Crawford v. Washington*** section below.

Business Records

General Laws c. 233, § 78, creates an exception to the rule prohibiting admission of hearsay evidence for official business records provided that (1) the entry, writing, or record was made in good faith; (2) in the regular course of business; (3) before the beginning of the civil or criminal proceeding in which it is offered; and (4) it was the regular course of such business to make such memorandum at the time of such act, transaction, occurrence, or event, or within a reasonable time thereafter." [831]

FEDERAL RULING: *CRAWFORD v. WASHINGTON*

The 2004 U.S. Supreme Court case of ***Crawford v. Washington***[832] reestablished the principle that **testimonial** out-of-court statements are inadmissible under the confrontation clause of the Sixth Amendment to the U.S. Constitution, regardless of local rules of evidence, unless the declarant is available at trial or the declarant formally is unavailable to testify and the defendant had a prior opportunity to cross-examine the declarant.

Testimonial Statements are Not Admissible if they Violate the Confrontation Clause

Statements "made in response to questioning by law enforcement agents are per se (automatically) testimonial, except where the questioning is meant to secure a volatile scene or to establish the need for or provide medical care."

Out-of-court statements made in response " 'to questions from people who are *not* law enforcement agents' and 'statements offered ... without prompting, regardless of who heard them,' are not testimonial per se (not automatically considered testimonial)." In addition, whether or not the statements are deemed testimonial is based on whether a reasonable person in the victim's position would not have anticipated that her statements would be used against the defendant in investigating and prosecuting a crime.

In ***Davis v. Washington***, the U.S. Supreme Court stated "statements are nontestimonial when made in the course of police interrogation under circumstances objectively indicating that the primary purpose of the interrogation is to enable police assistance to meet an **ongoing emergency**. They are testimonial when the circumstances objectively indicate that there is no such ongoing emergency, and that the primary purpose of the interrogation is to establish or prove past events potentially relevant to later criminal prosecution."[833]

The *Davis* Court then listed factors, including the existence of an ongoing emergency, which distinguished the testimonial statements in *Crawford*, from the nontestimonial statements in *Davis*. Those factors included:

1. whether the declarant was speaking about events as they were "actually happening, rather than describing past events";
2. whether any reasonable listener would recognize that the declarant was facing an "ongoing emergency";
3. whether what was asked and answered was necessary to resolve the present emergency rather than simply to learn what had happened in the past; and
4. the level of formality of the interview.

TRIAL ISSUES

---

[829] Mass. G. Evid. § 804(b)(2) (2013). See Commonwealth v. Vona, 250 Mass. 509, 511 (1925).
[830] Commonwealth v. Nesbitt, 452 Mass. 236, 249-251 (2008), quoting Crawford v.Washington, 541 U.S. 36, 56 n.6 (2004).
[831] Commonwealth v. Siny Van Tran, 460 Mass. 535, 548 (2011). See Mass. G. Evid. § 803(6)(A), at 259 (2011) ("This subsection is taken nearly verbatim from G. L. c. 233, § 78").
[832] *Commonwealth v. Washington,* 541 U.S. 36, 124 S.Ct. 1354, 158 L.Ed.2d 177 (2004).
[833] Davis v. Washington, 547 U.S. 813, 822 (2006).

Following *Davis*, the Court noted that these "indicia" help determine whether, objectively, the "primary purpose" of a statement may be said to be testimonial.[834]

Case example

- ***Com. v. Figueroa** (2011):* The defendant was a certified nursing assistant at the Fairlawn Nursing Home (Fairlawn) in Leominster. On October 13, 2003, Matthew Smith, was working the 3:00 to 11:00 P.M. shift as a certified nursing assistant (CNA) at Fairlawn. At approximately 10:30 P.M., Smith was assisting a patient into bed, and he determined that he needed the help of another CNA. Smith began to search for the defendant. While he looked down the hallway, Smith's attention was drawn to room number twenty-five (room 25) because the door was closed; CNAs were not ordinarily permitted to offer patient care behind closed doors. He went into room number twenty-seven and walked into the bathroom that was shared by room 25. When he entered the room he observed the defendant having sexual intercourse with the 86 year old victim, who was suffering from early on-set of dementia. Smith advised his supervisor. The victim was interviewed by the supervisor and the victim explained that the defendant keeps "doing that test to me." Through further inquiry the staff learned that the test consisted of the defendant putting his penis into her vagina. While explaining the incident the victim appeared scared and upset. Witnesses to the victim's statements testified at trial to what the victim had told them. The defendant was convicted. The Court permitted this testimony.

The Court explained that "the focus of the testimonial-in-fact inquiry is not on those who heard the statements but, rather, on an objective view of a reasonable person in the declarant's position. Thus, the fact that Miller knew she would have to notify the police about the assault is not ruling. Instead, a reasonable person in the victim's position would not have anticipated that her statements would be used against the defendant in investigating and prosecuting a crime" because she thought the defendant was performing "a test" and not committing a crime.

The Bar Only Applies to "Testimonial" Statements

This rule applies only to **testimonial** out-of-court statements, meaning statements that are made for *the purpose of establishing a case against the defendant.* The Confrontation Clause does not bar the admission of statements that a reasonable person in the position of the person making the statement would not objectively foresee as being used in the investigation or prosecution of a crime.

In other words if the statements were not made to be used as evidence against the suspect then they are most likely not testimonial in nature and will not be barred from trial, at least under the *Crawford* ruling.[835] However, the SJC has indicated that "statements elicited through questioning by law enforcement agents are per se testimonial."[836]

- In the 2005 case of ***Commonwealth v. Gonsalves,*** while the case was sent back to the District Court for more evidence, the SJC suggested that a young rape victim's statements to her mother before the police were called would probably be admissible (as they were not *testimonial).* However, those statements made to the police would not be admissible. The latter were not made to secure a volatile situation or to procure needed medical attention.[837]
- In ***Commonwealth v. Rodriguez,*** the Court held that a son's and daughter's out-of-court statements to the police regarding an alleged assault were per se testimonial and thus their admission into evidence violated their father's confrontation rights since neither child testified at trial.[838] The case involved a domestic violence assault by the father on his son. The son's and daughter's statements were made in response to police questioning at a secure scene. The son had no apparent injuries and did not want medical attention. Even though the trial court admitted the children's statements to the police under the "excited utterance" exception to the hearsay rule, the Sixth Amendment "trumps" that rule and precludes the admission of such statements.[839]

Statements made to meet and Ongoing Emergency are Not Testimonial

Statements made for the purpose meeting an ongoing emergency or securing a volatile scene are not barred by the Confrontation Clause providing there is still an "on-going emergency."

- In ***Commonwealth v. Foley***, the victim's responses to police officer's initial questions during a volatile scene were not testimonial, and thus their admission through officer's testimony did not violate defendant's right of confrontation. However, the victim's statements in response to police questioning after the scene had been secured

[834] Commonwealth v. Galicia, 447 Mass. 737, 743-744 (2006).
[835] *Davis v. Washington*, 547 U.S. 813, 822 (2006).
[836] *Commonwealth v. Gonsalves,* 445 Mass. 1, 833 N.E.2d 549 (2005).
[837] *Commonwealth v. Gonsalves,* 445 Mass. 1, 833 N.E.2d 549 (2005).
[838] *Commonwealth v. Rodriguez,* 445 Mass. 1003, 833 N.E.2d 134 (2005).
[839] See *Gonsalves, supra.*

were testimonial per se, and thus their admission at trial through officer's testimony without affording defendant opportunity to cross-examine victim violated Confrontation Clause.

- In the 2008 case of ***Commonwealth v. Nesbitt***, a statement by a domestic abuse stabbing victim during a 911 call was deemed by the Court not to be a testimonial statement for the purposes of *Crawford* but rather a call for help and intended to assist the police in meeting an ongoing emergency.[840]
- In the 2008 case of ***Commonwealth v. Lao***, the victim's statements made during 911 call reporting the defendant's alleged attempt to run over her with his vehicle were testimonial in nature under Crawford, and thus, admission of the statements violated the defendant's confrontation rights in his murder prosecution **because at the time of the 911 call the defendant had left and the victim was no longer in immediate peril.** However, the victim's statements to her daughter that the defendant had tried to run over her with his car were non-testimonial under Crawford, and thus, admission of the statements did not violate defendant's confrontation rights in his murder prosecution, given that statements were remarks to a relative, not to law enforcement officers, and there was nothing in the record to suggest that the victim had any reasonable expectation that these particular comments to her daughter would be used prosecutorially at some later date.[841]
- In the 2010 case of ***Commonwealth v. Simon***, the SJC ruled that a 911 call by a recent shooting victim calling for help for him and his injured brother was an ongoing emergency, and thus the answers to questions by the dispatcher were not testimonial as they were intended to meet an on-going emergency including questions about the identity of the perpetrator. The statements also qualified as excited utterances and thus were properly admitted at trial under that exception to the hearsay rule.

Statements made to Access Medical Care

Statements made in order to provide medical care will not be barred by the confrontation clause.

- In the 2006 case of ***Com .v. DeOliveira***, when a six year old victim reported sexual abuse to the doctors at an emergency room in the presence of police the statement were not deemed "testimonial per se" since the statements were not made in response to police questioning but rather to obtain medical treatment.[842]

Statements made to Co-Venturers

Statements made to cohorts in a criminal venture and overheard by a third party are generally not testimonial in nature.

- In the 2007 case of ***Commonwealth v. Burton***, a witness was permitted to testify to incriminating statements that she overheard three co-venturers make shortly after committing a murder. The court ruled that these statements were not the types which are reasonably foreseeable as being used in a criminal investigation or the prosecution of a crime. The witness who overheard the coventurer's statement testified and not the coventurer who made the statement, thus had the statement been reasonably foreseeable to be used in the prosecution the confrontation clause would have been violated. [843]

FEDERAL RULING: *MELENDEZ-DIAZ v. MASSACHUSETTS*

In 2009 the U.S. Supreme Court decided *Melendez-Diaz v. Massachusetts*, wherein the Supreme Court ruled that the admission of certificates of analysis into evidence of a criminal trial without testimony from the authoring analyst violates the Sixth Amendment right to confrontation. This is decision has had a serious impact of gun and drug cases in Massachusetts and will likely have an impact on other areas requiring certification of analysis.[844] The submission of a certificate of analysis from the lab is no longer sufficient to prove that the substance was a firearm, or drug, or other substance, without testimony from the lab technician.

However, proof "may be made by circumstantial evidence"[845] and by other methods such as witness statements and so on.

[840] *Commonwealth v. Nesbitt*, 452 Mass. 236 (2008).
[841] *Commonwealth v. Lao*, 450 Mass. 215, 877 N.E.2d 557 (2207)
[842] *Commonwealth v. DeOliveira*, 447 Mass. 56, 849 N.E.2d 218 (2006)
[843] *Commonwealth v. Burton*, 450 Mass. 55 (2007)
[844] *Melendez-Diaz v. Massachusetts*, 129 S.Ct. 2527, 2532, 2542 (2009).
[845] *Com. v. Dawson*, 399 Mass. 465,467 (1987)

THE "FIRST COMPLAINT" RULE

Despite the general prohibition on hearsay evidence, so-called "fresh complaint" evidence (statements made soon after a sexual assault) was admitted in sexual assault trials as an exception to the hearsay prohibition. This dates back to old English common law where it was believed that if a woman was sexually assaulted she would report it to someone else right away; [846] hence the term "fresh" complaint was termed.

In modern times the SJC indicated that "we cannot ignore the societal tendency to disbelieve sexual assault victims." The SJC felt it was necessary to permit out-of-court statements to be presented at trial to help corroborate the natural tendency of jurors to disbelieve sexual assault victims.[847]

Because of these exceptions to the general prohibition of hearsay evidence, it is vital that investigating officers properly record the statements of victims, and those whom the victim confided in, when investigating sexual assault crimes.

FRESH COMPLAINT BECOMES THE FIRST COMPLAINT

In the 2005 case of ***Commonwealth v. King***, the SJC revisited the "fresh complaint" rule. The Court acknowledged that research suggests that, in part because the harm suffered by sexual assault victims often consists of the psychological harm caused by the defendants' violation of a victim's body, such victims respond in a variety of ways to the trauma of the crime, and often do not promptly report or disclose the crime for a range of reasons, including shame, fear, or concern they will not be believed.

Despite the fact that the reasoning around the "freshness" of sexual assault complaints may not be accurate given recent studies, the Court determined that there was still a need to counterbalance the assumption that sexual assault victims fabricate their claims. The Court, in *King*, established the "First Complaint" rule, permitting the testimony of the first person whom the victim reports the assault to regardless of its "freshness."

ELEMENTS OF THE *FIRST COMPLAINT* RULE

Freshness is no longer required: A "delay" in disclosing a sexual assault is not a reason for excluding evidence of the initial complaint; the timing of a complaint is simply one factor the jury may consider in weighing the complainant's testimony.[848]

Multiple Complaint Witnesses are no longer permitted: The Court stated we "will no longer permit in evidence testimony from multiple complaint witnesses, limiting the testimony to that of one witness-- the first person told of the assault. The testimony of multiple complaint witnesses likely serves no additional corroborative purpose, and may unfairly enhance a complainant's credibility as well as prejudice the defendant by repeating for the jury the often horrific details of an alleged crime." However, multiple witnesses may be permitted when multiple offenses are involved.[849] See bullet D below:

Multiple "First Complaint" Witnesses Permitted Where Ongoing Abuse Occurs Involving Different Crimes

In situations where the victim is victimized over a period of years, involving escalating abuse (i.e. different crimes), more than one first complaint witness will be allowed.[850]

Exceptions: There are rare exceptions to the requirement that only the "first" person be allowed to testify:

a. **Bias or Hostile:** If the first person told of the assault is bias or hostile against the victim (i.e. the suspect's spouse) the Court may allow the second person told to serve as the first complaint witness.
b. **Incompetent:** If the first complaint is incompetent to serve as a witness at trial (e.g. a child or suffers from mental illness) the Court may allow the second person told to serve as the first complaint witness.

NO VIOLATION OF THE CONFRONTATION CLAUSE

There is no violation of the Confrontation Clause, in regards to the First Complaint witness, providing the victim testifies at trial granting the defendant the opportunity to cross examine the declarant.[851]

---

[846] *Commonwealth v. Bailey,* 370 Mass. 388 (1976).See *Commonwealth v. Peters,* 429 Mass. 22, 27 n. 6 (1999).
[847] *Commonwealth v. Licata*, 412 Mass. 654,658 (1992).
[848] *Commonwealth v. King*, 445 Mass. 217 (2005).
[849] *Commonwealth v. King*, 445 Mass. 217 (2005).
[850] *Commonwealth v. Kebreau*, SJC (July 2009).
[851] *Commonwealth v. King*, 445 Mass. 217 (2005).

PRIVILEGED COMMUNICATIONS

There are some communications made by the defendant that are inadmissible in court. Although these issues are typically a concern for the prosecution it is important to be familiar with them as it may guide your investigation.

Spousal Privilege

Under Chapter 233 § 20, a spouse generally cannot be compelled to testify against his/her husband or wife. There are some exceptions to this rule, for instance in any criminal proceeding in which one spouse is a defendant alleged to have committed a crime against the other spouse, in protective order proceedings, in cases involving child abuse and incest, a spouse can testify against his/her husband or wife.

Minor Child Privilege

Chapter 233 § 20 states that an unemancipated, minor child, living with a parent, shall not testify before a grand jury, trial of an indictment, complaint or other criminal proceeding, against his/her parent, where the victim in such proceeding is not a member of the minor child parent's family and who does not reside in the said parent's household. In other words, a child cannot testify against his/her parent, if the child lives with the parent, unless the victim is also a child living with the same parent.

For the purposes of this clause the term "parent" shall mean the natural or adoptive mother or father of the child.

Religious Privilege

Chapter 233 § 20 states that "a priest, rabbi or ordained or licensed minister of any church or an accredited Christian Science practitioner shall not, without the consent of the person making the confession, be allowed to disclose a confession made to him in his professional character, in the course of discipline enjoined by the rules or practice of the religious body to which he belongs; nor shall a priest, rabbi or ordained or licensed minister of any church or an accredited Christian Science practitioner testify as to any communication made to him by any person in seeking religious or spiritual advice or comfort, or as to his advice given thereon in the course of his professional duties or in his professional character, without the consent of such person."

Recently in the 2013 case of ***Commonwealth v. Vital***, the SJC affirmed that this privilege only applies to communications where a petinent religious or spiritual advice or comfort." It does not apply to other forms of communications with these religious practitioners.

GRAND JURY WITNESSES WARNINGS

The issuance of a summons requiring a witness to appear and give testimony before the grand jury is a form of compulsion. Because grand jury testimony is compelled, it ought to be ameliorated with an advisement of rights where there is a substantial likelihood that the witness may become an accused; that is where the witness is a "target" or is reasonably likely to become one.

Accordingly, the Court adopted a rule that where, at the time a person appears to testify before a grand jury, the prosecutor has reason to believe that the witness is either a "target" or is likely to become one, the witness must be advised, before testifying, that (1) he or she may refuse to answer any question if a truthful answer would tend to incriminate the witness, and (2) anything that he or she does say may be used against the witness in a subsequent legal proceeding. The rule is meant to discourage the Commonwealth from identifying a person as a likely participant in the crime under investigation, compelling his or her appearance and testimony at the grand jury without adequate warnings, and then using that testimony in a criminal trial.[852]

TRIAL ISSUES

[852] *Commonwealth v. Wood* (2014)

Section 5 MOTOR VEHICLE RELATED ISSUES

MOTOR VEHICLE STOPS

A MOTOR VEHICLE STOP IS A SEIZURE

SEIZURE

A *seizure* occurs under the Fourth Amendment and the Massachusetts Declaration of Rights whenever a motor vehicle is stopped by an agent of the government.[853] The temporary detention of individuals during the stop of an automobile by the police, even if only for a brief period and for a limited purpose, constitutes a *seizure* of persons under the Fourth Amendment.[854] Recall that a "seizure" of a person takes place, for purposes of the Massachusetts Constitution, if, under the circumstances, a reasonable person would have believed that he or she was not free to leave[855] (see Temporary Detentions Section for more).

JUSTIFICATION FOR THE STOP

Because stopping a motor vehicle and detaining its occupants is a "seizure" for Fourth Amendment purposes, the police must have a **reasonable suspicion that criminal activity is occurring** or **that a motor vehicle violation exists**, or has occurred, before they may stop a motor vehicle.[856]

- In ***Commonwealth v. Deramo***, a police officer had reasonable suspicion to stop a vehicle driven by the defendant, where the officer knew from contact two months before that the defendant's driver's license had been revoked for a period that would last at least two more years, the police officer recognized the vehicle as belonging to the defendant due to its distinctive door handles, and the officer testified that he recognized the defendant driving the vehicle before he made the stop.[857]
- In ***Commonwealth v. Smigliano***, an officer's reasonable belief that a motorist is lost, in the absence of complicating elements such as safety hazards, illness, suspicion of crime, or the like, is not sufficient to justify a seizure (stopping of motor vehicle).[858]

Criminal Activity

If a police officer has reasonable suspicion or probable cause that an occupant of a motor vehicle has committed (or is about to commit) a crime the officer may initiate a stop, just as if the suspect was walking on foot.

Traffic Violations

Chapter 90C § 2 and 3(A), authorize police to issue citations for motor vehicle *traffic* violations, including civil infractions.[859] Chapter 94C requires that a police officer issue a citation in-hand at the time of the violation (with few exceptions) this implies that police has the authority to stop the vehicle in order to comply with this requirement.

In ***Commonwealth v. Rodriguez*** (2015) the SJC stated "many of our traffic violation statutes regulate moving cars and relate directly to the promotion of public safety; even those laws that have to do with maintaining a vehicle's equipment in accordance with certain standards may also be safety-related. Permitting stops based on reasonable suspicion or probable cause that these laws may have been violated gives police the ability to immediately address potential safety hazards on the road. Thus, although a vehicle stop does represent a significant intrusion into an individual's privacy, the governmental interest in allowing such stops for the purpose of promoting compliance with our automobile laws is clear and compelling."

Attorney Hanrahan's Comment: The vast majority of motor vehicle violations are civil (i.e. non-criminal) violations of the law or rules of the road. However, a police detention infringes on the Fourth Amendment rights of the violator. The reason why the law permits a police officer to infringe on the Constitutional rights of citizen for a non-criminal civil violation is because it is necessary for public safety. The police would not be very effective at modifying driving behavior if they could not stop the violator and address the violation immediately. However, because the stop is based on a non-criminal violation the detention must be brief and limited to the purpose of the stop (i.e. issuing a citation or a warning) and, absent any indication of criminality; the violator should be allowed to carry on freely.

[853] *Commonwealth v. Rodriguez*, 430 Mass. 577, 722 N.E. 2d 429 (2000).
[854] *Commonwealth v. Rodriguez*, 430 Mass. 577, 722 N.E. 2d 429 (2000).
[855] *Commonwealth v. Redd*, 50 Mass.App.Ct. 904, 735 N.E.2d 1252 (2001).
[856] *Delaware v. Prouse*, 440 U.S. 648, 99 S.Ct. 1391 (1979).
[857] *Commonwealth v. Deramo*, 436 Mass. 40, 762 N.E.2d 815 (2002).
[858] *Commonwealth v. Smigliano*, 427 Mass. 490, 694 N.E. 2d 341 (1998).
[859] *Commonwealth v. Rodriguez*, SJC 2015

Non-Criminal Marijuana Citations

In 2015 case of *Commonwealth v. Rodriguez*, the SJC ruled that reasonable suspicion that the occupants of a motor vehicle possess non-criminal amounts of marijuana (in this case the reasonable suspicion stemmed from the odor of burnt marijuana) does not justify a vehicle stop.

Random motor vehicle stops

The U.S. Supreme Court case of ***Delaware v. Prouse,*** specifically held that police cannot randomly stop motorists to check the orderliness of license and registration papers.

However, randomly running license plates is permissible (there is no expectation of privacy in your license plate that is visible to the public).

Information from the registry of motor vehicles

Police officers may rely on information supplied by the Registry of Motor Vehicles in order to stop the operator of a motor vehicle.

- In ***Commonwealth v. Garden,*** the SJC permitted the stop of a motor vehicle where the registered owner had a suspended license even though the officer did not know whether or not the registered owner was actually operating the motor vehicle. It was not until the officer began to approach the vehicle that he could see that the operator was a man (the registered owner was a woman). The SJC held that even though reasonable suspicion evaporated when the officer realized the discrepancy he was still permitted to approach the driver and explain the reason for the stop.[860]

Officer's subjective intent

Generally, an officer's subjective intent or underlying motive will not invalidate an otherwise lawful motor vehicle stop.

- In ***Commonwealth v. Avellar***, the police began surveilling the defendant after receiving information from an informant that the defendant had purchased a large quantity of drugs. The police later stopped the vehicle for failing to use a turn signal. The Appeals Court ruled that stop as valid despite the officer's motive. The court stated "the law is that the officers' motive for stopping the vehicle is irrelevant."[861]

However, if the motivation is connected with the race, ethnicity or similar characteristic of the operator or occupants the stop would be unlawful.

PUBLIC SAFETY EXCEPTIONS

There are situations where police may stop a motor vehicle even without reasonable suspicion or the observation of a motor vehicle violation as long as the action was reasonable. These exceptions are in line with the Community Caretaking Doctrine and exigent/emergency circumstances discussed primarily in *the Temporary Detention Section* and other areas of this manual.

Drunk driver

An officer's community caretaking or emergency exception function may come into play when the police receive a report of a dangerous operator jeopardizing public safety. If the situation is deemed to be an emergency the reliability and basis of knowledge requirement of the reporting person normally required to establish reasonable suspicion to stop a motor vehicle may not be needed. Compare the following examples:

In ***Commonwealth v. Hurd***, the police received information from an anonymous caller that a man who appeared to be drunk was getting into a blue automobile with New Hampshire license plates in front of a package store. There were three small children in the automobile. The police responded to the call and, when they arrived at the location, they saw the automobile approaching the entrance to Route 128, a high speed highway. The court relaxed the basis of knowledge and reliability test because of the emergency presented.[862]

In the 2005 Appeals Court of ***Commonwealth v. Davis***, the court held that the police officer was justified under the emergency exception doctrine in making an investigatory stop of the defendant, even though the information

---

[860] *Commonwealth v. Garden*, 451 Mass. 43, 883 N.E.2d 905 (2008)
[861] *Commonwealth v. Avellar,* 70 Mass.App.Ct. 608, 875 N.E.2d 539 (2007)
[862] *Commonwealth v. Hurd*, 29 Mass.App.Ct. 929 (1990).

received by the officer was relayed from an anonymous tip, where the officer heard a radio dispatch of a potentially drunk driver with a description of the driver and the vehicle and the direction in which it was headed, and the officer saw the vehicle coming in his direction.[863]

Compare with:

In ***Commonwealth v. Lubiejewski,*** where a trooper arrested a motorist for operating under the influence and operating a motor vehicle negligently so as to endanger, the Appeals Court ruled that the community caretaking doctrine did not apply.[864] There the basis for the charge was an anonymous motorist's report that a truck was operating on the wrong side of Route 195. The trooper used the reported plate registration number and proceeded to the operator's residence. He observed the truck driving away but not improperly. He stopped the vehicle, had the operator perform a field sobriety test and concluded he had been operating under the influence. Because the reasonable inference was that the trooper was engaged in "the detection, investigation, or acquisition of evidence relating to the violation of a criminal statute,"[865] the court ruled that the community caretaking function could not be used to justify the stop.[866]

LENGTH OF THE DETENTION

The nature of the stop defines the scope of the initial inquiry.[867] The investigative detention must be temporary and last no longer than reasonably necessary to effectuate the purpose of the stop.[868] Absent indication of criminal activity, a routine motor vehicle stop should last no longer than is needed to issues the violator a citation or warning.

- In the 2009 case of ***Commonwealth v. Watts,*** a prolonged vehicle stop (approximately 1 hour) was justified when the driver produced a rental agreement that was expired by one day. The trooper phoned the rental company to inquire about the vehicle's status.[869] This inquiry justified the delay.

SCOPE OF THE INTERACTION WITH OPERATOR AND PASSENGERS

When a police officer stops a motor vehicle for a motor vehicle violation the scope of the interaction is limited to the violation unless the officer detects other criminal activity.[870] The Appeals Court has stated "if the driver produces a valid license and registration, there is ordinarily no reason for an officer to probe further. The officer should give the driver the citation for the traffic offense and then permit the vehicle to proceed on its way."[871] Additionally, passengers, who have not committed any criminal or motor vehicle violations, should be free from questioning or other aggressive police contact.

- In the 2006 case of ***Commonwealth v. Bettencourt,*** the court suppressed drugs found on a passenger during a "pat frisk" after the defendant was arrested on outstanding warrants. After the vehicle was stopped for a motor vehicle violation and the operator was arrested, the police pressed the passenger (defendant) for his information after he claimed not to have a license. The court ruled that the police had no authority to insist that the passenger provide his information. However, this case was argued by the Commonwealth on "reasonable ground to further investigation or precaution." The Commonwealth later attempted to change its argument on appeal claiming "community caretaking" because the police did not want to leave the vehicle unattended. The court did not hear this argument because it was not initially argued, however the court indicated that this may be a valid reason to obtain information from a passenger.[872]
- In the 2008 case of ***Commonwealth v. Goewey,*** the trooper was justified in asking the passengers of a vehicle for identification after stopping the vehicle for an expired inspection sticker because the passengers were not wearing seatbelts and the identification was necessary in order to issue the passengers citations.[873]

[863] *Commonwealth v. Davis*, 63 Mass.App.Ct. 88, 823 N.E.2d 411 (2005).
[864] *Commonwealth v. Lubiejewski*, 49 Mass.App.Ct. 212 (2000).
[865] *Cady v. Dombrowski*, supra.
[866] *Commonwealth v. Sondrini*, 48 Mass. App. Ct. 704, 724 N.E. 2d 748 (2000).
[867] *Commonwealth v. Bartlett,* 41 Mass.App.Ct. 468, 470-471, 671 N.E.2d 515 (1996)
[868] *Commonwealth v. Laaman,* 25 Mass.App.Ct. at 364, 518 N.E.2d 861 (1988).
[869] *Commonwealth v. Watts,* 22 Mass. App. Ct. 952 (2009).
[870] *Commonwealth v. Torres*, 424 Mass. 153,158 (1997).
[871] Commonwealth v. Bartlett, 41 Mass.App.Ct. 468, 471 (1996).
[872] *Commonwealth v. Bettencourt,* 447 Mass. 631, 856 N.E.2d 174 (2006)
[873] *Commonwealth v. Goewey*, 452 Mass. 399, 894 N.E.2d 1128 (2008).

ROAD BLOCKS/CHECK POINTS

Ordinarily, ''law enforcement officers must possess at least articulable suspicion before stopping a vehicle.''[874] There are, however, ''limited exceptions'' to the ''requirement that seizures be based on probable cause or reasonable suspicion.''[875] These include roadblocks to apprehend fleeing suspects as well as sobriety checkpoints.

Sobriety Roadblocks

The U.S. Supreme Court has upheld the constitutionality of sobriety roadblocks.[876] The US Supreme Court has stated "no one can seriously dispute the magnitude of the drunken driving problem or the States' interest in eradicating it. Media reports of alcohol-related death and mutilation on the Nation's roads are legion." The SJC stated "it is equally beyond question that the stop of a vehicle at a fixed roadblock, however brief, constitutes a warrantless seizure of that vehicle and its driver without individualized suspicion under the Fourth Amendment to the United States Constitution and art. 14 of the Massachusetts Declaration of Rights."[877] In determining whether such seizures are reasonable, we have recognized that we must balance the strong public interest in reducing the number of persons who die each year on our highways from alcohol-related accidents "against 'the individual's right to personal security free from arbitrary interference by law officers."[878]

Requirements

In the 1983 case of ***Commonwealth v. McGeoghegan,*** the Supreme Judicial Court discussed the lawfulness of a roadblock stop of vehicles for the purpose of detecting drunk drivers.[879] The Court stated, "for a roadblock to be permissible, it appears that:

1. The selection of motor vehicles to be stopped must not be arbitrary,
2. Safety must be assured,
3. Motorists' inconvenience must be minimized and
4. Assurance must be given that the procedure is being conducted pursuant to a written plan devised by law enforcement supervisory personnel.

The SJC stated that although advance notice is not a constitutional necessity, advance publication of the date of an intended roadblock, even without announcing its precise location, would have the virtue of reducing surprise, fear, and inconvenience.

Later in 1990, the SJC declared that each of the guidelines mentioned in *McGeoghegan* must be satisfied. Substantial compliance will not suffice.[880]

The brief intrusion on privacy is outweighed by the risk to society from drunk drivers. The courts conduct a so-called "balancing test" on whether or not the intrusion outweighs the public safety risk. This is why the Courts permit these brief detentions on less than reasonable suspicion in some rare circumstances.

No Discretion Permitted

Police officers may not, within the limits of the Fourth Amendment and art. 14, have discretion to target which vehicles to stop, such as in roving roadside checks, or fixed checkpoints in which cars are stopped according to no set pattern.[881] Because sobriety checkpoints, by their very nature, initially stop drivers without any individualized suspicion, giving police officers such discretion poses too high a risk that the discretion will be "standardless and unconstrained."[882] Instead, the SJC has required that sobriety checkpoints be governed by standard, neutral guidelines that clearly forbid the arbitrary selection of vehicles to be initially stopped.[883]

Reasonable suspicion required for further inquiry

Although reasonable suspicion is not required to briefly detain the operator of a motor vehicle during a sobriety checkpoint, reasonable suspicion is required in order to conduct more extensive field sobriety testing or to make a

[874] *Commonwealth v. Rodriguez,* 430 Mass. 577at 580, 722 N.E.2d 429, quoting from *United States v. Huguenin,* 154 F.3d 547, 553 (6th Cir. 1998).
[875] *Id.* at 579, 722 N.E.2d 429.
[876] See, *Michigan Department of State Police v. Sitz,* 496 U.S. 444, 110 S.Ct. 2481 (1990).
[877] Commonwealth v. Murphy, SJC-10287 quoting See United States v. Martinez-Fuerte, 428 U.S. 543, 556, 96 S.Ct. 3074, 49 L.Ed.2d 1116 (1976); Commonwealth v. McGeoghegan, 389 Mass. 137, 139, 449 N.E.2d 349 (1983).
[878] Commonwealth v. Murphy 2009
[879] *Commonwealth v. McGeoghegan,* 389 Mass. 138, 449 N.E.2d 349 (1983).
[880] *Commonwealth v. Cameron*, 407 Mass. 1005, 553 N.E.2d 897 (1990).
[881] See Delaware v. Prouse, 440 U.S. 648, 663, 99 S.Ct. 1391, 59 L.Ed.2d 660 (1979); Commonwealth v. Anderson, supra.
[882] Delaware v. Prouse, supra at 661, 99 S.Ct. 1391. See Commonwealth v. Shields, 402 Mass. 162, 165, 521 N.E.2d 987 (1988).
[883] See Trumble, supra at 89, 483 N.E.2d 1102; Commonwealth v. Anderson, supra at 348-349, 547 N.E.2d 1134.

request either for a license, registration or to exit the motor vehicle. Further interference requires reasonable suspicion that the operator is under the influence of either alcohol or drugs or is believed to have committed some other criminal offense or motor vehicle infraction.

- In ***Commonwealth v. Lovelace***, the defendant was approached by an officer as he passed through a sobriety checkpoint. The officer detected the odor of alcohol and instructed the driver to an area adjacent to the roadway for further inquiry. The defendant refused to produce his license and was arrested for violating M.G.L. 90 § 25. The court upheld the arrest.[884]
- In ***Commonwealth v. Bazinet***, the Appeals Court indicated that if an officer detects the odor of alcohol during contact with a motorist, that alone will justify directing the motorist to the screening area.[885]

Officer discretion in directing vehicles to secondary screening is not unconstitutional

A sobriety checkpoint plan that indicates that an officer/trooper "***may*** direct a vehicle from the normal flow of traffic to a secondary screening location" upon reasonable suspicion is not unconstitutional.[886] Although sobriety checkpoints must not be arbitrary and discretion must be reduced, the Court stated "we have never required an officer with reasonable suspicion to make a stop." The language in the plan which indicates that a trooper *may* direct the person to the secondary location "is not the type of discretion prohibited."

Roadside questioning does not require Miranda warnings

The Supreme Court has ruled that the roadside questioning of a motorist detained pursuant to a "routine" traffic stop does not constitute "custodial interrogation" for purposes of the Miranda rule as long as a reasonable person in the position of the motorist would reasonably have believed that he or she would be allowed to leave after a brief delay.[887] The same rule applies to brief detentions during a sobriety check point.

Plan which indicates officers should look for criminal activity permitted

A provision in the sobriety checkpoint written plan indicating that officers discovering "any observation of a crime that would amount to a felony or narcotic law violation" direct the vehicle for secondary screening does not turn an otherwise lawful sobriety checkpoint into an unlawful drug interdiction roadblock.

In ***Commonwealth v. Swartz,*** the defendant was arrested in the fall of 2006 at a roadblock established by the State police in Bridgewater as part of a sobriety checkpoint program to detect and deter drunk driving (sobriety checkpoint), and charged with operating a motor vehicle while under the influence of alcohol, third offense, in violation of G.L. c. 90, § 24. The roadblock was conducted pursuant to State police General Order TRF-15 (TRF-15), which sets forth protocols and guidelines governing sobriety checkpoints conducted in Massachusetts, supplemented by orders and instructions specific to this roadblock included in the saturation patrol and sobriety checkpoint operational plans and directives (operations plan). The plan indicated that "the following violations and/or observations warrant directing a motorist to drive to the check area:" and one of those provisions indicated "any observation of a crime that would amount to a felony or narcotic law violation." In upholding the conviction the Court noted that "nothing in our cases suggests that an officer participating in an initial lawful encounter with a driver must, or even should, turn a blind eye to contraband or evidence in plain view that provides reasonable suspicion that a crime has been, or is being, committed."[888]

Roadblocks Permissible For Apprehension of Dangerous Person

Following a shooting, or in situations involving other crimes where the police are attempting to apprehend fleeing, dangerous persons they may set up a roadblock along routes likely to be taken by such suspects. The usual rules requiring particularized suspicion before stopping a motor vehicle will not apply in such cases.

An emergency stop of numerous vehicles aimed at apprehending a fleeing, dangerous suspect requires a somewhat different constitutional analysis from a preplanned, "blueprinted" roadblock at a predetermined location, such as a sobriety checkpoint or a drug interdiction roadblock. Until the recent case of *Commonwealth v. Grant*, the emergency model roadblock had not been directly addressed by Massachusetts courts.[889]

- In ***Commonwealth v. Grant,*** the defendant was stopped as part of an early morning police roadblock in an attempt to apprehend one or more suspects who had been involved in a shooting incident. The defendant was questioned, and

---

[884] *Commonwealth v. Lovelace*, 26 Mass.App.Ct. 541 (1988).
[885] *Comm. v. Bazinet*, 76 Mass. App. Ct. 908 (2010).
[886] *Commonwealth v. Murphy*, SJC (2009).
[887] *Berkemer v. McCarthy*, 468 U.S. 420, 104 S.Ct. 3138 (1984).
[888] *Commonwealth v. Swartz*, SJC (July 2009).
[889] *Commonwealth v. Grant*, 57 Mass. App. Ct. 334, 783 N.E. 2d 455 (2003).

after police observed a weapon in his vehicle, he was arrested. In a jury-waived trial, he was found guilty of carrying a firearm without a license, G.L. c. 269, § 10(a), and defacing a firearm serial number, G.L. c. 269, § 11C. The Appeals Court affirmed the Superior Court conviction.

Drug Trafficking Road Blocks

Contraband (drug) interdiction roadblocks where citizens are stopped without probable cause or reasonable suspicion to look for evidence of criminal activity are unlawful. The risk that narcotics trafficking poses to the public is not immediate, as is the risk posed by a person operating while under the influence.[890] Therefore, drug trafficking roadblocks violate the Massachusetts Declaration of Rights article addressing searches and seizures.

ADMINISTRATIVE SCREENING STOPS AND SEARCHES

Stopping motor vehicles in the vicinity of potential terrorist targets requires the police to conform to constitutional requirements. The SJC has indicated that signs should be posted to allow motorists to seek alternate routes. This is similar to administrative inspections at court houses and similar public buildings. There must be a purpose other than to gather evidence for criminal prosecution.

- In the 2004 case of ***Commonwealth v. Carkhuff***[891], the Supreme Judicial Court addressed the ability of the police to stop motorists traveling near a public water supply shortly after the 9-11 attacks. The Court explained that without signs or similar notice, affording motorists the opportunity of taking an alternative route, such administrative stops (and searches) were a violation of this state's Constitution.

NOTE: In a 2004 non-administrative search case, the stopping of a truck in a state park at 1:00 a.m., where signs indicated the park closed at 8:00 p.m., was lawful.[892]

DISABLED MOTORISTS & BREAKDOWN LANES

There are certain interactions between police officers and citizens that do not require judicial justification. Local police officers are charged with "community caretaking functions, totally divorced from the detection, investigation, or acquisition of evidence relating to the violation of a criminal statute."[893]

Activation of cruiser lights

The SJC has stated that when the police activate their blue overhead lights when investigating criminal activity a seizure has taken place because a reasonable person would not feel that they were free to leave.[894]

However, when the overhead lights are used as a community caretaking function, such as checking on a disabled motorist, it does not "change the nature of the encounter into a seizure."[895] Using overhead lights at night at the side of a road is a safety measure. Also using the cruiser white lights to illuminate a motor vehicle is also not, by itself, a seizure.

- In ***Commonwealth v. Hill***, a police officer pulled behind the defendant's car, which was parked at 11:35 p.m. in the breakdown lane on a desolate highway with its directional light flashing. The court ruled that this did not constitute an impermissible seizure, even though the officer activated his vehicle's blue lights.[896] The court ruled that the officer was engaged in a community caretaker function, and the activation of blue lights was for the safety of the public, the officer and the defendant.
- In ***Commonwealth v. Briand***, the use of the cruiser's white "take down" lights to illuminate the interior of a stopped vehicle in a parking area did not constitute a seizure.[897]

Requesting license and registration

In ***Commonwealth v. Evans***, the SJC upheld the request of the defendant's license and registration while checking on a vehicle in the breakdown lane even though the operator indicated that he was not in need of assistance. The Court upheld the request stating there "several reasons justify an officer's actions in requesting a driver's license when performing community caretaking responsibilities. Quoting from a Wisconsin Court of

[890] *Commonwealth v. Rodriguez*, 430 Mass. 577, 722 N.E. 2d 429 (2000).
[891] *Commonwealth v. Carkhuff*, 441 Mass. 122, 804 N.E.2d 317 (2004).
[892] *Commonwealth v. Rousseau*, 61 Mass.App.Ct. 144, 807 N.E.2d 832 (2004).
[893] Cady v. Dombrowski, 413 U.S. 433, 441 (1973).
[894] *Commonwealth v. Smigliano*, 417 Mass. 490, 694 N.E.2d 341 (1998)
[895] *Commonwealth v. Evans*, 436 Mass. at 373, 764 N.E.2d 841 (2002).
[896] M.G.L.A. c.276, §1; *Commonwealth v. Hill*, 51 Mass. App. Ct. 598, 747 N.E.2d 1241 (2001).
[897] *Commonwealth v. Briand*,71 Mass.App.Ct. 160 (2008). Confirmed by SJC in Commonwealth v. Clark, 454 Mass. 1001

MOTOR VEHICLE STOPS

Appeals case, the SJC stated "In many cases, police officers are required to make a written report of contacts with citizens. An officer needs to know whom he or she is assisting in the event a citizen later complains about improper behavior on the part of the officer or makes any kind of legal claim against the officer. Moreover, even seemingly innocent activity, such as refueling a disabled car, could later turn out to be theft of a car that was left on the shoulder of a highway."[898]

REST AREAS

Although seemingly less dangerous and indicative of the need for assistance than stopping in a breakdown lane the SJC has indicated that police officers may check on motorists in rest areas to see if assistance is needed.

- In ***Commonwealth v. Murdough***, the Court ruled that officers may check on motorists parked in rest areas, especially in winter to ensure the occupants are not in need of assistance.[899]

Contact with the occupants

While checking on the well being of the occupants the officer may use his flashlight to illuminate the interior of the vehicle, rouse the motorist from sleep, ensure that the motorists is fit to drive[900] and even open the door to check on an unresponsive motorist.

- In ***Commonwealth v. Eckert***, the actions of a trooper in walking up to a parked vehicle at a roadside rest area, knocking on the vehicle's window, shining his flashlight inside, and asking whether the occupant, who was sleeping in the vehicle, was "all set", did not intrude on the defendant's constitutionally protected rights under the Fourth Amendment and this State's Constitution, as would require justification.[901] The trooper neither asserted nor implied that the occupant was not free at that moment to ignore the inquiry into his well-being, and nothing indicated that the trooper specifically targeted the vehicle for investigation. The actions of the trooper did not ripen into a search or seizure under the Fourth Amendment or Article 14 of this State's Constitution, until the occupant, who had responded to the trooper's initial inquiry by stating that he was all right was asked by the trooper whether he had been drinking and to get out of the vehicle and perform field sobriety tests.

Note: Although a written policy requiring that officers check on disabled motorists is recommended it is not constitutionally required.

Officer's subjective belief of criminal activity does not automatically negate community caretaking responsibility

Even if the officer harbors a subjective belief that criminal activity may be afoot, this does not negate the officer's community caretaking responsibility.

- In the 2003 case of ***Commonwealth v. McDevitt***, the Appeals Court ruled that a trooper's approach to the defendant's car in the breakdown lane falls within this community caretaking function.[902] It was after 10:30 P.M. on a high speed highway and the defendant was pulled over in a location normally associated with disabled vehicles, with the motor running and the headlights on. It was permissible, in these circumstances, for the Trooper to approach and check the stopped motor vehicle out of concern both for the occupants in the stopped car and for the public using the roadway. That the Trooper might have harbored a subjective belief, even a compelling one, that the operator was engaged in illegal behavior does not affect a court's decision. "An officer's motive does not invalidate objectively justifiable behavior."[903] The court stated that an officer may check on a stopped motor vehicle in the breakdown lane of a highway.[904] To except those who, while similarly situated, are also suspected of committing a crime would serve little purpose other than to jeopardize both the safety of those in the stopped car and the public using the road.

Roadside questioning

It is well established law that road side questioning during a routine traffic stop, including a question whether the driver has been drinking, do not require Miranda warnings as the stops are typically routine and brief in nature.[905] See the Interview & Interrogation section for more on this topic.

---

[898] State v. Ellenbecker, 159 Wis.2d 91 (Ct. App. 1990)

[899] *Commonwealth v. Murdough*, 428 Mass. 760, 762, 704 N.E.2d 1184 (1999).

[900] *Commonwealth v. Murdough*, 428 Mass. 760, 764 (1999) ("If the community caretaking function . . . means anything, surely it allows a police officer to determine whether a driver is in such a condition that if he resumes operation of the vehicle, in which he is seated at a highway rest stop, he will pose such an extreme danger to himself and others").

[901] *Commonwealth v. Eckert*, 431 Mass. 591, 728 N.E. 2d 312 (2000).

[902] *Commonwealth v. McDevitt*, 57 Mass. App. Ct. 733, 786 N.E.2d 404 (2003); *Commonwealth v. Dombrowski*, supra.

[903] *Commonwealth v. Murdough*, 428 Mass. at 762, 704 N.E.2d 1184, quoting from *Commonwealth v. Murdough*, 44 Mass.App.Ct.736, 740, 694 N.E.2d 15 (1998).

[904] *Commonwealth v. Evans*, 436 Mass. at 373, 764 N.E.2d 841

[905] *Commonwealth v. Sauer*,50 Mass.App.Ct. 299, 301, 737 N.E.2d 10 (2000). See also *Commonwealth v. McNelley*, 28 Mass.App.Ct. 985, 986, 554 N.E.2d 37 (1990); *Commonwealth v. D'Agostino*, 38 Mass.App.Ct.206, 208, 646 N.E.2d 767, *S.C.*, 421 Mass. 281, 281 n. 1, 657 N.E.2d 217 (1995).

PURSUITS

The Federal Rule concerning when a seizure occurs in a motor vehicle pursuit case is different from the Massachusetts Rule. Pursuit, for the purposes of Fourth Amendment analysis, begins only when action by the police would communicate to the reasonable person an attempt to capture or otherwise intrude on that person's freedom of movement. Following or observing someone without more, such as using a siren or lights, attempting to block or control an individual's path, direction, or speed, or commanding the individual to holt, is not a "seizure" for the purposes of Fourth Amendment analysis.[906]

In Massachusetts, a person is seized for purposes of this state's constitution's guarantee of freedom from unreasonable searches and seizures, when a police officer initiates a pursuit with the obvious intent of requiring the person to submit to questioning.[907]

Passengers: As regards to the passengers in a pursued motor vehicle, the rules in this state are slightly different than for drivers. A pursuit of a vehicle for a traffic violation does not constitute, without more, pursuit of a passenger, such that a passenger would be "seized" within meaning of this state's constitution.

- In ***Commonwealth v. Wilson,*** a police pursuit of a car passenger began, such that passenger was "seized" for purposes of the state constitution, when the officer left the patrol vehicle to chase the defendant as he fled from the stopped car, rather than when the officers had pursued the car for a traffic violation.[908]

RACIAL PROFILING

The U.S. Supreme Court has stated that "the use of automobiles is so heavily and minutely regulated that total compliance with traffic and safety rules is nearly impossible ... a police officer almost invariably will be able to catch any given motorist in a technical violation. This creates the temptation to use traffic stops as a pretext, or as a means of investigating other law violations, as to which no probable cause or even articulable suspicion exists." To guard against the potential for such abuse, the United States Supreme Court has routinely concluded that a stop is not constitutional if it is predicated on race alone. [909]

The SJC has also indicated that "it is unconstitutional for an officer to stop a vehicle based on the race or ethnicity of the person, or persons, in it."[910] The SJC has expanded the scope of the exclusionary rule to permit the suppression of contraband seized in the course of a traffic stop made for discriminatory reasons.[911]

However, a defendant cannot simply request an officer's stop data without showing that the basis of the stop was racially motivated. The preliminary showing required of the defendant seeking this type of discovery must contain reliable information, in affidavit form, demonstrating a reasonable basis to infer that profiling, and not a traffic violation alone, may have been the basis for the vehicle stop.[912]

- In ***Commonwealth v. Betances***, a trooper stopped the defendant's vehicle for speeding and marked lanes violations. During the stop the trooper detected the odor of burnt marijuana and observed small amounts of marijuana in the vehicle. A subsequent search of the vehicle revealed a large quantity of heroin. The defendant requested stop data pertaining to the trooper for a seven month period in preparation for a racial profiling defense. The defendant was Hispanic. The trial judge permitted the request and the Commonwealth appealed. The SJC overruled the request stating that a defendant must demonstrate a reasonable basis that the vehicle stop was based on racial profiling and not a traffic violation in order to compel the Commonwealth to produce the officer's stop data.[913]
- Also, in ***Commonwealth v. Thomas***, the SJC ruled that the Commonwealth is not required to produce agency data submitted in accordance with St. 2000, c. 228. "An Act providing for the collection of data relative to traffic stops" commonly referred to as the "Northeastern Study." The Court reasoned that the Commonwealth's obligation to furnish discovery is limited to facts and information that is relevant to the case and in the possession, custody, and control of the prosecution. The Court determined that this information is beyond the information held by agents of the prosecution team. [914]

MOTOR VEHICLE STOPS

[906] *Commonwealth v. Watson*, 430 Mass. 725, 723 N.E. 2d 501 (2000).
[907] *Commonwealth v. Wilson*, 52 Mass.App.Ct. 411, 754 N.E.2d 113 (2001).
[908] *Commonwealth v. Wilson, supra.*
[909] *U.S. v. Whren*, 51U.S. at 818-19 (1996)
[910] *Commonwealth v. Betances*, 451 Mass. 457, 886 N.E.2d 679 (2008).
[911] *Commonwealth v. Lora*, 451 Mass. 425, 886 N.E.2d 688 (2008).
[912] *Commonwealth v. Betances*, 451 Mass. 457, 886 N.E.2d 679 (2008).
[913] *Commonwealth v. Betances*, 451 Mass. 457, 886 N.E.2d 679 (2008).
[914] *Commonwealth v. Thomas,* 451 Mass. 457, 886 N.E.2d 679 (2008).

MOTOR VEHICLE SEARCHES & EXIT ORDERS

DIMINISHED EXPECTATION OF PRIVACY

The nature and scope of the protection of privacy afforded by the Fourth Amendment is often analyzed by determining what reasonable expectation of privacy a person has in the area or item to be searched. The courts have held that people have only a "diminished expectation of privacy" in automobiles.[915]

There are a number of reasons why persons have less of a reasonable expectation of privacy in an automobile than they would have in a house or apartment, their clothing or other personal items and effects.

A motor vehicle is primarily a means of transportation and (ordinarily) does not serve as one's private residence.

Also, it is used to only a limited extent as a repository for private effects.

Furthermore, much of the area inside an automobile is exposed and in plain view.[916]

Additionally, motor vehicles are used to travel public thoroughfares and are heavily regulated by motor vehicle laws and rules of the road, the very nature of which makes automobiles less private and autonomous than one's house, clothing or other personal property and effects. Because of the diminished expectation of privacy which a person has in a motor vehicle, warrantless searches of motor vehicles are more tolerable than would be the case for a house or apartment.

THE AUTOMOBILE EXCEPTION

Generally, the search of a motor vehicle must be consistent with general constitutional guidelines. However, the courts have carved out one major exception – The Automobile Exception.

The Fourth Amendment's automobile exception permits a warrantless search of an automobile as to which the police have probable cause, even when the officers have ample opportunity to obtain a warrant.[917] The bright-line rule established by the Fourth Amendment's automobile exception does not have a separate exigency requirement precluding the police from obtaining a warrant.[918]

No additional exigency required but public element is important

The traditional rule in Massachusetts had been that police may search an automobile where it is parked or where they have stopped it and do so without a warrant if they have probable cause *and* if exigent circumstances exist.

In its 1997 decision in ***Commonwealth v. Motta***, the Massachusetts Supreme Judicial Court appears to have abandoned this state's rule that had required some showing of exigency.[919] The court concluded that when an automobile is stopped in a public place with probable cause, no more exigent circumstances are required by Article 14 of the Massachusetts Constitution beyond the inherent mobility of an automobile itself to justify a warrantless search of the vehicle.

However, in order for this provision to be applied the vehicle must be lawfully stopped on a *public way* or is found parked in a *public place*; (a "public way" is more broadly defined than "public street")[920] and there is probable cause to believe the vehicle contains contraband or other evidence at the time the police begin their search of the vehicle.

Parked vehicles

In Public

The SJC ruled in 1997 that the apparent mobility of a vehicle parked in a public place was sufficient exigency to justify a warrantless search by the police.[921]

Private Property

There are circumstances where the police find a motor vehicle parked on private property and a warrant may be required, particularly if the car is immobilized.

- In the U.S. Supreme Court case of ***Coolidge v. New Hampshire***, the search of an automobile was illegal even though the police had both probable cause and a search warrant to search the house.[922] They knew, based on several days' observation, that the car would be parked in the driveway but did not seek a search warrant for the vehicle.

---

[915] *Cardwell v. Lewis*, 417 U.S. 583, 94 S.Ct. 2464 (1974); *U.S. v. Chadwick*, 433 U.S. 1, 97 S.Ct.2476 (1977); *Rakas v. Illinois*, 439, U.S. 128, 99 U.S. 421 (1978).
[916] *Commonwealth v. Lantigua*, 38 Mass. App. Ct. 526, 649 N.E.2d 1129 (1995).
[917] *Maryland v. Dyson*, 527 U.S. 465, 119 S.Ct. 2013, 144 L.Ed.2d. 442 (1999).
[918] *U.S. v. Ross*, 456 U.S. 798, 102 S.Ct. 2157, 72 L.Ed.2d. 572 (1982), *Pennsylvania v. Labron*, 518 U.S. 938, 116 S.Ct. 2485, 135 L.Ed.2d.1031 (1996).
[919] *Commonwealth v. Motta*, 424 Mass. 117, 676 N.E. 2d 795 (1997).
[920] *Commonwealth v. Wunder*, 407 Mass. 909, 556 N.E. 2d 65 (1990).
[921] *Commonwealth v. Gajka*, 425 Mass. 751, 682 N.E. 2d 1345 (1997).

- However, in a 1991 Massachusetts case of ***Commonwealth v. A Juvenile (No. 2)***, a search of an automobile in a private driveway was upheld.[923] Since the police did not know the location of the suspect (unlike *Coolidge* where he was in custody), the police had a need to secure the car to prevent the removal of evidence or having someone drive away with it.
- In ***Commonwealth v. Simmons,*** the Supreme Judicial Court upheld action taken by police in bringing a rape victim to a place where she could view her alleged assailant's automobile for identification purposes.[924] The car was parked next to the driveway of the defendant's mother-in-law's home. The driveway was adjacent to a public street and served as the primary path one would take in approaching the house. The Court held that no reasonable expectation of privacy is violated by the victim's looking at and into the car.

Attorney Hanrahan Recommendation: If there is no other urgency involved (other the fact that the car is potentially mobile) regarding a vehicle on private property it may be wise to utilize a warrant when the vehicle is located on private property.

SCOPE OF THE SEARCH

If probable cause justifies the search of a lawfully stopped vehicle, it justifies the search of every part of the vehicle and its contents *that may conceal the object of the search if the probable cause exists that the item sought is in the area searched.*[925]This includes containers within the vehicle capable of containing the item.

- A case from 1925 permitted the slashing of upholstery in search of whiskey (which was illegal at the time).

"The scope of a warrantless search of an automobile…is not defined by the nature of the container in which the contraband is secreted, but rather…by the object of the search and the places in which there is probable cause to believe that it may be found.[926]

Probable cause to search a vehicle "extends to all containers, open or closed, found within."[927]

Containers inside vehicle

The SJC has stated that "where police officers had probable cause and exigent circumstances to justify a warrantless stop and search of a motor vehicle for controlled substances, no further probable cause or exigent circumstances were needed, under either the Fourth Amendment to the United States Constitution or art. 14 of the Massachusetts Declaration of Rights, to justify a search of any closed container in the vehicle capable of holding the contraband.

- In ***Commonwealth v. Wunder***, Trooper John Walsh received information from a reliable informant that the defendant was anxious to sell a large amount of cocaine. According to the informant, Wunder had stated that he was going to sell the cocaine at 6 P.M. in the Grossman's parking lot on Route 114 in Danvers. The police set up surveillance and eventually stopped the suspect's van as it was about to exit the parking lot. The troopers searched the vehicle including a bag and cooler inside of the van both which contained drugs. The SJC upheld the search stating that the automobile exception includes closed containers.[928]
- In ***Commonwealth v. Bakoian***, the Massachusetts Supreme Judicial Court upheld the search under the hood — and even the removal of the vehicle's air filter — where the detective had probable cause to search the *entire* vehicle for narcotics.[929]

Locked Containers

If the police have probable cause that a container in the vehicle contains evidence or criminal contraband the police may search the container even if it is locked.

- In ***Commonwealth v. Moses***, it was permissible to open a locked suitcase located in the vehicle's trunk during a search for weapons and narcotics. [930]

[922]*Coolidge v.New Hampshire,* 403 U.S. 443, 478, 91 S.Ct. 2022, 29 L.Ed.2d 564 (1971).
[923]*Commonwealth v.A Juvenile (No. 2)*, 411 Mass. 157, 580 N.E.2d 1014 (1991).
[924]*Commonwealth v. Simmons,* 392 Mass. 45, 466 N.E.2d 85 (1984).
Commonwealth v. Pena, 69 Mass.App.Ct. 713, 718 (2007) [cited with approval in *Garden, supra* at 53])
[926]*Id.* at 906, 556 N.E.2d 69, quoting from *United States v. Ross,* 456 U.S. 798, 824, 102 S.Ct. 2157, 72 L.Ed.2d 572 (1982).See *Commonwealth v. Wunder,* 407 Mass. 909, 913-915, 556 N.E.2d 65 (1990).
[927]*Commonwealth v. Cast,* 407 Mass. 891, 908, 556 N.E.2d 69 (1990).
[928]*Commonwealth v. Wunder,* 407 Mass. 909 (1990)
[929]*Commonwealth v. Bakoian*, 412 Mass. 295, 588 N.E.2d 667 (1992).
[930]*Commonwealth v. Moses*, 408 Mass. 136, 557 N.E.2d 14 (1990).

Probable cause for specific container only

The traditional rule had been that, before stopping a vehicle, where the police have probable cause to believe that evidence or contraband is contained in a suitcase or closed container, they may seize it but must secure a warrant before opening it.[931] This holding was in line with earlier decisions of the U.S. Supreme Court.

- In ***Arkansas v. Sanders***, where the police had staked out an airport waiting for a suspect carrying a green suitcase, they should have obtained a warrant rather than stopping the taxi into which the suspect's companion placed the suitcase, and opening the suitcase.[932]
- In ***Chadwick v. U.S.***, where the police had probable cause to believe that contraband was inside a footlocker before the defendant claimed it and placed it in the trunk of a car at a railroad station, a warrant should have been obtained before opening the footlocker.[933]

The **more recent rule in Massachusetts is less stringent** with regard to when a warrant is required before opening a closed container in a vehicle where the probable cause is limited solely to a specific container. Only if the police observe a suspect place the container in a vehicle and never lose sight of the vehicle, thus precluding anyone from removing evidence or contraband from such container, will a warrant be required.

- In ***Commonwealth v. Cast,*** where the police — with probable cause for a gray suitcase — saw the defendant place the suitcase in his vehicle, but lost sight of the vehicle for several hours, no warrant was required. Since the defendant had time to hide the contents in other parts of the vehicle or switch the contents of the suitcase, probable cause then extended to the entire vehicle.[934]
- In ***Commonwealth v. Farinon,*** where the police did not see the defendant place a certain cooler in his vehicle, no search warrant was required even though the advance probable cause was limited to a specific cooler. In this case the court found that, based on the informant's information, money and contraband could also be found in other parts of the suspect's vehicle.[935]

Passengers

Evidence of a crime discovered on the passenger of a vehicle does not automatically extend to the vehicle absent some other connection, or nexus, aside from being a mere passenger.

- In ***Commonwealth v. Pena***, during a routine traffic stop in a high crime area the officers removed and pat frisked a passenger who was making furtive movements. During the pat frisk marijuana was discovered. The officers subsequently searched the motor vehicle and discovered firearms under a seat cushion. The court ruled that the automobile exception did not apply in this instance because the marijuana was only discovered on a passenger and there was no other connection to the vehicle. [936]

Additionally, when there is probable cause to search a car, the police have the authority to search the vehicle and its contents but the automobile exception **does not extend to the search of a person found in that automobile**.[937]

The Expansion of Probable Cause within the Vehicle

Once the police locate contraband or other evidence of a crime in a motor vehicle, they generally have probable cause to search for additional contraband or evidence in the "vicinity" of such evidence.[938]

However, it is important to note the scope is limited by the nature of the probable cause.

To justify the search of a trunk, there must be a connection between the vehicle and the criminal contraband/evidence.[939]

- In ***Commonwealth v. Pena,*** the Court ruled that there was no probable cause to search the entire vehicle based solely on finding of drugs on the passenger because this did not create a sufficient "connection between the car and the passenger's drugs."
- In ***Commonwealth v. Garden,*** the smell of burnt marijuana on the clothes of the automobile's occupants did not, in the absence of any physical evidence, give rise to the inference that marijuana had been smoked in the vehicle, and that marijuana might reasonably be found elsewhere in the vehicle.

---

[931] *Commonwealth v. Farinon*, 29 Mass. App. Ct. 945, 588 N.E.2d 1144 (1990).
[932] *Arkansas v. Sanders*, 442 U.S. 753, 99 S.Ct. 2586 (1977).
[933] *Chadwick v. U.S.*, 443 U.S. 1, 99 S.Ct. 2612 (1977).
[934] *Commonwealth v. Cast*, 407 Mass. 891, 556 N.E.2d 69 (1990).
[935] *Commonwealth v. Farinon*, 29 Mass. App. Ct. 945, 558 N.E.2d 1144 (1990).
[936] *Commonwealth v. Pena*, 69 Mass.App.Ct. 713, 871 N.E.2d 531 (2007)
[937] *Com. v. Griffin*, App.Ct (March 2011)
[938] *Commonwealth v. Crespo*, 59 Mass.App.Ct. 926, 798 N.E.2d 320 (2003).
[939] Commonwelath v. DeGray, Appeals Court 2010.

- In ***Commonwealth v. Villatoro****,* the discovery of a plastic bag containing marijuana on the driver, who was alone in the automobile, justified a comprehensive search of the vehicle, including the trunk.[940]
- In ***Commonwealth v. DeGray*****,** the court ruled that the discovery of even a small amount of contraband in the passenger compartment, which might only be for personal use, can extend the scope of the search to include the trunk.[941] The officers found two marijuana cigarettes and marijuana remnants inside the automobile; the Court noted that this established a connection between the contraband and the vehicle. In addition, the driver of the automobile admitted that he and his passengers had been smoking marijuana in the vehicle, and the officer smelled burnt marijuana in the vehicle.
- In ***Commonwealth v. Owens***, the defendant was **discovered with an unlawful firearm [revolver] in the passenger compartment** of a motor vehicle. In addition, the defendant had a magazine containing ammunition which did not fit the firearm. After seizing the revolver, the detective discovered that the defendant possessed ammunition that did not match the revolver, creating a suspicion that the defendant possessed other weapons. Discovery of an illegally possessed firearm and ammunition, which did not match the weapon, gave the detective probable cause to search the entire vehicle for other concealed objects and weapons.[942]
- In ***Commonwealth v. Jiminez***, the Massachusetts Appeals Court stated that once a firearm and contraband had been found in the passenger compartment; the police were justified in searching the trunk, "the trunk clearly being a 'part of the vehicle' capable of concealing 'the object of the search.
- In ***Commonwealth v. Moses***, the discovery of cocaine and a loaded firearm in the passenger compartment justified a further search extending into the trunk.[943]

Attorney Hanrahan's Note: Be sure to review the section regarding ***Commonwealth v. Cruz*** which indicated that the odor of marijuana alone no longer amounts to probable cause to search unless same other criminal activity is present.

DEVELOPING PROBABLE CAUSE TO SEARCH DURING A TRAFFIC STOP

There are a variety of ways of developing probable cause to search during a traffic stop. However, two of the most common are plan view observations and so-called plain smell observations.

Plain view during motor vehicle stops

A plain-view observation is not a search in the constitutional sense; it requires neither a warrant, nor an exception to the warrant requirement.[944] An officer making a stop for a traffic violation is not required to ignore what he or she sees, smells, or hears.

If an officer lawfully stops a motor vehicle and observes evidence or *criminal* contraband in plain view the officer could enter the vehicle and seize under the automobile exception.

- In ***Commonwealth v. Ciaramitaro***, following an officer's justified stop of the defendant for erratic driving and making an illegal left turn, the officer's plain-view observations of illegal weapons in the defendant's car, from a vantage point outside of the car, provided probable cause to arrest the defendant for illegal possession of a dangerous weapon, and probable cause to search the entire vehicle, as well as its compartments, for a weapon.[945]

The Plain View observation must be related to a crime. In the 2015 case of ***Commonwealth v. Sheridan***, the officer observed a bag of marijuana in a motor vehicle that he believed to be "about an ounce." The SJC ruled that the subsequent search was unlawful based on the officer's observations. Possession of "about an ounce" is not a criminal offense.

For a detailed analysis of Plain View see the Search section of this manual.

[940] *Commonwealth v. Villatoro*, 76 Mass.App.Ct. 645, 647-648 (2010)
[941] *Commonwealth v. DeGray*, decided June 25, 2010
[942] *Commonwealth v. Owens*, 414 Mass. 595 (1993).
[943] *Commonwealth v. Moses*, 408 Mass. 136 (1990).
[944] *Commonwealth v. Ciaramitaro*, 51 Mass. App. Ct. 638, 747 N.E.2d 1253 (2001).
[945] *Commonwealth v. Ciaramitaro*, 51 Mass. App. Ct. 638, 747 N.E.2d 1253 (2001).

Plain smell

For many decades the police often developed probable cause to search a vehicle when they detected the odor of burnt (or raw) marijuana. However, the odor of burnt marijuana *alone* no longer justifies an **exit order** or a **search of a motor vehicle**. With the passage of question 2 in 2008 (the decriminalization of possession of an ounce or less of marijuana) the *plain smell doctrine*, which previously indicated that the odor of burnt marijuana amounted to probable cause for the presence of marijuana (a crime at the time), and when involving a motor vehicle, permitted a search under the automobile exception, as we knew it, is no longer.

Burnt Marijuana

Commonwealth v. Cruz: On June 24, 2009, Boston Police Officers Christopher Morgan and Richard Diaz were patrolling in plain clothes and an unmarked Ford Crown Victoria automobile when the officers saw a vehicle parked in front of a fire hydrant. The vehicle's windows were rolled down and it was light outside. Inside, the officers could see a driver and the defendant, who was sitting in the front passenger seat. As the officers drove down the street, Officer Diaz saw the driver light a small, inexpensive cigar that is commonly known to mask the odor of marijuana smoke.

The officers approached the vehicle and detected a "faint odor" of marijuana. The driver appeared extremely nervous. When asked about the marijuana odor the driver stated that he had smoked earlier in the day. Both men were ordered out of the vehicle. Officer Diaz asked the defendant if he had anything on him and the defendant replied "a little rock for myself." A subsequent search revealed approximately four grams of crack cocaine. The defendant argued that the exit order was unlawful as the possession of small amounts of marijuana is no longer criminal. The Court ruled that the initiation of the stop was valid because the operator had committed a violation by parking in front of hydrant. However, the exit order was deemed unlawful. The Court explained that there are three scenarios in which an exit order issued to a passenger in a validly stopped vehicle is justified:

1. an exit order is justified if "a reasonably prudent man in the policeman's position would be warranted in the belief that the **safety** of the police or that of other persons was in danger."
2. Second, the officers could have developed reasonable suspicion (based on articulable facts) that the defendant was engaged in **criminal activity** separate from any offense of the driver.
3. Third, the officers could have ordered the defendant out of the car for **pragmatic reasons**, e.g., to facilitate an independently permissible warrantless search of the car under the automobile exception to the warrant requirement

The Commonwealth did not argue that the exit order was the result of safety concerns, so the first justification does not apply.

In the second instance, there must be reasonable suspicion of *criminal activity*, separate from any offense of the driver. Since the passing of Question 2 (the decriminalization of marijuana) the possession of an ounce or less of marijuana is no longer a criminal offense. Absent reasonable suspicion that more than an ounce of marijuana is present the *criminal* justification does not apply.

In the third instance, the police would have been justified to order the occupants out of the vehicle to facilitate a search under the motor vehicle exception. However, although the automobile exception permits a warrantless search for contraband (in addition to evidence), and marijuana is still contraband, the automobile exception is an exception to the search warrant requirement, therefore in order for the automobile exception to apply the officers would have to otherwise been able to apply for a search warrant. The Court ruled, citing a decision from 1859, that search warrants are "confined to cases of public prosecutions, *instituted and pursued for the suppression of* ***crime*** *or the detection and punishment of* ***criminals***." Therefore, a search would no longer permissible under the automobile exception as a search warrant could not be issued. The evidence was suppressed.

Attorney Hanrahan's Note: The impact on policing is obvious. As we all know many major drug cases began from a routine car stop with the odor of marijuana.

Raw/Unburnt Marijuana

The odor of raw marijuana may amount to reasonable suspicion of criminal activity but generally will not, alone, amount to probable cause of criminal activity. See the below very important cases this issue:

In the 2014 Appeals Court case of ***Commonwealth v. Fontaine***, the Court stated that the mere odor of raw marijuana *alone* does not amount to reasonable suspicion. However, when the odor of raw marijuana is detected by an ***experienced*** officer, the odor is ***overwhelming*** and ***pervasive*** (i.e. detected throughout the vehicle) there is **reasonable suspicion** that more than an ounce of marijuana is present. A police officer cannot lawfully search a car on reasonable suspicion (absent consent). However, reasonable suspicion would justify a further inquiry and detention. In this case, the officers noticed additional factors (i.e. packaging, lack of paraphernalia, and criminal history of drug dealing, and so on) which lead to the development of probable cause. Because probable cause was present the Court stated "it is therefore unnecessary for us to decide whether the 'overwhelming' odor of unburnt marijuana **alone** provided probable cause to support the issuance of the search warrant." This question was answered by the SJC later in 2014.

In the 2014, the question left open by the Appeals Court in *Fontaine* was answered. In ***Commonwealth v. Overmeyer***, the SJC ruled that the odor of unburnt marijuana alone *does not amount to probable cause* to believe criminal amounts of marijuana or evidence is present in the automobile.

Attorney Harahan's comment: Interestingly, in *Overmeyer*, the SJC stated "it is possible that training may overcome the deficiencies inherent in smell as a gauge of the weight of marijuana present…"

Federal Crime

In the 2014 case of ***Commonwealth v. Craan***, even though the possession of marijuana is a violation of **federal law** a Massachusetts police officer cannot search a vehicle under the automobile exception based solely on this fact. The Court reasoned the "general rule is that local police are not precluded from enforcing federal statutes," however "their authority to do so derives from state law." Where state police officers make an arrest for a violation of federal law, "the lawfulness of the arrest without a warrant is to be determined by reference to state law." The decriminalization of possession of an ounce or less of marijuana under state law removed police authority to arrest individuals for these civil violations and thus it also "must be read as curtailing police authority to enforce the federal prohibition of possession of small amounts of marijuana."

What are some other considerations when the odor of marijuana is detected in a motor vehicle?

OUI Drugs: Recently, the SJC ruled that the odor and possession of (small amounts) of marijuana alone will not justify an exit order and vehicle search for the purposes of an OUI drug investigation absent some indication that the operator is otherwise impaired. The officer must point to other factors that would amount to reasonable suspicion that the operator was impaired (e.g. slow motor movements, glassy eyes, slurred speech, etc.).

Case example

Commonwealth v. Clint Daniel (2013): On December 13, 2009, at 3:40 *A. M.*, Boston police officer Paul DeLeo, Jr., was patrolling alone, in a marked cruiser, on Adams Street in the Dorchester section of Boston. DeLeo noticed a Toyota sports utility vehicle without a functioning driver's-side headlight approaching from the opposite direction. When it reached the intersection, the Toyota made an abrupt left turn, passing directly in front of DeLeo's cruiser onto East Street without using a directional signal. DeLeo subsequently conducted a motor vehicle stop. DeLeo exited his cruiser and approached the passenger side of the vehicle. He observed the passenger (Clint DANIEL) making furtive movements. When the window was rolled down he detected a strong to moderate odor of marijuana. The operator and passenger admitted to smoking marijuana earlier at a party but denied smoking marijuana in the vehicle. When asked if there was any marijuana on them or in the vehicle, the operator (Tayetto) handed over two glassine baggies of marijuana. DANIEL later emptied his pockets revealing several items, including a folding knife. DeLeo subsequently ordered DANIEL and TAYETTO out of the vehicle. He searched both of them for weapons and drugs, finding nothing. He then went to the vehicle and opened the glove box finding a loaded semi-automatic pistol. Both were arrested for possession of the firearm, among other charges. The SJC ruled that the exit order and search of the vehicle

> was unlawful. At trial the Commonwealth elicited no testimony from the officer that TAYETTO showed any signs of impairment during their encounter. The officer did not testify that TAYETTO's eyes were red or glassy, that her speech or movements were unusual, or that her responses to questioning were inappropriate or uncooperative. He did not perform any tests to assess her physical and mental acuity. Thus there was no evidence to suspect TAYETTO of OUI drugs. Additionally, the officer had little, if any, information to suggest that the occupants of the vehicle were armed or dangerous, his extensive search was not "proportional to the degree of suspicion that prompted it."

Consent: Although further detainment during a routine motor vehicle stop to conduct a consent search is generally not justified, absent any indication of criminal behavior, a consent search to uncover contraband (i.e. marijuana) will most likely be upheld by the Court. General Law c. 94C §§ 32L-32N, although decriminalizing an ounce of less of marijuana, does call for the confiscation of the marijuana.

More than an Ounce: If there is probable cause that the vehicle contains more than an ounce of marijuana (i.e. informant tip, drug courier profile, etc) the exit order and/or search would be lawfully justified. Remember, possession of more than an ounce of marijuana is still a criminal offense.

Drugs Sales: Only **possession** of an ounce or less is no longer criminal. Had the police had reasonable suspicion that a drug sale, or possession with the intent to sell, or some similar offense, was involved the exit order would have been justified, and if probable cause existed a subsequent search would have been lawfully justified as well.

Search Based on Police Radio Dispatch

When a police officer stops and searches a motor vehicle pursuant to instructions and a description given from the radio dispatcher, "the police officer responsible for issuing the radio communication (must have) had reliable information that a crime had occurred and that the instrumentalities or evidence of that crime would be found in the vehicle described in the broadcast."[946]

- In ***Commonwealth v. Antobenedetto***, the police stopped a motor vehicle which fit a description given by the radio dispatcher of a car driven by a suspected bad check passer. However, it was not shown at trial that the radio dispatcher had received any information as to the reliability of the source of that information. The stop and search of the vehicle were, therefore, invalid, for lack of sufficient probable cause to believe that a crime had been committed and that the car was associated with the crime.[947]
- In ***Commonwealth v. Barbosa,*** officers had articulable facts sufficient to make an investigatory stop of a motor vehicle, where they received a radio dispatch describing the perpetrators of a robbery at a convenience store, the reliability of a dispatch message was substantiated by its detail, the officers observed a car parked behind another convenience store on the most direct route from the municipality in which the robbery occurred, and the clothing of two of the men in the car matched the description of the robbery suspects.[948]

DELAYS IN CONDUCTING THE MOTOR VEHICLE EXCEPTION SEARCH

Once the police establish probable cause to search a vehicle they can delay in conducting the search *if* the reason is **to further the investigation**, *but* if the delay in conducting the search is motivated by the desire to avoid the warrant requirement the automobile exception may not apply.[949]

The automobile exception may not be employed to justify an *unreasonable* delay between the time when the police have probable cause to search a vehicle and the time when the search is conducted. The question then becomes whether the police delayed execution of the search for an *unreasonably* long time without plausible justification for the delay.

The time between the establishment of probable cause and conducting the search may be *unreasonable* if the police have **no reasonable basis to expect that delay would produce any additional benefit**.

The SJC has indicated that a reasonable period to further the investigation may be permissible:

a. to *corroborate* information received;
b. because of an expectation that *additional evidence* will subsequently be located in the automobile; or
c. in anticipation that the suspect or another will *commit additional criminal acts.* [950]

[946] *Commonwealth v. Antobenedetto*, 366 Mass. 51, 315 N.E.2d 530 (1974).
[947] *See also,Commonwealth v. Gullick*, 386 Mass. 278, 435 N.E.2d 348 (1982).
[948] *Commonwealth v. Barbosa*, 49 Mass. App. Ct. 344, 729 N.E. 2d 650 (2000).
[949] *Commonwealth v. Eggleston*, 453 Mass. 554, (2009).
[950] *Commonwealth v. Eggleston*, 453 Mass. 554, (2009).

In the 2009 case of ***Commonwealth v. Eggleston,*** based on informant information, in December of 2004, the Berkshire County drug task force undertook an investigation of the defendant, who worked at a tire store. The investigation established that the defendant routinely sold drugs from the tire store parking lot or the neighboring car wash before work, during his lunch hour, and at the end of the work day. On January 7, 2005 the officers received information that the defendant was arranging to make a large sale of drugs after work. The officers conducted surveillance and waited for the defendant to enter his vehicle. They intended to follow the suspect and make the arrest once the transaction was completed but they reconsidered their plan due to the traffic conditions and the concern of a potential high speed pursuit. At the completion of his shift, when the defendant entered his vehicle, the police moved in and removed him from the vehicle and conducted a search of the car, under the automobile exception. The search resulted in 379 grams of crack cocaine and other evidence. The defendant argued that the police should have applied for a warrant because they had ample time to do so. The SJC ruled that although the police had ample opportunity to obtain a warrant, the delay in conducting the search was objectively reasonable.[951]

DEFERRED STATION SEARCH

If police have probable cause to search a motor vehicle at the scene where it is discovered or stopped, the Supreme Court has held that probable cause will continue to exist and the police may defer the search until the car is taken into custody.[952] The SJC has also followed this rule providing there is a valid reason for doing so.[953]

- In the 1984 case of ***Commonwealth v. Markou,*** the Supreme Judicial Court observed that the U.S. Supreme Court case of ***Chambers v. Moroney*** "reflects the reality of police work: in some circumstances it may be necessary to delay a search until it can be done in a safe, convenient, and risk-free place."[954]

The Court set these limitations on delayed searches of impounded vehicles:

a. **The search should be reasonably immediate.** An Oregon decision, cited with approval in *Markou*, invalidated a search which took place 22 hours after the car was impounded. In *Markou*, the search took place within two hours of the stop and was held valid.
b. **There must be circumstances at the time of the stop which suggest a risk associated with searching the car at the scene.** In *Markou*, this requirement was satisfied by the facts that the stop was made at 11:30 p.m. after a chase on rural roads and the town's only two on-duty officers would be required for the search if it were conducted on the side of the road.

In ***Commonwealth v. Agosto***, the police seized a vehicle and held it for 21 days and conducted several warrantless searches. The SJC concluded that the vehicle, because it was held in a police facility, was no longer mobile and that, therefore, the automobile exception did not apply.[955] No exigent circumstances or safety concerns existed.

SEARCH INCIDENT TO AN ARREST INVOLVING A MOTOR VEHICLE

Under a search incident to a lawful arrest analysis, once the police possess probable cause to arrest a defendant, they are entitled to search the immediate area, including his/her motor vehicle, for other evidence of the crime for which the arrest was made.[956] The intent of this search is to prevent the concealment or destruction of evidence related to the crime, as well as to prevent the arrestee from accessing a weapon.

However, once the arrestee is secured (i.e. handcuffed and placed into a cruiser) the search of the arrestee's immediate area is no longer permissible because the arrestee would be unable to access the area to conceal evidence; unless there is a *reason to believe* that evidence[957] is in the vehicle or unless someone else is present who may conceal/destroy evidence (see below).

- In the 2009 U.S. Supreme Court case of ***Arizona v. Gant,*** the police where acting on an anonymous tip that the residence at 2524 North Walnut Avenue was being used to sell drugs, Tucson police officers Griffith and

[951] *Commonwealth v. Eggleston*, 453 Mass. 554, (2009).
[952] *Texas v. White*, 423 U.S. 67, 96 S.Ct; 304 (1975); *Chambers v. Maroney*, 399 U.S. 42, 90 S.Ct. 1975 (1970).
[953] *Commonwealth v. Motta,* 424 Mass. 117, 676 N.E. 2d 795 (1997); *Commonwealth v. Lara*, 39 Mass. App. Ct. 546, 658 N.E.2d 692 (1995); *Commonwealth v. Rand*, 363 Mass. 554, 296 N.E.2d 200 (1973).
[954] *Commonwealth v. Markou,* 391 Mass. 27, 459 N.E.2d 1225 (1984).
[955] *Commonwealth v. Agosto,* 428 Mass. 31 (1998).
[956] *Commonwealth v. Ciaramitaro*, 51 Mass. App. Ct. 638, 747 N.E.2d 1253 (2001).
[957] *Commonwealth v. Perkins* SJC (2013) quoting from Arizona v. Gant.

Reed knocked on the front door and asked to speak to the owner. Gant answered the door and, after identifying himself, stated that he expected the owner to return later. The officers left the residence and conducted a records check, which revealed that Gant's driver's license had been suspended and there was an outstanding warrant for his arrest for driving with a suspended license. When the officers returned to the house that evening, they found a man near the back of the house and a woman in a car parked in front of it. After a third officer arrived, they arrested the man for providing a false name and the woman for possessing drug paraphernalia. Both arrestees were handcuffed and secured in separate patrol cars when Gant arrived. The officers recognized his car as it entered the driveway and Officer Griffith confirmed that Gant was the driver by shining a flashlight into the car as it drove by him. Gant parked at the end of the driveway, got out of his car, and shut the door. Griffith, who was about 30 feet away, called to Gant, and they approached each other, meeting 10-to-12 feet from Gant's car. Griffith immediately arrested Gant and handcuffed him. Because the other arrestees were secured in the only patrol cars at the scene, Griffith called for backup. When two more officers arrived, they locked Gant in the backseat of their vehicle. After Gant had been handcuffed and placed in the back of a patrol car, two officers searched his car: One of them found a gun, and the other discovered a bag of cocaine in the pocket of a jacket on the backseat. Gant was charged with two offenses—possession of a narcotic drug for sale and possession of drug paraphernalia (i.e., the plastic bag in which the cocaine was found). The Court held that the police are authorized to search a vehicle incident to a recent occupant's arrest only when the arrestee is unsecured and within reaching distance of the passenger compartment at the time of the search. The Court also concluded that circumstances unique to the vehicle context justify a search incident to a lawful arrest when it is "reasonable to believe evidence relevant to the crime of arrest might be found in the vehicle." The justification of the search-incident-to-arrest exception to the warrant requirement is justified by interests in officer safety and evidence preservation. Once the possibility of the arrestee accessing a weapon or evidence is no longer likely a search based on this reasoning would be unjustified.[958]

However, if a cohort at the location could gain access to the item a search-incident-to-an-arrest may still be permissible.

In the 2012 case of ***Commonwealth v. Young***, the SJC ruled that the police were justified in ordering passengers out of a vehicle to facilitate a search incident-to-an-arrest of an occupant who was observed with drugs in his shirt pocket during a routine traffic stop, even after the arrestee has been handcuffed and removed. The SJC distinguished this case from *Gant* because although the arrestee was removed and secured, other passengers remained in the vehicle and could have concealed or destroyed any evidence that may have been left behind.[959]

Attorney Hanrahan's Note: None of these search incident to an arrest issues affect a motor vehicle exception search. For instance, if you have probable cause that the vehicle contains evidence of a crime you could search the vehicle (providing the automobile exception otherwise applies), and even order any passengers out in order to facilitate the search of the vehicle. The Automobile exception would not be affected by the detainment of the arrestee. This only pertains to search incident an arrest authority where you would not otherwise have probable cause to search the vehicle. Additionally, the U.S. Supreme Court, in Gant, stated that a search of the vehicle would be justified, even though the arrestee was secured, as long as the police had a *reason to believe* that evidence was within. This same terminology was quoted by the SJC in the 2013 case of *Commonwealth v. Perkins*. By using the term *reason to believe* as opposed to *probable cause* the Court seemingly lowered the threshold requirement of searching a motor vehicle incident to an arrest.

For more information of Searches Incident to Arrest see the Warrantless Search section of this manual.

MOTOR VEHICLE CONSENT SEARCHES

Consent during routine motor vehicle stops

Generally, during a routine motor vehicle stop (i.e. traffic violation) the interaction must be limited to the reason from the stop. Requesting consent to search during a routine motor vehicle stop, absent some indication of criminal activity, will inevitably be deemed an unlawful detention by the courts. The stop cannot be prolonged, absent some reasonable justification, beyond the time it takes to address the underlying violation. However, if the police detect criminal activity during a routine motor vehicle stop consent to search may be permitted depending upon the circumstances.

[958] *Arizona v. Gant*, 540 U.S. 963, (2009).
[959] Commonwealth v. Young, Mass. Appeals Court January 2011

In the 2006 case of ***Commonwealth v. Gonsalves***, the SJC stated "a routine traffic stop… presents a situation where citizens, both the vehicle's driver and any passenger or passengers in the vehicle, expect a police officer to get the government's business done quickly, so those detained can go on their way. This expectation is a reasonable one. A passenger in the stopped vehicle may harbor a special concern about the officer's conduct because the passenger usually had nothing to do with the operation, or condition, of the vehicle which drew the officer's attention in the first place. Citizens do not expect that police officers handling a routine traffic violation will engage, in the absence of justification, in stalling tactics, obfuscation, strained conversation, or unjustified exit orders, to prolong the seizure in the hope that, sooner or later, the stop might yield up some evidence of an arrestable crime. That a small percentage of routine traffic stops may result in the detection of more serious crime is no reason to subject the vast majority of citizens to orders to get out of their vehicles.

Attorney Hanrahan's Note: The message the SJC sent in ***Commonwealth v. Gonsalves*** was that without any additional justification the prolonged detention of a vehicle, and its occupants, who has been stopped for a minor traffic violation will be unlawful.

Reasonable Suspicion

If the vehicle was stopped *based on reasonable suspicion of criminal activity* a request for consent to search would be lawful, in most circumstances. Additionally, if during a "routine traffic stop" the officer *develops reasonable suspicion* of criminal activity a prolonging of the stop, including a request for consent, would be lawful.

- In ***Commonwealth v. Lanoue***, responding to a radio dispatch, a police officer stopped a motor vehicle containing suspected burglars. The officer asked the driver if he would allow the officer to look in the trunk. The officer told the driver he didn't have to grant consent. After first refusing consent, the driver voluntarily opened the trunk. Inside, the police found a sledge hammer, tool box and chisel; the suspect was arrested and convicted of possession of burglarious tools.[960]

Typically a police officer is not required to have reasonable suspicion, or any other justification, to request consent from a citizen who is free to decline and walk away, however in the context of a motor vehicle stop the operator/occupant is not free to decline and leave. This is a key distinction between consent in general and consent during a routine traffic stop. Although there are no specific cases directly on point, presumably if a police officer, during a motor vehicle stop, makes it clear to the operator that the stop has ended and that he/she is free to go and then subsequently requests consent the lawfulness would be judged on the same basis as consensual searches not involving routine motor vehicle stops.

The Operator/Occupant Authority to Grant Consent

The driver of a motor vehicle ordinarily has authority to consent to a search of the vehicle as well as any locked containers in such vehicle.

Exceptions occur when the driver clearly lacks authority over certain locked containers belonging to others.[961]

- In the 1994 1st Circuit case of ***U.S. v. Infante-Ruiz,*** the Court concluded that it was not reasonable for the police to believe that the driver of an automobile in which the defendant was a passenger consented to a search of the defendant's briefcase, which was in the locked trunk, even though the driver consented to a search of the automobile and furnished the keys for the trunk. There the police officer did not notify the driver that he was looking for drugs, making it difficult to impute to the driver consent to search every container within the automobile which might contain drugs. Moreover, the driver told the officer, before opening and searching the briefcase, that the briefcase belonged to the defendant-passenger. The Court noted that a Fourth Amendment violation occurs when it is not objectively reasonable under the circumstances for a police officer to believe that the scope of a suspect's consent permitted the officer to open a particular container within the automobile. The Court suggested that since the passenger-owner was nearby, handcuffed in a cruiser, he should have been asked for permission.
- In the 1991 Supreme Court case of ***Florida v. Jimeno,*** one occupant of a rental car had no authority to consent to the search of another occupant's purse where there was no evidence of joint access to or shared control over the purse.[962] In *Jimeno*, the driver's general consent to search the vehicle was found sufficient to

[960] *Commonwealth v. Lanoue*, 356 Mass. 337, 251 N.E.2d 894 (1969).*See also,Commonwealth v. Egan*, 12 Mass. App. Ct. 658, 428 N.E.2d 342 (1981) .
[961] See *U.S. v. Infante-Ruiz*, 13 F.3d 498 (1st Cir. 1994).
[962] *Florida v. Jimeno*, 500 U.S. 248, 111 S.Ct. 1801, 114 L.Ed.2d 297 (1991).

authorize the search of a paper bag on the floorboard containing cocaine. The officer informed the suspect that he was under suspicion for carrying narcotics, and the suspect had not placed any explicit limitation on the scope of the search.

Scope of consent

Assuming consent is obtained voluntarily to search the interior of a motor vehicle, this consent extends to the contents of closed containers discovered inside the vehicle capable of holding the object for which the police were conducting the search, without having to ask the suspect for permission to open each container (unless he or she limited or revokes his or her consent, of course).[963]

Where a person gives a general consent to a police search of a motor vehicle, it is implied that he is consenting to a search of the trunk.[964]

For a full analysis of consent see the Warrantless search section of this manual.

SEARCH OF VEHICLE EXTERIOR

The police may make a plain view search of a motor vehicle as part of routine police work. If, during that plain view search, police come upon indications of criminal activity, probable cause to search may develop. If exigent circumstances are also present, (for example, if the car is parked in public and could be removed by the owner or others), police may conduct a warrantless search for evidence.

- In the U.S. Supreme Court case of ***Cardwell v. Lewis***, where police took control of an automobile after arresting the defendant for murder and they suspected that the automobile was used in the murder, they could make visual comparisons between the tire treads and casts of tire impressions taken from the murder scene. They could also take paint samples from the victim's automobile. [965]
- In ***Commonwealth v. Dolan***, the Supreme Judicial Court observed that the "inspection of the surface of (a) vehicle is not a search."[966] In that case, the police were led by the defendant to a stolen trailer. They inspected the underside of the trailer and noted the serial number located there.

Search of Damaged Vehicle after an Accident

Officers may remove a damaged vehicle from the roadway after an accident. A test to determine the cause of the accident is allowed since the owner has no reasonable expectation of privacy where the police have a duty to remove vehicles involved in serious accidents and attempt to pinpoint the causes.[967]

- In ***Commonwealth v. Mamacos***, while investigating a fatal motor vehicle accident the police were able to inspect and test the vehicle for mechanical failure even without consent or a warrant.[968]

VIN or Inspection Sticker

The Appeals Court, in the 2002 case of ***Commonwealth v. Starr***, recognized that motorists have a considerably reduced expectation of privacy in identification markings on a motor vehicle, such as a VIN number or an inspection sticker, than they have in personal items within the motor vehicle.[969]

In ***Commonwealth v. Starr*** , the Court approved the opening an unlocked vehicle in order to identify it through the vehicle identification number (VIN) on the door post as well as opening an unlocked vehicle to identify its general place of origin through the inspection station named on the inside of the inspection sticker - where such a search is justified because the car is associated with criminal activity, but not where the search of the VIN number or inspection sticker is a pretext for a general exploratory search of the vehicle.[970]

In ***New York v. Class***, the U.S. Supreme Court also approved of officers opening a vehicle door to move papers on the dashboard that obscured a vehicle's VIN.[971] While such officers must limit their "search" for the VIN, if they observe contraband (here a gun handle in plain view), it may be seized.

---

[963] *Florida v. Jimeno*, 111 S.Ct. 1801 (1991); *Commonwealth v. Lantigua*, 38 Mass. App. Ct. 526, 649 N.E.2d 1129 (1995).
[964] *U.S. v. Christian*, 371 F. Supp. 64 (D. Mass. 1978).
[965] *Cardwell v. Lewis*, 417 U.S. 583, 94 S.Ct. 2464 (1974); *Commonwealth v. Dolan*, 352 Mass. 432, 225 N.E.2d 910 (1967).
[966] *Commonwealth v. Dolan,* 352 MARS 432, 225 N.E.2d 910 (1967).
[967] *Commonwealth v. Mamacos*, 409 Mass. 635, 568 N.E.2d 1139 (1991).
[968] *Commonwealth v. Mamacos*, 409 Mass. 635, 568 N.E.2d 1139 (1991).
[969] *Commonwealth v. Starr,*55 Mass.App.Ct. 590, 773 N.E.2d 981 (2002). See also, *Commonwealth v. Hason*, 387 Mass. 169, 173, 439 N.E.2d 251 (1982); *Commonwealth v. Navarro*, 2 Mass.App.Ct. 214, 219-221, 310 N.E.2d 372 (1974); and, *Commonwealth v. Baldwin,* 11 Mass.App.Ct.386, 391, 416 N.E.2d 544 (1981).
[970] *See also*, *Commonwealth v. Hason*, 387 Mass. 169, 439 N.E.2d 251 (1982); *Commonwealth v. Baldwin*, 11 Mass. App. Ct. 386, 416 N.E.2d 544 (1981).
[971] *New York v. Class*, 475 U.S. 106, 106 S.Ct. 960, 89 L.Ed.2d 81 (1986).

In ***U.S. v. Sawyer***, the court ruled that officers may look for a VIN by looking at the underside of a truck using flashlights to illuminate the engine compartment.[972]

CANINE "SNIFF" OF VEHICLE'S EXTERIOR

Federal Law

The United State Supreme Court has held that a canine sniff of the exterior a vehicle is within constitutional limits as long as the as it does not extend the time necessary to complete the stop.[973]

Massachusetts Law

Massachusetts courts have concurred that the sniff of a vehicle's exterior is not a search, however, if a detention is unreasonable under the circumstances any subsequent sniff of the vehicle's exterior will be deemed unlawful.

See the K9 Search section of this manual for more on K9 issues.

WARRANT SEARCH OF MOTOR VEHICLE

When in possession of a properly issued warrant, the police may search a motor vehicle consistent with any restrictions the warrant may impose. Although many of the situations encountered by police regarding searches of motor vehicles are situations in which a warrantless search is permissible, police must be careful to follow proper warrant procedures in those situations where no exception to the Fourth Amendment warrant requirement is present.

Vehicle in Driveway or on Street

A motor vehicle found within the curtilage and owned or controlled by the owner of a residence for which the police have a search warrant may also be searched when executing a search warrant.[974]

However, a vehicle parked on a public street will not be considered within the curtilage of a residence. Unless proceeding under any exception to the warrant requirement, the police may not search a vehicle parked on a public street while executing a warrant for the adjacent premises where the vehicle is not specifically named in the warrant.[975] This is true even where the defendant lived in an apartment and there was no driveway or off-street parking.

For more information regarding the execution of a search warrant refer to the Search Warrant section of this Manual.

PAT FRISK OF VEHICLE OCCUPANTS AND EXIT ORDERS

The SJC has stated "it is settled that in appropriate circumstances a *Terry* type search may extend into the interior of an automobile."[976] "To justify either the search or the order to the occupants to exit the automobile, 'we ask ''whether a reasonably prudent man in the policeman's position would be warranted in the belief that the safety of the police or that of other persons was in danger.''[977]

Such a search of the automobile must be ''limited in scope to a protective end.''[978] A search of the automobile for evidence as opposed to weapons is not authorized by *Terry* principles.[979]

- In ***Commonwealth v. Prevost***, after lawfully stopping a motor vehicle for a traffic violation, a trooper's safety concerns justified his actions in opening the vehicle's passenger-side door and in searching the vehicle's passenger.[980] In that case, the trooper and police officers present had observed before leaving their cruiser that the passenger made unusual movements with his shoulders and arms and then bent over and was briefly out of sight. The trooper saw the passenger struggling to put on an overcoat as the trooper approached the vehicle. The passenger gave no explanation for putting on his coat. The trooper asked the passenger to open his overcoat, which he did. Then the trooper saw the outline of a handgun in the passenger's right leg area.

---

[972] *U.S. v. Sawyer*, 630 F.Supp. 889 (D. Mass. 1986).
[973] *Illinois v. Caballes*, 543 U.S 405 (2005).
[974] *Commonwealth v. Signorines*, 404 Mass. 400, 535 N.E.2d 601 (1989).
[975] *Commonwealth v. Santiago*, 410 Mass. 737, 575 N.E.2d 350 (1991).
[976] *Commonwealth v. Almeida*, 373 Mass. 266, 270, 366 N.E.2d 756 (1977).
[977] *Commonwealth v. Vazquez*, 426 Mass. 99, 102–103, 686 N.E.2d 993 (1997), quoting from *Commonwealth* v. S 125Santana, supra at 212–213, 649 N.E.2d 717. See *Commonwealth* v. Gonsalves, 429 Mass. 658, 661–662, 662–663, 711 N.E.2d 108 (1999).
[978] *Commonwealth v. Silva*, 366 Mass. 402, 408, 318 N.E.2d 895 (1974).
[979] See I*d*. at 410, 318 N.E.2d 895; *Commonwealthv. Almeida*, 373 Mass. at 272, 366 N.E.2d 756; *Commonwealthv. Santiago*, 53 Mass.App.Ct. 567, 570, 760 N.E.2d 800 (2002)
[980] *Commonwealth v. Prevost*, 44 Mass. App. Ct. 398, 691 N.E. 2d 592 (1998), *rev. den.*427 Mass. 1104, 695 N.E. 2d 667 (1998).

EXIT ORDERS

Federal law

The Federal standard mandated by the Fourth Amendment to the U.S. Constitution is not as stringent as the Massachusetts rule. Under the Federal Rule, when an automobile is properly stopped, the police officer may, as a matter of course, order the driver and any passengers to exit the vehicle.[981]

According to the 1977 U.S. Supreme Court case of ***Pennsylvania v. Mimms,*** the police may order a stopped motorist to alight from the vehicle to ensure the officer's safety.[982] The Court concluded that a police officer may order a stopped motorist to alight from the vehicle in order to reduce the chances of unobserved movements on the part of the motorist and also to allow the police officer to move off the highway and out of the way of traffic. The Court also cited a 1963 statistic that 30% of shootings of police occur when a police officer approaches a suspect seated in a stopped motor vehicle. In the *Mimms* case, a motorist was stopped for an expired license plate. When ordered to alight, the officer noticed a bulge in the suspect's sports jacket. A frisk uncovered a gun.

Massachusetts law

In the 2011 case of ***Com. v. Cruz,*** the SJC declared that there are three scenarios in which an exit order issued to an occupant in a validly stopped vehicle is justified:

1. **Safety**: an exit order is justified if "a reasonably prudent man in the policeman's position would be warranted in the belief that the **safety** of the police or that of other persons was in danger."
2. **Criminal Investigatory Purpose**: there is reasonable suspicion (based on articulable facts) that those ordered out are engaged in **criminal activity** (when it comes to passengers the suspicion must be separate from any offense solely of the driver).
3. **Facilitate A Lawful Search**: officers can order the occupants out of a car for "**pragmatic reasons"**, e.g., to facilitate an independently permissible warrantless search of the car under the automobile exception to the warrant requirement.

In the 2014 case of ***Commonwealth v. Fisher***, the Appeals Court indicated that an exit order would also be permissible for Community Caretaking purposes.

4. **Community Caretaking:** when a police officer reasonably believes that an operator may be impaired, even if not in a criminal sense (e.g. illness), and that the safety of the public may be in jeopardy an exit order would be justified.

Each of these issues are discussed in more detail below:

SAFETY CONCERNS

When police officers stop a vehicle for traffic violations, they are permitted to order the vehicle's occupants out of the vehicle if the officers reasonably fear for their own safety or the safety of others. It does not take much for a police officer to establish a reasonable basis to justify an exit order ... based on safety concerns."[983]

In the case of ***Commonwealth v. Gonsalves,*** the SJC interpreted art. 14 of the Declaration of Rights of the Massachusetts Constitution to require that "a police officer, in a routine traffic stop, must have a reasonable belief that the officer's safety, or the safety of others, is in danger before ordering a driver out of a motor vehicle."[984]

To determine whether such a belief is reasonable, the court will ask "whether a reasonably prudent man in the policeman's position would be warranted" in such a belief.[985] The court will look at the *totality of the circumstances* in determining whether or not an exit order is lawful.

Circumstances justifying an exit order during "routine" traffic stop for Safety Concerns

The SJC has declared "it does not take much for a police officer to establish a reasonable basis to justify an exit order or search based on safety concerns."[986] To establish the reasonableness of an officer's belief that someone's safety is in danger during a stop, the Commonwealth is not required to make the specific showing that a driver or passenger has a weapon.

[981] *Commonwealth v. Riche*, 50 Mass. App. Ct. 830, 741 N.E.2d 871 (2001).
[982] *Pennsylvania v. Mimms*, 434 U.S. 106, 98 S.Ct. 330 (1977).
[983] Commonwealth v. Goewey, 452 Mass. 399, 406-407 (2008)., quoting from Commonwealth v. Gonsalves, 429 Mass. 658, 664 (1999).
[984] See*Commonwealth v. Torres*, 433 Mass. 669, 673, 745 N.E.2d 945 (2001), officers conducting stop for routine traffic violation may order driver or passenger to leave vehicle, "but only if they have a reasonable belief that their safety, or the safety of others, is in danger"; *Commonwealth v. Gonsalves*, 429 Mass. 658, 662-663, 711 N.E.2d 108 (1999), *S.C.*, 432 Mass. 613, 739 N.E.2d 1100 (2000).
[985] *Commonwealth v. Vazquez*, 426 Mass. 99, 103, 686 N.E.2d 993 (1997), quoting *Commonwealth v. Santana, supra* at 212-213, 649 N.E.2d 717.
[986] *Commonwealth v. Gonsalves, supra*, at 664, 711 N.E.2d 108.

A "mere hunch" is not enough,[987] nor is nervousness or fidgeting on the part of the driver or passengers in a stopped vehicle an adequate reason to order them out of the car. [988]

"To support an order to a passenger to alight from a vehicle stopped for a traffic violation…the officer need not point to specific facts that the occupants are 'armed and dangerous.' Rather, the officer need point only to some fact or facts in the totality of the circumstances that would create in a police officer a heightened awareness of danger that would warrant an objectively reasonable officer in securing the scene in a more effective manner by ordering the passenger to alight from the car."[989]

- In ***Commonwealth v. Feyenord***, the officer conducted a threshold inquiry in which the driver could not produce a valid driver's license, produced a registration in another person's name, failed to identify himself, and appeared nervous. These circumstances justified an exit order and further inquiry.[990] ''Inability to produce a license or a registration reasonably gives rise to a suspicion of other offenses, such as automobile theft.''[991]
- In the 2005 Appeals Court case of ***Commonwealth v. Horton***, the court ruled that the police officers had reasonable suspicion of danger and thus, were justified in ordering the defendant out of the back seat of a vehicle stopped for a license-plate violation.[992] In this case, the defendant reached down below his leg and kicked at something, the stop occurred in the middle of the night in a high-crime area, and the defendant looked rapidly side to side at the officers.
- In the 2004 Appeals Court case of ***Commonwealth v. Rousseau***, the court found that the police officers were justified in ordering the driver and passenger to exit a pick-up truck they were driving at 1:00 a.m. in a state park where signs indicated the park was closed at 8:00 p.m.[993] The officers had minutes earlier seen the truck parked and, by using their flashlights, had seen a police duty belt on the seat. The court concluded it was reasonable for the officers to be fearful that a gun was somehow associated with the duty belt, so they were justified in ordering the suspects to exit their vehicle so the officers could conduct a search based on their safety concerns.
- In the 2013 case of ***Commonwealth v. Obiora***, the Appeals Court held that the exit order was valid based on the totality of the circumstances. In this case the officer was alone, late at night, with three detained persons, and was presented false identification.

Frisk for weapons

Police may order a motorist to alight and may conduct a protective frisk for weapons if they reasonably suspect the motorist has or may have a weapon. The same may be done with regard to passengers.[994] The standard for a pat frisk is the same as the standard required to justify an order to the occupants of a vehicle stopped for traffic violations to leave the vehicle. To justify a pat frisk, whether it occurs in the context of a routine traffic stop or in the context of a *Terry*-type stop, the Court asks whether a reasonably prudent person in the police officer's position would be warranted in the belief that the safety of the police or that of other persons was in danger.

- In ***Commonwealth v. Ciaramitaro***, a reasonable apprehension of danger justified a police pat frisk of a defendant, following an officer's justified stop of the defendant's car for erratic driving and making an illegal left turn, where the defendant had been driving erratically and made a sudden, illegal left turn, and when questioned by the police, reached into his jacket pocket and fumbled with an object.[995]
- In the 2013 case of ***Commonwealth v. Rosado***, the Appeals Court held that when a police officer sees something he thinks may be a weapon in a vehicle, but is not certain, he is not required to inquire before taking protective action.
- In a 1972 Supreme Court case of ***Adams v. Williams***, where a reliable informant told a police officer that a motorist seated in a nearby car was carrying narcotics and also had a gun tucked in at his waist, the officer was justified in approaching the motorist and asking him to open the door. When the motorist rolled down the window instead, the officer reached toward his waist and seized a loaded revolver from his waistband. The seizure of the revolver was a proper protective frisk for weapons.[996]

---

[987] *Commonwealth v. Silva, supra* at 406, 318 N.E.2d 895.
[988] *Commonwealth v. Torres,* 424 Mass. 153, 158-159, 674 N.E.2d 638 (1997). See *Commonwealth v. Davis,*41 Mass.App.Ct. 793, 796-797, 673 N.E.2d 879 (1996).
[989] *Commonwealth v. Gonsalves, supra* at 665, 711 N.E.2d 108, quoting *State v. Smith*, 134 N.J. 599, 618, 637 A.2d 158 (1994).
[990] See *Commonwealth v. Wilson*, 360 Mass. 557, 559–560, 276 N.E.2d 283 (1971) (defendant's incredible claim of ignorance about provenance of water pistol in vehicle justified further inquiry).
[991] *Commonwealth v. Lantigua*, 38 Mass.App.Ct. 526, 528, 649 N.E.2d 1129 (1995).
[992] *Commonwealth v. Horton*, 827 N.E.2d 1257, 63 Mass.App.Ct.571(2005).
[993] *Commonwealth v. Rousseau,* 61 Mass.App.Ct. 144, 807 N.E.2d 832 (2004).
[994] *See Commonwealth v. Pappalardo*, 10 Mass. App. Ct. 897, 409 N.E.2d 815 (1980).
[995] *Commonwealth v. Ciaramitaro*, 51 Mass. App. Ct. 638, 747 N.E.2d 1253 (2001).
[996] *Adams v. Williams*, 407 U.S. 143, 92 S.Ct. 1921 (1972).

Note: For a detailed discussion on pat frisks see *the Temporary Detention Section of this manual.*

Frisking the Vehicle (sometimes referred to as a *protective sweep* of the vehicle)

Once the police lawfully order the occupant(s) out of the vehicle the police can pat frisk the suspect for weapons and also conduct a *protective sweep* of the vehicle's interior, around where the suspect was seated, to ensure that no weapons are present prior to allowing the defendant back in the car. A protective sweep or "pat frisk" of a car must be justified by an officer's reasonable belief that his own safety or that of others is in danger.

In discussing stop and frisk and threshold searches of motorists and motor vehicles, the Supreme Judicial Court, in ***Commonwealth v. Silva,*** has declared that a "a *Terry* type of search may extend into the interior of an automobile as long as it is limited in scope to a protective end . . . which restricts the search to the area from within which . . . the suspect might gain possession of a weapon."[997]

A pat frisk may legitimately extend into the interior of an automobile, but police are confined to what is minimally necessary to learn whether the suspect is armed and to disarm him once the weapon is discovered.[998]

- In the 2012 case of ***Commonwealth v. Johnson***, Boston police officers Medina and Ball, along with Trooper Cameron, stopped Johnson's car for a red light violation. Off. Medina asked Johnson for his license and registration. Johnson would not make eye contact and appeared very nervous. Meanwhile, Off. Ball spoke to the passenger in the front seat and ascertained that she was Patricia Felix, the owner of the car. Felix also appeared nervous; she did not maintain eye contact, and she was breathing heavily and shallowly. The officers discovered that Johnson had an outstanding warrant for speeding and unauthorized use of a motor vehicle. The officers ordered both occupants from the vehicle and conducted a protective sweep of the car. A firearm was discovered. The SJC ruled that the protective sweep of the vehicle was not justified. The arrest warrant was for nonviolent motor vehicle offenses. The police officers had no reason to believe that either occupant had a history of weapons possession or dangerous crimes. They had no specific information that anyone in the car had a weapon. The occupants of the car kept their hands in sight of the officers. They made no furtive gestures suggesting that they might be reaching for or hiding weapons. The defendant's glances into the back of the car were ambiguous and not the equivalent of movements suggesting an attempt to conceal a weapon. Furthermore, when the pat frisk of the automobile was performed, Johnson was outside the car, under the watchful eyes of another officer. Finally, the officers outnumbered the occupants of the.

In *Johnson*, the SJC stressed "mere nervousness by the defendant is not enough and nervous or anxious behavior in combination with factors that add nothing to the equation will not support a reasonable suspicion that an officer's safety may be compromised."

- In ***Commonwealth v. Sumerlin,*** the Supreme Judicial Court ruled that an officer acted permissibly when he seized a bag carried into the car by a passenger.[999] The Court concluded that because the bag had been on the front seat, within the reach of the occupants, the officer's search had been reasonably limited to the scope necessary for his own protection. After seizing the bag and feeling something which turned out to be a revolver, the officer again acted permissibly by opening the bag. The revolver was admissible.

Scope of the Protective Frisk of the Vehicle's Interior

Generally, the protective frisk is limited to areas wherein the occupants could readily access a weapon.

In the 2013 case of ***Commonwealth v. Haynes***, the Appeals Court ruled that a protective frisk of a motor vehicle may extend to a suspected "hide," particularly if it is capable of housing a weapon.

A pat frisk must be "reasonably designed" to uncover threatening weapons, a concept that requires consideration of all the circumstances.[1000] In the 2009 case of ***Commonwealth v. Cruz-Rivera***, the Appeals Court ruled that the search of a small pill bottle located inside the center console of a motor vehicle during the pat frisk of the operator and his immediate area within the vehicle which subsequently uncovered illicit drugs was beyond the scope of a pat frisk of the vehicle. The court felt it was unreasonable to believe that a miniature weapon may be secreted in a pill bottle and that the operator would use it against the officers who were about to release him with only a citation.

[997] *Commonwealth v. Silva*, 366 Mass. 402, 318 N.E.2d 895 (1974).
[998] Com .v.Myers Appeals Ct (2012)
[999] *Commonwealth v. Sumerlin*, 393 Mass. 127, 469 N.E.2d 826 (1984).
[1000] *Commonwealth v. Cruz-Rivera*, Mass. App. Ct. (2009)

Pat frisk interior permitted even after occupants are removed

In ***Commonwealth v. Silva***, the Supreme Judicial Court noted that a police officer may search the vehicle even if the suspect is outside the car where "he was not in the custody of the police and could be expected to reenter the vehicle very soon."[1001]

Preventing Reentry

Officers may prevent reentry into the vehicle with proper justification, such as a concern for the officer's safety.

- In the 1995 case of ***Commonwealth v. Lantigua***[1002], the driver who had exited from the car told the officer that the registration was in the glove compartment and offered to get it.[1003] The Court held that the officer, in the interest of his own safety, could properly retrieve the registration from the place where the defendant said it would be, rather than have the defendant reenter the protective and partially concealing interior of the car, for the ostensible purpose of retrieving it himself.[1004] The court also noted that the inability to produce a license or registration reasonably gives rise to heightened suspicion of other offenses.

Passengers

A person who is merely present in a suspected car does not lose the immunities from the search of his or her person to which he or she would otherwise be entitled.

However, if the officer has a reasonable belief that the passenger poses a safety concern a passenger may be ordered from the vehicle and pat frisked.

- ***Commonwealth v. Barbosa***, after making a proper investigatory stop, officers were entitled, as a matter of reasonable precaution, to frisk the occupants of a car, since two of the occupants matched the description of robbery suspects and the reported robbery involved a firearm.[1005]

Additionally, there is no automatic right to search the companion of a person validly arrested.[1006]

Timing of the Exit Order

Generally, exit orders are given at the outset of the stop if circumstances dictate. However, in the 2002 case of ***Commonwealth v. Stampley***, the SJC pointed out that "justification for an exit order does not depend on the presence of an 'immediate threat' at the precise moment of the order, but rather on the safety concerns raised by the entire circumstances of the encounter."[1007] For instance, if a police officer develops a fear for his/her safety he/she should generally give the exit order at that moment. However, the circumstances may dictate otherwise. Perhaps the officer is awaiting back-up or some other reasonable justification to delay the exit order.

EXIT ORDER USED TO FURTHER CRIMINAL INVESTIGATORY PURPOSES – NO CONCERN FOR SAFETY REQUIRED

Police may order the occupants exit to further investigative efforts in some circumstances even without the need to show a fear for safety. This can occur when the vehicle is stopped because the occupants are suspected of being involved in criminal activity or when the vehicle is stopped for a traffic violation and the officer subsequently uncovers criminal behavior.

- In ***Commonwealth v. Bostock,*** while investigating the break-in of a motor vehicle the police located the suspect in a parked motor vehicle and ordered him out. There was no indication that the suspect was armed or dangerous. The SJC upheld the exit order reasoning that the fear of safety requirement related to routine traffic stops and does not extend to the investigation of criminal activity.[1008]
- In ***Commonwealth v. Riche***, the Appeals Court ruled in 2001 that an exit order was justified where "tender of a registration not crediting ownership of the vehicle to any occupant raised a question whether the car was

[1001] *Commonwealth v. Silva*, 366 Mass. 402, 318 N.E.2d 895 (1974).
[1002] *Commonwealth v. Lantigua*, 38 Mass.App.Ct. 526, 649 N.E.2d 1129 (1995).
[1003] *Id*. at 527, 649 N.E.2d 1129.
[1004] *Id*. at 529, 649 N.E.2d 1129. See *Commonwealth* v. Pagan, 440 Mass. 62, 68, 793 N.E.2d 1236 (2003).
[1005] *Commonwealth v. Barbosa*, 49 Mass. App. Ct. 344, 729 N.E. 2d 650 (2000).
[1006] *Commonwealth v. Prevost*, 44 Mass. App. Ct. 398, 691 N.E. 2d 592 (1997), *rev. den.*427 Mass. 1104, 695 N.E. 2d 667 (1998).
[1007] *Commonwealth v. Stampley*, 437 Mass. 323, 328, 771 N.E.2d 784 (2002).
[1008] *Commonwealth v. Bostock*, 450 Mass. 616, 880 N.E.2d 759 (2008)

stolen,'' and order served ''special practical purpose'' of ''separating those in a stopped car from each other to frustrate interchange or collaboration among them''[1009].

- In the 2005 Appeals Court case of ***Commonwealth v. San***, the court found that the officers had reasonable apprehension of danger to their safety following the stop of a van to justify: blocking of the van, a protective sweep of van, ordering the van's occupants to exit, and conducting a protective frisk of the van's occupants and the defendant, who was standing outside of the van.[1010] Here the officers had reasonable suspicion at time of the stop that occupants of the van might have been involved in a burglary, as within fifteen to thirty minutes following the burglary, and within a mile or two of the victims' residence, the police observed a man matching the description of the intruder standing alongside the van, which was similar to that seen circling the victim's neighborhood at the time the burglary occurred.
- In the 2013 case of ***Commonwealth v. Daniel***, the SJC ruled that the odor and possession of (small amounts) of marijuana alone will not justify an exit order and vehicle search for the purposes of an OUI drug investigation absent some indication that the operator is otherwise impaired.

PRAGMATIC REASONS FOR AN EXIT ORDER

Pragmatic (or practical) reasons arise when the police have the lawful authority to search the vehicle (e.g. the officer has probable cause that they vehicle contains evidence) and the officer orders the occupants out of the vehicle to facilitate the search of the vehicle. There must be legal justification for the search in order for the exit order to be lawful under this theory.

COMMUNITY CARETAKING CONCERNS

The community caretaking doctrine is applicable principally to a range of police activities involving motor vehicles in which there are objective facts indicating that a person may be need of medical assistance or some other circumstance exists apart from the investigation of criminal activity that supports police intervention to protect an individual or the public. The existence of objective grounds supporting police intervention for legitimate, noninvestigatory reasons excuses the need for a warrant, probable cause, or even reasonable suspicion.

So long as the officer's conduct at the outset and throughout the course of exercising a community caretaking function is justified by the doctrine, the law does not attach significance to the officer's subjective (i.e. ulterior) motives.

In the 2014 case of ***Commonwealth v. Fisher***, the Northampton police were dealing with a man who was unresponsive behind the wheel of a car. Although they did not detect any alcohol, the man was ordered out of the car after the officers observed a baggy containing white powder. The exit order was upheld because the Court ruled that the police had reasonable suspicion of criminal activity (i.e. the white powder coupled with the operator's condition), however the Court indicated that the exit order would also have been justified under the Community Caretaking doctrine given the man's condition.

[1009] *Commonwealth v. Riche*, 50 Mass.App.Ct. 830, 833–834, 741 N.E.2d 871 (2001).
[1010] *Commonwealth v. San*, 63 Mass.App.Ct.189, 824 N.E.2d 470 (2005).

IMPOUNDED VEHICLES AND INVENTORY SEARCHES

In order for the inventory search to be upheld the original impoundment (the tow) must be lawful. The legitimacy of an inventory search of an impounded vehicle involves two related, but distinct, inquiries:

1. whether the impoundment of the vehicle leading to the search meets constitutional strictures,

   and

2. whether the conduct and scope of the search itself meet those strictures.[1011]

The impoundment of a vehicle and an inventory search of such vehicle are not synonymous, and the constitutional analysis is different for each.[1012]

IMPOUNDMENT (i.e. towing)

Authority to Impoundment

Impoundment must be standard practice and all discretion must be removed. It must be based on specific criteria in the form of a written standardized procedure. This requirement is intended to eliminate/reduce discretion so that it is not used to circumvent the probable cause and search warrant requirements.

In ***US v. Donnelly***, where a police department's policy gave an officer discretion whether or not to impound a vehicle, without standardized criteria framing the exercise of that discretion, an inventory search conducted at the scene of a parked vehicle was invalid.[1013]

General justification for Impoundment

The impoundment of a vehicle for non-investigatory reasons is generally justified if supported by:

1. **Public safety concerns,** or
2. **The danger of theft or vandalism** to a vehicle left unattended.[1014]

"Where there is no practical available alternative, removal of a vehicle from a public roadway and inventory searches of it are constitutional."[1015]

Additionally, if the vehicle is heavily damaged as a result of a motor vehicle accident, or is otherwise prohibited from being on the roadway due to non-compliance with the law (e.g. unregistered, uninsured, OUI impoundment for breath test refusal, etc.) an impoundment, and subsequent inventory, would be lawful.

- In the 2005 case of ***Commonwealth v. Bienvenu***, neither defendant could lawfully drive the car. Bienvenu had been arrested and his passenger's license had been suspended.[1016] Additionally, the car was stopped at night alongside a two lane road. For public safety reasons, it would have been imprudent to allow the car to remain on the side of the road. The Court stated that reasonable concerns for public safety dictated that the car be removed from the two-lane road in accordance with clearly-defined Whitman Police Department policy. Impoundment was justified in this instance.

What Constitutes Proper Justification? It is not always clear.

The 2003 case of ***Commonwealth v. Brinson***, the SJC ruled that the government may not impound and conduct an inventory search of a car based on the arrest of the owner, where the car was lawfully parked in a privately owned parking lot and there was no evidence that the car constituted a safety hazard or was at risk of theft or vandalism. However, recently in the 2011 case of ***Com. v. Eddington***, the SJC upheld the impoundment of a motor vehicle that was otherwise lawfully parked. The SJC distinguished this decision from Brinson by explaining that in Brinson the owner of the vehicle had selected the location (the car had already been parked by the owner) but in Eddington the police pulled the vehicle over and thus it was the police who selected the

[1011] *Commonwealth v. Ellerbe,* 430 Mass. 769, 773, 723 N.E.2d 977 (2000); 60 Mass. App. Ct. 528, 803 N.E.2d 1274 (2004).
[1012] *Commonwealth v. Silva,* 61 Mass.App.Ct. 28, 807 N.E.2d 170 (2004).
[1013] *U.S. v. Donnelly,* 885 F.Supp. 300 (D. Mass. 1995).
[1014] *Commonwealth v. Daley*, 423 Mass. 747, 750, 672 N.E.2d 101 (1996).
[1015] Ibid. See, e.g., *Commonwealth v. Ellerbe*, 430 Mass. 769, 775-776, 723 N.E.2d 977 (2000).
[1016] *Commonwealth v. Bienvenu*, 63 Mass.App.Ct. 632, 828 N.E.2d.546 (2005).

location. In addition, unlike in Brinson, the actual owner of the vehicle was not present at the scene. In Eddington, the Appeals Court ruled that the police must offer evidence of a realistic risk of theft or vandalism in order to justify impounding a vehicle.[1017]

Attorney Hanrahan's Recommendation: If the vehicle is in a hazardous location (either a traffic hazard or located in a high crime area where the risk of theft/vandalism is high) and the vehicle cannot be quickly removed from the scene by either the owner or a duly licensed person, of the owner's choosing, an impoundment would most likely be upheld by the Courts, particularly if the officer dictated the location (e.g. pulled the vehicle over). If the vehicle is lawfully parked and there is no threat of theft/vandalism or no safety concerns involved and the owner approves the location or is able to arrange to have a duly licensed person take possession of the vehicle within a reasonable period of time, an impoundment would most likely not be justified absent some other justification (e.g. OUI – see below).

Pre-textual Inventory Searches are Unlawful

In the 2015 case of *Commonwealth v. Ortiz*, the Appeals Court ruled that pre-textual inventory searches are unlawful. In *Ortiz*, the defendant was under surveillance for suspected cocaine trafficking. The investigators knew that the defendant had a suspended driver's license for some time, however they devised a plan to wait until they suspected that he was in the process of trafficking cocaine to effect a vehicle stop and subsequent arrest. The officers intended to conduct an inventory search subsequent to the arrest for operating after suspension and to utilize the inventory inspection to uncover any drugs located within. The plan was successful; however the Court ruled that an inventory conducted for investigatory purposes is unlawful.

Impoundment From Private Property

Courts have upheld the impoundment of a car from the private lot associated with the arrest location when accompanied by such circumstances as threats of vandalism, parking restrictions, police liability concerns, or the inability of the defendant or another later to move the car[1018] and even to avoid an inconvenience to the property owner.

Case Examples (Federal cases):

- In ***U.S. v. Martin,*** lawful impoundment of car at parking lot where arrest occurred because no one was available to take custody of unlocked car with valuable equipment inside in plain view was permissible.
- In ***United States v. Kornegay***, the lawful impoundment at a parking lot associated with the building within which the driver was arrested because the defendant's identity was unknown, police had "reason to believe he would not be returning anytime soon," and threat of theft and vandalism.[1019]
- In ***Biggers v. State,*** the police were justified in impounding a car from a church parking lot where the arrest occurred because of expired registration plate and warning of weapon in car that posed danger to public. [1020]
- In the 2014 case of ***Commonwealth v. Crowley-Chester***, the Appeals Court approved the impoundment and subsequent inventory of a vehicle located in a private parking lot after the police arrested the operator for drug possession. The passenger was unlicensed and could not take charge of the vehicle. A folding knife was located within the vehicle. The location had a history of vandalism, break-ins and similar crimes. The court found that the impoundment was justified for both safety concerns (dangerous items that may be located within the vehicle) and for concerns of theft and vandalism due to the nature of the area.

Rental Car

In the 2005 case of ***Commonwealth v. Henley***, the Appeals Court ruled that the police were not constitutionally required to telephone either the car rental company or the individual who rented a car stopped in a lawful traffic stop prior to impounding the car for lack of any individual authorized to drive it, where the rental agreement specifically required written permission from the car rental company prior to the car being driven by anyone other than the individual who rented it.[1021]

[1017] Commonwealth v. Eddington, 76 Mass.App.Ct. 172 (2010)
[1018] See *United States v. Martin,*982 F.2d 1236, 1240 (8th Cir.1993).
[1019] *United States v. Kornegay,* 885 F.2d 713, 716 (10th Cir.1989).
[1020] *Biggers v. State,*162 Ga.App. 163, 164, 290 S.E.2d 159 (1982).
[1021] *Commonwealth v. Henley,*63 Mass.App.Ct. 1, 822 N.E.2d 313 (2005).

Operating Under The Influence Of Alcohol Arrest And Impoundment

With the passing of the 2007 so-called Melanie's Law, if a person refuses to take a (chemical) test under after an arrest for operating under the influence of alcohol, the police officer shall:

- Impound the vehicle being driven by the operator and arrange for the vehicle to be impounded for a period of 12 hours after the operator's **refusal**, with the costs for the towing, storage and maintenance of the vehicle to be borne by the operator.[1022]

INVENTORY SEARCH PROCEDURES

Police officers in the United States impound a tremendous number of motor vehicles every year. Many of these vehicles contain luggage, boxes, and other receptacles for storing personal items. Police have a duty to protect personal property in impounded vehicles. To care for this property, most police departments have developed a routine practice of inventorying and securing the contents of impounded automobiles.

Justification to conduct Inventory

The Supreme Court exempts inventory searches from the warrant requirement because these searches perform a caretaking function that is divorced from any investigatory motive. Although police may conduct inventory searches without a warrant, the inventory search still must be reasonable under the Fourth amendment.

The U.S. Supreme Court, in *South Dakato v. Opperman*, recognized three factors which justify warrantless inventory searches of motor vehicles:

1. Protect the law enforcement officer and the agency (and the tow company[1023]) from false claims of lost/stolen property from the vehicle that was towed;
2. Protect the person who owns the vehicle from having their property lost or stolen; and,
3. Protect law enforcement (and the public[1024]) from danger from items in the vehicle.

Written procedures are required

Inventory searches of automobiles *must* be conducted pursuant to **standard police procedures,** which must be in writing.[1025] The purpose for requiring written procedures by which inventory searches are to be conducted is to limit an officer's discretion to ''search at will, and so lessen the possibility that police will use inventory procedures as investigative searches.''[1026]

- In ***Commonwealth v. Ford***, where there was no established departmental procedure which was followed regularly, the Supreme Judicial Court has held that the opening of an automobile trunk by the Watertown Police Officer was unreasonable *per se* under article 14 of the Massachusetts Declaration of Rights.[1027] In that case, an officer opened the trunk to secure some music tapes found in the passenger compartment of an unregistered vehicle which was about to be towed. In the trunk, the officer observed a rifle. The rifle was suppressed from evidence because the court ruled that opening the trunk was an unreasonable search. The fact that the officer was not looking for anything when he opened the trunk was irrelevant. The court suggested that the search might have been lawful if carried out pursuant to an establish department policy which required a "storage search" of every vehicle which is towed. [1028]

The constitutional requirements of a written police policy to justify entry into a vehicle after impoundment, and the measurement of the scope of the ensuing search against such policy, apply not only to a police search to gather physical objects and things from within the vehicle, but also apply to a police search to gather documents, papers, or records from within a vehicle.[1029]

[1022] M.G.L. Ch. 90 § 24 (2007)
[1023] *Commonwealth v. Garcia*, 409 Mass. 675 (1991).
[1024] *Commonwealth v. Garcia*, 409 Mass. 675 (1991).
[1025] *Commonwealthv. Bishop*, 402 Mass. 449, 451, 523 N.E.2d 779 (1988).'' See *Colorado v. Bertine*, 479 U.S. 367, 376, 107 S.Ct. 738, 93 L.Ed.2d 739 (1987) (Blackmun, J., concurring); *Commonwealth v. Rostad*, 410 Mass. 618, 622, 574 N.E.2d 381 (1991).
[1026] *Commonwealthv.Garcia*, 409 Mass. at 681, 569 N.E.2d 385
[1027] *Commonwealth v. Ford*, 394 Mass. 421, 476 N.E.2d 560 (1985).
[1028] *Commonwealth v. Ford*, 394 Mass. 421, 476 N.E.2d 560 (1985).
[1029] *Commonwealth v. Silva*, 61 Mass.App.Ct. 28, 807 N.E.2d 170 (2004).

Container specific policy required

If police agencies want their officers to inventory the contents of closed containers the written policy must specify the parameters to eliminate, or at least reduce, officer discretion.

- In the 2004 Appeals Court case of ***Commonwealth v. Muckle***, the police department's written inventory policy delineated when an officer could impound a vehicle. However, the Court ruled that the police officers lacked authority to open a bag from a donut shop and a nylon laundry bag found in the defendant's vehicle during the inventory search of vehicle following the defendant's arrest for a license violation and the impoundment of his vehicle, as the police department's inventory procedure did not authorize the opening of closed but unlocked containers at all.[1030]
- Inventory policies which permit the inspection of closed containers includes the inspection of closed containers within closed containers. Specific wording, that closed containers within closed containers can be inspected, is not required.[1031]

Can a locked trunk be inventoried?

Inventory searches, as standard police practice, have been upheld even though they involved opening a locked trunk.[1032]

- In ***Cady v. Dombrowski***, the police knew that the car that had been impounded belonged to a police officer who was required to carry his service revolver which had not been found on his person. In light of that fact, the Court stressed the need for an inventory search of the car for public safety reasons to prevent an intruder from vandalizing the car and removing the revolver was proper. The car had been taken by police to a private garage that had no guard.

Locked Containers Cannot be Forced Open

As previously mentioned, one of the reasons the Courts permit law enforcement personnel to conduct inventory "searches" is to safeguard property. If thc property that is being safeguarded needs to be damages (i.e. broken open) it defeats one of the primary intents of the inventory search. Therefore, officers cannot force or break open containers for the purpose of inventorying the contents.[1033]

Although locked containers clearly cannot be forced or broken open, it appears that locked containers with a key readily accessible can be opened during an inventory search to inventory the contents of the container providing the intent is to safeguard and not circumvent warrant requirements.

- I***n Commonwealth v. Vanya V., a juvenile***, Officer Gallo of the Marblehead Police Department was in the process of transporting the defendant (a juvenile) to his home after witnessing the defendant trespassing (the defendant was not under arrest). Officer Gallo pat frisked the defendant before allowing the defendant into his cruiser. During the pat frisk the defendant struck Officer Gallo. The defendant was arrested and transported to the station. The defendant was carrying a locked bank bag on his person. The Marblehead police eventually cut open the canvas bank bag in order to inventory the contents of the bag. During the inventory a digital scale, plastic baggies, marijuana and cash were discovered. The defendant was charged with distribution of drugs among other charges. The Court ruled that "permitting an officer to destroy or break into a locked container runs counter to the very purpose of the inventory exception."[1034]

Attorney Hanrahan's Note: It is recommended that if police departments wish to have their officers inventory the contents of the trunk and locked containers it be specifically delineated in the department's inventory policy to eliminate discretion.

- In ***Commonwealth v. Difalco***, the police arrested the defendant on a warrant while he was seated in his vehicle. The officer then called for a tow truck and began to inventory the contents of the vehicle. The officer used the defendant's car keys to open the trunk. Inside the trunk was a small safe. Using the defendant's key ring the officer opened the safe. Inside was a handgun with defaced serial numbers. Department policy indicated that locked trunks and glove compartments should be unlocked and inventoried, however, the policy stated that locked containers "should be inventoried as a single unit" and "a search warrant should be obtained before the search of a locked container." The policy did not permit the opening of the locked container and thus the evidence was suppressed.[1035]

[1030] *Commonwealth v. Muckle*, 61 Mass.App.Ct. 678, 814 N.E.2d 7 (2004).
[1031] *Commonwealth v. Allen*, Mass.App.Ct. (2009).
[1032] *Cady v. Dombrowski*, 413 U.S. 433, 93 S.Ct. 2523 (1973).
[1033] *Commonwealth v. Vanya V.a juvenile*, MA App. Ct. (2009)
[1034] *Commonwealth v. Vanya V.a juvenile*, MA App. Ct. (2009)
[1035] *Commonwealth v. Difalco*, Mass.App.Ct. (2008).

Timing of search must be consistent with written policy

The Federal 1st Circuit Court has added the requirement that, in addition to an inventory policy detailing how such searches are to be performed, a department must also have a non-discretionary policy which specifies exactly *when* a car is to be impounded.[1036]

Location of search must be consistent with written policy

An inventory search of an impounded vehicle may be conducted on scene, at the station or other secure location so long as it is done pursuant to a written policy and procedure.[1037]

- In ***Commonwealth v. Tisserand,*** the police conducted an inventory search at the scene where the car was stopped.[1038] This was done pursuant to a department policy which required the police to make an inventory search of the vehicle before permitting it to be towed in order to secure any items of value that might be in the vehicle. (The on-the-scene inventory search revealed a revolver, a ski mask, checks and currency stolen in a recent armed robbery.)[1039]

Search cannot be for investigatory purposes

As stated in ***Commonwealth v. Alvarado***[1040]: ''Inventory searches are intended to be non investigatory and are for the purpose of protecting property which may be within the vehicle. A warrantless inventory search of a lawfully impounded vehicle meets constitutional requirements if carried out in accordance with standard procedures and if there is no suggestion that the procedure was a pretext concealing an investigatory motive.

The distinction between an inventory search and an investigatory search is found in the objective of each. The objective of an investigatory search is to gather evidence, whereas an inventory search is conducted for the purposes of ''safeguarding the car or its contents, protecting the police against unfounded charges of misappropriation, protecting the public against the possibility that the car might contain weapons or other dangerous instrumentalities that might fall into the hands of vandals, or a combination of such reasons.''[1041]

However, an officer's subjective beliefs would not render the inventory search impermissible.[1042] But, the police may not conduct an inventory search if they are acting in bad faith or if the search is done solely for investigative purposes.[1043]

- In ***Commonwealth v. Garcia,*** ''the fact that the searching officer may have harbored a suspicion that evidence of criminal activity might be uncovered as a result of the search should not vitiate his obligation to conduct the inventory''.

Because the intent of an inventory is for non-investigative purposes the use of a canine during an inventory would not be lawful.[1044]

[1036] *U.S. v. Donnelly*, 885 F.Supp. 300 (D. Mass. 1995).
[1037] See *Commonwealth v. Ford*, 394 Mass. 421, 476 N.E.2d 560 (1985); *Commonwealth v. Bishop*, 402 Mass. 449, 523 N.E.2d 779 (1988); *Commonwealth v. Solo*, 26 Mass. App. Ct. 766, 532 N.E.2d 1219 (1989).
[1038] *Commonwealth v. Tisserand*, 5 Mass. App. Ct. 383, 363 N.E.2d 530 (1977).
[1039] *See also, Commonwealth v. Caceres*, 413 Mass. 749, 604 N.E.2d 677 (1992).
[1040] *Commonwealth v. Alvarado*, 420 Mass. 542, 553, 651 N.E.2d 824 (1995).
[1041] *Commonwealthv. Muckle*, 61 Mass.App.Ct. 678, 682–683, 814 N.E.2d 7 (2004).See *Commonwealthv. Benoit*, 382 Mass. 210, 219, 415 N.E.2d 818 (1981), S.C., 389 Mass. 411, 451 N.E.2d 101 (1983).
[1042] See *Commonwealthv. Garcia*, 409 Mass. at 679, 569 N.E.2d 385, quoting from *Commonwealthv. Matchett*, 386 Mass. 492, 510, 436 N.E.2d 400 (1982).
[1043] *U.S. v. Donnelly*, 885 F.Supp. 3000 (D. Mass. 1995).
[1044] *Commonwealth v. Alvarado*, 420 Mass. 542, 553, 651 N.E.2d 824 (1995).

IDENTIFICATION PROCEDURES

OVERVIEW

In ***U.S. v. Wade*,**[1045] the U.S. Supreme Court discussed at length the dangers inherent in eyewitness identification and concluded, "The influence of improper suggestion upon identifying witnesses probably accounts for more miscarriages of justice than any other single factor — perhaps for more errors than all other factors combined." The police must, therefore, be careful to ensure that their eyewitness identification procedures are not conducted in an unnecessarily or impermissibly suggestive manner and that they do not contribute to mistaken identification.[1046]

In 2013, the SJC spearheaded a study on Eyewitness Identification. In that study the SJC recommended that the police comply with certain protocols. The report also suggests that failure to follow these protocols may result in the inadmissibility of the eyewitness identification.

General Best Practices (recommend by the 2013 SJC Study)

1. Every law enforcement agency should have a **written policy** on eyewitness identification.
2. Upon response to the scene of a crime, the police should make an effort to **prevent eyewitnesses from comparing their recollections** of the offender or the incident. The police often accomplish this by promptly separating the witnesses and interviewing each out of the earshot of the others. Witnesses should not participate in identification procedures together. For example, witnesses should not be transported together to view a suspect during a show up or allowed to view a suspect within earshot of each other.
3. Police officers should use caution when they interview eyewitnesses. Specifically, whenever possible, they should **avoid the use of leading questions**.
4. **Prior to asking an eyewitness to identify a suspect**, police officers should **obtain a detailed description** of the offender.
5. Police officers should **instruct eyewitnesses using standardized cards or forms** to insure that complete and accurate instructions are given. See model forms at the end of this section.
6. Police officers should **file a full report on every identification attempt**, whether an identification is made or not. Reports should include, at a minimum, the place where the procedure was conducted, who was present, the instructions given to the witness, any comments made to the witness before or after the identification, all comments made by the witness during or following the procedure, including any statement of certainty or confidence in any identification, and, in the case of a photo array, any steps taken to preserve the array. A copy of the array and the forms used and completed during the identification process should be included with the police report.

SHOW UPS

Where the police have received a sufficient description from a victim or a witness to a crime, they may confront a suspect with the eyewitness during or shortly after the criminal episode so that the eyewitness may identify the suspect as the perpetrator or as an innocent person.[1047]

The key factor is that the identification procedures must not be unnecessarily suggestive.

Temporary Detention

As part of a threshold inquiry under M.G.L. c.41, § 98, an officer may detain a person for a short amount of time to permit an eyewitness to be taken to the scene to view that person and possibly make an identification.[1048] Likewise, the police may take the suspect back to the crime scene to see if anyone can identify him or her.[1049]

- In ***Commonwealth v. Thompson***, it was permissible to bring the victims of a purse snatching in a cruiser to see if they could identify two persons the police had stopped (threshold inquiry) and observed two handbags and a wallet in the suspect's vehicle.[1050]

[1045] *U.S. v. Wade*, 388 U.S. 218, 87 S.Ct. 1926 (1967).
[1046] *Commonwealth v. Hicks*, 17 Mass. App. Ct. 574, 460 N. E. 2d 1053 (1984); see also, *Commonwealth v. Hill*, 64 Mass. App. Ct. 131, 831 N. E. 2d 923 (2005).
[1047] *Commonwealth v. Bumpus*, 354 Mass. 494, 238 N.E.2d 343, *cert. den.*393 U.S. 1034, 89 S.Ct. 649 (1968).
[1048] *Commonwealth v. Tosi*, 14 Mass. App. Ct. 901, 442 N.E.2d 419 (1982); *see, generally, Commonwealth v. Salerno*, 356 Mass. 642, 255 N.E.2d 318 (1970).
[1049] *Commonwealth v. Crowley*, 29 Mass. App. Ct. 1, 556 N.E.2d 1043 (1990).
[1050] *Commonwealth v. Thompson*, 427 Mass. 729, 696 N.E. 2d 105 (1998).

One-on-One Confrontations

Although one-on-one pretrial identifications may be disfavored generally,[1051] there is no due process violation unless the defendant meets his or her burden to show by a preponderance of the evidence that the show-up is **unnecessarily suggestive**.[1052]If the identification passes muster under this test, then it is for the jury to decide what weight to give to the identification.

The SJC has stated "we have repeatedly held that, although inherently suggestive, one-on-one confrontations in the immediate aftermath of a crime need not be suppressed.[1053] The advantages of such an immediate identification override the suggestiveness of the setting such that the procedure constitutes sound police practice. "Such confrontations permit the witnesses to view the suspect while recollection is fresh and before other images crowd in to distort the original picture. ..."[1054]

In reviewing whether an identification was "unnecessarily suggestive," the **key question** is whether police had "good reason" to follow such a procedure.

The SJC has listed the following factors to consider to justify one-on-one confrontations:

1. The nature of the crime involved and corresponding concerns for public safety;
2. The need for efficient police investigation in the immediate aftermath of a crime; and
3. The usefulness of prompt confirmation of the accuracy of investigatory information, which, if in error, will release the police quickly to follow another track.[1055]

In ***Commonwealth v. Coy***, the Court ruled that even where the victim is not near death or critically injured, a one-on-one confrontation between the victim and a suspect is permissible where the circumstances make it important for the suspect to be identified as the perpetrator (and arrested) or as an innocent person (and released) so that police can determine whether to continue their investigation or not.[1056]

Avoiding Suggestiveness

Police officers must make an effort to avoid making the identification overly suggestive. Comments never should be made to the witness suggesting the suspect's guilt. Comments regarding any admissions or confessions by the suspect, the suspect's criminal history, the identification of other suspects by other witnesses and so on could render the identification invalid.

Officers should use caution when restraining a suspect during a field interrogation. The use of handcuffs and the presence of many officers may influence the perception of the identifying witness since it may give the impression that the police have already determined that the suspect is the assailant. However, the use of handcuffs and other displays of detention will not automatically make the identification unnecessarily suggestive and the officers should not jeopardize their safety.

Attorney Hanrahan's Note: It is a good practice to lower the police radio to avoid any accidental suggestive exposure regarding the suspect (e.g. the suspect's BOP). Additionally, many agencies utilize a show-up identification checklist to help minimize the possibility of making the identification unnecessarily suggestive. See sample later in this section.

Case examples

- In ***Commonwealth v. Drane***, a show-up identification made by a robbery victim at the scene of the defendant's arrest was not impermissibly suggestive, despite the fact that the police illuminated the defendant's face with a flashlight.[1057] There the identification occurred promptly in the aftermath of the report of the crime and the defendant was apprehended shortly thereafter based on a strikingly similar description given by two robbery victims.
- In ***Commonwealth v. Rogers***, three men broke into an apartment on Marlborough Street in Boston and raped a sixty-seven year old woman while her son-in-law was held in his bedroom, face down on a pillow, with a knife to his neck. The victim's fifteen month old daughter was asleep in her bed. The men demanded money

[1051]See, e.g., *Commonwealth v. Moffett,* 383 Mass. 201, 213, 418 N.E.2d 585 (1981)
[1052]See *Commonwealth v. Leonardi,* 413 Mass. 757, 760-761, 604 N.E.2d 23 (1992); *Commonwealth v. Levasseur,* 32 Mass.App.Ct. 629, 635, 592 N.E.2d 1350 (1992), cert. denied, 506 U.S. 1053, 113 S.Ct. 978, 122 L.Ed.2d 132 (1993)
[1053]*Commonwealth v. Harris, 395 Mass. 296, 299 (1985).Commonwealth v. Barnett, 371 Mass. 87, 92 (1976).*
[1054]*Commonwealth* v. *Coy*, 10 Mass. App. Ct. 367, 371 (1980).

[1055]Commonwealth v. Austin, 421 Mass. 357 , 361 (1995)
[1056]*Commonwealth v. Coy*, 10 Mass. App. Ct. 367, 407 N.E.2d 1310.(1980); *Commonwealth v. Santos*, 402 Mass. 775, 525 N.E.2d 388 (1988).
[1057]*Commonwealth v. Drane*, 47 Mass. App. Ct. 913, 712 N.E. 2d 1162 (1999).

and jewelry and then fled. The police located three suspects using the victim's ATM card a short distance away. The suspects were brought back to Marlborough Street in handcuffs and shown to the victim. The court held that even if the police presented the suspects wearing handcuffs (the victim testified that she did not remember seeing any), we would not deem that procedure, in light of the totality of the circumstances, so unnecessarily suggestive as to require suppression of the identification.[1058]

Police not necessarily required to pursue other methods first

In the 2006 SJC case of ***Commonwealth v. Martin***, the defendant faulted the police for not asking him to agree to participate in a lineup or consent to be photographed after he was identified during a one-on-one show-up.[1059] The Court pointed out that failure of the police to pursue alternate identification procedures does not render an identification unduly suggestive. The question is whether the police acted permissibly. The answer is not governed by the availability of another approach.

Defendant has the burden

It is the defendant's burden to prove by a preponderance of the evidence that the show-up was "so unnecessarily suggestive and conducive to irreparable mistaken identification as to deny [him] due process of law."[1060]

SHOW UP BEST PRACTICES (recommend by the 2013 SJC Study)

1. **Showups are disfavored**. However, when they are conducted they **should not be conducted more than <u>two hours</u> after the witness's observation** of the suspect.
2. When transporting a witness to a showup, officers should **attempt to prevent the witness from hearing radio transmissions or other officer-to- officer conversations** related to the suspect or their investigation.
3. When conducting a showup, the police should **minimize suggestiveness**. Showups should not be conducted if the suspect is seated in the rear of a police cruiser, in a cell, or in any other enclosure associated with custody. If the suspect is handcuffed, he should be situated so that the handcuffs are not visible to the witness.
4. During a showup, the police should not tell the witness where the suspect was found or whether he did or said anything suspicious. Also, the police should not allow the witness to learn whether the suspect was found with items associated with the crime, such as the car used or a stolen purse. Once a witness has positively identified the suspect at a showup, the police should not conduct additional showups with the same suspect.
5. The **use of composites and sketches and the showing of mug files are disfavored**.
6. Officers should **avoid multiple identification procedures** featuring any one suspect with the same witness.

IDENTIFICATION BY PHOTOGRAPH AND LINE-UPS

Like the requirements for one-on-one identifications, line-ups and photo arrays must be constructed in such a way so that they are not unnecessarily suggestive.

What The Courts Look To In Order To Determine The Validity Of A Photo Identification

The SJC stated "In order to suppress a photographic identification, the defendant must show by a preponderance of the evidence that, in light of the totality of the circumstances, the procedures employed were so unnecessarily suggestive and conducive to irreparable misidentification as to deny the defendant due process of law."[1061]

- In the 1995 SJC case of ***Commonwealth v. Miles***,[1062] the defendant argued that an array of **nine photographs** was impermissibly suggestive simply because the other eight photographs depicted people who might arguably be a number of years older than the defendant. The Court found that the possible differences in age were inconsequential and did not rise to the level of impermissive suggestiveness.
- In ***Simmons v. U.S.***,[1063] Supreme Court fashioned a **two-pronged test** for the exclusion of identification based upon impermissibility suggestive photo arrays:

  1. Whether the identification procedure was impermissibly suggestive; (if not, the inquiry ends) if so,

[1058] *Commonwealth v. Rogers*, 38 Mass.App.Ct. 395 (1995).
[1059] *Commonwealth v. Martin*, 447 Mass. 274, 850 N.E. 2d 555 (2006).
[1060] *Commonwealth v. Odware*, 429 Mass. 231, 235, 707 N.E.2d 347 (1999), quoting *Commonwealth v. Otsuki*, 411 Mass. 218, 232, 581 N.E.2d 999 (1991).
[1061] *See also, Commonwealth v. Jackson*, 419 Mass. 716, 647 N.E.2d 1401 (1995); *Commonwealth v. Wallace*, 417 Mass. 126, 129, 627 N.E.2d 935 (1994); *Commonwealth v. Andrews*, 427 Mass. 434, 694 N.E. 2d 329 (1998).
[1062] *Commonwealth v. Miles* , 420 Mass. 67, 648 N.E. 2d 719 (1995).
[1063] *Simmons v. U.S.*, 390 U.S. 377, 88 S.Ct. 967, 19 L.Ed.2d 1247 (1968).

2. The court measures the reliability of the identification based on the *totality of the circumstances* according to a five-point index delineated in ***Neil v. Biggers***[1064] which include the following:
   - Witness's opportunity to view the suspect,
   - Degree of attention,
   - Accuracy of prior description,
   - Level of certainty, and
   - Time lapse between crime and identification.

- In ***Commonwealth v. Ross***, an array of photographs was fair and not unduly suggestive even though one witness said she made the identification due to the defendant's hair alone (seeing only a silhouette of a man in her room), where the room was dark and the other photos in the array did not have the same hairstyle.[1065] Negating the impact of these assertions were the photos themselves and the witness's earlier reports that the man was very thin with glasses and straight shaggy hair including bangs.[1066]

PHOTO ARRAY AND LINEUPS BEST PRACTICES (recommend by the 2013 SJC Study)

1. When assembling a photo array, officers should ensure they are using a current and accurate photograph of the suspect. In the case of arrays and lineups, they should select fillers based on their similarity to the witness's description of the offender, not to the appearance of the suspect. However, officers must also ensure that nothing about the suspect or his photo makes him stand out.
2. Photographic arrays and lineups must contain ***at least*** **five fillers** and only one suspect. The police must not repeat fillers with the same witness from one array or lineup to the next. **Note: the committee *recommends* 7 fillers.**
3. ***Blind administration:*** When showing a photo array or conducting a lineup, the police must use a technique that will ensure that no investigator present will know when the witness is viewing the suspect. The preference is that the police have an officer who does not know who the suspect is administer the array or lineup. With photo arrays, they may use a blinded technique such as the folder shuffle as an alternative.
4. Police officers **must** conduct photographic arrays and lineups by displaying the suspect and fillers **sequentially**.
5. Witnesses who ask to see a photo or lineup participant a second time should be shown the entire array or lineup, but no more than for a second time.
6. When an eyewitness identifies a photograph or person, the officer must immediately ask the witness how certain or confident he is of the identification.
7. When an officer is showing a photographic array or lineup to a subsequent witness in the same investigation, officers should shuffle the order so as to ensure that there could be no collusion between the two witnesses.
8. When submitting reports about photo arrays, officers should include copies of any instruction forms and a copy of the array.
9. Whenever practicable, the police **should videotape or audiotape** a photo array or lineup.

Documenting Photo Arrays

It is important to properly document the procedure used during a photo array in the event that the array is later challenged in court.

However, the SJC has stated "we recognize the importance of accurately documenting the identification procedure and the actual identification (or failure to identify), but also recognize that recording such a procedure is often not practicable and **do not require such a recording as a prerequisite to admissibility**."[1067] However, it is better practice to properly document the process whenever possible.

IDENTIFICATION PROCEDURES

[1064] *Neil v. Biggers*, 409 U.S. 188, 93 S.Ct. 375, 34 L.Ed.2d 401 (1972) (witness's opportunity to view the suspect, degree of attention, accuracy of prior description, level of certainty, and time lapse between crime and identification.) However, see *U.S. v. Boutho* F.2d 1506 (1st Cir. 1989) which refers to a two-part test that is applied in the First Circuit after determining that the identification was impermissibly suggestive.
[1065] *Commonwealth v. Ross*, 426 Mass. 555, 689 N.E. 2d 816 (1998).
[1066] *Commonwealth v. Ross*, 426 Mass. 555, 689 N.E. 2d 816 (1998).
[1067] *Commonwealth v. Silva-Santiago*, SJC (May 2009).

Single photos

Although showing a single photograph of the suspect, by itself, is strongly disfavored by the courts, there may be an emergency which justifies that practice, as when the victim is seriously wounded and near death and the perpetrator of the crime is still at large.[1068] Courts have also upheld single photograph identifications when they are presented shortly after the incident. Showing a single photograph of the suspect may also be condoned where numerous photographs have already been shown to the witness and showing "one more" photograph is part of an on-going process.[1069]

Whether a single photograph identification will be admitted is determined by examining the totality of the circumstances.[1070]

- A single photo shown to an undercover officer immediately following a drug transaction was not considered unduly suggestive. In ***Commonwealth v. Martinez***[1071] such a procedure was considered a necessary police investigatory function in order to identify the suspect while the image was still fresh in the officer's mind and to avoid arresting and charging the wrong person.
- In the 1995 case of ***Commonwealth v. Austin***, an identification stemming from a videotape containing only one individual is analogous to a one-on-one identification.

Unique characteristics

Unique characteristics may contribute to the determination that the photo array was unnecessarily suggestive. However, the presence of unique characteristics will not automatically deem the photo array invalid "if it is clear that the witness did not select the photograph on that basis." [1072]

- In ***Commonwealth v. Kent K.***, an array of photos in which a juvenile accused of murder was identified by eyewitnesses was not unduly suggestive when there were not a lot of youngsters with freckles similar to the juvenile.[1073] In that case, the array was shown to the eyewitnesses less than two hours after the shooting, and neither eyewitness indicated that the freckles, rather than the light skin, were relied upon in making the identification.
- In ***Commonwealth v. Melvin***, notwithstanding the fact that the defendant was the **only person in photographic array wearing a sling** (the suspect had fled from this B&E incident by leaping from a balcony), the identification procedure wherein victim was shown an array of the defendant and five other men of similar appearance was not impermissibly suggestive where victim identified defendant based solely on his observations at time of incident, and police officer did not coach victim in any way or suggest that photograph of defendant was in array.[1074]
- In ***Commonwealth v. Mobley***, where the police, on the day following an armed robbery, showed a witness, who had viewed the robber under bright lights for three to six minutes during the commission of the crime, a series of photographs, one of which depicted the defendant **wearing a hat similar to a hat worn by the robber while the others depicted people without hats**, the photographic identification procedures were **not so impermissibly suggestive** as to give rise to a very substantial likelihood of irreparable misidentification.[1075]
- In ***Commonwealth v. Thornley***, the defendant was picked out of a photo array and was the **only person in the array wearing glasses**. The glasses were "a major issue" in the case. SJC ruled that the Commonwealth was unable to show that the lineup and courtroom identification were based on a source independent of the suggestive photographic identification, it was error to admit that testimony.[1076]
- In ***Commonwealth v. Napolitano***, the fact that only three of the 44 photographs depicted heavy men with "scraggly" beards, a constant description of the assailant, did not render the photographic array impermissibly suggestive as several photographs closely resembled that of the defendant and the police officers in no way suggested to the witnesses which photograph was of the person under investigation.[1077]

[1068] *Commonwealth v. Nolin*, 373 Mass. 45, 364 N.E.2d 1224 (1977).
[1069] *Commonwealth v. Venios*, 378 Mass. 24, 389 N.E.2d 395 (1979).
[1070] *Commonwealth v. Day*, 42 Mass. App. Ct. 242, 676 N.E.2d 467 (1997).
[1071] *Commonwealth v. Martinez*, 67 Mass. App. Ct. 788, 857 N.E.2d 1096 (2006.
[1072] *Commonwealth v. Melvin*, 399 Mass. 201(1987).
[1073] *Commonwealth v. Kent K.*, 427 Mass. 754, 696 N.E. 2d 511 (1998)
[1074] *Commonwealth v. Melvin*, 399 Mass. 201, 503 N.E.2d 649 (1987)
[1075] *Commonwealth v. Mobley*, 369 Mass. 892 (1976).
[1076] *Commonwealth v. Thornley*, 400 Mass. 355 (1987).
[1077] *Commonwealth .v Napolitano*, 378 Mass. 599, 393 N.E.2d 338 (1979)

- In ***Commonwealth v. Hicks***, the defendant's picture, in a five photo array, was the **only one showing dark hair and dark complexion** that the witnesses had described to the police. The **judge held** that when the array was shown to the identifying witness, **"there was no impermissible indication or hint as to which one was the defendant."**[1078]
- In ***Commonwealth v. Jones***, the **Court permitted** the police to use photos depicting suspects with **both light and dark complexions** where the victim or witnesses gave no clear indication that the suspects were either light or dark in complexion.[1079]

The court will look at **the totality of circumstances,** thus if some photographs are deemed to be too dissimilar to the suspect it may be a safer course to include more rather than fewer photos. Some courts have noted that it is advisable to display at least ten photographs of persons fitting the same general description as the suspect.[1080]

Multiple arrays

The use of multiple arrays, even those which contain the same suspect in more than one array, will not automatically make the process unnecessarily suggestive. However, repeated exposure of a defendant by photograph may tend to overemphasize the defendant and create a danger of undue suggestiveness.[1081] The array must be composed in such a manner as not to dramatize the defendant's picture or to single out his picture from others, e.g., the defendant was the only one to wear glasses.[1082]

- In ***Commonwealth v. Wallace***, the police displayed an array of nine black and white photographs and a second array of color photographs to three witnesses. The defendant was depicted in each array. Each of the witnesses viewed the photos separately and each of the witnesses viewed only one array at a time. The defendant's photo was selected as being that of the suspect. The Court stated that where police duplicate the defendant's photo in one or more photographic arrays, it is not sufficient by itself to compel the suppression of a resulting identification.[1083]

It is also permissible to use filler photographs in more than one array.

- In ***Commonwealth v. Manning,*** a photographic identification procedure in which a victim was shown a photographic array consisting of nine photographs, with the defendant's photograph being the only one which had not been presented to the victim in the previous photographic array, was not unduly suggestive, where the victim testified that he did not realize that eight of the photographs were from the first array he had viewed.[1084]

Use of mug shots

A number of cases have ruled that any information or markings on a photograph, especially "mug shot" markings, which indicate that the person in the photograph has a criminal record, **must** be removed or completely hidden before the witness views the photograph.[1085] Front and side view photographs of the same person should be severed and shown separately.[1086]

In order to introduce a defendant's mug shot, and subsequent witness identification, in evidence, three criteria are required: (1) the prosecution must show some need to introduce the mug shot; (2) the mug shots, to the extent possible, should not indicate a prior record; and (3) the mug shots should not call attention to their origins and implications.[1087]

- In ***Commonwealth v. Hoilett***, a defendant's photograph picked out by a witness from a group of police photographs did not unfairly prejudice the defendant and the photograph was thus admissible at a murder trial where the judge instructed the jury that they should not draw any inference from the fact that the police

---

[1078] *Commonwealth v. Hicks*, 377 Mass. 1 (1979).
[1079] *Commonwealth v. Jones*, 375 Mass. 349 (1978).
[1080] *Commonwealth v. Caldwell*, 36 Mass. App. Ct. 570, 634 N.E.2d 124 (1994); *Commonwealth v. Otsuki*, 411 Mass. 218, 581 N.E.2d 999 (1991); *Commonwealth v. Lynes*, 6 Mass.App. 834, 372 N.E.2d 273 (1979).*See, Commonwealth v. Downey*, 407 Mass. 472, 553 N.E.2d 1303 (1990).
[1081] *U.S. v.Alexander*, 868 F.2d 492 (1st Cir. 1989), *cert. den.*493 U.S. 979, 110 S.Ct. 507 (1989); *Commonwealth v. Bowie*, 25 Mass. App. Ct. 70, 514 N.E.2d 1345 (1987).*U.S. v.Alexander*, 868 F.2d 492 (1st Cir. 1989), *cert. den.*493 U.S. 979, 110 S.Ct. 507 (1989); *Commonwealth v. Bowie*, 25 Mass. App. Ct. 70, 514 N.E.2d 1345 (1987).
[1082] *Commonwealth v. Thornley*, 406 Mass. 96, 546 N.E.2d 35E (1989); *Commonwealth v. Scott*, 408 Mass. 811, 564 N.E.2d 370 (1990).
[1083] *Commonwealth v. Wallace*, 417 Mass. 125 (1994).
[1084] *Commonwealth v. Manning*, 44 Mass. App. Ct. 695, 693 N.E. 2d 704 (1998).
[1085] *Commonwealth v. Cohen*, 412 Mass. 375, 589 N.E.2d 289 (1992); *Commonwealth v. Smith*, 29 Mass. App. Ct. 449, 561 N.E.2d 520 (1990); *U.S. v. Fosher*, 568 F.2d 207 (1st Cir. 1978) and *Commonwealth v. Washburn*, 5 Mass. App. Ct. 195, 360 N.E.2d 908 (1977).*Commonwealth v. Cohen*, 412 Mass. 375, 589 N.E.2d 289 (1992); *Commonwealth v. Smith*, 29 Mass. App. Ct. 449, 561 N.E.2d 520 (1990); *U.S. v. Fosher*, 568 F.2d 207 (1st Cir. 1978) and *Commonwealth v. Washburn*, 5 Mass. App. Ct. 195, 360 N.E.2d 908 (1977).
[1086] *Commonwealth v. Lockley*, 381 Mass. 156, 408 N.E.2d 834 (1980
[1087] *Commonwealth v. Smith*, 29 Mass. App. Ct. 449, 561 N.E. 2d 520 (1990);*Commonwealth v. McAfee*, 430 Mass. 483, 722 N.E. 2d 1 (2000).

possessed a photograph of the defendant, markings identifying the photograph as a mug shot were removed, and the witness who identified the defendant from the photograph knew the defendant.[1088]

Burden on defendant

In moving to suppress a photographic identification, the initial burden rests on the defendant to show, by a preponderance of the evidence, that, considering the totality of the circumstances attending the particular identification, the witness was subjected by the state to an identification so unnecessarily suggestive and conducive to irreparable misidentification as to deny the defendant due process.[1089]

Right to counsel

Unlike police line-ups, a suspect does not have a right to have counsel present when witnesses view a display of photographs which include a photograph of the suspect, even if the suspect has been formally charged.[1090]

LINEUPS

Although rarely used, line-ups may be utilized in order to have a victim identify a suspect. Because line-ups involve multiple people with similar appearances to the suspect they are generally less suggestive than one-on-one show ups.

Unnecessarily suggestive

As with one-on-one identifications line-ups should be constructed in a way that mitigates the suggestiveness of the procedure, meaning steps should be taken so that the other participants in the line-up are similar in appearance to the suspect.

- In ***Commonwealth v. Simmonds***, a lineup was deemed not to be unnecessarily suggestive where four of the seven participants had moustaches, even though the witnesses had described the assailant as clean shaven. In addition, several of the participants wore uniform police pants. The Court stated that "the participants' facial hair and wearing apparel are factors to be considered in determining the fairness of the confrontation, but they are not dispositive."[1091]

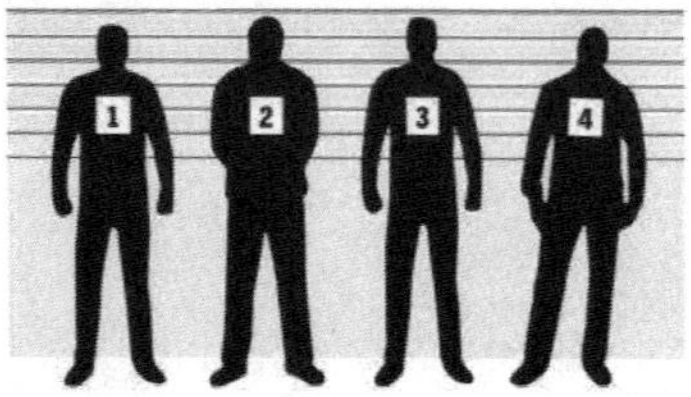

Manipulating the suspect's appearance

At a lineup, a suspect (and all other participants in the lineup) may be directed to wear certain clothing, to put on or take off certain clothing, to take certain positions, make specific gestures, speak words, walk or move in a given way.[1092]

Voice identification

The police may instruct those in the line-up to speak in order for the witness to attempt to identify the suspect's voice as well. However, do not ask those in the line-up recite the same exact words used during the crime. **See more on voice identifications later in this section.**

Presence of an attorney

The Sixth Amendment to the U.S. Constitution provides that suspects have a right to legal counsel. As to where in the legal process the right to an attorney becomes triggered, the U.S. Supreme Court as well as the Massachusetts SJC have

1088 *Commonwealth v. Hoilett*, 430 Mass. 369, 719 N.E. 2d 488 (1999).
1089 *Commonwealth v. Manning*, 44 Mass. App. Ct. 695, 693 N.E. 2d 704 (1998).
1090 *U.S. v. Ash*, 413 U.S. 300, 93 S.Ct. 2568 (1973); *Patterson v. Illinois*, 487 U.S. 285, 108 S.Ct. 2389 (1988).*See also, Commonwealth v. Carpinto*, 37 Mass. App. Ct. 51, 636 N.E.2d 1349 (1994) (also allows voice identifications by person who personally heard the call).
1091 *Commonwealth v. Simmonds*, 386 Mass. 234 (1982)
1092 *Commonwealth v. Odware,* 429 Mass. 231, 235, 707 N.E.2d 347 (1999), quoting *Commonwealth v. Otsuki,* 411 Mass. 218, 232, 581 N.E.2d 999 (1991).

held that a suspect does not have the right to have counsel present at a lineup **unless the suspect has been indicted, arraigned or formally charged and adversarial proceedings have been initiated**.[1093]

As with other constitutional rights, once a formally charged suspect has been advised of his or her constitutional right to have an attorney present at a lineup, he or she may waive that right and such a waiver will be valid if it is voluntarily, knowingly and intelligently made.[1094]

Although permitting the presence of an attorney prior to formally charging the defendant is not required the SJC has indicated it may be a better practice to permit an attorney to observe the procedure.

- In ***Commonwealth v. Clifford***,[1095] the defendant was arrested for murder and arson. He repeatedly requested the presence of an attorney. The police arranged for an attorney to respond. However, the attorney arrived after the line-up procedures had begun. The Supreme Judicial Court acknowledged that the "better practice would have been to give the attorney a . . . meaningful opportunity to become acquainted with the case and the prospective witnesses, even if this delayed the lineup a while."

VOICE IDENTIFICATIONS

The courts have cautioned that special care must be used in employing a voice identification procedure. It is recommended that you consult with the DA's office prior to conducting any voice identifications because of the legal complexity.

Some Important Points to Know:

- A voice identification may be conducted similar to a lineup, except that witnesses should not view the participants; rather, the witnesses should hear each participant speak, one by one.
- The words chosen for repetition should not be those heard by the victim at the scene. The suspect should not be asked at a visual show-up or a lineup to speak the words that were uttered by the perpetrator of the crime; rather, the police can engage the suspect in conversation unrelated to the crime.[1096]
- The procedure should be conducted as soon after the incident as possible. [1097]

Spontaneous Statements

If a suspect says something unprompted during a show-up, however, the witness's identification of the suspect's voice is generally admissible.

In ***Commonwealth v. Burgos***, a voice identification at show-up was admissible where the victim made visual identification and the defendant then said something without being prompted. [1098]

In ***Commonwealth v. Saunders***, a voice identification was admissible where the victim was unable to select the defendant at a show-up by his appearance, but the defendant spoke without being prompted.[1099]

IDENTIFYING PROPERTY

In addition to identifying suspects, show-ups are also possible to identify vehicles and other property used in the offense. But like show-ups the identification must not be unnecessarily suggestive.

- In ***Commonwealth v. Simmons***,**[1100]** the Supreme Judicial Court acknowledged that, in general, police may take a victim or witness to a place where the victim or witness can view a suspect's property for possible identification. In *Simmons*, a rape victim was taken to a place where she could view her alleged assailant's

[1093] *U.S. v. Wade*, 388 U.S. 218, 87 S.Ct. 1926 (1967); *Gilbert v. California*, 388 U.S. 263, 87 S.Ct. 1951 (1967).*See also,Messiah v. U.S.*, 377 U.S. 201, 84 S.Ct. 1199 (1964) and *Commonwealth v. Simmonds*, 386 Mass. 234, 434 N.E.2d 1270 (1982).
[1094] *Commonwealth v. Cooper*, 356 Mass. 74, 248 N.E.2d 253 (1969).
[1095] *Commonwealth v. Clifford*, 374 Mass. 293, 372 N.E.2d 1267 (1978).
[1096] *Commonwealth v. O'Loughlin*, 17 Mass. App. Ct. 972, 972 (1984)
[1097] *Commonwealth v. Miles*, 420 Mass. 67, 80 (1995); *Commonwealth v. Marini*, 375 Mass. 510, 516-19 (1978); *Commonwealth v. Gauthier*, 21 Mass. App. Ct. 585, 587-88 (1986).
[1098] *Commonwealth v. Burgos*, 36 Mass. App. Ct. 903, 904-05 (1994)

[1100] *Commonwealth v. Simmons*, 392 Mass. 45, 466 N.E.2d 85 (1981).

IDENTIFICATION PROCEDURES

motor vehicle. (However, the Court remanded the case for further proceedings to determine whether the defendant's reasonable expectation of privacy had been violated since his car was located on private property).

FIELD IDENTIFICATIONS

Distinguished from the highly suggestive one-on-one show-up in which attention is intentionally focused on the suspect, the field confrontation is conducted in an area occupied by enough people so as to prevent isolation of the suspect, but it must be void of suggestive comments or conduct that directs the witness's attention to the possible perpetrator.

In ***Commonwealth v. Eagles***, the SJC indicated that the police may take a witness to a place where he or she can informally observe a suspect who is not in police custody and who has not been formally charged, as long as the police officers do not make suggestive remarks or use words or actions which influence the witness' identification.[1101]

Case examples:

In the 2011 case of ***Com. v. Dyous,*** the police had the victim ride around the area to see if he recognized anyone. The Appeals Court upheld the identification by ruling it was not unnecessarily suggestive. The police officers did not indicate that the suspect would be in the area and there were others present on the street.

In ***Com. v. Walker***, at the request of police, two rape victims walked through the public park where they had been assaulted the previous day. The victims observed and identified the perpetrators, who were present in the park. The Appeals Court approved of the police procedure, stating that the "police did not walk with the victims or direct their attention to any particular spot."

ACCIDENTAL CONFRONTATIONS

When a witness accidentally encounters a suspect under circumstances that are coincidental and not prearranged by the police, a spontaneous and unsolicited identification by the eyewitness is valid.[1102] This is true even if the coincidental encounter and spontaneous identification occur at the police station.[1103]

- In ***Commonwealth v. Walker***, the manger of a Dunkin Donuts was robbed at gun point. Approximately two weeks later while working at a different Dunkin Donuts the manager observed the defendant enter the restaurant. After he left she phoned the police and he was detained a short distance away. The police brought him back to the Dunkin Donuts where he was identified by the manager. The defendant claimed that the one-on-one identification which occurred more than two weeks after the initial crime violated the principle behind permitting one-on-one identifications since the recollection was no longer fresh in the witnesses mind. The SJC upheld the chance identification as not unnecessarily suggestive. [1104]
- In the 2002 Appeals Court case of ***Commonwealth v. Brandwein,*** while perhaps not having sufficient reason to stop the defendant, the police acted after they saw a man running in a high crime area carrying a shiny object, which they thought could be a gun or other weapon. The man was wearing a sweatshirt and jeans, not typical clothes for February weather. After the stop, without any attempt by the police to exploit the detention, a woman unexpectedly appeared and identified the defendant as a man who had stolen her necklace.[1105] The Appeals Court ruled that the intervening circumstances and the absence of purposeful or flagrant conduct warranted the judge's denial of the motion to suppress the out-of-court identification.
- In ***Com v. Huan Lieu,*** a shooting victim's pretrial extrajudicial identification of the defendant as one of the assailants was not impermissibly suggestive and was admissible, where the victim spotted the defendant, an Asian man, outside the courtroom in the presence of other Asian men while waiting for a codefendant's probable cause hearing, and one week later at a rescheduled hearing, the victim once again identified the defendant outside the courtroom in a crowd that included other Asians and the defendant was not restrained or in custody.[1106]

However, if the police intentionally set into motion a plan they believe will cause a chance encounter between the suspect and a witness, the identification will likely be suppressed.[1107]

[1101] *Commonwealth v. Eagles*, 419 Mass. 825, 648 N.E.2d 410 (1995).
[1102] *Commonwealth v. Otsuki*, 411 Mass. 218, 581 N.E.2d 999 (1991); *Cefalo v. Fitzpatrick*, 434 F.2d 187 (1st Cir. 1970).
[1103] *Commonwealth v. Colon-Cruz*, 408 Mass. 533, 562 N.E.2d 797 (1990); *Commonwealth v. Calhoun*, 28 Mass. App. Ct. 949, 550 N.E.2d 896 (1990); *Commonwealth v. Leaster*, 352 N.E.2d 407, 287 N.E.2d 122 (1972) (saw suspect in police station parking lot); *Commonwealth v. D'Ambria*, 357 Mass. 260, 258 N.E.2d 74 (1970); *See, Commonwealth v. Santos*, 402 Mass. 775, 525 N.E.2d 388 (1988).
[1104] *Commonwealth v. Walker*, 421 Mass. 90 (1995).
[1105] *Commonwealth v. Brandwein*, 435 Mass. 623, 631–633, 760 N.E.2d 724 (2002) ("the 'target' of the exclusionary rule 'is official misconduct,' and the rule is not intended 'to discourage citizens from aiding…in the apprehension of criminals' ").
[1106] *Com v. Huan Lieu*, 50 Mass.App.Ct. 162, 735 N.E.2d 1263 (2000
[1107] *Commonwealth v. Frank*, 357 Mass. 250, 257 N.E.2d 919 (1970); *Commonwealth v. Redmond*, 357 Mass. 333, 258 N.E.2d 287 (1970); *Commonwealth v. Santos*, 402 Mass. 775, 525 N.E.2d 388 (1988); *Commonwealth v. McMaster*, 21 Mass. App. Ct. 722, 490 N.E.2d 464 (1988).

COMPOSITE SKETCHES

Earlier court decisions indicate that a sketch will be admissible in court as substantive identification evidence as long as it is not created in an unduly suggestive manner. [1108] Like the other identification procedures, however, composites will be deemed inadmissible if the pretrial identification process was so impermissibly suggestive as to give rise to a substantial likelihood of irreparable misidentification.

In order to ensure that the development of the composite is not suggestive, the person preparing the composite should:

a. Assess the ability of the witness to provide a description of the perpetrator;
b. Select the procedure to be used (artist or computer generated);
c. Avoid showing the witness any photographs immediately prior to the development of the composite;
d. Select an environment which minimizes distraction; and
e. Determine with the witness whether the composite is a reasonable representation of the perpetrator. Police should strive to conduct the procedure with each witness separately, though failure to do so does not automatically result in suppression of the composite. [1109]

The investigator or person conducting the procedure should explain to the witness -- without other persons present -- the type of composite technique being employed and how the composite will be used in the investigation. He or she should then advise the witness to think back to the event and his or her frame of mind at the time. The investigator should document in writing the procedure employed, the results of the procedure (including the witness's own words), and the items used to create the composite. Finally, the investigator should preserve any composite images.[1110]

Attorney Hanrahan's Note: In the recent 2013 SJC identification study the reports states that composite sketches are "disfavored."

Preparation of a composite is evidence of identity but, if possible, it should be combined with other identification procedures.[1111]

In the 2006 case of ***Com. v. Martin***, the victim gave the police a description of her attacker and she also aided in the composition of a sketch, in addition to looking through a mug book, viewing different suspects in the field, and viewing a photo array.

COURTROOM IDENTIFICATION

Whatever procedure may have been used to obtain an identification of the defendant prior to trial, at court the witness will be asked to identify the defendant again.[1112] If the pretrial identification was improperly conducted or if it was overly suggestive, the prosecutor will bear the difficult burden of proving that the in-court identification by the witness was not tainted by or a product of the improper or overly suggestive pretrial identification.[1113] For this reason, every precaution should be taken to ensure that eyewitness identifications are conducted correctly and free of suggestive elements.

[1108] Commonwealth v. Thornley, 400 Mass. 355, 359-60 (1987); Commonwealth v. Susi, 394 Mass. 784, 789 (1985); Commonwealth v. Weichell, 390 Mass. 62, 72 (1983); Commonwealth v. Poggi, 53 Mass. App. Ct. 685, 693 (2002).
[1109] *Commonwealth v. Thornley*, 400 Mass. 355, 359-60 (1987) and the 2011 Middlesex DA Law Guide
[1110] Eyewitness Evidence: A Guide for Law Enforcement, National Institute of Justice 18 (1999).
[1111] *Commonwealth v. Martin*, 447 Mass. 274, 276-84 (2006)
[1112] *Commonwealth v. Tyler*, 418 Mass. 143, 634 N.E.2d 912 (1994).
[1113] *Commonwealth v. Wilson*, 357 Mass. 49, 255 N.E.2d 744, *cert. den.*400 U.S. 823, 91 S.Ct. 44 (1970).

The factors to consider in determining if a witness's in-court identification of a defendant was independent of any taint from an allegedly suggestive identification are:

(1) the extent of the witness's opportunity to observe the defendant at the time of the crime; prior errors, if any,

(2) in description,

(3) in identifying another person or

(4) in failing to identify the defendant;

(5) the receipt of other suggestions, and

(6) the lapse of time between the crime and the identification.[1114]

ADMISSIBILITY OF IDENTIFICATIONS

Any identification which was accompanied by overly suggestive words or actions on the part of the police will be excluded at trial under the fruit of the poisonous tree doctrine.[1115] If the eyewitness' ability to identify the suspect does not have an independent basis (the most important factor being the witness' opportunity to observe the offender at the time of the offense), an impermissibly suggestive pretrial identification will also require that an in-court identification by the witness be excluded.[1116]

FACTORS CONSIDERED IN DECIDING THE ADMISSIBILITY OF AN IDENTIFICATION AFTER POLICE MISCONDUCT

Reliability and suggestiveness

There are two primary aspects the court considers in admitting a witness' identification. They are: the reliability of the witness' identification, and, the method employed by the police eliciting the witness' identification — e.g., line-up, photographs, one-on-one, as well as the conduct of the police in orchestrating the identification.

Reliability - generally

In determining the reliability of a witness' identification, the court will consider the detail of the person's unaided description of the suspect prior to the identification, along with his or her degree of certainty or uncertainty in making the identification.

Suggestiveness

As discussed earlier, courts view improper suggestiveness when making identifications to be one of the greatest miscarriages of justice in the entire judicial system.[1117] Realizing this concern, the SJC has indicated that it will be very critical in analyzing the procedures used in eliciting the identification.[1118] It did not, however, set down procedures or suggestions which would make admissibility more certain. Instead, it indicated that it would consider each situation on a case-by-case basis. Reviewing the cases, the decisions tend to focus on the existence or non-existence of a number of factors.

The factors most often considered are:

a. the amount of time between the incident and the identification;[1119]
b. the method used to make the identification;[1120]
c. the comments or conduct of the police — such as, indicating that other evidence implicates "that" individual, or "we think this is the man";
d. repeated showing of a suspect's photograph;
e. showing one suspect's photograph for a longer period of time than the others; and
f. indicating that one suspect has a criminal record whereas the others do not.[1121]

[1114] *Commonwealth v. Williams*, 58 Mass. App. Ct. 139, 788 N.E.2d 580 (2003).
[1115] *Commonwealth v. Johnson*, 420 Mass. 458, 650 N.E.2d 1257 (1995); *Commonwealth v. Guillory*, 356 Mass. 591, 254 N.E.2d 427 (1970).
[1116] *Commonwealth v. Wilson*, 357 Mass. 49, 255 N.E.2d 744, *cert. den.*400U.S. 823, 91 S.Ct. 44 (1970).
[1117] *U.S. v. Wade*, (cited above).
[1118] *Commonwealth v. Johnson*, 420 Mass. 458, 650 N.E.2d 1257 (1995).
[1119] *Commonwealth v. Freiberg*, 405 Mass. 282, 540 N.E.2d 1289 (1989).
[1120] *Simmons v. U.S.*, 390 U.S. 377, 88 S.Ct. 967 (1968).
[1121] *Commonwealth v. Riley*, 26 Mass. App. Ct. 550, 530 N.E.2d 181 (1988).

The less suggestive the identification is, the more likely the court will admit it at trial. Moreover, when the court finds that the identification was not suggestive, the court may spend less time analyzing the reliability of the witness.

Overcoming Suggestiveness

As a general rule, any identification which was accompanied by overly suggestive words or actions on the part of the police will be excluded at trial, with one exception. The court will, nonetheless, admit an identification if it can be shown that the witness would have made the same identification absent the suggestiveness. Following the reasoning in the U.S. Supreme Court case of ***Manson v. Brathwaite***,[1122] Massachusetts courts will allow the identification if the state can show, by clear and convincing evidence, that the suggestive aspects of that identification are outweighed by the high reliability of the witness' identification.[1123]

- In ***Commonwealth v. Odware***, where the identification of a defendant was made by a witness from a photo array several weeks after seeing a flyer containing the defendant's picture at the victim's funeral, the Court refused to suppress the identification.[1124] The flyer was found not to be unnecessarily suggestive, in view of the overwhelming evidence and the fact that the witness saw the defendant before, during and after the shooting.

The Independent Basis or Reliability Test

The *Manson* court, reaffirming the reliability test used in the earlier Supreme Court case of *Neal v. Biggers*,[1125] enunciated five factors which must be considered in determining whether the witness' identification is independently valid, notwithstanding the unnecessary suggestiveness.[1126]

The factors are:

- The witness' opportunity to view the criminal at the time of the crime;
- The witness' degree of attention;
- The accuracy of the witness' description of the suspect;
- The witness' level of certainty; and
- The time between the crime and the confrontation.

The most important factor is the witness' opportunity to view the criminal at the crime scene.[1127] The better the opportunity to view, the more weight that factor will be given.[1128] Likewise, if the witness had a very limited opportunity to see the suspect, whether because of poor eyesight, poor lighting, or a very short period of time in which he or she viewed the suspect, the court will be much less likely to admit the identification evidence.[1129]

The Requirement that the Identification Have a Source Independent from the Suggestive Activities

In addition to the five *Manson* identification reliability factors, the court will also consider whether the witness would have likely been able to give the same degree of detail of the suspect's appearance if he or she had not be subjected to the overly-suggestive conduct of the police. (Such as showing the suspect to the witness one-on-one while he or she is wearing handcuffs.) Stated another way, the court seeks to make sure that the untainted subsequent identification was entirely independent of the police misconduct.[1130]

For example, the court would likely find that an identification by an ex-spouse was independent of the police conduct because she was so very familiar with his appearance prior to the officer's overly-suggestive behavior.

To determine whether an independent basis does exist the court considers these individual factors:

a. The extent of the witness' opportunity to observe the defendant at the time of the crime,[1131]

b. as well as prior errors in description;

[1122] *Manson v. Brathwaite*, 432 U.S. 98, 97 S.Ct. 2243 (1977).
[1123] *Commonwealth v. Holland*, 410 Mass. 248, 571 N.E.2d 625 (1991); *Commonwealth v. Tanso*, 411 Mass. 640, 583 N.E.2d 1247 (1992); *Commonwealth v. Warren*, 402 Mass. 137, 526 N.E.2d 250 (1988).
[1124] *Commonwealth v. Odware*, 429 Mass. 231, 707 N.E. 2d 347 (1999).
[1125] *Neal v. Biggers*, 409 U.S. 188, 93 S.Ct. 375 (1972).
[1126] *See, Commonwealth v. Botelho*, 369 Mass. 860, 343 N.E.2d 876 (1976) (the Massachusetts Supreme Judicial Court, while using the *Manson* test, chooses to call its test the "independent basis" test rather than the commonly-referred "reliability test"). *See also*, *U.S. v. Ford*, 22 F.2d 374 (1st Cir. 1994) and *Commonwealth v. Tanso*, 411 Mass. 640, 583 N.E.2d 1247 (1992) (court acknowledged that reliability was the dispositive issue and name of test used was inconsequential).
[1127] *Commonwealth v. Riley*, 26 Mass. App. Ct. 550, 530 N.E.2d 181 (1988)
[1128] *Commonwealth v. Freiberg*, 405 Mass. 282, 540 N.E.2d 1289 (1989); *Commonwealth v. Thornley*, 406 Mass. 96, 546 N.E.2d 350 (1989); *Commonwealth v. Crowe*, 21 Mass. App. Ct. 550, 488 N.E.2d 780 (1988).
[1129] *Commonwealth v. Jones*, 25 Mass. App. Ct. 55, 514 N.E.2d 1337 (1987).
[1130] *Commonwealth v. Johnson*, 420 Mass. 458, 650 N.E.2d 1258 (1995).
[1131] *Commonwealth v. Botelho*, 369 Mass. 860, 343 N.E.2d 876 (1976), *as cited in Commonwealth v. Johnson*, 420 Mass. 458, 650 N.E.2d 1257 (1995).

c. Identifying another person (misidentifications);

d. Failing to identify the defendant;

e. the nature and degree of suggestions; and

f. The lapse of time between the crime and the identification.[1132]

- In ***Commonwealth v. Wen Chao,*** the identification of the defendant as the perpetrator of a robbery and assault and battery by a victim and witness had a sufficient independent source, even assuming that the one-on-one show-up procedure was unnecessarily suggestive, where the parking lot was well-lighted, the victim's interior light of his vehicle was on, and the witness with excellent eyesight was within thirty feet.[1133]

HEARING MAY BE REQUIRED WHEN THE BEST PRACTICES ARE NOT FOLLOWED

In the 2013 SJC study, the reported stated "the best police practices listed below should become standard operating procedures at all Massachusetts law enforcement agencies. Failure to adhere to these specific protocols carries a likelihood of tainting an identification by an eyewitness. A substantial failure in any category should warrant a hearing."

1. Police officers should not take an offender description from one eyewitness in the presence of another eyewitness in a case where the offender is a stranger to the witnesses.
2. A showup should not be conducted more than approximately two hours after the commission of the offense.
3. A showup should not be conducted where the suspect is seated in the rear of a police cruiser or in a cell. If the suspect is handcuffed he should be presented, if practicable, so that the handcuffs are not visible to the witness.
4. If showups are to be conducted with multiple witnesses, they should be conducted in such a way that one witness cannot see or hear the procedure or results of another witness.
5. When assembling a photographic array or line-up:
   a. fillers should fit the general description of the offender;
   b. to the extent possible, nothing about the suspect or his photo should make him stand out;
   c. each photographic array or line-up must contain at least five fillers;
   d. each array or line-up should contain only one suspect; and,
   f. the police should not repeat fillers with the same witness from one array or line-up to the next.
6. Prior to conducting a show-up, array, or line-up, police officers should instruct the witness that:
   a. The alleged wrongdoer may or may not be in the photograph.
   b. It is just as important to clear a person from suspicion as to identify a person as the wrongdoer.
   c. Individual depicted in the photographs may not appear exactly as they did on the date of the incident because features such as weight, head and facial hair are subject to change.
   d. Regardless of whether an identification is made, the investigation will continue; and
   e. The procedure requires the administrator to ask the witness to state, in his or own words, how certain he or she is of any identification.
7. When showing a photographic array or conducting a line-up, the police should use a technique that will ensure that no one present will know when the witness is viewing the suspect. This may be accomplished by having an officer unfamiliar with the suspect conduct the procedure (double blind) or by using a blinded technique.
8. Police officers should conduct photographic arrays and line-ups by displaying the suspect and fillers to the witness sequentially.
9. When an eyewitness identifies a photograph or person, the officer should immediately ask the witness how certain or confident he or she is of the identification.

[1132] *Commonwealth v. Rossi*, 361 Mass. 665, 282 N.E.2d 70 (1972).
[1133] *Commonwealth v. Wen Chao Ye*, 52 Mass. 850, 756 N.E.2d 640 (2001).

MODEL FORMS FOR USE BY MASSACHUSETTS POLICE DEPARTMENTS IN EYEWITNESS EVIDENCE PROCEDURES (Forms provided by the SJC Study Group on Eyewitness Identification)

FORM 1: OFFICER'S FIELD CARD FOR SHOW-UP IDENTIFICATIONS

A show-up should be conducted shortly after the commission of the crime or the witness's observation of the suspect. A person should only be detained when the officer has reasonable suspicion to believe the person could be a suspect.

Barring special circumstances, the witness should be transported to the suspect's location. When transporting a witness to a show-up, attempt to prevent the witness from hearing radio transmissions or other officer-to-officer conversations related to the suspect or the investigation.

A suspect should only be viewed by one witness at a time out of the presence and hearing of other witnesses. Talking among witnesses should not be allowed.

Minimize suggestiveness. Unless necessary for the safety of officers or others, show-ups should not be conducted if the suspect is seated in the rear of a police cruiser, in a cell, or in any other enclosure associated with custody. If the suspect is handcuffed, he should be turned so that the handcuffs are not visible to the witness.

Do not tell the witness where the suspect was found, whether the suspect said anything or did anything suspicious, or whether the suspect was found with items potentially related to the crime.

Once a witness has positively identified the suspect at a show-up, do not conduct additional show-ups with the same suspect.

If the witness fails to make an identification, or is not sure of an identification, and probable cause to arrest cannot be immediately developed, the person must be permitted to leave.

Instructions to be read aloud to the Witness:

1. You are going to be asked to view some people (even if only one person is shown).
2. The person you saw may or may not be among the people you are about to view.
3. It is just as important to clear innocent persons from suspicion as it is to identify the guilty.
4. Regardless of whether you identify someone, we will continue to investigate the incident.
5. If you identify someone, I will ask you to state, in your own words, how certain you are.
6. If you do select someone, please do not ask us questions about the person you have selected, because we cannot share that information with you at this time.
7. Regardless of whether you select a person, please do not discuss the procedure with any other witnesses in the case or the media.
8. Do you have any questions before we begin?

If an identification is made, ask: Without using a numerical scale, how certain are you?

FORM 2: Photo Array Instruction Form

1. You are being asked to view a set of photographs.

2. You will be viewing the photographs one at a time and in random order.

3. Please look at all of them. I am required to show you the entire series.

4. Please make a decision about each photograph before moving on to the next one.

5. The person you saw may or may not be in the set of photographs you are about to view.

6. You should remember that it is just as important to clear innocent persons from suspicion as to identify the guilty.

7. The officer showing the photographs does not know whether any of the people in the array are the person you saw.

8. The individuals in the photographs may not appear exactly as they did on the date of the incident because features such as head and facial hair are subject to change.

9. Regardless of whether or not you select a photograph, the police department will continue to investigate the incident.

10. If you select someone, the procedure requires the officer to ask you to state, in your own words, how certain you are.

11. If you do select a photograph(s), please do not ask the officer questions about the person you have selected, as no information can be shared with you at this stage of the investigation.

12. Regardless of whether you select a photograph(s), please do not discuss the procedure with any other witnesses in the case or the media.

13. Do you have any questions before we begin?

Witness Signature____ Date __________
Officer Signature ____ Date __________
Administrator Signature ____________________________________ Date __________

If an identification is made, ask: Without using a numerical scale, how certain are you?

FORM 3: LINE-UP INSTRUCTION FORM

1. You are being asked to view a group of people.

2. You will be viewing them one at a time in random order.

3. Please look at all of them. I am required to show you the entire series.

4. Please make a decision about each person before moving onto the next one.

5. The person who you saw may or may not be one of the people you are about to view.

6. You should remember that it is just as important to clear innocent persons from suspicion as to identify the guilty.

7. The officer who will be administering the line-up does not know whether any of the people in the line-up are the person you saw.

8. The individuals you view may not appear exactly as they did on the date of the incident because features such as head and facial hair are subject to change.

9. Regardless of whether or not you select someone, the police department will continue to investigate the incident.

10. If you select someone, the procedure requires the officer to ask you to state, in your own words, how certain you are.

11. If you do select someone, please do not ask the officer questions about the person you have selected.

12. Regardless of whether you select someone, please do not discuss the procedure with any other witnesses in the case or the media.

13. Do you have any questions before we begin?

Witness Signature ____ Date ____________
Officer Signature ____ Date ____________
Administrator Signature ____________________________________ Date ____________

If an identification is made, ask: Without using a numerical scale, how certain are you?

PAGE INTENTIONALLY LEFT BLANK

STATUTORY LAW

STATUTORY LAW

STATUTORY LAW

STATUTORY LAW

STATUTORY LAW

STATUTORY LAW

STATUTORY LAW

PAGE INTENTIONALLY LEFT BLANK

Section 2 STATUTORY LAW

IMPORTANT INFORMATION TO KNOW

Statutory Law is law created by the Legislature (and in rare circumstances through Court decisions or based on Common Law). These laws typically deal with the elements of an offense that must be proved in order to convict someone of an offense but there are also statutory laws that deal with a variety of other issues.

C. 274 § 1. FELONIES AND MISDEMEANORS

A crime punishable by death or imprisonment in the **state prison (F)** is a felony. All other crimes are misdemeanors.

PARTIES TO A CRIME

PRINCIPAL: The principal to the crime is the primary offender/actor of the particular crime.

JOINT VENTURER: Often the same crime is committed by more than one person, such as when a drive by shooting occurs – typically both the shooter and the driver are equally culpable. When more than one person act in concert with each other they both/all may face the same penalty as one principal offender.

The SJC stated in its 2009 case of *Commonwealth v. Zanetti,* "At its core, joint venture criminal liability has two essential elements":

1. that the defendant knowingly participated in the commission of the crime charged, and
2. that the defendant had or shared the required criminal intent.[1]

Such participation may take the form of:

a. personally committing the acts that constitute the crime, or
b. aiding or assisting another person in those acts, or
c. asking or encouraging another person to commit the crime, or
d. helping to plan the commission of the crime, or
e. agreeing to stand by, or near, the scene of the crime to act as lookout, or
f. agreeing to provide aid or assistance in committing the crime, or
g. agreeing to help in escaping if such help becomes necessary.

Presence alone not enough: Our law does not allow for guilt by association. Mere presence at the scene of the crime is not enough to find a defendant guilty. Presence alone does not establish a defendant's knowing participation in the crime, even if a person knew about the intended crime in advance and took no steps to prevent it. To find a defendant guilty, there must be proof that the defendant intentionally participated in some fashion in committing that particular crime and had or shared the intent required to commit the crime.

Under the "presence" branch of joint venture, "presence" is appropriately defined to mean "at or near the general vicinity of the crime . . . at some point during the joint venture".[2]

Withdrawal: The defendant is not guilty of a crime if he (she) withdrew from or abandoned it in a timely and effective manner. A withdrawal is effective only if it is communicated to the other persons involved, and only if it is communicated to them early enough so that they have a reasonable opportunity to abandon the crime as well. If the withdrawal comes so late that the crime cannot be stopped, it is too late and is ineffective.

AIDING and ABETTING: This is covered by statue (c. 274 § 2) and is essentially the same as joint venture in that "whoever aids in the commission of a **felony**… shall be punished **in the manner provided for the punishment of the principal**

[1] *Commonwealth v. Zanetti,* 454 Mass. 449 (2009).
[2] Commonwealth v.Serrano, 74 Mass. App. Ct. 1, 4, 904 N.E.2d 247 (2009)

felon."However, it also has an alternative way of **violating this statute in that** "whoever is accessory **before the fact** by **counseling, hiring or otherwise procuring** such felony to be committed...shall be punished **in the manner provided for the punishment of the principal felon.**

In the 2009 case of *Commonwealth v. Zanetti*, the SJC stated that Joint Venturer and Aiding and Abetting are the same and they elected to move forward with the term Aiding & Abetting .

ACCESSORIES AFTER THE FACT: This crime is also covered by statute (c. 274 § 4) and states:

- Whoever, after the commission of a **felony**,
  - harbors, conceals, maintains or assists the principal **felon** or accessory before the fact, or
  - gives such offender any other aid, knowing that he has committed a felony or has been accessory thereto before the fact,
- with intent that he shall avoid or escape detention, arrest, trial or punishment,
- shall be an accessory after the fact, and, except as otherwise provided, be punished by imprisonment in the **state prison (F)** for not more than 7 years or in jail for not more than 2½ years or by a fine of not more than $1,000.

Family Defense: The fact that the defendant is the husband or wife, or by consanguinity, affinity or adoption, the parent or grandparent, child or grandchild, brother or sister of the offender, shall be a defense to a prosecution under this section. If such a defendant testifies solely as to the existence of such relationship, he shall not be subject to cross examination on any other subject matter, nor shall his criminal record, if any, except for perjury or subornation of perjury, be admissible to impeach his credibility.

Unlike a participant, an accessory after the fact to a felony is not involved in the planning or execution of the crime, and need not have advance knowledge of it. An accessory after the fact "need merely [1] know the identity of the principal perpetrator and [2] have knowledge of the substantial facts of the felonious crime that the principal committed and, possessed of such knowledge, [3] aid the principal in avoiding punishment."[1]

A defendant who harbors a principal who has committed multiple felonies may be convicted of the same number of counts of being an accessory after the fact.[2]

A defendant cannot be convicted both of the substantive crime and as being an accessory after the fact to the same crime. [3]

Note: Accessories before and after only apply to felonies, not misdemeanors.

C. 274 § 6. ATTEMPTS TO COMMIT CRIMES

- The defendant attempts to commit a crime by:
- doing **any act** toward its commission,
- but fails in its perpetration, or is intercepted or prevented in its perpetration,

First, by imprisonment in the **state prison (F)** for not more than ten years, if he **attempts to commit a crime punishable with death**.

Second, by imprisonment in the **state prison (F)** for not more than 5 years or in a jail or HOC for not more than 2½ years, if he **attempts to commit a crime, except any larceny** under chapter 266 § 30, **punishable by imprisonment in the state prison (F) for life or for 5 years or more**.

Third, by imprisonment in a jail or HOC for not more than one year or by a fine of not more than $300, if he **attempts to commit a crime, except any larceny** under chapter 266 § 30, punishable by imprisonment in the **state prison (F)** for **less than 5 years** or by imprisonment in a jail or HOC or by a fine.

Fourth, by imprisonment in a jail or HOC for not more than 2½ years or by a fine, or by both such fine and imprisonment, if he **attempts to commit any larceny** punishable under chapter 266 § 30.

[1] Commonwealth v. Hoshi H., 72 Mass. App. Ct. 18, 19-21, 887 N.E.2d 1104, 1105-1106 (2008).
[22] Commonwealth v. Perez, 437 Mass. 186, 189-194, 770 N.E.2d 428, 433-434 (2002).
[3] Commonwealth v. Gajka, 425 Mass. 751, 754, 682 N.E.2d 1345, 1348 (1997); Commonwealth v. Berryman, 359 Mass. 127, 129, 268 N.E.2d 354, 356 (1971).

Attorney Hanrahan's Note: The attempt statute in Massachusetts requires some **overt act** toward the commission of the crime. Mere discussion and planning is not enough (conspiracy may be appropriate depending on the circumstances).

CASE LAW NOTE: Separated into its component parts, a conviction of attempt under G.L. c. 274, § 6, requires:

1. An intention to commit the underlying offense, [and]
2. An overt act toward its commission.
3. It also requires proof that the substantive crime was *not* achieved. [1]

In the 2014 case of ***Commonwealth v. Buswell***, the SJC ruled that to establish an attempt under G.L. c. 274, § 6, the Commonwealth must prove "an **intention** to commit the underlying offense, **and** also an **overt act** toward its commission." When the police have orchestrated the scene and no actual victim faces an immediate threat the defendant must come "**very close**" to committing the crime before he can be found guilty of an attempt.

C. 274 § 7. CONSPIRACY TO COMMIT A CRIME

Any person who commits the crime of conspiracy shall be punished as follows:

First, if the purpose of the conspiracy or any of the means for achieving the purpose of the conspiracy is a **felony punishable by death or imprisonment for life,** by a fine of not more than $10,000 or by imprisonment in the **state prison (F)** for not more than 20 years or in jail for not more than 2½ years, or by both such fine and imprisonment.

Second, if clause first does not apply and the purpose of the conspiracy or any of the means for achieving the purpose of the conspiracy is a **felony punishable by imprisonment in the state prison (F) for a maximum period exceeding ten years**, by a fine of not more than $10,000 or by imprisonment in the **state prison (F)** for not more than 10 years or in jail for not more than 2½ years, or by both such fine and imprisonment.

Third, if clauses first and second do not apply and the purpose of the conspiracy or any of the means for achieving the purpose of the conspiracy is a **felony punishable by imprisonment in the state prison (F) for not more than ten years**, by a fine of not more than $5,000 or by imprisonment in the **state prison (F)** for not more than 5 years or in jail for not more than 2½ years, or by both such fine and imprisonment.

Fourth, if clauses first through third do not apply and the purpose of the conspiracy or any of the means for achieving the purpose of the conspiracy is a crime, by a fine of not more than $2,000 or by imprisonment in jail for not more than 2½ years, or both.

Note: If a person is convicted of a crime of conspiracy for which crime the penalty is expressly set forth in any other section of the General Laws, the provisions of this section shall not apply to said crime and the penalty therefor shall be imposed pursuant to the provisions of such other section.

Attorney Hanrahan's note on CONSPIRACY:

What is conspiracy?: Conspiracy is an agreement between two or more people to commit a criminal act, or a lawful act for a criminal purpose.

No overt Act Required: Unlike attempt, no overt act is needed. The agreement is the crime.

Wharton's Rule: The rules says that if the crime requires two people to complete the crime, more than two people are needed to make the agreement (conspiracy), i.e. adultery

In the 2013 case of ***Commonwealth v. Rose***, the Appeals Court explained that a defendant can be convicted of both the crime of conspiracy and the substantive (underlying) crime. The conspiracy charge does not require proof of completion; the mere agreement is the crime.

Note: Also see Conspiracy to Violate the Drug Laws in the Drug Section of this manual

[1] *Commonwealth v. Ortiz,* 408 Mass. 463, 470 (1990) (absent evidence of overt act, evidence insufficient to support conviction of attempted assault and battery by means of dangerous weapon). Accord *Commonwealth v. Bell,* 455 Mass. 408, 412 (2009).

c. 265 § 13G. *COMMISSION OF A FELONY FOR HIRE*

- Whoever,
- for the payment of consideration or for the promise of the payment of such consideration,
- commits a felony,
- shall be punished as follows:

Penalty: imprisonment in the **state prison (F)** for not more than 5 years. The punishment imposed by this section shall be in addition to the punishment provided by law for the commission of a felony so committed.

POSSESSION

To prove constructive possession, the Commonwealth typically must establish the defendant's "**knowledge** coupled with the **ability and intention to exercise dominion and control**."

Essentially, in order to prove constructive possession, you must prove three elements:

1. The Defendant's knowledge of the item/substance's existence
2. The Defendant's ability to control it; and
3. The intent to control the item/substance.

Constructive possession includes more than being in the presence of the item or even operating a motor vehicle containing the item. The prosecution must show additional factors "that tip the scale" to prove constructive possession.[1]

"Proof of possession of contraband may be established by circumstantial evidence, and the inferences that can be drawn" from the circumstantial evidence. However, "presence alone cannot show the requisite knowledge, power, or intention to exercise control over [contraband], but presence, supplemented by other incriminating evidence, 'will serve to tip the scale in favor of sufficiency.' "

Knowledge: A defendant's knowledge is typically proved by "inference from all the facts and circumstances." For instance, the defendant's reaction to the presence of the police (i.e. running, or attempting to hide) may be indicative of the defendant's knowledge of any contraband present.

Ability and Intention to Control: in constructive possession cases, a defendant's presence alone is not enough to show knowledge, or the ability and intention to exercise control over the item, but "presence, supplemented by other incriminating evidence, 'will serve to tip the scale in favor of sufficiency.' "[2] For instance, the quantity of the contraband may be an indicator of the defendant's intent to exercise dominion and control. Two teenagers found sitting in the park alongside two open, partially consumed, cans of beer would likely be indicative that both teens exercised dominion and control over the beer absent some plausible explanation. The facts and circumstances of each case will have to be analyzed.

DUPLICATIVE CONVICTIONS & DOUBLE JEOPARDY

Where a defendant is charged with two criminal offenses based on the same conduct and where the Legislature has not declared its intent that a defendant be punished separately for both offenses, convictions of a greater and lesser offense are duplicative and barred by the prohibition against double jeopardy.[3]

A defendant may be convicted of and punished for multiple crimes based on the same act or single course of conduct provided that each crime requires proof of an element that the other does not.[4]

In ***Commonwealth v. Muller*** (2012), the defendant entered a convenience store, approached the cashier, and offered to "split the money" in the cash register with the cashier. When the cashier refused, the defendant removed a handgun from his jacket, placed the handgun on the counter, and demanded money. He was charged and convicted of assault by means of a dangerous weapon, G.L. c. 265, § 15B (*b*), and armed robbery, G.L. c. 265, § 17. The SJC upheld both convictions because "armed robbery has a required element--the theft of money or property--that is not required to prove assault by means of a dangerous weapon, and assault by means of a dangerous weapon has a required element--the use of a dangerous weapon to commit the assault--that is not required to prove armed robbery the two convictions are not duplicative.

[1] *Commonwealth v. Crapps*, Appeals Court (2013). Also see Commonwealth v. Romero, SJC (2013)
[2] *Com. v. Romero,* Appeals Court (2011)
[3] Luk v. Commonwealth, 421 Mass. 415, 419 (1995), citing North Carolina v. Pearce, 395 U.S. 711, 717 (1969)
[4] *Commonwealth v. Niels N., 73 MassApp.Ct. 689, 697 (2009)*

The "double jeopardy clause of the Fifth Amendment to the United States Constitution protects against three distinct abuses: a second prosecution for the same offense after acquittal; a second prosecution for the same offense after conviction; and multiple punishments for the same offense..."[1]

DEFENSES (Including self-defense and Entrapment)

USE OF DEADLY FORCE FOR SELF-DEFENSE

Before a defendant is entitled to imply self-defense with a dangerous weapon likely to cause serious injury or death, there must be evidence that he had a reasonable apprehension of great bodily harm or death and a reasonable belief that no other means would suffice to prevent such harm.... The defendant must also have actually believed that he was in imminent danger of serious harm or death. A person may not use force in self-defense until he has availed himself of all proper means to avoid physical combat, and must use no more force than reasonably necessary in all the circumstances. [2] The same holds true for self-defense non-involving deadly weapons. In order to be justified in using force for self-defense (at least in Massachusetts) you must make an effort to avoid the confrontation, including fleeing the area.

SELF-DEFENSE FOR NON-DEADLY FORCE

In the 2011 case of ***Commonwealth v. King,*** the SJC stated "where nondeadly force is used, a defendant is entitled to a self-defense instruction at trial if the evidence, viewed in the light most favorable to the defendant without regard to credibility, supports a reasonable doubt that (1) the defendant had reasonable concern for his personal safety; (2) he used all reasonable means to avoid physical combat; and (3) "the degree of force used was reasonable in the circumstances, with proportionality being the touchstone for assessing reasonableness."

However, a person generally is not required to flee a violent confrontation when in his/her own home. This is sometimes referred to as "the castle law" (i.e. your home is your castle). See chapter 278 § 8A below:

c. 278 § 8A	**KILLING OR INJURING A PERSON UNLAWFULLY IN A DWELLING**
In the prosecution of a person who is an occupant of a dwelling charged with killing or injuring one who was unlawfully in said dwelling, it shall be a defense that the occupant was in his dwelling at the time of the offense and that he acted in the reasonable belief that the person unlawfully in said dwelling was about to inflict great bodily injury or death upon said occupant or upon another person lawfully in said dwelling, and that said occupant used reasonable means to defend himself or such other person lawfully in said dwelling. There shall be no duty on said occupant to retreat from such person unlawfully in said dwelling.	
Attorney Hanrahan's Note: This is commonly referred to as the Castle Doctrine. Under most circumstances, a person is required to retreat, whenever possible, from an attack, in order to use self-defense as a defense. However, when a person is inside his dwelling he is <u>not</u> required to retreat before using force.	

ENTRAPMENT

Entrapment by law enforcement involves "implanting criminal ideas in innocent minds and thereby bringing about offenses that otherwise would never have been perpetrated."[3]

There are two elements of the entrapment defense:

(1) that the defendant was induced by a government agent or one acting at his direction and

(2) that the defendant lacked predisposition to engage in the criminal conduct of which he is accused.[4]

The defendant only bears an "initial burden 'of producing some evidence of inducement by the government.' ... The burden then shifts to the Commonwealth 'to prove beyond a reasonable doubt that (1) there was no government inducement *or* (2) the defendant was predisposed to commit the crime.'

[1] Luk v. Commonwealth, 421 Mass. 415, 419 (1995), citing North Carolina v. Pearce, 395 U.S. 711, 717 (1969)
[2] *Commonwealth v. Santos,* 454 Mass. 770, 772-773 (2009), citing *Commonwealth v. Harrington,* 379 Mass. 446, 450 (1980).
[3] *Commonwealth v. Shuman,* 391 Mass. 345, 351 (1984), quoting Perkins, Criminal Law 1031 (2d ed.1969)
[4] *Commonwealth v. Madigan,* 449 Mass. 702, 707 (2007), quoting from *Commonwealth v. Penta,* 32 Mass.App.Ct. 36, 47 (1992).

VENUE

Note: Many venue issues that pertain to specific crimes are noted in other parts of this manual along with the specific crimes. The below statutes deal with some general venue issues:

C. 277 § 57. Prosecutions of crimes committed near boundary line of counties, etc.; or at sea

A crime committed on or within one hundred rods of the boundary line of two counties may be alleged to have been committed, and may be prosecuted and punished, in either county; and if committed on or within fifty rods of the boundary line of two judicial districts, it may be alleged to have been committed, and may be prosecuted and punished, in either district. A crime committed upon the sea within one league of the shore may be prosecuted and punished in an adjacent county.

C. 277 § 57A. Venue in cases where crime was committed without county or territorial

A defendant shall not be discharged for want of jurisdiction if the evidence discloses that the crime with which he is charged was actually committed without the county or the territorial jurisdiction of the court in which he is being tried; provided, that the attorney general or the district attorney petitions to the court before proceeding with the trial for leave to proceed, stating that he is in doubt from the state of the evidence then in his possession as to whether or not the crime was committed within the county or the territorial jurisdiction of the court, and the court after hearing said petition orders the trial to proceed.

STATUTE OF LIMITATIONS

Crime	Limit	Chapter & Section(s)	Notes
All Crimes not listed below	**6 years** after the commission of the offense	Various	
Murder	**No Limit**	265 § 1	
Indecent A&B on a child under 14	**Any time** after the date of the commission of the offense; But any indictment or complaint found and filed more than **27 years** after the date of commission of the offense shall be supported by independent evidence that corroborates the victim's allegation. The independent evidence shall not consist exclusively of the opinions of mental health professionals.	265 § 13B, 265 § 13B½, 265 § 13B¾	Includes conspiracy to commit any of these offenses and accessory to any of these offenses. See notes below for victim under 16.
Indecent A&B on a person with an intellectual disability		265 § 13F	
Wanton and Reckless behavior creating a risk of serious bodily injury or sexual abuse to a child		265 § 13L	
Rape of a Child (force)		265 § 22A, 265 § 22B, 265 § 22C	
Rape of a Child (statutory rape)		265 § 23, 265 § 23A, 265 § 23B	
Assault of Child with Intent to Commit Rape		265 § 24B	
Assault with Intent to Commit Rape	**15 years** from the commission of the offense	265 § 24	Includes conspiracy to commit any of these offenses and accessory to any of these offenses
Rape		265 § 22	
Armed Robbery	**10 years** after the commission of the offense	265 § 17	Includes conspiracy to commit any of these offenses and accessory to any of these offenses
Assault with Intent to Rob or Murder		265 § 18	
Unarmed Robbery		265 § 19	
Stealing by Putting in Fear		265 § 21	

Suspect Residing outside of Massachusetts: Any period during which the defendant is not usually and publicly a resident within the commonwealth shall be excluded in determining the time limited.

Special Provisions for Child Victims:

If a victim of one of the crimes set forth below is under the age of 16 at the time the crime is committed, the period of limitation for prosecution shall not commence until the victim has reached the age of 16 or the violation is reported to a law enforcement agency, whichever occurs earlier.

Indecent A&B on a Child – 265 § 13B
Indecent A&B on a person with an intellectual disability – 265 § 13F
Indecent A&B on a person 14 or older – 265 § 13H
Rape (all forms) – 265 § 22, 22A & 23
Assault of Child with into to rape – 265 § 24B
Parental Kidnapping – 265 § 26A
Enticing a child for Marriage – 272 § 1
Enticing away person for prostitution or sexual intercourse – 272 § 2
Drugging Person for Sexual Intercourse – 272 § 3
Inducing person under 18 to have sexual intercourse – 272 § 4
Inducing a minor into prostitution – 272 § 4A
Living off earnings of a minor prostitute – 272 § 4B
Owner of place inducing person to resort in such place for sexual intercourse c. 272 § 6
Support from prostitute earnings – 272 § 7
Soliciting a prostitute – 272 § 8
Procuring person to practice…prostitution – 272 § 12
Detaining or drugging person for prostitution – 272 § 13
Incest – 272 § 17
Resorting to restaurants or taverns for immoral purposes – 272 § 26
Dissemination of harmful material to minors – 272 § 28
Posing child in nudity/sexual conduct – 272 § 29A
Dissemination of child porn – 272 § 29B
Exhibitions of Deformities – 272 § 33
Crimes against Nature – 272 § 34
Unnatural and lascivious acts – 272 § 35
Unnatural and lascivious acts with a child – 272 § 35A

MURDER/MANSLAUGHTER

C. 265 § 1	MURDER
Elements	
1st Degree	Murder committed with: • Deliberately **premeditated malice** aforethought, or • With **extreme atrocity or cruelty**, or • In the commission or attempted commission of a crime punishable with death or imprisonment for life (AKA "**Felony Murder**")
2nd Degree	Murder which does not appear to be in the first degree is murder in the second degree. Murder in the second degree is an unlawful killing with malice.[1]
Arrest Power, Penalties & Notes	
Power of Arrest	**Felony** – a police officer may effect a warrantless arrest for this offense provided he/she has probable cause that the suspect committed the offense.
Penalty	Imprisonment in the state prison for life. No eligibility for Parole under 1st degree murder. However, the sentence may be commuted by the Governor.
Related Statutes, Case Law & Other Important Information	
Jury decides	The degree of murder shall be found by the jury.
Premeditated Malice Aforethought	"Malice can be established by proving any of three facts, or 'prongs': 1) the defendant intended to cause the victim's death; 2) the defendant intended to cause grievous bodily harm to the victim; or 3) the defendant committed an intentional act which, in the circumstances known to the defendant, a reasonable person would have understood created a **plain and strong likelihood of death**."[2] In regards to first degree murder, there is additional requirement of *premeditation*, meaning there has to be some plan or thought process that occurred prior to the murder, even if only briefly before the killing.

[1] *Commonwealth v. Earle*, 458 Mass. 341, 346 (2010)
[2] *Commonwealth v. Daniel Horne*, SJC (2013).

C. 265 § 1 MURDER

Extreme Atrocity or Cruelty

Established law requires that a jury must find the presence of **one or more** of the following factors to convict a defendant of murder in the first degree based on extreme atrocity or cruelty (commonly referred to as the *Cunneen* factors): [1]

1. whether the defendant was indifferent to or took pleasure in the victim's suffering;
2. the consciousness and degree of suffering of the victim;
3. the extent of the victim's physical injuries;
4. the number of blows inflicted on the victim;
5. the manner and force with which the blows were delivered;
6. the nature of the weapon, instrument, or method used in the killing; and
7. the disproportion between the means needed to cause death and those employed."

Case Law Note:

In the 2011 case of ***Commonwealth v. Smith***, the SJC ruled that death by manual strangulation was sufficient to convict for murder in the first degree under theory of extreme atrocity and cruelty. Generally, the victim does not die right away and suffers as they are strangled.

Felony Murder

In the crime of felony-murder, a defendant's intent to commit the underlying felony stands in for the malice aforethought required for murder. For this theory to apply the nature of the felony must be such that an intent to commit that crime exhibits a conscious disregard for human life, hardness of heart, cruelty, recklessness of consequences and a mind regardless of social duty. The felony-murder rule thus requires that the predicate felony be either dangerous to life by its nature, or dangerous to life by the manner or method of its commission. A felony of this latter class--one that creates a foreseeable risk of death because of the peculiar circumstances of its commission--is a felony committed with conscious disregard of the risk to human life. [2]

The Legislature has provided that a killing constitutes felony-murder if the killing occurs "in the commission or attempted commission of" a predicate felony. G.L. c. 265, § 1. The SJC has interpreted this statutory language to mean that the killing must occur "in connection with the felony and at substantially the same time and place."[3] The killing and the predicate felony "need only to have occurred as part of one continuous transaction."[4]

The underlying felony must have a possible sentence of death or life imprisonment.

In felony-murder the conduct which constitutes the felony must be separate from the acts of personal violence which constitute a necessary part of the homicide itself. [5]

Attorney Hanrahan's Notes: the action that resulted in the death must have been committed by the defendant (or his accomplice). For instance, if a bank security guard in an effort to thwart a bank robbery fired a round at the robber and missed hitting a nearby teller causing her death would not result in the felony murder rule because the death was not caused directly by the defendant.

Case Law Note:

In the 2011 case of ***Commonwealth v. Lopez,*** the Court ruled that it is possible that a *weaponless* A&B committed during an unarmed robbery which results in death can rise to the level of first degree murder under the felony murder theory. In this case the defendant ordered a food delivery and when the delivery person arrived, standing on a staircase carrying the food, the defendant "sucker punched" the victim causing him to fall back, hitting his head on the concrete which resulted in his death.

---

[1] *Commonwealth v. Linton,* 456 Mass. 534, 546 n. 10 (2010).
[2] *Commonwealth v. Lopez,* 2011 Appeals Court
[3] Commonwealth v. Rolon, supra at 818 n. 11, quoting Model Jury Instructions on Homicide at 16, 17-18. See Commonwealth v. Gordon, 422 Mass. 816, 850 (1996); Commonwealth v. Ortiz, 408 Mass. 463, 466 (1990).
[4] Commonwealth v. Ortiz, supra. See Commonwealth v. Blackwell, 422 Mass. 294, 300-301 n. 2 (1996)
[5] *Commonwealth v. Gunter,* 427 Mass. 259, 272 (1989).

C. 265 § 1	MURDER
Attempted Murder **c. 265 § 16**	An attempt to commit murder by: • poisoning, drowning or strangling another person, or • any means not constituting an assault with intent to commit murder, **Penalty:** imprisonment in the **state prison (F)** for not more than 20 years or by a fine of not more than $1,000 dollars and imprisonment in jail for not more than 2½ years. **ARREST POWERS**: **Felony** – a police officer may effect an arrest for this offense committed in his/her presence or for an offense in the past, on probable cause.
Transferred Intent	A transferred intent theory provides that if a defendant intends to kill a person and in attempting to do so mistakenly kills another person, such as a bystander, the defendant is treated under the law as if he intended to kill the bystander. [1] The same principle of transferred intent applies to the element of premeditation: where a defendant decides after deliberation to kill one person and mistakenly kills another, the defendant's premeditation is transferred to the actual, unintended victim. [2] In ***Commonwealth v. Diaz***, the defendant was guilty of premeditated murder under doctrine of transferred intent where he planned to kill his former girl friend but mistakenly killed her sister.
Excessive Force in Self Defense	Excessive use of force in self-defense may mitigate a killing from murder to manslaughter. *Commonwealth v. Pring-Wilson*, 448 Mass. 718, 733 n. 15 (2007).
	Venue for Homicide Offenses
Injury in one county & death in another **c. 277 § 60**	If a mortal wound is given, or if other violence or injury is inflicted, or if poison is administered, in one county, by means whereof death ensues in another county, the homicide may be prosecuted and punished in either county.
Death at Sea **c. 277 § 61**	If a mortal wound is given, or if other violence or injury is inflicted, or if poison is administered, on the high seas or on land either within or without the commonwealth, by means whereof death ensues in any county thereof, the homicide may be prosecuted and punished in the county where the death happens.
Death in another State **c. 277 § 62**	If a mortal wound is given, or if other violence or injury is inflicted, or if poison is administered, in any county of the commonwealth, by means whereof death ensues without the commonwealth, the homicide may be prosecuted and punished in the county where the act was committed.

[1] Commonwealth v. Taylor (2012) referencing Commonwealth v. Shea, 460 Mass. 163, 172-174 & n. 7 (2011); Commonwealth v. Pitts, 403 Mass. 665, 669 & n. 6 (1989).
[2] Commonwealth v. Diaz, 431 Mass. 822, 831-832 (2000)

C. 265 § 13	MANSLAUGHTER
Manslaughter defined	Manslaughter is the taking of human life by an act not justified in law, but without malice aforethought which is necessary to constitute murder.[1]
Attorney Hanrahan's Note	Malice is the distinguishing factor between manslaughter and murder, meaning there was no preplan to kill. Although the elements are not defined in the actual statute, case law tells us that there are two types of Manslaughter (voluntary and involuntary).
Power of Arrest	**Felony** – a police officer may effect a warrantless arrest for this offense provided he/she has probable cause that the suspect committed the offense.
Penalty	Imprisonment in the **state prison (F)** for not more than 20 years or by a fine of not more than $1,000 and imprisonment in jail or a HOC for not more than 2½ years. **Enhanced Penalty**: Whoever commits manslaughter while involved in the following crimes: • Malicious Explosion (c. 266 § 101) • Throwing Explosives near person or property (c. 266 § 102) • Explosive Device Offenses (c. 266 § 102A & c. 266 102B) Penalty: Imprisoned in the **state prison (F)** for life or for any term of years.
	VOLUNTARY MANSLAUGHTER
Voluntary Manslaughter	Voluntary manslaughter is defined as a killing committed: 1. In "a sudden transport of passion or heat of blood, upon reasonable provocation and without malice, or 2. Upon sudden combat." [2] "Sudden combat" is "one of the events which may provoke the perturbation of mind that can end in a killing without malice." [3] Voluntary manslaughter may be based on a theory of the excessive use of force in self-defense.[4] A defendant is entitled to a jury instruction on voluntary manslaughter based on reasonable provocation if, viewing the evidence in the light most favorable to him, "there is evidence of provocation deemed adequate in law to cause the accused to lose his self-control in the heat of passion, and if the killing followed the provocation before sufficient time had elapsed for the accused's temper to cool."[5] "Insults and arguments are insufficient provocation for manslaughter."[6]
Attorney Hanrahan's Note on Voluntary Manslaughter	**Voluntary Manslaughter** occurs when the offender intended to kill the victim but was "adequately provoked" or the killing occurred "during the heat of passion," such as coming home and finding your wife in bed with another man. This would most likely rise to the level of a "heat of passion" defense preventing a murder charge. However, if there was a "cooling off period" the appropriate charge would be murder. For instance, if the offender comes home to find his wife in bed with another man and then leaves and poisons her drink the following day, the "heat of passion" would have ended and now the killing would be deemed murder.

[1] *Commonwealth v. Demboski*, 283 Mass. 315, 322, 186 N.E. 589, and cases cited. Note the legislature did not define the crime in the statute.
[2] *Commonwealth v. Burgess*,450 Mass. 422 (2008)
[3] *Commonwealth v. Peters*, 372 Mass. 319, 324 (1977).
[4] *Commonwealth v. Walden*, 380 Mass. 724, 729 (1980), citing *Commonwealth v. Kendrick*, 351 Mass. 203, 211-212 (1966).
[5] Commonwealth v. Andrade, 422 Mass. 236, 237 (1996), quoting Commonwealth v. Schnopps, 383 Mass. 178, 180 (1981), S. C., 390 Mass. 722 (1984).
[6] Commonwealth v. Burgess, 450 Mass. 422, 438 (2008).

C. 265 § 13 — MANSLAUGHTER

Related Statutes, Case Law & Other Important Information for Voluntary Manslaughter

Adequately Provoked for the purposes of Voluntary Manslaughter

The rule is "a reasonable person would have become sufficiently provoked and would not have 'cooled off' by the time of the homicide, and that in fact a defendant was provoked and did not cool off." *Commonwealth v. Groome*.[1]

Insults & Arguments:

Commonwealth v. Groome: **Verbal insults and arguments**, even if obscene or hostile, cannot constitute sufficient provocation, for a reasonable person 'can be expected to control the feelings aroused' thereby. [2]

Commonwealth v. Masello: A heated oral argument that escalated during the course of the evening, without more, does not constitute adequate provocation".[3]

Excessive Force:

In ***Commonwealth v. Bianchi,*** the Court ruled that a victim's offensive use of physical force against a defendant will not necessarily constitute "adequate provocation," particularly where the defendant responds with excessive force. In this case the Court ruled that there was no adequate provocation where the victim called the defendant an obscenity and punched the defendant in face, where the defendant was weightlifter, outweighed the victim by over 170 pounds, was armed with a fully loaded weapon, and was violating a protective order in pursuing victim.[4]

In ***Commonwealth v. Rembiszewski***, the Court states "it is an extravagant suggestion that scratches by the wife could serve as provocation for a malice- free but ferocious attack by the defendant with a deadly instrument".[5]

Although insults will not suffice a verbal revelation of infidelity may:

A sudden oral revelation of infidelity may be sufficient provocation to reduce murder to manslaughter. But the revelation which is said to have precipitated the homicide must constitute a "sudden discovery" in order to reduce the degree of culpability.[6]

INVOLUNTARY MANSLAUGHTER

Involuntary Manslaughter

Involuntary manslaughter is an unlawful homicide, unintentionally caused:

(1) In the commission of an unlawful act, *malum in se* (*malumn in se* is Latin referring to an act that is "wrong in itself," in its very nature being illegal because it violates the natural, moral or public principles of a civilized society not just because a law was passed) , not amounting to a felony nor likely to endanger life,

or

(2) By an act which constitutes such a disregard of probable harmful consequences to another as to constitute wanton or reckless conduct.

[1] *Commonwealth v. Groome*, 435 Mass. 201, 220 (2001), quoting *Commonwealth v. McLeod, supra* at 738.
[2] *Commonwealth v. Groome,* quoting *Commonwealth v. Estremera*, 383 Mass. 382, 392 (1981)
[3] *Commonwealth v. Masello*, 428 Mass. 446, 449 (1998).
[4] *Commonwealth v. Bianchi*, 435 Mass. 316, 329 (2001).
[5] *Commonwealth v. Rembiszewski*, 363 Mass. 311, 321 (1973), *S.C.*, 391 Mass. 123 (1984).
[6] *Commonwealth v. Andrade,* 422 Mass. 236, 237-238, 661 N.E.2d 1308 (1996). *Commonwealth v. Brown,* 387 Mass. 220, 228, 439 N.E.2d 296 (1982).

C. 265 § 13	MANSLAUGHTER
Attorney Hanrahan's Note on Involuntary Manslaughter	**Involuntary Manslaughter** occurs when the offender has a conscious disregard for the potential consequences of his actions, such as removing a stop sign at a busy intersection resulting in a deadly crash. Another way that involuntary manslaughter may be committed is when someone dies during the commission of a battery, such as the offender punches the victim who falls back and hits his head and dies. The third prong of Second degree murder (an act which causes a plain and likelihood of death – see section on Murder) and involuntary manslaughter can be difficult to distinguish. The SJC has stated "A fine line distinguishes murder in the second degree based on third prong malice from the lesser offense of involuntary manslaughter."[1] The difference between murder based on third prong malice and involuntary manslaughter "lies in the degree of risk of physical harm that a reasonable person would recognize was created by particular conduct, based on what the defendant knew." "The risk for the purposes of third prong malice is that there was a plain and strong likelihood of death.... The risk that will satisfy the standard for ... involuntary manslaughter 'involves a high degree of likelihood that substantial harm will result to another.' "[2]
Examples of Involuntary Manslaughter	• Bar owner who blocked doors resulting in death when a fire broke out • Failing to report a fire resulting in death • Driving recklessly causing death • Assisting in a suicide • Distributing drugs resulting in an overdose • Participating in Russian Roulette game • Failing to Act: in some cases, particularly involving parents, people have been convicted for failing to act, such as withholding medical treatment.
Related Statutes, Case Law & Other Important Information for Involuntary Manslaughter	
Shooting into a crowd may be Murder or Manslaughter depending on circumstances	In the 2013 case of ***Commonwealth v. Horne,*** the SJC stated "in decisions considering the level of risk created by the discharge of a firearm that results in the killing of another, we have concluded that it is only when a defendant has reason to believe that he is firing in the direction of a person or crowd of people that his conduct creates nothing less than a plain and strong likelihood of death." However, the SJC further stated "we have, however, limited that principle to circumstances where the defendant knowingly fires a weapon at a person or crowd, concluding that firing a weapon near, but not directed toward, a specific person or persons "is wanton and reckless behavior that may supply an element of murder in the second degree or of involuntary manslaughter." In ***Commonwealth v. Jenks,*** "firing a pistol seven times in a crowded room is more than wanton and reckless conduct risking substantial harm; it is malicious conduct in the plainest sense" and thus murder would be an appropriate charge as opposed to manslaughter. In ***Commonwealth v. Braley,*** the Court ruled that "firing rifle multiple times, directed toward specific individuals, creates nothing less than plain and strong likelihood of death." **Compare the above cases with**: ***Commonwealth v. Hawkins***, 157 Mass. 551, 553 (1893) where defendant fired pistol into dimly lit street at night and hit someone over 200 feet away, wounding her, on facts found by jury, defendant would have been guilty of manslaughter had victim died.

MURDER & MANSLAUGHTER

[1] *Commonwealth v. Lyons,* 444 Mass. 289, 293 (2005).
[2] Commonwealth v. Horne, SJC (2013)

C. 265 § 13	MANSLAUGHTER
Failure to seek medical care during child birth	In the 2012 case of *Commonwealth v. Pugh,* the SJC overturned the defendant's manslaughter conviction which originated from the defendant's failure to obtain medical assistance during child birth wherein her baby was being delivered in the breach position. The baby died as a result. The SJC stated "imposing a broad and ill-defined duty on all women to summon medical intervention during childbirth would trench on their "protected liberty interest in refusing unwanted medical treatment. Moreover, such a duty is inchoate and would be highly susceptible to selective enforcement.
Related Statutes, Case Law & Other Important Information	
Venue	See notes under Murder section for venue issues related to homicide.
Manslaughter by Motor Vehicle	Chapter 265 § 13½ provides a specialized form of Manslaughter (by motor vehicle). See the Motor Vehicle Law section of this manual for more information.

C. 265 § 28	POISON; USE WITH INTENT TO KILL/INJURE
Elements	
1.	The defendant does one of the following:
2.	• Mingles poison with food, drink or medicine with intent to kill or injure another person, or • Willfully poisons any spring, well or reservoir of water with such intent.
Arrest Power, Penalties & Notes	
Power of Arrest	**Felony** – a police officer may effect a warrantless arrest for this offense provided he/she has probable cause that the suspect committed the offense.
Penalty	Imprisonment in the **state prison (F)** for life or for any term of years.
Related Statutes, Case Law & Other Important Information	
Foods Containing Foreign Injury Causing Substances **c. 270 § 8A**	Whoever sells, gives, or distributes to anyone candy or other food or foodstuffs containing a foreign substance, which is intended or may reasonably be expected to cause injury to a person eating the same, shall be punished as follows: **Penalty**: by imprisonment in the **state prison (F)** for not more than 5 years. **ARREST POWERS**: **Felony** – a police officer may effect an arrest for this offense committed in his/her presence or for an offense in the past, on probable cause.

ASSAULT & BATTERY

C. 265 § 13A	ASSAULT and ASSAULT & BATTERY
	Misdemeanor Elements
1.	Commit an **Assault** or an **Assault & Battery** (be sure to review definitions below)
2.	Upon another
	Felony Elements
1.	Commit an **Assault** or an **Assault and Battery**
2.	(i) Upon another and by such assault and battery causes **serious bodily injury**; (ii) Upon another who is **pregnant at the time of such assault and battery**, knowing or having reason to know that the person is pregnant; or (iii) Upon another who he knows has an **outstanding temporary or permanent vacate, restraining or no contact order** or judgment issued pursuant to chapter 208 §§ 18, 34B or 34C (divorce proceedings), chapter 209 §s 32 (paternity proceedings), chapter 209A §§ 3, 4 or 5 (domestic violence), or c. 209C §§ 15 or 20 (child support), **in effect against him at the time of such assault or assault and battery**. *Attorney Hanrahan's Note*: The law, as written, does not cover harassment prevention orders pursuant to chapter 258E.
Serious Bodily Injury	For the purposes of this section, **"serious bodily injury"** shall mean bodily injury that results in a permanent disfigurement, loss or impairment of a bodily function, limb or organ, or a substantial risk of death. In ***Commonwealth v. Marinho*** (2013), the SJC ruled that facial fractures resulting in double-vision for three to four months met the serious bodily injury definition even though medical reports indicated that the victim's vision would return to normal. In **Commonwealth v. Baro** (2008), punches and kicks to head resulting in broken bones and temporary loss of sight for one and one-half months constitutes "serious bodily injury."[1] In ***Commonwealth v. Jean-Pierre*** (2005), punches resulting in a broken jaw and several weeks of tube-feeding constitutes "serious bodily injury".[2] In ***Commonwealth v. Scott*** (2013), punches to the abdomen resulting in a lacerated liver did not amount to serious bodily injury because there was no evidence that the laceration impacted the function of the liver.

[1] Commonwealth v. Baro, 73 Mass.App.Ct. 218, 219-220 (2008).
[2] Commonwealth v. Jean-Pierre, 65 Mass.App.Ct. 162, 162, 164 (2005).

C. 265 § 13A	ASSAULT and ASSAULT & BATTERY
Pregnant Victim A&B elements[1]	The elements of aggravated assault and battery on a pregnant woman are: 1. The defendant committed a touching, however slight; 2. The defendant intended to engage in the touching; 3. The touching was harmful or offensive; 4. It was committed without justification or excuse; 5. The victim was pregnant at the time; 6. The defendant knew, or had reason to know, the victim was pregnant.
Arrest Power, Penalties & Notes	
Power of Arrest	**Misdemeanor** – there is no statutory authority granting powers of arrest for this misdemeanor version of this offense unless it involves a specialized form of A&B (e.g. involves domestic violence, victim is in a protected class, etc.). However, if the offense is committed in public, in the officer's presence, and is creating a **breach of the peace** an arrest would be lawful. **Felony** – In the case of a felony level A&B the officer would warrantless arrest powers upon probable cause.
Penalty	**Misdemeanor** - imprisonment for not more than 2½ years in a HOC or by a fine of not more than $1,000. **Felony** - imprisonment in the **state prison (F)** for not more than 5 years or in the HOC for not more than 2½ years, or by a fine of not more than $5,000, or by both such fine and imprisonment.
Attorney Hanrahan's Comment	An assault and battery is the most frequently encountered violent crimes and there are many variations of this offense. It is important that police officers understand the various forms of A&B because it often effects the authority to effect a warrantless arrest.
Related Statutes, Case Law & Other Important Information	
Two Theories of *Assault*	**Two Theories of *Assault* under Massachusetts common law:** attempted battery and threatened battery. [2] • **Attempted battery:** A conviction of assault under a theory of attempted battery requires the prosecution to prove that the defendant "intended to commit a battery, took some overt step toward accomplishing that intended battery, and came reasonably close to doing so." [3] • **Threatened Battery:** A conviction of assault under a theory of threatened battery requires the prosecution to prove that the defendant engaged in conduct that a reasonable person would recognize to be threatening, that the defendant intended to place the victim in fear of an imminent battery, and that the victim perceived the threat. [4] The victim need not actually be in fear, but must apprehend the risk of an imminent battery.[5]

[1] Massachusetts Superior Court Criminal Practice Jury Instructions (2. Ed. 2013)
[2] *Commonwealth v. Richards,* 363 Mass. 299, 303 (1973). Also see Commonwealth v. Henson, 357 Mass. 686, 692-693 (1970).
[3] *Commonwealth v. Melton,* 436 Mass. 291, 295 (2002).
[4] *Commonwealth v. Chambers,*57 Mass.App.Ct. 47, 49, 51 (2003); *Commonwealth v. Musgrave,* 38 Mass.App.Ct. 519, 523-524 (1995), *S. C.,* 421 Mass. 610 (1996) (adopting opinion of Appeals Court).
[5] *Commonwealth v. Chambers*

C. 265 § 13A	ASSAULT and ASSAULT & BATTERY
Victim does not have to be in Fear	The **attempted battery** branch of assault does not require that the victim was aware of or feared the attempted battery.[1] The **threatened battery** branch of assault requires that the victim was aware of the defendant's objectively menacing conduct. Some older decisions seem to suggest that under the second branch of assault the victim must have feared as well as perceived the threatened battery. This may have resulted from the inherent ambiguity of the term "apprehend," which may signify either. The SJC in *Commonwealth v. Chambers*, concluded that subjective fear is not an element of either branch.[2] Other recent decisions appear to be in accord.[3]
Battery without an Assault?	**Attorney Hanrahan's Note:** Anytime there is a battery there is an assault. The "assault" could take place simultaneously or even after the battery in an A&B situation. For instance, hitting someone from behind when they were not aware of the pending attack would still be an Assault & Battery offense, even though the victim was not threatened (threatened battery) until the actual battery took place. In short, a completed battery is also an assault.
Two Theories & Three Types of Batteries	**Three *Battery* Theories in Massachusetts**: There are three theories of Battery: Harmful battery, reckless battery, and offensive battery.[4] They all have different material elements; along with the three theories, there are two categories – Intentional and Reckless **Intentional Batteries**: 1. **Harmful battery:** any touching 'with such violence that bodily harm is likely to result.' " 2. **Offensive battery**: "an offensive touching" which is an "affront to the victim's personal integrity." In order to establish offensive battery, the Commonwealth need only prove "that the defendant, without justification or excuse, intentionally touched the victim, and that the touching, *however slight,* occurred without the victim's consent." For instance, tickling could be considered an "offensive battery" yet it would not qualify as "physical force" capable of causing pain or injury. The same could be said for spitting. It is unlikely that spitting would cause injury; despite this intentionally spitting on another would meet the elements of Assault & Battery under the Offensive battery theory.[5] **Reckless Batteries**: 3. **Reckless battery**: a "wilful, wanton, and reckless act resulting in personal injury to another." For instance, stage diving in a crowded nightclub resulting in the injury of someone whom the defendant landed on would be considered a battery under this theory, even if the defendant did not intend on touching the victim. **Note**: for reckless battery there must be injury. The injury does not have to be serious but it must be more than "trifling or transient." See *Com. v. Hamilton* example below. **Note on indirect touching**: Under the different theories of battery, the "touching may be ... indirect, as by setting in motion some force or instrumentality" that causes the victim to be touched, such as where a defendant fires a gunshot that strikes the victim or intentionally or recklessly drives his vehicle into a vehicle occupied by the victim. [6] **Note on Consent**: Where the touching is physically harmful, "consent is immaterial," but "a nonharmful touching is a battery only if there is no consent." [7]

[1] Commonwealth v. Slaney, 345 Mass. 135, 138-139, 185 N.E.2d 919, 922 (1962); Commonwealth v. Richards, 363 Mass. 299, 303, 293 N.E.2d 854, 857-858 (1973); Commonwealth v. Gorassi, 432 Mass. 244, 248, 733 N.E.2d 106, 110 (2000).
[2] *Commonwealth v. Chambers*, 57 Mass. App. Ct. at 48-52, 78' N.E.2d at 39-42.
[3] See Commonwealth v. Melton, 436 Mass. 291, 295 n.4, 763 N.E.2d 1092, 1096 n.4 (2002); Gorassi, 432 Mass. at 248-249, 733 N.E.2d at 110; Commonwealth v. Gordon, 407 Mass. 340, 349, 553 N.E.2d 915, 920 (1990); Slaney, 345 Mass. at 139-141, 18 at 922-923; Richards, 363 Mass. at 303-304, 293 N.E.2d
[4] *Commonwealth v. Colon*, 958 Mass.App.Ct. 8 (2011).
[5] *Commonwealth v. Colon*, 958 Mass.App.Ct. 8 (2011).
[6] *Commonwealth v. Dixon,* 34 Mass.App.Ct. 653, 654 (1993). See *Commonwealth v. Burno, supra* at 628 ("a battery could occur although no force was applied to a person directly"); *Commonwealth v. Stratton,* 114 Mass. 303, 305-306 (1873
[7] *Commonwealth v. Burke,* 390 Mass. at 481.

C. 265 § 13A	ASSAULT and ASSAULT & BATTERY
Transferred intent	The Commonwealth need only prove intent as to one of the intended victims and does not have to prove intent specifically directed at each of the actual victims. *Commonwealth v. Melton*, 436 Mass. 291, 299 n.11, 763 N.E.2d 1092, 1099 n.11 (2002). "It is a familiar rule that one who shoots, intending to hit A., and accidentally hits and injures B., is liable for an assault and battery on B." *Commonwealth v. Hawkins*, 157 Mass. 551, 553, 32 N.E. 862, 863 (1893).
A&B by reckless conduct example	The 2015 case of ***Commonwealth v. Hamilton*** is an excellent example of why it is important to understand the concept of A&B by reckless means. In this case an officer was placing the defendant under arrest after he was discovered using heroin in a public bathroom. The officer asked him where the needle was and Hamilton responded "in my back pocket." The needle was actually in his hand and when the officer went to handcuff him he was stuck with the needle. Hamilton was convicted of assault & battery by means of a syringe under the theory of recklessness.
Multiple Victims	Where the defendant assaults multiple victims in a single act, the defendant may be convicted of multiple counts of assault and, in the judge's discretion, given consecutive sentences.[1] Example: Firing gun into house with several residents could result in multiple convictions of assault with a dangerous weapon.
Assault with intent to Commit a Felony **c. 265 § 29**	Whoever assaults another **with intent to commit a felony** shall be punished as follows: **Penalty:** if the punishment of such assault was not covered under another statute in chapter 265 - imprisonment in the **state prison (F)** for not more than 10 years or by a fine of not more than $1,000 and imprisonment in jail for not more than 2½ years. **ARREST POWERS**: **Felony** – a police officer may effect an arrest for this offense committed in his/her presence or for an offense in the past, on probable cause.
A&B Domestic Violence	Chapter 265 § 13M provides a specific Assault and Assault & Battery charge involving people involved in intimate relationships. See the domestic violence section for more.
Specialized A&B	There are numerous specialized versions of A&B, such as A&B on an elder, on a child, on an incompetent person, for the purposes of collecting a loan, A&B upon police officer or public employee (including a public transportation operator), and so one (see later in this section). Also See the below forms of assault which are covered in other sections of this manual: Assault with Intent to Rape (c. 265 § 14) - see Sex Crimes section of this manual. Assault with intent to Rob or Steal (c. 265 § 18) – See Robbery Offense section of this manual.
A&B involving Dangerous Weapons	See the Assault with Weapons later in this section for Assault and Assault & Battery with weapons offenses.

[1] Commonwealth v. Dello Iacono, 20 Mass. App. Ct. 83, 89-90, 478 N.E.2d 144, 148-149 (1985) (firing gun into house with several residents).

C. 265 § 13A	ASSAULT and ASSAULT & BATTERY
Intimate A&B **c. 265 § 13M**	In 2014 the legislature enacted/modified Chapter 265 § 13M creating a new criminal offense. This offense punishes an offender who assaults or commits an assault and battery on a family or household member, but for the purposes of this statute the legislature narrowed down the definition of family or household member to persons who: (a) are or were married to one another; (b) having a child in common regardless of whether they have ever married or lived together; (c) are or have been in a substantive dating or engagement relationship Note: under this definition the legislature removed the relations by marriage and those just living in the same household. This law does not override chapter 209A. Chapter 209A can still be utilized, however c. 265 § 13M should be utilized if the persons involved are in an intimate type relationship. See the Domestic Violence section of the manual for more on the offense.
Causing injury physical exercise training programs **c. 265 § 40**	Whoever, having the direct management or direct control over the conduct of physical exercise as part of a course of study or training program at any public or private institution, agency or entity, willfully, wantonly and recklessly causes serious bodily injury to a person participating in a course of study or training program involving physical exercise, shall be punished as follows: **Penalty:** a fine of not more than $5,000 or by imprisonment in a jail or HOC for not more than 2½ years or both.
Engaging in unauthorized prize fighting **c. 265 § 9**	Whoever, (except as provided in c. 147 § 32 through 50 - laws dealing with boxing, MMA and similar sports), by previous appointment or arrangement, engages in a fight with another person shall be punished by imprisonment in the **state prison (F)** for not more than 10 years or by a fine of not more than $5,000.
Affray (common law offense)	The crime of affray originates from British common law. "An Affray is a publick offense to the terror of the King's subjects, and ... so called, because it affrighteth and maketh men afraid...." No less now than historically, affray is an offense against the public, an aggravated disturbance of the public peace that arises when two or more people fight in public and cause terror to those present.[1] Whether at common law, or by codification, in most jurisdictions **the essential ingredients of affray are**: (1) fighting by or between two or more persons, (2) in some public place, (3) so as to cause alarm to the public. Affray is defined in c. 277 § 39 as "fighting together of two or more persons in a public place to the terror of the persons lawfully there." In the 2013 case of ***Commonwealth v. Nee***, the Appeals Court ruled that the common law crime of affray is not limited to *willing participants*. In this case the defendant was convicted of affray after the defendant, and a group of his friends, attacked an off-duty police officer and two of his companions. **Attorney Hanrahan's Note:** Although chapter 277 § 39 defines affray the statute does not regulate the prohibited conduct. This chapter and section simply provides definitions for indictment language. For a detailed explanation of common law see the Overview section of this manual.

[1] Commonwealth v. Matthew Nee (2013).

C. 265 § 15A	A&B BY MEANS OF A DANGEROUS WEAPON
	Elements
1.	An Assault and Battery committed
2.	By means (i.e. by the use of) a Dangerous Weapon
	Arrest Power, Penalties & Notes
Power of Arrest	**Felony** – a police officer may effect a warrantless arrest for this offense provided he/she has probable cause that the suspect committed the offense.
Penalty	Imprisonment in the **state prison (F)** for not more than 10 years or by a fine of not more than $1,000 r imprisonment in jail for not more than 2½ years. For A&B D/W on an elderly see A&B Special Populations section for enhanced penalty.
Aggravated A&B with a Dangerous Weapon	The penalty shall be enhanced (as noted below) when the defendant: (i) by means of a dangerous weapon, commits an assault and battery upon another and by such assault and battery **causes serious bodily injury**; (ii) by means of a dangerous weapon, commits an assault and battery upon another who is **pregnant** at the time of such assault and battery, knowing or having reason to know that the person is pregnant; (iii) by means of a dangerous weapon, commits an assault and battery upon another who he knows has an outstanding temporary or permanent vacate, **restraining or no contact order** or judgment issued pursuant to section 18, section 34B or section 34C of chapter 208, section 32 of chapter 209, section 3, 4 or 5 of chapter 209A, or section 15 or 20 of chapter 209C, in effect against him at the time of such assault and battery; or (iv) **is 18 years of age or older and**, by means of a dangerous weapon, commits an assault and battery **upon a child under the age of 14**; **Penalty**: imprisonment in the state prison for not more than 15 years or in the house of correction for not more than 2½ years, or by a fine of not more than $10,000, or by both such fine and imprisonment. **Definition**: For the purposes of this section, "serious bodily injury" shall mean bodily injury which results in a permanent disfigurement, loss or impairment of a bodily function, limb or organ, or a substantial risk of death.
	Related Statutes, Case Law & Other Important Information
Assault and Battery	See section on weaponless Assault and Assault and Battery for discussion on the various ways of committing an assault and an assault and battery.
Dangerous Weapon	A dangerous weapon could be a weapon that is "inherently" dangerous such as a knife or a gun (also referred to as per se dangerous), or an object could be dangerous as used, such as steel toed shoe. The shoe is not dangerous per se but if used to kick someone in the head it would be deemed a dangerous weapon. The courts have found a wide range of objects to be dangerous weapons. **Per se:** Weapons regarded as dangerous per se such as firearms, daggers, stilettos and brass knuckles are instrumentalities "designed and constructed to produce death or great bodily harm," and are classified in this manner "because they are designed for the purpose of bodily assault or defense." *Commonwealth v. Appleby*, 380 Mass. at 303 (1980). In the 2002 case of *Commonwealth v. Lord*, the Court ruled that a mace-spraying device was

C. 265 § 15A	A&B BY MEANS OF A DANGEROUS WEAPON
	dangerous per se. Weapons which are dangerous per se will qualify for c. 265 § 15A convictions when used to commit an assault and a battery of any kind, and without a jury determination that the weapon was dangerous as used. [1] **Neutral Objects**: Weapons which are not dangerous per se, but which may be used in a dangerous fashion, may also be "dangerous weapons."When a "neutral object is in fact used to inflict serious injury it would clearly be a dangerous weapon"[2]. For instance, a chair is not typically a dangerous weapon but it could become one when used to strike someone over the head. **The Judge/Jury decides**: The SJC has stated that "the question whether a weapon is dangerous as used is always one for the fact finder". [3]
Examples of Cases Wherein non-inherently dangerous items were determined to be Dangerous	*Commonwealth v. Farrell,* (1948).A lighted cigarette was a dangerous weapon. *Commonwealth v. LeBlanc,* (1975) - an automobile door used to strike police officer was a dangerous weapon. *Commonwealth v. Tarrant,* (1974) – a kitchen-type knife and German shepherd dog may both be used as "dangerous weapons". *United States v. Loman,* walking stick used with enough force to break it was a dangerous weapon. *United States v. Johnson,* (4th Cir. 1963) – a chair brought down upon victim's head was a dangerous weapon. *Bennett v. State,* 237 Md. 212, 216, 205 A.2d 393 (1964)- a microphone cord tied around victim's neck, causing inability to speak and marks on throat was a dangerous weapon. Some others include: • natural gas • footwear (shod foot - jury decides if the type of shoe is actually a dangerous weapon)[4] • a dog[5] • an aerosol can[6] • Duct tape (when used to cover mouth)[7] Even Items that can't be wielded can be determined to be a weapon: "Pavement and the ocean may be dangerous weapons despite inability of individual "to possess the ocean [or pavement] or exercise authority over it in a traditional sense." [8]
The Human Body	Human teeth and parts of the human body have been deemed not be dangerous weapons.
Multiple Victims in a single Assault	Where the defendant assaults multiple victims in a single act, the defendant may be convicted of multiple counts of assault and, in the judge's discretion, given consecutive sentences. *Commonwealth v. Dello Iacono,* 20 Mass. App. Ct. 83, 89-90, 478 N.E.2d 144, 148-149 (1985) (firing gun into house with several residents).

[1] *Commonwealth v. Appleby*, 380 Mass. at 307 (1980).
[2] *Commonwealth v. Tarrant*, 367 Mass. 411, 416 n. 4, 326 N.E.2d 710 (1975).
[3] *Commonwealth v. Appleby*, 380 Mass. at 307 (1980).
[4] Commonwealth v. Marrero, 19 Mass.App.Ct. (1984).
[5] Commonwealth v. Tarrant, 367 Mass. 411 (1975).
[6] Commonwealth v. Barrett, 12 Mass.App.Ct. 1001 (1981).
[7] *Comm. v. Mattei*, 455 Mass. 840 (2010)
[8] Commonwealth v. Sexton, 425 Mass. 146 (1996). Also see Commonwealth v. Mattei, 455 Mass. 840 (2010).

C. 265 § 15A	A&B BY MEANS OF A DANGEROUS WEAPON
Simultaneous assault and property destruction	A single act may support simultaneous convictions of assault by means of a dangerous weapon upon the victim who was assaulted and of malicious destruction of property (G.L. c. 266, § 127) with respect to the area where the victim was standing (i.e. firing gun in order to damage bar and frighten bartender).[1]
Lesser Included Offense	Simple assault is a lesser included offense of assault with a dangerous weapon, but assault and battery is not. *A Juvenile v. Commonwealth*, 404 Mass. 1001, 533 N.E.2d 1312 (1989).
Assault (only) with a Dangerous Weapon **c. 265 § 15B**	When no actual contact is made with the dangerous weapon but a dangerous weapon is used to otherwise assault the victim, chapter 265 § 15B would be the appropriate charge. • An assault upon another • By means of a dangerous weapon **Penalty**: imprisonment in the **state prison (F)** for not more than five years or by a fine of not more than $1,000 dollars or imprisonment in jail for not more than 2½ years. **ARREST POWERS**: **Felony** – a police officer may effect an arrest for this offense committed in his/her presence or for an offense in the past, on probable cause. **NOTE**: For Assault w D/W on an elderly see A&B Special Populations section for enhanced penalty.
Assault by means of a Hypodermic Syringe **Chapter 265 § 15C**	An **assault** upon another, by means of: • A hypodermic syringe, • A hypodermic needle, or • Any instrument adapted for the administration of controlled or other substances by injection, **Penalty:** imprisonment in the **state prison (F)** for not more than 10 years or in the HOC for not more than 2½ years, or by a fine of not more than $1,000, or by both such fine and imprisonment. If there is an Assault and Battery by means of a syringe the penalty would be imprisonment in the **state prison (F)** for not more than 15 years or in the HOC for not more than 2½ years, or by a fine of not more than $5,000, or by both such fine and imprisonment. **ARREST POWERS**: **Felony** – a police officer may effect an arrest for this offense committed in his/her presence or for an offense in the past, on probable cause. **Attorney Hanrahan's Note:** If a syringe is used it is best to use this specific statute because the penalty is stronger than basic Assault and Assault and Battery by means of a Dangerous Weapon.
Armed Assault in a Dwelling	Chapter 265 § 18A punishes someone who enters a home while armed and assaults someone inside the home. See the B&E and Burglary section of this manual for more.

[1] *Commonwealth v. Domingue*, see Model Jury Instructions

C. 265 § 15E	ASSAULT AND BATTERY BY DISCHARGING A FIREARM
	Elements
1.	The defendant commits an assault and battery
2.	upon another by discharging a firearm, large capacity weapon, rifle, shotgun, sawed-off shotgun or machine gun, as defined in chapter 140 § 121
	Arrest Power, Penalties & Notes
Power of Arrest	**Felony** – a police officer may effect a warrantless arrest for this offense provided he/she has probable cause that the suspect committed the offense.
Penalty	Imprisonment in the state prison for not more than 20 years or by imprisonment in the house of correction for not more than 2 ½ years or by a fine of not more than $10,000, or by both such fine and imprisonment.
Attorney Hanrahan's Comment	This law was enacted in 2014 and it essentially enhances the penalty for an act that was already covered under the A&B Dangerous weapon law. If the A&B is committed by means of a firearm, as opposed to another dangerous weapon (e.g. a baseball bat) the perpetrator faces a much stiffer penalty. Dance Spider Dance!
	Related Statutes, Case Law & Other Important Information
Attempted A&B by means of a firearm c. 265 § 13F	Whoever attempts to commit an assault and battery upon another by means of discharging a firearm, large capacity weapon, rifle, shotgun, sawed-off shotgun or machine gun, as defined in section 121 of chapter 140, shall be punished by imprisonment in the state prison for not more than 15 years or by imprisonment in the house of correction for not more than 2 1/2 years or by a fine of not more than $10,000, or by both such fine and imprisonment.

C. 265 § 13D ASSAULT & BATTERY ON A POLICE OFFICER/PUBLIC EMPLOYEE

Elements

1.	The defendant commits an Assault & Battery (see A&B section for A&B requirements)
2.	Upon a Police Officer or Public Employee
3.	Knowing that the victim is a Police Officer/Public Employee[1]
4.	When the police officer/public servant is engaged in the performance of his duties at the time of such assault and battery.

Arrest Power, Penalties & Notes

Power of Arrest	**Misdemeanor** – there is no statutory authority granting warrantless powers of arrest for this offense. However, if the offense is committed in public, in the officer's presence, and is creating a **breach of the peace** an arrest would be lawful. **Misdemeanor – if the victim is a public employee who was operating a public transit** vehicle – statutory authority exists to execute an arrest without a warrant upon probable cause. **Felony (attempt to disarm)** – a police officer may effect a warrantless arrest for this offense provided he/she has probable cause that the suspect committed the offense.
Penalty	Imprisonment for not less than 90 days nor more than 2½ years in a HOC or by a fine of not less than $500 nor more than $5,000.
Disarming a Police Officer FELONY	In 2014, the legislature included an enhanced penalty for those who commit and A&B on a police officer that involves an attempt to disarm a police officer. The statute states: Whoever commits an offense under this section and which includes an attempt to disarm a police officer in the performance of the officer's duties shall be punished by imprisonment in the state prison for not more than 10 years or by a fine of not more than $1,000 and imprisonment in a jail or house of correction for not more than 2½ years.
Attorney Hanrahan's Comment	Although there are more elements to prove (i.e. the defendant knew he was assaulting a police officer etc.) the benefit of pursuing this charge, as opposed to a basic A&B offense, is that it carries a minimum sentence of 90 days. There is not a specific charge for *Assault* on a Police Officer, only A&B.

Related Statutes, Case Law & Other Important Information

Public Transportation Operator	In 2015 the legislature modified this statute to permit the warrantless arrest of a defendant who commits an assault & battery upon a public employee who is in the process of operating a public transportation vehicle.
Reckless A&B on a PO possible	Assault and battery on a public employee may be done recklessly as well as intentionally; an intent to strike the public employee is not required under the recklessness analysis. *Commonwealth v. Correia*, 50 Mass. App. Ct. 455, 457-458, 737 N.E.2d 1264, 1266 (2000).
Resisting Arrest	A person is not permitted to resist arrest even if the arrest is unlawful, however, if excessive force is used the person may resist.
Mutual Aid Response	In *Commonwealth v. McCrohan*, a police officer was "engaged in the performance of his duty" while responding in a neighboring town pursuant to a mutual aid agreement under G.L. c. 40, § 8G.[2]

[1] *Commonwealth v. Moore,* 36 Mass. App. Ct. at 461, 632 N.E.2d at 1238.
[2] *Commonwealth v. McCrohan,* 34 Mass. App. Ct. 277, 282, 610 N.E.2d 326, 330 (1993)

C. 265 § 13D	ASSAULT & BATTERY ON A POLICE OFFICER/PUBLIC EMPLOYEE
Transferred Intent Does not Apply	In *Commonwealth v. Rosario*, the defendant who inadvertently struck police officer while intending to strike someone else may only be convicted of lesser included offense of assault and battery.[1]
A&B on a Correction or Jail Officer	General Laws c. 127, § 38B sets forth the separate offense of assault or assault and battery on a correctional officer. Any person in the custody of a correctional facility, including any jail, house of correction or state prison, who commits an assault or an assault and battery upon an officer or other employee, any volunteer or employee of a contractor in any such facility or any duly authorized officer or other employee of any such facility engaged in the transportation of a prisoner for any lawful purpose shall be punished by imprisonment for not more than 2 and one-half years in a jail or house of correction or for not more than 10 years in a state prison **(Felony).** Such sentence shall begin from and after all sentences currently outstanding and unserved at the time of said assault or assault and battery. Attorney Hanrahan's Note: The statute does not define "jail." An argument could be made that a police holding facility is a "jail", as the statute clearly differentiates between a house of correction and a jail, and therefore a defendant who is confined to a jail and subsequently assaults an officer could potentially be charged with this felony. You should confer with your local DA before pursuing this avenue.

C. 265 § 13I	ASSAULT OR A&B ON EMT/HEALTH CARE PROVIDER
	Elements
1.	The defendant commits an Assault or an Assault and Battery upon:
2.	• an emergency medical technician, • an ambulance operator, • an ambulance attendant, • health care provider
3.	While said technician, operator, attendant, or provider is treating or transporting, in the line of duty, a person.
	Arrest Power, Penalties & Notes
Power of Arrest	**Misdemeanor** – there is no statutory authority granting warrantless powers of arrest for this offense. However, if the offense is committed in public, in the officer's presence, and is creating a **breach of the peace** an arrest would be lawful.
Penalty	Imprisonment in the HOC for not less than 90 days nor more than 2½ years, or by a fine of not less than $500 nor more than $5,000, or both.
	Related Statutes, Case Law & Other Important Information
Interfering with a Firefighter	Consider chapter 268 § 32A (Interfering with a Firefighter) which is a felony offense. See the section of this manual on Fire Related Laws.

ASSAULT & BATTERY OFFENSES

[1] *Commonwealth v. Rosario*, 13 Mass. App.Ct. 920, 920, 430 N.E.2d 866, 866 (1982)

C. 265 § 39 A&B FOR PURPOSE OF INTIMIDATION (HATE CRIMES)

Elements	
1.	• Commit an assault or a battery upon a person, or • Damage the real or personal property of a person
2.	With the intent to intimidate such person because of such person's race, color, religion, national origin, sexual orientation, gender identity, or disability.
Arrest Power, Penalties & Notes	
Power of Arrest	**Misdemeanor** – there is no statutory authority granting powers of arrest for this offense. However, if the offense is committed in public, in the officer's presence, and is creating a **breach of the peace** an arrest would be lawful. However, see below for felony charges (injury or weapons). **Felony** – a police officer may effect a warrantless arrest for this offense provided he/she has probable cause that the suspect committed the offense.
Penalties	**Basic Penalty**: A fine of not more than $5,000 or by imprisonment in a HOC for not more than 2½ years, or by both such fine and imprisonment. The court may also order restitution to the victim in any amount up to three times the value of property damage sustained by the owners of such property. **Enhanced penalty for Bodily Injury:** fine of not more than $10,000 dollars or by imprisonment in the **state prison (F)** for not more than five years, or by both such fine and imprisonment. **Enhanced Penalty for use of certain weapons**: if armed with a **firearm, rifle, shotgun, machine gun or assault weapon** imprisonment in the **state prison (F)** for not more than 10 years or in the HOC for not more than 2½ years.
Mandatory Diversity Program	A person convicted under the provisions of this section shall complete a diversity awareness program designed by the secretary of the executive office of public safety in consultation with the Massachusetts commission against discrimination and approved by the chief justice for administration and management of the trial court. A person so convicted shall complete such program prior to release from incarceration or prior to completion of the terms of probation, whichever is applicable.
Related Statutes, Case Law & Other Important Information	
Disability Defined	For the purposes of this section, the term **"disability"** shall have the same meaning as "handicap" as defined in subsection 17 of section one of c. one hundred and fifty-one B; provided, however, that for purposes of this section, the term "disability" shall not include any condition primarily resulting from the use of alcohol or a controlled substance as defined in section one of c. ninety-four C.
Bodily Injury Defined	For purposes of this section, **"bodily injury"** shall mean substantial impairment of the physical condition, including, but not limited to, any burn, fracture of any bone, subdural hematoma, injury to any internal organ, or any injury which occurs as the result of repeated harm to any bodily function or organ, including human skin.
Sole motivation not required	In the 2015 case of ***Commonwealth v. Kelly***, the SJC ruled that the victim's characteristics (in this case race) do not have to be the sole motivating factor for the assault.
Deprivation of Civil Rights	G.L. c. 265 § 37 states "no person, whether or not acting under color of law, shall by force or threat of force, willfully injure, intimidate or interfere with, or attempt to injure, intimidate or interfere with, or oppress or threaten any other person in the free exercise or enjoyment of any right or privilege secured to him by the constitution or laws of the commonwealth or by the constitution or laws of the United States."

C. 265 § 13C — ASSAULT AND BATTERY TO COLLECT LOAN

Elements

1.	The defendant commits an Assault & Battery upon another
2.	For the purpose of collecting a loan

Arrest Power, Penalties & Notes

Power of Arrest	**Felony** – a police officer may effect a warrantless arrest for this offense provided he/she has probable cause that the suspect committed the offense.
Penalty	1st **offense:** imprisonment in the **state prison (F)** for not less than 3 nor more than 5 years or by imprisonment for not more than 2½ years in a jail or HOC; **2nd or subsequent offense**: imprisonment in the **state prison (F)** for not less than 5 nor more than 10 years.
Attorney Hanrahan's Note	This law was intended to penalize "leg-breaking" as it pertains to "loan sharking" or illegal gambling. However, it is not restricted to illegal loans. An A&B committed for the purpose of collecting a legal loan would also apply.

Related Statutes, Case Law & Other Important Information

Criminal Usury	See chapter 271 § 49 – criminal usury (AKA loan sharking) in Gaming section of this manual.

C. 265 § 15 — ASSAULT WITH INTENT TO MURDER OR MAIM

Elements

1.	The defendant commits an assault on another with intent to:
2.	• Commit murder, or • Maim or disfigure (as described in the Mayhem offense - chapter 265 §14)
Case Law Elements	The SJC , in the 2009 case of ***Commonwealth v. Moran***, listed the following elements for the crime of assault with intent to murder: • An assault • With a specific intent to kill, and • Malice, in the context of this crime, is the absence of justification, excuse or mitigation.

Arrest Power, Penalties & Notes

Power of Arrest	**Felony** – a police officer may effect a warrantless arrest for this offense provided he/she has probable cause that the suspect committed the offense.
Penalty	Imprisonment in the **state prison (F)** for not more than 10 years or by a fine of not more than $1,000 and imprisonment in jail for not more than 2½ years.

C. 265 § 15	ASSAULT WITH INTENT TO MURDER OR MAIM
Attorney Hanrahan's Comment	It is important to remember that when you decide to charge someone with assault with intent to murder you must point to evidence that the defendant actually intended to murder the victim. Typically statements made such as "I am going to kill you" and actions which infer an intent to murder (i.e. stabbing someone in the throat) are important factors to document. There are a variety of offenses that all seem to overlap, such as Assault with intent to Murder or Maim, Assault with intent to Murder or Rob, Attempted Murder and so on. All have slightly different elements (i.e. Assault with intent to Murder or Rob the defendant must have been armed) and penalties. You should analyze the facts of your case to the various elements for the most appropriate charge. This offense requires specific intent to kill or maim.
Related Statutes, Case Law & Other Important Information	
Case Example	In ***Commonwealth v. Smith***, during a struggle with correction officers, the defendant, a prison inmate, yelled that he had "HIV" and that "he was going to hurt one of [them]." The defendant then bit one of the officers' forearm and said, "I'm HIV positive. I hope I kill you and your fucking kids." Another correction officer testified that, during the incident, the defendant said, "I'm gonna kill you all. . . . You're all gonna die. . . . I have AIDS." The grand jury also heard testimony from a police officer that Dr. Barbara Werner of the department of health had told him that it would be possible for a person infected with the HIV virus to transmit the disease by biting someone, if they broke the skin and their gums contained blood, as in the case of poor gums. Based on the defendant's admission that he had HIV; the absence of any evidence of justification, excuse, or mitigation; and the defendant's statement that he intended to kill the officer by infecting him with HIV, coupled with his biting of his arm, the jury had sufficient evidence to return an indictment of assault with intent to murder.
Assault with intent to Murder or Rob	Chapter 265 § 18(b) Whoever, being armed with a dangerous weapon, assaults another with intent to rob or murder shall be punished by imprisonment in the state prison for not more than 20 years. Whoever, being armed with a firearm, shotgun, rifle, machine gun or assault weapon assaults another with intent to rob or murder shall be punished by imprisonment in state prison for not less than 5 years and not more than 20 years.

C. 265 § 15D	STRANGULATION and SUFFOCATION
Elements	
1.	The defendant strangles or suffocates
2.	another person
Arrest Power, Penalties & Notes	
Power of Arrest	**Felony** – a police officer may effect a warrantless arrest for this offense provided he/she has probable cause that the suspect committed the offense.
6 hour hold	Chapter 276 § 42A requires that a defendant, who has attained the age of 18 years, who has been arrested for this offense not be admitted bail sooner than 6 hours after arrest. A family/romantic relationship is not required for this rule to apply.

C. 265 § 15D	STRANGULATION and SUFFOCATION
Penalty	**Standard Penalty** Imprisonment in state prison for not more than 5 years or in the house of correction for not more than 2 1/2 years, or by a fine of not more than $5,000, or by both such fine and imprisonment **Aggravated Strangulation or Suffocation Penalty** Imprisonment in state prison for not more than 10 years, or in the house of correction for not more than 2½ years, and by a fine of not more than $10,000. **Aggravating factors** • strangles or suffocates another person and by such strangulation or suffocation causes **serious bodily injury**; • strangles or suffocates another person, who is **pregnant** at the time of such strangulation or suffocation, knowing or having reason to know that the person is pregnant; • **subsequent conviction**: defendant is convicted of strangling or suffocating another person after having been previously convicted of the crime of strangling or suffocating another person under this section, or of a like offense in another state or the United States or a military, territorial or Indian tribal authority; or • **Protective order**: the defendant strangles or suffocates another person, with knowledge that the individual has an outstanding temporary or permanent vacate, restraining or no contact order or judgment issued under sections 18 or 34B of chapter 208, section 32 of chapter 209, sections 3, 4 or 5 of chapter 209A or sections 15 or 20 of chapter 209C, in effect against such person at the time the offense is committed.
DEFINITIONS FOR THIS STATUTE	
Strangulation	"Strangulation", the intentional interference of the normal breathing or circulation of blood by applying substantial pressure on the throat or neck of another.
Suffocation	"Suffocation", the intentional interference of the normal breathing or circulation of blood by blocking the nose or mouth of another.
Serious bodily injury	"Serious bodily injury", bodily injury that results in a permanent disfigurement, loss or impairment of a bodily function, limb or organ or creates a substantial risk of death.
OTHER INFORMATION	
Attempted murder	Depending on the circumstances, the crime of attempted murder may be considered.

C. 265 § 14	MAYHEM
SPECIFIC PARTS	
1.	The defendant with malicious intent to maim or disfigure does anyone of the following acts to another:
2.	• Cuts out or maims the **tongue** • Puts out or destroys an **eye** • Cuts or tears off an **ear** • Cuts, slits or mutilates the **nose or lip** • Cuts off or disables a **limb or member**
GENERAL DISFIGUREMENT/CRIPPLING	
1.	With intent to maim or disfigure
2.	The offender assaults another person with a dangerous weapon, substance or chemical, and by such assault does one of the following: • Disfigures the victim, • Cripples the victim • Inflicts serious or permanent physical injury upon the victim
PRIVY TO MAYHEM	
Privy or is Present and Assists	• Whoever is privy to the intent to commit mayhem, or • Whoever is present and aids in the commission of such crime • Is also guilty of Mayhem.
Arrest Power, Penalties & Notes	
Power of Arrest	**Felony** – a police officer may effect a warrantless arrest for this offense provided he/she has probable cause that the suspect committed the offense.
Penalty	Imprisonment in the **state prison (F)** for not more than twenty years or by a fine of not more than $1,000 and imprisonment in jail for not more than 2½ years.
Attorney Hanrahan's Comment	This is a specific intent offense, meaning the offender must have the intent to cause a permanent disfigurement etc.; however, intent to inflict serious bodily harm may be used to show this intent.
Related Statutes, Case Law & Other Important Information	
Intent Required but may be inferred	The specific intent "to maim or disfigure" can be established by the showing of an intent to inflict "some serious bodily injury."[1] Malice may be inferred from the act.[2] The crime of mayhem is a greatly aggravated form of assault and battery. The intent to commit assault and battery, even with a dangerous weapon, falls short of the intent required to commit mayhem.[3] Under Massachusetts case law, "[t]he mental state required for conviction of mayhem ... is satisfied by

[1] *Commonwealth v. Farrell*, 322 Mass. 606, 619, 78 N.E.2d 697 (1948).
[2] *Commonwealth v. Lamothe*, 343 Mass. 417, 419-420, 179 N.E.2d 245 (1961).
[3] *Commonwealth v. Hogan*, 7 Mass.App.Ct. 236 (1979).

C. 265 § 14	MAYHEM
	direct or inferential proof that the assault was intentional, unjustified, and made with the reasonable appreciation on the assailant's part that a disabling or disfiguring injury would result."[1] Where the government lacks direct evidence of the requisite intent, as it often does, "[s]pecific intent may be inferred from the nature of the injuries as well as [from] evidence that 'the injuries arose from a sustained or atrocious attack.' "[2]
Length of Attack may Reveal Intent	The length of the attack may infer the offender's intent. However, a prolonged attack is not a necessary legal prerequisite to a finding of mayhem where a specific intent to maim or disfigure can be inferred from the circumstances of the attack and the severity of the inflicted injuries. See *Commonwealth v. Hap Lay,* 63 Mass.App.Ct. 27, 36 (2005). Contrast with *Commonwealth v. Johnson,* 60 Mass.App.Ct. 243, 246-247 (2003) (evidence insufficient to support conviction of mayhem where entire attack lasted no more than ninety seconds, and injuries resulted from single strike to victim's head with beer bottle that was intact before impact).
Crippling may apply even if victim may heal.	In *Commonwealth v. Farrell,* the court held that an injury could amount to a "crippling" within the meaning of the statute "even though there may be complete recovery in time," and we believe that this also holds true for disablement of the limbs.[3]
ABDW	A defendant may be convicted of both mayhem and assault and battery by means of a dangerous weapon for the same act.[4]
Case samples	***Commonwealth v. St. Pierre,*** 377 Mass. 650, 651-653 (1979) (defendants slammed steel cell door against victim's arm numerous times). ***Commonwealth v. Farrell,*** 322 Mass. 606, 618-619 (1948) (defendant repeatedly slashed victim with razor blade and burned his initials into her skin). ***Commonwealth v. Lazarovich,*** 28 Mass.App.Ct. 147, 153-155 (1989) (defendant beat victim into unconsciousness, causing fractures, multiple contusions, and retinal hemorrhages). ***Commonwealth v. Taghizadeh,*** 28 Mass.App.Ct. 52, 58 & n. 3 (1989) (defendant threw highly concentrated nitric acid in victim's face). ***Commonwealth v. Tucceri,*** 9 Mass.App.Ct. 844, 845 (1980) (defendant repeatedly rubbed handfuls of dirt into victim's eyes). In the 2014 case of ***Commonwealth v. Forbes***, the defendant, Timothy FORBES, was serving as the assistant coach for his sons' sixth grade basketball team. The team lost the championship game and as the teams were lining up to shake hands FORBES attacked the coach of the opposing team with warning. FORBES began punching and kicking the victim as the victim attempted to retreat. FORBES then grabbed the victim is a bear hug, trapping his arms and leaving his defenseless, while others attempted to free the victim. While trapping the victim FORBES bit the victim's ear tearing off a chunk of cartilage and flesh and then spit it onto the gymnasium floor. The entire attack lasted approximately 20-25 seconds. The Court indicated that even a **short attack** could be deemed mayhem. Additionally, the court stated the entire ear does not have to be torn off, a **substantial portion** may be sufficient.
Privy	There is no case law directly on point regarding this but according to Black's law dictionary the term privy means "to have knowledge or information about a matter that is considered to be a secret." Seemingly the legislature intended to punish those who are merely aware that someone secretly intends to maim another person and presumably does nothing to prevent it.

[1] *Commonwealth v. Davis,* 10 Mass.App.Ct. 190, 196 (1980).
[2] *Commonwealth v. Sparks,* 42 Mass.App.Ct. 915, 916 (1997).
[3] *Commonwealth v. Farrell,* 322 Mass. at 619, 78 N.E.2d at 704-705.
[4] *Commonwealth v. Hogan,* 7 Mass.App.Ct. 236 (1979).

A&B ON SPECIAL POPULATIONS (CHILDREN, ELDERLY & DISABLED)

C. 265 § 13J	ASSAULT & BATTERY ON A CHILD
	Elements
1.	An Assault and Battery
2.	Upon a child under the age of 14
3.	Causing bodily injury or substantial bodily injury
Exception	See discussion on Parental Discipline below
	Arrest Power, Penalties & Notes
Power of Arrest	**Felony** – a police officer may effect a warrantless arrest for this offense provided he/she has probable cause that the suspect committed the offense.
Penalty	**Penalty for bodily injury:** by imprisonment in the **state prison (F)** for not more than 5 years or imprisonment in the HOC for not more than 2½ years. **Penalty for *substantial* bodily injury:** by imprisonment in the **state prison (F)** for not more than 15 years or imprisonment in the HOC for not more than 2½ years.
Attorney Hanrahan's Comment	If someone were to assault a child and the child did not suffer any injury the offense would be a misdemeanor under chapter 265 § 13A.
	Related Statutes, Case Law & Other Important Information
Definitions	For the purposes of this section, the following words shall, unless the context indicates otherwise, have the following meanings: **"Bodily injury",** substantial impairment of the physical condition including any burn, fracture of any bone, subdural hematoma (Note: generally speaking, a subdural hematoma refers to bleeding on the brain), injury to any internal organ, any injury which occurs as the result of repeated harm to any bodily function or organ including human skin or any physical condition which substantially imperils a child's health or welfare. **"Substantial bodily injury",** bodily injury which creates a permanent disfigurement, protracted loss or impairment of a function of a body member, limb or organ, or substantial risk of death.
Parental Discipline	In the 2015 decision of ***Commonwealth v. Dorvill***, the SJC ruled that a parent or guardian may not be subjected to criminal liability for the use of force against a minor child under the care and supervision of the parent or guardian, provided that: 1. the force used against the minor child is reasonable; 2. the force is reasonably related to the purpose of safeguarding or promoting the welfare of the minor, including the prevention or punishment of the minor's misconduct; and 3. the force used neither causes, nor creates a substantial risk of causing, physical harm (beyond fleeting pain or minor, transient marks), gross degradation, or severe mental distress. Note: in the 2015 case of *Com. v. Packer*, the Appeals court ruled that the parental discipline privilege may extent to stepparents acting in "loco parentis," that is in the role of a parent. Other sources of law that recognize the right of a parent to use physical discipline: Additionally, the **Practice Jury Instructions** (1st Supp. 2003) proposes a jury instruction stating that "[a] parent, or one acting in the position of a parent and who has assumed the responsibilities of a parent, may use reasonable force to discipline (his/her) minor child. However, a parent may not use excessive force as a means of discipline or chastisement."

C. 265 § 13J	ASSAULT & BATTERY ON A CHILD
	In the 1999 case of ***Cobble v. Commissioner of the Dept. of Social Servs***., the SJC ruled that a parent's spanking of a nine year old child with a leather belt, delivering one or two (and no more than five) blows to the child's fully clothed buttocks in a nonviolent and controlled manner and not in anger, and leaving slightly pink marks with no bruising, combined with an explanation of the reason for the punishment and expressions of caring, did not constitute abuse as defined in the regulations of the Department of Social Services as set out in 110 Code Mass. Regs. § 2.00 (1996). The court noted that the regulations, promulgated pursuant to authority granted in G. L. c. 119, § 51B(8), "clearly draw a line between permissible physical discipline and prohibited abuse," as the regulations clearly specify the types of physical injuries that may not be inflicted on children. [1206]
Abuse Reporting	In most cases wherein a child is assaulted a report must be filed with DCF pursuant to chapter 199 § 51A. See Juvenile Law Section of this manual for more.

C. 265 § 13J	PERMITTING INJURY/A&B ON A CHILD
There are essentially two different theories on which someone can commit this offense.	
WANTONLY & RECKLESSLY PERMITTING BODILY INJURY TO A CHILD Elements	
1.	The offender had care & custody of the child (see discussion below)
2.	The child is under the age of 14 years
3.	The child suffered Bodily Injury or Substantial Bodily Injury
4.	The offender wantonly and recklessly permitted the injury to occur
WANTONLY & RECKLESSLY PERMITTING *ANOTHER TO COMMIT AN A&B* ON A CHILD Elements	
1.	The offender had care & custody of the child (see discussion below)
2.	The child is under the age of 14 years
3.	The child suffered Bodily Injury or Substantial Bodily Injury
4.	The defendant wantonly or recklessly permitted another to cause injury to the child by touching him/her without right to do so.
Arrest Power, Penalties & Notes	
Power of Arrest	**If the victim suffers bodily injury - Misdemeanor** – there is no statutory authority granting warrantless powers of arrest for this offense. However, if the offense is committed in public, in the officer's presence, and is creating a **breach of the peace** an arrest would be lawful. **If the victim suffers *substantial* bodily injury - Felony** – a police officer may effect a warrantless arrest for this offense provided he/she has probable cause that the suspect committed the offense.
Penalty	**Penalty for bodily Injury:** imprisonment for not more than 2½ years in the HOC. **Penalty for *substantial* bodily Injury:** imprisonment in the **state prison (F)** for not more than 5 years, or by imprisonment in a jail or HOC for not more than 2½ years

[1206] *Cobble v. Commissioner* of the Dept. of Social Servs., 430 Mass. 395 (1999)

C. 265 § 13J	PERMITTING INJURY/A&B ON A CHILD
Attorney Hanrahan's Comment	This law is designed to punish caregivers who fail to protect the children within their care whether from other people or from dangerous situations.
Related Statutes, Case Law & Other Important Information	
Care & Custody	Persons who have care and custody may include a parent, guardian, employee of a home or institution or any other person with equivalent supervision or care of a child, whether the supervision temporary or permanent.[1207]
Wantonly or Recklessly	It is not enough to prove that the defendant acted negligently — that is, in a manner that a reasonably careful person would not. It must be shown that the defendant's actions went beyond mere negligence and amounted to recklessness. The defendant acted recklessly if he/she knew, or should have known, that his/her actions were (or failure to act was) very likely to result in bodily harm to the victim but he/she ran that risk and went ahead anyway or failed to act anyway.[1208] It is not necessary that the defendant intended that the victim be harmed or that he/she foresaw the harm that resulted. If the defendant actually realized in advance that his/her conduct was very likely to result in bodily injury to the victim and decided to run that risk, such conduct would of course be reckless. But even if he/she was not conscious of the serious danger that was inherent in such conduct, it is still reckless conduct if a reasonable person, under the circumstances as they were known to the defendant, would have recognized that such actions were so dangerous that it was very likely that they would result in bodily harm to the victim.
Wantonly or Recklessly Permitting Death?	Case law indicates that death not does qualify as bodily injury but the actions which lead to death would most likely qualify. In *Commonwealth v. Chapman*, in a case wherein a baby died when left alone in a bathtub, the SJC ruled that the injury (asphyxiation) amounted to substantial bodily injury which lead to the death.
Definitions	For the purposes of this section, the following words shall, unless the context indicates otherwise, have the following meanings: **"Bodily injury",** substantial impairment of the physical condition including any burn, fracture of any bone, subdural hematoma (Note: generally speaking, a subdural hematoma refers to bleeding on the brain), injury to any internal organ, any injury which occurs as the result of repeated harm to any bodily function or <u>organ including human skin</u> or any physical condition which substantially imperils a child's health or welfare. **"Substantial bodily injury",** bodily injury which creates a permanent disfigurement, protracted loss or impairment of a function of a body member, limb or organ, or substantial risk of death.
Unconfirmed Abuser	It is possible to convict a defendant who has care and custody of a child under this offense even if it cannot be proven who caused the injury. In *Commonwealth v. Rodriques*, the mother of an infant who suffered physical abuse resulting in multiple fractures was convicted of this offense even though it was not certain whether the mother or her boyfriend, the only two people who had custody of the child, inflicted the abuse.[1209]

[1207] Model Jury Instructions May 2011
[1208] *Commonwealth v. Ford*, 424 Mass. 709, 711, 677 N.E.2d 1149, 1151 (1997) also see Model Jury Instructions May 2011
[1209] *Commonwealth v. Rodriques*, 78 Mass.App.Ct. 515 (2011).

C. 265 § 13L RECKLESS ENDANGERMENT TO A CHILD

Engages in Conduct Elements	
1.	Wantonly or recklessly
2.	**Engages in conduct**
3.	That creates a substantial **risk** of: a. serious bodily injury or b. sexual abuse
4.	To a child under the age of 18 years
Fails to Act Elements	
1.	Wantonly or recklessly
2.	**Fails to take reasonable steps** to alleviate a substantial **risk** of serious bodily injury or sexual abuse to a child under 18 years
3.	Where there is a duty to act.
Arrest Power, Penalties & Notes	
Power of Arrest	**Misdemeanor** – there is no statutory authority granting warrantless powers of arrest for this offense. However, if the offense is committed in public, in the officer's presence, and is creating a **breach of the peace** an arrest would be lawful.
Penalty	Imprisonment in the HOC for not more than 2½ years.
Attorney Hanrahan's Comment	What is the difference between this offense and c. 265 § 13J? There are few important distinctions. First, unlike § 13J, this offense does not require that the child actually become injured, only that the child was at **risk**. Additionally, this offense covers sexual abuse, § 13J only covers physical injury. For instance, a daycare worker who leaves a young child with a known sex offender with a history of sexually abusing children would most likely violate this offense. In most cases, § 13J would be a better offense to utilize (if the elements are met) because § 13J has the potential for a felony charge (see § 13J above for more).
Related Statutes, Case Law & Other Important Information	
Wanton & Reckless	For the purposes of this section, **wanton or reckless behavior** occurs when a person is aware of and consciously disregards a substantial and unjustifiable risk that his acts, or failure to act (where there is a duty to act), would result in serious bodily injury or sexual abuse to a child. The risk must be of such nature and degree that disregard of the risk constitutes a gross deviation from the standard of conduct that a reasonable person would observe in the situation.
Case Example	In *Commonwealth v. Hendricks* (2008), the defendant was convicted of this offense when he was involved in a high speed police chase with his 3 year old child in his car.

C. 265 § 13L	RECKLESS ENDANGERMENT TO A CHILD
Duty to Act	Legal custody of a child does not absolve every other caretaker of criminal liability for their own acts related to that child. In ***Commonwealth v. Figueroa*** (2013), the mother of the infant victim was only 14 years old and lived under the custody of her (the 14 year old girl's) mother (i.e. grandmother). Grandmother was found to have a duty to act (seek medical treatment for an infant who was intentionally dropped on his head onto a hard tile floor) and thus was convicted under this statute.
Serious Bodily Injury	Bodily injury which results in a permanent disfigurement, protracted loss or impairment of a bodily function, limb or organ, or substantial risk of death.
Sexual Abuse	An indecent assault and battery on a child under 14 (c. 265 § 13B); indecent assault and battery on a person age 14 or over (c. 265 § 13H); rape (c. 265 § 22); rape of a child under 16 with (c. 265 § 22A); rape and abuse of a child (c. 265 § 23); assault with intent to commit rape (c. 265 § 24); and assault of a child with intent to commit rape (c. 265 § 24B).
Lesser included Offenses	This offense is a lesser included offense of chapter § 13J (the failure to act version of the offense).[1210]
DCF report	In most cases a mandatory reporting to DCF will likely be required.

C. 265 § 44	COERCION OF CHILD UNDER 18 INTO CRIMINAL CONSPIRACY STREET GANG INITIATION (BEAT-INS)
	Elements
1.	The defendant commits an assault and battery
2.	On a child under the age of 18
3.	For the purpose of causing or coercing such child to join or participate in a criminal conspiracy in violation of c. 274 § 7 (general conspiracy statute), including but not limited to: • A criminal street gang or • Other organization of three or more persons which has a common name, identifying sign or symbol and whose members individually or collectively engage in criminal activity.
	Arrest Power, Penalties & Notes
Power of Arrest	**Felony** – a police officer may effect a warrantless arrest for this offense provided he/she has probable cause that the suspect committed the offense.
Penalty	**1st offense**: imprisonment in the **state prison (F)** for not less than 3 nor more than 5 years or by imprisonment in the HOC for not more than 2½ years; **2nd or subsequent offense**: imprisonment in the **state prison (F)** for not less than 5 nor more than 10 years.

[1210] *Commonwealth v. Roderiques. 462 mass. 415 (2012.)*

C. 265 § 13K	A&B ON AN ELDER OR DISABLED
	Elements
1.	An Assault and Battery upon
2.	• An elder (person aged 60 or older), or • Person with a disability (see definition below)
	Arrest Power, Penalties & Notes
Power of Arrest	**Felony** – a police officer may effect a warrantless arrest for this offense provided he/she has probable cause that the suspect committed the offense.
Penalty	**No injury** - imprisonment in the **state prison (F)** for not more than 3 years or by imprisonment in a HOC for not more than 2½ years, or by a fine of not more than $1,000, or both such fine and imprisonment. **Causing Bodily Injury**: imprisonment in the **state prison (F)** for not more than 5 years or in the HOC for not more than 2½ years or by a fine of not more than $1,000 or by both such fine and imprisonment. **Causing Serious Bodily Injury**: imprisonment in the **state prison (F)** for not more than 10 years or in the HOC for not more than 2½ years or by a fine of not more than $5,000 or by both such fine and imprisonment.
	Related Statutes, Case Law & Other Important Information
Bodily injury	Substantial impairment of the physical condition, including, but not limited to, any burn, fracture of any bone, subdural hematoma (bleeding on the brain), injury to any internal organ, or any injury which occurs as the result of repeated harm to any bodily function or organ, including human skin.
Serious bodily injury	Bodily injury which results in a permanent disfigurement, protracted loss or impairment of a bodily function, limb or organ, or substantial risk of death.
Person with disability	A person with a permanent or long-term physical or mental impairment that prevents or restricts the individual's ability to provide for his or her own care or protection.
A&B on a person with an Intellectual Disability	General Laws c. 265, § 13F also sets forth the separate offense of assault and battery on a person with an intellectual disability; "Whoever commits an assault and battery on a person with an intellectual disability knowing such person to have an intellectual disability shall for the first offense be punished by imprisonment in a house of correction for not more than two and one-half years or by imprisonment in the state prison (**Felony**) for not more than 5 years.
Assault with a Dangerous Weapon	Chapter 265 § 15B provides for an enhanced penalty to those who assault (no battery required) an elder (60 or older) with a dangerous weapon. **Penalty**: imprisonment in the **state prison (F)** for not more than 5 years or by a fine of not more than $1,000 or imprisonment in jail for not more than 2½ years. **2nd or subsequent**: imprisonment for not less than two years
Assault & battery by means of a Dangerous Weapon	Chapter 265 § 15A provides for an enhanced penalty to those who commit assault and battery upon an elder (60 or older) with a dangerous weapon. **Penalty:** imprisonment in the **state prison (F)** for not more than 10 years or by a fine of not more than $1,000 or imprisonment in jail for not more than 2½ years. **2nd or subsequent**: imprisonment for **not less than 2 years**.

C. 265 § 13K	CARETAKER COMMITS OR PERMITS ABUSE/MISTREATMENT/NEGLECT (ELDER OR DISABLED)
Elements	
1.	Being a caretaker of an elder (age 60 or older) or person with a disability
2.	The defendant wantonly or recklessly
3.	• Commits, or • Permits another to commit
4.	Abuse, neglect or mistreatment upon such elder or person with a disability
Exception	**Note**: Conduct shall not be construed to be wanton or reckless conduct under this section if directed by a competent elder or person with a disability, or for the sole reason that, in lieu of medical treatment, an elder or person with a disability is being furnished or relies upon treatment by spiritual means through prayer if such treatment is in accordance with the tenets and practices of the established religious tradition of such elder or person with a disability, and is provided at the direction of such elder or person with a disability, who shall be competent, or pursuant to the direction of a person who is properly designated a health care proxy under c. two hundred and one D.
Arrest Power, Penalties & Notes	
Power of Arrest	**Felony** – a police officer may effect a warrantless arrest for this offense provided he/she has probable cause that the suspect committed the offense.
Penalty	**Basic Penalty**: Imprisonment in the **state prison (F)** for not more than 3 years, or imprisonment in the HOC for not more than 2½ years, or by a fine of not more than $5,000, or by both such fine and imprisonment. **Causing Serious Bodily Injury** - imprisonment in the **state prison (F)** for not more than 10 years or by imprisonment in the HOC for not more than 2½ years or by a fine of not more than $10,000 or by both such fine and imprisonment.
Definitions for the Purposes of this Section	
Abuse	Physical contact which either harms or creates a substantial likelihood of harm.
Bodily injury	Substantial impairment of the physical condition, including, but not limited to, any burn, fracture of any bone, subdural hematoma, injury to any internal organ, or any injury which occurs as the result of repeated harm to any bodily function or organ, including human skin.
Caretaker	A person with responsibility for the care of an elder or person with a disability, which responsibility may arise as the result of a family relationship, or by a fiduciary duty imposed by law, or by a voluntary or contractual duty undertaken on behalf of such elder or person with a disability. A person may be found to be a caretaker under this section only if a reasonable person would believe that such person's failure to fulfill such responsibility would adversely affect the physical health of such elder or person with a disability. Minor children and adults adjudicated incompetent by a court of law may not be deemed to be caretakers under this section. (i) "**Responsibility arising from a family relationship**", it may be inferred that a husband, wife, son, daughter, brother, sister, or other relative of an elder or person with a disability is a caretaker if the person has provided primary and substantial assistance for the care of the elder

C. 265 § 13K	CARETAKER COMMITS OR PERMITS ABUSE/MISTREATMENT/NEGLECT (ELDER OR DISABLED)
	or person with a disability as would lead a reasonable person to believe that failure to provide such care would adversely affect the physical health of the elder or person with a disability. (ii) "**Responsibility arising from a fiduciary duty imposed by law",** it may be inferred that the following persons are caretakers of an elder or person with a disability to the extent that they are legally required to apply the assets of the estate of the elder or person with a disability to provide the necessities essential for the physical health of the elder or person with a disability: (i) a guardian of the person or assets of an elder or person with a disability; (ii) the conservator of an elder or person with a disability, appointed by the probate court pursuant to c. two hundred and one; and (iii) an attorney-in-fact holding a power of attorney or durable power of attorney pursuant to c. two hundred and one B. (iii) **"Responsibility arising from a contractual duty"**, it may be inferred that a person who receives monetary or personal benefit or gain as a result of a bargained-for agreement to be responsible for providing primary and substantial assistance for the care of an elder or person with a disability is a caretaker. (iv) **"Responsibility arising out of the voluntary assumption of the duties of caretaker"**, it may be inferred that a person who has voluntarily assumed responsibility for providing primary and substantial assistance for the care of an elder or person with a disability is a caretaker if the person's conduct would lead a reasonable person to believe that failure to provide such care would adversely affect the physical health of the elder or person with a disability, and at least one of the following criteria is met: (i) the person is living in the household of the elder or person with a disability, or present in the household on a regular basis; or (ii) the person would have reason to believe, as a result of the actions, statements or behavior of the elder or person with a disability, that he is being relied upon for providing primary and substantial assistance for physical care.
Mistreatment	The use of medications or treatments, isolation, or physical or chemical restraints which harms or creates a substantial likelihood of harm.
Neglect	The failure to provide treatment or services necessary to maintain health and safety and which either harms or creates a substantial likelihood of harm.
Person with disability	A person with a permanent or long-term physical or mental impairment that prevents or restricts the individual's ability to provide for his or her own care or protection.
Serious bodily injury	Bodily injury which results in a permanent disfigurement, protracted loss or impairment of a bodily function, limb or organ, or substantial risk of death.

C. 19A § 15	ELDER ABUSE: MANDATORY REPORTING
1.	A mandated reporter
2.	Who has **reasonable cause** to believe
3.	That an elderly person is suffering from or has died as a result of abuse,
4.	Shall immediately make a verbal report or cause a report to be made to the Department of Elder Affairs or its designated agency and file written notice within 48 hours.

Arrest Power, Penalties & Notes

Power of Arrest	There is no power of arrest for failing to report elder abuse.
Penalty	A fine of not more than $1,000.
Attorney Hanrahan's Comment	Most police officers are aware of the reporting requirements when they encounter a child who has been abused/neglected but many officers, inadvertently, overlook the reporting requirements when it comes to abused/neglected/exploited elders.

Related Statutes, Case Law & Other Important Information

Laws that offer additional Penalties	Many statutes offer enhanced penalties when the victim is an elder (typically 60 years or older). Specifically, chapter 265 § 15A (A&B DW) and 265 § 15B (A&B) create additional penalties for elder victims. Chapter 265 § 13K specifically protects elders and disabled persons from abuse.

Mandated Reporters	Physician	Nurse	**Policeman**	Coroner	Executive director of a licensed home health agency or executive director of a homemaker service agency
	Physician assistant	Family counselor	Firefighters & EMTs	Registered physical therapist &	
	Medical intern	Probation officer	Director of a Council on Aging	Registered occupational therapist	Outreach worker employed by a council on aging
	Dentist	Social worker	Psychologist	Podiatrists & Osteopath	Manager of an assisted living residence

Definitions for elder abuse statutes: chapter 19A § 14

Abuse	An **Act or Omission** which results in serious physical or emotional injury to an elderly person or financial exploitation of an elderly person; or the failure, inability or resistance of an elderly person to provide for him one or more of the necessities essential for physical and emotional well-being without which the elderly person would be unable to safely remain in the community; provided, however, that no person shall be considered to be abused or neglected for the sole reason that such person is being furnished or relies upon treatment in accordance with the tenets and teachings of a church or religious denomination by a duly accredited practitioner thereof.
Caretaker	The person responsible for the care of an elderly person, which responsibility may arise as the result of a family relationship, or by a voluntary or contractual duty undertaken on behalf of an elderly person, or may arise by a fiduciary duty imposed by law.
Conservator	A person who is appointed to manage the estate of a person.
Elderly person	An individual who is **sixty years of age or over**.

C. 19A § 15	ELDER ABUSE: MANDATORY REPORTING
Financial exploitation	An act or omission by another person, which causes a substantial monetary or property loss to an elderly person, or causes a substantial monetary or property gain to the other person, which gain would otherwise benefit the elderly person but for the act or omission of such other person; provided, however, that such an act or omission shall not be construed as financial exploitation if the elderly person has knowingly consented to such act or omission unless such consent is a consequence of misrepresentation, undue influence, coercion or threat of force by such other person; and, provided further, that financial exploitation shall not be construed to interfere with or prohibit a bona fide gift by an elderly person or to apply to any act or practice in the conduct of any trade or commerce declared unlawful by chapter 93A § 2.
Contacts	Elder Abuse Hotline: (800) 882-2003; Elder Information Hotline: (800) 922-2275
Disabled Abuse	If you have information that a disabled person is being abused it should be reported to the Disabled Persons Protection Commission (800) 426-9009. See chapter 19 § 5-13.
Child Abuse Reporting	See Juvenile Section of this Manual for child abuse reporting requirements.

DOMESTIC LAWS, PROTECTIVE ORDERS & FAMILY SUPPORT

Domestic Violence & Restraining Orders (209A)

Overview: Chapter 209A was designed to protect victims of domestic violence. This law provides protection to victims of domestic violence primarily by way of protective orders. The victim of abuse can apply for a protective order which will provide criminal sanctions on the defendant if he/she violates the provisions of the order. This law also provides the police warrantless arrest powers that they would not normally have in non-domestic abuse situations (i.e. an A&B involving domestic violence would be arrestable without a warrant even though it typically would not be in non-domestic situations). In addition to granting additional arrest powers the law also grants additional responsibilities when it comes to domestic violence, such as ensuring that the victim is safe.

This section also frequently references the **Massachusetts Domestic Violence Enforcement Guidelines**. Although these Guidelines are not necessarily "the law" the policy was established pursuant to Section 403 of the Acts of 1990. Pursuant to Section 15 of Chapter 403 of the Acts of 1990, law enforcement agencies SHALL adopt this policy or establish and implement specific operational guidelines consistent with the provisions of this policy.

C.209A § 1	DOMESTIC VIOLENCE LAW DEFINITIONS
	FAMILY OR HOUSEHOLD MEMBERS
Statutorily Definition of *Family or household members*	Chapter 209A is designed to protect persons who are family or household members from abuse. The statute protects persons who: (a) are or were married to one another; (b) are or were residing together in the same household; (c) are or were related by blood or marriage; (d) having a child in common regardless of whether they have ever married or lived together; (e) are or have been in a substantive dating or engagement relationship, which shall be adjudged by district, probate or Boston municipal courts consideration of the following factors: (1) the length of time of the relationship; (2) the type of relationship; (3) the frequency of interaction between the parties; and (4) if the relationship has been terminated by either person, the length of time elapsed since the termination of the relationship.
Intimate Violence **c. 265 § 13M**	In 2014 the legislature enacted/modified Chapter 265 § 13M creating a new criminal offense. This offense punishes an offender who assaults or commits an assault and battery on a family or household member, but for the purposes of this statute the legislature narrowed down the definition of family or household member to persons who: (a) are or were married to one another; (b) having a child in common regardless of whether they have ever married or lived together; (c) are or have been in a substantive dating or engagement relationship, which shall be adjudged by district, probate or Boston municipal courts consideration of the following factors: (1) the length of time of the relationship; (2) the type of relationship; (3) the frequency of interaction between the parties; and

C.209A § 1	DOMESTIC VIOLENCE LAW DEFINITIONS
	(4) if the relationship has been terminated by either person, the length of time elapsed since the termination of the relationship. Note: under this definition the legislature removed the relations by marriage and those just living in the same household. This law does not override chapter 209A. Chapter 209A can still be utilized, however c. 265 § 13M should be utilized if the persons involved are in an intimate type relationship. See this offense later in this section.
Family Members **Expanded under 209A**	In 2001 a civil case, ***Turner v. Lewis***, involving the application for a 209A restraining order was decided by the SJC. In *Turner*, the paternal grandmother of a ten year old child, whom she was raising, was assaulted by the child's drug addicted mother. The father of child and the mother of the child were never married. The grandmother sought a restraining order against the mother (her son's girlfriend) and was denied for lack of a "blood relationship." The grandmother appealed and the case was eventually heard by the SJC. The SJC determined that the two *were* related by "blood." "Here we conclude that the parties are related by blood." The paternal grandmother, through her son, is "related by blood" to the child. Likewise, the child and her mother are "related by blood." Thus, the child is "related by blood" to both parties, making the mother and grandmother "related by blood" through that child."
Household Members **refined under 209A**	In the 2014 case of ***Silva v. Carmel***, the SJC indicated that people who live together, but are not in a family like relationship, do not qualify as "household members" within the meaning of G.L. 209A § 1. The SJC stated "residing in the same household must be interpreted in the context of the statute's other definitions of family or household members which include people who are or have been married, have children together, are related by blood, or have been in a substantive dating or engagement relationship." In this case the two parties were residing together in a state-licensed residential facility that serves adults with intellectual disabilities. **Attorney Hanrahan's note**: Some people have interpreted this decision very narrowly, in that it only applies to people living in a state run facility. The rational the SJC uses would seem to apply more broadly, perhaps to college roommates, non-intimate roommates, and so on. Check with your local DA's office to see how they want your agency to proceed. Other cases worth noting: In ***Aguilar v. Hernandez-Mendez***, the girlfriend of the defendant's father and the defendant were deemed household members.[1211] In ***Sorgman v. Sorgman,*** the unadopted stepdaughter had the requisite relationship to mother's former husband to seek abuse prevention order against him.[1212]
Substantive Dating Relationship	In the 2004 case of ***C.O. v. M.M***, the SJC denied an abuse prevention order where the defendant, a 17 year old, offered to drive a 15 year old female classmate home from school and, along the way, stopped at his house, invited the young woman inside, and then forcibly sexually assaulted her in his bedroom. There was some evidence that the two "went out" but the extent of the relationship was unclear. In denying the order the SJC explained that the law requires a "substantive dating relationship." Note: Today a Harassment Prevention Order could be utilized. Substantive Dating Relationship includes relationships involving an individual or individuals who identify as gay, lesbian, bisexual or transgender.[1213] In ***Commonwealth v. Compton*** (2013), the SJC ruled that it is possible to establish a substantive dating relationship by way of electronic communication (i.e. Facebook, Skype, email, etc.).
Harassment Prevention	In 2010, the Legislature enacted Chapter 258E which now protects those who are harassed (similar to abuse) in non-family type relationships. See Harassment Prevention section.

[1211] *Aguilar v. Hernandez-Mendez*, 66 Mass.app.Ct. 367, 368-369 (2006).
[1212] *Sorgman v. Sorgman*, 49 Mass.App.Ct. 416, 417-418 (2000).
[1213] According to the 2009 Massachusetts Domestic Violence Enforcement Guidelines

C.209A § 1	DOMESTIC VIOLENCE LAW DEFINITIONS
	ABUSE DEFINITIONS
Statutorily Definition of *Abuse*	The occurrence of one or more of the following acts between **family or household members**: (a) attempting to cause or causing physical harm; (b) placing another in fear of imminent serious physical harm; (c) causing another to engage involuntarily in sexual relations by force, threat or duress. **Attorney Hanrahan's Note**: There are certain criminal offenses that are often associated with *Abuse* for the purpose of chapter 209A. For instance, assault and assault & battery are the most common forms of abuse under 209A. However, abuse can consist of other conduct which is not in and of itself a criminal offense (see notes that follow). Additionally, the crimes of stalking and witness intimidation are often present in the domestic violence context (these offenses are covered in other sections of this manual). Case Law Note: In ***Commonwealth v. Compton*** (2013), the SJC ruled that consensual sex between a teen who has reached the age of consent (16 years) and an adult is not abuse as defined by chapter 209A.
Assault and A&B	Assaults and Assault & Battery offenses tend to be the most frequent method of committing abuse under chapter 209A and chapter 265 § 13M. The common law crime of *assault* does not require any physical contact. It typically occurs when the assailant attempts to commit a battery and is unsuccessful **or** when the assailant places the victim in fear of an *imminent* battery, usually by way of an overt, threatening, or menacing gesture, which would cause a reasonable person to fear an imminent battery. See the Violent Crimes section of this manual for a detailed analysis of Assault and A&B.
Threatening	Although threats may serve as a valid basis to obtain a protective order, absent an active protective order, threatening alone does not justify *an arrest* for "abuse" under 209A, even though it seemingly meets the 209A definition of abuse. This stems from the 1995 case of ***Commonwealth v. Jacobsen*** wherein the SJC "warrantless arrests are not authorized for the offense of threatening to commit a crime. Rather, G.L. c. 275, § 3, provides that a warrant for that offense **may issue only after a complaint is filed** by the person threatened, and then only after a judge (or magistrate) examines the sworn testimony of the complainant, and any witnesses, and determines that there is "just cause to fear that such crime may be committed."[1214] **Assault Option:** In many cases involving threats related to domestic violence the crime of assault is often a possible charge which would permit a warrantless arrest. In *Jacobsen* the SJC stated "a warrantless arrest for 'abuse' properly may be made under G.L. c. 209A, § 6(7), if a police officer has reason to believe that a defendant's conduct with respect to a person protected under G.L. c. 209A, placed the person in fear of imminent serious physical harm. The appropriate complaint in such a circumstance would be one for assault under G.L. c. 265, § 13A."
Other Methods of Abuse: Words and aggressive actions may amount to abuse	Other actions, aside from an assault or A&B, can amount to abuse for the purposes of 209A. In *Com. v. Gordon* below, the defendant was convicted of violating a protective order, under a theory of not refraining from abusing his wife, by a variety of conduct, including name calling coupled with showing up unannounced and holding open a door as she attempted to close it. See case summary below: In the 1990 case ***Commonwealth v. Gordon***, the defendant was issued a 209A protective order ordering him not to abuse his wife and to vacate the home. The defendant showed up at the home on two different occasions and accosted his wife (Karen). The first visit involved a verbal outburst between the defendant and his wife in which the defendant called his wife a "bitch" and a "whore" (she later testified that she was "upset," and that she "didn't know what [the defendant] was going to

1214 *Commonwealth v. Kerns*, 449 Mass. 641 (2007).

C.209A § 1	DOMESTIC VIOLENCE LAW DEFINITIONS
	do next). At the next meeting between Karen and the defendant, five days later, the defendant arrived at the house unannounced, and when Karen refused to respond to the defendant's requests that she open the door, the defendant said that Karen was being "immature and ridiculous." Despite Karen's obvious unwillingness to speak with him, the defendant left his automobile when she appeared and prevented Karen from closing the front door by propping his back against it. The SJC ruled "in these circumstances, we cannot say that a jury could not conclude beyond a reasonable doubt that Karen entertained a reasonable apprehension that her husband might physically abuse her. The fact that the defendant had violated an order to remain away from the house, the evidence of the tension between the parties, the previous verbal abuse by the defendant, and the defendant's physical actions in holding open the door when Karen clearly desired to avoid contact could reasonably be combined by the jury to create a picture of a volatile situation in which the possibility of physical abuse was present." Similarly, in the 1995 case ***Commonwealth v. Robicheau***, the defendant's conviction for violating a protective order under a theory of abuse was upheld by the SJC when the defendant arrived at the victim's home unannounced, shouted to the victim to "shut the fuck up" and gave her the finger" when she told him to leave. He then drove away squealing his tires and subsequently called her stating that he would kill her. The SJC ruled that "this evidence was sufficient for a jury to find the essential elements of abuse beyond a reasonable doubt." The victim's relationship with the defendant was so tense that she had sought and obtained consecutive 209A orders against him. In light of this relationship and the other circumstances enumerated above, the jury were entitled to find that the defendant's belligerent words and conduct caused a reasonable apprehension in the victim that he intended to harm her."
Stalking and Criminal Harassment	See the Crimes Against the Person section of this manual.
Witness Intimidation	It is not uncommon for the abuser to attempt to thwart the victim's effort to summon help and/or intimidate the victim from providing information to the police or to testify later in court. See the Crimes Against Public Justice section of this manual.
Property Destruction	It is not uncommon for the abuser to destroy the personal property of the victim. See the Property Offenses Section of this manual.
Kidnapping	The crime of kidnapping in Massachusetts may not be necessarily what you think. Obviously, capturing someone and moving them and confining them against their will is kidnapping but kidnapping also includes merely **confining someone against their will,** even if only for a brief period. See kidnapping section for more.
	OTHER 209A DEFINITIONS
Law officer	Any officer authorized to serve criminal process
Protection order issued by another jurisdiction	Any injunction or other order issued by a court of another state, territory or possession of the United States, the Commonwealth of Puerto Rico, or the District of Columbia, or tribal court that is issued for the purpose of preventing violent or threatening acts or harassment against, or contact or communication with or physical proximity to another person, including temporary and final orders issued by civil and criminal courts filed by or on behalf of a person seeking protection.
Vacate order	Court order to leave and remain away from a premises and surrendering forthwith any keys to the premises to the plaintiff. NOTE: In the 1995 case ***Commonwealth v. Robicheau***, the Court held that an order to vacate implies an order not to return as well.
Utilities & Mail	The defendant shall not damage any of the plaintiff's belongings or those of any other occupant and shall not shut off or cause to be shut off any utilities or mail delivery to the plaintiff.

DOMESTIC LAWS

C. 265 § 13M

INTIMATE ASSAULT and ASSAULT & BATTERY

Elements	
1.	The defendant commits an assault or an assault and battery
2.	On a family or household member (as defined in this statute). Attorney Hanrahan's note: this definition is different from the *209A definition* of family or household member. This law narrows down the victim to those connected intimately (i.e. lovers). It does not apply to those related by blood (ex. siblings) or marriage (ex. in-laws) or those living together in non-intimate settings. If an A&B occurs among these other family or household members the basic A&B charge of c. 265 § 13A would be the appropriate charge and the arrest powers would stem from chapter 209A.

Arrest Power, Penalties & Notes	
Power of Arrest	**Misdemeanor**– a police officer may effect a warrantless arrest for this offense provided he/she has probable cause that the suspect committed the offense. Note: Chapter 265 § 13M does not provide warrantless arrest powers, however chapter 209A is still effective and will permit a warrantless arrest.
Penalty	**First offense:** imprisonment in the house of correction for not more than 2 ½ years, or by a fine of not more than $5,000, or by both such fine and imprisonment **Second or subsequent offense:** second or subsequent offense of assault or assault and battery on a family or household member shall be punished by imprisonment in the house of correction for not more than 2 1/2 years or by imprisonment in the state prison for not more than 5 years.
6 hour hold	Chapter 276 § 42A requires that a defendant, who has attained the age of 18 years, who has been arrested for this offense not be admitted bail sooner than 6 hours after arrest.
Batter's program required	For any violation of this section, or as a condition of a continuance without a finding, the court shall order the defendant to complete a certified batterer's intervention program unless, upon good cause shown, the court issues specific written findings describing the reasons that batterer's intervention should not be ordered or unless the batterer's intervention program determines that the defendant is not suitable for intervention.

DEFINITIONS FOR THIS STATUTE	
Family or household members	For the purposes of this law, "family or household member" shall mean persons who: (i) are or were married to one another, (ii) have a child in common regardless of whether they have ever married or lived together or (iii) are or have been in a substantive dating or engagement relationship; provided, that the trier of fact shall determine whether a relationship is substantive by considering the following factors: a. the length of time of the relationship; b. the type of relationship; the frequency of interaction between the parties; c. whether the relationship was terminated by either person; and d. the length of time elapsed since the termination of the relationship.
What about 209A?	This statute does not void chapter 209A's definition of family or household members, but it does narrow the parties who are eligible for prosecution under this statute and the required batterer's program. Other offenders who meet the family or household members under chapter 209A but not under chapter 265 § 13M can be charged under chapter 265 § 13A (the basic A&B offense) and would not be subject to the mandatory batterer's program (this is the primary distinction).

CRIMINAL OFFENSES OFTEN ENCOUNTERED DURING DOMESTIC VIOLENCE INCIDENTS	
OFFENSES	
Assault	See the Domestic Violence definitions section previously discussed in this section and the Crimes Against Persons section of this manual for more.
Assault & Battery	See the A&B section of this manual for more. Also see the felony second offense discussed later in this section.
A&B Domestic Second Offense	Chapter 265 § 13M provides a felony level penalty for a second offense A&B when related to domestic violence. However, there are specific timeframes involved. See the Domestic/Family Law related section of this manual for specifics.
Threats	See the **Domestic Violence definitions section** previously discussed in this section and the Threats & Terrorism section of this manual for more. Note: The crime of Threats is not arrestable without a warrant. Typically an assault charge may have also taken place. Before to review these areas before executing an arrest.
Strangulation or Suffocation c. 265 § 15D	Chapter 265 §. 13D makes it a felony to strangle or suffocate another person. For the purposes of this section the following words shall have the following meanings, unless the context clearly indicates otherwise: "Strangulation", the intentional interference of the normal breathing or circulation of blood by applying substantial pressure on the throat or neck of another. "Suffocation", the intentional interference of the normal breathing or circulation of blood by blocking the nose or mouth of another.
Criminal Violations of a Protective Order	The only *criminal* violations that may be prosecuted (under Section 7) are those relating to orders: a. to vacate, b. to refrain from abuse, or c. to have no contact (this includes "stay away" orders). d. failure to surrender firearms, ammunition and related licenses. See Section of Protective Order Violations (previously discussed in this section) for more.
Trespassing	If the offender was ordered from the property by way of a court order (i.e. protective order) and the offender fails to comply he/she would be committing a trespassing offense (see B&E & Burglary section of this manual for more).
Intimidation of a Witness	When the abuser attempts to prevent the victim (or any other person) from contacting the police, or from providing information to the police, the defendant can (and should) be charged with intimidation of a witness. See the Crimes Against Public Justice section of this manual.
Other crimes	Stalking, criminal harassment, harassing phone calls, kidnapping, sexual assault and destruction of property crimes are not uncommon offenses in domestic violence incidents.

C. 209A § 6 POLICE DUTIES INVOLVING DOMESTIC VIOLENCE INCIDENTS

Whenever any law officer has reason to believe that a family or household member has been abused or is in danger of being abused, such officer shall use all reasonable means to prevent further abuse. **The officer shall take, but not be limited to the following action:**

1.	**Remain on the scene** of where said abuse occurred or was in danger of occurring as long as the officer has reason to believe that at least one of the parties involved would be in immediate physical danger without the presence of a law officer. This shall include, but not be limited to remaining in the dwelling for a reasonable period of time;
2.	**Assist the abused person in obtaining medical treatment** necessitated by an assault, which may include driving the victim to the emergency room of the nearest hospital, or arranging for appropriate transportation to a health care facility, notwithstanding any law to the contrary;
3.	**Assist the abused person in locating and getting to a safe place**; including but not limited to a designated meeting place for a shelter or a family member's or friend's residence. The officer shall consider the victim's preference in this regard and what is reasonable under all the circumstances;
4.	**Give the person immediate and adequate notice of his or her rights**. The notice shall consist of handing the person a copy of the statement which follows below **and reading the same to the person**. Where the person's native language is not English, the statement shall be then provided in the person's native language whenever possible. "You have the right to appear at the Superior, Probate and Family, District or Boston Municipal Court, if you reside within the appropriate jurisdiction, and file a complaint requesting any of the following applicable orders: (a) an order restraining your attacker from abusing you; (b) an order directing your attacker to leave your household, building or workplace; (c) an order awarding you custody of a minor child; (d) an order directing your attacker to pay support for you or any minor child in your custody, if the attacker has a legal obligation of support; and (e) an order directing your attacker to pay you for losses suffered as a result of abuse, including medical and moving expenses, loss of earnings or support, costs for restoring utilities and replacing locks, reasonable attorney's fees and other out-of-pocket losses for injuries and property damage sustained. For an emergency on weekends, holidays, or weeknights the police will refer you to a justice of the superior, probate and family, district, or Boston municipal court departments. You have the right to go to the appropriate district court or the Boston municipal court and seek a criminal complaint for threats, assault and battery, assault with a deadly weapon, assault with intent to kill or other related offenses. If you are in need of medical treatment, you have the right to request that an officer present drive you to the nearest hospital or otherwise assist you in obtaining medical treatment. If you believe that police protection is needed for your physical safety, you have the right to request that the officer present remain at the scene until you and your children can leave or until your safety is otherwise ensured. You may also request that the officer assist you in locating and taking you to a safe place, including but not limited to a designated meeting place for a shelter or a family member's or a friend's residence, or a similar place of safety. You may request a copy of the police incident report at no cost from the police department." The officer shall leave a copy of the foregoing statement with such person before leaving the scene or premises.

C. 209A § 6	POLICE DUTIES INVOLVING DOMESTIC VIOLENCE INCIDENTS
5.	**Assist the person by activating the emergency judicial system** when the court is closed for business.
6.	**Inform the victim that the abuser will be eligible for bail** and may be promptly released.
7. (ARREST)	**ARREST any person a law officer witnesses or has probable cause to believe has violated** a temporary or permanent vacate, restraining, or no-contact order or judgment issued pursuant to: • Chapter 208 sections 18, 34B or 34C (certain Divorce Protective Orders) • Chapter 209 § 32 (Support Order issued by the Court among married people), • Chapter 209A § 3 & 3C (Abuse Prevention Order), § 3B (Firearm/License Surrender Order), § 4 (Temporary Abuse Prevention Order) or § 5 (Emergency Abuse Prevention Order) or • Chapter 209C § 15 or 20 (certain Child born out of Wedlock order) or • Similar protection order issued by another jurisdiction. When there are <u>no</u> vacate, restraining, or no-contact orders or judgments in effect, **arrest shall be the *preferred* response** whenever an officer witnesses or has probable cause to believe that a person: (a) has committed a **felony**; (b) has committed a misdemeanor involving **abuse** as defined in c. 209A § 1; (c) has committed an **assault and battery** in violation of c. 265 §13A. **Attorney Hanrahan's Note**: Not all violations of these orders are arrestable violations (at least without a without a warrant). Be sure to review the Violation of a Protective Order section later in this chapter.
Important Notes Regarding Arrests	
6 hour hold	Chapter 276 § 42A requires that a defendant, who has attained the age of 18 years, who has been arrested for a domestic violence related offense not be admitted bail sooner than 6 hours after arrest.
Victim Safety	The safety of the victim and any involved children shall be paramount in any decision to arrest.
Arrest Decision	The decision to arrest must be based on whether probable cause exists that crime occurred, not on whether the victim wishes to seek complaints or wishes to testify at a future date.[1215]
Dual Arrest	Any officer arresting both parties must submit a detailed, written report in addition to an incident report, setting forth the grounds for dual arrest. Dual arrests, like the issuance of mutual restraining orders, are **strongly discouraged** because they trivialize the seriousness of domestic abuse and increase the danger to victims. When both parties have used force against the other the police should try to determine whether the force was in self-defense or offensive in nature. If one of the persons acted entirely in self-defense, the situation should be treated as if there was a single offender. If neither party acted in self-defense and both parties have committed an act of domestic abuse, then the officers should determine who is the dominant aggressor.[1216] See Dominant Aggressor below.

[1215] The 2009 Massachusetts Domestic Violence Enforcement Guidelines.
[1216] The 2009 Massachusetts Domestic Violence Enforcement Guidelines

C. 209A § 6	POLICE DUTIES INVOLVING DOMESTIC VIOLENCE INCIDENTS
Dominant Aggressor	According to the 2009 Massachusetts Domestic Violence Enforcement Guidelines "It is important to determine the dominant aggressor." The dominant aggressor is "not who struck first, but who has a pattern of domination and control." Officers should consider the totality of the circumstances including: • The relative severity of the injuries and fear inflicted in the incident, • The relative use of force and intimidation in the incident, • Information available to the officers regarding prior incidents involving either party; or • The likelihood of either party to commit domestic violence in the near future.
Do not Threaten to Arrest All Parties	No law officer investigating an incident of domestic violence shall threaten, suggest, or otherwise indicate the arrest of all parties for the purpose of discouraging requests for law enforcement intervention by any party.
Court Official should inform Victim of Bail	When a judge or other person authorized to take bail bails any person arrested under the provisions of chapter 209A, he shall make reasonable efforts to inform the victim of such release prior to or at the time of the release.
	Confidentiality of Police Records
c. 209A § 8	Records involving minors or Plaintiff's address (including work) and telephone numbers are withheld from public inspection.
Confidentiality of all abuse related reports c. 47 § 97D	All reports of rape and sexual assault or attempts to commit such offenses, all reports of **abuse perpetrated by family or household members**, as defined in section 1 of chapter 209A, and all communications between police officers and victims of such offenses or abuse shall not be public reports and shall be maintained by the police departments in a manner that shall assure their confidentiality; provided, however, that all such reports shall be accessible at all reasonable times, upon written request, to: i. the victim, the victim's attorney, others specifically authorized by the victim to obtain such information, prosecutors and ii. victim-witness advocates as defined in section 1 of chapter 258B, domestic violence victims' counselors as defined in section 20K of chapter 233, sexual assault counselors as defined in section 20J of chapter 233, if such access is necessary in the performance of their duties; and provided further, that all such reports shall be accessible at all reasonable times, upon written, telephonic, facsimile or electronic mail request to law enforcement officers, district attorneys or assistant district attorneys and all persons authorized to admit persons to bail pursuant to section 57 of chapter 276. Communications between police officers and victims of said offenses and abuse may also be shared with the forgoing named persons if such access is necessary in the performance of their duties. A violation of this section shall be punished by imprisonment for not more than 1 year or by a fine of not more than $1,000, or both such fine and imprisonment.
Daily Log Confidentiality	Chapter 41 § 98F requires that the below information be withheld from daily log: i. any information concerning **responses to reports of domestic violence**, rape or sexual assault or ii. any entry concerning the **arrest of a person** for assault, assault and battery or violation of a protective order where the victim is a family or household member, as defined in section 1 of chapter 209A.

C. 209A § 6 POLICE DUTIES INVOLVING DOMESTIC VIOLENCE INCIDENTS

Related Statutes, Case Law & Other Important Information	
Liability	No law officer shall be held liable in any civil action regarding personal injury or injury to property brought by any party to a domestic violence incident for an arrest based on probable cause when such officer acted reasonably and in good faith and in compliance with chapter 209A and the statewide policy as established by the secretary of public safety.
Written Report Required	Whenever any law officer investigates an incident of domestic violence, the officer shall immediately file a written incident report in accordance with the standards of the officer's law enforcement agency and, wherever possible, in the form of the National Incident-Based Reporting System, as defined by the Federal Bureau of Investigation. The latter information may be submitted voluntarily by the local police on a monthly basis to the crime reporting unit of the criminal history systems board.
Copy of Report to Victim	The victim shall be provided a copy of the full incident report at no cost upon request to the appropriate law enforcement department.
Order Shall be Issued if charges pending and victim requests	When any person **charged with or arrested for a crime involving abuse** under chapter 209A is released from custody, the court or the emergency response **judge shall issue, upon the request of the victim, a written no-contact order** prohibiting the person charged or arrested from having any contact with the victim and shall use all reasonable means to notify the victim immediately of release from custody. The victim shall be given at no cost a certified copy of the no-contact order.
The Massachusetts Domestic Violence Enforcement Guidelines Related to Police Responsibility	
The Massachusetts Domestic Violence Enforcement Guidelines **call for certain action when a firearm is involved at the scene of a Domestic Violence incident**	When a firearm or other weapon is present at the scene of a domestic violence situation, officers **shall**: 1. Seize the firearm or weapon as evidence of the crime, if the responding officers are informed that a firearm or weapon has been involved in the dispute. 2. If the firearm or weapon is not reported to have been involved in the dispute: a) Request that the firearm or weapon be placed in their custody temporarily; b) Search for and take custody of the firearms or weapon if a party who lawfully resides there requests that the officer do so. A consent search is allowed in areas to which the victim has access, including joint access with the suspect; c) Take temporary custody of the firearm or weapon to alleviate the threat of serious violence. 3. Determine whether a firearm or weapon is lawfully possessed before returning the same. 4. If the officer determines that the firearm or weapon cannot be seized, the following actions can take place: a) A judge can order the defendant to surrender guns and licenses; and b) The chief who issued a license to carry may revoke or suspend the license. 5. In all domestic violence cases, the investigating department shall advise the licensing authority that the subject of the license is suspected of abuse.

DOMESTIC LAWS

C. 209A § 6	POLICE DUTIES INVOLVING DOMESTIC VIOLENCE INCIDENTS
Protection Procedures after the Call	Every effort shall be made to provide law enforcement protection and other safety measures to a victim domestic violence. These measures should be taken immediately following the report of an abusive incident, immediately preceding or following a criminal court date regarding the abuse, and at any other point at which the victim anticipates or is expecting prohibited contact or harassment from the abuser. Such protection shall include but not be limited to: • Drive-bys; • Welfare checks; • Arresting the abuser for violations of no-contact orders and any other offense committed; • Transporting the victim to a safe place when necessary; or • Ensuring victim contact with trained domestic violence advocates for safety planning.

Domestic Violence Venue & Jurisdiction Issues

C.209A § 2	DOMESTIC VIOLENCE VENUE: WHERE TO APPLY FOR AN ORDER
Plaintiff's residence	Proceedings shall be filed, heard and determined in the superior court department or the Boston municipal court department or respective divisions of the probate and family or district court departments having venue over the **plaintiff's residence**.
What if Plaintiff Flees Abuse?	If the plaintiff has left a residence or household to avoid abuse, the plaintiff shall have the option of commencing an action in the court having venue over the prior residence or household, or in the court having venue over the present residence or household.
Attorney Hanrahan's Comment	This statute addresses where a victim of abuse can apply for a protective order. Typically the victim must apply in the Court that has jurisdiction where the victim lives. However, if the victim flees his/her home because of the abuse the victim can apply in the jurisdiction where he/she relocated.

C.277 § 62A	DOMESTIC VIOLENCE JURISDICTION: WHERE TO PROSECUTE
Jurisdiction: Where to Prosecute?	Any criminal violation of chapter 209A may be prosecuted and punished in the territorial jurisdiction in which the **violation was committed** or in which the **original order under chapter 209A was issued**.
Violation Occurring in another State	Violations of out-of-state orders or Massachusetts orders violated in another state may be charged criminal as contempt of court (M.G.L. c. 220 § 14), in the Commonwealth of Massachusetts.[1217]
Attorney Hanrahan's Comment	If the defendant violates a 209A protective order (in Massachusetts), the defendant can be charge in the city or town where the violation was committed or where the order was issued. In cases where it is difficult to determine where the violation occurred, for instance when the defendant phones the plaintiff in violation of an order from an unknown location, it is easier to charge the defendant in the jurisdiction where the order was issued. If the defendant violates the order while out of state (i.e. while in New Hampshire) he may be charged in Massachusetts under a contempt of court offense. In this case you should coordinate with law enforcement in the other state in the event they are pursuing charges for violating the Massachusetts order in their state. If the other state is also pursuing charges for violating the Massachusetts order you should consult with your local DA's office before bring a contempt charge.

C.276 § 28	DOMESTIC VIOLENCE JURISDICTION: ARREST POWERS
Arrest for Offense in another jurisdiction	M.G.L. c. 276 § 28 states in part...Any officer authorized to serve criminal process may arrest, without a warrant, and detain a person: a. whom the officer has probable cause to believe has committed a misdemeanor by violating a (Massachusetts issued) temporary or permanent vacate, restraining, suspension and surrender, or no-contact order. b. whom the officer has probable cause to believe has committed a misdemeanor involving abuse as defined 209A or has committed an assault and battery against a family or household member.
Attorney Hanrahan's Comment	This does **not** grant police officers authority to **make arrests *outside* their jurisdiction**. It only permits officers to arrest someone in their jurisdiction who has committed a domestic violence offense even if the offense was committed in another jurisdiction.
Domestic Violence Enforcement Guidelines	According to the Massachusetts Domestic Violence Enforcement Guidelines, "when probable cause to arrest exists, and the suspect fled the scene: 1. Officers shall direct the dispatcher to advise area patrols, including other jurisdictions where the suspect is believed to be going, in order for those patrols to locate and arrest the suspect. 2. One department's statement that probable cause to arrest exists shall be honored by another department. The second department shall immediately attempt to effect the arrest as requested by the investigating department."

[1217] The 2009 Massachusetts Domestic Violence Enforcement Guidelines

PROTECTIVE ORDERS

Victims of abuse may seek protection, in the form of a protective order, from the court. This protective orders place the abuser on notice that he or she will face criminal sanctions if the conduct continues. These orders also grant law enforcement personnel the ability to make warrantless arrests in situations that they may not otherwise be authorized. There are three primary types of protective orders; 209A Abuse Prevention Orders, 208 Divorce Vacate Orders and 258E Harassment Prevention Orders. Harassment prevention orders are slightly different in that they prohibit harassment and thus are covered in a distinct section later in this section.

Divorce Vacate Orders (c. 208)

C.208 § 34B	ORDER TO VACATE MARITAL HOME
OVERVIEW	A Probate/Family Court may issue an order to vacate to one spouse and in many cases a violation of this vacate order can be enforced in the same manner as a 209A protection order.
Actual Statute language	• Any court with Divorce jurisdiction may, • Upon commencement of divorce action, • Order the husband or wife to vacate forthwith the marital home, • For a period of time not exceeding 90 days, • and upon further motion for such additional certain period of time, as the court deems necessary or appropriate if the court finds, after a hearing, that the health, safety or welfare of the moving party or any minor children residing with the parties would be endangered or substantially impaired by a failure to enter such an order.
3-Day Notice Required	The opposing party shall be given at least 3 days' notice of such hearing and may appear and be heard either in person or by his attorney.
Emergency Order to Vacate (no hearing)	If the moving party demonstrates a substantial likelihood of immediate danger to his or her health, safety or welfare or to that of such minor children from the opposing party, the court may enter a temporary order without notice, and shall immediately thereafter notify said opposing party and give him or her an opportunity to be heard as soon as possible but not later than five days after such order is entered on the question of continuing such temporary order.
Parties not residing together	The court may issue an order to vacate although the opposing party does not reside in the marital home at the time of its issuance, or if the moving party has left such home and has not returned there because of fear for his or her safety or for that of any minor children.

C.208 § 34C	MARITAL RESTRAINING ORDER PROCEDURES
Overview	In addition to a vacate order described above in section 34B, a Probate/Family Court may issue an order preventing "restraint on personal liberty." This statute describes the methods of serving these orders and the enforcement action and penalties that coincide.
General Provisions	Whenever a division of the probate and family court department issues: • an order to vacate or • an order prohibiting a person from imposing any restraint on the personal liberty of another person

C.208 § 34C	MARITAL RESTRAINING ORDER PROCEDURES
	The register shall transmit **two certified copies of each order forthwith to the appropriate law enforcement agency which shall serve one copy of each such order upon the defendant**. **Note:** Each such order issued shall contain the following statement: VIOLATION OF THIS ORDER IS A CRIMINAL OFFENSE. Any such violation may be enforced in the superior or district
Method of Service	Unless otherwise ordered by the court, service shall be by delivering a copy in hand to the defendant.
Law Enforcement Duties	Law enforcement officers shall use every reasonable means to enforce such order. Law enforcement agencies shall establish procedures adequate to insure that an officer at the scene of an alleged violation of such order may be informed of the existence and terms of such order.
Penalty	Any violation of such order shall be punishable by a fine of not more than $5,000 dollars or by imprisonment for not more than 2½ years in the HOC, or both such fine and imprisonment.
Arrest	Arrest powers come under chapter 209A.
Vacated Order	The court shall notify the appropriate law enforcement agency in writing whenever any such order is vacated by the court and shall direct the agency to destroy all records of such vacated order and such agency shall comply with the directive.

C. 209A § 3	209A DOMESTIC PROTECTIVE ORDER RELIEF OPTIONS
A person suffering from abuse from an adult or minor family or household member may file a complaint in the court requesting protection from such abuse**, including, but not limited to,** the following orders:	
No Abuse	(a) Ordering the defendant to **refrain from abusing the plaintiff**, whether the defendant is an adult or minor;
No Contact	(b) Ordering the defendant to **refrain from contacting the plaintiff**, unless authorized by the court, whether the defendant is an adult or minor;
Vacate	(c) Ordering the defendant to **vacate forthwith and remain away from the household**, multiple family dwelling, and workplace. **Note:** an order to vacate shall be for a fixed period of time, **not to exceed one year**, at the expiration of which time the court may extend the order upon motion of the plaintiff, with notice to the defendant, for such additional time as it deems necessary to protect the plaintiff from abuse. **Case Law Note**: In the 1995 case ***Commonwealth v. Robicheau***, the Court held that an order to vacate implies an order not to return as well as vacate the property.
Child Custody & Visitation	(d) Awarding the plaintiff **temporary custody of a minor child**; **Note on Visitation:** If ordering visitation to the abusive parent, the court shall provide for the safety and well-being of the child and the safety of the abused parent. The court may consider: (a) ordering an exchange of the child to occur in a protected setting or in the presence of an appropriate third party (e.g. police station); (b) ordering visitation supervised by an appropriate third party, visitation center or agency; (c) ordering the abusive parent to attend and complete, to the satisfaction of the court, a

DOMESTIC LAWS

C. 209A § 3	209A DOMESTIC PROTECTIVE ORDER RELIEF OPTIONS
	certified batterer's treatment program as a condition of visitation; (d) ordering the abusive parent to abstain from possession or consumption of alcohol or controlled substances during the visitation and for 24 hours preceding visitation; (e) ordering the abusive parent to pay the costs of supervised visitation; (f) prohibiting overnight visitation; (g) requiring a bond from the abusive parent for the return and safety of the child; (h) ordering an investigation or appointment of a guardian ad litem or attorney for the child; and (i) imposing any other condition that is deemed necessary to provide for the safety and well-being of the child and the safety of the abused parent.
Pay Support	(e) ordering the defendant **to pay temporary support for the plaintiff or any child** in the plaintiff's custody or both, when the defendant has a legal obligation to support such a person.
Pay for Losses	(f) ordering the defendant to **pay the person abused monetary compensation for the losses suffered** as a direct result of such abuse. **Note:** Compensatory losses shall include, but not be limited to, loss of earnings or support, costs for restoring utilities, out-of-pocket losses for injuries sustained, replacement costs for locks or personal property removed or destroyed, medical and moving expenses and reasonable attorney's fees.
Impound Record	(g) ordering **information in the case record to be impounded** in accordance with court rule;
Protect the Children	(h) ordering **the defendant to refrain from abusing or contacting the plaintiff's child, or child in plaintiff's care or custody,** unless authorized by the court;
Batterer's Program	(i) the **judge may recommend to the defendant that the defendant attend a batterer's intervention program** that is certified by the department of public health.
Pets c. 209 § 11(a)	The court may order the possession, care and control of any domesticated animal owned, possessed, leased, kept or held by either party or a minor child residing in the household to the plaintiff or petitioner. The court may order the defendant to refrain from abusing, threatening, taking, interfering with, transferring, encumbering, concealing, harming or otherwise disposing of such animal. Note: this applies to c. 258E as well.
Other Important Information	
Mutual Restraining Order	A court may issue a mutual restraining order or mutual no-contact order pursuant to any abuse prevention action **only if the court has made specific written findings of fact**. The court shall then provide a detailed order, sufficiently specific to apprise any law officer as to which party has violated the order, if the parties are in or appear to be in violation of the order.
Petition on behalf of others	A parent may petition the Court for a protective order on behalf of a minor child. Presumably, a guardian could petition the court for an order of protection on behalf of an incompetent person as well.
Time Limits, Extensions and Modifications	• **Initial Order:** Any relief granted by the court shall be for a fixed period of time **not to exceed one year**. • Every order shall on its face state the time and date the order is to expire and shall include the date and time that the matter will again be heard. • If the plaintiff appears at the court at the date and time the order is to expire, the court shall

C. 209A § 3	209A DOMESTIC PROTECTIVE ORDER RELIEF OPTIONS
	determine whether or not to extend the order for **any additional time** reasonably necessary to protect the plaintiff **or** to enter a **permanent order**. • When the expiration date stated on the order is on a weekend day or holiday, or a date when the court is closed to business, the order shall not expire until the next date that the court is open to business. • The plaintiff may appear on such next court business day at the time designated by the order to request that the order be extended. • The court may also extend the order upon motion of the plaintiff, for such additional time as it deems necessary to protect from abuse the plaintiff or any child in the plaintiff's care or custody. • **Further Abuse not Required for extension:** The fact that abuse has not occurred during the pendency of an order shall not, in itself, constitute sufficient ground for denying or failing to extend the order, of allowing an order to expire or be vacated, or for refusing to issue a new order. • The court may modify its order at any subsequent time upon motion by either party. • When the plaintiff's address is inaccessible to the defendant as provided in section 8 of this chapter and the defendant has filed a motion to modify the court's order, the court shall be responsible for notifying the plaintiff. In no event shall the court disclose any such inaccessible address.
Extension possible even if defendant is incarcerated	In the 2014 case of ***Callahan v. Callahan***, the Court ruled that an order could be extended even if the defendant will be incarcerated during the duration of the order.
No Compelled Mediation	No court shall compel parties to mediate any aspect of their case. Although the court may refer the case to the family service office of the probation department or victim/witness advocates for information gathering purposes, the court shall not compel the parties to meet together in such information gathering sessions.
No Denial for Un-timeliness	A court shall not deny any complaint filed under this chapter solely because it was not filed within a particular time period after the last alleged incident of abuse.
Order May be issued Without Notice to Defendant (*Ex-Parte*) **c. 209A § 4**	If the plaintiff **demonstrates a substantial likelihood of immediate danger of abuse**, the court may enter temporary relief orders without notice as it deems necessary to protect the plaintiff from abuse and shall immediately thereafter notify the defendant that the temporary orders have been issued. The court shall give the defendant an opportunity to be heard on the question of continuing the temporary order and of granting other relief as requested by the plaintiff **no later than 10 court business days after such orders are entered**. Notice shall be made by the appropriate law enforcement agency as provided in § 7 (notice served by law enforcement). **Note:** If the defendant does not appear at such subsequent hearing, the temporary orders shall continue in effect without further order of the court. Also, this relief shall not be contingent upon the filing of a complaint for divorce, separate support, or paternity action.

C. 209A § 3	209A DOMESTIC PROTECTIVE ORDER RELIEF OPTIONS
C. 209A § 5 EMERGENCY ORDERS WHEN COURT IS CLOSED OR PLAINTIFF IS UNABLE	
Emergency Order - off hours	• When the court is **closed for business** or • the plaintiff is unable to appear in court because of severe hardship due to the plaintiff's **physical condition**, • any justice of the superior, probate and family, district or Boston municipal court departments • may grant relief to the plaintiff if the plaintiff demonstrates a substantial likelihood of immediate danger of abuse.
Telephone Order	In the discretion of the justice, relief may be granted and communicated by telephone to an officer or employee of an appropriate law enforcement agency, who shall record such order on a form of order promulgated for such use by the chief administrative justice and shall deliver a copy of such order on the next court day to the clerk-magistrate of the court having venue and jurisdiction over the matter.
Plaintiff Must Appear Next Court Day	If relief has been granted (without the filing of a complaint pursuant to this section of this chapter, i.e. a telephone order), then the **plaintiff shall appear in court on the next available business day** to file the complaint. **A representative may appear for those physically unable**: If the plaintiff in such a case is unable to appear in court without severe hardship due to the plaintiff's physical condition, then a representative may appear in court on the plaintiff's behalf and file the requisite complaint with an affidavit setting forth the circumstances preventing the plaintiff from appearing personally. Notice to the plaintiff and defendant and an opportunity for the defendant to be heard shall be given as provided in said section four. Any order issued under this section and any documentation in support thereof shall be certified on the next court day by the clerk-magistrate or register of the court issuing such order to the court having venue and jurisdiction over the matter. Such certification to the court shall have the effect of commencing proceedings under this chapter and invoking the other provisions of this chapter but shall not be deemed necessary for an emergency order issued under this section to take effect.

C. 209A § 3B	ORDER TO SURRENDER FIREARMS & LICENSES
	Elements
Order Issued	Upon issuance of a temporary or emergency order the court shall, if the plaintiff demonstrates a substantial likelihood of immediate danger of abuse, do the following:
LTC & FID Card Surrendered	Order the immediate suspension and surrender of any license to carry firearms (LTC) and or firearms identification card (FID) which the defendant may hold; and they shall be surrendered to law enforcement personnel.
	And
Surrender Firearms	Order the defendant to surrender all firearms, rifles, shotguns, machine guns and ammunition which he then controls, owns or possesses in accordance
	Arrest Power & Penalties
Power of Arrest	**Misdemeanor** – Chapter 209A § 6 states, in part, that "a police officer **SHALL arrest** any person a law officer witnesses or has probable cause to believe has violated...Chapter 209A § 3B."
Penalty	Any violation of these orders shall be punishable by a fine of not more than $5,000 dollars, or by imprisonment for not more than 2½ in a HOC, or by both such fine and imprisonment.
	Additional Provisions
Police must take possession	Law enforcement officials, upon the service of the above surrender orders, shall immediately take possession of all firearms, rifles, shotguns, machine guns, ammunition, any license to carry firearms and any firearms identification cards in the control, ownership, or possession of the defendant.
Defendant has right to a hearing within 10 days	Any defendant aggrieved by an order of surrender or suspension (of firearm license) may petition the court which issued such suspension or surrender order for a review of such action and such petition **shall be heard no later than 10 court business days after the receipt of the notice of the petition by the court.** If said license to carry firearms or firearms identification card has been suspended upon the issuance of an ex-parte order or an emergency order, said petition may be heard contemporaneously with the hearing on the continuance of the order.
Firearm Needed for Employment: Right to hearing within 2 days	Upon the filing of an affidavit by the defendant that a firearm, rifle, shotgun, machine gun or ammunition is required in the performance of the defendant's employment, and upon a request for an expedited hearing, the **court shall order said hearing within 2 business days** of receipt of such affidavit and request but only on the issue of surrender and suspension of firearms and/or LTC and/or FID cards.
Firearm Storage	The law enforcement official may store, transfer or otherwise dispose of any such weapon in accordance with the provisions of Chapter 140 § 129D (transfer weapon to licensed dealer operating a bonded warehouse); provided however, that nothing herein shall authorize the transfer of any weapons surrendered by the defendant to anyone other than a licensed dealer.
Return of the Firearms	The firearms and licenses shall not be returned until the Abuse Prevention Order has been completely vacated or the firearms provision has been modified by order of the court. M.G.L. c. 140 §§ 129B, 131[1218]

DOMESTIC LAWS

[1218] The 2009 Massachusetts Domestic Violence Enforcement Guidelines

C. 209A § 3B	ORDER TO SURRENDER FIREARMS & LICENSES
	Related Statutes, Case Law & Other Important Information
Federal Law ***Restrictions on Firearm possession by RO defendants &Domestic Violence Convicts***	18 U.S.C. § 922 states in part "*It shall be unlawful for any person:* *8) who is subject to a court order that –* *a) was issued after a hearing of which such person received actual notice, and at which such person had an opportunity to participate;* *b) restrains such person from harassing, stalking, or threatening an intimate partner of such person or child of such intimate partner or person, or engaging in other conduct that would place an intimate partner in reasonable fear of bodily injury to the partner or child; and* *c) (i) includes a finding that such person represents a credible threat to the physical safety of such intimate partner or child; or* *(ii) by its terms explicitly prohibits the use, attempted use, or threatened use of physical force against such intimate partner or child that would reasonably be expected to cause bodily injury; or* 9) *who has* ***been convicted in any court of a misdemeanor crime of domestic violence****, to ship or transport in interstate or foreign commerce, or possess in or affecting commerce, any firearm or ammunition; or to receive any firearm or ammunition which has been shipped or transported in interstate or foreign commerce.*"
Slightest touch	In the 2014 US Supreme Court case of United ***States v. Castleman***, a conviction for a domestic offense involving "even the slightest of touching" meets the definition of a "crime of domestic violence" prohibiting the person from possessing a firearm under Title 18 U.S.C. § 922(g)(9).
Attorney Hanrahan's Comment	Although local and state law enforcement typically do not enforce federal law (that is the responsibility of federal law enforcement), the above federal law may be used to as a tool to prevent a domestic violence offender from retaining or receiving firearms.
Domestic Violence Law Enforcement Guidelines	The Domestic Violence Law Enforcement Guidelines calls for certain actions regarding the presence of firearms at the scene of a domestic violence incident. See the Police Officer Duties Section for more.
Licenses	According to the 2009 Massachusetts Domestic Violence Enforcement Guidelines the term "license" includes LTC Class A &B, FID Class C & D, Machine Gun Licenses, License to sell firearms and ammunition, and license to perform as a gunsmith.
Firearms	According to the 2009 Massachusetts Domestic Violence Enforcement Guidelines the term "firearms: includes firearms, rifles, shotguns, machine guns, ammunition, high capacity feeding devices, and antiques.

c. 209A § 5A	PROTECTION ORDER ISSUED BY ANOTHER JURISDICTION
Out of State Orders Enforceable	Any protection order issued by another jurisdiction (as defined below) shall be given full faith and credit throughout the commonwealth and enforced as if it were issued in the commonwealth for as long as the order is in effect in the issuing jurisdiction.
Police may Rely on Statement by Person Protected	A law enforcement officer may presume the validity of, and enforce (in accordance with Chapter 209A § 6), a copy of a protection order issued by another jurisdiction which has been provided to the law enforcement officer by any source; provided, however, that the officer is also provided with a statement by the person protected by the order that such order remains in effect. Law enforcement officers may rely on such statement by the person protected by such order.
Validity of the Order	According to the 2009 Massachusetts Domestic Violence Enforcement Guidelines "an order of protection is presumed valid if it gives the names of the parties involved, contains the date the order was issued, has not expired, specifies the terms and conditions set against the abuser, contains the name of the issuing court and is signed by the issuing authority.
Arrest Power, Penalties & Notes	
Power of Arrest	**Misdemeanor** – Chapter 209A § 6 states in part "a police officer shall arrest any person a law officer witnesses or has probable cause to believe has violated a ... protection order issued by another jurisdiction." However, the only criminal violations that may be prosecuted are those relating to orders: a. to vacate, b. to refrain from abuse, or c. to have no contact (this includes "stay away" orders). d. failure to surrender firearms, ammunition and related licenses See Violation of a Protective Order later in this section (c. 209A § 7)
Penalty	Any violation of protection order issued by another jurisdiction shall be punishable by a fine of not more than $5,000, or by imprisonment for not more than 2½ years in a house of correction, or by both such fine and imprisonment. In addition the court shall order persons convicted of a crime under this statute to pay a fine of $25 that shall be transmitted to the treasurer for deposit into the General Fund. **Batterer's Program**: For any violation of such order, the court shall order the defendant to complete a certified batterer's intervention program unless, upon good cause shown, the court issues specific written findings describing the reasons that batterer's intervention should not be ordered or unless the batterer's intervention program determines that the defendant is not suitable for intervention.
Definition: *Protection order issued by another jurisdiction* c. 209A § 1	"Protection order issued by another jurisdiction", includes any injunction or other order issued by a court of another state, territory or possession of the United States, the Commonwealth of Puerto Rico, or the District of Columbia, or tribal court that is issued for the purpose of preventing violent or threatening acts or harassment against, or contact or communication with or physical proximity to another person, including temporary and final orders issued by civil and criminal courts filed by or on behalf of a person seeking protection.
MA law governs	In the 2014 case of ***Commonwealth v. Shea,*** the SJC ruled that where an out-of-state abuse protection order is violated in Massachusetts and prosecuted under c. 209A, the violation is governed by Massachusetts law not the state that issued it.

C. 209A § 7	SERVING PROTECTIVE ORDERS
Service of Protective Order	Whenever the court orders [under Chapter 208 § 18, § 34B, or § 34C, Chapter 209 § 32, Chapter 209A § 3, § 4 and § 5, or Chapter 209C § 15], the defendant to: • vacate, • refrain from abusing the plaintiff; or • to have no contact with the plaintiff or the plaintiff's minor child The register or clerk-magistrate shall transmit two (2) certified copies of each such order and one (1) copy of the complaint and summons forthwith to the appropriate law enforcement agency which, unless otherwise ordered by the court, shall serve one (1) copy of each order upon the defendant, together with a copy of the complaint, order and summons and notice of any suspension or surrender ordered pursuant to Chapter 209S § 3B (firearms and license surrender). Law enforcement agencies shall establish adequate procedures to ensure that, when effecting service upon a defendant pursuant to this paragraph, a law enforcement officer shall, to the extent practicable: i. fully inform the defendant of the **contents of the order** and the available **penalties** for any violation of an order or terms thereof and ii. **provide the defendant with informational resources**, including, but not limited to, a list of certified batterer intervention programs, substance abuse counseling, alcohol abuse counseling and financial counseling programs located within or near the court's jurisdiction. The law enforcement agency shall promptly make its return of service to the court.
Massachusetts Domestic Violence Enforcement Guidelines	According to the 2009 Massachusetts Domestic Violence Enforcement Guidelines, service of orders shall be made **in hand** unless otherwise ordered by the court. 1. Orders shall be served promptly upon receipt. If service is initially unsuccessful, the department must continue to attempt service until it is completed. Service of orders will not be delayed in order to forward service by a specialized officer or unit. If an officer is unable to make service after numerous attempts, the officer should document in detail the service attempts on the "return of service" form and ***request*** **the court to allow service by leaving a copy of the order at the last known address of the defendan**t. 2. Service of orders may compromise victim safety. Victim safety should be considered in the timing of the service of the order. Officers should encourage the victim to contact an advocate (either through the D.A.'s Office, SAFEPLAN or the local domestic violence program) in order to develop a safety plan around the service of the order. [1219]
Police Must Take Action to Prevent Further Abuse	Law enforcement officers shall use every reasonable means to enforce such abuse prevention orders. Law enforcement agencies shall establish procedures adequate to insure that an officer on the scene of an alleged violation of such order may be informed of the existence and terms of such order.
Record of Service	Departments must keep a record of all attempts at service. [1220]
Return of Service	All returns of service, including service of Emergency Orders, must be sent to the court. [1221]
Plaintiff Delivers to PD	When a plaintiff brings an order to the department for service, officers should ensure that the department's responsibilities under c. 290A and the Domestic Violence Enforcement Guidelines are met. [1222]

[1219] The 2009 Massachusetts Domestic Violence Enforcement Guidelines
[1220] The 2009 Massachusetts Domestic Violence Enforcement Guidelines
[1221] The 2009 Massachusetts Domestic Violence Enforcement Guidelines

C. 209A § 7	SERVING PROTECTIVE ORDERS
	Additional Provisions & Other Important Information
Each abuse prevention order issued shall contain this statement:	VIOLATION OF THIS ORDER IS A CRIMINAL OFFENSE. Any violation of such order or a protection order issued by another jurisdiction shall be punishable by a fine of not more than $5,000 dollars, or by imprisonment for not more than 2½ years in a HOC, or by both such fine and imprisonment. In addition to, but not in lieu of, the forgoing penalties and any other sentence, fee or assessment, including the victim witness assessment in section 8 of chapter 258B, the court shall order persons convicted of a crime under this statute to pay a fine of $25 that shall be transmitted to the treasurer for deposit into the General Fund. For any violation of such order, the court shall order the defendant to complete a certified batterer's intervention program unless, upon good cause shown, the court issues specific written findings describing the reasons that batterer's intervention should not be ordered or unless the batterer's intervention program determines that the defendant is not suitable for intervention. The court shall not order substance abuse or anger management treatment or any other form of treatment as a substitute for certified batterer's intervention. If a defendant ordered to undergo treatment has received a suspended sentence, the original sentence shall be reimposed if the defendant fails to participate in said program as required by the terms of his probation. If the court determines that the violation was in retaliation for the defendant being reported by the plaintiff to the department of revenue for failure to pay child support payments or for the establishment of paternity, the defendant shall be punished by a fine of not less than $1,000 and not more than $10,000 and by imprisonment for not less than 60 days; provided, however, that the sentence shall not be suspended, nor shall any such person be eligible for probation, parole, or furlough or receive any deduction from his sentence for good conduct until he shall have served sixty days of such sentence.
Judge's Requirements	When considering a complaint filed under chapter 209A, a judge shall cause a search to be made of the records contained within the statewide domestic violence record keeping system maintained by the office of the commissioner of probation and shall review the resulting data to determine whether the named defendant has a civil or criminal record involving domestic or other violence. Upon receipt of information that an outstanding warrant exists against the named defendant, a judge shall order that the appropriate law enforcement officials be notified and shall order that any information regarding the defendant's most recent whereabouts shall be forwarded to such officials. In all instances where an outstanding warrant exists, a judge shall make a finding, based upon all of the circumstances, as to whether an imminent threat of bodily injury exists to the petitioner. In all instances where such an imminent threat of bodily injury is found to exist, the judge shall notify the appropriate law enforcement officials of such finding and such officials shall take all necessary actions to execute any such outstanding warrant as soon as is practicable.
Vacated Order	The court shall notify the appropriate law enforcement agency in writing whenever any such order is vacated and shall direct the agency to destroy all record of such vacated order and such agency shall comply with that directive.

[1222] The 2009 Massachusetts Domestic Violence Enforcement Guidelines

C. 209A § 7	VIOLATION OF A PROTECTIVE ORDER
Proof Required for a Protective Order Violation Conviction	In the ***Commonwealth v. Silva***, the SJC ruled "to establish a violation of G.L. c. 209A, § 7, the Commonwealth must prove that: 1) A valid G.L. c. 209A order was entered by a judge and was in effect on the date of the alleged violation; 2) The defendant violated the order; and 3) The defendant had knowledge of the order (see notes below)." [1223]
Only Vacate, No Contact, and Refrain from abuse, and fail to surrender are criminal violations	The only criminal violations that may be prosecuted (under Section 7) are those relating to orders: a. to vacate, b. to refrain from abuse, or c. to have no contact (this includes "stay away" orders). d. failure to surrender firearms, ammunition and related licenses (via § 6 see note below) In ***Com. v. Finase***, the SJC stated "It does not appear that *all* violations of any c. 209A order are criminalized. In *Commonwealth v. Delaney*, the Supreme Judicial Court held that only the offenses expressly set forth in G.L. c. 209A, Section 7, constituted criminal violations of the statute. In contrast, any other violation of a c. 209A order must be prosecuted as a criminal contempt.[1224] (See criminal contempt in Crimes Against Public Justice section) Section 3 authorizes the court to issue numerous other types of orders, such as ordering the defendant to pay temporary support for the plaintiff and ordering the defendant to pay the person abused monetary compensation for the losses suffered as a direct result of such abuse. The terms of Section 7 do not encompass these latter types of orders.[1225] These other violations may be charged under contempt of court. **NOTE**: c. 209A § 6 requires an arrest of the defendant who fails to surrender firearms, ammunition and licenses in violation of § 3B.
No Contact orders and "Stay away" orders	Pursuant to a "**stay away**" order, the defendant may not come within a specified distance of the protected party, usually stated in the order, but written or oral contact between the parties is not prohibited. By contrast, a "**no contact**" order mandates that the defendant not communicate by any means with the protected party, in addition to remaining physically separated. [1226] Thus, a "stay away" violation is arrestable because it is a type of no contact order.
Multiple Violations	In *Commonwealth v. Housen* (2013), the Appeals Court ruled that when a protective order protects more than one person (e.g. a mother and her children) the defendant can be convicted of multiple violations when he/she violates a stay away provision and in doing so has contact with multiple protected persons even if the contact occurs simultaneously.

[1223] *Commonwealth v. Silva,* 431 Mass. 401, 403 (2000)
[1224] *Com. v. Delaney* was quoting *Commonwealth v. Gordon,* 407 Mass. 340, 345, 553 N.E.2d 915 (1990).
[1225] *Commonwealth v. Finase,* 435 Mass. 310
[1226] *Commonwealth v. Finase,* 435 Mass. 310. Also see See *Commonwealth v. Butler,* **40 Mass.App.Ct. 906,** 907 (1996)

C. 209A § 7 VIOLATION OF A PROTECTIVE ORDER

<table>
<tr><th colspan="2">Arrest Power, Penalties & Notes</th></tr>
<tr><td>Power of Arrest</td><td>A Police Officer SHALL arrest any person a law officer witnesses or has probable cause to believe has violated a temporary or permanent vacate, restraining, or no-contact order or judgment issued pursuant to:
• Chapter 208 sections 18, 34B or 34C (certain Divorce Protective Orders)
• Chapter 209 § 32 (Support Order issued by the Court among married people),
• Chapter 209A § 3 & 3C (Abuse Prevention Order), § 3B (Firearm/License Surrender Order), § 4 (Temporary Abuse Prevention Order) or § 5 (Emergency Abuse Prevention Order)
or
• Chapter 209C § 15 or 20 (certain Child born out of Wedlock order)
or
• Similar protection order issued by another jurisdiction.
Attorney Hanrahan's Note: Not all violations are "criminal" violations. See explanation on above on criminal violations.</td></tr>
<tr><th colspan="2">Knowledge of the Order Issues</th></tr>
<tr><td>Failure to serve is not fatal</td><td>While failure to serve is " 'relevant to a determination as to whether the defendant possessed the knowledge required to convict him of violating the order' ... it is not fatal if the Commonwealth can demonstrate that the defendant had actual knowledge of the terms of the order." [1227]
Knowledge of the contents of a restraining order can be proven by demonstrating the defendant 'had actual or constructive knowledge of the order and its terms and conditions.'[1228]</td></tr>
<tr><td>Attorney Hanrahan's Comment</td><td>Although a defendant may still be convicted despite the fact that he was not served in-hand with the order, it still must be shown that he was aware of the order's existence. It is important to note any statements made by the defendant that would indicate the defendant's knowledge of the order because it is not an uncommon defense to later claim no knowledge of the order or its terms.</td></tr>
<tr><td>An order extension</td><td>Where there is actual service of an initial order that specifically informed the defendant of a hearing date for extension of that order, the defendant cannot escape being charged with knowledge that the initial order was extended (and the terms of the extended order) merely because he failed to attend the hearing on the extension of the order. [1229]</td></tr>
<tr><th colspan="2">Violation Issues</th></tr>
<tr><td>Protective order violations are non-bailable</td><td>Chapter 276 § 57 states in relevant part "a person arrested and charged with a violation of an order or judgment issued pursuant to chapter 208 § 8, 34B or 34C, chapter 209 § 32, chapter 209A § 3, 4, or 5, or chapter 209C § 15 or 20, or arrested and charged with a misdemeanor or felony involving abuse as defined in chapter 209A § 1 while an order of protection issued under said chapter 209A was in effect against said person, shall not be released out of court by a clerk of courts, clerk of a district court, bail commissioner or master in chancery."</td></tr>
</table>

DOMESTIC LAWS

[1227] *Commonwealth v. Welch*,58 Mass.App.Ct. 408, 410 (2003), quoting from *Commonwealth v. Delaney*, 425 Mass. 587, 593 (1997), cert. denied, 522 U.S. 1058 (1998).
[1228] *Commonwealth v. Crimmins*, 46 Mass.App.Ct. 489, 491-492 (1999).
[1229] See *Commonwealth v. Chartier*, 43 Mass.App.Ct. 758, 765, 686 N.E.2d 1055 (1997). See also *Commonwealth v. Delaney, supra* at 592, 682 N.E.2d 611, quoting *Commonwealth v. Olivo*, 369 Mass. 62, 69, 337 N.E.2d 904 (1975)

C. 209A § 7	VIOLATION OF A PROTECTIVE ORDER
Abuse	The refrain from abuse provision can be violated in many ways. The most common is perhaps an assault and battery. However, even a threat may be deemed abuse. In the 2012 case of ***Commonwealth v. Regil,*** the defendant was order not to abuse the plaintiff "by harming, threatening or attempting to harm the plaintiff physically or by placing the plaintiff in fear of imminent serious physical harm." The Appeals Court ruled that the defendant violated the no abuse provision by stating to the plaintiff (victim) "watch your back, because you're dead."
Cordial Contact is a Violation	In ***Commonwealth v. Tate***, the defendant was convicted for violating the no contact provision of a protective order when he sent flowers to the plaintiff in an effort to reconcile.
Plaintiff Actions & Behavior	**Attorney Hanrahan's Comment:** If the order is in effect the defendant must not violate its terms, even if the plaintiff invites the defendant to violate the order or even if the plaintiff makes the initial contact. Only the Court can amend or rescind the terms of the order. Additionally, the plaintiff *cannot* be charged with violating the order. Only the defendant is prohibited from engaging in the prescribed contact.
Victim Presence is not required	A "stay away" order (i.e. stay 100 yards from plaintiff's workplace) does not require that the plaintiff actually be at the location (unless the order specifically indicates) that the defendant is required to stay away from at the time of the violation, unless the order specifically states that the plaintiff must be present. The goal of a stay away order is "to create a safe haven" for the plaintiff.[1230]
Accidental Contact	In connection with an alleged violation of a G.L. c. 209A order the SJC has stated that the "long-standing common-law principle that, absent contrary indication from the Legislature, we assume that the Legislature did not intend `to make accidents and mistakes crimes.'" [1231] If a person subject to a restraining order happens upon a protected person whom he or she did not and could not reasonably know to be present at that time and place, the party subject to the order must make reasonable efforts to terminate the accidental encounter.[1232] When there is evidence that fairly raises the issue of accident, the burden falls on the Commonwealth to disprove it.[1233] **Attorney Hanrahan's Comment:** If the defendant accidentally or inadvertently encounters the plaintiff of the 209A order he/she will not have committed a violation absent some further effort to make contact, or to prolong the inadvertent contact. The defendant should remove himself/herself from the situation and not make any further contact (if the order prohibits contact).
Incidental Contact	If there is evidence that suggests that the alleged contact may have been incidental to a legitimate, lawful activity such as *(e.g., contacting a child, going to work, going to school)* , the Commonwealth must prove beyond a reasonable doubt that the alleged violation was not incidental to that permitted activity. Conduct that is incidental to legitimate, lawful activity is conduct which is connected to that activity — conduct which is purely or naturally a reasonable outgrowth or necessary part of that legitimate, lawful activity. For example, if a person subject to an abuse prevention order waited in the only public hallway of a courthouse for the start of a hearing, and the person protected by that order was waiting somewhere else in that same public hallway, that conduct would be incidental to a legitimate, lawful activity — attending the court hearing. Although there might be a stay away order in effect, there would be no violation of that order because the conduct was purely a natural and reasonable outgrowth of the scheduling of the hearing. On the other hand, if the subject entered the public hallway and intentionally stood directly next to the plaintiff when the subject could have stood

[1230] *Commonwealth v. Habenstreit*, 57 Mass.App.Ct. 785 (2003)
[1231] *Commonwealth v. Collier,* 427 Mass. 385, 388 (1998), quoting *Commonwealth v. Wallace,* 14 Mass.App.Ct. 358, 364 (1982).
[1232] *Commonwealth v. Stoltz,* 73 Mass. App. Ct. 642 (2009).
[1233] See *Commonwealth v. Zezima*, 387 Mass. 748, 756, 443 N.E.2d 1282 (1982); *Commonwealth v. Ferguson,* 30 Mass. App. Ct. 580, 583, 571 N.E.2d 411(1991) ("Where the evidence raises the possibility of accident, the defendant is, as matter of due process, entitled upon request to a jury instruction that the Commonwealth has the burden of proving beyond a reasonable doubt that the act was not accidental").

C. 209A § 7	VIOLATION OF A PROTECTIVE ORDER
	elsewhere, that would violate the order because it was not incidental or necessary to the lawful activity. The Commonwealth may prove that the defendant's conduct was not incidental to a lawful activity by proving that the alleged violation was not purely or naturally a reasonable outgrowth or necessary part of that legitimate, lawful activity. Put another way, the Commonwealth must prove that the defendant's conduct was not a good faith attempt by the defendant to do that which was permitted. In deciding whether there was any contact which violated the abuse prevention order, you may consider any evidence relevant to: (1) the nature and purpose of any contact; (2) the number of contacts over time; (3) the length of any contact; and (4) the substance and character of any statements made during any contact.[1234]
Third Party Contact	When it is claimed that a third party committed an act that would have violated c. 209A, § 7, if committed by the defendant, **there must be proof that the defendant intended the act that resulted in the violation**, but such proof may consist of circumstantial evidence.[1235] In the 2013 case of ***Commonwealth v. Vital***, the defendant, after sexually assaulting a 12 year old girl, contacted his priest and asked the priest to convince the girl's family not to pursue charges. The priest reached out to the family. The court found that this amounted to third party contact in violation of the order.
PENALTIES & RAMIFICATIONS OF A VIOLATION	
Penalty	A fine of not more than $5,000, or by imprisonment for not more than 2½ years in a HOC, or by both such fine and imprisonment. In addition to the court shall order persons convicted of a crime under this statute to pay a fine of $25 that shall be transmitted to the treasurer for deposit into the General Fund.
Attorney Hanrahan's Note	The defendant may also be charged with the underlying offense (e.g. trespassing, A&B etc.).
Batterer's Program	The court shall order the defendant to complete a certified batterer's intervention program unless, upon good cause shown, the court issues specific written findings describing the reasons that batterer's intervention should not be ordered or unless the batterer's intervention program determines that the defendant is not suitable for intervention. The court shall not order substance abuse or anger management treatment or any other form of treatment as a substitute for certified batterer's intervention. If a defendant ordered to undergo treatment has received a suspended sentence, the original sentence shall be reimposed if the defendant fails to participate in said program as required by the terms of his probation. When a defendant has been ordered to participate in a treatment program pursuant to this section, the defendant shall be required to regularly attend a certified or provisionally certified batterer's treatment program. To the extent permitted by professional requirements of confidentiality, said program shall communicate with local battered women's programs for the purpose of protecting the victim's safety. Additionally, it shall specify the defendant's attendance requirements and keep the probation department informed of whether the defendant is in compliance.

[1234] Model Jury Instructions revised 2011. *Commonwealth* v. *Silva*, 431 Mass. 194, 726 N.E.2d 408 (2000); *Commonwealth v. Consoli,* 58 Mass. App. Ct. 734, 738 (2003); *Commonwealth v. Stewart,* 52 Mass. App. Ct. 755, 756 N.E.2d 22 (2001); *Commonwealth v. Leger,* 52 Mass. App. Ct. 232, 752 N.E.2d 799 (2001); *Commonwealth v. Mendonca,* 50 Mass. App. Ct. 684, 687 n.8, 740 N.E.2d 799 n.8 (2001).
[1235] See *Commonwealth v. Collier,* 427 Mass. 385, 389, 693 N.E.2d 673 (1998)

C. 209A § 7	VIOLATION OF A PROTECTIVE ORDER
Child Support Retaliation	If the court determines that the violation was in retaliation for the defendant being reported by the plaintiff to the department of revenue for failure to pay child support payments or for the establishment of paternity, the defendant shall be punished by a fine of not less than $1,000 and not more than $10,000 and by imprisonment for not less than 60 days; provided, however, that the sentence shall not be suspended, nor shall any such person be eligible for probation, parole, or furlough or receive any deduction from his sentence for good conduct until he shall have served 60 days of such sentence.
Substance Abuse Program	In addition to, but not in lieu of, orders for treatment, if the defendant has a substance abuse problem, the court may order appropriate treatment for such problem. All ordered treatment shall last until the end of the probationary period or until the treatment program decides to discharge the defendant, whichever comes first. When the defendant is not in compliance with the terms of probation, the court shall hold a revocation of probation hearing. To the extent possible, the defendant shall be responsible for paying all costs for court ordered treatment.
GPS Monitoring	Where a defendant has been found in violation of an abuse prevention order under chapter 209A or a protection order issued by another jurisdiction, the court may, in addition to the penalties provided for in this section after conviction, as an alternative to incarceration and, as a condition of probation, prohibit contact with the victim through the establishment of court defined geographic exclusion zones including, but not limited to, the areas in and around the complainant's residence, place of employment, and the complainant's child's school, and order that the defendant to wear a global positioning satellite tracking device designed to transmit and record the defendant's location data. If the defendant enters a court defined exclusion zone, the defendant's location data shall be immediately transmitted to the complainant, and to the police, through an appropriate means including, but not limited to, the telephone, an electronic beeper or a paging device. The global positioning satellite device and its tracking shall be administered by the department of probation. If a court finds that the defendant has entered a geographic exclusion zone, it shall revoke his probation and the defendant shall be fined, imprisoned or both as provided in this section. Based on the defendant's ability to pay, the court may also order him to pay the monthly costs or portion thereof for monitoring through the global positioning satellite tracking system.
Restitution	In each instance where there is a violation of an abuse prevention order or a protection order issued by another jurisdiction, the court may order the defendant to pay the plaintiff for all damages including, but not limited to, cost for shelter or emergency housing, loss of earnings or support, out-of-pocket losses for injuries sustained or property damaged, medical expenses, moving expenses, cost for obtaining an unlisted telephone number, and reasonable attorney's fees.
Related Offense	
Criminal Contempt	In order to prove a defendant guilty of criminal contempt, the Commonwealth must prove beyond a reasonable doubt that: • there was a clear, outstanding order of the court, • that the defendant knew about the order, and • that the defendant clearly and intentionally disobeyed the order in circumstances in which he was able to obey it." [1236] See Crimes Against Public Justice section for more on this topic.

[1236] *Commonwealth v. Brogan*, 415 Mass. 169, 171, 612 N.E.2d 656 (1993), quoting *Furtado v. Furtado*, 380 Mass. 137, 145, 402 N.E.2d 1024 (1980).

CHILD & FAMILY SUPPORT

C. 273 § 1	ABANDONEMENT & NON-SUPPORT
Elements	
1.	A spouse or parent shall be guilty of a felony if he or she does any of the following:
2.	i. **Abandon within Massachusetts:** abandons his spouse or minor child without making reasonable provisions for the support of his/her spouse or minor child or both of them; or ii. **Abandon by leaving Massachusetts:** leaves Massachusetts and goes into another state without making reasonable provisions for the support of his/her spouse or minor child or both of them; or iii. **Abandon by entering Massachusetts:** enters Massachusetts from another state without making reasonable provisions for the support of his/her spouse or minor child, or both of them, living in another state; or iv. **Support Order Violation**: willfully and while having the financial ability or earning capacity to have complied, he/she fails to comply with an order or judgment for support in Massachusetts of similar laws of other states.
Arrest Power, Penalties & Notes	
Power of Arrest	**Felony** – a police officer may effect a warrantless arrest for this offense provided he/she has probable cause that the suspect committed the offense.
Penalty	HOC for not more than 2½ years or **state prison (F)** for not more than 5 years and/or a fine of up to $5,000. If the defendant left his/her family in Massachusetts or another state and failed to provide support the penalty increases to HOC for 2½ years or **state prison (F)** for not more than 10 years and/or a fine of up to $10,000.
Civil Proceeding no effect	A civil proceeding will not prevent a criminal prosecution under this statute.
Attorney Hanrahan's Note:	The Massachusetts Department of Revenue may seek an arrest warrant for non-compliance of a child support order when the defendant is 6 months or more behind in support payments.
Related Statutes, Case Law & Other Important Information	
Child Born out of Wedlock	See C. 273 § 15 later in this section.
Parental Support	See C. 273 § 20, which requires children to support needy parents, later in this section.
Disabled Child Support	C. 273 § 23 requires the mother and/or father of a needy disabled person to provide support. This is a misdemeanor offense with no statutory power of arrest.

C. 273 § 15	DUTY TO SUPPORT CHILD BORN OUT OF WEDLOCK
Elements	
1.	It is unlawful for a parent of a minor child born out of wedlock (whether or not the child was born in Massachusetts) to:
2.	• Willfully neglect or refuse to contribute reasonably to the support of the child • Leave Massachusetts and go into another state without making reasonable provision for the support of the child • Enter Massachusetts from another state without making reasonable provision for the support of the child domiciled in another state • Willfully and while having the financial ability or earning capacity to comply, fail to comply with an order or judgment for support from a Massachusetts court or entered pursuant to similar laws of other states
Arrest Power, Penalties & Notes	
Power of Arrest	**Felony** – a police officer may effect a warrantless arrest for this offense provided he/she has probable cause that the suspect committed the offense.
Penalty	HOC for not more than 2½ years or **state prison (F)** for not more than 5 years and/or a fine of up to $5,000. If the defendant left his/her family in Massachusetts or another state and failed to provide support the penalty increases to HOC for 2½ years or **state prison (F)** for not more than 10 years and/or a fine of up to $10,000.
Attorney Hanrahan's Comment	This offense is essentially the same as Chapter 273 § 1 however this offense specifically addresses children of unmarried parents.
Related Statutes, Case Law & Other Important Information	
Parental Support	See c. 273 § 20, which requires children to support needy parents, later in this section.
Disabled Child Support	Chapter 273 § 23 requires the mother and/or father of a needy disabled person to provide support. This is a misdemeanor offense with no statutory power of arrest.

C. 273 § 15B	CONCEALING ASSETS FOR THE PURPOSE OF AVOIDING PAYMENT
Elements	
1.	The defendant
2.	Receives or conceals an asset of another
3.	Knowing that the asset is being transferred for the purpose of concealing it to avoid payment of an order or judgment for support
Arrest Power, Penalties & Notes	
Power of Arrest	**Misdemeanor** – there is no statutory authority granting warrantless powers of arrest for this offense. However, if the offense is committed in public, in the officer's presence, and is creating a **breach of the peace** an arrest would be lawful.

C. 273 § 15B	CONCEALING ASSETS FOR THE PURPOSE OF AVOIDING PAYMENT
Penalty	A fine of not more than $5,000 or by imprisonment in a jail or HOC for not more than 2½ years, or by both such fine and imprisonment. The court may in the alternative to the foregoing punishment divert the defendant to a program as defined in c. 276A §1.
Attorney Hanrahan's Comment	This law punishes a third party who assists a father hide assets in an attempt to avoid paying court ordered support.

C. 273 § 20	NEGLECT OR REFUSAL TO SUPPORT PARENT
Elements	
1.	Any person, over 18 years old,
2.	Who, being possessed of sufficient means,
3.	Unreasonably neglects or refuses to provide for the support and maintenance of his parent, • whether father or mother • who resides in Massachusetts
4.	When such parent through misfortune and without fault of his/her own is destitute of means of sustenance and unable by reason of: • old age • infirmity, or • illness to support and maintain himself/herself
5.	Shall be punished
Exception	No such neglect or refusal shall be deemed unreasonable as to a child who shall not during his minority have been reasonably supported by such parent, if such parent was charged with the duty so to do, nor as to a child who, being one of two or more children, has made proper and reasonable contribution toward the support of such parent.
Arrest Power, Penalties & Notes	
Power of Arrest	**Misdemeanor** – there is no statutory authority granting warrantless powers of arrest for this offense. However, if the offense is committed in public, in the officer's presence, and is creating a **breach of the peace** an arrest would be lawful.
Penalty	A fine of not more than $200 or by imprisonment for not more than 1 year, or both.

STALKING/HARASSMENT

C. 265 § 43	STALKING
Elements	The defendant willfully and maliciously does the following: • Engages in a knowing pattern of conduct or series of acts (3 or more times) over a period of time, • Directed at a specific person, • Which seriously alarms or annoys that person and would cause a reasonable person to suffer substantial emotional distress, and • Makes a threat with the intent to place the person in imminent fear of death or bodily injury.
	Arrest Power, Penalties & Notes
Power of Arrest	**Felony** – a police officer may effect a warrantless arrest for this offense provided he/she has probable cause that the suspect committed the offense.
Penalty	Imprisonment in the **state prison (F)** for not more than 5 years or by a fine of not more than $1,000, or imprisonment in the HOC for not more than 2½ years or by both such fine and imprisonment.
	Related Statutes, Case Law & Other Important Information
Mail, Telephone and Electronic Stalking Possible	The conduct, acts or threats described in this subsection shall include, but not be limited to conduct, acts or threats conducted by: • Mail • By use of a telephonic or telecommunication device • Electronic communication device including, but not limited to any device that transfers signs, signals, writing, images, sounds, data, or intelligence of any nature transmitted in whole or in part by a wire, radio, electromagnetic, photo-electronic or photo-optical system, including, but not limited to: o electronic mail, o internet communications, o instant messages o facsimile communications
The Threat Requirement	The "threat" element "closely approximates the common law definition of the crime of assault" and should be so interpreted. *Commonwealth v. Matsos,* 421 Mass. 391, 394, 657 N.E.2d 467, 470 (1995). This threat requirement is the distinguishing element between stalking and criminal harassment. The threat does not necessarily need to be a direct threat, it can consist of conduct or statements that would put the victim in reasonable apprehension that force may be used (similar to the offense of criminal assault). In ***Commonwealth v. Matsos***, the defendant sent the victim more than forty letters during a ten-month period. These letters, which amounted to hundreds of pages, revealed the defendant's intense obsession with the victim and his anger at her rejection of him, and the letters chronicle a campaign of harassment mounted by him, which included a malicious attempt to interfere with the victim's employment. We disagree with the defendant's contention that the evidence did not provide a basis for a reasonable juror to conclude that the defendant had intentionally placed the victim in imminent fear of death or serious bodily injury. The defendant identified himself as "The Stalker" in a return address. Among other quite explicit threats, he warned the victim, "There is [going to come] a day when you are [going to] want to come and see me.... But you will never see me, your eyes will alway[s]

C. 265 § 43	STALKING
	be closed." He made references to guns and silencers, to dangerous friends, and to his own involvement in illegal activity. He made it clear that he was following the victim and would be able to find her, and he made an accusation against the victim's employer (the Salem Police Department) of drug use, this demonstrated that he was prepared to act on his threats of harassment and violence. The Court ruled that the jury could have found that the defendant intended to place the victim in fear of imminent bodily injury which would satisfy the threat element. In determining whether the "threat" element of a stalking violation is satisfied, the "court will look to the actions and *words* of the defendant in light of the attendant circumstances."[1237]
Threat must be aimed at victim	The threat component of the stalking statute specifically targets communications by the defendant that are *aimed at placing the victim in fear of physical violence*, whether or not the defendant actually intends to commit the threatened act of violence.[1238]
Social Media Posting	In the 2015 case of ***Commonwealth v. Walters***, the SJC ruled "where a defendant posted a threat to a Facebook page that meets the requirements of (the stalking statute) and has engaged in a series of acts or pattern of conduct (as described in the statute), the fact that the threat appears on the Internet is <u>not</u> a barrier to prosecution for stalking." However, it must be proven that the defendant intended the threat to reach the victim.
Imminent Fear	In the 2014 case of ***Commonwealth v. Gupta***, the SJC ruled that the crime of stalking aims to protect victims from fear itself, and not merely ultimate physical harm, therefore the *imminent* requirement in the law refers to *imminent* fear and not imminent physical harm. In this case, the defendant repeatedly phoned the victim from India threatening to harm her. Because he was in India at the time the harm was not imminent but the fear inflicted was.
"Series of Acts" means 3 or more	The statutory phrase "pattern of conduct or series of acts" appears to require three or more incidents. *Commonwealth* v. *Kwiatkowski,* 418 Mass. at 548.
Emotional Distress requirement	In the 2011 case of ***Com. v. Cullen,*** the SJC ruled that the requirement that a series of acts or pattern of conduct which results in alarm or annoyance and substantial emotional distress to a specific person *does <u>not</u> require each act in the series or pattern to produce alarm or annoyance and substantial emotional distress separately*, or to do so on each occasion.
Willful and malicious conduct	In *Commonwealth v. O'Neil*, the Court ruled that willful conduct must be intentional (as opposed to negligent) but does not require that the defendant intend its harmful consequences as well. The modern definition of "malice" does not require any showing of "cruelty, hostility or revenge, nor does it require an actual intent to cause the required harm, but merely that the conduct be "intentional and without justification or mitigation, and any reasonable prudent person would have foreseen the actual harm that resulted." [1239]

HARASSMENT & STALKING

[1237] *Commonwealth v. Matsos,* **421 Mass. 391**, 394-395 (1995), quoting *Commonwealth v. Gordon,* 407 Mass. 340, 349 (1990) (

[1238] See Commonwealth v. Matsos, 421 Mass. 391, 395 (1995) (to prove threat in furtherance of stalking, "Commonwealth need not prove that the defendant actually intended to harm the victim . . . [;] it need only prove that the defendant's threats were reasonably calculated to place the victim in imminent fear of bodily injury".

[1239] *Commonwealth v. O'Neil,* 67 Mass. App.Ct. 284, 290-293, 853 N.E.2d 576, 582-584 (2006) (criminal harassment)

C. 265 § 43	STALKING
Stalking in violation of a court order.	General Laws c. 265, § 43(b) creates an aggravated form of this offense with a mandatory minimum penalty if it is committed in violation of a temporary or permanent vacate, restraining or no-contact order or judgment issued pursuant to G.L. c. 208, §§ 18, 34B or 34C, G.L. c. 209, § 32, G.L. c. 209A, §§ 3-5, or G.L. c. 209C, §§ 15 or 20, or a protection order issued by another jurisdiction, or a temporary restraining order or preliminary or permanent injunction issued by the Superior Court. **Penalty: 1st Offense**: imprisonment in a jail or the **state prison (F)** for **not less than 1 year** and not more than 5 years. No sentence imposed under the provisions of this subsection shall be less than a **mandatory minimum** term of imprisonment of **one year**. **2nd or Subsequent Offense:** imprisonment in a jail or the **state prison (F)** for not **less than 2 years** and not more than ten years. No sentence imposed under the provisions of this subsection shall be less than a **mandatory minimum** term of imprisonment of **two years**.
Violation of c. 209A order is lesser included offense.	Violation of a 209A order (G.L. c. 209A, § 7) is a lesser included offense of stalking (G.L. c. 265, § 43), and therefore a defendant who has been convicted of violating a c. 209A order may not be convicted of stalking based upon the same conduct. *Edge v. Commonwealth*, 451 Mass. 74, 76-77, 883 N.E.2d 928, 931 (2008).
Venue	Violations of § 43 may be prosecuted wherever "an act constituting an element of the crime was committed." G.L. c. 277, § 62B.

c. 265 § 43A	CRIMINAL HARASSMENT
	Elements
1.	The defendant engaged in a knowing pattern of conduct or speech, or series of acts, on at least 3 separate occasions;
2.	The defendant intended to target the victim with the harassing conduct or speech, or series of acts, on each occasion;
3.	The conduct or speech, or series of acts, were of such a nature that they seriously alarmed the victim;
4.	The conduct or speech, or series of acts, were of such a nature that they would cause a reasonable person to suffer substantial emotional distress; and
5.	The defendant committed the conduct or speech, or series of acts, willfully and maliciously.
	Arrest Power, Penalties & Notes
Power of Arrest	**Misdemeanor** – although chapter 265 § 43A does not provide any warrantless arrest powers, Chapter 258E (the harassment prevention law) permits a police officer to arrest on probable cause via c. 258E § 8 (see harassment prevention orders for more).
Penalty	**1st offense**: Imprisonment in a HOC for not more than 2½ years or by a fine of not more than $1,000, or by both such fine and imprisonment. **2nd or subsequent**: imprisonment in a HOC for not more than 2½ years or by imprisonment in the **state prison (F)** for not more than 10 years.

c. 265 § 43A	CRIMINAL HARASSMENT
Attorney Hanrahan's Comment	The criminal harassment law was passed in response to a perceived loophole in the stalking statute. The stalking statute expressly includes "threatening" conduct or acts, those victims plagued by harassment that, although potentially dangerous, did not include an overt 'threat' and thus action could not be taken.
Related Statutes, Case Law & Other Important Information	
Includes mail, telephone and electronic methods	The conduct or acts described in this statute shall include, but not be limited to, conduct or acts conducted by **mail or by use of a telephonic or telecommunication device or electronic communication** device including, but not limited to, any device that transfers signs, signals, writing, images, sounds, data or intelligence of any nature transmitted in whole or in part by a wire, radio, electromagnetic, photo-electronic or photo-optical system, including, but not limited to, electronic mail, internet communications, instant messages or facsimile communications.
Directed at a specific person	In ***Commonwealth v. McDonald***, the SJC ruled for a conviction of Criminal Harassment (c. 265 § 43A) the conduct must be proven to be intentional and directed at a specific person.
Wilful and Malicious	Malicious acts are "done with an evil disposition, a wrong and unlawful motive or purpose; the wilful doing of an injurious act without lawful excuse". "Conduct is wilful when the actor intends both the conduct and its harmful consequences and may be wilful and malicious although its harmful consequences are neither substantial nor highly likely." *Commonwealth v. McDonald* (2012).
Harassment Prevention Orders	See Harassment Prevention order discussed later in this section.

C. 269 § 14A ANNOYING TELEPHONE CALLS/ELECTRONIC COMMUNICATION

Elements	
1.	• Whoever telephones another person or contacts another person by electronic communication, or • Causes any person to be telephoned or contacted by electronic communication,
2.	Repeatedly, (at least 3 times): • For the sole purpose of harassing, annoying or molesting such person or his family, whether or not conversation ensues or • Uses indecent or obscene language to such person.
Arrest Power, Penalties & Notes	
Power of Arrest	**Misdemeanor** – there is no statutory authority granting warrantless powers of arrest for this offense. However, if the offense is committed in public, in the officer's presence, and is creating a **breach of the peace** an arrest would be lawful.
Penalty	A fine of not more than $500 or by imprisonment for not more than three months, or both
Attorney Hanrahan's Comment	Modern technology, such as caller ID and private call blocking, has greatly reduced the frequency of this offense. However, what was once limited to telephone calls now covers other forms of contact (e.g. harassing emails).
Related Statutes, Case Law & Other Important Information	
Electronic Communication	For purposes of this section, **"electronic communication"** shall include, but not be limited to, any transfer of signs, signals, writing, images, sounds, data or intelligence of any nature transmitted in whole or in part by a wire, radio, electromagnetic, photo-electronic or photo-optical system.
Intent can be inferred	In ***Commonwealth v. Roberts***, the SJC ruled that "the jury could infer the required intent from the number of calls, the tenor of the calls, their sequence and timing, and the defendant's persistence in placing the calls despite repeatedly being asked to cease . . . ."*);*
Not motivated solely to harass = no violation	In ***Commonwealth v. Strahan** (1991),* the Court ruled that calling 11 times in 7 minutes, while perhaps partially motivated by a desire to harass, does not support conviction of § 14A where evidence suggests at least a partial motive was to reestablish a prior relationship with victim.
Anonymous telephone calls	"Anonymous telephone calls and acts . . . are, by their nature, not perceptibly linked to a particular individual. They are anonymous. Yet connections may be inferred through timing, mode of communication, content of the communication, similarity to identified conduct, and interpersonal relationships, particularly those involving grievances against the recipient of the unwanted communication." [1240]
Cannot annoy the Police	In ***Commonwealth v. Voight,*** the court ruled that this offense does not apply to a police department because a police department is not a "person" but the calls "could take on a tone so directed at the recipient [employee] as an individual as to constitute harassment under the statute". However, since that time the legislature has created § 14B (False Calls to 911 – See Public Justice Crimes Section of this manual).

[1240] *Commonwealth v. Wotan*, 37 Mass. App. Ct. at 730-734, 643 N.E.2d at 64-66 (1996).

Harassment Prevention Orders

Overview: In 2010, the Legislature created the harassment prevention laws (chapter 258E). These laws were designed to protect those people who were suffering from harassment but would not otherwise qualify for a 209A domestic violence protective order. The harassment prevention order is almost identical to a 209A protective order with a few major distinctions; one of those major distinctions involves the lack of domestic relationship and the other is the lack of authority, under chapter 258E, for the Court to issue a firearm surrender order. For this reason, and others (such as child custody and support matters), once a victim is eligible for both a harassment prevention order and a 209A domestic violence protection order, the 209A order would be the better option.

C. 258E § 1	DEFINITIONS FOR HARASSMENT PREVENTION ORDER
As used in this chapter the following words shall, unless the context clearly requires otherwise, have the following meanings:	
Abuse	Attempting to cause or causing physical harm to another or placing another in fear of imminent serious physical harm.
Harassment	• 3 or more acts of willful and malicious conduct • Aimed at a specific person • Committed with the intent to cause fear, intimidation, abuse or damage to property • And does in fact cause fear, intimidation, abuse or damage to property **Or** • An act that: (A) by force, threat or duress causes another to involuntarily engage in sexual relations; or (B) constitutes a violation of c. 265 § 13B (**Indecent A&B on a child under 14**), c. 265 § 13F (**A&B or Indecent A&B on a Mentally Retarded Person**), c. 265 § 13H (**Indecent A&B**), c. 265 § 22, 22A, 23 (**Rape and Statutory Rape**), c. 265 § 24, 24B (**Assault with Intent to Rape**), c. 265 § 26C (**child enticement**), c. 265 § 43(**Stalking**), c. 265 § 43A (**Criminal Harassment**), or c. 272 § 3 (**drugging a person for sexual assault**).
Court	The district or Boston municipal court, the superior court or the juvenile court departments of the trial court.
Law Officer	Any officer authorized to serve criminal process.
Malicious	Characterized by cruelty, hostility or revenge.
Protection order issued by another jurisdiction	An injunction or other order issued by a court of another state, territory or possession of the United States, the Commonwealth of Puerto Rico, or the District of Columbia, or a tribal court that is issued for the purpose of preventing violent or threatening acts, abuse or harassment against, or contact or communication with or physical proximity to another person, including temporary and final orders issued by civil and criminal courts filed by or on behalf of a person seeking protection.

C. 258E § 1	DEFINITIONS FOR HARASSMENT PREVENTION ORDER
Attorney Hanrahan's Comment	A frequent question asked by law enforcement personnel is "Do the three or more acts have to be reported to the police each time?" Although, absent forced sex or one of the specifically mentioned offenses, there must be at least three distinct acts to constitute harassment under this law, there is no requirement in the statute that each act must be reported individually to the police. Obviously three separate reports will make it easier to investigate (because of the timeliness) and it will likely make it easier to prosecute, however there is no legal requirement to do so.
Related Statutes, Case Law & Other Important Information	
Venue c. 258 § 2	Proceedings under this chapter shall be filed, heard and determined in the superior court department or the respective divisions of the district court department or the Boston municipal court department having venue over the **plaintiff's residence.** The juvenile court department shall have exclusive jurisdiction of proceedings under this chapter in which the defendant is under the age of 17. Such proceedings shall be filed, heard and determined in the division of the juvenile court department having venue over the plaintiff's residence.
Specific Person	It must be proven that the conduct is specifically aimed at the plaintiff. In the 2015 case of ***Commonwealth v. Quinn*** the Appeals Court found that although the conduct may be the type that would cause fear, intimidation, etc. there was no proof that the defendant's conduct was aimed at the plaintiff as the two did not even know each other. The defendant was caught on surveillance video repeatedly entering the plaintiff's barn and rearranging items within and similar type behavior.

C. 258 § 3	PROTECTION FROM HARASSMENT: AVAILABLE RELIEF
Available Protections	A person suffering from harassment may file a complaint in the appropriate court requesting protection from such harassment. A person may petition the court under this chapter for an order that the defendant: (i) **refrain from abusing or harassing** the plaintiff, whether the defendant is an adult or minor; (ii) **refrain from contacting** the plaintiff, unless authorized by the court, whether the defendant is an adult or minor; (iii) **remain away** from the plaintiff's household or workplace, whether the defendant is an adult or minor; and (iv) **pay the plaintiff monetary compensation** for the losses suffered as a direct result of the harassment; provided, however, that compensatory damages shall include, but shall not be limited to, loss of earnings, out-of-pocket losses for injuries sustained or property damaged, cost of replacement of locks, medical expenses, cost for obtaining an unlisted phone number and reasonable attorney's fees.
Petition Guidelines	
Impoundment	The court may order that information in the case record be impounded in accordance with court rules.
No Fees	No filing fee shall be charged for the filing of the complaint. The plaintiff shall not be charged for certified copies of any orders entered by the court, or any copies of the file reasonably required for future court action or as a result of the loss or destruction of plaintiff's copies.
Timeliness	The court **shall not deny any complaint** filed under chapter 258E **solely because it was not filed within a particular time period** after the last alleged incident of harassment.

C. 258 § 3	PROTECTION FROM HARASSMENT: AVAILABLE RELIEF
Must reveal Prior/Pending actions	A party filing a complaint under chapter 258E shall be required to disclose any prior or pending actions involving the parties; including, but not limited to, court actions, administrative proceedings and disciplinary proceedings.
Length of Order	Any relief granted by the court **shall not extend for a period exceeding 1 year**.
Hearing Requirements	Every order shall, on its face, state the time and date the order is to expire and shall include the date and time that the matter will again be heard. If the plaintiff appears at the court at the date and time the order is to expire, the court shall determine whether or not to extend the order for any additional time reasonably necessary to protect the plaintiff or to enter a permanent order.
Extensions	When the expiration date stated on the order is on a date when the court is closed to business, the order shall not expire until the next date that the court is open to business. The plaintiff may appear on such next court business day at the time designated by the order to request that the order be extended. The court may also extend the order upon motion of the plaintiff, for such additional time as it deems necessary to protect the plaintiff from harassment. The fact that harassment has not occurred during the pendency of an order shall not, in itself, constitute sufficient ground for denying or failing to extend the order, or allowing an order to expire or be vacated or for refusing to issue a new order.
Modification Requirements	The **court may modify its order at any subsequent time upon motion by either party**; provided, however, that the non-moving party shall receive sufficient notice and opportunity to be heard on said modification. When the plaintiff's address is inaccessible to the defendant as provided in section 10 and the defendant has filed a motion to modify the court's order, the court shall be responsible for notifying the plaintiff. In no event shall the court disclose any such inaccessible address.
No preclusion of other remedies	An action commenced under chapter 258E shall not preclude any other civil or criminal remedies.
	Related Statutes, Case Law & Other Important Information
Order may be issued without Defendant Notice **C. 258E § 5**	If the plaintiff demonstrates **a substantial likelihood of immediate danger of harassment**, the court may enter temporary relief orders **without notice** as it deems necessary to protect the plaintiff from harassment and shall immediately thereafter notify the defendant that the temporary orders have been issued. The court shall give the defendant an opportunity to be heard on the question of continuing the temporary order and of granting other relief as requested by the plaintiff **not later than 10 court business days after such orders are entered**.
Emergency Harassment Orders **c. 258E § 6**	**Court Closed or Plaintiff Physically Unable to Appear:** • When the court is closed for business or • the plaintiff is unable to appear in court because of severe hardship due to the plaintiff's physical condition, • the court may grant relief to the plaintiff if the plaintiff demonstrates a substantial likelihood of immediate danger of harassment.

HARASSMENT & STALKING

C. 258 § 3	PROTECTION FROM HARASSMENT: AVAILABLE RELIEF
	Telephonic Assessment In the discretion of the justice, relief may be granted and communicated by telephone to an officer or employee of an appropriate law enforcement agency, who shall record such order on a form of order promulgated for such use by the chief justice for administration and management and shall deliver a copy of such order on the next court day to the clerk or clerk-magistrate of the court having venue and jurisdiction over the matter. If relief has been granted without the filing of a complaint pursuant to this section, the plaintiff shall appear in court on the next available business day to file a complaint. **Plaintiff Incapable of Appearing in Court** If the plaintiff in such a case is unable to appear in court without **severe hardship due to the plaintiff's physical condition**, a representative may appear in court, on the plaintiff's behalf and file the requisite complaint with an affidavit setting forth the circumstances preventing the plaintiff from appearing personally. **Defendant Notice** Notice to the plaintiff and defendant and an opportunity for the defendant to be heard shall be given as provided in chapter 258E § 5 (see above).
Plaintiff Notification Nature of Proceedings **c. 258E § 4**	**Civil & Criminal:** Upon the filing of a complaint under this chapter, a complainant shall be informed that the **proceedings hereunder are civil in nature and that violations of orders issued hereunder are criminal in nature**. **Other Criminal Options:** A complainant shall be given information prepared by the appropriate district attorney's office that other criminal proceedings may be available and such complainant shall be instructed by such district attorney's office relative to the procedures required to initiate criminal proceedings including, but not limited to, a complaint for a violation of section 13B, 13F, 13H, 22, 22A, 23, 24, 24B, 26C, 43 and 43A of chapter 265 or section 3 of chapter 272. **Native Language:** Whenever possible, a complainant shall be provided with such information in the complainant's native language.
Foreign Orders **c. 258E § 7**	**Order Issued from a Foreign Jurisdiction is Enforceable** Any protection order issued by another jurisdiction shall be given full faith and credit throughout the commonwealth and enforced as if it were issued in the commonwealth for as long as the order is in effect in the issuing jurisdiction. **Plaintiff may file a Foreign Order with a Massachusetts Court** A person entitled to protection under a protection order issued by another jurisdiction may file such order with the appropriate court by filing with the court a certified copy of such order. Such person shall swear under oath in an affidavit, to the best of such person's knowledge, that such order is presently in effect as written. Upon request by a law enforcement agency, the clerk or clerk-magistrate of such court shall provide a certified copy of the protection order issued by the other jurisdiction.
Privacy Issues **c. 258E § 10**	**JUVENILE INVOLVEMENT:** The records of cases arising out of an action brought chapter 258E in which **the plaintiff or defendant is a minor** shall be **withheld from public inspection** except by order of the court; provided, however, that such records shall be open, at all reasonable times, to the inspection of the minor, such minor's parent, guardian and attorney and to the plaintiff and the plaintiff's attorney. **PLAINTIFF INFORMATION:** The plaintiff's **residential address, residential telephone number** and **workplace name, address** and **telephone number**, contained within the court records of cases arising out of an action brought by a plaintiff under chapter 258E, **shall be confidential and withheld from public inspection**, except by order of the court; provided, however, that the plaintiff's residential address and workplace address shall appear on the court order and be accessible to the defendant and the defendant's attorney unless the plaintiff specifically requests that this information be withheld from the order.

C. 258 § 3	PROTECTION FROM HARASSMENT: AVAILABLE RELIEF
	PLAINTIFF GRANTED ACCESS: All confidential portions of the records shall be accessible at all reasonable times to the plaintiff and plaintiff's attorney, to others specifically authorized by the plaintiff to obtain such information and to prosecutors, victim-witness advocates as defined in chapter 258B § 1, sexual assault counselors as defined in section 20J of chapter 233 and law officers, if such access is necessary in the performance of their duties. **APPLIES TO OUT-OF-STATE ORDERS:** These privacy protections shall apply to any protection order issued by another jurisdiction filed with a court of the commonwealth pursuant to chapter 258E §7. **EXEMPT FROM PUBLIC RECORDS**: The confidential portions of the court records shall not be deemed to be public records under chapter 4 § 7 clause 26th.

C. 258E § 8	PREVENTION OF FURTHER ABUSE OR HARASSMENT Police Officer Responsibility & Powers
Whenever a law officer has reason to believe that a person has been abused or harassed or is in danger of being abused or harassed, such officer shall use all reasonable means to prevent further abuse or harassment. Law officers shall make every reasonable effort to do the following as part of the emergency response:	
Assess Danger	Assess the immediate physical danger to the victim and provide assistance reasonably intended to mitigate the safety risk;
Encourage Medical Treatment	If there is observable injury to the victim or if the victim is complaining of injury, encourage the victim to seek medical attention and arrange for medical assistance or request an ambulance for transport to a hospital;
Sexual Assault Precautions	If a sexual assault has occurred, notify the victim that there are time-sensitive medical or forensic options that may be available, encourage the victim to seek medical attention and arrange for medical assistance or request an ambulance for transport to a hospital;
Provide Referrals	Provide the victim with referrals to local resources that may assist the victim in locating and getting to a safe place;
Provide Victim with Notice of Rights	Provide adequate notice to the victim of the victim's rights including, but not limited to, obtaining a harassment prevention order; provided, however, that the notice shall consist of **providing the victim with a copy** of the following statement before the officer leaves the scene or premises <u>and</u> **after reading the statement to the victim**; provided further, that if the victim's native language is not English, the statement shall be then provided in the victim's native language whenever possible: "You have the right to appear at the Superior, Juvenile (only if the attacker is under 17), District or Boston Municipal Court, if you reside within the appropriate jurisdiction, and file a complaint requesting any of the following applicable orders: (i) an order restraining your attacker from harassing or abusing you; (ii) an order directing your attacker to refrain from contacting you; (iii) an order directing your attacker to stay away from your home and your workplace; (iv) an order directing your attacker to pay you for losses suffered as a result of the harassment or abuse, including loss of earnings, out-of-pocket losses for injuries sustained or property damaged, costs of replacement of locks, medical expenses, cost for obtaining an unlisted phone number, and reasonable attorneys' fees. For an emergency on weekends, holidays or weeknights, the police will assist you in

HARASSMENT & STALKING

C. 258E § 8	PREVENTION OF FURTHER ABUSE OR HARASSMENT Police Officer Responsibility & Powers
	activating the emergency response system so that you may file a complaint and request a harassment prevention order. You have the right to go to the appropriate court and apply for a criminal complaint for sexual assault, threats, criminal stalking, criminal harassment, assault and battery, assault with a deadly weapon, assault with intent to kill or other related offenses. If you are in need of medical treatment, you have the right to request that an officer present drive you to the nearest hospital or otherwise assist you in obtaining medical treatment. If you believe that police protection is needed for your physical safety, you have the right to request that the officer present remain at the scene until you can leave or until your safety is otherwise ensured. You may also request that the officer assist you in locating and taking you to a safe place including, but not limited to, a designated meeting place for a shelter or a family member's or a friend's residence or a similar place of safety.
Emergency Judicial System	Assist the victim by activating the emergency judicial system when the court is closed for business;
Bail Notice	Inform the victim that the abuser will be eligible for bail and may be promptly released;
Mandatory Arrest	Arrest any person that a law officer witnessed or has probable cause to believe: • violated a temporary or permanent vacate, restraining, stay-away or no-contact order or judgment issued under chapter 258E or similar protection order issued by another jurisdiction;
Arrest Preferred	If there are no vacate, restraining, stay-away or no-contact orders or judgments in effect, arresting the person shall be the preferred response if the law officer witnessed or has probable cause to believe that a person: (i) has committed a felony; (ii) has committed a misdemeanor involving harassment or abuse as defined in c. 258E§ 1; or (iii) has committed an assault and battery in violation of c. 265 §13A (A&B)
Safety Paramount	The safety of the victim shall be paramount in any decision to arrest.
Attorney Hanrahan's Comment	There are a some who interpret this statute to mean that a warrantless arrest can be made for *any* assault & battery in violation of c. 265 § 13A. However, it would seem the legislature intended the arrest power to apply only to cases wherein the assault & battery involved harassment (considering that they inserted the language into the harassment prevention laws and neglected to amend chapter 265 § 13A). However, until this is interpreted by an Massachusetts Appellate Court or clarified by the legislature it is subject to debate. Prior to making an arrest for a non-harassment involved *simple* assault & battery in violation of c. 265 § 13A I recommend that you consult with your local District Attorney's Office.
	Penalties
Penalty	**Misdemeanor:** Any violation of such order or a protection order issued by another jurisdiction shall be punishable by a fine of not more than $5,000, or by imprisonment for not more than 2½ years in a house of correction, or both. **Victim/Witness Fee:** In addition to, but not in lieu of, the foregoing penalties and any other sentence,

C. 258E § 8	PREVENTION OF FURTHER ABUSE OR HARASSMENT Police Officer Responsibility & Powers
	fee or assessment, including the victim witness assessment in section 8 of chapter 258B, the court shall order persons convicted of a violation of such an order to pay a fine of $25 that shall be transmitted to the treasurer for deposit into the General Fund. **Mandatory Treatment Possible:** For any violation of such order, the court may order the defendant to complete an appropriate treatment program based on the offense. **Restitution:** In each instance in which there is a violation of a harassment prevention order or a protection order issued by another jurisdiction, the court may order the defendant to pay the plaintiff for all damages including, but not limited to, loss of earnings, out-of-pocket losses for injuries sustained or property damaged, cost of replacement locks, medical expenses, cost for obtaining an unlisted telephone number and reasonable attorney's fees.
Additional Provisions	
Report Required	Whenever a law officer investigates an incident of harassment, the officer **shall immediately file a written incident report** in accordance with the standards of the law officer's law enforcement agency and, wherever possible, in the form of the National Incident-Based Reporting System (NIBRS), as defined by the Federal Bureau of Investigation. The latter information may be submitted voluntarily by the local police on a monthly basis to the crime reporting unit of the state police crime reporting unit established in chapter 22C § 32.
Dual Arrest: Additional Report Required	If a law officer arrests both parties, the law officer shall submit a detailed, written report in addition to an incident report, setting forth the grounds for arresting both parties.
Civil Liability Protections	No law officer shall be held liable in a civil action for personal injury or property damage brought by a party to an incident of abuse or for an arrest based on probable cause when such officer acted reasonably and in good faith and in compliance with chapter 258E.
Victim's right to report	The victim shall be provided with a copy of the full incident report at no cost upon request to the appropriate law enforcement department.
Victim Notification Regarding Bail & Victim's Right to a Protective Order	When a judge or other person authorized to take bail bails any person arrested under chapter 258E, reasonable efforts shall be made to inform the victim of such release **prior to or at the time of the release**. When any person charged with or arrested for a crime involving harassment under chapter 258E is released from custody, the court or the emergency response judge shall issue, upon the request of the victim, a written no-contact order or stay-away order prohibiting the person charged or arrested from having any contact with the victim and shall use all reasonable means to notify the victim immediately of release from custody. The victim shall be provided, at no cost, with a certified copy of the no-contact or stay-away order.
Related Statutes, Case Law & Other Important Information	
Chapter 209A	See Chapter 209A for Domestic Related Protective Orders.

THREATS & TERRORISM RELATED OFFENSES

C. 272 § 2-4	THREAT TO COMMIT A CRIME
Elements[1241]	
1.	The defendant expressed an intent to injure a person, or property of another, now or in the future,
2.	The defendant intended that his/her threat be conveyed to a particular person,
3.	The injury that was threatened, if carried out, would constitute a crime,
4.	The defendant made the threat under circumstances which could reasonably have caused the person whom it was conveyed to fear that the defendant had both the intention and the ability to carry out the threat.
Arrest Power, Penalties & Notes	
Power of Arrest	Warrant only. No warrantless power of arrest.
Penalty	A fine of not more than $100 or by imprisonment for not more than 6 months. **Alternate disposition**: Instead of imposing sentence, the court or justice may order the person complained of to enter into a recognizance, with sufficient sureties, in such sum as the court or justice orders, to keep the peace toward all the people of the commonwealth, and especially toward the person requiring such security, for such term, not exceeding six months, as the court or justice may order. The court or justice may, for good cause, revoke such order or reduce the amount of the recognizance, or order that it be taken without surety.
Attorney Hanrahan's Comment	This is a very unique offense in that an arrest is expressly prohibited even if the crime created a breach of the peace and was committed in the presence of a police officer. Because the offense deals with speech and speech is protected by the First Amendment extra precautions have been implemented.
Related Statutes, Case Law & Other Important Information	
Arrest: Warrant Only	Threatening to Commit a Crime is a non-arrestable offense (absent a warrant) unless some other crime is also involved, such as an assault. An arrest can only be made for this offense upon the issuance of a warrant. See c. 275 § 3 below: **Chapter 275 § 3.** States "If, upon such examination, it is found there is just cause to fear that such crime may be committed, such court or justice shall issue a warrant, reciting the substance of the complaint, and requiring the officer to whom it is directed forthwith to apprehend the person complained of and take him before such justice or some other justice or court having jurisdiction of the cause." Threats are not typically arrestable even if involving a domestic violence situation (often times the crime of assault may be utilized, if the threat was made in person and involved a menacing gesture). However, if the threat violates the no abuse or not contact provision of a protective order an arrest would be permissible (even mandatory) under the arrest authority for violating the order. See domestic violence section of this manual for more.[1242]

[1241] *Commonwealth v. Sholley*, 432 Mass. 721, 725 (2000), cert. denied, 532 U.S. 980 (2001), quoting *Commonwealth v. Robicheau*, 421 Mass. 176, 183 (1995). See *Commonwealth v. Milo M.*, 433 Mass. 149, 154 (2001). See also *Commonwealth v. Chalifoux*, 362 Mass. 811, 816 (1973) (adopting said meaning of "threat" as first stated in *Robinson v. Bradley*, 300 F.Supp. 665, 668 [D. Mass.1969]).
[1242] c. 275, §§ 2-6 does not authorize warrantless arrest for threats. *Commonwealth v. Jacobsen*, 419 Mass. 269, 644 N.E.2d 213 (1995). Also see model Jury Instructions 2013 updated.

.C. 272 § 2-4	THREAT TO COMMIT A CRIME
Intent to reach victim	Actual receipt of the threat by the victim of the threat is not a necessary element; only the **intent** that the threat be conveyed to the target is required, whether or not it actually reached the victim.[1243] The requisite intent can be inferred where the circumstances indicate that the third party "would likely communicate the threatening statement to the ultimate target." [1244] In *Commonwealth v. Valentin V., a juvenile* (2013), a high school student made an announcement in a classroom, in the presence of several other students, his intent to do harm to another student who had just left the room. The Court ruled that the defendant's conduct was sufficient (for probable cause to bring charges) because the defendant likely made his remark with the intent that others pass it along to the victim.
Threatening to harm third person	The alleged victim of the threat, and of the threatened crime, need not be the same person. In ***Commonwealth v. Hamilton***, the defendant threatened a probation officer by threatening to do harm to her daughter. [1245]
Victim does not have to be scared	The test for victim apprehension is objective: "Whether the threat by its contents in the circumstances was such as would cause the target of the threat to fear that the threatened crime and injury might be inflicted." [1246]
Follow through not required	In ***Commonwealth v. Strahan***, the SJC stated "whether the defendant ultimately might not carry out the threat is not relevant to the question of the sufficiency of the Commonwealth's proof that a threat was in fact made."[1247]
Indirect Threats	In ***Commonwealth v. Milo***[1248], the SJC held that given the highly publicized incidence of school violence in this country, a drawing depicting a student pointing a gun at his teaching may constitute a criminal threat under c. 275 § 2. In ***Commonwealth v. Chou***, the defendant made a missing person flyer describing his ex-girlfriend in sexually offensive and abusive language and distributed the flyers throughout the school. The Court ruled that the flyer and distribution was a "true threat".[1249]
Threatening a place of worship **c. 266 § 127A**	The defendant threatens to burn, deface, mar, injure, or in any way destroy a church, synagogue or other building, structure, or place of worship. **Penalty:** a fine of not more than $1,500, or by imprisonment in a jail or HOC for not more than 1 year, or both.

THREATS & TERRORISM

[1243] *Commonwealth v. Maiden,* 61 Mass. App. Ct. 433, 436 , 810 N.E.2d 1279, 1281 (2004).
[1244] *Commonwealth v. James,* 73 Mass.App.Ct. 383, 386 (2008), citing *Commonwealth v. Simmons,* 69 Mass.App.Ct. 348, 351 (2007).
[1245] *Commonwealth v. Hamilton*, 459 Mass. 422, 428, 945 N.E.2d 877, 882 (2011).
[1246] *Commonwealth v. Maiden*, 61 Mass. App. Ct. at 436, 810 N.E.2d at 1282.
[1247] *Commonwealth* v. *Strahan*, 39 Mass. App. Ct. 928, 930, 657 N.E.2d 234 (1995).
[1248] *Commonwealth v. Milo*,433 Mass. 149 (2001).
[1249] *Commonwealth v. Chou,* 433 Mass. at 237, 741 N.E.2d at 23 (2001).

C. 265 § 25	EXTORTION
EXTORTION: Non-Public Employee Elements	
1.	The defendant verbally or by a written or printed communication does one of the following:
2.	• Maliciously threatens to accuse another of a crime or offence or • Maliciously threatens an injury to the person or property of another
3.	With intent to: • Extort money or any pecuniary advantage or • To compel any person to do any act against his will
EXTORTION: By Police Officer Elements	
1.	Any police officer or person having the powers of a police officer, or any officer, or employee of any licensing authority
2.	Who verbally or by written or printed communication
3.	Maliciously and unlawfully
4.	Uses or threatens to use against another the power or authority vested in him, • with intent to extort money or any pecuniary advantage, or • with intent to compel any person to do any act against his will.
Arrest Power, Penalties & Notes	
Power of Arrest	**Felony** – a police officer may effect a warrantless arrest for this offense provided he/she has probable cause that the suspect committed the offense.
Penalty	Imprisonment in the **state prison (F)** for not more than 15 years, or in the HOC for not more than 2½ years, or by a fine of not more than $5,000, or both.
Attorney Hanrahan's Comment	Some cases have indicated that if a police officer did not actually have the authority to carry out the threat the crime of extortion cannot occur.
Related Statutes, Case Law & Other Important Information	
Threatening a Third Party	In *Commonwealth v. Snow*, 269 Mass. 598 (1930), the SJC held that a person who attempts to extort money from one person by threatening to injure a different person may be found guilty of attempted extortion under G.L. c. 265, § 25.

C. 265 § 25	EXTORTION
Injury	Injury does not necessary have to be physical injury, it can also include emotional and psychological injury. Additionally, *property* has been broadly accepted by the court as well. In ***Commonwealth v. Miller*** (1982), a threat to expose a sexual relationship was sufficient to "injure" a person for the purpose of extortion. In ***Commonwealth v. Downey*** (1981), the Appeals Court held that a license to sell liquor was sufficient property for this offense.

C. 269 § 14	TERRORISTIC THREATS
	Elements
1.	The defendant, willfully communicates or causes to be communicated, either directly or indirectly, one of the below threats:
2.	1) That a firearm, rifle, shotgun, machine gun or assault weapon, an explosive or incendiary device, a dangerous chemical or biological agent, a poison, a harmful radioactive substance or any other device, substance or item capable of causing death, serious bodily injury or substantial property damage, will be used at a place or location, or is present or will be present at a place or location, whether or not the same is in fact used or present; 2) To hijack an aircraft, ship, or common carrier
3.	Thereby causing anxiety, unrest, fear, or personal discomfort to any person or group of persons.
Political Exception	Nothing in this section shall authorize the criminal prosecution of picketing, public demonstrations or other similar forms of expressing views.
	Arrest Power, Penalties & Notes
Power of Arrest	**Felony** – a police officer may effect a warrantless arrest for this offense provided he/she has probable cause that the suspect committed the offense.
Penalty	**Basic Penalty:** imprisonment in the **state prison (F)** for not more than 20 years or imprisonment in the HOC for not more than 2½ years, or by fine of not more than $10,000, or by both such fine and imprisonment. **Enhanced Penalty:** If the threat causes either the **evacuation or serious disruption** of a school, school related event, school transportation, or a dwelling, building, place of assembly, facility or public transport, or an aircraft, ship or common carrier, or **causes serious public inconvenience or alarm**, imprisonment in the **state prison (F)** for **not less than 3** years nor more than 20 years or imprisonment in the house of correction for **not less than 6 months** nor more than 2 years, or by fine of not less than $1,000 nor more than $50,000, or by both such fine and imprisonment.
	Related Statutes, Case Law & Other Important Information
Method of Communication	Communication may be made orally, in writing, by mail, by use of a telephone or telecommunication device including, but not limited to, electronic mail, Internet communications and facsimile communications, through an electronic communication device or by any other means.

C. 269 § 14	TERRORISTIC THREATS
Does not have to be communicated to target	In ***Commonwealth v. Kearns***, the SJC ruled that the threat (under § 14) does not have to be communicated t the intended target. The SJC ruled that the crime is committed when communicated to anyone other than an accomplice.[1250]
Definitions	For the purposes of this section, the following words shall have the following meanings:— **"Hijack",** to commandeer or to take control without authority. **"School",** any public or private preschool, headstart facility, elementary, vocational or secondary school, college or university. **"Serious bodily injury",** bodily injury which results in a permanent disfigurement, protracted loss or impairment of a bodily function, limb or organ, or substantial risk of death.
Restitution	The court may order restitution for the costs incurred as a result of the threat.
Use/Possession of Explosive Device and/or Weapons of Mass Destruction	See Weapons section for chapter 266 § 102 (use/deployment of an explosive device) and chapter 266 § 102A (possession/use of weapon of mass destruction)

[1250] *Commonwealth v. Kearns*, 449 Mass. 641 (2007).

ROBBERY RELATED OFFENSES

C.265 § 19	UNARMED ROBBERY
Elements	
1.	Rob, steal or take
2.	Money or other property which may be the subject of larceny
3.	From the person of another or from his immediate control,
4.	By force and violence, or by assault and putting in fear,
5.	Not being armed with a dangerous weapon
Arrest Power, Penalties & Notes	
Power of Arrest	**Felony** – a police officer may effect a warrantless arrest for this offense provided he/she has probable cause that the suspect committed the offense.
Penalty	Imprisonment in the **state prison (F)** for life or for any term of years. **Subsequent offense involving person over 60:** If the victim is 60 or over and the defendant commits a second or subsequent unarmed robber on a person 60 or shall be punished by imprisonment for **not less than two years**.
Attorney Hanrahan's Comment	There has to be some **use of force <u>or</u> fear** imposed for the offense to be a robbery. For, instance if a woman was sitting on a park bench with a her purse beside her and someone snuck up from behind and took the purse and ran, the crime would be larceny from a person (also a felony) and not robbery because there was no force or fear imposed.
Related Statutes, Case Law & Other Important Information	
Amount of Force Required	The force used does not have to be great. For instance, a suspect pulls a pocketbook out of the hand of a victim, even if the victim was not aware until the moment the item was grasped by the suspect, would generally amount to sufficient force to amount to robbery.[1251]
Robbery: retain stolen property	In the 2011 case of ***Com. v. Rogers,*** the SJC ruled that the crime of armed robbery (and unarmed robbery) includes the use of force applied *after* the initial theft in an effort to escape (in this case an initial shoplifting).
Larceny from the Person	If the theft does not involve force, fear or violence but the item is taken from the immediate control of the victim chapter 266 § 25, Larceny from the Person should be considered.
Multiple counts	Multiple counts is not based on the number of items taken but the number of victims. However, it is possible to rob the same person more than once particularly if the robberies occur at different times/different locations.[1252]

ROBBERY RELATED OFFENSES

[1251] *Commonwealth v. Brown*, 2 Mass.App.Ct. 883 (1974)
[1252] Commonwealth v. Clovicel Davis, Appeals Court (2015) and Commonwealth v. Tarrant, 14 Mass.App.Ct. 1020 (1982).

C. 265 § 17	ARMED ROBBERY
Elements	
1.	The defendant while armed with a dangerous weapon;
2.	• Applied actual force or violence to the victim or • By words or gestures put the victim in fear;
3.	Took money or the property of another;
4.	Did so with the intent to steal it.[1253]
Attorney Hanrahan's Note	Be sure to review additional clarifications in the unarmed robbery section of this manual.
Arrest Power, Penalties & Notes	
Power of Arrest	**Felony** – a police officer may effect a warrantless arrest for this offense provided he/she has probable cause that the suspect committed the offense.
Penalty	Imprisonment in the **state prison (F)** for life or for any term of years.
Enhanced Penalty for being masked	Any person who commits any offence described herein while masked or disguised or while having his features artificially distorted shall, for the first offence be sentenced to imprisonment for **not less than 5 years** and for any **subsequent offence** for **not less than 10 years**.
Enhanced penalty for Firearm	If armed with a firearm, shotgun, rifle, machine gun or assault weapon shall be punished by imprisonment in the **state prison (F) for not less than 5 years**. Any person who commits a **subsequent offense** while armed with a firearm, shotgun, rifle, machine gun or assault weapon shall be punished by imprisonment in the **state prison (F)** for not **less than 15 years**.
Related Statutes, Case Law & Other Important Information	
Robbery elements interpreted	In *Com. v. Christian*, the SJC interpreted the elements of robbery as "the crime of robbery is the (1) stealing or taking of personal property of another (2) by force and violence, or by assault and putting in fear." [1254]
Armed with a "dangerous weapon"	In order to commit the crime of armed robbery, the defendant must "be armed with a dangerous weapon" at the time of the robbery. The standard definition of "dangerous weapon" includes those items that are, by their nature, **capable of causing serious injury or death**, but also includes items that are used **or** displayed in a way such that they reasonably appear capable of causing serious injury or death. [1255]
***Appear* to be a Dangerous Weapon is generally sufficient**	If, an object that is, on closer inspection, incapable of inflicting serious injury or death can still be a dangerous weapon if, at the time of the offense, it would have been reasonable to believe that it was capable of inflicting such injury. **Case Examples**: In ***Commonwealth v. Nickologines,*** the SJC ruled that "on charge of armed robbery, the Commonwealth does not have to prove that defendant's gun was loaded."[1256] In ***Commonwealth v. Johnson,*** the victim's reasonable perception that the object in defendant's pocket

[1253] Commonwealth v. Benitez (SJC 2013) quoting Commonwealth v. Rogers, 459 Mass. 249, 252 n. cert. denied, 132 C.Ct. 813 (2012).
[1254] *Commonwealth v. Christian,* 430 Mass. 552, 556 (2000).
[1255] *Commonwealth v. Powell*, 433 Mass. 399 (2001) quoting from Commonwealth v. Tevlin, ante 305, 311 (2001); *Commonwealth v. Tarrant,* 367 Mass. 411 , 416-417 (1975).
[1256] *Commonwealth v. Nickologines,* 322 Mass. 274 , 277 (1948)

C. 265 § 17	ARMED ROBBERY
	was gun was sufficient to support a conviction of armed assault with intent to rob even though object was only hairbrush.[1257] In ***Commonwealth v. Garafolo,*** the defendant used a toy handgun to commit armed assault with intent to rob.[1258] In ***Commonwealth v. Nicholson,*** the Court ruled "armed robbery could be committed with a "fake plastic gun" if "it reasonably appeared capable of inflicting bodily harm".[1259] In ***Commonwealth v. Perry,*** an armed robbery was committed with a black plastic toy pistol.[1260]
Weapon not displayed	If the defendant is armed with a dangerous weapon at the time of the robbery, even if the weapon was never displayed, the defendant can still be found guilty of armed robbery. This is true even if the victim was not even aware of the weapon.[1261]
Armed Robbery with no weapon?	If a suspect claims to have a weapon it would be possible to convict him of armed robbery even if no object was ever observed. However, if a defendant claims to have a weapon by words alone (without the use of an object to resemble a weapon) but did not actually have one "a conviction of armed robbery is not warranted." For instance, of the suspect claimed to have a weapon during the robbery and then he flees after the robbery it would be possible to use his claim of a weapon to convict him. However, if he was caught in the act and found not to really have a weapon an *armed* robbery conviction would not be permissible.
BB gun not a firearm	In the 2015 case of *Com. v. Garrett*, the SJC ruled that a BB gun is not a firearm for the purposes of armed robbery. However, it possible that a BB gun may serve as a dangerous weapon for an armed robbery offense.

C. 265 § 21	STEALING BY CONFINING OR PUTTING IN FEAR
	Elements
1.	The defendant has an intent to commit larceny or any felony and does one of the following:
2.	• Confines, maims, injures or wounds, or attempts or threatens to kill, confine, maim, injure or wound, or • Puts any person in fear, for the purpose of stealing from a building, bank, safe, vault or other depository of money, bonds or other valuables, or • By intimidation, force or threats compels or attempts to compel any person to disclose or surrender the means of opening any building, bank, safe, vault or other depository of money, bonds, or other valuables.
Attorney Hanrahan's Note:	This law was designed cover more than your typical robbery; it covers conduct typically found in a bank robbery where the employees and patrons are threatened and/or injured in an effort to get a vault or similar depository of valuables opened. However, it is not limited to a bank; the courts have upheld convictions for this offense committed in a dwelling.
Power of Arrest	**Felony** – a police officer may effect a warrantless arrest for this offense provided he/she has probable cause that the suspect committed the offense.

1257 *Commonwealth v. Johnson,* 27 Mass.App.Ct. 746, 748-749 (1989)
1258 *Commonwealth v. Garafolo,* 23 Mass.App.Ct. 905, 907 (1986)
1259 *Commonwealth v. Nicholson,* 20 Mass.App.Ct. 9, 17 (1985)
1260 *Commonwealth v. Perry,* 6 Mass.App.Ct. 531, 533-536 (1978)
1261 Commonwealth v. Blackburn, 354 Mass. 200 (1968), Commonwealth v. Walker, 17 Mass.App.Ct. 194 (1983).

C. 265 § 21	STEALING BY CONFINING OR PUTTING IN FEAR
Penalty	Imprisonment in the **state prison (F)** for life or for any term of years.
Related Statutes, Case Law & Other Important Information	
"Building"	The term building includes a dwelling for the purposes of this statute.[1262]
"Confinement"	In the 1967 case of *Commonwealth v. Balakin*, removing a bank employee and restricting her to a location in the lobby of the bank was confinement for the purposes of this statute.

C. 265 § 21A	CARJACKING
Elements	
1.	The defendant has the intent to steal a motor vehicle and he/she does one of the following:
2.	• assaults, • confines, • maims or • puts any person in fear
3.	For the purpose of stealing a motor vehicle.
Arrest Power, Penalties & Notes	
Power of Arrest	**Felony** – a police officer may effect a warrantless arrest for this offense provided he/she has probable cause that the suspect committed the offense.
Penalty	**Penalty:** imprisonment in the **state prison (F)** for not more than 15 years or in a jail or HOC for not more than 2½ and a fine of not less than $1,000 nor more than $15,000 **Enhanced Penalty for Dangerous Weapon**: any person who commits this while being armed with a **dangerous weapon** shall be punished by imprisonment in the **state prison (F)** for not more than 20 years or in a jail or HOC for **not less than 1 year** nor more than 2½ years and a fine of not less than $5,000 nor more than $15,000. **Enhanced Penalty for Firearm**: whoever commits this offense while being armed with a **firearm, rifle, shotgun, machine gun or assault weapon**, shall be punished by imprisonment in the **state prison (F)** for **not less than 7 years** in **state prison (F)**.
Attorney Hanrahan's Comment	The defendant has not have to be successful. Meaning even if he does not succeed in stealing the vehicle he would still be guilty of this offense if he meets the elements. There is no requirement that he actually take possession of the car.
Related Statutes, Case Law & Other Important Information	
Larceny of Motor Vehicle	Chapter 266 § 28 addresses the theft of a motor vehicle (see Larceny section).

[1262] *Commonwealth v. Johnson*, 37 Mass.App.Ct. 940 (1994).

KIDNAPPING & HUMAN TRAFFICKING (also See Sex Crimes Section for Sex Trafficking)

C. 265 § 26	KIDNAPPING
	Elements
1.	Without lawful authority the defendant does one of the following:
2.	• Forcibly or secretly confines or imprisons another person within this Massachusetts against his will, or • Forcibly carries or sends a person out of Massachusetts, or • Forcibly seizes and confines or inveigles or kidnaps another person with intent either to cause him to be secretly confined or imprisoned in Massachusetts against his will or to cause him to be sent out of Massachusetts against his will or in any way held to service against his will.
	Arrest Power, Penalties & Notes
Power of Arrest	**Felony** – a police officer may effect a warrantless arrest for this offense provided he/she has probable cause that the suspect committed the offense.
Penalty	**Basic Penalty:** imprisonment in the **state prison (F)** for not more than 10 years or by a fine of not more than $1,000 and imprisonment in jail for not more than 2 years. **Child Kidnapping Penalty:** if the person kidnapped is under 16 years old - imprisonment in the state prison for not more than 15 years. The provisions of this statute shall not apply to the parent of a child under 16 years of age who takes custody of such child. **Penalty for Money Extortion**: Whoever commits any offence described in this section with the intent to extort money or other valuable thing thereby shall be punished by imprisonment in the state prison for life or for any term of years. **Enhanced Penalty for use of certain weapons:** Whoever commits any offense described in this section while armed with a firearm, rifle, shotgun, machine gun or assault weapon shall be punished by imprisonment in the state prison for not less than 10 years or in the HOC for not more than 2½ years. **Exception:** The provisions of the preceding sentence shall not apply to the parent of a child under 18 years of age who takes custody of such child. **Enhanced Penalty for Serious Bodily Injury or Sexual Assault:** Whoever commits any offense described in this section while **armed with a dangerous weapon** and: a. inflicts serious bodily injury thereby upon another person or b. who sexually assaults the person shall be punished by imprisonment in the state prison for **not less than 25 years.** **Definition:** For purposes of this paragraph the term "**serious bodily injury"** shall mean bodily injury which results in a permanent disfigurement, protracted loss or impairment of a bodily function, limb or organ or substantial risk of death. For purposes of this paragraph, the term **"sexual assault**" shall mean the commission of any act set forth in sections 13B, 13F, 13H, 22, 22A, 23, 24 or 24B.
Attorney Hanrahan's Comment	This crime is often committed in the course of another crime. For instance, most forcible rapes would also include the charge of kidnapping. However, the kidnapping cannot be merely incidental to the underlying offense (see notes below).

C. 265 § 26	KIDNAPPING
	Related Statutes, Case Law & Other Important Information
Confinement	Within the context of the crime of kidnapping, the concept of "confinement" has been broadly interpreted to mean any restraint of a person's movement. See *Commonwealth v. Titus,* 32 Mass.App.Ct. at 222, 587 N.E.2d 800 (the "[e]ssence [of kidnapping] is restraint, restraint of locomotion").
Kidnapping incidental to another crime	The kidnapping offense may be considered merely "incidental" to an underlying crime if the underlying crime cannot be completed without some type of confinement. There must be some evidence that kidnapping was separate and distinct from what was necessary to complete an underlying crime. In *Commonwealth v. Vasquez,* the evidence showed that the young victim was approached by the defendant at a bus station and taken to a room in an abandoned building and raped. The defendant claimed that the victim's confinement was merely incidental to the commission of the rape and therefore merged therein. The court held that "there was sufficient evidence concerning the defendant's confinement of the victim at the bus station and while on the way to the house some distance away to warrant the jury in finding that a kidnapping had occurred...."[1].
Attempted Kidnapping proof of intent required	The SJC ruled in the 2011 case of ***Com. v. Rivera***, that in order to convict a defendant for attempted kidnapping (c. 274 sec. 6), there must be evidence that the defendant intended to "forcibly or secretly confine," and in this case where the defendant pulled up to an 11 year old boy and stated "Get into the car" this was not enough to show that intent. However, in the 2013 case of ***Commonwealth v. Sullivan***, the Appeals Court ruled that a man who accosts an unknown woman on the street and demands that she enter his car can be found guilty of attempted kidnapping.
Sex Related offense	See the sex offense section of this manual for sex related crimes that are often connected to kidnapping.
Venue: where to bring charges	Chapter 265 § 27 states "a crime described in section 26 may be tried in the county where committed or in any county in or to which the person so seized, inveigled or kidnapped is confined, held, carried or brought; and upon the trial of any such crime, the consent thereto of the person so seized, inveigled, kidnapped or confined shall not be a defense unless the jury finds that such consent was not obtained by fraud or extorted by duress or threats."
Drugging for the Purpose of Kidnapping	Chapter 265 § 26B provides an additional offense when drugs are used to facilitate the kidnapping. If the defendant applies, administers to or causes to be taken by a person Any drug, matter or thing with intent to stupefy or overpower such person so as to commit the crime of kidnapping he/she can face an additional charge. **Penalty**: imprisonment in the **state prison (F)** for life or for any term of years not less than ten years. Whoever violates the provisions of this section with the intent to extort money or other valuable thing thereby shall be punished by imprisonment in the **state prison (F)** for life or for any term of years not less than 15 years.

1 *Commonwealth v. Vasquez,* **11 Mass.App.Ct. 261**, 268, **415 N.E.2d 858** (1981). See also *Commonwealth v. Rivera,* 397 Mass. 244, 245-247, 490 N.E.2d 1160 (1986).

C. 265 § 26A	CUSTODIAL INTERFERENCE
	"Parental Kidnapping" Elements
1.	The defendant is a relative of a child less than 18 years old,
2.	Without lawful authority the defendant does one of the following:
3.	• Holds or intends to hold such a child permanently or for a protracted period, or • Takes or entices such a child from his lawful custodian.
	Incompetent Person Elements
1.	The defendant (whether or not a relative) takes or entices from lawful custody any incompetent person or other person entrusted by authority of law to the custody of another person or institution.
	Arrest Power, Penalties & Notes
Power of Arrest	**Misdemeanor** – there is no statutory authority granting warrantless powers of arrest for this offense. However, if the offense is committed in public, in the officer's presence, and is creating a **breach of the peace** an arrest would be lawful. However, if the child is removed from Massachusetts or if the child/incompetent person is exposed to danger the crime becomes a felony and felony arrest powers would apply. **Felony** – a police officer may effect a warrantless arrest for this offense provided he/she has probable cause that the suspect committed the offense.
Penalty	**Basic Penalty**: imprisonment in the HOC for not more than 1year or by a fine of up to $1,000, or both. **Enhanced Penalty for Out of State or Exposure to Danger:** • Whoever commits this offense by taking or holding the child outside Massachusetts, or • Under circumstances which expose the person taken or enticed from lawful custody to a risk which endangers his/her safety **Enhanced Penalty:** fine of not more than $5,000, or by imprisonment in the **state prison (F)** for not more than 5 years, or by both such fine and imprisonment.
	Related Statutes, Case Law & Other Important Information
Married Parents with no court order in effect	If the parents are married and no court order is in effect, either parent has equal rights to the child, meaning the parent could not be convicted of this offense absent some court order to the contrary. "In making an order or judgment relative to the custody of children pending a controversy between their parents, or relative to their final possession, the rights of the parents shall, in the absence of misconduct, be held to be equal, and the happiness and welfare of the children shall determine their custody or possession." G.L. c. 208, § 31. A parent who takes minor children from the other spouse and removes them from the Commonwealth at a time when there were no pending proceedings concerning the marriage or their custody cannot be convicted under G.L. c. 265, § 26A. *Commonwealth v. Beals,* 405 Mass. 550, 541 N.E.2d 1011 (1989).

KIDNAPPING & ENTICEMENT

C. 265 § 26A	CUSTODIAL INTERFERENCE
Unmarried Parents with no order – Mom has custody	When it comes to unmarried parents with no court order regarding custody in effect the mother is granted custody of the child. "Prior to or in the absence of an adjudication or voluntary acknowledgment of paternity, the mother shall have custody of a child born out of wedlock." G.L. c. 209C, § 10(b). Also see model jury instructions 2009 edition. Additionally, G.L. c. 209C, § 10 (*b*) states that "the child's mother is vested with sole physical and legal custody, and that custody arrangement continues even after paternity is established until modified by a court." **Attorney Hanrahan's Note:** There is some question whether these statutes are Constitutional as some fathers have claimed these laws violate their Constitutional rights. Until this matter is resolved it is recommend that you follow the statutory law in these matters.
Parent who abandons child	A parent who abandons a child, or is otherwise absent from the child's life, cannot later claim that he/she has lawful authority over the child in a defense of the Parental Kidnapping statute.[1]
Interfering with visitation	Some legal scholars have suggested that the "takes or entices" branch of § 26A may be applied even to a parent with legal custody or joint legal custody who interferes with the visitation or joint custody rights of the other parent. Green, "The Crime of Parental Kidnapping in Massachusetts," 70 Mass. L. Rev.115 (1985). Also see model jury instructions 2009 edition.
Removal of child from Commonwealth after divorce	"A minor child of divorced parents who is a native of or has resided five years within this commonwealth and over whose custody and maintenance a probate court has jurisdiction shall not, if of suitable age to signify his consent, be removed out of this commonwealth without such consent, or, if under that age, without the consent of both parents, unless the court upon cause shown otherwise orders." G.L. c. 208, § 30.
Incompetent Person	General Laws c. 265, § 26A also punishes anyone, whether or not a relative, who "takes or entices from lawful custody any incompetent person or other person entrusted by authority of law to the custody of another person or institution."This branch of the statute would apparently apply to a non-relative's interference with child custody if a kidnapping charge (G.L. c. 265, § 26) is unavailable because the interference was consensual. See model jury instructions 2009 edition.
Venue: Where to charge	Chapter 265 § 27A states "a crime described in § 26A may be tried in the county where committed or in a county in or to which the person so taken or enticed is held, carried to, or brought."

[1] *Commonwealth v. Ernesto Gonzalez* (2012) SJC.

C. 265 § 26C ENTICEMENT OF CHILD UNDER AGE 16

Elements

1.	The defendant enticed: • A child under the age of 16, or • Someone he *believes* to be a child under the age of 16 (**Note:** this element includes undercover officers posing on the Internet as children and the like).
2.	To enter, exit or remain within any: • vehicle, dwelling, building, or other outdoor space
3.	With the intent that he or another person will violate one of the below statutes: • G.L. c. 265, § 13B Indecent assault and battery on a child under 14 • G.L. c. 265, § 13F Indecent assault and battery on a person with an intellectual disability • G.L. c. 265, § 13H Indecent assault and battery on a person 14 or older • G.L. c. 265, § 22 Rape; Aggravated rape • G.L. c. 265, § 22A Rape of a child under 16 with force • G.L. c. 265, § 23 Rape and abuse of a child under 16 (statutory rape) • G.L. c. 265, § 24 Assault with intent to rape • G.L. c. 265, § 24B Assault on a child under 16 with intent to rape • G.L. c. 272, § 4A Inducing a minor to prostitution • G.L. c. 272, § 16 Open and gross lewdness • G.L. c. 272, § 28 Disseminating matter harmful to a minor • G.L. c. 272, § 29 Disseminating or possessing to disseminate obscene matter • G.L. c. 272, § 29A Posing or exhibiting child under 18 in a state of nudity or sexual conduct • G.L. c. 272, § 29C Possessing child pornography • G.L. c. 272, § 35A Unnatural act with child under 16 • G.L. c. 272, § 53 Accost or annoy person of opposite sex, Common nightwalker, Common streetwalker, Disorderly conduct, Disturbing the peace, Indecent exposure, Keeping a noisy and disorderly house, Lewd, wanton and lascivious conduct. • G.L. c. 272, § 53A Sexual conduct for a fee, Paying or procuring for sexual conduct, Paying or procuring for sexual conduct with a child under 14 or • Any offense that has the use or attempted use of force as an element.

Arrest Power, Penalties & Notes

Power of Arrest	**Felony** – a police officer may effect a warrantless arrest for this offense provided he/she has probable cause that the suspect committed the offense.
Penalty	Imprisonment in the **state prison (F)** for not more than 5 years, or in the HOC for not more than 2½ years, or by both imprisonment and a fine of not more than $5,000

Related Statutes, Case Law & Other Important Information

"Entice"	In this section the term "**entice**" shall mean to **lure, induce, persuade, tempt, incite, solicit, coax** or **invite.**
Speech alone	The statute does not require an overt act but does require proof of specific intent to commit one or more of the enumerated crimes. It does not criminalize the mere sending of sexually explicit messages

C. 265 § 26C	ENTICEMENT OF CHILD UNDER AGE 16
	or indecent language, even to minors; in fact, the statute can be violated by enticing a child without making any verbal reference to sexual matters at all. *Commonwealth v. Disler,* 451 Mass. 216, 884 N.E.2d 500 (2008). In a prosecution for enticing a child with intent to kidnap, merely offering the victim a ride and then saying in a "more demanding" and "sort of loud" voice "Get in the truck" were insufficient to prove that the defendant intended to forcibly confine the victim. *Commonwealth v. LaPlante,* 73 Mass. App. Ct. 199, 897 N.E.2d 78 (2008).
Location selected by Defendant	In the 2011 case of ***Commonwealth v. Hall,*** the Appeals Court ruled that in order to be convicted of enticing a child, under c. 265 § 26C, there must be proof that the child was actually enticed "to enter, exit or remain within any vehicle, dwelling, building, or other outdoor space" not at a location selected by the victim. In this case, the defendant was accused of having enticed a child with the intent to pose the child in a state of nudity (a violation of G.L. c. 272, § 29A[*a*]), one of the offenses listed in the statute. However, he enticed the child to send him the photos via electronically media while she was at a location of her own choosing (mostly her home).
Victim choosing location	In the 2011 case of ***Commonwealth v. Hall,*** the Appeals Court ruled that in order to be convicted of enticing a child, under c. 265 § 26C, there must be proof that the child was actually enticed "to enter, exit or remain within any vehicle, dwelling, building, or other outdoor space" not at a location selected by the victim. In this case, the defendant was accused of having enticed a child with the intent to pose the child in a state of nudity (a violation of G.L. c. 272, § 29A[*a*]). However, he enticed the child to send him the photos via electronic media while she was at a location of her own choosing (mostly from own her home).

C. 265 § 26D	ENTICEMENT OF CHILD UNDER 18 BY ELECTRONIC COMMUNICATION
	Elements
1.	The defendant, by electronic communication,
2.	Knowingly entices a child under the age of 18 years (or attempts to entice), to engage in: • Prostitution in violation of chapter 272 § 50 or § 53A, • Human trafficking in violation of chapter 265 § 50, 51, 52 or 53 or • Commercial sexual activity as defined in chapter 265 § 49.
	Arrest Power, Penalties & Notes
Power of Arrest	**Felony** – a police officer may effect a warrantless arrest for this offense provided he/she has probable cause that the suspect committed the offense.
Penalty	**First Offense:** Imprisonment in a house of correction for not more than 2½ years or in the **state prison (F)** for not more than 5 years or by a fine of not less than $2,500, or by both such fine and imprisonment. **Subsequent Offense**: Whoever, after having been convicted of, or adjudicated delinquent by reason of a violation of this section, commits a second or subsequent such violation, shall be punished by imprisonment in the state prison for not less than 5 years and by a fine of not less than $10,000. Such sentence shall not be reduced to less than 5 years, or suspended, nor shall any person

C. 265 § 26D	ENTICEMENT OF CHILD UNDER 18 BY ELECTRONIC COMMUNICATION
	convicted under this subsection be eligible for probation, parole, work release or furlough or receive any deduction from the sentence for good conduct until that person has served 5 years of such sentence.
Attorney Hanrahan's Comment	What is the difference between this offense and enticing a child under 16 in c. 265 § 26C? Aside from the ages and the specific mention of electronic communication, section 26C requires that the child be "enticed" to a location (or to remain in a location). Section 26D only requires that the child be enticed to engage in one of the three listed offenses. There is no requirement that the child under 18 be enticed to any specific location just to engage in the prohibited conduct.
	Related Statutes, Case Law & Other Important Information
Entice	As used in § 26D, the term **"entice"** shall mean to lure, induce, persuade, tempt, incite, solicit, coax or invite.
Electronic Communication	As used in § 26D, the term **"electronic communication"** shall include, but not be limited to, any transfer of signs, signals, writing, images, sounds, data or intelligence of any nature transmitted in whole or in part by a wire, radio, electromagnetic, photo-electronic or photo-optical system.
Sex Crimes	See the sex crime section of this manual for more on the three listed offenses.

HUMAN TRAFFICKING

C. 265 § 51	TRAFFICKING OF PERSONS FOR FORCED SERVICES
	Elements
1.	The Defendant Knowingly does any of the following:
2.	(i) Subjects, or attempts to subject, another person to forced services, or (ii) Recruits, entices, harbors, transports, provides or obtains by any means, or attempts to recruit, entice, harbor, transport, provide or obtain by any means, another person, intending or knowing that such person will be subjected to forced services; or (iii) Benefits, financially or by receiving anything of value, as a result of a violation of clause (i).
	Arrest Power, Penalties & Notes
Power of Arrest	**Felony** – a police officer may effect a warrantless arrest for this offense provided he/she has probable cause that the suspect committed the offense.
Penalty	**Basic Penalty:** imprisonment in the **state prison (F)** for not less than 5 years but not more than 20 years and by a fine of not more than $25,000. Such sentence shall not be reduced to less than 5 years, or suspended, nor shall any person convicted under this section be eligible for probation, parole, work release or furlough or receive any deduction from his sentence for good conduct until he shall have served 5 years of such sentence. No prosecution commenced under this section shall be continued without a finding or placed on file. **Penalty if victim under 18:** whoever commits the crime of trafficking of persons for forced services upon a person **under 18 years** of age shall be imprisoned in the state prison for life or for any term of years, but not less than 5 years. No person convicted under this subsection shall be eligible for probation, parole, work release or furlough or receive any deduction from his sentence for good conduct until he shall have served 5 years of such sentence. **Penalty if committed by a Business:** A business entity that commits trafficking of persons for forced labor services shall be punished by a fine of not more than $1,000,000.
	Related Statutes, Case Law & Other Important Information
Definition of Forced Services	"**Forced services**", services performed or provided by a person that are obtained or maintained by another person who: (i) Causes or threatens to cause serious harm to any person; (ii) Physically restrains or threatens to physically restrain another person; (iii) Abuses or threatens to abuse the law or legal process; (iv) Knowingly destroys, conceals, removes, confiscates or possesses any actual or purported passport or other immigration document, or any other actual or purported government identification document, of another person; (v) Engages in extortion under chapter 265 § 25; or (vi) Causes or threatens to cause financial harm to any person.
Sexual Servitude	See Sex Crimes section of the manual for chapter 265 § 50. Trafficking of persons for sexual servitude.

C. 265 § 53	ORGAN TRAFFICKING
	Elements
1.	The defendant: (i) Recruits, entices, harbors, transports, delivers or obtains by any means, another person, intending or knowing that an **organ, tissue or other body part** of such person will be removed for sale, against such person's will; or (ii) Knowingly receives anything of value, directly or indirectly as a result of a violation of clause (i).
	Arrest Power, Penalties & Notes
Power of Arrest	**Felony** – a police officer may effect a warrantless arrest for this offense provided he/she has probable cause that the suspect committed the offense.
Penalty	**Basic Penalty:** imprisonment in the state prison for not more than 15 years or by a fine of not more than $50,000, or both. **Penalty victim under 18**: whoever commits the crime of organ trafficking upon a person under 18 years of age shall be punished by imprisonment in the state prison for 5 years. Such sentence shall not be reduced to less than 5 years, or suspended, nor shall any person convicted under this subsection be eligible for probation, parole, work release, or furlough or receive any deduction from such sentence for good conduct until having served 5 years of such sentence.

Hanrahan Consulting, LLC's
Firearm Licensing Quick Reference Guide

Note: this is only to be used as a quick field reference. There are many exemptions and exceptions. This should only be used as a general guide and then you should refer to the specific statute before making an arrest decision.

License Type	Firearm In Public	Large Capacity firearm in Public	Rifle or Shotgun In Public must be unloaded and in case unless hunting or similar lawful purpose	Large Capacity Rifle or Shotgun In Public must be unloaded and in case unless hunting or similar lawful purpose	Firearm in Home or Business	Large Capacity firearm in Home or Business	Rifle or Shotgun in Home or Business	Large Capacity Rifle or Shotgun in Home or Business
LTC Class A	Yes	Yes	Yes	Yes	Yes	Yes	Yes	Yes
Notes:	The local licensing authority may place certain restrictions, such as "target practice only." A violation of a restriction is not a violation of c. 269 § 10. It would result in a fine and likely the revocation of the license. See C. 140 § 131 for more.							
LTC Class B	Yes, but not concealed if loaded	No	Yes	Yes	Yes	No	Yes	Yes
Notes:	C. 269 § 10 would not apply for violating a restriction such as carrying concealed & loaded firearm, nor would it apply for carrying in violation of a restriction imposed by the local licensing authority (as mentioned above under LTC A notes) but it would result in a fine and most likely the revocation of the LTC.							
FID	No	No	Yes	No	Yes	No	Yes	No
Notes:	A holder of an FID who carries a large capacity rifle/shotgun or a firearm is subject to the provisions of chapter 269 § 10. However, the person would not be subject to the minimum mandatory sentence.							

Exemptions & Exceptions: there are many exemptions and exceptions that apply to chapter 140 (the firearm licensing laws) and c. 269 § 10 (the carrying a dangerous weapon law). For instance, people traveling through Massachusetts, people who have inherited firearms, people who recently moved into the Commonwealth etc. may be exempt. Always refer to chapter 140 for more, particularly if someone is claiming an exemption.

Machine Guns: You must have a special license to possess a machine gun and they are only issued to MPTC firearm instructors or a bona fide firearms collector. See chapter 140 § 131.

Silencers: can only be possessed by law enforcement. This is a felony offense – see c. 269 § 10A

Stun Guns: only law enforcement (and special teams in corrections) can lawfully possess electric weapons. It is a misdemeanor to possess or sell one in violation of the law. The law does provide the power of arrest on probable cause. See chapter 140 § 131J.

Sawed-off Shotguns and covert firearms: these are unlawful for anyone to possess. See chapter 269 § 10(c) and chapter 140 § 131N.

Pellet & BB guns: To possess in public or discharging in private – must be 18 or accompanied by an adult or the holder of a hunting or sporting license. No one can discharge one in public ("across a public way"). See chapters 269 § 12A and 269 § 12B.

Defense Spray: no licensing required for those who are 18 years or older.

IMPORTANT NOTE: Class A & B licenses are being phased out. In 2021 there will just be an LTC, no more class of license.

FIREARMS LICENSING LAWS

C.140 § 121	FIREARM LAW DEFINITIONS
The below definitions refer to the laws of Chapter 140 (Firearm Licensing Laws)	
Ammunition	Cartridges or cartridge cases, primers (igniter), bullets or propellant powder designed for use in any firearm, rifle or shotgun. The term "ammunition" shall also mean tear gas cartridges. **Attorney Hanrahan's Note**: With the exception of mace type products, it is generally understood that in order for the item to meet the definition of "ammunition" it must be designed to be used in conjunction with a firearm, rifle, or shotgun; even though the statute does specifically impose this requirement.
Assault Weapon	**"Assault weapon",** shall have the same meaning as a semiautomatic assault weapon as defined in the Federal Public Safety and Recreational Firearms Use Protection Act, 18 U.S.C. section 921(a)(30) as appearing in such section on September 13, 1994, and shall include, but not be limited to, any of the weapons, or copies or duplicates of the weapons, of any caliber, known as: (i) Avtomat Kalashnikov (AK) (all models); (ii) Action Arms Israeli Military Industries UZI and Galil; (iii) Beretta Ar70 (SC-70); (iv) Colt AR-15; (v) Fabrique National FN/FAL, FN/LAR and FNC; (vi) SWD M-10, M-11, M-11/9 and M-12; (iv) Steyr AUG; (vii) INTRATEC TEC-9, TEC-DC9 and TEC-22; (v) Revolving cylinder shotguns, such as, or similar to, the Street Sweeper and Striker 12; The term assault weapon **shall not include**: i. Any of the weapons, or replicas or duplicates of such weapons, specified in appendix A to 18 U.S.C. section 922 as appearing in such appendix on September 13, 1994, as such weapons were manufactured on October 1, 1993; ii. Any weapon that is operated by manual bolt, pump, lever or slide action; iii. Any weapon that has been rendered permanently inoperable or otherwise rendered permanently unable to be designated a semiautomatic assault weapon; iv. Any weapon that was manufactured prior to the year 1899; v. Any weapon that is an antique or relic, theatrical prop or other weapon that is not capable of firing a projectile and which is not intended for use as a functional weapon and cannot be readily modified through a combination of available parts into an operable assault weapon; vi. Any semiautomatic rifle that cannot accept a detachable magazine that holds more than five rounds of ammunition; or vii. Any semiautomatic shotgun that cannot hold more than five rounds of ammunition in a fixed or detachable magazine.
Conviction	A finding or verdict of guilt or a plea of guilty, whether or not final sentence is imposed.
Firearm	A pistol, revolver or other weapon of any description, loaded or unloaded, from which a shot or bullet can be discharged and of which the **length of the barrel or barrels is less than 16 inches** or **18 inches in the case of a shotgun** as originally manufactured; The term firearm **shall not include** any weapon that is: i. constructed in a shape that does not resemble a handgun, short-barreled rifle or short-

FIREARM LICENSING

C.140 § 121	FIREARM LAW DEFINITIONS
	barreled shotgun including, but not limited to, covert weapons that resemble key-chains, pens, cigarette-lighters or cigarette-packages; or ii. not detectable as a weapon or potential weapon by x-ray machines commonly used at airports or walk- through metal detectors.
Gunsmith	Any person who engages in the business of repairing, altering, cleaning, polishing, engraving, blueing or performing any mechanical operation on any firearm, rifle, shotgun or machine gun.
Imitation firearm	Any weapon which is designed, manufactured or altered in such a way as to render it incapable of discharging a shot or bullet.
Large capacity feeding device	i. a fixed or detachable magazine, box, drum, feed strip or similar device **capable of accepting**, or that **can be readily converted to accept**, **<u>more than 10</u> rounds of ammunition** or **<u>more than 5</u> shotgun shells**; or ii. a large capacity ammunition feeding device as defined in the federal Public Safety and Recreational Firearms Use Protection Act, 18 U.S.C. section 921(a)(31) as appearing in such section on September 13, 1994. The term "large capacity feeding device" **shall not include** an attached tubular device designed to accept, and capable of operating **only** with, **.22 caliber ammunition**. **Note**: the round in the chamber should not be included in the calculation because it is not "accepted" by the feeding device.
Large capacity weapon	Any firearm, rifle or shotgun: i. that is semiautomatic with a fixed large capacity feeding device; ii. that is semiautomatic and capable of accepting, or readily modifiable to accept, any detachable large capacity feeding device. **Important Note**: 501 CMR 7.02 indicates that "capable of accepting" or "readily modifiable to accept" means that the feeding device is fully or partially inserted, or attached to the weapon, or is under the direct control of a person who has direct control of a weapon capable of accepting the feeding device. iii. that employs a rotating cylinder capable of accepting more than ten rounds of ammunition in a rifle or firearm and more than five shotgun shells in the case of a shotgun or firearm; or iv. that is an assault weapon.
	Attorney Hanrahan's Note: EOPS periodically establishes a list of Large Capacity weapons (Large Capacity Weapons Roster). If the weapon is on the list it is a Large Capacity weapon. If it is not on the list can still be a large capacity weapon if it fits the definition. The most recent list of high capacity weapons can be found by visiting www..mass.gov/EOPS.
	The term "large capacity weapon" shall be a secondary designation and shall apply to a weapon in addition to its primary designation as a firearm, rifle or shotgun and **shall not include**: (i) any weapon that was manufactured in or **prior to the year 1899**; (ii) any weapon that operates by **manual bolt, pump, lever or slide action**; (iii) any weapon that is a **single-shot** weapon; (iv) any weapon that has been modified so as to render it **permanently inoperable** or otherwise rendered permanently unable to be designated a large capacity weapon; or (v) any weapon that is an **antique or relic**, **theatrical prop** or other weapon that is **not capable**

C.140 § 121	FIREARM LAW DEFINITIONS
	of firing a projectile and which is not intended for use as a functional weapon and cannot be readily modified through a combination of available parts into an operable large capacity weapon.
Barrel Length	**"Length of barrel" or "barrel length",** that portion of a firearm, rifle, shotgun or machine gun through which a shot or bullet is driven, guided or stabilized and shall include the chamber.
Licensing authority	**"Licensing authority",** the chief of police or the board or officer having control of the police in a city or town, or persons authorized by them.
Machine gun	A weapon of any description, by whatever name known, loaded or unloaded, from which a number of shots or bullets may be rapidly or automatically discharged by one continuous activation of the trigger, including a submachine gun.
Purchase & sale	**"Purchase" and "sale"** shall include exchange; the word "purchaser" shall include exchanger; and the verbs "sell" and "purchase", in their different forms and tenses, shall include the verb exchange in its appropriate form and tense.
Rifle	A weapon having a rifled bore with a barrel length equal to or greater than 16 inches and capable of discharging a shot or bullet for each pull of the trigger.
Sawed-off shotgun	any weapon made from a shotgun, whether by alteration, modification or otherwise, if such weapon *as modified* has: 1. One or more barrels **less than 18** inches in length, or 2. As modified has an overall length of **less than 26 inches.**
Semiautomatic	**"Semiautomatic",** capable of utilizing a portion of the energy of a firing cartridge to extract the fired cartridge case and chamber the next round, and requiring a separate pull of the trigger to fire each cartridge.
Shotgun	**"Shotgun",** a weapon having a smooth bore with a barrel length equal to or greater than 18 inches with an overall length equal to or greater than 26 inches, and capable of discharging a shot or bullet for each pull of the trigger.
Violent Crime	• Any crime punishable by imprisonment for a term exceeding one year, or • Any act of juvenile delinquency involving the use or possession of a deadly weapon that would be punishable by imprisonment for such term if committed by an adult, and • That: (i) has as an element involving the use, attempted use or threatened use of physical force or a deadly weapon against the person of another; (ii) is burglary, extortion, arson or kidnapping; (iii) involves the use of explosives; or (iii) Otherwise involves conduct that presents a serious risk of physical injury to another.
Weapon	Any rifle, shotgun or firearm.

C.140 § 121 — FIREARM LAW DEFINITIONS

The below definitions are not actually defined in c. 140 § 121 but they are important concepts to understand when reviewing the firearm licensing laws.

Possession vs. Carrying	It is important to understand the difference between *possession* and *carrying* when it comes to firearm violations. **Possession** simply means having the firearm under your immediate control. In most cases possession within your home or business is treated differently than possession in public. **Carrying** "a firearm occurs when the defendant knowingly has more than momentary possession of a working firearm and moves it from one place to another."[1265] It would not be deemed "carrying" to move the firearm within your own home or business; this would be considered mere possession because you are within your own property. However, carrying within the common area of the defendant's apartment complex was deemed to be carrying in *Commonwealth. v. Seay*. So the exemption for carrying within the home would seemingly apply only to property under the exclusive control of the resident (not common areas in a multi-unit dwelling). Additionally, when it comes to a public location the "moves" element may not be required, the mere possession of the firearm in public may be deemed to be carrying. [1266]
Nonresident vs. Alien	A nonresident is someone who is a U.S. citizen residing in a location other than Massachusetts. An alien is someone who is not a U.S. citizen.

[1265] *Commonwealth v. Albano*, 373 Mass. 132 (1977) also see *Commonwealth v. Seay*, 376 Mass. 735 (1978)
[1266] *Commonwealth v. Seay*, 376 Mass. 735 (1978) referencing Commonwealth v. Ballou, 350 Mass. 751 (1966) ("carrying" found where recited facts showed only stationary possession in public place).

LICENSE TO POSSESS

Overview: In nearly all cases a person must be properly licensed to possess or carry a firearm, rifle, shotgun or ammunition. This section deals with the varies license requirements and exemptions. However, when it comes to charging someone criminally for possessing a weapon, including firearms, rifles and shotguns, chapter 269 of the Massachusetts General Laws if often the correct source. You should refer to the Weapons section of this manual for information on charging someone who unlawfully possesses a weapon.

C. 140 § 129C	POSSESSION AND OWNERSHIP OF WEAPONS Licensing Requirements & Exceptions
	License Required
License Required to Possess Firearms, Rifles, Shotguns and Ammunition	• No person shall **own** or **possess** • Any firearm, rifle, shotgun or ammunition • **Unless** he has been issued a FIREARM IDENTIFICATION CARD (FID) or LICENSE TO CARRY (LTC) by the licensing authority, other than a **licensed dealer** or **an exempt person** (see below for exemptions below). **Attorney Hanrahan's note:** In short, you must have an FID or an LTC, or be either a licensed dealer or an exempt person (see below for exemptions) to own or possess a firearm, rifle, shotgun or ammunition. Depending on the type of weapon or ammunition the person possesses will dictate the appropriate criminal charge for those who are not in compliance with the law. See the weapons section of this manual for the appropriate charge.
Attorney Hanrahan's Note	It is important to understand the difference between *possession* and *carrying* when it comes to firearm violations. Some of the exemptions listed below apply to possession but not carrying. **Possession** simply means having the firearm under your immediate control. In most cases possession within your home or business is treated differently than possession in public. **Carrying** "a firearm occurs when the defendant knowingly has more than momentary possession of a working firearm and moves it from one place to another."[1267] It would not be deemed "carrying" to move the firearm within your own home or business; this would be considered mere possession because you are within your own property. However, carrying within the common area of the defendant's apartment complex was deemed to be carrying in *Commonwealth. v. Seay*. So the exemption for carrying within the home would seemingly apply only to property under the exclusive control of the resident (not common areas in a multi-unit dwelling). Additionally, when it comes to a public location the "moves" element may not be required, the mere possession of the firearm in public may be deemed to be carrying.[1268] In 1990, the Legislature removed the term "carry" from the former unlawful carrying law and simply made a crime to possess a firearm outside of the confines of the home or business. Despite the language change the concept remains.
	Exemptions **The provisions of chapter 140 § 129C (licensing requirements) shall <u>not</u> apply to the following exempted persons and uses:**
(a) Flare Gun & Construction Tools	Any device used exclusively for: a. **Signaling or distress** use and required or recommended by the United States Coast Guard or the Interstate Commerce Commission, or b. The firing of stud cartridges, explosive rivets or similar industrial ammunition.

[1267] *Commonwealth v. Albano*, 373 Mass. 132 (1977) also see *Commonwealth v. Seay*, 376 Mass. 735 (1978)
[1268] *Commonwealth v. Seay*, 376 Mass. 735 (1978) referencing Commonwealth v. Ballou, 350 Mass. 751 (1966) ("carrying" found where recited facts showed only stationary possession in public place).

C. 140 § 129C	POSSESSION AND OWNERSHIP OF WEAPONS Licensing Requirements & Exceptions
(b) Federal Dealers & Manufacturers	**Federally licensed firearms manufacturers or wholesale dealers, or persons employed** by them or by licensed dealers, or on their behalf, when possession of firearms, rifles or shotguns is necessary for manufacture, display, storage, transport, installation, inspection or testing.
(c) Voluntary Firearm Surrender	**To a person voluntarily surrendering a firearm, rifle or shotgun and ammunition therefor to a licensing authority, the colonel of the state police or his designee if prior written notice has been given** by said person to the licensing authority or the colonel of the state police, stating the place and approximate time of said surrender.
(d) Common Carrier	The regular and **ordinary transport of firearms, rifles or shotguns as merchandise by any common carrier**;
(e) Amusement Parks	Possession by **retail customers for the purpose of firing at duly licensed target concessions at amusement parks**, piers and similar locations, provided that the firearms, rifles or shotguns to be so used are firmly **chained or affixed** to the counter and that the proprietor is in possession of a FID or LTC.
(f) Out of State Hunters	Possession of rifles and shotguns and ammunition therefor by **nonresident hunters with valid** nonresident **hunting licenses during hunting season.** **Note:** no exemption for firearms (i.e. pistols). **Attorney Hanrahan's Note**: This exemption is seemingly unnecessary as exemption (p) allows nonresidents to carry rifles and shotguns as long as they are licensed in their home states.
(g) Out of State Residents at Range	Possession of rifles and shotguns and ammunition therefor **by nonresidents while on a firing or shooting range**. **Note:** no exemption for firearms (i.e. pistols). **Attorney Hanrahan's Note:** The legislature did not require the nonresident to be licensed in his/her home state (as exemption (p) so requires) when the possession takes place at a range.
(h) Non-resident traveling through Massachusetts	Possession of rifles and shotguns and ammunition therefor **by nonresidents traveling in or through the commonwealth**, **providing that any rifles or shotguns are unloaded and enclosed in a case**. **Attorney Hanrahan's Note**: the Massachusetts legislature did not grant such an exception for the transport of **firearms** through Massachusetts. However, federal law (18 USC § 926A – Interstate Transportation of Firearms) states in part a lawful gun owner "shall be entitled to transport a firearm for any lawful purpose from any place where he may lawfully possess and carry such firearm to any other place where he may lawfully possess and carry such firearm if, during such transportation the firearm is unloaded, and neither the firearm nor any ammunition being transported is readily accessible or is directly accessible from the passenger compartment of such transporting vehicle: Provided, that in the case of a vehicle without a compartment separate from the driver's compartment the firearm or ammunition shall be contained in a locked container other than the glove compartment or console." In short, a non-resident who lawfully possesses a firearm may transport the firearm through Massachusetts on his/her way to another state as long as it is unloaded and secured in the trunk. **Attorney Hanrahan's Note:** Oddly, the legislature did not require that the nonresident be able to lawfully possess the weapon in his/her home state (as exemption (p) so requires). It is unclear whether this was intentional or an oversight.

C. 140 § 129C	POSSESSION AND OWNERSHIP OF WEAPONS Licensing Requirements & Exceptions
(i) Non-resident at gun collector show	Possession of rifles and shotguns **by nonresidents while at a firearm showing or display organized by a regularly existing gun collectors' club or association.** **Note:** no such provision for firearms, only rifles and shotguns.
(j) New resident / Returning Resident has 60 days	• Any ***new* resident** moving into the Commonwealth, • Any resident of the Commonwealth **returning after having been absent from the Commonwealth for not less than 180 consecutive days,** or • **Any resident of the Commonwealth upon being released from active service with any of the armed services of the United States** With respect to any firearm, rifle or shotgun and any ammunition therefor then in his possession, for **60 days** after such **release, return** or **entry** into the Commonwealth. **Attorney Hanrahan's Note**: This provision only exempts a new resident/returning resident from needing a license to *possess* the weapon; this does not permit them to *carry* the weapon. In ***Commonwealth v. Wood*** (1986), the defendant was moving from Louisiana to his new residence in Malden, MA. On his way he was pulled over by the Cambridge Police. He had a revolver under the driver's seat. He was charged with unlawful carrying of a firearm. The SJC upheld the conviction stating that the exemption allows him to *possess* the firearm but not to *carry* it, even if the carrying is only to deliver it to his new residence. **Attorney Hanrahan's note:** In 1990 the legislature removed the term "carry" from the statute. In lieu of the carrying language they deciphered the crime which was formerly "carrying" and made it a violation to possess it outside of the home. Because of this change, based on the reasoning in ***Commonwealth v. Wood*** above, a new resident or a person returning to Massachusetts may be exempt from possessing the firearm without a license even outside of their home or business. This question won't be answered until it presented before the Court or the legislature clarifies their intent. Be sure to review the differences between possession and carrying explained at the beginning of this section.
(k) Military Personnel & Children under 15 while hunting	• Any person **under the age of fifteen with respect to the use of a rifle or shotgun by such person in hunting or target shooting**, provided that such use is otherwise permitted by law and is **under the immediate supervision of a person holding a firearm identification card or a license to carry firearms**, or • A (**Military Officer**) duly commissioned officer, noncommissioned officer or enlisted member of the United States Army, Navy, Marine Corps, Air Force or Coast Guard, or the National Guard or military service of the commonwealth or reserve components thereof, while **in the performance of his duty**;

C. 140 § 129C	POSSESSION AND OWNERSHIP OF WEAPONS Licensing Requirements & Exceptions
(l) **Movie Production**	The possession or utilization of any rifle or shotgun during the course of any **television, movie, stage or other similar theatrical production**, or by a **professional photographer or writer for examination purposes in the pursuit of his profession**, providing such possession or utilization is **under the immediate supervision of a holder of a firearm identification card or a license to carry firearms**. **Note:** Chapter 140 § 131F½ states "The carrying or possession of a firearm and blank ammunition therefor, during the course of any television, movie, stage or other similar theatrical production, by a person within such production, shall be authorized; provided, however, that such carrying or possession of such firearm shall be under the immediate supervision of a person licensed to carry firearms."
(m) **Temporary Inspection**	The **temporary holding, handling or firing of a firearm for examination, trial or instruction** in the presence of a holder of a license to carry firearms, or the temporary holding, handling or firing of a rifle or shotgun for examination, trial or instruction in the presence of a holder of a firearm identification card, or where such holding, handling or firing is for a lawful purpose. **Attorney Hanrahan's Note**: For example, this exemption would permit the holder of an LTC to take his/her spouse (whom does not have a license) to the range to instruct them on the use of the weapon.
(n) **Inheritance 180 days**	The **transfer of a firearm, rifle or shotgun upon the death of an owner to his heir or legatee** shall be subject to the provisions of this section, provided that said heir or legatee **shall within 180 of such transfer, obtain a firearm identification card or a license to carry firearms** if not otherwise an exempt person who is qualified to receive such or apply to the licensing authority for such further limited period as may be necessary for the disposition of such firearm, rifle or shotgun. Also see Chapter 140 § 128A for more on this exemption (sale of inherited weapons).
(o) **Military & Law Enforcement Personnel**	Persons in the **military** or **other service** of any state or of the United States, and **police officers** and other peace officers of any jurisdiction, **in the performance of their official duty** or **when duly authorized to possess them**. **Attorney Hanrahan's Note**: Exemption (k) specifically exempts *military officers*, this exemption (o) includes all persons in the military (not just officers) – when duly authorized or in the performance of their duties. This exemption also exempts police officers. Chapter 41 § 98 grants police officers the authority to carry agency authorized weapons.
(p) **Black Powder weapons**	Carrying or possession by residents or nonresidents of so-called **black powder rifles, shotguns, and ammunition** therefor as described in such paragraphs (A) and (B) of the third paragraph of section 121.
(p) **Nonresidents can *carry* rifles, shotguns & ammo if licensed to do so in their state**	The carrying or possession of **conventional rifles, shotguns, and ammunition** therefor by nonresidents who meet the requirements for such carrying or possession in the state in which they reside. **Attorney Hanrahan's Note**: the nonresident still has to comply with other related laws (i.e. you can't carry a loaded rifle in public unless hunting – see weapons sections for more).
	(There is no clause (q)).

C. 140 § 129C	POSSESSION AND OWNERSHIP OF WEAPONS Licensing Requirements & Exceptions
(r) Veteran's Organizations Parades & Ceremonies	Possession by **a veteran's organization** chartered by the Congress of the United States, chartered by the Commonwealth or recognized as a nonprofit tax-exempt organization by the Internal Revenue Service and possession by the members of any such organization when on **official parade duty** or **ceremonial occasions**.
(s) Museums	Possession by federal, state and local **historical societies, museums, and institutional collections open to the public**, provided such firearms, rifles or shotguns are unloaded, properly housed and secured from unauthorized handling.
(t) Bank Collateral	The possession of firearms, rifles, shotguns, machine guns and ammunition, by **banks or institutional lenders,** or their agents, servants or employees, when the same are **possessed as collateral** for a secured commercial transaction or as a result of a default under a secured commercial transaction.
(u) Nonresident (duly licensed) purchasing rifle or shotgun	Any **nonresident who is eighteen years of age or older at the time of acquiring a rifle or shotgun from a licensed firearms dealer**; provided, however, that **such nonresident must hold a valid firearms license from his state of residence**; provided, further, that the **licensing requirements of such nonresident's state of residence are as stringent as the requirements of the commonwealth** for a firearm identification card, as determined by the colonel of the state police who shall, annually, publish a list of those states whose requirements comply with the provisions of this clause.
Additional Exemptions	
Chapter 140 § 121	Chapter 140 § 121 states that "the provisions of sections 122 to 129D, inclusive, and sections 131, 131A, 131B and 131E **shall not apply to:** a) Any firearm, rifle or shotgun manufactured in or prior to the year 1899; b) Any replica of any firearm, rifle or shotgun described in clause (a) if such replica: i. Is not designed or redesigned for using rimfire or conventional centerfire fixed ammunition; or ii. Uses rimfire or conventional centerfire fixed ammunition which is no longer manufactured in the united states and which is not readily available in the ordinary channels of commercial trade; c) Manufacturers or wholesalers of firearms, rifles, shotguns or machine guns."
Additional Provisions, Related Statutes, Case Law & Other Important Information	
FID card does not permit person to CARRY a firearm	The possession of a FID shall not entitle any person to carry a firearm in violation of chapter 269 § 10 (carrying a firearm).
FID card does not permit person to possess any Large Capacity weapon/feeding device.	The possession of a FID card shall not entitle any person to possess any large capacity rifle or shotgun or large capacity feeding device violation of chapter 269 § 10(m).
Licensee must present license upon demand by a police officer (unless on own	On demand of a police officer or other law enforcement officer any person shall exhibit: • his license to carry firearms (LTC), or • his firearm identification card (FID) or

FIREARM LICENSING

C. 140 § 129C	POSSESSION AND OWNERSHIP OF WEAPONS Licensing Requirements & Exceptions
property)	• receipt for fee paid for the LTC or FID, or, • his valid hunting license issued to him **Exceptions**: This does not apply to a person who is within the limits of his own property or residence unless the property or residence is under lawful search. This also does not apply to a person who is exempt under chapter 140 § 129C (exemptions). **Failing to Comply:** Upon failure to do so such person may be required to surrender to the officer his firearm, rifle or shotgun which shall be taken into custody (as under the provisions of chapter 140 § 129D – surrender of licenses and weapons upon revocation of license), except that the firearm, rifle or shotgun shall be returned forthwith upon presentation within 30 days of the license to carry firearms, firearm identification card or receipt for fee paid for such card or hunting license as hereinbefore described. Any person subject to the conditions of this paragraph may, even though no firearm, rifle or shotgun was surrendered, be required to produce within 30 days said license to carry firearms, firearm identification card or receipt for fee paid for such card, or said hunting license, failing which the conditions of chapter 140 § 129D will apply.
Unlawful Carrying	See the Weapons section of this manual for various crimes related to those who carry weapons without proper licensing or authorization.

C. 140 § 131P	BASIC FIREARMS SAFETY CERTIFICATE
LTC/FID/PERMIT TO PURCHASE APPLCIANTS MUST TAKE SAFETY COURSE	
Safety Course Required	Any person making application for the issuance of a firearms identification card under section 129B, a Class A or Class B license to carry firearms under section 131 or 131F or a permit to purchase under section 131A **who was not licensed under the provisions of this chapter on June 1, 1998** shall, in addition to the requirements set forth in said section 129B, 131, 131A or 131F, submit to the licensing authority a basic firearms safety certificate No application for the issuance of a firearm identification card or license to carry shall be accepted or processed by the licensing authority without such certificate attached thereto.
Hunter education course substitution	A certificate issued by the division of law enforcement in the department of fisheries, wildlife and environmental law enforcement pursuant to the provisions of chapter 131 § 14 evidencing satisfactory completion of a hunter education course shall serve as a valid substitute for a basic firearms safety certificate required under this section.
June 1, 1998 exemption	Persons lawfully possessing a firearm identification card or license to carry firearms on June 1, 1998 shall be exempt from the provisions of this section upon expiration of such card or license and when applying for licensure as required under this chapter.

C. 140 § 131P	BASIC FIREARMS SAFETY CERTIFICATE
Government & Military Exemptions	The provisions of this section shall not apply to (i) any officer, agent or employee of the commonwealth or any state of the United States; (ii) any member of the military or other service of any state or of the United States; (iii) any duly authorized law enforcement officer, agent or employee of any municipality of the commonwealth; provided, however, that any such person described in clauses (i) to (iii), inclusive, is authorized by a competent authority to carry or possess the weapon so carried or possessed and is acting within the scope of his duties. A current member of the United States military or the Massachusetts National Guard who has not been prohibited under said section 129B from owning a firearm and has received adequate training while serving in the military shall be exempt from being required to submit a basic firearms safety certificate to the licensing authority upon submitting a copy of the member's most current military identification form.
INSTRUCTOR CERTIFICATIONS	
Certified Instructors	The colonel of state police shall promulgate rules and regulations governing the issuance and form of basic firearms safety certificates required by this section. The colonel shall certify certain persons as firearms safety instructors and shall certify safety course curriculum. Such certification shall be for a period of ten years, unless sooner revoked by reason of unsuitability, in the discretion of the colonel.
Qualifications	Firearms safety instructors shall be any person certified by a nationally recognized organization that fosters safety in firearms, or any other person in the discretion of said colonel, to be competent to give instruction in a basic firearms safety course. Applicants for certification as instructors under the provisions of this section shall not be exempt from the requirements of this chapter or any other law or regulation of the commonwealth or the United States.
Curriculum Requirements	Upon application to the colonel of state police, the colonel may, in his discretion, certify as a firearms safety instructor any person who operates a firearms safety course or program which provides in its curriculum: (a) the safe use, handling and storage of firearms; (b) methods for securing and childproofing firearms; (c) the applicable laws relating to the possession, transportation and storage of firearms; and (d) knowledge of operation, potential dangers and basic competency in the ownership and usage of firearms.
Fee	The department of state police may impose a fee of $50 for initial issuance of such certification to offset the cost of certifying instructors. The fee for certification renewal shall be $10.
ISSUANCE OF CERTIFICATES	
Instructor may issue certificate	Any firearms safety instructor certified under the provisions of this section may, in his discretion, issue a basic firearms safety certificate to any person who successfully completes the requirements of a basic firearms safety course approved by the colonel.
Student must meet minimum requirements	No firearms safety instructor shall issue or cause to be issued any basic firearms safety certificate to any person who fails to meet minimum requirements of the prescribed course of study including, but not limited to, demonstrated competency in the use of firearms. Instructors certified under the provisions of this section shall forward to the department of state police the names of those persons who have received basic firearms safety certificates.
Must Confirm Certificate prior license issue	Local licensing authorities, as defined in section 121, shall, upon receipt of an application for a firearm identification card or a Class A or Class B license to carry firearms, make inquiry to the department of state police to confirm the issuance to the applicant of a basic firearms safety certificate.

C. 140 § 131P	BASIC FIREARMS SAFETY CERTIFICATE
	INSTRUCTOR ISSUING FALSE CERTIFICATE
Penalty	Any firearms safety instructor who knowingly issues a basic firearms safety certificate to a person who has not successfully completed a firearms safety course approved by the colonel shall be punished by a fine of not less than $5,000 nor more than $10,000 or by imprisonment for not more than two years in a HOC, or by both such fine and imprisonment.
Power of Arrest	**Misdemeanor** – there is no statutory authority granting powers of arrest for this offense.
	FALSE CERTIFICATE SUBMITTED BY APPLICANT
Penalty	Any person applying for licensure under the provisions of this chapter who knowingly files or submits a basic firearms safety certificate to a licensing authority which contains false information shall be punished by a fine of not less than $1,000 nor more than $5,000 or by imprisonment for not more than 2 years in a HOC, or by both such fine and imprisonment.
Power of Arrest	**Misdemeanor** – there is no statutory authority granting powers of arrest for this offense.

C. 140 § 129B	FIREARM IDENTIFICATION CARDS
	A firearm identification card (FID) *shall* be issued subject to the following conditions and restrictions:
Residence, Place of Business or Federal Jurisdiction	• Any person **residing** or having a **place of business** within the jurisdiction of the licensing authority or • Any person **residing in an area of exclusive federal jurisdiction** located within a city or town • May submit to the licensing authority an application for a firearm identification card, or renewal of the same.
State Issued License Possible Ch. 140 § 121	Where the local licensing authority has the power to issue licenses or cards under chapter 140, but no such licensing authority exists, any resident or applicant may apply for such license or firearm identification card directly to the colonel of state police and said colonel shall for this purpose be the licensing authority.
	The licensing authority <u>shall</u> issue an FID, <u>unless</u>:
Section (i) Massachusetts Crimes	FID must be issued unless: The applicant has ever, in a court of the commonwealth, been convicted (or adjudicated a **youthful offender or delinquent child,** both as defined in section 52 of c. 119), for the commission of: a. a **felony;** b. a **misdemeanor** punishable by imprisonment for more than **2 years**; c. a **violent crime** as defined in chapter 140 § 121 (see definitions in the beginning of this section); d. **a violation of any law** regulating the use, possession, ownership, transfer, purchase, sale, lease, rental, receipt or transportation of **weapons or ammunition for which a imprisonment may be imposed**; or

C. 140 § 129B	FIREARM IDENTIFICATION CARDS
	e. a violation of any law regulating the use, **possession or sale of controlled substances**, as defined in chapter 94C § 1 including, but not limited to, a violation under chapter 94C. f. a misdemeanor **crime of domestic violence** as defined in 18 U.S.C. 921(a)(33).
	Exception –Except for the commission of a **felony**, a misdemeanor crime of **domestic violence**, a **violent crime** or a crime involving the **trafficking of controlled substances**, if the applicant has been so convicted or adjudicated or released from confinement, probation or parole supervision for such conviction or adjudication, whichever occurs last, for **5 or more years** immediately preceding such application, then the applicant's right or ability to possess a non-large capacity rifle or shotgun shall be deemed restored in the commonwealth with respect to such conviction or adjudication and that conviction or adjudication shall not disqualify the applicant for a firearm identification card.
Attorney Hanrahan 's Comment	As long as 5 years has passed since the applicant's last conviction or related sanction (parole, probation or incarceration) the crime will not disqualify the person from obtaining an FID card, *unless* the crime was a felony, a violent crime, a crime of domestic violence, or involved drug trafficking. These convictions will result in a lifetime disqualification. Oddly, gun trafficking will also disqualify the applicant for life **but** only if the charge occurred in another state or under federal jurisdiction (see below). Additionally, there is no "improper person" disqualifier for an FID as there is when it comes to an LTC.
Section (ii) Out-of-State and Federal Crimes	FID must be issued unless: The applicant has, in any **other state or federal jurisdiction**, been convicted (or adjudicated a youthful offender or delinquent child) for the commission of: (a) a **felony**; (b) a **misdemeanor** punishable by imprisonment for **more than 2 years;** (c) a **violent crime** as defined in section 121; (d) a violation of any law regulating the use, possession, ownership, transfer, purchase, sale, lease, rental, receipt or transportation of **weapons or ammunition for which a term of imprisonment may be imposed**; or (e) a violation of any law regulating the use, **possession or sale of controlled substances**, as defined in section 1 of c. 94C; (f) a misdemeanor **crime of domestic violence** as defined in 18 U.S.C. 921(a)(33). **Exception:** except for the commission a **felony**, a misdemeanor crime of **domestic violence**, a **violent crime** or a crime involving the **trafficking of weapons or controlled substances**, if the applicant has been so convicted or adjudicated or released from confinement, probation or parole supervision for such conviction or adjudication, whichever occurs last, **for 5 or more years** immediately preceding such application and the applicant's right or ability to possess a rifle or shotgun has been fully restored in the jurisdiction wherein the conviction or adjudication was entered, then the conviction or adjudication shall not disqualify such applicant for a firearm identification card.
Attorney Hanrahan 's Comment	Section (ii) has the same disqualifying factors as section (i) except section (ii) also imposes a lifetime disqualifier for those convicted of a crime involving gun trafficking in another state or under federal jurisdiction.

C. 140 § 129B	FIREARM IDENTIFICATION CARDS
Section (iii) Mental Illness & Substance abuse Disqualifications	FID must be issued unless: The applicant is or has been: a) committed pursuant to sections 35 or 36C of chapter 123, committed to any **hospital or institution for mental illness, alcohol or substance abuse**, unless after 5 years from the date of the confinement, the applicant submits with the application an affidavit of a licensed physician or clinical psychologist attesting that such physician or psychologist is familiar with the applicant's mental illness, alcohol or substance abuse and that in the physician's or psychologist's opinion the applicant is not disabled by a mental illness, alcohol or substance abuse in a manner that should prevent the applicant from possessing a firearm, rifle or shotgun; b) committed by an order of a court to any hospital or institution for mental illness, unless the applicant was granted a petition for relief of the court's order pursuant to said section 36C of said chapter 123 and submits a copy of the order for relief with the application; c) subject to an order of the probate court appointing a guardian or conservator for a incapacitated person on the grounds that that applicant lacks the mental capacity to contract or manage affairs, unless the applicant was granted a petition for relief pursuant to section 56C of chapter 215 and submits a copy of the order for relief with the application; or d) found to be a person with an alcohol use disorder or substance use disorder or both and committed pursuant to said section 35 of said chapter 123, unless the applicant was granted a petition for relief of the court's order pursuant to said section 35 of said chapter 123 and submits a copy of the order for relief with the application;
Section (iv) Under 15	FID must be issued unless: The applicant is at the time of the application is at the time of the application younger than 14 years of age; provided however that the applicant shall not be issued the card **until the applicant reaches the age of 15**.
Section (v) 15 to 17 with Parent Permission	FID must be issued unless: The applicant is at the time of the application **more than 14 but less than 18 years of age, unless the applicant submits with the application a certificate of a parent or guardian granting the applicant permission to apply for a card.**
Section (vi) Citizenship	FID must be issued unless: is an alien who does not maintain lawful permanent residency **Attorney Hanrahan's Note:** However, an alien may receive a permit to own/possess a rifle or shotgun from the Colonel of the State Police pursuant to chapter 140 § 131H. Also see chapter 120 § 131F – alien may receive a temporary LTC from Colonel.
Section (vii) Protective Order	FID must be issued unless: The applicant is currently subject to: a) an order for suspension or surrender issued pursuant to section 3B or 3C of chapter 209A (firearm surrender order for domestic protective order) or a similar order issued by another jurisdiction; or b) a permanent or temporary protection order issued pursuant to chapter 209A, a similar order issued by another jurisdiction, including an order described in 18 U.S.C. 922(g)(8).
Section (viii) Outstanding Warrant	FID must be issued unless: the applicant is currently the subject of an **outstanding arrest warrant** in any state or federal jurisdiction.
Section (ix) Dishonorable discharge	FID must be issued unless: the applicant has been discharged from the armed forces of the United States under dishonorable conditions.
Section (x) Fugitive	FID must be issued unless: the applicant is a fugitive from justice.

C. 140 § 129B	FIREARM IDENTIFICATION CARDS
Section (xi) Renounced US citizenship	FID must be issued unless: the applicant having been a citizen of the United States, has renounced that citizenship.
Licensing Authority may petition the Court for Unsuitable Person	a. The licensing authority may file a petition to request that an applicant be denied the issuance or renewal of a firearm identification card, or to suspend or revoke such a card in the district court of jurisdiction. If the licensing authority files any such petition it shall be accompanied by written notice to the applicant describing the specific evidence in the petition. Such petition shall be founded upon a written statement of the reasons for supporting a finding of unsuitability pursuant to subsection (d). b. Upon the filing of a petition to deny the issuance or renewal of a firearm identification card, the court shall within 90 days hold a hearing to determine if the applicant is unsuitable under subsection (d) of this paragraph. Such a petition shall serve to stay the issuance or renewal of the firearm identification card pending a judicial determination on such petition. c. Upon the filing of a petition to suspend or revoke a firearm identification card, the court shall within 15 days determine whether there is sufficient evidence to support a finding that the applicant is unsuitable. Such petition shall serve to effect the suspension or revocation pending a judicial determination on the sufficiency of evidence. If a court determines that insufficient evidence exists to support a finding of unsuitability, the licensing authority shall not file a petition under this subsection for the same applicant within 75 days of the licensing authority's previous petition for that applicant. If a court determines that sufficient evidence exists to support a finding of unsuitability, the court shall within 75 days hold a hearing to determine if the applicant is unsuitable under subsection (d); provided, however, that such initial suspension or revocation shall remain in effect pending a judicial determination thereon. d. A determination of unsuitability shall be based on a preponderance of evidence that there exists: I. reliable, articulable, and credible information that the applicant has exhibited or engaged in behavior to suggest the applicant could potentially create a risk to public safety; or II. existing factors that suggest that the applicant could potentially create a risk to public safety. If a court enters a judgment that an applicant is unsuitable the court shall notify the applicant in a writing setting forth the specific reasons for such determination. If a court has not entered a judgment that an applicant is unsuitable under this clause within 90 days for petitions under clause (ii) or within 75 days under clause (iii), the court shall enter a judgment that the applicant is suitable for the purposes of this paragraph.
FID RESTRICTIONS	
FID card not valid for firearms and large capacity rifles and shotguns with few exceptions.	A firearm identification card shall **not** entitle a holder thereof to possess: (i) A **large capacity** firearm or large capacity feeding device **Exception:** except **under a Class A license issued to a shooting club** as provided under section 131 or **under the direct supervision of a holder of a Class A license at an incorporated shooting club or licensed shooting range**; or (ii) A **non-large capacity firearm** or **large capacity rifle or shotgun** or large capacity feeding device **Exception:** except **under a Class A license issued to a shooting club** or **under the direct supervision of a holder of a Class A or Class B license at an incorporated shooting club or licensed shooting range**. (iii) An FID card shall not entitle a holder thereof to possess any rifle or shotgun that is, or in such manner that is, **otherwise prohibited by law**. (iv) Except as otherwise provided herein, a firearm identification card shall not be valid for the use,

C. 140 § 129B	FIREARM IDENTIFICATION CARDS
	possession, ownership, transfer, purchase, sale, lease, rental or transportation of a rifle or shotgun if such rifle or shotgun is a **large capacity weapon** (as defined in chapter 140 § 121).
FID card does not permit person to CARRY a firearm	Additionally, chapter 140 § 129C states that the possession of a FID shall not entitle any person to *carry* (i.e. possess outside of the home or business) a firearm in violation of c. 269 § 10(a) ("carrying" a firearm).
FID card does not permit person to possess any Large Capacity weapon/feeding device.	Additionally, chapter 140 § 129C states that the possession of a FID card shall not entitle any person to possess any large capacity rifle or shotgun or large capacity feeding device violation of chapter 269 § 10(m).
Chemical Spray	A firearm identification card **shall be valid for the purpose of purchasing and possessing chemical mace, pepper spray or other similarly propelled liquid, gas or powder** designed to temporarily incapacitate. Note: only persons under the age of 18 years require an FID card for defense sprays.
How c. 269 § 10 – Possession of a Weapon - Applies to those who have/had and FID	
Possession of non-large capacity rifle or shotgun after normal expiration is non-criminal	• Chapter 269 § 10 does not apply • if any person in possession of **a non-large capacity** rifle or shotgun • whose FID card issued under this section is invalid for the **sole reason that it has expired**, meaning after 90 days beyond the stated expiration date on the card, **Possession after expiration Penalty**: shall be subject to a civil fine of not less than $500 nor more than $5,000 and the provisions of chapter 269 § 10 shall not apply.
When c. 269 § 10 does apply to someone who once held an FID card	Chapter 269 § 10 (unlawful possession of a non-large capacity rifle or shotgun) <u>shall apply</u> if: (i) The FID card has been **revoked or suspended** Note: **unless** such revocation or suspension was caused by failure to give **notice of a change of address** as required under this section; (ii) Revocation or suspension of such firearm identification card is **pending**, **Note: unless** such revocation or suspension was caused by **failure to give notice of a change of address** as required under this section; or (iii) an application for renewal of such firearm identification card has been **denied**. **Law Enforcement Action for Suspension/Revocation involving Address Change Violation**: Any law enforcement officer who discovers a person to be in possession of a rifle or shotgun after such person's firearm identification card has expired, meaning after 90 days beyond the stated expiration date on the card, or has been revoked or suspended solely for failure to give notice of a change of address **shall confiscate any rifle or shotgun and such expired or suspended card then in possession**, and such officer shall forward such card to the licensing authority by whom it was issued as soon as practicable. **Return upon Renewal:** Any confiscated weapon shall be returned to the owner upon the renewal or reinstatement of such expired or suspended card within one year of such confiscation or such weapon may be otherwise disposed of in accordance with the provisions of section 129D. **Receipt alone Valid for 5 Days:** Pending the issuance of a renewed firearm identification card, a receipt for the fee paid, after five days following issuance, shall serve as a valid substitute and any rifle or shotgun so confiscated shall be returned, unless the applicant is disqualified. **Note:** The provisions of this paragraph shall not apply if such person has a valid license to carry firearms issued under section 131 or 131F. **See weapons section of this manual for more on carrying without a license.**

C. 140 § 129B	FIREARM IDENTIFICATION CARDS
	Application Issues
Application Format	The application for an FID card shall be made in a standard form provided by the commissioner of the department of criminal justice information services which shall require the applicant to affirmatively state, under the pains and penalties of perjury, that he is not disqualified on any of the grounds enumerated in clauses (i) to (ix) (see above), inclusive, from being issued such card.
Application Receipt	The licensing authority shall provide to the applicant a receipt indicating that it received the applicant's application. The receipt shall be provided to the applicant within 7 days by mail if the application was received by mail or immediately if the application was made in person; provided, however, that the receipt shall include the applicants' name, address, current firearm identification card number, if any, the current card's expiration date, if any, the date when the application was received by the licensing authority, the name of the licensing authority and its agent that received the application, the licensing authority's address and telephone number, the type of application and whether it is an application for a new card or for renewal of an existing card; and provided further, that a copy of the receipt shall be kept by the licensing authority for not less than 1 year and a copy shall be furnished to the applicant if requested by the applicant.
Time Limits	**Within 7 days** of the receipt of a completed application for a card, the licensing authority shall forward one copy of the application and one copy of the applicant's fingerprints to the colonel of state police, who shall, **within 30 days**, advise the licensing authority, in writing, of any disqualifying criminal record of the applicant arising from within or without the commonwealth and whether there is reason to believe that the applicant is disqualified for any of the foregoing reasons from possessing a card.
Databases Searched	In searching for any disqualifying history of the applicant, the colonel shall utilize, or cause to be utilized, files maintained by the department of mental health, department of probation and statewide and nationwide criminal justice, warrant and protection order information systems and files including, but not limited to, the National Instant Criminal Background Check System.
Decision Criteria and Time Limit	If the information available to the colonel does not indicate that the possession of a non-large capacity rifle or shotgun by the applicant would be in violation of state or federal law, he shall certify such fact, in writing, to the licensing authority **within such 30 day** period. The licensing authority may not prescribe any other condition for the issuance of a firearm identification card and shall, **within 40 days** from the date of application, either approve the application and issue the license or deny the application and notify the applicant of the reason for such denial in writing; provided, however, that no such card shall be issued unless the colonel has certified, in writing, that the information available to him does not indicate that the possession of a rifle or shotgun by the applicant would be in violation of state or federal law.
Penalty for False Application	Any person who knowingly files an application containing false information shall be punished by a fine of not less than $500 nor more than $1,000 or by imprisonment for not less than 6 months nor more than two years in a HOC, or by both such fine and imprisonment.

C. 140 § 129B	FIREARM IDENTIFICATION CARDS
	Expiration, Renewal & Relocate
Renewal	A firearm identification card shall be valid, unless revoked or suspended, for a period of **not more than 6 years** from the date of issuance, except that if the cardholder applied for renewal before the card expired, the card shall remain valid after the expiration date on the card for all lawful purposes, until the application for renewal is approved or denied. **Active duty military:** if the cardholder is on active duty with the armed forces of the United States on the expiration date of the card, the card shall remain valid until the cardholder is released from active duty and for a period of not less than **180 days** following such release, except that if the cardholder applied for renewal prior to the end of such period, the card shall remain valid after the expiration date on the card for all lawful purposes, until the application for renewal is approved or denied. A card issued on February 29 shall expire on March 1.
Notification of Expiration	The commissioner of criminal justice information services shall send electronically or by first class mail to the holder of a firearm identification card, a notice of the expiration of the card not less than **90 days before its expiration** and shall enclose with the notice a form for the renewal of the card. The form for renewal shall include an affidavit whereby the applicant shall verify that the applicant has not lost a firearm or had a firearm stolen from the applicant's possession since the date of the applicant's last renewal or issuance. The commissioner of criminal justice information services shall include in the notice all pertinent information about the penalties that may be imposed if the firearm identification card is not renewed. The commissioner of criminal justice information services shall provide electronic notice of expiration only upon the request of a cardholder. A request for electronic notice of expiration shall be forwarded to the department on a form furnished by the commissioner. Any electronic address maintained by the department to provide electronic notice of expiration shall be considered a firearms record and shall not be disclosed except as provided in section 10 of chapter 66.
Notification Requirements if the holder Relocates	A cardholder shall notify, in writing, the licensing authority that issued such card, the chief of police into whose jurisdiction such cardholder moves and the executive director of the criminal history systems board of any change of address. Such notification shall be made by certified mail **within 30 days** of its occurrence. Failure to so notify shall be cause for revocation or suspension of such card.
	Revocation & Denials
FID Revocation	A firearm identification card shall be revoked or suspended by the licensing authority or his designee upon the occurrence of **any event that would have disqualified the holder from being issued such card** or from having such card renewed or for a violation of a restriction provided under this section. Any revocation or suspension of a card shall be in writing and shall state the reasons therefor. Upon revocation or suspension, the licensing authority shall take possession of such card and receipt for fee paid for such card, and the person whose card is so revoked or suspended shall take all action required under the provisions of section 129D. No appeal or post-judgment motion shall operate to stay such revocation or suspension. Notices of revocation and suspension shall be forwarded to the commissioner of the department of criminal justice information services and the commissioner of probation and shall be included in the criminal justice information system. A revoked or suspended card may be reinstated only upon the termination of all disqualifying conditions.
Denial and Revocation Appeal	Any applicant or holder aggrieved by a denial, revocation or suspension of a firearm identification card, unless a hearing has previously been held pursuant to chapter 209A, may, within either **90 days** after receipt of notice of such denial, revocation or suspension or within 90 days after the expiration of the time limit in which the licensing authority is required to respond to the applicant, file a petition to obtain judicial review in the district court having jurisdiction in the city or town wherein the applicant filed for or was issued such card. A justice of such court, after a hearing, may direct that a card be issued or reinstated to the petitioner if the justice finds that such petitioner is not prohibited by law from possessing such card.

C. 140 § 129B	FIREARM IDENTIFICATION CARDS
	Format & Fees
FID card Format	**Standard FID:** A firearm identification card shall be in a standard form provided by the commissioner of the department of criminal justice information services in a size and shape equivalent to that of a license to operate motor vehicles issued by the registry of motor vehicles pursuant to section 8 of chapter 90 and shall contain an identification number, name, address, photograph, fingerprint, place and date of birth, height, weight, hair color, eye color and signature of the cardholder and shall be marked "Firearm Identification Card" and shall provide in a legible font size and style the phone numbers for the National Suicide Prevention Lifeline and the Samaritans Statewide Helpline. **Spray Only:** If a firearm identification card is issued for the sole purpose of purchasing or possessing chemical mace, pepper spray or other similarly propelled liquid, gas or powder designed to temporarily incapacitate, such card shall clearly state that such card is valid for such limited purpose only.
General Fee	Except an FID card solely for Defense Spray, the fee for an application for a firearm identification card shall be $100, which shall be payable to the licensing authority and shall not be prorated or refunded in the case of revocation or denial. The licensing authority shall retain $25 of the fee; $50 of the fee shall be deposited in the General Fund; and $25 of the fee shall be deposited in the Firearms Fingerprint Identity Verification Trust Fund. Notwithstanding any general or special law to the contrary, licensing authorities shall deposit quarterly that portion of the firearm identification card application fee which is to be deposited into the General Fund, not later than January 1, April 1, July 1 and October 1 of each year.
Fees for Chemical Spray	The application fee for a firearm identification card issued pursuant to clause (vi) of section 122D for the sole purpose of purchasing or possessing chemical mace, pepper spray or other similarly propelled liquid, gas or powder designed to temporarily incapacitate shall be $25, which shall be payable to the licensing authority and shall not be prorated or refunded in the case of revocation or denial. The licensing authority shall retain 50 per cent of the fee and the remaining portion shall be deposited in the General Fund. Notwithstanding any general or special law to the contrary, licensing authorities shall deposit quarterly that portion of the firearm identification card application fee which is to be deposited into the General Fund, not later than January 1, April 1, July 1 and October 1 of each year. There shall be no application fee for the renewal of a firearm identification card issued under this paragraph. A firearm identification card issued under this paragraph shall display, in clear and conspicuous language, that the card shall be valid only for the purpose of purchasing or possessing chemical mace, pepper spray or other similarly propelled liquid, gas or powder designed to temporarily incapacitate. Except as provided above, the fee for an application for a firearm identification card for any person under the age of 18 shall be $25, which shall be payable to the licensing authority and shall not be prorated or refunded in the case of revocation or denial. The licensing authority shall retain 50 per cent of the fee and the remaining portion shall be deposited into the General Fund. Notwithstanding any general or special law to the contrary, licensing authorities shall deposit quarterly that portion of the firearm identification card application fee which is to be deposited into the General Fund, not later than January 1, April 1, July 1 and October 1 of each year.
No Renewal Fee over 70	Any person over the age of 70 shall be exempt from the requirement of paying a renewal fee for a firearm identification card.
	OTHER REQUIREMENTS
Firearm Safety Course	Applicants must complete an authorized safety course. See Chapter 140 § 131P covered previously in this section.

LTC's

C. 140 § 131	LICENSE TO CARRY (LTC): CONDITIONS AND RESTRICTIONS
All licenses to carry firearms shall be designated Class A or Class B, and the issuance and possession of any such license shall be subject to the following conditions and restrictions:	
CLASS A License (LTC) ENTITLEMENTS AND RESTRICTIONS	
Large Capacity Firearms, Shotguns and Rifles	A **Class A** license shall entitle a holder thereof to purchase, rent, lease, borrow, possess and carry: i. **Firearms**, including large capacity firearms, and feeding devices and ammunition therefor, for all lawful purposes, subject to such restrictions relative to the possession, use or carrying of firearms as the licensing authority deems proper; and ii. **Rifles and shotguns**, including large capacity weapons, and feeding devices and ammunition therefor, for all lawful purposes.
Licensing Authority may Impose Restrictions	The licensing authority may impose such restrictions relative to the possession, use or carrying of large capacity rifles and shotguns as it deems proper.
Penalty for Restriction of License	A violation of a restriction imposed by the licensing authority under the provisions of this paragraph shall be cause for suspension or revocation and shall, unless otherwise provided, be punished by a fine of not less than $1,000 nor more than $10,000; provided, however, that the provisions of chapter 269 § 10 shall not apply to such violation. **Attorney Hanrahan's Note**: If the licensing authority (i.e. the Police Chief) places a restriction on the Class A LTC, for instance "target practice only", the license holder would not be guilty of carrying without a license (c. 269 § 10). He/she would only be subject to a fine and suspension/revocation of his/her LTC. No power of arrest for this violation.
Class A: Same entitlements as an FID	A Class A license is valid for the purpose of owning, possessing, purchasing and transferring non-large capacity rifles and shotguns, and for purchasing and possessing chemical mace, pepper spray or other similarly propelled liquid, gas or powder designed to temporarily incapacitate, consistent with the entitlements conferred by a firearm identification card issued under section 129B.

C. 140 § 131 LICENSE TO CARRY (LTC): CONDITIONS AND RESTRICTIONS

CLASS B License (LTC) ENTITLEMENTS AND RESTRICTIONS	
Non-Large Capacity Firearms and Large Capacity rifles and shotguns	A **Class B license** shall entitle a holder thereof to purchase, rent, lease, borrow, possess and carry: (i) **Non-large capacity** firearms and feeding devices and ammunition therefor, for all lawful purposes, subject to such restrictions relative to the possession, use or carrying of such firearm as the licensing authority deems proper; **Loaded and Concealed prohibited**: a Class B license shall not entitle the holder thereof to carry or possess a loaded firearm in a concealed manner in any public way or place; **Large Capacity firearm only at Gun Club or with Supervision**: a Class B license shall not entitle the holder thereof to possess a large capacity firearm, except under a Class A club license issued under c. 140 § 131 or under the direct supervision of a holder of a valid Class A license at an incorporated shooting club or licensed shooting range. (ii) **Rifles and shotguns, including large capacity** rifles and shotguns, and feeding devices and ammunition therefor, for all lawful purposes; provided, however, that the licensing authority may impose such restrictions relative to the possession, use or carrying of large capacity rifles and shotguns as he deems proper.
Licensing Authority may Impose Restrictions	The licensing authority may impose such restrictions relative to the possession, use or carrying of large capacity rifles and shotguns as he deems proper.
Violation of Restriction or Class	A violation of a restriction provided under this paragraph, or a restriction imposed by the licensing authority under the provisions of this paragraph, shall be cause for suspension or revocation and shall, unless otherwise provided, be punished by a fine of not less than $1,000 nor more than $10,000; provided, however, that the provisions of c. 269 § 10 shall not apply to such violation. **Attorney Hanrahan's Note**: a violation of a Class B restriction (i.e. carrying a large capacity firearm or carrying loaded and concealed) or a violation of a restriction put in place by the licensing authority (e.g. target practice only) would not be a violation of chapter 269 § 10 (unlawful carrying). The license holder would only be subject to a fine and suspension/revocation of his/her LTC. No power of arrest for this violation.
Class B: cannot purchase Large Capacity Firearm	A Class B license shall not be a valid license for the purpose of complying with any provision under this chapter governing the purchase, sale, lease, rental or transfer of any weapon or ammunition feeding device if such weapon is a large capacity firearm or if such ammunition feeding device is a large capacity feeding device for use with a large capacity firearm, both as defined in section 121.
Class B: Same entitlements as an FID	A Class B license is valid for the purpose of owning, possessing, purchasing and transferring non-large capacity rifles and shotguns, and for purchasing and possessing chemical mace, pepper spray or other similarly propelled liquid, gas or powder designed to temporarily incapacitate, consistent with the entitlements conferred by a firearm identification card issued under section 129B.
Licenses Classes are being phased out	The legislature passed legislation in 2014 phasing out the classes of licenses. In January of 2021 there will no longer be a Class A or Class B license just an LTC.
LTC NOT REQUIRED	
Signal (flare) guns	No license shall be required for the carrying or possession of a firearm known as a **detonator and commonly used on vehicles as a signaling and marking device**, when carried or possessed for such signaling or marking purposes.

C. 140 § 131	LICENSE TO CARRY (LTC): CONDITIONS AND RESTRICTIONS
Veteran's Organization	No license to carry shall be required for the possession of an **unloaded large capacity rifle or shotgun or an unloaded feeding device therefor by a veteran's organization** chartered by the Congress of the United States, chartered by the commonwealth or recognized as a nonprofit tax-exempt organization by the Internal Revenue Service, or by the members of any such organization when on official parade duty or during ceremonial occasions. For purposes of this subparagraph, an "unloaded large capacity rifle or shotgun" and an "unloaded feeding device therefor" shall include any large capacity rifle, shotgun or feeding device therefor loaded with a blank cartridge or blank cartridges, so-called, which contain no projectile within such blank or blanks or within the bore or chamber of such large capacity rifle or shotgun.
Attorney Hanrahan's Note	Additional exemptions exist for certain firearms, rifles and shotguns under the exemptions listed for an FID. See FID section previously in this section for more on these exemptions.
	LTC APPLICATION PROCEDURES AND RULES
To apply must be: Resident, Business owner or Law Enforcement	• Any person **residing** or having a **place of business** within the jurisdiction of the licensing authority or • Any **law enforcement officer** employed by the licensing authority or • Any person residing in an area of **exclusive federal jurisdiction** located within a city or town May submit to such licensing authority or the colonel of state police, an application for a Class A or Class B license to carry firearms, or renewal of the same.
State Issued License Possible Ch. 140 § 121	Where the local licensing authority has the power to issue licenses or cards under chapter 140, but no such licensing authority exists, any resident or applicant may apply for such license or firearm identification card directly to the colonel of state police and said colonel shall for this purpose be the licensing authority.
	REQUIREMENT TO GET AN LTC
Must be a Suitable Person with reason	The licensing authority or colonel may issue and LTC if it appears that the applicant is not a prohibited person, as set forth in this section (see below), to be issued a license and has good reason to fear injury to the applicant or the applicant's property or for any other reason, including the carrying of firearms for use in sport or target practice only, subject to the restrictions expressed or authorized under this section.
Firearm Safety Course	Applicants must complete an authorized safety course. See Chapter 140 § 131P covered previously in this section.
	DISQUALIFIERS FOR AN LTC (PROHIBITED PERSON)
(i) In-state conviction	A prohibited person shall be a person who has, in a court of the commonwealth, been convicted or adjudicated a youthful offender or delinquent child, both as defined in section 52 of chapter 119, for the commission of: a. a felony; b. a misdemeanor punishable by imprisonment for more than 2 years; c. a violent crime as defined in section 121; d. a violation of any law regulating the use, possession, ownership, transfer, purchase, sale, lease, rental, receipt or transportation of weapons or ammunition for which a term of imprisonment may be imposed; e. a violation of any law regulating the use, possession or sale of a controlled substance as defined in section 1 of chapter 94C including, but not limited to, a violation of said chapter 94C; or f. a misdemeanor crime of domestic violence as defined in 18 U.S.C. 921(a)(33);

C. 140 § 131	LICENSE TO CARRY (LTC): CONDITIONS AND RESTRICTIONS
(ii) **Foreign conviction**	A prohibited person shall be a person who has, in any other state or federal jurisdiction, been convicted or adjudicated a youthful offender or delinquent child for the commission of: a. a felony; b. a misdemeanor punishable by imprisonment for more than 2 years; c. a violent crime as defined in section 121; d. a violation of any law regulating the use, possession, ownership, transfer, purchase, sale, lease, rental, receipt or transportation of weapons or ammunition for which a term of imprisonment may be imposed; e. a violation of any law regulating the use, possession or sale of a controlled substance as defined in section 1 of chapter 94C including, but not limited to, a violation of said chapter 94C; or f. a misdemeanor crime of domestic violence as defined in 18 U.S.C. 921(a)(33);
(iii) **Mental Health and Substance Abuse**	A prohibited person shall be a person who is or has been: a. **committed to a hospital or institution for mental illness, alcohol or substance abuse**, except a commitment pursuant to chapter 123 § 35 or 36C, **unless after 5 years** from the date of the confinement, the applicant submits with the application an **affidavit** of a licensed physician or clinical psychologist attesting that such physician or psychologist is familiar with the applicant's mental illness, alcohol or substance abuse and that in the physician's or psychologist's opinion, the applicant is not disabled by a mental illness, alcohol or substance abuse in a manner that shall prevent the applicant from possessing a firearm, rifle or shotgun; b. committed by a court order to a hospital or institution for mental illness, unless the applicant was granted a petition for relief of the court order pursuant to chapter 123 § 35 or 36C and submits a copy of the court order with the application; c. subject to an order of the probate court appointing a guardian or conservator for a incapacitated person on the grounds that the applicant lacks the mental capacity to contract or manage the applicant's affairs, unless the applicant was granted a petition for relief of the order of the probate court pursuant to section 56C of chapter 215 and submits a copy of the order of the probate court with the application; or d. found to be a person with an alcohol use disorder or substance use disorder or both and committed pursuant to chapter 123 § 35, unless the applicant was granted a petition for relief of the court order pursuant to said section 35 and submits a copy of the court order with the application;
(iv) **Must be 21**	A prohibited person shall be a person who is younger than 21 years of age at the time of the application;
(v) **Alien**	A prohibited person shall be a person who is an alien who does not maintain lawful permanent residency; **NOTE**: see c. 140 § 131F, an alien may obtain a temporary license through the state police.
(v) **Protective Order**	A prohibited person shall be a person who is currently subject to: a. an order for suspension or surrender issued pursuant to chapter 209A § 3B or 3C (firearm **surrender order**) or a similar order issued by another jurisdiction; or b. a permanent or temporary **protection order** issued pursuant to said chapter 209A or a similar order issued by another jurisdiction, including any order described in 18 U.S.C. 922(g)(8);

C. 140 § 131	LICENSE TO CARRY (LTC): CONDITIONS AND RESTRICTIONS
(vii) Outstanding Warrant	A prohibited person shall be a person who is currently the subject of an **outstanding arrest warrant** in any state or federal jurisdiction;
(vii) Dishonorable Discharge	A prohibited person shall be a person who has been discharged from the armed forces of the United States under dishonorable conditions;
(ix) Fugitive from Justice	A prohibited person shall be a person who is a fugitive from justice.
(x) Renounced Citizenship	A prohibited person shall be a person who is having been a citizen of the United States, has renounced that citizenship.
General unsuitability	The licensing authority may deny the application or renewal of a license to carry, or suspend or revoke a license issued under this section if, in a reasonable exercise of discretion, the licensing authority determines that the applicant or licensee is unsuitable to be issued or to continue to hold a license to carry. A determination of unsuitability shall be based on: (a) reliable and credible information that the applicant or licensee has exhibited or engaged in behavior that suggests that, if issued a license, the applicant or licensee may create a risk to public safety; or (b) existing factors that suggest that, if issued a license, the applicant or licensee may create a risk to public safety.
Unsuitability notification	Upon denial of an application or renewal of a license based on a determination of unsuitability, the licensing authority shall notify the applicant in writing setting forth the specific reasons for the determination in accordance with the required processing deadlines listed below. Upon revoking or suspending a license based on a determination of unsuitability, the licensing authority shall notify the holder of a license in writing setting forth the specific reasons for the determination in accordance with revocation and suspension procedures listed later in this section. The determination of unsuitability shall be subject to judicial review.
APPLICATION PROCESS & TIMELINE	
Processing Deadlines	Within **7 days** of the receipt of a completed application for a license to carry or possess firearms, or renewal of same, the licensing authority shall forward one copy of the application and one copy of the applicant's fingerprints to the colonel of state police, who shall within **30 days** advise the licensing authority, in writing, of any disqualifying criminal record of the applicant arising from within or without the commonwealth and whether there is reason to believe that the applicant is disqualified for any of the foregoing reasons from possessing a license to carry or possess firearms.
40 days to approve or deny application	The licensing authority shall, within **40 days** from the date of application, either approve the application and issue the license or deny the application and notify the applicant of the reason for such denial in writing; provided, however, that no such license shall be issued unless the colonel has certified, in writing, that the information available to him does not indicate that the possession of a firearm or large capacity firearm by the applicant would be in violation of state or federal law.

C. 140 § 131	LICENSE TO CARRY (LTC): CONDITIONS AND RESTRICTIONS
Areas of permissible inquiry	In searching for any disqualifying history of the applicant, the colonel shall utilize, or cause to be utilized, files maintained by the **department of probation** and **statewide and nationwide criminal justice, warrant and protection order information systems** and files including, but not limited to, the National Instant Criminal Background Check System. The colonel shall inquire of the commissioner of the **department of mental health** relative to whether the applicant is disqualified from being so licensed. If the information available to the colonel does not indicate that the possession of a firearm or large capacity firearm by the applicant would be in violation of state or federal law, he shall certify such fact, in writing, to the licensing authority within said 30 day period. The licensing authority may also make inquiries concerning the applicant to: (i) The commissioner of the department of criminal justice information services relative to any disqualifying condition and records of purchases, sales, rentals, leases and transfers of weapons or ammunition concerning the applicant; (ii) The commissioner of probation relative to any record contained within the department of probation or the statewide domestic violence record keeping system concerning the applicant; (iii) The commissioner of the department of mental health relative to whether the applicant is a suitable person to possess firearms or is not a suitable person to possess firearms. The director or commissioner to whom the licensing authority makes such inquiry shall provide prompt and full cooperation for that purpose in any investigation of the applicant.
Licensing Authority Responsibilities upon issuance	Upon issuance of a license to carry or possess firearms under this section, the licensing authority shall forward a copy of such approved application and license to the commissioner of the department of criminal justice information services, who shall inform the licensing authority forthwith of the existence of any disqualifying condition discovered or occurring subsequent to the issuance of a license under this section.
Fraudulent application for an LTC	Any person who knowingly *files* an application containing false information shall be punished by a fine of not less than $500 nor more than $1,000 or by imprisonment for not less than 6 months nor more than two years in a HOC, or by both such fine and imprisonment. Note: No right of arrest powers enacted by statute. Attorney Hanrahan's Note: You may also want to consider a felony Perjury charge under chapter 268 § 1A which states "No written statement required by law shall be required to be verified by oath or affirmation before a magistrate if it contains or is verified by a written declaration that it is made under the penalties of perjury. Whoever signs and issues such a written statement containing or verified by such a written declaration shall be guilty of perjury and subject to the penalties thereof if such statement is wilfully false in a material matter."
Violation by licensing authority	Whoever knowingly *issues* a license in violation of this section shall be punished by a fine of not less than $500 nor more than $1,000 or by imprisonment for not less than 6 months nor more than two years in a jail or HOC, or by both such fine and imprisonment.

C. 140 § 131 LICENSE TO CARRY (LTC): CONDITIONS AND RESTRICTIONS

LTC RENEWAL PROCESS

LTC Duration & Renewal Requirements	A license to carry or possess firearms shall be valid, unless revoked or suspended, for a period of **not more than 6 years from the date of issue** and shall **expire on the anniversary of the licensee's date of birth** occurring not less than 5 years nor more than 6 years from the date of issue; provided, however, that, if the licensee applied for renewal before the license expired, the license shall remain valid after its expiration date for all lawful purposes until the application for renewal is approved or denied. **Military Personnel**: If a licensee is on active duty with the armed forces of the United States on the expiration date of the license, the license shall remain valid until the licensee is released from active duty and for a period not less than 180 days following the release; provided, however, that, if the licensee applied for renewal prior to the end of that period, the license shall remain valid after its expiration date for all lawful purposes until the application for renewal is approved or denied. Any renewal shall expire on the anniversary of the licensee's date of birth occurring not less than 5 years but not more than 6 years from the effective date of such license. Any license issued to an applicant born on February 29 shall expire on March 1. **Class B Renewal**: An application for renewal of a Class B license filed before the license has expired shall not extend the license beyond the stated expiration date; provided, that the Class B license shall expire on the anniversary of the licensee's date of birth occurring not less than 5 years nor more than 6 years from the date of issue.
State Sends Notice of pending expiration	The executive director of the criminal history systems board shall send electronically or by first class mail to the holder of each such license to carry firearms, a notice of the expiration of such license **not less than 90 days** prior to such expiration and shall enclose therein a form for the renewal of such license. The form for renewal shall include an affidavit in which the applicant shall verify that the applicant has not lost any firearms or had any firearms stolen from the applicant since the date of the applicant's last renewal or issuance. The commissioner of criminal justice information services shall provide electronic notice of expiration only upon the request of a cardholder. A request for electronic notice of expiration shall be forwarded to the department on a form furnished by the commissioner. Any electronic address maintained by the department for the purpose of providing electronic notice of expiration shall be considered a firearms record and shall not be disclosed except as provided in section 10 of chapter 66.
New Fingerprints are not required	The taking of fingerprints shall not be required in issuing the renewal of a license if the renewal applicant's fingerprints are on file with the department of the state police.

LTC EXPIRATION RAMIFICATIONS

Expired license does not result in Unlawful Possession of a Firearm violation under c. 269 § 10, unless revoked, suspended or denied.	• Any person in possession of a firearm, rifle or shotgun whose license issued under chapter 140 § 131 is invalid • For the **sole reason that it has expired** (possibly 90 days beyond the stated expiration date on the license) • But who shall not be disqualified from renewal upon application • Shall be subject to a civil fine of not less than $100 nor more than $5,000 and the provisions of ch. 269 § 10 shall not apply;

C. 140 § 131	LICENSE TO CARRY (LTC): CONDITIONS AND RESTRICTIONS
	However, the provisions of G. L. c. 269 § 10 (carrying a dangerous weapon) shall apply if: (i) The license has been **revoked or suspended**, **unless** such revocation or suspension was caused by **failure to give notice of a change of address** as required under this section; (ii) **Revocation or suspension** of such license is **pending**, unless such revocation or suspension was caused by failure to give notice of a change of address as required under this section (iii) An **application for renewal** of such license has been **denied**. **Police Action**: Any law enforcement officer who discovers a person to be in possession of a firearm, rifle or shotgun after such person's license has expired, meaning after 90 days beyond the stated expiration date on the license, has been revoked or suspended, solely for failure to give notice of a change of address, **shall confiscate such firearm, rifle or shotgun and the expired or suspended license** then in possession and such officer, shall forward such license to the licensing authority by whom it was issued as soon as practicable. The officer shall, at the time of confiscation, provide to the person whose firearm, rifle or shotgun has been confiscated, a written inventory and receipt for all firearms, rifles or shotguns confiscated and the officer and his employer shall exercise due care in the handling, holding and storage of these items. **Return to Owner upon Renewal/Reinstatement**: Any confiscated weapon shall be returned to the owner upon the renewal or reinstatement of such expired or suspended license within one year of such confiscation or may be otherwise disposed of in accordance with the provisions of section 129D. The provisions of this paragraph shall not apply if such person has a valid license to carry firearms issued under section 131F (non-resident temporary LTC's).
90 days for 269 § 10 violation	For the purposes of chapter 269 § 10, an expired license to carry firearms shall be deemed to be valid for a period not to exceed 90 days beyond the stated date of expiration, unless such license to carry firearms has been revoked.
	LICENSEE MUST REPORT CHANGE OF ADDRESS
30 days in writing	Any licensee who changes his/her address shall notify, in writing: 1. The licensing authority who issued the license, 2. The chief of police into whose jurisdiction the licensee moves, and 3. The executive director of the criminal history systems board. The notifications shall be made by certified mail within 30 days of its occurrence. Failure to so notify shall be cause for revocation or suspension of the license.
	LTC REVOCATIONS & SUSPENSIONS
Revocation & Suspension Of License	An LTC shall be revoked or suspended by the licensing authority, or his designee, upon the occurrence of any event that would have disqualified the holder from being issued such license or from having such license renewed. A license may be revoked or suspended by the licensing authority if it appears that the holder is **no longer a suitable person to possess such license**. Any revocation or suspension of a license shall be in writing and shall state the reasons therefor. Upon revocation or suspension, the licensing authority shall take possession of such license and the

C. 140 § 131	LICENSE TO CARRY (LTC): CONDITIONS AND RESTRICTIONS
	person whose license is so revoked or suspended shall take all actions required under the provisions of section 129D. No appeal or post-judgment motion shall operate to stay such revocation or suspension. Notices of revocation and suspension shall be forwarded to the commissioner of the department of criminal justice information services and the commissioner of probation and shall be included in the criminal justice information system. A revoked or suspended license may be reinstated only upon the termination of all disqualifying conditions, if any.
APPEAL PROCESS	
Judicial Review	Any applicant or holder aggrieved by a **denial, revocation, suspension** or **restriction** placed on a license, unless a hearing has previously been held pursuant to chapter 209A, may, within either 90 days after receiving notice of the denial, revocation or suspension or within 90 days after the expiration of the time limit during which the licensing authority shall respond to the applicant or, in the case of a restriction, any time after a restriction is placed on the license pursuant to this section, file a petition to obtain judicial review in the district court having jurisdiction in the city or town in which the applicant filed the application or in which the license was issued. If after a hearing a justice of the court finds that there was no reasonable ground for denying, suspending, revoking or restricting the license and that the petitioner is not prohibited by law from possessing a license, the justice may order a license to be issued or reinstated to the petitioner or may order the licensing authority to remove certain restrictions placed on the license.
Miscellaneous	
LTC Design	A license shall be in a standard form provided by the commissioner of the department of criminal justice information services in a size and shape equivalent to that of a license to operate motor vehicles issued by the registry of motor vehicles pursuant to chapter 90 § 8 and shall contain a license number which shall clearly indicate whether such number identifies a Class A or Class B license, the name, address, photograph, fingerprint, place and date of birth, height, weight, hair color, eye color and signature of the licensee. Such license shall be marked "License to Carry Firearms" and shall clearly indicate whether the license is Class A or Class B. The application for such license shall be made in a standard form provided by the commissioner of the department of criminal justice information services, which form shall require the applicant to affirmatively state under the pains and penalties of perjury that such applicant is not disqualified on any of the grounds enumerated above from being issued such license.
LTC Fees	The fee for the application shall be $100, which shall be payable to the licensing authority and shall not be prorated or refunded in case of revocation or denial. The licensing authority shall retain $25 of the fee; $50 of the fee shall be deposited into the general fund of the commonwealth and not less than $50,000 of the funds deposited into the General Fund shall be allocated to the Firearm Licensing Review Board, established in section 130B, for its operations and that any funds not expended by said board for its operations shall revert back to the General Fund; and $25 of the fee shall be deposited in the Firearms Fingerprint Identity Verification Trust Fund. For active and retired law enforcement officials, or local, state, or federal government entities acting on their behalf, the fee for the application shall be set at $25, which shall be payable to the licensing authority and shall not be prorated or refunded in case of revocation or denial. The licensing authority shall retain $12.50 of the fee, and $12.50 of the fee shall be deposited into the general fund of the commonwealth. Notwithstanding any general or special law to the contrary, licensing authorities shall deposit such portion of the license application fee into the Firearms Record Keeping Fund quarterly, not later than January 1, April 1, July 1 and October 1 of each year. Notwithstanding any general or special law to the contrary, licensing authorities shall deposit quarterly such portion of the license application fee as is to be deposited into the General Fund, not later than January 1, April 1, July 1 and October 1 of each year.

C. 140 § 131	LICENSE TO CARRY (LTC): CONDITIONS AND RESTRICTIONS
	Over 70 and Law Enforcement exempt: Any person over the age of 70 and any law enforcement officer applying for a license to carry firearms through his employing agency shall be exempt from the requirement of paying a renewal fee for a Class A or Class B license to carry. For the purposes of section 10 of chapter 269, an expired license to carry firearms shall be deemed to be valid for a period not to exceed 90 days beyond the stated date of expiration, unless such license to carry firearms has been revoked.
CMR's Permissible	The secretary of the executive office of public safety or his designee may promulgate regulations to carry out the purposes of this section.

C. 140 § 131f	TEMPORARY LTC FOR NON-RESIDENT
Temporary LTC for Competition Purposes	A Class A or Class B temporary license to carry firearms or feeding devices or ammunition therefor, within the commonwealth, may be issued by the colonel of state police, or persons authorized by him, to a nonresident or any person not falling within the jurisdiction of a local licensing authority or to an alien that resides outside the commonwealth **for purposes of firearms competition** and subject to such terms and conditions as said colonel may deem proper.
	PROVISIONS & RESTRICTIONS
Disqualifications	The same disqualifications for a standard LTC apply (see c. 140 § 131) plus these two additional disqualifiers: • not being a citizen or national of the United States, is illegally or unlawfully in the United States; or • not being a citizen or national of the United States, has been admitted to the United States under a nonimmigrant visa as defined in 8 U.S.C. 1101(a)(26), unless the person has been admitted to the United States for lawful hunting or sporting purposes or is in possession of a hunting license or permit lawfully issued in the United States or another exception set forth in 18 U.S.C. 922(y)(2) applies.
Duration	**Duration:** Such license shall be valid for a period of one year but the colonel may renew such license, if in his discretion, such renewal is necessary. **Special Extended Duration**: A license issued under the provisions of this section to a non-resident who is in the **employ of a bank, public utility corporation, or a firm engaged in the business of transferring monies**, or business of similar nature, or a firm licensed as **a private detective** under the provisions of c. one hundred and forty-seven, and whose application is endorsed by his employer, or who is a **member of the armed services and is stationed within the territorial boundaries of the commonwealth** and has the written consent of his commanding officer, **may be issued for any term not to exceed two years**, and said licenses shall expire in accordance with the provisions of section one hundred and thirty-one.
Conditions	The colonel may issue such license, subject to such terms and conditions as he deems proper, to any resident of the commonwealth for the purposes of sports competition.
Class A or B	Neither a large capacity firearm nor large capacity feeding device therefor may be carried unless such person has been issued a Class A license; provided, however, that the colonel may permit a Class A or Class B licensee to possess large capacity rifles or shotguns or both, and such entitlement shall be clearly indicated on such license.

C. 140 § 131f	TEMPORARY LTC FOR NON-RESIDENT
Format	A temporary license issued under this section shall be marked "Temporary License to Carry Firearms", shall clearly indicate whether it is Class A or Class B and shall not be used to purchase firearms in the commonwealth as provided under section 131E.
Fees	The fee for an application for the license shall be $100, which shall be payable to the licensing authority and shall not be prorated or refunded in case of revocation or denial. The licensing authority shall retain $25 of the fee; $50 of the fee shall be deposited into the general fund of the commonwealth; and $25 of the fee shall be deposited in the Firearms Fingerprint Identity Verification Trust Fund.
Temporary machine gun license	A license, otherwise in accordance with provisions of this section, may be issued to a nonresident employee, whose application is endorsed by his employer, of a **federally licensed Massachusetts manufacturer of machine guns** to possess within the commonwealth a machine gun for the **purpose of transporting or testing** relative to the manufacture of machine guns, and the license shall be marked "temporary license to possess a machine gun" and may be issued for any term not to exceed two years and shall expire in accordance with the provisions of section one hundred and thirty-one.

c. 140 § 131H	OWNERSHIP OR POSSESSION OF FIREARMS BY ALIENS
Alien (non US citizen) possession of firearms	No alien shall own or have in his possession or under his control a firearm except as provided in section 131F or a rifle or shotgun except as provided in this section or section 131F.
State Police Permit	The colonel of the state police may, after an investigation, issue a permit to an alien to own or have in his possession or under his control a rifle or shotgun; subject to such terms and conditions as said colonel may deem proper.
Local Authority Notification	Upon issuing such permit the colonel shall so notify, in writing, the chief of police or the board or officer having control of the police in the city or town in which such alien resides.
Expiration	Each such permit card shall expire at twelve midnight on December thirty-first next succeeding the effective date of said permit, and shall be revocable for cause by the colonel.
Revocation	In case of revocation, the fee for such permit shall not be prorated or refunded. Whenever any such permit is revoked, said colonel shall give notification as hereinbefore provided. The permit issued to an alien under this section shall be subject to sections one hundred and twenty-nine B and one hundred and twenty-nine C except as otherwise provided by this section.
Fee	The fee for the permit shall be $100, which shall be payable to the licensing authority and shall not be prorated or refunded in case of revocation or denial. The licensing authority shall retain $25 of the fee; $50 of the fee shall be deposited into the general fund of the commonwealth; and $25 of the fee shall be deposited in the Firearms Fingerprint Identity Verification Trust Fund.
Arrest Power, Penalties & Notes	
Power of Arrest	The director of law enforcement of the department of fisheries, wildlife and environmental law enforcement, deputy directors of enforcement, chiefs of enforcement, deputy chiefs of enforcement, environmental police officers and deputy environmental police officers, wardens as defined in chapter 131 § 1 and members of the state police in areas over which they have jurisdiction, and all officers qualified to serve criminal process **shall arrest, without a warrant, any person found with a firearm,**

c. 140 § 131H	OWNERSHIP OR POSSESSION OF FIREARMS BY ALIENS
	rifle or shotgun in his possession if they have reason to believe that he is an alien and if he does not have in his possession a valid permit as provided in this section.
Penalty	Violation of any provision of this section shall be punished by a fine of not less than $500 nor more than $1,000 dollars, and by imprisonment for not more than 6 months in a jail or HOC. **Attorney Hanrahan's Note**: In most cases chapter 269 § 10 (unlawful carrying) would be a more appropriate charge. Charging an alien under this offense would provide a lighter penalty for a foreign national than a U.S. citizen.
Forfeit of Firearm	Any firearm, rifle or shotgun owned by an alien or in his possession or under his control in violation of this section shall be forfeited to the commonwealth. Any such firearm, rifle or shotgun may be the subject of a search warrant as provided in chapter 276.
Citizen Defense	If, in any prosecution for violation of this section, the defendant alleges that he has been naturalized, or alleges that he is a citizen of the United States, the burden of proving the same shall be upon him.

C. 140 § 131	MACHINE GUN LICENSES
	Elements
Machine Gun Licensing	No person shall be issued a license to carry or possess a machine gun in the commonwealth, except that a licensing authority or the colonel of state police may issue a machine gun license to: i. A firearm instructor certified by the municipal police training committee for the sole purpose of firearm instruction to police personnel ii. A bona fide collector of firearms upon application or upon application for renewal of such license. The commissioner of the department of criminal justice information services shall promulgate regulations in accordance with Chapter 30A to establish criteria for persons who shall be classified as bona fide collectors of firearms.
	Additional Provisions
CMR's Permissible	The secretary of the executive office of public safety or his designee may promulgate regulations to carry out the purposes of this section.
Bona Fide Collectors of Firearms 501 CMR 6.02	A "*bona fide* collector of firearms," for the purpose of issuance of a machine gun license, shall be defined as an individual who acquires firearms for such lawful purposes as historical significance, display, research, lecturing, demonstration, test firing, investment or other like purpose. For the purpose of issuance of a machine gun license the acquisition of firearms for sporting use or for use as an offensive or defensive weapon shall not qualify an applicant as a *bona fide* collector of firearms. An individual licensed pursuant to 18 U.S.C. c. 44, §§ 921-929 and 27 CFR Part 178 shall be deemed a *bona fide* collector of firearms for the purpose of 501 CMR 6.00.
A temporary Machine Gun C. 140 § 131f	A temporary machine gun license may be issued by the Colonel of the State Police. See chapter 140 § 131F – Temporary LTC's for Nonresidents (early in this section).

SHOOTING CLUB LICENSES

C. 140 § 131	CLASS A SHOOTNG CLUB LICENSE
Issued by the Colonel of the State Police	The colonel of state police may, after an investigation, grant a Class A license to a club or facility with an on-site shooting range or gallery, which club is incorporated under the laws of the commonwealth for the possession, storage and use of large capacity weapons, ammunition therefor and large capacity feeding devices for use with such weapons on the premises of such club; provided, however, that not less than one shareholder of such club shall be qualified and suitable to be issued such license; and provided further, that such large capacity weapons and ammunition feeding devices may be used under such Class A club license only by such members that possess a valid firearm identification card issued under section 129B or a valid Class A or Class B license to carry firearms, or by such other persons that the club permits while under the direct supervision of a certified firearms safety instructor or club member who, in the case of a large capacity firearm, possesses a valid Class A license to carry firearms or, in the case of a large capacity rifle or shotgun, possesses a valid Class A or Class B license to carry firearms.
CLASS A SHOOTING CLUB ENTITLEMENTS AND RESTRICTIONS	
No Human Images	The club shall not permit shooting at targets that depict human figures, human effigies, human silhouettes or any human images thereof, except by public safety personnel performing in line with their official duties.
Restrictions on Removal of Weapons	No large capacity weapon or large capacity feeding device shall be removed from the premises except for the purposes of: (i) Transferring such firearm or feeding device to a licensed dealer; (ii) Transporting such firearm or feeding device to a licensed gunsmith for repair; (iii) Target, trap or skeet shooting on the premises of another club incorporated under the laws of the commonwealth and for transporting thereto; (iv) Attending an exhibition or educational project or event that is sponsored by, conducted under the supervision of or approved by a public law enforcement agency or a nationally or state recognized entity that promotes proficiency in or education about semiautomatic weapons and for transporting thereto and therefrom; (v) Hunting in accordance with the provisions of c. 131; or (vi) Surrendering such firearm or feeding device under the provisions of section 129D.
Weapons must Secured when not in Use	Any large capacity weapon or large capacity feeding device kept on the premises of a lawfully incorporated shooting club shall, when not in use, be secured in a locked container, and shall be unloaded during any lawful transport.
State Police Inspection	The colonel of state police or his designee, shall have the right to inspect all firearms owned or possessed by such club upon request during regular business hours and said colonel may revoke or suspend a club license for a violation of any provision of this chapter or chapter 269 relative to the ownership, use or possession of large capacity weapons or large capacity feeding devices.
Annual Reports must be Filed	The clerk or other corporate officer of such club shall annually file a report with the colonel of state police and the commissioner of the department of criminal justice information services listing all large capacity weapons and large capacity feeding devices owned or possessed under such license.
CMR's Permissible	The secretary of the executive office of public safety or his designee may promulgate regulations to carry out the purposes of this section.

SALES & PURCHASING OF FIREARMS

C. 140 § 122, 123	LICENSE TO SELL FIREARMS

Qualifications for a License to Sell	• The chief of police or the board or officer having control of the police in a city or town, or persons authorized by them, may,
	• after an investigation into the criminal history of the applicant to determine eligibility for a license
	• grant a license to sell, rent or lease firearms, rifles, shotguns or machine guns, or to be in business as a gunsmith
	• to any person except:
	  o an alien,
	  o a minor,
	  o a person who has been adjudicated a youthful offender, including those who have not received an adult sentence
	  o a person who has been convicted of:
	    ▪ a felony
	    ▪ the unlawful use, possession or sale of narcotic or harmful drugs.

Appeal to Colonel of State Police	Any person refused a license under this section may within 10 days thereafter apply to the colonel of state police for such license, who may direct that the licensing authorities grant the license, if, after a hearing, he is satisfied there were no reasonable grounds for the refusal to grant such license and that the applicant was not barred by the provisions of law from holding such a license.
Penalty for wrongful issuing of license	Whoever knowingly issues a license in violation of this section shall be punished by imprisonment for not less than 6 months nor more than 2 years in a jail or HOC.
LICENSE REQUIREMENTS	
Address	Every license shall specify the street and number of the building where the business is to be carried on, and the license shall not protect a licensee who carries on his business in any other place.
Fingerprints	The licensing authority to which such application is made shall cause one copy of said applicant's fingerprints to be forwarded to the department of the state police, who shall within a reasonable time thereafter advise such authority in writing of any criminal record of the applicant. The taking of fingerprints shall not be required in issuing a renewal of a license, if the fingerprints of said applicant are on file with the department of the state police. **Copy goes to CJIS**: The licensing authority to whom such application is made shall cause one copy of such application to be forwarded to commissioner of the department of criminal justice information services.
Licensing Authority Responsibility	The licensing authority to whom the application is made shall cause one copy of the application to be forwarded to commissioner of the department of criminal justice information services. Chapter 140 § 122A states that "the licensing authority, shall record all issued licenses in books, forms or electronic files kept for that purpose, and upon the granting of any such license or renewal thereof or renewal of an expired license **shall send notice thereof to the department of criminal justice information services**."

C. 140 § 122, 123	LICENSE TO SELL FIREARMS
Fees	The fee for an application for a license issued under this section shall be $100, which shall be payable to the licensing authority and shall not be prorated or refunded in case of revocation or denial. The licensing authority shall retain $25 of the fee; $50 of the fee shall be deposited into the general fund of the commonwealth; and $25 of the fee shall be deposited in the Firearms Fingerprint Identity Verification Trust Fund. A person licensed to sell, rent or lease firearms, rifles, shotguns or machine guns shall not be assessed any additional fee for a gunsmith's license.
Duration	Chapter 140 § 124 states that licenses issued under chapter 140 § 122 (License **to Sell Firearms**) shall expire 3 years from the date of issuance.

C. 140 § 123	CONDITIONS OF LICENSES TO SELL FIREARMS
	A License to Sell Firearms shall be subject to the following conditions:
1st Provisions must be Strictly Adhered to	The provisions in regard to the **nature of the license** and **the building in which the business may be carried on** under it shall be strictly adhered to.
2nd Record Keeping and Inspection	• Every licensee shall, • Before delivery of a firearm, rifle or shotgun, • Make or cause to be made a true, legible entry in a sales record book to be furnished by the commissioner of the department of criminal justice information services and to be kept for that purpose, • Specifying the complete description of the firearm, rifle or shotgun, including the make, serial number, if any, type of firearm, rifle or shotgun, and designation as a large capacity weapon, if applicable, whether sold, rented or leased, the date of each sale, rental or lease, • The license to carry firearms number or permit to purchase number and the identification card number in the case of a firearm or the identification card number or the license to carry firearms number in the case of a rifle or shotgun, • The sex, residence and occupation of the purchaser, renter or lessee, • And shall before delivery, as aforesaid, require the purchaser, renter or lessee personally to write in said sales record book his full name. • Said book shall be open at all times to the inspection of the police. **See 11th condition - Gunsmith exemptions.**
3rd License Displayed	The license or a copy thereof, certified by the official issuing the same, shall be displayed on the premises in a position where it can easily be read.
4th Firearms Not Visible from Exterior	No firearm, rifle or shotgun, or machine gun shall be displayed in any outer window of said premises or in any other place where it can readily be seen from the outside.
5th Report Sale	The licensee shall submit a record of all sales, rentals and leases forthwith at the time of such sale, rental or lease via electronic communication link to the commissioner of the department of criminal justice information services. **See 11th condition - Gunsmith exemptions.**

C. 140 § 123	CONDITIONS OF LICENSES TO SELL FIREARMS
6th Delivered Unloaded	Every firearm, rifle or shotgun shall be unloaded when delivered.
7th Delivery Restrictions	• No delivery of a firearm shall be made to any person not having a license to carry firearms • No delivery of a rifle or shotgun or ammunition be made to any minor nor to any person not having a license to carry firearms (LTC) or a firearm identification card (FID) • No delivery of any large capacity firearm or large capacity feeding device delivered to any person not having a Class A license to carry firearms • No delivery of a large capacity rifle or shotgun or large capacity feeding device delivered to any person not having a Class A or Class B license to carry firearms • Permit to Purchase and an FID will permit the delivery of a firearm by a licensee to purchaser's residence or place of business, subject to the restrictions imposed upon such permits.
8th Sale of a Firearm	• No firearm shall be sold, rented or leased to a minor • In order to purchase a firearm the purchaser must have either a permit to purchase and an FID or an LTC. • No large capacity firearm nor large capacity feeding device shall be sold, rented, leased or transferred to any person not having: (i) a Class A license to carry firearms issued under section 131 or (ii) a proper permit issued under section 131A and a firearm identification card issued under section 129B; • No large capacity rifle or shotgun nor large capacity feeding device shall be sold to any person not having a Class A or Class B license to carry firearms issued under said section 131; • No machine gun shall be sold, rented or leased to any person who has not a license to possess the same issued under section one hundred and thirty-one (Machine Gun license - bona fide collector or law enforcement instructor). • See Penalties later in this Section. **See 11th condition - Gunsmith exemptions.**
9th Document Submission requirements	**Permit to Purchase Sale:** upon the sale, rental or lease of a firearm, subject to a permit to purchase, the licensee shall take up such permit to purchase and shall endorse upon it the date and place of the sale, rental or lease, and shall transmit the same to the commissioner of the department of criminal justice information services. **Machine Gun Sale:** Upon the sale, rental or lease of a machine gun shall endorse upon the license to possess the same the date and place of said sale, rental or lease, and shall **within 7 days** transmit a notice thereof to the commissioner. **Sale to LTC/FID holder:** In case of a sale under to an LTC or FID holder the licensee shall write in the sales record book the number of the license to carry firearms issued the purchaser, or the number of the firearm identification card issued the purchaser, whichever is applicable under the provisions of condition Eighth of this section. **See 11th condition - Gunsmith exemptions.**
10th License Subject to Forfeiture	This license shall be subject to forfeiture as provided in §125 for breach of any of its conditions, and that, if the licensee hereunder is convicted of a violation of any such conditions, this license shall thereupon become void.

FIREARM LICENSING

C. 140 § 123	CONDITIONS OF LICENSES TO SELL FIREARMS
11th Gunsmith Exemptions	The second, fifth, eighth and ninth conditions shall not apply to a gunsmith with regard to repair or remodeling or servicing of firearms, rifles or shotguns unless said gunsmith has manufactured a firearm, rifle or shotgun for the purchaser, but said gunsmith shall keep records of the work done by him together with the names and addresses of his customers. Such records shall be kept open for inspection by the police at all times.
12th Records Must Be Kept	Any licensee shall keep records of each sale, rental or lease of a rifle or shotgun, specifying the description of said rifle or shotgun, together with the name and address of the purchaser, renter or lessee, and the date of such transaction.
13th Seller Must Verify Validity of License and May Seize it	**Verify License:** The current validity of any firearm identification card, license to carry firearms or permit to purchase, rent or lease firearms presented, and that the person presenting the card, license or permit is the lawful holder thereof, shall be verified by the licensee prior to any sale, rental or lease of a rifle, shotgun, firearm or large capacity feeding device; **Seize Invalid License:** Upon being presented with such card or license that is **expired, suspended or revoked**, the licensee shall notify the licensing authority of the presentment of such expired, suspended or revoked card, license or permit; and further, **the licensee may take possession of such card or license provided that, in such case, such licensee shall**: i. Issue a receipt, in a form provided by the commissioner of the department of criminal justice information services, to the holder thereof which shall state that the holder's card or license is expired, suspended or revoked, was taken by such licensee and forwarded to the licensing authority by whom it was issued and such receipt shall be valid for the date of issuance for the purpose of providing immunity from prosecution under chapter 269 § 10 for unlawfully possessing a firearm, rifle or shotgun or large capacity weapon; ii. Notify the cardholder or licensee of his requirement to renew said card or license; and iii. Forward such expired card or license to the licensing authority forthwith; provided, however, that such licensee shall be immune from civil and criminal liability for good faith compliance with the provisions herein.
14th Post Warning	The licensee shall conspicuously post at each purchase counter the following warning in bold type not less than one inch in height: "IT IS UNLAWFUL TO STORE OR KEEP A FIREARM, RIFLE, SHOTGUN OR MACHINE GUN IN ANY PLACE UNLESS THAT WEAPON IS EQUIPPED WITH A TAMPER-RESISTANT SAFETY DEVICE OR IS STORED OR KEPT IN A SECURELY LOCKED CONTAINER.", and that such licensee shall provide said warning, in writing, to the purchaser or transferee of any firearm, rifle, shotgun or machine gun in bold type not less than one-quarter inch in height. The licensee shall also conspicuously post and distribute at each purchase counter a notice providing information on **suicide prevention** developed and provided by the division on violence and injury prevention within the department of public health. The department of public health shall develop and make available on its website for download a sign providing the information on suicide prevention.
15th Permanent Place of Business/Non-Residential	All licensees shall maintain a permanent place of business that is not a residence or dwelling wherein all transactions described in this section shall be conducted and wherein all records required to be kept under this section shall be so kept.
16th Large Capacity Restriction	No licensee shall sell, lease, rent, transfer or deliver or offer for sale, lease, rent, transfer or delivery to any person **any assault weapon or large capacity feeding device** that was not otherwise lawfully possessed on September 13, 1994.

C. 140 § 123	CONDITIONS OF LICENSES TO SELL FIREARMS
17th Lost/Stolen Weapon	Any licensee from whom a rifle, shotgun, firearm or machine gun is lost or stolen shall report such loss or theft to the **licensing authority** and **the commissioner of the department of criminal justice information services *forthwith*.** Such report shall include a complete description of the weapon, including the make, model, serial number and caliber and whether such weapon is a large capacity weapon.
18th Condition of Weapons	No licensee shall sell, rent, lease, transfer or deliver or offer for sale, lease, transfer or delivery any firearm, to any purchaser in the commonwealth unless such sale is to a business entity that is primarily a firearm wholesaler and the sale, by its terms, prohibits the purchaser from reselling such firearm to a firearm retailer or consumer in the commonwealth if such firearm has a frame, barrel, cylinder, slide or breechblock that is composed of: (i) any metal having a melting point of less than 900 degrees Fahrenheit; (ii) any metal having an ultimate tensile strength of less than 55,000 pounds per square inch; or (iii) any powdered metal having a density of less than 7.5 grams per cubic centimeter. **Exceptions & testing Requirements:** This clause shall not apply to any make and model of firearm for which a sample of three firearms in new condition all pass the following test: Each of the three samples shall fire 600 rounds, stopping every 100 rounds to tighten any loose screws and to clean the gun if required by the cleaning schedule in the user manual, and as needed to refill the empty magazine or cylinder to capacity before continuing. For any firearm that is loaded in a manner other than via a detachable magazine, the tester shall also pause every 50 rounds for ten minutes. The ammunition used shall be the type recommended by the firearm manufacturer in its user manual or, if none is recommended, any standard ammunition of the correct caliber in new condition. A firearm shall pass this test if it fires the first 20 rounds without a malfunction, fires the full 600 rounds with not more than six malfunctions and completes the test without any crack or breakage of an operating part of the firearm. The term "crack" or "breakage" shall not include a crack or breakage that does not increase the danger of injury to the user. For purposes of evaluating the results of this test, malfunction shall mean any failure to feed, chamber, fire, extract or eject a round or any failure to accept or eject a magazine or any other failure which prevents the firearm, without manual intervention beyond that needed for routine firing and periodic reloading, from firing the chambered round or moving a new round into position so that the firearm is capable of firing the new round properly. "Malfunction" shall not include a misfire caused by a faulty cartridge the primer of which fails to detonate when properly struck by the firearm's firing mechanism.
19th Quality Testing Required	No licensee shall sell, rent, lease, transfer or deliver or offer for sale, lease, transfer or delivery any firearm to any purchaser in the commonwealth unless such sale is to a business entity that is primarily a firearms wholesaler, and the sale, by its terms, prohibits such purchaser from reselling such firearm to a firearm retailer or consumer in the commonwealth if such firearm is prone to accidental discharge which, for purposes of this clause, shall mean any make and model of firearm for which a sample of five firearms in new condition all undergo, and none discharge during, the following test: **Each of the five sample firearms shall be**: (a) test loaded; (b) set so that the firearm is in a condition such that pulling the trigger and taking any action that must simultaneously accompany the pulling of the trigger as part of the firing procedure would fire the handgun; and (c) dropped onto a solid slab of concrete from a height of one meter from each of the following positions: (i) normal firing position; (ii) upside down;

C. 140 § 123	CONDITIONS OF LICENSES TO SELL FIREARMS
	(iii) on grip; (iv) on the muzzle; (v) on either side; and (vi) on the exposed hammer or striker or, if there is no exposed hammer or striker, the rearmost part of the firearm. If the firearm is designed so that its hammer or striker may be set in other positions, each sample firearm shall be tested as above with the hammer or striker in each such position but otherwise in such condition that pulling the trigger, and taking any action that must simultaneously accompany the pulling of the trigger as part of the firing procedure, would fire the firearm. Alternatively, the tester may use additional sample firearms of the same make and model, in a similar condition, for the test of each of these hammer striker settings.
20th Defective Weapon Sales	No licensee shall sell, rent, lease, transfer or deliver or offer for sale, lease, transfer or delivery, any firearm to any purchaser in the commonwealth unless such sale is to a business entity that is primarily a firearm wholesaler, and the sale, by its terms, prohibits the purchaser from reselling such firearm to a firearm retailer or consumer in the commonwealth if such firearm is prone to: (i) firing more than once per pull of the trigger; or (ii) explosion during firing.
21st Short Barrel Accuracy	No licensee shall sell, rent, lease, transfer or deliver or offer for sale, lease, transfer or delivery any firearm to any purchaser in the commonwealth unless such sale is to a business entity that is primarily a firearm wholesaler and the sale, by its terms, prohibits the purchaser from reselling such firearm to a firearm retailer or consumer in the commonwealth if such firearm has a barrel less than three inches in length, unless the licensee discloses in writing, prior to the transaction, to the prospective buyer, lessee, deliveree or transferee the limitations of the accuracy of the particular make and model of the subject firearm, by disclosing the make and model's average group diameter test result at seven yards, average group diameter test result at 14 yards and average group diameter test result at 21 yards. For purposes of this clause, "average group diameter test result" shall mean the arithmetic mean of three separate trials, each performed as follows on a different sample firearm in new condition of the make and model at issue. Each firearm shall fire five rounds at a target from a set distance and the largest spread in inches between the centers of any of the holes made in a test target shall be measured and recorded. This procedure shall be repeated two more times on the firearm. The arithmetic mean of each of the three recorded results shall be deemed the result of the trial for that particular sample firearm. The ammunition used shall be the type recommended by the firearm manufacturer in its user manual or, if none is recommended, any standard ammunition of the correct caliber in new condition. No licensee shall sell any rifle or shotgun, contrary to the provisions of section one hundred and thirty or section 131E. **Exclusions:** Clauses Eighteenth to Twenty-first, inclusive, of the first paragraph shall not apply to: I. a firearm lawfully owned or possessed under a license issued under this chapter on or before October 21, 1998; II. a firearm designated by the secretary of public safety, with the advice of the gun control advisory board, established pursuant to section 131 1/2of chapter 140, as a firearm solely designed and sold for formal target shooting competition; or III. a firearm designated by the secretary of public safety, with the advice of the gun control advisory board, established pursuant to section 131 1/2of chapter 140, as a firearm or pistol solely designed and sold for Olympic shooting competition. The secretary of public safety shall compile lists, on a bi-annual basis, of firearms designated as "formal target shooting firearms" and "Olympic competition firearms" in accordance with this paragraph. Such lists shall be made available for distribution by the executive office of public safety and security.

C. 140 § 123 CONDITIONS OF LICENSES TO SELL FIREARMS

Minors and Aliens: No person licensed under the provisions of section 122 or section 122B shall sell, rent, lease, transfer or deliver any rifle, shotgun or firearm or ammunition or ammunition feeding device contrary to the provisions of section 130 or section 131E;

Proof of Proper License Required: no such licensee shall sell, rent, lease, transfer or deliver any rifle, shotgun or firearm or ammunition or ammunition feeding device to any person who does not have in his possession the required firearm identification card or proof of exemption therefrom, license to carry firearms or permit to purchase, rent or lease firearms and who does not present such card, proof, license or permit to the licensee in person at the time of purchase, rental or lease. No person licensed under the provisions of section 122 or section 122B shall fill an order for such weapon, ammunition or ammunition feeding device that was received by mail, facsimile, telephone or other telecommunication unless such transaction or transfer includes the in-person presentation of the required card, proof, license or permit as required herein prior to any sale, delivery or any form of transfer of possession of the subject weapon, ammunition or ammunition feeding device. Transactions between persons licensed under section 122 or between federally licensed dealers shall be exempt from the provisions of this paragraph.

Annual Inspection: The licensing authority shall enter, one time per calendar year, during regular business hours, the commercial premises owned or leased by any licensee, wherein such records required to be maintained under this section are stored or maintained, and inspect, in a reasonable manner, such records and inventory for the purpose of enforcing the provisions of this section. If such records and inventory contain evidence of violations of this section, the inspecting officer shall produce and take possession of copies of such records and, in the event that the licensee subject to inspection does not possess copying equipment, the inspecting officer shall arrange to have copied, in a reasonable time and manner, such records that contain evidence of such violations and the costs for such copying shall be assessed against the owner of such records. Licensees found to be in violation of this section shall be subject to the suspension or permanent revocation of such license issued under section 122 and to the provisions of section 128. Nothing herein shall prohibit the licensing authority or the department of state police from conducting such inspections pursuant to a valid search warrant issued by a court of competent jurisdiction.

Collectors & Gun Shows Exceptions: Notwithstanding the provisions of this section, a person licensed under the provisions of section one hundred and twenty-two, or section one hundred and twenty-two B, may sell or transfer firearms, rifles, shotguns, machine guns or ammunition at any regular meeting of an incorporated collectors club or at a gun show open to the general public; provided, however, that all other provisions of this section are complied with and that such sale or transfer is in conformity with federal law or regulations applicable to the transfer or sale of firearms, rifles, shotguns, machine guns or ammunition, including the restrictions imposed upon firearm identification cards issued under section 129B, licenses to carry firearms issued under section 131 and permits to purchase, lease or rent firearms.

Arrest Power, Penalties & Notes

C. 140 § 128: Penalty for violating certain provisions of a license to sell firearms

- Any licensee under a license described in C. 140 § 123 (license to sell firearms), and any employee or agent of the licensee,
- who violates any provision of C. 140 § 123 required to be expressed in the 2nd, 4th, 6th 7th, 8th, 9th, 16th, 17th, 18th, 19th, 20th, or 21st condition of the license, and
- any person who, without being licensed properly licensed, sells, rents or leases a firearm, rifle, shotgun or machine gun or is engaged in business as a gunsmith, (except as provided in chapter 140 § 128A - selling to a licensed dealer or a resident who sells not more than 4 in a year – see § 128A below),
- shall be punished as follows:

Penalty: a fine of not less than $1,000 nor more than $10,000, or by imprisonment for **not less than one year** nor more than 10 years **(Felony),** or by both such fine and imprisonment.

C. 140 § 123	CONDITIONS OF LICENSES TO SELL FIREARMS
	Powers of Arrest: felony – a warrantless arrest is authorized on probable cause. **Prima Facie Evidence for Machine Gun Sales**: Evidence that a person sold or attempted to sell a machine gun without being licensed under § 123 shall, in a prosecution under this section, constitute prima facie evidence that such person is engaged in the business of selling machine guns.
Related Statutes, Case Law & Other Important Information	
C. 140 § 128A. Sale of Firearm by a non-licensee to a dealer.	**The provisions of section 128 (sale of firearm condition penalties) shall not apply to:** Any person who, (who is not properly licensed to sell firearms) sells or transfers a firearm, rifle or shotgun to: • a person properly licensed to sell firearms, or • to a federally licensed firearms dealer or • to a federal, state or local historical society, museum or institutional collection open to the public. **Attorney Hanrahan's Note**: However, the non-licensed seller cannot sell more than 4 guns in a calendar year. See *Sale & Transfer of Firearms* Section later in this section for more.
Chapter 140 § 130 makes it a felony to sell to minors	Chapter 140 § 130 makes it a felony to sell firearms, rifles and shotguns to minors (with some exceptions). See the *Sale & Transfer of Firearms* section later in this manual for more.
Forfeiture or suspension of licenses to sell firearms **Chapter 140 § 125**	The officials authorized to issue a license under chapter 140 § 122 (license to sell firearms), after due notice to the licensee and reasonable opportunity for him to be heard, may declare his license forfeited, or may suspend his license for such period of time as they may deem proper, upon satisfactory proof that he has: • violated or permitted a violation of any condition of the license • or has violated any provision of this chapter, • or has been convicted of a felony. **License may be Forfeited Prior to Court Proceeding:** The pendency of proceedings before a court shall not suspend or interfere with the power to declare a forfeiture. If the license is declared forfeited, the licensee shall be disqualified to receive a license for one year after the expiration of the term of the license so forfeited. The commissioner of the department of criminal justice information services shall be notified in writing of any forfeiture under this section.
Transfer of licenses to sell firearms **Chapter 140 § 127**	The officials authorized to issue a license under C. 140 § 122 (license to sell firearms) **may transfer licenses from one location to another within the city or town** in which the licenses are in force, but such transfer shall be granted only to the original licensee and upon the same terms and conditions upon which the license was originally granted. **Note:** The commissioner of the department of criminal justice information services shall be notified in writing of any transfers made under this section.

C. 140 § 122B	LICENSE TO SELL AMMUNITION
Must be Licensed	No person shall sell ammunition in the commonwealth unless duly licensed.
Qualifications for a License to Sell	• The chief of police or the board or officer having control of the police in a city or town, or persons authorized by them, may, • after an investigation into the criminal history of the applicant to determine eligibility for a license • grant a license to ammunition • to any person except: ○ an alien, ○ a minor, ○ a person who has been adjudicated a youthful offender, including those who have not received an adult sentence ○ a person who has been convicted of: ▪ a felony ▪ the unlawful use, possession or sale of narcotic or harmful drugs.
Appeal to District Court	Any person refused a license under this section or once issued a license under this section has had said license suspended or revoked may obtain a judicial review of such refusal, suspension or revocation by filing within 30 days of such refusal, suspension or revocation a petition for review thereof in the **District Court** having jurisdiction in the city or town in which the applicant filed for such license, and a justice of said court, after a hearing, may direct that a license be issued the applicant if satisfied there was no reasonable ground for refusing such license and that the applicant was not prohibited by law from holding the same.
Penalty for wrongful issuing of license	Whoever not being duly licensed, sells ammunition within the commonwealth shall be punished by a fine of not less than $500 nor more than $1,000 or by imprisonment for not less than 6 months nor more than 2 years
Revocation	The licensing authority may revoke or suspend a license to sell ammunition for violation of any provision of chapter 140.
	LICENSE REQUIREMENTS
Address	Every license shall specify the street and number of the building where the business is to be carried on.
Fingerprints	The licensing authority to which such application is made shall cause one copy of said applicant's fingerprints to be forwarded to the department of the state police, who shall within a reasonable time thereafter advise such authority in writing of any criminal record of the applicant. The taking of fingerprints shall not be required in issuing a renewal of a license, if the fingerprints of said applicant are on file with the department of the state police.
Licensing Authority Responsibility	The licensing authority to whom the application is made shall cause one copy of the application to be forwarded to commissioner of the department of criminal justice information services. Who shall within a reasonable time thereafter advise the authority in writing of any criminal record disqualifying the applicant. If a license is issued, the licensing authority to whom such application is made shall cause one copy of any approved application to be forwarded to the department of criminal justice

C. 140 § 122B	LICENSE TO SELL AMMUNITION
	information services. Chapter 140 § 122A states that "the licensing authority, shall record all issued licenses in books, forms or electronic files kept for that purpose, and upon the granting of any such license or renewal thereof or renewal of an expired license **shall send notice thereof to the department of criminal justice information services**."
Fees	The fee for an application for a license to sell ammunition shall be $100, which shall be payable to the licensing authority and shall not be prorated or refunded in case of revocation or denial. The licensing authority shall retain $25 of the fee; $50 of the fee shall be deposited into the general fund of the commonwealth; and $25 of the fee shall be deposited in the Firearms Fingerprint Identity Verification Trust Fund.
Duration	Chapter 140 § 124 states that licenses issued under chapter 140 §123B (**License to sell ammunition)** shall expire 3 years from the date of issuance.
Shooting Club License	Any lawfully incorporated sporting or shooting club shall, upon application, be licensed to sell or supply ammunition for regulated shooting on their premises, as for skeet, target or trap shooting; provided, however, that such club license shall, in behalf of said club, be issued to and exercised by an officer or duly authorized member of the club who himself possesses a firearm identification card or a license to carry a firearm and who would not be disqualified to receive a license to sell ammunition in his own right.

C. 140 § 122C	ILLEGAL SALE OF DEFENSE SPRAY
Must be Licensed	Whoever, not being licensed as provided in section 122B, sells self-defense spray shall be punished by a fine of not more than $1,000 or by imprisonment in a house of correction for not more than 2 years.
Illegal to sell to person under 18	Whoever sells self-defense spray to a person younger than 18 years of age, if the person younger than 18 years of age does not have a firearms identification card, shall be punished by a fine of not more than $300.
ADDITIONAL INFORMATION	
Defense Spray definition	As used in this section and section 122D, "self-defense spray" shall mean chemical mace, pepper spray or any device or instrument which contains, propels or emits a liquid, gas, powder or other substance designed to incapacitate.
Must be 18 to possess defense spray	A person under 18 years of age who possesses self-defense spray and who does not have a firearms identification card shall be punished by a fine of not more than $300.

FIREARM SALES

LAWS RELATED TO SALE & TRANSFER OF FIREARMS

Sale, Give, or Loan a Firearm
Chapter 140 § 129C

Receiver must be qualified	• No person (who is not a licensed dealer) shall • sell, give away, loan or otherwise transfer • a rifle or shotgun or ammunition other than (a) by operation of law, or (b) to an exempt person as hereinafter described, or (c) to a licensed dealer, or (d) to a person who displays his firearm identification card, or license to carry a pistol or revolver.
Reporting Requirements	A seller shall, **within 7 days**, report all such transfers to the commissioner of the department of criminal justice information services according to the provisions set forth in § 128A. Failure to so report shall be cause for suspension or permanent revocation of such person's firearm identification card or license to carry firearms, or both, and shall be punished by a fine of not less than $200 nor more than $1,000 for a first offense and by a fine of not less than $1,000 nor more than $5,000 for a second offense.

Limitations on Sale and Transfers by Non-Licensed Sellers
Chapter 140 § 128A

C. 140 § 128A. Limit on gun sales by non-licensed seller – no more than 4 guns in calendar year.	• Any resident of the commonwealth (who is not licensed to sell firearms), • Cannot sell or transfer, other than a federally licensed firearms dealer or an authorized organization, more than **4 firearms**, including **rifles** and **shotguns** in any **one calendar year**. **Additional Provisions** Provided, however, that the seller has an FID card or an LTC, is an exempt person under the conditions of clauses (n), (o), (r) and (s) of the fourth paragraph of section one hundred and twenty-nine C, or is permitted to transfer ownership under the conditions of section 129 D and the purchaser has, in the case of sale or transfer of a firearm, a permit to purchase issued under the provisions of section 131A and a firearm identification card issued under section 129B, or has such permit to purchase and is an exempt person under the provisions of section 129C, or has been issued a license to carry firearms under the provisions of section 130, or in the case of sale or transfer of a rifle or shotgun, the purchaser has a firearm identification card or a license to carry firearms or is an exempt person as hereinbefore stated; and **Reporting Requirements** Provided, further, that such resident reports within **7 days**, in writing to the commissioner of the department of criminal justice information services on forms furnished by said executive director, the names and addresses of the seller and the purchaser of any such large capacity feeding device, firearm, rifle or shotgun, together with a complete description of the firearm, rifle or shotgun, including its designation as a large capacity weapon, if applicable, the caliber, make and serial number and the purchaser's license to carry firearms number, permit to purchase number and identifying number of such documentation as is used to establish exempt person status in the case of a firearm or the purchaser's license to carry number or firearm identification card number or said document identity number, in the case of a rifle or shotgun. **Attorney Hanrahan's Note**: the penalties for a violation of a condition on a license to sell firearms in chapter 140 § 128A, (e.g. record keeping requirements) only apply to those who have a license to sell firearms. A private citizen (i.e. non-licensed seller) who sells a firearm is not subject to the same provisions. Also, the 4 gun limit does not apply if the weapons are sold to a licensed dealer or authorized institution (e.g. museum). See Firearm Sales License section for more on this exemption.

LAWS RELATED TO SALE & TRANSFER OF FIREARMS

UNLAWFUL FIREARM & AMMUNITION SALES

Unlawful transfer of weapon **Chapter 269 § 10(h)(1)**	• Whoever owns, possesses or **transfers** • a firearm, rifle, shotgun or ammunition • without complying with the provisions of c. 140 § 129C • shall be punished as follows: **Penalty:** imprisonment in a jail or house of correction for not more than 2 years or by a fine of not more than $500. **2nd or subsequent violation** of this paragraph shall be punished by imprisonment in a house of correction for not more than 2 years or by a fine of not more than $1,000, or both. **ARREST POWERS – Misdemeanor:** Any officer authorized to make arrests may arrest without a warrant any person whom the officer has probable cause to believe has violated this paragraph. **Attorney Hanrahan's note**: if the purchaser is a juvenile or an alien the better charge would be under chapter 140 § 130. If the weapon is a large capacity weapon chapter 269 § 10F may be a more appropriate charge. (See more later in this section).
Trafficking in Firearms (illegal sale of 1 or more) **Chapter 269 § 10E**	• Whoever, (except as provided by law, in a single transaction or occurrence or in a series of transactions) • within a 12 month period, • knowingly or intentionally • distributes, sells, or transfers possession of a quantity of firearms, rifles, shotguns, machine guns, or any combination thereof, shall, if the quantity of firearms, rifles, shotguns, machine guns, or any combination thereof is: 1. **1 or more**, but less than 3, be punished by a term of imprisonment of not more than 10 years in the state prison or by a fine of not more than $50,000, or by both such imprisonment and fine; 2. **3 or more**, but less than 10, be punished by a term of imprisonment, not to exceed 20 years in the state prison; provided, however, that said sentence shall not be less than a mandatory minimum term of imprisonment of 5 years; and provided further, that said sentence may include and a fine of not more than $100,000, which shall not be in lieu of the mandatory minimum term of imprisonment; 3. **10 or more**, be punished by a term of imprisonment up to life imprisonment in the state prison; provided, that said sentence shall not be less than a mandatory minimum term of imprisonment of 10 years; and provided further, that said sentence may include a fine of not more than $150,000, which shall not be in lieu of the mandatory minimum term of imprisonment. A prosecution commenced under this section shall not be placed on file or continued without a finding and the sentence imposed upon a person convicted of violating this section shall not be reduced to less than the mandatory minimum term of imprisonment, as established in the first paragraph, nor shall any sentence of imprisonment imposed upon any person be suspended or reduced until such person shall have served said mandatory minimum term of imprisonment. **ARREST POWERS**: **Felony** – a police officer may effect an arrest for this offense committed in his/her presence or for an offense in the past, on probable cause.

LAWS RELATED TO SALE & TRANSFER OF FIREARMS	
Illegal Sale/Transfer of Large Capacity Weapons **Chapter 269 § 10F.**	**Receiver 18 years of Age or Older** • Any person who **sells, keeps for sale, or offers or exposes for sale, gives or otherwise transfers** • any **large capacity weapon or large capacity feeding device** (both as defined in of chapter 140 § 121) • **to a person 18 years of age or over**, (except as permitted under this section or chapter 140) • shall be punished as follows: **Penalty:** imprisonment in a **state prison (F)** for **not less than 2½ years** nor more than ten years. Any person who commits a second or subsequent such crime shall be punished by imprisonment in a **state prison (F)** for not less than 5 years nor more than 15 years. **Receiver under 18 years** • Any person who **transfers, sells, lends or gives** • a **large capacity weapon or large capacity feeding device** • to a person **under the age of 18** (except as permitted under the provisions of chapter 140), • shall be punished as follows: **Penalty**: imprisonment in a **state prison (F)** for **not less than 5** nor more than 15 years. **ARREST POWERS**: **Felony** – a police officer may effect an arrest for this offense committed in his/her presence or for an offense in the past, on probable cause.
Sale of Large Capacity Feeding Device Prohibitions by non-licensed person **c. 140 § 131M**	No person shall sell, offer for sale, transfer or possess an assault weapon or a large capacity feeding device that was not otherwise lawfully possessed on September 13, 1994. **Penalty for person not licensed under 140 § 122: 1st offense**: a fine of not less than $1,000 nor more than $10,000 or by imprisonment for not less than 1 year nor more than 10 years, or by both such fine and imprisonment. **2nd offense**, a fine of not less than $5,000 nor more than $15,000 or by imprisonment for not less than 5 years nor more than 15 years, or by both such fine and imprisonment. The provisions of this section shall not apply to: (i) the possession by a law enforcement officer; or (ii) the possession by an individual who is retired from service with a law enforcement agency and is not otherwise prohibited from receiving such a weapon or feeding device from such agency upon retirement.

LAWS RELATED TO SALE & TRANSFER OF FIREARMS

Sale of Firearms, Rifles, Shotguns, Machine guns, or ammunition to a minor **Chapter 140 § 130**	**Firearms & Large Capacity Weapons: Must be 21+** • It is unlawful to sell or furnish • To any person under **21 years** of age • A firearm or large capacity rifle or shotgun or ammunition (i.e. ammunition for firearm or a large capacity weapon) **Non-Large Capacity Rifles & Shotguns: Must be 18+** • It is unlawful to sell or furnish [except as provided in this section (§130) or §131E] • To any alien or any person under **18 years** of age • A rifle, shotgun, machine gun or ammunition **Penalty:** a fine of not less than $1,000 nor more than $10,000, or by imprisonment in a **state prison (F)** for not more than 10 years or by imprisonment in a HOC for not more than 2½ years, or by both such fine and imprisonment. **License to Sell Suspension:** an offender shall have his license to sell firearms, rifles, shotguns, machine guns and or ammunition revoked and shall not be entitled to apply for such license for ten years from the date of such revocation. **ARREST POWERS**: **Felony** – a police officer may effect an arrest for this offense committed in his/her presence or for an offense in the past on probable cause. **Exceptions:** **Parent Supervision – 15+:** Nothing in this section or § 131E shall be construed to prohibit a parent or guardian from allowing his child or ward, who has not attained age 15, the supervised use of a rifle or shotgun or ammunition therefor, according to the provisions of § 129C, nor from furnishing such child or ward, who has attained age 15, with a rifle or shotgun that is not a large capacity weapon or ammunition; provided, however, that the child or ward, being 15 years of age or older, has been issued a valid firearm identification card or alien permit to possess a rifle or shotgun which is in his possession. **Instruction**: Nothing in this section shall be construed to prohibit an instructor from furnishing rifles or shotguns or ammunition therefor to pupils; provided, however, that said instructor has the **consent of a parent** or guardian of a pupil **under the age of 18 years**. **Attorney Hanrahan's Note**: Chapter 140§ 129C permits a child to use a rifle or shotgun for target or hunting purposes as long as the child is properly supervised. See exemptions in firearms licensing section for more.
Sale or furnishing weapons or ammunition to alien who does not possess license **Chapter 140 § 130**	• The defendant • Sells or furnishes a rifle, shotgun or ammunition • To any alien 18 years of age or older • who does not hold a permit card issued to him under § 131H (temporary alien license). **Penalty:** a fine of not less than $1,000 nor more than $10,000, or by imprisonment in a **state prison (F)** for not more than 10 years or by imprisonment in a HOC for not more than 2½ years, or by both such fine and imprisonment. **License to Sell Suspension:** an offender shall have his license to sell firearms, rifles, shotguns, machine guns and or ammunition revoked and shall not be entitled to apply for such license for ten years from the date of such revocation. **Arrest powers**: **Felony** – a police officer may effect an arrest for this offense committed in his/her

LAWS RELATED TO SALE & TRANSFER OF FIREARMS

	presence or for an offense in the past on probable cause. **Attorney Hanrahan's Note**: Chapter 140§ 129C permits a person to hold, handle and even fire a rifle or shotgun when properly supervised. See exemptions in firearms licensing section for more.
Exceptions for juveniles **c. 140 § 130 ½**	Notwithstanding section 130 or any general or special law to the contrary, it shall be lawful to furnish a weapon to a minor for hunting, recreation, instruction and participation in shooting sports while under the supervision of a holder of a valid firearm identification card or license to carry appropriate for the weapon in use; provided, however, that the parent or guardian of the minor granted consent for such activities.
Leaving a weapon unattended with intent to transfer **Chapter 269 § 10(h)(2)**	Any person who leaves a firearm, rifle, shotgun or ammunition unattended with the intent to transfer possession of such firearm, rifle, shotgun or ammunition to any person not licensed under c. 140 § 129C or c. 140 § 131 for the purpose of committing a crime or concealing a crime shall be punished as follows: **Penalty**: imprisonment in a house of correction for not more than 2½ years or in state prison for not more than 5 years. **Arrest Powers**: **Felony** – a police officer may effect an arrest for this offense committed in his/her presence or for an offense in the past, on probable cause.

Related Statutes, Case Law & Other Important Information

License to Sell	For regulations governing the sale of firearms by licensed sellers see chapter 140 § 128 under the *License to Sell* section of this manual.
Advertising is evidence of unlawful sales **Chapter 140 § 126**	If there is exposed from, maintained in or permitted to remain on any vehicle or premises any placard, sign or advertisement purporting or designed to announce that firearms, rifles, shotguns or machine guns are kept in or upon such vehicle or premises or that an occupant of any vehicle or premises is a gunsmith, it shall be prima facie evidence that firearms, rifles, shotguns or machine guns are kept in or upon such vehicle or premises for sale or that the occupant is engaged in business as a gunsmith.
Restrictions on Sale to Minors **Chapter 140 § 129C**	**Chapter 140 § 129C states in relevant part:** Nothing in this section shall permit the sale of **rifles or shotguns or ammunition** therefor to a minor **under the age of eighteen.** **No firearm** may be sold to: • a person **under the age of 21** nor • to any person who is not licensed to carry unless he presents a valid FID and a permit to purchase, or presents such permit to purchase and is a properly documented exempt person.
Air rifles; sale/furnish to minors **c. 269 § 12A**	Whoever sells to a minor under the age of 18 or whoever, not being the parent, guardian or adult teacher or instructor, furnishes to a minor under the age of 18 an air rifle or so-called BB gun, shall be punished by a fine of not less than $50 nor more than $200 or by imprisonment for not more than 6 months. **Arrest Powers**: **Misdemeanor** – there is no statutory authority granting powers of arrest for this offense. However, if the offense is committed in public, in the officer's presence, and is creating a **breach of the peace** an arrest would be lawful.

LAWS RELATED TO SALE & TRANSFER OF FIREARMS	
Punishment for failing to keep/report record of sale **Chapter 269 § 10(g)**	Whoever, within this commonwealth, produces for sale, delivers or causes to be delivered, orders for delivery, sells or offers for sale, or fails to keep records regarding, any **rifle or shotgun** without complying with the requirement of a serial number, (as provided c. 140 § 129B) shall be punished as follows: **Penalty:** imprisonment in a jail or house of correction for not more than 2 years or by a fine of not more than $500. **2nd or subsequent violation** of this paragraph shall be punished by imprisonment in a house of correction for not more than 2 years or by a fine of not more than $1,000, or both. **Arrest Powers**: **Misdemeanor** – there is no statutory authority granting powers of arrest for this offense. However, if the offense is committed in public, in the officer's presence, and is creating a **breach of the peace** an arrest would be lawful.
Sale or Manufacture of Firearms or large capacity weapons without safety devices **Chapter 140 § 131K**	Any firearm or large capacity weapon, both as defined in §121, sold within the commonwealth without a safety device designed to prevent the discharge of such weapon by unauthorized users and approved by the colonel of state police including, but not limited to, mechanical locks or devices designed to recognize and authorize, or otherwise allow the firearm to be discharged only by its owner or authorized user, by solenoid use-limitation devices, key activated or combination trigger or handle locks, radio frequency tags, automated fingerprint identification systems or voice recognition, provided, that such device is commercially available, shall be defective and the sale of such a weapon shall constitute a breach of warranty under section 2-314 of c. 106 and an unfair or deceptive trade act or practice under chapter 93A § 2. Any entity responsible for the manufacture, importation or sale as an inventory item or consumer good, both as defined in section 9-102 of c. 106, of such a weapon that does not include or incorporate such a device shall be individually and jointly liable to any person who sustains personal injury or property damage resulting from the failure to include or incorporate such a device. If death results from such personal injury, such entities shall be liable in an amount including, but not limited to, that provided under c. 229. Contributory or comparative negligence shall not be valid defenses to an action brought under this section in conjunction with chapter 93A § 2 or section 2-314 of c. 106 or both; provided, however, that nothing herein shall prohibit such liable parties from maintaining an action for indemnification or contribution against each other or against the lawful owner or other authorized user of said weapon. Any disclaimer, limit or waiver of the liability provided under this section shall be void. **Liability**: No entity responsible for the manufacture, importation or sale of such a weapon shall be liable to any person for injuries caused by the discharge of such weapon that does not include or incorporate a safety device as required under this section if such injuries were: (i) self-inflicted, either intentionally or unintentionally, unless such injuries were self-inflicted by a person less than 18 years of age; (ii) inflicted by the lawful owner or other authorized user of said weapon; (iii) inflicted by any person in the lawful exercise of self-defense; or (iv) inflicted upon a co-conspirator in the commission of a crime. **Exceptions:** This section shall not apply to any weapon distributed to an officer of any law enforcement agency or any member of the armed forces of the United States or the organized militia of the commonwealth; provided, however, that such person is authorized to acquire, possess or carry such a weapon for the lawful performance of his official duties; and provided further, that any such weapon so distributed is distributed solely for use in connection with such duties. This section shall not apply to any firearm manufactured in or prior to the year 1899, or to any replica of such a firearm if such replica is not designed or redesigned for using rimfire or conventional centerfire fixed ammunition.

PURCHASING OF FIREARMS

FIREARM PURCHASING REQUIREMENTS

Chapter 140 § 131E states: Any resident of the commonwealth may purchase firearms, rifles, shotguns and ammunition feeding devices from any dealer licensed under § 122, or from such person as shall be qualified under § 128A, or ammunition from a licensee under § 122B, subject to the following conditions and restrictions:

Purchase of rifles, shotguns and feeding devices **Chapter 140 § 131E**	RIFLES, SHOTGUNS AND FEEDING DEVICES (for rifles & shotguns) may be purchased only upon presentment of: i. a valid **Firearm Identification card** issued under section 129B; or ii. a valid **Class A or Class B license** to carry firearms issued under section 131; or iii. valid proof of **exempt status** under section 129C; provided, however, that large capacity rifles and shotguns and large capacity feeding devices therefor may be so purchased only upon presentment of a Class A or Class B license to carry firearms issued under said §131; **Restrictions on Large Capacity**: Nothing in chapter 140 § 129C shall permit the sale or transfer of any **large capacity rifle or shotgun** or large capacity **feeding device** to any person not in possession of a Class A or Class B license to carry firearms, Nothing in this section shall permit the sale or transfer of any **large capacity firearm or large capacity feeding device therefor** to any person not in possession of a **Class A license** to carry firearms. **Related law:** Chapter 140 § 129C permits certain exceptions for rifles, shotguns and ammunition: Any person, exempted by clauses (o) and (p) of Chapter 140 § 129C: (o) - Police Officers, Military personnel in the performance of their duties and (p) - non-residents carrying or possessing rifles, shotguns and ammo who meet the requirements in their state Purchasing a rifle or shotgun or ammunition shall submit to the seller such full and clear proof of identification, including shield number, serial number, military or governmental order or authorization, military or other official identification, other state firearms license, or proof of nonresidence, as may be applicable.
Purchase of firearms and feeding devices **Chapter 140 § 131E**	FIREARMS AND FEEDING DEVICES (for firearms): may be purchased only upon presentment of: (i) a valid **Class A or Class B** license to carry firearms issued under section 131; or (ii) a valid **firearm identification card** issued under section 129B **together with a valid permit to purchase a firearm** issued under section 131A; or (iii) a **valid permit to purchase a firearm** issued under section 131A together with valid proof of **exempt status** under section 129C; <u>LARGE CAPACITY</u> FIREARMS AND FEEDING DEVICES may be so purchased only upon presentment of: (i) a valid **Class A license** to carry firearms issued under section 131; or (ii) a valid **firearm identification card** issued under section 129B **together with** a valid and proper **permit to purchase a firearm** issued under section 131A; or (iii) a valid and proper **permit to purchase a firearm** issued under section 131A **together with**

FIREARM LICENSING

FIREARM PURCHASING REQUIREMENTS

	valid proof of **exempt status** under section 129C; **Restrictions:** Neither a firearm identification card issued under §129B, nor proof of exempt status under §129C, shall be valid for the purpose of purchasing any firearm or ammunition feeding device without being presented together with a valid and proper permit to purchase issued under §131A; An alien permit to possess a rifle or shotgun shall not be valid for the purpose of purchasing firearms or ammunition or ammunition feeding devices No firearm or ammunition or ammunition feeding device therefor shall be sold to any person less than 21 years of age.
PURCHASE REPORTING REQUIREMENTS	
Reporting requirements when purchasing from non-dealer or out of state **Chapter 140 § 128B**	• Any resident of the commonwealth who purchases or obtains a firearm, rifle or shotgun or machine gun from any source (whether in Massachusetts or outside of Massachusetts), other than from a Massachusetts licensed dealer or a person authorized to sell firearms under chapter 140 § 128A and • Any nonresident of the commonwealth who purchases or obtains a firearm, rifle, shotgun or machine gun from any source within or without the commonwealth, other than such a licensee or person, and receives such firearm, rifle, shotgun or machine gun, within the commonwealth • Shall within **7 days** after receiving such firearm, rifle, shotgun or machine gun, report, in writing, to the commissioner of the department of criminal justice information services: o the name and address of the seller or donor and the buyer or donee, o together with a complete description of the firearm, rifle, shotgun or machine gun, including the caliber, make and serial number. **Penalty: 1st Offense**: a fine of not less than $500 nor more than $1,000. **A subsequent offense** by imprisonment in the **state prison (F)** for not more than ten years. **ARREST POWERS**: **Misdemeanor (1st offense)** – there is no statutory authority granting powers of arrest for this offense. **2nd or Subsequent offense** – felony – arrest on probable cause.

PERMITS TO PURCHASE
Chapter 140 § 131E

Permit to purchase: MA residents	A licensing authority, upon the application of a person qualified to be granted a license thereunder by such authority, may grant to such a person, other than a minor, **a permit to purchase, rent or lease a firearm** if it appears that such purchase, rental or lease is for a proper purpose, and may revoke such permit at will.
Permit to purchase: non-residents	The colonel of the state police or a person authorized by him, upon the application of a person licensed section 131F (non-residents with temporary LTC), may grant to such licensee, other than a minor, a permit to purchase, rent or lease a firearm, rifle or shotgun, or to purchase ammunition therefor, if it appears that such purchase, rental or lease is for a proper purpose, and may revoke such permit at will.
Duration	The permit to purchase shall be issued on forms furnished by the commissioner of the department of criminal justice information services, it shall be valid for not more than 10 days after issue, and a copy of every such permit so issued shall within one week thereafter be sent to the said commissioner.
Restrictions	The licensing authority may impose restrictions relative to the caliber and capacity of the firearm to be purchased, rented or leased as he deems proper.

FIREARM PURCHASING REQUIREMENTS	
Penalty for wrongful issuance of a Permit to Purchase	Whoever knowingly issues a permit in violation of this section shall be punished by a fine of not less than $500 nor more than $1,000 and by imprisonment for not less than 6 months nor more than 2 years in a jail or HOC.
Permit to Purchase Fees	The fee for the permits shall be $100, which shall be payable to the licensing authority and shall not be prorated or refunded in case of revocation or denial. The licensing authority shall retain $25 of the fee; $50 of the fee shall be deposited into the general fund of the commonwealth; and $25 of the fee shall be deposited in the Firearms Fingerprint Identity Verification Trust Fund.
Related Statutes, Case Law & Other Important Information	
Penalty for purchasing for another or for unlawful resale **Chapter 140 § 131E**	Any person who uses his/her license to carry firearms or firearm identification card for the purpose of purchasing a firearm, rifle or shotgun for the unlawful use of another, or for resale to or giving to an unlicensed person, shall be punished by a fine of not less than $1,000 nor more than $50,000, or by imprisonment for not less than 2½ years nor more than ten years in a **state prison (F)**, or by both such fine and imprisonment. **Arrest Powers**: **Felony** – a police officer may effect an arrest for this offense committed in his/her presence or for an offense in the past on probable cause. **Revocation**: A conviction of a violation of this section shall be reported forthwith by the court to the licensing authority which issued the license or firearm identification card, which shall immediately revoke the license or firearm identification card of such person. No new license or firearm identification card under §139B or §131 shall be issued to any such person within 2 years after the date of said revocation.

FRAUD INVOLVING FIREARMS

C. 140 § 129	FICTITIOUS INFORMATION REGARDING PURCHASE/RENT
Elements	
1.	The defendant
2.	• in **purchasing**, **renting** or **hiring** a firearm, rifle, shotgun or machine gun, or • in **making application** for any form of license or permit issued in connection therewith, or • in **requesting that work** be done by a gunsmith,
3.	• gives a **false or fictitious name or address**, or • knowingly **offers or gives false information** concerning the date or place of birth, his citizenship status, occupation, or criminal record
Arrest Power, Penalties & Notes	
Power of Arrest	**Misdemeanor** – there is no statutory authority granting warrantless powers of arrest for this offense. However, if the offense is committed in public, in the officer's presence, and is creating a **breach of the peace** an arrest would be lawful.

FIREARM LICENSING

C. 140 § 129	FICTITIOUS INFORMATION REGARDING PURCHASE/RENT
Penalty	**1st Offense:** a fine of not less than $500 nor more than $1,000 dollars, or by imprisonment for not more than 1 year, or both; **2nd or subsequent offense,** shall be punished by imprisonment for not less than 2½ years nor more than five years in the **state prison (F)**.
Related Statutes, Case Law & Other Important Information	
Fraudulent application for an LTC C. 140 § 131(H)	Any person who knowingly files an application containing false information (for an LTC) shall be punished by a fine of not less than $500 nor more than $1,000 or by imprisonment for not less than 6 months nor more than 2 years in a HOC, or by both such fine and imprisonment.

C. 140 § 131I	COUNTERFEIT LTC/FID
Elements	
1.	• Falsely make, alter, forge or counterfeit or procure, or • Assist another to falsely make, alter, forge or counterfeit
2.	A license to carry a firearm (LTC) or a firearm identification card (FID)
Arrest Power, Penalties & Notes	
Power of Arrest	**Felony** – a police officer may effect a warrantless arrest for this offense provided he/she has probable cause that the suspect committed the offense.
Penalty	Imprisonment in a **state prison (F)** for not more than 5 years or in a jail or HOC for not more than 2 years, or by a fine of not less than $500, or both such fine and imprisonment.
Forgery of an FID/LTC	
Forgery related to an LTC/FID Chapter 130 § 131I	Whoever forges or without authority uses the signature, facsimile of the signature, or validating signature stamp of the licensing authority or its designee, or whoever possesses, utters, publishes as true or in any way makes use of a falsely made, altered, forged or counterfeited license to carry a firearm or a firearm identification card. Same punishment/arrest power as above.

ADDITIONAL REQUIREMENTS & PROVISIONS

C. 140 § 129C	MUST PRESENT FID/LTC WHEN DEMANDED BY A POLICE OFFICER
Must Present Upon Demand	Any person shall on demand of a police officer or other law enforcement officer, exhibit: • his license to carry firearms, • or his firearm identification card • or receipt for fee paid for such FID card, • or, exhibit a valid hunting license issued to him
Exception	This does not apply to a person who is exempt as previously described nor to a person within the limits of his own property or residence (unless such person's property or residence is under lawful search).
Arrest Power, Penalties & Notes	
Power of Arrest	There is no statutory authority granting warrantless powers of arrest for this offense.
Penalty	Upon failure to present upon demand the person may be required to surrender to the officer the firearm, rifle or shotgun which shall be taken into custody. However, the firearm, rifle or shotgun shall be returned forthwith upon presentation **within 30** of said license to carry firearms, firearm identification card or receipt for fee paid for such card or hunting license as hereinbefore described.

C. 140 § 129D	FIREARMS AND LICENSES MUST BE SURRENDERED UPON REVOCATION, SUSPENSION OR DENIAL
Must turn in guns	Upon revocation, suspension or denial of an application for a firearm identification card pursuant to the conditions of § 129B, or of any firearms license if said firearms identification card is not then in force or of any machine gun license, the person whose application was so revoked, suspended or denied shall without delay deliver or surrender, to the licensing authority where he resides, all firearms, rifles, shotguns and machine guns and ammunition which he then possesses unless an appeal is pending.
1 Year to Transfer Weapons to Lawful Person	The person or the person's legal representative shall have the right, at any time up to 1 year after the delivery or surrender, to transfer the firearms, rifles, shotguns and machine guns and ammunition to any licensed dealer or any other person legally permitted to purchase or take possession of the firearms, rifles, shotguns and machine guns and ammunition and, upon notification in writing by the purchaser or transferee and the former owner, the licensing authority shall within 10 days deliver the firearms, rifles, shotguns and machine guns and ammunition to the transferee or purchaser and the licensing authority shall observe due care in the receipt and holding of any such firearm, rifle, shotgun or machine gun and ammunition; provided, however, that the purchaser or transferee shall affirm in writing that the purchaser or transferee shall not in violation of section 129C transfer the firearms, rifles, shotguns or machine guns or ammunition to the former owner. The licensing authority shall at the time of delivery or surrender inform the person in writing of the authority's ability, within 1 year after delivery or surrender, to transfer the firearms, rifles, shotguns and machine guns and ammunition to any licensed dealer or other person legally permitted to purchase or take possession.;
Storage Procedures for Licensing Authority	The licensing authority, after taking possession of any firearm, rifle, shotgun, machine gun or ammunition by any means, may transfer possession of such weapon for storage purposes to a federally and state licensed dealer of such weapons and ammunition who operates a bonded warehouse on the licensed premises that is equipped with a safe for the secure storage of firearms and a weapon box or

C. 140 § 129D	FIREARMS AND LICENSES MUST BE SURRENDERED UPON REVOCATION, SUSPENSION OR DENIAL
taking possession of Weapons	similar container for the secure storage of other weapons and ammunition; provided, however, that the licensing authority shall not transfer to such dealer possession of any weapon that is or may be evidence in any current or pending criminal case concerning a violation of any general or special law, rule or regulation governing the use, possession or ownership of such weapon. Any such dealer that takes possession of a weapon under the provisions of this section shall: (i) inspect such weapon; (ii) issue to the owner a receipt indicating the make, model, caliber, serial number and condition of each weapon so received; and (iii) store and maintain all weapons so received in accordance with such regulations, rules or guidelines as the secretary of the executive office of public safety may establish under this section. The owner shall be liable to such dealer for reasonable storage charges and may dispose of any such weapon as provided under this section by transfer to a person lawfully permitted to purchase or take possession of such weapon.
Sale by Auction	Firearms, rifles, shotguns or machine guns and ammunition not disposed of after delivery or surrender according to the provisions of this section shall be sold at public auction by the colonel of the state police to the highest bidding person legally permitted to purchase and possess said firearms, rifles, shotguns or machine guns and ammunition and the proceeds shall be remitted to the state treasurer. Any such weapon that is stored and maintained by a licensed dealer as provided under this section may be so auctioned at the direction of: i. the licensing authority at the expiration of one year following initial surrender or delivery to such licensing authority; or ii. the dealer then in possession, if the storage charges for such weapon have been in arrears for 90 days; provided, however, that in either case, title shall pass to the licensed dealer for the purpose of transferring ownership to the auctioneer; and provided further, that in either case, after deduction and payment for storage charges and all necessary costs associated with such surrender and transfer, all surplus proceeds, if any, shall be immediately returned to the owner of such weapon; provided, however, that no firearm, rifle, shotgun or machine gun or ammunition classified as having been used to carry out a criminal act pursuant to section 131Q shall be sold at public auction pursuant to this section. If the licensing authority cannot reasonably ascertain a lawful owner within 180 days of acquisition by the authority, the authority may, in its discretion, trade or dispose of surplus, donated, abandoned or junk firearms, rifles, shotguns or machine guns or ammunition to properly licensed distributors or firearms dealers. The proceeds of the sale or transfer shall be remitted or credited to the municipality in which the authority presides to purchase weapons, equipment or supplies or for violence reduction or suicide prevention; provided, however, that no firearm, rifle, shotgun or machine gun or ammunition classified as having been used to carry out a criminal act pursuant to section 131Q shall be considered surplus, donated, abandoned or junk for the purposes of this section. The secretary of the executive office of public safety may make and promulgate such rules and regulations as are necessary to carry out the provisions of this section.
See c. 269 § 10(i)	Chapter 269 § 10(i) makes it a misdemeanor for failing to turn-in suspended/revoked LTC/FID. (see later in this section)

C. 269 § 10(i)	FAILING TO DELIVER OR SURRENDER A REVOKED/SUSPENDED LTC/FID
	Elements
1.	The defendant knowingly
2.	Fail to deliver or surrender a revoked or suspended: • license to carry or possess firearms or machine, • firearm identification card, • receipt for the fee for an FID card, • a firearm, rifle, shotgun or machine gun, as provided in c. 140 § 129D,
Exception	Unless an appeal is pending
	Arrest Power, Penalties & Notes
Power of Arrest	**Misdemeanor** – there is no statutory authority granting warrantless powers of arrest for this offense. However, if the offense is committed in public, in the officer's presence, and is creating a **breach of the peace** an arrest would be lawful.
Penalty	Imprisonment in a jail or house of correction for not more than 2½ years or by a fine of not more than $1,000.

C. 140 § 129C	REPORT OF LOST, STOLEN, OR RECOVERED WEAPON
Must report immediately	In the case of loss, theft or recovery of any firearm, rifle, shotgun or machine gun, a report shall be made **forthwith** to both the **commissioner of the department of criminal justice information services** and **the licensing authority** in the city or town where the owner resides.
	Arrest Power, Penalties & Notes
Power of Arrest	There is no statutory authority granting warrantless powers of arrest for this offense.
Penalty	Failure to so report (sale, transfer, loss or theft) shall be cause for suspension or permanent revocation of such person's firearm identification card or license to carry firearms, or both, and shall be punished by a fine of not less than $200 nor more than $1,000 for a first offense and by a fine of not less than $1,000 nor more than $5,000 for a second offense, a fine of not less than $7,500 and not more than $10,000, imprisonment for not less than 1 year and not more than 5 years of both for a third or subsequent offense.
1st offense fail to report not cause for suspension or revocation	Failure to so report shall be a cause for suspension or permanent revocation of a person's firearm identification card or license to carry firearms, or both. Notwithstanding this paragraph or any general or special law to the contrary, no person, who in good faith, reports a loss or theft under this paragraph for the first time shall be subject to suspension, revocation or be considered unsuitable under section 131 for the renewal of a lawfully held firearm identification card or license to carry firearms; provided, however, that persons reporting loss or theft under this paragraph or under section 129B on a second or subsequent occasion may be subject to suspension, revocation or be considered unsuitable under said section 131 for the renewal of a lawfully held firearm identification card or license to carry firearms.

C. 140 § 131B	PENALTY FOR LOAN OF MONEY SECURED BY WEAPONS
Guns cannot be used as collateral	Whoever loans money secured by mortgage, deposit or pledge of a firearm, rifle, shotgun or machine gun shall be punished by a fine of not more than $500 or by imprisonment for not more than 1 year, or by both
Exception for Banks	Nothing herein shall prohibit a bank or other institutional lender from loaning money secured by a mortgage, deposit, or pledge of a firearm, rifle, shotgun or machine gun to a manufacturer, wholesaler, or dealer of firearms, rifles, or shotguns.
Bank doesn't need license to sell guns	The provisions of §123 (gun seller license) shall not be applicable to any such mortgage, deposit or pledge unless or until the lender takes possession of the collateral upon default or the collateral is removed from the premises of the debtor.

C. 140 § 131O	STATEWIDE FIREARMS SURRENDER PROGRAM
Surrender Program	Notwithstanding any general or special law, rule or regulation to the contrary, the colonel of state police, in conjunction with the secretary of the executive office of public safety, shall promulgate rules and regulations implementing a statewide firearms surrender program.
Immune from unlawful possession offenses	In conjunction with this program only, any citizen of the commonwealth who complies with the policies set forth by the colonel shall **not** be asked for identification and shall be immune from prosecution for possession of such firearm; provided, however, that nothing herein shall prohibit the prosecution of any person for the unlawful possession of a firearm who is not in compliance with the conditions and procedures established by the colonel; and provided further, that nothing herein shall prohibit the prosecution of any person for any other offense committed within the commonwealth.
Firearm disposition	Any firearm surrendered in accordance with the provisions of this program that is reported stolen shall be returned to its lawful owner; provided, however, that any firearm suspected to be evidence in a crime shall remain in the custody and control of the department of state police in the same manner as any other such firearm lawfully seized by the department of state police. The department of state police may test-fire and preserve any and all firearms voluntarily surrendered. All weapons that have been voluntarily surrendered that are not suspected to be evidence of criminal activity and have not been reported stolen shall be disposed of in accordance with procedures established by the colonel.

WEAPON OFFENSES

COMMITTING CRIMES WITH WEAPONS/BODY ARMOR	
Use of firearms while committing a felony c. 265 § 18B	The defendant, while in the commission of or the attempted commission of a **felony**, has in his possession or under his control a firearm, rifle or shotgun. **Penalty:** in addition to the penalty for the underlying offense imprisonment in the state prison (F) for **not less than 5 years**; **Enhanced Penalty for Large Capacity or Machine Gun:** if such firearm, rifle or shotgun is a large capacity weapon, or a machine gun, shall be punished by imprisonment in the **state prison (F) for not less than 10 years**.
Tear gas use in commission of a crime c. 269 § 10C	The defendant uses tear gas cartridges, or any device or instrument which contains a liquid, gas, powder, or any other substance designed to incapacitate for the purpose of committing a crime. **Penalty**: imprisonment in the **state prison (F)** for not more than 7 years. Attorney Hanrahan's note: the underlying crime can be a misdemeanor or a felony.
Body armor use in commission of a felony c. 269 § 10D	The defendant, while in the commission or attempted commission of a **felony**, uses or wears any body armor, so-called, or any protective covering for the body or any parts thereof, made of resin-treated glass-fiber cloth, or of any other material or combination of materials, designed to prevent, deflect or deter the penetration thereof by ammunition, knives or other weapons. **Penalty:** imprisonment in the **state prison (F)** for not less than 2½ years nor more than 5 years or for **not less than 1 year** nor more than 2½ years in a jail or HOC.
Arrest Power, Penalties & Notes	
Power of Arrest	**All of the above offenses are felonies** – a police officer may effect a warrantless arrest for this offense provided he/she has probable cause that the suspect committed the offense.

C. 140 § 131Q	STATISTIC REPORTING REQUIRED
Licensing Authority must report weapons used in criminal activity	A firearm, rifle or shotgun, large capacity weapon, machine gun or assault weapon used to carry out a criminal act shall be traced by the licensing authority for the city or town in which the crime took place. The licensing authority shall report statistical data, when the data is readily available as determined by the chief of police, including, but not limited to: (i) the make, model, serial number and caliber of the weapon used; (ii) the type of crime committed; (iii) whether an arrest or conviction was made; (iv) whether fingerprint evidence was found on the firearm; (v) whether ballistic evidence was retrieved from the crime scene; (vi) whether the criminal use of the firearm was related to known gang activity; (vii) whether the weapon was obtained illegally; (viii) whether the weapon was lost or stolen; and (ix) whether the person using the weapon was otherwise a prohibited person. The data shall be reported to the commonwealth fusion center or the criminal firearms and trafficking unit within the division of investigation and intelligence in the department of state police established pursuant to section 6 of chapter 22C. The colonel of state police shall produce an annual report by December 31 of each year regarding crimes committed in the commonwealth using firearms, rifles or shotguns, large capacity weapons, machine guns or assault weapons, including all of the categories of data contained in this section, and shall submit a copy of the report to the joint committee on public safety and homeland security, the clerks of the house of representatives and the senate and, upon request, to criminology, public policy and public health researchers and other law enforcement agencies.

C. 269 § 10G	ARMED CAREER CRIMINAL ACT
	ENHANCED PENALTIES FOR REPEAT OFFENSES
Section a	Whoever, having been **previously convicted of a violent crime or of a serious drug offense**, both as defined herein, violates the provisions of paragraph (a), (c) or (h) of c. 269 § 10 shall be punished by imprisonment in the **state prison (F)** for **not less than three years** nor more than 15 years.
Section b	Whoever, having been previously convicted of **two violent crimes, or two serious drug offenses or one violent crime and one serious drug offense, arising from separate incidences**, violates the provisions of said paragraph (a), (c) or (h) of said section 10 shall be punished by imprisonment in the **state prison (F)** for **not less than ten years** nor more than 15 years.
Section c	Whoever, having been previously convicted of **three violent crimes or three serious drug offenses, or any combination thereof totaling three, arising from separate incidences**, violates the provisions of said paragraph (a), (c) or (h) of said section 10 shall be punished by imprisonment in the **state prison (F)** for **not less than 15 years** nor more than 20 years.
	Related Statutes, Case Law & Other Important Information
Minimum sentences	The sentences imposed upon such persons **shall not be reduced to less than the minimum, nor suspended, nor shall persons convicted under this section be eligible for probation, parole, furlough, work release or receive any deduction from such sentence for good conduct until such person shall have served the minimum number of years of such sentence**; provided, however, that the commissioner of correction may, on the recommendation of the warden, superintendent or other person in charge of a correctional institution or the administrator of a county correctional institution, grant to such offender a temporary release in the custody of an officer of such institution for the following purposes only: (i) to attend the funeral of a spouse or next of kin; (ii) to visit a critically ill close relative or spouse; or (iii) to obtain emergency medical services unavailable at such institution. **No CWOF's or Placed on File:** Prosecutions commenced under this section shall neither be continued without a finding nor placed on file. The provisions of section 87 of c. 276 relative to the power of the court to place certain offenders on probation shall not apply to any person 17 years of age or over charged with a violation of this section.
Definition	For the purposes of this section, **"violent crime"** shall have the meaning set forth in Chapter 140 § 121.
Attorney Hanrahan's Note	In order to sustain a conviction under the Massachusetts armed career criminal act the Commonwealth must prove that the defendant has been previously convicted of **at least one** "violent crime." For purposes of the Massachusetts ACCA, a "violent crime" is defined as:[1269] "any crime punishable by imprisonment for a term exceeding one year ... that: I. has as an element the use, attempted use or threatened use of **physical force** or a **deadly weapon** against the person of another; II. is **burglary, extortion, arson** or **kidnapping**; III. involves the use of **explosives**; or IV. otherwise involves **conduct that presents a serious risk of physical injury to another**." In short, the crime must have an "element of the use of **physical force**" which is capable of causing pain or injury. For the purposes of this section, **"serious drug offense"** shall mean an offense under the federal Controlled Substances Act, 21 U.S.C. 801, et seq., the federal Controlled Substances Import and Export

[1269] *Commonwealth v. Colon*, SJC 2011

C. 140 § 131Q	STATISTIC REPORTING REQUIRED
	Act, 21 U.S.C. 951, et seq. or the federal Maritime Drug Law Enforcement Act, 46 U.S.C. App. 1901, et seq. for which a maximum term of imprisonment for ten years or more is prescribed by law, or an offense under c. 94C involving the manufacture, distribution or possession with intent to manufacture or distribute a controlled substance, as defined in section 1 of said c. 94C, for which a maximum term of ten years or more is prescribed by law.
A&B offense not automatically a "violent crime"	In the 2011 case of ***Com. v. Colon,*** the SJC ruled that a conviction of assault & battery does not automatically amount to a violent crime under the Armed Career Criminal Act because an A&B conviction can occur as the result of reckless conduct and not necessarily violent action. Evidence must be introduced at court that the A&B involved violence. However, the Court also ruled that a conviction of A&B on a police does automatically amount to a violent crime because the involvement in even a minor dispute with a civilian distracts from the officer's duties, the offense **creates a public risk**.
Deadly vs. Dangerous Weapon	In the 2015 case of ***Commonwealth v. Rezendes,*** the Appeals Court ruled that, for the purposes of this statute, the weapon must be a deadly weapon and not just a dangerous weapon. Deadly connotes an *inevitability of death* or at least a *higher certainty of death* than does dangerous.

CARRYING OFFENSES

c. 269 § 10(a)	UNLAWFUL POSSESSION OUTSIDE OF HOME OR BUSINESS (i.e. "CARRYING") OF A *FIREARM*
	Elements[1270]
1.	The defendant knowingly possessed, or had under his/her control in a motor vehicle, a firearm (with a barrel under 16 inches),
2.	The defendant does not have a valid license to possess the firearm outside of his/her home or office; and
3.	The defendant does not qualify for one of the statutory exemptions from the licensing requirements (see exemptions below).
	Arrest Power, Penalties & Notes
Power of Arrest	**Felony** – a police officer may effect a warrantless arrest for this offense provided he/she has probable cause that the suspect committed the offense.
Penalty	Imprisonment in the **state prison (F)** for not less than 2½ years nor more than 5 years, or for not less than 18 months nor more than 2½ years in a jail or house of correction. **Minimum Mandatory Sentence:** The sentence imposed on such person shall not be reduced to less than 18 months, nor suspended, nor shall any person convicted under this subsection be eligible for probation, parole, work release, or furlough or receive any deduction from his sentence for good conduct **until he shall have served 18 months of such sentence**. **No Placing on File or CWOF**: Prosecutions commenced under this subsection shall neither be continued without a finding nor placed on file. See additional penalty (below) if firearm is loaded.

WEAPON VIOLATIONS

[1270] *Commonwealth v. White,* 452 Mass. 133, 136, 891 N.E.2d 675, 678 (2008).

c. 269 § 10(a)	UNLAWFUL POSSESSION OUTSIDE OF HOME OR BUSINESS (i.e. "CARRYING") OF A *FIREARM*
	Subsequent Offenses – chapter 269 § 10(d): Whoever, after having been convicted of any of the offenses set forth in paragraph (a), (b) or (c) (unlawful carrying of a firearm, rifle, shotgun, per se dangerous weapon, machine gun or sawed-off shotgun) commits a like offense or any other of the said offenses: **2nd Offense:** state prison for **not less than 5 years** nor more than 7 years; **3rd Offense**: state prison for **not less than 7 years** nor more than 10 years; **4th Offense**: state prison for **not less than 10 years** nor more than 15 years. **No Suspended sentences or Probation:** The sentence imposed upon a person, who after a conviction of an offense under paragraph (a), (b) or (c) of chapter 269 commits the same or a like offense, shall not be suspended, nor shall any person so sentenced be eligible for probation or receive any deduction from his sentence for good conduct. **Attorney Hanrahan's Note:** the subsequent penalty to possession of dangerous weapons (non-firearm related) as well.
Attorney Hanrahan's Comment	Be sure to read the explanation on the differences between "carrying" and mere possession below despite the terminology used in the statute.
	Related Statutes, Case Law & Other Important Information
Possession inside home or Business	If unlicensed possession occurs inside home or business see Chapter 269 § 10(h) later in this section.
Multiple Convictions possible for same act	In the 2013 case of ***Commonwealth v. Horne***, the defendant was convicted of two counts of carrying a rifle outside of his home in violation of c. 269 § 10(a) when, during the same incident, he twice left his home carrying a rifle prior to murdering the victim. The defendant argued that it was a continuous course of conduct and that he should only be convicted for one offense. The SJC that the crux of the offense is being outside of your home or business with the weapon; therefore "an individual who returns to his residence with a rifle that he has been carrying (or relinquishes possession of that rifle), and then goes back outside with the rifle, has committed a second violation."
The statute exempts a defendant who:[1271]	1) is present in or on <u>*his*</u> residence or place of business; or 2) has in effect a license to carry firearms (LTC) issued under c. 140 § 131; or 3) has in effect a license to carry firearms issued under 140 § 131F (temp LTC for alien/non-resident); or 4) has complied with the provisions of 140 § 129C and 131G (see list below): **C. 140 § 20C exemptions:** (b) licensed dealers transporting firearms, (c) surrendering a firearm with prior written permission, (d) transportation by a common carrier (e) amusement park when chained (j) is an out-of-state resident moving to Massachusetts (m) examining a firearm or receiving instruction from a licensed person (n) transfer to a descendent upon the death of the licensed owner (o) police officer or military official (r) authorized veterans event (s) museum or historical exemption (t) bank holding as collateral. **C. 130 § 131G exemptions:** collectors meeting or exhibition, hunting, pistol competition.

[1271] Model Jury Instructions (updated 2013).

c. 269 § 10(a)	UNLAWFUL POSSESSION OUTSIDE OF HOME OR BUSINESS (i.e. "CARRYING") OF A *FIREARM*
	5) has complied as to possession of an air rifle or BB gun with the requirements imposed by § 12B; Note: General Laws c. 278, § 7 places on the defendant the burden of producing evidence of one of these exemptions; the Commonwealth must then disprove beyond a reasonable doubt the applicability of the claimed exemption. Until there is such evidence, the exemptions are not at issue.[1272]
Additional Crime if firearm is loaded **c. 269 s 10(n)**	Chapter 269 § 10(n) states whoever violates paragraph (a) – carrying firearm/rifle/shotgun, or paragraph (c) – possession of machine gun, by means of a loaded firearm, loaded sawed off shotgun or loaded machine gun shall be **further** punished by imprisonment in the house of correction for not more than 2½ years, which sentence shall begin from and after the expiration of the sentence for the violation of paragraph (a) or paragraph (c). **Note:** For purposes of this section, loaded shall mean that ammunition is contained in the weapon or within a feeding device attached thereto.
Unlawful carrying of a *Large Capacity* Weapon or Feeding device **c. 269 § 10(m)**	Notwithstanding (despite) the provisions of paragraph (a) - unlawful carrying a firearm - or (h) - unlawful possession of a firearm, rifle shotgun or ammunition- of Chapter 269 § 10, any person not exempted by statute who knowingly has in his possession, or knowingly has under his control in a vehicle, a **large capacity weapon** or **large capacity feeding device** who does not possess a valid **Class A or Class B** license to carry firearms issued under section 131 or 131F of c. 140, except as permitted or otherwise provided under this section or c. 140, shall be punished as follows: **Penalty**: imprisonment in a **state prison (F)** for **not less than 2½ years** nor more than ten years. The sentence imposed upon such person shall not be reduced to less than one year, nor suspended, nor shall any person convicted under this subsection be eligible for probation, parole, furlough, work release or receive any deduction from his sentence for good conduct until he shall have served such minimum term of such sentence. **Arrest powers**: **Felony** – a police officer may effect an arrest for this offense committed in his/her presence or for an offense in the past, on probable cause. **FID is no defense:** The possession of a valid firearm identification card issued under section 129B shall not be a defense for a violation of this subsection; provided, however, that any such person charged with violating this paragraph and holding a valid firearm identification card **shall not be subject to any mandatory minimum sentence** imposed by this paragraph. **EXCEPTIONS**: The provisions of this paragraph shall not apply to the possession of a large capacity weapon or large capacity feeding device by: (i) any officer, agent or employee of the commonwealth or any other state or the United States, including any federal, state or local law enforcement personnel; (ii) any member of the military or other service of any state or the United States; (iii) any duly authorized law enforcement officer, agent or employee of any municipality of the commonwealth; (iv) any federal, state or local historical society, museum or institutional collection open to the public; provided, however, that any such person described in clauses (i) to (iii), inclusive, is authorized by a competent authority to acquire, possess or carry a large capacity semiautomatic weapon and is acting within the scope of his duties; or (v) any gunsmith duly licensed under the applicable federal law. **Attorney Hanrahan's Note:** This offense makes it a crime to carry or possess a large capacity weapon (firearm, rifle or shotgun) or feeding device without a Class A or B license (other than exempt as listed above (i) through (v) or exempt by another law. An FID will only prevent the mandatory 1 year

[1272] *Commonwealth v. Seay*, 376 Mass. 735, 738, 383 N.E.2d 828, 830 (1978) (former statute); *Commonwealth v. Jones*, 372 Mass. 403, 406-407, 361 N.E.2d 1308, 1310-1311 (1977) (same); *Commonwealth v. Davis*, 359 Mass. 758, 270 N.E.2d 925 (1971) (same); *Commonwealth v. Baker*, 10 Mass. App. Ct. 852, 853, 407 N.E.2d 398, 399 (1980) (lack of license need not be charged in complaint).

c. 269 § 10(a)	UNLAWFUL POSSESSION OUTSIDE OF HOME OR BUSINESS (i.e. "CARRYING") OF A *FIREARM*
	sentence.
Defendant bears burden to prove licensed	The reason why the defendant is faced with the burden of proving some evidence that he has a license as opposed to the Commonwealth is because this state does not have a central register of firearm licenses. Therefore, the defendant is in a unique position to know whether or not he is properly licensed, information that the prosecution may not have access to. This is referred to as an affirmative defense.[1273]
Carrying v. Possession	It is important to understand the difference between *possession* and *carrying* when it comes to firearm violations. Some of the exemptions listed below apply to possession but not carrying. **Possession** simply means having the firearm under your control within your home or business. **Carrying** "a firearm occurs when the defendant knowingly has more than momentary possession of a working firearm and moves it from one place to another."[1274] It would not be deemed "carrying" to move the firearm within your own home or business. However, carrying within the common area of the defendant's apartment complex was deemed to be carrying in *Commonwealth. v. Seay*. So the exemption for carrying within the home would apply only to property under the exclusive control of the resident (not common areas in a multi-unit dwelling). Additionally, when it comes to a public location the "moves" element may not be required, the mere possession of the firearm in public may be deemed to be carrying. [1275] **Important Attorney Hanrahan's Note**: The legislature later removed the term "carrying" from this statute but deciphered this offense [269 § 10(a)] from [269 § 10(h)(1)] *unlawful possession of a firearm, rifle, shotgun, or ammunition in the home or business*, by including the additional element of "outside of the home or business." Despite this legislative change the case law deciphering the difference between carrying and possession are still viable and noteworthy. In common terminology most in the criminal justice field still refer to this as *carrying.*
Weapon in the car	Presence of a firearm in a vehicle owned or operated by the defendant does not automatically mean that the defendant possessed or carried the item. There must also be proof that the defendant knew of the weapons presence, had the ability to control it, and had the intention to control it.[1276]
Probable cause	Possession of a firearm, standing alone and without indication that the person was involved in criminal activity does not provide probable cause to believe that the person was unlicensed to carry that firearm.[1277] However, additional evidence of criminal activity and flight would provide such probable cause.[1278] See Investigative Detention section of this manual for more.
Residence or Place of Business	A person's "residence" or "place of business" does not include common areas of an apartment or office building, but only areas that are under that person's exclusive control. It includes "all areas in and around a defendant's property, including outside areas, over which defendant retains exclusive control," but not including "public streets, sidewalks, and common areas to which occupants of multiple dwellings have access."[1279]

1273 *Commonwealth v. Humphries*, SJC (2013).
1274 *Commonwealth v. Albano*, 373 Mass. 132 (1977) also see *Commonwealth v. Seay*, 376 Mass. 735 (1978).
1275 *Commonwealth v. Seay*, 376 Mass. 735 (1978) referencing Commonwealth v. Ballou, 350 Mass. 751 (1966) ("carrying" found where recited facts showed only stationary possession in public place).
1276 Commonwealth v. Romero, SJC (2013).
1277 *Commonwealth v. Couture,* 407 Mass. 178, 552 N.E.2d 538, cert. denied, 498 U.S. 951, 111 S.Ct. 372 (1990).
1278 *Commonwealth v. Brookins,* 416 Mass. 97, 104, 617 N.E.2d 621, 625 (1993).
1279 *Commonwealth v. Coren*, 437 Mass. 723, 734, 774 N.E.2d 623, 632 (2002)

c. 269 § 10(a)	UNLAWFUL POSSESSION OUTSIDE OF HOME OR BUSINESS (i.e. "CARRYING") OF A *FIREARM*
Under control in a vehicle	The defendant must know that the firearm is there, and that he/she has both the ability and the intention to exercise control over the firearm, although this does not have to be exclusive control. Where the issue is constructive possession rather than actual physical possession, the Commonwealth must prove that "in addition to knowledge and the ability to exercise control over the firearm, the defendant must have the intention to do so." [1280] Simply being in a vehicle that also has a firearm in it is not enough.
Carrying outside of Class	No person having in effect a license to carry firearms (LTC) for any purpose, issued under chapter 140 § 131 or §131F of shall be deemed to be in violation of this section. **Attorney Hanrahan's Note**: this means that if a person with a Class B license is carrying in violation of his/her class (e.g. carrying concealed) would not be deemed to be carrying in violation of c. 269 § 10(a). See next block and chapter 140 § 131 under the firearms licensing section of this manual.
Violation of *Restriction* or *Class* c. 140 § 131	A violation of a restriction provided under this paragraph, or a restriction imposed by the licensing authority under the provisions of this paragraph, shall be cause for suspension or revocation and shall, unless otherwise provided, be punished by a fine of not less than $1,000 nor more than $10,000; provided, however, that the provisions of c. 269 § 10 shall not apply to such violation. **Attorney Hanrahan's Note**: a violation of a Class B restriction (i.e. carrying a large capacity firearm or carrying loaded and concealed) or a violation of a restriction put in place by the licensing authority (e.g. target practice only) would not be a violation of chapter 269 § 10 (unlawful carrying). The license holder would only be subject to a fine (see above) and suspension/revocation of his/her LTC. No power of arrest for this violation.
Notice of license revocation	To prove notice of license revocation by certified mail requires proof of receipt.[1281] However, if a defendant purposefully or wilfully evades notice of license revocation sent by certified mail he/she has constructive notice of the license revocation.[1282]
Necessity defense	The Supreme Judicial Court has assumed that a threat of death or serious injury, if it is direct and immediate, may excuse momentary carrying of a firearm. [1283]
Air rifles and BB guns.	In decisions under the earlier version of G.L. c. 269, § 10(a), air guns, BB guns and CO2 guns were held to be regulated solely by G.L. c. 269, § 12B and not by § 10(a).[1284] The current text of § 10(a) applies to anyone who carries "a firearm . . . without . . . having complied as to possession of an air rifle or BB gun with the requirements imposed by [§ 12B]." Thus, compliance with § 12B is a defense to a prosecution under § 10(a), just as the possession of a firearm license would be.[1285]
Flare guns	A flare gun is not a "firearm" for purposes of G.L. c. 269, § 10(a). [1286]

1280 *Commonwealth v. Costa*, 65 Mass. App. Ct. 227, 838 N.E.2d 592 (2005); *Commonwealth v. Sann Than,* 442 Mass. 755, 748, 817 N.E.2d 705 (2004).
1281 See *Police Comm'r of Boston v. Robinson*, 47 Mass. App. Ct. 767, 773, 774, 716 N.E. 2d 652, 656 (1999).
1282 *Commonwealth v. Hampton*, 26 Mass. App. Ct. 938, 940, 525 N.E.2d 1341, 1343 (1988).
1283 *Commonwealth v. Lindsey,* 396 Mass. 840, 843-845, 489 N.E.2d 666, 668-669 (1986). See *Commonwealth v. Iglesia*, 403 Mass. 132, 135-136, 525 N.E.2d 1332, 1333-1334 (1988); *Commonwealth v. Franklin,* 376 Mass. 885, 888 n.2, 385 N.E.2d 227, 230 n.2 (1978). See Instruction 9.240 (Necessity or Duress).
1284 *Commonwealth v. Fenton,* 395 Mass. 92, 94-95, 478 N.E.2d 949, 950-951 (1985); *Commonwealth v. Rhodes,* 389 Mass. 641, 644, 451 N.E.2d 1151, 1153 (1983).
1285 Model Jury Instructions referencing *Commonwealth v. Sayers,* 438 Mass. 238, 240, 780 N.E.2d 24, 26 (2002).
1286 *Commonwealth v. Sampson,* 383 Mass. at 753-761, 422 N.E.2d at 452-456.

c. 269 § 10(a)	UNLAWFUL POSSESSION OUTSIDE OF HOME OR BUSINESS (i.e. "CARRYING") OF A *FIREARM*
FID or other Exemption Required to possess Firearm in Home/Office	The provisions of this subsection shall not affect the licensing requirements of c. 140 § 129C which require every person not otherwise duly licensed or exempted to have been issued a firearms identification card in order to possess a firearm, rifle or shotgun in his residence or place of business.
Firearm	The weapon must be a firearm. In short, it must be capable of discharging a shot or bullet and it must have a barrel length of less than 16 inches (otherwise see carrying rifle shotgun offense). The term "barrel length" refers to "that portion of a firearm . . . through which a shot or bullet is driven, guided or stabilized, and [includes] the chamber." G.L. c. 140, § 121. Note: The weapon need not be loaded.[1287]
Must be capable of discharging round	A weapon that was originally a firearm (or rifle or shotgun) may become so defective or damaged that it will no longer fire a projectile, and then the law no longer considers it to be a firearm (or rifle or shotgun). But a weapon remains a firearm (or rifle or shotgun) within the meaning of the law when a slight repair, replacement or adjustment will again make it an effective weapon.[1288]
License must be presented	Chapter 140 § 129C requires that a holder of an FID or LTC present his FID or LTC to a police officer upon demand (except when on his own property).
Probation not an Option	The provisions of section c. 276 § 87 shall not apply to any person 17 years of age or older, charged with a violation of this subsection, or to any child between ages 14 and 17 so charged, if the court is of the opinion that the interests of the public require that he should be tried as an adult for such offense instead of being dealt with as a child.
Effects of an FID	Chapter 140 § 129C states that the possession of a FID shall not entitle any person to carry a firearm in violation of c. 269 § 10 (carrying of a dangerous weapon) and, the possession of a FID card shall not entitle any person to possess any *large capacity* rifle or shotgun or large capacity feeding device violation of c. 269 § 10(m).
Carrying of firearms by non-residents **c. 140 § 131G**	Any person who is not a resident of the commonwealth may carry a pistol or revolver **in or through the Commonwealth** for the purpose of: • Taking part in a pistol or revolver competition • Attending any meeting or exhibition of any organized group of firearm collectors • For the purpose of hunting; Provided, that such person is a resident of the United States and has a permit or license to carry firearms issued under the laws of any state, district or territory thereof which has licensing requirements which prohibit the issuance of permits or licenses to persons who have been convicted of a felony or who have been convicted of the unlawful use, possession or sale of narcotic or harmful drugs; provided, further, that in the case of a person traveling in or through the commonwealth for the purpose of hunting, he has on his person a hunting or sporting license issued by the commonwealth or by the state of his destination. **Law Enforcement:** Police officers and other peace officers of any state, territory or jurisdiction within the United States duly authorized to possess firearms by the laws thereof shall, for the purposes of this section, be deemed to have a permit or license to carry firearms as described in this section.

[1287] *Commonwealth v. Williams*, 422 Mass. 111, 120, 661 N.E.2d 617, 624 (1996)
[1288] *Commonwealth v. Rhodes*, 21 Mass. App. Ct. 968, 969- 970, 489 N.E.2d 216, 217 (1986) (not a firearm where bent part rendered inoperable until repaired).

c. 269 § 10(a)	UNLAWFUL POSSESSION OUTSIDE OF HOME OR BUSINESS (i.e. "CARRYING") OF A *FIREARM*
The Federal Safe Passage Act	**18 USCA § 926A – *"SAFE PASSAGE ACT" (FEDERAL LAW)*** Notwithstanding (despite) any other provision of any law or any rule or regulation of a State or any political subdivision thereof, any person who is not otherwise prohibited by this chapter from transporting, shipping, or receiving a firearm **shall be entitled to**: • Transport a firearm for any lawful purpose • From any place where he may lawfully possess and carry such firearm • To any other place where he may lawfully possess and carry such firearm • If, during such transportation the firearm is: ▪ Unloaded, and ▪ Neither the firearm nor any ammunition being transported is readily accessible or is directly accessible from the passenger compartment of such transporting vehicle: NOTE: in the case of a vehicle without a compartment separate from the driver's compartment the firearm or ammunition shall be contained in a locked container other than the glove compartment or console. This section applies to any person not prohibited under federal law from possessing firearms. Such persons may transport firearms from any place where they can lawfully possess and carry such firearms to any other place where they can lawfully possess and carry such firearms. For example a Florida gun owner may lawfully drive through Massachusetts to his ultimate destination in Vermont provided he or she complies with the requirements of the federal "Safe Passage" act. Note, however, that it is not clear whether this act applies to transportation of firearms through the District of Colombia (Washington, D.C.). NR 218 It was signed into law by President George W. Bush on July 22, 2004 This Act may be cited as the `Law Enforcement Officers Safety Act of 2004.
Federal Law Exempting Law Enforcement Personnel Chapter 44 of title 18, United States Code	**SEC. 2. Exemption of qualified law enforcement officers from state laws prohibiting the carrying of concealed firearms (Federal Law)** Chapter 44 of title 18, United States Code, is amended by inserting after section 926A the following: Sec. 926B. Carrying of concealed firearms by qualified law enforcement officers (a) Notwithstanding any other provision of the law of any State or any political subdivision thereof, an individual who is a qualified law enforcement officer and who is carrying the identification required by subsection (d) may carry a concealed firearm that has been shipped or transported in interstate or foreign commerce, subject to subsection (b). (b) This section shall not be construed to supersede or limit the laws of any State that: (i) permit private persons or entities to prohibit or restrict the possession of concealed firearms on their property; or (ii) prohibit or restrict the possession of firearms on any State or local government property, installation, building, base, or park. (c) As used in this section, the term `**qualified law enforcement officer'** means an employee of a governmental agency who: 1) is authorized by law to engage in or supervise the prevention, detection, investigation, or

c. 269 § 10(a)	**UNLAWFUL POSSESSION OUTSIDE OF HOME OR BUSINESS (i.e. "CARRYING") OF A *FIREARM***
	prosecution of, or the incarceration of any person for, any violation of law, and has statutory powers of arrest; 2) is authorized by the agency to carry a firearm; 3) is not the subject of any disciplinary action by the agency; 4) meets standards, if any, established by the agency which require the employee to regularly qualify in the use of a firearm; 5) is not under the influence of alcohol or another intoxicating or hallucinatory drug or substance; and 6) is not prohibited by Federal law from receiving a firearm. (d) The identification required by this subsection is the photographic identification issued by the governmental agency for which the individual is employed as a law enforcement officer. (e) As used in this section, the term `firearm' does not include-- 1) any machinegun (as defined in section 5845 of the National Firearms Act); 2) any firearm silencer (as defined in section 921 of this title); and **3)** any destructive device (as defined in section 921 of this title).
Federal Law Exempting *Retired* Law Enforcement Personnel Chapter 44 of title 18, United States Code	**SEC. 3. Exemption of qualified retired law enforcement officers from state laws prohibiting the carrying of concealed firearms (FEDERAL LAW)** Chapter 44 of title 18, United States Code, is further amended by inserting after section 926B the following: Sec. 926C. Carrying of concealed firearms by qualified retired law enforcement officers (a) Notwithstanding any other provision of the law of any State or any political subdivision thereof, an individual who is a **qualified retired law enforcement officer** and **who is carrying the identification** required by subsection (d) may carry a concealed firearm that has been shipped or transported in interstate or foreign commerce, subject to subsection (b). (b) This section shall not be construed to supersede or limit the laws of any State that: (iii) permit private persons or entities to prohibit or restrict the possession of concealed firearms on their property; or (iv) prohibit or restrict the possession of firearms on any State or local government property, installation, building, base, or park. (c) As used in this section, the term `**qualified retired law enforcement officer'** means an individual who: (1) Retired in good standing from service with a public agency as a law enforcement officer, other than for reasons of mental instability: (2) Before such retirement, was authorized by law to engage in or supervise the prevention, detection, investigation, or prosecution of, or the incarceration of any person for, any violation of law, and had statutory powers of arrest; (3) (A) before such retirement, was regularly employed as a law enforcement officer for an aggregate of 15 years or more; or (B) retired from service with such agency, after completing any applicable probationary period of such service, due to a service-connected disability, as determined by such agency; (4) Has a nonforfeitable right to benefits under the retirement plan of the agency;

c. 269 § 10(a)	UNLAWFUL POSSESSION OUTSIDE OF HOME OR BUSINESS (i.e. "CARRYING") OF A *FIREARM*
	(5) During the most recent 12-month period, has met, at the expense of the individual, the State's standards for training and qualification for active law enforcement officers to carry firearms; (6) Is not under the influence of alcohol or another intoxicating or hallucinatory drug or substance; and (7) Is not prohibited by Federal law from receiving a firearm. (d) The identification required by this subsection is: (1) a photographic identification issued by the agency from which the individual retired from service as a law enforcement officer that indicates that the individual has, not less recently than one year before the date the individual is carrying the concealed firearm, been tested or otherwise found by the agency to meet the standards established by the agency for training and qualification for active law enforcement officers to carry a firearm of the same type as the concealed firearm; or (2) (A) a photographic identification issued by the agency from which the individual retired from service as a law enforcement officer; and (B) a certification issued by the State in which the individual resides that indicates that the individual has, not less recently than one year before the date the individual is carrying the concealed firearm, been tested or otherwise found by the State to meet the standards established by the State for training and qualification for active law enforcement officers to carry a firearm of the same type as the concealed firearm. (e) As used in this section, the term `firearm' does not include-- 1) any machine gun (as defined in section 5845 of the National Firearms Act); 2) any firearm silencer (as defined in section 921 of this title); and 3) any destructive device (as defined in section 921 of this title).
Weapon Forfeiture	Chapter 269 § 10(e) states "upon conviction of a violation of c. 269 §10, the firearm or other article shall, unless otherwise ordered by the court, be confiscated by the commonwealth. The firearm or article so confiscated shall, by the authority of the written order of the court be forwarded by common carrier to the colonel of the state police, who, upon receipt of the same, shall notify said court or justice thereof. Said **colonel may sell or destroy the same**, except that any firearm which may not be lawfully sold in the commonwealth shall be destroyed, and in the case of a sale, after paying the cost of forwarding the article, shall pay over the net proceeds to the commonwealth." **Chapter 269 § 10(f) Exception For Lost Or Stolen Weapon:** The court shall, if the firearm or other article was lost by or stolen from the person lawfully in possession of it, order its return to such person. **Attorney Hanrahan's Note**: this forfeiture provision applies to all weapons violations in chapter 269 § 10 (i.e. rifles, shotguns, etc. and even non-firearm type weapons, such as metallic knuckles.

C. 269 § 10(a)	UNLAWFUL POSSESSION OUTSIDE OF HOME OR BUSINESS (i.e. "CARRYING") OF A *RIFLE OR SHOTGUN*
Elements	
1.	The defendant knowingly possessed (outside or his home or business), or had under his/her control in a motor vehicle, a rifle or shotgun (whether loaded or unloaded),
2.	The defendant does not have a valid license to lawfully possess the rifle or shotgun outside of his/her home or office; and
3.	The defendant does not qualify for one of the statutory exemptions from the licensing requirements (see exemptions below).
Arrest Power, Penalties & Notes	
Power of Arrest	**Felony** – a police officer may effect a warrantless arrest for this offense provided he/she has probable cause that the suspect committed the offense.
Penalty	Imprisonment in the **state prison (F)** for not less than 2½ years nor more than 5 years, or for not less than 18 months nor more than 2½ years in a jail or house of correction. **Minimum Mandatory Sentence:** The sentence imposed on such person shall not be reduced to less than 18 months, nor suspended, nor shall any person convicted under this subsection be eligible for probation, parole, work release, or furlough or receive any deduction from his sentence for good conduct **until he shall have served 18 months of such sentence**. **No Placing on File or CWOF**: Prosecutions commenced under this subsection shall neither be continued without a finding nor placed on file.
Related Statutes, Case Law & Other Important Information	
The statute exempts a defendant who:[1289]	1) Is present in or on his residence or place of business; or 2) has in effect a license to carry firearms issued under section 140 § 131; or 3) has in effect a license to carry firearms issued under 140 § 131F; or 4) has in effect a firearms identification card issued under c. 140 § 129B; or 5) has complied with the requirements imposed c. 140 § 120C upon ownership or possession of rifles and shotguns (see list below); or **C. 140 § 20C exemptions:** (a) flare guns and construction tools (b) licensed dealers transporting firearms, (c) surrendering a firearm with prior written permission, (d) transportation by a common carrier (e) amusement park when chained (f) nonresident hunters (g) nonresident at firing range (h) nonresident traveling through Massachusetts (i) nonresident partaking in a gun show (j) is an out-of-state resident moving to Massachusetts (k) person under 15 under the supervision of a properly licensed person (l) theatrical production or writer or photographer inspection (m) examining a firearm or receiving instruction from a licensed person (n) transfer to a descendent upon the death of the licensed owner (o) police officer or military official (p) black powder exception (r) authorized veterans event (s) museum or historical exemption (t) bank holding as collateral (u) nonresident purchasing from a dealer license and a foreign state 6) having complied as to possession of an air rifle or BB gun with the requirements imposed by c. 140 §12B.

1289 Model Jury Instructions (updated 2013).

C. 269 § 10(a)	UNLAWFUL POSSESSION OUTSIDE OF HOME OR BUSINESS (i.e. "CARRYING") OF A *RIFLE OR SHOTGUN*
Important Information	Be sure to read the additional information section of unlawful carrying of firearms (carrying v. possession, prohibition on large capacity, etc.) as most of the same provisions apply to the carrying of a rifle or shotgun. For the purposes of brevity they have not been repeated in this section. For unlicensed possession in the home or business see Chapter 269 § 10(h) later in this section.
Non-Resident Exceptions	Chapter 140 § 129C(p) permits non-resident possession of a rifle , shotgun and ammunition, as long as his/she can lawfully possess them in his/her home state (see Firearm Licensing section for more). Chapter 140 §129C(h) permits possession of those traveling through Massachusetts (see Firearm Licensing section for more).
Rifle defined	A weapon having a rifled bore with a barrel length equal to or greater than 16", capable of discharging a shot or bullet for each pull of the trigger.
Shotgun Defined	A weapon having a smooth bore with a barrel length equal to or greater than 18" with an overall length equal to or greater than twenty-six inches, capable of discharging a shot or bullet for each pull of the trigger.
Barrel Length	The term "barrel length" refers to "that portion of a firearm . . . through which a shot or bullet is driven, guided or stabilized, and includes the chamber.
FID Card	A "firearms identification card" (FID) is not the same thing as a "license to carry a firearm." When a person has a valid firearms identification card, that card gives him the right to possess a firearm within his residence or place of business. But it does not give him the right to possess it outside of his/her home or business, which requires a license to possess a firearm. G.L. c. 140, §§ 129B-129D. An FID is a defense to a charge of carrying a rifle or shotgun, but not other firearms. G.L. c. 269, § 10(a).
How 269 § 10 applies to those who once had an FID card. **c. 140 § 129B**	**Possession after normal expiration is non-criminal:** Chapter 269 § 10 (unlawful possession/carrying of a rifle/shotgun) does not apply if any person in possession of **a non-large capacity** rifle or shotgun whose firearm identification card issued under chapter 140 is invalid for the **sole reason that it has expired**, (note: the card shall remain valid after the expiration date on the card for all lawful purposes, until the application for renewal is approved or denied). **Possession after expiration Penalty**: shall be subject to a civil fine of not less than $100 nor more than $5,000 and the provisions of c. 269 § 10 shall not apply; **Criminal penalties for someone previously holding an FID:** C. 269 § 10(a) shall apply if: i. such firearm identification card has been revoked or suspended, **unless** such revocation or suspension was caused by failure to give **notice of a change of address** as required under this section; ii. revocation or suspension of such firearm identification card is pending, **unless** such revocation or suspension was caused by **failure to give notice of a change of address** as required under this section; or iii. an application for renewal of such firearm identification card has been denied. **Law Enforcement Action for Suspension/Revocation involving Address Change Violation**: Any law enforcement officer who discovers a person to be in possession of a rifle or shotgun after such person's firearm identification card has expired, meaning after 90 days beyond the stated expiration date on the card, or has been revoked or suspended solely for failure to give notice of a change of address **shall confiscate any rifle or shotgun and such expired or suspended card then in possession**, and such officer shall forward such card to the licensing authority by whom it was issued as soon as practicable. **Return upon Renewal:** Any confiscated weapon shall be returned to the owner upon the renewal or reinstatement of such expired or suspended card within one year of such confiscation or such weapon

C. 269 § 10(a)	UNLAWFUL POSSESSION OUTSIDE OF HOME OR BUSINESS (i.e. "CARRYING") OF A *RIFLE OR SHOTGUN*
	may be otherwise disposed of in accordance with the provisions of section 129D. **Receipt alone Valid for 5 Days:** Pending the issuance of a renewed firearm identification card, a receipt for the fee paid, after five days following issuance, shall serve as a valid substitute and any rifle or shotgun so confiscated shall be returned, unless the applicant is disqualified. **Note:** The provisions of this paragraph shall not apply if such person has a valid license to carry firearms issued under section 131 or 131F. **See more on Chapter 140 § 129C in the Firearms License Section for more.**

C. 269 § 12D	CARRYING A *LOADED* RIFLE OR SHOTGUN ON A PUBLIC WAY
	Elements
Loaded Weapon Prohibited	No person shall carry on his person (except as exempted or provided by law) on any public way a loaded rifle or shotgun having cartridges or shells in either the magazine or chamber thereof.
Enclosed Case	No person shall carry on his person (except as exempted or provided by law) on any public way an unloaded rifle or shotgun, unless such rifle or shotgun is enclosed in a case.
Exceptions	The enclosed case restriction shall not apply to drills, parades, military reenactments or other commemorative ceremonies, color guards or memorial service firing squads, so-called, as permitted by law. The provisions of this section shall not apply to the carrying of a loaded or unloaded rifle or shotgun on a public way by: (i) any officer, agent or employee of the commonwealth or any other state or the United States, including any federal, state or local law enforcement personnel; (ii) any member of the military or other service of any state or the United States, including members of the national guard, reserves and junior reserve officer training corps; (iii) any duly authorized law enforcement officer, agent or employee of any municipality of the commonwealth; **Note:** provided, however, that any such person described in clauses (i) to (iii), inclusive, shall be authorized by a competent authority to so carry a loaded or unloaded rifle or shotgun on a public way and such person is acting within the scope of his duties or training; or (iv) a person who is **lawfully engaged in hunting and is the holder of a valid hunting or sporting license** issued pursuant to c. 131. **Shooting Gallery**: this section shall not apply to the operation of a shooting gallery, licensed and defined under the provisions of section 56A of c. 140, nor to persons using the same.
	Arrest Power, Penalties & Notes
Power of Arrest	**For Loaded Weapon: Misdemeanor** – anyone violating this provision may be arrested without a warrant. **For unloaded weapon not in a secure case: Misdemeanor** - statutory authority permits a police may effect an arrest for this offense committed in his/her presence only.

C. 269 § 12D	CARRYING A *LOADED* RIFLE OR SHOTGUN ON A PUBLIC WAY
Penalty for Loaded Rifle or Shotgun in Public	**Penalty Non-large capacity:** A fine of not less than $500 nor more than $5,000 or by imprisonment in the HOC for not more than 2 years, or by both such fine and imprisonment. **Penalty Large capacity:** A fine of not less than $1,000 nor more than $10,000 or by imprisonment for **not less than one year** nor more than ten years, or by both such fine and imprisonment, and may be arrested without a warrant.
Penalty for not being in enclosed case	**Non-Large Capacity - Penalty:** a fine of not less than $100 nor more than $1,000. **Large Capacity - Penalty**: if such unloaded rifle or shotgun is a large capacity weapon and is **carried simultaneously with a fully or partially loaded large capacity feeding device**, such person shall be punished by a fine of not less than $1,000 nor more than $10,000 or by imprisonment for not less than 1 year nor more than 10 years, or by both such fine and imprisonment.
Attorney Hanrahan's Comment	This law is intended for those who are otherwise lawfully permitted to carry rifles and shotguns (i.e. they are licensed). It prohibits the carrying of loaded rifles and shotguns, unless exempted by law (i.e. in an area authorized for hunting).
Related Statutes, Case Law & Other Important Information	
Confiscation of Weapon	Upon a conviction of a violation of any provision of this section, such rifle or shotgun shall be confiscated by the commonwealth and, upon written order of the court, such weapon shall be forwarded to the colonel of the state police, who may dispose of such weapon in the manner prescribed in section 10.
Definition of a loaded rifles or shotgun	For purposes of this section, **"loaded shotgun or loaded rifle"** shall mean any shotgun or rifle having ammunition in **either the magazine or chambe**r thereof, such ammunition including a live cartridge, primer (igniter), bullet or propellant powder designed for use in any firearm, rifle or shotgun and, in the case of a muzzle loading or black powder shotgun or rifle, containing powder in the flash pan, a percussion cap and shot or ball; but the term "loaded shotgun or loaded rifle" shall not include a shotgun or rifle loaded with a blank cartridge, which contains no projectile within such blank or within the bore or chamber of such shotgun or rifle.

C. 140 § 131C	CARRYING OF WEAPONS IN A VEHICLE
Elements	
§a CLASS A Restriction in Motor Vehicle	No person carrying a ***loaded*** **firearm** under a Class A license (issued under section 131 or 131F) shall carry the firearm in a vehicle unless such firearm while carried therein is **under the direct control of such person**. **Penalty:** A fine of $500.
§b CLASS B Firearm MV Restriction	No person carrying a firearm under a Class B license (issued under section 131 or 131F) shall possess the same in a vehicle **unless such weapon is *unloaded* and contained *within the locked trunk*** of such vehicle or in a ***locked case*** or other secure container. **Penalty:** A fine of $500. Note: this provision will be eliminated on January 1, 2021.

WEAPON VIOLATIONS

C. 140 § 131C	CARRYING OF WEAPONS IN A VEHICLE
§c Rifle or Shotgun in MV	No person possessing a **large capacity rifle or shotgun** under a **Class A or Class B** license shall possess the same in a vehicle unless such weapon is ***unloaded*** **and contained *within the locked trunk*** of such vehicle or **in a *locked case*** or other secure container. **Penalty:** A fine of not less than $500 nor more than $5,000.
§d Exemptions to the above Restrictions	The provisions of this section shall not apply to: i. any **officer, agent or employee of the Commonwealth or any state or the United States**; ii. any member of the **Military** or other service of any state or of the United States; iii. any duly authorized **law enforcement officer**, agent or employee of any municipality of the commonwealth; Provided, however, that any such person described in clauses (i) to (iii), inclusive, is authorized by a competent authority to carry or possess the weapon so carried or possessed and is acting within the scope of his duties.
§e Revocation	A conviction of a violation of this section shall be reported forthwith by the court or magistrate to the licensing authority who shall immediately revoke the card or license of the person so convicted. No new such card or license may be issued to any such person until one year after the date of revocation.
Arrest Power, Penalties & Notes	
Power of Arrest	**Misdemeanor** – there is no statutory authority granting warrantless powers of arrest for this offense. However, if the offense is committed in public, in the officer's presence, and is creating a **breach of the peace** an arrest would be lawful.
Attorney Hanrahan's Comment	This statute applies to those who have a Class A or B license. Obviously if someone was transporting a firearm in a vehicle without a license c. 269 § 10 would be the appropriate law to utilize.
Related Statutes, Case Law & Other Important Information	
***Commonwealth v. Reyes* (2013)**	A defendant cannot be convicted of unlawful carrying a firearm in a motor vehicle, G.L. c. 140, § 131C (*a*) (carrying statute), when he is not himself in the vehicle. The SJC stated "once the defendant left his motor vehicle and the firearm in it, he became subject to the storage statute (but not the carrying statute) because he was storing or keeping his firearm in a "place" neither on his person nor "under the control of the owner or other lawfully authorized user." G.L. c. 140, § 131L (*a*)."
Safe Passage Law	Be sure to review the *Carrying* a Firearm section of this manual for a detailed explanation of exemptions for those who are traveling through (and in some cases to) Massachusetts.
See c. 269 § 12D	Chapter 269 § 12D restricts the **Carrying of a loaded rifle or shotgun on a public way.**

C. 269 § 10H CARRYING LOADED FIREARM WHILE UNDER THE INFLUENCE

Elements	
1.	The defendant, having in effect a license to carry firearms issued under section 131 or 131F of c. 140, carries on his person, or has under his control in a vehicle, a **loaded firearm**, (as defined in section chapter 140 § 121),
2.	While under the influence of intoxicating liquor or marijuana, narcotic drugs, depressants or stimulant substances, all as defined in chapter 94C § 1, or the vapors of glue.

Arrest Power, Penalties & Notes	
Power of Arrest	**Misdemeanor** – there is no statutory authority granting warrantless powers of arrest for this offense. However, if the offense is committed in public, in the officer's presence, and is creating a **breach of the peace** an arrest would be lawful.
Penalty	A fine of not more than $5,000 or by imprisonment in the HOC for not more than 2½ years, or by both such fine and imprisonment
Attorney Hanrahan's Comment	Interestingly, the legislature narrowed this statute down only to those who have LTC's. So, for instance, a police officer carrying on his badge could theoretically carry while under the influence (not recommended). Also, this *prevents* an additional penalty to unlicensed carriers to be additionally punished for being under the influence (probably an oversight by the legislature).

C. 269 § 10(b) CARRYING A DANGEROUS WEAPON

Carrying Specifically Listed Weapons Elements	
1.	The defendant, except as provided by law, carries on his person, or carries on his person or under his control in a vehicle, any of the following:
2.	• **Certain Knives:** stiletto, dagger or a device or case which enables a knife with a locking blade to be drawn at a locked position, any ballistic knife, or any knife with a detachable blade capable of being propelled by any mechanism, dirk knife, any knife having a double-edged blade, or a switch knife, or any knife having an automatic spring release device by which the blade is released from the handle having a blade of over one and one-half inches - Note: In regards to the carrying of knives, the intent of the law is to outlaw the carrying of those knives which are primarily designed for stabbing human beings or for other unlawful objectives.[1290]), • a slung shot, • blowgun, • blackjack (small heavy billy club type weapon), • Metallic knuckles or knuckles of any substance which could be put to the same use with the same or similar effect as metallic knuckles, • **So-called Nun chucks:** nunchaku, zoobow, also known as klackers or kung fu sticks, or any similar weapon consisting of two sticks of wood, plastic or metal connected at one end by a length of rope, chain, wire or leather, • **Throwing Stars:** a shuriken or any similar pointed starlike object intended to injure a person when

[1290] *Commonwealth v. Miller*, 22 Mass.App.Ct. 694 (1986).

C. 269 § 10(b)	CARRYING A DANGEROUS WEAPON
	thrown, • **Studded Arm/Fist wraps**: any armband, made with leather which has metallic spikes, points or studs or any similar device made from any other substance or a cestus or similar material weighted with metal or other substance and worn on the hand, • **Ball and Chain type Weapon:** a manrikigusari or similar length of chain having weighted ends.
Carrying Specifically "Other" Dangerous Weapons when Arrested Elements	
1.	The defendant, **when arrested upon a warrant** for an alleged crime, or **when arrested while committing a breach or disturbance of the public peace**, is armed with or has on his person the following:
2.	A billy or <u>other dangerous weapon other than those herein mentioned</u> (not on the above list of specific weapons)" The Courts have interpreted the "dangerous weapon" term in the second portion to refer to the common law definition; Under the common law of Massachusetts, dangerous weapons include those objects that are: 1. **Dangerous per se**--"designed and constructed to produce death or great bodily harm" and "for the purpose of bodily assault or defense," 2. **Dangerous as used**--items that are not dangerous per se but "become dangerous weapons because they 'are used in a dangerous fashion.' See notes below.
Arrest Power, Penalties, & Notes	
Power of Arrest	**Felony** – a police officer may effect a warrantless arrest for this offense provided he/she has probable cause that the suspect committed the offense.
Penalty	Imprisonment for not less than 2½ years nor more than 5 years in the **state prison (F),** or for not less than 6 months nor more than 2½ years in a jail or house of correction. **Exception**: if the court finds that the defendant has not been previously convicted of a felony, he may be punished by a fine of not more than $50.00 or by imprisonment for not more than 2½ years in a jail or house of correction. **Subsequent Offenses – chapter 269 § 10(d):** Whoever, after having been convicted of any of the offenses set forth in paragraph (a), (b) or (c) (unlawful carrying of a firearm, rifle, shotgun, per se dangerous weapon, machine gun or sawed-off shotgun) commits a like offense or any other of the said offenses: **2nd Offense:** state prison for **not less than 5 years** nor more than 7 years; **3rd Offense**: state prison for **not less than 7 years** nor more than 10 years; **4th Offense**: state prison for **not less than 10 years** nor more than 15 years.
Attorney Hanrahan's Comment	The possession of a dangerous weapon **c. 269 § 10(b),** has two separate parts. The first part punishes the possession of a specifically listed dangerous weapon and provides a list of specific items that are prohibited (i.e. daggers, dirk knives, throwing stars etc). The second portion of 269 § 10(b) states "whoever, **when arrested upon a warrant** for an alleged crime, or **when arrested while committing a breach or disturbance of the public peace**, is armed with or has on his person ... a billy <u>or other dangerous weapon other than those herein mentioned</u>... shall be

punished…". The Courts have interpreted the "dangerous weapon" term in the second portion to refer to the common law definition;

Under the common law of Massachusetts, dangerous weapons include those objects that are:

1. **Dangerous per se**--"designed and constructed to produce death or great bodily harm" and "for the purpose of bodily assault or defense,"
2. **Dangerous as used**--items that are not dangerous per se but "become dangerous weapons because they are <u>used</u> in a dangerous fashion.' [1291]

"The essential question, when an object which is not dangerous per se is alleged to be a dangerous weapon, is whether the object, as used by the defendant, is capable of producing serious bodily harm."[1292]

Under the second portion of 169 § 10(b) a person carrying a Samurai sword, for instance, while placed under arrest for disturbing the peace could also be charged with 269 § 10(b) even though a Samurai sword is not specifically listed on the list of items because it would fit the common law definition (designed to inflict death or serious bodily harm) **AND** the suspect was arrest for a breach of the peace offense (or a warrant). However, simply carrying a Samurai sword when not arrested on a warrant or arrested for a breach of the peace would not violate this statute.

Case Law Note: *Commonwealth v. Turner*, 59 Mass. App. Ct.974 (2003), ruled that when arrested **on a warrant**, the arrestee must actually ***use*** a weapon (which is not dangerous *per se*) in order for this charge to apply. For instance, carrying a steak knife, alone, when arrested on a warrant would not violate this law because a steak knife is designed to cut steak, not inflict death or great bodily injury."

The *<u>use</u>* of the weapon is broadly interpreted. Carrying an item, intended for self defense, that is readily available, can be considered *used* for the purposes of this statute.[1293]

Case Example

In the 2014 case of ***Commonwealth v. Bradshaw***, the defendant, Christopher Bradshaw, sexually assaulted a young boy while visiting the boy's mother. A warrant was issued for his arrest and Det. Beth Halloran of the Cambridge Police Department contacted Bradshaw and asked to meet with him and discuss "some paperwork." Bradshaw chose the location and asked to meet the detective alone. The two were familiar with each other as they had met and spoken during the investigation.

Bradshaw arrived at the chosen location and approached Det. Halloran and informed her to keep walking. When Halloran asked where they were walking to Bradshaw indicated that they were going to the train tracks. At this point, another detective approached and the two detectives took Bradshaw to the ground. The detectives noticed a large knife protruding from the backpack that Bradshaw was wearing. The knife was later identified as a large kitchen knife, measuring more than 14", with a 9" blade. Bradshaw never held the knife during the incident. He was charged, and later convicted of, with carrying a dangerous weapon. He argued that a kitchen knife was not inherently dangerous.

The Court stated Bradshaw "is correct that merely carrying a kitchen knife, without more, would not be prohibited by the statute." But, "the manner in which the defendant carried the knife and the circumstances surrounding his carrying the knife defeat any suggestion that he was doing so with an innocent purpose." He had positioned a large kitchen knife such that its handle was protruding from the top of his backpack, both making it visible and providing the defendant easy access to an unsheathed knife even without removing the backpack he was wearing. He was planning on meeting a police officer, at a remote location of his choosing, and in his belief the officer would be alone.

The Court stated "under the circumstances, even though the defendant never wielded the knife, there was sufficient evidence for the jury to conclude that the defendant used the knife in a manner that was capable of causing serious harm, placing him within the ambit of the statute."

[1291] Commonwealth v, Turner, 59 Mass.App.ct. 825, 827 (2003), quoting from Commonwealth v. Thompson, 15 Mass.App.Ct. 974, 971 (1983)
[1292] Commonwealth v. Marrero, 19 Mass. App. Ct. 921, 922 (1984).
[1293] Commonwealth v. Bradshaw, Appeals Court (2014).

C. 269 § 10(b) CARRYING A DANGEROUS WEAPON

Related Statutes, Case Law & Other Important Information

Arrested on a warrant	The arrest must have been made for the warrant, for the "other dangerous weapon" provision to apply. If the defendant is arrested, a non-listed dangerous weapon is found, and then the police discover a warrant is outstanding this statute will not apply.[1294]
Dirk Knife Defined	The leading case in Massachusetts on the definition of "dirk knife" is *Commonwealth v. Miller.*[1295] That case noted that Webster's Third New International Dictionary 642 (1971) defined a " 'dirk knife' as a 'clasp knife,' ... having a large blade like that of a dirk.' "  Currently, Webster's Third New International Dictionary 642 (2002) also defines "dirk knife" as a "clasp knife having a large blade like that of a dirk." "Dirk" is defined as "a long straight blade dagger ..." or "a short sword....". A "clasp knife" is, in turn, defined as "a large pocketknife the blade or blades of which fold or shut into the handle." Webster's Third New International Dictionary 416 (2002). However, in *Miller*, the Court ruled that intent of the law is to **prohibit weapons that are designed for stabbing** humans and the knife in *Miller*, although seemingly meeting the definition of a dirk knife was not prohibited. The knife was only 5 inched and the blade was not **tapered** for stabbing. The Court did state that they were <u>not</u> saying that a 5" blade could never be deemed a dangerous weapon.
Blade that locks into place	Under the provision regarding "a knife with a locking blade to be drawn at a locked position," a knife is not prohibited merely because it has a blade that locks into position. There must be an additional device or case that allows the blade to be drawn in the locked position.[1296]
Dagger Defined	A dagger is any blade of relatively short length primarily designed or modified for stabbing. This definition excludes common household items such as a steak knife which are designed primarily for utilitarian purposes.[1297] In the 2012 case of ***Commonwealth v. Garcia,*** the Appeals Court ruled that a weapon referred to as a "pimp cane" with a long thin knife type weapon concealed inside to be a dagger.
Forfeiture of weapon **c. 269 § 10(e)**	Upon conviction of a violation of c. 269 §10, the firearm or other article shall, unless otherwise ordered by the court, be confiscated by the commonwealth. The firearm or article so confiscated shall, by the authority of the written order of the court be forwarded by common carrier to the colonel of the state police, who, upon receipt of the same, shall notify said court or justice thereof. Said **colonel may sell or destroy the same**, except that any firearm which may not be lawfully sold in the commonwealth shall be destroyed, and in the case of a sale, after paying the cost of forwarding the article, shall pay over the net proceeds to the commonwealth. Chapter **269 § 10(f) provides an exception to the forfeiture requirement for a lost or stolen weapon:** "the court shall, if the firearm or other article was lost by or stolen from the person lawfully in possession of it, order its return to such person."
Manufacturing and selling knives, slung shots, swords, bludgeons and similar weapons	Chapter 269 § 12 prohibits the manufacture and sale of certain non-firearm weapons: "whoever manufactures or causes to be manufactured, or sells or exposes for sale, an instrument or weapon of the kind usually known as: • a dirk knife, a switch knife or any knife having an automatic spring release device by which the blade is released from the handle, having a blade of over one and one-half inches or a device or case which enables a knife with a locking blade to be drawn at a locked position, any ballistic knife, or any knife with a detachable blade capable of being propelled by any mechanism, • slung shot, sling shot, bean blower,

[1294] Commonwealth v. Ford, Appeals Court (2014)
[1295] Commonwealth v. Miller, 22 Mass.App.Ct. 694 (1986).
[1296] Commonwealth v. Higgins, Appeals Court (2014)
[1297] Commonwealth v. Ismael Garcia, the Appeals Court (2012).

C. 269 § 10(b)	CARRYING A DANGEROUS WEAPON
	• sword cane, pistol cane, bludgeon, blackjack, • nunchaku, zoobow, also known as klackers or kung fu sticks, or any similar weapon consisting of two sticks of wood, plastic or metal connected at one end by a length of rope, chain, wire or leather, • a shuriken or any similar pointed starlike object intended to injure a person when thrown, or a manrikigusari or similar length of chain having weighted ends; • metallic knuckles or knuckles of any other substance which could be put to the same use and with the same or similar effect as metallic knuckles, shall be punished as follows: **Penalty:** a fine of not less than $50 nor more than $1,000 or by imprisonment for not more than 6 months. **Arrest powers**: **Misdemeanor** – there is no statutory authority granting powers of arrest for this offense. However, if the offense is committed in public, in the officer's presence, and is creating a **breach of the peace** an arrest would be lawful. **Exception:** sling shots may be manufactured and sold to clubs or associations conducting sporting events where such sling shots are used. **Attorney Hanrahan's Note**: Oddly, this list is not the exact same as the per se list of dangerous weapons in c. 269 § 10(b).
City ordinance	Some cities/towns prohibit the carrying of certain knives and weapons not listed under the state statute. For instance, the City of Salem prohibits the carrying of knives with a blade over 2.5 inches. In some cities/towns the carrying of these prohibited weapons may even subject the carrier to arrest (via. C. 272 § 59). Refer to the particular ordinance before taking action.
Defense spray c. 140 § 122C	A person under 18 years of age who possesses self-defense spray and who does not have a firearms identification card shall be punished by a fine of not more than $300.

C. 269 § 10(j)	CARRYING DANGEROUS WEAPONS ON SCHOOL GROUNDS
	Elements
1.	The defendant, not being a law enforcement officer,
2.	Carries on his person a firearm (loaded or unloaded) or other dangerous weapon,
3.	In any building or on the grounds of any elementary or secondary school (i.e. high school level), college or university,
4.	Without the written authorization of the board or officer in charge of the school.
	Arrest Power, Penalties & Notes
Power of Arrest	**Firearm (as defined by statute) - misdemeanor** – a police officer may effect a warrantless arrest for this offense provided he/she has probable cause that the suspect committed the offense. **Non-firearm weapon - misdemeanor** – there is no statutory authority granting powers of arrest for this misdemeanor version of this offense unless it involves a specialized form of A&B (e.g. involves domestic violence, victim is in a protected class, etc.). However, if the offense is committed in public, in the officer's presence, and is creating a **breach of the peace** an arrest would be lawful.

C. 269 § 10(j)	CARRYING DANGEROUS WEAPONS ON SCHOOL GROUNDS
Penalty	A fine of not more than $1,000 or by imprisonment for not more than 2 years, or both.
Attorney Hanrahan's Comment	This law applies to anyone who is not a law enforcement officer (and the statute does not define that term), even if otherwise properly licensed. Also, the law's definition of a firearm includes a weapon capable of discharging a pellet, which would seemingly cover pellet and paintball guns.
Related Statutes, Case Law & Other Important Information	
"Other Dangerous Weapon"	In the 2011 case of ***Commonwealth v. Wynton W., a juvenile,*** the SJC ruled that when the legislature fails to include a definition of a term in the statute (as it failed to define dangerous weapon in this statute) the court will presume that they intended the common law definition (**note:** the term common law refers law developed by the courts through their previous court decisions or the ancient law of England based on customs and practices). Under the common law of Massachusetts, dangerous weapons include those objects that are: 1. **Dangerous per se**--"designed and constructed to produce death or great bodily harm" and "for the purpose of bodily assault or defense," or 2. **Dangerous as used**--items that are not dangerous per se but become dangerous weapons because they are used in a dangerous fashion. Case Facts: On April 1, 2009, Officer Michael Gough of the Marlborough police department was dispatched to Assabet Valley Regional High School on a report that a student, the juvenile, had been found in possession of a knife. When Officer Gough met with the juvenile in the dean's office, the juvenile admitted that the knife in question was his and that his father had given it to him three days before on the occasion of his sixteenth birthday. The knife had fallen out of his pocket in shop class and had been seen on the floor by the instructor who reported the juvenile to the dean. The knife was a small folding knife with a blade approximately two inches long with a black plastic and metal handle. The juvenile's father confirmed for Officer Gough that the knife had indeed been a recent birthday present. The SJC ruled that because the knife did not meet the common law definition it did not violate the statute.
Firearm	The statute provides a definition for a firearm so you must base this offense on this definition: "for the purpose of this paragraph, "firearm" shall mean any pistol, revolver, rifle or smoothbore arm from which a shot, bullet or **<u>pellet</u>** can be discharged by whatever means."
Failure to Report Violation	Any officer in charge of an elementary or secondary school, college or university or any faculty member or administrative officer of an elementary or secondary school, college or university failing to report violations of this paragraph shall be guilty of a **misdemeanor** and punished by a fine of not more than $500. No right of arrest.

C. 269 § 12F(b)	ENTERING A SECURE AREA OF AN AIRPORT WITH WEAPON
Elements	
1.	The defendant occupies, or attempts to enter or occupy, a secure area of an airport or the cabin of an airplane,
2.	Knowingly having in his possession or in his control and knowingly concealing, • a cutting device, or • a prohibited weapon, notwithstanding any license to possess such a weapon or device.
Arrest Power, Penalties & Notes	
Power of Arrest	**Felony** – a police officer may effect a warrantless arrest for this offense provided he/she has probable cause that the suspect committed the offense.
Penalty	Imprisonment in the HOC for not more than 2½ years or by imprisonment in the **state prison (F)** for not more than 5 years or by a fine of not more than $5,000, or by both such fine and imprisonment.
Related Statutes, Case Law & Other Important Information	
Entering a secure area of an airport w/weapon with intent to commit a felony c. 269 § 12F(c)	The defendant, with intent to commit a felony, occupies, or attempts to enter or occupy, a secure area of an airport or the cabin of an airplane knowingly having in his possession or in his control a cutting device or a prohibited weapon. **Penalty:** imprisonment in the HOC for not more than 2 years or by imprisonment in the **state prison (F)** for not more than 10 years or by a fine of not more than $10,000, or by both such fine and imprisonment. Attorney Hanrahan's Note: the slight difference between this offense and §12F(b) above is that this offense does not require that the weapon be concealed and 12F(b) does not require a specific intent to commit a felony.
Placing a weapon in a secure area c. 269 § 12F(d)	The defendant, with intent to commit a felony, places, attempts to place or attempts to have placed within a secure area of an airport or the cabin of an airplane, a prohibited weapon or cutting device, notwithstanding any license to possess such a weapon or device. **Penalty:** imprisonment in the HOC for not more than 2½ years or by imprisonment in the **state prison (F)** for not more than 10 years or by a fine of not more than $10,000, or by both such fine and imprisonment.
Additional Penalties	Whoever willfully and without regard for the safety of human life, or with reckless disregard for the safety of human life, violates subsection (b), (c) or (d) shall be punished by imprisonment in the **state prison (F)** for not more than 20 years or by a fine of not more than $20,000, or by both such fine and imprisonment.
Possession or placement of a cutting device or prohibited weapon at an airport definitions & Exceptions	**Exemptions:** This section shall not apply to: 1) Any law enforcement officer of a state or political subdivision of a state, an officer or employee of the United States government or United States military personnel authorized to carry prohibited weapons or cutting devices in an official capacity; 2) A duly licensed individual transporting an unloaded, lawful weapon or cutting device in baggage not accessible to a passenger in flight and, in the case of a lawful weapon, if the air carrier was informed of the presence of the weapon; 3) A cutting device, which is otherwise lawfully possessed, ordinarily used in the course of the holder's employment, trade or occupation, while the holder is authorized to conduct such employment, trade or occupation within a secure area of an airport or airplane cabin.

WEAPON VIOLATIONS

C. 269 § 12F(b)	ENTERING A SECURE AREA OF AN AIRPORT WITH WEAPON
Definitions	For the purposes of this section, the following words shall have the following meanings:— **"Airplane",** an aircraft operated by an air carrier holding a certificate issued under 49 U.S.C. 41101 or any aircraft ordinarily used to transport passengers or cargo for hire. **"Cutting device",** any knife, cutlery, straight razor, box cutter or other device containing a fixed, folding or retractable blade, which is not included in the list of weapons set forth in paragraph (b) of section 10. **"Prohibited weapon",** any infernal machine as defined in section 102A of c. 266, any stun gun as defined in section 131J of c. 140, any rifle, shotgun or firearm as defined in section 121 of c. 140 or any weapon included in the list of weapons set forth in paragraph (b) of section 10. **"Secure area",** any area of an airport to which access is restricted through security measures by the airport authority or a public agency and the area beyond a passenger or property screening checkpoint at an airport. "Airplane cabin", **any passenger or flight crew area within an airplane while the airplane is on the ground in the commonwealth or over the commonwealth.**

TRANSPORTATION OF FIREARMS

c. 269 § 10I	UNLAWFUL TRANSPORTATION OF A FIREARM
	Elements
Transportation into Mass. to *use* in Mass.	Whoever transports a firearm, rifle, shotgun, machine gun or sawed-off shotgun into the commonwealth to **use the weapon for the commission of criminal activity** shall be punished by imprisonment in the state prison for not less than 5 years nor more than 10 years.
Transportation into Mass. to *unlawfully distribute*	Whoever transports a firearm, rifle, shotgun, machine gun or sawed-off shotgun into the commonwealth to **unlawfully distribute, sell or transfer possession** of the weapon **to a prohibited person**, as defined in chapter 140 § 131, shall be punished by imprisonment in the state prison for not less than 10 years nor more than 20 years.
Transportation into Mass. to *unlawfully distribute and causes death*	Whoever transports a firearm, rifle, shotgun, machine gun or sawed-off shotgun into the commonwealth to **unlawfully distribute**, sell or transfer the weapon to a prohibited person, as defined in chapter 140 § 131, and if the weapon is **subsequently used to cause the death** of another, shall be punished by imprisonment in the state prison for not less than 20 years.
	Arrest Power & Notes
Power of Arrest	**Felony** – a police officer may effect a warrantless arrest for this offense provided he/she has probable cause that the suspect committed the offense.
Prohibited person c. 140 § 131	The actual definition of a prohibited person can be found in the Firearm licensing section of this manual. However, in summary, a prohibited person is someone who would not qualify for a License to Carry.

POSSESSION (i.e. non-carrying) OFFENSES: note these offense do not require public "carrying".

C. 269 § 10(h)(1)	UNLAWFUL *POSSESION or TRANFER*: FIREARM, RIFLE, SHOTGUN, or AMMUNITION
	Elements
1.	The defendant owns, possesses or transfers,
2.	A firearm, rifle, shotgun or ammunition,
3.	Without complying with the provisions of c. 140 § 129C
	Arrest Power, Penalties & Notes
Power of Arrest	**Misdemeanor:** Any officer authorized to make arrests may arrest without a warrant any person whom the officer has probable cause to believe has violated this provision.
Penalty	Imprisonment in a jail or house of correction for not more than 2 years or by a fine of not more than $500. **2nd or subsequent violation** of this paragraph shall be punished by imprisonment in a house of correction for not more than 2 years or by a fine of not more than $1,000, or both.
Attorney Hanrahan's Comment	This offense covers those who possess firearms, rifles shotguns without a license while within the confines of their home. If they are in public the *carrying* charge should be used. This offense also covers the unlawful possession of ammunition (anywhere) and the unlawful transfer of these items.
	Related Statutes, Case Law & Other Important Information
Ammunition Defined	For purposes of this section, "ammunition" shall mean cartridges or cartridge cases, primers (igniter), bullets or propellant powder designed for use in any firearm, rifle or shotgun.
Cartridge Casings	In the 2010 case of ***Commonwealth v. Truong,*** the court ruled that possession of cartridge casings themselves is illegal under G.L. c. 269, § 10(h). The court noted, however, that it was not reaching the question of whether possession of casings for certain purposes, e.g., souvenirs, scrap metal, etc., was also illegal under the statute.
Mace and OC products no longer covered	In 2006 the legislature added the definition of ammunition to 269 § 10(n) (above) previously the court would look to chapter 140 for the ammunition definition. The court will no longer look to chapter 140 for the definition of ammunition because of this. This definition, as you can see, does not include **mace and OC type products**.
Loaded weapon	In the 2011 case of ***Com. v. Johnson,*** the SJC ruled that a defendant cannot be convicted of both possession of a loaded firearm and possession of ammunition if the ammunition used to convict the defendant for possession of ammunition is the same ammunition to convict him of possession of a loaded weapon.
Important Information	Be sure to review the previous section on unlawful *carrying* a firearm, particularly the exemptions for those traveling through Massachusetts and those who are in, or retired from, Law Enforcement.
Nonresident exemption	See Chapter 141 § 129C in the firearm licensing section of this manual for nonresident exemptions.

UNLAWFUL PURCHASSE/POSSESSION OF DEFENSE SPRAY

Under 18 c. 140 § 122C	A person under 18 years of age who possesses self-defense spray and who does not have a firearms identification card shall be punished by a fine of not more than $300. No right of arrest but would be arrestable if it involved a breach of the peace and was committed in the officer's presence.
Disqualified person c. 140 § 122D	Whoever purchases or possesses self-defense spray in violation of this section (see disqualifications listed below) shall be punished by a fine of not more than $1,000 or by imprisonment in a house of correction for not more than 2 years or both such fine and imprisonment. No right of arrest but would be arrestable if it involved a breach of the peace and was committed in the officer's presence.
Arrest power	**Misdemeanor** – there is no statutory authority granting powers of arrest for this offense. However, if the offense is committed in public, in the officer's presence, and is creating a **breach of the peace** an arrest would be lawful.

DISQUALIFICATIONS

Crime within Massachusetts	In a court of the commonwealth, the person has been convicted or adjudicated a youthful offender or delinquent child as defined in section 52 of chapter 119 for the commission of: a. a felony; b. a misdemeanor punishable by imprisonment for more than 2 years; c. a violent crime as defined in section 121; d. a violation of a law regulating the use, possession, ownership, transfer, purchase, sale, lease, rental, receipt or transportation of weapons or ammunition for which a term of imprisonment may be imposed; or e. a violation of a law regulating the use, possession or sale of a controlled substance as defined in section 1 of chapter 94C including, but not limited to, a violation under said chapter 94C; provided, however, that except for the commission of a violent crime or a crime involving the trafficking of controlled substances, if the person has been so convicted or adjudicated or released from confinement, probation or parole supervision for such conviction or adjudication, whichever occurs last, for 5 or more years immediately preceding the purchase or possession, that person may purchase or possess self-defense spray;
Crime outside of Massachusetts	In another state or federal jurisdiction, the person has been convicted or adjudicated a youthful offender or delinquent child for the commission of: a. a felony; b. a misdemeanor punishable by imprisonment for more than 2 years; c. a violent crime as defined in section 121; d. a violation of a law regulating the use, possession, ownership, transfer, purchase, sale, lease, rental, receipt or transportation of weapons or ammunition for which a term of imprisonment may be imposed; or e. a violation of a law regulating the use, possession or sale of a controlled substance as defined in section 1 of chapter 94C; provided, however, that, except for the commission of a violent crime or a crime involving the trafficking of weapons or controlled substances, if the person has been so convicted or adjudicated or released from confinement, probation or parole supervision for such conviction or adjudication, whichever occurs last, for 5 or more years immediately preceding the purchase or possession and that applicant's right or ability to possess a rifle or shotgun has been fully restored in the jurisdiction wherein the subject conviction or adjudication was entered, then

UNLAWFUL PURCHASSE/POSSESSION OF DEFENSE SPRAY	
	that person may purchase or possess self-defense spray;
Mental illness	The person has been **committed to any hospital or institution for mental illness** unless the person obtains, prior to purchase or possession, an affidavit of a licensed physician or clinical psychologist attesting that such physician or psychologist is familiar with the applicant's mental illness and that in the physician's or psychologist's opinion the applicant is not disabled by such an illness in a manner that shall prevent the applicant from possessing self-defense spray;
Substance abuse	The person is or has been in recovery from or committed based upon a finding that the person is a person with an alcohol use disorder or a substance use disorder or both unless a licensed physician or clinical psychologist deems such person to be in recovery from such condition, in which case, such person may purchase or possess self-defense spray after 5 years from the date of such confinement or recovery; provided, however, that prior to such purchase or possession of self-defense spray, the applicant shall submit an affidavit issued by a licensed physician or clinical psychologist attesting that such physician or psychologist knows the person's history of treatment and that in that physician's or psychologist's opinion the applicant is in recovery;
Under 15	The person is at the time of the application (for an FID), is younger than 15 years of age;
Between 15 and 18 need parent permission	At the time of the application (for and FID), the person is at least 15 years of age but less than 18 years of age unless the applicant submits with the application a certificate from the applicant's parent or guardian granting the applicant permission to apply for a card;
Alien	The person is an alien who does not maintain lawful permanent residency or is an alien not residing under a visa pursuant to 8 U.S.C § 1101 (a)(15)(U), or is an alien not residing under a visa pursuant to 8 U.S.C. § 1154 (a)(1)(B)(ii)(I) or is an alien not residing under a visa pursuant to 8 U.S.C. § 1101 (a)(15)(T)(i)(I)-(IV);
Protective order	The person is currently subject to: 1. an order for suspension or surrender issued pursuant to section 3B or 3C of chapter 209A or section 7 of chapter 258E; or 2. a permanent or temporary protection order issued pursuant to chapter 209A or section 7 of chapter 258E; or
Warrant	The person is currently the subject of an outstanding arrest warrant in any state or federal jurisdiction.

C. 269 § 10(C)	UNLAWFUL POSSESSION OF A MACHINE GUN
Elements	
1.	The defendant unlawfully possesses a machine gun, as defined in c. 140 § 121,
2.	Without authority under C. 140 § 131 (must be a **bona fide collector** or a **Law Enforcement Instructor**).
Arrest Power, Penalties & Notes	
Power of Arrest	**Felony** – a police officer may effect a warrantless arrest for this offense provided he/she has probable cause that the suspect committed the offense.
Penalty	**1st offense**: **state prison (F)** for life, or for any term of years provided that any sentence imposed under the provisions of this paragraph shall be subject to the minimum requirements of paragraph (a) **(18 months)**. **2nd offense:** state prison for **not less than 5 years** nor more than 7 years; **3rd offense**: state prison for **not less than 7 years** nor more than 10 years; **4th offense**: state prison for **not less than 10 years** nor more than 15 years. **No Suspended sentences or Probation:** The sentence imposed upon a person, who after a conviction of an offense under paragraph (a), (b) or (c) of chapter 269 commits the same or a like offense, shall not be suspended, nor shall any person so sentenced be eligible for probation or receive any deduction from his sentence for good conduct.
Other Important Information	
Machine Gun Defined	"Machine gun", a weapon of any description, by whatever name known, loaded or unloaded, from which a number of shots or bullets may be rapidly or automatically discharged by one continuous activation of the trigger, including a submachine gun.
Additional Crime if machine gun is loaded **c. 269 s 10(n)**	Chapter 269 § 10(n) states whoever violates paragraph (a) – carrying firearm/rifle/shotgun, or paragraph (c) – possession of machine gun, by means of a loaded firearm, loaded sawed off shotgun or loaded machine gun shall be **further** punished by imprisonment in the house of correction for not more than 2½ years, which sentence shall begin from and after the expiration of the sentence for the violation of paragraph (a) or paragraph (c). **Note:** For purposes of this section, loaded shall mean that ammunition is contained in the weapon or within a feeding device attached thereto.

C. 269 § 10(C)	UNLAWFUL POSSESSION OF A SAWED-OFF SHOTGUN
	Elements
1.	The defendant owns, possesses or carries on his person, or carries on his person or under his control in a vehicle,
2.	A sawed-off shotgun, as defined in c. 140 § 121.
	Arrest Power, Penalties & Notes
Power of Arrest	**Felony** – a police officer may effect a warrantless arrest for this offense provided he/she has probable cause that the suspect committed the offense.
Penalty	1st **offense**: **state prison (F)** for life, or for any term of years provided that any sentence imposed under the provisions of this paragraph shall be subject to the minimum requirements of paragraph (a) **(18 months**). 2nd **offense:** state prison for **not less than 5 years** nor more than 7 years; 3rd **offense**: state prison for **not less than 7 years** nor more than 10 years; 4th **offense**: state prison for **not less than 10 years** nor more than 15 years. **No Suspended sentences or Probation:** The sentence imposed upon a person, who after a conviction of an offense under paragraph (a), (b) or (c) of chapter 269 commits the same or a like offense, shall not be suspended, nor shall any person so sentenced be eligible for probation or receive any deduction from his sentence for good conduct.
	Other Important Information
Sawed-off shotgun	"Sawed-off shotgun", any weapon made from a shotgun, whether by alteration, modification or otherwise, if such weapon as modified has one or more barrels less than 18 inches in length or as modified has an overall length of less than 26 inches.
Additional Crime if saw-off shotgun is loaded **c. 269 s 10(n)**	Chapter 269 § 10(n) states whoever violates paragraph (a) – carrying firearm/rifle/shotgun, or paragraph (c) – possession of machine gun, by means of a loaded firearm, loaded sawed off shotgun or loaded machine gun shall be **further** punished by imprisonment in the house of correction for not more than 2½ years, which sentence shall begin from and after the expiration of the sentence for the violation of paragraph (a) or paragraph (c). **Note:** For purposes of this section, loaded shall mean that ammunition is contained in the weapon or within a feeding device attached thereto.

C. 140 § 131M	UNLAWFUL POSSESSION OF AN ASSAULT WEAPON or LARGE CAPACITY FEEDING DEVICE
Elements	
1.	No person shall sell, offer for sale, transfer or possess an **assault weapon** or a **large capacity feeding device** that was not otherwise lawfully possessed on September 13, 1994.
Exception	The provisions of this section shall not apply to: (i) the possession by **a law enforcement officer**; or (ii) the possession by an individual who is **retired from service with a law enforcement agency** and is not otherwise prohibited from receiving such a weapon or feeding device from such agency upon retirement.
Arrest Power, Penalties & Notes	
Power of Arrest	**Felony** – a police officer may effect a warrantless arrest for this offense provided he/she has probable cause that the suspect committed the offense.
Penalty	1st offense: a fine of not less than $1,000 nor more than $10,000 or by imprisonment for not less than 1 year nor more than 10 years, or by both such fine and imprisonment, and for a second offense, by a fine of not less than $5,000 nor more than $15,000 or by imprisonment for not less than 5 years nor more than 15 years, or by both such fine and imprisonment.
Attorney Hanrahan's Comment	Review definitions section in the firearms licensing section of this manual for a more detailed explanation of assault weapons and large capacity feeding devices.
Related Statutes, Case Law & Other Important Information	
Assault Weapon Defined c. 140 § 121	"Assault weapon", shall have the same meaning as a semiautomatic assault weapon as defined in the federal Public Safety and Recreational Firearms Use Protection Act, 18 U.S.C. section 921(a)(30) as appearing in such section on September 13, 1994, and shall include, but not be limited to, any of the weapons, or copies or duplicates of the weapons, of any caliber, known as: (i) Avtomat Kalashnikov (AK) (all models); (ii) Action Arms Israeli Military Industries UZI and Galil; (iii) Beretta Ar70 (SC-70); (iv) Colt AR-15; (v) Fabrique National FN/FAL, FN/LAR and FNC; (vi) SWD M-10, M-11, M-11/9 and M-12; (vi) Steyr AUG; (vii) INTRATEC TEC-9, TEC-DC9 and TEC-22; and (viii) revolving cylinder shotguns, such as, or similar to, the Street Sweeper and Striker 12; provided, however, that the term assault weapon shall not include: (i) any of the weapons, or replicas or duplicates of such weapons, specified in appendix A to 18 U.S.C. section 922 as appearing in such appendix on September 13, 1994, as such weapons were manufactured on October 1, 1993; (ii) any weapon that is operated by manual bolt, pump, lever or slide action; (iii) any weapon that has been rendered permanently inoperable or otherwise rendered permanently unable to be designated a semiautomatic assault weapon; (iv) any weapon that was manufactured prior to the year 1899; (v) any weapon that is an antique or relic, theatrical prop or other weapon that is not capable of firing a projectile and which is not intended for use as a functional weapon and cannot be readily modified through a combination of available parts into an operable assault weapon; (vi) any semiautomatic rifle that cannot accept a detachable magazine that holds more than five rounds of ammunition; or (vii) any semiautomatic shotgun that cannot hold more than five rounds of ammunition in a fixed or detachable magazine.
Large capacity feeding device c. 140 § 121	"Large capacity feeding device", (i) a fixed or detachable magazine, box, drum, feed strip or similar device capable of accepting, or that can be readily converted to accept, more than ten rounds of ammunition or more than five shotgun shells; or (ii) a large capacity ammunition feeding device as defined in the federal Public Safety and Recreational Firearms Use Protection Act, 18 U.S.C. section 921(a)(31) as appearing in such section on September 13, 1994. The term "large capacity feeding device" shall not include an attached tubular device designed to accept, and capable of operating only with, .22 caliber ammunition.

C. 140 § 131J	POSSESSION/SALE OF ELECTRICAL WEAPONS (STUN GUNS)
Elements	
Possession Prohibited	No person shall possess a portable device or weapon from which an electrical current, impulse, wave or beam may be directed, which current, impulse, wave or beam is designed to incapacitate temporarily, injure or kill.
Sales Prohibited	No person shall sell or offer for sale such device or weapon, except to federal, state or municipal law enforcement agencies. A device or weapon sold under this section shall include a mechanism for tracking the number of times the device or weapon has been fired.
Exception: these persons and entities may lawfully possess	(1) a federal, state or municipal law enforcement officer, or member of a special reaction team in a state prison or designated special operations or tactical team in a county correctional facility, acting in the discharge of his official duties who has completed a training course approved by the secretary of public safety in the use of such a devise or weapon designed to incapacitate temporarily; or (2) a supplier of such devices or weapons designed to incapacitate temporarily, if possession of the device or weapon is necessary to the supply or sale of the device or weapon within the scope of such sale or supply enterprise.
Arrest Power, Penalties & Notes	
Power of Arrest	**Misdemeanor** – A law enforcement officer may arrest without a warrant any person whom he has probable cause to believe has violated this section.
Penalty	A fine of not less than $500 nor more than $1,000 or by imprisonment in the HOC for not less than 6 months nor more than 2½ years, or by both such fine and imprisonment
2nd Amendment	In the 2015 case of *Com. v. Caetano*, the SJC ruled that the ban on stun guns does not violate the 2nd Amendment.

C. 140 § 131N	COVERT WEAPONS; SALE, TRANSFER OR POSSESSION
Elements	
1.	No person shall sell, offer for sale, transfer or possess,
2.	Any weapon, capable of discharging a bullet or shot, that is: (i) Constructed in a shape that does not resemble a handgun, short-barreled rifle or short-barreled shotgun including, but not limited to, covert weapons that resemble key-chains, pens, cigarette-lighters or cigarette-packages; or (ii) Not detectable as a weapon or potential weapon by x-ray machines commonly used at airports or walk-through metal detectors.
Arrest Power, Penalties & Notes	
Power of Arrest	**Felony** – a police officer may effect a warrantless arrest for this offense provided he/she has probable cause that the suspect committed the offense.
Penalty	**1st Offense**: a fine of not less than $1,000 nor more than $10,000 or by imprisonment for not less than 1 year nor more than 10 years, or by both such fine and imprisonment. **2nd Offense**: a fine of not less than $5,000 nor more than $15,000 or by imprisonment for not less than 5 years nor more than 15 years, or by both such fine and imprisonment.
Attorney Hanrahan's Note	There is no exception to this provision. For instance, even law enforcement personnel would be precluded from possessing one of these weapons.

C. 265 § 58	POSSESSION OF A DECEPTIVE WEAPON DEVICE
Elements	
Deceptive Device	Any person who is in possession of a deceptive weapon device as defined in chapter 140 § 121 during the commission of a violent crime as defined in said chapter 140 § 121 shall be deemed to be armed and shall be punishable by penalties set forth in chapter 265.
Arrest Power, Penalties & Notes	
Power of Arrest	**Felony** – a police officer may effect a warrantless arrest for this offense provided he/she has probable cause that the suspect committed the offense.
Penalty	The penalty is dependent upon the underlying violent crime.
Deceptive Weapon Device § 121	"Deceptive weapon device", any device that is intended to convey the presence of a rifle, shotgun or firearm that is used in the commission of a violent crime, as defined in § 121, and which presents an objective threat of immediate death or serious bodily harm to a person of reasonable and average sensibility.
Violent Crime definition according to c. 140 § 121	"Violent crime", shall mean any crime punishable by imprisonment for a term exceeding one year, or any act of juvenile delinquency involving the use or possession of a deadly weapon that would be punishable by imprisonment for such term if committed by an adult, that: (i) has as an element the use, attempted use or threatened use of physical force or a deadly weapon against the person of another; (ii) is burglary, extortion, arson or kidnapping; (iii) involves the use of explosives; or (iv) otherwise involves conduct that presents a serious risk of physical injury to another.

C. 269 § 10A	POSSESSION/SALE/USE OF SILENCERS
	Elements
1.	The defendant, • sells or keeps for sale, or offers, or gives or disposes of by any means other than submitting to an authorized law enforcement agency, or • uses or possesses
2.	Any instrument, attachment, weapon or appliance for causing the firing of any gun, revolver, pistol or other firearm to be silent or intended to lessen or muffle the noise of the firing of any gun, revolver, pistol or other firearm.
Exception	This law does not apply to: • A federally licensed firearms manufacturer, • An authorized agent of the Municipal Police Training Committee, or • A duly authorized sworn law enforcement officer while acting within the scope of official duties and under the direct authorization of the police chief or his designee, or the colonel of the state police.
	Arrest Power, Penalties & Notes
Power of Arrest	**Felony** – a police officer may effect a warrantless arrest for this offense provided he/she has probable cause that the suspect committed the offense.
Penalty	By imprisonment for not more than 5 years in **state prison (F)** or for not more than 2½ years in a jail or HOC.
	Related Statutes, Case Law & Other Important Information
Federally Licensed dealers may sell to Law Enforcement	Nothing contained herein shall be construed to prohibit a federally licensed firearms manufacturer from selling such instrument, attachment, weapon or appliance to authorized law enforcement agencies for law enforcement purposes or to the municipal police training committee for law enforcement training.
Confiscation of Silencer	Upon conviction of a violation of this section, the instrument, attachment or other article shall be confiscated by the commonwealth and forwarded, by the authority of the written order of the court, to the colonel of the state police, who shall destroy said article.

C. 269 § 11C	POSSESSION OF A FIREARM WITHOUT A SERIAL NUMBER
Elements	
1.	The defendant receives a firearm
2.	With knowledge that its serial number or identification number has been removed, defaced, altered, obliterated or mutilated in any manner.
Arrest Power, Penalties & Notes	
Power of Arrest	**Misdemeanor** – there is no statutory authority granting warrantless powers of arrest for this offense. However, if the offense is committed in public, in the officer's presence, and is creating a **breach of the peace** an arrest would be lawful.
Penalty	A fine of not more than $200 or by imprisonment for not less than one month nor more than 2½ years.
Related Statutes, Case Law & Other Important Information	
Definitions c. 269 § 11A	For the purposes of this section and §11B, §11C and §11D, the following words shall have the following meanings:— **"Firearm",** a firearm as defined in section chapter 140 § 121, or a rifle or shotgun. **"Serial number",** the number stamped or placed upon a firearm by the manufacturer in the original process of manufacture. **"Identification number",** the number stamped or placed upon a firearm by the colonel of the state police under authority of section 11D.
Possession of firearm w/number mutilated, during a felony c. 269 § 11B	The defendant, while in the commission or attempted commission of a felony, has in his possession or under his control a firearm the serial number or identification number of which has been removed, defaced, altered, obliterated or mutilated in any manner. **Penalty**: imprisonment in the **state prison (F)** for not less than 2½ nor more than five years, or in a jail or HOC for not less than six months nor more than 2½ years. **Arrest Powers**: **Felony** – a police officer may effect an arrest for this offense committed in his/her presence or for an offense in the past, on probable cause. **Destruction of Weapon**: Upon a conviction of a violation of this section, said firearm or other article, by the authority of the written order of the court, shall be forwarded to the colonel of the state police, who shall cause said weapon to be destroyed.
Removal or mutilation of serial or identification numbers of firearms c. 269 § 11C	The defendant, by himself or another, removes, defaces, alters, obliterates or mutilates in any manner the serial number or identification number of a firearm, or in any way participates therein. **Penalty:** by a fine of not more than $200 or by imprisonment for not less than 1 month nor more than 2½ years. **Arrest Powers**: **Misdemeanor** – there is no statutory authority granting powers of arrest for this offense. However, if the offense is committed in public, in the officer's presence, and is creating a **breach of the peace** an arrest would be lawful.

STORAGE OFFENSES

c. 140 § 131L	IMPROPER FIREARM STORAGE
	Elements
Requirements	It shall be unlawful to store or keep any firearm, rifle or shotgun including, but not limited to, large capacity weapons, or machine gun in any place unless such weapon is: a. Secured in a locked container. or b. Equipped with a tamper-resistant mechanical lock. or c. Equipped with some other safety device, properly engaged so as to render such weapon inoperable by any person other than the owner or other lawfully authorized user.
Under Control Exception	For purposes of this section, such **weapon shall not be deemed stored or kept if carried by or under the control** of the owner (see case law notes below) or other lawfully authorized user.
	Arrest Power, Penalties & Notes
Power of Arrest	**If the weapon is not large capacity or is not accessible to a person under 18: Misdemeanor** – there is no statutory authority granting powers of arrest for this offense. However, if the offense is committed in public, in the officer's presence, and is creating a **breach of the peace** an arrest would be lawful. **If weapon is accessible to person under 18 or if the weapon is a large capacity weapon: Felony** – a police officer may effect a warrantless arrest for this offense provided he/she has probable cause that the suspect committed the offense.
Penalties When Weapon Is <u>Not</u> <u>Accessible</u> to Person Under 18	**Non-Large Capacity Penalty:** A violation of this section shall be punished, in the case of a firearm, rifle or shotgun that is not a large capacity weapon, by a fine of not less than $1,000 nor more than $7,500 or by imprisonment for not more than 1½ years, or by both such fine and imprisonment. **Large Capacity weapon or Machine Gun Penalty:** by a fine of not less than $2,000 nor more than $15,000 or by imprisonment for not less than 1½ years nor more than 12 years, or by both such fine and imprisonment.
Penalties When Weapon <u>Is</u> <u>Accessible</u> to Person Under 18	**Non-large Capacity**: A violation of this section shall be punished, in the case of a rifle or shotgun that is not a large capacity weapon and such weapon was stored or kept in a place where a person under the age of 18 who does not possess a valid firearm identification card issued under section 129B may have access without committing an unforeseeable trespass, by a fine of not less than $2,500 nor more than $15,000 or by imprisonment for not less than 1 ½ years nor more than 12 years, or by both such fine and imprisonment. **Large Capacity**: A violation of this section shall be punished, in the case of a rifle or shotgun that is a large capacity weapon, firearm or machine gun was stored or kept in a place where a person under the age of 18 may have access, without committing an unforeseeable trespass, by a fine of not less than $10,000 nor more than $20,000 or by imprisonment for not less than 4 years, nor more than 15 years, or by both such fine and imprisonment.
Attorney Hanrahan's Comment	This offense has been strictly interpreted in recent months. Be sure t use extreme caution when your weapon is not on your person.
	Related Statutes, Case Law & Other Important Information
Wanton and Reckless Evidence	A violation of the provisions of this section shall be evidence of wanton or reckless conduct in any criminal or civil proceeding if a person under the age of 18 who was not a trespasser or was a foreseeable trespasser acquired access to a weapon, unless such person possessed a valid firearm identification card issued under section 129B and was permitted by law to possess such weapon, and such access results in the personal injury to or the death of any person.

c. 140 § 131L	IMPROPER FIREARM STORAGE
Exceptions for certain weapons	This section shall not apply to the storage or keeping of any firearm, rifle or shotgun with matchlock, flintlock, percussion cap or similar type of ignition system manufactured in or prior to the year 1899, or to any replica of any such firearm, rifle or shotgun if such replica is not designed or redesigned for using rimfire or conventional centerfire fixed ammunition.
Legislative Intent	Legislative history leaves no doubt that the measure was intended to prevent accidental injuries and deaths resulting from firearms falling into the hands of children and other unauthorized users, by criminalizing negligent storage.[1298]
"Under Control" Defined	In the 2011 case of ***Com. v. Patterson,*** the Appeals Court ruled that whether or not the firearm was under the control of the defendant is a case by case basis but consideration should be given to: (1) the firearm's location, (2) its proximity to the authorized user or owner, and (3) that person's ability to *immediately* reach the gun.
What qualifies as a secure container?	***Commonwealth v. Parzick***, the door lock that was easily defeatable by using "bobby pin" did not prevent access to unauthorized persons other than owner and therefore was "not secure."[1299] What qualifies as a securely locked container? At a minimum, to be secure, any qualifying container must be capable of being unlocked only by means of a key, combination, or other similar means.[1300] In ***Com. v. Reyes*** (2013), the SJC stated "statutory and regulatory references to acceptable containers include safes, weapon boxes, locked cabinets, gun cases, lock boxes, and locked trunks of vehicles. This is not to say that locked containers beyond those types referenced in statutes do not qualify as secure under the storage statute. Ultimately, the matter is one of fact for a properly instructed fact finder to determine at trial."
Federal Law	Federal law governing civil liability for unsafe firearm storage provides that "secure gun storage or safety device" means "a safe, gun safe, gun case, lock box, or other device that is designed to be or can be used to store a firearm and that is designed to be unlocked only by means of a key, a combination, or other similar means" (emphasis added). 18 U.S.C. § 921(a)(34)(C) (2006). A person in lawful possession of a handgun who uses one of these devices is entitled to immunity from a qualified civil liability action. See 18 U.S.C. § 922(z)(3)(A) (2006).
Unusual Container may suffice	***Comm. v. Lojko,*** the defendant stored his firearm in a cooler in his back yard. The cooler had a cable with a lock. The Court ruled that although it could be easily carried away it was still "secured in a locked container" as required by the statute.[1301]
Stored in a vehicle	In the 2013 case of ***Commonwealth v. Reyes***, the SJC upheld the conviction of a correction officer who stored his firearm in the *unlocked* glove box of his *locked* car. The SJC stated ": a locked glove box might qualify as a secure container depending on the particular factual circumstances including the nature of the locking mechanism, whether the motor vehicle was also locked and alarmed, and ultimately whether in the circumstances it was adequate to "deter all but the most persistent from gaining access."
Locked Home	In the 2013 case of ***Commonwealth v. Cantelli***, the Appeals Court upheld the improper storage conviction of the defendant who was home alone in his locked apartment but had licensed firearms strewn about the apartment outside of his reach. The police entered in response to a gas leak.

[1298] *Commonwealth v. Reyes,* (2013) SJC
[1299] Commonwealth v. Parzick, 64 Mass.App.Ct. 846, 850 (2005).
[1300] Com. v. Reyes, referencing 18 U.S.C. § 921(a)(34)(C) (2006) (requiring "secure gun storage or safety device" be designed to unlock only by means of key, combination, or other similar means).
[1301] *Comm. v. Lojko,* 77 Mass. App. Ct. 82 (2010).

C. 269 § 12E	DISCHARGE OF A FIREARM WITHIN 500 FEET OF A DWELLING OR OTHER BUILDING IN USE
Elements	
1.	The defendant discharges a firearm, a rifle or shotgun,
2.	Within 500 feet of a dwelling or other building in use
Exception	Discharge is permissible with the consent of the owner or legal occupant thereof. Additionally, the provisions of this section shall not apply to: a) the lawful defense of life and property; b) any law enforcement officer acting in the discharge of his duties; c) persons using underground or indoor target or test ranges with the consent of the owner or legal occupant thereof; d) persons using outdoor skeet, trap, target or test ranges with the consent of the owner or legal occupant of the land on which the range is established; e) persons using shooting galleries, licensed and defined under the provisions of chapter 140 § 56A; and f) the discharge of blank cartridges for theatrical, athletic, ceremonial, firing squad, or other purposes in accordance with section chapter 148 § 39.
Arrest Power, Penalties & Notes	
Power of Arrest	**Misdemeanor** – there is no statutory authority granting warrantless powers of arrest for this offense. However, if the offense is committed in public, in the officer's presence, and is creating a **breach of the peace** an arrest would be lawful.
Penalty	A fine of not less than $50.00 nor more than $100 or by imprisonment in a jail or HOC for not more than 3 months, or both.
Related Statutes, Case Law & Other Important Information	
Discharge Firearm or Release Arrow across Way C. 131 § 58	A person shall not discharge any firearm or release any arrow upon or across any state or hard surfaced highway, or within 150 feet, of any such highway, or possess a loaded firearm or hunt by any means on the land of another within 500 feet of any dwelling in use, except as authorized by the owner or occupant thereof. **Arrest powers**: **Misdemeanor** – there is no statutory authority granting powers of arrest for this offense. However, if the offense is committed in public, in the officer's presence, and is creating a **breach of the peace** an arrest would be lawful. **Note:** see the Hunting & Fishing Section for more.

PELLET AND AIR GUNS

C. 269 § 12B	PELLET AND AIR GUN LAWS
	Minors Possessing Air Rifles **Elements**
1.	No minor under the age of 18 shall have an air rifle or so-called BB gun in his **possession** while in any place to which the public has a right of access, unless:
2.	• he/she is accompanied by an adult or • he/she is the holder of a sporting or hunting license and has on his person a permit from the chief of police of the town in which he resides granting him the right of such possession.
	Shooting air rifles **Elements**
Any age	No person shall discharge a BB shot, pellet or other object from an air rifle or so-called BB gun, into, from or across any street, alley, **public way** or railroad or railway right of way.
Minors	**No minor under the age of 18** shall discharge a BB shot, pellet or other object from an air rifle or BB gun unless he is accompanied by an adult or is the holder of a sporting or hunting license.
Attorney Hanrahan's Note	No one can shoot an air rifle on or across a public way and a minor cannot shoot one <u>anywhere</u>, unless accompanied an adult of is the holder of a sporting/hunting license.
	Arrest Power, Penalties & Notes
Power of arrest	**Misdemeanor** – there is no statutory authority granting powers of arrest for this offense. However, if the offense is committed in public, in the officer's presence, and is creating a **breach of the peace** an arrest would be lawful.
Penalty	A fine of not more than $100, and the air rifle or BB gun or other weapon shall be confiscated.
Air Rifle Forfeiture	Upon a conviction of a violation of this section the air rifle or BB gun or other weapon shall, by the written authority of the court, be forwarded to the colonel of the state police, who may dispose of said article in the same manner as prescribed in section 10.

	Related Statutes, Case Law & Other Important Information
Air rifles; sale/furnish to minors c. 269 § 12A	Whoever sells to a minor under the age of 18 or whoever, not being the parent, guardian or adult teacher or instructor, furnishes to a minor under the age of 18 an air rifle or so-called BB gun, shall be punished by a fine of not less than $50 nor more than $200 or by imprisonment for not more than 6 months. **Arrest Powers**: **Misdemeanor** – there is no statutory authority granting powers of arrest for this offense. However, if the offense is committed in public, in the officer's presence, and is creating a **breach of the peace** an arrest would be lawful.
Air rifles and air guns	In the 2015 case of *Com. v. Garrett*, the SJC reiterated that. "absent indication of contrary legislative intent, a BB gun is akin to an "air rifle," and we have considered definitions of air rifles, and air guns as interchangeable."
Not a firearm	In the 2015 case of *Com. v. Garrett*, the SJC clarified that a BB gun is not a firearm for the purposes of the firearm licensing requirements and carrying/weapons offenses.

WEAPON VIOLATIONS

BOMBS and DANGEROUS SUBSTANCES & MATERIALS

C. 266 § 102	POSSESSION/CONTROL OF EXPLOSIVE, CHEMICAL, BIOLOGICAL OR NUCLEAR WEAPONS, INGREDIENT
	Possession of Explosive or Destructive Device or Substance **Elements**
1.	The defendant, without lawful authority, has in his possession or under his control
2.	Any explosive or any destructive or incendiary device or substance.
	Arrest Power, Penalties & Notes
Power of Arrest	**Felony** – a police officer may effect a warrantless arrest for this offense provided he/she has probable cause that the suspect committed the offense.
Penalty	Imprisonment for not more than 2½ years in the house of correction or for **not less than 10 years** nor more than 20 years in the state prison or by a fine of not more than $25,000, or by both such fine and imprisonment.
Attorney Hanrahan's Note	This offense does not require an "intent" to use the item, just mere possession is sufficient.
	Possession of Materials with Intent **Elements**
1.	The defendant, without lawful authority, has in his possession or under his control one of the following substances/with the required intent:
2.	any substance, material, article, explosive or ingredient which, alone or in combination, could be used to make a destructive or incendiary device or substance **and who intends to make a destructive or incendiary device or substance**; or any substance, material, article, explosive or ingredient which, alone or in combination, could be used to make a chemical, biological or nuclear weapon **and who intends to make a chemical, biological or nuclear weapon**.
	Arrest Power, Penalties & Notes
Power of Arrest	**Felony** – a police officer may effect a warrantless arrest for this offense provided he/she has probable cause that the suspect committed the offense.
Penalty	Imprisonment in the house of correction for not more than 2½ years or in **state prison (F)** for **not less than 5 years** nor more than 10 years or by a fine of not more than $25,000, or by both such fine and imprisonment.
Note: Not all necessary materials are required	It shall not be a defense to a violation of this subsection that the defendant did not possess or have under his control every substance, material, article, explosive or ingredient, or combination thereof, required to make a complete and functional destructive or incendiary device or substance or chemical, biological or nuclear weapon.
	Related Statutes, Case Law & Other Important Information
Definitions **c. 266 § 102**	**Biological weapon**", any microorganism, virus, infectious substance or biological product that may be engineered as a result of biotechnology, or any naturally occurring or bioengineered component of any such microorganism, virus, infectious substance or biological product, except if intended for a purpose not prohibited under this chapter or c. 265, specifically prepared in a manner to cause death, disease or other biological malfunction in a human, animal, plant or another living organism, deterioration of food,

C. 266 § 102	POSSESSION/CONTROL OF EXPLOSIVE, CHEMICAL, BIOLOGICAL OR NUCLEAR WEAPONS, INGREDIENT
	water, equipment supplies or material of any kind, or deleterious alteration of the environment. **Black powder**, a compound or mixture of sulfur, charcoal and an alkali nitrate including, but not limited to, potassium or sodium nitrate. **Chemical weapon**, (i) a toxic chemical or substance, including the precursors to any toxic chemical or substance; and (ii) ammunition or a device designed to cause death or bodily harm by means of the release of a toxic chemical or substance. **Nuclear weapon**, a device designed for the purpose of causing bodily injury, death or denial of access through the release of radiation or radiological material either by propagation of nuclear fission or by means of any other energy source.
Possession or use of biological, chemical, or nuclear weapon or delivery system **c. 266 § 102C**	**Elements**: The defendant, without lawful authority, knowingly develops, produces, stockpiles, acquires, transports, possesses, controls, places, secretes or uses any biological, chemical or nuclear weapon or delivery system, with the intent to cause death, bodily injury or property damage. **Penalty:** Imprisonment in the HOC for not more than 2½ years or by imprisonment in the **state prison (F)** for not more than 20 years or by a fine of not more than $20,000, or by both such fine and imprisonment. **Arrest Powers**: **Felony** – a police officer may effect an arrest for this offense committed in his/her presence or for an offense in the past, on probable cause. **Definitions**: For the purposes of this section (§102C), the following words shall have the following meanings: "**Biological weapon**", any microorganism, virus, infectious substance or biological product that may be engineered as a result of biotechnology, or any naturally occurring or bioengineered component of any such microorganism, virus, infectious substance or biological product, except if intended for a purpose not prohibited under this chapter or chapter 265, specifically prepared in a manner to cause death, disease or other biological malfunction in a human, animal, plant or another living organism, deterioration of food, water, equipment supplies or material of any kind, or deleterious alteration of the environment. "**Chemical weapon**", (i) a toxic chemical or substance, including the precursors to any toxic chemical or substance; and (ii) ammunition or a device designed to cause death or bodily harm by means of the release of a toxic chemical or substance. "**Nuclear weapon**", a device designed for the purpose of causing bodily injury, death or denial of access through the release of radiation or radiological material either by propagation of nuclear fission or by means of any other energy source. "**Delivery system**", any equipment designed or adapted for use in connection with the deployment of chemical, biological or nuclear weapons.

C. 266 § 102A	***USE/DEPLOYMENT* OF AN EXPLOSIVE OR DESTRUCTIVE DEVICE OR SUBSTANCE**
Elements	
1.	The defendant, without lawful authority, secretes, throws, launches or otherwise places,
2.	An explosive or a destructive or incendiary device or substance,
3.	With the intent to: • Cause fear, panic or apprehension in any person; or • Ignite, explode or discharge such explosive or such destructive or incendiary device or substance; or • Release or discharge any chemical, biological or nuclear weapon.
Arrest Power, Penalties & Notes	
Power of Arrest	**Felony** – a police officer may effect a warrantless arrest for this offense provided he/she has probable cause that the suspect committed the offense.
Penalty	Imprisonment for not more than 2½ years in the house of correction or for **not less than 10** years nor more than 25 years in the **state prison (F)** or by a fine of not more than $25,000, or by both such fine and imprisonment.
Related Statute	
Discharge or ignition of destructive device or substance **c. 266 § 102B**	The defendant, without lawful authority, willfully discharges, ignites or explodes any destructive or incendiary device or substance. **Penalty**: imprisonment in the **state prison (F)** by **not less than 15** years nor more than 25 years or by a fine of $50,000 or by both such fine and imprisonment. **Arrest Powers**: **Felony** – a police officer may effect an arrest for this offense committed in his/her presence or for an offense in the past, on probable cause.

C. 266 § 102(b)	**USE/POSSESSION OF A HOAX DEVICE**
Elements	
1.	The defendant, without lawful authority,
2.	• Has in his possession or uses or places, or • Causes another to knowingly or unknowingly possess, use or place,
3.	Any hoax explosive, hoax destructive or incendiary device or substance or any hoax chemical, biological or nuclear weapon,
4.	With the intent that such hoax explosive, device or substance or weapon be used to cause anxiety, unrest, fear or personal discomfort to any person or group of persons.
Arrest Power, Penalties & Notes	
Power of Arrest	**Felony** – a police officer may effect a warrantless arrest for this offense provided he/she has probable cause that the suspect committed the offense.

C. 266 § 102(b)	USE/POSSESSION OF A HOAX DEVICE
Penalty	Imprisonment in the house of correction for not more than 2½ years or by imprisonment in the **state prison (F)** for not more than 5 years or by a fine of not more than $10,000, or by both.
Related Statutes, Case Law & Other Important Information	
Definitions	**Hoax explosive**, "hoax destructive or incendiary device or substance" or "hoax chemical, biological or nuclear weapon", any device, article or substance that would cause a person to reasonably believe that such device, article or substance is: a. an explosive; b. a destructive or incendiary device or substance; or c. a chemical, biological or nuclear weapon, harmful radioactive substance or poison capable of causing bodily injury which is actually an inoperable facsimile. See chapter 266 § 102 (c) and (a) for additional definitions.
Possession, transportation, use or placement of hoax devices **c. 266 § 102A½**	**Elements:** The defendant possesses, transports, uses or places (or causes another to knowingly or unknowingly possess, transport, use or place) any hoax device or hoax substance with the intent to cause anxiety, unrest, fear or personal discomfort to any person or group of persons. **Penalty:** imprisonment in a HOC for not more than 2½ years or by imprisonment in the **state prison (F)** for not more than 5 years or by a fine of not more than $5,000, or by both such fine and imprisonment. **Definitions for C. 266 § 102A½:** For the purposes of this section, the term "**hoax device**" shall mean any device that would cause a person reasonably to believe that such device is an infernal machine. For the purposes of this section, the term "**infernal machine**" shall mean any device for endangering life or doing unusual damage to property, or both, by fire or explosion, whether or not contrived to ignite or explode automatically. For the purposes of this section, the words "**hoax substance**" shall mean any substance that would cause a person reasonably to believe that such substance is a harmful chemical or biological agent, a poison, a harmful radioactive substance or any other substance for causing serious bodily injury, endangering life or doing unusual damage to property, or both. **Exception:** This section shall not apply to any law enforcement or public safety officer acting in the lawful discharge of official duties.

SEX CRIMES & SEX OFFENDERS

Rape & Indecent Assaults

C. 265 § 22	RAPE
Elements	
1.	Compelling a person to submit by force and against his will (see case law notes below) or Compelling a person to submit by threat of bodily injury
2.	To engage sexual intercourse or unnatural sexual intercourse with a person (see definitions below)
Arrest Power, Penalties & Notes	
Power of Arrest	**Felony** – a police officer may effect a warrantless arrest for this offense provided he/she has probable cause that the suspect committed the offense.
Penalty	**1st Offense**: Imprisonment in the **state prison (F)** for not more than 20 years **2nd or Subsequent Offense**: Imprisonment in the **state prison (F)** for life or for any term or years. **Enhanced Penalty for Certain Weapons**: Whoever commits this offense while being armed with a firearm, rifle, shotgun, machine-gun or assault weapon, shall be punished by imprisonment in the **state prison (F)** for not less than 10 years. Whoever commits a second or subsequent such offense shall be punished by imprisonment in the **state prison (F)** for life or for any term of years, but not less than 15 years. **Also See aggravated rape below.**
Attorney Hanrahan's Comment	Be sure to read the different variations of force and the definitions of natural and unnatural sexual intercourse.
Case Law, Definitions & Other Important Information	
Force	The "force" requirement does not have to be significant. In fact, in situations where the victim is unable to consent due to intoxication, or physical impairment, the minimal amount of force required to accomplish penetration may be enough.
Constructive Force	The proof of force element of rape ... may be established by physical force or constructive force. **Constructive force** may be "by threatening words or gestures and operates on the mind" to instill fear in the victim in order for the defendant to achieve his goal. Stated differently, there must be proof that the victim was afraid or that she submitted to the defendant because his conduct intimidated her. In the 2011 case of ***Commonwealth v. Newcomb***, the Appeals Court ruled that rape by force (via the theory of constructive force) of an adult victim may be proven by the defendant's rape of the victim as a child with the defendant's unbroken course of regularly raping the victim into adulthood. **Deceit:** Typically, deception would not amount to force. In ***Com. v. Feijoo***, the defendant, a karate instructor, convinced his 17 year old male student that he must engage in sex with him in order to be a Ninja warrior. However, constructive force can be accomplished in varied ways, particularly when the defendant is in a position of authority and the victim is young and submissive. In the 2013 case of ***Commonwealth v. Dumas***, The victim, a child of Hmong refugees from Laos, testified that at the time of the assaults she practiced a religion called Houplle. Pursuant to the tenets of Houplle, the victim believed that the spirits of her ancestors watched over her and possessed great influence over her life. The victim's

SEX RELATED CRIMES

C. 265 § 22	RAPE
	testimony indicated that the defendant (a religious leader) was aware of her religious beliefs, and that he preyed on those beliefs by telling her that if she did not submit to his sexual demands her ancestors would hurt her and her family. The Appeals Court upheld the defendant's rape conviction. **Attorney Hanrahan's Note:** You should not confuse the *Dumas* case with rape by "trickery", as in when a perpetrator convinces a victim to submit to sexual advances in promise of a recording contract or some similar promise that does not exist. That type of scenario typically would not be considered "constructive force" for the purposes of rape, and thus typically would not be a rape. In this case, although the victim was tricked, she was tricked into believing she was in danger if she did not comply; a significant distinction.
Against Victim's Will	The "against his will" simple means without consent.
Intoxication and its effect on consent	In the 2010 case of ***Commonwealth v. LeBlanc,*** the SJC ruled that intoxication *can* negate consent to sexual intercourse.[1] If a victim is too intoxicated to consent the act will be deemed against the victim's will. However, if the lack of consent is based on the victim's level of intoxication it must be proven that the defendant was aware of the victim's level of intoxication and the defendant's own intoxication may effect his/her ability to comprehend the victim's incapacitation.[2]
Withdrawn Consent	In ***Commonwealth v. Enimpah*** (2012), the Appeals Court ruled that failure to end sexual intercourse after one party withdraws consent is rape, even if consent was originally given.
Penetration	For rape to occur some penetration, even slight penetration, must exist. The requirement is different depending on the body part penetrated. **Female genitalia**: Even slight penetration is typically sufficient for sexual intercourse. For instance in ***Com. v. Baldwin***[3], the defendant was convicted of rape even though he was unsuccessful in penetrating into the vaginal orifice after attempting penetration for 10 minutes and applying petroleum jelly to the vulva and labia. The Court Ruled "Intrusion into the vagina itself is not required to make out the wrongful penetration. Touching by the male of the vulva or labia, as may surely be inferred from spreading Vaseline and ten minutes or so of attempted penile penetration, is intrusion enough." In the 2013 case of ***Commonwealth v. Olmonde***, the Appeals Court ruled that manipulation of the clitoris may constitute enough penetration for rape. **Buttocks:** In ***Com. v. Nylander***, insertion of the penis between the buttocks (butt cheeks), without penetration into the anus, was insufficient for a rape conviction. However, in ***Com. v. Lawton*** (2012), penetration of into the anus by way of the defendant's tongue was sufficient to prove rape of a child. **The victim does not have to be the one penetrated**. In ***Com. v. Hackett,*** [4]the defendant committed rape when he performed fellatio on a teenage boy. In ***Com. v. Guy***[5], a rape occurred when a female was forced to perform cunnilingus on another female. **Defendant does not have to actually perform the act**. In ***Com. v. Nuby***, the defendant forced his girlfriend's young sons to penetrate their mother's vagina with their tongues.

[11] *Com .v Leblanc (SJC Feb 2010)*
[2] Cmmonwealth v. Mountry, (2012) SJC
[3] *Com. v. Baldwin*, 24 Mass.App.Ct. 200 (1987)
[4] *Com. v. Hackett*, 383 Mass. 888 (1981)
[5] *Com. v. Guy*, 24 Mass.App.Ct. 783 (1987)

C. 265 § 22	RAPE
Natural Sexual Intercourse	Natural Sexual Intercourse refers to the insertion of the penis into the vagina, even if only slightly. Ejaculation is not required.
Unnatural Sexual Intercourse	This includes oral sex such as fellatio (oral penetration with the penis), cunnilingus (oral contact with the female genitalia) providing some penetration took place (even if only of the vulva or labia) and anal intercourse.[1] It also includes insertion of an object (i.e. finger, stick, tongue or other object) into the anus or female genitalia. In. ***Com. v. Baldwin*** (1987), the Appeals Court ruled intrusion into the vagina orifice is not required penetration by the defendant of the vulva or labia was sufficient for a conviction. In ***Com. v. Edward,*** rape was committed when the defendant placed his lips on the 15 year old babysitter's vulva or labia because a jury could find that some penetration took place.[2] In ***Com. v. Guy,*** unnatural sexual intercourse occurred when a female performed cunnilingus on another female.[3] In ***Com. v. Cifizzari,*** insertion of a mop handle into the vagina was deemed to be rape.[4] In ***Com. v. Basey*** (2012), the defendant was convicted of aggravated rape when he stuck a stick into another man's anus rupturing his bowel after beating him unconscious. In a rape prosecution, "unnatural sexual intercourse" includes female-to-female cunnilingus; [5] In a rape prosecution, "unnatural sexual intercourse" includes digital contact with vagina, vulva or labia.[6]
Victim Privacy	Chapter 265 § 24C prohibits the police from releasing the name of a rape victim. A violation can result in a fine of $2,500 up to $10,000.
Related Statutes	
Statutory Rape	See chapter 265 § 22A
Indecent A&B	Indecent A&B is a lesser included offense of rape. However, convictions of both the greater and lesser offenses are permitted as long as they "rest on separate distinct acts." In ***Commonwealth v. Rodriguez*** (2013), the defendant kidnapped the victim licked her breasts and rubbed her genitals over the clothing before raping her and he was convicted of both offenses. See Chapter 265 § 13H and 265 § 13B (child) for more.
Drugging for sex	See Chapter 272 § 3
Sex offense venue c. 265 § 24A	The person against whom the crime is alleged to have been committed has been conveyed from one county or judicial district into another, the crime may be alleged to have been committed, and may be prosecuted and punished, in the county or judicial district where committed or from which the person was so conveyed.

SEX RELATED CRIMES

[1] *Comm. v. Gallant*, 373 Mass. 577 (1977)
[2] *Com. v. Edward*, 34 Mass.App. Ct. 521 (1993).
[3] *Com. v. Guy*, 24 Mass.App.Ct. 783 (1987).
[4] *Com. v. Cifizzari*, 397 Mass. 560 (1986).
[5] *Commonwealth v. Guy*, 24 Mass. App. Ct. 783, 785-787, 513 N.E.2d 701, 702-704 (1987).
[6] *Commonwealth v. Baldwin*, 24 Mass. App. Ct. 200, 204-205, 509 N.E.2d 4, 7 (1987).

C. 265 § 22	RAPE
Rape victim's name; confidentiality **c. 265 § 24C**	That portion of the records of a court or any police department of the commonwealth or any of its political subdivisions, which contains the name of the victim in an arrest, investigation or complaint for rape or assault with intent to rape or an arrest, investigation or complaint for trafficking of persons chapter 265 § 50, shall be withheld from public inspection, except with the consent of a justice of such court where the complaint or indictment is or would be prosecuted. Said portion of such court record or police record shall not be deemed to be a public record. Except as otherwise provided in this section, it shall be unlawful to publish, disseminate or otherwise disclose the name of any individual identified as an alleged victim of any of the offenses described in the first paragraph. A violation of this section shall be punishable by a fine of not less than $2,500 nor more than $10,000.
Rape: department requirements **c. 41 § 97B**	**Every municipal police department shall have a rape reporting and prosecution unit** which shall be designed to improve the quality of rape reporting, counseling, and prosecution. **Rape Training Required** These units shall consist of police investigators who shall have completed a course of training in the counseling of victims of rape and the prosecution of alleged perpetrators of the crime of rape which shall be approved and funded by the MPTC. **Same Sex Reporting** Each department **shall make efforts to employ women police officers** to serve in these units. A victim of rape who is male shall, whenever possible, be interviewed initially by a male police officer, and a victim of rape who is female shall, whenever possible, be interviewed initially by a woman police officer. Each unit shall in addition make use of such counselors, attorneys, and medical personnel as are necessary to provide a broad range of therapeutic services for victims of rape. **Rape Kit** Each unit shall provide personnel with training in the use of a standardized kit for the collection and preservation of evidence in rape cases. Such kit shall be designed by the MPTC and shall include instructions, standardized reporting forms, and appropriate receptacles for the collection and preservation of evidence for laboratory and police use. Each kit shall also include medically and factually accurate written information prepared by the commissioner of public health about emergency contraception. A hospital shall inform a victim of rape that the **evidence of rape preserved in a rape kit shall be kept** for a period of **at least 6 months** upon the written request of the victim at the time the evidence is obtained upon forms provided to such victim by such hospital.
Special telephone exchange **c. 41 § 97C**	**Each Department must have Special Rape Reporting Line:** Each rape reporting and prosecution unit **shall establish a special telephone exchange** for the reporting of rape which may be utilized at any hour of day or night and shall widely publicize this number and information concerning the activities of the unit throughout the city or town.
Rape Report is Confidential	All reports of rape and sexual assault or attempts to commit such offenses and all conversations between police officers and victims regarding these offenses shall not be public reports and shall be maintained by the police departments in a manner which will assure their confidentiality. **Penalty:** Whoever violates any provision of this section shall be punished by imprisonment for not more than 1year or by a fine of not more than $1,000, or both.

C. 265 § 22(a)	AGGRAVATED RAPE
Elements	
1.	The defendant Rape (see Rape offense) coupled with one of the following:
2.	• It results in or is committed with acts resulting in **serious bodily injury,** or • is committed by a **joint enterprise**, (more than one suspect), or • is committed during the commission or attempted commission of one of the following felonies: c. 265 § 15A (**A&B dangerous weapon**), c. 265 § 15B (**Assault by means of a dangerous weapon**), c. 265 § 17 & 19 **(robbery/unarmed robbery)**, c. 265 § 26 (**kidnapping**), c. 266 § 14, 15 (**burglary offenses**), c. 266 § 16, 17 & 18 (**B&E offenses**), and c. 269 § 10 (**unlawful carrying of a dangerous weapon**)
Arrest Power, Penalties & Notes	
Power of Arrest	**Felony** – a police officer may effect a warrantless arrest for this offense provided he/she has probable cause that the suspect committed the offense.
Penalty	Imprisonment in the **state prison (F)** for life or for any term of years.
Related Statutes, Case Law & Other Important Information	
Aggravated Statutory Rape	See Chapter 265 § 22B

C. 265 § 24	ASSAULT WITH INTENT TO COMMIT RAPE
Elements	
1.	The defendant committed an assault
2.	With intent to commit rape
Arrest Power, Penalties & Notes	
Power of Arrest	**Felony** – a police officer may effect a warrantless arrest for this offense provided he/she has probable cause that the suspect committed the offense.
Penalty	**Penalty:** shall be punished by imprisonment in the **state prison (F)** for not more than twenty years or by imprisonment in a jail or HOC for not more than 2½ years; and whoever commits a second or subsequent such offense shall be punished by imprisonment in the **state prison (F)** for life or for any term of years. **Enhanced Penalty**: Whoever commits this offense **while armed with a firearm, rifle, shotgun, machine gun or assault weapon** shall be punished by imprisonment in the **state prison (F)** for not less than 5 years. 2nd or subsequent offense: imprisonment in the **state prison (F)** for life or for any term of years, but not less than 20 years.
Attorney Hanrahan's Comment	This offense can be used when the perpetrator accosts the victim and his goal is to rape but he is unsuccessful. For instance, the suspect jumps from a bush and grabs a female jogger, tries to pull her into the woods and rip off her clothes but she is able to break free. A simple A&B charge would not be

SEX RELATED CRIMES

C. 265 § 24	ASSAULT WITH INTENT TO COMMIT RAPE
	a sufficient punishment. Although the elements require merely an "assault" it certainly would also apply if the act involved and "assault and battery" with the same intent, as every battery includes an assault.
	Related Statutes, Case Law & Other Important Information
Sexual overtones	Often the offender's conduct is accompanied by sexual overtones. This is often sufficient to show the intent to rape. In ***Com. v. Rossi,***[1] the offender entered the victim's home and awoke her from sleep and ordered to take off her clothes, referring to her as a whore. When she failed to comply he began to beat her. He then fled. His conduct was sufficient to show an intent to rape. In ***Com. v. Santiago***[2], the defendant pulled alongside the female victim as she walked and tried to convince her to get into his car. When she refused he made statements such as "you're breaking my heart." He then displayed a weapon. The victim ran off. His conduct amounted to an assault with intent to rape.
Sex offense venue **c. 265 § 24A**	The person against whom the crime is alleged to have been committed has been conveyed from one county or judicial district into another, the crime may be alleged to have been committed, and may be prosecuted and punished, in the county or judicial district where committed or from which the person was so conveyed.

C. 272 § 3	DRUGGING PERSONS FOR SEXUAL INTERCOURSE
	Elements
1.	The defendant applies, administers to or causes to be taken by a person
2.	Any drug, matter or thing with intent to stupefy or overpower the person
3.	So as to thereby enable any person to have sexual intercourse or unnatural sexual intercourse with the person
	Arrest Power, Penalties & Notes
Power of Arrest	**Felony** – a police officer may effect a warrantless arrest for this offense provided he/she has probable cause that the suspect committed the offense.
Penalty	Imprisonment in the **state prison (F)** for life or for any term of years not less than 10 years.
Attorney Hanrahan's Comment	This offense can be committed by someone who doesn't even take part in the sex act or even if the act is not completed. For instance, the defendant slips a "roofie" in the drink of girl so that his friend can take sexual advantage of the victim. The elements have been met even if the scheme was unsuccessful.
	Case Law & Other Important Information
Substance	The substance used can be any substance (whether a drug or not) as long as it was intended to "stupefy or overpower." For instance, in ***Com. v. Odell*** (1993), seasickness medication qualified under this statute.

[1] *Com. v. Rossi*, 19 Mass.App.Ct. 257 (1985).
[2] *Com. v. Santiago*, 53 Mass.App.Ct. 567 (2002).

C. 265 § 13H	INDECENT ASSAULT AND BATTERY (14 or older)
	Elements
1.	The defendant commits an indecent assault & battery
2.	On a person age 14 or older
	Arrest Power, Penalties & Notes
Power of Arrest	**Felony** – a police officer may effect a warrantless arrest for this offense provided he/she has probable cause that the suspect committed the offense.
Penalty	**Penalty:** imprisonment in the **state prison (F)** for not more than 5 years, or by imprisonment for not more than 2½ years in a jail or HOC. **Enhanced Penalty for Elder or Disabled Person**: **1st offense**: imprisonment in the **state prison (F)** for not more than 10 years, or by imprisonment for not more than 2½ years in a jail or HOC. **2nd or subsequent offense:** shall be punished by imprisonment in the **state prison (F)** for not more than 20 years.
	Related Statutes, Case Law & Other Important Information
Indecent	"Indecent" assault and battery typically involves touching of the genitals, buttocks, or female breasts. However, in some cases indecent assault and battery was found where there was touching of the stomach and thigh with sexual overtones, and even forced tongue kissing has been found to qualify as an indecent assault and battery.
Lack of Consent	Although it does not specifically state it lack of consent is required. At least for the 14+ version of this offense. An A&B is, by definition, either a harmful or an offensive touching which would imply lack of consent.
14+ years	Although the age of consent for sexual intercourse is 16 years. A teen, aged 14 or 15, may engage in consensual sexual fondling (short of penetration – see rape definitions). However, the teen must still have the capacity to consent and the age of the person is a factor to consider when determining whether consent existed.[1] For instance, if a 14 year old girl "permitted" sexual fondling by a much older adult male who was also an authority figure it may still be deemed a non-consensual act based on the circumstances.
No indecent assault (must be a battery)	In the 2010 case of ***Com. v. Marzilli,*** the SJC ruled that there is no crime of "indecent assault" only indecent assault & battery. In this case the defendant did not actually touch the victim. However, a charge of attempt to commit a crime (c. 274 § 6), with the attempted crime being Indecent A&B, would still apply.
Indecent assault and battery on mentally retarded person c. 265 § 13F	The defendant commits an indecent assault and battery on a person with an intellectual disability knowing the person has intellectual disability. **Penalty: 1st Offense:** imprisonment in the **state prison (F)** for not less than five years or not more than ten years. **2nd or subsequent offense**, by imprisonment in the **state prison (F)** for not less than ten years. **Arrest Powers**: **Felony** – a police officer may effect an arrest for this offense committed in his/her presence or for an offense in the past, on probable cause. **Exception:** This section shall not apply to the commission of an indecent assault and battery by a mentally retarded person upon another mentally retarded person.
Sex offense venue c. 265 § 24A	The person against whom the crime is alleged to have been committed has been conveyed from one county or judicial district into another, the crime may be alleged to have been committed, and may be prosecuted and punished, in the county or judicial district where committed or from which the person was so conveyed.

[1] *Com. v. Burke*, 390 Mass. 480 (1983).

SEX CRIMES INVOLVING SPECIAL POPULATIONS (Children, Elderly & Disabled)

C. 265 § 22A	RAPE OF CHILD WITH FORCE (UNDER 16)
Elements	
1.	The defendant has sexual intercourse or unnatural sexual intercourse with a child under 16
2.	And compels the child to submit by: • force and against his will, or • threat of bodily injury.
Arrest Power, Penalties & Notes	
Power of Arrest	**Felony** – a police officer may effect a warrantless arrest for this offense provided he/she has probable cause that the suspect committed the offense.
Penalty	Imprisonment in the **state prison (F)** for life or for any term of years. A prosecution commenced under this section shall neither be continued without a finding nor placed on file.
Attorney Hanrahan's Comment	This offense is the same as Adult Rape however the victim is under 16. Review the adult version of this offense for more particulars of the crime.
Related Statutes, Case Law & Other Important Information	
Aggravated rape of a child **c. 265 § 22B**	Whoever has sexual intercourse or unnatural sexual intercourse with a child **under 16,** and compels such child to submit by force and against his will or compels such child to submit by threat of bodily injury **and**: (a) the sexual intercourse or unnatural sexual intercourse is committed during the commission or **attempted commission of any of the following offenses**: (1) armed burglary as set forth in c. 266 § 14; (2) unarmed burglary as set forth in c. 266 § 15 ; (3) breaking and entering as set forth in c. 266 § 16; (4) entering without breaking as set forth in c. 266 § 17; (5) breaking and entering into a dwelling house as set forth in c. 266 § 18; (6) kidnapping as set forth in c. 265 § 26; (7) armed robbery as set forth in c. 265 § 17; (8) unarmed robbery as set forth in c. 265 § 19; (9) assault and battery with a dangerous weapon or assault with a dangerous weapon as set forth in c. 265 §15A § 15B; (10) home invasion as set forth in section c. 265 § 18C; (11) results in substantial bodily harm; or (11) posing or exhibiting child in state of nudity or sexual conduct as set forth in c. 272 § 29A; (c) the sexual intercourse or unnatural sexual intercourse is committed while the victim is **tied, bound or gagged**; (d) the sexual intercourse or unnatural sexual intercourse is committed after the **defendant administered, or caused to be administered, alcohol or a controlled substance by injection, inhalation, ingestion, or any other means to the victim without the victims consent;** (e) the sexual intercourse or unnatural sexual intercourse is committed by a **joint enterprise**; or (f) the sexual intercourse or unnatural sexual intercourse was committed in a manner in which **the victim could contract a sexually transmitted disease or infection** of which the defendant knew or

C. 265 § 22A	RAPE OF CHILD WITH FORCE (UNDER 16)
	should have known he was a **carrier**. **Penalty:** imprisonment in the **state prison (F)** for life or for any term of years, but **not less than 15 years**. The sentence imposed on such person shall not be reduced to less than 15 years, or suspended, nor shall any person convicted under this section be eligible for probation, parole, work release or furlough or receive any deduction from his sentence for good conduct until he shall have served 15 years of such sentence. Prosecutions commenced under this section shall neither be continued without a finding nor placed on file.
Statutory Rape **c. 265 § 23**	The defendant unlawfully has sexual intercourse or unnatural sexual intercourse, and abuses a child under 16 years of age. **Penalty:** imprisonment in the **state prison (F)** for life or for any term of years or, except as otherwise provided, for any term in a jail or HOC. A prosecution commenced under this section shall neither be continued without a finding nor placed on file. **Arrest powers**: **Felony** – a police officer may effect an arrest for this offense committed in his/her presence or for an offense in the past, on probable cause. **Attorney Hanrahan's Note**: A child under the age of 16 cannot legally consent to sexual intercourse. This is considered a strict liability crime, meaning even if the defendant thought the victim was 16 or older this would not be a defense.
Aggravated Statutory Rape **c. 265 § 23A**	Statutory Rape and one of the following: • the victim is under 12 and more than 5 years separate the age of the victim and defendant; • the victim is 12, 13, 14 or 15 and more than 10 years separate the age of the victim and defendant; • the defendant is a mandated reporter. **Penalty:** punishable by up to life imprisonment with a minimum mandatory sentence of 10 years. 2nd offense has a minimum mandatory sentence of 15 years.
Fictitious child	In *Commonwealth v. Buswell* (2012), the Appeals Court ruled that the crime of attempted rape of a child and attempted indecent assault & battery on a child may be proven even though the child is fictitious.
Sex offense venue **c. 265 § 24A**	The person against whom the crime is alleged to have been committed has been conveyed from one county or judicial district into another, the crime may be alleged to have been committed, and may be prosecuted and punished, in the county or judicial district where committed or from which the person was so conveyed.

C. 265 § 23	STATUTORY RAPE OF A CHILD
Elements	
1.	The defendant unlawfully has sexual intercourse or unnatural sexual intercourse, and abuses a child under 16 years of age.
Arrest Power, Penalties & Notes	
Power of Arrest	**Felony** – a police officer may effect a warrantless arrest for this offense provided he/she has probable cause that the suspect committed the offense.
Penalty	imprisonment in the **state prison (F)** for life or for any term of years or, except as otherwise provided, for any term in a jail or HOC. A prosecution commenced under this section shall neither be continued without a finding nor placed on file.
Attorney Hanrahan's Comment	A child under the age of 16 cannot legally consent to sexual intercourse. This is considered a strict liability crime, meaning even if the defendant thought the victim was 16 or older this would not be a defense.
Related Statutes, Case Law & Other Important Information	
Aggravated Statutory Rape c. 265 § 23A	Statutory Rape and one of the following: • the victim is under 12 and more than 5 years separate the age of the victim and defendant; • the victim is 12, 13, 14 or 15 and more than 10 years separate the age of the victim and defendant; • the defendant is a mandated reporter. **Penalty:** punishable by up to life imprisonment with a minimum mandatory sentence of 10 years. 2nd offense has a minimum mandatory sentence of 15 years.

C. 265 § 24B	ASSAULT OF CHILD (UNDER 16) WITH INTENT TO COMMIT RAPE
Elements	
1.	The defendant assaults a child under 16
2.	with intent to commit a rape.
Arrest Power, Penalties & Notes	
Power of Arrest	**Felony** – a police officer may effect a warrantless arrest for this offense provided he/she has probable cause that the suspect committed the offense.
Penalty	**Penalty:** imprisonment in the **state prison (F)** for life or for any term of years. **Subsequent Offense:** if the defendant is over the age of 18 and commits a subsequent such offense shall be punished by imprisonment in the **state prison (F)** for life or for any term of years but not less than 5 years. **Enhanced Penalty for certain Weapons:** Whoever commits any offense described in this section while being armed with a **firearm, rifle, shotgun, machine gun or assault weapon** shall be punished by imprisonment in the **state prison (F)** for life or for any term of years, but not less than ten years. Whoever over the age of 18 commits a second or subsequent such offense shall be punished by imprisonment in the **state prison (F)** for life or for any term of years, but not less than 15 years.
Related Statutes, Case Law & Other Important Information	
Important Information	This is the same offense as the adult version however the victim is under 16. See the adult version of this offense for more.

C. 265 § 24B	ASSAULT OF CHILD (UNDER 16) WITH INTENT TO COMMIT RAPE
Aggravated Indecent Assault on a Child **c. 265 § 13B½**	The following are "aggravating factors" in regards to the crime of Indecent assault and battery: the offense was committed during the commission, or attempted commission, of: • Armed or unarmed burglary • Breaking and entering, • Entering without breaking, • Breaking and entering or breaking without entering in the nighttime, • Breaking and entering a home in the nighttime, • Kidnapping, • Armed and unarmed robbery, • Assault or assault and battery with a dangerous weapon, • Armed assault in a dwelling, • Posing or exhibiting a child in a state of nudity Or the offense was committed by a **mandatory reporter**. **Penalty** if Aggravating Factors where involved: **Minimum Mandatory 10 year sentence**, up to life imprisonment.

C. 265 § 13B	INDECENT ASSAULT AND BATTERY ON CHILD UNDER 14
	Elements
1.	The defendant commits an indecent assault and battery on a child under the age of 14.
	Arrest Power, Penalties & Notes
Power of Arrest	**Felony** – a police officer may effect a warrantless arrest for this offense provided he/she has probable cause that the suspect committed the offense.
Penalty	1st offense: imprisonment in the **state prison (F)** for not more than 10 years, or by imprisonment in the HOC for not more than 2½ years. 2nd offense: up to life with a minimum mandatory sentence of 15 years. A prosecution commenced under this section shall neither be continued without a finding nor placed on file.
Attorney Hanrahan's Comment	"Indecent" assault and battery typically involves touching of the genitals, buttocks, or female breasts. However, in some cases indecent assault and battery was found where there was touching of the stomach and thigh with sexual overtones, and forced tongue kissing has been found to qualify as an indecent assault and battery.
	Related Statutes, Case Law & Other Important Information
Under 14 incapable of consent	In a prosecution under this section, a child under the age of 14 years shall be deemed incapable of consenting.
Indecent	An indecent act is one that is fundamentally offensive to contemporary standards of decency. An assault and battery may be "indecent" if it involves touching portions of the anatomy commonly thought private, such as a person's genital area or buttocks, or the breasts of a female. However, it is no limited to the touching of these areas. "A touching is indecent when, judged by the normative standard of societal mores, it is violative of

SEX RELATED CRIMES

C. 265 § 13B	INDECENT ASSAULT AND BATTERY ON CHILD UNDER 14
	social and behavioral expectations in a manner which [is] fundamentally offensive to contemporary moral values . . . [and] which the common sense of society would regard as immodest, immoral and improper."[1]
Kissing	The mouth and its interior are an intimate part of the body. *Commonwealth v. Rosa*, 62 Mass. App. Ct. 622, 625, 818 N.E.2d 621, 624 (2004) (insertion of thumb into mouth, coupled with other suggestive circumstances, found indecent). "An unwanted kiss on the mouth has been held to constitute indecent conduct, at least in circumstances involving the forced insertion of the tongue, when coupled with surreptitiousness and a considerable disparity in age and authority between the perpetrator and the victim. We do not read our cases, however, as requiring that there always be tongue involvement for an act that might be characterized as a kiss to be found indecent, as other facts and circumstances may allow the trier of fact rationally to determine that the kiss was an indecent act . . . . [I]n most situations it would not be appropriate to criminalize a brief kiss on the mouth that did not involve the insertion or attempted insertion of the tongue [except where] the kiss could be viewed as having improper, sexual overtones, violative of social and behavioral expectations." *Commonwealth v. Vasquez,* 65 Mass. App. Ct. 305, 307, 839 N.E.2d 343, 346 (2005) (internal quotations omitted).

C. 265 § 13L	RECKLESS SEXUAL ENDANGERMENT TO A CHILD
	Engages in Conduct **Elements**
1.	Wantonly or recklessly
2.	**Engages in conduct**
3.	That creates a substantial **risk** of: c. serious bodily injury, or **d. sexual abuse**
4.	To a child under the age of 18 years
	Fails to Act **Elements**
1.	Wantonly or recklessly
2.	**Fails to take reasonable steps** to alleviate a substantial **risk** of serious bodily injury or **sexual abuse** to a child under 18 years
3.	Where there is a duty to act
	Arrest Power, Penalties & Notes
Power of Arrest	**Misdemeanor** – there is no statutory authority granting warrantless powers of arrest for this offense. However, if the offense is committed in public, in the officer's presence, and is creating a **breach of the peace** an arrest would be lawful.

[1] *Commonwealth v. Vasquez,* 65 Mass. App. Ct. 305, 306, 839 N.E.2d 343, 346 (2005) (internal quotations omitted). See *Commonwealth v. Bishop,* 296 Mass. 459, 462, 6 N.E.2d 369, 370 (1937).

C. 265 § 13L	RECKLESS SEXUAL ENDANGERMENT TO A CHILD
Penalty	Imprisonment in the HOC for not more than 2½ years
	Related Statutes, Case Law & Other Important Information
Wanton & Reckless	For the purposes of this section, **wanton or reckless behavior** occurs when a person is aware of and consciously disregards a substantial and unjustifiable risk that his acts, or failure to act (where there is a duty to act), would result in serious bodily injury or sexual abuse to a child. The risk must be of such nature and degree that disregard of the risk constitutes a gross deviation from the standard of conduct that a reasonable person would observe in the situation.
Sexual Abuse	An indecent assault and battery on a child under 14 (c. 265 § 13B); indecent assault and battery on a person age 14 or over (c. 265 § 13H); rape (c. 265 § 22); rape of a child under 16 with (c. 265 § 22A); rape and abuse of a child (c. 265 § 23); assault with intent to commit rape (c. 265 § 24); and assault of a child with intent to commit rape (c. 265 § 24B).
Lesser included Offenses	This offense is a lesser included offense of chapter § 13J (the failure to act version of the offense).[1]

C. 265 § 26C	ENTICEMENT OF CHILD UNDER AGE 16
	Elements
1.	The defendant entices,
2.	• A child under the age of 16, or • Someone he *believes* to be a child under the age of 16 (**Attorney Hanrahan's Note:** this element includes undercover officers posing on the Internet as children and the like),
3.	To enter, exit or remain
4.	Within any vehicle, dwelling, building, or other outdoor space
5.	With the intent that he or another person will violate one of the following laws: • G.L. c. 265, § 13B Indecent assault and battery on a child under • G.L. c. 265, § 13F Indecent assault and battery on a person with an intellectual disability • G.L. c. 265, § 13H Indecent assault and battery on a person 14 or older • G.L. c. 265, § 22 Rape; Aggravated rape • G.L. c. 265, § 22A Rape of a child under 16 with force • G.L. c. 265, § 23 Rape and abuse of a child under 16 (statutory rape) • G.L. c. 265, § 24 Assault with intent to rape • G.L. c. 265, § 24B Assault on a child under 16 with intent to rape • G.L. c. 272, § 4A Inducing a minor to prostitution • G.L. c. 272, § 16 Open and gross lewdness • G.L. c. 272, § 28 Disseminating matter harmful to a minor or any offense that has the use or attempted use of force as an element, • G.L. c. 272, § 29 Disseminating or possessing to disseminate obscene matter • G.L. c. 272, § 29A Posing or exhibiting child under 18 in a state of nudity or sexual conduct

SEX RELATED CRIMES

[1] *Commonwealth v. Roderiques.* 462 mass. 415 (2012.)

C. 265 § 26C	ENTICEMENT OF CHILD UNDER AGE 16
	• G.L. c. 272, § 35A Unnatural act with child under 16 • G.L. c. 272, § 53 Accost or annoy person of opposite sex ▪ Common nightwalker ▪ Common streetwalker ▪ Disorderly conduct ▪ Disturbing the peace ▪ Indecent exposure ▪ Keeping a noisy and disorderly house ▪ Lewd, wanton and lascivious conduct • G.L. c. 272, § 53A Sexual conduct for a fee 7.480 ▪ Paying or procuring for sexual conduct ▪ Paying or procuring for sexual conduct with a child under 14 • "Any offense that has as an element the use or attempted use of force"
Arrest Power, Penalties & Notes	
Power of Arrest	**Felony** – a police officer may effect a warrantless arrest for this offense provided he/she has probable cause that the suspect committed the offense.
Penalty	Imprisonment in the **state prison (F)** for not more than 5 years, or in the HOC for not more than 2½ years, or by both imprisonment and a fine of not more than $5,000.
Related Statutes, Case Law & Other Important Information	
Entice	In this section the term "**entice**" shall mean to **lure, induce, persuade, tempt, incite, solicit, coax** or **invite**.
Speech alone	The statute does not require an overt act but does require proof of specific intent to commit one or more of the enumerated crimes. It does not criminalize the mere sending of sexually explicit messages or indecent language, even to minors; in fact, the statute can be violated by enticing a child without making any verbal reference to sexual matters at all.[1] In a prosecution for enticing a child with intent to kidnap, merely offering the victim a ride and then saying in a "more demanding" and "sort of loud" voice "Get in the truck" were insufficient to prove that the defendant intended to forcibly confine the victim.[2]
Age Issues	The Commonwealth need not prove that the defendant knew the exact age of the victim, but must prove that the defendant intended to direct his sexual advances to an underage victim, i.e., to do a criminal act. Intending to have consensual sexual relations with another adult would not provide the requisite criminal specific intent for the fifth element, even if it turned out that the object of the defendant's advances was in fact a child. *Commonwealth v. Filopoulos,* 451 Mass. 234, 884 N.E.2d 514 (2008); *Commonwealth v. Disler,* 451 Mass. 216, 884 N.E.2d 500 (2008).
Electronic Enticement Of Child under 18 C. 265 § 26D	The defendant, by electronic communication, knowingly entices a child under the age of 18 years (or attempts to entice), to engage in: • Prostitution in violation of chapter 272 § 50 or § 53A, • Human trafficking in violation of chapter 265 § 50, 51, 52 or 53 , or • Commercial sexual activity as defined in chapter 265 § 49. For more on this offense see the Kidnapping & Enticement section of the manual.

[1] *Commonwealth v. Disler,* 451 Mass. 216, 884 N.E.2d 500 (2008).
[2] *Commonwealth v. LaPlante,* 73 Mass. App. Ct. 199, 897 N.E.2d 78 (2008).

C. 272 § 35A UNNATURAL AND LASCIVIOUS ACTS WITH CHILD UNDER 16

Elements	
1.	The defendant commits
2.	Any unnatural and lascivious act
3.	With a child under 16 years old
Arrest Power, Penalties & Notes	
Power of Arrest	**Felony** – a police officer may effect a warrantless arrest for this offense provided he/she has probable cause that the suspect committed the offense.
Penalty	A fine of not less than $100 nor more than $1,000 or by imprisonment in the **state prison (F)** for not more than 5 years or in jail or the HOC for not more than 2½ years. **2nd or subsequent offense**: if the defendant is over the age of 18 commits a second or subsequent such offence shall be sentenced to imprisonment in the **state prison (F)** for a term of **not less than 5 years.**
Attorney Hanrahan's Comment	The adult version of this offense requires a public element. However, the public element is not required when it involves conduct with a child.
Related Statutes, Case Law & Other Important Information	
Unnatural and lascivious act	The term "unnatural and lascivious act" includes: anal intercourse, fellatio, or oral sex involving contact between the mouth of one person and the penis of another person, cunnilingus, or oral sex involving contact between the mouth of one person and the female sex organs — the vagina, vulva or labia — of another person, masturbation of another person, or any other intrusion of a part of one person's body or some other object into the genital or anal opening of another person's body. Cunnilingus is an "unnatural and lascivious act" and, except in a rape prosecution, does not require proof of penetration of the genital opening.[1] The statute includes public fellatio and oral-anal contact.[2]

SEX RELATED CRIMES

[1] *Commonwealth v. Benoit*, 26 Mass. App. Ct. 641, 646-648, 531 N.E.2d 262, 265-266 (1988).
[2] *Commonwealth v. Sefranka*, 382 Mass. 108, 116, 414 N.E.2d 602, 607 (1980).

LEWDNESS & MORAL INDECENCY

C. 272 § 16	OPEN AND GROSS LEWD AND LASCIVIOUS BEHAVIOR
Elements	
1.	The defendant intentionally exposed his/her genitals, buttocks or female breast
2.	The defendant did so "openly," that is, either he/she intended public exposure (or exposure to another), or he/she recklessly disregarded a substantial
3.	The defendant's actions were done in such a way as to produce alarm or shock
4.	One or more persons were in fact alarmed or shocked by the exposure.
Arrest Power, Penalties & Notes	
Power of Arrest	**Felony** – a police officer may effect a warrantless arrest for this offense provided he/she has probable cause that the suspect committed the offense.
Penalty	Imprisonment in the **state prison (F)** for not more than three years or in jail for not more than two years or by a fine of not more than $300.
Related Statutes, Case Law & Other Important Information	
Crime can be committed in a private home	In *Commonwealth v. Wardell,* a salesman exposed himself in private home to minor children. The requirement that act be "open" refers to defendant's intent that act be seen by one or more unwilling persons present and does not require that it be done in a public place.[1]
Victim	A police officer can serve as the person who is "shocked or alarmed" by the defendant's act.[2]
No exposure intended	In *Commonwealth v. Catlin,* the SJC ruled the statute inapplicable to sexual acts reasonably expected to be private but accidentally observed through broken window.[3]
Attempt to avoid public exposure must be legit	In *Commonwealth v. Cummings,* the SJC ruled that consensual homosexual conduct in a public toilet coupled with ineffective attempts at concealment do not prevent the act from being "open" if committed in a place where there can be no real privacy.[4]
Masturbating	*Commonwealth v. Adams,* 389 Mass. 265, 272, 450 N.E.2d 149, 153 (1983) (masturbating in a public place "certainly falls within the common understanding" of the offense.[5] Attorney Hanrahan's note: the Courts seem to be uncertain whether there must be exposure in addition to masturbation. When in doubt summons, hopefully the Courts will clarify this at some point soon.
"Buttocks" or "female breasts."	Open and gross lewdness is not limited to exposure of the genitals, and may include exposure of the "buttocks" or "female breasts." *Commonwealth v. Quinn*, 439 Mass. 492, 501, 789 N.E.2d 138, 146 (2003); *Commonwealth v. Ora, supra.*

[1] *Commonwealth v. Wardell,* 128 Mass. 52, 53-54 (1880).
[2] Commonwealth v. Manuel Pereira (2012) Appeals Court.
[3] *Commonwealth v. Catlin,* 1 Mass. 8, 10 (1804).
[4] *Commonwealth v. Cummings,* 273 Mass. 229, 231-232, 173 N.E. 506, 507 (1930).
[5] *Commonwealth v. Adams,* 389 Mass. 265, 272, 450 N.E.2d 149, 153 (1983).

C. 272 § 16	OPEN AND GROSS LEWD AND LASCIVIOUS BEHAVIOR
Single penalty for one act with multiple victims	Where there is a single incident of open and gross lewdness resulting in shock and alarm to more than one person, the legislature intended that only a single penalty attach to the conduct. For double jeopardy purposes, the "unit of prosecution" is conduct-based, not victim based. [1]
What if no exposure?	In ***Commonwealth v. Quinn,*** 439 Mass. 492 (2003), the SJC concluded that thong clad buttocks violated this statute. The key to this charge, and the key difference between this offense and indecent exposure, is that the defendant's lewd conduct produced "shock or alarm" to another. Up until *Quinn*, it was generally restricted to the full exposure of genitalia, female breasts, and buttocks. However, in *Quinn*, the SJC seemed to expand the conduct punishable by this statute. Seemingly, any lewd and lascivious conduct which produces shock and alarm can violate this statute. Below is a list of some conduct (and the cases from which they came) referenced in the *Quinn* decision that would violate this statute: a. Masturbating in automobile - *Commonwealth v. Poillucci*, 46 Mass.App.Ct. 300, 302 (1999) b. Oral sex - *Commonwealth v. Gray*, 40 Mass.App.Ct. 901, 901 (1996) c. Masturbating through his pants and without exposure of penis - (see notes below) Cf. *State v. Maunsell*, 170 Vt. 543, 547 (1999) d. Standing in window of apartment and masturbating - *Commonwealth v. Montez*, 45 Mass.App.Ct. 802, 806 (1997) However, in the 2010 Appeals Court case of ***Commonwealth v. Blackmer, III,*** the Appeals Court ruled that *Quinn* did not eliminate the exposure requirement but merely left open the possibility that non-exposed masturbation may violate c. 272 § 16. **Attorney Hanrahan's Note**: Although *Quinn* seemed to eliminate the exposure requirement of this offense, the Appeals Court has subsequently interpreted the *Quinn* decision to mean something else. In short, until something changes, the five elements listed above must be met in order to secure a conviction for this offense. **If exposure of genitals, buttocks, or females breasts are not present consider Lewd, Wanton and Lascivious Persons offense**.
Semi-transparent clothing	In the 2014 case of ***Commonwealth v. Coppinger***, the defendant entered a Target store in Kingston wearing white "see through" compression shorts. He had a visible erection and his pink flesh could be seen through his shorts. The Appeals Court ruled that this violated the statute.
Indecent Exposure **c. 272 § 53**	In 1937, the SJC decided ***Commonwealth v. Bishop***, which spelled out three elements to this crime: 1. Intentional 2. Exposure of genitals or female breasts to one or more persons 3. One or more persons were offended by the exposure **Attorney Hanrahan's Note:** This crime is almost identical to Open and Gross however Indecent Exposure does not require the "shock and alarm" element, additionally flashing the buttocks does not violate the indecent exposure law but even thong clad buttocks could violate the open and gross law. **Power of Arrest - Misdemeanor:** c. 272 § 54 authorizes a warrantless arrest for disorderly conduct offenses committed in the officers presence. **Indecent exposure is lesser included offense.** Indecent exposure (G.L. c. 272, § 53) is a lesser included offense of open and gross lewdness[2]. However, indecent exposure may be used to prosecute only exposure of the genitals and not exposure of non-genital pubic areas.[1]

[1] *Commonwealth v. Botev*, 79 Mass. App. Ct. 281,___ N.E.2d ___ (2011).
[2] *Commonwealth v. Alvin B. Fields*, 71 Mass. App.Ct. 1116, 883 N.E.2d 343, 2008 W L 859686 (No. 07-P-895, Apr. 1, 2008) (unpublished opinion under Appeals Court Rule 1:28).

C. 272 § 53	LEWD, WANTON AND LASCIVIOUS PERSONS
	Elements[2]
1.	The defendant committed, or publicly solicited another person to commit, a sexual act
2.	The sexual act involved touching the genitals or buttocks, or the female breasts
3.	The defendant did this either for the purpose of sexual arousal or gratification, or for the purpose of offending other people; and
4.	The sexual act was, or was to be, committed in a public place; that is, a place where the defendant either intended public exposure, or recklessly disregarded a substantial risk of public exposure at that time and under those circumstances, to others who might be offended by such conduct.
Exception	The defendant cannot be found guilty of this offense if he/she desired privacy for a sexual act.
	Arrest Power, Penalties & Notes
Power of Arrest	**Misdemeanor** – c. 272 § 54 authorizes a warrantless arrest for disorderly conduct offenses committed in the officers presence.
Penalty	Imprisonment in a jail or HOC for not more than 6 months, or by a fine of not more than $200, or by both such fine and imprisonment.
Attorney Hanrahan's Comment	This offense is very similar to c. 272 § 35 (lascivious acts) if the act is actually performed (as opposed to proposed) c. 272 § 35 may be a better option because it imposes felony penalties.
	Related Statutes, Case Law & Other Important Information
Public Element	In *Commonwealth v. Roy,* the SJC ruled that the statute cannot be applied to solicitation for sexual conduct where it is unclear whether it was to occur in a public or private place.[3] In *Commonwealth v. Beauchemin,* the SJC ruled that the statute cannot be applied to sexual conduct in location where little likelihood of being observed by casual passersby.[4] *Commonwealth v. Kelley,* the place need not be one "to which the public or a substantial group has access," but "judges, in the interest of caution, would be well advised to charge that the offense requires either that the defendant 'intended public exposure or recklessly disregarded a substantial risk of exposure to one or more persons'".[5]

[1] *Commonwealth v. Arthur,* 420 Mass. 535, 650 N.E.2d 787 (1995).
[2] *Commonwealth v. Sefranka,* 382 Mass. 108, 117-118, 414 N.E.2d 602, 608 (1980).
[3] *Commonwealth v. Roy,* 420 Mass. 1, 647 N.E.2d 1179 (1995).
[4] *Commonwealth v. Beauchemin,* 410 Mass. 181, 183-184, 571 N.E.2d 395, 397 (1991).
[5] *Commonwealth v. Kelley,* 25 Mass. App. Ct. 180, 516 N.E.2d 1188 (1987).

C. 272 § 35	UNNATURAL AND LASCIVIOUS ACTS
Elements	
1.	The defendant committed an unnatural and lascivious act with another person.
2.	The defendant committed that act intentionally; and
3.	The sexual act was done in a public place; that is, a place where the defendant either intended public exposure, or recklessly disregarded a substantial risk of public exposure at that time and under those circumstances, to others who might be offended by such conduct. Note: public element not required if consent is lacking
Arrest Power, Penalties & Notes	
Power of Arrest	**Felony** – a police officer may effect a warrantless arrest for this offense provided he/she has probable cause that the suspect committed the offense.
Penalty	A fine of not less than $100 nor more than $1,000 or by imprisonment in the **state prison (F)** for not more than five years or in jail or the HOC for not more than 2½ years.
Attorney Hanrahan's Comment	The purpose of the statute is to prevent public sexual conduct that might give offense to persons present in a place that is frequented by members of the public. This offense is very similar to c. 272 § 53 (lewd, wanton and lascivious person) however to be convicted of this offense the defendant must have actually engaged in the act, which would make it a felony; under 272 § 53 merely asking another to engage in the conduct would be sufficient.
Related Statutes, Case Law & Other Important Information	
Unnatural and lascivious act	The term "unnatural and lascivious act" includes: anal intercourse, fellatio, or oral sex involving contact between the mouth of one person and the penis of another person, cunnilingus, or oral sex involving contact between the mouth of one person and the female sex organs — the vagina, vulva or labia — of another person, masturbation of another person, or any other intrusion of a part of one person's body or some other object into the genital or anal opening of another person's body. Cunnilingus is an "unnatural and lascivious act" and, except in a rape prosecution, does not require proof of penetration of the genital opening.[1] The statute includes public fellatio and oral-anal contact.[2]
Non-consensual conduct – public element not required	The statute may be applied to non-consensual conduct, in which case the public nature of the act is not an element of the offense, but absence of consent is.[3]
Person under 16	See chapter 272 § 35A in the juvenile sex crime section for this offense involving a child under 16.

[1] *Commonwealth v. Benoit*, 26 Mass. App. Ct. 641, 646-648, 531 N.E.2d 262, 265-266 (1988).
[2] *Commonwealth v. Sefranka*, 382 Mass. 108, 116, 414 N.E.2d 602, 607 (1980).
[3] Commonwealth v. *Balthazar*, (1974) 366 Mass. at 302-303, 318 N.E.2d at 481.

C. 272 § 35	UNNATURAL AND LASCIVIOUS ACTS
Private Conduct	The statute does not apply to the private, consensual conduct of adults. The defendant cannot be found guilty of this charge if he (she) desired privacy for a sexual act with a consenting adult and took reasonable measures in order to secure that privacy.[1] The Commonwealth must prove that the likelihood of being observed by casual passersby must have been reasonably foreseeable to the defendant, or stated otherwise, that the defendant acted upon an unreasonable expectation that his conduct would remain secret".[2] The key to this statute is that is the act was conducted in a place where the possibility of public view is eliminated. Thus, acts conducted in secluded public locations may not be punishable under this statute if it was highly unlikely that another member of the public may come across the act.

C. 272 § 17	INCESTUOUS MARRIAGE OR SEXUAL ACTIVITIES
Elements	
1.	Persons within degrees of consanguinity within which marriages are prohibited or declared by law to be incestuous and void who do any of the following:
2.	• Intermarry or have sexual intercourse with each other, or • Engage in sexual activities with each other, including but not limited to oral or anal intercourse, fellatio, cunnilingus, or other penetration of a part of a person's body, or insertion of an object into the genital or anal opening of another person's body, or the manual manipulation of the genitalia of another person's body.
Arrest Power, Penalties & Notes	
Power of Arrest	**Felony** – a police officer may effect a warrantless arrest for this offense provided he/she has probable cause that the suspect committed the offense.
Penalty	Imprisonment in the **state prison (F)** for not more than 20 years or in the HOC for not more than 2½ years.
Related Statutes, Case Law & Other Important Information	
Marriage Restrictions c. 207 § 1-2	No man shall marry his mother, grandmother, daughter, granddaughter, sister, stepmother, grandfather's wife, grandson's wife, wife's mother, wife's grandmother, wife's daughter, wife's granddaughter, brother's daughter, sister's daughter, father's sister or mother's sister. No woman shall marry her father, grandfather, son, grandson, brother, stepfather, grandmother's husband, daughter's husband, granddaughter's husband, husband's grandfather, husband's son, husband's grandson, brother's son, sister's son, father's brother or mother's brother.

[1] 2009 Massachusetts ModelJury Instructions.
[2] *Commonwealth v. Ferguson*, 384 Mass. 13, 16, 422 N.E.2d 1365, 1367 (1981).

C. 272 § 17	INCESTUOUS MARRIAGE OR SEXUAL ACTIVITIES
Adultery c. 272 § 14	A married person who has sexual intercourse with a person not his spouse or an unmarried person who has sexual intercourse with a married person shall be guilty of adultery and shall be punished by imprisonment in the **state prison (F)** for not more than 3 years or in jail for not more than 2 years or by a fine of not more than $500. **Arrest Powers**: **Felony** – a police officer may effect an arrest for this offense committed in his/her presence or for an offense in the past, on probable cause **Attorney Hanrahan's Note**: Although this crime is still technically a felony it has not been prosecuted in recent time.
Polygamy c. 272 § 15	Whoever, having a former husband or wife living, marries another person or continues to cohabit with a second husband or wife in the commonwealth shall be guilty of polygamy, and be punished by imprisonment in the **state prison (F)** for not more than five years or in jail for not more than 2½ years or by a fine of not more than $500; **Exception:** this section shall not apply to a person whose husband or wife has continually remained beyond sea, or has voluntarily withdrawn from the other and remained absent, for seven consecutive years, the party marrying again not knowing the other to be living within that time, nor to a person who has been legally divorced from the bonds of matrimony. **Arrest Powers**: **Felony** – a police officer may effect an arrest for this offense committed in his/her presence or for an offense in the past, on probable cause.

C. 272 § 34	BEASTIALITY
	Elements
1.	The defendant commits the abominable and detestable crime against nature, either with mankind or with a beast.
	Arrest Power, Penalties & Notes
Power of Arrest	**Felony** – a police officer may effect a warrantless arrest for this offense provided he/she has probable cause that the suspect committed the offense.
Penalty	Imprisonment in the state prison for not more than 20 years.

DISSEMINATION OF HARMFUL MATTER & CHILD PORNOGRAPHY OFFENSES

C. 272 § 29	DISSEMINATION OR POSSESSION OF OBSCENE MATTER
	Elements
1.	The defendant disseminates or has in his possession with intent to disseminate
2.	Matter that is in evidence is obscene (see definitions below)
3.	The defendant knows that it is obscene
Exception	It shall be a defense under this section if the evidence proves that the defendant was a bona fide **school, museum or library**, or was acting in the course of his employment as an employee of such organization or of a **retail outlet affiliated with and serving the educational purpose** of such organization.
	Arrest Power, Penalties & Notes
Power of Arrest	**Felony** – a police officer may effect a warrantless arrest for this offense provided he/she has probable cause that the suspect committed the offense.
Penalty	Imprisonment in the **state prison (F)** for not more than 5 years or in a jail or HOC for not more than 2½ years or by a fine of not less than $1,000 nor more than $10,000 for the first offense. **2nd Offense:** not less than $5,000 nor more than $20,000 or by both fine and the above imprisonment **3rd or subsequent offense**: not less than $10,000 nor more than $30,000, or by both fine and the above imprisonment. A prosecution commenced under this section shall not be continued without a finding nor placed on file.
	Related Statutes, Case Law & Other Important Information
Matter **c. 272 § 31**	"Matter", any handwritten or printed material, visual representation, live performance or sound recording including, but not limited to, books, magazines, motion picture films, pamphlets, phonographic records, pictures, photographs, figures, statues, plays, dances, or any electronic communication including, but not limited to, electronic mail, instant messages, text messages, and any other communication created by means of use of the Internet or wireless network, whether by computer, telephone, or any other device or by any transfer of signs, signals, writing, images, sounds, data, or intelligence of any nature transmitted in whole or in part by a wire, radio, electromagnetic, photo-electronic or photo-optical system.
Obscene **c. 272 § 31**	Any such material is obscene if, taken as a whole, it meets all three of the following requirements: *[1]* it appeals to the prurient interest of an average citizen of this county; *[2]* it shows or describes sexual conduct in a way that is patently offensive to an average citizen of this county; and *[3]* it has no serious value of a literary, artistic, political or scientific kind. For something to be obscene is that, taken as a whole, it must appeal to the prurient interest of an average adult person in this county. You are to determine this by applying the contemporary standards in this county on the date of the alleged offense. "Prurient interest" means "a shameful or morbid interest in nudity, sex, or excretion," an unhealthy interest about sexual matters which is repugnant to prevailing moral standards.[1]

[1] *Roth v. United States,* 354 U.S. 476, 487 n.20, 77 S.Ct. 1304, 1310 n.20 (1957), quoting from Model Penal Code § 207.10(2) (Tent. Draft No. 6, 1957); *Commonwealth v. Dane Entertainment Servs., Inc. (No. 2),* 397 Mass. 201, 204, 490 N.E.2d 785, 787 (1986) (community standards to be applied are those at time of act, not those at time of trial).

C. 272 § 29	DISSEMINATION OR POSSESSION OF OBSCENE MATTER
	The fact finder must look to the matter as a whole and see whether its dominant theme depicts hard core sexual conduct that goes substantially beyond customary limits of candor and appeals to an unhealthy, shameful or morbid interest in sex.[1]
Disseminate	"Disseminate", to import, publish, produce, print, manufacture, distribute, sell, lease, exhibit or display. c. 272 § 31
Commercial Distribution not required	In the 2011 case of ***Commonwealth v. Dodgson***, the Appeals Court ruled that the crime of dissemination of obscene material (c. 272 §§ 29 and 31) does not require *public or commercial* distribution. Simply distributing the material to one person is sufficient.

C. 272 § 28	DISSEMINATION OF MATTER HARMFUL TO MINORS
	Elements
1.	The defendant • disseminates to a minor (person under 18) or someone he believes is a minor, or • has in his possession with the intent to disseminate to a minor
2.	Any matter harmful to minors (see definition below),
3.	Knowing it to be harmful to minors
	Arrest Power, Penalties & Notes
Power of Arrest	**Felony** – a police officer may effect a warrantless arrest for this offense provided he/she has probable cause that the suspect committed the offense.
Penalty	**Penalty:1st Offense:** imprisonment in the **state prison (F)** for not more than 5 years or in a jail or HOC for not more than 2½ years, or by a fine of not less than $1,000 nor more than $10,000 **2nd Offense**: imprisonment in the **state prison (F)** for not more than 5 years or in a jail or HOC for not more than 2½ years, or by fine of not less than $5,000 nor more than $20,000, or by both such fine and imprisonment. **3rd of Subsequent Offense:** imprisonment in the **state prison (F)** for not more than 5 years or in a jail or HOC for not more than 2½ years, or by fine of not less than $10,000 nor more than $30,000, or by both such fine and imprisonment. A prosecution commenced under this section shall not be continued without a finding nor placed on file.
	Related Statutes, Case Law & Other Important Information
Harmful to Minors	**"Harmful to minors",** matter is harmful to minors if it is obscene or, if taken as a whole, it (1) describes or represents nudity, sexual conduct or sexual excitement, so as to appeal predominantly to the prurient interest of minors; (2) is patently contrary to prevailing standards of adults in the county where the offense was committed as to suitable material for such minors; and (3) lacks serious literary, artistic, political or scientific value for minors.

[1] *Commonwealth v. 707 Main Corp.*, 371 Mass. 374, 384, 357 N.E.2d 753, 760 (1976); *Commonwealth v. United Books, Inc.*, 18 Mass. App. Ct. 948, 949, 468 N.E.2d 283, 285 (1984); *Commonwealth v. Dane Entertainment Servs., Inc.*, 13 Mass. App. Ct. 931, 932, 430 N.E.2d 1231, 1233 (1982).

C. 272 § 28	DISSEMINATION OF MATTER HARMFUL TO MINORS
Matter **c. 272 § 31**	"Matter", any handwritten or printed material, visual representation, live performance or sound recording including, but not limited to, books, magazines, motion picture films, pamphlets, phonographic records, pictures, photographs, figures, statues, plays, dances, or any electronic communication including, but not limited to, electronic mail, instant messages, text messages, and any other communication created by means of use of the Internet or wireless network, whether by computer, telephone, or any other device or by any transfer of signs, signals, writing, images, sounds, data, or intelligence of any nature transmitted in whole or in part by a wire, radio, electromagnetic, photo-electronic or photo-optical system.
Computer display	In ***Commonwealth v. Washburn***, a high school teacher was convicted of c. 272 § 28 when he displayed pornography on his computer screen to his 15 year old student.[1]
Disseminate **c. 272 § 31**	"Disseminate", to import, publish, produce, print, manufacture, distribute, sell, lease, exhibit or display.
Defense	It shall be a defense in any prosecution under this section that the defendant was in a **parental or guardianship relationship with the minor**. It shall also be a defense in any prosecution under this section if the evidence proves that the defendant was a bona fide **school, museum or library**, or was acting in the course of his employment as an employee of such organization or of a retail outlet affiliated with and serving the educational purpose of such organization.

C. 272 § 29C	KNOWINGLY PURCHASE/POSSESS CHILD PORNOGRAPHY
	Elements
1.	The defendant knowingly purchases or possess
2.	A negative, slide, book, magazine, film, videotape, photograph or other similar visual reproduction, or depiction by computer, of any child whom the person knows or reasonably should know to be **under the age of 18 years** of age and such child is: (i) actually or by simulation engaged in any act of sexual intercourse with any person or animal; (ii) actually or by simulation engaged in any act of sexual contact involving the sex organs of the child and the mouth, anus or sex organs of the child and the sex organs of another person or animal; (iii) actually or by simulation engaged in any act of masturbation; (iv) actually or by simulation portrayed as being the object of, or otherwise engaged in, any act of lewd fondling, touching, or caressing involving another person or animal; (v) actually or by simulation engaged in any act of excretion or urination within a sexual context; (vi) actually or by simulation portrayed or depicted as bound, fettered, or subject to sadistic, masochistic, or sadomasochistic abuse in any sexual context; or (vii) depicted or portrayed in any pose, posture or setting involving a lewd exhibition of the unclothed genitals, pubic area, buttocks or, if such person is female, a fully or partially developed breast of the child;
3.	with knowledge of the nature or content thereof

[1] *Commonwealth v. Washburn*, 55 Mass.App.Ct. 493 (2002).

C. 272 § 29C	KNOWINGLY PURCHASE/POSSESS CHILD PORNOGRAPHY
Arrest Power, Penalties & Notes	
Power of Arrest	**Felony** – a police officer may effect a warrantless arrest for this offense provided he/she has probable cause that the suspect committed the offense.
Penalty	1st Offense: Imprisonment in the state prison for not more than 5 years or in a jail or house of correction for not more than 2½ years or by a fine of not less than $1,000 nor more than $10,000, or by both such fine and imprisonment. 2nd Offense: not less than 5 years in a state prison or by a fine of not less than $5,000 nor more than $20,000, or by both such fine and imprisonment. 3rd or more: not less than 10 years in a state prison or by a fine of not less than $10,000 nor more than $30,000, or by both such fine and imprisonment.
Related Statutes, Case Law & Other Important Information	
Dost Factors	In deciding whether a particular exhibition of the naked body is lewd, the courts have utilized the so-called Dost factors as a starting point for analysis, recognizing that they are not dispositive or comprehensive, but aids to further analysis.[1] Those factors are as follows: 1. whether the focal point of the visual depiction is on the child's genitalia or pubic area; 2. whether the setting of the visual depiction is sexually suggestive, i.e., in a place or pose generally associated with sexual activity; 3. whether the child is depicted in an unnatural pose, or in inappropriate attire, considering the age of the child; 4. whether the child is fully or partially clothed, or nude; 5. whether the visual depiction suggests sexual coyness or a willingness to engage in sexual activity; 6. whether the visual depiction is intended or designed to elicit a sexual response in the viewer.
Nudity alone	The depiction of mere nudity is not enough to support a conviction under c. 272 § 29A.[2] In the 2014 case of ***Commonwealth v. Rex***, the defendant, an inmate at MCI, was found to be in the possession of photos of children who were naked but engaged in everyday activities (National Geographic type images). The SJC ruled reiterated that naked images alone do not qualify.
Cell Phone and/or Computer Images	In a case involving photographs received on a cell phone, the Appeals Court described the following four elements of possession of child pornography: "The Commonwealth must present evidence that the defendant (1) knowingly possessed a photograph or other similar visual reproduction or depiction by computer; (2) depicting a child that the defendant knew or reasonably should have known was under the age of eighteen; (3) in a pose of a lewd or sexual nature as defined in the statute; and (4) with knowledge of the nature or content of the material." *Commonwealth v. Hall*, 80 Mass. App. Ct. 317, 327, 952 N.E.2d 951, 959 (2011).

[1] Commonwealth v. Mark Sullivan (2012) Appeals Court
[2] *Commonwealth v. Bean*, 435 Mass. 708, 715 n.17, 761 N.E.2d 501, 508 n.17 (2002).

c. 272 § 29A	**POSING/EXHIBITING CHILD IN STATE OF NUDITY OR SEXUAL CONDUCT (Creating Child Pornography)**
Elements	
1.	The defendant either with knowledge that a person is a child under 18 years of age or with knowledge of facts that he should have reason to know that such person is a child under 18 years of age,
2.	With lascivious (sexual arousal or gratification) intent,
3.	▪ Hires, coerces, solicits or entices, employs, procures, uses, causes, encourages to do one of the below, or ▪ Knowingly permits the child to do one of the below:
4.	a. To **pose or be exhibited in a state of nudity** for the purpose of representation or reproduction in any visual material, or b. To **participate or engage in any act** that depicts, describes, or represents **sexual conduct** for the purpose of representation or reproduction in any visual material; or c. To engage in any **live performance** involving sexual conduct
Arrest Power, Penalties & Notes	
Power of Arrest	**Felony** – a police officer may effect a warrantless arrest for this offense provided he/she has probable cause that the suspect committed the offense.
Penalty	Imprisonment in the **state prison (F)** for a term of not less than 10 nor more than 20 years, or by a fine of not less than $10,000 nor more than $50,000, or by both such fine and imprisonment.
Related Statutes, Case Law & Other Important Information	
Strict Liability	In a prosecution under this section, a minor shall be deemed incapable of consenting to any conduct of the defendant for which said defendant is being prosecuted.
Evidence	The determination whether the person in any visual material prohibited in this statute is under 18 years of age may be made by the **personal testimony** of the person, by the testimony of a person who produced, processed, published, printed or manufactured such visual material that the child therein was known to him to be under 18 years of age, or by **expert medical testimony** as to the age of the person based upon the person's physical appearance, by **inspection of the visual material**, or by any other method authorized by any general or special law or by any applicable rule of evidence.
Lascivious intent	**"Lascivious intent",** a state of mind in which the sexual gratification or arousal of any person is an objective. For the purposes of prosecution under this chapter, proof of lascivious intent may include, but shall not be limited to, the following: (1) whether the circumstances include sexual behavior, sexual relations, infamous conduct of a lustful or obscene nature, deviation from accepted customs and manners, or sexually oriented displays; (2) whether the focal point of a visual depiction is the child's genitalia, pubic area, or breast area of a female child; (3) whether the setting or pose of a visual depiction is generally associated with sexual activity; (4) whether the child is depicted in an unnatural pose or inappropriate attire, considering the child's

c. 272 § 29A	POSING/EXHIBITING CHILD IN STATE OF NUDITY OR SEXUAL CONDUCT (Creating Child Pornography)
	age; (5) whether the depiction denotes sexual suggestiveness or a willingness to engage in sexual activity; (6) whether the depiction is of a child engaging in or being engaged in sexual conduct, including, but not limited to, sexual intercourse, unnatural sexual intercourse, bestiality, masturbation, sado-masochistic behavior, or lewd exhibition of the genitals.
Nudity	**"Nudity",** uncovered or less than opaquely covered human genitals, pubic areas, the human female breast below a point immediately above the top of the areola, or the covered male genitals in a discernibly turgid state. For purposes of this definition, a female breast is considered uncovered if the nipple or areola only are covered.
Sexual Conduct and Excitement **c. 272 31**	**"Sexual conduct",** human masturbation, sexual intercourse, actual or simulated, normal or perverted, any lewd exhibitions of the genitals, flagellation or torture in the context of a sexual relationship, any lewd touching of the genitals, pubic areas, or buttocks of the human male or female, or the breasts of the female, whether alone or between members of the same or opposite sex or between humans and animals, and any depiction or representation of excretory functions in the context of a sexual relationship. Sexual intercourse is simulated when it depicts explicit sexual intercourse which gives the appearance of the consummation of sexual intercourse, normal or perverted. **"Sexual excitement"**, the condition of human male or female genitals or the breasts of the female while in a state of sexual stimulation or the sensual experiences of humans engaging in or witnessing sexual conduct or nudity
Live Performance	Encouraging a sex act over live video (i.e. Skype, Facetime, Video gaming, etc.) is a *live performance* for the purposes of G.L. chapter 272 § 29A (posing or exhibiting child in state of nudity or sexual conduct).[1]

C. 272 § 29B	DISSEMINATION OF CHILD PORNOGRAPHY
	Elements
1.	The defendant, with lascivious (sexual arousal or gratification) intent, disseminates, or has in his possession with intent to disseminate,
2.	Any visual material that contains: • a representation or reproduction of any posture or exhibition in a **state of nudity** involving the use of a child who is under 18 years of age, or • a representation or reproduction of any act that depicts, describes, or represents **sexual conduct** participated or engaged in by a child who is under 18 years of age.
3.	Knowing the contents of the material/reproduction or having sufficient facts in his possession to have knowledge of the contents.

PORNOGRAPHY

[1] *Commonwealth v. Bundy*, SJC (2013).

C. 272 § 29B	DISSEMINATION OF CHILD PORNOGRAPHY
Arrest Power, Penalties & Notes	
Power of Arrest	**Felony** – a police officer may effect a warrantless arrest for this offense provided he/she has probable cause that the suspect committed the offense.
Penalty	**State prison (F)** for a term of not less than 10 nor more than 20 years or by a fine of not less than $10,000 nor more than $50,000 or 3 times the monetary value of any economic gain derived from said dissemination, whichever is greater, or by both such fine and imprisonment.
Attorney Hanrahan's Comment	The same definitions (e.g. disseminate, lascivious, etc.) apply to all of these pornography type offenses.
Related Statutes, Case Law & Other Important Information	
Exception for School, Museum, or Library	Proof that dissemination of any visual material that contains a representation or reproduction of sexual conduct or of any posture or exhibition in a state of nudity involving the use of a child who is under eighteen years of age was for a bona fide scientific, medical, or educational purpose for a bona fide school, museum, or library may be considered as evidence of a lack of lascivious intent.
Strict Liability	In a prosecution under this section, a minor shall be deemed incapable of consenting to any conduct of the defendant for which said defendant is being prosecuted.
Evidence	The determination whether the person in any visual material prohibited in this statute is under 18 years of age may be made by the **personal testimony** of the person, by the testimony of a person who produced, processed, published, printed or manufactured such visual material that the child therein was known to him to be under 18 years of age, or by **expert medical testimony** as to the age of the person based upon the person's physical appearance, by **inspection of the visual material**, or by any other method authorized by any general or special law or by any applicable rule of evidence.

PROSTITUTION OFFENSES

C. 272 § 53A	SEXUAL CONDUCT FOR A FEE
The Prostitute Elements	
1.	The defendant either engaged, or agreed to engage, or offered to engage, in sexual conduct with another person; and
2.	That the sexual conduct was, was to be, done in return for a fee.
Penalty for the prostitute	Imprisonment in the house of correction for not more than 1 year or by a fine of not more than $500, or by both such imprisonment and fine, whether such sexual conduct occurs or not.
The Customer Elements	
1.	That the defendant, paid, agreed to pay, or offered to pay, another person; and
2.	The payment was in exchange for that person's engaging in sexual conduct, or for that person's agreeing to engage in sexual conduct, with the defendant, or another person.
Penalty for the customer	Imprisonment in the house of correction for not more than 2 and one-half years or by a fine of not less than $1,000 and not more than $5,000, or by both such imprisonment and fine, whether such sexual conduct occurs or not.
Arrest Power	
Power of Arrest	**Misdemeanor** – c. 272 § 54 authorizes a warrantless arrest for all sex for a fee offenses committed in the officers presence in a public place.
Related Statutes, Case Law & Other Important Information	
Sexual Conduct and Activity	The term "sexual conduct" includes (sexual intercourse) (anal intercourse) (fellatio, or oral sex involving contact between the mouth of one person and the penis of another person) (cunnilingus, or oral sex involving contact between the mouth of one person and the female sex organs —the vagina, vulva or labia — of another person) (masturbation of another person) (or) (any other intrusion of a part of one person's body or some other object into the genital or anal opening of another person's body).[1] The term "'sexual activity' . . . encompass[es] all acts commonly understood to be described by the term, including masturbation" of another as well as sexual intercourse and deviate sexual intercourse, and is not unconstitutionally vague. Commonwealth v. *Walter,* 388 Mass. at 463, 465-466, 446 N.E.2d at 709-710.
Prostitute under 18 years Felony	Whoever pays, agrees to pay or offers to pay any person with the intent to engage in sexual conduct with a child under the age of 18, or whoever is paid, agrees to pay or agrees that a third person be paid in return for aiding a person who intends to engage in sexual conduct with a child under the age of 18, shall be punished by imprisonment in the state prison for not more than 10 years, or in the house of correction for not more than 2 and one-half years and by a fine of not less than $3,000 and not more than $10,000, or by both such imprisonment and fine, whether such sexual conduct occurs or not; provided, however, that a prosecution commenced under this section shall not be continued without a finding or placed on file.

PROSTITUTION OFFENSES

[1] 2009 Model Jury Instructions.

C. 272 § 53A	SEXUAL CONDUCT FOR A FEE
Selective prosecution of females	The Massachusetts Equal Rights Amendment (art. 106 of the Articles of Amendment to the Massachusetts Constitution) requires that a § 53A charge against a female defendant be dismissed with prejudice upon an appropriate showing that the particular police department or prosecutor's office consistently prosecutes female prostitutes but not their male customers. [1]
	ADDITIONAL PROSTITUTION RELATED OFFENSES
Soliciting a Prostitute **AKA Pimping** **G.L. c. 272 § 8**	The defendant solicits or receives compensation for soliciting for a prostitute. **Penalty**: imprisonment in a house of correction for not more than 2½ years, or by a fine of not less than $1,000 and not more than $5,000 or by both such imprisonment and fine. **Attorney Hanrahan's Note**: consider the Human Trafficking offenses or deriving support from the earning of a prostitute as they impose much greater penalties.
Deriving Support from earnings of a Prostitute **c. 272 § 7**	The defendant knowing a person to be a prostitute, • lives or derives support or maintenance, in whole or in part, from the earnings or proceeds of his prostitution, from moneys loaned, advanced to or charged against him by any keeper or manager or inmate of a house or other place where prostitution is practiced or allowed, or • shares in the earnings, proceeds or moneys. **Penalty:** imprisonment in the **state prison (F)** for a period of 5 years and by a fine of $5,000. This statute requires a mandatory minimum sentence of 2 years. **Arrest Powers**: **Felony** – a police officer may effect an arrest for this offense committed in his/her presence or for an offense in the past, on probable cause. In *Commonwealth v. Thetonia,* the Court ruled that a friend chauffeuring who was a prostitute in exchange for occasional gas money and drugs was insufficient; since the statute is aimed at pimping, a minor indirect financial benefit not sufficient to convict.[2]
Deriving Support from Earnings of Minor Prostitute **c. 272 § 4B**	The defendant lives or derives support or maintenance, in whole or in part, from the earnings or proceeds of prostitution committed by a minor (under 18), knowing the same to be earnings or proceeds of prostitution, or shares in such earnings, proceeds or monies, shall be punished by imprisonment in the **state prison (F)** for **not less than 5 years** and by a fine of $5,000.
Inducing Minor into Prostitution **c. 272 § 4A**	The defendant induces a minor (under 18) to become a prostitute, or knowingly aids and assists in such inducement, **Penalty**: by imprisonment in the **state prison (F)** for not more than 5, nor less than 3 years, and by a fine of $5,000. **Case Law Note:** In order to secure a conviction for this offense the Commonwealth must show that the minor was not already a prostitute but that the defendant actually *induced* the minor to become a prostitute.[3]

[1] *An Unnamed Defendant,* 22 Mass. App. Ct. at 233-236, 492 N.E.2d at 1186-1188. See *Commonwealth v. Hackett,* 383 Mass. 888, 888-889, 421 N.E.2d 769, 771 (1981); *King,* 374 Mass. at 17-22, 372 N.E.2d at 204-207.
[2] *Commonwealth v. Thetonia,* 27 Mass. App. Ct. 783,543 N.E.2d 700 (1989).
[3] *Commonwealth v. Matos,* decided January 11, 2011

C. 272 § 53A	SEXUAL CONDUCT FOR A FEE
House of Prostitution **c. 272 § 6**	The defendant, being the owner of a place or having or assisting in the management or control thereof induces or knowingly suffers a person to resort to or be in or upon such place, for the purpose of unlawfully having sexual intercourse for money or other financial gain. **Penalty:** imprisonment in the **state prison (F)** for a period of 5 years and a $5,000 fine.
Keeping house of ill fame **c. 272 § 24**	The defendant keeps a house of ill fame which is used for prostitution or lewdness. **Penalty**: imprisonment for not more than 2 years. **Arrest Powers**: **Misdemeanor** – statutory authority, via c. 272 § 10, permits a police may effect an arrest for this offense committed in his/her presence or for an offense in the past on "reasonable cause."
Detaining, or Drugging to Detain, Person In Place For Prostitution **c. 272 § 13**	The defendant, for any length of time, unlawfully detains or attempts to detain a person, or aids or abets in unlawfully detaining or attempting to detain a person, or provides or administers or aids or abets in providing or administering any drug or liquor for the purpose of detaining a person in a house of ill fame or other place where prostitution is practiced or allowed. **Penalty:** imprisonment in the **state prison (F)** for not more than 5 years or in the HOC for not less than one nor more than 2½ years or by a fine of not less than $100 nor more than $500.

C. 265 § 50	TRAFFICKING OF PERSONS FOR SEXUAL SERVITUDE
	Elements
1.	The defendant knowingly does any of the following:
2.	• Subjects, Attempts to subject, Causes, Recruits, entices, Harbors, Transports, Provides or Obtains by any means, or Attempts to recruit, entice, harbor, transport, provide or obtain by any means, another person to engage in any of the following: (a) a commercial sexual activity, (b) a sexually-explicit performance (c) the production of unlawful pornography in violation of chapter 272, (d) causes a person to engage in commercial sexual activity, a sexually-explicit performance (e) the production of unlawful pornography in violation of said chapter 272; • Benefits, financially or by receiving anything of value, as a result of a violation of the above activities.
	Arrest Power, Penalties & Notes
Power of Arrest	**Felony** – a police officer may effect a warrantless arrest for this offense provided he/she has probable cause that the suspect committed the offense.
Penalty	**Penalty victim 18 plus:** imprisonment in the state prison for not less than 5 years but not more than 20 years and by a fine of not more than $25,000. Such sentence shall not be reduced to less than 5 years, or suspended, nor shall any person convicted under this section be eligible for probation, parole, work release or furlough or receive any deduction from his sentence for good conduct until he shall have

PROSTITUTION OFFENSES

C. 265 § 50	TRAFFICKING OF PERSONS FOR SEXUAL SERVITUDE
	served 5 years of such sentence. No prosecution commenced under this section shall be continued without a finding or placed on file. **Penalty victim under 18**: whoever commits the crime of trafficking of persons for sexual servitude upon a person under 18 years of age shall be punished by imprisonment in the state prison for life or for any term of years, but not less than 5 years. No person convicted under this subsection shall be eligible for probation, parole, work release or furlough or receive any deduction from his sentence for good conduct until he shall have served 5 years of such sentence. **Penalty for a business:** A business entity that commits trafficking of persons for sexual servitude shall be punished by a fine of not more than $1,000,000.
	Related Statutes, Case Law & Other Important Information
Definitions for sections c. 265 § 50 via c. 265 § 49	The following words shall, unless the context clearly requires otherwise, have the following meanings: "**Commercial sexual activity",** any sexual act on account of which anything of value is given, promised to or received by any person. "**Forced services**", services performed or provided by a person that are obtained or maintained by another person who: (i) causes or threatens to cause serious harm to any person; (ii) physically restrains or threatens to physically restrain another person; (iii) abuses or threatens to abuse the law or legal process; (iv) knowingly destroys, conceals, removes, confiscates or possesses any actual or purported passport or other immigration document, or any other actual or purported government identification document, of another person; (v) engages in extortion under section 25; or (vi) causes or threatens to cause financial harm to any person. "**Services**", acts performed by a person under the supervision of or for the benefit of another including, but not limited to, commercial sexual activity and sexually-explicit performances. "**Sexually-explicit performance**", an unlawful live or public act or show intended to arouse or satisfy the sexual desires or appeal to the prurient interests of patrons.
Civil Remedy	A victim may bring an action in tort in the superior court in any county wherein a violation of subsection (a) occurred, where the plaintiff resides or where the defendant resides or has a place of business. Any business entity that knowingly aids or is a joint venturer in trafficking of persons for sexual servitude shall be civilly liable for an offense under this section.
Forced Services	See the Kidnapping section for non-sex related human trafficking offenses.

SEX OFFENDER LAWS

C. 6 § 178H	SEX OFFENDER FAIL TO REGISTER, VERIFY INFORMATION OR PROVIDE NOTICE OF CHANGE OF ADDRESS; PROVIDING FALSE INFORMATION
Elements	
Registration and Reporting Violations	A sex offender required to register pursuant to this chapter who knowingly: i. fails to register; ii. fails to verify registration information; iii. fails to provide notice of a change of address; or iv. who knowingly provides false information
Arrest Power, Penalties & Notes	
Power of Arrest	**Arrest Powers:** Whenever a police officer has probable cause to believe that a sex offender has failed to comply with the registration requirements.....such officer shall have the right to arrest such sex offender without a warrant and to keep such sex offender in custody.
Penalty	**Penalty (F):** A first conviction under this subsection shall be punished by imprisonment for not less than 6 months and not more than 2½ years in a HOC nor more than 5 years in a **state prison (F)** or by a fine of not more than $1,000 or by both such fine and imprisonment. Important exception: **UNLESS the sex offender is homeless than the first offense is only a misdemeanor.**
Attorney Hanrahan's Comment	The sex offender laws seem to be constantly changing. They are frequently challenged in court as unconstitutional and as a result the Board often modifies the regulations and registration requirements, be sure to check the most current regulations before making an arrest. Also, all registrations/notifications must be done using a Board approved form under the pains and penalties of perjury.
REGISTRATION/NOTIFICATION REQUIREMENTS	
Violations involving INITIAL registration.	
§ 178E (a).	Any level Sex Offender must register by mailing to the Sex Offender Registry Board, at least 2 days before **release from custody (jail/prison)**.
§ 178E (b) or (c).	Any level sex offender must register by mailing to the Sex Offender Registry Board within 2 days **after receiving notice** of the requirement or release from custody.
§ 178E(g).	*If defendant is a **level 1** sex offender:* register by **mailing** to the Sex Offender Registry Board within 2 days after **moving to Massachusetts**.
§§ 178E(g) and 178F½.	*If defendant is a **level 2 or 3** sex offender:* register **in person** with the police department by completing and delivering within 2 days after **moving to Massachusetts** a Board-approved form that includes all of the required information.
§ 178E(o)	Any level sex offender must register by mailing to the Sex Offender Registry Board, **within 10 days** before commencing employment or enrollment at an institution of higher education.
§ 178E(q).	Any level sex offender who is a non-resident and is attending an education institution in Massachusetts must register by mailing to the Sex Offender Registry Board, within 10 days of attending an educational institution as a **nonresident** of Massachusetts.

SEX OFFENDERS

C. 6 § 178H	SEX OFFENDER FAIL TO REGISTER, VERIFY INFORMATION OR PROVIDE NOTICE OF CHANGE OF ADDRESS; PROVIDING FALSE INFORMATION
Violations involving reporting status changes	
§ 178E(h).	*If defendant is a **level 1** sex offender:* he must notify by mailing to the Sex Offender Registry Board, **at least 10 days before moving to a different town.**
§§ 178E(h) & 178F½.	*If defendant is a **level 2 or 3** sex offender:* he must notify by reporting in person to the police department of the town where he/she resides **at least 10 days before moving** to a different town.
§ 178E(h).	*If defendant is a **level 1** sex offender:* he must notify the Sex Offender Registry Board in writing at least 10 days before **moving within a town**.
§§ 178E(h) & 178F½.	*If defendant is a **level 2 or 3** sex offender:* he must notify by reporting in person, **at least 10 days before moving within a town**, to the police department of that town.
§ 178E(l)	*If defendant is a **level 1** offender:* he must notify the Sex Offender Registry Board at least 10 days before moving out of Massachusetts.
§§ 178E(l) & 178F½.	*If defendant is a **level 2 or 3** sex offender:* he must notify by reporting **in person** to the police department of the town where he resides **at least 10 days before moving out** of Massachusetts.
§ 178E(j).	*If defendant is a **level 1** sex offender:* he must notify the Sex Offender Registry Board in writing at least 10 days before **changing work address**.
§§ 178E(j) & 178F½.	*If defendant is a **level 2 or 3** sex offender:* He must notify by reporting in person to the police department of the town where he resides, at least 10 days before **changing work address**.
178E(p)	He must notify by mailing to the Sex Offender Registry Board, at least 10 days before he transfers from, or stops attending, an institution of higher education.
Violations involving periodic verification.	
§ 178F.	*If defendant is a **level 1** sex offender:* he must verify **annually** by mailing to the Sex Offender Registry Board, within 5 days of receipt of notice from the Board.
§§ 178F & 178F½.	*If defendant is a **level 2 or 3** sex offender:* he shall **verify annually** by reporting **in person** to the police department of the town where he resides within 5 days of receipt of notice from the Sex Offender Registry Board.
§ 178F1/2	As a **sexually violent predator**, verify **every 45 days** by appearing in person at the police department of the town where he resides and verifying under the penalties of perjury that all information remained true and accurate.
Related Statutes, Case Law & Other Important Information	
Homeless	All sex offenders residing at a homeless shelter must verify registration data every 30 days.[1349]
Out of State Sex Offenders working in MA	Sex offenders residing in locations outside of Massachusetts, but who are employed in the Commonwealth, must register within 2 days of beginning employment. A person is working in Massachusetts if he comes into Massachusetts to work at a full-time or part-time job for a period of time exceeding 14 days or for an aggregate period of time exceeding 30 days during any calendar year, whether compensated or uncompensated.[1350]

[1349] SORB Website 2013
[1350] SORB Website 2013

C. 6 § 178H	SEX OFFENDER FAIL TO REGISTER, VERIFY INFORMATION OR PROVIDE NOTICE OF CHANGE OF ADDRESS; PROVIDING FALSE INFORMATION
Board Form and Required Information	All registrations/notifications must be completed by utilizing a Board approved form. The Board-approved form requires that the sex offender provide his or her name, date of birth, home address or intended home address (and, if the offense occurred on or after 7/1/2006, any secondary addresses or intended secondary addresses), work address or intended work address, and the name and address of any institution of higher learning where the sex offender is or intends to become an employee or student. The form must be signed under the penalties of perjury.
Annual Registration begins after year of initial registration	The sex offender annual registration requirement begins after the calendar year wherein the sex offender has otherwise registered. In ***Com. v. Loring***, the defendant was classified as a level two sex offender and as a result of the classification he registered with the Brockton Police Department on June 20, 2008. His birthday was three months later in September of 2008. He failed to register again in September, during the month of his birth and he was charged with failing to register. The Appeals Court ruled that he was not required to register again until next calendar year.[1351]
No intent to deceive required	In a prosecution for providing false information, the Commonwealth is not required to prove that the defendant intended to deceive the Sex Offender Registry Board *Commonwealth* v. *Fondakowski*, 62 Mass. App. Ct. 939, 821 N.E.2d 481 (2005).
Secondary Addresses	Secondary addresses are: *First,* the addresses of all places where a sex offender lives, abides, lodges, or resides for a period of **14 or more days** in the aggregate during any **calendar year** and which is not a sex offender's primary address; and *Second,* any place where a sex offender routinely lives, abides, lodges, or resides for a period of **4 or more consecutive or non-consecutive days** in any **month** and which is not a sex offender's permanent address, including any out-of-state address.
Sex Offenders Prohibited from convalescent Homes	It is a crime for a Level 3 sex offender to "knowingly and willingly" live in any convalescent or nursing home, infirmary maintained in a town, rest home, charitable home for the aged or intermediate care facility for the mentally retarded which meets the requirements of the DPH under G.L. c. 111, § 71. Penalties for committing this crime are as follows: First conviction: imprisonment for not more than 30 days in a jail or house of correction; Second conviction: imprisonment for not more than 2 ½ years in a jail or house of correction nor more than 5 years in a state prison or by a fine of not more than $1,000, or by both such fine and imprisonment; and Third and subsequent conviction: imprisonment in a state prison for not less than 5 years; provided, however, that the sentence imposed for such third or subsequent conviction shall not be reduced to less than 5 years, nor suspended.
Ice Cream Vendor Restriction	Chapter 265 § 48 makes it a crime for a sex offender to engage in ice cream truck vending. Penalty: **misdemeanor** - imprisonment in the house of correction for not more than 2½ years or by a fine of $1,000, or by both such fine and imprisonment. **Arrest Power**: A police officer or officer authorized to serve criminal process may arrest, without a warrant, any person whom he has probable cause to believe has violated this section.
Level 0	The Sex Offender Registry Board refers to out-of-state sex offenders who have yet to be classified after moving to Massachusetts as Level 0.

SEX OFFENDERS

[1351] Com. v. Loring, Appeals Court 2012.

C. 6 § 178H	SEX OFFENDER FAIL TO REGISTER, VERIFY INFORMATION OR PROVIDE NOTICE OF CHANGE OF ADDRESS; PROVIDING FALSE INFORMATION
State not required to inform out-of-state sex offender of requirement	In ***Commonwealth v. Bell*** (2013), the SJC ruled that it is not required that the State notify an out-of-state sex offender of his/her requirement to register when entering Massachusetts in order to prove that the defendant "knowingly" failed to register.
Attorney Hanrahan's Comment	Many people have the misconception that a sex offender's daily activities are restricted in some way. However, generally this is not the case. For instance, it is not uncommon for a parent who recognizes a sex offender near their child's school to frantically phone the police. However, absent any restrictions placed by probation, parole or bail terms, a sex offender is generally not prohibited from any particular area or activity, with the few exceptions noted (e.g. ice cream truck vending). The intent of the sex offender registration is more for monitoring purposes. In some cases, the sex offender may be required to wear a GPS tracking device. However, the SJC recently ruled that a JV sex offender cannot be required to wear a tracking bracelet.[1352] Additionally, the sex offender laws and rules seem to be constantly changing. Many of the provisions are frequently challenged on Constitutional grounds. It is best to check the most recent change in this area when investigating a sex offender case.

PUBLIC DISSIMENATION OF SEX OFFENDER INFORMATION

Some, but not all, Sex Offender information is accessible to the public. In some situations the police must actively warn the public. In some situations the information is prohibited from public release (see CORI section of the manual). Below depicts the type of information that can and cannot be released.

Sex Offender Type	Public Release	Additional information
Level 1	No public dissemination permitted.	The SORB deems these offenders as low risk of reoffending.
Level 2	Public dissemination permitted – see additional information.	Up until 2013 level 2 sex offender information was limited those who specifically requested the information and it was limited to a geographical radius and it had to be for the protection of the requester or the requesters children. However, the law was modified in 2013 to permit level 2 sex offender information to be public disseminated without a specific request. There have been some challenges to this change regarding its retroactivity. Those classified level 2 before the law change argue that they are exempt. Some of these cases are still being litigated. At the time of the printing of this manual the CMR regarding this still indicated that the information must be specifically requested. Contact the SORB for guidance. The SORB deems level 2 sex offenders as moderate risks.
Level 3 & Sexually Violent Predators	Active dissemination required	The SORB deems level 3 sex offenders at a high risk of reoffending. 803 CMR 1.33 states in part "The police department shall notify organizations in the community that are likely to encounter an offender Finally Classified as a Level 3 Offender or a sexually violent predator, and notify individual members of the public who are likely to encounter such an offender. Organizations in the community that are likely to encounter the sex offender include, but are not limited to, public and private organizations, areas and establishments which provide services of any type to children, the elderly, or other vulnerable members of the population.." Community notification shall require notification by the police department to all schools in the community...The chief of the police department, in his discretion, may notify other organizations, such as day care centers, youth/recreational programs, and organizations providing elder services, as deemed necessary to protect the public safety."

[1352] Commonwealth v. Hanson H., a juvenile, (SJC 2013).

B&E UNLAWFULL ACCESS OFFENSES

Overview: There is a variety of burglary and B&E offenses, many are very similar. If the crime you are investigating fits more than one offense you may elect to charge the crime which carries the greatest penalty, you may be able to charge for more than one offense (see the Important Information to Know section at the start of the Statutory law section of this manual for duplicative convictions), or you may elect to charge the offense which will be easiest to prove. In practice, it is often best to make the arrest (if applicable), or otherwise conduct your investigation, and then consult with the DA's office for the most appropriate charge.

Nighttime: For the purposes of burglary (and B&E) offenses, nighttime begins 1 hour after sunset and ends 1 hour before sunrise the next day. This is set by statute chapter 278 § 10. **Note:** For the purpose of executing a search warrant, case law tells us that nighttime is from 10 pm to 6 am.

Breaking: a breaking typically occurs when someone uses force to move an obstruction to gain entrance, even if the exertion of force is minor. But it can also occur when someone enters by a means not intended for entry, such as climbing through a window, down a chimney etc. in these cases the exertion of physical force is not required. A breaking can also occur through a so-called "constructive" breaking; such as when the perpetrator gains entry by threats or fraud or if an accomplice let the defendant in or if the defendant convinced an innocent person by trick or threat to allow him/her to enter.[1]

Entering: An entry occurs when any part of the suspect's body crosses the plane into the protected space. It also occurs when the suspect utilizes an object to break the plane, such as when the suspect uses a long stick to reach into an open window in order to pull out a woman's purse by its handle. For the purposes of B&E related crimes the entry must be unprivileged, or in other words unlawful, to meet this element of the offense.

Intent: An important factor when charging a suspect with a B&E related offense is what was the suspect's intent when he/or she committed the offense. In short, all B&E's and Burglaries are felonies unless the suspect had only the intent to commit a misdemeanor. If the suspect breaks into a building in the nighttime it can be inferred that his intent was to commit a larceny absent some evidence to the contrary. A larceny from a building, therefor in most B&E's involving buildings and dwellings it can be presumed that the suspect's intent was to commit a felony.[2] Additionally, when someone breaks in by using force it can presumed," in the absence of evidence to the contrary, that his intent is to steal."[3]

B&E vs. Burglary: The key difference between these offenses is that under common law a burglary can only occur in a dwelling and in the nighttime. For instance, if a defendant broke into a dwelling during the daytime it would be a B&E offense, not burglary; or if the defendant broke into a building (non-dwelling) in the nighttime it would be a B&E offense, not burglary.

A **Dwelling** is a place where someone lives (and it is intended and designed for someone to live - e.g. even if someone lived in their car it would not be considered a dwelling). See the following case law notes on dwellings:

- A hotel/motel can be deemed a dwelling.[4]
- The common hallway of an apartment building can be deemed a dwelling. [5]
- The key to a building being a dwelling is that someone lives there, it must be inhabited. If the house is abandoned than it is not a dwelling.

[1] *Commonwealth v. Lowrey,* 158 Mass. 18, 19-20, 32 N.E. 940, 941 (1893) (accomplice); *Commonwealth v. Labare,* 11 Mass. App. Ct. 370, 377, 416 N.E.2d 534, 538 (1981) (phony name).
[2] *Commonwealth v. McGovern,* 397 Mass. 863, 868, 494 N.E.2d 1298, 1301 (1986); *Commonwealth v. Hughes,* 380 Mass. 596, 602-604, 404 N.E.2d 1246, 1250-1251 (1980) (dwelling); *Commonwealth v. Wygrzywalski,* 362 Mass. 790, 792, 291 N.E.2d 401, 402-403 (1973) (store);
[3] Commonwealth v. Eppich, 342 Mass. 487 (1961).
[4] *Com. v. Correia* (1983) 17 Mass.App.Ct. 233
[5] *Com. v. Goldoff* (1987) 24 Mass.App.Ct. 458

BURGLARIES & HOME INVASIONS

c. 266 § 15	BURGLARY
Elements	
1.	The defendant, in the **nighttime**:
2.	• Breaks and enters a dwelling house with intent to commit a felony or • After having entered with intent to commit a felony, breaks such dwelling house
Arrest, Penalties, Attempts & Notes	
Power of Arrest	**Felony** – a police officer may effect an arrest on probable cause.
Penalty	Imprisonment in the state prison (F) for not more than 20 years. If the defendant has been previously convicted for not less than 5 years.
Attorney Hanrahan's Comment	How could someone break after entering? This could occur in a number of ways, for instance the suspect enters through an open door (no break) but once inside he then breaks into a bed room.
Related Statutes & Case Law	
Nighttime	Nighttime begins 1 hour after sunset and ends 1 hour before sunrise the next day
Be sure to review comments on dwellings, nighttime, etc. at the beginning of the B&E and Burglary section of this manual.	

C.266 § 14	ARMED BURGLARY; ASSAULT ON OCCUPANTS "AGGRAVATED BURGLARY"
Elements	
1.	The defendant, in the **nighttime**:
2.	• Breaks and enters a dwelling house with intent to commit a felony or • After having entered with intent to commit a felony, breaks such dwelling house
3.	Another person is lawfully in the dwelling, and
4.	• the offender being armed with a dangerous weapon at the time of such breaking or entry, or • arms himself while inside, or • makes an actual assault on a person lawfully therein.
Arrest, Penalties, Attempts & Notes	
Power of Arrest	**Felony** – a police officer may effect an arrest for this offense on probable cause
Penalty	**1st Offense:** Imprisonment in the state prison (F) for life or for any term of not less than 10 years.

C.266 § 14	ARMED BURGLARY; ASSAULT ON OCCUPANTS "AGGRAVATED BURGLARY"
	Subsequent offense: imprisonment in the state prison (F) for life or for any term of years, but not less than 20 years. **If Armed with a firearm, rifle, shotgun, machine gun or assault weapon:** not less than 15.
Attorney Hanrahan's Comment	With this offense the defendant commits a burglary 1. while being armed (or arms himself once inside) – even if the weapon is not used or 2. assaults an occupant (even without having a weapon).
Related Statutes, Case Law & Important Information	
Nighttime	Chapter 278 § 10 defines nighttime begins 1 hour after sunset and ends 1 hour before sunrise the next day
Only one offense per entry	Even if the defendant enters a dwelling and assaults multiple people inside he has only committed this offense once. In the 2014 case of ***Commonwealth v. Bolden***, the SJC ruled that 266 § 14 permits only one burglary conviction per dwelling.
Be sure to review comments on dwellings, nighttime, etc. at the beginning of the B&E and Burglary section of this manual.	

C.265 § 18A	ARMED ASSAULT IN DWELLING HOUSE
Elements	
1.	The defendant being armed with a **dangerous weapon**
2.	Enters a dwelling house
3.	And, while inside assaults another with intent to commit a felony
Arrest, Penalties, Attempts & Notes	
Power of Arrest	Felony – a police officer may effect an arrest for this offense committed in his/her presence or for an offense in the past, on probable cause.
Penalty	Imprisonment in the **state prison (F)** for life, or for a term of not less than 10 years. No parole in less than 5 years. If the defendant was armed with a firearm, shotgun or rifles no parole in less than 10 years.
Attorney Hanrahan's Comment	The assault must be designed to commit a felony other than the assault itself or the entry. For instance, a suspect enters a dwelling while armed and assaults the home owner with the intent of intimidating the occupant who is serving as a witness in a criminal case. The underlying felony would be Intimidation of a Witness.
Related Statutes & Case Law	
Invited Guest	***Com. v. Fleming*** (1999): The Court ruled "An entry, i.e., going in, by an armed person into a dwelling in response to an invitation from a person living there rather obviously is not a violation of the statute." The entry must be unprivileged, or in other words unlawful.

C.265 § 18C	HOME INVASION
Elements	
1.	The defendant knowingly enters the dwelling place of another
2.	• Knowing or having reason to know that one or more persons are present within, or • Remains in the dwelling place knowing or having reason to know that one or more persons are present within
3.	While armed with a dangerous weapon
4.	• Uses force or threatens the imminent use of force upon any person within such dwelling place whether or not injury occurs, or • Intentionally causes any injury to any person within such dwelling place
Arrest, Penalties, Attempts & Notes	
Power of Arrest	Felony – a police officer may effect an arrest on probable cause.
Penalty	Imprisonment in the state prison (F) for life or for any term of not less than 10 years.
Attorney Hanrahan's Comment	Unlike burglary, this offense does not require a nighttime entry. Also, the suspect is not required to have a felonious intent at the time of entry.
Related Statutes, Case Law & Other Important Information	
Must be armed at the of Entry	In ***Com. v. Ruiz*** (1998), the SJC ruled "the statute applies only where a defendant is armed at the time of entry."
Applies to victim who enters dwelling after the defendant	In ***Commonwealth v. Martinez***, the victim, a neighbor, came to the aid of resident after a home invasion began and was assaulted by the defendant (who was already inside). The Court ruled that the victim qualified as an "occupant."
Consent to enter	Consent to enter a home – in and of itself – is not a defense to a charge of armed home invasion. In *Commonwealth v. Maher*, someone inside the home had opened the door and allowed the defendant to enter before the defendant, who was wielding a machete, attacked the homeowners. The SJC ruled that "when consent to enter is given to someone, in circumstances presented here, the consent cannot be considered legally significant unless the occupant has been made aware that the person at the door is armed with a dangerous weapon and is about to commit an assault on someone inside."[1]
What is the difference between c. 265 § 18A and 265 § 18C?	C. 265 § 18C (Armed Home Invasion) imposes a more severe penalty than C. 265 § 18A (Armed Assault in a Dwelling). Under 18C it must be proven that the defendant **knew or had reason to know** that one or more persons were present within the dwelling house **at the time of entry** or that the defendant gained such knowledge **after entry but nevertheless remained there** for some period of time prior to attacking or threatening the person. These knowledge requirements are not present in 18A. Under 18A the defendant may not know that anyone is home until the time he commits the assault. Therefor, if the defendant entered a dwelling without knowing or having reason to know of the presence of others, to prosecute under § 18C the Commonwealth would have to establish that, some appreciable time prior to the assault, the defendant remained there, and presumably could have chosen to leave, after realizing that others were in the dwelling house. 18A also requires that the defendant have an intent to commit a felony at the time of the assault, 18C does not have this requirement. [2]
Nighttime	Chapter 278 § 10: nighttime begins 1 hour after sunset and ends 1 hour before sunrise the next day.

[1] *Com. v. Maher*, 430 Mass. 643 (2000)
[2] See *Com. v. Ruiz* (1998).

BREAKING & ENTERING

C.266 § 16A	B&E with INTENT to COMMITT a MISDEMEANOR
Elements	
1.	The defendant
2.	In the nighttime or daytime
3.	Breaks and Enters
4.	A building, ship, vessel or vehicle
5.	With intent to commit a misdemeanor
Arrest, Penalties, Attempts & Notes	
Power of Arrest	**Misdemeanor** – there is no statutory authority granting powers of arrest for this offense. However, if the offense is committed in public, in the officer's presence, and it is creating a breach of the peace an arrest would be lawful.
Penalty	A fine of not more than $200 or by imprisonment for not more than 6 months, or both.
Attorney Hanrahan's Comment	Most B&E offenses are felonies unless the intent of the suspect was only to commit a misdemeanor. It is often difficult to determine what the intent of the defendant is at the time of the offense. If the B&E involved a building it can usually be assumed, absent some evidence to the contrary, that the intent was to commit a larceny, and a larceny in a building would be a felony. There are some situations wherein the intent of the defendant would be obvious, such as in the case of a homeless man who B&E's into a building on a frigid night to escape the elements. His intent would be a misdemeanor (i.e. to trespass). Some investigation typically needs to be conducted in order to determine the intent
Related Statutes, Case Law & Other Important Information	
C. 266 § 16 B&E into a Depository	B&E into a Depository with intent to commit a larceny (or felony) may also be an appropriate charge in some cases, such as when someone breaks into a locked car to steal the contents. This would clear up any power of arrest issues as this charge would be a felony (see statute).
Intent presumed	Established case law indicates that larcenous intent may be inferred from the act of breaking and entering [see *Commonwealth v. Maia*, 429 Mass. 585, 587-588 (1999)]; and larceny from a building is a felony. A locked vehicle can be deemed a depository, especially if it contains valuables, and B&E into a depository with intent to commit a larceny is a felony, even if the value of the item is less than $250 (see B&E Depository offense). See intent at the beginning of this section for more on this topic.
Be sure to review comments on dwellings, nighttime, etc. at the beginning of the B&E and Burglary section of this manual.	

C.266 § 16	B&E into a DEPOSITORY with INTENT to COMMIT a LARCENY or FELONY
Elements	
1.	The defendant, with intent to commit a larceny or felony,
2.	Attempts or does
3.	Break, burn, blow up or otherwise injure or destroy
4.	A **safe**, **vault** or other **depository** of money, bonds or other valuables, located within any building, vehicle or place.
Arrest, Penalties, Attempts & Notes	
Power of Arrest	**Felony** – a police officer may effect an arrest on probable cause.
Penalty	Imprisonment in the **state prison (F)** for not more than 20 years or in a jail or HOC for not more than 2½ years.
Attorney Hanrahan's Comment	This would be the appropriate offense if someone breaks into (or tries to break into) a safe or similar container of valuables. It could also be applied to a locked automobile if valuables were secured within (see below).
Related Statutes, Case Law & Other Important Information	
Depository	A depository is typically a place where something is deposited especially for safekeeping. In the 1976 case of ***Com. v. Armenia***, the Appeals Court ruled that the trunk of a car can be found to be a depository. In the 1984 case of ***Com. v. Dreyer***, the Appeals Court ruled that "a locked passenger automobile can be inferred a depository." In the 2013 case of ***Commonwealth v. Doyle***, the Appeals Court ruled that an ATM was a depository.
Lock not a depository	In ***Commonwealth v. Hogan*** (1996), the Appeals Court held that bolt cutters, which were used on a lock in an attempt to remove a bicycle affixed to a parking meter, was not a burglarious tool because the lock (and parking meter) was not a "depository."
Be sure to review comments on dwellings, nighttime, etc. at the beginning of the B&E and Burglary section of this manual.	

C.269 § 10J	B&E WITH INTENT TO STEAL A FIREARM
Elements	
1.	The defendant in the nighttime or the daytime,
2.	breaks and enters a building, ship, vessel or vehicle
3.	to steal a firearm
Arrest, Penalties, Attempts & Notes	
Power of Arrest	**Felony** – a police officer may effect an arrest on probable cause.
Penalty	Imprisonment in the state prison for not more than 5 years or by imprisonment in the house of correction for not more than 2½ years or by a fine of not more than $10,000, or by both such fine and imprisonment.
Enhanced penalty if intended to distribute to prohibited person	Whoever in the nighttime or the daytime breaks and enters a building, ship, vessel or vehicle to steal a firearm to **distribute to a prohibited person**, as defined in section 131 of chapter 140 shall be punished by imprisonment in the state prison for not more than 10 years or by imprisonment in the house of correction for not more than 2½ years or by a fine of not more than $10,000, or by both such fine and imprisonment.
Enhanced penalty for causing injury	Whoever in the nighttime or the daytime breaks and enters a building, ship, vessel or vehicle to steal a firearm and **in the process causes injury of another** shall be punished by imprisonment in the state prison for not more than 10 years or by imprisonment in the house of correction for not more than 2 1/2 years or by a fine of not more than $10,000, or by both such fine and imprisonment.
Related Statutes, Case Law & Other Important Information	
Vehicle forfeited	Any motor vehicle lawfully owned or operated by any person convicted pursuant to this section shall be forfeited pursuant to section 24W of chapter 90. All proceeds from the auction of the vehicle shall be deposited into the Public Safety Training Fund established under section 2JJJJ of chapter 29.

C.269 § 10K	B&E TO FIREARM RETAILER
Elements	
1.	The defendant in the nighttime or the daytime
2.	breaks and enters any building in which a firearm retailer, wholesaler or manufacturer conducts business
Arrest, Penalties, Attempts & Notes	
Power of Arrest	**Felony** – a police officer may effect an arrest on probable cause.
Penalty	Imprisonment in the state prison for not more than 10 years or by imprisonment in the house of correction for not more than 2½ years or by a fine of not more than $10,000, or by both such fine and imprisonment.
Additional element option: intent to obtain a weapon	Whoever in the nighttime or the daytime breaks and enters any building in which a firearm retailer, wholesaler or manufacturer conducts business **with the intent to unlawfully obtain a firearm, rifle, shotgun, machine gun or ammunition** shall be punished by imprisonment in the state prison for not more than 10 years or by imprisonment in the house of correction for not more than 2½ years or by a fine of not more than $10,000, or by both such fine and imprisonment. **Attorney Hanrahan's note**: Oddly, the legislature included an alternative version of this offense which includes the additional element of the *intent to unlawfully obtain a firearm, rifle, shotgun, machine gun or ammunition* but the penalty is the same. A conviction would be easier to obtain without adding in

B&E & BURGLARY OFFENSES

C.269 § 10K	B&E TO FIREARM RETAILER
	this additional element.
Enhanced penalty if weapon is actually obtained	Whoever unlawfully **obtains** a firearm, rifle, shotgun, machine gun or ammunition by means of breaking and entering, in the nighttime or the daytime, any building in which a firearm retailer, wholesaler or manufacturer conducts business and who unlawfully distributes said firearm, rifle, shotgun, machine gun or ammunition shall be punished by imprisonment in the state prison for not more than **20 years** or by imprisonment in the house of correction for not more than 2½ years or by a fine of not more than $10,000, or by both such fine and imprisonment.

C.266 § 18	B&E in the DAYTIME with intent to commit a FELONY
Elements	
1.	Breaks and Enters
2.	In the Daytime
3.	A building, ship, vessel, or vehicle
4.	With the intent to commit a Felony
Arrest, Penalties, Attempts & Notes	
Power of Arrest	**Felony** – a police officer may effect an arrest on probable cause.
Penalty	Imprisonment in the state prison (F) for not more than 10 years or by a fine of not more than $500 and imprisonment in jail for not more than 2 years. **Enhanced Penalty Firearms**: imprisonment in the state prison (F) for not less than 5 years or by imprisonment in the HOC for not more than 2½ years.
Attorney Hanrahan's Comment	B&E during the day and the perpetrator has the intent to commit a felony. If it occurs at night use chapter 266 § 16.
Related Statutes, Case Law & Other Important Information	
B&E without felony intent	If the B&E occurs either during the day or night and the intent was only to commit a misdemeanor use chapter 266 § 16A. See the notes on intent at the beginning of this section.
Intent to Commit a Felony	Established case law indicates that larcenous intent may be inferred from the act of breaking and entering [see *Commonwealth v. Maia*, 429 Mass. 585, 587-588 (1999)]; and larceny from a building is a felony. A locked vehicle can be deemed a depository, especially if it contains valuables, and B&E into a depository with intent to commit a larceny is a felony, even if the value of the item is less than $250 (see B&E Depository offense). See intent at the beginning of this section for more on this topic.
Enter in the day without breaking	If the suspect enters in the day without breaking the proper charge, oddly, would be only trespassing and whatever other corresponding charge if another crime was committed while inside, as there is no charge for *entering a dwelling in the day* (unless by false pretenses). If the person was armed at the time of entry chapter 265 § 18C (Home Invasion) or chapter 265 §18A (Armed Assault in a Dwelling) may be an appropriate charge.
B&E railroad car	Chapter 266 § 19 makes it a felony to B&E into a railroad car with the intent to commit a felony.
Truck/Trailer	Chapter 266 § 20A makes it a felony to B&E or just to Enter into a truck, tractor, trailer or freight container with an intent to commit a felony.

C.266 § 17	B&E in the DAYTIME with intent to commit a FELONY and Person Put in Fear
Elements	
1.	Breaks and Enters
2.	In the Daytime
3.	A building, ship, vessel, or vehicle
4.	With the intent to commit a Felony
5.	The owner or any other person lawfully inside being put in fear
Arrest, Penalties, Attempts & Notes	
Power of Arrest	**Felony** – a police officer may effect an arrest on probable cause.
Penalty	Imprisonment in the **state prison (F)** for not more than 10 years. **Enhanced Penalty Firearms:** If armed with a firearm, rifle, shotgun, machine gun or assault weapon shall be punished by imprisonment in the **state prison (F)** for not less than 7 years or by imprisonment in the HOC for 2 years and not more than 2½ years.
Related Statutes, Case Law & Other Important Information	
Intent to instill fear not needed	The crime of B&E in the daytime with intent to commit a felony and placing an occupant in fear, c. 266 § 17, does not require that the defendant intend to place the occupant in fear.[1]
No Fear or No Break	If no one was put in fear and/or no break occurred use c. 266 § 18.
Be sure to review comments on dwellings, nighttime, etc. at the beginning of the B&E and Burglary section of this manual.	

[1] Commonwealth v. Santana (2012) Appeals Court

C. 266 § 16	B&E in the NIGHTTIME with Intent to commit a FELONY
Elements	
1.	In the nighttime
2.	Breaks and Enters
3.	A building, ship, vessel or vehicle
4.	With intent to commit a Felony
Arrest, Penalties, Attempts & Notes	
Power of Arrest	**Felony –** a police officer may effect an arrest on probable cause.
Penalty	Imprisonment in the state prison (F) for not more than 20 years or in a jail or HOC for not more than 2½ years.
Attorney Hanrahan's Comment	This is the offense to use for a B&E at night for non-dwellings.
Related Statutes, Case Law & Other Important Information	
Nighttime	Chapter 278 § 10 defines nighttime begins 1 hour after sunset and ends 1 hour before sunrise the next day
Intent to Commit a Felony	Established case law indicates that larcenous intent may be inferred from the act of breaking and entering [see *Commonwealth v. Maia*, 429 Mass. 585, 587-588 (1999)]; and larceny from a building is a felony. A locked vehicle can be deemed a depository, especially if it contains valuables, and B&E into a depository with intent to commit a larceny is a felony, even if the value of the item is less than $250 (see B&E Depository offense). See intent at the beginning of this section for more on this topic.
What is a Building?	Typically property that is secured within a structure with expectation that it will be protected against theft is "under the protection of the building." Often times a key component is that the structure has a roof. However, in the 2010 case of ***Commonwealth v. Rudenko,*** the court ruled that the delivery hall of a fenced-in storage area used to house overstocked items and items prepared for delivery of a Home Depot was protected by this statute even though it did not have a roof; it did connect directly with the roofed-in portion of the Home Depot store.
Be sure to review comments on dwellings, nighttime, etc. at the beginning of the B&E and Burglary section of this manual.	

C.266 § 18	DWELLING NIGHTTIME ENTERY WITHOUT BREAKING
	Elements
1.	Enters a dwelling house
2.	Without breaking
3.	In the Nighttime
4.	With the intent to commit a Felony
	Arrest, Penalties, Attempts & Notes
Power of Arrest	**Felony** – a police officer may effect an arrest on probable cause.
Penalty	Imprisonment in the state prison (F) for not more than 10 years or by a fine of not more than $500 and imprisonment in jail for not more than 2 years. **Enhanced Penalty Firearms**: imprisonment in the state prison (F) for not less than 7 years or by imprisonment in the HOC for 2 years but not more than 2½ years.
Attorney Hanrahan's Comment	How does someone enter without breaking? This occurs when the entry may have been made through an open (propped open) door where the offender needed to do nothing more than to walk through the threshold (if he physically moved something, liked opened the door, a breaking could have occurred).
	Related Statutes, Case Law & Other Important Information
Breaking	If a breaking also is involved use 266 § 18.

C.266 § 17	DWELLING NIGHTTIME ENTERY WITHOUT BREAKING & PERSON PUT IN FEAR
	Elements
1.	Enters a dwelling house
2.	Without breaking
3.	In the Nighttime
4.	With the intent to commit a Felony
5.	The owner or any other person lawfully inside being put in fear.
	Arrest, Penalties, Attempts & Notes
Power of Arrest	**Felony** – a police officer may effect an arrest on probable cause.
Penalty	Imprisonment in the **state prison (F)** for not more than 10 years. **Enhanced Penalty Firearms:** If armed with a firearm, rifle, shotgun, machine gun or assault weapon shall be punished by imprisonment in the **state prison (F)** for not less than 5 years or by imprisonment in the HOC for not more than 2½ years.
	Related Statutes, Case Law & Other Important Information
Intent to instill fear not needed	The crime of B&E in the daytime with intent to commit a felony and placing an occupant in fear, c. 266 § 17, does not require that the defendant intend to place the occupant in fear.[1]
No Fear	If no one was put in fear use c. 266 § 18

[1] Commonwealth v. Santana (2012) Appeals Court

C.266 § 18A	ENTERING BY FALSE PRETENSES
Elements	
1.	Enters a dwelling house
2.	By False Pretenses
3.	• With intent to commit a felony, or • After entering commits a larceny
Arrest, Penalties, Attempts & Notes	
Power of Arrest	**Felony** – a police officer may effect an arrest on probable cause.
Penalty	Imprisonment in the **state prison (F)** for not more than 10 years or by a fine of not more than $5,000 and imprisonment in a HOC for not more than 2 years, or by both fine and imprisonment.
Attorney Hanrahan's Comment	This statute was designed to address those who pose as salesmen, or utility workers, or use some similar ruse to gain entrance and then once inside commit a larceny or some other crime. But it also applies to just those who enter with the intent to commit a felony once inside even if the felony was never accomplished.
Impersonating a Gas or Electric Worker **c. 164 § 126A**	The defendant falsely assumes, pretends to be or holds himself out as an officer or servant of a gas or electric company for the purpose of gaining access to any premises shall be punished by imprisonment in a HOC for not more than 2 years or by a fine of not more than $1,000, or both such fine and imprisonment.
Be sure to review comments on dwellings, nighttime, etc. at the beginning of the B&E and Burglary section of this manual.	

C.266 § 49	BURGLARIOUS TOOLS
Elements	
1.	The defendant: • Makes or mends, or begins to make or mend, or • Knowingly has in his possession
2.	An engine, machine, tool or implement adapted and designed for cutting through, forcing or breaking open a **building, room, vault, safe** or **other depository**
3.	• In order to steal therefrom money or other property, or • To commit any other crime
4.	Knowing the item to be adapted and designed for this purpose, with intent to use or employ or allow the same to be used or employed for such purpose
Arrest, Penalties, Attempts & Notes	
Power of Arrest	A police officer may effect an arrest for this offense on probable cause
Penalty	Imprisonment in the **state prison (F)** for not more than 10 years or by a fine of not more than $1,000 dollars and imprisonment in jail for not more than 2½ years
Attorney Hanrahan's Comment	Common tools such as screwdrivers and crow bars can qualify but in these case the defendant would, in most cases, have to be actually using the item during a B&E for these elements to be met (or at least proven). When it comes to tools specifically designed to break-in the actual use is <u>not</u> required, although you would still have to prove that is was designed to commit a break.
Related Statutes, Case Law & Other Important Information	
Must be a Depository, building, vault, etc.	In ***Commonwealth v. Hogan*** (1996), the Appeals Court held that bolt cutters, which were used on a lock in an attempt to remove a bicycle affixed to a parking meter, was not a burglarious tool because the lock (and parking meter) was not a "depository."
A Motor Vehicle can be a depository	In C***ommonwealth v. Aleo*** (1984), the Appeals Court held that the passenger's compartment of a motor vehicle was a "depository." In ***Commonwealth v. Armenia*** (1976), the Appeals Court ruled that a trunk of a motor vehicle was a "depository."
Mere possession of tool during a break does not qualify. It must be intended to facilitate the actual break.	In ***Commonwealth v. Redmond,*** the Court explained that the Commonwealth needs to prove that the defendant possessed the implement with the intent to use it to break into the building (or depository etc.), as opposed to having possessed it with the intent to steal (or commit some other crime). The intent required under G.L. c. 266, Section 49, is the **intent to use the implement to effectuate the break-in**. Otherwise a felon who carries an ordinary implement such as a pocketknife during an intended breaking and entering, but who intends to accomplish the breaking and entering by entering a closed but unlocked door could stand convicted of possession of burglarious implements although he never intended to use the pocketknife to accomplish the break.
Not required to prove intent to use at a particular place	In *Commonwealth v. Faust* (2012), the Appeals Court ruled that in order to convict a defendant of possession of burglarious tools the Commonwealth must prove that the defendant intended to use the tools to break into a building, room, vault, safe or place for keeping valuables but the Commonwealth does not need to prove intent to use them in a particular place.
Be sure to review comments on dwellings, nighttime, etc. at the beginning of the B&E and Burglary section of this manual.	

TRESPASSING OFFENSES

C.266 § 120	TRESPASSING
Elements	
1.	The defendant
2.	Without right
3.	**Enters** or **remains**
4.	in or upon the dwelling house, buildings, boats or improved or enclosed land, wharf, or pier of another, or enters or remains in a school bus
5.	• after having been forbidden so to do by the person who has lawful control of the premises (whether directly or by notice posted) or • in violation of a court order pursuant to C. 208 § 34B (divorce decree) or c. 209A § 3 & 4 (domestic restraining order)
Exception Landlord/Tenant issues	**Landlord must evict through civil process:** This does not apply to tenants or occupants of residential premises who, having rightfully entered said premises at the commencement of the tenancy or occupancy, remain therein after such tenancy or occupancy has been or is alleged to have been terminated. The owner or landlord of said premises may recover possession thereof only through appropriate civil proceedings.
Arrest, Penalties, Attempts & Notes	
Power of Arrest	**Misdemeanor** – A person who is found committing such trespass may be arrested by a sheriff, deputy sheriff, constable or police officer
Penalty	A fine of not more than $100 or by imprisonment for not more than 30 days or both.
Related Statutes, Case Law & Other Important Information	
Put on Notice	A person can be notified either directly (verbally or in writing) by someone in-charge of the property (i.e. homeowner, security guard, etc) or the person could be put on notice by posted signs (i.e. No Trespassing, Keep Out, Park Closes at 10:00 PM, etc.). Notice can also be made by the design and nature of the property (sometimes referred to as ***constructive notice*)**. For instance, a fence or stone wall around the property of a building, without any unrestricted passageway, is notice to others that they are not welcome on the property.[1362]
No need to prove defendant saw sign	As long as the trespass notice is posted in a conspicuous place there is no actual requirement to prove that the defendant saw the sign.[1363]
Lawful Control of Property	In ***Commonwealth v. Greene*** (2012). The SJC ruled that in order to convict someone of trespassing it must be proven that the person who trespassed the defendant had lawful control of the property. Attorney Hanrahan's Note: It is not required that the person be the actual property owner, just that they had authority of the property owner to trespass the defendant.
Landlord Trespass is trumped by invitation by lawful resident	A trespass order issued from the landlord of a private residence, or even from a public housing authority, cannot prevent *invited* guests from visiting a resident who resides on the housing authority property.[1364]

[1362] *Commonwealth v. A Juvenile*, 6 Mass.App.Ct. 106 (1978).
[1363] *Fitzgerald v. Lewis*, 164 Mass. 495 (1895)
[1364] *Commonwealth v. Nelson*, Mass.App.Ct. (2008).

C.266 § 120	TRESPASSING
Attorney Hanrahan's Comment on Landlord Issue	When officers locate a person on public housing authority property, or even from a multi-unit private residence, who has been trespassed some form of investigation needs to be conducted to see if the person is an "invited guest" before making an arrest or charging the person. Simply asking the person if he or she has been invited to a particular apartment and then following up with the resident to confirm should be enough in most cases. A trespass order can be used to prevent the visitor from hanging around the common areas of the property but it can't be used to regulate visitors to the tenant's home. If the visitor needs to access common areas of the property in order to access the apartment the visitor cannot be convicted of trespass if he/she used the common area to access the apartment (when properly invited).
Public Property	Just because a property is government owned does not mean that any citizen can enter that property whenever they wish. Access to public property can be regulated and restricted.[1365] In ***Commonwealth v. Egleson***, the SJC held that 'another' in c. 266, § 120, includes the State and municipalities.
State Property	Chapter 266 § 123 prohibits trespassing on state property, including state colleges, state hospitals and even Houses of Correction.
Time Restriction	It is possible to restrict access during specific times. In *Commonwealth v. Einarson,* the Court that in order to convict a defendant for trespassing on public property after a specified time the municipal ordinance or regulation forbidding trespass after dark must be introduced in evidence.[1366]
Steps leading to building	In ***Commonwealth v. Wolf***, the Court ruled that an external deck or porch, or steps leading to the front door, are properly regarded as part of a building for purposes of the trespass statute.
Airspace: not trespassing	In ***Commonwealth v. Santos***, the Court overturned a conviction by the lower court of the defendant who was involved in an ongoing neighbor dispute, where she hired a crane operator to move cement blocks on her property and at one point the crane and block(s) was suspended over the neighbors land during the move. The Appeals Court stated "we find it implausible that the average citizen would understand that the type of 'entry' that G.L. c. 266, § 120, prohibits extends to the unusual, technical circumstance of momentarily conveying an object through airspace over someone's property without causing the slightest harm to that property or any interference with or danger to anyone's use of the property."
Trespassing by Agent	A trespass can occur as the result of an agent relationship.[1367] For example, a business owner who directs an employee to enter onto someone's property after being informed not to enter may be guilty of trespass.
Removing a trespass sign	c. 266 § 122 imposes a $25 fine for removing a trespass sign.
Trespassing by Motor Vehicle	There is a specific charge when trespassing involves a motorized vehicle. See chapter 266 § 121A later in this section.
Abutting property owners permitted to trespass to care for property: Chapter 266 § 120B	• Whoever, being the owner of land abutting that of another, • The building or buildings on which are so close to the land of such other person as to require an entry on said abutting land for the purpose of maintaining or repairing said building or buildings in order to prevent waste, • Shall not be deemed guilty of trespass or liable civilly for damages,

[1365] *Commonwealth v. Egleson,* 355 Mass. 259 (1969)
[1366] *Commonwealth v. Einarson,* 6 Mass. App. Ct. 835, 372 N.E.2d 278,279 (1978)
[1367] *Commonwealth v. Santos,* 58 Mass.App.Ct. 701 (2003)

C.266 § 120	TRESPASSING
	• Provided that such entry is made expeditiously and in the exercise of due care and that no damage is caused by such entry to the land or buildings of said abutting owner. **Prior Police Notification Required**: Before such entry said owner shall notify the chief or other officer in charge of the police department of the city or town in which the land is located that he has requested permission to enter on adjoining land from the owner or occupants thereof for the purpose of maintaining or repairing a building or buildings and that such permission has been refused, and that he intends to enter under the provisions of this section. **Bond Required:** Before entering on said land, said owner shall post bond with the chief of police in the amount of $1,000 dollars to protect the adjoining land owner from damage caused by said entry. **8 hour/30 day limit:** No person so entering on land of another shall store material or tools thereon for more than eight hours in any one day nor shall he continue to enter thereon for more than thirty days in the aggregate in any calendar year. **Restoration:** After said entry, said owner shall in all respects restore said adjoining land to the condition in which it was prior to said entry.
Surveyors may Trespass: Chapter 266 § 120C	Whenever a duly registered land surveyor (registered under c. 112) deems it reasonably necessary to enter upon adjoining lands to make surveys of any description included under "Practice of land surveying" (as defined in c. 112 § 81D) for any private person, excluding any public authority, public utility or railroad, the land surveyor or his authorized agents or employees may, after reasonable notice, enter upon lands, waters and premises, not including buildings, in the commonwealth, within a reasonable distance from the property line of the land being surveyed, and such entry shall not be deemed a trespass. Nothing in this act shall relieve a land surveyor of liability for damage caused by entry to adjoining property, by himself or his agents or employees.

C.266 § 121	ENTRY ON LAND WITH FIREARMS
	Elements
1.	The defendant entered the land of another (without right)
2.	With firearms
3.	With intent to fire or discharge them while on the property
4.	Having been requested by the owner or occupant of such land or by his agent to leave
5.	Remained on the land
	Arrest, Penalties & Notes
Power of Arrest	**Misdemeanor** – there is no statutory authority granting powers of arrest for this offense. However, if the offense is committed in public, in the officer's presence, and is creating a **breach of the peace** an arrest would be lawful.
Penalty	A fine of not more than $200 or by imprisonment for not more than two months, or both.
Attorney Hanrahan's Comment	The fine and jail time is doubled compared to the standard trespassing offense, but in this instance the offender must also have the intent to discharge the firearms and the offender must be requested to leave (posted sign is likely not enough).

C.266 § 121A	TRESPASS INVOLVING MOTORIZED VEHICLES
Elements	
1.	The defendant, without right, enters upon the private land of another
2.	Whether or not such land be posted against trespass
3.	And in so entering makes use of or has in his immediate possession or control any vehicle, machine, or device which includes an internal combustion engine or other source of mechanical power
Exceptions	The provisions of this section shall not apply to such an entry at the junction of a public way with a paved private roadway, unless said private roadway is distinguished from the public way by a sign, gatepost, or the display of a street number or the name of the occupant of the premises, or by the improvement of adjacent land, the type of construction of the roadway, or other distinguishing feature, or unless such entry has been forbidden by the person having lawful control of said private roadway. Nothing herein shall in any way restrict the operation of power boats on waterways not otherwise restricted
Arrest Power & Penalties	
Power of Arrest	**Misdemeanor** – there is no statutory authority granting powers of arrest for this offense. However, if the offense is committed in public, in the officer's presence, and is creating a **breach of the peace** an arrest would be lawful.
Penalty	$250 fine
Related Statutes, Case Law & Other Important Information	
Parking	Chapter 266 § 120A indicates that one can commit a trespass by parking on the "private way or upon improved or enclosed land" and that it is prima facie evidence that the registered owner trespassed.
Operation where not permitted; c. 90 § 16	No person shall **operate a motor vehicle**, nor shall any owner of such **vehicle permit it to be operated**, in or over **any way, public or private**, which **motor vehicles are prohibited from using**, provided notice of such (notice) is conspicuously posted at the entrance to such way. **Penalty:** $50 fine

C. 266 § 120F	UNAUTHORIZED ACCESS TO COMPUTER SYSTEM
	Elements
1.	The defendant, without authorization:
2.	• Knowingly accesses a computer system by any means, or • After gaining access to a computer system by any means knows that such access is not authorized and fails to terminate such access
	Arrest Power, Penalties & Notes
Power of Arrest	**Misdemeanor** – there is no statutory authority granting warrantless powers of arrest for this offense. However, if the offense is committed in public, in the officer's presence, and is creating a **breach of the peace** an arrest would be lawful.
Penalty	Imprisonment in the HOC for not more than 30 days or by a fine of not more than $1,000, or both.
	Related Statutes, Case Law & Other Important Information
Password	The requirement of a password or other authentication to gain access shall constitute notice that access is limited to authorized users.
C. 277 § 58A½. Computer offenses; place of prosecution	The crimes described in chapter 266 § 102F , chapter 266 § 33A and chapter 266 § 127 when the personal property involved is electronically processed or stored data, either tangible or intangible, and data while in transit, may be prosecuted and punished in any county where the defendant was physically located at the time of the violation, or where the electronic data was physically located at the time of the violation.

DESTRUCTION OF PROPERTY

OVERVIEW: There are numerous individual laws relating to the destruction and defacement of various specific properties and items (e.g. Damage to Goal Posts). However, c. 266 § 162A provides a broad definition and may be used for almost any type of vandalism type offense. However, some district courts are particular on how they choose to proceed with these type of offenses so it is best to consult with your local DA's office on which charges to bring involving vandalism and property destruction offenses.

C. 266 § 126A	DEFACEMENT/DAMAGE OF PROPERTY
Elements	
1.	The defendant intentionally
2.	Willfully and maliciously, or wantonly, (see notes below)
3.	Paints, marks, scratches, etches or otherwise marks, injures, mars, defaces or destroys;
4.	The real (real estate type fixed property) or personal property (items) of another, including **but not limited to** a wall, fence, building, sign, rock, monument, gravestone or tablet,
Arrest Power, Penalties & Notes	
Power of Arrest	**Felony** – a police officer may effect a warrantless arrest for this offense provided he/she has probable cause that the suspect committed the offense.
Penalty	Imprisonment in a **state prison (F)** for a term of not more than 3 years or by imprisonment in a HOC for not more than 2 years or by a fine of not more than $1,500 or not more than 3 times the value of the property effected, whichever is greater, or both imprisonment and fine. **Enhanced Penalty for Veteran Memorial:** If the property marked, injured, marred, defaced or destroyed is a war or veterans' memorial, monument or gravestone, the fine under this section shall be doubled and the person convicted shall be ordered to perform not less than 500 hours of court-approved community service.
RMV Action	Upon conviction for said offense the individual's driver's license shall be suspended for 1 year. If the individual convicted of defacing or vandalizing the real or personal property of another is under the age of 16 then 1 year shall be added to the minimum age eligibility for driving.
Attorney Hanrahan's Comment	Many police officers mistakenly believe that this offense is limited to a "wall, fence, etc." but the statute is not so limited. It covers *any* personal property or real estate related property. Additionally, the statute does <u>not</u> require any type of permanent damage. Simply defacing is enough to complete this felony. For instance, is someone were to smear dog feces on an enemy's car it would be safe to say that the car had been defaced even if it could be washed off.
Related Statutes, Case Law & Other Important Information	
Throwing into building or vessel a noxious substance c. 266 § 103c	The defendant willfully, intentionally and without right throws into, against or upon a dwelling house, office, shop or other building, or vessel, or puts or places therein or thereon oil of vitriol, coal tar or other noxious or filthy substance, with intent unlawfully to injure, deface or defile such dwelling house, office, shop, building or vessel, or any property therein, shall be punished. **Penalty**: imprisonment in the **state prison (F)** for not more than 5 years or in jail for not more than 2½ years or by a fine of not more than $300. **Arrest Powers: Felony** – a police officer may effect an arrest for this offense committed in his/her presence or for an offense in the past, on probable cause.
Specialized forms of Property Damage Offenses	There are dozens of specialized forms of property damage/destruction offenses. However, this offense (§126A) can be used in most cases. See later in this section for some of the specialized forms of property damage/destruction offenses.

C. 266 § 127	DESTRUCTION OF PROPERTY
	Elements
1.	The defendant injured or destroyed the, personal property, dwelling house, or building of another;
2.	That the defendant did so: • Wantonly or • Wilfully and Maliciously
	Arrest Power & Penalties
Power of Arrest	**If act was willful and malicious- Felony** – a police officer may effect an arrest for this offense committed in his/her presence or for an offense in the past, on probable cause. **If act was wanton - Misdemeanor** – there is no statutory authority granting warrantless powers of arrest for this offense. However, if the offense is committed in public, in the officer's presence, and is creating a **breach of the peace** an arrest would be lawful. **Important**: see Attorney Hanrahan's Note below.
Wantonly Penalty	**Damage $250 or less -** if the value of the property so destroyed or injured is not alleged to exceed $250, the punishment shall be by a fine of three times the value of the damage or injury to such property or by imprisonment for not more than 2½ months; provided, however, that where a fine is levied pursuant to the value of the property destroyed or injured, the court shall, after conviction, conduct an evidentiary hearing to ascertain the value of the property so destroyed or injured. ***Damage over $250** - a fine of $1,500 or three times the value of the property so destroyed or injured, whichever is greater, or by imprisonment for not more than 2½ years.
Wilful and Malicious Penalty	*Imprisonment in the state **prison (F)** for not more than 10 years or by a fine of $3,000 or three times the value of the property so destroyed or injured, whichever is greater and imprisonment in jail for not more than 2½ years. Note: the statute is poorly constructed and has created great confusion as to whether or not the value of damage or the intent dictates whether or not a felony or misdemeanor.
Attorney Hanrahan's Comment	*It is commonly believed that the value of the property dictates whether or not the crime is a felony. However, the statute tends to read as if the intent of the offender is what dictates. If the act was "willful and malicious" the offense is seemingly a felony no matter what the value of the damage. If the act was done "wantonly" the offense is a misdemeanor, no matter the value of the damage. This was recently interpreted this way in the 2012 case of *Commonwealth v. James Gordon* - see footnote 5. However, earlier cases have indicated that the value dictates. In the 2001 case of *Commonwealth v. Beale*, the SJC stated to prove the felony branch of this offense, the Commonwealth must additionally prove that "the value of the property so destroyed or injured" is over $250.[1368] This may be partly based on the fact that the Commonwealth presented the value of damage as part of its case. Additionally, this statute states "whoever destroys or injures the personal property...in any manner or by any means not particularly described or mentioned in this chapter," indicating that if there is another specialized form of property destruction offense you should charge the specific offense in lieu of this statute. Most of the specialized property destruction offenses are listed later in this section. I offer two suggestions: if you wish to pursue a felony charge and the value is $250 or less use c. 266 § 126A (which is always a felony) or consult with your local DA's office on how they would prefer you proceed.

[1368] Commonwealth v. Beale, 434 Mass. 1024, 751 N.E.2d 845 (2001); Commonwealth v. Lauzier, 53 Mass. App. Ct. 626, 633 n.10, 760 N.E.2d 1256 (2002).

C. 266 § 127	DESTRUCTION OF PROPERTY
	Related Statutes, Case Law & Other Important Information
Distinction between "wilful and malicious" and "wanton" destruction	Wilful and malicious property destruction is a specific intent crime requiring proof that the defendant intended both the conduct and its harmful consequences, while wanton property destruction requires only a showing that the actor's conduct was indifferent to, or in disregard of, the probable consequences. [1369] "The forcible entry into an office will, without doubt, result in some destruction of property, but a messy thief is not necessarily malicious within the meaning of the statute." The essence of the distinction "appears to lie in the fact that a wilful actor intends both his conduct and the resulting harm, whereas a wanton or reckless actor intends his conduct but not necessarily the resulting harm."[1370] As an example, if youths throw rocks from a bridge and one strikes a car passing below, the act is wanton if the rocks were thrown casually, without thought of striking any cars, but the act is wilful and malicious if the rocks were aimed at passing cars. "It is worth noting that destruction of property which accompanies even violent crime may not by that token alone qualify as wilful and malicious."[1371]
Wilful and Malicious	The offense requires proof of cruel, hostile or vengeful intent in addition to intentional doing of the unlawful act.[1372] Malice requires a showing that defendant was motivated by "cruelty, hostility or revenge".[1373] In *Commonwealth v. DaVilla,* malice not inferable from sawing through jail window incident to escape attempt.[1374] In the 2013 case of *Commonwealth v. Doyle*, the Appeals Court overturned the defendant's conviction for malicious destruction of property when he used a cutting tool to access an ATM in order to steal the money inside. The Court ruled "it was clear that the damage was done in an effort to steal from the ATM and not with a state of mind infused with cruelty, hostility or revenge."
Wantonly Explained	An act of destruction is "wanton" if the person was reckless or indifferent to the fact that his conduct would probably cause substantial damage. Someone acts "wantonly" when he consciously disregards, or is indifferent to, an immediate danger of substantial harm to other people or their property. It is not enough to prove that the defendant acted negligently — that is, acted in a way that a reasonably careful person would not. The Commonwealth must prove that the defendant's actions went beyond mere negligence and amounted to recklessness. The defendant acted wantonly if he/she knew, or should have known, that such actions were likely to cause substantial harm to other people or their property, but he/she recklessly ran that risk and went ahead anyway.
Lesser included offense	Wanton property destruction is not a lesser included offense of wilful and malicious property destruction, since wanton conduct requires proof that the likely effect of the defendant's conduct was substantial harm, but wilful and malicious conduct does not. [1375]
Vandalism to MV	Malicious damage to a motor vehicle or trailer is punishable also under G.L. c. 266, § 28.
Value	Where the damage is repairable, the value of the property is to be measured by the pecuniary loss (usually the reasonable repair or replacement cost), and not by the fair market value of the whole property or of the damaged portion. "Of course, in certain circumstances a seemingly minor type of damage may effectively destroy the value of an entire property, such as a tear in a valuable painting or a chip in an antique cup."[1376] **Attorney Hanrahan's Note**: In other words, the value is based on the cost of repair or only the value of the section of the property damaged. For instance, if the defendant smashed a car window the value would be the value of the window, or the cost to replace the window, not the value of the car.

[1369] .*Commonwealth v. Armand,* 411 Mass. 167, 170-171, 580 N.E.2d 1019, 1022 (1991);
[1370] *Commonwealth v. Smith,* 17 Mass. App. Ct. 918, 920, 456 N.E.2d 760, 763 (1983).
[1371] *Commonwealth v. Cimino*, 34 Mass. App. Ct. 925, 927, 611 N.E.2d 738, 740-741 (1993).
[1372] Commonwealth v. O'Neil, 67 Mass.App.Ct. 284, 291, 853 N.E.2d 576, 583 (2006).
[1373] Commonwealth v. Peruzzi, 15 Mass. App. Ct. 437, 440-444, 446 N.E.2d 117, 119-121 (1983).
[1374] Commonwealth v. Victor Davila, Jr., 24 Mass. App. Ct. 1105, 507 N.E.2d 1067 (May 18, 1987) (unpublished decision under Appeals Court Rule 1:28)
[1375] Commonwealth v. Schuchardt, 408 Mass. 347, 352, 557 N.E.2d 1380, 1383 (1990).
[1376] Commonwealth v. Deberry, 441 Mass. 211, 221-222, 804 N.E.2d 911 (2004), rev'g 57 Mass. App. Ct. 93, 751 N.E.2d 858 (2003).

C. 266 § 126B	TAGGING
Elements	
1.	The defendant sprays or applies paint or places a sticker,
2.	Upon a building, wall, fence, sign, tablet, gravestone, monument or Other object or thing on a public way or adjoined to it, or in public view, or on private property.
Arrest Power, Penalties & Notes	
Power of Arrest	**Misdemeanor** – A police officer may arrest any person for commission of the offenses prohibited by this section without a warrant if said police officer has probable cause to believe that said person has committed the offenses prohibited by this section.
Penalty	Imprisonment in a HOC for not more than 2 years or by a fine of not less than $1,500 or not more than 3 times the value of such damage to the property so defaced, marked, marred, damaged or destroyed, whichever is greater, or both fine and imprisonment.
Restitution	The defendant shall also be required to pay for the removal or obliteration of such "tagging" or to obliterate such "tagging"; provided, however that when a fine is levied pursuant to the value of the property marred, defaced, marked, damaged or destroyed or where the cost of removal or obliteration is assessed the court shall, after conviction, conduct an evidentiary hearing to ascertain the value of the property so defaced, marked, marred, damaged or destroyed or to ascertain the cost of the removal or obliteration.
RMV Action	Upon conviction for said offense the individual's driver's license shall be suspended for 1 year. If the individual convicted of defacing or vandalizing the real or personal property of another is under the age of 16 then 1 year shall be added to the minimum age eligibility for driving.

SPECIALIZED FORMS OF VANDALISM/PROPERTY DESTRUCTION	
Motor vehicle malicious damage **c. 266 § 28**	The defendant maliciously damages a motor vehicle or trailer shall be punished. **Penalty**: 1st offense: imprisonment in the **state prison (F)** for not more than 15 years or by imprisonment in a jail or HOC for not more than 2 1/2 years or by a fine of not more than $15,000, or by both such fine and imprisonment. 2nd or subsequent offense: results in a minimum mandatory sentence of 1 year. No CWOF's or placed on file permitted. **RMV Action**: License revocation: 1st offense - 1 year. 2nd Offense 5 years. **Arrest Powers: Felony** – a police officer may effect an arrest for this offense committed in his/her presence or for an offense in the past, on probable cause. **Prima Facie Evidence**: Evidence that an identifying number or numbers of a motor vehicle or trailer or part thereof has been intentionally and maliciously removed, defaced, altered, changed, destroyed, obliterated, or mutilated, shall be prima facie evidence that the defendant knew or had reason to know that the motor vehicle, or trailer or part thereof had been stolen. See Larceny section for other aspects of this statute.

SPECIALIZED FORMS OF VANDALISM/PROPERTY DESTRUCTION

Destruction or injury to buildings **c. 266 § 104**	The defendant willfully, intentionally and without right destroys, injures, defaces or mars a dwelling house or other building, whether upon the inside or outside, shall be punished. **Penalty**: imprisonment for not more than 2 months or by a fine of not more than $50.00. **Arrest Powers**: Misdemeanor – there is no statutory authority granting powers of arrest for this offense. However, if the offense is committed in public, in the officer's presence, and is creating a breach of the peace an arrest would be lawful.
Destruction of place of worship **c. 266 § 127A**	The defendant willfully, intentionally and without right, or wantonly and without cause, destroys, defaces, mars, or injures a church, synagogue or other building, structure or place used for the purpose of burial or memorializing the dead, or a school, educational facility or community center or the grounds adjacent to and owned or leased by any of the foregoing or any personal property contained in any of the foregoing shall be punished. **Penalty:** a fine of not more than $2,000 or not more than three times the value of the property so destroyed, defaced, marred or injured, whichever is greater, or by imprisonment in a HOC for not more than 2½ years, or both. **Arrest Powers**: **Misdemeanor** – there is no statutory authority granting powers of arrest for this offense. However, if the offense is committed in public, in the officer's presence, and is creating a breach of the peace an arrest would be lawful. **Value over $5,000**: if the damage to or loss of such property exceeds $5,000, such person shall be punished by a fine of not more than three times the value of the property so destroyed, defaced, marred or injured or by imprisonment in a **state prison (F)** for not more than 5 years, or both. **Arrest Powers**: Felony – a police officer may effect an arrest for this offense committed in his/her presence or for an offense in the past, on probable cause. **NOTE**: Also see Threats to a Place of Worship in the Threats section of this manual
Malicious destruction or injury to historical monuments **c. 266 § 95**	The defendant willfully or maliciously removes, displaces, destroys, defaces, mars or injures any monument, tablet or other device erected to mark an historic place or to commemorate an historic event shall be punished. **Penalty**: fine of not more than $1,000or by imprisonment for not more than 2 years. **Arrest Powers: Misdemeanor** – there is no statutory authority granting powers of arrest for this offense. However, if the offense is committed in public, in the officer's presence, and is creating a breach of the peace an arrest would be lawful. **Note**: Any person convicted under the provisions of this section shall, in addition to any fine assessed, reimburse the commonwealth for the total amount of damage incurred.
Defacement or injury to a schoolhouse or church **c. 266 § 98**	The defendant willfully, intentionally and without right, or wantonly and without cause, destroys, defaces, mars or injures a schoolhouse, church or other building erected or used for purposes of education or religious instruction, or for the general diffusion of knowledge, or an outbuilding, fence, well or appurtenance of such schoolhouse, church or other building, or furniture, apparatus or other property belonging thereto or connected therewith, shall be punished. **Penalty**: a fine of not more than $1,000, or by imprisonment for not more than 2 years, or both. **Arrest Powers: Misdemeanor** – there is no statutory authority granting powers of arrest for this offense. However, if the offense is committed in public, in the officer's presence, and is creating a breach of the peace an arrest would be lawful.

SPECIALIZED FORMS OF VANDALISM/PROPERTY DESTRUCTION	
Destruction of Library Materials	The willful alteration or destruction of library ownership records, electronic or catalog records retained apart from or applied directly to the library materials or property shall be punished. **Penalty**: imprisonment in the **state prison (F)** for not more than 5 years or by a fine of not less than $1,000 nor more than $25,000, or both, and shall pay the replacement value of such library materials or property, including all reasonable processing costs, as determined by the governing board having jurisdiction. **Arrest Powers: Felony** - c. 266 § 100 grants the police the power to make a warrantless arrest for any violation of this section (99A) whether in the officer's presence or not.
Libraries; mutilation or destruction of materials or property **c. 266 § 100**	The defendant willfully, maliciously or wantonly writes upon, injures, defaces, tears, cuts, mutilates or destroys any library material or property, shall make restitution in full replacement value of the library materials or property, and, in addition, shall be punished by imprisonment in a HOC for not more than 2 years or by a fine of not less than $100 nor more than $1,000, or both. **Arrest Powers: Misdemeanor**: A law enforcement officer may arrest without warrant any person he has probable cause to believe has violated the provisions of c. 266 § 99A and this section. **Probable Cause**: The statement of an employee or agent of the library, eighteen years of age or older, that a person has violated the provisions of said section ninety-nine A and this section shall constitute probable cause for arrest by a law enforcement officer authorized to make an arrest in such jurisdiction. The activation of an electronic anti-theft device shall constitute probable cause for believing that a person has violated the provisions of this section. **Poster Requirement**: A library shall prepare posters to be displayed therein in a conspicuous place. Said posters shall contain a summary and explanation of section 99A and this section.
Destruction, defacement to public park or equipment c. 266 § 98A	The defendant willfully, intentionally and without right, or wantonly and without cause destroys, defaces, mars or injures any playground apparatus or equipment located in a public park or playground shall be punished by a fine of not more than $1,000. **Arrest Powers: Misdemeanor** – there is no statutory authority granting powers of arrest for this offense. However, if the offense is committed in public, in the officer's presence, and is creating a breach of the peace an arrest would be lawful.
c. 266 § 104A Destruction goal posts	The defendant willfully and without right destroys, injures or removes a goal post on a football field shall be punished. **Penalty**: a fine of not less than $50 nor more than $200. **Arrest Powers: Misdemeanor** – there is no statutory authority granting powers of arrest for this offense. However, if the offense is committed in public, in the officer's presence, and is creating a breach of the peace an arrest would be lawful.

SPECIALIZED FORMS OF VANDALISM/PROPERTY DESTRUCTION

Intentional injury or destruction of utility property c. 166 § 38	The defendant unlawfully and intentionally injures, molests or destroys any line, wire, pole, pier or abutment, or any of the materials or property of any street railway company, of any electric railroad company, or of any city or town engaged in the manufacture and sale of electricity for light, heat or power or of any company, owner or association described in sections twenty-one and forty-three. **Penalty:** a fine of not more than $500 or by imprisonment for not more than 2 years, or both; **Enhanced Penalty**: whoever does any act prohibited by this section between the hours of **4 o'clock in the afternoon (PM) and 7 o'clock in the forenoon (7AM)** shall be punished by a fine of not more than $1,000 or by imprisonment for not more than 4 years, or both. **Arrest Powers**: **Misdemeanor** – there is no statutory authority granting powers of arrest for this offense. However, if the offense is committed in public, in the officer's presence, and is creating a **breach of the peace** an arrest would be lawful. Note: between 4PM-7AM – felony.

C. 272 § 73 VANDALIZING/TAMPERING WITH A VETERAN/POLICE/FIRE MEMORIAL

Elements	
1.	The defendant does any of the following:
2.	Wilfully destroys, mutilates, defaces, injures or removes a tomb, monument, gravestone, American flag, veteran's grave marker, metal plaque, veteran's commemorative flag holder, commemorative flag holder representing service in a police or fire department, veteran's flag holder that commemorates a particular war, conflict or period of service or flag, or other structure or thing which is placed or designed for a memorial of the dead, or a fence railing, curb or other thing which is intended for the protection or ornament of a structure or thing before mentioned or of an enclosure for the burial of the dead, or Wilfully removes, destroys, mutilates, cuts, breaks or injures a tree, shrub or plant placed or being within such enclosure, or Wantonly or maliciously disturbs the contents of a tomb or a grave.
Arrest Power, Penalties & Notes	
Power of Arrest	**Felony** – a police officer may effect a warrantless arrest for this offense provided he/she has probable cause that the suspect committed the offense.
Penalty	Imprisonment in the state prison for not more than 5 years or by imprisonment in the jail or house of correction for not more than 2½ years and by a fine of not more than $5,000.
Attorney Hanrahan's Comment	This law was modified in 2015 to include Police and Fire memorials. The previous version was limited to veteran memorials.
Related Statutes, Case Law & Other Important Information	
C. 272 § 73B	Sale of a commemorative grave marker.

FIRE PREVENTION & Related Crimes (Including Fireworks & Explosives)

Arson & Related Crimes (Also See Weapons Section for Explosive devices and Hoax Devices)

C. 266 § 1	BURNING OR AIDING IN BURNING A DWELLING HOUSE
	Elements
1.	The defendant willfully and maliciously
2.	• Set fire to, burn, or cause to be burned, or • Aid, counsel or procure the burning of,
3.	• A dwelling house, or a building adjoining or adjacent to a dwelling house, or • A building by the burning whereof a dwelling house is burned,
4.	Whether the house or other building is the property of himself or another and whether the same is occupied or unoccupied.
	Arrest Power, Penalties & Notes
Power of Arrest	**Felony** – a police officer may effect a warrantless arrest for this offense provided he/she has probable cause that the suspect committed the offense.
Penalty	Imprisonment in the **state prison (F)** for not more than 20 years, or by imprisonment in a jail or HOC for not more than 2½ years, or by a fine of not more than $10,000, or by both such fine and imprisonment.
Attorney Hanrahan's Comment	This offense covers the burning, or helping someone burn, a house, or a building next to a house and the house gets burned as a result. The crime is still committed even if it is the house of the person causing the fire or his helper's house. No one has to be home.
	Related Statutes, Case Law & Other Important Information
Dwelling	The words "dwelling house", as used in this section, shall mean and include all buildings used as dwellings such as apartment houses, tenement houses, hotels, boarding houses, dormitories, hospitals, institutions, sanatoria, or other buildings where persons are domiciled. In ***Commonwealth v. DeStefano***, the Court ruled that the home does not actual require that someone is currently residing in the home, only that is capable of being used as dwelling.[1377]
Extent of burning	The entire structure does not have to be destroyed, a partial burning of the structure would suffice (even if no significant damage occurred). [1378]
Intent to defraud	Also see chapter 266 § 10 intent to defraud an insurer (later in this section). A defendant can be convicted of both chapter 266 § 1 and 266 § 10 intent to defraud an insurer.
No Dwelling Involved	If the building was not a dwelling and/or a dwelling was not affected chapter 266 § 2 may be an appropriate charge (see next).
Firefighter injuries resulting from criminal offenses	See chapter 265 § 13D½ in the *Crimes Against Firefighters & Fire Equipment* section of this manual, which provides for additional penalties for injuries suffered by firefighters.

[1377] ***Commonwealth v. DeStefano***, 16 Mass.App.Ct. 208 (1983).
[1378] ***Commonwealth v. Tucker***, 110 Mass. 403 (1872).

C. 266 § 2	BURNING A BUILDING (NON-DWELLING)
Elements	
1.	The defendant willfully and maliciously
2.	• Set fire to, burn, or cause to be burned, or • Aid, counsel or procure the burning of,
3.	• A meeting house, church, court house, town house, college, academy, jail or other building which has been erected for public use, or • A banking house, warehouse, store, manufactory, mill, barn, stable, shop, outhouse or other building, or an office building, lumber yard, ship, vessel, street car or railway car, or a bridge, lock, dam, flume, tank, or • **Any building or structure or contents thereof**, not included or described in the preceding section (burning a dwelling),
4.	Whether the property is his or another and whether the same is occupied, unoccupied or vacant.
Arrest Power, Penalties & Notes	
Power of Arrest	**Felony** – a police officer may effect a warrantless arrest for this offense provided he/she has probable cause that the suspect committed the offense.
Penalty	Imprisonment in the **state prison (F)** for not more than ten years, or by imprisonment in a jail or HOC for not more than 2½ years.
Related Statutes, Case Law & Other Important Information	
Chapter 266 § 5	Chapter 266 § 5 prohibits the burning of other personal property (non-buildings)
Firefighter injuries resulting from criminal offenses	See chapter 265 § 13D½ in the *Crimes Against Firefighters & Fire Equipment* section of this manual, which provides for additional penalties for injuries suffered by firefighters.

ARSON & FIRE RELATED LAWS

C. 266 § 5	WILFUL AND MALICIOUS BURNING
Elements	
1.	The defendant wilfully and maliciously
2.	• Sets fire to, or burn or otherwise destroy or injure by burning, or • Causes to be burned or otherwise so destroyed or injured, or • Aids, counsels or procures the burning of,
3.	• A pile or parcel of wood, boards, timber or other lumber, or any fence, bars or gate, or a stack of grain, hay or other vegetable product, or any vegetable product severed from the soil and not stacked, or any standing tree, grain, grass or other standing product of the soil, or the soil itself, **of another**. or • Any personal property of whatsoever class or character exceeding a value of $25.00, **of another.** or • Any boat, motor vehicle as defined in section one of chapter ninety, or other conveyance, whether of himself or another.
Arrest Power, Penalties & Notes	
Power of Arrest	**Felony** – a police officer may effect a warrantless arrest for this offense provided he/she has probable cause that the suspect committed the offense.
Penalty	Imprisonment in the state prison for not more than 3 years, or by a fine of not more than $500 and imprisonment in a jail or house of correction for not more than 1 year.
Attorney Hanrahan's Comment	This is the catch-all arson statute. However, the value of the property must be worth more than $25. You could also consider the general destruction of property statutes if appropriate. Also, you can burn your own property as long as it is not a vehicle, boat, or building.
Related Statutes, Case Law & Other Important Information	
Attempted Arson	See chapter 265 § 5A for attempted arson.
Insurance Fraud	See chapter 266 § 10 for conduct related to arson and insurance fraud (later in this section).
Negligent destruction by fire	See chapter 266 § 8 for negligent conduct which results in fire damage.
Destruction of Property	See the Destruction of Property section of this manual for various offenses related to the damage of property whether by fire or otherwise.
Damage to Wood Chapter 266 § 7	Chapter 266 § 7 states **"**Whoever by wantonly or recklessly setting fire to any material, or by increasing a fire already set, causes injury to, or the destruction of, **any growing or standing wood of another** shall be punished by a fine of not more than $1,000 or by imprisonment for not more than 2 years."

C. 266 § 5A	ATTEMPTED ARSON
	Elements
1.	Willfully and maliciously
2.	• Attempt to set fire to, or attempt to burn, or • Aid, counsel or assist in an attempt to set fire to or burn,
3.	Any of the buildings, structures or property mentioned in: • Chapter 266 § 1 (dwellings) • Chapter 266 § 2 (buildings) or • Chapter 266 § 5 (Property of another or vehicles or boats).
4.	Or commits any act preliminary thereto or in furtherance thereof
	Arrest Power, Penalties & Notes
Power of Arrest	**Felony** – a police officer may effect a warrantless arrest for this offense provided he/she has probable cause that the suspect committed the offense.
Penalty	Imprisonment in the **state prison (F)** for not more than 20 years, or by imprisonment in a jail or HOC for not more than 2½ years or by a fine of not more than $1,000.
Actions constituting Attempted Arson	The law states "the placing or distributing of any flammable, explosive or combustible material or substance or any device in or against any building, structure or property mentioned in the foregoing sections in an arrangement or preparation with intent eventually to willfully and maliciously set fire to or burn such building, structure or property, or to procure the setting fire to or burning of the same shall, for the purposes of this section, constitute an attempt to burn such building, structure or property. "
Attorney Hanrahan's Comment	Oddly, *completing* the malicious burning in §5 is a 3 year felony but *attempting* to do it is a 10 year felony.

ARSON & FIRE RELATED LAWS

C. 266 § 8	FIRE NEGLIGENCE
Elements	
1.	• The defendant, not being a tenant thereof, sets or increases a fire upon land of another whereby the property of another is injured, or • The defendant negligently or willfully suffers any fire upon his own land to extend beyond the limits thereof whereby the woods or property of another are injured.
Arrest Power, Penalties & Notes	
Power of Arrest	**Misdemeanor** – there is no statutory authority granting warrantless powers of arrest for this offense. However, if the offense is committed in public, in the officer's presence, and is creating a **breach of the peace** an arrest would be lawful.
Penalty	A fine of not more than $1,000 or by imprisonment for not more than 2 years, and the town where such fire occurred may recover in an action of tort, brought within 2 years after the cause of action accrues, against any such person the expense of extinguishing such fire.
Related Statute	
Lighted cigarettes: throwing from vehicles or placing on forest/lands/ fields	Chapter 148 § 54 states "whoever drops or throws from any vehicle while the same is upon a public or private way running along or near forest land or open fields, or, except as permitted by law, drops, throws, deposits or otherwise places in or upon forest land, any lighted cigarette, cigar, match, live ashes or other flaming or glowing substance, or any substance or thing which in and of itself is likely to cause a fire, shall be punished by a fine of not more than $100 or by imprisonment for not more than 30 days."

C. 266 § 10	INSURED PROPERTY; BURNING WITH INTENT TO DEFRAUD
Elements	
1.	Willfully and with intent to defraud or injure the insurer
2.	• Set fire to, or • Attempt to set fire to, or • Cause to be burned, or • Aid, counsel or procure the burning of
3.	A building, or any goods, wares, merchandise or other chattels, belonging to himself or another,
4.	Which are at the time insured against loss or damage by fire.
Arrest Power, Penalties & Notes	
Power of Arrest	**Felony** – a police officer may effect a warrantless arrest for this offense provided he/she has probable cause that the suspect committed the offense.
Penalty	Imprisonment in the **state prison (F)** for not more than 5 years or in a jail or HOC for not more than 2½ years.
Related Statutes, Case Law & Other Important Information	
Burning motor vehicle; owner's statement	Chapter 266 § 29B states "whenever a motor vehicle is burned, the owner of record of such vehicle shall submit to the appropriate fire department a statement signed under the penalties of perjury containing such information concerning the burning of such vehicle as the state fire marshall shall require. "

C. 148 § 2A	REPORTING REQUIREMENTS FOR UNAUTHORIZED FIRE IGNITION WITHIN SCHOOL PROPERTY

The principal of any public or private school that provides instruction to pupils in any of grades 1 to 12, inclusive, **shall immediately report** any incident involving the **unauthorized ignition of any fire** within the school building or on school grounds to the local fire department. The principal shall submit a **written report** of the incident to the head of the fire department **within 24 hours** on a form furnished by the department of fire services. The report shall be filed without regard to the extent of the fire or whether there was a response by the fire department.

CRIMES AGAINST FIREFIGHTERS AND FIRE EQUIPMENT

C. 268 § 32A	INTERFERENCE WITH FIRE FIGHTING OPERATIONS
Elements	
1.	Willfully
2.	Obstruct, interfere with or hinder
3.	A fire fighter/fire fighting force in the lawful performance of his/its duty
Arrest Power, Penalties & Notes	
Power of Arrest	**Felony** – a police officer may effect an arrest for this offense committed in his/her presence or for an offense in the past, on probable cause.
Penalty	A fine of not less than $100 nor more than $1,000 or by imprisonment in a jail or HOC for not less than 30 days nor more than 2½ years or by imprisonment in the **state prison (F)** for not more than 5 years, or by both the fine and imprisonment in a jail or HOC.
Related Statutes, Case Law & Other Important Information	
Refusing to leave a Burning Structure	In the 2013 case of ***Commonwealth v. Joyce***, the Appeals court ruled that the defendant's refusal to leave a burning building, which caused the fire chief to attempt to physically remove him, was sufficient to convict him of this offense. The Court noted that a fire is handled differently when someone is inside as opposed to a vacant building. However, the act still must be *willful.*

C. 265 § 13D½	FIREFIGHTERS, INJURIES RESULTING FROM CRIMINAL OFFENSES
Elements	
1.	The commission of one of the following offenses:
2.	• Arson (c. 266 § 1) • willful burning of a structure (c. 266 § 2) • burning of personal property over $25.00 (c. 266 § 5) • recklessly increasing a fire (c. 266 § 7)
3.	Which results in injury to a firefighter in the performance of his duty
Arrest Power, Penalties & Notes	
Power of Arrest	**Felony** – a police officer may effect a warrantless arrest for this offense provided he/she has probable cause that the suspect committed the offense.
Penalty	Imprisonment in the **state prison (F)** for not more than 10 years, or by a fine of not more than $1,000 and imprisonment in a jail or HOC for not more than 2½ years.

C. 266 § 11	DAMAGING A FIRE ALARM OR EQUIPMENT BEFORE A FIRE
	Elements
1.	Willfully, intentionally and without right
2.	Within **24 hours** prior to the burning of a building or other property
3.	• Cut or remove a bell rope or a wire or conduit connected with a fire alarm signal system, or • Injure or disable any fire alarm signal box or any part of the system in the vicinity of the building or property, or • Cut, injure or destroy an engine, hose or other fire apparatus in the vicinity
	Arrest Power, Penalties & Notes
Power of Arrest	**Misdemeanor** – there is no statutory authority granting warrantless powers of arrest for this offense. However, if the offense is committed in public, in the officer's presence, and is creating a **breach of the peace** an arrest would be lawful.
Penalty	A fine of not more than $500 or by imprisonment for not more than 2 years
	Related Statutes, Case Law & Other Important Information
Malicious Destruction of Property	You may want to consider a charge under Chapter 266 § 126A which would make the offense a felony. See Property Destruction section of this manual.

C. 266 § 12	INJURING FIRE EQUIPMENT DURING FIRE TO HINDER
	Elements
1.	During the burning of a building or other property
2.	• Willfully and maliciously cut or remove a bell rope or a wire or conduit connected with a fire alarm signal system, or • Injure or disable any fire alarm signal box or any part of such system in the vicinity of such building or property, or • Otherwise prevent an alarm being given, or • Cut, injure or destroy an engine, hose or other fire apparatus, in said vicinity, or • Otherwise willfully and maliciously prevent or obstruct the extinction of a fire
	Arrest Power, Penalties & Notes
Power of Arrest	**Felony** – a police officer may effect a warrantless arrest for this offense provided he/she has probable cause that the suspect committed the offense.
Penalty	Imprisonment in the **state prison (F)** for not more than 7 years or in jail for not more than 2½ years or by a fine of not more than $1,000.
	Related Statutes, Case Law & Other Important Information
Injury to Fire Engine c. 266 § 13	Whoever wantonly or maliciously injures a fire engine or other fire apparatus shall be punished by a fine of not more than $500 or by imprisonment for not more than 2 years, and shall be further ordered to recognize with sufficient surety or sureties for his good behavior during such term as the court shall order. No statutory power of arrest.

EXPLOSIVES (Also see weapons section of this manual for bombs and bomb making material offenses)

C. 266 § 101	MALICIOUS EXPLOSION
Elements	
1.	Willfully, intentionally and without right
2.	• Unlawfully damage or destroy property, or • Unlawfully injure a person
3.	By the explosion of gunpowder or of any other explosive.
Arrest Power, Penalties & Notes	
Power of Arrest	**Felony** – a police officer may effect a warrantless arrest for this offense provided he/she has probable cause that the suspect committed the offense.
Penalty	By imprisonment in the **state prison (F)** for not more than 20 years or in jail for not more than 2½ years or by a fine of not more than $1,000.
Related Statutes, Case Law & Other Important Information	
Explosive Defined in relation to c. 266 § 101	"**Explosive**", any element, compound or mixture that is manufactured, designed or used to produce an explosion and that contains an oxidizer, fuel or other ingredient, in such proportion, quantity or packing that an ignition by fire, friction, concussion, percussion or detonation of the element or of any part of the compound or mixture may cause such a sudden generation of highly heated gases that the resultant gaseous pressures, release of heat or fragmentation is capable of producing destructive effects on contiguous objects or of destroying life or causing bodily harm including, but not limited to, all material which is classified as division 1.1, 1.2, 1.3, 1.4, 1.5 or 1.6 explosives by the United States Department of Transportation or listed pursuant to 18 USC 841(d) and 27 CFR 555.23. **NOTE:** Explosive shall not include: • **a pyrotechnic:** which is defined as any commercially manufactured combustible or explosive composition or manufactured article designed and prepared for the purpose of producing an audible effect or a visible display and regulated by c. 148 including, but not limited to: (i) fireworks, firecrackers; (ii) flares, fuses and torpedoes, so-called, and similar signaling devices. • **small arms ammunition**, which is defined as any shotgun, rifle, pistol, or revolver cartridge, and cartridges for propellant-actuated power devices and industrial guns. • **small arms ammunition primers** • smokeless powder weighing less than 50 pounds and black powder weighing less than 5 pounds, unless possessed or used for an illegal purpose.
Terroristic Threats	See chapter 269 § 14, located in the *Threats* section of this manual.
Possession of Explosives	See Chapter 148 § 35 later in this section.
Hoax and Destructive Device offenses	**See Threats and Terrorism Section of this Manual for related offenses such as:** chapter 266 § 102A. ***Use of an explosive or destructive or incendiary device or substance*** chapter 266 § 102(b). ***Use/possession of a hoax device*** chapter 266 § 102(c). ***Possession of destructive or incendiary device***

C. 148 § 35	POSSESSION OF BOMBS OR EXPLOSIVES IN VIOLATION OF REGULATIONS
Elements	
1.	No person shall have in his possession or under his control
2.	Any bomb or other high explosive [as defined by the rules and regulations made under **section 9 (see below),** contrary to the provisions of this chapter or of any rule or regulation made thereunder].
Arrest Power, Penalties & Notes	
Power of Arrest	**Misdemeanor** – Any officer qualified to serve criminal process may arrest without a warrant any person violating this section.
Penalty	A fine of not more than $1,000, or by imprisonment for not more than 2½ years, or both, and any bomb or explosive found in his possession or under his control on such violation shall be forfeited to the commonwealth.
Attorney Hanrahan's Comment	This charge would be more appropriate for in a commercial setting (e.g. construction contractor without the proper permits). If someone possess explosive material and has bad intentions a charge such as chapter 266 § 102 (possession of an incendiary device) would be a more appropriate charge. See the *Threats and Terrorism* section of this manual.
Related Statutes, Case Law & Other Important Information	
Regulations relative to explosives and inflammable materials **c. 148 § 9**	The board shall make rules and regulations for the keeping, storage, use, manufacture, sale, handling, transportation or other disposition of **gunpowder, dynamite, crude petroleum or any of its products, or explosive or inflammable fluids or compounds, tablets, torpedoes or any explosives of a like nature, or any other explosives, fireworks, firecrackers, or any substance having such properties that it may spontaneously, or acting under the influence of any contiguous substance, or of any chemical or physical agency, ignite, or inflame or generate inflammable or explosive vapors or gases to a dangerous extent**, and may prescribe the location, materials and construction of buildings to be used for any of the said purposes. Such rules and regulations shall require persons keeping, storing, using, selling, manufacturing, handling or transporting dynamite or other high explosives to make reports to the department in such particulars and in such detail that the quantity and location thereof will always be a matter of authentic record in the department. Cities and towns may also make and enforce ordinances and by-laws, not inconsistent with said rules and regulations, relative to the subject matter of this section. Each city or town shall submit a copy of each such ordinance or by-law to the board within ten days after the passage thereof. Any ordinance or by-law regulating blasting operations, or the use, handling, transportation or storage of dynamite or gunpowder, shall not take effect until such ordinance or by-law is approved by the board, except that any such ordinance or by-law that has not been approved or disapproved by the board within ninety days after the receipt thereof shall be deemed to have been approved.
Explosive golf balls **c. 148 § 55**	Whoever manufactures or sells or knowingly uses, or has in possession for the purpose of sale, any golf ball containing any acid, fluid, gas or other substance tending to cause the ball to explode and to inflict bodily injury shall for the first offence be punished by a fine of not more than $500, and for any subsequent offence by a fine of not more than $1,000 or by imprisonment for not more than 1 year, or both.
Fireworks	See next section for Firework offenses.
Hoax and Destructive Device offenses	**See Weapons & Bombs Section of this Manual for related offenses such as:** chapter 266 § 102A. ***Use of an explosive or destructive or incendiary device or substance*** chapter 266 § 102(b). ***Use/possession of a hoax device*** chapter 266 § 102(c). ***Possession of destructive or incendiary device***

FIREWORKS

C. 148 § 39	COMBUSTIBLE MATERIALS FOR EFFECT (AKA FIREWORKS)
	General Restrictions
1.	No person shall
2.	• Sell, or keep or offer for sale, or • Have in his possession, or under his control, or • Use, or explode, or cause to explode,
3.	Any combustible or explosive composition or substance, or any combination of such compositions or substances, or any other article
4.	Which was prepared for the purpose of producing a visible or audible effect by combustion, explosion, deflagration, or detonation.
	Arrest Power, Penalties & Notes
Power of Arrest	**Misdemeanor** – Any officer qualified to serve criminal process may arrest without a warrant any person who shall **sell or keep for sale or offer for sale** any fireworks in violation of this section and any fireworks found in his possession or under his control upon conviction of such a violation shall be forfeited to the commonwealth. **Attorney Hanrahan's note**: if the offense involves mere possession with no intent to sell there is no warrantless arrest power. Confiscate the fireworks and summons. However, if the offender is setting off the fireworks (and creating a breach of the peace) a warrantless offense would be lawful if committed in your presence.
Penalty	**Sale Violation**: A fine of not less than $100 nor more than $1,000 or by imprisonment for not more than 1 year or both. **Possession Violation**: a fine of not less than $10.00 nor more than $100.
	Related Statutes, Case Law & Other Important Information
Seize Fireworks and turn over to Fire Marshall	Any officer qualified to serve criminal process shall seize all of the fireworks mentioned herein without a warrant, and the fireworks seized shall, upon conviction of such violation, be forfeited to the commonwealth. Notice of such seizure of the fireworks shall immediately be sent to the marshal by the officer making the seizure, and the fireworks seized shall be held and securely stored by that department until the marshal or his authorized representative takes them into his possession for disposal.
Fireworks defined	**"Fireworks"** shall include compositions, substances or other articles and shall also include blank cartridges or toy cannons in which explosives are used, the type of toy balloon which requires fire underneath to propel the same, firecrackers, cherry bombs, silver salutes, M-80's, torpedoes, sky-rockets, Roman candles, sparklers, rockets, wheels, colored fires, fountains, mines, serpents, or other fireworks of like construction or any fireworks containing any explosive or flammable compound, or any tablets or other device containing any explosive substance.
Non-Fireworks	**The term "fireworks" as used herein shall not include**: toy pistols, toy canes, toy guns or other devices in which paper caps or plastic caps containing twenty-five hundredths grains or less of explosive compound are used, if they are so constructed that the hand cannot come in contact with the cap when in place for the explosion, or toy pistol paper caps or plastic caps which contain less than twenty hundredths grains of explosive mixture, the sale and use of which shall be permitted at all times.

C. 148 § 39	COMBUSTIBLE MATERIALS FOR EFFECT (AKA FIREWORKS)
Exceptions to the fireworks prohibition	This section shall not apply 1) To the sale of any fireworks to be shipped directly out of the commonwealth, or 2) To the sale of any such article for the use of, and its use by, persons having obtained a permit for a supervised display of such fireworks from the marshal or some officer designated by him therefor, under any provision of section thirty-nine A, or 3) To the sale of flares, lanterns or fireworks for the use of, and their use by, railroads, railways, boats, motor vehicles or other transportation agencies, or other activity, lawfully permitted or required to use any or all of such articles for signal purposes, illumination or otherwise, or 4) To the sale or use of blank cartridges for a duly licensed show or theatre or for signal or ceremonial purposes in athletics or sports, or to the sale of special blank cartridges and their use in the proper operation of industrial tools and equipment only, or 5) To experiments at a factory for explosives, or 6) To the sale of blank cartridges for the use of, or their use by, the militia or any organization of war veterans or other organizations authorized by law to parade in public, a color guard armed with firearms, or 7) In teaching the use of firearms by experts, or 8) To the sale of shells for firearms, cartridges, gunpowder, and for the purpose of using, and their use, or in connection with the hunting of game or in target practice with firearms, or 9) To farmers and fruit growers who, having obtained a permit under chapter 48 § 13, use firecrackers for the control of damage to their crops by birds.
Regulations for permits for displays of fireworks **c. 148 § 39A**	The board shall make rules and regulations for the granting of permits for supervised displays of fireworks by municipalities, fair associations, amusement parks and other organizations or groups of individuals. Such rules and regulations shall provide in part that: a) Every such display shall be handled by a competent operator to be approved by the chief of the fire department or officer or officers having similar powers and duties, of the municipality in which the display is to be held and shall be of such a character, and so located, discharged or fired as, in the opinion of the chief of the fire department or the officer or officers having similar powers and duties, after proper inspection, not to be hazardous to property or to endanger any person or persons, b) Application for permits shall be made in writing at least fifteen days in advance of the date of the display, and c) No permit so granted shall be transferable. The fee for such permits shall be set by the chief of the fire department or the officer or officers having similar powers and duties of the municipality in which the display is to be held, but in no event shall any such fee be greater than $25.
Notify State Fire Marshall	Confiscated fireworks are supposed to be turned over to the State Fire Marshall by calling 1-800-682-9229 or 978-567-3365.

Larceny Overview

Chapter 266 § 30 incorporates three forms of larceny: general larceny, larceny by false pretenses and embezzlement into the same statute. There are also specific forms of larceny, such as larceny from a building, larceny from a person, larceny of rental property and others.

C. 266 § 30	GENERAL LARCENY (AKA Larceny By Stealing)
Elements	
1.	The defendant steals (see definition below)
2.	The *property* of another (see definition below)
Arrest Power, Penalties & Notes	
Power of Arrest	If the theft involves property over $250 or it is a firearm or trade secret, the crime would be a felony and the suspect could be arrested with probable cause. However, **anytime a police officer witnesses a theft statutory arrest powers apply**. Chapter 276 § 28 states in part "any officer authorized to serve criminal process may arrest, without a warrant, and detain a person found in the act of stealing property in the presence of the officer regardless of the value of the property stolen…"
Penalty	**MISDEMEANOR PENALTIES:** **Penalty for property $250 or less:** imprisonment in jail for not more than one year or by a fine of not more than $300 **Penalty if Property was from a Common Carrier (i.e. UPS):** if the property was stolen from the conveyance of a common carrier or of a person carrying on an express business: **1st Offense:** imprisonment for not less than 6 months nor more than 2½ years, or by a fine of not less than $50.00 nor more than $600.00, or both **2nd or Subsequent Offense:** a subsequent offence, by imprisonment for not less than 18 months nor more than 2½ years, or by a fine of not less than $150 nor more than $600, or both. **FELONY PENALTIES:** **Penalty if Firearm or over $250:** if the property stolen is a **firearm**, or, if the value of the property stolen **exceeds $250**, be punished by imprisonment in the **state prison (F)** for not more than 5 years, or by a fine of not more than $25,000 and imprisonment in jail for not more than 2 years. **Penalty if Property is a Trade Secret:** Whoever steals, or with intent to defraud obtains by a false pretense, or whoever unlawfully, and with intent to steal or embezzle, converts, secretes, unlawfully takes, carries away, conceals or copies with intent to convert any trade secret of another, regardless of value, whether such trade secret is or is not in his possession at the time of such conversion or secreting, shall be guilty of larceny, and shall be punished by imprisonment in the **state prison (F)** for not more than 5 years, or by a fine of not more than $25,000 and imprisonment in jail for not more than 2 years. **Victim 60 or older:** if the value of the property **exceeds $250,** imprisonment in the **state prison (F)** for not more than 10 years or in the HOC for not more than 2½ years, or by a fine of not more than $50,000 or by both such fine and imprisonment; or if the value of the property does not exceed $250, imprisonment in the HOC for not more than 2½ years or by a fine of not more than $1,000 or by both such fine and imprisonment. The court may order, regardless of the value of the property, restitution to be paid to the victim commensurate with the value of the property.

C. 266 § 30	GENERAL LARCENY (AKA Larceny By Stealing)
	Definitions, Related Statutes, Case Law & Other Important Information
Larceny from a person 65 or over	Although chapter 266 § 30 provides for an enhanced penalty when the victim is 60 years old older. Chapter 266 § 25 states "whoever commits larceny by stealing from the person of a person 65 years or older shall be punished." Penalty 1st offense: imprisonment in the state prison (F) for not more than 5 years or in jail for not more than 2½ years. 2nd or subsequent offense: imprisonment for not less than two years. 1 year minimum mandatory. Attorney Hanrahan's Note: Under c. 266 § 25 the crime is a felony no matter the value of the property stolen. This is not the case under 266 § 30, even when the victim is 60 (through 64).
Stealing	The statute does not define stealing but chapter 277 § 39 defines stealing as: the criminal taking, obtaining or converting of personal property, with intent to defraud or deprive the owner permanently of the use of it; including all forms of larceny, criminal embezzlement and obtaining by criminal false pretences. In short, stealing involves the **taking of property** of **another** with the **intent to permanently deprive** the owner of the item. A temporary taking would not constitute stealing. **Attorney Hanrahan's Note**: The intent to permanently deprive can be shown by indifference to the owner (e.g. throwing the victim's purse in the trash).
Taking and Carrying Away required	The taking must also involve some type of "carrying away." Taking and carrying away is accomplished if the defendant physically transferred the property from the other person's control to his/her own. It does not matter if the transfer involved only slight movement, or if it lasted only for a short time. *Commonwealth v. Fielding*, 371 Mass. 97, 117, 353 N.E.2d 719, 731-732 (1976) (any separation of property from victim's dominion, even if brief in space and time, sufficient); *Commonwealth v. Salerno*, 356 Mass. 642, 648, 255 N.E.2d 318, 321 (1970) (taking can be proved by circumstantial evidence); *Commonwealth v. Luckis*, 99 Mass. 431, 433 (1868) (wallet need not be removed from victim's pocket, but defendant "must for an instant at least have had perfect control of the property"); *Commonwealth v. Stephens*, 14 Mass. App. Ct. 994, 994-995, 440 N.E.2d 777, 777 (1982) (sufficient that victim put property in bag at defendant's orders, though defendant never touched it); *Commonwealth v. Bradley*, 2 Mass. App. Ct. 804, 805, 308 N.E.2d 772, 772 (1974) (momentary transfer sufficient); *Commonwealth v. Flowers*, 1 Mass. App. Ct. 415, 418-419, 298 N.E.2d 898, 900-901 (1973) (transfer of property from victim's control to thief's sufficient, since literal "carrying away" not required; transfer may be through agent or victim).
Property	The term **"property",** as used in the section, shall include **money**, **personal chattels** (this means personally owned tangible items), a bank note, bond, promissory note, bill of exchange or other bill, order or certificate, a book of accounts for or concerning money or goods due or to become due or to be delivered, a deed or writing containing a conveyance of land, any valuable contract in force, a receipt, release or defeasance, a writ, process, certificate of title or duplicate certificate issued under chapter 185, a public record, anything which is of the realty or is annexed thereto, a security deposit received pursuant to chapter 186 § 15B, electronically processed or stored data, either tangible or intangible, data while in transit, telecommunications services, and any **domesticated animal**, including dogs, or a beast or bird which is ordinarily kept in confinement.

C. 266 § 30	**GENERAL LARCENY** **(AKA Larceny By Stealing)**
Property "of another"	G.L. c. 278, § 9 indicates that the "owner" includes anyone in actual or constructive possession. The identity of owner need not be proved, only that it was not defendant.[1379] The "owner" includes anyone with a possessory or property interest.[1380] It is even possible to steal from a thief.[1381]
Attorney Hanrahan's Comment	Massachusetts does not have a theft of services statute. However, there are a variety of specific statutes covering theft of what would otherwise be services. See below and the Fraud section of this manual for more.
***Services* are not property for the purpose of this statute**	In ***Commonwealth v. Rivers*** (1991), the Court ruled that dumping in a landfill without payment does not meet the definition of "property" under the statute. In ***Commonwealth v. Geane*** (2001), the Court ruled that arranging for labor services and then neglecting to pay for the labor is not property for the purposes of c. 266 § 30.
Trade Secret	The term "trade secret" as used in this statute means and includes anything tangible or intangible or electronically kept or stored, which constitutes, represents, evidences or records a secret scientific, technical, merchandising, production or management information, design, process, procedure, formula, invention or improvement.
Property of "another"	**Not True Owner**: The person from whom the property is taken from does not have to be the actual owner of the property. In fact, in ***Commonwealth v. Finn*** (1871), the SJC indicated that stealing from a thief is larceny. **Unknown owner**: It is also possible to charge someone with larceny even if the true owner is not known as long as probable cause exists that the property is actually stolen.[1382]
Establishing property value	The value of the property stolen is important because it often determines whether a felony or misdemeanor has occurred. **Commonsense and life experience** can be used to determine the value of the property.[1383]
Continuous course of theft (single scheme) can be combined to establish value	If the defendant is involved in an ongoing theft spree, it is possible to combine the value of the various thefts for the purpose of establishing a felony charge.[1384] The Commonwealth must prove beyond a reasonable doubt that during that period of time the defendant acted out of a single, continuing intent to steal; that even though time elapsed between incidents, they were not separately motivated but were part of one general scheme or plan to steal.[1385] The value of successive larcenies in single scheme may be added together to charge "grand larceny."[1386] Distinct larcenies may be presented in multiple counts; stealing at one time of articles belonging to several owners may be charged either as one larceny or as distinct larcenies.[1387] But in *Commonwealth v. Donovan* the Court ruled that only one count of larceny, not seven, was required where defendant mounted imitation deposit lock box over the real one at a bank, obtaining seven bank deposits from different depositors.[1388] However, *Donovan* inapplicable where circumstances involve more than one

THEFT OFFENSES

[1379] *Commonwealth v. Souza*, 397 Mass. 236, 238-239, 490 N.E.2d 1173, 1175 (1986)
[1380] *Commonwealth v. Kiernan*, 348 Mass. 29, 50-51, 201 N.E.2d 504, 516 (1964), cert. denied sub nom. *Gordon v. Mass.*, 380 U.S. 913 (1965)
[1381] *Commonwealth v. Finn*, 108 Mass. 466, 467 (1871).
[1382] *Commonwealth v. Dottin* 233 N.E.2d 304 (1968) & *Commonwealth v. Souza* 397 Mass. 236 (1986)
[1383] *Commonwealth v. LaFontaine*, 32 Mass.App.Ct. 529 (1992).
[1384] *Commonwealth v. Pina*, 1 Mass.App.Ct. 411 (1973)
[1385] 2009 Model Jury Instructions.
[1386] *Commonwealth v. England*, 350 Mass. 83, 86-87, 213 N.E.2d 222, 224-225 (1966)
[1387] Commonwealth v. *Sullivan*, 104 Mass. at 553 (see 2009 Model Jury Instruction).
[1388] see *Commonwealth v. Donovan*, 395 Mass. 20, 29, 478 N.E.2d 727, 734 (1985).

C. 266 § 30	GENERAL LARCENY (AKA Larceny By Stealing)
	discrete offense, such that different property is taken at different times and from different locations.[1389]
Venue	According to chapter 277 § 58 larceny, whether at common law or as defined by c. 266 § 30, may be prosecuted and punished in any county where the defendant had possession of the property alleged to have been stolen.
Attempt	Chapter 274 § 6 dictates that any attempted larceny under c. 266 § 30 is only a misdemeanor.
Receiving stolen property	A defendant cannot be convicted both of stealing and receiving the same goods.[1390] Although a defendant cannot be convicted of both crimes, a defendant may be *charged* with both crimes; if the evidence would support either, it is for the jury to decide "under clear and precise instructions" of which to convict.[1391] For buying or receiving stolen property use chapter 266 § 60.
Mistaken theft?	Where a defendant claims as an affirmative defense a mistake of fact concerning the ownership of property or abandonment (i.e. "I thought this scrap metal was trash."), such mistaken belief must be honestly held but does not have to be reasonable under the circumstances.[1392]
Larceny of a motor vehicle	For larceny of a motor vehicle use c. 266 § 28 or c. 90 § 24 for Using without Authority.
"Chew and Screw"	For consuming food and beverage without paying see chapter 140 § 12 in the fraud section of this manual.
Taxi Fare Evasion	See chapter 159A § 16 later in this section.
Leased or Rented Property	Use chapter 266 § 87 if the stolen property was leased or rented.
Theft of Public Records	Chapter 266 § 145 provides "any person who intentionally conceals upon his person or otherwise any record of the commonwealth or a political subdivision thereof, with the intention of permanently depriving said commonwealth or said political subdivision of its use shall be punished by a fine of not more than $500. Detain: A custodian of such records or his agent who has probable cause to believe that a person has violated the provisions of this section may detain such person in a reasonable manner and for a reasonable time. Power of Arrest: Misdemeanor - A law enforcement officer may arrest without warrant any person he has probable cause to believe has violated the provisions of this section. Probable Cause: The statement of a custodian of such records or his agent that a person has violated the provisions of this section shall constitute probable cause for arrest by a law enforcement officer authorized to make an arrest in such jurisdiction.

[1389] *Commonwealth v. Baldwin*, 52 Mass. App. Ct. 404, 407, 754 N.E.2d 121, 124 (2001)
[1390] *Commonwealth v. Dellamano*, 393 Mass. 132, 134, 469 N.E.2d 1254, 1255 (1984).
[1391] *Commonwealth v. Ross*, 339 Mass. 428, 430-432, 159 N.E.2d 330, 332-334 (1959); *Kelley*, 333 Mass. at 195, 129 N.E.2d at 903; *Commonwealth v. Obshatkin*, 2 Mass. App. Ct. 1, 4-5, 307 N.E.2d 341, 343-344 (1974).
[1392] *Commonwealth v. Liebenow*, SJC (2014).

C.266 § 30	LARCENY BY FALSE PRETENSES
Elements	
1.	The defendant, with intent to defraud,
2.	Obtains property of another
3.	By false pretense. Note: for the element of false pretense to be met the defendant must have made a false statement of fact, knowing that the statement was false at the time it was made, and that the defendant intended the victim to rely on the false statement and the victim did rely on and in turn parted with his/her personal property.
Exception	This statute shall not apply to a purchase of property by means of a false pretence relative to the purchaser's means or ability to pay, if, by the terms of the purchase, payment therefor is not to be made upon or before the delivery of the property purchased, unless such pretence is made in writing and is signed by the person to be charged. (c. 266 § 35)
Arrest Power, Penalties & Notes	
Power of Arrest	If the theft involves property over $250 or it is a firearm, the crime would be a felony and the suspect could be arrest with probable cause. However, **anytime a police officer witnesses a theft statutory arrest powers apply**.
Penalty	See larceny by stealing for penalties.
Related Statutes, Case Law & Other Important Information	
False Pretenses	False pretenses means "false representations made by word or act of such a character, or made under such circumstances and in such a way, with the intention of influencing the action of another, as to be punishable".[1393] Absurd, irrational or incredible misrepresentation may not suffice.[1394] Opinions and beliefs are not false representations unless speaker creates impression that he is asserting knowledge of fact rather than opinion or judgment.[1395] The intent to permanently deprive of property not an element of offense and intent to repay not a defense.[1396] The deceptive intent can be inferred from evidence that nonperformance was intended, e.g. that defendant knew that performance was impossible. [1397] Similarly, entering into a contract with the intent not to fulfill it constitutes false representation.[1398]
Statement must be false at the time it was made.	In *Commonwealth v. McCauliffe* (2012), the SJC overturned the defendant's conviction because it was not proven that the defendant made a false statement at the time he obtained the victim's money. However, once he received the money he repeatedly told lies about when he would return it. This did not satisfy the elements of the offense.
Use of an Agent	Misrepresentation can be communicated through agent.[1399]
Obtaining signature on by false Pretenses	The separate offense of obtaining a signature on a written instrument by false pretenses (G.L. c. 266, § 31) has four elements: "(1) obtaining the signature of a person to a written instrument (2) the false making whereof would be a forgery (3) by a false pretense (4) with intent to defraud." [1400]

THEFT OFFENSES

[1393] G.L. c. 277, § 39 and *Commonwealth v. Schackenberg,* 356 Mass. 65, 73, 248 N.E.2d 273, 278 (1969) (definition of false pretenses)
[1394] *Commonwealth v. Louis Constr. Co.,* 343 Mass. 600, 605, 180 N.E.2d 83, 86-87 (1962).
[1395] *Commonwealth v. Anthony,* 306 Mass. 470, 474-475, 28 N.E.2d 542, 544 (1940).
[1396] *Commonwealth v. Hildreth,* 30 Mass. App. Ct. 963, 965, 572 N.E.2d 18,20-21 (1991).
[1397] *Commonwealth v. Edgerly,* 6 Mass. App. Ct. 241, 261-264, 375 N.E.2d 1, 14-16 (1978).
[1398] *Commonwealth v. Wright,* 5 Mass. App. Ct. 860, 861, 365 N.E.2d 836, 837 (1977).
[1399] *Commonwealth v. Camelio,* 1 Mass. App. Ct. 296, 299, 295 N.E.2d 902, 905 (1973).
[1400] *Commonwealth v. Levin,* 11 Mass. App. Ct. 482, 495, 417 N.E.2d 440, 447 (1981).

C.266 § 30	LARCENY BY FALSE PRETENSES
Venue	Larceny by false pretenses may be prosecuted wherever "the false pretence was made, written or used, or in or through which any of the property obtained was carried, sent, transported or received by the defendant." G.L. c. 277, § 59. There is no requirement that it be prosecuted where the false representation was relied on. *Commonwealth v. Abbott Eng'g, Inc.*, 351 Mass. 568, 579, 222 N.E.2d 862, 870 (1967). Where the defendant made phone calls from Suffolk County to the homes of Norfolk County residents, who then delivered money to the defendant in Suffolk County, the offense could properly be prosecuted in Norfolk County. [1401]
Banking related larceny by false pretenses **c. 266 § 33**	Whoever, with intent to defraud, obtains by a false pretence the making, acceptance or endorsement of a bill of exchange or promissory note, the release or substitution of collateral or other security, an extension of time for the payment of an obligation, or the release or alteration of the obligation of a written contract, shall be guilty of larceny.
Fraud	There are numerous fraud related larceny type crimes covered in the Fraud section of this manual. See the Fraud section for similar offenses.
IMPORTANT: Be sure to review the general larceny section for important definitions and concepts regarding all larcenies.	

C. 266 § 30	LARCENY BY EMBEZZLEMENT
Elements	
1.	The defendant, while in a position of trust or confidence, was entrusted with possession of personal property belonging to another person or entity;
2.	The defendant took that property, or hid it, or converted it to his/her own use, without the consent of the owner; and
3.	The defendant did so with the intent to deprive the owner of the property permanently
Arrest Power, Penalties & Notes	
Power of Arrest	If the theft involves property over $250 or it is a firearm, the crime would be a felony and the suspect could be arrest with probable cause. However, **anytime a police officer witnesses a theft statutory arrest powers apply**.
Penalty	See general larceny for penalties.
Related Statutes, Case Law & Other Important Information	
Plan to Repay	It is not a defense that defendant intended to repay misappropriated money.[1402]
Illegal Purpose	It is not a defense that money was entrusted to defendant for illegal purpose.[1403]
Carrying not required	Unlike general larceny, embezzlement does not require asportation (carrying away), but does require that property be received in relationship of trust or confidence.[1404]
Converts to own	A defendant who obtains money legally and then forms intent to keep it is embezzler.[1405]
Continuous Course	A systematic course of embezzlement by single scheme constitutes one offense.[1406]

[1401] *Commonwealth v. Price*, 72 Mass. App. Ct. 280, 891 N.E.2d 242 (2008).
[1402] *Commonwealth v. O'Connell*, 274 Mass. 315, 319-320, 174 N.E. 665, 667 (1931).
[1403] *Commonwealth v. Cooper*, 130 Mass. 285, 288 (1881).
[1404] *Commonwealth v. Hays*, 80 Mass. 62, 64-65 (1859).
[1405] *Commonwealth v. Kenneally*, 10 Mass. App. Ct. 162, 176-177, 406 N.E.2d 714, 724-725 (1980) aff'd on other grounds, 383 Mass. 269, 418 N.E.2d 1224, cert. denied, 454 U.S. 849 (1981).
[1406] *Slater v. United States Fidelity & Guar. Co.*, 7 Mass. App. Ct. 281, 285, 386 N.E.2d 1058, 1061 *S.C.*, 379 Mass. 801, 400 N.E.2d 1256 (1979).

C. 266 § 30	LARCENY BY EMBEZZLEMENT
Embezzlement by fiduciary	Fiduciary embezzlement requires a showing that the defendant: (1) was a fiduciary during the relevant time period; (2) had in his possession money, goods, or property for the use or benefit either in whole or in part of some other person; (3) converted or appropriated the money or property to his own use or benefit or the benefit of a third person without the consent of the beneficiaries and without the legal right or legal authority to do so; and (4) took such action with fraudulent intent.[1407] Note: The **fiduciary** manages the assets for the benefit of the other person rather than for his or her own profit.
Embezzlement by municipal official	Embezzlement by a municipal or county officer (G.L. c. 266, § 51) has the same essential elements as embezzlement under G.L. c. 266, § 30, with two additional elements: (1) the status of the perpetrator (i.e., a municipal or county officer) and (2) the identity of the owner whose property is embezzled (i.e., the municipality or county).[1408]
Larceny by inducement (fraud) C. 266 § 34	Whoever, with intent to defraud and by a false pretense, induces another to part with property of any kind or with any of the benefits described in the preceding section shall be guilty of larceny. Arrest powers and penalties would be the same as the standard larceny offense. **NOTE**: this section shall not apply to a purchase of property by means of a false pretence relative to the purchaser's means or ability to pay, if, by the terms of the purchase, payment therefor is not to be made upon or before the delivery of the property purchased, unless such pretence is made in writing and is signed by the person to be charged. (c. 266 § 35).

C. 266 § 25	LARCENY FROM THE PERSON
	Elements
1.	The defendant took and carried away property
2.	The property was owned or possessed by someone other than the defendant;
3.	The defendant took the property from the person of someone who owned or possessed it or from the person's area of control in his/her presence;
4.	The defendant did so with the intent to deprive that person of the property permanently
	Arrest Power, Penalties & Notes
Power of Arrest	**Felony** – a police officer may effect a warrantless arrest for this offense provided he/she has probable cause that the suspect committed the offense.
Penalty	Imprisonment in the **state prison (F)** for not more than 5 years or in jail for not more than 2½ years.
Attorney Hanrahan's Comment	This crime occurs when the item is stolen from the person's immediate control but no force or fear is used as in a robbery conviction - common example is a pickpocket.
	Related Statutes, Case Law & Other Important Information
Robbery	If forced was used, even slight force, robbery may be the more appropriate charge.

[1407] *Commonwealth v. Garrity*, 43 Mass. App. Ct. 349, 353-354, 682 N.E.2d 937, 941 (1997).
[1408] *Commonwealth v. Mahoney*, 68 Mass. App. Ct. 561, 564, 863 N.E.2d 951, 955 (2007).

C. 266 § 20	LARCENY FROM A BUILDING
Elements	
1.	The defendant took and carried away property
2.	At the time the property was being kept safe by virtue of being in a building (or a ship, vessel or railroad car)
3.	The property belonged to someone other than the defendant
4.	The defendant took the property with the intent to deprive the owner of it permanently[1409]
Arrest Power, Penalties & Notes	
Power of Arrest	**Felony** – a police officer may effect a warrantless arrest for this offense provided he/she has probable cause that the suspect committed the offense.
Penalty	Imprisonment in the **state prison (F)** for not more than 5 years or by a fine of not more than $500 or by imprisonment in jail for not more than 2 years.
Attorney Hanrahan's Comment	These elements were established through case law. The actual statute simply states whoever steals in a building…shall be punished. The statute also prohibits theft from a "ship, vessel, and railroad car."
Related Statutes, Case Law & Other Important Information	
Building must be protecting the property	The Commonwealth must prove that the property was being protected and kept safe by virtue of being in the building rather than being under the watchful eye or personal care of someone in the building.[1410]
Value of property stolen immaterial	Larceny in a building is a felony regardless of the value of the property stolen. *Commonwealth v. Graham*, 62 Mass. App. Ct. 642, 647, 818 N.E.2d 1069, 1074 (2004).
Shoplifting does not apply	Larceny from a building would not be an appropriate charge for shoplifting, must use shoplifting statute.[1411]
B&E & Burglary	See the B&E and Burglary section for related statutes.

[1409] *Commonwealth v. Sollivan*, 40 Mass. App. Ct. 284, 287, 663 N.E.2d 580, 582-583 (1996) (approving model instruction).
[1410] 2009 Model Jury Instructions
[1411] McDermott v. W.T. Grant Co., 313 Mass. 736 (1943).

C. 266 § 37	LARCENY BY CHECK
	Elements
1.	The defendant did one of the following: • Wrote a check • Cashed a check • Passed a check • Delivered a check
2.	By doing the above act obtained money, property or services
3.	That when the defendant wrote, cashed, passed or delivered the check, he/she knew that there were insufficient funds or credit at the bank on which the check was drawn to cover the check; and
4.	The defendant did so with the intent to defraud the bank or someone who received the check
	Arrest Power, Penalties & Notes
Power of Arrest	**Misdemeanor** – there is no statutory authority granting warrantless powers of arrest for this offense. However, if the offense is committed in public, in the officer's presence, and is creating a **breach of the peace** an arrest would be lawful.
Penalty	See general larceny statute for penalties. If no property, money or services were obtained the defendant will be guilty of **attempted larceny**. If property, *services*, or money is obtained the defendant will be guilty of **larceny**.
	Related Statutes, Case Law & Other Important Information
Fail to repay within two days of notice is prima facie evidence	Unless the offender pays the bank the amount due, together with all costs and fees, within two days after receiving notice that such check, draft or order has not been paid. The submitted check etc. will be prima facie evidence against the defendant. Failure to pay within two days after notice of dishonor is not an element of the offense, but only a trigger for the statutory prima facie effect.[1412] Note that the prima facie provision is available only against the "maker or drawer" of a check. Oral notice of dishonor is sufficient, including notice communicated through the other depositor to a joint account.[1413]
Credit	The word "credit" means an arrangement or understanding with the bank to pay the check, such as a line of credit.
Intent can be proven by actions	In *Commonwealth v. Dunnington* the defendant who ordered secretary to make out the check was the "drawer." The account was overdrawn before and after check presented, and the defendant's repeated unfulfilled promises to cover it, supported an inference of fraudulent intent.[1414]
Civil Remedy	Civil penalties. General Laws c. 93, § 40A permits, "in addition to any criminal penalties," a civil suit to recover the face amount of a bounced check "and for additional damages, as determined by the court, but in no event . . . less than one hundred nor more than five hundred dollars" if a specified form of written demand goes unanswered for 30 days.

THEFT OFFENSES

[1412] *Commonwealth v. Klein*, 400 Mass. At 312-313, 509 N.E.2d at 267.
[1413] *Commonwealth v. Ohanian.*
[1414] *Commonwealth v. Dunnington*, 390 Mass. 472, 474-476, 457 N.E.2d 1109, 1111-1112 (1987)

C. 266 § 87	LARCENY OF LEASED OR RENTED PROPERTY
Elements	
1.	The defendant leased or rented personal property
2.	The defendant subsequently did one of the following: • Concealed some or all of that property • Aided or abetted in concealing some or all of that property • Failed or refused to return such property to its owner within 10 days after the lease or rental agreement had expired • Sold, conveyed or pledged some or all of that property without the written consent of its owner.
3.	The defendant did so with the intention to place such property beyond the control of its owner.
Arrest Power, Penalties & Notes	
Power of Arrest	**Misdemeanor** – there is no statutory authority granting warrantless powers of arrest for this offense. However, if the offense is committed in public, in the officer's presence, and is creating a **breach of the peace** an arrest would be lawful.
Penalty	A fine of not more than $1,000 or imprisonment of not more than 1 year, or both. A person found guilty shall be ordered to make restitution to the owner for any financial loss.
Attorney Hanrahan's Comment	No matter what the value of the property is the law only provides for a misdemeanor penalty. However, if evidence exists that the defendant intended to steal the item at the time of the rental a general larceny charge under 266 § 30 may be appropriate.
Related Statutes, Case Law & Other Important Information	
Aid and Abet	The words "aid and abet" comprehend all assistance rendered by acts, words of encouragement or support, or presence, actual or constructive, or the readiness to render assistance, should it become necessary, and no particular acts are necessary.
Bona fide purchasers	In order to protect bona fide purchasers, G.L. c. 266, §87 provides that "it shall be a defense to prosecution for conversion of leased or rented property that the defendant was unaware the property belonged to another or that he had a right to acquire or dispose of the property as he did."
Restitution mandatory	Upon the defendant's conviction under § 87, the statute requires the judge, in addition to any sentence imposed, to order restitution to the owner for any financial loss.
Prima Facie Evidence	It shall be prima facie evidence of intent to place such property beyond the control of the owner when a person in obtaining such property: • Presents identification or information which is materially false, fictitious, misleading or not current with respect to such person's name, address, place of employment or any other material matter; or • Fails to return such property to the owner or his representative within ten days after proper notice (certified or registered mail) to return such property.

C. 266 § 60	BUYING OR RECEIVING STOLEN PROPERTY
	Elements[1415]
1.	The property is stolen
2.	The defendant knew that the property had been stolen
3.	The defendant knowingly did one of the following: • Had the stolen property in his/her possession • Bought the stolen property • Aided in concealing the stolen property
	Arrest Power, Penalties & Notes
Power of Arrest	**$250 or Less Misdemeanor** – there is no statutory authority granting warrantless powers of arrest for this offense. However, if the offense is committed in public, in the officer's presence, and is creating a **breach of the peace** an arrest would be lawful. **Felony** – a police officer may effect a warrantless arrest for this offense provided he/she has probable cause that the suspect committed the offense.
Penalty	**$250 or less – misdemeanor:** if the value of such property does not exceed $250, be punished for a first offense by imprisonment in jail or HOC for not more than 2½ years, or by a fine of not more than $1,000. **More than $250 - felony:** if for a second or subsequent offense, or if the value of such property **exceeds $250**, be punished by imprisonment in the **state prison (F)** for not more than 5 years, or by imprisonment in a jail or HOC for not more than 2½ years or by a fine of not more than $5,000. **Note:** Unless first offense and restitution is made (see c. 266 § 61). Note: Chapter 266 § 61 provides an option for defendant to avoid prosecution is full restitution is made.
	Related Statutes, Case Law & Other Important Information
Property under the control of law enforcement	In 2015, the Legislature modified this statute to include property within the control of law enforcement and not actually "stolen." This would permit police to conduct sting type operations. The statute states in relevant part: whoever, intending to deprive the property's rightful owner permanently of the use and enjoyment of the property, obtains or exerts control over property: a. That is in the custody of either any law enforcement agency or any individual acting on behalf of a law enforcement agency, and b. That any law enforcement officer or individual acting on behalf of a law enforcement agency explicitly represented to such person that the property is stolen.
Distinct Offenses	Buying, receiving, or aiding in the concealment of stolen property are disjunctive, alternate ways of violating the statute. *Commonwealth v. Ciesla*, 380 Mass. 346, 347, 403 N.E.2d 381, 382 (1980). A complaint drawn in the language of G.L. c. 277, § 79 (that the defendant did "buy, receive, and aid in the concealment of" stolen property) is sufficient, even though G.L. c. 266, § 60 is phrased in the disjunctive, and the defendant may be convicted upon proof of any one of the three branches. *Commonwealth v. Valleca*, 358 Mass. 242, 244-245, 263 N.E.2d 468, 469 (1970).
Knowledge Requirement	The defendant cannot be found guilty unless the Commonwealth has proved that he/she actually knew that the property was stolen, or at least believed that it was stolen. Even if the defendant did not know

[1415] 2009 Model Jury Instructions.

C. 266 § 60	BUYING OR RECEIVING STOLEN PROPERTY
	that the property was stolen at the time when he/she received it, the defendant is still guilty of receiving stolen property if he (she) subsequently learned that the property had been stolen, and at that point decided to keep it and to deprive the owner of its use.[1416] The defendant's subjective knowledge that the property was stolen is required; a negligent or reckless failure to inquire is not enough.[1417] The defendant's knowledge can be inferred from circumstantial evidence.[1418] Possession can be proven by joint occupancy of apartment where goods trafficked openly.[1419] Suspicious circumstances of sale which would satisfy a reasonable person that goods were stolen may satisfy the knowledge requirement.[1420] The possession of unusually large quantity of goods in defendant's home may prove knowledge.[1421] An improbable explanation; a steeply discounted price and a cash payment requirement may prove knowledge.[1422]
Receive	A person "receives" property by knowingly taking custody or control of it. It is not necessary that the defendant personally possessed the stolen property; as long as it is proved that he/she knowingly exerted control over it in some way.[1423]
No Personal Benefit is no Defense	It is irrelevant whether the defendant intended to derive personal benefit from receiving the goods, *Commonwealth v. Bean*, 117 Mass. 141, 142 (1875) (receiver doing personal favor for another equally guilty).
Possession	Constructive possession is enough. *Commonwealth v. Carroll*, 360 Mass. 580, 586, 276 N.E.2d 705, 710 (1971) (items held by others in a joint criminal enterprise); *Commonwealth v. Smith*, 3 Mass. App. Ct. at 146, 324 N.E.2d at 926 (dominion and control is equivalent of possession).
"Stolen" property	The Commonwealth must prove that the property was in fact stolen. *Commonwealth v. Budreau*, 372 Mass. 641, 643-644, 363 N.E.2d 506, 508-509 (1977). It is not necessary to prove who the thief was, or that the defendant received the goods directly from the thief. *Commonwealth v. Grossman*, 261 Mass. 68, 70-71, 158 N.E. 338, 339 (1927). Circumstantial evidence can suffice to demonstrate that the goods were stolen. *Commonwealth v. Ryan*, 11 Mass. App. Ct. 906, 414 N.E.2d 1020 (1981). Additionally, there is no requirement to prove who the victim was as long as it can otherwise be proven that the property was stolen.
Statute of limitations	Concealing stolen property is not a continuing offense if the defendant took no further actions after the initial concealment, and the statute of limitations runs from the initial concealment date. However the limitations period begins to run anew from the date of any specific, subsequent affirmative act in aid of the continued purposeful concealment.[1424]

[1416] Commonwealth v. *Sandler*, 368 Mass. at 740-741, 335 N.E.2d at 911; *Commissioner of Pub. Safety v. Treadway*, 368 Mass. 155, 160, 330 N.E.2d 468, 472 (1975); *Kirkpatrick*, 26 Mass. App. Ct. at 599, 530 N.E.2d at 365.
[1417] *Commonwealth v. Boris*, 317 Mass. 309, 315-317, 58 N.E.2d 8, 12-13 (1944);
[1418] See, e.g., *Commonwealth v. Imbruglia*, 377 Mass. 682, 693-694, 387 N.E.2d 559, 566-568 (1979).
[1419] *Commonwealth v. Matheson*, 328 Mass. 371, 373-374, 103 N.E.2d 714, 715 (1952).
[1420] *Commonwealth v. Boris,* 317 Mass. at 316, 58 N.E.2d at 11
[1421] *Commonwealth v. Billings*, 167 Mass. 283, 285-286, 45 N.E. 910, 910-911 (1897).
[1422] *Commonwealth v. Santucci*, 13 Mass. 933, 934, 430 N.E.2d 1239, 1241 (1982)
[1423] 2009 Model Jury Instructions
[1424] *Commonwealth v. Ciesla.*

C. 266 § 60	BUYING OR RECEIVING STOLEN PROPERTY
Stealing and receiving same property	A defendant cannot be convicted both of stealing and receiving the same goods, since receipt of stolen property requires that the property already be stolen at the time of receipt.[1425] A defendant may be charged with both crimes; if the evidence would support either, it is for the jury to decide "under clear and precise instructions" of which to convict. However, a conviction for receipt of stolen property does not require the Commonwealth to preclude the possibility that the defendant was the thief. If there is sufficient evidence to support a conviction for receipt of stolen property, such a conviction may stand even if there is also evidence that the defendant may be, or is in fact, the thief, since the jury is free to reject the evidence tending to prove theft and to infer receipt from the fact of possession.[1426]
Receiving stolen property not duplicative of B&E	While a defendant cannot be convicted both of larceny and of receiving the same stolen property, a defendant may be convicted both of breaking and entering in the nighttime to commit larceny (G.L. c. 266, § 16) and of receiving (G.L. c. 266, § 60) the same stolen property. *Commonwealth v. Cabrera*, 449 Mass. 825, 874 N.E.2d 654 (2007).
Venue	Venue lies either where the goods were stolen or where they were received. G.L. c. 277, § 58A. The place of receipt can be established by circumstantial evidence. *Obshatkin*, 2 Mass. App. Ct. at 3, 307 N.E.2d at 343. The Commonwealth is not required to allege or prove either the place of the theft or the place of receipt. *Commonwealth v. Parrotta*, 316 Mass. 307, 308-309, 55 N.E.2d 456, 457 (1944). Chapter 277 § 58A states that buying, receiving, or aiding in the concealment of this stolen or embezzled property may be prosecuted and punished in the same jurisdiction in which the larceny or embezzlement of any property involved in the crime may be prosecuted and punished.
Stolen property; restitution prevents incarceration	Chapter 266 § 61 states "if, upon a first conviction of receiving stolen property (c. 266 § 60), it is shown that the act of stealing the property was a simple larceny, and if the person convicted makes restitution to the person injured to the full value of the property stolen and not restored, he shall not be imprisoned in the state prison."

[1425] *Dellamano*, 393 Mass. at 134, 469 N.E.2d at 1255; *Commonwealth v. Haskins*, 128 Mass. 60, 61 (1880);
[1426] 2009 Model Jury Instructions.

C. 272 § 73B	SALE OF A COMMEMORATIVE GRAVE MARKER
Elements	
1.	Whoever sells or attempts to sell
2.	A commemorative grave marker that has been stolen and the person knows or should know the commemorative grave marker to be stolen.
Arrest Power, Penalties & Notes	
Power of Arrest	**Misdemeanor** – there is no statutory authority granting warrantless powers of arrest for this offense. However, if the offense is committed in public, in the officer's presence, and is creating a **breach of the peace** an arrest would be lawful.
Penalty	A fine of not more than $5,000 for a first offense and for a second or subsequent offense by imprisonment in a state prison for not more than 5 years or by imprisonment in a jail or house of correction for not more than 2½ years and by a fine of not more than $5,000.
Attorney Hanrahan's note	This law was enacted to provide an enhanced punishment to those who steal grave markers belonging to veterans, police and fire personnel, usually in the form of valuable metals to trade in for cash.
Related Statutes, Case Law & Other Important Information	
Definition	For purposes of this section, "commemorative grave marker" shall mean a grave marker, headstone, monument, structure, medallion or other object designed to commemorate the grave of a veteran, police officer or firefighter.
Receiving stolen commemorative grave marker	This statute also punishes someone who knowingly receives a stolen commemorative grave marker. The statute states: whoever receives, retains or disposes of a commemorative grave marker that the person knows or should know to be stolen, shall be punished by a fine of not more than $5,000. Exception: however, that no such penalty shall be imposed upon: (i) a person who receives or retains the commemorative grave marker with the intent to return it to a cemetery, a member of law enforcement, a member of a fire department, a member of the department of veterans' services, a non-profit veterans' services group or a veterans' agent of a city or town; or (ii) a person who in fact disposes of the commemorative grave marker by returning it to a cemetery, a member of law enforcement, a member of a fire department, a member of the department of veterans' services, a non-profit veterans' services group or a veterans' agent of a city or town.

C. 266 § 28	LARCENY OF A MOTOR VEHICLE & RELATED STATUTES
Elements	
1.	The defendant does any of the following:
2.	• Steals a motor vehicle or trailer • Maliciously damages a motor vehicle or trailer • Buys, receives, possesses, conceals, or obtains control of a motor vehicle or trailer, knowing or having reason to know the same to have been stolen • Takes a motor vehicle without the authority of the owner and steals from it any of its parts or accessories
Arrest Power, Penalties & Notes	
Power of Arrest	**Felony** – a police officer may effect a warrantless arrest for this offense provided he/she has probable cause that the suspect committed the offense.
Penalty	**1st Offense:** imprisonment in the **state prison (F)** for not more than 15 years or by imprisonment in a jail or HOC for not more than 2½ years or by a fine of not more than $15,000, or by both such fine and imprisonment. **2nd or subsequent offense:** results in a minimum mandatory sentence of 1 year. No CWOF's or placed on file permitted.
RMV Action	License revocation: 1st offense: 1 year. 2nd Offense: 5 years.
Case Law & Other Important Information	
Prima Facie Evidence	Evidence that an identifying number or numbers of a motor vehicle or trailer or part thereof has been intentionally and maliciously removed, defaced, altered, changed, destroyed, obliterated, or mutilated, shall be prima facie evidence that the defendant knew or had reason to know that the motor vehicle, or trailer or part thereof had been stolen.
Venue	Chapter 277 § 58A states that buying, receiving, or aiding in the concealment of this stolen or embezzled property may be prosecuted and punished in the same jurisdiction in which the larceny or embezzlement of any property involved in the crime may be prosecuted and punished.
ATV is a Motor Vehicle	In *Commonwealth v. Gonsalves,* 56 Mass.App.Ct. 506, 509, 778 N.E.2d 997 (2002), the Court affirmed the defendant's conviction for receipt of a stolen motor vehicle, an ATV.
Related Statutes	
Special requirements for vehicle theft c. 266 § 29	**Signature Required**: Whenever a motor vehicle is stolen or misappropriated, the owner of record shall sign and submit to the appropriate police authority a statement under the penalties of perjury on a form containing such information relating to the theft or misappropriation of the vehicle as is prescribed by the registrar of motor vehicles. **Recovery:** Whenever a stolen or misappropriated motor vehicle is recovered by law enforcement the police department shall notify: • the RMV, • the owner of record • the storage facility (if any) as soon as possible after the identity of the owner is determined. Such notification may be made by letter, telephone call or personal visit to the owner and shall include information as to the location of the recovered vehicle. **Storage Charges**: In the event the vehicle is placed in a garage or other storage facility, the owner of the storage facility shall lose his lien for the reasonable charges for storage and towing unless he notifies the owner of record of the vehicle by certified mail and return receipt requested within 5 of the date of the recovery or upon learning the identity of the owner of record. The notice shall contain the information on the location of the vehicle and the amount of charge due on said vehicle.

C. 266 § 28	LARCENY OF A MOTOR VEHICLE & RELATED STATUTES
MV Insurance Fraud **c. 266 § 27A**	Whoever, with intent to defraud the insurer, removes or conceals a motor vehicle or trailer belonging to himself or another which is at the time insured against theft, or whoever, aids or abets (with the same intent) in the removal or concealment, shall be punished. **Penalty:** by imprisonment in the **state prison (F)** for not more than 5 years or by imprisonment in jail or HOC for not less than 1 year nor more than 2½ years, and a fine of not less than $500 or more than $5,000. **Arrest Powers**: **Felony** – a police officer may effect an arrest for this offense committed in his/her presence or for an offense in the past, on probable cause.
Theft of Registration Plate **c. 266 § 139**	Whoever takes and carries away the registration plate that is attached to the vehicle of another or is assigned by the registry of motor vehicles to another shall be punished. **Penalty:** a fine of not less than $500 nor more than $1,000 or imprisonment in the HOC for not more than 2½ years, or both. **Arrest Powers**: **Misdemeanor** – statutory authority permits a police to effect an arrest for this offense when committed in his/her presence, or for this offense in the past on probable cause.
Handicap Placard theft and fraud	Chapter 90 § 24B makes it a felony to falsely make, **steal**, alter, forge or counterfeit or procure or to assist another to falsely make, steal, alter, forge or counterfeit a special parking identification disability placard.
Possession of a master key to a motor vehicle **c. 266 § 49**	Whoever knowingly has in his possession a master key designed to fit more than one motor vehicle, with intent to use or employ the same to steal a motor vehicle or other property therefrom, shall be punished by imprisonment in the **state prison (F)** for not more than 10 years or by a fine of not more than $1,000 and imprisonment in jail for not more than 2½ years. **Arrest Powers**: **Felony** – a police officer may effect an arrest for this offense committed in his/her presence or for an offense in the past, on probable cause.
Sale or offer for sale of master keys **c. 266 § 140**	Whoever sells or offers to sell or solicits offers to purchase a master key designed to fit more than one motor vehicle knowing, or having reasonable cause to believe, that said key will be used for an illegal purpose shall be punished. **Penalty**: a fine of not more than $500 or by imprisonment for not more than 1 year, or both. **Arrest Powers**: **Misdemeanor** – there is no statutory authority granting powers of arrest for this offense. However, if the offense is committed in public, in the officer's presence, and is creating a **breach of the peace** an arrest would be lawful.
Concealing a motor vehicle thief **c. 266 § 28**	Whoever conceals any motor vehicle or trailer thief knowing him to be such, shall be punished. **Penalty:** imprisonment for not more than 10 years or by imprisonment in jail or HOC for not more than 2½ years or by a fine of not more than $5,000, or both. **Arrest Powers**: **Felony** – a police officer may effect an arrest for this offense committed in his/her presence or for an offense in the past, on probable cause. **RMV Action:** license suspension - 1st offense - 1 year. 2nd Offense - 5 years.
Stolen leased or rented motor vehicle reporting requirements **c. 266 § 87A**	The owner or lessee of a leased or rented motor vehicle which has been stolen or placed beyond his control shall report the loss of the same to the police department of the city or town wherein said vehicle was leased or rented or stolen. Notwithstanding any provision of law to the contrary, a police department receiving a report of said stolen vehicle shall list the same as stolen and shall, by the use of radio, teletype, computer or other communication, disseminate the information concerning said stolen vehicle using the same standards as applicable to other stolen motor vehicles.
MV Repossession **c. 255B § 20C**	Any creditor obtaining possession of a motor vehicle under the provisions of this chapter shall, within one hour after obtaining such possession, notify the police department of the city or town in which such possession occurred, giving such police department a description of the vehicle involved.

C. 90 § 24(2)(a)	USING A MOTOR VEHICLE WITHOUT AUTHORITY
Elements	
1.	The defendant **used** a motor vehicle;
2.	That at the time he/she used that motor vehicle, he/she did so **without the permission** of the owner, or the permission of some other person who possessed the legal right of control ordinarily exercised by the owner; and
4.	That at the time he/she used the motor vehicle, the defendant **knew** that he/she was not authorized to use that vehicle.
Arrest Power, Penalties & Notes	
Power of Arrest	G.L. c. 90 § 21 authorizes a warrantless arrest for using without authority when committed in the officer's presence.
Penalty	**1st Offense:** a fine of not less than \$50.00 nor more than \$500.00 or by imprisonment for not less than 30 days nor more than 2 years, or both. **2nd Offense:** imprisonment in the **state prison (F)** for not more than 5 years or in a HOC for not less than 30 days nor more than 2½ years, or by a fine of not more than \$1,000, or by both such fine and imprisonment. **3rd or Subsequent Offense:** Committed within 5 years of the earliest of his two most recent prior offenses shall be punished by a fine of not less than \$200 nor more than \$1,000 or by imprisonment for not less than 6 months nor more than 2½ years in a HOC or for not less than 2½ years nor more than 5 years in the **state prison (F)** or by both fine and imprisonment.
RMV sanctions	**RMV Action:** 1st Offense: 1 year license revocation. 2nd or subsequent offense: 3 year revocation.
Related Statutes, Case Law & Other Important Information	
Applies to passengers	A person "uses" a motor vehicle within the meaning of the law if he rides in it, either as the driver or as a passenger. It is not necessary that the defendant personally drove or controlled the vehicle, only that he/she **rode** in it while it moved.[1427]
Public way not required	This statutes does not require the vehicle to be used on public way.[1428]
Lesser included offense of MV larceny	Use of a motor vehicle without authority is a lesser included offense of larceny of a motor vehicle (G.L. c. 266, § 28), without the element of intending to deprive the owner of possession permanently.[1429]
Rental Vehicle	Generally, once a rental agreement has expired the operator/user is considering using without authority.[1430] Note: it is recommended that you contact the rental company before taking action.

THEFT OFFENSES

[1427] District Court Jury Instructions 5.660, also Commonwealth v. Linder, 17 Mass. App. Ct. 967, 967, 458 N.E.2d 744, 745 (1983).
[1428] Commonwealth v. Morris M., 70 Mass. App. Ct. 688, 876 N.E. 2d 462, 488 (2007) (rejecting dictum in Commonwealth v. Giannino, 371 Mass. at 702, suggesting that "in a public way" is a fourth element of offense
[1429] Commonwealth v. Giannino, 371 Mass. 700, 703, 358 N.E.2d 1008, 1010 (1977); Commonwealth v. Linder, 17 Mass. App. Ct. 967, 967, 458 N.E.2d 744, 745 (1983).
[1430] Commonwealth v. Watts, 74 Mass.App.Ct. 514 (2009).

C. 159A § 16 TAXI FARE EVASION

Elements	
1.	The suspect fraudulently evades or attempts to evade the payment of a fare lawfully established by a common carrier (duly licensed under the provisions of this chapter), by one of the following:
2.	• Giving a false answer to the collector of the fare, or • By travelling beyond the point to which he has paid the same, or • By leaving the motor vehicle without having paid the fare lawfully established for the distance travelled.
Arrest Power, Penalties & Notes	
Power of Arrest	**Power of Arrest: NONE** – this is a civil offense and is only mentioned here because of the frequency in which police officers deal with this type of incident.
Penalty	Forfeit not less than $5.00 nor more than $20.00. **The court shall treat a violation of this section as a civil infraction**. A person complained of for such civil infraction shall be adjudicated responsible upon such finding by the court and shall neither be sentenced to a term of incarceration nor be entitled to appointed counsel pursuant to chapter 211D.
Attorney Hanrahan's Comment	Massachusetts does not have a theft of services statute. However, there are a variety of specific statutes covering theft of what would otherwise be services. This being one of them. See the Fraud section of this manual for more.
Related Statutes, Case Law & Other Important Information	
Payment may be demanded	Whoever does not upon demand first pay such fare shall not be entitled to be transported for any distance, and may be ejected from such a motor vehicle.
Fraudulent Hiring of Media Transportation c. 266 § 64	Some agencies use c. 266 § 64 to criminally prosecute taxi fare evasion. Although c. 159A § 16 is seemingly more on point, Chapter 266 § 64 states in part: "whoever hires a horse, carriage or **other vehicle**, and, with intent to cheat or defraud the owner thereof, makes to him or to his agent at the time of such hiring a false statement of the distance which he proposes to travel with such horse, carriage or other vehicle, or whoever, with such intent, makes to the owner or his agent, after the use of a horse, carriage or other vehicle, a false statement of the distance which he has actually traveled with such horse, carriage or other vehicle, and whoever, with such intent, refuses to pay for the use of a horse, carriage or other vehicle the lawful fare established therefor by any town, shall be punished by a fine of not more than $20 or by imprisonment for not more than 2 months, or both."

C. 266 § 146 ILLEGAL DUMPING

Elements	
1.	The defendant willfully and without right
2.	Deposits solid waste in a commercial disposal container of another without the consent of the owner or other person who has legal custody, care or control thereof
Arrest Power, Penalties & Notes	
Power of Arrest	**Misdemeanor** – there is no statutory authority granting warrantless powers of arrest for this offense. However, if the offense is committed in public, in the officer's presence, and is creating a **breach of the peace** an arrest would be lawful.
Penalty	A fine of not less than $100, nor more than $1,000.
Solid Waste	For purposes of this section "solid waste" shall mean garbage, refuse, trash, rubbish, sludge, residue or by-products of processing or treatment of discarded material, and any other solid, semi-solid or liquid discarded material resulting from domestic, commercial, mining, industrial, agricultural, municipal, or other sources or activities, but shall not include solid or dissolved material in domestic sewage

UNIQUE AND SPECIALIZED THEFT LAWS

Below are some of the many specialized forms of larceny which are rarely utilized.

Libraries; theft of materials or property **c. 266 § 99A**	Whoever willfully conceals on his person or among his belongings any library materials or property and removes said library materials or property, **Penalty if value over $250**: by imprisonment in the **state prison (F)** for not more than 5 years, or by a fine of not less than $1,000 nor more than $25,000, or both. **Penalty if value $250 or under:** punished by imprisonment in jail for not more than 1 year or by a fine of not less than one hundred nor more than $1,000, or both, **Note on Library Materials**: "Library materials and property", include any book, plate, picture, portrait, photograph, broadside, engraving, painting, drawing, map, specimen, print, lithograph, chart, musical score, catalog card, catalog record, statue, coin, medal, computer software, film, periodical, newspaper, magazine, pamphlet, document, manuscript, letter, archival material, public record, microform, sound recording, audio-visual material in any format, magnetic or other tape, tape recorder, film projector or other machinery or equipment, electronic data-processing record, artifact or other documentary written or printed material regardless of the physical form or characteristics which is a constituent element of a library's collection or any part thereof, belonging to, on loan to or otherwise in the custody of any library. Library materials and property shall also include the walls, wainscotting or any part of the library, or any other building or room used for library business or the appurtenances thereof, including furnishings. **Arrest:** c. 266 § 100 grants the police the power to make a warrantless arrest for any violation of this section (99A) whether in the officer's presence or not. **Restitution:** The offender shall be ordered to pay the replacement value of such library materials or property, including all reasonable processing costs, as determined by the governing board of said library.
Failure to return library materials **c. 266 § 99A**	Any person who has properly charged out any library materials or property, and who, upon neglect to return the same within the time required and specified in the by-laws, rules or regulations of the library owning the property, after receiving notice from the librarian or other proper custodian of the property that the same is overdue, shall willfully fail to return the same within 30 days from the date of such notice shall pay a fine of not less than $100 nor more than $500 and shall pay the replacement value of such library materials or property, including all reasonable processing costs, as determined by said governing board. **Note**: Each piece of library property shall be considered a separate offense. **Arrest:** c. 266 § 100 grants the police the power to make a warrantless arrest for any violation of this section (99A) whether in the officer's presence or not.
Embezzlement of property at fire **c. 266 § 23**	Whoever steals, conveys away or conceals any furniture, goods, chattels, merchandise or effects of persons whose houses or buildings are on fire or are endangered thereby, and does not, within 2 days thereafter, restore the same or give notice of his possession thereof to the owner, if known, or if unknown, to the mayor or one of the aldermen, selectmen or firewards of the place, shall be guilty of larceny. Note: the same penalties and arrest powers for basic larceny will apply.
Stealing at a fire **c. 266 § 24**	Whoever steals in a building which is on fire, or steals property which has been removed in consequence of an alarm caused by fire, shall be punished. **Penalty:** imprisonment in the **state prison (F)** for not more than five years or by a fine of not more than five hundred dollars and imprisonment in jail for not more than two years. **ARREST POWERS**: **Felony** – a police officer may effect an arrest for this offense committed in his/her presence or for an offense in the past, on probable cause.

UNIQUE AND SPECIALIZED THEFT LAWS	
Stealing tools of contractors, builders or mechanics **c. 266 § 27**	Whoever steals any tool belonging to any contractor, builder or mechanic from any building during the course of its construction, completion, alteration or repair, shall be punished. **Penalty:** a fine of not more than one hundred dollars or by imprisonment for not more than six months, or both. **Arrest Powers**: **Misdemeanor** – there is no statutory authority granting powers of arrest for this offense. However, if the offense is committed in public, in the officer's presence, and is creating a **breach of the peace** an arrest would be lawful.
Refusal to surrender stolen property **c. 266 § 21**	Whoever, having been convicted, either as principal or accessory, of **burglary or robbery**, or of any of the crimes described in sections 17-20, inclusive, of c. 265, or of **breaking and entering or of entering a building with intent to commit robbery or larceny,** has in his possession or control money, goods, bonds or bank notes, or any paper of value, or any property of another, which was obtained or taken by means of such crime, and, upon being requested by the lawful owner thereof to deliver the same to him, refuses or fails so to do while having power to deliver the same, shall be punished by imprisonment in the **state prison (F)** for not more than 5 years or in jail or HOC for not more than 2 years.
Common and notorious thief **c. 266 § 40**	Whoever, having been convicted, upon indictment, of larceny or of being accessory to larceny before the fact, afterward commits a larceny or is accessory thereto before the fact, and is convicted thereof upon indictment, and whoever is convicted at the same sitting of the court, as principal or accessory before the fact, of three distinct larcenies, shall be adjudged a common and notorious thief, and shall be punished by imprisonment in the **state prison (F)** for not more than 20 years or in jail for not more than 2½ years. **Attorney Hanrahan's Note:** What this means is that a 2nd conviction of larceny or a conviction of 3 distinct larcenies in the same proceeding results in an added penalty and the title of Common and Notorious Thief!
Larceny of bicycles; second conviction is a felony **c. 266 § 41**	Whoever is convicted of a second offence of the larceny of a bicycle shall, if the value of the bicycle stolen exceeds $10.00, be punished by imprisonment in the **state prison (F)** for not more than 5 years or by a fine of not more than $200 or by imprisonment in jail for not more than 2 years.
Larceny of a Handicap Placard/Plate	Chapter 90 § 24B makes it a felony to falsely make, steal, alter, forge or counterfeit or procure or to assist another to falsely make, steal, alter, forge or counterfeit a special parking identification disability placard.
Theft of Electricity **c. 164 § 127**	Summary: The defendant tampers with a electricity meter or does a variety of other actions designed to utilize electricity without payment. Misdemeanor.
Interference with Gas Meter **c. 164 § 126**	Summary: The defendant tampers with a gas meter or does a variety of other actions designed to utilize electricity without payment. Misdemeanor.
Duty of arresting officers to secure stolen goods **c. 266 § 48**	An officer who arrests a person charged as principal or accessory in a robbery or larceny shall secure the property which is alleged to have been stolen, annex a schedule thereof to his return and be answerable for the same; and, upon conviction of the offender, it shall be restored to the owner.

C. 266 § 30A	SHOPLIFTING
	Shoplifting by Asportation **Elements**
1.	The defendant intentionally takes possession of, carries away, transfers or causes to be carried away or transferred,
2.	Any merchandise displayed, held, stored or offered for sale by any store or other retail mercantile establishment
3.	With the intention of depriving the merchant of the possession, use of benefit of such merchandise or converting the same to the use of such person
4.	Without paying to the merchant the value thereof
	Shoplifting by Concealment **Elements**
1.	The defendant intentionally conceals upon his person or otherwise
2.	Any merchandise offered for sale by any store or other retail mercantile establishment
3.	With the intention of depriving the merchant of proceeds, use or benefit of such merchandise or converting the same to the use of such person
4.	Without paying to the merchant the value thereof
	Shoplifting by Altering Price Tag **Elements**
1.	The defendant intentionally
2.	Alters, transfers or removes;
3.	Any label, price tag or marking indicia of value or any other markings which aid in determining value affixed to any merchandise displayed, held, stored or offered for sale by any store or other retail mercantile establishment,
4.	To attempt to purchase such merchandise personally or in consort with another at less than the full retail value,
5.	With the intention of depriving the merchant of all or some part of the retail value thereof.
	Shoplifting by Changing Containers **Elements**
1.	The defendant intentionally transfers
2.	Any merchandise displayed, held, stored or offered for sale by any store or other retail mercantile establishment from the container in or on which the same shall be displayed to any other container
3.	With intent to deprive the merchant of all or some part of the retail value thereof

C. 266 § 30A	SHOPLIFTING
Shoplifting by Recording Lower Price Elements	
1.	The defendant intentionally
2.	Records a value for the merchandise which is less than the actual retail value
3.	with the intention of depriving the merchant of the full retail value thereof
Stealing a Shopping Cart Elements	
1.	The defendant intentionally
2.	Removes a shopping cart from the premises of a store or other retail mercantile establishment, without the consent of the merchant given at the time of such removal,
3.	With the intention of permanently depriving the merchant of the possession, use or benefit of cart.
Arrest Power, Penalties & Notes	
Power of Arrest	**Misdemeanor** – Law enforcement officers may arrest **without warrant** any person he has probable cause for believing has committed the offense of shoplifting as defined in this section.
Penalty	**Less than $100:** where the retail value of the goods obtained is less than $100, **1st** offense fine not to exceed $250. **2nd Offense**: a fine of not less than $100 nor more than $500. **3rd or subsequent offense**: a fine of not more than $500 or imprisonment in a jail for not more than 2 years, or by both such fine and imprisonment. **$100 or more ("aggravated shoplifting")**: a fine of not more than $1,000 or by imprisonment in the HOC for not more than 2½ years, or by both such fine and imprisonment.
Related Statutes, Case Law & Other Important Information	
"Conceal"	To "conceal" means to cover an object to keep it from being seen or to withdraw an object from view to prevent its discovery. To conceal is to take an action that makes it more difficult for the owner to discover the property or that makes discovery or identification of the property more difficult.[1431]
Retail merchandise	Retail merchandise means products or goods that are offered for sale in relatively small quantities directly to consumers. It refers to the type of merchandise sold in an ordinary store open to the public, as opposed to goods sold in bulk to merchants but not directly to the public.
Larceny charge in lieu of Shoplifting	*Commonwealth v. Hudson,* held that theft of retail merchandise may be prosecuted either under the shoplifting statute (G.L. c. 266, § 30A) or under the general larceny statute (G.L. c. 266 § 30). However, § 30A was amended by St. 1996, c. 430 (effective December 9, 1996) to provide that "[i]f the retail value of the goods obtained is less than $100.00, this section shall apply to the exclusion of section thirty." This appears to provide that shoplifting goods worth less than $100 may now be prosecuted *only* under § 30A and may not be prosecuted under § 30.[1432]
Merchant statement amounts to Probable Cause	The statement of a merchant or his employee or agent that a person has violated a provision of this section shall constitute probable cause for arrest by any law enforcement officer authorized to make an arrest in such jurisdiction.
Merchant Detention	Chapter 231 § 85R½ immunes merchants from liability for detention of shoplifters provided it is reasonable under the circumstances.

[1431] *Commonwealth v. Balboni,* 26 Mass. App. Ct. 750, 532 N.E.2d 706 (1989).
[1432] *Commonwealth v. Hudson*, 404 Mass. 282, 285-289, 535 N.E.2d 208, 210-212 (1989).

C. 266 § 30C RETAIL RECEIPT/PRICE TAG FRAUD

Elements	
1.	A person who, with intent to cheat or defraud a retailer;
2.	Possess, uses, utters, transfers, makes, alters, counterfeits or reproduces;
3.	A retail sales or return receipt, price ticket or universal product code label (UPC).

Arrest Power, Penalties & Notes	
Power of Arrest	**Felony** – a police officer may effect a warrantless arrest for this offense provided he/she has probable cause that the suspect committed the offense.
Penalty	2 ½ years in the house of correction or state prison for not more than 5 years or by a fine of more than $10,000, or by both such fine and imprisonment.
Attorney Hanrahan's Comment	This law covers the growing trend of thieves who obtain receipts (in various ways) and then grab an item off the shelf of a retail store (that is reflected on the receipt) and then returns the item for cash or credit. In many situations this conduct may not have technically violated the shoplifting statute. Now this conduct will amount to a felony offense, irrespective of the value.

Related Statutes, Case Law & Other Important Information	
266 § 30A	See the shoplifting statute for similar violations

C. 266 § 30B THEFT DETECTION SHEILDING DEVICE OFFENSES

(a) Distribution of Theft Detection Shielding Devices Elements	
1.	Knowingly manufacture, sell, offer for sale or distribute,
2.	A laminated or coated bag or other device intended to shield merchandise from detection by an electronic or magnetic theft detector.

(b) Unlawful Possession of Theft Detection Shielding Devices Elements	
1.	Knowingly possess,
2.	A laminated or coated bag or device intended to shield merchandise from detection by an electronic or magnetic theft detector,
3.	With the intent to commit, aid or abet a theft.

RETAIL THEFT OFFENSES

C. 266 § 30B	THEFT DETECTION SHEILDING DEVICE OFFENSES
	(c) Unlawful Possession of Theft Detection Deactivator or Remover Elements
1.	Knowingly possess,
2.	Any tool or device designed or adapted to either: (i) allow the deactivation of a theft detection device, with the intent to use such tool or device to deactivate a theft detection device on merchandise without the permission of the merchant or person owning or lawfully holding said merchandise; or (ii) allow the removal of a theft detection device from merchandise, with the intent to use such tool or device to remove a theft detection device from merchandise without the permission of the merchant or person owning or lawfully holding said merchandise.
	(d) Unlawful Distribution of Theft Detection Deactivator or Remover Elements
1.	Knowingly manufacturer, sell, offer for sale or distribute,
2.	A tool or device designed or adapted to allow the deactivation of a theft detection device or to allow the removal of a theft detection device from merchandise,
3.	Without the permission of the merchant or person owning or lawfully holding said merchandise.
	(e) Unlawful Deactivation or Removal of a Theft Detection Device Elements
1.	The person intentionally deactivate or remove a theft detection device from merchandise prior to purchase,
2.	In a retail establishment,
3.	With the intent to steal said merchandise.
	Arrest Power, Penalties & Notes
Power of Arrest	**Felony** – a police officer may effect a warrantless arrest for this offense provided he/she has probable cause that the suspect committed the offense.
Penalty	A violation of this section shall be punished by imprisonment in a house of correction for not more than 2½ years or by imprisonment in the state prison for not more than 5 years or by a fine of not more than $25,000, or by both such fine and imprisonment.
Attorney Hanrahan's Comment	These laws were passed to address the growing trend of professional type retail theft. Instead of utilizing the basic shoplifting statute to prosecute those who commit retail theft by way of aluminum foil coated and similar type bags or who utilize theft detection devices these felony level offenses can now be used.

c. 266 § 30D(b)	ORGANIZED RETAIL THEFT
	Elements
1.	The defendant, acting in concert with 2 or more persons and within a 180 day period
2.	Steals, embezzles or obtains by fraud, false pretense or other illegal means
3.	Retail merchandise valued at more than $2,500 to resell or otherwise reenter such retail merchandise into commerce.
	Arrest Power, Penalties & Notes
Power of Arrest	**Felony** – a police officer may effect a warrantless arrest for this offense provided he/she has probable cause that the suspect committed the offense.
Penalty	A violation of this subsection shall be punished by imprisonment in a state prison for not more than 10 years. ***Aggravated*** Organized Retail Theft: if the property stolen is valued at more than $10,000 imprisonment in a state prison for not more than 15 years.
	Related Statutes, Case Law & Other Important Information
Thefts may be aggregated	A series of thefts from 1 or more mercantile establishments may be aggregated.
Retail Merchandise	For purposes of this section, "retail merchandise" shall mean 1 or more items of tangible personal property displayed, held, stored or offered for sale in a retail establishment.
Venue	The defendant may be prosecuted in any county where a theft from a mercantile establishment occurred.
Leader of an Organized Retail Theft Enterprise **c. 266 § 30D(d)**	A person shall be a leader of an organized retail theft enterprise if the person conspires with others as an organizer, supervisor, financier or manager, to commit an organized retail crime or an aggravated organized retail crime. A leader of organized retail crime may be punished by a fine of not more than $250,000 or 5 times the retail value of the merchandise seized at the time of the arrest, whichever is greater, or imprisonment in state prison for not more than 20 years, or both such fine and imprisonment.

FRAUD RELATED OFFENSES (SEE MOTOR VEHICLE FRAUD FOR RMV & LICENSE FRAUD)

C. 266 § 37E	**IDENTITY FRAUD**
	Posing as Another for PERSONAL GAIN Elements[1]
1.	The defendant posed as another person
2.	Without the person's express authorization
3.	The defendant used the person's identifying information to: • Obtain, or attempt to obtain, money, credit, goods, services, something of value, an identification card or other evidence of the person's identity.
4.	The defendant did so with the intent to defraud.
	Posing as Another in order to HARASS Elements
1.	The defendant obtained personal identifying information about another person with the intent to: • Pose as that person or • To assist someone else to pose as that person
2.	The defendant did so without the express authorization of that person; and
3.	That the defendant did so with the specific intent to harass another person
	Arrest Power, Penalties & Notes
Power of Arrest	**Misdemeanor** – statutory authority permits a police may effect an arrest for this offense committed in his/her presence or for an offense in the past on probable cause.
Penalty	A fine of not more than $5,000 or imprisonment in a HOC for not more than 2½ years, or by both such fine and imprisonment.
Restitution	A person found guilty of violating any provisions of this section shall, in addition to any other punishment, be **ordered to make restitution for financial loss sustained by a victim** as a result of such violation. Financial loss may include any costs incurred by such victim in correcting the credit history of such victim or any costs incurred in connection with any civil or administrative proceeding to satisfy any debt or other obligation of such victim, including lost wages and attorney's fees.
Attorney Hanrahan's Comment	Most police officers are aware of identity theft in the terms of obtaining something of value but many are unaware the "harass" prong of this statute. With the prevalence of social networking many people, particularly children and teens, are being harassed (i.e. tormented) by others who create phony accounts posing as the target in order to humiliate and harass.

[1] 2009 Model Jury Instructions.

C. 266 § 37E	IDENTITY FRAUD
	Related Statutes, Case Law & Other Important Information
Report Jurisdiction	A law enforcement officer **shall accept a police incident report** from a victim and shall provide a copy to such victim, if requested, within 24 hours. Such police incident reports may be filed in **any county** where a **victim resides**, or in any county where the **owner or license holder of personal information stores or maintains said personal information**, the **owner's or license holder's principal place of business** or any county in which the **breach of security occurred**.
Definitions	For purposes of c. 266 § 37E, the following words shall have the following meanings: **"Harass"**, willfully and maliciously engage in an act directed at a specific person or persons, which act seriously alarms or annoys such person or persons and would cause a reasonable person to suffer substantial emotional distress. **"Pose"**, to falsely represent oneself, directly or indirectly, as another person or persons. **"Victim"**, any person who has suffered financial loss or any entity that provided money, credit, goods, services or anything of value and has suffered financial loss as a direct result of the commission or attempted commission of a violation of this section.
Willful	An act is "willful" if it is done intentionally and by design, in contrast to an act which is done accidentally.
Malice	An act is done with "malice" if it is intentional and without justification or mitigation, and any reasonably prudent person would have foreseen the actual harm that resulted. In the criminal harassment statute (G.L. c. 265, §43A), the requirement of malice does not require a showing of cruelty, hostility or revenge, nor does it require an actual intent to cause the required harm, but merely that the conduct be "intentional and without justification or mitigation, and any reasonable prudent person would have foreseen the actual harm that resulted." [1]
Personal identifying information	Personal identifying information. While the statute specifically identifies particular types of personal information that would fall within the definition of personal identifying information (specifically name, address, telephone number, driver's license number, social security number, place of employment, employee identification number, mother's maiden name, demand deposit account number, savings account number, credit card number, and computer password identification), the statute does not indicate that they are exclusive. G.L. c. 266, §37E(a).

FRAUD, FORGERY & LIES

[1] *Commonwealth v. O'Neil,* 67 Mass. App. Ct. 284, 290-293, 853 N.E>2d 576, 582-584 (2006). Accord, *Commonwealth v. Paton,* 63 Mass. App. Ct. 215, 219, 824 N.E.2d 887, 891 (2005); *Commonwealth v. Giavazzi,* 60 Mass. App. Ct. 374, 375-376, 802 N.E.2d 589 (2004).

C. 268 § 34A	FALSE NAME OR SOCIAL SECURITY NUMBER AFTER ARREST
Elements	
1.	The defendant knowingly and willfully
2.	Furnishes a false name or Social Security number to a law enforcement officer or law enforcement official
3.	Following an arrest
Arrest Power, Penalties & Notes	
Power of Arrest	He/she is already arrested.
Penalty	A fine of not more than $1,000 or by imprisonment in a HOC for not more than one year or by both such fine and imprisonment. **From and After:** The sentence shall run from and after any sentence imposed as a result of the underlying offense.
Restitution	The court may order that restitution be paid to persons whose identity has been assumed and who have suffered monetary losses as a result of a violation of this section.
Related Case Law	
Name Change	The law permits a person to change his/her name at will, without resort to legal proceedings, merely by adopting another name, as long as he/she is not using that name for a dishonest purpose. For purposes of this charge, a false name is one that a person has assumed for a dishonest purpose.[1]

SPECIALIZED VARIOUS FORMS OF FRAUD	
There are numerous fraud related crimes dealing with specific forms of fraud.	
Defrauding a common victualler (food seller) AKA "chew and screw" c. 140 § 12	Whoever, without having an express agreement for credit, with intent to cheat or defraud procures food or beverage from a common victualler without paying therefore shall be punished. **Penalty:** by a fine of not more than $500 or by imprisonment for not more than 3 months. **Arrest Powers**: **Misdemeanor** – there is no statutory authority granting powers of arrest for this offense. However, if the offense is committed in public, in the officer's presence, and is creating a **breach of the peace** an arrest would be lawful.
Defrauding an innkeeper c. 140 § 12	Whoever puts up at a hotel, motel, inn, lodging house or boarding house and, without having an express agreement for credit, with intent to cheat or defraud the owner or keeper procures food, entertainment or accommodation without paying therefor, or obtains credit at a hotel, motel, inn, lodging house or boarding house for such food, entertainment or accommodation by means of any false show of baggage or effects or removes or causes to be removed any baggage or effects from a hotel, motel, or inn while a lien exists thereon for the proper charges due from him for fare and board furnished therein, shall be punished. **Penalty**: If the value exceeds $100: imprisonment in a jail or HOC for not more than 2 years, or by a fine of not more than $600. If the value does not exceed $100: imprisonment for not more than 1 year or by a fine of not more than $1,000. **Arrest Powers**: **Misdemeanor** – there is no statutory authority granting powers of arrest for this offense. However, if the offense is committed in public, in the officer's presence, and is creating a **breach of the peace** an arrest would be lawful.

[1] *Commonwealth v. Clark*, 446 Mass. 620, 846 N.E.2d 765 (2006).

SPECIALIZED VARIOUS FORMS OF FRAUD	
Obtaining goods under false pretences **c. 266 § 73**	Whoever, with intent to defraud, by a false pretence of carrying on business and dealing in the ordinary course of trade, obtains from any person goods or chattels, shall be punished. **Penalty:** imprisonment in the **state prison (F)** for not more than 5 years or by a fine of not more than $500 and imprisonment in jail for not more than 2 years. **Arrest Powers**: **Felony** – a police officer may effect an arrest for this offense committed in his/her presence or for an offense in the past, on probable cause.
Obtaining property by trick **c. 266 § 75**	Whoever, by a game, device, sleight of hand, pretended fortune telling or by any trick or other means by the use of cards or other implements or instruments, fraudulently obtains from another person property of any description shall be punished as in the case of larceny of property of like value. Arrest powers and penalties would be the same as the standard larceny offense.
Obtaining credit by false pretenses **c. 266 § 33**	Whoever, with intent to defraud, by a false statement in writing respecting the financial condition, or means or ability to pay, of himself or of any other person, obtains credit from any bank or trust company or any banking institution or any retail seller of goods or services accustomed to give credit in any form whatsoever shall be guilty of larceny. Arrest powers and penalties would be the same as the standard larceny offense.
Obtaining signature under false pretenses **c. 266 § 31**	Whoever by a false pretence, with intent to defraud, obtains the signature of a person to a written instrument, the false making whereof would be a forgery, shall be punished. **Penalty**: imprisonment in the **state prison (F)** for not more than 10 years, or by a fine of not more than $500 and imprisonment in the jail for not more than t2 years. **ARREST POWERS**: **Felony** – a police officer may effect an arrest for this offense committed in his/her presence or for an offense in the past, on probable cause. **NOTE**: this section shall not apply to a purchase of property by means of a false pretence relative to the purchaser's means or ability to pay, if, by the terms of the purchase, payment therefor is not to be made upon or before the delivery of the property purchased, unless such pretence is made in writing and is signed by the person to be charged. (c. 266 § 35) **Venue:** Chapter 277 § 59 states "the crime of obtaining money or a personal chattel by a false pretence, and the crime described in c. 226 § 31, may be alleged to have been committed, and may be prosecuted and punished, in any county where the false pretence was made, written or used, or in or through which any of the property obtained was carried, sent, transported or received by the defendant.
Giving false information to library **c.266 § 99A**	The giving of a false identification or fictitious name, address or place of employment with the intent to deceive, or borrowing or attempting to borrow any library material or property by the use of a library card issued to another without the other's consent; the use of a library card knowing that it is revoked, canceled or expired; or, the use of a library card knowing that it is falsely made, counterfeit or materially altered shall be punished by a fine of not less than $100 nor more than $1,000. **Arrest Powers**: c. 266 § 100 grants the police the power to make a warrantless arrest for any violation of this section (99A) whether in the officer's presence or not.

SPECIALIZED VARIOUS FORMS OF FRAUD	
Presentation of false claims against government agency **c. 266 § 67B**	Whoever makes or presents to any employee, department, agency or public instrumentality of the commonwealth, or of any political subdivision thereof, any claim upon or against any department, agency, or public instrumentality of the commonwealth, or any political subdivision thereof, knowing such claim to be false, fictitious, or fraudulent, shall be punished **Penalty**: a fine of not more than $10,000 dollars or by imprisonment in the **state prison (F)** for not more than 5 years, or in the HOC for not more than 2½ years, or both. **Arrest Powers**: **Felony** – a police officer may effect an arrest for this offense committed in his/her presence or for an offense in the past, on probable cause.
Burning insured property with intent to defraud **c. 266 § 10**	Whoever, willfully and with intent to defraud or injure the insurer, sets fire to, or attempts to set fire to, or whoever causes to be burned, or whoever aids, counsels or procures the burning of, a building, or any goods, wares, merchandise or other chattels, belonging to himself or another, and which are at the time insured against loss or damage by fire, shall be punished. **Penalty:** imprisonment in the **state prison (F)** for not more than 5 years or in a jail or HOC for not more than 2.5 years. **Arrest Powers**: **Felony** – a police officer may effect an arrest for this offense committed in his/her presence or for an offense in the past, on probable cause.
Motor vehicle insurance policies fraudulent claims **c. 266 § 111B**	Whoever in connection with, or in support of, any application for or claim under any motor vehicle, theft or comprehensive insurance policy, with intent to injure, defraud or deceive knowingly presents to the insurer, or aids or abets in or procures to present to the insurer, any notice, statement, or proof of loss, knowing that it contains any false or fraudulent statement or representation of any fact or thing material to such application or claim, shall be punished. **Penalty** by imprisonment in the **state prison (F)** for not more than 5 years or by imprisonment in the HOC for not less than 6 months nor more than 2½ years or by a fine of not less than $1,000 nor more than $10,000, or by both such fine and imprisonment. **Arrest Powers**: **Felony** – a police officer may effect an arrest for this offense committed in his/her presence or for an offense in the past, on probable cause. **Enhanced Penalty for Appraiser or Repairman:** A person licensed as a motor vehicle damage appraiser or registered as a motor vehicle repair shop who fraudulently inflates an appraisal of damage to a motor vehicle or the charges for repairing a damaged motor vehicle, shall be punished by the additional penalty of revocation of such license or registration for a period not to exceed 2 years. **Restitution:** A person found guilty shall, in all cases, upon conviction, in addition to any other punishment, be ordered to make restitution to the insurer for any financial loss sustained as a result of the commission of the crime.
Acting as runner **c. 266 § 111C**	Whoever knowingly acts as a runner (see definition below) or uses, solicits, directs, hires or employs another to act as a runner for the purpose of defrauding an insured or an insurance carrier shall be punished. **Penalty:** imprisonment in the **state prison (F)** for not more than 5 years, by imprisonment in a jail or HOC for not less than 6 months nor more than 2½ years or by a fine of not less than $1,000 nor more than $4,000. **ARREST POWERS**: **Felony** – a police officer may effect an arrest for this offense committed in his/her presence or for an offense in the past, on probable cause. **Definitions:** **"Runner",** a person who, for a pecuniary benefit, procures or attempts to procure a client, patient or customer at the direction of, request of, or in cooperation with a provider whose purpose is to seek to fraudulently obtain benefits under a contract of insurance or fraudulently assert a claim against an insured or an insurance carrier for providing services to the client,

SPECIALIZED VARIOUS FORMS OF FRAUD

	patient or customer. Exception: "Runner" shall not include a person who procures or attempts to procure clients, patients or customers for a provider through public media or a person who refers clients, patients or customers to a provider as otherwise authorized by law. **"Provider",** an attorney, a health care professional licensed pursuant to c. 112, an owner or operator of a health care practice or facility, any person who creates the impression that he or his practice or facility can provide legal or health care services, or any person employed or acting on behalf of any of the aforementioned persons. **"Public media",** telephone directories, professional directories, newspapers and other periodicals, radio and television, billboards and mailed or electronically transmitted written communications that do not involve in-person contact with a specific prospective client, patient or customer.
Degrees; pretending to hold **c. 266 § 89**	Whoever, in a book, pamphlet, circular, advertisement or advertising sign, or by a pretended written certificate or diploma, or otherwise in writing, knowingly and falsely pretends to have been an officer or teacher, or to be a graduate or to hold any degree, of a college or other educational institution of this commonwealth or elsewhere, which is authorized to confer degrees, or of a public school of this commonwealth, shall be punished. **Penalty:** a fine of not more than $1,000 dollars or by imprisonment for not more than one year, or both. Any individual, school, association, corporation or institution of learning, not having lawful authority to confer degrees, using the designation of "university" or "college" shall be punished by a fine of $1,000 dollars; but this shall not apply to any educational institution whose name on July ninth, nineteen hundred and nineteen, included the word "university" or "college". **Arrest Powers**: **Misdemeanor** – there is no statutory authority granting powers of arrest for this offense.
Conferring a degree without authority **c. 266 § 89**	Whoever, without having lawful authority to confer degrees, offers or confers degrees as a school, college or as a private individual, alone or associated with others, shall be punished. **Penalty:** a fine of not more than $1,000 or by imprisonment for not more than 1 year, or both. Any individual, school, association, corporation or institution of learning, not having lawful authority to confer degrees, using the designation of "university" or "college" shall be punished by a fine of $1,000 dollars; but this shall not apply to any educational institution whose name on July ninth, nineteen hundred and nineteen, included the word "university" or "college". **Arrest Powers**: **Misdemeanor** – there is no statutory authority granting powers of arrest for this offense.
Animals; obtaining or giving false pedigree **c. 266 § 93**	Whoever, by a false pretence, obtains from any club, association, society or company for improving the breed of cattle, horses, sheep, swine or other domestic animals, the registration, or a certificate thereof, of any animal in the herd register, or any other register of such club, association, society or company, or a transfer of such registration, or whoever knowingly makes, exhibits or gives a false pedigree in writing of any animal, shall be punished by imprisonment for not more than 2 years or by a fine of not more than $500, or both. **Arrest Powers**: **Misdemeanor** – there is no statutory authority granting powers of arrest for this offense.

SPECIALIZED VARIOUS FORMS OF FRAUD	
Tampering with odometer of motor vehicle **c. 266 § 141**	Whoever advertises for sale, sells, uses, installs or has installed any device which causes an odometer to register any mileage other than the true mileage driven, or whoever resets, or alters the odometer of any motor vehicle with the intent to change the number of miles indicated thereon, or whoever, with the intent to defraud, operates a motor vehicle on any street or highway knowing that the odometer of such vehicle is disconnected to nonfunctional, shall be liable in a civil action of tort or contract in an amount equal to the sum of three times the amount of actual damages sustained or $1,500, whichever is the greater, plus the costs of the action together with reasonable attorney fees as determined by the court. **Note:** Nothing in this section and section one hundred and forty-one A shall prevent the service, repair or replacement of an odometer, provided the mileage indicated thereon remains the same as before the service, repair or replacement. Where the odometer is incapable of registering the same mileage as before such service, repair or replacement, the odometer shall be adjusted to read zero and a notice in writing shall be attached to the left door frame of the vehicle by the owner or his agent specifying the mileage prior to repair or replacement of the odometer and the date on which it was repaired or replaced.
Misrepresentation of mileage of motor vehicle by turning back odometer **c. 266 § 141A**	Whoever, with the intent to misrepresent to a prospective or eventual purchaser the number of miles traveled by a motor vehicle, turns back or readjusts the speedometer or odometer thereof shall be punished. **Penalty:** a fine of not less than $500 nor more than $1,000, or by imprisonment in a jail or HOC for not less than 30 days nor more than 2 years, or both. **Note:** Evidence that a dealer, as defined in section one of c. ninety, or a person required to be licensed under the provisions of section fifty-nine of c. one hundred and forty, by himself or by another turned back or readjusted the speedometer or odometer shall constitute prima facie evidence of such intent to misrepresent.
Transitional Assistance "Welfare" Theft, Fraud & Embezzlement **c. 18 § 5K**	Whoever embezzles, steals or obtains by fraud any funds, assets or property provided by the department of transitional assistance and whoever receives, conceals or retains such funds, assets or property for his own interest knowing such funds, assets or property have been embezzled, stolen or obtained by fraud shall be punished. **Penalty:** **$100 or more:** a fine of not more than $25,000 or by imprisonment in a jail or house of correction for not more than 2½ years, or imprisonment in the state prison for not more than 5 years, or both such fine and imprisonment **(Felony).** **Less than $100**: a fine of not more than $1,000 or by imprisonment in a jail or house of correction for not more than 1 year, or both such fine and imprisonment **(Misdemeanor).** **NOTE: see miscellaneous crimes section for more welfare related crimes. See computer crime section for computer services by fraud.**
Telecommunication service; fraud **c. 166 § 42A**	**Telecommunication Theft Under $5,000** The defendant, with intent to defraud, obtains, or attempts to obtain, or aids or abets another in obtaining, any **telecommunications services** valued **less than $5,000** by any false representation, false statement, or stratagem, by unauthorized charging to the account of another, by installing or tampering with any facilities or equipment or by any other means. **Penalty:** by a fine of not more than $3,000 or by imprisonment for not more than 2½ years in a HOC, or both. **If the theft is equal to or greater than $5,000.** **Penalty:** by a fine of not more than $10,000 or by imprisonment for not more than 10 years in a **state prison (F)**, or both. As used in this section, the words "telecommunication service" shall include the transmission of

SPECIALIZED VARIOUS FORMS OF FRAUD	
	intelligence by a community antenna television system licensed pursuant to the provisions of chapter166A.
Fraudulently avoiding charges for telecommunication service **c. 166 § 42B**	The defendant makes any instrument, apparatus, equipment or device which is designed, adapted or which is used to fraudulently obtain telecommunication service in the manner prohibited by section forty-two A or which is used to conceal, or to assist another to conceal, or from any lawful authority, the existence or place of origin or of destination of any telecommunication; or whoever possesses any such instrument, apparatus, equipment or device with the intent to use or employ the same in violation of this section or section forty-two A, or whoever sells, gives transport, or otherwise transfers to another, or offers to advertisers for sale, any such instrument apparatus, equipment, or device, or any plans or instructions for making or assembling the same, with the intent to use or employ such apparatus, equipment, or device, or to allow the same to be used or employed, for a purpose described in this section or whoever, knowing or having reason to believe that the same is intended to be used, or that said plans or instructions are intended to be used for making or assembling such apparatus, equipment or device, or whoever publishes plans or instructions for making or assembling or using any such apparatus, equipment or device, intending that such be used or employed in violation of this section or section forty-two A. **Penalty**: a fine of not more than $30,000 or by imprisonment in the **state prison (F)** for not more than 15 years, or by both.
Obtaining Computer Services by Fraud **c .266 § 33A**	The defendant, with intent to defraud, Obtains, or attempts to obtain, or aids or abets another in obtaining, any commercial computer service by false representation, false statement, unauthorized charging to the account of another, by installing or tampering with any facilities or equipment by any other means. **Penalty:** Imprisonment in the HOC for not more than 2½ years or by a fine of not more than $3,000, or both.
C. 277 § 58A½. Computer offenses; place of prosecution	The crimes described in chapter 266 § 102F, chapter 266 § 33A and chapter 266 § 127 when the personal property involved is electronically processed or stored data, either tangible or intangible, and data while in transit, may be prosecuted and punished in any county where the defendant was physically located at the time of the violation, or where the electronic data was physically located at the time of the violation.
Police Officer filing False Reports **c. 268 § 6A**	The defendant, being an officer or employee of the commonwealth or of any political subdivision thereof or of any authority created by the general court, in the course of his official duties executes, files or publishes any false written report, minutes or statement, knowing the same to be false in a material matter. **Penalty**: A fine of not more than $1,000 or by imprisonment for not more than 1 year, or by both such fine and imprisonment.

C. 268 § 33 IMPERSONATING A POLICE OFFICER/GOVERNMENT OFFICIAL

Elements	
1.	The defendant falsely assumes or pretends to be: • Law Enforcement: police officer, sheriff, deputy sheriff, constable, probation officer • Justice of the peace, or notary public, • Medical examiner, Associate Medical examiner • Examiner, investigator or other officer appointed by the registrar of motor vehicles, • Inspector, investigator or examiner of the department of public utilities, the department of telecommunications and cable, • Investigator or other officer of the alcoholic beverages control commission, • Investigator or other official of the bureau of special investigations, • Examiner, investigator or other officer of the department of revenue
2.	And • Acts as such, or • Requires a person to aid or assist him in a matter pertaining to the duty of such officer.
Arrest Power, Penalties & Notes	
Power of Arrest	**Misdemeanor** – there is no statutory authority granting warrantless powers of arrest for this offense. However, if the offense is committed in public, in the officer's presence, and is creating a **breach of the peace** an arrest would be lawful.
Penalty	A fine of not more than $400 or by imprisonment for not more than 1 year.
Related Statutes, Case Law & Other Important Information	
Blue lights on vehicles c. 90 § 7E.	Chapter 90 § 7E establishes strict rules on the type of vehicles that are permitted to display red and blue lights. See the Motor Vehicle Section of this manual for details.
Impersonating a Gas or Electric Worker c. 164 § 126A	The defendant falsely assumes, pretends to be or holds himself out as an officer or servant of a gas or electric company for the purpose of gaining access to any premises shall be punished by imprisonment in a HOC for not more than 2 years or by a fine of not more than $1,000, or both such fine and imprisonment.

C. 272 § 106

STOLEN VALOR

Elements

1.	The person knowingly, with the intent to obtain money, property or any other tangible benefit,
2.	Fraudulently represents such person to be an active member or veteran of the United States Navy, Army, Air Force, Marines or Coast Guard, including armed forces reserves and National Guard: a. through the unauthorized manufacture, sale or use of military regalia or gear, including the wearing of military uniforms, or b. the use of falsified military identification and obtains money, property or another tangible benefit through such fraudulent representation; or Fraudulently represents such person to be a recipient of the Congressional Medal of Honor, Distinguished Service Cross, Navy Cross, Air Force Cross, Silver Star, Purple Heart, Combat Infantryman Badge, Combat Action Badge, Combat Medical Badge, Combat Action Ribbon or Air Force Combat Action Medal *and obtains money, property or another tangible benefit* through such fraudulent representation.

Arrest Power, Penalties & Notes

Power of Arrest	**Misdemeanor** – there is no statutory authority granting warrantless powers of arrest for this offense. However, if the offense is committed in public, in the officer's presence, and is creating a **breach of the peace** an arrest would be lawful.
Penalty	Imprisonment in a house of correction for not more than 1 year or by a fine of $1,000, or both such fine and imprisonment.
Attorney Hanrahan's Comment	The defendant must commit this act with the intent to obtain some type of tangible benefit, (e.g. a free meal, a discount, etc.), simply bragging by making false claims to impress others would not violate the statute.

CREDIT CARD FRAUD OFFENSES

C. 266 § 37B/C	CREDIT CARD FRAUD
Chapter 266 § 37B depicts the misdemeanor credit card offenses. Chapter 266 § 37C depicts the felony level credit card offenses. Below are the MISDEMEANOR CREDIT CARD OFFENSES in c. 266 § 37B.	
FRAUDULENT APPLICATION FOR CREDIT CARD	
(a)	The defendant, with intent to defraud, makes or causes to be made, either directly or indirectly, any false statement as to a material fact **in writing**,
	Knowing it to be false and with intent that it be relied on, respecting his **identity** or that of any other person, or his **financial condition** or that of any other person,
	For the **purpose of procuring the issuance of a credit card**
OBTAINING OR STEALING CREDIT CARD OF ANOTHER	
(b)	The defendant, with intent to defraud, takes a credit card from the person, possession, custody or control of another without the cardholder's consent by any conduct which would constitute larceny or The defendant, with knowledge that it has been so taken, receives the credit card with intent to use it or to sell it, or to transfer it to a person other than the issuer or cardholder.
RETAINING A LOST CREDIT CARD WITH INTENT TO USE	
(c)	The defendant, with intent to defraud, receives a credit card that he knows to have been lost, mislaid, or delivered under a mistake as to the identity or address of the cardholder, and retains possession with intent to use it or to sell it or to transfer it to a person other than the issuer or the cardholder.
BUYING OR SELLING A CREDIT CARD	
(d)	Whoever being a person other than the issuer or his authorized agent, sells a credit card, or buys a credit card from a person other than the issuer or his authorized agent.
UNLAWFUL SIGNING OF A CREDIT CARD	
(e)	The defendant being a person other than the cardholder or a person authorized by him, signs a credit card.
USING A LOST OR STOLEN, UNLAWFULLY OBTAINED CREDIT CARD	
(f)	The defendant uses, for the purpose of obtaining money, goods, services or anything else of value, a credit card obtained or retained in violation of clauses (b) to (e)(unlawfully possessed credit cards), inclusive, or a credit card which he knows is forged, expired or revoked, where the value of money, goods or services obtained in violation of this section is not in excess of $250.
UNLAWFUL USE OF A CREDIT CARD	
(g)	The defendant obtains money, goods, services or anything else of value by representing without the consent of the cardholder that he is said cardholder or by representing that he is the holder of a card and such card has not in fact been issued, where the value of money, goods or services obtained is not in excess of $250.

C. 266 § 37B/C	CREDIT CARD FRAUD
	PROVIDING GOODS/SERVICES KNOWING THE CARD IS UNLAWFULLY BEING USED
(h)	The defendant, being a person authorized by an issuer to furnish money, goods, services or anything else of value upon presentation of a credit card by the cardholder, or any agent or employees of such person, furnishes money, goods, services or anything else of value upon presentation of a credit card which he knows was obtained or retained in violation of clauses (b) to (e) (unlawfully obtained credit cards), inclusive, or a credit card which he knows is forged, expired or revoked where the value of the goods or services obtained is not in excess of $250.
	OVERCHARGING A CREDIT CARD
(i)	The defendant, being a person who is authorized by an issuer to furnish money, goods, services or anything else of value upon presentation of a credit card by the cardholder, or any agent or employee of such person, fails to furnish money, goods, services or anything else of value which he represents in writing to the issuer that he has furnished, and the difference between the value of all money, goods, services and anything else of value actually furnished and the value represented to the issuer to have been furnished does not exceed $250
	OBTAINING GOODS/SERVICES IN VIOLATION OF CLAUSES (F) to (I)
(j)	The defendant receives money, goods, services or anything else of value obtained in violation of clauses (f) to (i), inclusive.
	FALSE REPORT OF STOLEN CREDIT CARD
(k)	The defendant makes a false statement in reporting a credit card to be lost or stolen.
	POSSESSION OF 4 OR MORE STOLEN CREDIT CARDS
(L)	The defendant has in his possession or under his control stolen credit cards issued in the names of four or more other persons shall be presumed to have violated clause (b) (obtaining stolen credit cards/stealing credit cards).
	Arrest Power, Penalties for Chapter 266 § 37B **Misdemeanor Credit Card Offenses**
Power of Arrest	Whoever is **discovered by a police officer in the act of violating this section**, while such officer is lawfully at or within the place where such violation occurs, **may be arrested without a warrant** by such police officer.
Penalty	**Penalty for all credit cards offenses in this section (§37B)**: a fine of not more than $500 or by imprisonment in a jail or HOC for not more than 1 year or both.

C. 266 § 37B/C	CREDIT CARD FRAUD
	FELONY CREDIT CARD OFFENSES ARE LISTED BELOW **Chapter 266 § 37C**
	OBTAINING CONTROL OF A CREDIT CARD AS A SECURITY FOR A DEBT
(a)	The defendant with intent to defraud obtains control over a credit card as a security for a debt.
	WRONGFULLY RECEIVES CREDIT CARD
(b)	The defendant receives a credit card which he knows was taken or retained under circumstances which constitute credit card theft or a violation of clauses (a) or (d) of section 37B or clause (a) of this section.
	FALSELY CREATES OR UTTERS A FALSE CREDIT CARD
(c)	The defendant with intent to defraud falsely makes or embosses a purported credit card or utters such card. Note: whoever has in his possession or under his control **4 or more** credit cards which are falsely embossed shall be presumed to have violated this clause.
	OBTAINS MONEY, GOODS, SERVICES OR ANYTHING ELSE OF VALUE BY USE OF A CREDIT CARD OVER $250
(d)	The defendant obtains money, goods, services or anything else of value by use of a credit card obtained or retained in violation of clauses (b) to (e), inclusive, of section 37 B, or by use of a credit card which he knows is forged, expired or revoked, where the value of the money, goods or services obtained in violation of this section is in excess of $250.
	FALSELY USES CREDIT CARD OVER $250
(e)	The defendant obtains money, goods or services or anything else of value by representing without the consent of the cardholder that he is said cardholder or by representing that he is the holder of a card and such card has not in fact been issued, where the value of money, goods or services obtained in violation of this section is in excess of $250.
	UNLAWFULLY ACCEPTING A CREDIT CARD (VALUE OVER $250)
(f)	The defendant being a person authorized by an issuer to furnish money, goods, services or anything else of value upon presentation of a credit card which he knows was obtained in violation of subsections (b) to (e), inclusive, of section 37B, or a credit card which he knows is forged, expired or revoked, when the value of the money, goods or services obtained is in excess of $250.
	UNLAWFULLY CHARGING A CREDIT CARD (VALUE OVER $250)
(g)	The defendant being a person authorized by an issuer to furnish money, goods, services or anything else of value upon presentation of a credit card by the cardholder or any agent or employee of such person, fails to furnish money, goods or services or anything else of value which he represents in writing to the issuer that he has furnished, and the difference between the value of all money, goods, services and anything else of value actually furnished and the value represented to the issuer to have been furnished exceeds $250.
	RECEIVING GOODS/SERVICES FROM UNLAWFULLY USED CREDIT CARD
(h)	The defendant receives money, goods, services or anything else of value obtained in violation of subsections (f) or (g) of section 37B.

C. 266 § 37B/C	CREDIT CARD FRAUD
	POSESSION OF INCOMPLETE CREDIT CARDS
(i)	The defendant possesses one or more incomplete credit cards, intending to complete them without the consent of the issuer.
	UNLAWFUL POSSESSION OF CREDIT CARD MAKING EQUIPMENT
(j)	The defendant possesses, with knowledge of its character, machinery, plates or any other contrivance designed to reproduce instruments purporting to be the credit cards of an issuer who has not consented to the preparation of such credit cards.
	ARREST POWER, PENALTIES FOR CHAPTER 266 § 37C FELONY CREDIT CARD OFFENSES
Power of Arrest	**Felony** - A police officer may effect an arrest for this offense committed in his/her presence or for an offense in the past, on probable cause.
Penalty	**Penalty for all credit cards offenses in this section (§37C)**: a fine of not more than $2,000, or by imprisonment in a jail or HOC for not more than 2½ years or in the state prison (F) for not more than 5years, or by both such fine and imprisonment.
	Other Important Information
Definitions	**"Cardholder",** the person named on the face of a credit card to whom or for whose benefit the credit card is issued by an issuer. **"Credit card",** any instrument or device, whether known as a credit card, credit plate, or by any other name, issued with or without fee by an issuer for the use of the cardholder in obtaining money, goods, services or anything else of value on credit. **Case Law Note:** In the 2011 case of ***Com. v. Ryan***, the Appeals Court ruled that a debit card was a credit card for the purpose of the misuse of credit card laws in chapter 266 § 37. **"Expired credit card",** a credit card which is no longer valid because the term shown on its face has elapsed. **"Falsely embosses",** completion of a credit card, without the authorization of the named issuer, by adding any of the matter, other than the signature of the cardholder, which an issuer requires to appear on the credit card before it can be used by a cardholder. **"Falsely makes",** making or drawing, in whole or in part, a device or instrument which purports to be the credit card of a named issuer but which is not such a credit card because the issuer did not authorize the making or drawing, or altering a credit card which was validly issued. **"Incomplete credit card",** a credit card that does not contain all of the matter that must be stamped, embossed, imprinted or written on said card other than the signature, as required by the issuer before it can be used by a cardholder. **"Issuer",** the business organization or financial institution which issues a credit card or his duly authorized agent. **"Receives" or "receiving",** acquiring possession or control or accepting as security for a loan. "Revoked credit card", **a credit card which is no longer valid because permission to use it has been suspended or terminated by the issuer.**

FORGERY & UTTERING

C. 267 § 1	FORGERY
Elements[1]	
1.	The defendant did one or more of the following: • Falsified one or more significant parts of the document in question • Altered one or more significant parts of the document in question • Counterfeited the document in question to make it appear to be genuine
2.	The defendant did so with the intent to injure or to defraud someone.
Arrest Power, Penalties & Notes	
Power of Arrest	**Felony** – a police officer may effect a warrantless arrest for this offense provided he/she has probable cause that the suspect committed the offense.
Penalty	Imprisonment in the state prison (F) for not more than 10 years or in jail for not more than 2 years.
Attorney Hanrahan's Comment	The document forged must be a document of *legal significance*. For instance, a child who forged his mother's signature relating to his failed math test would not rise to the level of legal significance in order to justify a forgery charge.
Related Statutes, Case Law & Other Important Information	
Specific Documents that can be the subject of forgery	• A public record, • A certificate, return or attestation of a clerk or register of a court, public register, notary public, justice of the peace, town clerk or any other public officer, in relation to a matter wherein such certificate, return or attestation may be received as legal proof; • A charter, deed, will, testament, bond or writing obligatory, power of attorney, policy of insurance, bill of lading, bill of exchange or promissory note; • An order, acquittance or discharge for money or other property or a credit card or an instrument described as a united states dollar traveler's check or cheque, purchased from a bank or other financially responsible institution, the purpose of which is a source of ready money on cashing the instrument without identification other than the signature of the purchaser; • An acceptance of a bill of exchange, or an endorsement or assignment of a bill of exchange or promissory note for the payment of money; • An accountable receipt for money, goods or other property; • A stock certificate, • Any evidence or muniment of title to property; • A certificate of title, duplicate certificate of title, certificate issued in place of a duplicate certificate, the registration book, entry book, or any indexes provided for by chapter 185, or the docket of the recorder;
Must relate to the document	To have a forgery, something relating to a legal document itself, as distinguished from its contents, must be false. Making a false statement in a document is a separate crime under some circumstances, but it is not the offense of forgery, which is concerned with the genuineness of the document itself, rather than the truth of its contents.
Forgery can be committed in three ways	The first is to counterfeit or produce what appears to be a genuine legal document, but which is in fact a **phony document.** The second way is to **falsely fill in one or more important parts** of a genuine document — for example, by forging someone else's signature on a check or a bill of sale. The third way is closely related to the second: **altering in a significant way one or more parts** of a genuine document that has already been made out — for example, changing the amount on a check.[1]

[1] 2009 Model Jury Instructions. Commonwealth v. O'Connell, 438 Mass. 658, 664 n.9, 783 N.E.2d 417, 424 n.9 (2003) (elements offorgery); Commonwealth v. Apalakis, 396 Mass. 292, 486 N.E.2d 669 (1985); Commonwealth v.Segee, 218 Mass. 501, 504, 106 N.E. 173, 174 (1914); Commonwealth v. Baldwin, 11 Gray 197, 198 (1858).

C. 267 § 1	FORGERY
Claim of Authority	Lack of authority is not an element of the offense of forgery, but if a claim of authority is properly raised, the Commonwealth must prove the absence of authority beyond a reasonable doubt in order to prove the element of fraudulent intent.
Forged MV Document	See Chapter 90 § 24B for prohibited conducted related to forged motor vehicle documents.
Forged Prescriptions	See chapter 94C § 33(b) in the Drug Laws Section of this Manual for forgery offenses related to prescriptions for drugs.

C. 267 § 5	UTTERING
	Elements[2]
1.	That the defendant passed or attempted to pass as true and genuine one of the following: • a check or other order for money • a promissory note • an order for other property
2.	The check, promissory note, order for property was: • Falsely made, or • Forged, or • Altered
3.	The defendant knew it was falsely made, forged, altered; and
4.	The defendant passed or attempted to pass it with the specific intent to injure or defraud someone.
	Arrest Power, Penalties & Notes
Power of Arrest	**Felony** – a police officer may effect a warrantless arrest for this offense provided he/she has probable cause that the suspect committed the offense.
Penalty	Imprisonment in the state prison (F) for not more than 10 years or in jail for not more than 2 years.
Attorney Hanrahan's Comment	Forgery is the creation of the false document. Uttering is the presentation, or passing, of the forged document knowing that it is forged.
	Related Statutes, Case Law & Other Important Information
Checks	Uttering a false, forged or altered check may be prosecuted under G.L. c. 267, § 5 because a check is "an order . . . for money" (G.L. c. 267, § 1). A check is "a draft, other than a documentary draft, payable on demand and drawn on a bank" and is an order if, among other things, it is "an unconditional promise or order to pay a fixed amount of money". An attempt to negotiate a false check will support a conviction for attempted larceny (G.L. c. 266, § 30). Commonwealth v. Green, 66 Mass. App. Ct. 901, 845 N.E.2d 392 (2006).
Bank Card	A bank signature card could be uttered. *Commonwealth v. Murphy* 59 Mass. 571 (2003).

FORGERY & UTTERING

[1] 2009 Model Jury Instructions.
[2] Commonwealth v. O'Connell, 438 Mass. 658, 664 n.9, 783 N.E.2d 417, 424 n.9 (2003) (elements of uttering); also see the 2009 Model Jury Instructions.

C. 267 § 5	UTTERING
Intent to defraud	The defendant must have intended to defraud someone, but not necessarily any particular person.[1] It is not necessary that the intended victim have been misled by forgery.[2]
Larceny by False Pretenses	Uttering not a lesser included offense of larceny by false pretenses, therefore a defendant could be convicted of both offense if the circumstances dictate.[3]
Uttering via an Agent	Uttering may be accomplished through innocent agent.[4]

C. 267 § 12	FALSE, FORGED or COUNTERFEIT BILLS
	Elements
1.	The defendant brings into this commonwealth or has in his possession
2.	A false, forged or counterfeit bill or note, in the similitude of the bills or notes, payable to the bearer thereof or to the order of any person, issued by or for any bank or banking company, or an instrument described as a United States Dollar Traveller's Check or Cheque, purchased from a bank or other financially responsible institution, the purpose of which is a source of ready money on cashing the instrument without identification other than the signature of the purchaser,
3.	With intent to utter or pass the same or to render the same current as true, **knowing** the same to be false, forged or counterfeit,
	Arrest Power, Penalties & Notes
Power of Arrest	**Felony** – a police officer may effect a warrantless arrest for this offense provided he/she has probable cause that the suspect committed the offense.
Penalty	Imprisonment in the state prison for not more than 5 years, or by a fine of not more than $1,000 and imprisonment in jail for not more than 1 year.
Attorney Hanrahan's Comment	The Secret Service has primary jurisdiction in relation to counterfeit U.S. currency. You should contact the Secret Service prior to formerly charging the defendant.
	Related Statutes, Case Law & Other Important Information
US Secret Service	Contact the US Secret Service, Boston Office, 10 Causeway Street #447, Boston, MA 0222. Phone number: (617) 565-5640. www.secretservice.gov
Counterfeiting Bank Bills	Chapter 267 § 8 states "no person may engage in the act of counterfeiting."

[1] Commonwealth v. Analetto, 326 Mass. 115, 118, 93 N.E.2d 390 (1950).
[2] Commonwealth v. Bond, 188 Mass. 91, 74 N.E. 293 (1905).
[3] Commonwealth v. Crocker, 384 Mass. 353, 358, 424 N.E.2d 524, 528 (1981).
[4] Commonwealth v. Hill, 11 Mass. 136, 136-137 (1814).

C. 267A § 2	MONEY LAUNDERING
	Elements
1.	The Defendant knowingly does one of the following:
2.	transports or possesses a monetary instrument or other property that was derived from criminal activity with the intent to promote, carry on or facilitate criminal activity; or
3.	Engages in a transaction involving a monetary instrument or other property known to be derived from criminal activity: I. with the intent to promote, carry on or facilitate criminal activity; or II. knowing that the transaction is designed in whole or in part either to: a. conceal or disguise the nature, location, source, ownership or control of the property derived from criminal activity; or b. avoid a transaction reporting requirement of this chapter, of the United States, or of any other state; or
4.	Directs, organizes, finances, plans, manages, supervises or controls the transportation of, or transactions in, monetary instruments or other property known to be derived from criminal activity or which a reasonable person would believe to be derived from criminal activity.
	Arrest Power, Penalties & Notes
Power of Arrest	**Felony** – a police officer may effect a warrantless arrest for this offense provided he/she has probable cause that the suspect committed the offense.
Penalty	Imprisonment in the state prison for not more than 6 years or by a fine of not more than $250,000 or twice the value of the property transacted, whichever is greater, or by both such imprisonment and fine. 2nd or subsequent such offense: imprisonment in the state prison for not less than 2 years, but not more than 8 years or by a fine of not more than $500,000 or 3 times the value of the property transacted, whichever is greater, or by both such imprisonment and fine.
	DEFINITIONS (c. 267A § 1)
Criminal Activity	Activity which constitutes a criminal offense punishable under the laws of the commonwealth by imprisonment in a state prison or a criminal offense committed in another jurisdiction punishable under the laws of that jurisdiction as a felony.
Monetary instrument	The currency and coin of the United States or any foreign country; any bank check, money order, stock, investment security, or negotiable instrument in bearer form or otherwise in such form that title passes upon delivery; gold, silver or platinum bullion or coins; diamonds, emeralds, rubies or sapphires; any negotiable instrument including, bank checks, cashier's checks, traveler's checks or monetary orders made payable to the order of a named party that have not been endorsed or which bear restrictive endorsements; poker chips, vouchers or other tokens exchangeable for cash by gaming entities; and credit cards, debit cards, gift cards, gift certificates or scrips.

C. 267A § 2	MONEY LAUNDERING
Financial institution	(1) a bank as defined in section 1 of chapter 167; (2) a national banking association, bank, savings and loan association, savings bank, cooperative bank, building and loan or credit union organized under the laws of the United States; (3) a banking association, bank, savings and loan association, savings bank, cooperative bank, building and loan or credit union organized under the laws of any state; (4) an agency, agent or branch of a foreign bank; (5) a currency dealer or exchange; (6) a person or business engaged primarily in the cashing of checks; (7) a person or business regularly engaged in the issuing, selling or redeeming of traveler's checks, money orders or similar instruments; (8) a broker or dealer in securities or commodities; (9) a licensed transmitter of funds or other person or business regularly engaged in the transmission of funds to a foreign nation for others; (10) an investment banker or investment company; (11) an insurer; (12) a dealer in precious metals, stones or jewels; (13) a pawnbroker or scrap metal dealer; (14) a telegraph or other communications company; (15) a personal property or real estate broker; (16) a dealer in vehicles including, but not limited to, automobiles, aircraft and vessels; (17) an operator of a betting or gaming establishment; (18) a travel agent; (19) a thrift institution, as defined in section 1 of chapter 167F; (20) an operator of a credit card system; or (21) a loan or finance company.
Transaction	A purchase, sale, loan, pledge, gift, transfer, delivery or other disposition and, with respect to a financial institution, including, but not limited to, a deposit, withdrawal, bailment, transfer between accounts, exchange of currency, loan, extension of credit, purchase or sale of any stock, bond, certificate of deposit or other monetary instrument, use of a safe deposit box or any other payment, transfer or delivery by, through or to a financial institution, by whatever means effected.

SERIAL NUMBER OFFENSES (for offenses involving VIN's see Motor Vehicle Section)

C. 266 § 139A	REMOVING/ALTERING SERIAL NUMBERS
Elements	
1.	The defendant: • Removes, defaces, alters, changes, destroys, obliterates or mutilates, or • Causes to be removed or destroyed or in any way defaced, altered, changed, obliterated or mutilated,
2.	The identifying number or numbers of any machine or any electrical or mechanical device;
3.	With intent thereby to: • Conceal its identity, • Defraud the manufacturer, seller, or purchaser, • Hinder competition in the areas of sales and servicing, or • Prevent the detection of a crime;
Arrest Power, Penalties & Notes	
Power of Arrest	**Misdemeanor** – there is no statutory authority granting powers of arrest for this offense. However, if the offense is committed in public, in the officer's presence, and is creating a breach of the peace an arrest would be lawful.
Penalty	A fine of not more than $500 or by imprisonment in a jail or HOC for not more than 1 year or by both such fine and imprisonment.
Related Statutes, Case Law & Other Important Information	
Possession Prima Facie Evidence	Possession of any machine or electrical or mechanical device the identifying number or numbers of which have been so removed, defaced, altered, changed, destroyed, obliterated or mutilated shall be prima facie evidence of a violation of the foregoing provision.
Selling	This chapter and section also punishes those who sell items without identifying numbers. It states "whoever sells or otherwise disposes of or attempts to sell or otherwise dispose of a machine or an electrical or a mechanical device, knowing or having reason to believe that the identifying number or numbers of the same have been so removed, defaced, altered, changed, destroyed, obliterated or mutilated shall be punished." Same penalty imposed.
MV serial number offenses	See the motor vehicle section of this manual for crimes related to motor vehicle serial numbers.

INTELLECTUAL PROPERTY (INCLUDING UNLAWFUL RECORDINGS ETC.)

C. 266 § 143A	UNAUTHORIZED TRANSFER OF SOUND RECORDINGS
Elements	
1.	The defendant directly or indirectly transferred or caused to be transferred sounds that had been recorded on a: • Phonograph record • Disc • Wire • Tape • Film • Video cassette • Sound recording;
2.	The defendant knew he/she was transferring such sounds;
3.	That the defendant did so without the consent of the owner of the master recording from which the transferred sounds were derived; and
4.	The defendant intended to sell (or did actually sell) or to rent or to transport the recorded copy, or to play it in a public performance for profit, or intended to cause one of those things to happen.
Arrest Power, Penalties & Notes	
Power of Arrest	**Misdemeanor** – If the number of recordings do not meet the felony level (see Penalty Section) there is no statutory authority granting warrantless powers of arrest for this offense. However, if the offense is committed in public, in the officer's presence, and is creating a **breach of the peace** an arrest would be lawful. **Felony** – a police officer may effect a warrantless arrest for this offense provided he/she has probable cause that the suspect committed the offense.
Penalty	**Misdemeanors:** **1-99 Sound Recordings** or **1-6 Audio Visual Recordings**: - imprisonment for not more than 1 year in the HOC or by a fine of not more than $25,000, or by both such fine and imprisonment; **100 to 999 Unlawful Sound Recordings** or **7 to 64 Unlawful Audio Visual Recordings**: imprisonment in the HOC for not more than 2 years or by a fine of not more than $100,000, or by both such fine and imprisonment . **Felony:** **1,000 or more Unlawful Sound Recordings** or **65 or more Unlawful Audio Visual Recordings**: imprisonment in **state prison (F)** for not more than 5 years or by a fine of not more than $250,000, or by both such fine and imprisonment.
Attorney Hanrahan's Comment	This law is designed to punish those who sell bootleg copies of music and videos. However, there are also specific statutes (below) which prohibit recording of live performances and movies at a movie theater.

C. 266 § 143A	UNAUTHORIZED TRANSFER OF SOUND RECORDINGS
	Related Statutes, Case Law & Other Important Information
Unauthorized Reproduction and Sale Of Live Performances **c. 266 § 143B**	The defendant for commercial advantage or private financial gain records or causes to be recorded a **live performance** with knowledge that such recording is without the consent of the owner, or advertises, sells, rents, transports or causes to be advertised, sold, rented or transported, or possesses for any of such purposes, a recording of a live performance with the knowledge that the live performance was recorded without the consent of the owner, shall be punished. The same punishment and arrest powers as § 143A (above).
Packaging Not Bearing Reproducer's Name and Address **c. 266 § 143C**	The defendant for commercial advantage or private financial gain knowingly manufactures, rents, sells, transports, or causes to be manufactured, rented, sold or transported, or possesses for purposes of sale, rental or transport, any recorded device the outside packaging of which does not clearly and conspicuously bear the true name and address of the transferor of the sounds or images contained thereon shall be punished. The same punishment and arrest powers as § 143A (above).
Exceptions to § 143 TO 143C **c. 266 § 143D**	Nothing in sections 143A to 143C, inclusive, shall be construed to apply to any person lawfully entitled to use or who causes to be used such sound or images for profit through public performance, or who transfers or causes to be transferred any such sound or images as part of a radio or television broadcast or for archival preservation. Nothing in section 143A to 143C, inclusive, shall be construed to apply to local, state or federal law enforcement officers employing an audiovisual recording function during the lawful exercise of law enforcement duties.
Unlawful recording of motion picture in motion picture theater **c. 266 § 143F**	Any person, in a motion picture theater while a motion picture is being exhibited, who knowingly operates an audiovisual recording function, with the intent to unlawfully record the motion picture and without the consent of the owner or lessee of the motion picture theater, shall be punished as follows: **1st Offense**: imprisonment in the HOC for not more than 2 years or by a fine of not more than $100,000, or by both such fine and imprisonment **2nd or subsequent conviction**, by imprisonment in the state prison (F) for not more than 5 years or by a fine of not more than $250,000, or by both such fine and imprisonment. **Arrest Powers**: Misdemeanor – there is no statutory authority granting powers of arrest for this offense. However, if the offense is committed in public, in the officer's presence, and is creating a breach of the peace an arrest would be lawful. **Exception**: Nothing in this section shall be construed to apply to local, state or federal law enforcement officers employing an audiovisual recording function during the lawful exercise of law enforcement duties. **C. 266 § 143G. Persons Detained For Possible Violation Of Sec. 143f** In an action for false arrest or false imprisonment brought by any person, by reason of having been detained for questioning or awaiting the arrival of law enforcement, on or in the immediate vicinity of a motion picture theater, if such person was detained in a reasonable manner and for not more than a reasonable length of time by a person authorized to make arrests or by the owner or his agent or servant authorized for such purpose and if there were reasonable grounds to believe that the person so detained was committing or attempting to commit any violation of section 143F, it shall be a defense to such action.

C. 266 § 143A	UNAUTHORIZED TRANSFER OF SOUND RECORDINGS
Definitions	As used in sections 143A to 143H, inclusive, the following words shall have the following meanings: **"Article"** or "recorded device", the tangible medium upon which sounds or images are recorded or otherwise stored, and shall include any original phonograph record, disc, wire, tape, audio or video cassette, film or other medium now known or later developed on which sounds or images may be recorded or otherwise stored, or any copy or reproduction which duplicates, in whole or in part, the original. **"Audiovisual recording function"**, the capability to record or transmit visual images or soundtrack, including any portion thereof, from a motion picture. **"Motion picture theater"**, movie theater, screening room, or other venue if used primarily for the exhibition of motion pictures. **"Owner"**, the person or other entity who owns a master phonograph record, master disc, master tape, master film or other device used for reproducing recorded visual images or sounds on a phonograph record, disc, tape, film, video cassette or other article on which visual images or sound is recorded, and from which the transferred recorded images or sounds are directly or indirectly derived.

TICKET SCALPING LAWS	
Ticket Scalping c. 140 § 185A	Reselling tickets without being properly licensed is unlawful in Massachusetts. See Commonwealth v. Sovrensky, 269 Mass. 460 (1929). Arrest Power: none.
Ticket Scalping Violation 140 § 185F	Whoever violates any provision of section 185A to section 185G, inclusive, or any rule or regulation of the commissioner made under section 185E, shall be punished by a **fine of not more than $500 (for 1st and 2nd offense). 3rd and Subsequent Offense:** punished by such find and by imprisonment in a jail or HOC for not more than one year.

DRUGS

C. 94C § 1	DRUG LAW DEFINITIONS
Controlled Substance	A drug, substance, or immediate precursor in any schedule or class referred to in chapter 94C.
Counterfeit Substance	A substance which is represented to be a particular controlled drug or substance, but which is in fact not that drug or substance.
Deliver	To transfer, whether by actual or constructive transfer, a controlled substance from one person to another, whether or not there is an agency relationship.
Drug Paraphernalia Defined	All equipment, products, devices and materials of any kind which are primarily intended or designed for use in planting, propagating, cultivating, growing, harvesting, manufacturing, compounding, converting, producing, processing, preparing, testing, analyzing, packaging, repackaging, storing, containing, concealing, ingesting, inhaling or otherwise introducing into the human body a controlled substance in violation of chapter 94C. It includes, but is not limited to: 1) Kits used, primarily intended for use or designed for use in planting, propagating, cultivating, growing or harvesting of any species of plant which is a controlled substance or from which a controlled substance can be derived; 2) Kits used, primarily intended for use or designed for use in manufacturing, compounding, converting, producing, processing or preparing controlled substances; 3) Isomerization devices used, primarily intended for use or designed for use in increasing the potency of any species of plant which is a controlled substance; 4) Testing equipment used, primarily intended for use or designed for use in identifying or in analyzing the strength, effectiveness or purity of controlled substances; 5) Scales and balances used, primarily intended for use or designed for use in weighing or measuring controlled substances; 6) Diluents and adulterants, such as quinine hydrochloride, mannitol, mannite, dextrose and lactose, used, primarily intended for use or designed for use in cutting controlled substances; 7) Separation gins and sifters used, primarily intended for use or designed for use in removing twigs and seeds from or in otherwise cleaning or refining marihuana; 8) Blenders, bowls, containers, spoons and mixing devices used, primarily intended for use or designed for use in compounding controlled substances; 9) Capsules, balloons, envelopes and other containers used, primarily intended for use or designed for use in packaging small quantities of controlled substances; 10) Containers and other objects used, primarily intended for use or designed for use in storing or concealing controlled substances; 11) There is no clause 11 12) Objects used, primarily intended for use or designed for use in ingesting, inhaling, or otherwise introducing marihuana, cocaine, hashish or hashish oil into the human body, such as: a) metal, wooden, acrylic, glass, stone, plastic or ceramic pipes, which pipes may or may not have screens, permanent screens, hashish heads or punctured metal bowls; b) water pipes; c) carburetion tubes and devices; d) smoking and carburetion masks; e) roach clips; meaning objects used to hold burning material, such as a marihuana cigarette that has become too small or too short to be held in the hand; f) miniature cocaine spoons and cocaine vials;

C. 94C § 1	DRUG LAW DEFINITIONS
	g) chamber pipes; h) carburetor pipes; i) electric pipes; j) air-driven pipes; k) chillums; l) bongs; m) ice pipes or chillers; n) wired cigarette papers; o) cocaine freebase kits.
Factors used to determine drug paraphernalia	In determining whether an object is drug paraphernalia, a court or other authority should consider, in addition to all other logically relevant factors, the following: (a) the proximity of the object, in time and space, to a direct violation of this chapter; (b) the proximity of the object to controlled substances; (c) the existence of any residue of controlled substances on the object; (d) instructions, oral or written, provided with the object concerning its use; (e) descriptive materials accompanying the object which explain or depict its use; (f) national and local advertising concerning its use; (g) the manner in which the object is displayed for sale; (h) whether the owner, or anyone in control of the object, is a supplier of like or related items to the community, such as a licensed distributor or dealer of tobacco products; (i) direct or circumstantial evidence of the ratio of sales of the object to the total sales of the business enterprise; (j) the existence and scope of legitimate uses for the object in the community; (k) expert testimony concerning its use.
Related Statutes, Case Law & Other Important Information	
Distribution of Counterfeit Substance	Chapter 94C § 32G makes it a crime (misdemeanor) to sell a counterfeit controlled substance (see later in this section).
Sale of Drug Paraphernalia	Chapter 94C § 32I makes it a misdemeanor to sell drug paraphernalia. It becomes a felony when sold to someone under the age of 18 (see later in this section).

DRUG USE AND POSSESSION

C. 270 § 18	INHALING VAPORS FOR EFFECT (HUFFING)
Elements	
1.	No person shall intentionally smell or inhale (or possess with the intent to smell or inhale)
2.	The fumes of any substance having the property of releasing toxic vapors
3.	For the purpose of causing a condition of intoxication, euphoria, excitement, exhilaration, stupefaction, or dulled senses or nervous system.
Arrest Power, Penalties & Notes	
Power of Arrest	**Misdemeanor -** Any person who is discovered by a police officer or special police officer in the act of violating this section may be arrested without a warrant.
Penalty	A fine of not more than $200 or by imprisonment for not more than 6 months, or both.
Attorney Hanrahan's Comment	Although this statute is not limited to controlled substances, in fact it most often used when the substance is not a controlled substance, many of those who violate this statute are also involved with illicit drug use.
Related Statutes, Case Law & Other Important Information	
Glue or Cement Sale to Minors c. 270 § 19	Any person who sells glue or cement to a minor shall require such minor to properly identify himself and write his name and address legibly in a permanently bound register. The seller shall keep such register available for police inspection for a period of **6 months** after the last sale is recorded therein. **Note:** No such glue or cement shall be sold to a minor unless it contains allyl isothiocyanate (oil of mustard) or some other equally effective and safe deterrent against smelling or inhaling the fumes of such glue or cement. **Penalty:** a fine of not more than $200 or by imprisonment for not more than 6 months, or both.
OUI c. 90 § 24	Chapter 90 § 24 prohibits the operation of a motor vehicle while under the intoxicating effects of glue.
Carrying a firearm c. 269 § 10H	Chapter 269 § 10H prohibits the carrying of a firearm while under the intoxicating effects of glue or similar substances.

The Concept of Possession

Possession is easy to prove when a defendant is holding an item or secreting it on his/her person, however possession may be proved without the item actually being in the defendant's possession. This is typically referred to as **constructive possession**.

To prove constructive possession, the Commonwealth typically must establish the defendant's "**knowledge** coupled with the **ability and intention to exercise dominion and control**."

Essentially, in order to prove constructive possession, you must prove two elements:

1. The Defendant's knowledge of the item/substance's existence
2. The Defendant's ability to control it; and
3. The intent to control the item/substance.

Constructive possession includes more than being in the presence of the item or even operating a motor vehicle containing the item. The prosecution must show additional factors "that tip the scale" to prove constructive possession.[1]

Knowledge: A defendant's knowledge is typically proved by "inference from all the facts and circumstances." For instance, the defendant's reaction to the presence of the police (i.e. running, or attempting to hide) may be indicative of the defendant's knowledge of any contraband present.

Dominion and Control: in constructive possession cases, a defendant's presence alone is not enough to show knowledge, or the ability and intention to exercise control over the item, but "presence, supplemented by other incriminating evidence, 'will serve to tip the scale in favor of sufficiency.' "[2] For instance, the quantity of the contraband may be an indicator of the defendant's intent to exercise dominion and control. Two teenagers found sitting in the park alongside two open, partially consumed, cans of beer would likely be indicative that both teens exercised dominion and control over the beer absent some plausible explanation. The facts and circumstances of each case will have to be analyzed.

Admission of Use can be used to Prove Possession

Admission of recent drug use may provide sufficient evidence of constructive possession.

In the 2015 SJC case of ***Commonwealth v. Cullity***, the admission of a passenger in a motor vehicle wherein PCP was found, coupled with the passenger's visible signs of impairment, was used to prove that the passenger constructively possessed the PCP found in the vehicle where he was merely a passenger.

[1] *Commonwealth v. Crapps*, Appeals Court (2013).
[2] *Com. v. Romero*, Appeals Court (2011)

C. 94C § 32L	MARIJUANA - POSSESSION OF AN OUNCE OR LESS – CIVIL
Civil Offense	The possession of **1 ounce or less** of marihuana shall only be a civil offense.
Arrest Power, Penalties & Notes	
Power of Arrest	No Arrest Power. Civil offense.
Penalty: 18 years old and older	A civil penalty of $100 and forfeiture of the marihuana. (**Note:** City/Town receives fine revenues.)
Penalty: 17 years old and younger	• A civil penalty of $100 and forfeiture of the marihuana • The Minor must complete a drug awareness program with one year • The parents or legal guardian shall be notified **Failure to Complete Drug Awareness Program**: If an offender under the age of 18 fails within one year of the offense to complete both a drug awareness program and the required community service, the civil penalty may be increased $1,000 and the offender and his or her parents shall be jointly and severally liable to pay that amount.
Attorney Hanrahan's Comment	Although it is no longer a criminal offense to possesses an ounce or less of marijuana, it is still a criminal offense to distribute marijuana in any amount. This law does not affect other offenses such as those related to OUI, cultivating, selling, manufacturing or trafficking. However, this law has had a major impact on criminal procedure issues, particularly in the area of search and seizure (see the criminal procedure section of this manual for more on this topic). Additionally, cities and towns may pass local ordinances and by-laws prohibiting the public consumption of marijuana.
Additional Provisions	
No other Sanctions May be Imposed	Neither the Commonwealth nor any of its political subdivisions or their respective agencies, authorities or instrumentalities may impose any form of penalty, sanction or disqualification on an offender for possessing an ounce or less of marihuana (other than possible delinquency proceedings against a juvenile who does not complete drug awareness program - see section 32M below). **For example**: possession of one ounce or less of marihuana shall not provide a basis to deny an offender student financial aid, public housing or any form of public financial assistance including unemployment benefits, to deny the right to operate a motor vehicle or to disqualify an offender from serving as a foster parent or adoptive parent.
No CORI	Information concerning the offense of possession of one ounce or less of marihuana shall not be deemed "criminal offender record information," "evaluative information," or "intelligence information" as those terms are defined in chapter 6 § 167 and shall not be recorded in the Criminal Offender Record Information system.
Possession includes *internal possession*:	As used herein, "possession of one ounce or less of marihuana" includes possession of one ounce or less of marihuana or tetrahydrocannabinol and having cannabinoids or cannibinoid metabolites in the urine, blood, saliva, sweat, hair, fingernails, toe nails or other tissue or fluid of the human body. **Attorney Hanrahan's Note:** Many people are confused as to why internal possession was included into the this law. It would appear that *internal possession* was added into the law to prevent those who test positive from having employment sanctions placed on them, as opposed creating an avenue to fine people who are high (although some agencies have done so).

C. 94C § 32L	MARIJUANA - POSSESSION OF AN OUNCE OR LESS – CIVIL
	Related Statutes, Case Law & Other Important Information
Offender Under 18: Copy must be delivered to parent **c. 94C § 32N**	A second copy of the notice delivered to an offender under the age of eighteen shall be mailed or delivered to at least one of that offender's parents having custody of the offender, or, where there is no such person, to that offender's legal guardian at said parent or legal guardian's last known address.
Drug Awareness Requirement **c. 94C § 32M**	The failure of the offender to complete a drug awareness program may be a basis for **delinquency proceedings** for persons under the age of 18 at the time of their offense. The drug awareness program (approved by DYS) must provide at **least 4 hours** of classroom instruction or group discussion and **10 hours of community service**. The subject matter of such drug awareness programs shall be specific to the use and abuse of marihuana and other controlled substances with particular emphasis on early detection and prevention of abuse of substances.
Parent must file Drug Awareness Certificate with Court **c. 94C § 32N**	If an offender under the age of 18, a parent or legal guardian fails to file with the Clerk of the appropriate Court a certificate that the offender has completed a drug awareness program in accordance within one year of the relevant offense, the Clerk shall notify the offender, parent or guardian and the enforcing person who issued the original notice to the offender of a hearing to show cause why the civil penalty should not be increased to $1,000. Factors to be considered in weighing cause shall be limited to: 1. Financial capacity to pay any increase, 2. The offender's ability to participate in a compliant drug awareness program and 3. The availability of a suitable drug awareness program. **Fines go to the City/Town:** Any civil penalties imposed under the provisions of "An Act Establishing A Sensible State Marihuana Policy" shall inure to the city or town where the offense occurred.
Police Department Requirements **c. 94C § 32N**	The person in charge of each police department shall direct the department's public safety officer or another appropriate member of the department to function as a liaison between the department and persons providing drug awareness and the Clerk-Magistrate's office of the District Court. The person in charge shall also issue books of non-criminal citation forms to the department's officers which conform with the provisions Chapter 40 § 21D
Public consumption	Currently, no state law prohibits public consumption of marijuana. However, some municipalities have passed ordinances/by-laws prohibiting public consumption.
Weight unknown	In the 2014 case of ***Commonwealth v. Overmeyer***, the Court stated "In cases where the weight of seized marijuana is not immediately evident, we not that the executive office of Public Safety and Security has advised that, if 'portable scales are not available, (police) have the option of taking the suspect's information and releasing him while also instructing him that he will receive something in the mail. When police return to the station, they may weigh the marijuana. If the weight is more than an ounce, the suspect may be summonsed to court on a criminal complaint. If the weight is an ounce of less, a citation may be mailed to the suspect within 15 days of the offense.'"
No MV stop permitted	In 2015 case of ***Commonwealth v. Rodriguez***, the SJC ruled that reasonable suspicion that the occupants of a motor vehicle possess non-criminal amounts of marijuana (in this case the reasonable suspicion stemmed from the odor of burnt marijuana) does <u>not</u> justify a vehicle stop.

C. 94C § 32L	MARIJUANA - POSSESSION OF AN OUNCE OR LESS – CIVIL
Must be *more than an ounce* to be criminal	In the 2015 case of ***Commonwealth v. Sheridan***, the officer observed a bag of marijuana in a motor vehicle that he believed to be "about an ounce." The SJC ruled that the subsequent search was unlawful based on the officer's observations. Possession of "about an ounce" is not a criminal offense.
Marijuana & Motor Vehicles	See the Motor Vehicle Stops and Motor Vehicle Search sections in the Criminal Procedure section of this manual for more on marijuana and motor vehicle related issues.
Medical Marijuana	See medical marijuana law for additional exemptions below.

c. 369	MEDICAL MARIJUANA[1]
Medical Use now permitted	In November 2012, Massachusetts voters approved a ballot question that allows a qualifying patient with a debilitating medical condition to obtain and possess marijuana for medical use beginning January 1, 2013.
Who's covered	A patient must obtain a written certification from a physician for a debilitating medical condition. The law specifies: cancer, glaucoma, AIDS, hepatitis C, amyotrophic lateral sclerosis (ALS), Crohn's disease, Parkinson's disease, multiple sclerosis and other conditions as determined in writing by a qualifying patient's physician.
What can they posses	The law allows a qualifying patient to possess up to a 60-day supply of marijuana for his or her personal medical use. The regulations define a 60-daysupply as up to 10 ounces.
Medical Marijuana Cards	There are three types of ID cards: 1) Patient; 2) Personal Caregiver; and 3) RMD Agent. Each ID card contains the individual's name, photograph, the type of registrant, their registration number, the ID card expiration date, and five different security features. <u>Important:</u> The "ID card expiration date" is NOT the date that the individual's registration expires. Registrations must be renewed annually, whereas new ID cards are issued every three years. To find out whether an individual has an active registration with the MMJ, run the "MMJ" query from CJIS Web or CJIS Messenger and observe whether the individual has an "Active" or "Inactive" status next to "Registration Status". Additional information about the MMJ program, as well as the sample images below can be found on the Department of Public Health's website. Questions regarding the MMJ query in CJIS can be directed to the CJIS Support Services Unit at 617.660.4710.

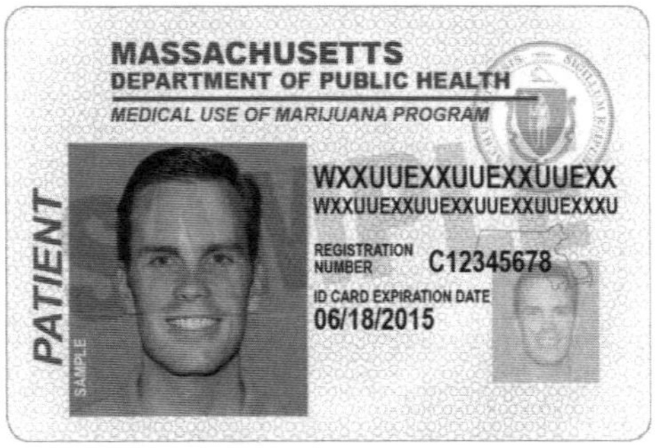

[1] http://www.mass.gov/eohhs/gov/departments/dph/programs/hcq/medical-marijuana/

c. 369	MEDICAL MARIJUANA[1]
No penalty for possession	Any person meeting the requirements under this law shall not be penalized under Massachusetts law in any manner, or denied any right or privilege, for such actions. A qualifying patient or a personal caregiver shall not be subject to arrest or prosecution, or civil penalty, for the medical use of marijuana provided he or she: a. Possesses no more marijuana than is necessary for the patient's personal, medical use, not exceeding the amount necessary for a sixty-day supply; and b. Presents his or her registration card to any law enforcement official who questions the patient or caregiver regarding use of marijuana.
Cultivation Registration	The Department shall issue a cultivation registration to a qualifying patient whose access to a medical treatment center is limited by: 1. verified financial hardship, 2. a physical incapacity to access reasonable transportation, or 3. the lack of a treatment center within a reasonable distance of the patient's residence. The Department may deny a registration based on the provision of false information by the applicant. Such registration shall allow the patient or the patient's personal caregiver to cultivate a limited number of plants, sufficient to maintain a 60-day supply of marijuana, and shall require cultivation and storage only in an enclosed, locked facility. The department shall issue regulations consistent with this section within 120 days of the effective date of this law. Until the department issues such final regulations, the written recommendation of a qualifying patient's physician shall constitute a limited cultivation registration.
Search warrants for Cultivation	In the 2015 case of ***Commonwealth v. Canning***, the SJC ruled that the police should have determined whether or not the defendant was the holder of a medical marijuana card before executing a search warrant for cultivation. See search warrant section form more.
Protection Against Forfeiture and Arrest	The lawful possession, cultivation, transfer, transport, distribution, or manufacture of medical marijuana as authorized by this law shall not result in the forfeiture or seizure of any property. No person shall be arrested or prosecuted for any criminal offense solely for being in the presence of medical marijuana or its use as authorized by this law.
Limitations of the Law	a. Nothing in this law allows the operation of a motor vehicle, boat, or aircraft while under the influence of marijuana. b. Nothing in this law requires any health insurance provider, or any government agency or authority, to reimburse any person for the expenses of the medical use of marijuana. c. Nothing in this law requires any health care professional to authorize the use of medical marijuana for a patient. d. Nothing in this law requires any accommodation of any on-site medical use of marijuana in any place of employment, school bus or on school grounds, in any youth center, in any correctional facility, or of smoking medical marijuana in any public place. e. Nothing in this law supersedes Massachusetts law prohibiting the possession, cultivation, transport, distribution, or sale of marijuana for nonmedical purposes. f. Nothing in this law requires the violation of federal law or purports to give immunity under federal law. g. Nothing in this law poses an obstacle to federal enforcement of federal law.

c. 369	MEDICAL MARIJUANA[1]
Fraudulent Activity	The fraudulent use of a medical marijuana registration card or cultivation registration shall be a misdemeanor punishable by up to 6 months in the house of correction, or a fine up to $500, but if such fraudulent use is for the distribution, sale, or trafficking of marijuana for non-medical use for profit it shall be a felony punishable by up to 5 years in state prison or up to 2½ years in the house of correction.
	DEFINITIONS
Personal Caregiver	"Personal caregiver" shall mean a person who is at least twenty-one (21) years old who has agreed to assist with a qualifying patient's medical use of marijuana. Personal caregivers are prohibited from consuming marijuana obtained for the personal, medical use of the qualifying patient.
Enclosed, locked facility	"Enclosed, locked facility" shall mean a closet, room, greenhouse, or other area equipped with locks or other security devices, accessible only to dispensary agents, patients, or personal caregivers.

C. 94C § 34	UNLAWFUL POSSESSION OF CONTROLLED SUBSTANCES
	Elements
1.	No person shall knowingly or intentionally
2.	Possess a controlled substance (this law does not apply to possession of 1 ounce or less of marijuana or to medical marijuana – see medical marijuana section)
3.	Unless such substance was obtained directly, or pursuant to a valid prescription or order, from a practitioner while acting in the course of his professional practice, or except as otherwise authorized by the provisions of chapter 94C.
	Arrest Power, Penalties & Notes
Power of Arrest	Whether **Felony or Misdemeanor** statutory authority permits a police officer to effect an arrest for this offense provided the officer has probable cause that the defendant committed the offense.
	Penalties
All Drugs except Heroin, Marijuana, & Class E	Imprisonment for not more than 1 year or by a fine of not more than $1,000, or by both such fine and imprisonment.
Marihuana (more than one ounce) or Class E	Imprisonment in a house of correction (HOC) for not more than 6 months or a fine of $500, or both.
Heroin	**1st Offense**: imprisonment in a HOC for not more than 2 years or by a fine of not more than $2,000, or both. **2nd or subsequent offense**: imprisonment in the **State Prison (F)** for not less than 2½ years nor more than 5 years or by a fine of not more than $5,000 and imprisonment in a jail or HOC for not more than 2½ years.
2nd or Subsequent Offense or Previous Related Conviction (other than heroin or Class E)	One or more convictions of a violation of this section (§34 – unlawful possession) or of a felony under any other provisions of chapter 94C, or of a corresponding provision of earlier law relating to the sale or manufacture of a narcotic drug as defined in said earlier law, shall be punished by imprisonment in a HOC for not more than 2 years or by a fine of not more than $2,000, or both.

DRUG POSSESSION & USE

C. 94C § 34	UNLAWFUL POSSESSION OF CONTROLLED SUBSTANCES
	Related Statutes, Case Law & Other Important Information
Good Samaritan Exception	Chapter 94C § 34A "Medical assistance for persons experiencing drug-related overdose" sometimes referred to by the media as "The 911 Good Samaritan Law." The law essentially prohibits the prosecution, for a drug possession crime, of someone who is suffering from a drug overdose. It also prohibits the same prosecution of someone who is in the possession of illegal drugs but summons medical assistance for someone else who is suffering an overdose emergency. **Attorney Hanrahan's Note**: It is often not clear what has triggered the medical emergency, in these cases it may be prudent to charge the suspect and let them raise this as a defense.
First Offense Marijuana or Class E – Probation & Record gets Sealed	Any person who is convicted for the first time under chapter 94C § 34 for the possession of marihuana or a controlled substance in Class E and who has not previously been convicted of any offense pursuant to the provisions of chapter 94C, or any provision of prior law relating to narcotic drugs or harmful drugs as defined in said prior law shall be placed on probation unless such person does not consent thereto, or unless the court files a written memorandum stating the reasons for not so doing. **Upon successful completion of said probation, the case shall be dismissed and records shall be sealed.**
First Offense with no other drug related convictions: Dismissal and Record Sealed	If any person who is charged with a violation of chapter 94C § 34 has not previously been convicted of a violation of any provision of chapter 94C or other provision of prior law relative to narcotic drugs or harmful drugs as defined in said prior law, or of a felony under the laws of any state or of the United States relating to such drugs, has had his case continued without a finding to a certain date, or has been convicted and placed on probation, and if, during the period of said continuance or of said probation, such person does not violate any of the conditions of said continuance or said probation, then upon the expiration of such period the court may dismiss the proceedings against him, and may order sealed all official records relating to his arrest, indictment, conviction, probation, continuance or discharge pursuant to this section; provided, however, that departmental records which are not public records, maintained by police and other law enforcement agencies, shall not be sealed; and provided further, that such a record shall be maintained in a separate file by the department of probation solely for the purpose of use by the courts in determining whether or not in subsequent proceedings such person qualifies under this section.
Sealed Record	Any conviction, the record of which has been sealed under this section, shall not be deemed a conviction for purposes of any disqualification or for any other purpose.
Defendant Can Claim No Priors once record is sealed	No person as to whom such sealing has been ordered shall be held thereafter under any provision of any law to be guilty of perjury or otherwise giving a false statement by reason of his failure to recite or acknowledge such arrest, indictment, conviction, dismissal, continuance, sealing, or any other related court proceeding, in response to any inquiry made of him for any purpose.
Therapeutic Defense	It shall be a prima facie defense to a charge of possession of marihuana under chapter 94C § 34 that the defendant is a patient certified to participate in a therapeutic research program described in chapter 94D, and possessed the marihuana for personal use pursuant to such program.
Ch. 94C § 44. Dismissal of sec. 34 sealing of records	If any person is found not guilty of the violation of any provision of section thirty-four (possession offense) or if a complaint against him is dismissed or an indictment nol prossed for a violation of said section, the court shall order all official records relating to his arrest, indictment, conviction, continuance or discharge to be sealed; **Exception**: Departmental records maintained by police and other law enforcement agencies which are not public records shall not be sealed. **Person Can Later Deny Charge:** No person as to whom such sealing has been ordered shall be held thereafter under any provision of any law to be guilty of perjury or otherwise making a false statement by reason of his failure to recite or acknowledge such arrest, indictment, disposition, sealing or any other related court proceeding, in response to any inquiry made of him for any purpose.

C. 94C § 35	UNLAWFUL PRESENCE OF HEROIN
	Elements
1.	It is unlawful for any person to knowingly be:
2.	• Present at a place where heroin is unlawfully kept or deposited or • In the company of a person, knowing that the person is in unlawful possession of heroin
	Arrest Power, Penalties & Notes
Power of Arrest	**Misdemeanor** – statutory authority permits a police officer to effect an arrest for this offense provided the officer has probable cause that the defendant committed the offense.
Penalty	Imprisonment for not more than 1 year or by a fine of not more than $1,000 dollars, or both.
Attorney Hanrahan's Comment	This tends to be an underutilized statute. It can be effective tool to take action against those who are not found in "possession" of the heroin but otherwise are aware of its existence. However, discretion should be used. For instance, although a technical violation of the law it probably would not be appropriate to arrest a teenage child of a heroin user who is aware that his/her parent stores heroin in the house for personal use.

DRUG PARAPHERNALIA LAWS

C. 94C § 32I	SALE OR MANUFACTURING DRUG PARAPHERNALIA
	Elements
1.	No person shall
2.	1. **Sell** 2. Possess or purchase with **intent to sell** 3. **Manufacture** with intent to sell
3.	Drug paraphernalia (see definition at the beginning of this section).
4.	Knowing, or under circumstances where one reasonably should know, that it will be used to: plant, propagate, cultivate, grow, harvest, manufacture, compound, convert, produce, process, prepare, test, analyze, pack, repack, store, contain, conceal, ingest, inhale, or otherwise introduce into the human body; A controlled substance.
	Arrest Power, Penalties & Notes
Power of Arrest	**Misdemeanor** – chapter 94C § 41 permits a police officer to effect an arrest for this offense committed in his/her presence. **If the person purchasing is under 18**: **Felony** – a police officer may effect a warrantless arrest for this offense provided he/she has probable cause that the suspect committed the offense.

DRUG POSSESSION & USE

C. 94C § 32I	SALE OR MANUFACTURING DRUG PARAPHERNALIA
Penalty	**Penalty for Selling Drug Paraphernalia to Someone 18 years or older – Misdemeanor:** Imprisonment in jail or HOC for not less than one nor more than 2 years, or by a fine of not less than $500 nor more than $5,000 dollars, or both. **Penalty for Selling Drug Paraphernalia to Someone under 18 - Felony**: imprisoned in the state prison for **not less than 3** nor more than 5 years, or by a fine of not less than $1,000 nor more than $5,000 dollars, or both.
Attorney Hanrahan's Comment	There is not a criminal offense for merely possessing drug paraphernalia, only for the sale of it or the intent to sell it. However, some cities and towns have enacted drug paraphernalia ordinances and by-laws. Although mere possession of paraphernalia is not a criminal offense in some cases it may be useful evidence to prove possession, distribution, cultivation and so on; although under routine circumstances the state lab will not process residue, the paraphernalia may have sufficient drug "residue" to help prove the nature of the substance.
Related Statutes, Case Law & Other Important Information	
Sale of hypodermic syringes or hypodermic needles c. 94C § 27	Hypodermic syringes or hypodermic needles for the administration of controlled substances by injection **may be sold** in the commonwealth, but **only to persons who have attained the age of 18 years** and only by: 1. a licensed pharmacist or wholesale druggist, 2. a manufacturer of or dealer in surgical supplies or 3. a manufacturer of or dealer in embalming supplies. When selling hypodermic syringes or hypodermic needles **without a prescription**, a pharmacist or wholesale druggist **must require proof of identification that validates the individual's age**.
Sale of cigarette rolling papers to minors c. 270 § 6A	The defendant sells cigarette rolling papers to any person under the age of 18 **Penalty:** a fine of not less than $25 for the first offense, not less than $50 for the second offense and not less than $100 for a third or subsequent offense. **Arrest Powers**: **Misdemeanor** – there is no statutory authority granting powers of arrest for this offense. **Attorney Hanrahan's Note**: Although this offense is not arrestable the sale of drug paraphernalia is a felony, see c. 94C § 34I.
Sale of rolling papers: must post warning sign. c. 94C § 32I	On any premises where tobacco rolling papers are sold, the person in control of the premises shall display in a prominent place within, a printed warning that rolling papers shall not be used in conjunction with the possession of a controlled substance the possession of which is punishable by a fine or imprisonment. **Penalty for Failing to Post**: a fine of not less than $50 nor more than $200. **Note:** This statute **shall not apply to the sale of hypodermic syringes** or hypodermic needles to persons **over the age of 18.** **ARREST POWERS**: **Misdemeanor** – chapter 94C § 41 permits a police officer to effect an arrest for any violation of chapter 94C when committed in his/her presence.

DISTRIBUTION & MANUFACTURING

DISTRIBUTION: For the purposes of 94C distribution offenses, an actual *sale* is not required. Merely handing someone else a controlled substance will amount to distribution. In the 2007 case of *Com. v. Lawrence*, the Appeals Court reiterated the fact that *sharing* a controlled substance is *distributing*.[1] However, when two or more people purchase the drug together with the intent of consume it together the sharing among the co-purchasers will not amount to distribution.[2]

Note: The SJC has recently ruled that the social sharing of marijuana is not a violation of the distribution statute as it violates the intent of the people as reflected in the passage of Question 2 and the de-criminalization of marijuana.

C. 94C § 32-32D	UNLAWFUL DISTRIBUTION OF A CONTROLLED SUBSTANCE
Elements	
1.	The defendant knowingly or intentionally;
2.	• Manufactures, Distributes, Dispenses, or Cultivates, or • Possesses with intent to manufacture, distribute or dispense, or cultivate
3.	A Controlled Substance
Class A Chapter 94C § 34	
Power of Arrest	**Felony** – a police officer may effect a warrantless arrest for this offense provided he/she has probable cause that the suspect committed the offense.
Penalty	**1st Offense**: imprisonment in the **state prison (F)** for not more than 10 years or in a jail or HOC for not more than 2½ years or by a fine of not less than $1,000 nor more than $10,000, or by both such fine and imprisonment. **2nd or subsequent Offense**: minimum mandatory of **5 years and** a fine of not less than $2,500 nor more than $25,000 **but** no more than 15 years.
Class B Chapter 94C § 34A	
Power of Arrest	**Felony** – a police officer may effect a warrantless arrest for this offense provided he/she has probable cause that the suspect committed the offense.
Penalty	**1st Offense**: Imprisonment in the **state prison (F)** for not more than 10 years, or in a jail or HOC for not more than 2½ years, or by a fine of not less than $1,000 nor more than $10,000, or both such fine and imprisonment. **2nd or subsequent Offense**: minimum mandatory of **3 years and** a fine of not less than $2,000 nor more than $25,000 **but** no more than 10 years.
Enhanced Penalty for Phencyclidine (PCP), Methamphetamines, and Cocaine	Imprisonment in the **state prison (F)** for not less 2½ years nor more than 10 years or by imprisonment in a jail or HOC for **not less than 1** nor more than 2½ years. No sentence imposed under the provisions of this section shall be for less than a **mandatory minimum term of imprisonment of 1 year** and a fine of not less than $1,000 nor more than $10,000, may be imposed but not in lieu of the mandatory minimum 1year term of imprisonment.

DRUG DISTRIBUTION

[1] *Comm. v. Lawrence*, 69 Mass. App. Ct. 596 (2007).
[2] *United States v. Wright*, 593 F.2d 105 (1979)

C. 94C § 32-32D	UNLAWFUL DISTRIBUTION OF A CONTROLLED SUBSTANCE
Class C Chapter 94C § 34B	
Power of Arrest	**Felony** – a police officer may effect a warrantless arrest for this offense provided he/she has probable cause that the suspect committed the offense.
Penalty	**1st Offense**: Imprisoned in **state prison (F)** for not more than 5 years or in a jail or HOC for not more than 2½ years, or by a fine of not less than \$500 nor more than \$5,000, or both such fine and imprisonment. **2nd or subsequent Offense: state prison (F)** for not less than 2½ years nor more than 10 years, or by imprisonment in a jail or HOC for not less than 2 years nor more than 2½ years. No sentence imposed under the provisions of this section shall be for less than a **mandatory minimum term of imprisonment of 2 years** and a fine of not less than \$1,000 nor more than \$10,000 may be imposed, but not in lieu of the mandatory minimum term of imprisonment.
Class D Chapter 94C § 34C	
Power of Arrest	**Misdemeanor** – statutory authority permits a police officer to effect an arrest for this offense on probable cause.
Penalty	**1st Offense:** imprisoned in a jail or HOC for not more than 2 years or by a fine of not less than \$500 nor more than \$5,000, or both such fine and imprisonment. **2nd or subsequent offense:** imprisonment in a jail or HOC for not less than 1 nor more than 2½ years, or by a fine of not less than \$1,000 nor more than \$10,000, or both such fine and imprisonment.
Class E Chapter 94C § 34D	
Power of Arrest	**Misdemeanor** – statutory authority permits a police officer to effect an arrest for this offense on probable cause.
Penalty	**1st Offense:** imprisoned in a jail or HOC for not more than 9 months, or by a fine of not less than \$250 nor more than \$2,500, or both such fine and imprisonment. **2nd or subsequent offense:** imprisonment in a jail or HOC for not more than 1½ years, or by a fine of not less than \$500 nor more than \$5,000, or both such fine and imprisonment.
Related Statutes, Case Law & Other Important Information	
Attorney Hanrahan's Note	Distributing Class D & E always amounts to only a misdemeanor offense even for multiple convictions (unless involving a school zone or park).
Out of State Convictions	Previous convictions include other states and territories of the US, including federal convictions.
"Distribute"	Chapter 94C § 1 defines "Distribute, to deliver other than by administering or dispensing a controlled substance." This distinguishes this illegal act from those who are lawfully permitted to administer or dispense, such as medical professionals and pharmacists.

C. 94C § 32-32D	UNLAWFUL DISTRIBUTION OF A CONTROLLED SUBSTANCE
Social Sharing of Marijuana	Before the passing of Question 2 (the decriminalization of an ounce or less of marijuana) if two people were caught smoking marijuana together they would be charged with unlawful possession. The SJC ruled to now charge people sharing marijuana with a more serious crime (distributing) seems to violate the will of the people. Therefore, the social sharing of a marijuana cigarette is not a violation of G.L. chapter 94C § 32C(a) (drug distribution).[1]
Criminal Distribution	In interpreting the distribution statute in situations where a defendant purchases drugs and then gives them to others, the SJC has distinguished between "circumstances where a defendant facilitates a transfer of drugs from a seller to a buyer," which can constitute the crime of distribution even if the defendant intends to share some of the drug with the buyer,[2] and "the passing of a drug between joint possessors who simultaneously acquire possession at the outset for their own use," which does not constitute distribution. The unifying principle underlying these types of cases is that a defendant who gives drugs to others "distributes" those drugs whenever the defendant serves as "a link in the chain" between supplier and consumer.[3]
Distribution without being present	It is possible to convict a defendant for distribution even if he/she is not present at the scene of the transaction on a theory of *constructive transfer* as long as it can be proven that the defendant had the ability and intent to exercise dominion and control over the drug and participated in its sale (e.g. arranged for it to be delivered).[4]
Can a doctor be convicted of this offense?	The SJC ruled in *Commonwealth v. Brown*, the SJC concluded that a physician who "for no legitimate medical purpose and not in the usual course of his professional practice, delivers a controlled substance by issuing a prescription to a patient seeking the substance for illicit ends" may be prosecuted for unlawfully *distributing* the substance pursuant to G.L. c. 94C, §§ 32-32H.
Attorney Hanrahan's note on "Intent to Distribute"	The intent to distribute can often be proven by the circumstances present. Observations of a sale or an attempted sale, information from a reliable informant, large amounts of the substance, and admissions, are some of the more obvious factors. However, although each situation is unique, the intent to distribute can often be determined by the method of packaging, the presence of scales or similar measuring devices, ledgers, large amounts of cash and similar indications of distribution. Additionally, the SJC ruled that although c. 94C § 32L decriminalized small amounts of marijuana it did not impact the amount of marijuana required for a charge of distribution (i.e. someone could be convicted for *distributing* any amount, even less than an ounce, of marijuana).[5] For these reasons careful documentation and evidence gathering is very important.
Quantity may indicate intent	A large amount of drugs alone can support an inference of an intent to distribute. In ***Commonwealth v. Ridge***, the Appeals Court ruled that 636.8 grams of cocaine alone is sufficient to warrant inference beyond reasonable doubt that defendant intended to distribute cocaine.[6]

DRUG DISTRIBUTION

[1] Commonwealth v. Jackson, SJC 2013.
[2] *Commonwealth v. Fluellen*, 456 Mass. 517, 524-525 (2010).
[3] Commonwelath v. Palmer, SJC 2013
[4] Commonwealth v. Mgaresh (2013) Appeals Court
[5] Commonwealth v. Keefer, SJC 2012.
[6] Commonwealth v. Ridge, 37 Mass.App.Ct. 943, 945 (1994)

C. 94C § 32-32D	UNLAWFUL DISTRIBUTION OF A CONTROLLED SUBSTANCE
Packaging and packaging material may indicate intent	In ***Commonwealth v. Acosta***, five twists bags *alone* were not enough to prove intent. Similarly, in ***Commonwealth v. Humberto*** (2013) possession of five small bags of marijuana, with no other evidence, was not enough to establish probable cause for distribution. Compare with: In ***Commonwealth v. Pratt***, numerous bags of heroin bundled into groups of ten and wrapped together in packages of fifty was sufficient to prove intent. [1] In ***Commonwealth v. Gonzales***, the bundling of ten packets with elastic band was sufficient to prove intent.[2] In ***Commonwealth v. Ridge***, the defendant had drug paraphernalia, including cutting powder, digital scale, bag sealer, and box of small baggies; this could be used to prove intent.[3] In ***Commonwealth v. LaPerle***, cutting powder, wrapping paper, and scale with cocaine residue on pan was used to prove intent. [4]
Large amounts of cash may show intent	The amount of money found on a person may imply an intent to distribute. A large amount of cash certainly is probative of an intent to distribute. In ***Commonwealth v. Sendele***, bundles of worn bills, mostly ten- and twenty-dollar bills, but also some fifties and hundreds, totaling $33,020, was used to prove intent. Particularly if the defendant is unemployed. In ***Commonwealth v. Gonzales***, $167 on the unemployed defendant supported the inference of distribution.[5]
Absence of a "smoking device" or other instrument to introduce to body	In the 2014 case of ***Commonwealth v. Sepheus***, the absence of a smoking device may support an inference of an intent to distribute; it is a weak inference, particularly in the absence of other factors.
Attorney Hanrahan's note on "Intent to Distribute"	The intent to distribute can often be proven by the circumstances present. Observations of a sale or an attempted sale, information from a reliable informant, large amounts of the substance, and admissions, are some of the more obvious factors. However, although each situation is unique, the intent to distribute can often be determined by the method of packaging, the presence of scales or similar measuring devices, ledgers, large amounts of cash and similar indications of distribution. However, simply possessing drugs which are individually packaged would not, without more, prove that the defendant had the intent to distribute. In most cases, additional evidence would be required.[6] In ***Commonwealth v. Acosta*** (2012), five small bags of cocaine, alone, was not enough to prove intent to distribute. Similarly, in ***Commonwealth v. Humberto*** (2013) possession of five small bags of marijuana, with no other evidence, was not enough to establish probable cause for distribution. Additionally, the SJC ruled that although c. 94C § 32L decriminalized small amounts of marijuana it did not impact the amount of marijuana required for a charge of distribution (i.e. someone could be convicted for *distributing* any amount, even less than an ounce, of marijuana).[7] For these reasons careful documentation and evidence gathering is very important.

[1] *Commonwealth v. Pratt*, 407 Mass. 647, 652-653 (1990)
[2] Commonwealth v. Gonzales, 33 Mass.App.Ct. 728, 731 (1992)
[3] Commonwealth v. Ridge, 37 Mass.App.Ct. 943, 945 (1994)
[4] Commonwealth v. LaPerle, 19 Mass.App.Ct. 424, 427 (1985)
[5] Commonwealth v. Gonzales, 33 Mass.App.Ct. 728, 731 (1992)
[6] Commonwealth v. Acosta, MassApp.Ct. 2012.
[7] Commonwealth v. Keefer, SJC 2012.

C. 94C § 32-32D	UNLAWFUL DISTRIBUTION OF A CONTROLLED SUBSTANCE
Cultivate	In the 2013 case of ***Commonwealth v. Palmer***, the SJC looked to the dictionary to define term cultivate. The SJC referred to the American Heritage Dictionary of English Language in that stating: "the word 'cultivate' has plain, ordinary meaning: 'To grow or tend (a plant or crop).'"
Decriminalization of marijuana and the effects on cultivation	In the 2013 case of ***Commonwealth v. Palmer***, the SJC ruled that the decriminalization of an ounce or less of marijuana has no effect on the unlawfulness of cultivating marijuana, even if the amount cultivated (e.g. grown) is less than an ounce or is intended only for personal use. However, the recent passing of the medical marijuana laws may also play a role. The new medical marijuana laws, permits a holder of a medical marijuana card to cultivate their own marijuana, in some circumstances. See section on medical marijuana for more.
Cultivate	This means "to grow or tend (a plant or crop)."[1]
Cultivate Marijuana	Cultivating marijuana in any amount (even an ounce or less and even for only personal use) is a violation of this statute. [2]
Search warrants for Cultivation	In the 2015 case of ***Commonwealth v. Canning***, the SJC ruled that the police should have determined whether or not the defendant was the holder of a medical marijuana card before executing a search warrant for cultivation. See search warrant section form more.
Manufacture **c. 94C § 1**	"Manufacture", the production, preparation, propagation, compounding, conversion or processing of a controlled substance, either directly or indirectly by extraction from substances of natural origin, or independently by means of chemical synthesis, including any packaging or repackaging of the substance or labeling or relabeling of its container.
Counterfeit Substance	Chapter 94C § 32G makes it a crime (misdemeanor) to sell a counterfeit controlled substance.
School Zone & Parks	Chapter 94C § 32J provides an enhanced penalty for those who distribute within certain school zones and parks (see later in this section).
Trafficking	Chapter 94C § 32E provides enhanced penalties for those who "traffic" in controlled substances (see later in this section).
Drug Classifications	Below is a list of some of the more *common* encountered drugs: **Class A:** Heroin, Morphine, Gamma Hydroxy Butric Acid (GHB), Ketamine **Class B**: Cocaine, Methadone, Oxycontin, LSD, MDMA ("Ecstasy"), Fentanyl **Class C**: Valium, Mescaline, Peyote, Bath Salts. **Class D**: Marijuana. **Class E**: most other prescription drugs not listed in the other classes. See drug classification section later in this section for a complete list of drugs and their classification.
Distribution involving minors	See the *Special Protections for Minors* section later in this chapter for specific crimes involving the distribution to minors and inducing minors to distribute.

[1] Commonwealth v. Palmer, SJC 2013
[2] Commonwealth v. Palmer, SJC 2013

C. 94C § 32G	COUNTERFEIT SUBSTANCES; CREATION & DISTRIBUTION
	Elements
1.	The defendant knowingly or intentionally;
2.	• Manufactures, Distributes, Dispenses, or • Possesses with intent to manufacture, distribute or dispense,
3.	A Counterfeit Substance
	Arrest Power, Penalties & Notes
Power of Arrest	**Misdemeanor** – chapter 94C § 41 permits a police officer to effect an arrest for this offense committed in his/her presence.
Penalty	Imprisonment in a jail or HOC for not more than 1year or by a fine of not less than $250 nor more than $2,500, or both such fine and imprisonment.
Attorney Hanrahan's Comment	This law is designed to punish those who sell substances wherein the buyer believes the substance to be a controlled substance (i.e. a bag of oregano purported to be marijuana).
	Related Statutes, Case Law & Other Important Information
Chapter 94C § 1 defines a Counterfeit Substance	"Counterfeit substance", a substance which is represented to be a particular controlled drug or substance, but which is in fact not that drug or substance.

C. 94C § 32E	DRUG TRAFFICKING
	Elements
1.	The defendant knowingly or intentionally
2.	• Manufacture, Distribute, Dispense, or Cultivate or • Possess with intent to manufacture, distribute, dispense, or cultivate or • Bring into the Commonwealth
3.	A controlled substance with a net weight as noted below
	MARIJUANA
Marijuana Amounts & Penalties	(1) **50 lbs or more but less than 100 lbs:** imprisonment in the **state prison (F)** for not less than 2½ nor more than 15 years or by imprisonment in a jail or HOC for not less than 1 nor more than 2½ years. **Mandatory minimum term of imprisonment of one year** and a fine of not less than $500 nor more than $10,000. (2) **100 lbs or more, but less than 2,000 lbs**, imprisonment in the **state prison (F)** for not less than 2 nor more than 15 years. **Mandatory minimum term of imprisonment of 2 years** and a fine of not less than

C. 94C § 32E	DRUG TRAFFICKING
	$2,5000 nor more than $25,000 may be imposed but not in lieu of the mandatory minimum term of imprisonment, as established herein. (3) **2,000 lbs or more, but less than 10,000** lbs: imprisonment in the **state prison (F)** for not less than 3½ nor more than 15 years. **Mandatory minimum term of imprisonment of 3½ years** and a fine of not less than $5,000 nor more than $15,000 may be imposed but not in lieu of the mandatory minimum term of imprisonment, as established herein. (4)**10,000 lbs or more:** imprisonment in the **state prison (F)** for not less than 8 nor more than 15 years. **Mandatory minimum term of imprisonment of 8 years** and a fine of not less than $20,000 nor more than $200,000 may be imposed but not in lieu of the mandatory minimum term of imprisonment, as established herein. **Note:** weight includes mixture which contains marijuana (i.e. fillers)
COCAINE	
Cocaine Amounts & Penalties	(1) **18 grams or more but less than 36 grams**: imprisonment in the **state prison (F)** for not less than 2 nor more than 15 years. **Minimum term of imprisonment of 2 years**, and a fine of not less than $2,500 nor more than $25,000 may be imposed but not in lieu of the mandatory minimum term of imprisonment, as established herein. (2) **36 grams or more, but less than 100 grams:** imprisonment in the **state prison (F)** for not less than 3½ nor more than 20 years. **Mandatory minimum term of imprisonment of** 3½ **years,** and a fine of not less than $5,000 nor more than $50,000 may be imposed but not in lieu of the mandatory minimum term of imprisonment, as established herein. (3) **100 grams or more, but less than 200 grams:** imprisonment in the **state prison (F)** for not less than 8 nor more than 20 years. **Mandatory minimum term of imprisonment of 8 years** and a fine of not less than $10,000 nor more than o$100,000 may be imposed but not in lieu of the mandatory minimum term of imprisonment, as established herein. (4) **200 grams or more**: imprisonment in the **state prison (F)** for not less than 12 nor more than 20 years. **Mandatory minimum term of imprisonment of 12 years** and a fine of not less than $50,000 nor more than $500,000 may be imposed but not in lieu of the mandatory minimum term of imprisonment, as established herein. **Note:** weight includes mixture which contains cocaine (i.e. fillers)
HEROIN	
Heroin and Opiate Amounts & Penalties	(1) **18 grams or more but less than 36 grams:** be punished by a term of imprisonment in the **state prison (F)** for not less than 3½ nor more than 20 years. No sentence imposed under the provisions of this clause shall be for less than a **mandatory minimum term of imprisonment of 3½ years** and a fine of not less than $5,000 nor more than $50,000 may be imposed but not in lieu of the mandatory minimum term of imprisonment, as established herein. (2) **36 grams or more but less than 100 grams**: be punished by a term of imprisonment in the **state prison (F)** for not less than 5 nor more than 20 years. No sentence imposed under the provisions of this clause shall be for less than a **mandatory minimum term of imprisonment of 5 years** and a fine of not less than $5,000 nor more than $50,000 may be imposed, but not in lieu of the mandatory minimum term of imprisonment, as established herein. (3) **100 grams or more but less than 200 grams:** be punished by a term of imprisonment in the **state prison (F)** for not less than 8 nor more than 20 years. **Mandatory minimum term of imprisonment of 8 years**, and a fine of not less than $10,000 nor more than $100,000 dollars may be imposed but not in lieu of the mandatory minimum term of imprisonment, as established therein. (4) **200 grams or more:** imprisonment in the **state prison (F)** for not less than 12 nor more than 20

C. 94C § 32E	DRUG TRAFFICKING
	years. **Mandatory minimum term of imprisonment of 12 years** and a fine of not less than $50,000 nor more than $500,000 may be imposed but not in lieu of the mandatory minimum term of imprisonment, as established therein. **Note:** Prohibited substance includes heroin or any salt thereof, morphine or any salt thereof, opium or any derivative thereof (or a mixture containing these substances).
FENTANYL	
Fentanyl and its derivatives	A net weight of **more than 10 grams** of fentanyl shall be subject to imprisonment in state prison for not more than 20 years.
Arrest Power & Notes	
Power of Arrest	**Felony** – a police officer may effect a warrantless arrest for this offense provided he/she has probable cause that the suspect committed the offense.
Attorney Hanrahan's Comment	Many drug dealers include additives to the drug to increase profits and/or to facilitate the effect. The weights for trafficking include mixtures, meaning additives that are added to the illegal substance can be included as part of the weight for the purpose of trafficking.
Related Statutes, Case Law & Other Important Information	
Possession with intent to distribute	Chapters 94C § 32-32D prohibits the possession of these substances with the intent to distribute. If the weight does not amount to a trafficking charge in most cases the amount will be evidence of the intent to distribute because most users do not store large quantities for personal use.
Definition of Fentanyl	For purposes of this subsection, "fentanyl" shall include any derivative of fentanyl and any mixture containing more than 10 grams of fentanyl or a derivative of fentanyl.

SPECIAL PROTECTIONS FOR MINORS

C. 94C § 32F	UNLAWFUL DISTRIBUTION OF CLASS A, B, OR C TO MINORS
	Elements
1.	The defendant knowingly or intentionally
2.	• Manufacture, distribute, or dispense, or • Possess with intent to manufacture, distribute, or dispense;
3.	A controlled substance in Class **A**, Class **B**, or Class **C** drug
4.	To a person under the age of **18 years**
	Arrest Power, Penalties & Notes
Power of Arrest	**Felony** – a police officer may effect a warrantless arrest for this offense provided he/she has probable cause that the suspect committed the offense.
Penalty	**Class A drug:** imprisonment in the **state prison (F)** for not less than 5 nor more than 15 years. **Minimum Mandatory Sentence**: imprisonment for 5 years and a fine of not less than $1,000 nor more than $25,000 may be imposed but not in lieu of the mandatory minimum term of imprisonment. **Class B drug:** imprisonment in the **state prison (F)** for not less than 3 nor more than 15 years. **Minimum Mandatory Sentence**: imprisonment of 3 years and a fine of not less than $1,000 nor more than $25,000 may be imposed but not in lieu of the mandatory minimum term of imprisonment, as established herein. **Enhanced Penalty for crack cocaine:** imprisonment in the **state prison (F)** for **not less than 5** nor more than 15 years. **Class C drug:** imprisonment in the **state prison (F)** for **not less than 2½** nor more than 15 years or in a jail or HOC for not less than 2 nor more than 2½ years. **Minimum Mandatory Sentence** imprisonment of 2 years and a fine of not less than $1,000 nor more than $25,000 may be imposed but not in lieu of the mandatory minimum 2 year term of imprisonment, as established herein.
Attorney Hanrahan's Comment	This would not be an additional charge, for instance if someone sold heroin to a 17 year old you would not charge both 94C § 32B and this statute (94C § 32F); you would choose to charge one or the other (unless the transaction also included a Class D or E substance. This law provides no additional penalty for those who sell Class D & E drugs to minors.
	Related Statutes, Case Law & Other Important Information
School and Park Zone violations	See chapter 94C § 32J, later in this section, for additional penalties for those who sell drugs in prohibited areas.
Paraphernalia Sales	Chapter 94C § 32I makes it a felony to sell drug paraphernalia to people under the age of 18.

DRUG LAWS

C. 94C § 32J	DISTRIBUTION NEAR SCHOOL OR PARK
	Elements
1.	Any person who violates the provisions of chapter 94C § 32, 32A, 32B, 32C, 32D, 32E, 32F, or 32I (**distribution related offense for all classes of drugs including paraphernalia**),
2.	• while in or on, or within **300 feet** of the real property comprising a public or private accredited preschool, accredited headstart facility, elementary, vocational, or secondary school if the violation occurs between **5:00 a.m. and midnight**, whether or not in session, or • within **100 feet** of a public park or playground
3.	Shall be punished
	Arrest Power, Penalties & Notes
Power of Arrest	**Felony** – a police officer may effect a warrantless arrest for this offense provided he/she has probable cause that the suspect committed the offense.
Penalty	Imprisonment in the **state prison (F)** for **not less than 2½** nor more than 15 years or by imprisonment in a jail or HOC for **not less than 2** nor more than 2½ years. No sentence imposed under the provisions of this section shall be for **less than a mandatory minimum term of imprisonment of 2 years**. A fine of not less than $1,000 nor more than $10,000 dollars may be imposed but not in lieu of the mandatory minimum two year term of imprisonment as established herein. **Sentencing Note**: the sentence shall begin **from and after** the expiration of the sentence for the underlying drug violation.
Knowledge of Boundary	Lack of knowledge of school boundaries shall not be a defense to any person who violates the provisions of this section.
Attorney Hanrahan's Note	In the 1992 case of ***Commonwealth v. Roucoulet*** the SJC stated that the school violation is committed "when one of the identified drug crimes is committed (a) in a school; (b) on school property; or (c) within (300) feet of school property." Recent legislative changes would now require that these elements take place between 5:00 AM and midnight.
	Related Statutes, Case Law & Other Important Information
Secondary School Defined	The term secondary school generally refers to high school level schools. In ***Commonwealth v. Bell***, the Court stated a secondary school is "a school more advanced in grade than an elementary school and offering general, technical, vocational, or college-prepatory courses."[1]
***All* School Land**	In ***Commonwealth v. Paige***, the Court stated "As long as the property belongs to the school, it qualifies under the school zone statute. It is not contradictory to the spirit of the school zone law that adjacent, undeveloped school land be treated as school property...because, by its very nature, it may attract the children who attend school."[2]

[1] *Commonwealth v. Bell*, 442 Mass. 118 (2004).
[2] *Commonwealth v. Paige*, 54 Mass.App. Ct. 840 (2002).

C. 94C § 32J	DISTRIBUTION NEAR SCHOOL OR PARK
Park Defined	Although the legislature did not define "park or playground" the Court, in ***Commonwealth v. Davie,*** looked to other sources of law to define the terms. Below are the sources that the *Davie* court looked to: In ***Cohen v. Lynn***, the Court stated "[T]he term 'park' usually signifies an open or inclosed tract of land set apart for the recreation and enjoyment of the public; or, 'in the general acceptance of the term, a public park is said to be a tract of land, great or small, dedicated and maintained for the purposes of pleasure, exercise, amusement, or ornament; a place to which the public at large may resort to for recreation, air, and light.' " [1] Chapter 45 § 1, defines park as including "a city or town common dedicated to the use of the public." The *Davie* court stated the intent of the law involves "discouraging distribution of illegal drugs near children, the invitation to public recreation inherent in these common definitions of 'park' suggests the likelihood of the presence of children." Note: The above elements and concepts should be considered when deciphering whether or not the violation you are investigating involved a "park or playground."
Public *owned* park only	In the 2014 case of ***Commonwealth v. Gopaul***, the Appeals Court ruled that the this law only applies to *public owned* parks, not privately owned parks even if open to the public.
How to measure distance	***Commonwealth v. Spano***, indicated that the measurement should be take in a straight line from location of the sale to the school or park property.[2]
Possession with intent within the area is enough – even if the actual sale takes place elsewhere	In the 1992 case of ***Commonwealth v. Roucoulet,*** the SJC stated "the possession with intent to distribute cocaine, do(es) not require...that a defendant ha(s) an intent to *distribute* within any specific area." Meaning possession with intent to distribute while located within the protected area completes the crime, even if the intent is to make the actual sale at a different location not within the protected zone.

DRUG LAWS

[1] *Cohen v. Lynn*, 33 Mass.App.Ct. 271, 278, 598 N.E.2d 682 (1992), quoting from *Salem v. Attorney Gen.*, 344 Mass. 626, 630, 183 N.E.2d 859 (1962).
[2] *Commonwealth v. Spano*, 414 Mass. 178 (1993)

C. 94C § 32K	INDUCING MINOR TO DEAL DRUGS
Elements	
1.	The defendant knowingly
2.	Causes, Induces, or Abets
3.	A person under the age of 18 years
4.	• To **distribute, dispense** or **possess with the intent** to distribute or dispense any **controlled substance,** or • To **accept, deliver or possess money** used or intended for use in the procurement, manufacture, compounding, processing, delivery, distribution or sale of any controlled substance.
Arrest Power, Penalties & Notes	
Power of Arrest	**Felony** – a police officer may effect a warrantless arrest for this offense provided he/she has probable cause that the suspect committed the offense.
Penalty	Imprisonment in the **state prison (F)** for **not less than 5 years** nor more than 15 years. Mandatory minimum term of imprisonment of 5 years and a fine of not less than $1,000 nor more than $100,000 may be imposed but not in lieu of the mandatory minimum 5 year term of imprisonment established herein.
Attorney Hanrahan's Comment	This law applies to *all classes* of drugs.
Related Statutes, Case Law & Other Important Information	
No Need to Prove Defendant knew child's age	In the 2000 case of ***Commonwealth v. Montalvo,*** the Appeals Court stated "we conclude by comparing § 32K with other provisions in the General Laws that § 32K **does** **not** require the prosecution to prove that the defendant knew the age of the youth employed in drug dealing; it is sufficient to prove the age of that youth."

C. 94C § 36	PROTECTIVE CUSTODY OF CHILDREN FOUND PRESENT WHERE CLASS A, B, or C is KEPT
Elements	
1.	• If a police officer finds a child present where the officer finds a substance which he reasonably believes to be a **Class A, B, or C** controlled substance kept or possessed unlawfully, and • If the police officer reasonably believes that the child has not reached his 18 birthday **(17 and under)** and • That the child knew of the presence of the controlled substance
2.	The police officer may lawfully take such child into protective custody
3.	For a period **not to exceed 4 hours**.
Arrest Power, Penalties & Notes	
Power of Arrest & Penalty	**This is not a criminal offense. This is not Considered an Arrest**: A child detained pursuant to the provisions of this section shall not be considered to have been arrested or to have a criminal record for any purpose; however, only a departmental record of custody shall be made by the officer indicating the circumstances of custody.
Notify Parents	The persons having custody of a child shall make reasonable efforts to notify the child's parent or guardian or other person having lawful custody
No Liability	Those involved in taking custody of the child shall be considered to be acting in the conduct of their official duties and shall not be held criminally or civilly liable for such acts.
Attorney Hanrahan's Comment	This law is designed to remove children from dangerous environments. It is not a criminal offense, however it does not preclude charging juveniles who are in possession of the controlled substance.
Related Statutes, Case Law & Other Important Information	
Presence of Heroin	Chapter 94C § 35 makes it a criminal offense to knowingly be in the presence of heroin.

DRUG RELATED FRAUD & THEFT

C. 94C § 37	THEFT OF CONTROLLED SUBSTANCES
Elements	
1.	The defendant steals
2.	A controlled substance
3.	From a registered manufacturer, wholesale druggist, pharmacy or other person authorized to dispense or possess any controlled substance.
Arrest Power, Penalties & Notes	
Power of Arrest	**Felony** – a police officer may effect a warrantless arrest for this offense provided he/she has probable cause that the suspect committed the offense.
Penalty	Imprisonment in the **state prison (F)** for not more than 10 years or in a jail or HOC for not more than 2½ years or by a fine of not more than $500.
Attorney Hanrahan's Comment	This law is limited to theft from those who are duly authorized to distribute drugs, it would not apply to someone who stole drugs from a criminal drug dealer; in that situation the general larceny statute could be used, as well as drug possession and distribution statutes.
Related Statutes, Case Law & Other Important Information	
False Prescription	Chapter 94C § 33 makes it a felony to utter a false prescription or to obtain a controlled substance by false pretenses. See later in this section.
Larceny	Chapter 266 § 30 covers the theft of most tangible property.

C. 94C § 33	UTTERING A FALSE PRESCRIPTION
Elements	
1.	No person shall
2.	Utter a false prescription for a controlled substance from a practitioner
Arrest Power, Penalties & Notes	
Power of Arrest	**Felony** – a police officer may effect a warrantless arrest for this offense provided he/she has probable cause that the suspect committed the offense.
Penalty	Imprisonment in the **state prison (F)** for not more than 4 years or in a HOC for not more than 2½ years or by a fine of not more than $20,000 dollars, or by both such fine and imprisonment. **Enhanced Penalty for Prior Convictions:** Whoever violates any provision of this section (§ 33) after one or more prior convictions of a violation of this section, or of a felony under any other provision of chapter 94C, or under a provision of prior law relative to the sale or manufacture of a narcotic drug or a harmful drug as defined in said earlier law shall be punished by imprisonment in the **state prison (F)** for not more than 8 years or in a jail or HOC for not more than 2½ , or by a fine of not more than $30,000 or by both such fine and imprisonment.
Attorney Hanrahan's Comment	This offense covers the mere passing of a false prescription. There is no requirement that the controlled substance actually be obtained, the passing (or attempt to obtain) is enough to meet the elements.
Related Statutes, Case Law & Other Important Information	
Ch. 94C § 1 defines *Practitioner*	a) A physician, dentist, veterinarian, podiatrist, scientific investigator, or other person registered to distribute, dispense, conduct research with respect to, or use in teaching or chemical analysis, a controlled substance in the course of professional practice or research in the commonwealth;

C. 94C § 33	UTTERING A FALSE PRESCRIPTION
	b) A pharmacy, hospital, or other institution registered to distribute, dispense, conduct research with respect to or to administer a controlled substance in the course of professional practice or research in the commonwealth. c) An optometrist authorized by sections 66 and 66B of chapter 112 and registered pursuant to paragraph (h) of section 7 to utilize and prescribe therapeutic pharmaceutical agents in the course of professional practice in the commonwealth.

C. 94C § 33	OBTAINING BY FALSE PRETENSE
Elements	
1.	No person shall
2.	Knowingly or intentionally acquire or obtain possession of a controlled substance
3.	By means of forgery, fraud, deception or subterfuge,
4.	Including but not limited to: • the forgery or falsification of a prescription, or • the nondisclosure of a material fact in order to obtain a controlled substance from a practitioner.
Arrest Power, Penalties & Notes	
Power of Arrest	**Felony** – a police officer may effect a warrantless arrest for this offense provided he/she has probable cause that the suspect committed the offense.
Penalty	Imprisonment in the **state prison (F)** for not more than 4 years or in a HOC for not more than 2½ years or by a fine of not more than $20,000, or by both such fine and imprisonment. **Enhanced Penalty for Prior Convictions:** Whoever violates any provision of this section (§ 33) after one or more prior convictions of a violation of this section, or of a felony under any other provision of chapter 94C, or under a provision of prior law relative to the sale or manufacture of a narcotic drug or a harmful drug as defined in said earlier law shall be punished by imprisonment in the **state prison (F)** for not more than 8 years or in a jail or HOC for not more than 2½ , or by a fine of not more than $30,000 or by both such fine and imprisonment.
Fictitious registration number	Chapter 94C § 33 also states: No person shall knowingly or intentionally use in the course of the manufacture or distribution of a controlled substance a registration number which is fictitious, revoked, suspended, or issued to another person. A violation of this provision is a felony offense.
Attorney Hanrahan's Comment	This offense covers more than just the forgery of a prescription. The statute uses the terms "fraud" and "deception." This covers a wide array of behavior including falsifying claims of illness or injury in order to obtain a controlled substance. However, as the statute dictates, the controlled substance must actually be obtained. If the substance is not obtained an attempt charge may be appropriate (see *attempt to commit a crime* in the beginning of the Statutory section of this manual).

DRUG LAWS

MISCELLANEOUS DRUG LAWS

C. 94C § 40	CONSPIRACY TO VIOLATE THE DRUG LAWS
Elements	
1.	Conspire
2.	With another person
3.	To violate any provision of chapter 94C
Arrest Power, Penalties & Notes	
Power of Arrest	Whether **Felony or Misdemeanor** – statutory authority permits a police officer to effect an arrest for this offense provided the officer has probable cause that the defendant committed the offense.
Penalty	Imprisonment or fine, or both, which punishment shall not exceed the maximum punishment prescribed for the offense, the commission of which was the object of the conspiracy.
Attorney Hanrahan's Comment	When two or more people *agree* to do anything that violates any provision of chapter 94C those involved have committed this offense. The punishment depends upon the underlying offense that the parties agreed to commit. Unlike attempt, completion of the crime will not prevent an additional conspiracy charge.
Related Statutes, Case Law & Other Important Information	
Conspiracy	A conspiracy is simply an agreement. The basis of the conspiracy offense is the unlawful agreement, "the unlawful confederacy to do an unlawful act, or even a lawful act for unlawful purposes . . . ." [1]
Buyer-seller relationship	In the 2015 case of ***Commonwealth v. Doty***, the Appeals Court ruled that a buyer-seller relationship, without more, does not constitute a conspiracy to distribute a controlled substance. In a conspiracy the parties must agree to the same act. In a buyer-seller relationship one party is agreeing to *buy* drugs the other is agreeing to *sell* drugs, thus no conspiracy exists.
Wharton's Rule does not apply	In ***Commonwealth v. Cantres,*** the SJC ruled that Whartons's Rule does not apply to chapter 94C § 30. Wharton's Rule provides "that an agreement by two persons to commit a particular crime cannot be prosecuted as a conspiracy when the crime is of such a nature as necessarily to require the participation of two persons for its commission."[2]
No overt act required	The law of the Commonwealth does not require an overt act to complete a conspiracy. [3]
Defendant can be convicted of both conspiracy and substantive offense	In the 2013 case of ***Commonwealth v. Rose***, the Appeals Court ruled that a defendant can be convicted of both the crime of conspiracy and the underlying drug offense if the evidence is sufficient. There are no double-jeopardy concerns because both crimes will have different elements. In this case, the defendant was present in the car and assisted in handing over drugs to a buyer. The Court ruled that because the defendant arrived in the car with drug dealer with obvious knowledge that the drug sale was about to take place and participated in the transaction there was sufficient evidence that conspiracy was formed prior to the transaction.
Conspiracy often proven by Circumstantial Evidence	"A conspiracy may be proved by circumstantial evidence, and this is the usual mode of proving it, since it is not often that direct evidence can be had. The acts of different persons who are shown to have known each other, or to have been in communication with each other, directed towards the accomplishment of the same object, especially if by the same means or in the same manner, may be satisfactory proof of a conspiracy." [4]

[1] *Commonwealth v. Judd*, 2 Mass. 329, 336 (1807).
[2] *Commonwealth v. Cantres*, 405 Mass. 238 (1989).
[3] *Commonwealth v. Harris*, 232 Mass. 588, 591 [122 N.E. 749] (1919).
[4] *Commonwealth v. Beneficial Fin. Co.*, 360 Mass. 188, 251, 275 N.E.2d 33 (1971), cert. denied sub nom.

C. 94C § 41	SPECIAL ARREST POWERS FOR 94C VIOLATIONS
	A police officer shall have the authority to arrest without a warrant:
In-presence	Any person committing in **his presence** *any* controlled substance related offense;
Felony	Any person who he has probable cause to believe has committed or is committing a **felony** set forth under the provisions of this chapter;
Probable Cause – designated offenses	Any person who he has **probable cause** to believe has committed or is committing: a. Possession with Intent to Distribute Class A, B, C, D, or E b. Trafficking in a controlled substance c. Distributing Class A, B, or C to a minor (under 18) d. Uttering a False Prescription e. Unlawful Possession of controlled substance (except an ounce of less of marijuana) f. Knowingly being present where heroin is kept g. Stealing a controlled substance from a manufacturer, pharmacy or druggist h. Conspiracy to violate the controlled drug laws
	Related Statute
Ch. 94C § 45. Photographing and fingerprinting of persons charged with drug felony	Any person arrested for or charged with the criminal **violation of any controlled substance offense** which **constitutes a felony** may at the time of arrest or as soon thereafter as is practicable be **photographed and fingerprinted** according to the system of the state bureau of identification, and upon conviction any such fingerprints and photographs shall be made a part of permanent records of the police department of the municipality where the arrest took place, and **without delay two copies of the fingerprints and photographs shall be forwarded**, with such other description as may be required and a written history of the offense, **to the state bureau of identification.**

C. 94C § 30	ADMINISTRATIVE INSPECTION OF CONTROLLED PREMISES
Businesses that are engaged in the manufacture and distribution of controlled substances are subject to close regulations for obvious reasons. These businesses are subject to inspections to ensure compliance with the law. Chapter 94C § 30 sets the scope of these inspections.	
Administrative Warrant Requirements	An administrative inspection warrant shall issue only upon affidavit sworn to before the court, or justice establishing the grounds for issuing the warrant. If the court or justice is satisfied that grounds for the issuance of such warrant exists or that there is probable cause to believe they exist, he shall issue such warrant identifying the area, premises, buildings or conveyances to be inspected, the purpose of the inspection, and, if appropriate, the type of property to be inspected, if any. **Such warrant shall:** 1) **Be directed to** the commissioner or his designee, except in the case of a pharmacy to the commissioner or to the designee of the board of registration in pharmacy, **or to a police officer**; 2) **Command the person to whom it is directed to inspect the area,** premises, buildings or conveyances identified for the purpose specified and, if appropriate, direct the seizure of the property specified; 3) **Describe the item or types of property to be inspected or seized**, if any; 4) Direct that it be served during **normal business hours**.
Administrative Probable Cause	For the purposes of the issuance of administrative inspection warrants, probable cause exists upon a showing of a reasonable and valid public interest in the effective enforcement of chapter 94C or rules or regulations hereunder under a general plan sufficient to justify administrative inspection of an area, premises, buildings or conveyances in the circumstances specified in the application or such warrant.
Gaining Entry	When authorized by an administrative inspection warrant (the person authorized) ... upon showing such warrant to the owner, operator, or agent in charge, may enter controlled premises for the purpose of conducting an administrative inspection. **A person executing an administrative inspection warrant may**: 1) **Use reasonable force** and means to execute the warrant; 2) **Inspect and copy records** required by this chapter to be kept; 3) **Inspect,** within reasonable limits and in a reasonable manner, controlled premises and all pertinent equipment, finished and unfinished material, containers and labeling found therein, (except financial, sales & shipping data), all other things therein, including records, files, papers, processes, controls, and facilities bearing on violation of this chapter; and 4) **Inventory any stock of any controlled substance** therein and obtain samples thereof.
Entry without a Warrant	This section shall not prevent entries and administrative inspections, including seizures of property, without a warrant: 1) If the owner, operator, or agent in charge of the controlled premises **consents**; 2) In situations presenting **imminent danger to health or safety;** 3) In situations involving inspection of conveyances if there is reasonable cause to believe that the **mobility of the conveyance makes it impracticable to obtain a warrant**; 4) In any other **exceptional or emergency circumstance** where time or opportunity to apply for a warrant is lacking; or 5) In all other situations in which a warrant is **not required by the laws and constitution of the commonwealth or of the United States**.
Excluded Areas	An inspection authorized by this section shall not extend to **financial data, sales data, other than shipment data, or pricing data unless** the owner, operator, or agent in charge of the controlled premises **consents in writing**.

C. 94C § 30	ADMINISTRATIVE INSPECTION OF CONTROLLED PREMISES
Inventory Required if Property Seized	If property is seized pursuant to the warrant, a copy of the inventory shall be given to the person from whose premises the property is taken, together with a receipt for the property taken. The inventory shall be made in the presence of the person executing such warrant and of the person from whose possession or premises the property was taken, if present. A copy of the inventory shall be delivered to the person from whom or from whose premises the property was taken and to the applicant for such warrant at the time it is returned to a court.
Return Requirements	An administrative inspection warrant issued and executed pursuant to the provisions of this section shall be: • Returned to the issuing court, (unless it was issued by the superior court then it shall be returned to any court named in such warrant), • Within **10 days** of the date of issuance thereof unless, upon a showing of a need for additional time, the court or justice orders otherwise.
Jurisdiction to Issue Administrative Inspection Warrants	A district court or justice or superior court justice may, upon proper oath or affirmation by the commissioner or his designee except in the case of a pharmacy, by the commissioner or his designee or by the designee of the board of registration in pharmacy, **or by a police officer showing probable cause**, issue warrants for the purpose of conducting administrative inspections authorized by this chapter or rules hereunder, and seizures of property if appropriate to the inspections.
Definitions	
Administrative inspection warrants	**"Administrative inspection warrants"** are warrants for the purpose of **inspecting, copying and verifying the correctness of records, reports or other documents** required to be kept by a registrant on controlled premises and for the seizure of property appropriate to such inspection.
Commissioner	"**Commissioner**", the commissioner of public health.
Controlled premises	**"Controlled premises"** means any place or area, including but not limited to any building, conveyance, warehouse, factory, or establishment, in which persons registered under the provisions of this chapter or required thereunder to keep records, are **permitted to hold, manufacture, compound, process, distribute, deliver, dispense, or administer any controlled substance** or in which such persons make or maintain records pertaining thereto.

CLASSIFICATIONS

C. 94C § 31

CLASSES OF CONTROLLED SUBSTANCES

CLASS A

Unless specifically excepted or unless listed in another schedule, any of the following opiates, including their isomers, esters, ethers, salts, and salts of isomers, esters and ethers, whenever the existence of such isomers, esters, ethers and salts is possible within the specific chemical designation:

(1) Acetylmethadol	(12) Dextromoramide	(23) Etoxeridine	(34) Phenadoxone
(2) Allylprodine	(13) Dextrorphan	(24) Furethidine	(35) Phenampromide
(3) Alphacetylmethadol	(14) Diampromide	(25) Hydroxypethidine	(36) Phenomorphan
(4) Alphameprodine	(15) Diethylthiambutene	(26) Ketobemidone	(37) Phenoperidine
(5) Alphamethadol	(16) Dimenoxadol	(27) Levomoramide	(38) Piritramide
(6) Benzethidine	(17) Dimepheptanol	(28) Levophenacylmorphan	(39) Proheptazine
(7) Betacetylmethadol	(18) Dimethylthiambutene	(29) Morpheridine	(40) Properidine
(8) Betameprodine	(19) Dioxaphetylbutyrate	(30) Noracymethadol	(41) Racemoramide
(9) Betamethadol	(20) Dipipanone	(31) Norlevorphanol	(42) Trimeperidine
(10) Betaprodine	(21) Ethylmethylthiambutene	(32) Normethadone	
(11) Clonitazene	(22) Etonitazene	(33) Norpipanone	

Unless specifically excepted or unless listed in another schedule, any of the following opium derivatives, their salts, isomers, and salts of isomers whenever the existence of such salts, isomers, and salts of isomers is possible within the specific chemical designation:

(1) Acetorphine	(8) Dihydromorphine	(15) Morphine methylsulfonate	(22) Thebacon
(2) Acetyldihydrocodeine	(9) Etorphine	(16) Morphine-N-Oxide	
(3) Benzylmorphine	(10) Heroin	(17) Myrophine	
(4) Codeine methylbromide	(11) Hydromorphinol	(18) Nicocodeine	
(5) Codeine-N-Oxide	(12) Methyldesorphine	(19) Nicomorphine	
(6) Cyprenorphine	(13) Methylhydromorphine	(20) Normorphine	
(7) Desomorphine	(14) Morphine methylbromide	(21) Pholcodine	

Unless specifically excepted or unless listed in another schedule, any material, compound, mixture or preparation that contains any quantity of the following substances including its salts, isomers and salts of isomers whenever the existence of such salts, isomers and salts of isomers is possible within the specific chemical designations:

(1) Flunitrazepam	(2) Gamma Hydroxy Butyric Acid	(3) Ketamine	

C. 94C § 31

CLASSES OF CONTROLLED SUBSTANCES

CLASS B

Unless specifically excepted or unless listed in another schedule, any of the following substances whether produced directly or indirectly by extraction from substances of vegetable origin, or independently by means of chemical synthesis, or by a combination of extraction and chemical synthesis:

(1) Opium and opiate, and any salt, compound, derivative, or preparation of opium or opiate

(2) Any salt, compound, derivative, or preparation thereof which is chemically equivalent or identical with any of the substances referred to in paragraph (1) except that these substances shall not include the isoquinoline alkaloids of opium.

(3) Opium poppy and poppy straw

(4) Coca leaves and any salt, compound, derivative, or preparation of coca leaves, and any salt, compound, derivative, or preparation thereof which is chemically equivalent or identical with any of these substances, except that the substances shall not include decocainized coca leaves or extraction of coca leaves, which extractions do not contain cocaine or ecgonine.

(5) Phenyl-2-Propanone (P2P)	(6) Phenylcyclohexylamine (PCH)	(7) Piperidinocyclohexanecarbonitrile (PCC)	(8) 3,4-methylenedioxy methamphetamine (MDMA).

Unless specifically excepted or unless listed in another schedule, any of the following opiates, including isomers, esters, ethers, salts, and salts of isomer, esters, and ethers, whenever the existence of such isomers, esters, ethers and salts is possible within the specific chemical designation:

(1) Alphaprodine	(9) Levorphanol	(15) Pethidine-Intermediate-A, 4-cyano-1-methyl-4-phenylpiperidine	
(2) Anileridine	(10) Metazocine	(16) Pethidine-Intermediate-B, ethyl-4-phenylpiperidine-4-carboxylate	
(3) Bezitramide	(11) Methadone	(17) Pethidine-Intermediate-C, 1-methyl-4-phenylpiperidine-4-carbox-ylic acid	
(4) Dihydrocodeine	(12) Methadone-Intermediate, 4-cyano-2-dimethylamino-4, 4-diphenyl butane		(18) Phenazocine
(5) Diphenoxylate	(13) Moramide-Intermediate, 2-methyl-3 morpholine-1, 1-diphenyl-propane carboxylic acid		(19) Piminodine
(6) Fentanyl	(14) Pethidine	(20) Racemethorphan	
(7) Isomethadone		(21) Racemorphan	
(8) Levomethorphan			

Unless specifically excepted or unless listed in another schedule, any material, compound, mixture, or preparation which contains any quantity of the following substances having a stimulant effect on the central nervous system:

(1) Amphetamine, its salts, optical isomers and salts of its optical isomers.

(2) Any substance which contains any quantity of methamphetamine, including its salts, isomers and salts of isomers.

(3) Phenmetrazine and its salts.	(4) Methylphenidate.

Unless specifically excepted or unless listed in another schedule, any material, compound, mixture or preparation which contains any quantity of the following substances having a depressant effect on the central nervous system:

(1) Any substance which contains any quantity of a derivative of barbituric acid, or any salt of a derivative of barbituric acid.

(2) Any substance which contains any quantity of methaqualone, or any salt or derivative of methaqualone.

C. 94C § 31

CLASSES OF CONTROLLED SUBSTANCES

Unless specifically excepted or listed in another schedule, any material, compound, mixture, or preparation, which contains any quantity of the following hallucinogenic substances or which contains any of their salts, isomers, and salts of isomers whenever the existence of such salts, isomers, and salts of isomers is possible within the specific chemical designation:

(1) Lysergic acid	(2) Lysergic acid amide	(3) Lysergic acid diethylamide	(4) Phencyclidine.

CLASS C

Unless specifically excepted or unless listed in another schedule, any material, compound, mixture, or preparation which contains any quantity of the following substances having a depressant effect on the central nervous system:

(1) Chlordiazepoxide	(5) Diazepam	(9) Methyprylon	(13) Sulfonethylmethane
(2) Chlorhexadol	(6) Flurazepam	(10) Oxazepam	(14) Sulfonmethane
(3) Clonazepam	(7) Glutethimide	(11) Prazepam	(15) Temazepam.
(4) Clorazepate	(8) Lorazepam	(12) Sulfondiethylmethane	Nalorphine

Unless specifically excepted or unless listed in another schedule, any material, compound, mixture, or preparation containing limited quantities of any of the following narcotic drugs, or any salts thereof:

(1) Not more than 1.8 grams of codeine per 100 milliliters or not more than 90 milligrams per dosage unit with an equal or greater quantity of an isoquinoline alkaloid of opium.

(2) Not more than 1.8 grams of codeine per 100 milliliters or not more than 90 milligrams per dosage unit, with one or more active, nonnarcotic ingredients in recognized therapeutic amounts.

(3) Not more than 300 milligrams of dihydrocodeinone per 100 milliliters or not more than 15 milligrams per dosage unit, with a fourfold or greater quantity of an isoquinoline alkaloid of opium.

(4) Not more than 300 milligrams of dihydrocodeinone per 100 milliliters or not more than 15 milligrams per dosage unit, with one or more active nonnarcotic ingredients in recognized therapeutic amounts.

(5) Not more than 1.8 grams of dihydrocodeine per 100 milliliters or not more than 90 milligrams per dosage unit, with one or more active nonnarcotic ingredients in recognized therapeutic amounts.

(6) Not more than 300 milligrams of ethylmorphine per 100 milliliters or not more than 15 milligrams per dosage unit with one or more active nonnarcotic ingredients in recognized therapeutic amounts.

(7) Not more than 500 milligrams of opium per 100 milliliters or per 100 grams, or not more than 25 milligrams per dosage unit, with one or more active, nonnarcotic ingredients in recognized therapeutic amounts.

(8) Not more than 50 milligrams of morphine per 100 milliliters or per 100 grams with one or more active nonnarcotic ingredients in recognized therapeutic amounts.

Unless specifically excepted or listed in another schedule, any material, compound, mixture, or preparation, which contains any quantity of the following hallucinogenic substances, or which contains any of their salts, isomers, and salts of isomers whenever the existence of such salts, isomers, and salts of isomers is possible within the specific chemical designation:

(1) 3, 4-methylenedioxy amphetamine	(9) Mescaline	(17) 3, 4 - methylenedioxymethcathinone, MDMC	(25) 3-methoxymethcathinone
(2) 5-methoxy-3, 4-methylenedioxy amphetamine	(10) Peyote	(18) 3, 4 - methylenedioxypyrovalerone, MDPV	(26) 4-methyl-alpha-pyrrolidinobutyrophenone

C. 94C § 31	CLASSES OF CONTROLLED SUBSTANCES		
(3) 3, 4, 5-trimethoxy amphetamine	(11) N-ethyl-3-piperidyl benzilate	(19) 4 - methylmethcathinone, 4-MMC	(27) 2-(methylamino)-1-phenylpropan-1-one
(4) Bufotenine	(12) N-methyl-3-piperidyl benzilate	(20) 4 - methoxymethcathinone, bk-PMMA, PMMC	(28) 4-ethylmethcathinone
(5) Diethyltryptaminc	(13) Psilocybin	(21) 3, 4 - fluoromethcathinone, FMC	(29) 3,4-Dimethylmethcathinone
(6) Dimethyltryptamine	(14) Psilocyn	(22) Napthylpyrovalerone, NRG-1	(30) alpha-Pyrrolidinopentiophenone
(7) 4-methyl-2, 5-dimethoxyamphetamine	(15) Tetrahydrocannabinols	(23) Beta-keto-N-methylbenzodioxolylpropylamine	(31) beta-Keto-Ethylbenzodioxolylbutanamine
(8) Ibogaine	(16) 4-Bromo-2, 5-Dimethoxy-amphetamine.	(24) 2-(methylamino)-propiophenone; OR alpha-(methylamino) propiophenone	(32) 3,4-methylenedioxy-N-ethylcathinone.

CLASS D

(1) Barbital	(4) Ethchlorvynol	(7) Meprobamate	(10) Petrichloral
(2) Chloral betaine	(5) Ethinamate	(8) Methylphenobarbital	(11) Phenobarbital
(3) Chloral hydrate	(6) Methohexital	(9) Paraldehyde	

Unless specifically excepted or unless listed in another schedule, any material, compound, mixture, or preparation, which contains any quantity of the following substances, or which contains any of their salts, isomers, and salts of isomers whenever the existence of such salts, isomers, and salts of isomers is possible within the specific chemical designation:

(1) Marihuana	(2) Butyl Nitrite	(3) Isobutyl Nitrite	(4) 1-Nitrosoxy-Methyl-Propane.

CLASS E

Any compound, mixture, or preparation containing any of the following limited quantities of narcotic drugs, which shall include one or more nonnarcotic active medicinal ingredients in sufficient proportion to confer upon the compound, mixture, or preparation valuable medicinal qualities other than those possessed by the narcotic drug alone:

(1) Not more than 200 milligrams of codeine per 100 milliliters or per 100 grams

(2) Not more than 100 milligrams of dihydrocodeine per 100 milliliters or per 100 grams

(3) Not more than 100 milligrams of ethylmorphine per 100 milliliters or per 100 grams

(4) Not more than 2.5 milligrams of diphenoxylate and not less than 25 micrograms of atropine sulfate per dosage unit

(5) Not more than 100 milligrams of opium per 100 milliliters or per 100 grams

Prescription drugs other than those included in Classes A, B, C, D, and subsection (a) of this Class.

ALCOHOL/LIQUOR LAWS

The laws involving alcohol are somewhat archaic and in some areas have yet to evolve to modern standards, particularly in the area of transportation and search issues, many seem tied to the days of prohibition. Despite this, the laws are in effect and must be enforced, particularly those designed to protect minors. The alcohol section of the manual is broken down into three sections; general provisions, licensed establishment requirements, and minors with alcohol.

The Alcohol Beverage Control Commission can be a valuable resource when dealing with alcohol issues. They can be contacted by phone at (617) 727-3040 (for general inquiries use ext. 10 for the Investigative Unit use ext. 772).

Alcoholic Beverages Control Commission
239 Causeway St.
Boston MA, 02114
617-727-3040

General Provisions

C.138 § 56	SPECIAL ARREST POWERS FOR ALCOHOL VIOLATIONS
	Provisions
Certain law enforcement officials	A deputy sheriff, chief of police, deputy chief of police, city marshal, deputy or assistant marshal, police officer including a state police officer, or constable, or, in the county of Dukes or Nantucket, the sheriff anywhere within his county, or any investigator of the commission,
Arrest for certain Prohibited Conduct	May without a warrant arrest any person whom he finds in the act of illegally: • **S**elling • **E**xporting, • **E**xposing, • **K**eeping, • **M**anufacturing, • **I**mporting, • **S**toring, • **T**ransporting Alcoholic beverages or alcohol
Seize alcohol, vessels & implements	The law enforcement officer may seize the beverages or alcohol and any vessels and implements of manufacture or sale in the possession of such person, and detain them until warrants can be procured against such person, and for the seizure of said beverages or alcohol, vessels and implements.
Enforcement required	"Such officers shall enforce or cause to be enforced the penalties provided by law against every person who is guilty of a violation of chapter 138 of which they can obtain reasonable proof, and shall make all needful and appropriate investigations for the said purpose."
	Related Statute
General penalty for alcohol offenses c. 138 § 62.	A violation by any person of any provision of chapter 138 for **which a specific penalty is not provided** or a violation by a licensee or permitted of any provision of his license or permit or of any regulation made under authority of this chapter shall be punished by a fine of not less than $50 nor more than $500 or by imprisonment for not less than 1 month nor more than 1 year, or both.

c. 138 § 22	TRANSPORT ALCOHOL (Max Amounts)
Elements	
1.	Any person
2.	May transport alcoholic beverages or alcohol (but only for his own use and that of his family and guests)
3.	Without a license or permit
4.	But not exceeding in amount, at any one time, the following amounts: 20 gallons of malt beverages (e.g. beer) 3 gallons of any other alcoholic beverage (i.e. "hard liquor"), or 1 gallon of alcohol (i.e. pure grain alcohol)
Exception:	**Moving:** No permit is required and no limit is placed when transporting from place of residence to a new place of residence established by him if the alcohol and the beverages were manufactured by him for his own private use. **Salesman:** a salesman licensed under c. 138 § 19 may transport up to 24 gallons of alcohol or alcoholic beverages with a proper permit. **Delivery:** delivery services and caterers may transport larger amount with proper permits.
ARREST, PENALTIES & NOTES	
Power of Arrest	**Misdemeanor** – statutory authority permits a police officer to effect an arrest for this offense committed in his/her presence only via c. 138 § 56 (SEEKMIST- Transporting)
Penalty	A fine of not more than $2,500 or by imprisonment for not more than 6 months, or both.
Attorney Hanrahan's Comment	If you do the math the most beer that can be transported without a permit is 8.88 cases of beer, based on 12 ounce cans in a 24 can case of beer.
Related Laws	
c. 138 § 22	See special transport provisions for licensees under the Licensed Establishment Requirement Section.
c. 138 § 34	See minor transportation of alcohol under the minors with alcohol section

C. 272 § 59	VIOLATION OF A PUBLIC DRINKING ORDINANCE
	Elements
1.	Whoever is in a street or elsewhere in a town
2.	In willful violation of an ordinance or by-law of such town or of any rule or regulation for the government or use of any public reservation, parkway or boulevard made under authority of law by any department, officer or board in charge thereof,
3.	The substance of which is the drinking or possession of alcoholic beverage.
	Arrest Power, Penalties & Notes
Power of Arrest	The offender may be arrested without a warrant by an officer authorized to serve criminal process in the place where the offence is committed and kept in custody until he can be taken before a court having jurisdiction of the offence.
Penalty	See local ordinance for fine amounts. Chapter 40 sec. 21D states that the paying of a City Ordinance fine shall not be deemed a criminal violation.
Attorney Hanrahan's Comment	This only applies when the city or town has a local ordinance/by-law that specifically prohibits public drinking or possession of alcohol. This is a state law that allows police to arrest for violations of local alcohol possession/drinking rules. You must be guided by the local ordinance/by-law/rule so be sure to be familiar with the local rules/laws before executing an arrest. This law does not prohibit public drinking by itself, a local ordinance must exist.

Licensed Establishment Requirements

204 CMR 4.00	PROHIBITION OF CERTAIN PRACTICES
	Elements
204 CMR 4.03	No licensee or employee or agent of a licensee shall:
Prohibited Practices	a. Offer or deliver any free drinks to any person or group of persons; b. Deliver more than two drinks to one person at one time; c. Sell, offer to sell or deliver to any person or group of persons any drinks at a price less than the price regularly charged for such drinks during the same calendar week, except at private functions not open to the public; d. Sell, offer to sell or deliver to any person an unlimited number of drinks during any set period of time for a fixed price, except at private functions not open to the public; e. Sell, offer to sell or deliver drinks to any person or group of persons on any one day at prices less than those charged the general public on that day, except at private functions not open to the public; f. Sell, offer to sell or deliver malt beverages or mixed drinks by the pitcher except to two or more persons at any one time; g. Increase the volume of alcoholic beverages contained in a drink without increasing proportionately the price regularly charged for such

204 CMR 4.00	PROHIBITION OF CERTAIN PRACTICES
	drink during the same calendar week; h. Encourage or permit, on the licensed premises, any game or contest which involves drinking or the awarding of drinks as prizes.
No Advertising These Practices	No licensee shall advertise or promote in any way, whether within or without the licensed premises, any of the practices prohibited under 204 CMR 4.03.
Licensee Definition	Licensee: means any person, club, partnership, corporation or other entity licensed under the provisions of M.G.L. c. 138 to sell alcoholic beverages to be served and drunk on the premises.
Exceptions	Nothing contained in 204 CMR 4.03 shall be construed to prohibit licensees from offering **free food or entertainment** at any time; or to prohibit licensees from including **a drink as part of a meal package**; or to prohibit the sale or delivery of **wine by the bottle or carafe** when sold with meals or to more than one person; or to prohibit those licensed under M.G.L. c. 138, § 15, from offering free wine tastings; or to prohibit those licensed under M.G.L. c. 138, § 12, from offering room services to registered guests.
Other Important Information	
Required Records	All licensees shall maintain a **schedule of the prices charged** for all drinks to be served and drunk on the licensed premises or in any room or part thereof. Such prices **shall be effective for not less than one calendar week.**
Enforcement	The provisions of 204 CMR 4.00 shall be deemed to be **a condition of every license** issued under M.G.L. c. 138 to sell alcoholic beverages to be drunk on the premises, and said provisions may be enforced by the local licensing authorities or their agents by the Alcoholic Beverage Control Commission or its investigators.

C. 138 § 69	SALE OR DELIVERY TO INTOXICATED PERSONS
Elements	
Applies to Licensed Premises	No alcoholic beverage shall be sold or delivered on any premises licensed under chapter 138 to an intoxicated person
Arrest, Penalties & Notes	
Power of Arrest	**Misdemeanor** – because this violation involves a sale it would be arrestable under c. 138 § 56 if committed in the officer's presence.
Penalty	A fine of not less than $50 nor more than $500 or by imprisonment for not less than 1 month nor more than 1 year, or both. See chapter 138 § 62.

C.138 § 34B	LIQUOR IDENTIFICATION CARDS
SPECIFICATIONS	
Who Can Apply for a Liquor ID	• Any person 21 or older • that does not hold a valid operator's license issued by the RMV • may apply for a liquor purchase identification card
Methods of Verifying Age	An entity that reasonably relies on one of the following documents to prove age shall not be punished or criminally liable for the delivery/sale of alcohol: [1471] • A Massachusetts Liquor Identification card • A Massachusetts Identification Card • A Massachusetts Driver's License • A valid Passport issued by the US government or a foreign government recognized by the US • A valid US military identification card
Duration	The cards are valid for 5 years.
Note:	See C. 90 § 8E in the Motor Vehicle Section of this manual for RMV identification cards for those who do not have driver's licenses.
Attorney Hanrahan's Comment	If a licensed establishment relies on any other form of id and it turns out that the id is phony, or otherwise not valid, they will have no defense to sanctions. Also see Licenses, ID's and Right to Operate in the Motor Vehicle Section for more information on licenses and identifications.

C.138 § 34B	REQUIREMENT TO PRODUCE ID AT LIQUOR ESTABLISHMENT
Elements	
1.	Whoever
2.	Upon the request of an agent of: 1. the Liquor Commission or 2. the local licensing authority
3.	While in a licensed premises (a business licensed to sell alcohol)
4.	a. Refuses to state his name, age or address, or b. States a false name, age, or address (including a name or address which is not his name or address in ordinary use)
5.	Shall be punished.
ARREST, PENALTIES & NOTES	
Power of Arrest	**Misdemeanor** – Any person who is discovered by a police officer or special police officer in the act of violating the provisions of this section (e.g. refusing) may be arrested without a warrant by such police officer or special police officer.
Penalty	$500 fine
Attorney Hanrahan's Comment	This offense is not limited to minors. Everyone inside a licensed establishment must provide this information when requested.

[1471] ABCC Advisory issued (9/4/2012)

C.138 § 63A	HINDERING AN AGENT OF THE LIQUOR COMMISSION OR THE LOCAL LICENSING AUTHORITY
Elements	
1.	Any person
2.	• Who **hinders or delays** any investigator/agent of the Liquor Commission or Local Licensing authority in the performance of his duties • Who **refuses to admit to or locks out** investigator/agent of the Liquor Commission or Local Licensing authority, or • Who **refuses to give to information** that may be required for the proper enforcement of chapter 138 to an investigator/agent of the Liquor Commission or Local Licensing authority.
3.	Shall be punished
Arrest, Penalties & Notes	
Power of Arrest	**Misdemeanor –** there is no statutory authority granting powers of arrest for this offense. However, if the offense is committed in public, in the officer's presence, and is creating a breach of the peace an arrest would be lawful.
Penalty	A fine of not less than $50 nor more than $200 or by imprisonment for not more than 2 months, or both
Attorney Hanrahan's Comment	Obviously, this only applies if these officials are acting in the performance of their duties. Additionally, many municipal police officers are agents of the local licensing authority – check with your agency.
Related Statutes & Case Law	
c. 138 § 34B ID required	Chapter 138 § 34B requires that a patron identify himself while in a licensed establishment.
c. 138 § 63 Inspection of Licensed Establishments	The **local licensing authorities or their agents** may at **any time enter upon the premises** of a person who is licensed by them, and the commission or its agents may enter upon the premises of any holder of a license, permit or certificate of fitness under this chapter, **to ascertain the manner in which he conducts the business carried on under such license,** permit or certificate. Such licensing authorities or their agents **may at any time take samples for analysis from any beverages or alcohol kept on such premises, and the vessel or vessels containing** such samples shall be sealed on the premises in the presence of the holder of such license, permit or certificate or one of his employees, and shall remain so sealed until presented to the state department of public health for analysis, and duplicate samples shall be left with such holder.

c. 138 § 22	TRANSPORT ALCOHOL (Max Amounts) LICENSED SELLERS
Elements	
1.	Licensees for the sale of alcoholic beverages or alcohol
2.	May transport and deliver anywhere in the Commonwealth alcoholic beverages or alcohol
3.	Lawfully bought or sold by them
4.	In vehicles owned or leased by them or their employees
5.	If each vehicle used for such transportation and delivery is covered by a permit issued by the Liquor Commission
Limitations	• Vehicles owned or leased by holders of permits under 138 § 19A (salesmen) may be used only for the transportation of samples or of no more than 24 gallons of alcoholic beverages or alcohol; provided, further, that the salesperson possesses the proper invoice and that a record of these deliveries is kept available by the wholesaler for commission inspection. • Hawking and peddling of alcohol from a vehicle is prohibited.
Arrest, Penalties & Notes	
Power of Arrest	**Misdemeanor** – statutory authority permits a police officer to effect an arrest for this offense committed in his/her presence only via c. 138 § 56 (SEEKMIST - Transporting)
Penalty	A fine of not more than $2,500 or by imprisonment for not more than 6 months, or both.
Attorney Hanrahan's Comments	Corporations, shipping companies, and caterers may obtain permits to transport larger amounts of alcohol in furtherance of their business. The permit (or a certified copy) must be carried during transport.

C. 138 § 34D	POSTING NOTICES OF OUI/OPEN CONTAINER REQUIREMENTS
REQUIREMENTS	
Alcohol consumed on premises: OUI notice required	Any establishment which sells alcoholic beverages to be drunk on the premises, shall post a copy of the penalties set forth in subdivision (1) of chapter 90 § 24 for driving under the influence.
Liquor Store: Open Container Notice	Any establishment which sells alcoholic beverages not to be drunk on the premises shall post a copy of the penalties set forth in chapter 90 § 24I for operating a motor vehicle while drinking from an open container of alcohol.
Signs Requirements	The copies shall be posted conspicuously. They must be printed in letters not less in size than 18 point capitals, boldface, and shall be prepared by the commission and distributed to business establishments which sell, serve or otherwise dispense alcohol or alcoholic beverages to the general public.
ARREST, PENALTIES & NOTES	
Power of Arrest	None
Penalty for not posting required sign	a fine of not more than $50
Penalty for removing sign	Any person unlawfully removing a copy posted shall be punished by a fine of $50.

MINORS WITH ALCOHOL

c. 138 § 34	SALE/DELIVERY/FURNISH ALCOHOL TO PERSONS UNDER 21
	Elements
Prohibited Acts	The below acts are prohibited in the specific locations noted.
Sale or Delivery prohibited Anywhere	It is illegal to make a **sale** or **delivery** of any alcoholic beverage or alcohol to any person under 21 (either for the use of the person or a parent).
Procure while a Patron of a Liquor Store, Tavern, Winery or Brewery	**It is illegal to deliver, procure, or procure to be delivered** (i.e. has waiter bring a drink) to any person he *knows* or *has reason to believe* is under 21 years of age, (either for his own use or for the use of his parent or any other person). While the person under 21 is a patron of: a. an establishment license under section 12 (**tavern, restaurant etc. essentially a public place where alcohol is consumed on premises**), b. an establishment license under section 15 (**liquor store**) c. an establishment license under section 19B (**Winery**) d. an establishment license under section 19C (**Brewery Farm**) e. an establishment license under section 19D (**Brewery**)
Furnishing on property owned or controlled by person charged	It is unlawful to **furnish** any alcoholic beverage or alcohol to a person under 21 years of age. **Important note**: the word "furnish" shall mean to knowingly or intentionally *supply, give, or provide to or allow* a person under 21 years of age to possess alcoholic beverages on premises or property *owned or controlled by the person charged*.
Exceptions	**Procuring alcohol:** A parent, ward or spouse may procure alcohol for a person under 21 who is their child or spouse from all locations above except for an establishment licensed under section 12 (Tavern/Restaurant – place where alcohol consumed on premises). **Note:** The SJC has stated that parents are immune from criminal liability for delivering alcoholic beverage to their children despite the legislature only listing "procuring" as exempt.[1472] **Furnishing:** A parent or grandparent can furnish alcohol to their children/grandchildren **Employment**: Nothing in this section shall be construed to prohibit any person licensed under chapter 138 from employing any person 18 years of age or older for the direct handling or selling of alcoholic beverages or alcohol. An employee under 18 cannot directly handle, sell, mix or serve alcohol or alcoholic beverages.
	ARREST, PENALTIES & NOTES
Power of Arrest	**Misdemeanor** – statutory authority permits a police officer to effect an arrest for this offense committed in his/her presence only via c. 138 § 56 (SEEKMIST) **if it involves a sale or delivery in a non-dwelling** (see definition below involving a delivery/sale). If the alcohol is possessed by the minor, the minor can be arrested under c. 138 § 134C. Furnishing would **not be arrestable** unless a sale was also involved.
Penalty	A fine of not more than $2,000 or by imprisonment for not more than 1 year or both.
Delivery in non-dwelling is evidence of a sale	Chapter 138 § 41 defines a sale as: "The delivery of alcoholic beverages in or from a building, booth, stand or other place, **except a private dwelling house**, or in or from a private dwelling house if any part thereof or its dependencies is used as an inn, eating house or shop of any kind, or other place of common resort, such delivery in either case being to a person not a resident therein, shall be prima facie evidence that such delivery is a sale."

[1472] *Commonwealth v. Parent*, SJC (2013).

c. 138 § 34	SALE/DELIVERY/FURNISH ALCOHOL TO PERSONS UNDER 21
Attorney Hanrahan's Comment	A person does not have to be 21 or older in order to be guilty of furnishing; therefore a person under 21 who hosts an underage drinking party and *furnishes* alcohol to people under 21 may be guilty of this offense.
	Case Law Notes
Com. v. Sueiras	In *Sueiras*, the Court upheld the warrantless entry of a police officer into a private dwelling under the exigent circumstances exception when the officer had probable cause that underage children were actively, and unlawfully, consuming alcoholic beverages.
Alcohol Search Warrants	When it comes to obtaining a search warrant for alcohol evidence special provisions are required. See c. 138 § 142 in the Search Warrant chapter of the Criminal Procedure section of this manual.

C.138 § 34C	MINOR TRANSPORT/POSSESSION OF ALCOHOL
	Elements
1.	The defendant being under 21 years of age (and not accompanied by a parent or legal guardian)
2.	Knowingly • possesses, or • transports, or • carries on his person Any alcohol or alcoholic beverages
Exception	This does not apply to a person between the ages of 18 and 21who knowingly possesses, transports, or carries on his person, alcohol or alcoholic beverages in the course of his employment.
	ARREST, PENALTIES & NOTES
Power of Arrest	**Misdemeanor** – statutory authority permits a police officer to make an arrest for this offense committed in his/her presence.
Penalty	1st offense: a fine of not more than $50.00 2nd or Subsequent offense: a fine of not more than $150.00
RMV Action	A conviction of a violation of this section shall be reported forthwith to the registrar of motor vehicles by the court, and said registrar shall thereupon suspend for a period of **90 days** the license of such person to operate a motor vehicle.
Attorney Hanrahan's Comment	The only exceptions to a minor transporting/possessing alcohol occurs when the child is accompanied by their parent/guardian or during the course of employment. For instance, an 18 year old who is driving a car with alcohol inside, accompanied by her 21 year old boyfriend, would be unlawfully transporting alcohol, even though her boyfriend is of legal age.
	Related Case Law
Constructive Possession	Case law indicates that possession includes construction possession, meaning the person does not have to be actually holding the alcohol in his hand but may otherwise have control and easy access to it. See more on Constructive possession in the **Important Information to Know** section of this manual.

C.138 § 34A	MINOR PURCHASE OR ATTEMPT TO PURCHASE ALCOHOL
Elements	
1.	Any person under 21 years of age who
2.	• **purchases or attempts** to purchase alcoholic, or • makes **arrangements** with any person to purchase or procure alcohol, or • willfully **misrepresents his age** with the intent of purchasing alcoholic beverages ,or • in any way **alters, defaces** or otherwise **falsifies** his **identification** offered as proof of age *with the intent of purchasing alcoholic beverages*
3.	Either for his own use or for the use of any other person
4.	Shall be punished
ARREST, PENALTIES & NOTES	
Power of Arrest	**Misdemeanor** – there is no statutory authority granting powers of arrest for this offense. However, if the offense is committed in public, in the officer's presence, and is creating a breach of the peace an arrest would be lawful. **Other Options**: if the person under 21 is successful and obtains the alcohol he/she may be arrested for unlawful transportation/possession via § 56. You may also consider c. 90 § 24B if the license if altered which would allow a warrantless felony arrest (see related statutes notes below).
Penalty	$300 fine
RMV Action	A conviction of a violation of this section shall be reported forthwith to the RMV *by the court*. Upon receipt of such notice the RMV shall suspend for **180 days** the defendant's license or right to operate a motor vehicle.
Attorney Hanrahan's Comment	This statute covers a wide array of methods that a minor may attempt to obtain alcohol, including asking someone to purchase alcohol for him/her ("makes arrangements"), claiming to be older ("misrepresents age") or by falsifying identification.
Related Statutes & Case Law	
c. 90 § 24B **Phony Document**	When the attempt involves an altered or imitation license the officer may elect to charge the minor with c. 90 § 24B which would make the offense a felony. See Motor Vehicle Law section for more on this topic.
c. 138 § 34B **ID of another**	Chapter 138 § 34B makes it arrestable to alter an ID card/license, or to use another's ID, or to falsely apply for the ID of another – even without the intent to obtain alcohol. See below.

C.138 § 34B	MISUSE, POSSESSION OR APPLICATION OF LIQUOR CARD/LICENSE
Elements	
1.	Any person who
2.	• transfers, alters or defaces any Massachusetts liquor identification card or license, or makes, uses, carries, sells or distributes a false identification card or license, or • uses the identification card or motor vehicle license of another, or • furnishes false information in obtaining such card or license
3.	shall be guilty of a misdemeanor and shall be punished
ARREST, PENALTIES & NOTES	
Power of Arrest	**Misdemeanor** – Any person who is discovered by a police officer or special police officer in the act of violating the provisions of this section may be arrested without a warrant by such police officer or special police officer.
Penalty	A fine of not more than $200 or by imprisonment for not more than 3 months
Attorney Hanrahan's Comment	This offense covers much of the same conduct as c. 138 § 34A, however there is no need to prove that the intent was to obtain alcohol, nor is there a requirement that the offender be under the age of 21 years.
Case Law Notes	
c. 138 § 34A	Section 34A closes mirrors this statue with slight variations.
c. 90 § 24B Phony Document	When the attempt involves an altered or imitation license the officer may elect to charge the minor with c. 90 § 24B which would make the offense a felony. See Motor Vehicle Law section for more on this topic.

c. 138 § 34A	FALSE STATEMENT TO PROCURE ALCOHOL FOR A MINOR
Elements	
1.	Knowingly make (or induce to be made)
2.	A false statement as to the age of a person who is under 21 years of age
3.	In order to procure a sale or delivery of such beverages or alcohol to the person under 21
4.	Either for the use of the person under 21 years of age or for the use of some other person
ARREST, PENALTIES & NOTES	
Power of Arrest	**Misdemeanor** – there is no statutory authority granting powers of arrest for this offense. However, if the offense is committed in public, in the officer's presence, and is creating a **breach of the peace** an arrest would be lawful.
Penalty	Fine of $300
RMV Action	A conviction of a violation of this section shall be reported forthwith to the RMV by the court. Upon receipt of such notice the RMV shall thereupon suspend for **180 days** the defendant's license or right to operate a motor vehicle.

MISCELLANEOUS ALCOHOL LAWS

C.268 § 26	DELIVERING ALCOHOLIC BEVERAGES TO PRISONERS
Elements	
1.	The defendant
2.	• **gives, sells or delivers** alcoholic beverages to: b. a **person confined** in any correctional institution or other place of confinement, or c. to a **person in** the **custody** of a sheriff, constable, police officer, superintendent of a correctional institution, or other superintendent or keeper of a place of confinement • or, has in his **possession**, within the precincts of any prison or other place of confinement, any such beverages, **with intent** to convey or deliver them to any person confined therein
Exception	This does not apply to someone acting under the direction of the physician appointed to attend to the prisoner
Arrest, Penalties & Notes	
Power of Arrest	**Misdemeanor** – no statutory power of arrest, however if the violation involves a sale it would arrestable under c. 138 § 56 if committed in the officer's presence
Penalty	A fine of not more than $50 or by imprisonment for not more than 2 months.

C. 272 § 40A	ALCOHOL POSSESSION ON SCHOOL PREMISES
Elements	
1.	The defendant gives, sells, delivers or has in his possession
2.	Any alcoholic beverage, except for medicinal purposes,
3.	In any public school building, or on any premises used for public school purposes and under the charge of a school committee or other public board or officer.
Exception	A school committee of a city, town or district may authorize a public or nonprofit organization using a public school building with its permission during non school hours to possess and sell alcoholic beverages therein provided such nonprofit organization is properly licensed under the provisions of chapter 138 § 14..
Arrest Power, Penalties & Notes	
Power of Arrest	**Misdemeanor** – if a violation involves a SEEKMIST violation it would arrestable under c. 138 § 56 if committed in the officer's presence.
Penalty	Imprisonment for not more than 30 days or by a fine of not more than $100 or both.

111B § 8	PROTECTIVE CUSTODY
CRITERIA TO DETAIN	
PC Criteria	• Any person • who is **incapacitated** (alcohol only - see definition below) • may be assisted by a police officer • with or without his consent to: 1. his residence, or 2. to a facility (see definition below), or 3. to a police station
DEFINITIONS	
Definitions c. 111B § 3	**"Facility",** any public or private place, or portion thereof, providing services especially designed for the detoxification of intoxicated persons or alcoholics. **"Incapacitated",** the condition of an intoxicated person who, by reason of the consumption of intoxicating liquor is (1) unconscious, (2) in need of medical attention, (3) likely to suffer or cause physical harm or damage property, or (4) disorderly. **"Juvenile",** any person who is between seven and 17 years of age.
Attorney Hanrahan's Comment	The Protective custody law under chapter 111B only applies to those who are affected by alcohol, not drugs. A person cannot be detained, at least consistent with G.L. c. 111B, for drug impairment. In this case it is often based to seek medical treatment.
RIGHTS OF THOSE IN PROTECTIVE CUSTODY	
Right to Breathalyzer	A PC shall have the **right**, and be informed *in writing* of this right**,** to request and be administered a **breathalyzer test**.
Right to Phone Call	Any person presumed intoxicated and to be held in protective custody at a police station **shall, immediately after being presumed intoxicated, have the right and be informed of a right to make one phone call** at his own expense and on his own behalf. Any person assisted by a police officer to a facility under this section shall have **the right to make one phone call** at his own expense on his own behalf and shall be informed forthwith upon arriving at the facility.
Maximum Detention Period	No person assisted to a police station shall be held in protective custody against his will, unless a suitable treatment at a facility is not available. If a treatment facility is not available, an incapacitated person may be held in protective custody at a police station **until he is no longer incapacitated** or **for a period of not longer than 12 hours**, whichever is shorter.
IMPORTANT INFORMATION	
FTS's Can be used	To determine whether or not a person is intoxicated, the police officer may request the person to submit to reasonable tests of coordination, coherency of speech, and breath.
Standard of Belief to order FST's	In ***Com. v. McCaffrey***, the Court ruled that **reasonable suspicion** that the person is "incapacitated" is required in order to detain a person for further testing. [1473]
Reasonable Force may be used	A police officer acting in accordance with the provisions of this section may use such force as is reasonably necessary to carry out his authorized responsibilities.
Police Required to Seek Services from Nearest Facility	If any incapacitated person is assisted to a police station, the officer in charge or his designee shall notify forthwith the nearest facility that the person is being held in protective custody. If suitable treatment services are available at a facility, the department shall thereupon arrange for the transportation of the person to the facility.

[1473] *Commonwealth v. McCaffrey*, 49 Mass.App.Ct. 713, 716 (2000)

111B § 8	PROTECTIVE CUSTODY
BAC of .10% Presumed intoxicated	Any person who is administered a breathalyzer test shall be **presumed intoxicated** if evidence from said test indicates that the percentage of alcohol in his blood is **.10% or more and shall be placed in protective custody** at a police station or transferred to a facility.
BAC .05% or less must release	Any person who is administered a breathalyzer test, under this section, shall be presumed not to be intoxicated if evidence from said test indicates that the percentage of alcohol in his blood is **.05% or less and shall be released** from custody forthwith.
BAC more than .05% but less than .10%	If any person who is administered a breathalyzer test, under this section, and evidence from said test indicates that the percentage of alcohol in his blood is **more than .05% and is less than .10%** there shall be no presumption made based solely on the breathalyzer test. In such instance **a reasonable test of coordination or speech coherency must be administered to determine if said person is intoxicated**. Only when such test of coordination or speech coherency indicates said person is intoxicated shall he be placed in protective custody at a police station or transferred to a facility.
Search for Weapons Only	If the police officer *reasonably believes* that his safety or the safety of other persons present so requires, he may search the PC and his immediate surroundings, but only to the extent necessary to discover and seize any dangerous weapons which may on that occasion be used against the officer or other person present.
Inventory Searches are Permitted	If a person is held in protective custody at a police station all valuables and all articles which may pose a danger to the person or to others may be taken from him for safekeeping and if so taken shall be inventoried.
Record *Required* but Not Considered an Arrest	A person assisted to a facility or held in protective custody by the police shall not be considered to have been arrested or to have been charged with any crime. An entry of custody shall be made indicating the date, time, place of custody, the name of the assisting officer, the name of the officer in charge, whether the person held in custody exercised his right to make a phone call, whether the person held in custody exercised his right to take a breathalyzer test, and the results of the breathalyzer test if taken, which entry shall not be treated for any purposes, as an arrest or criminal record.
	SPECIAL RULES FOR JUVENILES HELD IN PC
Same rights for JV's	All rights afforded any person under chapter 111B shall apply to juveniles. chapter 111B § 10
Parent Notification Required	The **parent or guardian** of any person, **under the age of 18**, to be held in protective custody at a police station **shall be notified forthwith** upon his arrival at said station or as soon as possible thereafter.
Release to Parent Required c. 111B § 10	Any person **under the age of 18** who is a patient at a facility for protective custody, or held in protective custody at a police station, upon request of his parent or guardian, shall be released to the custody of the parent or guardian.
No Cell Detainment for 17 & under	Only those age 18 and older may be placed in a cell for the purposes of protective custody.
Juvenile Consent requires Parent	Any provisions of chapter 111B requiring the consent of a person shall, if the person is a juvenile, require the consent of both the juvenile and his parent or guardian. c. 111B § 10
	LIABILITY
c. 111B § 13	Police officers, facility administrators or other persons acting in a reasonable manner and pursuant to the provisions of chapter 111B shall not be held criminally or civilly liable for such acts (detaining someone in protective custody).

C. 123 § 35	COMMITMENT of ALCOHOLICS & SUBSTANCE ABUSERS
Commitment Order	• Any **police officer**, physician, spouse, blood relative, guardian or court official • may petition *in writing* any district court or any division of the juvenile court department • for an order of commitment of a person whom he has reason to believe is **an alcoholic or substance abuser**.
IMPORTANT INFORMATION	
Summons issued before warrant	The court shall immediately schedule a hearing on the petition and shall cause a summons and a copy of the application to be served upon the person. In the event of the person's failure to appear at the time summoned, the court may issue a warrant for the person's arrest.
Arrest only when Court is in Session	No arrest shall be made on such warrant unless the person may be presented immediately before a judge of the district court. The court shall order examination by a qualified physician or a qualified psychologist.
Up to 30 Day Commitment	If, after a hearing, the court based upon competent medical testimony finds that the person is an alcoholic or substance abuser and there is a likelihood of serious harm as a result of his alcoholism or substance abuse, it may order the person to be committed for a period not to exceed 30 days.
Court must notify DCJIS for FID/LTC purposes	The court, in its order, shall specify whether such commitment is based upon a finding that the person is a person with an alcohol use disorder, substance use disorder, or both. The court, upon ordering the commitment of a person found to be a person with an alcohol use disorder or substance use disorder pursuant to this section, **shall transmit the person's name and nonclinical identifying information, including the person's social security number and date of birth, to the department of criminal justice information services**. The court shall notify the person that such person is prohibited from being issued a firearm identification card pursuant to section 129B of chapter 140 or a license to carry pursuant to sections 131 and 131F of said chapter 140 unless a petition for relief pursuant to this section is subsequently granted. After 5 years from the date of commitment, a person found to be a person with an alcohol use disorder or substance use disorder and committed pursuant to this section may file a petition for relief with the court that ordered the commitment requesting that the court restore the person's ability to possess a firearm, rifle or shotgun.
DEFINITIONS (c. 123 § 35)	
Alcoholic	A person who chronically or habitually consumes alcoholic beverages to the extent that: 1) such use substantially injures his health or substantially interferes with his social or economic functioning, or 2) he has lost the power of self-control over the use of such beverages.
Substance abuser	A person who chronically or habitually consumes or ingests controlled substances to the extent that: 1) such use substantially injures his health or substantially interferes with his social or economic functioning, or 2) he has lost the power of self-control over the use of such controlled substances.
Free Legal help	There is a 24/7 resource with volunteer attorneys who will sometimes go as far as accompanying families to court to assist with § 35. If they are not able to service the caller, they should be able to refer them to someone who will meet their needs. Massachusetts Bar Association Hotline: 1-844-843-6221 or email: HelpUs@MassBar.org

PUBLIC PEACE OFFENSES

C.272 § 53	DISORDERLY CONDUCT & DISTURBING THE PEACE and its many variations
Overview	The disorderly conduct statute, as drafted by the legislature, was archaic, vague and incorporated a wide variety of conduct (see actual statutory language below). However, various court decisions have sculpted the various aspects of this crime. This crime covers a wide array of criminal behavior from disturbing the peace, to peeping tom, to prostitution, to indecent exposure.
Actual Statutory Language	Common night walkers, common street walkers, both male and female, persons who with offensive and disorderly acts or language accost or annoy another person, lewd, wanton and lascivious persons in speech or behavior, keepers of noisy and disorderly houses, and persons guilty of indecent exposure shall be punished...
ELEMENTS	
SJC Adopts the Model Penal Code	In 1975, the SJC adopted the **Model Penal Code definition of the offense of disorderly conduct** which provides: A person is guilty of disorderly conduct if, with purpose to cause *public* inconvenience, annoyance or alarm, or recklessly creating a risk thereof, he does any of the following: (a) Engages in **fighting or threatening, or in violent or tumultuous behavior**; or (b) Makes **unreasonable noise or offensively coarse utterance, gesture or display, or addresses abusive language to any person** present; or (c) **Creates a hazardous or physically offensive condition by any act which serves <u>no legitimate purpose</u> of the actor.** **Additional Public Element** In addition to the above the defendant's conduct must be **reasonably likely to affect the public** (or a substantial group) and that the defendant either intended to cause public inconvenience, annoyance or alarm, or recklessly created a risk of public inconvenience, annoyance or alarm.
Attorney Hanrahan's Note	Think of the above as three distinct offenses. 1. Violent, threatening & fighting behavior. 2. Unreasonable noise and bothering others. 3. Hazardous or physically offensive condition (with no legitimate purpose). For example if the person is violent and tumultuous the legitimate purpose aspect is not a defense. It would only be a defense if they created a hazardous or physically offensive condition. The following sections have been broken into the three distinct variations of this offense and the court decisions that have analyzed the various behaviors as it pertains to this statute. Additionally, there are a variety of "offenses" that are often treated as separate and distinct offenses but are actually various versions of violating the disorderly conduct statute, many of which have their own distinct elements that have evolved through common law (i.e. court decisions), such as *disturbing the peace, indecent exposure* and *accosting persons of the opposite sex*.
FIGHTING, THREATENING, VIOLENT OR TUMULTUOUS BEHAVIOR	
Flailing arms not enough	In ***Commonwealth v. Lopiano***, the Court found no violent or tumultuous behavior where the defendant, upon being told by police that he would be summoned to court for assault and battery, began to flail his arms and shout at police.[1]

[1] *Commonwealth v. Lopiano*, 60 Mass. App. Ct. 723,725-726, 805 N.E.2d 522, 525 (2004).

C.272 § 53	**DISORDERLY CONDUCT & DISTURBING THE PEACE and its many variations**
Failing to Obey a Police Order	In ***Commonwealth v. Marcarvage*** (2009), the Appeals Court ruled that "tumultuous behavior, for the purposes of § 53, includes the refusal to obey a police order." In this case the defendant was preaching, by way of a megaphone, in the face of passerbies. The police warned the defendant to stop but he persisted. The officers then attempted to confiscate the megaphone and the defendant resisted, eventually going limp as he clutched the megaphone bringing the officers to the ground with him. The court added "it is also significant to note that the police order by no means prevented the defendant from disseminating his message; rather, it was directed only at the manner of the defendant's delivery."
Threatening Behavior	In ***Commonwealth v. Milo***, a student was convicted of disorderly conduct for drawing pictures of his school teacher being shot.
Attorney Hanrahan's Note:	Basically, anytime someone is exhibiting violent or so-called "tumultuous" behavior in public this aspect of disorderly conduct has likely been violated.
UNREASONABLE NOISE AND DISTURBING OTHERS	
Offensive Language	General Laws c. 272, § 53 cannot constitutionally be applied to language and expressive conduct, even if it is offensive and abusive, unless it falls outside the scope of First Amendment protections, i.e. it constitutes "fighting words which by their very utterance tend to incite an immediate breach of the peace."[1]
Disturbing the Peace	Although § 53 mentions *disturbers of the peace* it does not define this crime so we turn to case law. In 1977, the SJC decided ***Commonwealth v. Orlando***, 371 Mass. 732. In this decision the Court analyzed these two elements: 1. Conduct which "tends to annoy all good citizens" 2. Did in fact annoy (or "infringe on one's right to be undisturbed") at least one person present **Note:** In a later Appellate Court decision, the court added the "intentional" element to the disturbing the peace offense. **Factors to Consider:** To amount to disturbing the peace, the defendant's acts must have been voluntary, unnecessary, and contrary to normal standards of conduct. Important factors to consider include: **Time and place** are factors to be considered in determining whether activities are 'unreasonably disruptive.' For instance, playing loud music at 2 in the afternoon is much different from playing loud music at 2 in the morning. **People affected:** The defendant disturbed the tranquility of at least one person in the area or interfered with at least person's normal activity. In *Commonwealth v. Piscopo*, the Court ruled that the fact that police were called will support inference that citizens of neighborhood were disturbed.[2] In ***Commonwealth v. Orlando***, the SJC ruled that "loud speech may be constitutionally proscribed when uttered late at night in a residential neighborhood, so that people are disturbed in their homes by the noise." [3] **Attorney Hanrahan's Note:** To convict someone of disturbing the peace you must show that someone was actually disturbed. It is not required to identify someone by name but it must be shown that at least one person's peace was disturbed.

[1] Commonwealth v. Richards, 369 Mass. 443, 445-450, 340 N.E.2d 892, 894-897 (1976); A Juvenile, 368 Mass. at 587- 595, 334 N.E.2d at 622-627; Commonwealth v. Sinai, 47 Mass. App. Ct. 544 at 546, 714 N.E.2d at 833. See Lewis v. New Orleans, 415 U.S. 130, 94 S.Ct. 970 (1974)
[2] *Commonwealth v. Piscopo*, 11 Mass. App. Ct. 905, 905, 414 N.E.2d 630, 631 (1981).
[3] *Commonwealth v. Orlando*, 371 Mass. 732, 733-736, 359 N.E.2d 310, 311-313 (1977).

C.272 § 53	DISORDERLY CONDUCT & DISTURBING THE PEACE and its many variations
Keeper of a disorderly house	The statutory language mentions the language *keepers of noisy and disorderly houses.* Many police departments tasked with policing college areas utilize this part of the statute to take action against students who repeatedly hold large, disturbing house parties.
Indecent Exposure	Chapter 272 § 53 does not define this crime but court decisions have determined that this crime falls within this statute. In 1937, the SJC decided ***Commonwealth v. Bishop***, which spelled out three elements to this crime: 1. Intentional 2. Lewd exposure of genitals to one or more persons 3. One or more persons were offended by the exposure **Attorney Hanrahan's note:** This crime is almost identical to Open and Gross however Indecent Exposure does not require the "shock and alarm" element. Open & Gross Lewdness is a felony. **See Sex Crime Section** of this manual for more on this offense and similar offenses.
Accost or annoy the opposite sex with offensive and disorderly acts	There are five elements to this offense:[1] 1. The defendant knowingly engaged in an offensive and disorderly act (or acts), or offensive and disorderly language (see definitions below). 2. The defendant intended to direct that conduct to the victim. 3. The victim was aware of the defendant's offensive and disorderly conduct. 4. The conduct was offensive to a reasonable person. 5. The person was of the opposite sex. The Appeals Court analyzed this aspect of the crime in its 2011 decision in ***Commonwealth v. Moran***. The defendant approached a nanny who was pushing a baby carriage on a public sidewalk. He yelled "Hey, nanny" and then began simulating masturbation with his hand by his groin area. The court provided the following definitions: c. An **"offensive" act** is one that causes "displeasure, anger or resentment; especially one that is repugnant to the prevailing sense of what is decent or moral." d. **"Disorderly" acts** include those that involve "threatening ... behavior." The threat need not involve physical contact, and "sexually explicit language, when directed at particular individuals in settings in which such communications are inappropriate and likely to cause severe distress, may be inherently threatening." The Court found that the defendant's conduct clearly was both offensive and disorderly. The Court also ruled that although the statute uses the plural term "acts," more than one act is not required to violate this law. **A single act sufficient.** The statute originally penalized "persons who with offensive and disorderly act or language accost or annoy persons of the opposite sex." In 1983, the word "act" was changed to "acts." St. 1983, c. 66, § 1. Nevertheless, "the change had no impact on the statute's meaning," *Commonwealth v. Moran*, 80 Mass. App. Ct. 8, 13, 951 N.E.2d 356, 360-361 (2011), and proof of a single disorderly and offensive act is sufficient. **Public or private.** The offense may be committed in public or in private.[2]

[1] The 2009 Model Jury Instructions (this law updated 2013).
[2] *Commonwealth v. Cahill*, 64 Mass. App. Ct. 911, 834 N.E.2d 1238 (2005) and *Commonwealth v. Chou*, 433 Mass. 229, 741 N.E.2d 12 (2001)

C.272 § 53	DISORDERLY CONDUCT & DISTURBING THE PEACE and its many variations
Lewd, Wanton and Lascivious Behavior	The SJC stated that the vague language in the statute was unconstitutionally clear. However, in a 1980 decision (***Com. v. Sefranka***) the SJC established the following elements for this offense: This statute prohibits: • The commission of conduct in a public place, or the public solicitation of conduct to be performed in a public place • When the conduct committed or solicited involves the **touching of the genitals, buttocks, or female breasts**, • for purposes of sexual arousal, gratification, or offense, • By a person who knows or should know of the presence of a person or persons who may be offended by the conduct. **See Sex Crimes Section for more on this and similar offenses**.
HAZARDOUS OR PHYSICALLY OFFENSIVE CONDITION (with no legitimate purpose)	
"Physically offensive condition"	If the act was physically offensive, it need not also be threatening, and vice versa. In *Commonwealth v. Chou*, the Court ruled that the distribution of sexually derogatory flyers concerning the victim was not physically offensive but was threatening. "Offensive acts are those that cause 'displeasure, anger or resentment; esp., repugnant to the prevailing sense of what is decent or moral.'" [1]
Peeping Tom	In ***Commonwealth v. LePore***, 40 Mass.App.Ct. 543 (1996), the Court ruled that a peeping tom (peering into the home of another where privacy would be expected) met the definition of disorderly conduct.
Creating a Traffic Hazard	In ***Com. v. Bosk***, the operator of a motor vehicle was guilty of disorderly conduct when he refused to re-enter his vehicle while on a major thoroughfare, insisting that he view the trooper's radar unit. He was creating a hazardous situation by forcing vehicles to pass around him, and insisting on looking at the officer's radar was not a legitimate purpose.
Legitimate Purpose Issues	A hazardous or physically offensive condition" branch of the statute cannot be applied to political protesters who block passage. In ***Com. v. Feigenbaum***, political protestors sat in the road and were arrested for disorderly conduct (creating a hazardous or physically offensive condition**)**. The SJC ruled although their actions may have been criminal, it was done for a legitimate purpose (political protest) and their convictions were overturned.[2] A disorderly conduct prosecution of political protesters is maintainable only under the first of the two branches. "[A]lthough conduct that is designed to call attention to a political cause, and may therefore have a legitimate purpose, may nevertheless be criminal under the common law or by some statute, it does not constitute disorderly conduct under the violent and tumultuous prong of G.L. c. 272, § 53" because it does serve a legitimate purpose of the actor.[3] In ***Com. v. Zettel***, a mother obstructing traffic in order to pick her child up at school was not guilty of disorderly conduct because her actions weren't tumultuous and she had a legitimate purpose (picking up her child).
Arrest Power, Penalties & Important Notes	
Power of Arrest	**Misdemeanor:** c. 272 § 54 authorizes a warrantless arrest for disorderly conduct offenses when "the offender is found in a public way or other public place." This terminology should be interpreted as committed in the officer's presence and in public (see "public" comments below).

[1] *Cahill*, 446 Mass. at 781, 847 N.E.2d at 346, quoting Black's Law Dictionary 1113 (8th ed. 2004).
[2] *Commonwealth v. Feigenbaum*, 404 Mass. 471, 536 N.E.2d 325 (1989).
[3] *Commonwealth v. Feigenbaum*, 404 Mass. 471, 536 N.E.2d 325 (1989).and 2009 Model Jury Instructions.

C.272 § 53	DISORDERLY CONDUCT & DISTURBING THE PEACE and its many variations
Penalty	***Disorderly persons*** **and** ***disturbers of the peace***: 1st offense a fine of not more than $150. **2nd offense**: imprisonment in a jail or house of correction for not more than 6 months, or by a fine of not more than $200, or by both such fine and imprisonment. **All other offenses (prostitution, lewdness, etc.) punished under c. 272 § 53**: Imprisonment in a jail or HOC for not more than 6 months, or by a fine of not more than $200, or by both such fine and imprisonment.
The Public Requirement of Disorderly Conduct	*Public* means affecting or likely to affect persons in a place to which the public or a substantial group has access,' quoted in ***Alegata v. Commonwealth,*** 353 Mass. at 304, 231 N.E.2d 201 at 211 (1967). The conduct does not have to occur in public it just has to be likely to affect persons nearby. In one case, ***Commonwealth v. Collins*** (1994) the police station booking area was deemed a public place, and in ***Com. v. Ormonde***, kicking the door of a cruiser and spitting, while at the station, was deemed disorderly conduct.

C. 277 § 39	AFFRAY
	Elements
1.	Fighting by or between two or more persons
2.	In some public place
3.	So as to cause alarm to the public
	Arrest Power, Penalties & Notes
Power of Arrest	**Misdemeanor** – there is no statutory authority granting warrantless powers of arrest for this offense. However, if the offense is committed in public, in the officer's presence, and is creating a **breach of the peace** an arrest would be lawful.
Penalty	Since the General Laws do not specify a penalty for common law affray, a convicted defendant should be punished under G.L. c. 279 § 5, which provides for "such sentence, according to the nature of the crime, as conforms to the common usage and practice in the commonwealth." See *Com. v. Nee*, 83 Mass. App. Ct. 441, 447 (2013)
Attorney Hanrahan's Comment	The crime of affray originates from British common law. "An Affray is a publick offense to the terror of the King's subjects, and ... so called, because it affrighteth and maketh men afraid...." No less now than historically, affray is an offense against the public, an aggravated disturbance of the public peace that arises when two or more people fight in public and cause terror to those present.[1]
	Related Statutes, Case Law & Other Important Information
No limited to willing participants	In the 2013 case of ***Commonwealth v. Nee***, the Appeals Court ruled that the common law crime of affray is not limited to *willing participants*. In this case the defendant was convicted of affray after the defendant, and a group of his friends, attacked an off-duty police officer and two of his companions.

[1] Commonwealth v. Matthew Nee (2013).

C. 269 § 1	RIGHT TO DISPERSE AN UNLAWFUL ASSEMBLY
Right to Disperse	○ If 5 or more persons, being armed with clubs or other dangerous weapons, or ○ if 10 or more persons, whether armed or not, • are unlawfully, riotously or tumultuously assembled in a city or town, • the mayor and each of the aldermen of such city, each of the selectmen of such town, every justice of the peace living in any such city or town, any member of the city, town, or state police and the sheriff of the county and his deputies • shall go among the persons so assembled, or • as near to them as may be with safety, • and in the name of the commonwealth command all persons so assembled immediately and peaceably to disperse; • and if they do not thereupon immediately and peaceably disperse, • each of said magistrates and officers shall command the assistance of all persons there present in suppressing such riot or unlawful assembly and arresting such persons.
UMass Amherst	For the purposes of this section, the University of Massachusetts at Amherst shall be considered to be a town.
Attorney Hanrahan's Note	This chapter and section authorizes police to disperse groups unlawfully assembled. Caution should be used as to not infringe on someone's First Amendment rights. However, if the people are armed "with dangerous weapons" you may have a 269 § 10(b) violation.
Arrest Power, Penalties & Notes	
Power of Arrest	**See Chapter 269 § 2 below**

C. 269 § 2	REFUSING TO DISPERSE OR TO ASSIST IN THE DISPERSAL OF AN UNLAWFUL ASSEMBLY
Elements	
1.	The defendant being present and being commanded: ▪ to assist in arresting rioters or persons so unlawfully assembled, or ▪ in suppressing such riot or unlawful assembly
2.	• refuses or neglects to obey the command, or • if required by a magistrate or officer to depart from the place, refuses or neglects so to do
3.	shall be considered one of the rioters or persons unlawfully assembled
Arrest Power, Penalties & Notes	
Power of Arrest	**Misdemeanor** – there is no statutory authority granting powers of arrest for this offense. However, if the offense is committed in public, in the officer's presence, and is creating a **breach of the peace** an arrest would be lawful.
Penalty	Imprisonment for not more than one year or by a fine of not less than $100 or more $500, or both.
Attorney Hanrahan's Comment	This offense carries a more severe penalty than disorderly conduct and it may be a more appropriate charge if the circumstances warrant.

C. 272 § 40	DISTURBANCE OF SCHOOLS OR ASSEMBLIES
	Elements
1.	The defendant willfully
2.	Interrupts or disturbs
3.	A school or other assembly of people met for a lawful purpose
	Arrest Power, Penalties & Notes
Power of Arrest	**Misdemeanor** – there is no statutory authority granting powers of arrest for this offense. However, if the offense is committed in public, in the officer's presence, and is creating a **breach of the peace** an arrest would be lawful.
Penalty	Imprisonment for not more than 1 month or by a fine of not more than $50.00. **Minimum Mandatory**: If *within one year after being twice convicted* of a violation of this section, again violates the provisions of this section shall be punished by imprisonment for 1 month, and the sentence imposing such **imprisonment shall not be suspended**.
Attorney Hanrahan's Comment	Because of the potential for a more severe penalty this offense may be a better option that disorderly conduct if the circumstances warrant.
	Related Statutes, Case Law & Other Important Information
Defacing a Schoolhouse	See Chapter 266 § 98 (Property Destruction section)
Threats – School	See Chapter 269 § 14 (Threat Crimes Section)

C. 272 § 41	DISTURBANCE OF LIBRARIES
	Elements
1.	The defendant willfully disturb persons assembled in a public library, or a reading room connected to a the library
2.	By making a noise or in any other manner
3.	During the time when such library or reading room is open to the public
	Arrest Power, Penalties & Notes
Power of Arrest	**Misdemeanor** – there is no statutory authority granting warrantless powers of arrest for this offense. However, if the offense is committed in public, in the officer's presence, and is creating a **breach of the peace** an arrest would be lawful.
Penalty	Imprisonment for not more than 30 days or by a fine of not more than $100, or both.

C. 272 § 42	DISTURBANCE OF FUNERAL PROCESSION
Elements	
1.	The defendant willfully interrupt
2.	• by fast driving, or • in any other way disturbs
3.	a funeral assembly or procession
Arrest Power, Penalties & Notes	
Power of Arrest	**Misdemeanor** – there is no statutory authority granting warrantless powers of arrest for this offense. However, if the offense is committed in public, in the officer's presence, and is creating a **breach of the peace** an arrest would be lawful.
Penalty	Imprisonment for not more than 1 month or by a fine of not more than $50.00. **Minimum Mandatory**: If *within one year after being twice convicted* of a violation of this section, again violates the provisions of this section shall be punished by imprisonment for 1 month, and the sentence imposing such **imprisonment shall not be suspended**.
Related Statutes, Case Law & Other Important Information	
Funeral right to use parkway	See Chapter 85 § 14A (in the Motor Vehicle Law section of this manual)

C. 272 § 42A	DISTURBANCE OF FUNERAL SERVICES
Elements	
1.	Picket, loiter or otherwise create a disturbance
2.	**within 500 feet** of a funeral home, church or temple or other building where funeral services are being held
Arrest Power, Penalties, Notes & Related Statutes	
Power of Arrest	**Misdemeanor** – there is no statutory authority granting warrantless powers of arrest for this offense. However, if the offense is committed in public, in the officer's presence, and is creating a **breach of the peace** an arrest would be lawful.
Penalty	a fine of not more than $1,000 dollars or by imprisonment for not more than 1 year in a HOC, or both.
Attorney Hanrahan's Comment	This offense could be used to address those groups who picket and disrupt the funerals of fallen soldiers. However, caution should be used not to be drawn into a First Amendment right violation. Oddly, the law was drafted to require a building ("or other building") to be involved for this offense to apply. They may protest but the law indicates they must do so from 500 feet away from the church, temple, funeral home or "building." This would not apply to the cemetery unless a building was near-by.

C. 272 § 42A	DISTURBANCE OF FUNERAL SERVICES
Disturbing of a Military funeral	Chapter 272 § 48B offers a harsher penalty for those who disturb a military funeral. The statute states: Whoever willfully pickets, loiters or otherwise creates a disturbance within 500 feet of a funeral home, church, temple, **burial** or other building where military funeral services are being held, shall be punished by a fine of NMT $2,000 or by imprisonment for not more than 2 years in a HOC, or both. **Attorney Hanrahan's note**: section 42A the 500 foot zone is limited to a building or other structure but section 42B (military funeral) also protects the burial site.
Removing flowers, flags & memorials c. 272 § 75	Whoever, without authority, removes flowers, flags or memorial tokens from any grave, tomb, monument or burial lot in any cemetery or other place of burial shall be punished by a fine of not more than $1,000 or by imprisonment for not more than six months.
Injuring tombs, graves, etc. c. 272 § 73	Whoever wilfully destroys, mutilates, defaces, injures or removes a tomb, monument, gravestone, veteran's grave marker or metal plaque, veteran's flag holder that commemorates a particular war, conflict or period of service or flag, or other structure or thing which is placed or designed for a memorial of the dead, or a fence railing, curb or other thing which is intended for the protection or ornament of a structure or thing before mentioned or of an enclosure for the burial of the dead, or wilfully removes, destroys, mutilates, cuts, breaks or injures a tree, shrub or plant placed or being within such enclosure, or wantonly or maliciously disturbs the contents of a tomb or a grave, shall be punished by imprisonment in the state prison for not more than 5 years or by imprisonment in the jail or house of correction for not more than two and one-half years and by a fine of not more $5,000.
Disinterring bodies c. 272 § 71	Whoever, not being lawfully authorized by the proper authorities, wilfully digs up, disinters, removes or conveys away a human body, or the remains thereof, or knowingly aids in such disinterment, removal or conveying away, and whoever is accessory thereto either before or after the fact, shall be punished by imprisonment in the state prison for not more than 3 years or in jail for not more than 2½ years or by a fine of not more than $4,000.

C. 272 § 43	DISORDERLINESS IN PUBLIC CONVEYANCES
	Elements
1.	Being disorderly, or disturb or annoy travelers by profane, obscene or indecent language, or by indecent behavior
2.	While in or upon a railroad carriage, steamboat or other public conveyance (buses, trolleys etc)
	Arrest Power, Penalties & Notes
Power of Arrest	**Misdemeanor** – there is no statutory authority granting warrantless powers of arrest for this offense. However, if the offense is committed in public, in the officer's presence, and is creating a **breach of the peace** an arrest would be lawful.
Penalty	Imprisonment for not more than 1 month or by a fine of not more than $50.00. **Minimum Mandatory**: If *within one year after being twice convicted* of a violation of this section, again violates the provisions of this section shall be punished by imprisonment for 1 month, and the sentence imposing such **imprisonment shall not be suspended**.
Attorney Hanrahan's Comment	First offense disorderly conduct no longer has the possibility of jail time so this offense may be appropriate if the circumstances warrant.
	Related Statutes, Case Law & Other Important Information
Related Offenses	**Smoking in Public conveyance** (see Chapter 272 § 43A) **Blasting Tunes on Public Conveyance (**See Chapter 265 § 42)

PUBLIC PEACE OFFENSES

C. 272 § 43	DISORDERLINESS IN PUBLIC CONVEYANCES
Throwing or Shooting Missiles or Interfering with a Conductor **c. 159 § 104**	• The defendant willfully throws or shoots a missile at a locomotive engine, or railroad or railway car or train, or at a motor bus or trackless trolley vehicle, or at a school bus, or at a person on such engine, car, train, motor bus or trackless trolley vehicle, or school bus, or • The defendant in any way assaults or interferes with a conductor, engineer, brakeman, motorman or operator while in the performance of his duty on or near such engine, car, train, motor bus or trackless trolley vehicle, or school bus. **Penalty:** by a fine of not more than $500 or by imprisonment for not more than 1 year, or both. **Arrest Powers**: **Misdemeanor** – If such person commits such offense in the presence of such officer and refuses to state his name and address at the request of such officer, he may be arrested without a warrant.

C. 265 § 42	USE OF RADIOS PUBLIC CONVEYANCES
	Elements
1.	Using a radio or boom box, or similar broadcasting equipment
2.	without the use of earphones or other apparatus
3.	on a public conveyance used for the common carriage of persons (buses, trolleys etc)
	Arrest Power, Penalties & Notes
Power of Arrest	**Misdemeanor** – there is no statutory authority granting warrantless powers of arrest for this offense. However, if the offense is committed in public, in the officer's presence, and is creating a **breach of the peace** an arrest would be lawful.
Penalty	A fine of not less than $100 nor more than $500 or by imprisonment for not more than 1 month
Item seized and sold	Evidence seized pursuant to this section shall be sold at public auction and the proceeds therefrom may be applied against outstanding fines and court costs.

C. 272 § 43A	SMOKING IN PUBLIC CONVEYANCES AND TERMINALS
	Elements
1.	Smoking or carrying an open flame or lighted match, cigar, cigarette, or pipe
2.	• in or upon a railroad carriage, steamboat, or other public conveyance (buses, trolleys etc), or • in a terminal or other facility of the Massachusetts Bay Transportation Authority
	Arrest Power, Penalties & Notes
Power of Arrest	**Misdemeanor** – there is no statutory authority granting warrantless powers of arrest for this offense other than the provision noted below. However, if the offense is committed in public, in the officer's presence, and is creating a **breach of the peace** an arrest would be lawful. **Note:** c. 161A § 42 provides enforcement power to this statute. c. 161A § 42 states in part: If, after an officer delivers a notice to an offender, the offender continues to violate said section 43A of said c. 272, an officer *of the authority* **may arrest such offender without a warrant**. Any offender arrested under this section shall be subject to the fines and penalties provided under the provisions of c. 272 S 43A.
Penalty	Imprisonment for not more than 10 days or by a fine of not more than $100, or both such fine and imprisonment

C. 265 § 35	THROWING OR DROPPING OBJECTS ONTO PUBLIC WAY
Elements	
1.	The defendant willfully or negligently
2.	Drops, throws or otherwise releases any object, missile or other article
3.	Onto any way as defined in c. 90 §1, the turnpike as defined in clause (*b*) of chapter 354 § 4 of the acts of 952 or the tunnels as defined in clause (*d*) of 598§ 1 of the acts of 1958 (**in short a public way or a way open to the public)**
4.	So that the lives or safety of the public might be endangered
Arrest Power, Penalties & Notes	
Power of Arrest	**Misdemeanor** – there is no statutory authority granting warrantless powers of arrest for this offense. However, if the offense is committed in public, in the officer's presence, and is creating a **breach of the peace** an arrest would be lawful.
Penalty	A fine of not more than $100, or by imprisonment for not more than 1 year, or both.
Attorney Hanrahan's Comment	If damage results from throwing objects into the public way you may also have a malicious destruction of property charge – see chapter 266 § 126A and chapter 266 § 127.

C. 265 § 36	THROWING/DROPPING OBJECTS AT SPORTING EVENTS
Elements	
1.	Willfully drop, throw or otherwise release any object, missile or other article
2.	at any sporting event
3.	with the intent to injure any person at the event
Arrest Power, Penalties & Notes	
Power of Arrest	**Misdemeanor** – there is no statutory authority granting warrantless powers of arrest for this offense. However, if the offense is committed in public, in the officer's presence, and is creating a **breach of the peace** an arrest would be lawful.
Penalty	a fine of not more than $500 or by imprisonment in the HOC for not more than 1 year, or both.
Related Statutes	
Damaging a Goal Post	See Chapter 266 § 104A (crimes against property section)
Abuse of Participants & Officials at Sporting Event c. 272 S 36A	Whoever, having arrived at the age of 16 years, directs any profane, obscene or impure language or slanderous statement at a participant or an official in a sporting event, shall be punished by a fine of not more than $50.

PUBLIC HEALTH

C. 111 § 111C	UNPROTECTED EXPOSURE TO INFECTIOUS DISEASE
Exposure requires completion of trip form	• Any person, including without limitation, a police officer, fire fighter, emergency medical technician, corrections officer, ambulance operator or attendant • who, while acting in his professional capacity, • attends, assists, or transports a person or deceased person to a health care facility licensed under c. 111 § 51, and who sustains an unprotected exposure capable of transmitting an infectious disease dangerous to the public health, • shall immediately, upon arrival at such facility, provide to the admitting agent or other appropriate employee of the said facility a standardized trip form. • The department shall prepare and distribute said standardized trip form, which shall include, but need not be limited to the names of persons who believe they have had such unprotected exposure, and the manner in which such exposure occurred.
Facility required to notify person exposed	Any health care facility licensed under c. 111 § 51 which, after receiving a transported individual or deceased person, diagnoses the individual or deceased person as having an infectious disease dangerous to the public health as defined pursuant to the provisions of this section, shall notify orally within **48 hours** after making such a diagnosis, and in **writing within 72 hours** of such diagnosis, any individual listed on the trip report who has sustained an unprotected exposure which, in the opinion of the health care facility is capable of transmitting such disease. Such response shall include, but not be limited to, the appropriate medical precautions and treatments which should be taken by the party who has sustained the unprotected exposure; provided, however, that the identity of the patient suspected of having such disease shall not be released in such response, and shall be kept confidential in accordance with the provisions of section seventy. The department shall determine the method by which the response to the trip report is conveyed, and shall assure the patient or deceased person's legal representative or next of kin, if there is no legal representative is informed of those individuals who have been notified of his disease pursuant to this section, and that the response is directed only to those parties who have sustained an unprotected exposure to an infectious disease.
Definitions & Other Important Information	
Definitions	"**Infectious diseases dangerous to the public health**" shall be defined by department regulations which shall be promulgated pursuant to this section. "**Unprotected exposure capable of transmitting an infectious disease dangerous to the public health**" shall be defined in regulations promulgated by the department and shall include, but not be limited to, instances of direct mouth-to-mouth resuscitation, or the co-mingling of the blood of the patient and the person who has transported the patient to the health care facility.

C. 270 § 16	LITTERING
Elements	
1.	The defendant places, throws, deposits or discharges or whoever causes to be placed, thrown, deposited or discharged,
2.	Trash, bottles or cans, refuse, rubbish, garbage, debris, scrap, waste or other material of any kind: • on (or within 20 yards of) a public highway • on any other public land • in or upon (or within 20 yards of) coastal or inland waters • on property of another (without permission) • on lands dedicated for open space purposes
Exception	The provisions of this section shall not be applicable to any dumping ground approved under section 150A A of c. 111 or by other appropriate public authority.
Arrest Power, Penalties & Notes	
Power of Arrest	**Chapter 270 § 16A**: An officer may request the offender (who litters) to state his name and address. If the offender refuses to state his name and address, or if he states a false name and address or a name and address which is not his name and address in ordinary use, he may be arrested without a warrant.
Penalty	**Littering**: 1st Offense: fine of not more than $5,500. 2nd or Subsequent Offense: a fine not to exceed $15,000. **Penalty for refusing or providing false information**: a fine of not less than $50 nor more than $100.
Attorney Hanrahan's Comment	There are a variety of statutes that address littering however this particular statute covers most situations (i.e. "on any public land" and "on property of another"). Additionally, it provides for RMV sanctions (if involving a vehicle) and arrest powers (under certain circumstances).
Related Statutes, Case Law & Other Important Information	
Littering involving a motor vehicle c. 270 § 16	If a motor vehicle is used (to litter); and the unlawful disposal consists of more than 7 cubic feet of trash etc. and the motor vehicle is observed while the offense is in progress by an officer, the officer may seize the vehicle and remove and store it or otherwise immobilize it by a mechanical device until: 1) Payment is made to the enforcing authority of a fine set by such enforcing authority up to the maximum fine which may be imposed under this section, 2) The illegally disposed of material is removed and legally disposed of, and 3) Payment is made to the enforcing authority of its reasonable towing and storage charges, if any, for the seized vehicle. **RMV Action** (if vehicle is used): 30 day license suspension and if the owner committed the offense the registration may be suspended for 30 days. **RMV Action**: C. 90 § 22 authorizes the RMV, after a hearing, to suspend for a period not exceeding seven days the license or permit to operate motor vehicles or the right of a person to operate motor vehicles in the commonwealth of any person who litters, or who knowingly permits, as the operator, occupants of his vehicle to litter, public or private property through the disposal of trash or garbage from his/her motor vehicle
Lighted cigarettes: throwing from vehicles or placing on forest/lands/ fields	Chapter 148 § 54 states "whoever drops or throws from any vehicle while the same is upon a public or private way running along or near forest land or open fields, or, except as permitted by law, drops, throws, deposits or otherwise places in or upon forest land, any lighted cigarette, cigar, match, live ashes or other flaming or glowing substance, or any substance or thing which in and of itself is likely to cause a fire, shall be punished by a fine of not more than $100 or by imprisonment for not more than 30 days."
Disposal in Containers Placed Along Highways c. 270 § 17	Whoever disposes of household or commercial garbage or refuse by placing it in a trash barrel placed on a public highway by the commonwealth, or by any political subdivision thereof for the convenience of the traveling public shall be punished by a fine of not less than $200. Note: ½ of any fine paid into a court shall be paid over to the city or town where the offense occurred.

PUBLIC HEALTH LAWS

C. 270 § 16	LITTERING
Disposal of rubbish: arrest without a warrant **c. 272 § 60**	Whoever commits a misdemeanor, as defined by a by-law, regulation or ordinance of a town or authority therein, in the presence of a police officer or an officer authorized to serve criminal process, the substance of which misdemeanor is the placing on or in or throwing into a public way, the sidewalk of a public way or a public alley, filth, rubbish or other substance, and, being requested by such officer forthwith to remove it, refuses or neglects so to do, and if the identity of such person is unknown to the officer, may be arrested by such officer and detained in a safe place without a warrant until his identity is ascertained. Reasonable diligence shall be exercised by the arresting officer in ascertaining the identity of the offender and when identified he shall be released from arrest unless a warrant has issued against him.
Illegal dumping **c. 266 § 146**	Whoever willfully and without right deposits solid waste in a commercial disposal container of another without the consent of the owner or other person who has legal custody, care or control thereof shall be punished by a fine of not less than $100, nor more than $1,000. **Definition**: For purposes of this section "**solid waste**" shall mean garbage, refuse, trash, rubbish, sludge, residue or by-products of processing or treatment of discarded material, and any other solid, semi-solid or liquid discarded material resulting from domestic, commercial, mining, industrial, agricultural, municipal, or other sources or activities, but shall not include solid or dissolved material in domestic sewage.
Glass; throwing in public streets and beaches **c. 265 § 32**	The defendant throws or drops glass on a public way, or on or near a bathing beach, or on a public way, sidewalk or reservation in the immediate neighborhood of a bathing beach. **Penalty:** a fine of not more than $100 or by imprisonment for not more than 1 month.
Willful defilement of sources of water supply **c. 111 § 171**	Willfully deposit excrement or foul or decaying matter in water used for domestic water supply, or upon the shore thereof within 5 rods of the water, or whoever bathes in such water. **Penalty:** a fine of not more than $50 or by imprisonment for not more than 1 month. **Arrest Powers:** A police officer or constable of a town where such water is wholly or partially situated, acting within the limits of such town, and any executive officer or agent of a water board, board of water commissioners, public institution or water company furnishing water or ice for domestic purposes, acting upon ... and not more than five rods from the water, may without a warrant arrest any person found in the act of violating this section.

C. 270 § 14	EXPECTORATING (SPITTING IN PUBLIC)
	Elements
1.	The defendant expectorates or spits,
2.	upon any public sidewalk, or upon any place used exclusively or principally by pedestrians, or, except in receptacles provided for the purpose, in or upon any part of any city or town hall, any court house or court room, any public library or museum, any church or theatre, any lecture or music hall, any mill or factory, any hall of any tenement building occupied by 5 or more families, any school building, any ferry boat or steamboat, any railroad car or elevated railroad car, except a smoking car, any street railway car, any railroad or railway station or waiting room, or on any track, platform or sidewalk connected therewith, and included within the limits thereof.
	Arrest Power, Penalties & Notes
Power of Arrest	Chapter 270 § 15 states **"any person detected in the act of violating the preceding section (spitting) may,** if his name is unknown to the officer**, be** arrested without a warrant **by any officer authorized to serve criminal process in the place where the offence is committed and kept in custody until he can be taken before a court having jurisdiction of such offence."**
Penalty	a fine of not more than $20.

C. 123 § 12	EMERGENCY RESTRAINT OF DANGEROUS PERSONS (AKA SECTION 12/PINK SLIP)
	3 Day Commitment
3 Day Hospitalization	Any physician or a qualified psychologist who after examining a person has **reason to believe** that the failure to hospitalize the person would **create a likelihood of serious harm** by reason of **mental illness** may restrain or authorize the restraint of such person and apply for the hospitalization of such person for a three day period at a public or private facility.
Emergency Involuntary Committal	If an **examination is not possible** because of the emergency nature of the case and because of the refusal of the person to consent to such examination, the physician, qualified psychologist or qualified psychiatric nurse mental health clinical specialist on the basis of the facts and circumstances may determine that hospitalization is necessary and may apply for an **involuntary committal**.
A Police Officer May Restrain in an Emergency	In an emergency situation, if a physician, qualified psychologist or qualified psychiatric nurse mental health clinical specialist is not available, **a police officer**, who believes that failure to hospitalize a person would **create a likelihood of serious harm by reason of mental illness** may restrain such person and apply for the hospitalization of such person for a three day period at a public facility or a private facility authorized for such purpose by the department.
Any Person may *apply* for a Warrant of Apprehension	**Any person** may make application to a district court justice or a justice of the juvenile court department for a three day commitment to a facility of a mentally ill person whom the failure to confine would cause a likelihood of serious harm.
Discharge	A person shall be discharged at the end of the three day period unless the superintendent applies for a commitment under the provisions of sections seven and eight of this chapter or the person remains on a voluntary status.
	Related Statutes, Case Law & Other Important Information
Likelihood of serious harm	Chapter 123 § 1 defines "likelihood of serious harm" as: (1) a substantial risk of physical harm to the person **himself** as manifested by evidence of, **threats of, or attempts** at, suicide or serious bodily harm; (2) a substantial risk of physical harm to **other persons** as manifested by evidence of homicidal or other violent behavior or evidence that others are placed in reasonable fear of violent behavior and serious physical harm to them; or (3) a very substantial risk of physical impairment or injury to the person **himself** as manifested by evidence that such person's judgment is so affected that he is **unable to protect himself** in the community and that reasonable provision for his protection is not available in the community.
Civil Liability Protections C. 123 § 22	Physicians, qualified psychologists, qualified psychiatric nurse mental health clinical specialists and police officers shall be immune from civil suits for damages for restraining, transporting, applying for the admission of or admitting any person to a, if the physician, qualified psychologist, qualified psychiatric nurse mental health clinical specialist or police officer acts pursuant to chapter 123.
Substance Abuser Commitment	Chapter 123 § 35 provides a method of forcing a substance abuser into treatment. **See the Alcohol section of this manual for more information.**
Emergency Entry	In ***McCabe v. Life-Line Ambulance Service***, regarding a warrantless entry to take custody of a mentally ill person, under a section 12. The 1st Circuit upheld the entry as a "special needs" entry.[1] See the Warrantless Search Section of the manual for more on this topic.

MENTAL HEALTH

[1] *McCabe v. Life-Line ambulance Service*, 77 F.3d 540

Public Justice Offenses

CRIMINAL CONTEMPT OF COURT	
Elements	
Criminal Contempt (Common Law Offense)	In order to prove a defendant guilty of criminal contempt, the Commonwealth must prove beyond a reasonable doubt that: • There was a clear, outstanding order of the court, • That the defendant knew about the order, and • That the defendant clearly and intentionally disobeyed the order in circumstances in which he was able to obey it." [1485]
Attorney Hanrahan's Note	The crime of criminal contempt is a common law offense meaning that it was not enacted by the legislature but rather through case law or precedent.
Arrest Power, Penalties & Notes	
Power of Arrest	In most cases a warrant would have to be sought in order to make an arrest for contempt.
Related Statutes, Case Law & Other Important Information	
Fail to Appear **c. 276 § 26**	If a defendant properly summoned to court fails, without reasonable cause, to appear and abide the orders of the court or justice, he shall be considered in contempt of court, and may be punished by a fine of not more than $20. A warrant, if necessary, may be issued at any time after the issue of such summons, whether it has been served or not.
Failure to appear in court after release on bail or recognizance **c. 276 § 82A**	A person who is released by court order or other lawful authority on bail or recognizance on condition that he will appear personally at a specified time and place and who fails without sufficient excuse to so appear shall be punished. **Penalty**: a fine of not more than $10,000 or by imprisonment in a HOC for not more than 1 year, or both, in the case of a misdemeanor, and by a fine of not more than $50,000 and imprisonment in a **state prison (F)** for not more than 5 years, or a HOC for not more than 2½ years, or by fine and imprisonment, in the case of a felony. **Arrest Powers: Felony** – a police officer may effect an arrest for this offense committed in his/her presence or for an offense in the past, on probable cause. A term of imprisonment imposed under this section shall be consecutive to any other sentence of imprisonment for the offense for which the prisoner failed to appear.

[1485] *Commonwealth v. Brogan,* 415 Mass. 169, 171, 612 N.E.2d 656 (1993), quoting *Furtado v. Furtado,* 380 Mass. 137, 145, 402 N.E.2d 1024 (1980).

C. 268 § 1	PERJURY
Elements	
1.	• The defendant, being lawfully required to depose the truth in a judicial proceeding or in a proceeding in a course of justice, willfully swears or affirms falsely in a matter material to the issue or point in question, or • The defendant, being required by law to take an oath or affirmation, willfully swears or affirms falsely in a matter relative to which such oath or affirmation is required.
Arrest Power, Penalties & Notes	
Power of Arrest	**Felony** – a police officer may effect a warrantless arrest for this offense provided he/she has probable cause that the suspect committed the offense.
Penalty	Whoever commits perjury on the trial of an indictment for a capital crime shall be punished by imprisonment in the **state prison (F)** for life or for any term of years, and whoever commits perjury in any other case shall be punished by imprisonment in the state prison (F) for not more than 20 years or by a fine of not more than $1,000 or by imprisonment in jail for not more than 2½ years, or by both such fine and imprisonment in jail.
Related Statutes, Case Law & Other Important Information	
Statements containing declaration relative to penalties of perjury **c. 268 § 1A**	No written statement required by law shall be required to be verified by oath or affirmation before a magistrate if it contains or is verified by a written declaration that it is made under the penalties of perjury. Whoever signs and issues such a written statement containing or verified by such a written declaration shall be guilty of perjury and subject to the penalties thereof if such statement is willfully false in a material matter.
Subornation of perjury **c. 268 § 2**	Whoever is guilty of subornation of perjury, by procuring another person to commit perjury, shall be punished as for perjury.
Attempt to procure another to commit perjury **c. 268 § 3**	The defendant attempts to incite or procure another person to commit perjury, although no perjury is committed. **Penalty:** imprisonment in the **state prison (F)** for not more than 5 years or in jail for not more than 1 year.
Perjury involving statements alleging motor vehicle theft **c. 268 § 39**	The defendant knowingly makes a false written statement on a form bearing notice that false statements made therein are punishable under the penalty of perjury, to a police officer, police department or the registry of motor vehicles alleging the theft or conversion of a motor vehicle. **Penalty: 1st Offense**: imprisonment not less than 5 months, nor more than 2 years, or a fine of not less than $250 and not more than $2,500, or both. **2nd or subsequent offense:** shall be punished by imprisonment **not less than 1**, nor more than 5 years, or a fine of not less than $500 and not more than $5,000, or both. No CWOF or place on file permitted for this offense. **Note:** although this state does not specifically mention state prison, a second offense would be deemed a **felony** as it imposes a 5 year sentence and the HOC is limited to a maximum 2½ year sentence. **Arrest Powers**: **Misdemeanor** – there is no statutory authority granting powers of arrest for this offense. However, if the offense is committed in public, in the officer's presence, and is creating a **breach of the peace** an arrest would be lawful.
Police Officer filing False Reports	The defendant, being an officer or employee of the commonwealth or of any political subdivision thereof or of any authority created by the general court, in the course of his official duties executes, files or publishes any false written report, minutes or statement, knowing the same to be false in a material matter. **Penalty**: A fine of not more than $1,000 or by imprisonment for not more than 1 year, or by both such fine and imprisonment.

C. 268A § 2	BRIBERY/PUBLIC CORRUPTION
	Solicit/Accept a Bribe Elements
1.	The defendant, being a state, county or municipal employee or a member of the judiciary or a person selected to be such an employee or member of the judiciary, directly or indirectly,
2.	Corruptly asks, demands, exacts, solicits, seeks, accepts, receives or agrees to receive anything of value for himself or for any other person or entity, in return for one of the following:
3.	a) Being influenced in his performance of any official act or any act within his official responsibility, or b) Being influenced to commit or aid in committing, or to collude in, or allow any fraud, or make opportunity for the commission of any fraud, on the commonwealth or on a state, county or municipal agency, or c) Being induced to do or omit to do any acts in violation of his official duty;
	Offer a Bribe Elements
1.	The defendant, directly or indirectly, corruptly gives, offers or promises anything of value to any state, county or municipal employee (or any other person or entity), with intent to do any of the following:
2.	a) To influence any official act or any act within the official responsibility of such employee or member of the judiciary or person who has been selected to be such employee or member of the judiciary, or b) To influence such an employee or member of the judiciary or person who has been selected to be such an employee or member of the judiciary, to commit or aid in committing, or collude in, or allow, any fraud, or make opportunity for the commission of any fraud on the commonwealth or a state, county or municipal agency, or c) To induce such an employee or member of the judiciary or person who has been selected to be such an employee or member of the judiciary to do or omit to do any act in violation of his lawful duty;
	Offer Bribe to Influence Testimony Elements
1.	The defendant, directly or indirectly, corruptly gives, offers or promises anything of value to any person, or offers or promises such person to give anything of value to any other person or entity,
2.	**With intent to influence the testimony under oath or affirmation** of such first-mentioned person or any other person as a witness upon a trial, or other proceeding, before any court, any committee of either house or both houses of the general court, or any agency, commission or officer authorized by the laws of the commonwealth to hear evidence or take testimony, or with intent to influence such witness to absent himself therefrom.
	Solicit or Agree to Influence Testimony Elements
1.	The defendant, directly or indirectly, corruptly asks, demands, exacts, solicits, seeks, accepts, receives or agrees to receive anything of value for himself or for any other person or entity,
2.	In return for influence upon the testimony under oath or affirmation of himself or any other person as a witness upon any such trial, hearing or other proceeding or in return for the absence of himself or any other person therefrom.
	Arrest Power, Penalties & Notes
Power of Arrest	**Felony** – a police officer may effect a warrantless arrest for this offense provided he/she has probable cause that the suspect committed the offense.

C. 268A § 2	BRIBERY/PUBLIC CORRUPTION
Penalty	A fine of not more than $100,000, or by imprisonment in the state prison for not more than 10 years, or in a jail or HOC for not more than 2½ years, or both; and in the event of final conviction shall be incapable of holding any office of honor, trust or profit under the commonwealth or under any state, county or municipal agency.
Related Statutes, Case Law & Other Important Information	
Witness Intimidation	See Witness Intimidation later in this section.
Extortion	See extortion in threats section of this manual

C. 268 § 13E	TAMPERING WITH COURT PROCEEDINGS/EVIDENCE
Elements	
1.	The defendant alters, destroys, mutilates, or conceals (or attempts to do so)
2.	a record, document, or other object,
3.	with the intent to impair the record, document or object's integrity or availability for use in an official proceeding, whether or not the proceeding is pending at that time.
Arrest Power, Penalties & Notes	
Power of Arrest	**Felony** – a police officer may effect a warrantless arrest for this offense provided he/she has probable cause that the suspect committed the offense.
Penalty	(i) A fine of not more than $10,000, or by imprisonment in the state prison for not more than 5 years, or in a jail or house of correction for not more than 2½ years, or both, or (ii) if the official proceeding involves a violation of a criminal statute, by a fine of not more than $25,000, or by imprisonment in the state prison for not more than 10 years, or in a jail or house of correction for not more than 2½ years, or both.
Attorney Hanrahan's Comment	This offense can be used when someone tampers with evidence. The infamous Annie Dookhan, a state Crime Lab chemist, who falsified evidence testing was charged with this offense, among others, and subsequently convicted.
Related Statutes, Case Law & Other Important Information	
Definition	"Official proceeding", a proceeding before a court or grand jury, or a proceeding before a state agency or commission, which proceeding is authorized by law and relates to an alleged violation of a criminal statute or the laws and regulations enforced by the state ethics commission, the state secretary, the office of the inspector general, or the office of campaign and political finance, or an alleged violation for which the attorney general may issue a civil investigative demand.
Venue	A prosecution under this section may be brought in the county where the official proceeding was or would have been convened or where the alleged conduct constituting an offense occurred.
Evidentiary value not required	The record, document, or other object need not be admissible in evidence or free of a claim of privilege.

MANDATORY REPORTING OF CRIMES

Reports of crimes to law enforcement officials Chapter 268 § 40	
1.	Whoever knows that another person is a victim of one the following crimes: • Rape or aggravated rape, • Murder or manslaughter • Armed robbery and is at the scene of said crime,
2.	shall, to the extent that said person can do so without danger or peril to himself or others, report said crime to an appropriate law enforcement official as soon as reasonably practicable.
Arrest Power & Penalties	
Power of Arrest	No right of arrest.
Penalty	Any person who violates this section shall be punished by a fine of not less than $500 nor more than $2,500
Mandatory Reporting of Injuries Chapter 112 § 12A	
Gun Shot Wounds Must be Reported **c 112 § 12A**	Every physician attending or treating a case of bullet wound, gunshot wound, powder burn or any other injury arising from or caused **by the discharge** of a gun, pistol, **BB gun**, or other **air rifle** or firearm shall report such case at once to the **colonel of the state police and to the police of the town** where such physician, hospital, sanatorium or institution is located
Burn Injuries Must Be Reported **c 112 § 12A**	Every physician attending or treating a person with a **burn injury affecting 5% or more** of the surface area of his body notification shall be made at once to the state fire marshal and to the police of the town where the burn injury occurred. Note: if person is being treated at hospital, sanatorium or other institution, the manager, superintendent or other person in charge shall make the report.
Knife/Sharp Instrument Wounds **c 112 § 12A**	Every physician attending or treating a case of wound or injury caused by a knife or sharp or pointed instrument shall, if in his opinion a criminal act was involved, report such case forthwith to the police authorities of the town in which he attended or treated such wound or injury.
Additional Information related to **c. 112 § 12A**	**Penalty for failing to report any of the above** injuries: a fine of not less than $50.00 nor more than $100.00. **Arrest Powers**: there is no statutory authority granting powers of arrest for this offense. **Exception:** This section shall not apply to such wounds, burns or injuries received by any member of the armed forces of the United States or of the commonwealth while engaged in the actual performance of duty.
Hazing Reporting Required **c. 269 § 18**	Whoever knows that another person is the victim of hazing as defined in section seventeen and is at the scene of such crime shall, to the extent that such person can do so without danger or peril to himself or others, report such crime to an appropriate law enforcement official as soon as reasonably practicable. Whoever fails to report such crime shall be punished by a fine of not more than $1,000.

OFFENSES RELATED TO ARRESTS

C. 268 § 32B	RESISTING ARREST & other laws related to arrests
Elements	
1.	A person commits the crime of resisting arrest if he knowingly prevents or attempts to prevent a police officer, acting under color of his official authority, from effecting an arrest of the actor or another, by:
2.	(1) using or threatening to use physical force or violence against the police officer or another; or (2) using any other means which creates a substantial risk of causing bodily injury to such police officer or another.
Arrest Power, Penalties & Notes	
Power of Arrest	**Misdemeanor** – there is no statutory authority granting warrantless powers of arrest for this offense. However, if the offense is committed in public, in the officer's presence, and is creating a **breach of the peace** an arrest would be lawful.
Penalty	Imprisonment in a jail or HOC for not more than 2½ years or a fine of not more than $500, or both.
Attorney Hanrahan's Note	The officer must actually be effecting an arrest. This will not apply if someone is resisting during a threshold inquiry. Once the person is already arrested, this charge will not apply, such as misbehavior which occurs in the booking room.
Case Law & Other Important Information	
Definitions	The term "police officer" as used in this section shall mean a police officer in uniform or, if out of uniform, one who has identified himself by exhibiting his credentials as such police officer while attempting such arrest.
Unlawful Arrest is not a Defense	It shall not be a defense to a prosecution under this section that the police officer was attempting to make an arrest which was unlawful, if he was acting under color of his official authority, and in attempting to make the arrest he was not resorting to unreasonable or excessive force giving rise to the right of self-defense.
Good Faith	A police officer acts under the color of his official authority when, in the regular course of assigned duties, he is called upon to make, and does make, a judgment in good faith based upon surrounding facts and circumstances that an arrest should be made by him.
Only applies to actions taken while "effecting" an arrest	The crime of resisting arrest is committed, if at all, at the time of the "effecting" of an arrest.'[1486] An arrest is effected when there is (1) 'an actual or constructive seizure or detention of the person, [2] performed with the intent to effect an arrest and [3] so understood by the person detained.' [1487]
Threshold inquiries	In the 2010 case of ***Com. v. Quintos Q.***, a juvenile, the SJC ruled that fleeing during a threshold inquiry does not amount to a charge of resisting arrest because the flight prevented the police from a effecting a stop and not an arrest.

PUBLIC JUSTICE

[1486] Commonwealth v. Grandison, 433 Mass. 135, 145.
[1487] Ibid., quoting from Commonwealth v. Cook, 419 Mass. 192, 198 (1994).

C. 268 § 32B	RESISTING ARREST & other laws related to arrests
Knowledge of the arrest	In order to be convicted it must be proven that the defendant was aware that an arrest was being executed. The standard for determining whether a defendant understood that he was being arrested is objective--whether a reasonable person in the defendant's circumstances would have so understood."[1488] The most common scenario is when the officer advises the arrestee that he is about to be arrested. However, the circumstances may be enough to put the offender on notice that an arrest is taking place. In ***Commonwealth v. Soun*** (2012), the Appeals Court ruled that an order by police to "turn around and place your hands behind your back" would be sufficient to notify the person that an arrest is taking place. In ***Commonwealth v. Portee (***2012), the Appeals Court ruled that a threshold inquiry with active physical resistance from the suspect can rise to the level of an arrest justifying a resisting arrest conviction, even though the suspect cannot be convicting of resisting arrest for his/her actions during only a threshold inquiry. In this case the defendant punched the officer during the threshold inquiry. After that point, his continued physical resistance would amount to resisting arrest even if the officer did not advise him that he was being arrested because one could presumed he would be arrested under such circumstances.
Completed Arrests	Conduct after the arrest has been completed (i.e. in the booking room) does not constitute resisting arrest.[1489] *Effecting an arrest* is a process that begins when the [three arrest] criteria are present and ends when the person is **fully detained by his submission to official force or placed in a secure location** from which he can neither escape nor harm the police officer or others nearby.[1490] In ***Com. v. Knight***, the defendant, while in handcuffs, kicked at officers before they were able to secure him in a patrol car. This was deemed resisting arrest.[1491] In ***Com. v. Katykhin***, the defendant was handcuffed but stiffened his body "like a plank of wood" preventing the officers from getting him into the patrol car. This was sufficient for resisting.[1492]
Creating a substantial risk	In ***Commonwealth v. Montoya,*** the defendant created a substantial "risk" by jumping over fence into canal (20 foot drop) when being chased by the police even though the officers did not follow him into canal. It is the creation of the risk that is vital to this charge. The officer does not have to actually be injured.
Running alone not enough	Flight from the arrest, alone, does not create a substantial risk of bodily injury. However, the circumstances of the flight can create such a risk.[1493]
Resisting handcuffs	In ***Commonwealth v. Grandison***[1494], the defendant stiffened and pulled his arms free as officers were attempting to handcuff him. The defendant's actions "especially at the moment he freed his arm" was sufficient to conclude that the defendant by "any other means...created a substantial risk of causing injury to the police officers." Additionally, in ***Commonwealth v. Lender***, "the defendant's resistance to being handcuffed and paced in the cruiser was sufficient to amount to...a means creating a substantial risk of causing bodily injury to the arresting officer."[1495]
Third parties	This offense is not limited to the person being placed under arrest. A third party who intervenes in an arrest can also be convicted of resisting arrest.

[1488] Commonwealth v. Grant, 71 Mass.App.Ct. 205, 208 (2008).
[1489] *Commonwealth v. Dobbins*, Appeals Court 2011
[1490] Commonwealth v. Hart, (2012) Appeals Court.
[1491] Commonwealth v. Knight, 75 Mass.App.Ct. 735 (2009).
[1492] ***Com. v. Katykhin, 59 Mass.App.Ct. 261 (2003).***
[1493] Commonwealth v. Michael Sylvia, Appeals Court 2015
[1494] *Commonwealth v. Grandison*, 433 Mass. 135, 144-145 (2001).
[1495] ***Commonwealth v. Lender***, 66 Mass.App.Ct. 303, 306 (2006).

C. 268 § 32B

RESISTING ARREST
& other laws related to arrests

Related Statutes

Failure to Stop	Chapter 90 § 25 provides a criminal penalty to MV operators who refuse to stop when signaled by a police officer. See the Motor Vehicle section of this manual for more.
Arrest: False Information c. 268 § 34A	The defendant knowingly and willfully furnishes a false name or Social Security number to a law enforcement officer or law enforcement official following an arrest. **Penalty**: a fine of not more than $1,000 or by imprisonment in a HOC for not more than one year or by both such fine and imprisonment.
Escapes from jail **c. 268 § 15A**	The defendant, after lawfully being placed in custody in a jail of a city or town, escapes from any such **jail**. **Penalty:** imprisonment in a jail or HOC for not more than 2½ years, or by a fine of not more than $500, or both. In ***Com. v. Porter*** (2015), the Appeals Court ruled that failing to return to the house of correction for weekend confinement violation the statute (c. 268 § 16) **Attorney Hanrahan's Note**: G.L. c. 126, § 4. "Jails may also be used for the detention of persons arrested without a warrant and not admitted to bail pending appearance before the district court" instead of a local lock-up.
Refusal/delay to execute process resulting in escape **c. 268 § 23**	An officer who, being authorized to serve process, willfully and corruptly refuses to execute a lawful process directed to him and requiring him to apprehend or confine a person convicted of or charged with crime, or willfully and corruptly omits or delays to execute such process, whereby such person escapes, shall be punished. **Penalty:** a fine of not more than $500 or by imprisonment for not more than 1 year.
Delay service of warrants **c. 268 § 22**	An officer who willfully delays service of warrant of arrest or a search warrant committed to him for service shall be punished by a fine of not more than $50.
Neglect or refusal to assist officer or watchman **c. 268 § 24**	The defendant, being required in the name of the commonwealth by a sheriff, deputy sheriff, constable, police officer or watchman, neglects or refuses to assist him in one of the following situations: • in the execution of his office in a criminal case, • in the preservation of the peace • in the apprehension or securing of a person for a breach of the peace, • in a case of escape or rescue of persons arrested upon civil process. **Penalty**: a fine of not more than $50 or by imprisonment for not more than 1 month.
False Arrest **c. 263 § 2**	An officer who arrests or takes into or detains in custody a person, pretending to have a process if he has none, or pretending to have a different process from that which he has, shall be punished by a fine of not more than $1,000 or by imprisonment for not more than 1 year.
A&B on a police officer **c. 265 § 13D**	A&B on a police officer often accompanies a resisting arrest charge when force is used to prevent the arrest. This statute was also amended to include a felony version for attempting to disarm a police officer. See the Assault & Battery section of this manual for more.

REPORTS OF CRIMES & EMERGENCIES

FALSE REPORTS OF CRIMES & EMERGENCIES	
	Elements
False reports to police officers **c. 269 § 13A**	The defendant intentionally and knowingly makes or causes to be made a false report of a crime to police officers. **Penalty**: a fine of not less than $100 nor more than $500 or by imprisonment in a jail or HOC for not more than 1 year, or both. **Arrest Powers**: **Misdemeanor** – there is no statutory authority granting powers of arrest for this offense. However, if the offense is committed in public, in the officer's presence, and is creating a breach of the peace an arrest would be lawful. **Case Law Note:** In the 2011 case of ***Commonwealth v. Fortuna,*** the Appeals Court ruled that c.269 § 13A is not limited to those who seek out the police to report a crime but also to those who report false criminal activity when questioned by the police.
Police Officer filing False Reports **c. 268 § 6A**	The defendant, being an officer or employee of the commonwealth or of any political subdivision thereof or of any authority created by the general court, in the course of his official duties executes, files or publishes any false written report, minutes or statement, knowing the same to be false in a material matter. **Penalty**: A fine of not more than $1,000 or by imprisonment for not more than 1 year, or by both such fine and imprisonment.
Interference or tampering with police signal system **c. 268 § 32**	The defendant opens a **police signal box** for the purpose of causing a false alarm, or interferes in any way with such box by breaking, cutting, injuring or defacing or whoever, without authority, opens, tampers or meddles with such box, (includes parts and wires connect to the signal) **Penalty:** a fine of not less than $500 nor more than $1,000, or by imprisonment for not more than 2 years, or both. **Arrest: Misdemeanor** - this offense subjects the suspect to "immediate arrest."
Interference or tampering with fire signal system **c. 268 § 32**	The defendant, for the purpose of causing a false alarm, wantonly and without cause tampers or meddles with a signal box connected with a **fire signal system** or with any part or thing connected therewith. **Penalty:** a fine of not less than $500 nor more than $1,000, or by imprisonment for not more than 2 years, or both. **Arrest: Misdemeanor** - this offense subjects the suspect to "immediate arrest."
False alarms of fire **c. 269 § 13**	The defendant, without reasonable cause, by outcry or the ringing of bells, or otherwise, makes or circulates or causes to be made or circulated a false alarm of fire. **Penalty:** a fine of not less than $100 nor more than $500, or by imprisonment in a jail or HOC for not more than 1 year. **ARREST POWERS**: **Misdemeanor** – there is no statutory authority granting powers of arrest for this offense. However, if the offense is committed in public, in the officer's presence, and is creating a **breach of the peace** an arrest would be lawful.
False use of motorist call box **c. 268 § 32**	The defendant opens a motorist highway emergency aid call box on any state highway connected with a highway emergency signal system for the purpose of giving or causing to be given a false call for aid, or interferes in any way with the box by breaking, cutting, injuring or defacing the same; or, without authority, opens, tampers or meddles with such box, (including any part or parts or anything connected). **Penalty:** shall be punished by a fine of not less than $100 nor more than $500 (no statutory right of arrest).

C. 269 § 14B	FALSE REPORTS TO EMERGENCY SERVICES PROVIDER
	FALSE CALLS **Elements**
1.	The defendant willfully and maliciously communicates with a PSAP (or causes a communication to be made to a PSAP),
2.	• Which communication transmits information which the person knows or has reason to know is false; and • Which results in the dispatch of emergency services to a nonexistent emergency or to the wrong location of an actual emergency.
	SILENT CALLS **Elements**
1.	The defendant willfully and maliciously,
2.	• Makes or causes to be made **3 or more silent** calls to any PSAP, **and** • Hereby causes emergency services to be dispatched 3 or more times
	Arrest Power, Penalties & Notes
Power of Arrest	**Misdemeanor** – there is no statutory authority granting warrantless powers of arrest for this offense. However, if the offense is committed in public, in the officer's presence, and is creating a **breach of the peace** an arrest would be lawful.
Penalty	**1st offense:** Imprisonment in the HOC for not more than 2½ years or by a fine of not more than $1,000. **2nd or subsequent** :imprisonment in the HOC for not more than 2½ years or by imprisonment in the state prison (F) for not more than 10 years or by a fine of not more than 5,000, or by both such fine and imprisonment.
	Other Important Information
Definitions for this Section	**Emergency response services provider**, a police department, fire department, emergency medical service provider, PSAP, public safety department, private safety department or other public safety agency. **PSAP**, a facility assigned the responsibility of receiving 911 calls and, as appropriate, directly dispatching emergency response services or transferring or relaying emergency 911 calls to other public or private safety agencies or other PSAPs. **Silent call**, a call or other communication made to a PSAP in which the initiating party fails to provide information regarding his or her identity or location or the nature of the emergency. The initiating party shall not be considered to have provided any information that is automatically transmitted by a communication device or network upon connection with a PSAP including, but not be limited to, automatic location information and automatic number information.
Restitution	Upon any conviction of this section, the court shall conduct a hearing to ascertain the extent of costs incurred, and damages and financial loss sustained by any emergency response services provider as a result of the violation and shall order the defendant to make restitution to the emergency response services provider or providers for any such costs, damages or loss.
Venue	Chapter 277 § 59A provides that this crime may be prosecuted and punished in the territorial jurisdiction in which the communication originates or is received.

C. 268 § 13B	WITNESS INTIMIDATION/MISLEADING A POLICE OFFICER
Elements	
1.	The defendant directly or indirectly, does one of the following: • Threatens, or attempts or causes physical injury, emotional injury, economic injury or property damage to another person, • Conveys a gift, offer or promise of anything of value to another person, • Misleads, intimidates or harasses another person,
2.	That other person is: a) A **witness or potential witness** at any stage of a **criminal** investigation, grand jury proceeding, trial or other criminal proceeding of any type; b) A person who is or was **aware of information**, records, documents or objects that relate to a violation of a criminal statute, or a violation of conditions of probation, parole or bail; c) A judge, juror, grand juror, prosecutor, **police officer**, federal agent, investigator, defense attorney, clerk, court officer, probation officer or parole officer; d) A person who is furthering a **civil** or **criminal** proceeding, including criminal investigation, grand jury proceeding, trial, other criminal proceeding of any type, probate and family proceeding, juvenile proceeding, housing proceeding, land proceeding, clerk's hearing, court ordered mediation, any **other civil proceeding of any type**; e) A person who is or was attending or had made known his intention to attend a **civil or criminal proceeding**, including criminal investigation, grand jury proceeding, trial, other criminal proceeding of any type, probate and family proceeding, juvenile proceeding, housing proceeding, land proceeding, clerk's hearing, court-ordered mediation, any other civil proceeding of any type with the intent to impede, obstruct, delay, harm, punish or otherwise interfere thereby, or do so with reckless disregard, with such a proceeding.
3.	The defendant did so with the specific intent to impede/obstruct/delay or otherwise interfere with a criminal investigation/criminal proceeding/grand jury or trial, or acted in reckless disregard that his/her conduct with have such an impact.[1496]
Arrest Power, Penalties & Notes	
Power of Arrest	**Felony** – a police officer may effect a warrantless arrest for this offense provided he/she has probable cause that the suspect committed the offense.
Penalty	Imprisonment for not more than 2½ years in a jail or HOC or not more than 10 years in a **state prison (F)**, or by a fine of not less than $1,000 nor more than $5,000.
Attorney Hanrahan's Comment	This is very powerful statute that can assist in many investigations. Anytime someone provides false information or otherwise tries to hinder an investigation this statute can be used to punish the offender, or at least direct them to the truth by pointing out the consequences of their actions.
Other Important Information	
Definitions	As used in this section, **"investigator"** shall mean an individual or group of individuals lawfully authorized by a department or agency of the federal government, or any political subdivision thereof, or a department or agency of the commonwealth, or any political subdivision thereof, to conduct or engage in an investigation of, prosecution for, or defense of a violation of the laws of the United States or of the commonwealth in the course of his official duties. As used in this section, **"harass"** shall mean to engage in any act directed at a specific person or persons, which act seriously alarms or annoys such person or persons and would cause a reasonable person to suffer substantial emotional distress. Such act shall include, but not be limited to, an act conducted by mail or by use of a telephonic or telecommunication device or electronic communication device including but not limited to any device that transfers signs, signals, writing,

[1496] 2014 Model Jury Instruction

<table>
<tr><th>C. 268 § 13B</th><th>WITNESS INTIMIDATION/MISLEADING A POLICE OFFICER</th></tr>
<tr><td></td><td>images, sounds, data, or intelligence of any nature transmitted in whole or in part by a wire, radio, electromagnetic, photo-electronic or photo-optical system, including, but not limited to, electronic mail, internet communications, instant messages or facsimile communications.</td></tr>
<tr><td>Jurisdiction</td><td>A prosecution under this section may be brought in the county in which the criminal investigation, grand jury proceeding, trial or other criminal proceeding is being conducted or took place, or in the county in which the alleged conduct constituting an offense occurred.</td></tr>
<tr><td colspan="2">Related Case Law</td></tr>
<tr><td>Intimidation</td><td>In the 2010 case of Commonwealth v. Rivera, the court ruled the Commonwealth need not prove that the victim was in fact intimidated, only that the defendant intended to intimidate the victim.

It is not necessary that the defendant's statement or conduct refer directly to a pending court case in order to constitute intimidation.[1497]

Photographing the victim's family near the victim's home on the day of a court hearing is sufficient for the jury to infer intent to intimidate. Commonwealth v. Robinson, 444 Mass. 102, 110, 825 N.E.2d 1021, 1028 (2005).

It is not required that the defendant specifically articulated a warning against speaking to the police or other criminal investigator. The fact finder may evaluate the circumstances in which a statement was made, including its timing, to determine whether the defendant in fact intended to intimidate the victim. In Commonwealth v. King, the court ruled that it was inferable that defendant's statement that "if he saw the victim on TV News he was going to come back and kill him" was a shorthand warning against reporting a robbery to the police."[1498]</td></tr>
<tr><td>Intimidation does not have to be threatening</td><td>In the 2013 case of Commonwealth v. Vital, the defendant, after sexually assaulting a 12 year old girl, contacted his priest and asked the priest to convince the girl's family not to pursue charges. The priest reached out to the family, who were also members of the same parish. The court found that this amounted to intimidation.</td></tr>
<tr><td>Crime can be Committed before formal Proceedings begin</td><td>In the 2014 case of Commonwealth v. Gomez (non-published opinion), the suspect, while still on scene but after being placed under arrest for sexual assault, and waiting for transportation to the station, stated to one of the officers that if it was "those homos [who had reported the crime] . . . he would take care of them" referring to the son of the victim, and his boyfriend, who phoned the police to report the on-going assault. The Court stated the witness intimidation statute is "aimed at deterring interference with future communication of information."[1499] The statute was violated by the defendant's words/actions.</td></tr>
<tr><td>On-going Preceding</td><td>In the 2011 case of Commonwealth v. Hamilton, the SJC ruled that the conduct must involve an on-going investigation, not one that has already been fully adjudicated. In this case the defendant had already completed his sentence.

However, four days after the Hamilton case, the SJC decided Hrycenko v. Commonwealth. In this case the recently convicted defendant sent a letter from jail to the judge who handled his case. The judge felt the letter was threatening and contacted the state police. The defendant argued that he could not be charged with intimidation of a witness because there were no pending criminal proceedings. However, six days after sending the letter he filed a motion for a reduced sentence. The SJC ruled that "there is no requirement there be a pending criminal proceeding. Rather it requires intent to interfere in a criminal proceeding of any type." The Court ruled that the post trial motion clearly falls within the statute's language.

The trial does not end when the verdict is announced.[1500]. In Commonwealth v. Robinson, the Court ruled "when a show cause hearing was held and the application was either allowed or no decision had yet been announced, the proceeding was still ongoing." [1501]

In Commonwealth v. Isle, the defendant ripped the cord out of the wall in order to prevent the</td></tr>
</table>

PUBLIC JUSTICE

[1497] *Commonwealth v. Drumgoole*, 49 Mass. App. Ct. 87, 91, 726 N.E.2d 440, 443 (2000).
[1498] *Commonwealth v. King*, 69 Mass. App. Ct 113, 120, 866 N.E.2d 938, 944 (2007)
[1499] *Commonwealth* v. *Burt*, 40 Mass. App. Ct. 275, 278, 663 N.E.2d 271 (1996), quoting from *United States* v. *San Martin*, 515 F.2d 317, 320 (5th Cir. 1975). See *Commonwealth* v. *Belle Isle*, 44 Mass. App. Ct. 226, 228-229, 694 N.E.2d 5 (1998); *Commonwealth* v. *King*, 69 Mass. App. Ct. 113, 121-122, 866 N.E.2d 938 (2007).
[1500] *Commonwealth v. Cathy C.*, 64 Mass. App. Ct. 471, 474, 833 N.E.2d 1189, 1191 (2005).
[1501] *Commonwealth v. Robinson*, 444 Mass. 102, 109, 825 N.E.2d 1021, 1028 (2005).

C. 268 § 13B	WITNESS INTIMIDATION/MISLEADING A POLICE OFFICER
	victim from calling the police. The Court held this a violation of the statute even though it was not an "on-going investigation" because the victim was attempting to report a criminal incident.
Witness	The statute is applicable to any potential witness, whether or not actually called to testify, who has any relevant and material information, whether or not it bears directly on an essential element of the crime.[1502] A court interpreter is not a "witness" within the meaning of § 13B.[1503]
Victim can be charged	In the 2011 case of ***Commonwealth v. Fortuna***, the Appeals Court ruled that this statute also applies to a victim who intentionally misleads an officer regarding the nature of his/her injuries.
Misleading[1504]	Under the misleading prong, the statute punishes whoever directly or indirectly: 1. Willfully misleads 2. A police officer 3. With the intent to impede, obstruct, delay, harm, punish, or otherwise interfere thereby with a criminal investigation. Misleading conduct comprises: a. Knowingly making a false statement b. intentionally omitting information from a statement and thereby causing a portion of such statement to be misleading, or intentionally concealing a material fact, and thereby creating a false impression by such statement; c. with intent to mislead, knowingly submitting or inviting reliance on a writing or recording that is false, forged, altered, or otherwise lacking in authenticity; d. with intent to mislead, knowingly submitting or inviting reliance on a sample, specimen, map, photograph, boundary mark, or other object that is misleading in a material respect; or e. knowingly using a trick, scheme, or device with intent to mislead.
Must have intent to mislead, denial not enough	In the 2014 case of ***Commonwealth v. Morse***, the Court also stated "absent additional evidence of **specific intent**, such exculpatory denials, standing alone, rarely will permit a reasonable inference that a defendant possessed the specific intent necessary to establish a violation of § 13B." **Case examples** In ***Commonwealth v. Figueroa***, "a parole officer was investigating a possible violation of her directive that the defendant remain home after 6 P.M. on Halloween to avoid congregating with children who were out trick-or-treating.... On being asked why he left his home, the defendant told his parole officer that he had attended an Alcoholics Anonymous meeting in Framingham and that the global positioning system (GPS) information reflecting that he had been in an apartment complex must have arisen from a 'glitch' in the GPS system. He intentionally concealed his visit to his girl friend's] apartment and his trick-or-treating activities with her children." In ***Commonwealth v. Lopez***, (2013) (unpublished), police believed that an individual illegally possessing a firearm was present in the defendant's house. The defendant falsely represented to police that the individual was not there, even after being told that police had seen the individual in his house and would arrest the defendant for interfering with a police investigation if he did not cooperate. In ***Commonwealth v. Fortuna***[1505], the defendant told police that he had been shot from far away by unknown shooter, but subsequent observation of gunshot residue around wound revealed that shooter had been in very close proximity to defendant. In ***Commonwealth v. Mantello***[1506], after he had used excessive force against victim, defendant, who was a police officer, prepared and filed a police report falsely stating that the victim had assaulted

[1502] *Commonwealth v. Burt*, 40 Mass. App. Ct. 275, 277-278, 663 N.E.2d 271, 273-274 (1996).
[1503] *Commonwealth v. Belete*, 37 Mass. App. Ct. 424, 426, 640 N.E.2d 511, 512 (1994).
[1504] Commonwealth v. Morse, SJC (2014)
[1505] Commonwealth v. Fortuna, 80 Mass.App.Ct. 45, 47 (2011)

C. 268 § 13B	WITNESS INTIMIDATION/MISLEADING A POLICE OFFICER
	him, resulting in baseless assault charges against victim. **Attorney Hanrahan's note**: It is not a enough for a suspect to deny involvement in a criminal offense. For example, "did you break into the drug store last night?" and the defendant replies "no" even though he was the perpetrator, this would be insufficient. But if the suspect replied that he saw a suspect flee the scene, gave a false description and vehicle involved, this would be enough to violate the statute because he had the intent to mislead, not merely deny.
Subjective opinion not enough for misleading	In the 2014 case of ***Commonwealth v. Morse***, the defendant was piloting a boat when he struck a kayak killing a 10 year boy and seriously injuring the boy's father. When interviewed by police the trooper asked "did you consume any-are you on any kids of medication?" and the Morse said "nope." The trooper then asked "did you consume any other, you know, substance that could've impaired your ability to, you know, be aware of what was going on around you?" Morse replied "no." It was later learned that Morse had smoked marijuana shortly before the accident. The Court ruled that Morse's denial was not misleading because it was a subjective opinion – i.e. Morse could have felt marijuana was not a medication and did not affect his ability to be aware of was going on around him. A better question would have been "did you consume marijuana?" or "did you consume any illicit substances?"
Future cooperation with police	There is no requirement that the victim must be furnishing information on the day that the intimidating action is taken or statement made. It is enough that the jury reasonably concludes from the surrounding circumstances that "it was likely that the victim would furnish to an official investigating authority information pertaining to the crime and that the defendant intended to discourage that communication."[1507]
Separate threats or inducements in same communication	Separate and distinct threats or inducements may be charged as separate offenses even if they are contained within a single telephone call, letter or personal confrontation. *Commonwealth v. Lester*, 70 Mass. App. Ct. 55, 68, 872 N.E.2d 818, 829 (2007) (a "person seeking to influence a witness may, in one telephone call, threaten physical harm to the witness, threaten to kill a family member, or offer varying inducements").
Related Statutes	
Disguises to obstruct execution of law, performance of duties, or exercise of rights **c. 268 § 34**	The defendant disguises himself with intent to obstruct the due execution of the law, or to intimidate, hinder or interrupt an officer or other person in the lawful performance of his duty, or in the exercise of his rights under the constitution or laws of the commonwealth, whether such intent is effected or not. **Penalty**: a fine of not more than $500 or by imprisonment for not more than 1 year and may if imprisoned also be bound to good behavior for one year after the expiration of such imprisonment. **Arrest Powers:** there is no statutory authority granting powers of arrest for this offense. However, if the offense is committed in public, in the officer's presence, and is creating a breach of the peace an arrest would be lawful.
Compounding or concealing felonies **c. 268 § 36**	The defendant, having knowledge of the commission of a felony, takes money, or a gratuity or reward, or an engagement therefor, upon an agreement or understanding, express or implied, to compound or conceal such felony, or not to prosecute therefor, or not to give evidence thereof. **Penalty:** if such crime is punishable with death or imprisonment in the **state prison (F)** for life, be punished by imprisonment in the **state prison (F)** for not more than 5 years or in jail for not more than 1 year; and if such crime is punishable in any other manner, by a fine of not more than $500 or by imprisonment in jail for not more than 2 years. **Arrest Powers**: **Felony** – a police officer may effect an arrest for this offense committed in his/her presence or for an offense in the past, on probable cause

[1506] Commonwealth v. Mantello, 79 Mass.App.Ct. 1112 (2011) (unpublished)
[1507] *Commonwealth v. King*, 69 Mass. App. Ct 113, 120, 866 N.E.2d 938, 944 (2007)

C. 268 § 13B	WITNESS INTIMIDATION/MISLEADING A POLICE OFFICER
Interfering with a Police Officer **(common law offense)**	Some police agencies have regularly utilized the common law offense of *interfering with a police officer*. The Massachusetts Legislature has never enacted an offense entitled *interfering with a police officer*. In the 2003-2004 legislative session, Rep. Bruce J. Ayers proposed HB109 to make it a crime to "knowingly and willfully obstruct, resist, interfere with, or oppose any police officer ... in the lawful performance of his duties."[1508] But this bill has remained stalled in the House Committee on Steering Policy and Scheduling since then. Despite this some police agencies continue to utilize this charge. In the ***District Court Complaint Language Manual***, under the Common Law Offenses, is listed: "Police Officer, interfere with: On [date of offense] did intimidate, hinder or interrupt a police officer in the lawful performance of his or her duty, in violation of the Common Law (penalty from G.L. c. 279, § 5: 'according to the nature of the crime, as conforms with the common usage and practice in the commonwealth')."[1509] The fact that the offense shows up in the *District Court Complaint Language Manual* is indicative that the offense is recognized at least to some extent. It is listed as a *common law offense*; meaning that it has been established not by the Legislature but has been adopted by court decisions and/or old English law. However, there is very little Massachusetts case law regarding this offense. In a non-published opinion by the Appeals Court in 2012 (*Commonwealth v. Shave*, 81 Mass.App.Ct. 1131) the court seemed to acknowledge the existence of this offense (although the case did not provide details/elements of the offense). The elements listed in the District Court Complaint Language Manual are very similar to the elements of the Witness Intimidation statute, with the exception of the term "interrupts." If the circumstances permit, a charge of intimidation (c. 268 §13B) would be a better route to take. Unless your District Court readily accepts the common law offense of interfering with a police officer. Because this crime and its elements are not clearly recognized/established in Massachusetts it is recommended that you avoid its use and try to utilize other statutes, such as c. 268 § 13B. See the Overview section at the beginning of this manual for a discussion on Common law. Also see, MassBar Association Lawyers Journal: *Interfering with a police officer: a common law offense*. Molly Ryan Strehorn, March 2013. For an excellent discussion on this "offense."
Obstruction of Justice (common law offense)	In the 1997 case of ***Commonwealth v. Tripplett***, the SJC ruled that the common law offense of Obstruction of Justice was not an indictable offense when someone makes an effort to hamper a criminal investigation. The SJC ruled that the charge can only been used for those attempting to interfere with a judicial proceeding. In the 2014 case of ***Commonwealth v. Morse***, the Court reiterated that "there is no general obstruction of justice statute in Massachusetts, as there is in the Federal system and in a number of other States...instead Massachusetts utilizes a patchwork of statutes in an effort to combat crimes against justice." Note: The intimidation of a witness statute is often the most common. See the Overview section at the beginning of this manual for a discussion on Common law. In the 2015 case of ***Forlizzi v. Commonwealth***, the SJC referred to c. 268 § 13B as "obstruction of justice."

1508 2003 House Doc. No. 109

1509 The District Court Complaint Language Manual is not a legal device. The Administrative Office of the District Court serves an administrative function, taking no position on the binding authority of the manual, as it is not even reviewed by a committee.

ANIMAL CRUELTY & PROTECTION LAWS

C. 272 § 77	CRUELTY TO ANIMALS
Elements	
1.	The defendant does any of the following:
2.	▪ Overdrives, overloads, drives when overloaded, overworks, tortures, torments, deprives of necessary sustenance, cruelly beats, mutilates or kills an animal, ▪ Causes or procures an animal to be overdriven, overloaded, driven when overloaded, overworked, tortured, tormented, deprived of necessary sustenance, cruelly beaten, mutilated or killed; ▪ Uses in a cruel or inhuman manner in a race, game, or contest, or in training therefor, as lure or bait a live animal, except an animal if used as lure or bait in fishing; ▪ Having the charge or custody of an animal, either as owner or otherwise, inflicts unnecessary cruelty upon it, or unnecessarily fails to provide it with proper food, drink, shelter, sanitary environment, or protection from the weather, ▪ As owner, possessor, or person having the charge or custody of an animal, cruelly drives or works it when unfit for labor, or willfully abandons it, or carries it or causes it to be carried in or upon a vehicle, or otherwise, in an unnecessarily cruel or inhuman manner or in a way and manner which might endanger the animal carried thereon, ▪ Knowingly and willfully authorizes or permits it to be subjected to unnecessary torture, suffering or cruelty of any kind
Arrest Power, Penalties & Notes	
Power of Arrest	**Felony** – a police officer may effect a warrantless arrest for this offense provided he/she has probable cause that the suspect committed the offense.
Penalty	Imprisonment in the **state prison (F)** for not more than **7 years** or imprisonment in the HOC for not more than 2½ years or by a fine of not more than $5,000, or by both fine and imprisonment.
Forfeit Animal upon Conviction	In addition to any other penalty provided by law, upon conviction for any violation of this section (or of sections 77A, 78, 78A, 79, 79B, 80C, 80D, 80F, 86, 86A, 86B, or 94 – these are specific forms of animal cruelty, such as dying baby chickens) the defendant shall forfeit to the custody of any society, incorporated under the laws of the commonwealth for the prevention of cruelty to animals or for the care and protection of homeless or suffering animals, the animal whose treatment was the basis of such conviction.
Attorney Hanrahan's Comment	This statute essentially covers any, and all, cruel acts that can be inflicted upon an animal.
Related Statutes, Case Law & Other Important Information	
MSPCA Police	The MSPCA has a sworn police force charged with investigating animal abuse and similar offenses. They can be a valuable resource. Contact number: (617) 522-6008.
Wild Animals	In the 2011 case of ***Com. v. Linares***, the Appeals Court ruled that this statue applies to wild animals as well as domesticated animals.
No Specific Intent to Inflict Harm Required	Also in the 2011 case of ***Com. v. Linares*** the specific intent to cause harm is not required, only that the defendant knowingly and intentionally committed an act which was plainly of the nature to inflict unnecessary pain.
c. 272 § 82	Chapter 272 § 82 states that "the person making an arrest (for animal cruelty under § 77) with or without a warrant shall use reasonable diligence to give notice to the owner of animals found in the charge or custody of the person arrested, shall properly care and provide for such animals until the owner thereof takes charge of them, not, however, exceeding 60 from the date of said notice, and shall have a lien on said animals for the expense of such care and provision. "
c. 272 § 84	Requires that "police officers **shall** prosecute all violations" or animal cruelty offenses. This statute removes officer discretion when it comes to enforcement.

C. 272 § 77	CRUELTY TO ANIMALS
c. 272 § 104	Chapter 272 § 104 permits animals being treated cruelly to be seized. The owner is permitted to have a hearing within 30 days.
Specialized Animal Cruelty	Chapter 277 includes numerous specialized statutes which protect animals from various types of abuse. Many of these statutes involve prohibited conduct by those is the business of selling and boarding animals.
Surgical Devocalization of Cats &Dogs **c. 272 § 80 ½**	It is a felony to remove, or caused to be removed, the vocal cords of a dog or cat. **Exceptions:** This restriction shall not apply if: 1) the person performing such devocalization is licensed under c. 112 § 55; and 2) surgical devocalization of a dog or cat is medically necessary to treat or relieve an illness, disease or injury or to correct a congenital abnormality that is causing or may cause the animal physical pain or harm; or 3) the person who causes a devocalization procedure to be performed is relying upon the opinion of a person licensed under section 55 of c. 112 that surgical devocalization of the dog or cat is medically necessary to treat or relieve an illness, disease or injury or to correct a congenital abnormality that is causing or may cause the animal physical pain or harm.
Striking a Dog or Cat (with car) **c. 272 § 80H**	The operator of a motor vehicle that strikes and injures or kills a dog or cat shall forthwith report such an accident to the owner or custodian of the dog or cat or to a police officer in the town wherein such accident has occurred. **Penalty**: $50 fine
Mandatory reporting	Chapter 272 § 77, requires veterinarians whom in their normal course of business observe an animal whom they suspect of being abused to report the abuse to the police.
Wrongful removal of Dog collar **c. 266 § 47**	Whoever wrongfully removes the collar from a dog which is licensed and collared as provided in chapter 147 shall be punished by a fine of not more than $100, or by 6 months' imprisonment, or both. No statutory right of arrest.
Killing & Fighting Animals	See statues related to killing/poisoning animals and also the statutes related to fighting animals.
c. 119 § 85	A DCF investigator investigating a 51A complaint who uncovers animal cruelty must report discovery to police within 2 working days.

C. 272 § 77B	EXHIBITION OF WILD ANIMALS
	Elements
Prohibited	No person shall exhibit or sponsor an exhibition of any wild animal for the purpose of attracting trade at or for any place of amusement, recreation or entertainment.
Exception	This section shall not be deemed to prevent the exhibition of any wild animal in a zoological garden or in connection with any theatrical exhibition or circus or by any educational institution or wild animal farm, whether on or off the premises of such educational institution or wild animal farm.
Power of Arrest	**Misdemeanor** – there is no statutory authority granting warrantless powers of arrest for this offense. However, if the offense is committed in public, in the officer's presence, and is creating a **breach of the peace** an arrest would be lawful.
Penalty	A fine of not more than $200 or by imprisonment for not more than 30 days.

C. 266 § 112	MALICIOUS KILLING, MAIMING, POISONING DOMESTIC ANIMALS
Elements	
1.	It is unlawful to:
2.	• willfully and maliciously **kill, maim or disfigure** any horse, cattle or other animal of another person or • willfully and maliciously administer or expose **poison** with intent that it shall be taken or swallowed by any such animal
Arrest Power, Penalties & Notes	
Power of Arrest	**Felony** – a police officer may effect a warrantless arrest for this offense provided he/she has probable cause that the suspect committed the offense.
Penalty	Imprisonment in the **state prison (F)** for not more than **5 years** or by imprisonment in the HOC for not more than 2½ years or by a fine of not more than $2,500, or by both such fine and imprisonment.
Related Statutes, Case Law & Other Important Information	
No Specific Owner	There is no need to prove that the animal was owned by only one specific person. In the 2011, case of ***Com. .v Epifania,*** the defendant was convicted of killing a cat which was cared for by a variety of tenants within an apartment complex.

C. 272 § 77A	INJURING/INTERFERE A POLICE DOG OR HORSE
Elements	
1.	The defendant willfully
2.	Tortures, torments, beats, kicks, strikes, mutilates, injures, disables or otherwise mistreats
3.	A dog or horse owned by a police department or police agency of the commonwealth or any of its political subdivisions
or	
1.	The defendant willfully
2.	By any action whatsoever
3.	Interferes with the lawful performance of such dog or horse
Arrest Power, Penalties & Notes	
Power of Arrest	**Misdemeanor:** Persons violating this section may be arrested without a warrant by any officer qualified to serve criminal process provided said offense is committed in his presence.
Penalty	A fine of not less than $100 and not more than $500 or by imprisonment for not more than 2½ years or both.
Attorney Hanrahan's Comment	The statutory language of "by any action whatsoever" grants police great latitude in charging (and arresting in presence) anyone who interferes with a police dog/horse even if the animal is not abused.

C. 140	KILLING DOGS
KILLING AGGRESSIVE DOGS	
c. 140 § 156	Any person **may kill a dog:** • **which suddenly assaults** him while he is peaceably standing, walking or riding outside the enclosure of its owner or keeper; • found out of the enclosure of its owner or keeper and not under his immediate care in the act of worrying, wounding or killing persons, live stock or fowls.
Liability	The person shall not be held liable for cruelty to the dog unless it shall be shown that he intended to be cruel to the dog, or that he acted with a wanton and reckless disregard for the suffering of the dog. Prompt killing of a wounded dog, or a prompt report to the owner or to a dog officer of the wounding of the dog, shall be considered evidence of sufficient regard for the suffering of the dog.
KILLING UNRESTRAINED DOGS OR DOGS IN A WILD STATE	
c. 140 § 158	Any police officer, constable or dog officer **shall kill a dog** which the selectmen of a town, chief of police of a city, or the county commissioners, or, upon review, the district court, shall have **ordered to be restrained if such dog is again found outside the enclosure** of its owner or keeper and not under his immediate care, **and may kill a dog which is living in a wild state.**
Attorney Hanrahan's Comment	Although the statute says that a police officer "shall" kill a dog living in the wild or which has become loose after being order to by the City/Town to be restrained, I recommend seeking another option if the animal is not otherwise a danger.

FIGHTING ANIMALS

C. 272 § 89	EXHIBITION PLACE OF FIGHTING ANIMALS
Elements	
Warrantless Entry Permitted & Arrest All Present	• Any officer authorized to serve criminal process, or any special police officer duly appointed by the colonel of the state police at the request of the Massachusetts Society for the Prevention of Cruelty to Animals, or any municipal officer involved with animal control • May, **without a warrant**, *enter any place or building* • In which there is an exhibition of any fighting birds, dogs or other animals, preparations are being made for such an exhibition, or birds, dogs or other animals are owned, possessed, kept, trained, bred, loaned, sold, exported or otherwise transferred in violation of c. 272 § 94 (fighting animal prohibition law). • Any such officer may arrest all persons there present and take possession of and remove from the place of seizure such animals there found in violation of said section 94, and hold the same in custody subject to the order of court as hereinafter provided.
Attorney Hanrahan's Comment	This is a very unique statute in that it is one of the only statutes that allow a warrantless and the power to arrest *everyone* who is present. It is, in a sense, statutorily enacted exigent circumstances.
Related Statutes, Case Law & Other Important Information	
c. 272 § 94	c. 272 § 94 prohibits owning, possessing or training fighting animals and other related acts.
c. 272 § 88	Authorizes a judge to issue a search warrant for fighting animal violations "at any hour of the day or night."

C. 272 § 94	OWNING, POSSESSING, OR TRAINING FIGHTING ANIMALS
Elements	
1.	It is unlawful to:
2.	• **own, possess, keep or train** any bird, dog or other animal, with the intent that it shall be engaged in an **exhibition of fighting;** • **establish or promote an exhibition of the fighting** of any birds, dogs or other animals; • **loan, sell, export or otherwise transfer** any bird, dog or other animal for the purpose of animal fighting; • **own, possesses or keep** any bird, dog or other animal for the purpose of breeding such animal with the **intent that its offspring be used for animal fighting**
Arrest Power, Penalties & Notes	
Power of Arrest	**Felony** – a police officer may effect a warrantless arrest for this offense provided he/she has probable cause that the suspect committed the offense.
Penalty	Imprisonment in the **state prison (F)** for not more than **5 years** or in the HOC for not more than 1 year, or by a fine of not more than $1,000 or by both such fine and imprisonment.
Related Statutes, Case Law & Other Important Information	
c. 272 § 89	Section 89 authorizes a warrantless entry and an all person warrantless arrest provision.
c. 272 § 91	Section 91 enables the district court to order the destruction of these animals with 24 hours.

C. 272 § 95	AIDING OR BEING PRESENT AT EXHIBITION OF FIGHTING ANIMALS
Elements	
1.	It is unlawful to: a. be present at b. aid in c. contribute to
2.	Any place, building or tenement where preparations are being made for an exhibition of the fighting of birds, dogs or other animals
3.	With intent to be present at such exhibition
Arrest Power, Penalties & Notes	
Power of Arrest	**Felony** – a police officer may effect a warrantless arrest for this offense provided he/she has probable cause that the suspect committed the offense.
Penalty	A fine of not more than $1,000 or by imprisonment in the **state prison (F)** for not more than **5 years** or imprisonment in the HOC for not more than 2½ years or by both such fine and imprisonment.

POLICE TRAINING REQUIREMENTS

Police training schools; supervisory training requirements **c. 41 § 96B**	**Full-time Officers Must receive Training:** Every person who receives an **appointment to a position on a full-time basis** in which he will exercise police powers in the police department of any city or town, shall, **prior to exercising police powers,** be assigned to and satisfactorily complete a prescribed course of study approved by the municipal police training committee. **Student Officers not covered by Civil Service or Collective Bargaining**: any person so attending such a school shall be deemed to be a student officer and shall be exempted from the provisions of c. thirty-one and any collective bargaining agreement for that period during which he is assigned to a municipal police training school, provided that such person shall be paid the regular wages provided for the position to which he was appointed and such reasonable expenses as may be determined by the appointing authority and be subject to the provisions of c. one hundred and fifty-two. **In-service Training Required:** Every police officer on a full-time basis in any municipal police department, shall be assigned to and shall attend a prescribed course of study approved by the municipal police training committee for in-service officers training at such intervals and for such periods as said department may determine. **In-service upon Promotion:** Upon promotion to a higher rank the promoted officer shall complete any training required by the MPTC and while attending the training shall be paid his regular wages as a police officer and shall receive such reasonable expenses as may be determined by the appointing authority. **Reserve/Intermittent Police must be trained**: Each person appointed as a reserve, or intermittent police officer, in a city or town shall, prior to exercising police powers, satisfactorily complete a course of study prescribed by said committee. **MPTC may waive training requirements**: Upon petition by the appointing authority required training may be exempted by the MPTC, in whole or in part, from the provisions of this section prior to his exercising police powers. The requirement that training be completed prior to exercising any police powers may be waived by said committee. **Failure to meet training requirements may result in removal**: Failure of an appointed person to comply with training requirements (without a waiver) prior to his exercising police powers, **shall result** in the appointed person's removal by the appointing authority. Failure of an appointed person to **satisfactorily** complete the prescribed course of study **may** result in his removal by the appointing authority.
Police; training in suicide detection, intervention and prevention **c. 40 § 36C**	All members of municipal police departments, and all uniformed members of the state police shall be trained in the detection, intervention and prevention of suicide. The training shall include training in: 1. the nature and symptomatology of suicide, 2. in communicating with suicidal detainees, and 3. in appropriate suicide prevention techniques and emergency procedures. The training shall be approved and coordinated by the municipal police training committee, and shall be included in the curriculum of all police training schools and academies, including the state police academy. **In-service:** In-service training shall be provided for police officers having previous basic recruit training. **Upon Promotion:** Completion of a refresher seminar in suicide prevention **shall be a condition of promotion** for all police officers affected by the provisions of this act. **Written Procedures Required:** All police lockup facilities shall establish written procedures to be followed in any situation which threatens or may threaten the safety of persons detained therein.

POLICE TRAINING REQUIREMENTS

First aid training of emergency personnel **c. 111 § 201**	**Members of police and fire departments**, members of the state police participating in highway patrol, persons appointed permanent or temporary lifeguards by the commonwealth or any of its political subdivisions, and members of emergency reserve units of a volunteer fire department or fire protection district **shall be trained to administer first aid, including, but not limited to, cardiopulmonary resuscitation**. The training shall meet the standards for first aid training prescribed by the department and shall not be less than the standards established by the Committee on Cardiopulmonary Resuscitation and Emergency Cardiac Care of the American Heart Association, and shall be satisfactorily completed by them as soon as practical, but in no event more than one year after the date of their employment. Satisfactory completion of a **refresher course** approved by the department in **cardiopulmonary resuscitation** each year and in other **first aid every three years** shall also be required. The training and equipment for automatic or semi-automatic cardiac defibrillation shall meet standards prescribed by the department. **Exception:** This section **shall not apply to** police officers, fire fighters and persons engaged in police and fire work whose **duties are primarily clerical or administrative**.
Emergency Care and civil liability **c. 112 § 12V**	Any person, whose usual and regular duties **do not include the provision of emergency medical care,** and who, in good faith, attempts to render emergency care including, but not limited to, cardiopulmonary resuscitation or defibrillation, **and does so without compensation**, shall not be liable for acts or omissions, other than gross negligence or willful or wanton misconduct, resulting from the attempt to render such emergency care
Police officers attending law enforcement courses at accredited college or university for degree **c. 41 § 108M**	A city or town which employs a permanent police officer who is enrolled as a student in good standing in a police, law enforcement, criminal justice or police career oriented course of study at a college or university accredited by the New England Association of Colleges and Secondary Schools, Inc., or the board of higher education, shall, **subject to the approval of the appointing authority, and chief of police or any other officer having similar duties**, pay said police officer his full weekly salary during the normal thirty-two weeks such college or university is in session; provided, that he is enrolled for at least sixteen hours of classroom instruction, works twenty-four hours a week on regular duty as a police officer in said city or town and during regularly scheduled school vacations works his regular tour of duty; and provided, further, that he is studying for a baccalaureate, master's or higher degree. Each officer who is enrolled in a college or university under the provisions of this section shall enter into an agreement providing that he shall remain in full-time employment as a police officer in such city or town after completion of such course of study for as many years as he has been aided under this section.

POLICE ELIGIBILITY REQUIREMENTS

Residence requirements **c. 41 § 99A**	Any member of the regular **police or fire department** shall reside within **15 miles** of the limits of the city or town employed measured from the closest border employed to the closest border limits of the city or town in which the employee lives; **Attorney Hanrahan's Note:** by-law or collective bargaining agreement will supersede this law.
Felons disqualified **c. 41 § 96A**	no person who has been **convicted of any felony** shall be appointed as a police officer of a city, town or district.

POLICE ELIGIBILITY REQUIREMENTS

Police officers or firefighters; tobacco prohibited **c. 41 § 101A**	Effective January 1, 1988, no person who smokes any tobacco product shall be eligible for appointment as a police officer or firefighter in a city or town and no person so appointed after said date shall continue in such office

POLICE OFFICER & AGENCY POWERS, RESPONSIBILITIES & RESTRICTIONS

Firefighter duties; performance by police **c. 41 § 97F**	**City cannot require Police to work as firefighter:** No city or town shall require a member of its police department, or other employee with police powers, to perform the duties of a firefighter during his tour of duty. **Police Officer cannot work as Firefighter during a Labor Dispute:** No police officer, or other employee with police powers, shall, in connection with any industrial or labor dispute, perform the duties of a firefighter or any duties other than those regularly assigned to him. **Exception:** this shall not prohibit any officer from serving as a call or volunteer firefighter, or from responding to an emergency in the normal course of his duties.
Powers and duties **c. 41 § 98**	**General Police Powers/Duties** The chief and other police officers of all cities and towns shall have all the powers and duties of constables **except** serving and executing civil process. The Police shall suppress and prevent all disturbances and disorder. **Power to Carry Firearms** Massachusetts Police **may carry within Massachusetts department authorized weapons.** Any **law enforcement officer of another state or territory** of the United States may, while on official business within Massachusetts, **carry authorized weapons.** **Investigative Detentions** • The Police may examine all persons abroad whom they have reason to suspect of unlawful design, and • may demand of them their business abroad and whither they are going; • they may disperse any assembly of **three or more persons**, • and may enter any building to suppress a riot or breach of peace therein. **Right to Arrest:** Persons so suspected who do not give a satisfactory account of themselves (NOTE: this provision has been deemed unconstitutionally vague and not enforceable), persons so assembled and who do not disperse when ordered, and persons making, aiding and abetting in a riot or disturbance may be arrested by the police. **Right to Fingerprint:** Whoever is arrested and charged with any offense committed during a **riot, disturbance or mass demonstration** may be fingerprinted, and may be photographed. **Right to Frisk for Weapons**: If a police officer stops a person for questioning pursuant to this section and **reasonably suspects that he is in danger of life or limb**, he may search such person for a **dangerous weapon**. If he finds such weapon or any other thing the possession of which may constitute a crime, he may take and keep it until the completion of the questioning, at which time he shall return it, if lawfully possessed, or he shall arrest such person.

POLICE OFFICER & AGENCY POWERS, RESPONSIBILITIES & RESTRICTIONS	
Foot patrol **c. 41 § 98B**	In every city or town which has a population of **40,000 or more** and (which accepts the provisions of this section) there shall be **at all times a minimum of one police officer on foot patrol for every 10,000** inhabitants.
Badges; identification by name or number **c. 41 § 98C**	In any city or town *which accepts the provisions of this section* no uniformed police officer, and no other uniformed person empowered to make arrests, employed by such city or town **shall be required to wear a badge, tag or label of any kind which identifies him by name**, but any such officer or other person employed by such city or town who does not wear any such badge, tag or label **shall wear a badge, tag or label which identifies him by number**.
Police identification cards **c. 41 § 98D**	Each city or town shall issue to every full time police officer employed by it an identification card bearing his photograph and the municipal seal. Such card **shall be carried on the officer's person, and shall be exhibited upon lawful request for purposes of identification**.
Public solicitations **C. 41 § 98E**	**No person or persons shall solicit the public** in any manner or form **using the word "police" or "firefighter"** or any derivative thereof **without using the name or names of the city or town police or firefighters organization sponsoring such solicitation**.
MPA Attendance **c. 41 § 100G½**	Members of the police department may be excused from duty without loss of compensation while in attendance of meetings of the executive board of the MPA, when such regular meetings are held during the regular tour of duty of such member. **Note**: only if the City accepts this requirement
Female police officers; equality of compensation **c. 41 § 108K**	A **female regular police officer** in a city or town **shall receive compensation equal,** in all respects, to the **compensation** received by a male regular police officer of equal rank and seniority.
Serving a summons **c. 276 § 25**	A summons shall require the defendant to appear before the court at a stated time and place on the return day and shall be served by an officer authorized to serve criminal process by giving to the defendant in hand or by leaving at his dwelling house or last and usual place of abode with some person of suitable age and discretion then residing therein an attested copy not less than 24 hours before the return day, or by mailing an attested copy to the defendant's last known address

PUBLIC RECORDS and CORI

PUBLIC RECORDS LAW

PUBLIC RECORD: All records held by a state or local agency are open to public inspection

What is a "Public Record"? c. 4 § 7	"Public records" shall mean *all:* • books, • papers, • maps, • photographs, • recorded tapes, • financial statements, • statistical tabulations, or • **other documentary materials or data regardless of physical form or characteristics**, **Made** or **received** by any officer or employee of any agency, executive office, department, board, commission, bureau, division or authority of the commonwealth, or of **any political subdivision** thereof, or of any authority established by the general court to serve a public purpose, Unless such materials or data fall within certain exemptions - see exemptions later in this manual. In short – pretty much everything associated with your police agency is a public record unless it falls within one of the 18 specified exemptions.
Attorney Hanrahan's Note	The Public Records Law only applies to *records.* A records custodian is not required by the Public Records Law to answer questions or create a record in response to a request, but may do so at his or her discretion.

PUBLIC RECORD EXEMPTIONS

Exemption A Exempt by Statute	This exemption applies when there is a law that either **exempts** the information from being a public record or the law **prohibits** the information from being released to the public. If the law exempts the information the government agency is not compelled to release it; essentially it is the option of the agency whether or not release the information, but it most cases it is best not to release exempt information. If the law prohibits the release of the information the agency cannot release the information. In some cases the law is not always clear on whether or not the information is exempt or prohibited, this is why it is best, in most cases, to refrain from releasing exempt information. Here is a *sampling* of relevant Statutorily Exempt and Prohibited records that can be withheld from public inspection: • **Victim information protected PROHIBITED:** Chapter 66 § 10 also exempts "the home address and telephone number or place of employment or education of victims of **adjudicated crimes**, of victims of **domestic violence** and of **persons providing or training in family planning services** and the name and home address and telephone number, or place of employment or education of **a family member** of any of the foregoing shall not be public records in the custody of a government agency which maintains records identifying such persons as falling within such categories and shall not be disclosed."

PUBLIC RECORDS LAW

- **Sex Victim and Rape report information PROHIBITED:** Chapter 265 § 24C states that any record "which contains the name of the victim in an arrest, investigation or complaint for rape of assault with intent to rape...or a complaint for human trafficking of persons" (for sexual servitude) shall be withheld from public records. Chapter 41 § 97D also states that rape reports shall not be open to the public.
- **Domestic Violence Reports PROHIBITED: All domestic violence reports and associated documents can only be released to the victim, victim's attorney, and a few select others. See the actual statutory language below:**

  All reports of rape and sexual assault or attempts to commit such offenses, all reports of abuse perpetrated by family or household members, as defined in c. 209A sec. 1, and all communications between police officers and victims of such offenses or abuse shall not be public reports and shall be maintained by the police departments in a manner that shall assure their confidentiality; provided, however, that all such reports shall be accessible at all reasonable times, upon **written request**, to:

  (i) the victim, the victim's attorney, others specifically authorized by the victim to obtain such information,

  (ii) prosecutors,

  (iii) victim-witness advocates as defined in section 1 of chapter 258B,

  (iv) domestic violence victims' counselors as defined in section 20K of chapter 233,

  (v) sexual assault counselors as defined in section 20J of chapter 233, if such access is necessary in the performance of their duties;

  (vi) and provided further, that all such reports shall be accessible at all reasonable times, **upon written, telephonic, facsimile or electronic mail** request to law enforcement officers, district attorneys or assistant district attorneys and

  (vii) all persons authorized to admit persons to bail pursuant to section 57 of chapter 276.

  Communications between police officers and victims of said offenses and abuse may also be shared with the forgoing named persons if such access is necessary in the performance of their duties. A violation of this section shall be punished by imprisonment for not more than 1 year or by a fine of not more than $1,000, or both such fine and imprisonment.

- **Harassment Order Plaintiff PROHIBITED:** Chapter 258E § 10 exempts "The **plaintiff's residential address, residential telephone number and workplace name, address and telephone number**, contained within the court records of cases arising out of an action brought by a plaintiff ."
- **Immediate Threat Report EXEMPT:** Chapter 90 § 22I states "a report made under this section shall not be a public record."
- **Firearm information PROHIBITED**: Chapter 66 §10 the names and home addresses of those who have applied for LTC and FID licenses shall not be released, including the names and addresses of those who possess firearms.
- **Law Enforcement & Court Personnel Personal information EXEMPT**: Although the definition of Public Record in c. 4 § 7 exempts personnel information of public employees Chapter 66 § 10 also **exempts** the home address and phone numbers of law enforcement personnel, corrections personal and other criminal justice professionals (including their families).

PUBLIC RECORDS LAW

	• **Child Requiring Assistance** (formerly CHINS) **PROHIBITED**: Chapter 119 states that records pertaining to a Child Requiring Assistance shall be confidential and not open to the public. • **Juvenile Delinquency Case Records PROHIBITED:** Chapter 119 § 60A indicates that juvenile delinquency records shall not be open to the public (under age 18). • **Requests for Sex Offender information PROHIBITED:** Chapter 6 § 178I states that people who request sex offender information shall be kept confidential. • **Nude/partially nude without knowledge/consent of victim EXEMPT**: Images of someone taken in violation of chapter 272 § 105 are not public record. Note: this would also be PROHIBITED as the person in the photo would also be a victim. • **Search Warrants and Affidavits EXEMPT:** Search warrants and associated affidavits are exempt from public record until the search warrant has been returned to the court. However, in most cases this information would jeopardize a criminal investigation and could be withheld under Exemption F (see exemption F for more). • **Registry of Motor Vehicle Information PROHIBITED**: the Driver's Privacy Protection Act is a Federal Law that prohibits the disclosure of personal information gathered by state registry of motor vehicle departments. There are many exceptions to the release of this information, most importantly: o "For any government agency to carry out its functions" o "For use by insurance companies" o "When written consent of the individual is provided." Refer to the actual Federal Law for other exceptions. • **Criminal Offender Record Information (CORI) PROHIBITED:** this information is exempt from public records (and other laws make it a criminal offense to release) with few exceptions (see CORI section more information). The CORI laws can be very complex and often at odds with other laws. Because of this, a special section on CORI has been added at the end of this manual.
Exemption B Internal Rules and Practices	"Information related solely to internal personnel rules and practices of the government unit, provided however, that such records shall be withheld only to the extent that proper performance of necessary governmental functions requires such withholding." **Attorney Hanrahan's Notes:** There are no authoritative Massachusetts decisions interpreting this exemption. For Exemption B to apply in Massachusetts, a records custodian must demonstrate not only that the records relate solely to the internal personnel practices of the government entity, but also that proper performance of necessary government functions will be inhibited by disclosure. Example: Procedures used by the police department during shift change, which if released may be used by a criminal element to reduce the likelihood of being captured, would likely be exempt under this exemption.

PUBLIC RECORDS LAW

Exemption C Privacy	"Personnel and medical files or information; also any other materials or data relating to a specifically named individual, the disclosure of which may constitute an unwarranted invasion of personal privacy." **Attorney Hanrahan's Notes:** **Personal Privacy:** is limited to "intimate details of a highly personal nature." Examples of "intimate details of a highly personal nature" include marital status, paternity, substance abuse, government assistance, family disputes and reputation. Portions of records containing such information are exempt unless there is a paramount public interest in disclosure. "Other personal information such as social security numbers and the like should also be withheld to prevent identity theft and similar problems from arising. **Medical Information:** As a general rule, medical information will always be of a sufficiently personal nature to warrant exemption. **Personnel Information:** The Appeals Court of Massachusetts distinguished "personnel records" from "internal affairs" records. Information used to determine employment decisions fall within this exemption. Examples include employment applications, resumes employee work evaluations, disciplinary documentation and promotion, demotion and termination information. **Internal Affairs Records:** A 2003 Appeals Court case (Worcester Telegram & Gazette v. Chief of Police of Worcester) ruled that officer reports, witness interview summaries, and the internal affair report itself do not fall within and the internal affairs report itself do not fall within the personnel information exemption, as these documents relate to the workings and determinations of the internal affairs process whose quintessential purpose is to inspire public confidence. Also See: **950 CMR 33.16 - Invasion of Personal Privacy:** General Rule Personal data the disclosure of which may constitute an invasion of personal privacy is not a public record. In general, it is an invasion of personal privacy under M.G.L. c. 214, § 1B, as appearing in St. 1973, c. 1114, § 62, to disclose personal data where such disclosure will result in an unreasonable, substantial or serious interference with the privacy of a data subject unless the data subject or his authorized representative consents to such disclosure.
Exemption D Deliberative Process	"Inter-agency or intra-agency memoranda or letters relating to policy positions being developed by the agency; but this subclause shall not apply to reasonably completed factual studies or reports on which the development of such policy positions has been or may be based"
Exemption E Personal Employee Notes	"Notebooks and other materials prepared by an employee of the commonwealth which are personal to him and not maintained as part of the files of the governmental unit" **Note:** This is limited to notes that are personal to the employee. The notes are not public if they were personal in nature, kept by the employee merely to assist him in preparing reports, were not shared with anyone in the department and were not maintained as part of the department's files.
Exemption F Investigatory Exemption	"Investigatory materials necessarily compiled out of the public view by law enforcement or other investigatory officials the disclosure of which materials would probably so prejudice the possibility of effective law enforcement that such disclosure would not be in the public interest" Attorney Hanrahan's note - this exemption essentially covers three areas: 1. **Ongoing investigations**: Information that may alert suspects, or otherwise jeopardize an ongoing investigation, may be withheld.

PUBLIC RECORDS LAW	
	2. **Future Investigations:** Confidential investigative techniques may be withheld that would jeopardize future investigative efforts. 3. **Confidentiality**: information may be withheld to provide an assurance of confidentiality to private citizens so that they will speak openly about matters under investigation. Accordingly, any details in witness statements, which if released create a grave risk of directly or indirectly identifying a private citizen who volunteers as a witness are indefinitely exempt. **Example from A Guide to Massachusetts Public Records Law:** If a requested incident report contains witness statements, can a police department use Exemption (f) to withhold the requested report in its entirety? No. Generally, a police incident report may be released to a requester after the records custodian has redacted the exempt portions from the record, such as, medical information [Exemption (c) and witness statements (Exemption (f)]. If, however, the requester is familiar with the individuals who were involved in the incident(s) noted in the report, then the department may withhold the entire record because it would not be possible for the records custodian to redact the report in a manner as to avoid indirect identification of the voluntary witness and complainant.
Exemption G Trade Secrets	"Trade secrets or commercial or financial information voluntarily provided to an agency for use in developing governmental policy and upon a promise of confidentiality; but this subclause shall not apply to information submitted as required by law or as a condition of receiving a governmental contract or other benefit"
Exemption H Closed Bids	"Proposals and bids to enter into any contract or agreement until the time for the opening of bids in the case of proposals or bids to be opened publicly, and until the time for the receipt of bids or proposals has expired in all other cases; and inter-agency or intra-agency communications made in connection with an evaluation process for reviewing bids or proposals, prior to a decision to enter into negotiations with or to award a contract to, a particular person"
Exemption I Property Appraisals	"Appraisals of real property acquired or to be acquired until (1) a final agreement is entered into; or (2) any litigation relative to such appraisal has been terminated; or (3) the time within which to commence such litigation has expired"
Exemption J LTC & FID Information	"The names and addresses of any persons contained in, or referred to in, any applications for any licenses to carry or possess firearms issued pursuant to chapter one hundred and forty or any firearms identification cards issued pursuant to said chapter one hundred and forty and the names and addresses on sales or transfers of any firearms, rifles, shotguns, or machine guns or ammunition therefor, as defined in said chapter one hundred and forty and the names and addresses on said licenses or cards" This only restricts the name and address of individuals.
No exemption K	
Exemption L Exam Information	"Questions and answers, scoring keys and sheets and other materials used to develop, administer or score a test, examination or assessment instrument; provided, however, that such materials are intended to be used for another test, examination or assessment instrument"

PUBLIC RECORDS LAW	
Exemption M Hospital Contracts	"Contracts for hospital or related health care services between (i) any hospital, clinic or other health care facility operated by a unit of state, county or municipal government and (ii) a health maintenance organization arrangement approved under chapter one hundred and seventy-six I, a nonprofit hospital service corporation or medical service corporation organized pursuant to chapter one hundred and seventy-six A and chapter one hundred and seventy-six B, respectively, a health insurance corporation licensed under chapter one hundred and seventy-five or any legal entity that is self insured and provides health care benefits to its employees. "
Exemption N Facility Security	"Contracts for hospital or related health care services between (i) any hospital, clinic or other health care facility operated by a unit of state, county or municipal government and (ii) a health maintenance organization arrangement approved under chapter one hundred and seventy-six I, a nonprofit hospital service corporation or medical service corporation organized pursuant to chapter one hundred and seventy-six A and chapter one hundred and seventy-six B, respectively, a health insurance corporation licensed under chapter one hundred and seventy-five or any legal entity that is self insured and provides health care benefits to its employees. "
Exemption O Home Addresses and Telephone Numbers of Government Employees	The home address and home telephone number of an employee of the judicial branch, an unelected employee of the general court, an agency, executive office, department, board, commission, bureau, division or authority of the commonwealth, or of a political subdivision thereof or of an authority established by the general court to serve a public purpose, in the custody of a government agency which maintains records identifying persons as falling within those categories; provided that the information may be disclosed to an employee organization under chapter 150E, a nonprofit organization for retired public employees under chapter 180, or a criminal justice agency as defined in section 167 of chapter 6.
Exemption P Family Member Info of Government Employees	"The name, home address and home telephone number of a family member of a commonwealth employee, contained in a record in the custody of a government agency which maintains records identifying persons as falling within the categories listed in subclause (o). "
Exemption Q Adoption Records	(q) Adoption contact information and indices therefore of the adoption contact registry established by section 31 of chapter 46.
Exemption R Child Advocate Information	"Information and records acquired under chapter 18C by the office of the child advocate. "

PUBLIC RECORDS LAW

Exemption S Energy Supplier Trade Secret	"Trade secrets or confidential, competitively-sensitive or other proprietary information provided in the course of activities conducted by a governmental body as an energy supplier under a license granted by the department of public utilities pursuant to section 1F of chapter 164, in the course of activities conducted as a municipal aggregator under section 134 of said chapter 164 or in the course of activities conducted by a cooperative consisting of governmental entities organized pursuant to section 136 of said chapter 164, when such governmental body, municipal aggregator or cooperative determines that such disclosure will adversely affect its ability to conduct business in relation to other entities making, selling or distributing electric power and energy; provided, however, that this subclause shall not exempt a public entity from disclosure required of a private entity so licensed. Any person denied access to public records may pursue the remedy provided for in section ten of chapter sixty-six.

Important Information

Record Custodian Response Requirements	A records custodian must respond as soon as practicable, without reasonable delay and within 10 days. Chapter 66 § 10 states that "a custodian of a public record shall, within 10 days following receipt of a request for inspection or copy of a public record, comply with such request. A request may be delivered in hand to the office of the custodian or mailed via first class mail.

C. 22A § 4

CRIMINAL OFFENDER RECORD INFORMATION (CORI)

The CORI laws are designed to protect the criminal records of individuals from public dissemination by Criminal Justice Agencies. However, there are many exceptions and exemptions.

What is CORI information? c. 6 § 167

Criminal offender record information (CORI) is:

- Records and data in any communicable form
- Compiled by a Massachusetts **criminal justice** agency
- which concern an **identifiable individual** and relate to
  - the nature or disposition of a criminal charge,
  - an arrest,
  - a pre-trial proceeding,
  - other judicial proceedings,
  - sentencing,
  - incarceration,
  - rehabilitation, or
  - release

Such information shall be restricted to that recorded as the result of the initiation of criminal proceedings or any consequent proceedings related thereto.

C. 22A § 4	CRIMINAL OFFENDER RECORD INFORMATION (CORI)
Penalty for misuse or wrongful dissemination	The provisions of Massachusetts General Laws, c. 6, §§ 167-178B, of which sections 177-178 provide that it is a criminal offense to willfully disclose to any unauthorized person or agency any criminal offender record information concerning an individual or to willfully falsify any criminal offender record information. Unauthorized access to or dissemination of criminal offender record information is punishable by a fine of not more than five thousand dollars ($5,000.00), or imprisonment in jail or house of correction for not more than one year, or both. Any such dissemination also subjects me to a suit for civil damages and/or a civil fine of up to five hundred dollars ($500.00) for each such willful violation.
	Exceptions to the Prohibition of CORI Records Release
Exemptions under c. 6 § 176 and c. 6 § 175	**STATISTICS:** Criminal offender record information shall not include evaluative information, statistical and analytical reports and files in which individuals are not directly or indirectly identifiable, or intelligence information. **NO INCARCERATION POSSIBLE – Not CORI**: Criminal offender record information shall not include information concerning any offenses which are not punishable by incarceration. **UNDER 18:** Criminal offender record information shall be limited to information concerning persons who have attained the age of 18 and shall not include any information concerning criminal offenses or acts of delinquency committed by any person before he attained the age of 18; provided, however, that if a person under the age of 18 is adjudicated as an adult, information relating to such criminal offense shall be criminal offender record information. **Note:** Juvenile information is protected by c. 119 § 160A. Which states in part: "The records of a youthful offender proceeding conducted pursuant to an indictment shall be open to public inspection in the same manner and to the same extent as adult criminal court records. All other records of the court in cases of delinquency arising under sections fifty-two to fifty-nine, inclusive, shall be withheld from public inspection except with the consent of a justice of such court."
Written waiver and follow-up	There are various statutes which permit the dissemination of CORI information but for the most part these exemptions apply to dissemination by the Department of Criminal Justice Information Services (not the police). For instance, the law permits (actually requires) CORI information to be disseminated to schools regarding taxi employees hired to transport pupils. However, this information must be provided by the Department of Criminal Justice Information Services. Under the law, the police should not be providing this information to the school. According to DCJIS if an individual has been authorized (i.e. by way of a waiver of the criminal offender) to obtain CORI information the person seeking the information **must get the information from DCJIS**, police agencies cannot release BOP's. However, if the person seeking information has been granted access to the BOP information they may obtain additional information that is in possession of the law enforcement agency (i.e. the actual police report – providing it does not contain other protected information, such as the identity of a sexual assault victim).[1] **For example**, an Army Recruiter arrives at the police station looking for a criminal report on an Army applicant. The recruiter presents a signed waiver. The recruiter should be directed to DCJIS for BOP information. Once DCJIS confirms the waiver and releases the information the recruiter may return to the police agency and request additional information related to the applicant's CORI record.

[1] Information received verbally from DCJIS support line. Relayed by General Counsel to phone operator after consultation. 11/8/2012.

C. 22A § 4	CRIMINAL OFFENDER RECORD INFORMATION (CORI)
Inspection of own records	803 CMR 7.10(6) states in part "Pursuant to M.G.L. c. 6, § 175, a CJA (Criminal Justice Agency) may disseminate CORI to the individual to whom it pertains, or to the individual's attorney, with a signed release from the individual. The CORI provided shall be limited to information compiled by the CJA, such as a police report prepared by the CJA. A CJA may not provide an individual with any CORI obtained through CJIS."
Daily Police Logs **c. 41 § 98**	Each police department and each college or university to which officers have been appointed shall make, keep and maintain a daily log, written in a form that can be easily understood, recording, in chronological order: 1. all responses to valid complaints received, 2. crimes reported, 3. the names, addresses of persons arrested and the charges against such persons arrested. All entries in said daily logs shall, unless otherwise provided in law, be public records available without charge to the public during regular business hours and at all other reasonable times; provided, however, that the following entries shall be kept in a separate log and shall not be a public record nor shall such entry be disclosed to the public, or any individual not specified in section 97D: (i) any entry in a log which pertains to a handicapped individual who is physically or mentally incapacitated to the degree that said person is confined to a wheelchair or is bedridden or requires the use of a device designed to provide said person with mobility, (ii) any information concerning responses to reports of domestic violence, rape or sexual assault or (iii) any entry concerning the arrest of a person for assault, assault and battery or violation of a protective order where the victim is a family or household member, as defined in section 1 of chapter 209A. **Attorney Hanrahan's note:** although CJ agencies generally cannot release arrest information it is permissible, in fact it is required, that this information be recorded in the daily log which is accessible to the public.
Criminal Investigations **803 CMR 2.04 (5)**	The Police may release CORI information "that is specifically related to and contemporaneous with an investigation or prosecution." See below: **803 CMR 2.04 (5) Authorization for public dissemination of CORI.** (a) A criminal justice agency with official responsibility for a **pending criminal investigation or prosecution** <u>may disseminate CORI</u> that is specifically related to and contemporaneous with an investigation or prosecution; (b) A criminal justice agency may disseminate CORI that is specifically related to and contemporaneous with **the search for or apprehension of any person**, or with a disturbance at a penal institution; **Important Case:** In ***Bellin v. Kelley*** (2001), Kelley Consultants, Inc., a small company consisting of approximately 6 employees was broken into. The officer surmised that the perpetrator was familiar with the layout and an "inside job" was suspected. Bellin was the only employee with a criminal record. The officer called in Bellin for an interview. The officer asked Bellin to take a polygraph and Bellin refused. The officer then warned the company President, Frederick Kelley, about Bellin's criminal history. Bellin was fired. Bellin sued arguing that the police wrongfully disclosed his criminal history.

C. 22A § 4	CRIMINAL OFFENDER RECORD INFORMATION (CORI)
	The SJC ruled: The challenged regulation, 803 Code Mass. Regs. Section 2.04 (5) (a), represents the board's reasonable determination that, **during the course of an investigation, law enforcement agencies often need to reveal CORI that is related to that investigation**. The statute implicitly allows criminal justice agencies to use CORI to perform their criminal justice duties, and the board's regulation simply authorizes the use of such information for that fundamental law enforcement purpose....Here, the officer investigating the crime suspected that the perpetrator was an employee of the victim. Notifying the employer of those suspicions (and the bases for those suspicions) allowed the employer to take precautions to protect himself and his company from any further criminal acts of a possibly disloyal insider. Leaving a victim in ignorance in such circumstances, and thus completely vulnerable to further criminal acts, would have been viewed as irresponsible on the part of the police.
Media Releases	Many Law Enforcement agencies will issue press releases regarding the arrest and capture of high profile criminals. Although this seemingly appears to be contrary to CORI restrictions DCJIS has stated that this is "within the agency's discretion" under previously mentioned 803 CMR 2.04 (5) Authorization for public dissemination of CORI.[1]
CJ agencies and the Military c. 6 § 172	**Chapter 6 § 172** permits the dissemination of CORI information to: (a) **criminal justice agencies**; (b) such other agencies and individuals required to have access to such information by statute including: i. **United States Armed Forces recruiting offices** for the purpose of determining whether a person enlisting has been convicted of a felony; ii. to the **active or organized militia of the commonwealth** (i.e. National Guard) for the purpose of determining whether a person enlisting has been convicted of a felony, and (c) any other agencies and individuals where it has been determined that the public interest in disseminating such **information to these parties clearly outweighs the interest in security and privacy.** **Note:** For access under clause (c), the criminal history systems board (now DCJIS - established by G.L.c. 6, Section 168) (board) must first determine and certify by a two-thirds majority "that the public interest in disseminating such information to such party clearly outweighs the interest in security and privacy." G.L. c. 6, Section 172. From *Bellin v. Kelley*, 435 Mass. 261 (2001). **Attorney Hanrahan's Comment:** be sure to obtain a written waiver before releasing records to a military recruiter.
Crime Victims c. 6 § 178A	A victim of crime, witness, or family member of a homicide victim upon request, may receive criminal offender record information, must relate to the offense in which the person was involved. Criminal justice agencies may also disclose to such persons additional information, including but not limited to evaluative information, as such agencies determine, in their discretion, is reasonably necessary for the security and wellbeing of such persons.

PUBLIC RECORDS & CORI

[1] Email correspondence from Georgia Critsley, DJIS General Counsel – June 19, 2013.

C. 22A § 4	CRIMINAL OFFENDER RECORD INFORMATION (CORI)
DCF and DYC release	Exceptions for DCF & DYS - C. 6 § 172B. This law permits the release of: a. Conviction data, b. Arrest data c. Sealed record data, and d. Juvenile arrest or conviction data To DCF (the department of children and families) and DYS (the department of youth services), for the purpose of evaluating foster homes and adoptive homes (including public or private agencies), in order to further the protection of children.
Department of early Education - c. 6 § 172F	Conviction & Arrest data available to the department of early education - C. 6 § 172F. This law permits the release of: **a.** Conviction data, **b.** Arrest Data **c.** Sealed record data, and **d.** Juvenile arrest or conviction data Available to the department of early education and care ▪ for the purposes of evaluating any residence, facility, program, system or other properly licensed entity (public or private), or ▪ any non-relative, in-home child care provider that receives federal or state funding in order to further the protection of children. **Attorney Hanrahan's note:** this information generally should be provided by DCJIS and not local law enforcement agencies.
Community Based Justice c. 12 § 187B	This law requires the local DA's office to conduct weekly meetings in conjunction with schools, local law enforcement, probation, DCF and similar agencies in order to identify juveniles who are most likely to pose a threat to the community. Although the law does not specifically mention the authority to release CORI type information it seems to be implied in the law. Also, CORI does not include children under the age of 18. Criminal information regarding juveniles is covered under chapter 119 § 60A which also does not specifically authorize the release of criminal information in this setting. It is recommended that you defer to the prosecutor assigned to the particular workgroup for guidance on what information can be released and what information cannot, as the law appoints the prosecutor assigned to the group as the group coordinator.
Death	The restrictions on the dissemination of CORI shall cease to exist at the death of the individual. c. 6 § 178
Sex Offender c. 6 § 178C-178Q	The sex offender laws permit, and in some cases require, public dissemination of an offender's criminal history. **Level 1 – no dissemination permitted.** **Level 2 – dissemination upon proper request (and proactive dissemination in some cases).** **Level 3 – proactive dissemination.** **See sex crimes section for more on sex offenders.**

GAMBLING & LOAN SHARKING

NOTE ON GAMING OFFENSES: There are numerous gaming statutes in Massachusetts, many of which are very narrowly defined and archaic. For this reason, many were not included in this manual. If you have a gaming investigation we recommend that you refer to the specific statutes. All are available on the mass.gov website.

CASE LAW NOTE: As the Supreme Judicial Court has long recognized, "lottery" encompasses a large variety of activities, which include three elements:

1) the payment of a price for
2) the possibility of winning a prize, depending upon
3) hazard or chance. [1]

C. 271 § 10A	GAMING VIOLATIONS: ARREST WITHOUT WARRANT
Warrantless Arrest	Any person who is discovered by a police officer in the act of violating section: • Chapter 271 § 7 (unlawful lotteries), • Chapter 271 § 8 (hosting illegal lottery), • Chapter 271 § 9 (unlawful lottery tickets), • Chapter 271 § 12 (false lottery tickets), • Chapter 271 § 16 (sale/possession of unlawful lottery tickets), • Chapter 271 § 17 (registering bets or pools) , • Chapter 271 § 17A (telephone use for gaming), • Chapter 271 § 18 (lottery rules involving shops) or • Chapter 271 § 22 (receiving delivery of illegal lottery/gaming items), while such officer is lawfully at or within the place where such violation occurred, may be **arrested without a warrant** by such police officer, and held in custody, in jail or otherwise, until a complaint be made against him for such offense, unless previously admitted to bail, which complaint shall be made as soon as practicable and in any case within twenty-four hours, Sundays and legal holidays excepted

C. 271 § 2	GAMING OR BETTING IN PUBLIC (OR IN PRIVATE WHILE TRESPASSING)
	Elements
1.	In a public conveyance or public place, or in a private place upon which he is trespassing:
2.	• Plays at cards, dice or any other game for money or other property, or • Bets on the sides or hands of those playing, or • Sets up or permits such a game
	Arrest Power, Penalties & Notes
Power of Arrest	**Misdemeanor** – If discovered in the act, the violator may be arrested without a warrant by a sheriff, deputy sheriff, constable or any officer qualified to serve criminal process.

[1] *Commonwealth v. Lake*, 317 Mass. 264, 267 (1944), citing *Commonwealth v. Wall*, 295 Mass. 70, 72 (1936), and *Commonwealth v. Plissner*, 295 Mass. 457, 463 (1936).

C. 271 § 2	GAMING OR BETTING IN PUBLIC (OR IN PRIVATE WHILE TRESPASSING)
Penalty	**Participating**: Forfeit not more than $50 or be imprisoned for not more than 3 months. **Set up or Permit**: a fine of not less than $50 nor more than $100 or by imprisonment for not less than 3 nor more than 12 months.
Related Statutes, Case Law & Other Important Information	
Chapter 4 § 7 defines "Illegal Gaming"	"Illegal gaming," a banking or percentage game played with cards, dice, tiles or dominoes, or an electronic, electrical or mechanical device or machine for money, property, checks, credit or any representative of value, but excluding: (i) a lottery game conducted by the state lottery commission, under sections 24, 24A and 27 of chapter 10; (ii) a game conducted under chapter 23K; (iii) pari-mutuel wagering on horse races under chapters 128A and 128C and greyhound races under said chapter 128C; (iv) a game of bingo conducted under chapter 271; and (v) charitable gaming conducted under said chapter 271.
Gaming House Chapter 271 § 5	Whoever, except as permitted under chapter 23K, keeps or assists in keeping a common gaming house, or building or place occupied, used or kept for the purposes described in section twenty-three, or is found playing or present as provided in said section, or commonly keeps or suffers to be kept, in a building or place actually used and occupied by him, tables or other apparatus for the purpose of playing at an unlawful game or sport for money or any other valuable thing, shall be punished by a fine of not more than $50 or by imprisonment for not more than 3 months.
Illegal Lottery Chapter 271 § 7	Whoever sets up or promotes a lottery for money or other property of value, or by way of lottery disposes of any property of value, or under the pretext of a sale, gift or delivery of other property or of any right, privilege or thing whatever disposes of or offers or attempts to dispose of any property, with intent to make the disposal thereof dependent upon or connected with chance by lot, dice, numbers, game, hazard or other gambling device that is not taking place in a gaming establishment licensed pursuant to chapter 23K, whereby such chance or device is made an additional inducement to the disposal or sale of said property, and whoever aids either by printing or writing, or is in any way concerned, in the setting up, managing or drawing of such lottery, or in such disposal or offer or attempt to dispose of property by such chance or device, shall be punished by a fine of not more than $3,000 or by imprisonment in the state prison **(Felony)** for not more than 3 years, or in jail or the house of correction for not more than 2½ years.
Possession of Illegal Lottery Tickets Chapter 271 § 9	Whoever, for himself or for another, sells or offers for sale or has in his possession with intent to sell or offer for sale, or to exchange or negotiate, or aids or assists in the selling, exchanging, negotiating or disposing of a ticket in such lottery, or a share of a ticket, or any such writing, certificate, bill, token or other device, or a share or right in such disposal or offer, as is mentioned in §7, shall be punished by a fine of not more than $2,000 or by 1 year.
Hosting a Lottery Chapter 271 § 8	Whoever owns, occupies or is in control of a house, shop or building and knowingly permits the establishing, managing or drawing of a lottery, or the disposal or attempt to dispose of property, or the sale of a lottery ticket or share of a ticket, or any other writing, certificate, bill, token or other device purporting or intended to entitle the holder, bearer or any other person to a prize or to a share of or an interest in a prize to be drawn in a lottery, or in the disposal of property, and whoever knowingly allows money or other property to be raffled for or won by throwing or using dice or by any other game of chance that is not being conducted in a gaming establishment licensed under chapter 23K, shall be punished by a fine of not more than $2,000 or by imprisonment in the house of correction for not more than 1 year.

C. 271 § 49	CRIMINAL USURY (AKA LOAN SHARKING)
Elements	
1.	In exchange for either a loan of money or other property
2.	Knowingly contracts for, charges, takes or receives, directly or indirectly, interest and expenses
3.	The aggregate of which exceeds an amount greater than 20% per annum upon the sum loaned or the equivalent rate for a longer or shorter period.
Exception	The provisions of this section shall not apply to any loan the rate of interest for which is regulated under any other provision of general or special law or regulations promulgated thereunder or to any lender subject to control, regulation or examination by any state or federal regulatory agency.
Arrest Power, Penalties & Notes	
Power of Arrest	**Felony** – a police officer may effect a warrantless arrest for this offense provided he/she has probable cause that the suspect committed the offense.
Penalty	Imprisonment in the **state prison (F)** for not more than 10 years or by a fine of not more than $10,000, or by both such fine and imprisonment.
Attorney Hanrahan's Comment	This law only applies to non-regulated lending institutions (e.g. the local bookie). This is an abbreviated version of the actual statute.
Related Statutes, Case Law & Other Important Information	
A &B to Collect a Loan	See chapter 265 § 13C in the Assault & Battery Offenses section of this manual.

HUNTING & FISHING

Note: This section only includes a small selection of Hunting & Fishing laws. There are numerous laws and regulations that deal with hunting and fishing, most of which the average police officer does not encounter.

C. 131 § 58	SHOOTING UPON/ACROSS HIGHWAY; HUNTING NEAR DWELLING
Elements	
1.	A person shall not discharge any firearm or release any arrow
2.	• Upon or across any state or hard surfaced highway, or • Within 150 feet, of any highway (as described above), or • Possess a loaded firearm or hunt by any means on the land of another within 500 of any dwelling in use except as authorized by the owner or occupant thereof.
Arrest Power, Penalties & Notes	
Power of Arrest	**Misdemeanor** – there is no statutory authority granting warrantless powers of arrest for this offense. However, if the offense is committed in public, in the officer's presence, and is creating a **breach of the peace** an arrest would be lawful.
Penalty	A fine of not less than fifty nor more than one hundred dollars, or by imprisonment for not more than thirty days, or both such fine and imprisonment (see c. 131 § 9 for more)
Related Statutes, Case Law & Other Important Information	
Chapter 269 § 12E	Chapter 269 § 12E prohibits the discharge of a firearm within 500 feet of a dwelling. See firearms/weapons section of this manual.
Chapter 131 § 65A	Chapter 131 § 65A criminalizes (misdemeanor) on-line shooting or spearing.
Chapter 131 § 64	A person shall not use for hunting purposes any type of full automatic firearm, machine gun or submachine gun, or any crossbow, except as provided in section 69, nor use any tracer or incendiary ammunition for hunting or outdoor target shooting purposes except on a skeet, trap, or target range.
Bows and Arrows for Hunting	Chapter 131 § 69 regulates the use of bows and arrows for the purposes of hunting. For instance, crossbows can only be used by persons who are permanently disabled.
Hunting while Intoxicated	Chapter 131 § 62 states "A person, while under the influence of intoxicating liquor or of drugs shall not hunt or carry a firearm, bow and arrow or other weapon while engaged in hunting or target shooting."
Careless or negligent use of weapons causing injury or death to another	Chapter 131 § 60 states "A person shall not use any firearm, bow and arrow or other weapon or article in a careless or negligent manner so as to cause bodily injury or death to another while engaged in hunting or target shooting. Any person, while so engaged, who causes injury or death to any other person by reason of the use of any firearm, bow and arrow or other weapon or article and any person having knowledge of such injury or death shall immediately report the same to the state or local police who shall in turn submit a copy of such report to the director of law enforcement. Any person found guilty of, or convicted of, any violation of the first sentence of this section or any person failing to make the report required by this section who is the holder of any hunting or sporting license issued under the provisions of this chapter shall forthwith lose any rights thereunder, and said license shall be surrendered to any officer empowered to enforce the provisions of this chapter and no other hunting or sporting license shall be granted to him for a period of 5 years."

C. 131 § 58	SHOOTING UPON/ACROSS HIGHWAY; HUNTING NEAR DWELLING
Hunting on Sundays	Chapter 131 § 57 states "Every Sunday shall be a closed season. Except as otherwise provided in sections four, thirty-one and thirty-seven, a person, on Sunday, shall not hunt any bird or mammal or carry on that day on his person a rifle, shotgun or bow and arrow or, unless otherwise permitted by law, a pistol or revolver, in any place where birds or mammals might be found. This section shall not render unlawful the possession or carrying of a rifle, shotgun, pistol, revolver or bow and arrow, for the purpose of using the same on a skeet, trap or target range, nor for the purpose of using the same for sport target shooting at artificial targets by an owner or lessee, or his guest, upon his own or leased property, or by members or guests of clubs or associations on supervised firing ranges, nor shall it prohibit the taking of mammals by means of traps, nor the training of falcons or protected species, nor the exercising of such falcons as regulated by the director."
Penalties	Chapter 131 § 90 provides the penalties for most hunting violations.
Arrest Powers	Chapter 131 § 87 provides the power of a warrantless arrest for nearly all hunting violations (committed in presence) in chapter 131. However, the statute seems to limit the power to environmental and state police.
Searches, seizures and arrests without warrant for Fishing Violations	Chapter 130 § 9: The director, the deputy directors of enforcement, chiefs of enforcement, deputy chiefs of enforcement and all environmental police officers and deputy environmental police officers or a member of the state police may, without a warrant, search any boat, vessel, fish car, bag, box, locker, package, crate, any building other than a dwelling house, any motor vehicle as defined in section one of c. ninety, or other vehicle, or any other personal property in which he has reasonable cause to believe, and does believe, that fish taken, held, kept, possessed, transported or held for transportation or sale in violation of law, may be found, and may seize any such fish there found, and may seize any boat, vessel, fish car, bag, box, locker, package, crate, any motor vehicle as defined in section one of c. ninety, or other vehicle, or any other personal property used in a violation of the laws relative to marine fisheries and hold the same for forfeiture. Any such person or officer may arrest without a warrant any person found violating any provision of this chapter or of any ordinance, rule or regulation made under authority thereof, or any other provision of law relative to marine fisheries. **Editor's Note:** this law does not include municipal police officers.

HUNTING & FISHING OFFENSES

INVASION OF PRIVACY

C. 272 § 99 INTERCEPTION OF WIRE AND ORAL COMMUNICATIONS

Summary: This law prohibits the interception of wire or oral communications without knowledge of the parties and without a warrant. This portion of the manual does not include the entire statute. For a more detailed analysis of this statute and its exceptions see the criminal procedure section of this manual.

Elements	
1.	In regards to any wire or oral communication the defendant unlawfully does any of the following:
2.	• Willfully commits an interception • Procures any other person to commit an interception • Attempts to commit an interception
Arrest Power, Penalties & Notes	
Power of Arrest	**Felony** – a police officer may effect a warrantless arrest for this offense provided he/she has probable cause that the suspect committed the offense.
Penalty	A fine of not more than $10,000, or imprisoned in the **state prison (F)** for not more than 5 years, or imprisoned in a jail or house of correction for not more than 2½ years, or both so fined and given one such imprisonment.
Attorney Hanrahan's Comment	Be sure to see a detailed analysis of this offense in the surveillance section of the Criminal Procedure part of this manual. There are some instances wherein someone may lawfully intercept communications.
Other Important Information	
Prima Facie evidence	Proof of the installation of any intercepting device by any person under circumstances evincing an intent to commit an interception, which is not authorized or permitted by this section, shall be prima facie evidence of a violation of this subparagraph.

C. 272 § 105	PHOTOGRAPHING, VIDEOTAPING OR ELECTRONICALLY SURVEILING SOMEONE NUDE/PARTIALLY NUDE or SEXUAL INTIMATE PARTS
	Surveil Nude or Partially Nude Victim **Elements**
1.	The defendant willfully,
2.	Photographs, videotapes or electronically surveils another person who is nude or partially nude,
3.	With the intent to secretly conduct or hide such activity,
4.	When the other person in such place and circumstance would have a reasonable expectation of privacy in not being so photographed, videotaped or electronically surveilled,
5.	Without the person's knowledge or consent.
	Surveil Sexual Intimate Parts (AKA "up-skirting) **Elements**
1.	The defendant willfully
2.	Photographs, videotapes or electronically surveils
3.	The sexual or other intimate parts of a person under or around the person's clothing
4.	To view, or attempt to view, the person's sexual or other intimate parts without the knowledge or consent of the person
5.	When a reasonable person would believe that the person's sexual or intimate parts would not be visible to the public
6.	And without the person's knowledge and consent.
	Arrest Power, Penalties & Notes
Power of Arrest	**Misdemeanor** - A sheriff, deputy sheriff or police officer may arrest without a warrant, a person whom he has probable cause to believe has violated this section.
Penalty	Imprisonment in the HOC for not more than 2½ years or by a fine of not more than $5,000, or by both such fine and imprisonment. **Victim under 18 (F)**: if the victim is under the age of 18 HOC for not more than 2 1/2 years, by imprisonment in the state prison for not more than 5 years, or by a fine of not more than $10,000, or by both such fine and imprisonment. **Important note**: the under 18 felony provision only applies to the "up-skirting" offense not the secret surveiling of someone in the nude or partial nude. This is seemingly an oversight by the legislature as the quickly modified this statute after a high profile court dismissal of an "up-skirting" event. Nonetheless, as written the under 18 felony aspect is limited to the "up-skirting" provision only.

C. 272 § 105	PHOTOGRAPHING, VIDEOTAPING OR ELECTRONICALLY SURVEILING SOMEONE NUDE/PARTIALLY NUDE or SEXUAL INTIMATE PARTS
Exceptions to the above offenses	(a) This section shall not apply to a merchant that electronically surveils a customer changing room, provided that signage warning customers of the merchant's surveillance activity is conspicuous posted at all entrances, and in the interior of any changing room electronically surveilled. (b) This section shall not apply to a law enforcement officer when acting within the scope of the officer's authority under applicable law, or by an order or warrant issued by a court.
Related Statutes, Case Law & Other Important Information	
Dissemination	Chapter 272 § 105(c) punishes whoever willfully disseminates the visual with knowledge that such visual image was unlawfully obtained in violation 272 § 105 and without consent of the person so depicted. **Penalty:** by imprisonment in the house of correction for not more than 2½ years or in **state prison (F)** for a period of not more than 5 years, or by a fine of not more than $10,000, or by both such fine and imprisonment. If image is of person under the age of 18 years house of correction for not more than 2 1/2 years or in the state prison for not more than 10 years or by a fine of not more than $10,000, or by both such fine and imprisonment **Arrest Powers**: **Felony** – a police officer may effect an arrest for this offense committed in his/her presence or for an offense in the past, on probable cause.
Image not Public Record	Any photograph, videotape or other recorded visual image, depicting a person who is nude or partially nude that is part of any court record arising from a prosecution under this section, shall not be open to public inspection and shall only be made available for inspection by court personnel to any law enforcement officer, prosecuting attorney, defendant's attorney, defendant, or victim connected to such prosecution, unless otherwise ordered by the court.
Definitions	**"Electronically surveils"** or "**electronically surveilled",** to view, obtain or record a person's visual image by the use or aid of a camera, cellular or other wireless communication device, computer, television or other electronic device. **"Partially nude"** the exposure of the human genitals, buttocks, pubic area or female breast below a point immediately above the top of the areola. "**Sexual or other intimate parts**", human genitals, buttocks, pubic area or female breast below a point immediately above the tip of the areola, whether naked or covered by clothing or undergarments.

CONSTITUTIONAL RIGHTS VIOLATIONS

C. 265 § 37	VIOLATIONS OF CONSTITUTIONAL RIGHTS
Elements	
1.	No person, whether or not acting under color of law, shall by force or threat of force, do the following:
2.	• Willfully injure, intimidate or interfere with, or • Attempt to injure, intimidate or interfere with, or • Oppress or threaten
3.	Any other person in the free exercise or enjoyment of any right or privilege secured to him by the constitution or laws of the commonwealth or by the constitution or laws of the United States.
Arrest Power, Penalties & Notes	
Power of Arrest	**No bodily injury - Misdemeanor** – there is no statutory authority granting powers of arrest for this offense. However, if the offense is committed in public, in the officer's presence, and is creating a **breach of the peace** an arrest would be lawful. However, see below for felony charge: **If Bodily Injury Results then crime becomes a Felony:** a police officer may effect an arrest for this offense committed in his/her presence or for an offense in the past, on probable cause.
Penalty	No bodily Injury - A fine of not more than $1,000 dollars or imprisoned not more than 1 year or both. **If Bodily Injury Results then crime becomes a Felony:** if bodily injury results, shall be punished by a fine of not more than $10,000 or by imprisonment for not more than 10 years, or both.
Case Law & Important Information	
Distinctions between Federal Law and State Law	General Laws c. 265, § 37 offers a scope of protection that is similar in many respects to 42 U.S.C.§ 242 (the Federal criminal statute governing civil rights violations), and to 42 U.S.C. § 1983 (the Federal civil statute governing civil rights violations). General Laws c. 265, § 37 differs from both Federal statutes in two significant ways: 1. It applies whether or not a defendant was acting under color of law, and therefore encompasses not only private rights secured against the government but also relations between private parties. *O'Connell v. Chasdi,* 400 Mass. 686, 692, 511 N.E.2d 349, 352 (1987); *Bell v. Mazza,* 394 Mass. 176, 182, 474 N.E.2d 1111, 1115 (1985) (statutory phrase "whether or not acting under color of law" is superfluous); *Batchelder v. Allied Stores Corp.,* 393 Mass. 819, 822-823, 473 N.E.2d 1128, 1131 (1985); *United States Jaycees v. Massachusetts Comm'n Against Discrimination,* 391 Mass. 594, 609 n.9, 463 N.E.2d 1151, 1160 n.9 (1984). 2. It requires proof of force or threat of force, and is limited to certain specific prohibited acts (e.g., "injure," "intimidate," etc.). *Commonwealth v. Stephens,* 25 Mass. App. Ct. 117, 122 n.5, 515 N.E.2d 606, 609 n.5 (1987). In addition, the Massachusetts statute, unlike 42 U.S.C. § 1983, requires that the violation have been "willful," *Redgrave v. Boston Symphony Orchestra, Inc.,* 399 Mass. 93, 99-100, 502 N.E.2d 1375, 1379, *S.C.,* 831 F.2d 339 (1st Cir. 1987), 855 F.2d 888 (1st Cir. 1988) (en banc).

C. 265 § 37	VIOLATIONS OF CONSTITUTIONAL RIGHTS
Threat	The "threat" is "acts or language by which another is placed in fear of injury or damage".[1]
Education rights	Under Federal and state law, public school students have a right to attend school and to be educated without discrimination or segregation on account of race. U.S. Const., Amend. 14. *Brown v. Board of Education,* 347 U.S. 483, 74 S.Ct. 686 (1954). Mass. Const., Pt. 1, art. 1. G.L. c. 76, § 5.
Employment rights	The right to work without discrimination because of race color, religious creed, national origin or ancestry is a right and privilege of all inhabitants of the Commonwealth. St. 1946, c. 368. It is an unlawful discriminatory practice for any employer or his agent to discriminate against an applicant or employee in compensation, terms, conditions or privileges of employment because of race, color, religious creed, national origin, sex, age or ancestry, or for any person to aid, abet, incite, compel or coerce such discrimination. G.L. c. 151B, § 4. See *Radvilas v. Stop & Shop, Inc.,* 18 Mass. App. Ct. 431, 466 N.E.2d 832 (1984) (employment discrimination because of sex and age). **Sexual harassment** in the workplace violates both art. 1 of the Massachusetts Declaration of Rights, *O'Connell,* 400 Mass. at 693, 511 N.E.2d at 353, and G.L. c. 151B, § 4(1), *College-Town, Div. of Interco, Inc. v. Massachusetts Comm'n Against Discrimination,* 400 Mass. 156, 162, 508 N.E.2d 587, 591 (1987).
Housing rights	The right to own, rent and occupy housing without discrimination because of race, color, religion, sex, or national origin is guaranteed by the federal Fair Housing Act of 1968. 42 U.S.C. § 3601 et seq. *Trafficante v. Metropolitan Life Ins. Co.,* 409 U.S. 205, 93 S.Ct. 364 (1972). The right to occupy and enjoy housing is protected against racially motivated interference, whether by the property owners or by third persons unconnected to the property owner. *Metropolitan Hous. Dev. Corp. v. Village of Arlington Heights,* 558 F.2d 1283, 1294 (7th Cir. 1977), cert. denied, 434 U.S. 1025 (1978).
Mental patients' rights	A mental patient has a constitutional right to basically safe and humane living conditions, which includes protection from assaults. *Harper v. Cserr,* 544 F.2d 1121, 1123 (1st Cir. 1976). See *Goodman v. Parwatikar,* 570 F.2d 801, 804 (8th Cir. 1978).
Personal security rights	All persons have the same right to the full and equal benefit of all laws and proceedings for the security of persons and property that is enjoyed by white citizens. 42 U.S.C. § 1981. This right is violated by racially motivated violence. *Mahone v. Waddle,* 564 F.2d 1018 (3d Cir. 1977), cert. denied, 438 U.S. 904 (1978).
Prisoners' rights	**Prisoners' rights**. While officials such as police or corrections officers may use reasonable force to overcome resistance by a person whom they are taking into custody or holding in custody, the constitutional right to due process includes the right not to be subjected to unreasonable, unnecessary or unprovoked force by such officers. Arresting officers may use only such force as is reasonably necessary to effect an arrest or to defend themselves. It is a violation of the Fourteenth Amendment to hold and physically punish a person and thereby deprive him of liberty without due process of law.[2] Reasonable force is that which an ordinary prudent person would deem necessary under the circumstances. *Powers v. Sturtevant,* 199 Mass. 265, 266, 85 N.E. 84, 84 (1908). This is a jury question. *Commonwealth v. Young,* 326 Mass. 597, 603, 96 N.E.2d 133, 136 (1950).

[1] *Delaney v. Chief of Police of Wareham,* 27 Mass. App. Ct. 398, 409, 539 N.E.2d 65, 72 (1989)

[2] *Ingraham v. Wright,* 430 U.S. 651, 674, 97 S.Ct. 1401, 1414 (1977); *Screws,* 325 U.S. at 106, 111, 65 S.Ct. at 1038, 1040; *United States v. McQueeney,* 674 F.2d 109, 113 (1st Cir. 1982); *Landrigan v. Warwick,* 628 F.2d 736, 741-742 (1st Cir. 1980); *United States v. Villarin Gerena,* 553 F.2d 723, 724 (1st Cir. 1977); *Human Rights Comm'n of Worcester v. Assad,* 370 Mass. 482, 487, 349 N.E.2d 341, 344-345 (1976). G.L. c. 111B, § 8, sixth par. (protective custody statute); G.L. c. 124, § 1(b), (g). 103 Code Mass. Regs. §§ 505.05(5), 505.06.

C. 265 § 37	VIOLATIONS OF CONSTITUTIONAL RIGHTS
Private establishments open to the public	Privately-owned facilities (such as stores, restaurants, taverns, gas stations, theaters and arcades) which are open to the public and which solicit or accept the patronage of the general public are also places of public accommodation covered by the Massachusetts Public Accommodations Law, *(see below).* See also 804 Code Mass. Regs. § 5.01.
Public accommodations rights	The Massachusetts Public Accommodations Law guarantees to all persons the full and equal use of all places of public accommodation free from any distinction, discrimination or restriction on account of race, color, religious creed, national origin, sex, deafness, blindness, ancestry, or any physical or mental disability. Public facilities such as parks, playgrounds, government buildings, public beaches, highways, streets and sidewalks are all places of public accommodation covered by the law. G.L. c. 272, §§ 92A, 98.
Religious exercise rights	The right to free exercise of religion is guaranteed by Articles 2 and 3 of the Declaration of Rights of the Massachusetts Constitution and by the First Amendment to the United States Constitution. This right protects religious worship, religious practices, meetings for those purposes, and ownership and use of buildings and other property for religious purposes. It protects the religious activities of individuals, congregations, and their spiritual leaders. Mass. Const., Pt. 1, arts. 2, 3; U.S. Const., Amends. 1, 14.
Travel rights	Under the United States Constitution, all persons have a right to travel freely between the states, and to use the highways and other avenues of interstate commerce in doing so. *Griffin v. Breckenridge,* 403 U.S. 88, 91 S.Ct. 1790 (1971); Public transportation vehicles (such as MBTA buses, subway cars, and streetcars), bus stops, and subway stations and platforms are all places of public accommodation under the Massachusetts Public Accommodations Law.
Voting rights	The right to elect public officials and to be elected to public office is guaranteed by the Federal Constitution, *United States v. Classic,* 313 U.S. 299, 314, 61 S.Ct. 1031, 1035 (1941), and by Article 9 of the Massachusetts Declaration of Rights, *Batchelder v. Allied Stores Int'l,* 388 Mass. 83, 445 N.E.2d 590 (1983).
Civil Action **c. 12 § 11H**	Chapter 12 § 11H permits the issuance of a civil injunction for violations of civil and constitutional rights. The statute states "whenever any person or persons, whether or not acting under color of law, interfere by threats, intimidation or coercion, or attempt to interfere by threats, intimidation or coercion, with the exercise or enjoyment by any other person or persons of rights secured by the constitution or laws of the United States, or of rights secured by the constitution or laws of the commonwealth, the attorney general may bring a civil action for injunctive or other appropriate equitable relief in order to protect the peaceable exercise or enjoyment of the right or rights secured. Said civil action shall be brought in the name of the commonwealth and shall be instituted either in the superior court for the county in which the conduct complained of occurred or in the superior court for the county in which the person whose conduct complained of resides or has his principal place of business."

C. 265 § 39	A&B/PROPERTY DESTRUCTION HATE CRIME
Elements	
1.	The defendant: • Commits an assault or a battery upon a person, or • Damages the real or personal property of a person
2.	With the intent to intimidate such person because of such person's race, color, religion, national origin, sexual orientation, gender identity, or disability.
Arrest Power, Penalties & Notes	
Power of Arrest	**Misdemeanor** – there is no statutory authority granting powers of arrest for this offense. However, if the offense is committed in public, in the officer's presence, and is creating a **breach of the peace** an arrest would be lawful. However, if bodily injury results or weapons are used. **Felony** warrantless arrest powers would apply.
Penalty	**Penalty – No Bodily Injury:** a fine of not more than $5,000 or by imprisonment in a HOC for not more than 2½ years, or by both such fine and imprisonment. The court may also order restitution to the victim in any amount up to 3 times the value of property damage sustained by the owners of such property. **Enhanced penalty for Bodily Injury:** fine of not more than $10,000 or by imprisonment in the **state prison (F)** for not more than 5 years, or by both such fine and imprisonment. **Enhanced Penalty for use of certain weapons**: Whoever commits any offense described in this subsection while armed with a **firearm, rifle, shotgun, machine gun or assault weapon** shall be punished by imprisonment in the **state prison (F)** for not more than 10 years or in the HOC for not more than 2½ years.
Related Statutes, Case Law & Other Important Information	
Definitions	For the purposes of this section, the term **"disability"** shall have the same meaning as "handicap" as defined in c. 151B § 17; provided, however, that for purposes of this section, the term "disability" shall not include any condition primarily resulting from the use of alcohol or a controlled substance as defined in c. 94C § 1. For purposes of this section, **"bodily injury"** shall mean substantial impairment of the physical condition, including, but not limited to, any burn, fracture of any bone, subdural hematoma, injury to any internal organ, or any injury which occurs as the result of repeated harm to any bodily function or organ, including human skin.
Mandatory Diversity Program	A person convicted under the provisions of this section shall complete a diversity awareness program designed by the secretary of the executive office of public safety in consultation with the Massachusetts commission against discrimination and approved by the chief justice for administration and management of the trial court. A person so convicted shall complete such program prior to release from incarceration or prior to completion of the terms of probation, whichever is applicable.

C. 266 § 120E½

IMPEDING ACCESS TO REPRODUCTIVE HEALTH CARE FACILITY

Elements & Variations

Law Enforcement withdrawal order (Section b)	A law enforcement official may order the immediate withdrawal of 1 or more individuals who have on that day substantially impeded access to or departure from an entrance or driveway to a reproductive health care facility. A withdrawal order issued pursuant to this section shall be in writing and shall include the following statements: (i) the individual or individuals have substantially impeded access to or departure from the reproductive health care facility; (ii) the individual or individuals so ordered shall, under the penalty of arrest and prosecution, immediately withdraw and cease to stand or be located within at least 25 feet of an entrance or driveway to the reproductive health care facility; and (iii) the order shall remain in place for 8 hours or until the close of business of the reproductive health facility, whichever is earlier. This subsection shall apply during the business hours of a reproductive health care facility. This subsection shall also apply only if the 25 foot boundary is clearly marked and subsections (a) through (c), inclusive, of this section are posted outside of the reproductive health care facility. **Penalty:** A person who fails to comply with a withdrawal order pursuant to subsection (b) shall be punished, for the first offense, by a fine of not more than $500 or not more than 3 months in a jail or house of correction or by both such fine and imprisonment and, for each subsequent offense, by a fine of not less than $500 nor more than $5,000 or not more than 2 ½ years in a jail or house of correction or by both such fine and imprisonment.
Threatening, Intimidating or Injuring (section d)	A person who, by force, physical act or threat of force, intentionally injures or intimidates or attempts to injure or intimidate a person who attempts to access or depart from a reproductive health care facility shall be punished. **Penalty: 1st offense** - a fine of not more than $2,000 or not more than 1 year in a jail or house of correction or by both such fine and imprisonment and, for each subsequent offense, by a fine of not less than $10,000 nor more than $50,000 or not more than 2½ years in a jail or house of correction or not more than 5 years in a state prison or by both such fine and imprisonment. For the purpose of this subsection, "intimidate" shall mean to place a person in reasonable apprehension of bodily harm to that person or another.
Impeding by Force or Intimidation (section e)	A person who impedes a person's access to or departure from a reproductive health care facility with the intent to interfere with that person's ability to provide, support the provision of or obtain services at the reproductive health care facility shall be punished. **Penalty : 1st offense** - a fine of not more than $1,000 or not more than 6 months in a jail or house of correction or by both such fine and imprisonment and, for each subsequent offense, by a fine of not less than $5,000 nor more than $25,000 or not more than 2½ years in a jail or house of correction or not more than 5 years in the state prison or by both such fine and imprisonment.

C. 266 § 120E½	IMPEDING ACCESS TO REPRODUCTIVE HEALTH CARE FACILITY
Knowingly Impeding a vehicle (section f)	A person who knowingly impedes or attempts to impede a person or a vehicle attempting to access or depart from a reproductive health care facility shall be punished. **Penalty: 1st offense** - a fine of not more than $500 or not more than 3 months in a jail or house of correction or by both such fine and imprisonment and, for each subsequent offense, by a fine of not less than $1,000 nor more than $5,000 or not more than 2½ years in a jail or house of correction or by both such fine and imprisonment.
Recklessly Impeding a Vehicle (section g)	A person who recklessly interferes with the operation of a vehicle that attempts to enter, exit or park at a reproductive health care facility shall be punished, for the first offense, by a fine of not more than $500 or not more than 3 months in a jail or house of correction or by both such fine and imprisonment and, for each subsequent offense, by a fine of not less than $1,000 nor more than $5,000 or not more than 2½ years in a jail or house of correction or by both such fine and imprisonment.
	Arrest Power, Penalties & Notes
Power of Arrest	**Misdemeanor** – a person who fails to comply with a dispersal order (section b above) or is found violating any of the other provisions (sections c, d, e, or f) may be arrested without a warrant.
Attorney Hanrahan's Comment	An earlier version of this offense (c. 266 § 120E) created an automatic 35 foot buffer zone. However, in 2014 the U.S. Supreme Court ruled the statute unconstitutional. The legislature reacted by enacting this statute.
	Other Important Information
Definitions	"Driveway", an entry from a public street to a public or private parking area used by a reproductive health care facility. "Entrance", a door to a reproductive health care facility that directly abuts the public sidewalk; provided, however, that if the door does not directly abut the public sidewalk, the "entrance" shall be the point at which the public sidewalk intersects with a pathway leading to the door. "Impede", to obstruct, block, detain or render passage impossible, unsafe or unreasonably difficult. "Law enforcement official", a duly authorized member of a law enforcement agency, including a member of a municipal, metropolitan or state police department, sheriffs or deputy sheriffs. "Reproductive health care facility", a place, other than within or upon the grounds of a hospital, where abortions are offered or performed including, but not limited to, the building, grounds and driveway of the facility and a parking lot in which the facility has an ownership or leasehold interest.
Civil Action Remedies	If a person or entity fails to comply with a withdrawal order pursuant to subsection (b) or who is found in violation of subsection (c), (d), (e), (f) or (g), an aggrieved person or entity or the attorney general or both may commence a civil action. The civil action shall be commenced either in the superior court for the county in which the conduct complained of occurred or in the superior court for the county in which the person or entity complained of resides or has a principal place of business. In such a civil action a court may award as remedies: (1) temporary, preliminary and permanent injunctive relief; (2) compensatory and punitive damages; and (3) costs, attorneys' fees and expert witness fees. In an action brought by the attorney general pursuant to subsection (i), the court may also award civil penalties against each defendant in an amount not exceeding: (A) $5,000 for a nonviolent violation and $7,500 for other first violations; and (B) $7,500 for a subsequent nonviolent violation and $12,500 for any other subsequent violation.

MISCELLANEOUS STATUTES

LOST PROPERTY

C. 134 § 1. ***Report of lost money or goods by finder***

- Any person who finds
- **lost money or goods** of the value of **$3.00 or more**,
- the owner of which is unknown,
- shall within 2 days
- report the finding thereof to the officer in charge at a police station in the town where said property was found,
- or, if there is no police station, post notice thereof in two public places therein,
- or, instead of such report or posting, cause notice thereof to be advertised in a newspaper published therein.

C. 134 § 3. Restitution of property

If, within **3 months after the finding of stray beasts**, or **within 1 year after the finding of lost money or goods**, the owner appears and pays all reasonable expenses incurred by the finder in keeping such goods or beasts and in complying with this chapter, **he shall have restitution of the money, goods or beasts**.

C. 134 § 4. ***Rights of finder if no owner appears***

If the owner of lost money or goods does not appear within one year after the finding thereof, they shall enure (it becomes property of the finder) to the finder, provided he has complied with section one (report to police or make public notice).

WITNESSS ISSUES & EXEMPTIONS

C. 233 § 13C ***Exemption from arrest and process of witnesses from outside state***

If a person comes into this commonwealth **in obedience to a summons or order directing him to attend and testify in a criminal proceeding or grand jury investigation** or proceeding in this commonwealth **he shall not, while in this commonwealth pursuant to such summons or order, be subject to arrest or the service of process,** civil or criminal, in connection with matters which arose before his entrance into this commonwealth under the summons or order.

If a person **passes through this commonwealth while going to another state in obedience to a summons or order to attend and testify in a criminal proceeding or grand jury investigation or proceeding in that state, or while returning therefrom**, he shall **not,** while so passing through this commonwealth, **be subject to arrest** or the service of process, civil or criminal, in connection with matters which arose before his entrance into this commonwealth under the summons or order.

Nothing in this section or either of the two preceding sections shall preclude action under sections twelve and thirteen or under similar reciprocal provisions of law in other states.

C. 233 § 20. ***Competency of witnesses; husband and wife; criminal defendant; parent and child***

Any person of sufficient understanding, although a party, may testify in any proceeding, civil or criminal, in court or before a person who has authority to receive evidence, **except as follows**:

First, neither husband nor wife shall testify as to <u>private conversations</u> with the other.

> **Exceptions:** a. proceedings involving a contract made by a married woman with her husband, b. any criminal proceeding in which one spouse is a defendant alleged to have committed a crime against the other spouse or to have violated protective order and c. a proceeding involving abuse of a person under the age of eighteen, including incest,

Second, neither husband nor wife shall be compelled to testify in the trial of an indictment, complaint or other criminal proceeding against the other;

MISCELLANEOUS LAWS

Exceptions: in any proceeding relating to child abuse, including incest,

Third, The defendant in the trial of an indictment, complaint or other criminal proceeding shall, at his own request, but not otherwise, be allowed to testify; but his neglect or refusal to testify shall not create any presumption against him.

Fourth, An **unemancipated, minor child, living with a parent, shall not testify** before a grand jury, trial of an indictment, complaint or other criminal proceeding, **against said parent, where the victim in such proceeding is not a member of said parent's family and who does not reside in the said parent's household**. For the purposes of this clause the term "parent" shall mean the natural or adoptive mother or father of said child.

§ 278:16D. Child witness testimony; videotaping or transmission by simultaneous electronic means in certain cases

(a) For the purposes of this section, the following words shall have the following meanings:

"Child witness", a person who is under the age of fifteen years and who is alleged to have been a victim of, or a witness to an alleged violation of section thirteen B, 13B½, 13B 3/4, thirteen F, thirteen H, twenty-two, twenty-two A, 22B, 22C, twenty-three , 23A, 23B, twenty-four, 24B or 50 of chapter two hundred and sixty-five, or section two, three, four, four A, four B, five, six, seven, eight, twelve, thirteen, sixteen, seventeen, twenty-four, twenty-eight, twenty-nine, twenty-nine A, twenty-nine B, thirty-three, thirty-four or thirty-five A of chapter two hundred and seventy-two.

"Simultaneous electronic means", any device capable of projecting a live visual and aural transmission such as closed-circuit television.

(b) (1) At any time after the issuance of a complaint or indictment alleging an offense punished by any of the statutes listed herein, the court on its own motion or on motion of the proponent of a child witness, and after a hearing, may order the use of a suitable alternative procedure for taking the testimony of the child witness, in proceedings pursuant to said complaint or indictment, provided that the court finds by a preponderance of the evidence at the time of the order that the child witness is likely to suffer psychological or emotional trauma as a result of testifying in open court, as a result of testifying in the presence of the defendant, or as a result of both testifying in open court and testifying in the presence of the defendant. If the court orders the use of a suitable alternative for taking the testimony of a child witness pursuant to this section, the court shall make and enter specific findings upon the record describing with particularity the reasons for such order.

(2) An order issued under paragraph (1) shall provide that the testimony of the child witness be recorded on videotape or film to be shown in court at a later time or that the testimony be transmitted to the courtroom by simultaneous electronic means.

(3) Testimony taken by an alternative procedure pursuant to an order issued under paragraph (1) shall be taken in the presence of the judge, the prosecutor, defense counsel and such other persons as the court may allow. The defendant shall also have the right to be present unless the court's order under paragraph (1) is based wholly or in part upon a finding that the child witness is likely to suffer trauma as a result of testifying in the presence of the defendant. If the order is based on such a finding, the testimony of the child witness shall not be taken in the presence of the defendant except as provided in paragraph (4).

(4) Testimony taken by an alternative procedure pursuant to an order issued under paragraph (1) shall be taken in a suitable setting outside the courtroom, except that an order based only on a finding that the child witness is likely to suffer trauma as a result of testifying in the presence of the defendant may provide that the testimony be taken in a suitable setting inside the courtroom in a manner so that the child witness is not able to see or hear the defendant.

(5) When testimony is taken by an alternative procedure pursuant to an order issued under paragraph (1), counsel shall be given the opportunity to examine or cross-examine the child witness to the same extent as would be permitted at trial, and the defendant shall be able to see and hear the child witness and to have constant private communication with defense counsel.

(6) The film, videotape or transmission of testimony taken by an alternative procedure pursuant to an order issued under paragraph (1) shall be admissible as substantive evidence to the same extent as and in lieu of live testimony by the child witness in any proceeding for which the order is issued or in any related criminal proceeding against the same defendant when consistent with the interests of justice, provided that such an order is entered or re-entered based on current findings at the time when or within a reasonable time before the film, videotape or transmission is offered into evidence. Subsequent testimony of a child witness in any such proceeding shall also be taken by a suitable alternative procedure pursuant to this section.

(7) Whenever pursuant to an order issued under paragraph (1), testimony is recorded on videotape or film or is transmitted to the courtroom by simultaneous electronic means, the court shall ensure that:

(a) The recording or transmitting equipment is capable of making an accurate recording or transmission and is operated by a competent operator;

(b) The recording or transmission is in color and the witness is visible at all times;

(c) Every voice on the recording or transmission is audible and identified;

(d) The courtroom is equipped with monitors which permit the jury and others present in the courtroom to see and hear the recording or transmission;

(e) In the case of recorded testimony, the recording is accurate and has not been altered;

(f) In the case of recorded testimony, each party is afforded the opportunity to view the recording before it is shown in the courtroom.

(8) Nothing in this section shall be deemed to prohibit the court from using other appropriate means, consistent with this section and other laws and with the defendant's rights, to protect a child witness from trauma during a court proceeding.

LAWS DEALING WITH INNS AND HOTELS

C. 140 § 12. *Defrauding an innkeeper*

Defrauding an Innkeeper

- Whoever puts up at a hotel, motel, inn, lodging house or boarding house
- and, without having an express agreement for credit,
- with intent to cheat or defraud the owner or keeper
- procures food, entertainment or accommodation without paying therefor,
- or
- obtains credit at a hotel, motel, inn, lodging house or boarding house for such food, entertainment or accommodation by means of any false show of baggage or effects
- or
- removes or causes to be removed any baggage or effects from a hotel, motel, or inn while a lien exists thereon for the proper charges due from him for fare and board furnished therein,
- shall be punished by as follows:

Penalty: If the value exceeds $100: imprisonment in a jail or HOC for not more than 2 years, or by a fine of not more than $600.

If the value does not exceed $100: imprisonment for not more than 1 year or by a fine of not more than $1,000 dollars;

ARREST POWERS: **Misdemeanor** – there is no statutory authority granting powers of arrest for this offense. However, if the offense is committed in public, in the officer's presence, and is creating a **breach of the peace** an arrest would be lawful.

C. 140 § 12B. *Removal of guest from hotel*

An innkeeper may remove or cause to be removed from a hotel a guest or other person who:

- refuses or is unable to pay for accommodations or services;
- while on the premises of the hotel:
  - acts in an obviously intoxicated or disorderly manner, destroys or threatens to destroy hotel property,
  - causes or threatens to cause a disturbance;
  - violates a rule of the hotel that is clearly and conspicuously posted at or near the front desk and on the inside of the entrance door of every guest room.

If the guest has paid in advance, the innkeeper shall tender to the guest any unused portion of the advanced payment at the time of removal.

MISCELLANEOUS LAWS

C. 140 § 12C. *Refusal of accommodation in hotel to persons acting in disorderly manner*

An innkeeper may refuse to admit or refuse service or accommodation in the hotel to a person who:

while on the premises of the hotel:

- acts in an obviously intoxicated or disorderly manner, destroys or threatens to destroy hotel property, or causes or threatens to cause a public disturbance;
- refuses or is unable to pay for the accommodations or services.

An innkeeper may require the prospective guest to demonstrate an ability to pay. An innkeeper may require a parent or guardian of a minor to accept liability for the proper charges for the minor's accommodation, board, room, or lodging; and any damages to the guest room or its furniture or furnishings caused by the minor, and provide a credit card to cover the charges. When the parent or guardian cannot provide a credit card, the innkeeper may require the parent or guardian to make an advance cash deposit in an amount not exceeding $100 for payment of any additional charges by the minor or any damages to the guest room or its furnishings. The innkeeper shall refund the damage deposit to the extent it is not used to cover any reasonable charges or damages.

Note: An innkeeper may limit the number of persons who may occupy a particular guest room in the hotel.

C. 140 § 27. Register; entry of names; condition precedent to occupancy; retention; inspection

Summary: Inn Keepers must keep a log of all registered guests which is subject to inspection by the police.

- Every innholder, and every lodging house keeper, and every person who shall conduct, control, manage or operate, directly or indirectly, any recreational camp, overnight camp or cabin, motel or manufactured housing community
- shall keep or cause to be kept, in permanent form,
- a register in which shall be recorded the name and the residence of every person engaging or occupying a private room (averaging less than 400 Square Feet)
- for any period of the day or night in any part of the premises controlled by the licensee, together with a true and accurate record of the room assigned to such person and of the day and hour when such room is assigned.
- The entry of the names of the person engaging a room **and of the occupants of said room** shall be made by said person engaging said room or by an occupant

Exception: except that when five or more members of a business, fraternal, or social group or other group having a common interest are engaging rooms, they may designate one person to make said entry on their behalf and prior to occupancy.

No Room until entered in Log: Until the entry of such name and the record of the room have been made, such person shall not be allowed to occupy privately any room upon the licensed premises.

Open for Inspection: Such register shall be retained by the holder of the license for a period of **at least 1 year** after the date of the last entry therein, and shall be open to the inspection of the licensing authorities, their agents and **the police**.

Penalty: Whoever violates any provision of this section shall be punished by a fine of not less than one hundred nor more than five hundred dollars or by imprisonment for not more than three months, or both.

ARREST POWERS: **Misdemeanor** – there is no statutory authority granting powers of arrest for this offense.

C. 266 § 13A. *Duty of hotel manager to notify fire department and sound alarm*

The manager of a hotel or family hotel or such other person as may be in charge of the premises in the absence of the manager, shall, as soon as he becomes aware that there is a fire therein, notify the fire department and, if such fire, or heat, smoke or gas therefrom, threatens to spread to rooms occupied by guests, sound the alarm system required by the state building code.

Penalty: Whoever violates any provision of this section shall be punished by imprisonment in a jail or HOC for not more than two and a half years or by a fine of not more than $1,000 dollars.

ARREST POWERS: **Misdemeanor** – there is no statutory authority granting powers of arrest for this offense. However, if the offense is committed in public, in the officer's presence, and is creating a **breach of the peace** an arrest would be lawful,

WELFARE RELATED CRIMES

C. 18 § 5I: *Transitional Assistance Funds – Alcohol, Tobacco and Lottery Restrictions by Recipient*

- Eligible recipients of direct cash assistance (a.k.a. transitional assistance or "welfare") shall not use direct cash assistance funds for the purchase of:
  - alcoholic beverages, or
  - lottery tickets, or
  - tobacco products
- An eligible recipient of direct cash assistance who makes a purchase in violation of this section shall reimburse the department for such purchase.

C. 18 § 5J: *EBT Cards cannot be used for Alcohol, Tobacco and the Lottery*

- An individual or store owner
- shall not accept direct cash assistance funds held on electronic benefit transfer cards (EBT cards)
- for the purchase of:
  - alcoholic beverages, or
  - lottery tickets or
  - tobacco products

Penalty: An individual or store owner who knowingly accepts electronic benefit transfer cards in violation of this section shall be punished by a fine of not more than $500 for the first offense, a fine of not less than $500 nor more than $1,000 for the second offense and a fine of not less than $1,000 for the third or subsequent offense.

ARREST POWERS: **Misdemeanor** – there is no statutory authority granting powers of arrest for this offense. However, if the offense is committed in public, in the officer's presence, and is creating a **breach of the peace** an arrest would be lawful.

RARELY ENCOUNTERED CRIMES

C. 268B § 8. *Retribution for engaging in commission proceedings (whistle blowing)*

- No officer or employee of the commonwealth or of any county, city or town
- shall discharge an officer or employee, or change his official rank, grade or compensation, or deny him a promotion, or threaten so to do,
- for filing a complaint with or providing information to the commission or testifying in any commission proceeding.

C. 268 § 8B. *Compulsion or coercion to refuse appointment or promotion*

- Any appointing authority or appointing officer
- by himself or by some other person acting on his behalf,
- compels, or induces by the use of threats or other form of coercion,
- any person on an eligible list, as defined in c. thirty-one,
- to refuse an appointment or promotion by such authority or officer to any position in the classified civil service
- shall be punished as follows:

Penalty: a fine of not less than $50 nor more than two hundred dollars or by imprisonment in a jail or HOC for not more than two months, or by both such fine and imprisonment.

ARREST POWERS: **Misdemeanor** – there is no statutory authority granting powers of arrest for this offense.

C. 269 § 15. *Sale of stink bombs*

The defendant sells or offers for sale a stink bomb

Penalty: by a fine of not less than ten nor more than $200.

Note: As used in this section the words **"stink bomb"** shall mean a small bomb that gives off a foul odor on bursting or any compound or device prepared for the primary purpose of generating a foul odor and sold or offered for sale for such purpose.

C. 264 § 1. *Treason*

Treason against the commonwealth shall consist only in levying war against it, or in adhering to the enemies thereof, giving them aid and comfort; it shall not be bailable.

Notes: this offense carries a life imprisonment. Also, person cannot be convicted unless two witnesses testify, or accused confesses in court.

C. 266 § 39. *Wills; destruction or concealment*

- Whoever
- steals or for any fraudulent purpose destroys, mutilates or conceals
- a will, codicil or other testamentary instrument
- shall be punished as follows:

Penalty: imprisonment in the **state prison (F)** for not more than five years or in the HOC for not more than two years.

ARREST POWERS: **Felony** – a police officer may effect an arrest for this offense committed in his/her presence or for an offense in the past, on probable cause.

Note: An indictment for a violation of this section need not contain any allegation of value or ownership; and in the trial of such an indictment, no disclosure made by any person under section fourteen of c. one hundred and ninety-one shall be used in evidence against him.

DEATH &MEDICAL EXAMINERS REQUIRMENTS

C. 38 § 3. DUTY TO REPORT DEATHS; FAILURE TO REPORT

Any person having knowledge of a death which occurs under the circumstances below shall immediately to notify the ME's office of the known facts concerning the time, place, manner, circumstances and cause of such death:

(1) death where **criminal violence** appears to have taken place, regardless of the time interval between the incident and death, and regardless of whether such violence appears to have been the immediate cause of death, or a contributory factor thereto;

(2) death by **accident or unintentional injury**, regardless of time interval between the incident and death, and regardless of whether such injury appears to have been the immediate cause of death, or a contributory factor thereto;

(3) **suicide**, regardless of the time interval between the incident and death;

(4) death **under suspicious or unusual circumstances**;

(5) death following an **unlawful abortion**;

(6) death related to **occupational illness or injury**;

(7) death **in custody**, in any jail or correctional facility, or in any mental health or mental retardation institution;

(8) death where **suspicion of abuse of a child, family or household member**, **elder person or disabled person** exists;

(9) death **due to poison or acute or chronic use of drugs or alcohol**;

(10) **skeletal remains**;

(11) death associated with **diagnostic or therapeutic procedures**;

(12) sudden death when the **decedent was in apparent good health**;

(13) death within **twenty-four hours of admission to a hospital or nursing home**;

(14) death in any **public or private conveyance**;

(15) **fetal death**, as defined by section two hundred and two of c. one hundred and eleven, where the period of gestation has been twenty weeks or more, or where fetal weight is three hundred and fifty grams or more;

(16) **death of children under the age of 18 years from any** cause;

(17) **any person found dead**;

(18) **death in any emergency treatment facility, medical walk-in center, child care center, or under foster care**; or

(19) deaths occurring under such other circumstances as the chief medical examiner shall prescribe in regulations promulgated pursuant to the provisions of c. thirty A.

Penalty: A physician, **police officer**, hospital administrator, licensed nurse, department of children and families social worker, or licensed funeral director, within the commonwealth, who, having knowledge of such an unreported death, fails to notify the office of the chief medical examiner of such death shall be punished by a **fine of not more than $500**. Such failure shall also be reported to the appropriate board of registration, where applicable.

C. 38 § 4. INVESTIGATION; TRANSPORTATION OF BODIES

If the chief medical examiner or such designee is of the opinion that the death was **due to violence or other unnatural means or to natural causes** that require further investigation, **he shall take jurisdiction.**

The body of the deceased **shall not be moved,** and **the scene where the body is located shall not be disturbed, until either the medical examiner or the district attorney** or his representative **either arrives at the scene or gives directions as to what shall be done at the scene**.

In such cases of unnatural or suspicious death where the district attorney's office is to be notified, the medical examiner shall not disturb the body or the scene without permission from the district attorney or his representative.

The medical examiner shall be responsible for making arrangements for transport of the body. The district attorney or his law enforcement representative shall direct and control the investigation of the death and shall coordinate the investigation with the office of the chief medical examiner and the police department within whose jurisdiction the death occurred. Either the medical examiner or the district attorney in the jurisdiction where death occurred may order an autopsy. Cases requiring autopsy shall be subject to the jurisdiction of the office for such purpose. As part of his investigation, the chief medical examiner or his designee may, in his discretion, notwithstanding any other provision of law, cause the body to be tested by the department of public health for the presence of any virus, disease, infection, or syndrome which might pose a public health risk.

If the medical examiner is unable to respond and take charge of the body of the deceased in an expeditious manner, the chief of police of the city or town wherein the body lies, or his representative, may, after conferring with the appropriate district attorney, move the body to another location until a medical examiner is able to respond. Before moving the body the police shall document all facts relevant to the appearance, condition and position of the body and every fact and circumstance tending to show the cause and circumstances of death.

In carrying out the duties prescribed by this section, the chief medical examiner or his designee shall be entitled to review and receive copies of medical records, hospital records, or information which he deems relevant to establishing the cause and manner of death.

Liability: No person or hospital shall be subject to liability of any nature for providing such records or information in good faith at the request of the office. The chief medical examiner shall notify the local district attorney of the death of a child immediately following receipt of a report that such a death occurred.

C. 38 § 4A. Death resulting from single-vehicle accident; blood sample analysis

- If the medical examiner (ME) is of the opinion that **death may have resulted from injuries sustained in a motor vehicle accident**,

and

- that the **death occurred within four hours of such accident**,
- that the **deceased was the operator and sole occupant** of the motor vehicle,

and

- **that no other individuals were involved in the accident**,
- the **ME shall submit to the state police laboratory a sample of blood from the deceased**

If such chemical analysis indicates the presence of a controlled substance or alcohol, **such sample shall be preserved for no less than 120** days from the date the sample is taken to permit an independent analysis. Such independent analysis shall be done upon the written request and at the expense of the next of kin of the decedent. No independent analysis of blood performed after sixty days pursuant to this section shall be admissible as evidence of the level of alcohol or controlled substance in any legal proceeding. The medical examiner shall not be civilly or criminally liable for any action taken in compliance with this section.

C. 38 § 5. COOPERATION WITH OFFICE OF CHIEF MEDICAL EXAMINER

All law enforcement officers, district medical examiners, hospitals and other medical facilities, and other state, county and local officials **shall cooperate with the office of chief medical examiner** in the investigation of medicolegal cases.

C. 38 § 7. ATTORNEY GENERAL; NOTICE OF CIRCUMSTANCES OF DEATH

- If the medical examiner is of the opinion that **the death may have been caused by the act or negligence of another**
- he **shall at once notify the district attorney**
- He shall also make available to the district attorney any and all records pertaining to such investigation.
- He shall in all cases forthwith certify to the city or town clerk or registrar in the place where the deceased died, the name and address, if known, or otherwise a description as full as may be of the deceased, and the cause and manner of death.

Notwithstanding any other provision of law, such certification may indicate that the death was caused by auto-immune deficiency syndrome, so-called.

In cases of homicide, after indictment and arraignment, and while the defendant is in custody or subject to the jurisdiction of the court, upon his request, a copy of the official autopsy report and a copy of the inquest report, if any, shall be made available to him by the district attorney in accordance with the provisions of the Massachusetts Rules of Criminal Procedure.

C. 38 § 15. PERSONAL PROPERTY OF DECEASED; DISPOSITION

- A medical examiner responding to the scene of a death **shall take charge of any money or other personal property of the deceased found on or near the body,** or may request the police department to do so.
- The medical examiner or police department shall, unless such money or property is required as evidence, **deliver it to the person entitled to its custody or possession, or, if not claimed within 60, to a public administrator**.

  Penalty: A medical examiner or police officer who **fraudulently refuses to deliver such property within 10 after demand or who converts such property to his own use shall be punished** by a fine of not more than $1,000 or by imprisonment for not more than two years.

JUVENILE LAW

NOTE: Many laws that may be considered "JUVENILE" laws, such statutory rape and A&B on a child, are covered in other parts of this manual.

PAGE INTENTIONALLY LEFT BLANK

Section 3 JUVENILE LAW

Important Note: Many juvenile issues are handled elsewhere within this manual. For instance, Miranda involving juveniles is covered in the Interview & Interrogation Section of this manual. Most crimes committed against children are covered in the Crimes against the Person section. This section covers areas that police officers may need to be familiar with but are not covered in other sections of this manual.

CHILD PROTECTION & ABUSE

C. 119 § 21. *Definitions applicable to child protection laws*

DEFINITIONS

As used in sections 21 to 51H, inclusive, the following words shall have the following meanings, unless the context clearly otherwise requires:--

"51A report", a report filed with the department under section 51A that details suspected child abuse or neglect.

"Advocate", an employee of a governmental or non-governmental organization or entity providing appropriate services, or a similar employee of the department of children and families who has been trained to work and advocate for the needs of sexually exploited children.

"Appropriate services", the assessment, planning and care provided by a state agency or nongovernmental organization or entity, through congregate care facilities, whether publicly or privately funded, emergency residential assessment services, family-based foster care or the community, including food, clothing, medical care, counseling and appropriate crisis intervention services, provided: (i) that such agency, organization or entity has expertise in providing services to sexually exploited children or children who are otherwise human trafficking victims; and (ii) that such services are provided in accordance with such regulations that the department of children and families may adopt or the policies of such department.

"Child", a person under the age of 18.

"Commissioner", the commissioner of children and families.

"Custody", the power to: (1) determine a child's place of abode, medical care and education; (2) control visits to a child; and (3) consent to enlistments, marriages and other contracts otherwise requiring parental consent. If a parent or guardian objects to the carrying out of any power conferred by this paragraph, that parent or guardian may take application to the committing court and the court shall review and make an order on the matter.

"Department", the department of children and families.

"Mandated reporter", a person who is:

(i) a physician, medical intern, hospital personnel engaged in the examination, care or treatment of persons, medical examiner, psychologist, emergency medical technician, dentist, nurse, chiropractor, podiatrist, optometrist, osteopath, allied mental health and human services professional licensed under section 165 of c. 112, drug and alcoholism counselor, psychiatrist or clinical social worker;

(ii) a public or private school teacher, educational administrator, guidance or family counselor, child care worker, person paid to care for or work with a child in any public or private facility, or home or program funded by the commonwealth or licensed under c. 15D that provides child care or residential services to children or that provides the services of child care resource and referral agencies, voucher management agencies or family child care systems or child care food programs, licensor of the department of early education and care or school attendance officer;

(iii) a probation officer, clerk-magistrate of a district court, parole officer, social worker, foster parent, firefighter, police officer;

(iv) a priest, rabbi, clergy member, ordained or licensed minister, leader of any church or religious body, accredited Christian Science practitioner, person performing official duties on behalf of a church or religious body that are recognized as the duties of a priest, rabbi, clergy, ordained or licensed minister, leader of any church or religious body, accredited Christian Science practitioner, or person employed by a church or religious body to supervise, educate, coach, train or counsel a child on a regular basis;

(v) in charge of a medical or other public or private institution, school or facility or that person's designated agent; or

(vi) the child advocate.

"Parent", a mother or father, unless another relative has been designated as a parent as defined in section 1 of c. 118 for the purposes of receiving benefits from the department of transitional assistance.

"Relative", the father or mother of a child; a stepfather, stepmother, stepbrother, stepsister, or any blood relative of a child, including those of the half blood, except cousins who are more distantly related than first cousins; any adoptive relative of equal propinquity to the foregoing; or a spouse of any such persons.

"Serious bodily injury", bodily injury which involves a substantial risk of death, extreme physical pain, protracted and obvious disfigurement or protracted loss or impairment of the function of a bodily member, organ or mental faculty.

"Sexually exploited child", any person under the age of 18 who has been subjected to sexual exploitation because such person:

(1) is the victim of the crime of sexual servitude pursuant to section 50 of chapter 265 or is the victim of the crime of sex trafficking as defined in 22 United States Code 7105;

(2) engages, agrees to engage or offers to engage in sexual conduct with another person in return for a fee, in violation of subsection (a) of section 53A of chapter 272, or in exchange for food, shelter, clothing, education or care;

(3) is a victim of the crime, whether or not prosecuted, of inducing a minor into prostitution under by section 4A of chapter 272; or

(4) engages in common night walking or common streetwalking under section 53 of chapter 272.

"Young adult", a person between the ages of 18 and 22.

C. 119 § 51A	MANDATORY ABUSE REPORTING REQUIREMENTS
Reporting Requirements	A mandated reporter who, in his professional capacity, has reasonable cause to believe that a child is suffering physical or emotional injury resulting from: I. abuse inflicted upon him which causes harm or substantial risk of harm to the child's health or welfare, including sexual abuse; II. neglect, including malnutrition; III. physical dependence upon an addictive drug at birth, IV. being a sexually exploited child V. being a human trafficking victim Shall **immediately** communicate with the department **orally** and, within **48 hours**, shall file a **written report** with the department detailing the suspected abuse or neglect.
Special Provision for Employees of Certain Facilities:	If a mandated reporter is a member of the staff of a medical or other public or private institution, school or facility, the mandated reporter **may instead notify the person or designated agent in charge of such institution, school or facility** who shall become responsible for notifying the department in the manner required by this section.
Police Notification	A mandated reporter may, **<u>in addition</u>** to filing a report under this section, contact local law enforcement authorities or the child advocate about the suspected abuse or neglect.
Required Information	A report filed under this section shall contain: i. the names and addresses of the child and the child's parents or other person responsible for the child's care, if known; ii. the child's age; iii. the child's sex; iv. the nature and extent of the child's injuries, abuse, maltreatment or neglect, including any evidence of prior injuries, abuse, maltreatment or neglect; v. the circumstances under which the person required to report first became aware of the child's injuries, abuse, maltreatment or neglect; vi. whatever action, if any, was taken to treat, shelter or otherwise assist the child; (vii) the name of the person or persons making the report; vii. any other information that the person reporting believes might be helpful in establishing the cause of the injuries; viii. the identity of the person or persons responsible for the neglect or injuries; and ix. other information required by the department.
Penalties	
Penalty for failing to Report	**Penalty for failing to Report:** a fine of not more than $1,000. **Penalty for Failing to Report knowing abuse/neglect resulted in serious bodily harm or death**: a fine of up to $5,000 or imprisonment in the HOC for not more than 2½ years or by both such fine and imprisonment; and, upon a guilty finding or a continuance without a finding, the court shall notify any appropriate professional licensing authority of the mandated reporter's violation of this paragraph.

C. 119 § 51A	MANDATORY ABUSE REPORTING REQUIREMENTS
Penalty for filing a Frivolous Report	**Penalty for Knowingly Filing a Frivolous Report:** Whoever knowingly and willfully files a frivolous report of child abuse or neglect under 51A shall be punished by: (i) a fine of not more than $2,000 for the first offense; (ii) imprisonment in a HOC for not more than 6 months and a fine of not more than $2,000 for the second offense; and (iii) imprisonment in a HOC for not more than 2½ years and a fine of not more than $2,000 for the third and subsequent offenses.
Related Statutes, Case Law & Other Important Information	
DCF Reporting	During office hours, contact the local DCF office. After hours, call the hotline: 1-800-792-5200. Officers should file 51A child abuse reports against the offender abusing or neglecting the child.
Abuse 110 CMR 2.00	Abuse means the non-accidental commission of any act by a caretaker upon a child under age 18 which causes, or creates a substantial risk of physical or emotional injury, or constitutes a sexual offense under the laws of the Commonwealth or any sexual contact between a caretaker and a child under the care of that individual. Abuse is not dependent upon location (i.e., abuse can occur while the child is in an out-of-home or in-home setting.) **Verbal sexual abuse**: In the 2001 case of ***John D. v. DCF***, the Appeals Court ruled that "verbal sexual contact" is abuse even though the victim is not touched. In this case the defendant (father) had explicit sexual discussions with his 15 year old daughter. **Attorney Hanrahan's Note**: DCF's Abuse and Neglect Reporting Guide for Mandated Reports states that a 51A should be filed when "the alleged perpetrator coerced the child to participate in or witness the abuse of a caretaker."
Physical injury 110 CMR 2.00	Death; or fracture of a bone, a subdural hematoma, burns, impairment of any organ, and any other such nontrivial injury; or soft tissue swelling or skin bruising depending upon such factors as the child's age, circumstances under which the injury occurred, and the number and location of bruises; or addiction to drug at birth; or failure to thrive. **See Assault and Battery section of this manual for discussion Parental Discipline**.
Emotional Injury 110 CMR 2.00	Emotional Injury means an impairment to or disorder of the intellectual or psychological capacity of a child as evidenced by observable and substantial reduction in the child's ability to function within a normal range of performance and behavior.
Neglect 110 CMR 2.00	Failure by a caretaker, either deliberately or through negligence or inability, to take those actions necessary to provide a child with minimally adequate food, clothing, shelter, medical care, supervision, emotional stability and growth, or other essential care; provided, however, that such inability is not due solely to inadequate economic resources or solely to the existence of a handicapping condition. This definition is not dependent upon location (i.e., neglect can occur while the child is in an out-of-home or in-home setting.)

C. 119 § 51A	MANDATORY ABUSE REPORTING REQUIREMENTS
Caretaker	110 CMR 2.00 defines a CARETAKER as: (a) parent (b) stepparent (c) guardian (d) any household member entrusted with the responsibility for a child's health or welfare (e) any other person entrusted with the responsibility for a child's health or welfare whether in the child's home, a relative's home, a school setting, a day care setting (including babysitting), a foster home, a group care facility, or any other comparable setting. As such "caretaker" includes (but is not limited to) school teachers, babysitters, school bus drivers, camp counselors, etc. The "caretaker" definition is meant to be construed broadly and inclusively to encompass any person who is, at the time in question, entrusted with a degree of responsibility for the child. This specifically includes a caretaker who is him/herself a child (i.e. a babysitter under 18 years of age).
Hospital Staff May Take Photographs	Hospital personnel may have photographs taken of the areas of trauma visible on the child without the consent of the child's parents or guardians. These photographs or copies thereof shall be sent to DCF with the report. If hospital personnel collect physical evidence of abuse or neglect of the child, the local district attorney, local law enforcement authorities, and DCF shall be immediately notified. The physical evidence shall be processed immediately.
Death Requires DA & ME Notification	A mandated reporter who has reasonable cause to believe that a child has died as a result of any of abuse or neglect shall report the death to the district attorney for the county in which the death occurred and the office of the chief medical examiner. **Penalty for Failing to Notify DA & ME:** a fine of not more than $1,000.
Reporters are Immune from Liability for Good Faith Reports	No mandated reporter shall be liable in any civil or criminal action for filing a report under this section or for contacting local law enforcement authorities or the child advocate, if the report or contact was **made in good faith**, was not frivolous, and the reporter did not cause the abuse or neglect. No other person filing a report under this section shall be liable in any civil or criminal action by reason of the report if it was made in good faith and if that person did not perpetrate or inflict the reported abuse or cause the reported neglect. **No Immunity if Reporter Inflicted the Abuse:** Any person filing a report under this section may be liable in a civil or criminal action if the department or a district attorney determines that the person filing the report may have perpetrated or inflicted the abuse or caused the neglect. **Employer cannot take adverse action against a Reporter who Files:** No employer shall discharge, discriminate or retaliate against a mandated reporter who, in good faith, files a report under 51A, testifies or is about to testify in any proceeding involving child abuse or neglect. **Penalty against Employer for violation**: Any employer who discharges, discriminates or retaliates against that mandated reporter shall be liable to the mandated reporter for treble damages, costs and attorney's fees.

C. 119 § 51A	MANDATORY ABUSE REPORTING REQUIREMENTS
Privileged Communications Do Not Apply	Any privilege relating to confidential communications, established for Health Professionals and members of the Clergy, shall not prohibit the filing of a report under 51A or a care and protection petition under section 24. However, a priest, rabbi, clergy member, ordained or licensed minister, leader of a church or religious body or accredited Christian Science practitioner need not report information solely gained in a confession or similarly confidential communication in other religious faiths. Nothing in the general laws shall modify or limit the duty of a priest, rabbi, clergy member, ordained or licensed minister, leader of a church or religious body or accredited Christian Science practitioner to report suspected child abuse or neglect under this section when the priest, rabbi, clergy member, ordained or licensed minister, leader of a church or religious body or accredited Christian Science practitioner is acting in some other capacity that would otherwise make him a mandated reporter.
DCF must inform reporter of results within 30 Days:	Within **30 days** of receiving a report from a mandated reporter, the department shall notify the mandated reporter, in writing, of its determination of the nature, extent and cause or causes of the injuries to the child and the services that the department intends to provide to the child or the child's family.
Training Required	A mandated reporter who is professionally licensed by the commonwealth shall complete training to recognize and report suspected child abuse or neglect
Parental Discipline	In the 2015 decision of ***Commonwealth v. Dorvill***, the SJC ruled that a parent or guardian may not be subjected to criminal liability for the use of force against a minor child under the care and supervision of the parent or guardian, provided that: 1. the force used against the minor child is reasonable; 2. the force is reasonably related to the purpose of safeguarding or promoting the welfare of the minor, including the prevention or punishment of the minor's misconduct; and 3. the force used neither causes, nor creates a substantial risk of causing, physical harm (beyond fleeting pain or minor, transient marks), gross degradation, or severe mental distress. Note: in the 2015 case of *Com. v. Packer*, the Appeals court ruled that the parental discipline privilege may extent to stepparents acting in "loco parentis," that is in *the role of a parent*.

C. 119 § 51B	DCF RESPONSIBILITIES UPON RECEIVING REPORT
DCF Responsibilities upon receiving abuse report	Upon receipt of a report filed under section 51A, DCF shall investigate the suspected child abuse or neglect, provide a written evaluation of the household of the child, including the parents and home environment and make a written determination relative to the safety of and risk posed to the child and whether the suspected child abuse or neglect is substantiated. The investigation shall include: (a) a home visit at which the child is viewed, if appropriate; (b) a determination of the nature, extent and cause or causes of the injuries; (c) the identity of the person or persons responsible therefore; (d) the name, age and condition of other children in the same household; (e) an evaluation of the parents and the home environment; and (f) all other pertinent facts or matters. The department shall coordinate with other agencies to make all reasonable efforts to minimize the number of interviews of any potential victim of child abuse or neglect.
Written Findings Required	Upon completion of the investigation and evaluation, the department shall make a written determination relative to: (i) the safety of the child and risk of physical or emotional injury to that child and the safety of and risk thereto of any other children in the household; and (ii) whether the suspected child abuse or neglect is substantiated.
Immediate Danger Requires Immediate Action	If DCF has reasonable cause to believe a child's health or safety is in immediate danger from abuse or neglect, DCF shall take a child into immediate temporary custody if it has reasonable cause to believe that the removal is necessary to protect the child from abuse or neglect. The investigation and evaluation shall commence **within 2 hours** of initial contact and an interim report with an initial determination regarding the child's safety and custody shall be completed as soon as possible but **not more than 24 hours after initial contact**. The final report shall be complete within 5 business days of initial contact. If a child is taken into immediate temporary custody, the department shall make a written report stating the reasons for such removal and shall file a care and protection petition under section 24 on the next court day.
No Immediate Danger	If DCF does not have reasonable cause to believe that a child's health or safety is in immediate danger from abuse or neglect, the **investigation and evaluation shall commence within 2 business days** of initial contact and a **determination shall be made within 15 business days**, unless a waiver has been approved by the area director or requested by law enforcement.

C. 119 § 51B	DCF RESPONSIBILITIES UPON RECEIVING REPORT
Police & DA Notification	DCF shall immediately report to the district attorney and local law enforcement authorities when early evidence indicates there is reasonable cause to believe that 1 of the conditions listed below resulted from abuse or neglect: a. a child has died or has suffered brain damage, loss or substantial impairment of a bodily function or organ, substantial disfigurement, or serious physical injury including, but not limited to, a fracture of any bone, a severe burn, an impairment of any organ or an injury requiring the child to be placed on life-support systems; b. a child has been sexually assaulted c. a child has been sexually exploited, which shall include a violation of chapter 272 § 4A, 4B or 29A or is a sexually exploited child or a child who is otherwise a human trafficking victim **d.** any other disclosure of physical abuse involving physical evidence which may be destroyed, any current disclosure by a child of sexual assault, or the presence of physical evidence of sexual assault.
Related Statutes, Case Law & Other Important Information	
Custody of injured child pending transfer to department or Hearing **c. 119 § 51C**	If a parent or other person requests the release from a hospital of a child reported under 51A, the presiding judge of the juvenile court of the judicial district in which such hospital is located may, if he believes such release would be detrimental to the child's health or safety, authorize the hospital and the attending physician, by any means of communication, to keep such a child in the hospital until custody is transferred to DCF or until a hearing may be held relative to the care and custody of such child. Any other physician treating a child reported pursuant to 51A may be so authorized by the court to keep the child in his custody until such time as the custody of the child has been transferred to the department or until a hearing may be held relative to the care and custody of the child.

C. 119 § 39	ABANDONMENT OF INFANT UNDER AGE OF TEN
Elements	
1.	The defendant abandons an infant under the age of 10 years old
OR	
2.	Being its parent, or being under a legal duty to care for it, and having made a contract for its board or maintenance, absconds or fails to perform such contract, and for 4 weeks after such absconding or breach of his contract, if of sufficient physical and mental ability, neglects to visit or remove such infant or notify DCF of his inability to support such infant.
Arrest Power, Penalties & Notes	
Power of Arrest	**If child does not die - Misdemeanor** – there is no statutory authority granting warrantless powers of arrest for this offense. However, if the offense is committed in public, in the officer's presence, and is creating a **breach of the peace** an arrest would be lawful. **If child dies - Felony** – a police officer may effect a warrantless arrest for this offense provided he/she has probable cause that the suspect committed the offense.
Penalty	**In child does not die:** imprisonment in a jail or HOC for not more than 2 years; **If child dies:** if the infant dies by reason of such abandonment, by imprisonment in a jail or HOC for not more than 2½ years or in the **state prison (F)** for not more than 5 years.
Attorney Hanrahan's Comment	Case law indicates that the parent/guardian must have an *intent to abandon the child*, leaving the child alone for a brief period of time will generally not violate this statute. For instance, leaving the child in a car while the parent went shopping, although possibly neglectful, would not meet the elements of this statute because there was no intent to abandon.

C. 119 § 39½	VOLUNTARY ABANDONMENT OF AN INFANT
Infant Drop Off	DCF shall accept for placement into foster care any newborn infant **7 days of age or less** that is voluntarily placed with a "designated facility" by a parent of the newborn infant. A "**designated facility**" includes: a hospital, a police department or a manned fire station.
No Criminal Charges	Voluntary placement as mentioned above shall not by itself constitute either a finding of abuse or neglect or a violation of any criminal statue for child abuse or neglect or for abandonment.
Notify DCF	The designated facility receiving a newborn infant shall **immediately** notify DCF of the placement of the newborn infant at the facility. Upon receipt of such notice, the department shall take immediate custody of the newborn infant and shall initiate all actions authorized by law to achieve the safety and permanent placement of the newborn infant in a manner that is consistent with the best interests of the child.

C. 119 § 39½	VOLUNTARY ABANDONMENT OF AN INFANT
Attempt to Obtain Information	The person accepting a newborn infant at a designated facility shall make every effort to solicit the following information from the parent placing the newborn infant: a. the name of the newborn infant; b. the name and address of the parent placing the newborn infant; c. the location of the newborn infant's birthplace; d. information relative to the newborn infant's medical history and his or her biological family's medical history, if available; and e. any other information that might reasonably assist the department or the court in current or future determinations of the best interests of the child, including whether the parent or guardian plans on returning to seek future custody of the child. The person receiving the newborn infant shall encourage the parent to provide the information but the parent shall not be required to provide such information.
Attorney Hanrahan's Comment	This law was created to prevent the many cases of unwanted newborns being discarded, and in some cases murdered. The parent can drop the child off at a designated facility without any penalty.

C. 22A § 4	ENTRY OF INFORMATION RELATIVE TO MISSING CHILDREN
Enter as Missing	Whenever a parent, guardian, or governmental unit responsible for a child, reports to any police officer or law enforcement official that a child is missing, the officer **shall immediately enter the child's information into the central register** (i.e. CJIS/NCIC). Attorney Hanrahan's note: in 2015 c. 22A was modified to specifically reference the federal missing person law and to require the same information that is required in the federal law to be gathered and entered into CJIS as is required under the federal law. See the federal law requirements below.
Attempt to Locate	The officer must also **immediately** try to locate the child**.**
Information Access	Police officers shall have access to the fingerprints and other data and information concerning the missing child on file with the central register.
Missing Child Defined	Any person **under the age of 18 years** missing from his normal and ordinary place of residence and whose whereabouts cannot be determined by the person responsible for such child's care (c. 22A § 1). **Note**: Federal law requires that anyone under 21 who is reported missing be entered into the appropriate database.
The Federal Missing Child Law	**Federal Law 42 U.S.C. § 5780 - state requirements** Each State reporting under the provisions of this section and section 5779 of this title shall: 1. ensure that no law enforcement agency within the State establishes or maintains any policy that requires the observance of any waiting period before accepting a missing child or unidentified person report; 2. ensure that no law enforcement agency within the State establishes or maintains any policy that requires the removal of a missing person entry from its State law enforcement system or the National Crime Information Center computer database based solely on the age of the person;

C. 22A § 4 ENTRY OF INFORMATION RELATIVE TO MISSING CHILDREN

3. provide that each such report and all necessary and available information, which, with respect to each missing child report, shall include-
   a. the name, date of birth, sex, race, height, weight, and eye and hair color of the child;
   b. a recent photograph of the child, if available;
   c. the date and location of the last known contact with the child; and
   d. the category under which the child is reported missing;

   the information is entered **within 2 hours** of receipt into the State law enforcement system and the National Crime Information Center computer networks and made available to the Missing Children Information Clearinghouse within the State or other agency designated within the State to receive such reports; and

   Attorney Hanrahan's Note: the information above (paragraph 3) *must* be entered into the database per the new version of the Massachusetts Missing Child Law (c. 22A § 2).
4. provide that after receiving reports as provided in paragraph (3), the law enforcement agency that entered the report into the National Crime Information Center shall:
   a. **no later than 30 days** after the original entry of the record into the State law enforcement system and National Crime Information Center computer networks, verify and **update such record** with any additional information, including, where available, medical and dental records and **a photograph** taken during the previous 180 days;
   b. institute or assist with appropriate search and investigative procedures;
   c. notify the National Center for Missing and Exploited Children of each report received relating to a child reported missing from a foster care family home or childcare institution;
   d. maintain close liaison with State and local child welfare systems and the National Center for Missing and Exploited Children for the exchange of information and technical assistance in the missing children cases; and
   e. grant permission to the National Crime Information Center Terminal Contractor for the State to update the missing person record in the National Crime Information Center computer networks with additional information learned during the investigation relating to the missing person.

Related Statutes, Case Law & Other Important Information

Release of medical and dental records **c. 22A § 6**	When any person makes a report of a missing person to law enforcement, the law enforcement agency shall request a member of the family or next of kin to authorize the release of the medical and dental records of the missing person **Note:** The state police shall compare the dental records received from the medical examiner to dental records of missing persons on file with the department. The state police shall submit the results of the comparison to the medical examiner and if a tentative or positive identification is made, to the law enforcement authority which submitted the report of the missing person.

C. 22A § 4	ENTRY OF INFORMATION RELATIVE TO MISSING CHILDREN
Marking of school records; notification requirements **c. 22A § 9**	Upon receipt of a report of a missing child the police shall notify the last known elementary or secondary school in which such child had been enrolled If the police have reason to believe that a missing child or person has been enrolled in a specific school in Massachusetts, the police shall notify the school about the disappearance. **School responsibility**: Upon notification by a law enforcement authority of a child's disappearance, each elementary and secondary school, either public or private, in which such child is currently or was previously enrolled shall mark the record of such child in such a manner that whenever a copy of or information regarding the record is requested, said school shall be alerted to the fact that the record is that of a missing child. The school shall immediately report to the appropriate law enforcement authority any request concerning such marked records or knowledge as to the whereabouts of such missing child. Notification Upon learning that a missing child has been located, such law enforcement authority shall notify any school previously informed of such child's disappearance that such child has been located, and the school shall remove such mark from the record of such child.
"Child"	In Massachusetts, a child is typically deemed anyone under the age of 18 years. However, federal law requires that anyone **under 21** who is reported missing be entered into the appropriate database (CJIS/NCIC).
The AMBER Alert Plan c. 22C § 71	There are 3 criteria that must be met before the State Police will activate the plan: 1. A child, 17 years of age or younger, has been abducted; 2. The child is in danger of serious bodily harm, injury or death; and 3. There is enough descriptive information to believe that an AMBER Alert may help locate the child. Note: The AMBER Alert plan is not legally mandated. However, law enforcement personnel should be familiar with the plan as it can be a very helpful tool.
Contact Number	The Massachusetts State Police makes the final decision whether or not to issue an Amber Alert. State police amber alert contact number: (508) 820-2121

C. 119 § 63A	AIDING, CONCEALING, OR HARBORING A CHILD
	Elements
1.	The defendant is 19 years of age or older and he/she:
2.	a. knowingly and willfully aids or abets a child under the age of 18 to violate an order of a juvenile court; or b. knowingly and willfully conceals or harbors a child who has taken flight from the custody of the court, a parent, a legal guardian, DCF or DYS.
	Arrest Power, Penalties & Notes
Power of Arrest	**Misdemeanor** – there is no statutory authority granting warrantless powers of arrest for this offense. However, if the offense is committed in public, in the officer's presence, and is creating a **breach of the peace** an arrest would be lawful.

C. 119 § 63A	AIDING, CONCEALING, OR HARBORING A CHILD
Penalty	A fine of not more than $500 or by imprisonment in the HOC for not more than 1 year, or by both such fine and imprisonment.
Related Statutes, Case Law & Other Important Information	
Statutorily Prescribed Defense	It shall be a defense if the defendant concealed or harbored a child in the reasonable good faith belief that the child would be at risk of physical or sexual abuse if the child returned to his custodial residence, unless the defendant concealed or harbored such child with intent to abuse the child or if the defendant committed abuse on that child.
Jurisdiction Note	The divisions of the juvenile court department shall, within their respective territorial limits, have exclusive jurisdiction over complaints alleging a violation of this section.

C. 119 § 63	CONTRIBUTING TO THE DELINQUENCY OF A MINOR
Offense	Any person who caused, induced, abetted, or encouraged or contributed toward the delinquency of a child, or who acted in any way tending to cause or induce such delinquency.
Arrest Power, Penalties & Notes	
Power of Arrest	**Misdemeanor** – there is no statutory authority granting warrantless powers of arrest for this offense. However, if the offense is committed in public, in the officer's presence, and is creating a **breach of the peace** an arrest would be lawful.
Penalty	A fine of not more than $500 or by imprisonment of not more than 1 year, or both
Attorney Hanrahan's Comment	"Delinquency" means that the child committed a criminal act. The offender must contribute or induce the child to commit a criminal act.
Related Statutes, Case Law & Other Important Information	
Jurisdiction Note	The divisions of the juvenile court department shall, within their respective territorial limits, have exclusive jurisdiction over complaints alleging violations of this section.
Providing alcohol to a minor	In the 2013 case of ***Commonwealth v. Parent***, the SJC held that a parent could not be found guilty of *contributing to the delinquency of a minor* for delivering alcohol to a minor because chapter 138 § 34 provides an exemption for parents. However, the defendant was convicted of *contributing to the delinquency of a minor* for provided alcohol to his daughter's underage friend.

CHILD LABOR	
Street Vending Restrictions for Children Under 12 **149 § 69**	No boy or girl under 12 shall sell, expose or offer for sale any magazines, periodicals or any other articles of merchandise of any description, or exercise the trade of bootblack or scavenger, or any other trade, in any street or public place. **Penalty:** Any newspaper which willingly and knowingly employs any boy or girl contrary to the provisions of this section shall be subject to a fine of not less than $250 nor more than $500. **Arrest Powers**: **Misdemeanor** – there is no statutory authority granting powers of arrest for this offense. However, if the offense is committed in public, in the officer's presence, and is creating a **breach of the peace** an arrest would be lawful.
Newspaper Delivery 9 Years Old And Up **149 § 69**	A boy or girl 9 years of age or older may engage or be employed in the sale or delivery of newspapers **Additional Requirements:** • The publisher or distributor of the newspapers must provide the boy or girl with written policies regarding the activities and responsibilities of the boy or girl and of the publisher or distributor; • The publisher or distributor must provide an orientation and training program for the boy or girl before he or she undertakes responsibility for newspaper sales or delivery; • The boy or girl must provide the publisher or distributor with a written statement of permission to sell or deliver newspapers from a parent or guardian, said parent or guardian having previously reviewed the policies of the newspaper relative to sales or delivery. • No child shall be so employed **during the hours that the public schools** in the city or town in which such boy or girl resides are in session **nor before 6 o'clock in the morning nor after 8 o'clock in the evening**. **Penalty:** Any newspaper which willingly and knowingly employs any boy or girl contrary to the provisions of this section shall be subject to a fine of not less than $250 nor more than $500. **Arrest Powers**: **Misdemeanor** – there is no statutory authority granting powers of arrest for this offense. However, if the offense is committed in public, in the officer's presence, and is creating a **breach of the peace** an arrest would be lawful.
Employing or permitting a minor under 15 to beg **c. 272 § 58**	A parent or other person who employs a minor under 15 in begging or who, having the care or custody of such minor, permits him to engage in such employment shall be punished as follows: **Penalty**: fine of not more than $200 or by imprisonment for not more than 6 months. **Arrest Powers**: **Misdemeanor** – there is no statutory authority granting powers of arrest for this offense. However, if the offense is committed in public, in the officer's presence, and is creating a **breach of the peace** an arrest would be lawful

TOBACCO & MINORS

Tobacco; Sale Or Gift To Minors **c. 270 §6**	The defendant sells or gives a cigarette, chewing tobacco, snuff or any tobacco in any of its forms to any person under the age of 18. **Penalty:** a fine of not less than $100 for the first offense, not less than $200 for a second offense and not less than $300 for any 3rd or subsequent offense. **Arrest Powers**: **Misdemeanor** – there is no statutory authority granting powers of arrest for this offense. **Exception:** A parent or guardian is exempt from this statute. **Note:** A retailer who sells tobacco must post a copy of this law ($50 fine for non-compliance).
City Ordinances	It is possible for Cities and Towns to place further restrictions on the sale of tobacco. For instance, in 2015 the City of Boston passed an ordinance prohibiting the sale of tobacco products to persons under the age of 21. Refer to your local City ordinances/Town by-laws for more.
Sale of cigarette rolling papers to minors **c. 270 § 6A**	The defendant sells cigarette rolling papers to any person under the age of 18 **Penalty:** a fine of not less than $25 for the first offense, not less than $50 for the second offense and not less than $100 for a third or subsequent offense. **Arrest Powers**: **Misdemeanor** – there is no statutory authority granting powers of arrest for this offense. **Attorney Hanrahan's Note**: Although this offense is not arrestable the sale of drug paraphernalia is a felony, see c. 94C § 34I.
Cities & Towns cannot impose restrictions	Notwithstanding the provisions of any civil ordinance or by-law or regulation to the contrary, which is in effect on the effective date of this section, no city, town, department, board or other political subdivision or agency of the commonwealth may impose any requirements, restrictions or prohibitions pertaining to the sale of cigarette rolling papers, in addition to those in this section.

C. 119	CHILD REQUIRING ASSISTANCE (CRA)
Summary: Significant changes to M.G.L. Chapter 119 took effect in November of 2012. These changes eliminate Child in Need of Services (CHINS) and create what is now called Child Requiring Assistance (CRA). Although many of these changes do not have an impact of police operations and duties, some of these changes do. Below is a summary of the pertinent parts of the law that impact how police officers handle Child Requiring Assistance incidents (formerly CHINS).	
Child Requiring Assistance c. 119 § 21	"Child requiring assistance", a child between the ages of 6 and 18 (i.e. 6 years to one day before 18th birthday) who: (i) **repeatedly runs away** from the home of the child's parent, legal guardian or custodian; (ii) **repeatedly fails to obey** the lawful and reasonable commands of the child's **parent, legal guardian or custodian**, thereby interfering with their ability to adequately care for and protect the child; (iii) **repeatedly fails to obey** the lawful and reasonable regulations of the child's **school** (up to 16th birthday); (iv) is **habitually truant** (up to 16th birthday); or (v) is a **sexually exploited child**.
Custodial Protection c. 119 § 39H	A child may be taken into **custodial protection** (arrest no longer permitted) for engaging in the behavior described in the definition of "Child requiring assistance" in section 21 (above), only if: a. the child has **failed to obey a summons** issued pursuant to §39E, or b. if the law enforcement officer initiating such custodial protection has **probable cause** to believe that the child has **run away from the home** of his parents or guardian and **will not respond to a summons**. Attorney Hanrahan's note: for non-runaway related orders (e.g. truancy) it is recommended that you only execute the custodial protection "warrant" when the juvenile court is in session, as the child should be brought directly to the court in these instances.
Notification Requirements c. 119 § 39H	After a law enforcement officer has taken a child into custodial protection, the officer shall immediately notify: a. the parent, or b. other person legally responsible for the child's care, or c. the person with whom the child is domiciled, That the child is under the custodial protection of the officer. **DCF Notification:** The officer shall also notify a representative of the department of children and families (DCF), if the law enforcement officer has reason to believe that the child is or has been in the care or custody of such department, and shall inquire into the case. **Attorney Hanrahan's note**: Chapter 119 § 67 indicates that whenever a child is "arrested" the probation officer who has jurisdiction over the arrest shall be notified. Although custodial protection is not "an arrest" it is recommended that you also contact the probation officer, unless the probation department says otherwise. Chapter 119 § 39H also makes reference to ***consulting probation***.

C. 119	CHILD REQUIRING ASSISTANCE (CRA)
Transfer of Custody **c. 119 § 39H**	The law enforcement officer, in consultation with the probation officer*, shall then immediately make all reasonable diversion efforts so that such child is delivered to the following types of placements, and in the **following order of preference**: (i) **FIRST PRIORITY – Parent/Guardian**: Deliver the child to one of the child's parents, or to the child's guardian or other responsible person known to the child, or to the child's legal custodian including the department of children and families or the child's foster home **upon the written promise**, without surety, of the person to whose custody the child is released that such parent, guardian, person or custodian will bring the child to the court on the next court date; (ii) **SECOND PRIORITY – Shelter Facility**: Forthwith and with all reasonable speed take the child directly and **without first being taken to the police station house**, to a temporary shelter facility licensed or approved by the department of early education and care, a shelter home approved by a temporary shelter facility licensed or approved by said department of early education and care or a family foster care home approved by a placement agency licensed or approved by said department of early education and care (link to list of shelters http://www.eec.state.ma.us/ChildCareSearch/RPMap.aspx; or (iii) **LAST RESORT – Directly to JV Court but only after the first and second priorities above were unsuccessful**: Take the child directly to the juvenile court in which the act providing the reason to take the child into custodial protection occurred if the officer affirms on the record that the officer attempted to exercise the options identified in clauses (i) and (ii), was unable to exercise these options and the reasons for such inability. **Attorney Hanrahan's note:** The child should not be "booked." In fact the child should generally not be brought to the police station. However, there may be circumstances wherein a parent/guardian cannot be raised, a shelter (as described above) is not immediately available, and the juvenile court is closed. In these cases it is recommended that you contact DCF for guidance. If the child is brought to the station (because there is nowhere else to bring the child) he/she should not be held in a secure area (absent criminal charges otherwise authorizing secure detention) and immediate steps should be taken to turn the child over to a parent/guardian or DCF.
Runaway Assistance Program (RAP)	The Runaway Assistance Program (RAP) is available to assist officers with the placement of runaway children during hours when the court is closed. Police can access RAP by contacting Mass211, a statewide 24/7 information and referral program, by dialing "**2-1-1**" from any phone.

CHILD REQUIRING ASSISTANCE

C. 119	CHILD REQUIRING ASSISTANCE (CRA)
Child Cannot be Handcuffed or Held in Locked Facility c. 119 § 39H	A child in custodial protection may not be confined in **shackles or similar restraints** or in a court lockup facility in connection with any proceedings under sections 39E to 39I, inclusive. A child who is the subject of an application for assistance shall not be placed in: a) A locked facility, or b) A facility designated or operated for juveniles who are alleged to be delinquent or who have been adjudicated delinquent. **Exception:** The child may be placed in a facility which operates as a group home to provide therapeutic care for juveniles, regardless of whether juveniles adjudicated delinquent are also provided care in such facility. **Medical Treatment:** Notwithstanding the foregoing requirements for placement, any such child who is taken into custodial protection shall, if necessary, be taken to a medical facility for treatment or observation. **Attorney Hanrahan's note:** If the child is also being charged criminally (e.g. he commits an A&B on the officer during the custodial protection) the use of handcuffs would, in most cases, be appropriate. However, if the child is strictly being held in "custodial protection" handcuffs cannot be used.
Applying for an Application For A Child Requiring Assistance C. 119 § 39E	**A Misbehaved Child**: A parent, legal guardian, or custodian of a child having custody of the child, may initiate an application for assistance stating that: a) The child repeatedly runs away from the home of the parent or guardian; or b) The child repeatedly refuses to obey the lawful and reasonable commands of the parent or guardian resulting in the parent's or guardian's inability to adequately care for and protect the child. **Note**: police officer can no longer apply. **Truancy & School Misbehavior**: Only the School can Apply: A school district may initiate an application for assistance in stating that the child: a) Is not excused from attendance in accordance with the lawful and reasonable regulations of such child's school, has willfully failed to attend school for more than 8 school days in a quarter; or b) Repeatedly fails to obey the lawful and reasonable regulations of the child's school. **Note on Sexually Exploited Children:** Chapter 119 § 39L indicates that "a parent or a police officer may file a child in need of services petition under § 39E" when a child is sexually exploited. However, the legislature neglected to modify § 39L when they amended § 39E (eliminating CHINS and created a Child Requiring Assistance). It is unclear whether the legislature intended to permit police officers to continue to apply for Child Requiring Services when a child has been sexually exploited. In any event, anytime a police officer has information that a child has been sexually exploited DCF should be immediately notified.

C. 119	CHILD REQUIRING ASSISTANCE (CRA)
Child may be placed in DCF custody **c. 119 § 39H**	If the court finds that a child stated to require assistance by reason of repeatedly refusing to obey the lawful and reasonable commands of such child's parents, legal guardian or custodian or is likely not to appear at the fact finding or disposition hearing, the court may order the child to be released upon such terms and conditions as it determines to be reasonable or, if the standards below are met, may place the child in the temporary custody of the department of children and families. Prior to the court granting temporary custody to the department of children and families, the court shall make a written certification and determination that it is contrary to the best interests of the child for the child to be in the child's home or current placement and that the department of children and families has made reasonable efforts to prevent removal of the child from the child's home or the existing circumstances indicate that there is an immediate risk of harm or neglect which precludes the provision of preventative services as an alternative to removal. An order placing a child with the department under this section shall be valid for not more than 15 days upon which the child and the child's parents, legal guardians or custodians, represented by counsel, shall be brought again before the court for a hearing on whether such order should be continued for another 15 day period based on the preponderance of the evidence. If the court decides to continue said order, it shall note in writing the detailed reasons for its decision; provided, however that no child shall be placed with the department under this section for more than 45 days.

DELINQUENT CHILDREN

C. 119 § 54	ENFORCEMENT ACTION AGAINST JUVENILES
Child Under 12: Summons First	If the child is under 12 years of age, the court shall **first issue a summons** requiring him to appear. A warrant may be issued if the court believes that the child will not appear or if a summons had previously been issued and the child failed to appear.
Youthful Offender c. 119 § 52	A person who is alleged to have committed an offense against a law of Massachusetts while between the ages of 14 and 18 (ages 14, 15 , 16 & 17) which, if he were an adult, would be punishable by imprisonment in the state prison **(i.e. the child committed a felony)**, and • the person has **previously been committed** to the department of youth services (DYS), or • the offense involves the **infliction or threat of serious bodily harm** in violation of law, or • the person has committed a violation of c. 269 §10 (a), (c) or (d) (**possession of a firearm, rifle, shotgun, sawed-off shotgun, or machine gun**) or c. 269 § 10E (**trafficking in guns**). Case law note: the distribution of heroin does not qualify as "the infliction or threat of serious bodily harm" for the purposes of the youthful offender law.[1]
Delinquent	A Child between the ages of 7 and 18 (i.e. one day before 18th birthday) who commits offense and, who does not qualify as a Youthful Offender, is deemed a delinquent child.
Attorney Hanrahan's Note	A "youthful offender" can be indicted as opposed to a delinquent child who proceeds only through the juvenile complaint process. The youthful offender may also be sentenced in accordance with the "adult" penalties imposed by the statute except he/she would remain in DYS custody until the age of 21 before being placed in an adult prison/jail. See chapter 119 § 58 for more.
Related Statutes, Case Law & Other Important Information	
Attorney Hanrahan's Note on ages.	Common law indicates that children under 7 years old are deemed to be incapable of forming criminal intent. Also a person 18 years of age is an adult for the purposes of criminal conduct.
Summoning of parent or guardian	If a child (under 18) has been summoned to appear or is brought before such court upon a warrant a summons shall be issued to at least one of its parents or guardians, if either of them is known to reside within the Commonwealth. If a parent or guardian does not live with the child in Massachusetts an adult living with the child shall be summoned, or the court may appoint a guardian
Method of Service c. 119 § 55	The summons shall be served by a constable or police officer, by delivering it personally to the person to whom addressed, or by leaving it with a person of proper age to receive the same, at the place of residence or business of such person; and said constable or officer shall immediately make return to the court of the time and manner of the service

[1] Felix F., a juvenile v. Commonwealth SJC 2015

DETENTION OF JUVENILES

C. 119 § 67	ARREST/DETENTION OF CHILDREN REQUIREMENTS & ISSUES
Parent & Probation Notification	Whenever a child between 7 and 18 years of age (one day before 18th birthday) is arrested the officer in charge of the police station where the child has been taken shall immediately notify: • the probation officer within whose judicial district such child was arrested and • at least one of the child's parents/guardian.
Release Requirements	The child shall be released to the parent/guardian upon receipt of: • A written promise of the parent, guardian (or any other reputable person to be responsible for the presence of such child), and • A request by the probation officer.
Hold for Court	If the arresting officer **requests in writing** that a child between 14 and 18 years of age be detained, **and** if **the court issuing a warrant** for the arrest of a child between 14 and 18 years of age **directs** in the warrant that such child shall be held in safekeeping pending his appearance in court, **or**, if the **probation officer shall so direct**, the child shall be detained in a police station or town lockup, or place of temporary custody commonly referred to as a detention home of the department of youth services, or any other home approved by the department of youth services pending his appearance in court. **Attorney Hanrahan's Note:** The child may still be eligible for bail. This just means that child is not turned over on the parent's promise.
	Related Statutes, Case Law & Other Important Information
Important Notes on Secured Juvenile Detentions See EOPPS Guidelines later in this section	• Federal law prohibits the secure detention (**cell** or **handcuffed to fixed object**) of a child under 14. • A child between the ages of 14 and 18 shall not be held in an **adult** lock-up and shall be sight and sound separated from adults. • If a child (between the ages of 14 and 18) offender is secured in a police lock-up the child must be visually inspected at reasonable intervals and the locked detention **cannot exceed 6 hours**. • **Status Offenders** [Child Requiring Assistance, curfew or alcohol related offenses (including protective custody) by a child under 18] shall not be placed in a jail cell or secured to a fixed object. Reminder: Children Requiring Assistance cannot be handcuffed at all. • No child between 14 and 18 years of age shall be detained in a police station or town lockup unless the detention facilities for children at such police station or town lockup have received the approval in writing of the **commissioner of youth services**. • The department of youth services shall make inspection **at least annually** of police stations or town lockups wherein children are detained.
Where do you put them?	If a juvenile is arrested/detained and they cannot be placed in a secure lock-up they must be housed in an unlocked, multi-purpose area (i.e. an area not used for detention). Some departments have created so-called "juvenile watch rooms" (unlocked rooms with furnishings, etc.), others use report rooms, dispatch center, lobby, break room, etc.

C. 119 § 67	ARREST/DETENTION OF CHILDREN REQUIREMENTS & ISSUES
Documenting	EOPS now requires that an entry be made into CJIS when a juvenile is placed in secured lock-up and also document, in CJIS, when the juvenile is released from lock-up.
IMPORTANT NOTES on "STATUS OFFENDERS"	A so called status offender is anyone, under the age of 18, who commits a Child Requiring Assistance offense, violates a youth curfew, or possesses alcohol. The term status offense comes from Juvenile Justice and Delinquency Prevention Act of 2002 which essentially classifies offenses committed by juveniles which would not be offenses if committed by an adult as so-called status offenses. The 2002 reauthorization of the Juvenile Justice and Delinquency Prevention (JJDP) Act re-affirmed the four core protections: 1. Deinstitutionalization of Status Offenders 2. Separation of Juveniles from adults in institutions 3. Removal of juveniles from adult jails and lockups 4. Reduction of disproportionate minority contact This Act provides funding to States, which develop and implement a strategy for achieving and maintaining compliance with these four core protections.
Transportation of children in patrol wagons **c. 119 § 34**	A child involved in any proceeding shall not be transported in a patrol wagon from his home or from any other place to any court or institution, but if a conveyance is necessary shall convey him in such other suitable vehicle as shall be provided or designated by the department. **Penalty:** a fine of not less than $25 nor more than $50 or by imprisonment for not more than 3 months.
ESCAPE FROM DYS **c. 120 § 13**	The Department of Youth Services (DYS) may issue a warrant for the arrest of any person committed to it who has escaped from a facility or who has been released on parole and broken the conditions. **Arrest:** Such person may be arrested with or without such warrant by a police officer, sheriff, deputy sheriff, constable or person employed or authorized by DYS and may be kept in custody in a suitable place and there detained until such person may be returned to the custody of the department.
Escape or attempt to escape; assisting child in escape **c. 120 § 26**	The defendant escapes, or attempts to escape from DYS (note: the escape does not have to be from a lock-up facility) or aids or assists a child in the custody of the DYS to escape or attempt to escape. **Penalty:** a fine of not more than $500 or by imprisonment for not more than 2 years.

** PLEASE POST **

JUVENILE LOCKUP LAWS & PROCEDURES

I. Status offenders cannot be securely detained for any amount for time.

- Federal JJDP Act Section 223(a)(14)
- **See MGL Chapter 119, Section 39H (as amended) for State law regarding Child Requiring Assistance (CRA): CRA youth should not be brought back to the station.**
- *Status Offender* = Child Requiring Assistance (runaways, stubborn child, habitual school offenders, habitual truants) and youth curfew violators. A child in protective custody, a non-offense, shall be accorded the same treatment as a status offender.
- *Securely detained* is defined as physically detained or confined in a room, set of rooms, or a cell that has the ability to lock an individual within. Secure detention can result either from being placed in such a room and/or from being physically secured to a stationary object such as a cuffing rail/bench.

II. Youth charged with delinquency offenses shall not be held in a police lockup or otherwise securely detained for any longer than six hours.

(Juveniles may be securely detained only for purposes related to identification, processing, and releasing the offender to his/her parent(s)/guardian(s) or transporting the accused offender to court or an appropriate alternative lockup program.) Under state law juveniles should not be placed in a cell unless it has been certified by the Department of Youth Services.

- Federal JJDP Act Section 223(a)(14).
- 28 CFR Part 31.303(d)(1)(i)

III. Juveniles must be sight and sound separate from adults in custody.

- Federal JJPD Act Section 223(a)(13).
- MGL Chapter 119, Section 67.

IV. Juveniles are constitutionally afforded the right to bail.

- Please ensure that the practice of contacting a bail magistrate occurs for all juveniles that probation informs the officer to "hold."

Revised: February 2014

Note: this notice is published by the Executive Office of Public Safety.

PUBLIC SCHOOL LAWS

Student Behavior

C. 71 § 37H 1/2. DELINQUENCY COMPLAINT AGAINST STUDENT; SUSPENSIONS & EXPULSIONS

Suspension for Felony Charge: Upon the issuance of a **criminal complaint charging** a student with a **felony** or upon the issuance of a felony delinquency complaint against a student, the principal or headmaster of a school in which the student is enrolled may suspend such student for a period of time determined appropriate by the principal or headmaster if the principal or headmaster determines that the student's continued presence in school **would have a substantial detrimental effect on the general welfare of the school**.

Expulsion for Conviction: Upon a student being **convicted of a felony** or upon an adjudication or admission in court of guilt with respect to such a felony or felony delinquency, the principal or headmaster of a school in which the student is enrolled **may expel** the student if such principal or headmaster determines that the **student's continued presence in school would have a substantial detrimental effect on the general welfare of the school**.

Appeal Process: The student shall have the right to appeal the expulsion to the superintendent. The student shall notify the superintendent, in writing, of his request for an appeal no later than **5 calendar days** following the effective date of the expulsion. The superintendent shall hold a hearing with the student and the student's parent or guardian within three calendar days of the expulsion.

Note: Upon expulsion of such student, no school or school district shall be required to provide educational services to such student.

Bullying

C. 71 § 37O BULLYING IN SCHOOLS

Definitions:

(a) As used in this section the following words shall, unless the context clearly requires otherwise, have the following meaning:

"Approved private day or residential school", a school that accepts, through agreement with a school committee, a child requiring special education pursuant to section 10 of c. 71B.

"Bullying", the repeated use by one or more students of a written, verbal or electronic expression or a physical act or gesture or any combination thereof, directed at a victim that: (i) causes physical or emotional harm to the victim or damage to the victim's property; (ii) places the victim in reasonable fear of harm to himself or of damage to his property; (iii) creates a hostile environment at school for the victim; (iv) infringes on the rights of the victim at school; or (v) materially and substantially disrupts the education process or the orderly operation of a school. For the purposes of this section, bullying shall include cyber-bullying.

"Charter school", commonwealth charter schools and Horace Mann charter schools established pursuant to section 89 of c. 71.

"Cyber-bullying", bullying through the use of technology or any electronic communication, which shall include, but shall not be limited to, any transfer of signs, signals, writing, images, sounds, data or intelligence of any nature transmitted in whole or in part by a wire, radio, electromagnetic, photo electronic or photo optical system, including, but not limited to, electronic mail, internet communications, instant messages or facsimile communications. Cyber-bullying shall also include (i) the creation of a web page or blog in which the creator assumes the identity of another person or (ii) the knowing impersonation of another person as the author of posted content or messages, if the creation or impersonation creates any of the conditions enumerated in clauses (i) to (v), inclusive, of the definition of bullying. Cyber-bullying shall also include the distribution by electronic means of a communication to more than one person or the posting of material on an electronic medium that may be accessed by one or more persons, if the distribution or posting creates any of the conditions enumerated in clauses (i) to (v), inclusive, of the definition of bullying.

"Collaborative school", a school operated by an educational collaborative established pursuant to section 4E of c. 40.

"Department", the department of elementary and secondary education.

"Hostile environment", a situation in which bullying causes the school environment to be permeated with intimidation, ridicule or insult that is sufficiently severe or pervasive to alter the conditions of the student's education.

"Plan", a bullying prevention and intervention plan established pursuant to subsection (d).

"Perpetrator", a student who engages in bullying or retaliation.

"School district", the school department of a city or town, a regional school district or a county agricultural school.

"School grounds", property on which a school building or facility is located or property that is owned, leased or used by a school district, charter school, non-public school, approved private day or residential school, or collaborative school for a school-sponsored activity, function, program, instruction or training.

"Victim", a student against whom bullying or retaliation has been perpetrated.

BULLYING SHALL BE PROHIBITED:

(i) on school grounds, property immediately adjacent to school grounds, at a school-sponsored or school-related activity, function or program whether on or off school grounds, at a school bus stop, on a school bus or other vehicle owned, leased or used by a school district or school, or through the use of technology or an electronic device owned, leased or used by a school district or school

and

(ii) at a location, activity, function or program that is not school-related, or through the use of technology or an electronic device that is not owned, leased or used by a school district or school, **if the bullying creates a hostile environment at school** for the victim, infringes on the rights of the victim at school or materially and substantially disrupts the education process or the orderly operation of a school. Nothing contained herein shall require schools to staff any non-school related activities, functions, or programs.

Retaliation against a person who reports bullying, provides information during an investigation of bullying, or witnesses or has reliable information about bullying shall be prohibited.

BULLY PREVENTION CURRICULUM:

Each school district, charter school, approved private day or residential school and collaborative school shall provide age-appropriate instruction on bullying prevention in each grade that is incorporated into the curriculum of the school district or school. The curriculum shall be evidence-based.

BULLY PREVENTION PLAN:

Each school district, charter school, non-public school, approved private day or residential school and collaborative school shall develop, adhere to and update a plan to address bullying prevention and intervention in consultation with teachers, school staff, professional support personnel, school volunteers, administrators, community representatives, local law enforcement agencies, students, parents and guardians.

The consultation shall include, but not be limited to notice and a public comment period; provided, however, that a non-public school shall only be required to give notice to and provide a comment period for families that have a child attending the school.

The plan shall be updated **at least biennially** (every two years).

PLAN CONTENTS:

Each plan shall include, but not be limited to:

(i) descriptions of and statements prohibiting bullying, cyber-bullying and retaliation;

(ii) clear procedures for students, staff, parents, guardians and others to report bullying or retaliation;

(iii) a provision that reports of bullying or retaliation may be made anonymously; provided, however, that no disciplinary action shall be taken against a student solely on the basis of an anonymous report;

(iv) clear procedures for promptly responding to and investigating reports of bullying or retaliation;

(v) the range of disciplinary actions that may be taken against a perpetrator for bullying or retaliation; provided, however, that the disciplinary actions shall balance the need for accountability with the need to teach appropriate behavior;

(vi) clear procedures for restoring a sense of safety for a victim and assessing that victim's needs for protection;

(vii) strategies for protecting from bullying or retaliation a person who reports bullying, provides information during an investigation of bullying or witnesses or has reliable information about an act of bullying;

(viii) procedures consistent with state and federal law for promptly notifying the parents or guardians of a victim and a perpetrator; provided, further, that the parents or guardians of a victim shall also be notified of the action taken to prevent any further acts of bullying or retaliation; and provided, further, that the procedures shall provide for immediate notification pursuant to regulations promulgated under this subsection by the principal or person who holds a comparable role to the local law enforcement agency when criminal charges may be pursued against the perpetrator;

(ix) a provision that a student who knowingly makes a false accusation of bullying or retaliation shall be subject to disciplinary action;

and

(x) a strategy for providing counseling or referral to appropriate services for perpetrators and victims and for appropriate family members of said students. The plan shall afford all students the same protection regardless of their status under the law.

A school district, charter school, non-public school, approved private day or residential school or collaborative school may establish separate discrimination or harassment policies that include categories of students. Nothing in this section shall prevent a school district, charter school, non-public school, approved private day or residential school or collaborative school from remediating any discrimination or harassment based on a person's membership in a legally protected category under local, state or federal law.

The plan for a school district, charter school, approved private day or residential school and collaborative school shall include a provision for ongoing professional development to build the skills of all staff members, including, but not limited to, educators, administrators, school nurses, cafeteria workers, custodians, bus drivers, athletic coaches, advisors to extracurricular activities and paraprofessionals, to prevent, identify and respond to bullying. The content of such professional development shall include, but not be limited to: (i) developmentally appropriate strategies to prevent bullying incidents; (ii) developmentally appropriate strategies for immediate, effective interventions to stop bullying incidents; (iii) information regarding the complex interaction and power differential that can take place between and among a perpetrator, victim and witnesses to the bullying; (iv) research findings on bullying, including information about specific categories of students who have been shown to be particularly at risk for bullying in the school environment; (v) information on the incidence and nature of cyber-bullying; and (vi) internet safety issues as they relate to cyber-bullying. The department shall identify and offer information on alternative methods for fulfilling the professional development requirements of this section, at least 1 of which shall be available at no cost to school districts, charter schools, approved private day or residential schools and collaborative schools.

The plan shall include provisions for informing parents and guardians about the bullying prevention curriculum of the school district or school and shall include, but not be limited to: (i) how parents and guardians can reinforce the curriculum at home and support the school district or school plan; (ii) the dynamics of bullying; and (iii) online safety and cyber-bullying.

The department shall promulgate rules and regulations on the requirements related to a principal's duties under clause (viii) of the second paragraph of this subsection; provided, that school districts, charter schools, approved private day or residential schools and collaborative schools shall be subject to the regulations. A non-public school shall develop procedures for immediate notification by the principal or person who holds a comparable role to the local law enforcement agency when criminal charges may be pursued against the perpetrator.

(e)(1) Each school district, charter school, non-public school, approved private day or residential school and collaborative school shall provide to students and parents or guardians, in age-appropriate terms and in the languages which are most prevalent among the students, parents or guardians, annual written notice of the relevant student-related sections of the plan.

(2) Each school district, charter school, non-public school, approved private day or residential school and collaborative school shall provide to all school staff annual written notice of the plan. The faculty and staff at each school shall be trained annually on the plan applicable to the school. Relevant sections of the plan relating to the duties of faculty and staff shall be included in a school district or school employee handbook.

(3) The plan shall be posted on the website of each school district, charter school, non-public school, approved private day or residential school and collaborative school.

(f) Each school principal or the person who holds a comparable position shall be responsible for the implementation and oversight of the plan at his school.

(g) A member of a school staff, including, but not limited to, an educator, administrator, school nurse, cafeteria worker, custodian, bus driver, athletic coach, advisor to an extracurricular activity or paraprofessional, shall immediately report any instance of bullying or retaliation the staff member has witnessed or become aware of to the principal or to the school official identified in the plan as responsible for receiving such reports or both. Upon receipt of such a report, the school principal or a designee shall promptly conduct an investigation. If the school principal or a designee determines that bullying or retaliation has occurred, the school principal or designee shall (i) notify the local law enforcement agency if the school principal or designee believes that criminal charges may be pursued against a perpetrator; (ii) take appropriate disciplinary action; (iii) notify the parents or guardians of a perpetrator; and (iv) notify the parents or guardians of the victim, and to the extent consistent with state and federal law, notify them of the action taken to prevent any further acts of bullying or retaliation.

(h) If an incident of bullying or retaliation involves students from more than one school district, charter school, non-public school, approved private day or residential school or collaborative school, the school district or school first informed of the bullying or retaliation shall, consistent with state and federal law, promptly notify the appropriate administrator of the other school district or school so that both may take appropriate action. If an incident of bullying or retaliation occurs on school grounds and involves a former student under the age of 21 who is no longer enrolled in a local school district, charter school, non-public school, approved private day or residential school or collaborative school, the school district or school informed of the bullying or retaliation shall contact law enforcement consistent with the provisions of clause (viii) of the second paragraph of subsection (d).

(i) Nothing in this section shall supersede or replace existing rights or remedies under any other general or special law, nor shall this section create a private right of action.

(j) The department, after consultation with the department of public health, the department of mental health, the attorney general, the Massachusetts District Attorneys Association and experts on bullying shall: (i) publish a model plan for school districts and schools to consider when creating their plans; and (ii) compile a list of bullying prevention and intervention resources, evidence-based curricula, best practices and academic-based research that shall be made available to schools. The model plan shall be consistent with the behavioral health and public schools framework developed by the department in accordance with section 19 of c. 321 of the acts of 2008. The resources may include, but shall not be limited to, print, audio, video or digital media; subscription based online services; and on-site or technology-enabled professional development and training sessions. The department shall biennially update the model plan and the list of the resources, curricula, best practices and research and shall post them on its website.

C. 269 § 17	HAZING
Elements	
1.	Any conduct or method of initiation into any student organization, whether on public or private property, which willfully or recklessly endangers the physical or mental health of any student or other person.
2.	Such conduct or method of initiation includes: ○ whipping, ○ beating, ○ branding, ○ forced calisthenics, ○ exposure to the weather, ○ forced consumption of any food, liquor, beverage, drug or other substance, or • Any other brutal treatment or forced physical activity which is **likely to adversely affect the physical health or safety** of any such student or other person, or • Conduct which subjects such student or other person to **extreme mental stress**, including extended **deprivation of sleep or rest or extended isolation**.
Arrest Power, Penalties & Notes	
Power of Arrest	**Misdemeanor** – there is no statutory authority granting warrantless powers of arrest for this offense. However, if the offense is committed in public, in the officer's presence, and is creating a **breach of the peace** an arrest would be lawful.
Penalty	Whoever is a **principal organizer or participant** in the crime of hazing shall be punished by a fine of not more than $3,000 or by imprisonment in a HOC for not more than 1 year, or both such fine and imprisonment.
Attorney Hanrahan's Comment	You may have felonious charges as well depending on the conduct which would trigger arrest powers.
Related Statutes, Case Law & Other Important Information	
Consent is no Defense	Consent shall not be available as a defense to any prosecution under this action.
Failure to Report Hazing c. 269 § 18	Whoever **knows** that another person is the victim of hazing and is **at the scene of such crime** shall, to the extent that such person can do so without danger or peril to himself or others, **report such crime** to an appropriate law enforcement official as soon as reasonably practicable. **Penalty:** whoever fails to report such crime shall be punished by a fine of not more than $1,000. **Note:** Each institution of secondary education and each public and private institution of post secondary education shall issue to every student group, student team or student organization which is part of such institution or is recognized by the institution or permitted by the institution to use its name or facilities or is known by the institution to exist as an unaffiliated student group, student team or student organization, a copy of the hazing laws.

SCHOOL ATTENDANCE

C. 76 § 1 SCHOOL ATTENDANCE; REQUIREMENTS AND EXCEPTIONS

Children Required to Attend School:

Every child between the minimum and maximum ages established for school attendance by the board of education, shall, attend a public day school, or some other day school approved by the school committee, during the number of days required by the board of education in each school year, unless the child attends school in another town, for said number of days, under sections six to twelve, inclusive, or attends an experimental school project established under an experimental school plan,

Notable Exceptions:

- a child whose physical or mental condition is such as to render attendance inexpedient or impracticable
- a child granted an employment permit by the superintendent of schools when such superintendent determines that the welfare of such child will be better served through the granting of such permit,
- a child who is being otherwise instructed in a manner approved in advance by the superintendent or the school committee.

Note there are numerous exceptions to this requirement - refer to the entire statute for your particular case

Excused Absences:

The superintendent, or teachers authorized by him or by the school committee, may excuse cases of necessary absence for other causes **not exceeding 7 day sessions or 14 half day sessions in any period of 6 months**.

C. 76 § 2. DUTIES OF PARENTS

Every person in control of a child shall cause him to attend school as therein required, and, if he fails so to do for **7 day sessions** or **14 half day sessions** within any period of **6 months**, he shall, on complaint by a supervisor of attendance, be punished by a fine of not more than $20 dollars.

C. 76 § 4: INDUCING ABSENCES

- Whoever
- induces or attempts to induce
  - a minor to absent himself unlawfully from school, or
  - unlawfully employs him (while school is in session and the child is absent), or
  - harbors a minor (while school is in session and the child is absent)
- shall be punished by a fine of not more than $200.

C. 76 § 19. SUPERVISORS OF ATTENDANCE

Every school committee shall appoint....**one or more supervisors of attendance**, who may be either male or female, and who shall meet such standards of qualifications for such work as shall be established by the department of education; provided, that such supervisors shall have attained the age of 21. The committees of two or more towns may employ the same supervisors of attendance.

C. 76 § 20. POWERS AND DUTIES OF SUPERVISORS OF ATTENDANCE

Supervisors of attendance shall inquire into cases involving failure to attend school and may apply for petitions .... They may apprehend and take to school without a warrant any truant or absentee found wandering in the streets or public places.

Miscellaneous School Law

C. 272 § 40A. *Alcoholic beverages on public school premises*

- Whoever
- gives, sells, delivers

or

- has in his possession any alcoholic beverage (except for medicinal purposes),
- in any public school building,

or

- on any premises used for public school purposes (and under the charge of a school committee or other public board or officer)
- shall be punished as follows:

Penalty: imprisonment for not more than 30 days or by a fine of not more than $100, or both.

ARREST POWERS: **Misdemeanor** – there is no statutory authority granting powers of arrest for this offense. However, if the offense is committed in public, in the officer's presence, and is creating a **breach of the peace** an arrest would be lawful.

Exception: The school committee of a city, town or district may authorize a public or nonprofit organization using a public school building with its permission during non school hours to possess and sell alcoholic beverages therein provided such nonprofit organization is properly licensed.

71:37L. *Mandatory Reporting of Weapons*

Personnel Must Report to Supervisor: Any school department personnel shall report **in writing to their immediate supervisor** an incident involving a student's possession or use of a dangerous weapon on school premises at any time.

Must report to Police & DCF: Supervisors who receive such a weapon report shall file it with the superintendent of said school, who shall file copies of said weapon report with the local chief of police, the department of children and families, the office of student services or its equivalent in any school district, and the local school committee.

Assessment Required: The superintendent, police chief, and representative from the department of children and families, together with a representative from the office of student services or its equivalent, shall arrange an assessment of the student involved in said weapon report.

Student Counseling: The student shall be referred to a counseling program; provided, however, that said counseling shall be in accordance with acceptable standards as set forth by the board of education. Upon completion of a counseling session, a follow-up assessment shall be made of said student by those involved in the initial assessment.

A student transferring into a local system must provide the new school system with a complete school record of the entering student. Said record shall include, but not be limited to, any incidents involving suspension or violation of criminal acts or any incident reports in which such student was charged with any suspended act.

C. 71 § 37H. *Student handbook requirements*

The superintendent of every school district shall publish the district's policies pertaining to the conduct of teachers and students. These policies shall:

- Prohibit the use of **any tobacco** products within the school buildings, the school facilities or on the school grounds or on school buses by any individual, including school personnel.
- Restrict operators of school buses and personal motor vehicles, including students, faculty, staff and visitors, from **idling such vehicles on school grounds**.

- The policies shall also **prohibit bullying** and shall include the student-related sections of the bullying prevention and intervention plan required by said section 37O. Copies of these policies shall be provided to any person upon request and without cost by the principal of every school within the district.

Each school district's policies pertaining to the conduct of students shall include the following:

- disciplinary proceedings, including procedures assuring due process;
- standards and procedures for suspension and expulsion of students;
- procedures pertaining to discipline of students with special needs;
- standards and procedures to assure school building security and safety of students and school personnel;
- the disciplinary measures to be taken in cases involving the possession or use of illegal substances or weapons, the use of force, vandalism, or violation of a student's civil rights.

Codes of discipline, as well as procedures used to develop such codes shall be filed with the department of education for informational purposes only

Notwithstanding any general or special law to the contrary, **all student handbooks shall contain** the following provisions:

(a) Any student who is found on school premises or at school-sponsored or school-related events, including athletic games, in possession of a **dangerous weapon**, including, but not limited to, a gun or a knife; or a **controlled substance**, including, but not limited to, marijuana, cocaine, and heroin, may be **subject to expulsion** from the school or school district by the principal.

(b) Any student who **assaults** a principal, assistant principal, teacher, teacher's aide or other **educational staff** on school premises or at school-sponsored or school-related events, including athletic games, may be **subject to expulsion** from the school or school district by the principal.

(c) Any student who is charged with a violation of either paragraph (a) or (b) shall be notified in writing of an opportunity for a hearing; provided, however, that the student may have representation, along with the opportunity to present evidence and witnesses at said hearing before the principal.

After said hearing, a principal may, in his discretion, decide to suspend rather than expel a student who has been determined by the principal to have violated either paragraph (a) or (b).

(d) Any student who has been expelled from a school district pursuant to these provisions shall have the right to appeal to the superintendent. The expelled student shall have ten days from the date of the expulsion in which to notify the superintendent of his appeal. The student has the right to counsel at a hearing before the superintendent. The subject matter of the appeal shall not be limited solely to a factual determination of whether the student has violated any provisions of this section.

(e) When a student is expelled under the provisions of this section, no school or school district within the commonwealth shall be required to admit such student or to provide educational services to said student. If said student does apply for admission to another school or school district, the superintendent of the school district to which the application is made may request and shall receive from the superintendent of the school expelling said student a written statement of the reasons for said expulsion.

MISCELLANEOUS JUVENILE LAWS

C. 85 § 11B½. *Mandatory helmet use for persons 16 years of age or younger*

- Any person 16 years of age or younger operating:
    - in line skates,
    - a skate board,
    - a scooter
    - or other manually-propelled wheeled vehicle
- or riding as a passenger on any such manually-propelled vehicle
- on a public way, bicycle path or on any other public right-of-way
- shall wear a helmet.

Such helmet shall fit the person's head and be secured by straps at all times while operating in line skates, scooters, skate board or other manually-propelled wheeled vehicle and shall meet the standards for helmets established by the American National Standards Institute (ANSI Z 90.4) or subsequent standards or the Snell Memorial Foundation's 1984 standard for use in bicycling or subsequent standards. A violation of this section shall not be used as evidence of contributory negligence in a civil action.

A city or town shall not adopt any by-laws or ordinances to change the standards required by this section.

MOTOR VEHICLE LAW

Section 4 MOTOR VEHICLE LAW

In 2010, Justice Green wrote the following statement in the *Commonwealth v. Velasquez* decision: "wading through the various provisions of chapter 90 is akin to driving a car without windshield wipers on a dirt road on the side of a mountain at night during a blizzard." This section will hopefully clear off your windshield.

20 OF THE MOST COMMON MV OFFENSES

VIOLATIONS/OFFENSE	PENALTY	ARREST POWER	STATUTE
OPERATING UNDER THE INFLUENCE	CRIMINAL	Yes, on probable cause	c.90 § 24
OPERATING AFTER SUSPENSION/REVOCATION	CRIMINAL	Yes, if in presence on public way only.	c. 90 § 23
OPERATING WITHOUT A LICENSE	CRIMINAL	Yes, if in presence on public way only.	c. 90 § 10
SPEEDING (POSTED – C. 90 §S 18, NOT POSTED C. 90 §S 17)	$50, plus $10 for each M.P.H. in excess of 10 M.P.H. over limit, plus $50 head injury surcharge	No	c. 90 § 17 §18
STOP SIGN/RED LIGHT	$100 Plus $5 Public Safety Surcharge	No	c. 89 § 9
INSPECTION VIOLATION	$50 Plus $5 Public Safety Surcharge	No	c.. 90 § 20
UNREGISTERED MOTOR VEHICLE	$100 Plus $5 Public Safety Surcharge	No	c. 90 § 9
UNINSURED MOTOR VEHICLE	CRIMINAL	No	c. 90 § 34J
MARKED LANES VIOLATION	$100 Plus $5 Public Safety Surcharge	No	c. 89 § 4A
SEAT BELT VIOLATION	$25 Plus $5 Public Safety Surcharge	No	c. 90 § 13A
DEFECTIVE EQUIPMENT	$35 Plus $5 Public Safety Surcharge	No	c. 90 § 7
PEDESTRIAN IN CROSSWALK	$200 Plus $5 Public Safety Surcharge	No	c. 89 § 11
CITY/TOWN MV By-law Violation	$20	No	c. 85 § 10
BLOCKING AN INTERSECTION	$100 Plus $5 Public Safety Surcharge	No	c. 89 § 9
LICENSE/REGISTRATION NOT IN POSSESSION	$35	No, unless non-MA resident without license in possession	c. 90 § 11
FAILURE TO REPORT ADDRESS CHANGE: license/Reg. 30 days	$35 Plus $5 Public Safety Surcharge	No	c. 90 § 26A
ONE WAY STREET VIOLATION: must use by-law violation	$20 (City/Town may charge up to $50)	No	c. 85 § 10
FAILURE TO DISPLAY REGISTRATION DECAL	$35	No	540 CMR 2.05
WINDOW TINT IMPROPER	$250 Plus $5 Public Safety Surcharge	No	c. 90 § 9D
FAILURE TO DIM HEADLIGHTS	$35	No	540 CMR 22.05(2)

Important Note on Citation Amounts: Although the various statutes assigned various monetary penalties to the various offenses the fines on citations must be consistent with the Court's **Scheduled Assessment amounts**. See the citation fine reference at the end of this manual for the scheduled assessment for various violations.

Fineless Statutes: according to c. 90 § 20, any violation of chapter 90 **which does not specifically state a fine amount** shall result in a **$35.00 for the first offense**. See c. 90 § 20 for more information.

CITATIONS PROCEDURES & REQUIREMENTS

C. 90C § 2. CITATIONS AND CITATION BOOKS

Chief's Responsibilities:

Each police chief **shall issue citation books** to each permanent full-time police officer of his department whose duties may or will include traffic duty or traffic law enforcement, or directing or controlling traffic, and to such other officers as he at his discretion may determine.

Each police chief **shall obtain a receipt** from each officer to whom a citation book has been issued. Each police chief **shall also maintain citation books at police headquarters** for the recording of automobile law violations by police officers to whom citation books have not been issued.

Issuing of Citations:

Any police officer assigned to traffic enforcement duty shall, whether or not the offense occurs within his presence, record the occurrence of automobile law violations upon a citation and shall inform the violator of the violation and shall give a copy of the citation to the violator. Such citation **shall be signed by said police officer and by the violator**, and whenever a citation is given to the violator in person that fact shall be so certified by the police officer.

The **violator shall be requested to sign** the citation in order to acknowledge that is has been received. If a written warning is indicated, no further action need be taken by the violator. No other form of notice, except as provided in this section, need be given to the violator.

Failure to Give Copy to Violator:

A **failure to give a copy** of the citation to the violator at the time and place of the violation **shall constitute a defense in any court proceeding for such violation**, except:

- where the violator **could not have been stopped** or
- where additional time was reasonably necessary to **determine the nature of the violation**, or
- where additional time was reasonably necessary the **identity of the violator,** or
- where the court finds that a circumstance justifies the failure.

NOTE: If a person later dies as a result of a motor vehicle collision, the delay in issued the citation would be justified. See *Commonwealth v. Nadworthy*, 30 Mass. App. Ct. 912 (1991).

In such case the violation shall be recorded upon a citation **as soon as possible after such violation** and the citation shall be **delivered to the violator or mailed to him** at his residential or mail address or to the address appearing on his license or registration as appearing in registry of motor vehicles records.

NOTE: The burden is on the police to justify the delay. Also, giving citation to agent of violator is permissible.

Off-Duty Officer without Ticket Book:

In the 2013 case of ***Commonwealth v. Correia***, the Appeals Court ruled that an off-duty police officer who observes a civil motor vehicle infraction can issue a citation when he/she returns to duty and it will not impact the "in-hand" provision of chapter 90C § 2. A similar ruling was made by the SJC in the 1970 case of ***Commonwealth v. Pizzano***. And in the 1997 case of ***Commonwealth v. Cameron***, the SJC upheld the delay of issuing a citation when an off-duty police officer came upon a motor vehicle accident where a young boy was seriously injured. The officer then went on days off and returned two days later to issue the citation. The SJC stated that the delay was justified.

Procedure after having been issued:

At or before the completion of his tour of duty, a police officer to whom a citation book has been issued and who has recorded the occurrence of an automobile law violation upon a citation **shall deliver to his police chief or to the person duly authorized by said chief all remaining copies of such citation**, duly signed, **except the police officer's copy which shall be retained by him**. If the police officer has directed that a written warning be issued, the part of the citation designated as the registry of motor vehicles record shall be forwarded forthwith by the police chief or person authorized by him to the registrar and shall be kept by the registrar in his main office.

If the police officer has not directed that a written warning be issued and has not arrested the violator, the police chief or a person duly authorized by him shall retain the police department copy of each citation, and **not later than the end of the sixth business day after the date of the violation**:

(a) in the case of citations alleging only one or more **civil motor vehicle infractions**, shall cause all remaining copies of such citations to be **mailed or delivered to the registrar**; or

(b) in the case of citations alleging one or more **criminal automobile law violations**, shall cause all remaining copies of such citations to be delivered to the clerk-magistrate of the district court for the judicial district where the violation occurred.

VOIDED CITATION:

If a citation is spoiled, mutilated or voided, it shall:

- be endorsed with a full explanation why by the police officer voiding such citation,
- be returned to the registrar forthwith
- be duly accounted for upon the audit sheet for the citation book from which said citation was removed.

C. 90C § 9. DISPOSAL OF CITATION, COPY OR RECORD OF ISSUANCE

It shall be unlawful and official misconduct to dispose of a citation or copies thereof, or of the record of the issuance of same in a manner other than as required by the provisions of this chapter.

C. 90C § 10. PENALTY FOR FALSIFICATION OR DISPOSAL OF CITATION

Whoever knowingly falsifies a citation or copies thereof or a record of the issuance of same, or disposes of such citation, copy, or record, in a manner other than as required by the provisions of this chapter, or attempts so to falsify or dispose, or attempts to incite or procure another so to falsify or dispose shall be punished by a fine of not more than $500 or by imprisonment for a term not to exceed one year, or both such fine and imprisonment

Definitions & Auto Types

<table>
<tr><th>90 § 1</th><th>AUTO TYPES</th></tr>
<tr><td>Hybrid Vehicle</td><td>"Hybrid vehicle", a vehicle:
(a) which draws propulsion energy from onboard sources of stored energy which are both:
1) an internal combustion or heat engine using combustible fuel; and
2) a rechargeable energy storage system; or
(b) which, in the case of a passenger vehicle, medium duty passenger vehicle or light truck:
1) for model year 2002 and later model year vehicles, has received a certificate of conformity under the Clean Air Act and meets or exceeds the equivalent qualifying California low emission vehicle standard adopted under section 243(e)(2) of said Clean Air Act for that make and model year;
2) for model year 2004 and later model vehicles, has received a certificate that the vehicle meets or exceeds the Tier II Bin 5 emission level established in regulations prescribed by the Administrator of the United States Environmental Protection Agency under section 202(i) of said Clean Air Act for that make and model year vehicle; and
3) achieves an increase of 25 per cent fuel efficiency as compared to the average vehicle of its class as defined by the United States Environmental Protection Agency.</td></tr>
<tr><td>Low-speed vehicle</td><td>"Low-speed motor vehicle" or "low-speed vehicle", a motor vehicle which is:
a. 4-wheeled,
b. whose speed attainable in 1 mile is more than 20 miles per hour and not more than 25 miles per hour on a paved level surface; and
c. whose gross vehicle weight rating is less than 3,000 pounds.
All low-speed motor vehicles shall comply with the standards established in 49 C.F.R. § 571.500, as amended, and pursuant thereto, shall be equipped with:
• headlamps,
• front and rear turn signal lamps,
• tail lamps,
• stop lamps,
• an exterior mirror mounted on the driver's side of the vehicle and
• either an exterior mirror mounted on the passenger's side of the vehicle or an interior mirror,
• a parking brake,
• a windshield that conforms to the federal standards on glazing materials,
• a vehicle identification number that conforms to the requirements of 49 C.F.R. pt 565 for such numbers, a Type 1 or Type 2 seat belt assembly conforming to 49 C.F.R. § 571.209,
• installed at each designated seating position and reflex reflectors; provided, that 1 reflector is red on each side as far to the rear as practicable and 1 reflector is red on the rear.
A low speed motor vehicle that meets the requirements of 49 C.F.R. § 571.500, as amended, and is equipped as herein provided, may be registered in the commonwealth, subject to inspection and insurance requirements.</td></tr>
<tr><td>Motorcycle</td><td>"Motorcycle", any motor vehicle having a seat or saddle for the use of the rider and designed to travel on not more than three wheels in contact with the ground, including any bicycle with a motor or driving wheel attached, except for the following:
• a tractor or a motor vehicle designed for the carrying of golf clubs and not more than four persons,
• an industrial three-wheel truck,
• a motor vehicle on which the operator and passenger ride within an enclosed cab,
• a motorized bicycle</td></tr>
</table>

Motorized Bicycle	**"Motorized bicycle"(Moped)**, 1. a **pedal bicycle which has a helper motor**, or 2. a **non-pedal bicycle which has a motor.** The moped includes the following characteristics: • with a cylinder capacity **not exceeding fifty cubic centimeters**, • an **automatic transmission**, and • capable of a **maximum speed of no more than 30 miles per hour**.
	"Motorized scooter", any 2 wheeled tandem or 3 wheeled device, that has handlebars, designed to be stood or sat upon by the operator, powered by an electric or gas powered motor that is capable of propelling the device with or without human propulsion. The definition of "motorized scooter" shall not include: • a motorcycle or • motorized bicycle or • a 3 wheeled motorized wheelchair
Motor Vehicle	**"Motor vehicles"**, all vehicles constructed and designed for propulsion by power other than muscular power including such vehicles when pulled or towed by another motor vehicle, **except:** • railroad and railway cars, • vehicles operated by the system known as trolley motor or trackless trolley under chapter one hundred and sixty-three or section ten of chapter 544 of the acts of 1947, • vehicles running only upon rails or tracks, • vehicles used for other purposes than the transportation of property and incapable of being driven at a speed exceeding twelve miles per hour and which are used exclusively for the building, repair and maintenance of highways or designed especially for use elsewhere than on the travelled part of ways, • wheelchairs owned and operated by invalids • vehicles which are operated or guided by a person on foot • motorized bicycles In doubtful cases, the registrar may determine whether or not any particular vehicle is a motor vehicle as herein defined. If he determines that it should be so classified, he may require that it be registered, but such determination shall not be admissible as evidence in any action at law arising out of the use or operation of such vehicle previous to such determination.
Antique motor car"	**"Antique motor car"**, any motor vehicle **over 25 years old** which is maintained solely for use in exhibitions, club activities, parades and other functions of public interest and which is not used primarily for the transportation of passengers or goods over any way.
Way	**"Way"**, any public highway (including municipal streets and roads), private way laid out under authority of statute, way **dedicated to public use**, or way under the control of park commissioners or body having like powers. **NOTE on PUBLIC USE**: the public use element exists when the public has a right of access or when members of the public have access as invitees or licensees. An **invitee** is a person who has been invited to the location by the owner for the mutual benefit of both, such as a shopping mall or restaurant parking lot. A **licensee** is a person who is in a place with only the passive permission of the owner and usually for the licensee's benefit. **NOTE on PROOF:** Common methods of proving the public nature of a way include: a. certification from the municipality (with this nothing more is needed), b. official municipal/government records, c. testimony (i.e. police officer testimony of public nature and features).
Operation	Although not defined in G.L. chapter 90 § 1, case law has indicated that operation typically includes any act which can set the vehicle in motion. For a detailed, description see the OUI section of this manual.
Child Passenger Restraint	**"Child Passenger restraint"**, a specifically designed seating system which meets the United States Department of Transportation Federal Motor Vehicle Safety Standards, as established in 49 C.F.R. 571.213, which is either permanently affixed to a motor vehicle or is affixed to such vehicle by a safety belt or a universal attachment system.

EQUIPMENT & SAFETY

GENERAL EQUIPMENT REQUIREMENTS		
Source of Law/Rule	VIOLATION/OFFENSES	PENALTY
Lock & Key 90 § 7	Every motor vehicle operated on a way shall be provided with a **lock, key** or other device to prevent such vehicle from being set in motion by unauthorized persons, or otherwise contrary to the will of the owner or person in charge thereof.	1ST OFF: $35 Plus $5 Public Safety Surcharge 2ND OFF: $75 Plus $5 Public Safety Surcharge 3RD OFF: $150 Plus $5 Public Safety Surcharge
Horn 90 § 7	Every motor vehicle operated on a way shall be provided with a suitable **bell, horn** or **other means of signaling**	1ST OFF: $35 Plus $5 Public Safety Surcharge 2ND OFF: $75 Plus $5 Public Safety Surcharge 3RD OFF: $150 Plus $5 Public Safety Surcharge
Muffler 90 § 7	Every motor vehicle operated on a way shall be provided with a **muffler** or other suitable device to prevent unnecessary noise.	1ST OFF: $35 Plus $5 Public Safety Surcharge 2ND OFF: $75 Plus $5 Public Safety Surcharge 3RD OFF: $150 Plus $5 Public Safety Surcharge
Suitable lamps 90 § 7	Every motor vehicle operated on a way shall be provided with **suitable lamps**	1ST OFF: $35 Plus $5 Public Safety Surcharge 2ND OFF: $75 Plus $5 Public Safety Surcharge 3RD OFF: $150 Plus $5 Public Safety Surcharge
Miscellaneous Equipment 90 § 7	**EQUIPMENT VIOLATION, MISCELLANEOUS MV** • Audible alarm on dump truck, no audible alarm on flammables tanker, • Mud guards violation on commercial motor vehicle • Overhang +4 ft without flag/light reflector violation • Motor vehicle safety chains viol on trailer • Seat belt missing • Slow moving emblem viol	1ST OFF: $35 Plus $5 Public Safety Surcharge 2ND OFF: $75 Plus $5 Public Safety Surcharge 3RD OFF: $150 Plus $5 Public Safety Surcharge

Inspection Requirements

C. 90 § 20	INSPECTION REQUIREMENTS	
Law/Rule	VIOLATION/OFFENSES	PENALTY
Motor Vehicle not displaying valid Sticker	Any person who owns and fails to have inspected a motor vehicle owned by him, or any person who operates or permits a motor vehicle owned by him to be operated without a certificate of inspection or a certificate of rejection displayed shall be punished by a fine. **NOTE:** 540 CMR 4.07 permits the continued operation of a motor vehicle for 60 days with a rejection sticker provided the safety issues have been corrected (20 days for a motorcycle). Therefore, operation permissible for 60 days with rejection sticker if only emissions failure.	$50 Plus $5 Public Safety Surcharge
Safety Violation	Any person who operates or owns and permits to be operated a motor vehicle or trailer that fails to meet the safety standards shall be punished. **Note:** the way this statute is constructed is that a vehicle which has a safety issue even if otherwise properly inspected is subject to a fine.	$25 Plus $5 Public Safety Surcharge
	Important Information	
Testing	Safety or Safety/Emissions testing is performed annually or upon transfer of ownership of the vehicle.	

C. 90 § 20	INSPECTION REQUIREMENTS
Possible to have Sticker that doesn't match Reg.	It is possible for a vehicle to display a valid Certificate of Inspection, indicating a different number plate on the face of the sticker. However, the VIN should always match the sticker. Instances where the number plate might not match the registration include:[1] a. Plate swap (where ownership has ***not*** changed) b. Newly issued vanity/reserve/special plates (where ownership has not changed).
Permissible to stop vehicle with rejection sticker	The Appeals Court recently ruled "while it is possible that the driver of a car with a rejection sticker has corrected the underlying safety issues and has merely neglected to get the car reinspected, the police officer was not required to "exclude all possible innocent explanations of the facts and circumstances." Operation of a car with a red rejection sticker will give the police reasonable grounds to believe that the car is being driven in current violation of the civil traffic laws.[2]

NOISE & POLLUTANTS

NOISE & POLLUTANTS		
Law/ Rule	**Violation/Offense**	**Penalty**
Harsh Objectionable Noise c. 90 § 16	No person operating a motor vehicle shall sound a **bell, horn** or **other device,** nor **operate** in any manner, so as to make a **harsh, objectionable or unreasonable noise.** In ***Com. v. Young*** (2012), the Court upheld the stop of a vehicle for "screeching" tires.	$50 Plus $5 Public Safety Surcharge
Unnecessary Pollutants c. 90 § 16	No person operating a motor vehicle shall permit to escape from such vehicle smoke or pollutants in such amounts or at such levels as may violate motor vehicle air pollution control regulations adopted under the provisions of chapter 111.	$50 Plus $5 Public Safety Surcharge
Muffler Noise c. 90 § 16	No person shall operate a motor vehicle, nor shall any owner of such vehicle permit it to be operated upon any way, (except fire department and fire patrol apparatus), unless the motor vehicle: • is equipped with a muffler to prevent excessive or unnecessary noise, • has a muffler is in good working order and in constant operation, and • has a muffler that complies with the minimum standards for construction and performance as the registrar may prescribe.	$50 Plus $5 Public Safety Surcharge
Muffler Modification c. 90 § 16	• No person shall use a muffler cut-out or by-pass. • No person shall operate a motor vehicle on any way which motor vehicle is equipped: 1) with a muffler from which the baffle plates, screens or other original internal parts have been removed and not replaced; or 2) with an exhaust system which has been modified in a manner which will amplify or increase the noise emitted by the exhaust.	$50 Plus $5 Public Safety Surcharge

[1] Official Notification from MassDOT Judith Dupille, Vehicle Safety and Compliance Services 12.17.12
[2] *Commonwealth v. Rivas,* App.Ct. July 6, 2010

NOISE & POLLUTANTS		
Idling Motor Vehicle over 5 minutes c. 90 § 16A	No person shall cause, allow, or permit the unnecessary operation of the engine of a motor vehicle while said vehicle is stopped for a foreseeable period of time in excess of **5 minutes.** **This section shall not apply to:** a. Vehicles **being serviced**, provided that operation of the engine is essential to the proper repair b. Vehicles **engaged in the delivery or acceptance of goods**, wares, or merchandise for which engine assisted **power is necessary** and substitute alternate means cannot be made available, or c. Vehicles engaged in an operation for which the engine power is necessary for an associate power need other than movement and substitute alternate power means cannot be made available provided that **such operation does not cause or contribute to a condition of air pollution**.	1ST OFF: $100 Plus $5 Public Safety Surcharge 2ND OFF: $250 Plus $5 Public Safety Surcharge
Idling Motor Vehicle on School Property C. 90 § 16A	Idle Engine of Stopped MV on School Property	1ST OFF: $100 Plus $5 Public Safety Surcharge 2ND OFF: $500 Plus $5 Public Safety Surcharge
c. 90 § 7U	Motorcycle too loud (see motorcycle section of this manual)	1ST OFF: $35 +5 2ND OFF: $75 +5 3RD OFF: $150 +5

LIGHTING & REFLECTORS

LIGHTING & REFLECTORS		
Law/ Rule	**Violation/Offense**	**Penalty**
LIGHTS ON VEHICLES c. 85 § 15	A vehicle, **whether stationary or in motion**, on a public way, shall have attached to it headlights and taillights which shall be turned on by the vehicle operator and so displayed as to be visible from the front and rear during the period of **1/2 hour after sunset to 1/2 hour before sunrise**; provided, however, that such headlights and taillights shall be turned on by the vehicle operator **at all other times** when, due to insufficient light or unfavorable atmospheric conditions, visibility is reduced such that persons or vehicles on the roadway are **not clearly discernible at a distance of 500 feet** or when the vehicle's **windshield wipers are needed .** **Exceptions**: this section shall not apply to a vehicle which is designed to be **propelled by hand**; and provided further, that a vehicle carrying hay or straw for the purpose of transporting persons on a **hayride** shall display only electrically operated lights which shall be 2 flashing amber lights to the front and 2 flashing red lights to the rear, each of which shall be at least 6 inches in diameter and mounted 6 feet from the ground. **RMV Exemption:** Upon the written application of the owner of a vehicle and the presentation of reasons therefor the department may, in writing, in such form and subject to such requirements as it may elect, and without expense to the applicant, exempt said vehicle from the provisions of this section for such period of time as said department may elect.	$5

LIGHTING & REFLECTORS

USE OF LIGHTS **c. 90 § 7**	Every automobile **operated** ○ during the period from one half an hour after sunset to one half an hour before sunrise, and ○ during any other period when visibility is **reduced by atmospheric conditions** so as to render dangerous further operation without lights being displayed (i.e. Rain), • shall display at least two lighted white headlamps with at least one mounted at each side of the front of the vehicle or • **if parked** within the limits of a way ○ at least one white or amber light on the side of the automobile nearer the center of the way, **NOTE:** motorcycles must have least one white headlamp and if it has a sidecar attached, in addition, one such light on the front of the sidecar. **Lights must comply with RMV:** No headlamp or rear lamp shall be used on any motor vehicle so operated unless such headlamp or rear lamp is of a type complying with such minimum standards for construction and performance as the registrar may prescribe. **Case Law Note:** A motor vehicle with its headlights on during the daylight hours, when not required by law, may still be stopped for a violation of this chapter if the lights are not functioning properly.[1]	1ST OFF: $35 Plus $5 Public Safety Surcharge 2ND OFF: $75 Plus $5 Public Safety Surcharge 3RD OFF: $150 Plus $5 Public Safety Surcharge
FAILURE TO DIM LIGHTS 540 CMR 22.05(2)	540 CMR 22.05(2) requires that so-called high beams shall be dimmed when the vehicle is **within 500 feet of another vehicle** (the light cannot raise above 42 inches from the surface of the road when measured 75 feet or more ahead of the vehicle).	1ST OFF: $35 2ND OFF: $75 3RD OFF: $150
AFTERMARKET LIGHTING 540 CMR 22.07	**Aftermarket Lighting:** No person shall mount or display any lighting device which does not comply with Federal Motor Vehicle Safety Regulations, 49 CFR Part 571, unless specifically allowed by M.G.L. c. 90, §7. Such prohibited devices shall include, but not be limited to, neon undercarriage lighting. (540 CMR 22.07).	1ST OFF: $35 2ND OFF: $75 3RD OFF: $150
ALTERNATING HEADLIGHTS 540 CMR §22.05(5)	**Alternating Flashing Headlights** 540 CMR §22.05(5) (AKA "wigwag" lights) Note: exception for government vehicles and private ambulances "for the benefit of public safety."	1ST OFF: $35 2ND OFF: $75 3RD OFF: $150
REAR LIGHTS REQUIRED **90 § 7**	Every motor vehicle and trailer operated on a way shall be equipped **with two rear lights mounted one at each side of the rear of the vehicle** so as to show two red lights from behind and a white light to illuminate and not obscure the rear number plate. **Exceptions special vehicles:** A two-wheeled motorcycle, an antique motor car, and a farm tractor only need one rear red light and one suitable stop light in addition to the number plate illuminator; **Exception trailer:** a trailer having a gross weight of 3,000 pounds or less which does	1ST OFF: $35 Plus $5 Public Safety Surcharge 2ND OFF: $75 Plus $5 Public Safety Surcharge

[1] *Commonwealth v. Feyenord,* 445 Mass. 72 (2004)

LIGHTING & REFLECTORS

	not obscure the required lights of the towing vehicle need be equipped with only one such rear red light and one white light so arranged as to illuminate and not obscure the rear number plate. **NOTE on THIRD BRAKE LIGHT:** The common third brake light is not required by this statute.	3RD OFF: $150 Plus $5 Public Safety Surcharge
PLATE LIGHT 90 § 6	Plate must be illuminated plainly visible from 60 feet.	1ST OFF: $35 +5 2ND OFF: $75 +5 3RD OFF: $150 +5
RED/BLUE LIGHT 90 § 7E	Only authorized vehicles permitted to display red and blue lights (see emergency vehicle section of this manual).	$300 Plus $5 Public Safety Surcharge
PURPLE LIGHT 85 §14A	Authorized vehicles in a funeral procession may use (but are not required) to use purple oscillating lights during a funeral procession. Only purple can be used.	See c. 90 § 7
SPOT LIGHT 90 § 16	No person shall use on or in connection with any motor vehicle a spot light; the rays from which shine more than **2 feet above the road at a distance of 30 feet** from the vehicle. **Exceptions to Spot Light restrictions:** • a spot light may be used for the purpose of reading signs • as an auxiliary light in cases of necessity when the other lights required by law fail to operate.	$50 Plus $5 Public Safety Surcharge
HAZARD LIGHTS 90 § 7	Every motor vehicle registered in Massachusetts shall be equipped with a device to permit the front and rear directional signals to flash simultaneously these lights shall **only be operated only when the vehicle is disabled or stopped in the event of emergency** on or at the side of any way.	1ST OFF: $35 +5 2ND OFF: $75 +5 3RD OFF: $150 +5
AMBER LIGHT ON EXTREME LEFT 90 § 7	Every motor truck, trailer and commercial motor vehicle having a carrying capacity of three tons or over, must have an amber light attached to the extreme left of the front of the vehicle, attached and adjusted as to indicate the extreme left lateral extension of the vehicle or load, which shall be visible not less than 200 feet in the direction toward which the vehicle is proceeding or facing **Exception**: this is not required when parked within the limits of a way in a space in which unlighted parking is permitted by the rules or regulations of the board or officer having control of such way.	1ST OFF: $35 Plus $5 Public Safety Surcharge 2ND OFF: $75 Plus $5 Public Safety Surcharge 3RD OFF: $150 Plus $5 Public Safety Surcharge
OSCILLATING LIGHTS 90 § 7	No motor vehicle operated on a way shall mount or display a flashing, rotating or oscillating light in any direction (except pursuant to chapter 90 § 7E – emergency vehicles, school buses etc and c. 85 § 14A purple funeral lights).	1ST OFF: $35 +5 2ND OFF: $75 +5 3RD OFF: $150 +5

LIGHTING & REFLECTORS		
AMBER OSCILLATING LIGHTS 540 CMR 22	No person shall mount or display a flashing, rotating or oscillating amber light on a motor vehicle operated on the way, except as provided below: a. emergency or service purposes operated by members or employees of an auxiliary police force, b. charitable organizations, c. private burglar alarm companies, d. private detective and private security agencies, e. agencies of the Commonwealth or its political subdivisions, f. persons and garages providing motorists assistance services or towing services, g. public and private utility companies for emergency or service purposes, h. persons and companies that are transporting human blood or organs for emergency purposes, oxygen, explosives or other hazardous materials i. Permit issued by RMV, the owner's name must be displayed on vehicle on each side of vehicle and the permit must be carried by operator.	The RMV must order the violator to remove the light. Failure to remove the light would be a violation of 90 § 20 inspection violation.
Operator must allow inspection	The operator of a motor vehicle shall permit any police officer or motor vehicle investigator and examiner to inspect and test the head lighting equipment of such motor vehicle to determine compliance with the provisions of M.G.L. c. 90, § 7 and 540 CMR 22.05.	540 CMR 2205(4)
FOG LIGHTS PERMISSIBLE 540 CMR 22.05(3)	Whenever reflection from fog, snow or other atmospheric conditions make it impossible for the operator of a motor vehicle to see clearly substantial objects for the prescribed distances, the headlamps may be regulated as to give the driver the maximum visibility under the circumstances and, for this purpose, auxiliary headlamps may be used in conjunction with, or in place of the headlamps otherwise required.	

TIRES

TIRES & MUDGUARDS		
Law/ Rule	**Violation/Offense**	**Penalty**
TIRE PROTRUDING BEYOND FENDER 90 § 19	No passenger motor vehicle shall be operated on any way if such vehicle has the **side wall or thread of any tire projecting outward beyond the outer portion of the fender or side body panel**, unless such vehicle is equipped with four-wheel drive or is otherwise modified and intended for off-the-way use.	$100 Plus $5 Public Safety Surcharge
Wheel Track 540 CMR 6.04	The wheel track may be increased by the use of tires and rims for a maximum total increase of **4 inches beyond** the original manufacturer's specification. Cite for violation of c. 90 § 7.	1ST OFF: $35 +5 2ND OFF: $75 +5 3RD OFF: $150 +5

TIRES & MUDGUARDS		
STUDDED TIRES 90 § 16	No person, shall operate a motor vehicle equipped with metal studded tires upon a public way between May 1st and November the 1st **Exceptions:** This law does not apply to a duly authorized person driving an emergency fire vehicle, Additionally, the registrar may authorize the use of such tires before November 1st if weather conditions require the use thereof.	$50 Plus $5 Public Safety Surcharge
TIRE TREAD DEPTH VIOLATION 90 § 7Q	2/32 inch is the minimum tire depth permitted. Note: the statute requires that the violator *knows* about the deficiency.	1st Off: $35 +5 2nd Off: $75 +5 3rd Off: $150 +5
MATCHING TIRES REQUIRED 90 § 20	Tire size shall be the same on each side of the front and/or rear axle. Tire size may be different between front and rear axles as determined by vehicle manufacturer. (see **540 CMR 4.04 – safety requirements).**	$25 Plus $5 Public Safety Surcharge
MUDGUARDS 90 § 7	Every motor vehicle or trailer operated in or upon any way shall be equipped with suitable guards which will effectively reduce the spray or splash to the rear of mud, water or slush caused by the rear wheels. **NOTE:** The above does not pertain to passenger vehicles unless the tires extend beyond the fenders or body of the vehicle.	1st Off: $35 Plus $5 Public Safety Surcharge 2nd Off: $75 Plus $5 Public Safety Surcharge 3rd Off: $150 Plus $5 Public Safety Surcharge

WINDSHIELDS & WINDOWS

WINDSHIELDS, WINDOWS & MIRRORS		
Law/ Rule	**Violation/Offense**	**Penalty**
SAFETY GLASS REQUIRED 90 § 9A	No person shall operate any motor vehicle, and the owner or custodian of a motor vehicle shall not permit the same to be operated with partitions, doors, windows or windshields of glass unless such glass is of a type known as safety glass. The term "safety glass", as used herein, shall include any glass designed to minimize the likelihood of personal injury from its breaking or scattering when broken. This section shall not apply to motor vehicles manufactured prior to January 1st, 1966.	1st Off: $35 Plus $5 Public Safety Surcharge 2nd Off: $75 Plus $5 Public Safety Surcharge 3rd Off: $150 Plus $5 Public Safety Surcharge
WINDOW OBSTRUCTIONS & TINT 90 § 90D	No person shall operate any motor vehicle upon any public way or upon any way to which the public shall have the right of access with any of the following affixed thereto: (1) **a sign, poster or sticker,** in such a manner so as to obstruct, impede or distort the vision of the operator, on the: a. front windshield, b. the side windows immediately adjacent to the operator's seat and the front passenger seat,	$250 Plus $5 Public Safety Surcharge

EQUIPMENT & SAFETY

WINDSHIELDS, WINDOWS & MIRRORS

c. the side windows immediately to the rear of the operator's seat and

d. the front passenger seat and the rear window.

(2) **(Window tint)** nontransparent or sunscreen material, window application, reflective film or nonreflective film used in any way so as to make such windshield and window glass areas in any way nontransparent or obscured from either the interior or exterior. This applies to the following areas:

a. front windshield,

b. the side windows immediately adjacent to the right and left of the operator's seat,

c. the side windows immediately to the rear of the operator's seat and the front passenger seat and the rear window.

This section **shall not apply to**:

(1) motor vehicles manufactured with windshields and window glass areas equipped in accordance with specifications of 49 Code of Federal Regulations 571.205 as authorized by 15 USC 1407.

(2) the use of draperies, louvers, or other special window treatments, except those specifically designated in this section, **on the rear window**, or a side window to the rear of the driver **if the vehicle is equipped with two outside mirrors**, one on each side, adjusted so that the driver has a clear view of the highway behind the vehicle.

(3) federal, state and local **law enforcement agencies**, watch guard or patrol agencies licensed under the provisions of section twenty-five of c. one hundred and forty-seven and college, university and hospital police agencies appointed under the provisions of section sixty-three of c. twenty-two C utilizing K-9 teams in a motor vehicle while in the regular performance of their duties provided said motor vehicle is equipped with two outside mirrors, one on each side, adjusted so that the driver has a clear view of the highway behind the vehicle.

(4) the use of nontransparent or sunscreen material or window application which has a total visible light reflectance of not more than 35% or a visible light transmittance of not less than 35% on the side windows immediately adjacent to the right and left of the operator's seat, the side windows immediately to the rear of the operator's seat and the front passenger seat or on the rear window if the vehicle is equipped with two outside mirrors, one on each side, adjusted so that the driver has a clear view of the highway behind the vehicle.

(5) the use of any transparent material limited to the **uppermost 6" along the top of the windshield**, provided such strip does not encroach upon the driver's direct forward viewing area as more particularly described and defined in applicable Federal Motor Vehicle Safety Standards.

(6) a vehicle registered in another **state, territory or another country or province**.

(7) the use of nontransparent or sunscreen material, window application, reflective film or nonreflective film used in any way to cover or treat the side windows immediately to the rear of the operator's seat and the front passenger seat and the rear window so as to make such window glass areas in any way nontransparent or obscured from either the interior or exterior thereof of a private passenger motor vehicle registered under the provisions of this chapter for public livery and hired for that purpose for any period of time which exclusion shall not include a taxicab.

RMV Sanction

Subsequent offense results in 90 license suspension

WINDSHIELDS, WINDOWS & MIRRORS

	(8) special window treatment or application determined necessary by a licensed physician, for the protection of the owner or operator of a private passenger motor vehicle who is determined to be light or photosensitive. Must have proper medical documentation. **Unlawful to Sell Vehicle in Violation of this Statute:** No person shall manufacture, sell, offer for sale or trade, equip or operate a motor vehicle in the commonwealth in violation of the provisions of this section; provided, however, that nothing in this section shall be construed to prohibit the manufacture or sale of reflective or nonreflective film in the commonwealth. Case law note: In ***Commonwealth v. Baez***, the Court ruled that officers could conduct a motor vehicle stop based on the officer's observation of the dark window tint.[1]	
Windshield Defects 540 CMR 4.04	Windshields having any of the following defects will be rejected for a safety inspection: 1. Any broken glass with sharp or jagged edges inside or outside. 2. Any stone bruise, star break, or bulls eye, damage in excess of one inch in diameter within the critical viewing area or larger than two inches outside the critical viewing area, or multiple such damage. 3. Single line cracks which extend more than three inches into the critical viewing area. 4. Multiple cracks, having one or more which extends into the critical viewing area. 5. Wiper scrape(s) in excess of ¼ inch wide within the critical viewing area. 6. Clouding extending more than three inches within the perimeter of the exposed glass. 7. No poster, sticker decal or any other item shall be attached to the windshield in such a manner so as to obstruct the vision of the operator. 8. Any tinting or reflective material applied by brush, spray, or adhesive which is below the uppermost six inches of the windshield or which may encroach upon the drivers direct forward viewing area. (All such tinting provided by the original manufacturer in compliance with applicable Federal Motor Vehicle Safety Standards is acceptable.) (d) Rear Windows. Rear windows, if originally equipped, must allow an unobstructed view to the rear, unless the vehicle is equipped with two outside rear view mirrors.	$25 Safety Violation Pursuant to 90 § 20 Note: some cite this violation at a general equipment violation under 90 § 7. However, 90 § 7 does <u>not</u> address windshields. So the proper way to fine is under the generic safety violation of 90 § 20.
Mirrors 90 § 7	Every motor vehicle shall be equipped with at least one mirror so placed and adjusted as to afford the operator a clear, reflected view of the highway to the **rear and left side** of the vehicle.	1ST OFF: $35 +5 2ND OFF: $75 +5 3RD OFF: $150 +5

EQUIPMENT & SAFETY

[1] Commonwealth v. Baez, MassApp.Ct. 115 (1999)

BRAKES

BRAKES		
Law/ Rule	**Violation/Offense**	**Penalty**
Brakes Must Be In Good Working Order **90 § 7**	Every motor vehicle operated in or upon any way shall be provided with brakes adequate to control the movement of such vehicle such brakes shall at all times be maintained in good working order. **NOTE:** 540 CMR 4.04 (3) requires that brakes on a pleasure vehicle be capable of stopping the vehicle within 30 feet, and 40 feet for most trucks and buses, when traveling at 20 MPH.	1ST OFF: $35 Plus $5 Public Safety Surcharge 2ND OFF: $75 Plus $5 Public Safety Surcharge 3RD OFF: $150 Plus $5 Public Safety Surcharge
At Least Two Braking Systems **90 § 7**	One shall be the service brake system, and the other shall be the parking brake system, each with a separate means of application, each operating directly or indirectly on at least two wheels and each of which shall suffice alone to stop said automobile within a proper distance **Note:** 540 CMR 4.04(3) indicates that a parking brake shall be capable of stopping all vehicles traveling 20 MPH within 80 feet.	1ST OFF: $35 Plus $5 Public Safety Surcharge 2ND OFF: $75 Plus $5 Public Safety Surcharge 3RD OFF: $150 Plus $5 Public Safety Surcharge
Set Brake **90 § 13**	Must set brake when vehicle left unattended.	1ST OFF: $35 Plus $5 Public Safety Surcharge 2ND OFF: $75 Plus $5 Public Safety Surcharge 3RD OFF: $150 Plus $5 Public Safety Surcharge

HEIGHT & WIDTH

C. 90 § 19	HEIGHT, LENGTH & WIDTH REQUIREMENTS	
Except as otherwise provided in sections 19F and 19G, or when a vehicle has **been authorized by permit** to transport an irreducible load, the **following provisions shall apply**:		
Law/ Rule	**Violation/Offense**	**Penalty**
MAXIMUM WIDTH AND LENGTH OF MOTOR VEHICLE	No motor vehicle or trailer shall have (without a permit) an outside **width of which is more than 102"** or an extreme **overall length of more than 33 feet**. The 102" width restriction **does not include**: • load-induced tire bulge, • rearview mirrors, • turn signal lamps, • shade awnings on auto homes and house trailers, • hand-holds for cab entry and egress and • splash and spray suppressant devices; Provided, however, that such mirrors and other devices are mounted so as **not to cause a hazard to pedestrians** on or adjacent to any way.	$100 Plus $5 Public Safety Surcharge

C. 90 § 19	HEIGHT, LENGTH & WIDTH REQUIREMENTS	
MAXIMUM LENGTH OF OTHER VEHICLES MOTOR VEHICLE	• Truck, or house trailer: 40 feet • Motor bus or auto home: 45 feet • Articulated bus: 60 feet • Traditional automobile transporter, a traditional boat transporter and a truck-trailer boat transporter: 65 feet (not including load overhang which shall not exceed three feet beyond the foremost part of the front transporting vehicle or more than four feet beyond the rear bed of the body) • Stringer-steered automobile transporter or stringer-steered boat transporter: 75 feet (not including load overhang which shall not exceed three feet beyond the foremost part of the front transporting vehicle or more than four feet beyond the rear bed of the body) • Semi-trailer in a semi-trailer unit or trailer in a tractor-trailer unit: 53 feet **Note:** For more lengths and specifications for other types of specialty vehicles refer to the actual statue	$100 Plus $5 Public Safety Surcharge
TIRE PROTRUDING BEYOND FENDER	No passenger motor vehicle shall be operated on any way if such vehicle has the **side wall or thread of any tire projecting outward beyond the outer portion of the fender or side body panel**, unless such vehicle is equipped with four-wheel drive or is otherwise modified and intended for off-the-way use.	$100 Plus $5 Public Safety Surcharge
MAXIMUM VEHICLE HEIGHT	No vehicle shall exceed a height of **13' 6"** without a special permit.	$100 Plus $5 Public Safety Surcharge
Maximum height and weight alteration **c. 90 § 7P**	No person shall alter, modify or change the height of a motor vehicle with an original manufacturer's gross vehicle weight rating of up to and including ten thousand pounds, by elevating or lowering the chassis or body by more than **two inches** above or below the original manufacturer's specified height by use of so-called "shackle lift kits" for leaf springs or by use of lift kits for coil springs, tires, or any other means or device.	**1ST OFF: $35** Plus $5 Public Safety Surcharge **2ND OFF: $75** Plus $5 Public Safety Surcharge **3RD OFF: $150** Plus $5 Public Safety Surcharge
REQUIREMENT FOR VEHICLES OVER 10 FEET	No motor vehicle which has a total height exceeding 10' (excluding the height of any load on the vehicle) shall be operated on any way unless the total height is painted or printed in letters and numerals at least 4' high in a conspicuous place upon the side or front of such vehicle. **Exception:** the length shall not apply to any vehicle or combination of vehicles being towed because of disablement or emergency	$100 Plus $5 Public Safety Surcharge

C. 90 § 19	HEIGHT, LENGTH & WIDTH REQUIREMENTS	
MAXIMUM TRAILER WEIGHT	No trailer which with its load weighs more than 5,000 pounds shall be operated or drawn on any way without a permit, other than: • a semitrailer, • a heavy duty platform trailer, • a cable-reel trailer, a house trailer, • a trailer having at least two axles and used to collect and carry bulk milk from dairy farms to processing plants, • a trailer which is an apparatus or other object on wheels not used to transport other things for delivery, • or a trailer having at least two axles which, when used for agricultural purposes with its load weighs not more than $10,000 pounds; Provided, however, that the gross weight of such vehicle as operated does not exceed the gross vehicle weight rating as established by the original manufacturer of the trailer. **Penalty (general weight violations):** $40 per 1000 lbs. or fraction thereof overweight up to 10,000 lbs; $80 per 1000 lbs or fraction overweight over 10,000 lbs. **Note**: c. 85 § 35 holds the owner of an overweight vehicle for damage caused to a bridge.	$40 per 1000 lbs. or fraction thereof overweight up to 10,000 lbs; $80 per 1000 lbs or fraction overweight over 10,000 lbs Plus $5 Public Safety Surcharge
IRREDUCIBLE LOAD	Weight Violation With Irreducible Load	$10 per 1000 lbs. or fraction thereof overweight, but not more than $500 Plus $5 Public Safety Surcharge
REFUSAL TO BE WEIGHED	Refusing to be Weighed	$500 Plus $5 Public Safety Surcharge
Note: These dimensions of width, length and height shall be inclusive of the load and load-holding devices		

GENERAL SAFETY ISSUES & EQUIPMENT

GENERAL SAFETY EQUIPMENT & REQUIREMENTS

Law/ Rule	Violation/Offense	Penalty
MUST STOP ENGINE AND REMOVE KEY 90 § 13	No person having control or charge of a motor vehicle shall allow his/her vehicle to stand in any way and remain unattended without: stopping the engine of the vehicle, effectively setting the brakes and locking and removing the key from the locking device and from the vehicle. **Case law note**: In the civil case of *West v. Kendall*, the Court stated "G.L. c. 90, § 13 only applies to a vehicle left unattended in 'any way.' A way is defined in G.L. c. 90, § 1 as, 'any public highway, private way laid out under authority of statute, (or) way dedicated to public use....' We believe that a private parking lot does not fit within this definition of a 'way' and, therefore, that the statute was not violated."[1]	1ST OFF: $35 Plus $5 Public Safety Surcharge 2ND OFF: $75 Plus $5 Public Safety Surcharge 3RD OFF: $150 Plus $5 Public Safety Surcharge
MUST BE EQUIPPED WITH SAFETY BELTS 90 § 7	Every motor vehicle registered in Massachusetts which is privately owned and operated and designed for the carriage of passengers and which is used primarily for pleasure or for pleasure and business (including every such vehicle furnished for hire by a rental car agency but excluding every such vehicle used for public or commercial purposes) shall be equipped with two seat safety belts for the use of occupants of the front seats. **Cannot Remove Belts:** No safety belt installed in a motor vehicle in accordance with the provisions of this section or in accordance with the provisions of federal law or the rules or regulations issued by the United States Department of Transportation, shall be removed from said motor vehicle except for the purpose of repairs.	1ST OFF: $35 Plus $5 Public Safety Surcharge 2ND OFF: $75 Plus $5 Public Safety Surcharge 3RD OFF: $150 Plus $5 Public Safety Surcharge
UNCOVERED LOAD 85 § 36	No person shall drive or move a motor vehicle on any way, nor shall the owner or person in charge of any vehicle require or permit the vehicle to be driven or moved on any way, unless the vehicle **is constructed or loaded so as to prevent any of its load from dropping, sifting, leaking or otherwise escaping** and if it is loaded with sand, gravel, loam, dirt, stone, rubbish or debris that could fall on other vehicles or on the highway and create litter or potential hazards to other vehicles, unless its load is fully and adequately covered.	$200
RED FLAG/LIGHT FOR EXTENDED LOAD 90 § 7	Every motor vehicle or trailer operated on a way which carries a load or object extending **4 feet or more** beyond the cab or body shall display at the extreme rear end of such load or object **a red light** plainly visible from a distance of at least **500 feet** to the sides and rear, or during the period when motor vehicles are not required to display lights a red flag or cloth not less than **12" square.**	1ST OFF: $35 +5 2ND OFF: $75 +5 3RD OFF: $150 +5
Plow and Hitch removal 90 § 19K	Between May 15 and October 15 of each year, any vehicle with a gross weight of less than 26,000 pounds which is equipped with a plow shall be required to have removed the plow and hitching mechanism used with the plow. Vehicles equipped with an apparatus that allows the hitching mechanism to be folded flat leaving no protruding surfaces, shall only be required to have the plow itself removed; if the hitching mechanism is in the folded flat position while the vehicle is in operation. If snowfall occurs before October 25 or after May 15 vehicles subject to this act may be re-equipped with the plow and any apparatus necessary for clearing snow. Vehicles shall be required to abide by this section within 72 hours of the conclusion of snowfall.	1ST OFF: warning 2ND OFF: $250 +5 3RD OFF: $500 +5

[1] West v. Kendall, 1989 Mass.App.Div. 20 (1989).

COMMERCIAL VEHICLES SAFETY & EQUIPMENT ISSUES

COMMERCIAL VEHICLES SAFETY & EQUIPMENT ISSUES		
Law/ Rule	**Violation/Offense**	**Penalty**
FLARES; USE BY CERTAIN COMMERCIAL VEHICLES 85 § 14B	Whenever any commercial vehicle having a gross weight in excess of 5,000 pounds (other than a motor bus or taxicab, or any automobile service truck) becomes disabled or stops to load or unload any motorized equipment from such vehicle or from a trailer upon the traveled portion of any street or highway the operator of such vehicle shall, during the time when lights are required to be displayed on motor vehicles, place **3 flares** on the traveled part of the way in the following positions: • one flare in the center of the traffic lane in which such disabled vehicle remains and distant approximately 100 feet from such vehicle in the direction of traffic approaching in that lane; • one flare not less than 100 feet from such vehicle in the opposite direction in said lane; and • one flare at the traffic side of such vehicle, not nearer than 10 feet from the front or rear of such vehicle; **Exceptions for Obstructed View**: if such vehicle is disabled or stopped to load or unload any motorized equipment from such vehicle or from a trailer upon the traveled portion of any street or highway **within 300 feet of** • a curve, • crest of a hill, • or other place where the view of such vehicle is obstructed, The flare in that direction shall be so placed as to afford ample warning to other persons using such way, and in no case less than 100 feet, nor more than 300 feet, from the disabled vehicle. The word "flare" as used in this section shall mean either a lighted pot torch, a lighted red electric lamp, or a warning device meeting the requirements of Federal Motor Vehicle Safety Standard No. 125. **Exclusion:** Flare requirement shall not apply to street railway cars and trackless trolley vehicles	$50 **RMV Action:** the RMV may, in the case of a motor vehicle not equipped with at least 3 flares, suspend for not more than 15 days the certificate of registration of such vehicle.
FLARES MUST BE CARRIED AT ALL TIMES 85 § 14B	Every motor vehicle to which this section applies, when operated on any street or highway, shall carry at all times not less than three flares in a position where they are easily accessible to any person desiring to use the same and to any officer or official authorized to inspect said vehicle.	$50

COMMERCIAL VEHICLES SAFETY & EQUIPMENT ISSUES

AUDIBLE WARNING SIGNAL 90 § 7	**Dump Truck** Every motor vehicle truck with dump bodies shall be equipped with an adequate audible warning system to alert the operator when the dump body is in an upright and elevated position. **Flammable Material Delivery** Every bulk tank carrier delivering gasoline or other flammable material, or trailer weighing, with its load, more than 12,000 lbs, and used to deliver gasoline or other flammable material, shall be equipped with an audible warning system when the vehicle's transmission is in reverse.	1ST OFF: $35 Plus $5 Public Safety Surcharge 2ND OFF: $75 Plus $5 Public Safety Surcharge 3RD OFF: $150 Plus $5 Public Safety Surcharge
TRAILER SAFETY CHAINS 90 § 7	Every trailer (except a semi-trailer), shall, in addition to a regular hitch, be fastened by safety chains to prevent it from breaking away from the towing vehicle. Such chains shall comply with such minimum standards for construction and performance as the registrar may prescribe. **US DOT compliance deemed to be in compliance**: Notwithstanding the preceding provisions of this section, any commercial motor vehicle, semi-trailer or trailer, used in interstate commerce, which shall conform as to its equipment with the regulations established from time to time by the bureau of motor carrier safety of the United States department of transportation, shall be deemed to conform to the requirements of this section.	1ST OFF: $35 Plus $5 Public Safety Surcharge 2ND OFF: $75 Plus $5 Public Safety Surcharge 3RD OFF: $150 Plus $5 Public Safety Surcharge
CHOCK BLOCKS REQUIRED 90 § 13	Whenever one of the below vehicles • a bus having a seating capacity of more than 7 passengers, • a truck weighing, unloaded, more 4,000 lbs, • or a tractor, trailer, semi-trailer or combination thereof, is parked on a way, on a grade sufficient to cause such vehicle to move of its own momentum, and is left unattended by the operator, one pair of adequate wheel safety chock blocks shall be securely placed against the rear wheels of such vehicle so as to prevent movement thereof. **Exception:** This shall not apply to a vehicle equipped with positive spring-loaded air parking brakes.	1ST OFF: $35 Plus $5 Public Safety Surcharge 2ND OFF: $75 Plus $5 Public Safety Surcharge 3RD OFF: $150 Plus $5 Public Safety Surcharge

See License section for Commercial License Disqualifiers.

OPERATION/RULES OF THE ROAD

C. 90 § 25	REFUSAL TO SUBMIT TO POLICE OFFICER	
Law/ Rule	**Violation/Offense**	**Penalty**
FAILURE TO SUBMIT TO A POLICE OFFICER	The defendant, while **operating** or **in charge** of a motor vehicle, when requested by a police officer: • **Refuses to give his name and address** or the name and address of the owner of such motor vehicle; • **Gives a false name or address** • **Refuses or neglects to stop** when signaled to stop by any police officer who is in uniform or who displays his badge conspicuously* on the outside of his outer coat or garment; ***note**: by utilizing lights and siren in marked cruiser, or displaying badge against window in an unmarked cruiser, have been found to satisfy this requirement.[1] • **Refuses to produce his license or his certificate of registration**, or • **Refuses to permit such officer to take the license or certificate in hand** for the purpose of examination, or • Refuses, on demand of such officer, **to sign his name in the presence of the officer.** **Attorney Hanrahan's Note:** the purpose of the signing requirement is to assist with the identification of the operator; it is not intended to punish a violator who refuses to acknowledge a citation. Also, it only applies to the operator or person in charge of the vehicle. **It does not apply to passengers of the vehicle.**	$100 Criminal **Arrestable**: this offense is arrestable via C. 90 subsection 21 when the offense is committed in the officer's presence **RMV sanction**: License Suspension: 60 days
REFUSAL TO SURRENDER LICENSE OR REGISTRATION	The defendant without a reasonable excuse fails to deliver his license to operate motor vehicles or the certificate of registration of any motor vehicle operated or owned by him or the number plates furnished by the registrar for said motor vehicle, or who refuses or neglects to produce his license when requested by a court or trial justice.	$100 Arrestable: see above **RMV sanction**: License Suspension: 60 days

Noteworthy Cases	
Must be in active control	In ***Commonwealth v. Schiller*** (1979), the Court ruled that the defendant was not in control of his vehicle when he was visited by an officer investigating a report of erratic operation that occurred the day before. Even though the defendant was at his front door and his vehicle was in his driveway he was not "in control" of his vehicle, at least for the purposes of this statute.

[1] *Commonwealth v. Ross*, 73 Mass. App. Ct. 181 (2008) and *Commonwealth v. Gray*, 423 Mass. 293 (1996).

C. 90 § 25	REFUSAL TO SUBMIT TO POLICE OFFICER
Compliance required even if Operator does not believe reason for stop legitimate	In ***Commonwealth v. Coleman***, the defendant and another driver separately called the police after being involved in an altercation on the highway. When the police began their investigation by speaking with the other driver, the defendant became impatient and told the officers that he could not wait. Despite being directed to remain at the scene, the defendant engaged his vehicle and prepared to leave. One of the officers pronounced the defendant under arrest for disorderly conduct and used the handle of his weapon in an unsuccessful attempt to break the defendant's car window, prompting the defendant to flee and lead the officers on a high-speed chase. Eventually, the defendant was apprehended and charged failure to stop for a police officer (G. L. c. 90, § 25) among numerous other offenses. The Court ruled that the statutory requirement that motorists stop for police allows "no exception -- even for a driver who reasonably believes that police detention is unjustified. If there is no legitimate basis for the stop, the driver's recourse is not through flight with its attendant risks to others, but through the orderly judicial process." [1]

INTERFERENCE WITH SAFE OPERATION

INTERFERENCE WITH SAFE OPERATION (including Texting and Mobile Devices)

Law/ Rule	Violation/Offense	Penalty
TEXTING WHILE DRIVING C. 90 § 13B	**No operator of a motor vehicle shall use a mobile telephone, or any handheld device capable of accessing the internet, to manually compose, send or read an electronic message while operating a motor vehicle.** **Stationary off-road Exception:** an operator shall not be considered to be operating a motor vehicle if the vehicle is stationary and not located in a part of the public way intended for travel. **Non-surchargeable**: A penalty under this section shall not be a surchargeable offense under section 113B of chapter 175. **NOTE:** See Reckless & Negligent Operation section for Texting Causing Death offense.	1ST OFF: $100 Plus $5 Public Safety Surcharge 2ND OFF: $250 Plus $5 Public Safety Surcharge 3RD OFF: $500 Plus $5 Public Safety Surcharge
OPERATION OF MOBILE ELECTRONIC DEVICES BY JUNIOR OPERATORS C. 90 § 8M	**No person under 18 years of age shall use a mobile telephone, hands-free mobile telephone or mobile electronic device while operating a motor vehicle on any public way.** **RMV Action:1st Offense**: license or permit suspended for 60 days and shall not be eligible for license reinstatement until he also completes a program selected by the registrar that encourages attitudinal changes in young drivers; **2nd offense**: license or permit suspended for 180 days; **3rd or subsequent offense**: license or permit suspended for 1 year.	1ST OFF: $100 Plus $5 Public Safety Surcharge

SAFE OPERATION

[1] Commonwealth v. Coleman, 64 Mass. App. Ct. 558 (2005).

INTERFERENCE WITH SAFE OPERATION
(including Texting and Mobile Devices)

	Note: The law (Chapter 155 of the Acts of 2010) defines a "**mobile electronic device**" as any hand-held or other portable electronic equipment capable of providing data communication between two or more persons, including, without limitation, a mobile telephone, a text messaging device, a paging device, a personal digital assistant, a laptop computer, electronic equipment that is capable of playing a video game or digital video disk, equipment on which digital photographs are taken or transmitted or any combination thereof, or equipment that is capable of visually receiving a television broadcast. Mobile electronic device shall **not** include any audio equipment or any equipment installed, or affixed, either temporarily or permanently, in a motor vehicle for the purpose of providing navigation or emergency assistance to the operator of such motor vehicle or video entertainment to the passengers in the rear seats of such motor vehicle. **Exceptions/Defenses:** **STATIONARY OFF OF PUBLIC WAY**: For the purposes of this section, a junior operator shall not be considered to be operating a motor vehicle if the vehicle is stationary and not located in a part of the public way intended for travel. **EMERGENCY:** It shall be an affirmative defense for a junior operator to produce evidence that the use of a mobile telephone, hands-free mobile telephone or mobile electronic device that is the basis of the alleged violation was for emergency purposes. For the purpose of this section, an emergency shall mean that the junior operator used the hands-free mobile telephone or mobile electronic device to communicate with another to report any of the following: (i) The motor vehicle was disabled; (ii) Medical attention or assistance was required; (iii) Police intervention, fire department or other emergency service was necessary for the personal safety of the operator or a passenger; or (iv) A disabled vehicle or an accident was present in the public way. Note: A penalty under this subsection shall not be a surchargeable offense under chapter 175 §113B.	2ND OFF: $250 Plus $5 Public Safety Surcharge 3RD OFF: $500 Plus $5 Public Safety Surcharge
MOBILE ELECTRONIC DEVICE USE BY PUBLIC TRANSPORTATION OPERATORS C. 90 § 12A	**No operator of a vehicle or vessel used in public transportation shall use a mobile telephone, hands-free mobile telephone or other mobile electronic device (while operating the vehicle or vessel) including:** • **a train,** • **passenger bus,** • **school bus or other vehicle used to transport pupils,** • **passenger ferry boat, water shuttle or other equipment used in public transportation owned by, or operated under the authority of the Massachusetts Bay Transportation Authority, the Woods Hole, Martha's Vineyard and Nantucket Steamship Authority, Massachusetts Port Authority, or the Massachusetts Department of Transportation,** **Non-Moving Violation**: A violation of this section shall not be a moving violation for	$500 Plus $5 Public Safety Surcharge

INTERFERENCE WITH SAFE OPERATION
(including Texting and Mobile Devices)

	purposes of the safe driver insurance plan under section 113B of chapter 175. **Hands Free/Performance of Duty exception:** this section shall not apply to the operator of a vehicle or vessel used in public transportation using a mobile telephone, hands-free mobile telephone or mobile electronic device in the performance of the operator's official duties; provided, however, that in order for the use of any such device to be made "in the performance of the operator's official duties," such use must have been made in conformance with applicable written guidelines issued by a public entity listed in this paragraph relative to circumstances when operators are permitted to use said devices in the performance of their official duties or pursuant to directives from federal authorities having regulatory jurisdiction over such public entity's operations. **Emergency Exception:** It shall be an affirmative defense for an operator under this section to produce evidence that the use of a mobile telephone that is the basis of the alleged violation was in the case of an emergency. For the purpose of this paragraph, an emergency shall mean that the operator needed to communicate with another to report any of the following: (1) that the vehicle or vessel was disabled; (2) that medical attention or assistance was required on the vehicle or vessel; (3) that police intervention, fire department or other emergency services was necessary for the personal safety of a passenger or to otherwise ensure the safety of the passengers; or (4) that a disabled vehicle or an accident was present on a roadway.	
SAFETY PRECAUTIONS FOR PROPER OPERATION (IMPEDED OPERATION) **C. 90 § 13**	**Generic Restrictions** No person when operating a motor vehicle shall permit to be on or in the vehicle or on or about his person **anything** which may interfere with or impede the proper operation of the vehicle or any equipment by which the vehicle is operated or controlled. **Exception:** A person may operate a motor vehicle while using a federally licensed **2-way radio** or **mobile telephone** (except as provided in sections 8M, 12A and 13B – Texting/Cell phone restrictions) as long as one hand remains on the steering wheel at all times. **Case Law Notes:** Courts have found the following distractions to violate this statute: • Reading a Newspaper while Driving[1] • Vehicle overloaded with Passengers[2] • Obscured Windshield[3] • Dog riding on lap of operator[4]	1ST OFF: $35 Plus $5 Public Safety Surcharge 2ND OFF: $75 Plus $5 Public Safety Surcharge 3RD OFF: $150 Plus $5 Public Safety Surcharge

1 Levin v. Ginsberg, Massachusetts 1961.
2 Seymour v. Dunsville, 265 Mass. 78 (1928).
3 Commonwealth v. Arone, 265 Mass. 128 (1928).
4 Morse v. Sturgis, 262 Mass. 612 (1928).

INTERFERENCE WITH SAFE OPERATION (including Texting and Mobile Devices)

Law/Rule	Violation/Offense	Penalty
NO TELEVISION FORWARD THE DRIVER **C. 90 § 13**	No person shall drive any motor vehicle equipped with any **television viewer, screen or other means of visually receiving a television broadcast** which is located in the motor vehicle at any point forward of the back of the driver's seat, or which is visible to the driver while operating such motor vehicle.	1ST OFF: $35 Plus $5 Public Safety Surcharge 2ND OFF: $75 Plus $5 Public Safety Surcharge 3RD OFF: $150 Plus $5 Public Safety Surcharge
HEADPHONES **C. 90 § 13**	No person shall operate a motor vehicle while wearing headphones, unless said headphones are used for communication in connection with controlling the course or movement of said vehicle.	1ST OFF: $35 Plus $5 Public Safety Surcharge 2ND OFF: $75 Plus $5 Public Safety Surcharge 3RD OFF: $150 Plus $5 Public Safety Surcharge

TRAFFIC CONTROL DEVICES & YIELD REQUIREMENTS

TRAFFIC CONTROL DEVICES & YIELD REQUIREMENTS

Law/Rule	Violation/Offense	Penalty
TOWN MV BY-LAW VIOLATION **85 § 10**	Summarized: Towns may make ordinances and by-laws...regulating the passage of street cars, or other vehicles... **Attorney Hanrahan's Note**: this statute can be used to cite those who violate locally erected signs/rules designed to regulate traffic (e.g. no left turns).	$20
ONE-WAY VIOLATION **85 § 10**	There is actually no state law regulating one-way streets (aside from state highways – 720 CMR 9.05). In order to cite for a violation of a one-way street you have to cite under a Town ordinance or by-law (see above).	$20
FLASHING RED LIGHT/STOP SIGN **89 § 9**	Except when directed to proceed by a police officer, every driver of a vehicle approaching a stop sign or a flashing red signal shall stop a. At a clearly marked stop line, but if none, b. Before entering the crosswalk on the near side of the intersection, or, if none, c. At the point nearest the intersecting roadway where the driver has a view of approaching traffic on the intersecting roadway before entering it. After having stopped, the driver shall yield the right of way to any vehicle in the intersection or approaching on another roadway so closely as to constitute an immediate hazard during the time when such driver is moving across or within the intersection or junction of roadways. **Attorney Hanrahan's Note**: This is the statute that is also used to cite an operator who runs through a "solid" red light. Although technically the language of the statute does not specifically cover that violation.	1ST OFF: $100 Plus $5 Public Safety Surcharge SUBSQ. OFF: $150 Plus $5 Public Safety Surcharge

TRAFFIC CONTROL DEVICES & YIELD REQUIREMENTS

RIGHT TURN/LEFT TURN ON RED SIGNAL **89 § 8**	At any intersection in which vehicular traffic is facing a steady red light the driver of a vehicle which is stopped may make either: a. a right turn, or b. if on a one-way street may make a left turn to another one-way street, but shall yield the right-of-way to pedestrians and other traffic signals (including signals prohibiting the above turns).	$35 Plus $5 Public Safety Surcharge
YIELD SIGN **89 § 89**	The driver of a vehicle approaching a yield sign shall slow down to a speed reasonable for the existing conditions and, if required for safety, stop: a. at a clearly marked stop line, but if none, b. before entering the crosswalk on the near side of the intersection, or, if none, c. at the point nearest the intersecting roadway where the driver has a view of approaching traffic on the intersecting roadway before entering it. After slowing or stopping, the driver shall yield the right of way to any vehicle in the intersection or approaching on another roadway so closely as to constitute an immediate hazard during the time such driver is moving across or within the intersection or junction of roadways **Prima Facie Evidence:** if the driver is involved in a collision with a vehicle in the intersection or junction of roadways, after driving past a yield sign without stopping, such collision shall be deemed prima facie evidence of his failure to yield the right of way.	1st Off: $100 Plus $5 Public Safety Surcharge Subsq. Off: $150 Plus $5 Public Safety Surcharge
Following too closely **85 § 10**	There is no state law or CMR that specifically address following another vehicle too closely. Many cities and towns have enacted their own ordinance/by-law (85 § 10). Driving negligently may also be an option if the circumstances warrant.	$20
RIGHT-OF-WAY AT INTERSECTING WAYS **89 § 8**	**VEHICLE ON LEFT MUST YIELD TO VEHICLE ON THE RIGHT:** • When two vehicles approach or enter an intersection at approximately the same instant, • The operator of the vehicle on the left shall yield the right-of-way to the vehicle on the right. **LEFT TURN MUST YIELD** Any operator intending to turn left, in an intersection, across the path or lane of vehicles approaching from the opposite direction shall, before turning, yield the right-of-way until such time as the left turn can be made with reasonable safety. **MUST YIELD WHEN ENTERING A ROTARY** Any operator of a vehicle entering a rotary intersection shall yield the right-of-way to any vehicle already in the intersection. **Exception to the above Requirements:** The foregoing provisions of this section shall not apply when an operator is otherwise directed by a police officer, or by a traffic regulating sign, device or signal lawfully erected.	$35 Plus $5 Public Safety Surcharge

TRAFFIC CONTROL DEVICES & YIELD REQUIREMENTS		
BLOCKING AN INTERSECTION 89 § 9	The driver of a motor vehicle shall not cross or enter an intersection, which it is unable to proceed through without stopping and thereby blocking vehicles from traveling in a free direction. The driver must wait another cycle of the signal light, if necessary **Note:** A green light is no defense to blocking the intersection. For the purposes of this section the word, "vehicle", shall include a trackless trolley.	1ST OFF: $100 Plus $5 Public Safety Surcharge SUBSQ. OFF: $150 Plus $5 Public Safety Surcharge

PASSING

Law/Rule	Violation/Offense	Penalty
RULES FOR PASSING A VEHICLE ON THE LEFT 89 § 2	The driver of a vehicle passing another vehicle traveling in the same direction shall drive a safe distance to the left of such other vehicle and shall not return to the right until safely clear of the overtaken vehicle. If it is not possible to overtake a bicycle or other vehicle at a safe distance in the same lane, the overtaking vehicle shall use all or part of an adjacent lane if it is safe to do so or wait for a safe opportunity to overtake.	$100 Plus $5 Public Safety Surcharge
RULES FOR VEHICLE BEING PASSED ON LEFT 89 § 2	If the way is of sufficient width for the two vehicles to pass, the driver of the leading one shall not unnecessarily obstruct the other. Except when overtaking and passing on the right is permitted, the driver of an overtaken vehicle shall give way to the right in favor of the overtaking vehicle on visible signal and shall not increase the speed of his vehicle until completely passed by the overtaking vehicle.	$100 Plus $5 Public Safety Surcharge
PASSING ON THE RIGHT 89 § 2	The driver of a vehicle may, if the roadway is free from obstruction and of sufficient width for two or more lines of moving vehicles, overtake and pass upon the right of another vehicle when the vehicle overtaken is: a) making or about to make a left turn, b) upon a one-way street, or c) upon any roadway on which traffic is restricted to one direction of movement.	$100 Plus $5 Public Safety Surcharge

LANE REQUIREMENTS

LANE REQUIREMENTS		
Law/ Rule	**Violation/Offense**	**Penalty**
MARKED LANE VIOLATION 89 § 4A	When any way has been divided into lanes, the driver of a vehicle shall drive entirely within a single lane, and he shall not move from the lane in which he is driving until he has first ascertained if such movement can be made with safety. Note: the tires must drive over the line(s), merely making contact with the line is not a violation.[1]	$100 Plus $5 Public Safety Surcharge
VEHICLES MUST OPERATE IN THE RIGHT LANE 89 § 4B	Upon all ways the driver of a vehicle shall drive in the lane nearest the right side of the way when such lane is available for travel, except : • when overtaking another vehicle or • when preparing for a left turn. **Exceptions:** When the right lane has been constructed or designated for purposes other than ordinary travel, a driver shall drive his vehicle in the lane adjacent to the right lane except when overtaking another vehicle or when preparing for a left or right turn; provided, however, that a driver may drive his vehicle in such right lane if signs have been erected by the department of highways permitting the use of such lane.	$100 Plus $5 Public Safety Surcharge
KEEPING TO RIGHT WHILE VIEW OBSTRUCTED 89 § 4	Whenever on any way (public or private) there is not a clear view of the road for at least 400 feet, the driver of every vehicle shall keep his vehicle on the right of the middle of the traveled part of the way whenever it is safe and practicable so to do. **Exception:** the department of highways may alter this provision by the use of restrictive pavement markings in areas of limited sight distance, at intersections and at obstructions in the highway, on state highways, on ways leading thereto and on all main highways between cities and towns; and may by permit, revocable upon notice, authorize cities and towns to alter said provision by the use of such restrictive pavement markings; provided, that such markings shall be in accordance with accepted standards of engineering practice	$100 Plus $5 Public Safety Surcharge
SLOW MOVING VEHICLE EXTREME RIGHT REQUIREMENT 89 § 4	On any highway with more than one passing lane in the same direction, all heavy commercial vehicles (as defined below), shall be restricted in ordinary operation to the right-hand travel lane, and in overtaking and passing shall be restricted to the next adjacent passing or travel lane and shall not use any other lanes except in an emergency. **Definition**: for the purpose of this section, heavy commercial vehicles shall be defined as those in excess of 2½ tons used for transportation of goods, wares, and merchandise. Buses are exempt from this requirement.	$100 Plus $5 Public Safety Surcharge

SAFE OPERATION

[1] *Commonwealth v. O'Brien*, 2013 WL 708877 non-published opinion Mass.App.Ct.

LANE REQUIREMENTS		
HEAVY TRUCKS; DRIVING IN RIGHT-HAND LANE ON MULTI-LANE HIGHWAYS 89 § 4C	On any highway with more than one passing lane in the same direction, all heavy commercial vehicles (as defined below), shall be restricted in ordinary operation to the right-hand travel lane, and in overtaking and passing shall be restricted to the next adjacent passing or travel lane and shall not use any other lanes except in an emergency. **Definition**: for the purpose of this section, heavy commercial vehicles shall be defined as those in excess of 2½ tons used for transportation of goods, wares, and merchandise. Buses are exempt from this requirement.	$100 Plus $5 Public Safety Surcharge
MEETING VEHICLES KEEP RIGHT 89 § 1	When persons traveling with vehicles meet on a way, each shall reasonably drive his vehicle to the right of the middle of the traveled part of such way, so that the vehicles may pass without interference, **Exceptions**: the department of highways may modify such restriction by pavement markings on state highways, on ways leading thereto and on all main highways between cities and towns. The department may by permit, revocable upon notice, authorize cities and towns to modify such restriction by pavement markings. The provisions of this section shall not be construed as prohibiting a vehicle from crossing a solid center pavement marking line or lines in making a left turn into or from a private way.	$100 Plus $5 Public Safety Surcharge

TURNING REQUIREMENTS

TURNING & SIGNALING REQUIREMENTS		
Law/Rule	**Violation/Offense**	**Penalty**
RIGHT TURN RIGHT SIDE OF ROAD 90 § 14	When turning to the right, an operator shall do so: • in the lane of traffic nearest to the right-hand side of the roadway and • as close as practicable to the right-hand curb or edge of roadway.	1ST OFF: $35 Plus $5 Public Safety Surcharge 2ND OFF: $75 Plus $5 Public Safety Surcharge 3RD OFF: $150 Plus $5 Public Safety Surcharge
TURNING LEFT 90 § 14	When approaching for a left turn on a two-way street, an operator shall do so in the lane of traffic to the right of and nearest to the center line of the roadway and the left turn shall be made by passing to the right of the center line of the entering way where it enters the intersection from his left. **Yield to on-coming traffic:** When turning to the left within an intersection or into an alley, private road or driveway an operator shall **yield the right of way to any vehicle approaching from the opposite direction**, including a bicycle on the right of the other approaching vehicles, which is within the intersection or so close thereto as to constitute an immediate hazard. **One-way Street:** When approaching for a left turn on a one-way street, an operator shall do so in the lane of traffic nearest to the left-hand side of the roadway and as close as practicable to the left-hand curb or edge of roadway.	1ST OFF: $35 Plus $5 Public Safety Surcharge 2ND OFF: $75 Plus $5 Public Safety Surcharge 3RD OFF: $150 Plus $5 Public Safety Surcharge

TURNING & SIGNALING REQUIREMENTS

TURN & STOP SIGNALS REQUIRED 90 § 14B	Every person operating a motor vehicle, • before stopping their vehicle or • making any turning movement which would affect the operation of any other vehicle, Shall give a plainly visible signal by activating the brake lights or directional lights or appropriate signal.	$25 Plus $5 Public Safety Surcharge
HAND SIGNALS **90 § 14B**	In the event electrical or mechanical signals are not operating or not provided on the vehicle, a plainly visible signal by means of the hand and arm shall be made. Hand and arm signals shall be made as follows: 1. An intention to **turn to the left** shall be indicated by hand and arm extended horizontally. 2. An intention to **turn to the right** shall be indicated by hand and arm extended upward. 3. An intention to **stop or decrease speed** shall be indicated by hand and arm extended downward	$25 Plus $5 Public Safety Surcharge
RIGHT TURN NEAR BICYCLIST 90 § 14	No person operating a vehicle that overtakes and passes a bicyclist proceeding in the same direction shall make a right turn at an intersection or driveway unless the turn can be made at a safe distance from the bicyclist at a speed that is reasonable and proper. **NOTE:** It shall not be a defense for a motorist causing an accident with a bicycle that the bicycle was to the right of vehicular traffic.	1ST OFF: $35 Plus $5 Public Safety Surcharge 2ND OFF: $75 Plus $5 Public Safety Surcharge 3RD OFF: $150 Plus $5 Public Safety Surcharge

SPECIAL PRECAUTIONS

SPECIAL PRECAUTIONS REQUIRED

Law/ Rule	Violation/Offense	Penalty
REQUIREMENTS TO SLOW DOWN 90 § 14	**Obstructed View:** The person operating a motor vehicle on any way or a **curve or a corner** where his **view is obstructed** shall slow down and keep to the right. **Intersection:** The person operating a motor vehicle on any way upon approaching any junction with an **intersecting way** shall, before entering the same, slow down and keep to the right of the center line.	1ST OFF: $35 Plus $5 Public Safety Surcharge 2ND OFF: $75 Plus $5 Public Safety Surcharge 3RD OFF: $150 Plus $5 Public Safety Surcharge
APPROACHING A SCHOOL BUS 90 § 14	When approaching a vehicle which displays a sign bearing the words "SCHOOL BUS" and which is equipped with front and rear alternating flashing red signal lamps which are flashing, and which has been stopped to allow pupils to alight from or board the same, a person operating a motor vehicle or trackless trolley shall:	1ST OFF: $250 Plus $5 Public Safety Surcharge

SAFE OPERATION

SPECIAL PRECAUTIONS REQUIRED

	• bring **vehicle** (or trackless trolley) **to a full stop** before reaching said school bus • not proceed until the warning signals are deactivated **Exceptions:** • Vehicles approaching from the opposite direction on a divided highway are not required to stop. • Vehicles directed to the contrary by a police officer duly authorized to control the movement of traffic. **RMV action:** A 2nd, 3rd or subsequent conviction: the registrar who shall revoke immediately the license or right to operate of the person so convicted and no appeal, motion for a new trial or exceptions, shall operate to stay the revocation of the license or right to operate; provided, however, that no license or right to operate shall be issued to any person convicted of a second such offense until 6 months after the date of revocation following said conviction or to any person convicted of a third or subsequent such offense until 1 year after the date of revocation following said conviction. **NOTE**: if the prosecution against such person has terminated in his favor the registrar shall forthwith reinstate his license or right to operate.	2ND OFF: $1,000 Plus $5 Public Safety Surcharge 3RD OFF: $2,000 Plus $5 Public Safety Surcharge
TRAVELING BEHIND A SCHOOL BUS 90 § 14	No person shall operate a motor vehicle **within a distance of 100 feet** behind a school bus. Every school bus shall have the words "keep back 100 feet" prominently displayed on the back of the bus, in type large and dark enough so that the words are legible at a distance of 100 feet.	1ST OFF: $35 Plus $5 Public Safety Surcharge 2ND OFF: $75 Plus $5 Public Safety Surcharge 3RD OFF: $150 Plus $5 Public Safety Surcharge
OPERATION NEAR AN ANIMAL 90 § 14	Every person operating a motor vehicle shall bring the vehicle and the motor propelling it **immediately to a stop** when approaching a **cow, horse or other draft animal** being led, ridden or driven, if such animal **appears to be frightened** and if the person in **charge thereof shall signal so to do** and if traveling in the opposite direction to that in which such animal is proceeding, said vehicle shall remain stationary so long as may be reasonable to allow such animal to pass; or, if traveling in the same direction, the person operating shall use reasonable caution in thereafter passing such animal.	1ST OFF: $35 Plus $5 Public Safety Surcharge 2ND OFF: $75 Plus $5 Public Safety Surcharge 3RD OFF: $150 Plus $5 Public Safety Surcharge
PASSING A BICYCLIST 90 § 14	In approaching or passing a person on a bicycle the operator of a motor vehicle shall slow down and pass at a safe distance and at a reasonable and proper speed.	1ST OFF: $35 Plus $5 Public Safety Surcharge 2ND OFF: $75 Plus $5 Public Safety Surcharge 3RD OFF: $150 Plus $5 Public Safety Surcharge
APPROACHING A STREET CAR 90 § 14	In approaching or passing a car of a street railway which has been stopped to allow passengers to alight from or board the same, the person operating a motor vehicle shall not drive such vehicle **within eight feet** of the running board or lowest step of the car then in use by passengers for the purpose of alighting or boarding, except by the express direction of a traffic officer or except at points where passengers are protected by safety zones.	1ST OFF: $35 Plus $5 Public Safety Surcharge 2ND OFF: $75 Plus $5 Public Safety Surcharge 3RD OFF: $150 Plus $5 Public Safety Surcharge

SPECIAL PRECAUTIONS REQUIRED

PRECAUTIONS AT RAILROAD CROSSINGS 90 § 15	**Slow Upon Approach of RR Crossing** Except as hereinafter otherwise provided, every person operating a motor vehicle, upon approaching a railroad crossing at grade, shall reduce the speed of the vehicle to a reasonable and proper rate before proceeding over the crossing, and shall proceed over the crossing at a rate of speed and with such care as is reasonable and proper under the circumstances. **RR Crossing Flashing Lights** Every person operating any motor vehicle, upon approaching at grade a railroad crossing protected by red lights which flash as a warning, shall bring his vehicle to a **full stop not less than 15 feet and not more than 50 feet from the nearest track** of said railroad and shall not proceed to cross until said lights stop flashing. **RR Crossing Lowered Gate** Every person operating any motor vehicle, upon approaching at grade a railroad crossing protected by a lowered automatic gate, shall bring his vehicle to a **full stop not less than 15 feet and not more than 50 feet from the nearest track** of said railroad and shall not proceed to cross until said automatic gate is raised. **RR Crossing Employee Waiving Red Flag** Every person operating any motor vehicle, upon approaching at grade a railroad crossing protected by a railroad employee waving a red flag or white lantern, **shall bring his vehicle to a full stop not less than 15 feet and not more than 50 feet from the nearest track** of said railroad and shall not proceed to cross until said railroad employee signals that it is safe to do so. **Warning Signal** A railroad train approaching within approximately **1,500 feet of a highway crossing** shall emit a warning signal audible from such distance.	$200 or $500: If the vehicle is carrying explosive substances or flammable liquids as a cargo or part of a cargo. Plus $5 Public Safety Surcharge
SCHOOL BUS PRECAUTIONS AT RAILROAD CROSSINGS 90 §S 15	**School Bus must Come to Complete Stop and Open Service Door** Every person operating a school bus, or any motor vehicle carrying explosive substances or flammable liquids as a cargo, or part of a cargo, upon approaching a railroad crossing at grade, shall bring his vehicle to a full stop **not less than 15 feet and not more than 50 feet from the nearest track** of said railroad, and shall not proceed to cross until it is safe to do so. The operator of a school bus, in addition to bringing his vehicle to a full stop, as aforesaid, **shall open the service door**, ascertain if he may cross safely and thereupon close said door before proceeding.	$500 Plus $5 Public Safety Surcharge
OPENING CAR DOOR 90 § 14	No person shall open a door on a motor vehicle unless it is reasonably safe to do so without interfering with the movement of other traffic, including bicyclists and pedestrians.	$100 Plus $5 Public Safety Surcharge

SPEEDING

Law/Rule	Violation/Offense	Penalty
Speed Greater than Posted 90 § 18	If the speed limit is posted issue citation under chapter 90 § 18. This statute grants cities and towns the authority to post signs regulating speed.	**$50, plus $10 for each M.P.H. in excess of 10 M.P.H. over limit, plus $50 head injury surcharge +5**
Speed Greater than Reasonable (Not Posted) 90 § 17	**General Rule:** No person operating a motor vehicle on any way shall run it at a rate of speed greater than is reasonable and proper, having regard to traffic and the use of the way and the safety of the public. Unless a way is otherwise posted, it shall be prima facie evidence of a rate of speed greater than is reasonable and proper under the following conditions: (1) if a motor vehicle is operated on a **divided highway** outside a thickly settled or business district at a rate of speed exceeding **50 MPH** for a distance of a **quarter of a mile**, or (2) on **any other way outside a thickly settled or business district** at a rate of speed exceeding **40 MPH** for a distance of a **quarter of a mile**, or (3) **inside a thickly settled or business district** at a rate of speed exceeding **30 MPH** for a distance of **one-eighth of a mile**.	**$50, plus $10 for each M.P.H. in excess of 10 M.P.H. over limit, plus $50 head injury surcharge** Plus $5 Public Safety Surcharge
Speeding in Construction Zone 90 § 17	Any person in violation of this section, while operating a motor vehicle through the parameters of a marked construction zone or construction area, **at a speed which exceeds the posted limit**, or **at a speed that is greater than is reasonable and proper**, shall be subject to **a fine of 2 times the amount** currently in effect for the violation issued.	**$100, plus $20 for each M.P.H. in excess of 10 M.P.H. over limit, plus $50 head injury surcharge** Plus $5 Public Safety Surcharge
Speeding in School Zone 90 § 17	Operating within **a school zone** which may be established by a city or town at a rate of speed exceeding **20 MPH.**	**$50, plus $10 for each M.P.H. in excess of 10 M.P.H. over limit, plus $50 head injury surcharge.** Plus $5 Public Safety Surcharge.
School Bus Speeding 90 § 17	**School Bus:** Except on a limited access highway, no person shall operate a school bus at a rate of speed **exceeding 40 MPH**, while actually engaged in carrying school children.	**$50, plus $10 for each M.P.H. in excess of 10 M.P.H. over limit, plus $50 head injury surcharge.** Plus $5 Public Safety Surcharge.
Hawkers & Peddler Speeding 90 § 17	**Vehicles used for Hawking & Peddling:** Operation of a motor vehicle at a speed in excess of **15 MPH** within one-tenth of a mile of a vehicle used in hawking or peddling merchandise and which displays flashing amber lights shall likewise be prima facie evidence of a rate of speed greater than is reasonable and proper.	**$50, plus $10 for each M.P.H. in excess of 10 M.P.H. over limit, plus $50 head injury surcharge.** Plus $5 Public Safety Surcharge.
Speed Of Heavy Vehicles With Metallic Tires 85 § 31	No vehicle which with its load weighs more than four tons shall, when equipped with **metallic tires**, travel upon any public way at a speed **greater than 4 MPH.**	$100
Moped Speeding 90 § 1B	Motorized bicycles cannot travel faster than 25 MPH.	**1ST OFF: $25 +5** **2ND OFF: $50 +5** **3RD OFF: $100 +5**

SPEEDING

Scooter Speeding 90 § 1E	Motorized Scooter cannot travel faster than 20 MPH	1ST OFF: $25 +5 2ND OFF: $50 +5 3RD OFF: $100 +5

Related Statutes, Case Law & Other Important Information

Arrest Without Warrant For Driving at Excessive Speed 85 § 11	Whoever violates an **ordinance or by-law** prohibiting persons from **riding or driving at a rate of speed inconsistent with public safety** or convenience **may be arrested without a warrant** by an officer authorized to make arrests and kept in custody not more than twenty-four hours, Sunday excepted; and within such time he shall be brought before a proper magistrate and proceeded against according to law. **Attorney Hanrahan's Note:** This is restricted to cities and towns that have ordinances/by-laws which restrict speeding. Although this law exists an arrest is typically not advised unless the operation of the vehicle rises to the level of operating to endanger.
Road Hazard 90 § 17	Every person operating a motor vehicle shall decrease the speed of the vehicle when a special hazard exists with respect to pedestrians or other traffic, or by reason of weather or highway conditions.
Prima Facie Evidence 90 § 17	If a speed limit has been duly established upon any way, operation of a motor vehicle at a rate of speed in excess of such limit shall be prima facie evidence that such speed is greater than is reasonable and proper.
RMV Action	3 responsible speeding violations with a 1 year period will result in a 30 day license suspension.
Arrest for speeding?	Chapter 85 § 11 states that an arrest may be made, without a warrant, for speeding. However, in ***Commonwealth v. Suggs*** (2007), the Appeals Court stated that this statute "appears to be inoperative and may have been repealed by implication by virtue of…chapter 90."

SAFE OPERATION

RACING

Law/Rule	Violation/Offense	Penalty
Drag Racing 90 § 17B	No person shall operate a motor vehicle, nor shall any owner of such vehicle permit it to be operated, in a manner where the owner or operator accelerates at a high rate of speed in competition with another operator, (whether or not there is an agreement to race) causing increased noise from skidding tires and amplified noise from racing engines. **Penalty:** imprisonment in the house of correction for not more than 2½ years or by a fine of not more than $1,000. **RMV Action:** The RMV shall suspend such violator's license for a period of not less than 30 days for a first offense and for not less than 180 days for any subsequent violation. Note: junior operators who violate this section are handled differently – see below.	**Criminal**
Junior Operator Drag Racing 90 § 17B	A holder of a junior operator's license or learners permit who commits a violation of this section shall **1st Offense:** License/permit suspension for 1 year ($500 reinstatement fee). **2nd Offense**: License/permit suspension for 3 years ($1,000 reinstatement fee). Must complete the state courts against road rage program sponsored by the trial court and the department of state police.	**1ST OFF: $500** Plus $5 Public Safety Surcharge. **2ND OFF: $1000** Plus $5 Public Safety Surcharge.
Drag Racing or Attempting to Set a Record 90 § 24(2)(a)	The defendant upon any way or in any place to which the public has a right of access, or any place to which members of the public have access as invitees or licensees, upon a bet or wager or in a race, or operates a motor vehicle for the purpose of making a record. **Arrest Powers**: **Misdemeanor** – there is no statutory authority granting powers of arrest for this offense. However, if the offense is committed in public, in the officer's presence, and is creating a **breach of the peace** an arrest would be lawful.	Criminal a fine of not less than $20 nor more than $200 or by imprisonment for not less than 2 weeks nor more than 2 years, or both.

RECKLESS & NEGLIGENT OPERATION (Including MV Homicide Offenses)

C. 90 § 24	OPERATING RECKLESSLY OR NEGLIGENTLY "OPERATING TO ENDANGER"
	Elements
1.	The defendant operated a motor vehicle;
2.	On a way, *or* in a place where the public has a right of access, *or* in a place where members of the public have access as invitees or licensees;
3.	That he (she) did so in a negligent or reckless manner so that the lives or safety of the public might have been endangered.
	Arrest Power, Penalties & Notes
Power of Arrest	**Misdemeanor** – there is no statutory authority granting warrantless powers of arrest for this offense. However, if the offense is committed in public, in the officer's presence, and is creating a **breach of the peace** an arrest would be lawful.
Penalty	A fine of not less than $20 nor more than $200 or by imprisonment for not less than 2 weeks nor more than 2 years, or both. Plus a $250 head injury fund fee.
Attorney Hanrahan's Comment	Many officers are under the assumption that there are two distinct offenses, operating negligently and operating recklessly. In fact, there is only one statute that addresses this offense. It is easier to show that a person acted negligently (did not operate reasonably thus placing others in danger) than it is to show that someone operated recklessly (consciously acted is a dangerous manner). The key is that the offender operated in such a way as "to place the lives and safety of the public in danger."
	Related Statutes, Case Law & Other Important Information
Negligently	A person acts negligently when he fails to use due care, that is, when he acts in a way that a reasonable person would not act. This can happen either by doing something that a reasonably prudent person would not do under those circumstances, or by failing to do something that a reasonably prudent person would do. The defendant's subjective **intent is irrelevant**; the issue is whether or not he/she drove as a reasonable person would have under the circumstances.
Recklessly	A person is reckless if he consciously disregards, or is indifferent to, a significant possibility of serious injury to anyone else who might be on the road. The defendant **must have intended his /her acts**, in the sense that they were not accidental. But it is not necessary that the defendant intended or foresaw the consequences of those acts, as long as a reasonable person would know that they were so dangerous that death or serious injury would probably result.
Considerations	In determining whether the defendant drove negligently or recklessly in a manner that might have endangered the public, you should take into account all the facts of the situation: the defendant's rate of speed and manner of operation, the defendant's physical condition and how well he/she could see and could control his/her vehicle, the condition of the defendant's vehicle, what kind of a road it was and who else was on the road, what the time of day, the weather and the condition of the road were, what any other vehicles or pedestrians were doing, and any other factors that you think are relevant.

C. 90 § 24	OPERATING RECKLESSLY OR NEGLIGENTLY "OPERATING TO ENDANGER"
Desolate area	Reckless operation can occur even on deserted street.[1] The potential for others to be place in danger is the key; there is no requirement that someone actually be placed in danger.
Speed	Speeding is not negligence per se but can be considered with other evidence in determining negligence. *Commonwealth v. Campbell*, 394 Mass. 77, 83 n.5 & 87, 474 N.E.2d 1062, 1067 n.5 & 1069 (1985). Speed is relevant factor. *Commonwealth v. Charland*, 338 Mass. 742, 744, 157 N.E.2d 538, 539 (1959).
Case Example	In *Commonwealth v. Ferreira*, a conviction was upheld where the defendant backed out of parking space in shopping center parking lot and then accelerated forward at about 20 m.p.h., causing the wheels to spin and the back end to fishtail, while the vehicle made a screeching noise.[2]

C. 90 § 24L	OUI <u>AND</u> OPERATING TO ENDANGER CAUSING SERIOUS BODILY INJURY
	Elements
1.	The defendant operated a motor vehicle;
2.	On a way, *or* in a place where the public has a right of access, *or* in a place where members of the public have access as invitees or licensees;
3.	In a negligent or reckless manner so that the lives or safety of the public might have been endangered
4.	• with a **BAC of .08**% or greater, or • while **under the influence** of intoxicating liquor, or marihuana, narcotic drugs, depressants, or prohibited stimulant, or the vapors of glue,
5.	**And;** causes serious bodily injury
	Arrest Power, Penalties & Notes
Power of Arrest	**Felony** – a police officer may effect a warrantless arrest for this offense provided he/she has probable cause that the suspect committed the offense.
Penalty	Imprisonment in the **state prison (F)** for not less than 2½ years nor more than 10 years and by a fine of not more than $5,000, or by imprisonment in a jail or HOC for **not less than 6 months** nor more than 2½ years and by a fine of not more than $5,000. (CWOF and placed on file prohibited).
RMV Action	The RMV shall revoke the license or right to operate of a person convicted for a period of **2 years** after the date of conviction. No appeal, motion for new trial or exception shall operate to stay the revocation of the license or the right to operate; provided, however, such license shall be restored or such right to operate shall be reinstated if the prosecution of such person ultimately terminates in favor of the defendant.

[1] *Commonwealth v. Horsfall*, 213 Mass. 232, 235, 100 N.E. 362, 363 (1913).
[2] *Commonwealth v. Ferreira*, 70 Mass. App. Ct. 32, 872 N.E.2d 808 (2007).

C. 90 § 24L OUI AND OPERATING TO ENDANGER CAUSING SERIOUS BODILY INJURY

Related Statutes, Case Law & Other Important Information	
Serious Bodily Injury	For the purposes of this section "serious bodily injury" shall mean bodily injury which creates a substantial risk of death or which involves either total disability or the loss or substantial impairment of some bodily function for a substantial period of time.
OUI Offenses	If the operator was OUI and caused injury, but was not otherwise reckless, the offense would be a misdemeanor. See the OUI section of this manual for this offense.

C. 90 § 24G(a) HOMICIDE BY MOTOR VEHICLE (Drunk and Reckless)

Elements	
1.	The defendant operated a motor vehicle;
2.	On a way, *or* in a place where the public has a right of access, *or* in a place where members of the public have access as invitees or licensees;
3.	In a negligent or reckless manner so that the lives or safety of the public might have been endangered
4.	• with a **BAC of .08%** or greater, or • while **under the influence** of intoxicating liquor, or marihuana, narcotic drugs, depressants, or prohibited stimulant, or the vapors of glue,
5.	**And**; causes the death of another person.

Arrest Power, Penalties & Notes	
Power of Arrest	**Felony** – a police officer may effect a warrantless arrest for this offense provided he/she has probable cause that the suspect committed the offense.
Penalty	Imprisonment in the **state prison (F)** for not less than 2½ years or more than 15 years and a fine of not more than $5,000, or by imprisonment in a jail or HOC for not less than 1 year nor more than 2½ years and a fine of not more than $5,000. **Minimum Mandatory Sentence:** The sentence imposed upon such person shall not be reduced **to less than one year**, nor suspended, nor shall any person convicted under this subsection be eligible for probation, parole, or furlough or receive any deduction from his sentence until such person has served at least one year of such sentence; Prosecutions shall neither be CWOF nor placed on file.
RMV Action	**1st Offense:** The registrar shall revoke the license or right to operate of a person convicted for a period of 15 years after the date of conviction for a first offense. **2nd Offense**: Revocation of license for life.

Related Statutes, Case Law & Other Important Information	
Manslaughter by Motor Vehicle	Chapter 265 § 13 ½ (Manslaughter by Motor Vehicle) imposes a stiffer penalty for essentially the same offense as above. **Penalty**: imprisonment in the **state prison (F)** for **not less than 5 years** and not more than 20 years, and by a fine of not more than $25,000. See notes under Drunk or Reckless section for more.
Multiple deaths	Multiple deaths, even involving a single incident, may result in multiple convictions.

C. 90 § 24G(b)	HOMICIDE BY MOTOR VEHICLE (Drunk or Reckless)
Elements	
1.	The defendant operated a motor vehicle;
2.	On a way, *or* in a place where the public has a right of access, *or* in a place where members of the public have access as invitees or licensees;
3.	• with a **BAC of .08**% or greater, or • while **under the influence** of intoxicating liquor, or marihuana, narcotic drugs, depressants, or prohibited stimulant, or the vapors of glue, or • in a **negligent or reckless manner** so that the lives or safety of the public might have been endangered.
4.	**And**; causes the death of another person.
Arrest Power, Penalties & Notes	
Power of Arrest	**Misdemeanor – If OUI** - statutory authority permits a police may effect an arrest for this offense committed in his/her presence or for an offense in the past on probable cause. **Misdemeanor – If not OUI -** there is no statutory authority granting warrantless powers of arrest for this offense. However, if the offense is committed in public, in the officer's presence, and is creating a **breach of the peace** an arrest would be lawful.
Penalty	Imprisonment in a jail or HOC for not less than 30 days nor more than 2½ years, or by a fine of not less than $300 nor more than $3,000, or both.
RMV Action	**1st Offense:** The registrar shall revoke the license or right to operate of a person convicted for a period of 15 years after the date of conviction for a first offense. **2nd Offense**: Revocation of license for the life of such person.
Related Statutes, Case Law & Other Important Information	
Multiple deaths	Multiple deaths, even involving a single incident, may result in multiple convictions.

C. 90 § 24G(a)	HOMICIDE BY MOTOR VEHICLE (Drunk <u>and</u> Reckless)
OUI Manslaughter by Motor Vehicle	Chapter 265 § 13½ (Manslaughter by Motor Vehicle while OUI) imposes a stiffer penalty for essentially the same offense as above (c. 90 § 24G). In fact, this law does not require the reckless or negligent element. **Elements**: the defendant commits manslaughter while operating a motor vehicle in violation of c. 90 § 24 (1)(a) (OUI) or chapter 90B § 8A (OUI via boat).(The penalty imposed under c. 265 § 13 ½ is as follows: **Penalty**: imprisonment in the **state prison (F)** for **not less than 5 years** and not more than 20 years, and by a fine of not more than $25,000. **RMV Action:** The RMV may suspend the license or right to operate for any extended period up to life, provided that such suspension be **at least a 15 year period**. **Appeal permitted**: A person aggrieved by a decision of the registrar pursuant to this section may file an appeal in the superior court of the trial court department. If the court determines that the registrar abused his discretion, the court may vacate the suspension or revocation of a license or right to operate and reduce the period of suspension or revocation as ordered by the registrar, but in no event may the reduced period of suspension be for less than 15 years.

C. 90 § 24	NEGLIGENT OPERATION WHILE TEXTING/MOBILE PHONE USE
	Elements
1.	The defendant operated a motor vehicle;
2.	On a way, *or* in a place where the public has a right of access, *or* in a place where members of the public have access as invitees or licensees;
3.	negligently so that the lives or safety of the public might be endangered in violation of section 8M (Junior Operator using mobile device), 12A (Electronic Mobile Device by Public Transportation Operator) or 13B (Texting while Driving),
4.	**and** such violation is the proximate cause of injury to any other person, vehicle or property.
	Arrest Power, Penalties & Notes
Power of Arrest	**Misdemeanor** – c. 90 § 21 permits an arrest for this offense if the offense is committed in the officer's presence.
Penalty	A fine of not less than $20 nor more than $200 or by imprisonment for not less than 2 weeks nor more than 2 years, or both.

OUI & RELATED LAWS

C. 90 § 24	OPERATING UNDER THE INFLUENCE
	Elements
1.	**Operate** a motor vehicle
2.	• Upon any **way** (see notes on "way" below), or • In any place to which the (*motoring*) public has a right of access (see notes below), or • Upon any way or in any place to which members of the public have access as invitees or licensees (see notes below on invitees and licensees).
3.	• With a percentage, by weight, of alcohol in their blood of **.08** or greater (*per se* impaired), or • **While under the influence** of: 1. intoxicating liquor 2. marijuana 3. narcotic drugs (as defined in chapter 94C § 1) 4. depressants or stimulant substances (as defined in chapter 94C § 1) 5. the vapors of glue
	OUI Arrest Power & Penalties
Power of Arrest	Whether **Felony** or **Misdemeanor** – statutory authority permits a police may effect an arrest in presence or for an offense in the past on probable cause.
Penalty	**1st offense:** a fine of not less than $500 nor more than $5,000 or by imprisonment for not more than 2½ years, or both such fine and imprisonment. **1 year License Suspension.** Hardship license possible within 3 months. **Alternative Disposition**: In lieu of above penalty the offender may be assigned to an alcohol education program and receive 2 years probation and a reduced license suspension. **21+ years**: 45-90 days. **Under 21**: 210 days. Note offender between 16-21 years must complete a 14 day residential program. Hardship license possible in 3 days.
	2nd Offense: If the defendant has been previously convicted, or assigned to an alcohol or controlled substance education, treatment, or rehabilitation program by a Massachusetts court or any other jurisdiction because of an OUI offense, the defendant shall be punished by a fine of: not less than $600 nor more than $10,000 and by imprisonment for not less than 60 nor more than 2½ years. **Minimum mandatory sentence of 30 days.** **2 year License Suspension.** Hardship license possible in 1 year. Ignition interlock device required. **Alternative Disposition**: 2 years probation and 14 days in a residential treatment facility.
	3rd Offense: If the defendant has been previously convicted or assigned to an alcohol or controlled substance education, treatment, or rehabilitation program by a Massachusetts court, or any other jurisdiction because of a like offense two times preceding the date of the commission of the offense for which he has been convicted, the defendant shall be punished by a fine of not less than $1,000 nor more than $15,000 and by imprisonment for not less than one 180 nor more than 2½ years or the same fines in addition to imprisonment in the **state prison (F)** for not less than 2½ years nor more than 5 years. **Minimum mandatory sentence of 150 days.** **8 year License Suspension.** Hardship possible in 2 years. Ignition interlock device required.

C. 90 § 24	OPERATING UNDER THE INFLUENCE
	4th Offense: If the defendant has been previously convicted or assigned to an alcohol or controlled substance education, treatment, or rehabilitation program by Massachusetts court or any other jurisdiction because of a like offense three times preceding the date of the commission of the offense for which he has been convicted the defendant shall be punished by a fine of not less than $1,500 nor more than $25,000 and by imprisonment for not less than 2 years nor more than 2½ years, or the same fines in addition to imprisonment in the **state prison (F)** for not less than 2½ years nor more than 5 years. **Minimum mandatory sentence of 12 months.** **10 year license suspension.** Hardship possible in 5 years. Ignition interlock device required. Vehicle forfeiture possible.
	5 or more offenses: If the defendant has been previously convicted or assigned to an alcohol or controlled substance education, treatment or rehabilitation program by a Massachusetts court or any other jurisdiction because of a like offense four or more times preceding the date of the commission of the offense for which he has been convicted, the defendant shall be punished by a fine of not less than $2,000 nor more than $50,000 and by imprisonment for not less than 2½ years or by a fine of not less than two thousand nor more than fifty thousand dollars and by imprisonment in the **state prison (F)** for not less than 2½ years nor more than 5 years. **Minimum mandatory sentence of 24 months.** **Lifetime license suspension.** No hardship and vehicle forfeiture possible.
Like Offense	The increase penalties for multiple offenses includes "like offenses" in other jurisdictions. In the 2013 case of ***Scheffler v. MV Board of Appeals*** the Appeals Court ruled that being assigned to an alcohol program in lieu of a conviction in another jurisdiction is a "like offense" for the purpose of receiving RMV sanctions for multiple offenses.
Additional Fees	**Additional fines for each offense**: $250 against a person who is convicted, is placed on probation, or is granted a CWOF (continuance without a finding), or pleads guilty to or admits to a finding of sufficient facts of OUI (including OUI drugs). An additional assessment of $50 shall go to the Victims of Drunk Driving Fund. There is also reinstatement fees involved.
Souza v. RMV	In the 2012 case of *Souza v. RMV,* the SJC ruled Pleading to sufficient facts to a charge of OUI (c. 90 § 24) and receiving a continuance without a finding (CWOF) does not amount to a previous conviction for the purposes receiving an enhanced license suspension for a subsequent OUI arrest and chemical test refusal.
	OPERATION
Any act which sets vehicle in Motion	In the 1928 case of ***Commonwealth v. Uski*** the SJC ruled that "a person operates a motor vehicle within the meaning of G.L. c. 90, § 24, when, in the vehicle, he intentionally does any act or makes use of any mechanical or electrical agency which alone or in sequence will set in motion the motive power of that vehicle." In ***Commonwealth v. McGillivary*** (2011), the defendant, who was under the influence of intoxicating liquor and was found slumped over the wheel, operated a motor vehicle by putting the keys in the ignition and turning the electricity on, **but not turning the engine on**. The Appeals Court ruled inserting and turning the ignition key to the on position is the "first step" in making the vehicle move. In the 1926 case of ***Commonwealth v. Clarke,*** the SJC ruled that a vehicle which is shifted into gear causing the vehicle to roll is sufficient to prove operation even if the engine is not running.

C. 90 § 24	OPERATING UNDER THE INFLUENCE
Attorney Hanrahan's Comment	You do not have to actually see the defendant operating. Many cases are proven by circumstantial evidence. For instance, a registered who owner is found intoxicated standing next to his vehicle which has struck a tree with no other persons present would, in most cases, be enough to convince a jury that the registered owner was the operator, absent some plausible explanation.[1] In the 1986 case of ***Commonwealth v. Hilton***, two Reading police officers were on routine patrol during the early hours of the morning. The officers observed an automobile at the intersection of Grove Street and Lowell Street parked half on the street and half on the sidewalk. The automobile lights and engine were off. The police officers approached the automobile. Hilton was alone inside the vehicle, half sitting and half lying on the front seat, her feet on the floor near the brake and accelerator pedals, her head toward the passenger side of the front seat, facing forward in the automobile. Hilton appeared to be asleep. In an attempt to awaken her, the police officers yelled and pounded on the windows and the roof of the automobile for about five minutes. Finally, she was roused. When she opened the door, one officer removed the keys from the ignition switch. One of the officers asked Hilton where she was coming from. She said she was coming from Lynn. He asked where she was going. Again, she said Lynn. She stated that she had dropped off a friend in Reading. She found to be intoxicated and placed under arrest. The Appeals Court stated "the evidence introduced by the Commonwealth does not prove directly that Hilton drove the automobile or that, if she drove the automobile, she was intoxicated at that time. The evidence is circumstantial." However, the Court ruled, based on circumstantial evidence, "the trier of fact would be justified in concluding that Hilton, in fact, drove the automobile to the intersection of Grove and Lowell Streets. She was found alone in the front seat of the automobile. She occupied a position in the seat consistent with that she might have occupied had she been a recent operator of the vehicle; her feet remained near the brake and accelerator pedals. The jury could infer that she lay down in that position directly from her position sitting in the driver's seat. The keys were in the ignition. Perhaps most convincing were her statements, in response to the officer's questions, that she had come from Lynn, she had dropped off a friend in Reading, and she was going back to Lynn.
Operation of a "Motor Vehicle"	Chapter 90 § 1 defines a motor vehicle as "all vehicles constructed and designed for propulsion by power other than muscular power including such vehicles when pulled or towed by another motor vehicle...". The definition specifically excludes "motorized bicycles" among other specific specialized vehicles, from the definition of a *motor vehicle*. Despite this, in the 1984 case of ***Commonwealth v. Griswold,*** the Appeals Court ruled that a **motorized bicycle** (moped) was a motor vehicle for the purpose of OUI.[2] The Court referenced chapter 90 § 1B (motorized bicycle law) which states in part an operator is "subject to the traffic laws and regulations of the commonwealth." The Court said by making the operator of a moped subject to traffic laws "the Legislature manifested its intention to make those portions of c. 90 that are concerned with operation, such as G.L. c. 90, § 24(1)(a), also apply to operators of motorized bicycles." **ATV:** In 2011 of ***Com .v Soldega***, the Appeals Court ruled that an ATV was a vehicle for the purposes of 90 § 24 when it was driven on a public way because ATV's are designed to be driven off-road, once the operator chose to drive it on the public way the nature of vehicle changed and it was no longer, by definition, an ATV. Chapter 90 § 1 specifically exempts those motor vehicles that cannot exceed twelve miles per hour *and* are "designed especially for use elsewhere than on the traveled parts of ways." The Court ruled "here, the ATV was powered by a motor and was being operated at speeds estimated at sixty miles per hour on a public highway. Therefore, although the ATV may indeed have been a " recreational vehicle," in these circumstances it also fell into the category of a 'motor vehicle' subject to G.L. c. 90, § 24(1)(*a*)."

[1] *Commonwealth v. Wood,* 261 Mass. 458 (1927).
[2] *Commonwealth v. Griswold,* 17 Mass.App.Ct. 461 (1984).

C. 90 § 24	OPERATING UNDER THE INFLUENCE
	"WAY" for the purposes of OUI
Way	For the purposes of an OUI charge, the "way" requirement is relatively broad. Essentially, any area designed to accommodate motor vehicles *and* that is open, or at least appears to be open, to the general public will, in most circumstances, be considered a *way* for the purpose of OUI. **Chapter 90 § 1 defines as *way*** as "any public highway (including municipal streets and roads), private way laid out under authority of statute, way **dedicated to public use**, or way under the control of park commissioners or body having like powers." **Note on public use**: the public use element exists when the public has a right of access or when members of the public have access as invitees or licensees. An **invitee** is a person who has been invited to the location by the owner for the mutual benefit of both, such as a shopping mall or restaurant parking lot. A **licensee** is a person who is in a place with only the passive permission of the owner and usually for the licensee's benefit. It is sufficient if the physical circumstances of the way are such that members of the public may reasonably conclude that it is open for travel to invitees or licensees. The usual "indicia of accessibility to the public," includes street lights, paving, curbing, abutting houses or businesses, crossroads, traffic, street signs, or hydrants. [1]
Attorney Hanrahan's Comment	Most of the Court decisions wherein the public nature of the way has been challenged have indicated that if the area was designed for vehicular traffic and the public was not specifically excluded from the area (e.g. a gated community) the area has been deemed to meet the *way* element for the purposes of OUI. Features such as paved roadways, street signs, street lights, curbing and the absence of signage or gates restricting access to the general public will typically qualify as a *way* for the purposes of OUI. The key is whether the area appears to be open to the general public even if it is otherwise privately owned.
Proof of Public Nature of way for Court Purposes	Common methods of proving the public nature of a way include: a. certification from the municipality (with this nothing more is needed), b. official municipal/government records, c. testimony (i.e. police officer testimony of public nature and features).
Examples of Cases wherein a *way* was satisfied for an OUI conviction	In the 2003 case of ***Commonwealth v. Kriss***, the Appeals Court ruled that a strip mall parking lot was a *way* for the purposes of an OUI conviction even though the stores were closed. There were other features such as an ATM, pay telephone and a newspaper distribution box which could be used by members of the public therefore the parking lot was open to members of the public. In the 1988 case of ***Commonwealth v. Hart***, the defendant was found by Woburn Police operating on the private portion of Dragon Way. Part of Dragon Way is a public road and then it transitions into a private way. The Court noted "no gate or sign marks the transition of Dragon Court from public to private way... It is the status of the way, not the status of the driver, which the statute defines. No specific license or invitation need be granted to the particular driver charged with violating the statute, i.e., it is sufficient if the physical circumstances of the way are such that members of the public may reasonably conclude that it is open for travel to invitees or licensees of the abutters." The conviction was upheld.

OUI & RELATED LAWS

[1] *Commonwealth v. Hart*, 26 Mass.App.Ct. 235 (1988).

C. 90 § 24	OPERATING UNDER THE INFLUENCE
Examples of cases wherein the area was <u>not</u> found to be a *way* for the purposes of OUI.	In the 2009 case of ***Commonwealth v. Stoddard***, the Appeals Court ruled that a private camping area with a gate limiting access was not a way that was accessible to the public within the meaning of the statute. The presence of a gate severely restricting general access to the campground was of great significance. In the 2011 case of ***Commonwealth v. Virgilio,*** the Appeals Court ruled that a driveway between two private dwellings was not a way for the purpose of OUI. In the 1990 case of ***Commonwealth v. George***, the defendant was driving while impaired on the baseball field of the West Junior High School in Brockton. SJC ruled that "because the baseball field was not a place to which the public has a right of access *by motor vehicle*, we conclude that there was insufficient evidence…". The fact that the land is accessible to the public is not sufficient; it must be open to the *motoring public.* **Attorney Hanrahan's Note**: There are times when you may find an impaired operator on land that is not open to the motoring public; in these cases a careful investigation may show that the impaired operator traveled on land *that was open to the motoring public* in order to access the land wherein he/she was found. A thorough investigation may prove that the operator was impaired when he/she traveled on the public way prior to landing on the non-motoring public land. Remember, an OUI conviction may be based on circumstantial evidence. [1]
	UNDER THE INFLUENCE
The person must be adversely affected	In ***Commonwealth v. Connolly,***[2] the SJC stated "to be driving while under the influence of liquor a person need not be drunk…to obtain a conviction under G.L. c. 90, § 24, the Commonwealth need not prove the defendant actually drove unskillfully or carelessly…the statute says that the intake of alcohol must adversely affect the person."
Per Se	If an operator's blood alcohol content (BAC) registers .08% or higher the operator is presumed to be impaired by alcohol.
Proof of impairment	Although Field Sobriety testing is often a key factor in proving that the operator's ability to drive was adversely affected, field sobriety testing is not required. Officer observations, driving behavior and admissions often play a key role. In the 2015 case of ***Commonwealth v. Rarick***, despite the fact that the defendant was not swaying or staggering and was not even asked to perform field sobriety testing his conviction was upheld after he admitted to consuming 6 beers coupled with the officer's observation that his eyes were bloodshot and glassy. Additionally, chemical testing is one of the most effective means of evidence in an OUI prosecution. Chemical testing is described in greater detail later in this section.
Drug Impairment	The statute list four other substances, aside from alcohol, which can cause impairment in violation of the law: 1. marijuana 2. narcotic drugs* (*see below) 3. depressants or stimulant substances* (*see below) 4. the vapors of glue

[1] *Commonwealth v. Wood,* 261 Mass. 458 (1927).
[2] *Commonwealth v. Connolly,* 394 Mass. 169 (1985).

C. 90 § 24	OPERATING UNDER THE INFLUENCE
Law applies only to drugs listed in chapter 94C § 1	In ***Commonwealth v. Ferola,*** the Appeals Court ruled "the crime...does not criminalize operation under the influence of *all narcotics*, stimulants, or depressants, but only those "defined in section one of chapter ninety-four C". Absent proof that the defendant's operation was impaired by a drug, depressant, or stimulant that is among those so defined, no statutory violation arises." (See drug section of this manual for list of prohibited drugs).[1] **Attorney Hanrahan's Note**: For instance if someone was driving under the influence from injecting Liquid Drano into his veins he could not be convicted of OUI because Drano is not a controlled substance. However, driving to endanger or a similar charge may be utilized if appropriate.
The burden is on the prosecution to prove substance is prohibited	In ***Commonwealth v. Green***, the Commonwealth was required to prove that codeine was a prohibited substance. As the Court noted "section 1 defines a 'narcotic drug' to include derivatives of opium, but it says nothing about codeine itself." The SJC ruled that the judge could take *judicial notice* is he or she so chooses. The SJC also ruled that "the Commonwealth could have easily met its burden of proof that codeine was a derivative of opium by presenting *expert testimony*. A similar issue was raised in ***Commonwealth v. Finegan***, the Appeals Court stated "section 1 defines a 'narcotic drug' to include derivatives of opium, but it says nothing about heroin itself." **Attorney Hanrahan's Note**: as noted in *Green*, there are essentially three ways to prove the substance in question is prohibited by c. 94C § 1: 1. The Judge could take judicial notice; 2. The defendant could stipulate to the facts; and 3. Expert testimony could be introduced.
Prescribed drugs: defendant must be *aware* of possible effects	The Legislature did not intend to penalize a person (for operating a motor vehicle while under the influence of an intoxicant) who drives after consuming a therapeutic dose of a prescription drug *unaware of its possible effects*. [2] However, even with prescribed drugs, if the defendant was aware of the risk and chose to operate the defendant can be found guilty of OUI.[3]
Drugs & Alcohol Combined	**OUI Alcohol Conviction Proper when alcohol enhanced by *illegal* drugs**: It is well established that a defendant who combines alcohol with *illegal* drugs, thus diminishing his/her ability to operate a vehicle safely, may be found guilty of operating under the influence of alcohol, if alcohol was one contributing cause of her diminished ability. Alcohol need not have been the sole or exclusive cause.[4] In the 1988 case of *Commonwealth v. Stathopoulos*, the SJC stated "it is enough if the defendant's capacity to operate a motor vehicle is diminished because of alcohol, even though other, concurrent causes contribute to that diminished capacity." The focus is on whether or not the consumption of liquor was one of the causes of the defendant's diminished capacity to operate safely. "The mixture of alcohol with another substance is not a separate theory of culpability." [5] **OUI Alcohol Conviction Proper when alcohol enhanced by *legal prescription* drugs:** "In the case of alcohol, our cases posit that 'the effects of liquor upon the mind and actions of men are well known to everybody.' "[6] The same thing may be said about the effects of *combining* alcohol and drugs, *even prescription drugs*.[7] "When the defendant is charged with operating while under the influence of intoxicating liquor, it is immaterial whether the driver is under the influence of intoxicating liquor and other substances.... [In]

[1] *Commonwealth v. Ferola, Mass. App. Ct. (2008)*
[2] *Commonwealth v. Reynolds* referencing *Commonwealth v. Wallace,* 14 Mass.App.Ct. 358, 365 (1982).
[3] *Commonwealth v. Reynolds* 67 Mass.App.Ct. 215 (2006).
[4] *Commonwealth v.Bishop*, 78 Mass.App.Ct. 90 (2010).
[5] *Commonwealth v. Lampron*, 65 Mass.App.Ct. 340, 348 (2005).
[6] *Commonwealth v. Wallace*, 14 Mass.App.Ct. at 361 n. 7, quoting from *Commonwealth v. Taylor*, 263 Mass. 356, 362 (1928).
[7] *Commonwealth v.Bishop*, 78 Mass.App.Ct. 90 (2010).

C. 90 § 24	OPERATING UNDER THE INFLUENCE
	order to find guilt, the jury need only to find that the liquor contributed to the defendant's impairment."[1] **Attorney Hanrahan's Note**: The defendant is entitled to an acquittal if his/her intoxication was caused *solely* by his/her prescription medication, taken as prescribed, and she did not know or have "reason to know of the possible effects of the drug on [his/her] driving abilities." If alcohol is a factor, there is no requirement to prove that the defendant had to know that the alcohol would be enhanced by the prescribed drugs. This additional knowledge of effects requirement only pertains to those who are impaired solely by prescribed drugs.
Vapors of Glue	In the 2015 case of ***Commonwealth v. Sousa***, the Appeals Court ruled that the defendant was not guilty of OUI when he was operating under the influence of computer aerosol (e.g. Dust-Off). He was prosecuted under the theory of OUI under the vapors of glue. However, computer aerosol is not glue.
	REASONABLE SUSPICION FOR STOPPING/TESTING AND PROBABLE CAUSE TO ARREST
Reasonable Suspicion required for Field Sobriety Testing	In order for a police officer to order an operator from a motor vehicle to perform field sobriety tests the officer must have reasonable suspicion based on specific and articulable facts that the operator is driving under the influence.[2] However, it often does not take much to establish reasonable suspicion (see below).
Alcohol Odor Alone is enough for FTS's	In the 2010 case of *Com .v. Bazinet* the Appeals Court ruled that during a Sobriety Checkpoint, if an officer detects the odor of alcohol during contact with a motorist, that alone will justify directing the motorist to the screening area.[3] Using the logic in *Com. v. Bazinet*, the odor of alcohol along would justify an officer to request the operator perform FST's during a routine traffic stop.
Probable Cause to Arrest	• There is no requirement that a police officer perform a field sobriety test at the time of arrest.[4] • Probable Cause may be determined based on the officer's observations even if field sobriety tests are not performed. • In the 1998 of *Commonwealth v. Blais*, the SJC concluded that the officer had probable cause to arrest the defendant for the offense of operating a vehicle while under the influence of alcohol, when the officer observed that the defendant's speech was slurred, his eyes red and glassy, and he detected a strong odor of alcohol. Because the defendant was the only person in the automobile that was enough to give the officer probable cause to arrest. • Although Field Sobriety Testing (FST) is not required to establish probable cause for the arrest it is often compelling evidence and FST's should be offered whenever possible. • Field sobriety tests "measure a person's sense of balance, coordination, and acuity of mind in understanding and following simple instructions. A lay juror understands that intoxication leads to diminished balance, coordination, and mental acuity from common experience and knowledge."[5]
Officer Opinion	A police officer who observed the defendant may offer an opinion as to the level of intoxication arising from the consumption of alcohol, but may not offer an opinion as to whether the defendant's intoxication impaired his ability to operate a motor vehicle.[6]

[1] *Commonwealth v. Stathopoulos,* 401 Mass. at 457, quoting from *State v. West,* 416 A.2d 5, 9 (Me.1980). *See Commonwealth v. Lampron,* 65 Mass.App.Ct. at 348.
[2] Commonwealth.v. Blais SJC (1998)
[3] *Comm. v. Bazinet,* 76 Mass. App. Ct. 908 (2010).
[4] *Commonwealth v. Ames,* 410 Mass. 603, 609 (1991).
[5] *Commonwealth v. Sands,* 424 Mass. 184, 188 (1997). See *Commonwealth v. McGrail,* 419 Mass. 774, 777 n. 7 (1995) (" Field sobriety tests are dexterity tests").
[6] *Commonwealth v. Canty*, SJC (2013).

C. 90 § 24	OPERATING UNDER THE INFLUENCE
NHTSA OUI Driving Indicators	**According to NHTSA's study on DWI (i.e. OUI) there are 4 categories of indicators that someone may be impaired:** **Problems Maintaining Proper Lane Position** • Weaving • Weaving across lane lines • Straddling a lane line • Swerving • Turning with a wide radius • Drifting • Almost striking a vehicle or other object **Speed and Braking Problems** • Stopping problems (too far, too short, or too jerky) • Accelerating or decelerating for no apparent reason • Varying speed • Slow speed (10+ mph under limit) **Vigilance Problems** • Driving in opposing lanes or wrong way on one-way • Slow response to traffic signals • Slow or failure to respond to officer's signals • Stopping in lane for no apparent reason • Driving without headlights at night • Failure to signal or signal inconsistent with action **Judgment Problems** • Following too closely • Improper or unsafe lane change • Illegal or improper turn (too fast, jerky, sharp, etc.) • Driving on other than the designated roadway • Stopping inappropriately in response to officer • Inappropriate or unusual behavior (throwing, arguing, etc.) • Appearing to be impaired
HGN	The HGN test measures the onset of the phenomenon known as nystagmus. Nystagmus is "[a]n abnormal and involuntary movement of the eyeballs from side to side or up and down, but usually from side to side. It is a sign of a number of ailments, usually of a nervous origin. It may, however, "be due to simple fatigue of the eye muscles, as when watching a tennis game."[1] Intoxicants, such as alcohol, interrupt various tracking and focusing functions of the retina which can be observed through a series of simple tests. Expert testimony on the scientific theory is needed if the subject of expert testimony is beyond the common knowledge or understanding of the lay juror. HGN test relies on an underlying scientific proposition and therefore expert testimony is required in order for the evidence to be admissible at trial.[2] The mechanics of the HGN test contrast distinctly from those of ordinary field sobriety tests. These tests measure a person's sense of balance, coordination, and acuity of mind in understanding and following simple instructions. A lay juror understands that intoxication leads to diminished balance, coordination, and mental acuity from common experience and knowledge. The testimony of the result of an HGN test relies on an underlying assumption that there is a strong correlation between

[1] *Commonwealth v. Sands*, 424 Mass. 184 (1997)
[2] *Commonwealth v. Sands*, 424 Mass. 184 (1997)

C. 90 § 24	OPERATING UNDER THE INFLUENCE
	intoxication and nystagmus. That underlying assumption is not within the common experience of jurors.[1]
	CHEMICAL TESTING
Implied Consent **Alcohol**	Whoever operates a motor vehicle upon any way or in any place to which the public has right to access, or upon any way or in any place to which the public has access as invitees or licensees, shall be deemed to have consented to submit to a chemical test or analysis of his breath or blood in the event that he is arrested for operating a motor vehicle while under the influence of **intoxicating liquor**.
Implied consent: Blood Test	**Blood Test**: There is no implied consent for a blood test unless the arrestee has been brought for treatment to a licensed medical facility.[2] **Exceptions**: no person who is afflicted with hemophilia, diabetes or any other condition requiring the use of anticoagulants shall be deemed to have consented to a withdrawal of blood. See blood sample procedures later in this section. See Blood Testing notes later in this section.
Drugs: Implied Consent	**There is no implied consent for those arrested for OUI drugs.**
Police Officer Direction	The alcohol test shall be administered at the direction of a police officer having reasonable grounds to believe that the person arrested has been operating a motor vehicle upon such way or place while under the influence of **intoxicating liquor**.
Test Refusal not Admissible	Police Officers cannot testify to the fact that the defendant refused to take either Field Sobriety Tests or BAC testing. If this testimony is inadvertently revealed a mistrial is the most likely outcome. In ***Commonwealth v. McGrail***, the SJC stated "a prosecutor wants to admit evidence that the defendant refused to take a field sobriety test so that the jury may infer that it is the equivalent of his statement, "I have had so much to drink that I know or at least suspect that I am unable to pass the test." Such refusal evidence, therefore, would be relevant to show that the defendant believed that the test results would tend to incriminate him. Because the refusal, in essence, constitutes testimony concerning the defendant's belief on a central issue to the case, we conclude that the evidence of the defendant's refusal to submit to a field sobriety test constitutes testimonial or communicative evidence." The SJC went on to say "allowing such refusal evidence to be admissible at trial would compel defendants to choose between two equally unattractive alternatives: 'take the test and perhaps produce potentially incriminating real evidence; refuse and have adverse testimonial evidence used against him at trial.'"[3] In the 2012 case of ***Commonwealth v. Gibson***, the Appeals Court ruled that a judge cannot instruct a jury that a person can refuse a breath test when the jury inquires about why there was no test.
Once agree to Testing statements related to testing are admissible	In the 2013 case of *Commonwealth v. Brown*, the Appeals Court ruled that although a refusal to submit to testing was not admissible (because it puts the defendant in a "catch 22") any statements the defendant makes related to his ability to successfully complete the test would be admissible. In this case, after the defendant began to attempt the tests he stated "I can't do this." The Court ruled that these statements were admissible.
Breathalyzer Requirements **90 § 24K**	**EOPS can create Rules and Procedures for Test Administration:** The secretary of public safety shall promulgate rules and regulations regarding satisfactory methods, techniques and criteria for the conduct of such (breath) tests, and shall establish a statewide training and certification program for all operators of such devices and a periodic certification program for such breath testing devices; provided, however, that the secretary may terminate or revoke such certification at his discretion.

[1] *Commonwealth v. Sands*, 424 Mass. 184 (1997)
[2] 90 § 24(1)(f)(1)
[3] Com.v.. McGrail, 419 Mass. 774 (1995).

Must Comply with CMR otherwise likely to be inadmissible

General Laws c. 90, § 24K, inserted by St.1986, c. 620, § 17, requires that a chemical analysis of the breath of a person charged with a violation under c. 90 "shall not be considered valid ... unless such analysis has been performed by a certified operator, using infrared breath-testing devices according to methods approved by the secretary of public safety." Section 24K further directs the Secretary of Public Safety to "promulgate rules and regulations regarding satisfactory methods, techniques and criteria for the conduct of such tests."

15 Minute Observation Period: A common tactic of the defense is to attack the 15 minute observation period.

501 CMR 2.13

> (3) The BTO shall observe the arrestee for no less than 15 minutes immediately prior to the administration of the breath test. If the BTO has reason to believe the arrestee has introduced any item into his or her mouth, the 15 minute observation period shall be restarted. Also, if during the test sequence, the breath test device reports the presence of mouth alcohol, the test sequence shall end. The 15 minute observation period shall be restarted and a new test sequence shall be started. This observation period is designed to allow the dissipation of mouth alcohol.

The purpose of the fifteen-minute waiting period is to ensure that the defendant has not brought any substance into his mouth, such as food, drink, or regurgitation by burping or by hiccoughing, that would have had a contaminating impact on the accuracy of the results, and to permit a sufficient lapse in time to allow such possible contaminants to clear.[1]

A new period of observing the arrestee would be necessary upon the detection of such a contaminating event.

The regulation does not preclude observation of an arrestee by the breathalyzer operator outside the breathalyzer room; however, the observation must be uninterrupted and continuous.[2]

Maintenance Requirements

In order for the BAC results to be admissible the machine must be maintain in accordance with EOPS regulations. These regulations tend to change from time to time, particularly depending on the type of machine your agency is utilizing. Be sure to refer to the particular maintenance requirements for your particular machine.

Certified Operator Required: Chemical analysis of the breath of a person charged with a violation of this chapter shall not be considered valid unless it was performed by a certified operator, using infrared breath-testing devices according to methods approved by the secretary of public safety.

Mere Deviations

The Supreme Judicial Court has stated that 'mere 'deviations from meticulous compliance' [with the regulation]... are inadequate to justify suppression of the results of the breathalyzer test.' [3] However, many OUI cases have been lost because the Executive Office of Public Safety (EOPS) guidelines were not followed.

In ***Commonwealth v. Kelley,*** the Court ruled that the fact that an officer other than the test operator entered the defendant's breath test results into the device's use and maintenance log was not a sufficient ground on which to exclude the test results, notwithstanding the requirement of 501 Code Mass. Regs. § 2.57 (1987) that the test operator must do so.[4]

[1] *Commonwealth v. Kelley,* **39 Mass.App.Ct. 448**, 452 n. 5 (1995), citing 501 Code Mass. Regs. § 2.55 (1987).
[2] *Commonwealth v. Pierre,* 72 Mass.App.Ct. 230 (2008)
[3] *Commonwealth v. Zeininger,* 459 Mass. 775, 792, cert. denied, 132 S.Ct. 462 (2011) (citation omitted).
[4] *Commonwealth v. Kelley,* 39 Mass.App.Ct. 448, 452-453 (1995).

C. 90 § 24	OPERATING UNDER THE INFLUENCE
General Admissibility	In the 2011 case of ***Com. v. Lopes,*** the SJC reiterated that breathalyzer test results "shall be admissible and deemed relevant" only if the defendant actually consented to the test; was properly notified of the right to an independent medical examination under § 5A; and if the test's administrator promptly provided the defendant with the results of the test. The prosecution must also establish, as a predicate to admissibility, conformity with regulations governing annual certification and periodic testing of the breathalyzer machine.
No right to Breath Test	An OUI arrestee is not entitled to a police-administered blood alcohol content (BAC) test.[1] However, it is often the deciding factor in many OUI cases. When BAC evidence is presented at trial it is very compelling evidence, and in many cases the defendant will plea to the charges if BAC evidence is secured.
Breathalyzer reading	Breath samples must be within 0.02% of each other in order to be admissible. The lower reading is BAC that is used.[2]
Immediate Action for high BAC levels	If a person's blood alcohol percentage is not less than .08 or the person is under 21 years of age and his blood alcohol percentage is not less than .02, the police officer shall do the following: • immediately take custody the drivers license or permit (if issued by the Massachusetts RMV); • provide a written notification of suspension • immediately report action taken to the RMV
BAC results	**Criminal** **.00-05% –** Release no charges (unless drugs have enhanced effects). **.06-.07% -** Charges possible, must show impairment by other means. **.08 or higher –** Presumed intoxicated. **RMV Sanctions Only** **.02% - .05% –** RMV sanctions imposed if <u>under 21 years</u> **.04% - .05% –** RMV sanctions imposed for <u>CDL operator</u>. If any alcohol is present CDL operator should be placed out of service for 24 hours.
Sabotaging the Test	The Appeals Court recently, in ***Com. v. Curley***, ruled that although refusing to submit to tests is not admissible, once an arrestee consents to take a test (in this case a breathalyzer) and then intentionally tries to sabotage the test (i.e. failing to properly blow into the machine) his actions will be admissible.[3]
BAC within 3 hours	In ***Commonwealth v. Colturi***, 448 Mass. 809 (2007), the SJC ruled that the passage of up to three hours between (BAC) testing and operation is a reasonable time (for the admission of evidence without requiring expert testimony on retrograde extrapolation). The facts and circumstances in particular cases may establish that a lesser or greater time period ought to be applied. Such determinations fall within the sound discretion of the trial judge.[4] Because the statute reads that the operator cannot *operate* with a BAC of .08% or greater (for a *per se* violation) it becomes difficult to prove what the operator's BAC was at the time of operation when the test is performed a significant time after the arrest. For this reason the SJC set a three hour limit, however the three hour timeframe can be overcome with expert testimony on the retrograde extrapolation (dissipation and/or increase of alcohol overtime). The SJC also left open the door for the judge to allow some deviation in the three hour limit in appropriate circumstances without the need for expert testimony.

[1] *Commonwealth v. Alano*, 388 Mass. 871, 877, 448 N.E.2d 1122 (1983).
[2] 501 CMR 2.14
[3] *Commonwealth v. Curley*, October 25, 2010
[4] *Commonwealth v. Colturi*, 448 Mass. 809 (2007).

C. 90 § 24	OPERATING UNDER THE INFLUENCE
License Suspension immediate for failure or Refusal	**License Suspension Immediate**: The license suspension shall become effective immediately. The license to operate a motor vehicle shall remain suspended until the disposition of the offense for which the person is being prosecuted, but in no event shall such suspension exceed 30 days. **License Seizure & Suspension:** If the person refuses or registers a BAC of .08% or greater; or for a person under the age of 21 years who registers a BAC of .02% or higher the license shall be immediately seized. The suspension of a license or right to operate shall become effective immediately upon receipt of the notification of suspension from the police officer. A suspension for a refusal of either a chemical test or analysis of breath or blood shall run consecutively and not concurrently, both as to any additional suspension periods arising from the same incident, and as to each other. For a person under the age of twenty-one who has not been charged with a criminal violation but only for having a BAC of .02% or higher the suspension will be an RMV administrative suspension.
Reporting requirements	The police officer before whom the refusal was made shall, within 24 hours, prepare a report of such refusal (in practice this is typically done electronically via the breathalyzer machine).
Police Officer Actions Upon Refusal	If a person refuses to take a test, the police officer shall: a. immediately, on behalf of the registrar, take custody of such person's license or right to operate issued by the commonwealth; b. provide to each person who refuses such test, on behalf of the registrar, a written notification of suspension in a format approved by the registrar; and c. impound the vehicle being driven by the operator and arrange for the vehicle to be impounded for a period of 12 hours after the operator's refusal, with the costs for the towing, storage and maintenance of the vehicle to be borne by the operator.
Arrestee's Actions and Refusals	If arrestee tries to "cheat" the test he/she may be deemed a refusal. In the 2012 Appeals Court case of *Kasper v. RMV*, the defendant was deemed a refusal after blowing one sample resulting in a .18 BAC. He blew five more samples and none of them were sufficient to register a reading, even though the machine was working properly.
PBT	PBT evidence is not admissible in a criminal proceeding for OUI. OUI evidence, as it relates to breathalyzer testing, is regulated by 501 CMR and the breath test must be the strict requirements of 501 CMR in order to be admissible. If a PBT is used, it should be used after all other standardized field sobriety tests as to not taint the officer's opinion regarding the other tests.

C. 90 § 24. OPERATING UNDER THE INFLUENCE

Refusal of Chemical Test Consequences

From the RMV Driver's Manual

License Suspension Periods for Refusing a Chemical Test

Note: For this table, a prior operating under the influence (OUI) offense refers to a court conviction for OUI or a court-ordered assignment to an alcohol education program. Chemical test refusals do not count as prior OUI offenses.

AGE	LICENSE SUSPENSION	
Drivers over age 21	No Prior OUI Offenses	180 days
	One Prior OUI Offense	Three years
	Two Prior OUI Offenses	Five years
	Three or More Prior OUI Offenses	Lifetime
Drivers age 18 to 21	No Prior OUI Offenses	Three years + 180 days
	One Prior OUI Offense	Three years + 180 days
	Two Prior OUI Offenses	Five years + 180 days
	Three or More Prior OUI Offenses	Lifetime

Note: The additional 180-day suspension for drivers under age 21 is designed to get youths charged with OUI who refuse a chemical test to undergo alcohol education. It does not matter what happens with your court case. **Even if you win the case, it will not change the requirement for you to take an alcohol education course.** If this is your first OUI case, the 180-day suspension can be waived upon entry into a Department of Public Health (DPH) approved alcohol education program.

AGE	LICENSE SUSPENSION	
Drivers under age 18	No Prior OUI Offenses	Three years + One year
	One Prior OUI Offense	Three years + One year
	Two Prior OUI Offenses	Five years + One year
	Three or More Prior OUI Offenses	Lifetime

Note: The additional one-year suspension for drivers under age 18 is designed to get youths charged with OUI who refuse a chemical test to undergo alcohol education. It does not matter what happens with your court case. **Even if you win the case, it will not change the requirement for you to take an alcohol education course**. If this is your first OUI case, the one-year suspension can be reduced to 180 days upon entry into a Department of Public Health (DPH) approved alcohol education program.

C. 90 § 24	OPERATING UNDER THE INFLUENCE
	BLOOD TESTING ISSUES
Implied consent: Blood Test	**Blood Test**: There is no implied consent for a blood test **<u>unless</u> the arrestee has been brought for treatment to a licensed medical facility**. **Exceptions**: no person who is afflicted with hemophilia, diabetes or any other condition requiring the use of anticoagulants shall be deemed to have consented to a withdrawal of blood. See blood sample procedures later in this section.
If arrestee consents	The blood must be drawn at the direction of the officer by a medical doctor, registered nurse, or a certified medical technician.[1]
Non-alcohol swabs	Ensure that non-alcohol swabs are used to prep the skin.[2]
Two test Tubes	Two tubes of blood should be drawn containing a powdered anticoagulant. Shake the tubes once received to active the anticoagulant.[3]
Submit to state lab	Properly mark the samples and refrigerate samples until they can be submitted to the state lab. Call (508) 358-3155 to arrange submission of evidence.
Refusal Testimony	Although a defendant's refusal to submit to testing is not admissible in court, the defendant's refusal to permit medical personnel to take blood (which was not prompted by the police but down for medical purposes), can be introduced at trial through the officer's testimony. See *Com. v. Arruda* (2008).
Obtaining Medical Blood evidence	If blood is drawn by medical staff, even if only for medical purposes, it would, under most circumstances, be deemed evidence to the charge of OUI. In these cases a ***search warrant*** may be sought to obtain the alcohol content. Some agencies successfully use the ***subpoena*** process.[4] If it is anticipated that this medical evidence may be sought for evidentiary purposes the police should put the medical facility on notice. This is sometimes referred to as a "**preservation notice**." Generally, the DA's office prosecuting the case should subpoena the evidence as the role of the prosecutor is to gather evidence for court. **Attorney Hanrahan's note:** The RMV will only suspend the operator's license based on a police initiated blood test, not a medical blood test.
	HOW TO PROCESS AN OUI DRUG OFFENSE
No Implied Consent to Chemical Testing	**Commentary:** OUI drug offenses are very difficult to prosecute. There is no implied consent to chemical testing when it comes to drug impairment (only with alcohol). In any event, a breathalyzer would not detect drugs, and blood testing is not permissible unless the person is otherwise being treated at a medical facility when suspected of OUI alcohol. Absent an admission, witness testimony of drug ingestion, drugs located on the suspect, or some other type of substantial evidence, a conviction is unlikely. Additionally, the law requires that not the Commonwealth must not only prove that the operator was impaired but also the Commonwealth must prove the drug ingested is listed in chapter 94C § 1. When probable cause exists that an operator is impaired by drugs careful documentation of the operator's impairment and all other evidence is crucial. A careful search may uncover physical evidence. Additionally an interrogation (review the Interview and Interrogation section) may also play a key role. Lastly, contacting a Drug Recognition Expert (DRE) is recommended. A DRE is trained to recognize indicators of drugs impairment; they are also trained in collecting urine samples (given with consent) that may be submitted for testing.

[1] Massachusetts State Police Guidelines for drawing blood. Revised January 2008
[2] Massachusetts State Police Guidelines for drawing blood. Revised January 2008.
[3] Massachusetts State Police Guidelines for drawing blood. Revised January 2008
[4] See Commonwealth v.Dyer, 77 Mass. App. Ct. 850 (2010). Commonwealth v. McLaughlin, 79 Mass. App. Ct. 670 (2011).

C. 90 § 24	OPERATING UNDER THE INFLUENCE
DRE	Although there is very limited Massachusetts case law on DRE (Drug Recognition Expert) evidence and its admissibility in Court, it is almost certain that it will be treated similarly to HGN testing (see additional OUI issues later in this section). In order for the evidence to be admissible it must be introduced along with expert testimony. For a list of DRE's in your area visit www.massdre.org The admission of expert testimony lies 'largely in the discretion of the trial judge.[1] 'The crucial issue,' in determining whether a witness is qualified to give an expert opinion, 'is whether the witness has sufficient "education, training, experience and familiarity" with the subject matter of the testimony.' " [2] Note: Expert testimony is required when introducing breathalyzer results and the defendant is being charged under the "impairment" theory. Expert testimony is not required when charging under the "*per se*" theory.
Attorney Hanrahan's Comment	OUI Drug offenses are perhaps the most difficult offenses to prosecute. Not only must you prove impairment but you must prove the substance causing impairment is regulated by chapter 94C. Often times admissions made by the offender are critical in prosecuting these offenses.
	Additional OUI Issues
Independent Medical Exam	A person who has been arrested for OUI has the right to have an independent medical exam at his expense and at his request. The person arrested shall be given a copy of M.G.L. c. 263, § 5A, unless a copy is conspicuously posted in the station or place of detention. Section 5A requires that the police officer in charge of the police station or other place of detention inform a person held in custody in such a place and charged with operating a motor vehicle while under the influence of intoxicating liquor, immediately on being booked, that he has the right "at his request and at his expense, to be examined immediately by a physician selected by him." Section 5A further requires that the police afford that person a reasonable opportunity to exercise that right. On being booked, a person must also be given a copy of § 5A unless a copy is posted in a conspicuous place to which the person has access. **Invoking right to medical exam**: The police are not required to transport the arrestee to the hospital if he/she requests an independent medical exam. Basically, the only requirement is that the police arrange to have the person promptly bailed. **Invocation of 263 § 5A rights typically requires that the police arrange for prompt bail:** The right to a prompt bail hearing intersects with the § 5A right: a defendant ordinarily will be unable to exercise his right to an independent medical examination without being promptly released to bail. Normally, a defendant must go to a hospital if he wishes an independent medical examination because of the difficulty of finding medical personnel willing to come to a police station to draw blood for a blood test. [3] Because the evidence that may be obtained through the blood test is fleeting, such a test must be conducted promptly; thus, the bail hearing must be conducted promptly. If the defendant is denied his/her right to an independent medical exam it may result in the dismissal of charges. Even the bail commissioner's action can lead to evidence suppression under 263 § 5A if there is an unreasonable delay. When a defendant exercises his/her right to an independent medical exam the police must contact the bail commissioner without delay. The SJC stated "because of the fleeting nature of the evidence that might be obtained as a result of the medical examination, the bail hearing in such a case ***must be held as promptly as possible***... In cases where the defendant has <u>not</u> asserted his § 5A right, the general rule of promptness, loosely delimited by the **six-hour guideline**, still holds."

[1] *Commonwealth v. Hudson*, **417 Mass. 536**, 540, **631 N.E.2d 50** (1994), quoting *Commonwealth v. Maltais*, **387 Mass. 79**, 93, **438 N.E.2d 847** (1982).
[2] *McLaughlin v. Selectmen of Amherst*, supra at 361-362, 664 N.E.2d 786, quoting *Letch v. Daniels*, 401 Mass. 65, 68, 514 N.E.2d 675 (1987). See *Leibovich v. Antonellis*, 410 Mass. 568, 571-573, 574
[3] *Commonwealth v. Finelli*,; *Commonwealth v. Chistolini*, 422 Mass. 854, 858, 665 N.E.2d 994 (1996).

C. 90 § 24	OPERATING UNDER THE INFLUENCE
	See Commonwealth v. King, 429 Mass. 169 (1999). However, the SJC has indicated that the dismissal of the charges is inappropriate if the evidence against the defendant is overwhelming. [1] **Other important notes:** The independent medical exam right only applies to those who are arrested for OUI alcohol, not OUI drugs.[2] Police may insist that all booking components be completed before granting independent medical evaluation rights.[3]
Leasing Motor Vehicles To Intoxicated 90 § 32C	No person engaged in the business of leasing motor vehicles shall lease any vehicle for operation on any public way by any person whom he knows or has reason to believe to be under the influence of intoxicating liquor or of any drug. No lessor shall lease any motor vehicle or trailer until the lessee shows that he or his authorized operator is the holder of a duly issued license to operate the type of motor vehicle or trailer which is being leased.
Court Inquiry	Chapter 90 § 24J requires the Court to inquiry of every defendant conviction of OUI (alcohol) whether he/she was served alcohol in a licensed establishment, including the name and location, prior to the offense. The information will be turned over to the ABCC, the Attorney General and the DA's office.
OAS for OUI issues	Operating after suspension for OUI convictions – 60 day minimum mandatory sentence. An operator with a hardship license is not operating after suspension (90 § 23), the proper charge would be operating without a license (90 § 10). See *Commonwealth v. Murphy*, 69 Mass. App. Ct. 152 (2007).
OUI Boats	**BOATS**: Chapter 90B § 8 – criminalizes OUI while operating a "vessel: (i.e. a boat), on the waters of the Commonwealth. There is an implied consent for OUI Boat. **Arrest powers**: all 90B violations authorize a warrantless arrest provided the officer has probable cause. See c. 90B § 13
Recreational Vehicle OUI	**RECREATION VEHICLES**: Chapter 90B § 26A provides a penalty (fine only) for OUI while operating a recreational vehicle (ATV's, dirt bikes, snow vehicles, etc. – vehicles designed for off road use). Operators may lose right to operate for I year (first offense). There is no implied consent for recreation vehicles; therefore if the operator refuses they are not subject to RMV sanctions. The penalty is only a $500 fine. NOTE: a driver's license is not required for snow and recreation vehicles. **Arrest powers**: all 90B violations authorize a warrantless arrest provided the officer has probable cause. See c. 90B § 13

[1] *Commonwealth v. Andrade,* supra at 877-878, 453 N.E.2d 415.
[2] *Commonwealth v. Mandell,* 61 Mass.App.Ct. 526 (2004).
[3] Commonwealth v. Lively, 30 Mass.App.Ct. 970 (1991).

LICENSE SUSPENSION PERIODS FOR FAILED CHEMICAL TESTS

All drivers will fail a chemical test if they have a Blood Alcohol Content (BAC) of .08 or greater. Drivers under 21 have the same standard for criminal purposes, but will face administrative sanctions for tests with a BAC as low as .02.

AGE	LICENSE SUSPENSION
Driver 21 and over	License is suspended for 30 days or until the conclusion of the court case, whichever is shorter. The suspension will end if the case is concluded either before or during the 30-day period. If the court finds the defendant guilty, the defendant will then face whatever sanctions ordered by the court.
Drivers age 18 to 21	License is suspended for 30 days, plus an additional 180 days, pursuant to MGL c.90, s. 24P. If this is the defendant's first operating under the influence case, the 180-day suspension can be waived upon entry into a Department of Public Health (DPH) approved alcohol education program.
Drivers under age 18	License is suspended for 30 days, plus an additional one year, pursuant to MGL c.90, s. 24P. If this is your first operating under the influence case, the one-year suspension can be reduced to 180 days upon entry into a Department of Public Health (DPH) approved alcohol education program.

Note: The additional 180-day or one-year suspension for drivers under age 21 is designed to get youths charged with operating under the influence, or with having a BAC of .02 or higher, to undergo alcohol education. **It does not matter what happens with your court case. Even if you win the case, it will not change the requirement for you to take the alcohol education course.**

C. 90 § 24V — OUI CHILD ENDANGERMENT

Elements

1.	Whoever commits an OUI offense
2.	With a child 14 years of age or younger in the motor vehicle or vessel
3.	Shall also be guilty of child endangerment while operating a motor vehicle or vessel under the influence.

Arrest Power, Penalties & Notes

Power of Arrest	The OUI offense would grant the authority to arrest.
Penalty	**1st Offense**: a fine of not less than $1,000 nor more than $5,000 and by imprisonment in the HOC for **not less than 90 days** nor more than 2½ years. **2nd Offense:** If a defendant has previously violated this subsection or a like offense in another jurisdiction preceding the date of the commission of the offense for which he has been convicted, he shall be punished by a fine of not less than $5,000 nor more than $10,000 and by imprisonment in the HOC for **not less than 6 months** nor more than 2½ years or by imprisonment in **state prison (F)** for not less than 3 years but not more than 5 years. **Note**: Any penalty for this offense will run after the underlying offense, not concurrently.

C. 90 § 24V	OUI CHILD ENDANGERMENT
RMV Action	The RMV shall suspend the license or right to operate for a period of 1 year for a first offense, and for a period of 3 years for a second or subsequent violation.
Attorney Hanrahan's Comment	This is an additional offense to the underlying OUI offense; it is not one or the other. The defendant can be convicted of both for the same act.
Related Statutes, Case Law & Other Important Information	
Child Abuse & Neglect	In most cases the officer should also file a report to the Department of Children and Families (DCF) in accordance with chapter 119 § 51A.
Important Statistic	**In 2010, 211 children were killed in drunk driving crashes. Out of those 211 deaths, 131 (62 percent) were riding with the drunk driver.** (National Highway Traffic Safety Administration. "Traffic Safety Facts 2010: Alcohol Impaired Driving" Washington DC: National Highway Traffic Safety Administration, 2011.)

C. 90 § 24L	OUI CAUSING SERIOUS BODILY INJURY
Elements	
1.	Operate a motor vehicle
2.	Upon any way or in any place to which the public has a right of access, or upon any way or in any place to which members of the public have access as invitees or licensees
3.	• with a **BAC of .08%** or greater, or • while **under the influence** of intoxicating liquor, or marihuana, narcotic drugs, depressants, or prohibited stimulant, or the vapors of glue,
4.	And causes serious bodily injury
Note	If the above elements are met the defendant has committed a misdemeanor. However, if in addition to the above elements the defendant also "operates a motor vehicle **recklessly or negligently** so that the lives or safety of the public might be endangered" the defendant has committed a felony.
Arrest Power, Penalties & Notes	
Power of Arrest	**Misdemeanor (without being reckless or negligent)** – statutory authority permits a police may effect an arrest for this offense committed in his/her presence or for an offense in the past on probable cause. **Felony (also being reckless and negligent)** – a police officer may effect a warrantless arrest for this offense provided he/she has probable cause that the suspect committed the offense.

C. 90 § 24L	OUI CAUSING SERIOUS BODILY INJURY
Penalty	**Without being reckless or negligent**: Imprisonment in a jail or HOC for not more than 2½ years, or by a fine of not less $3,000, or both. **With being reckless and negligent**: imprisonment in the **state prison (F)** for not less than 2½ years nor more than 10 years and by a fine of not more than $5,000 dollars, or by imprisonment in a jail or HOC for **not less than 6 months** nor more than 2½ years and by a fine of not more than $5,000 dollars. (CWOF and placed on file prohibited).
RMV Action	The RMV shall revoke the license or right to operate of a person convicted for a period of **2 years** after the date of conviction. No appeal, motion for new trial or exception shall operate to stay the revocation of the license or the right to operate; provided, however, such license shall be restored or such right to operate shall be reinstated if the prosecution of such person ultimately terminates in favor of the defendant.
Serious Bodily Injury	For the purposes of this section "serious bodily injury" shall mean bodily injury which creates a substantial risk of death or which involves either total disability or the loss or substantial impairment of some bodily function for a substantial period of time.
Related Statutes, Case Law & Other Important Information	
Homicide by Motor Vehicle Drunk and Reckless or Negligent	Chapter 90 § 24G includes the same elements as the **felony** version of c. 90 § 24L listed above (the conduct must include the reckless or negligent element) but includes the additional element that the operation **causes the death of another**. **Note:** Chapter 90 § 24G also has a misdemeanor version of this offense. If the operator is drunk or reckless/negligent, even death results, the offense is only a misdemeanor. When death results and the operator is both drunk and reckless/negligent the offense is a felony, as described above. **IMPORTANT: If reckless or negligence was involved see the safe operation section of this manual for more.**
OUI Manslaughter by Motor Vehicle	Chapter 265 § 13½ (Manslaughter by Motor Vehicle while OUI) imposes a stiffer penalty for essentially the same offense as above (c. 90 § 24G). In fact, this law does not require the reckless or negligent element. Elements: the defendant commits manslaughter while operating a motor vehicle in violation of c. 90 § 24 (1)(a) (OUI) or chapter 90B § 8A (OUI via boat).(The penalty imposed under c. 265 § 13 ½ is as follows: **Penalty**: imprisonment in the **state prison (F)** for **not less than 5 years** and not more than 20 years, and by a fine of not more than $25,000. **RMV Action:** The RMV may suspend the license or right to operate for any extended period up to life, provided that such suspension is **at least for a 15 year period**. **Appeal permitted**: A person aggrieved by a decision of the registrar pursuant to this section may file an appeal in the superior court of the trial court department. If the court determines that the registrar abused his discretion, the court may vacate the suspension or revocation of a license or right to operate and reduce the period of suspension or revocation as ordered by the registrar, but in no event may the reduced period of suspension be for less than 15 years.

IGNITION LOCK REQUIREMENTS & VIOLATIONS

MANDATORY USE
Chapter 90 § 24½

Previous Conviction Requires Interlock Device	No person whose license has been suspended in the commonwealth or any other jurisdiction by reason of: ▪ an assignment to an alcohol or controlled substance education, treatment or rehabilitation program; or ▪ a conviction for violating paragraph (a) of subdivision (1) of section 24, subsection (a) of section 24G, operating a motor vehicle with a percentage by weight of blood alcohol of eight one-hundredths or greater, or while under the influence of intoxicating liquor in violation of subsection (b) of said section 24G, section 24L, section 13 ½ of c. 265, subsection (a) of section 8 of c. 90B, section 8A or 8B of c. 90B or, in the case of another jurisdiction, for any like offense, No Person shall be issued a new license or right to operate or have his license or right to operate restored if he has previously been so assigned or convicted, unless: ▪ a certified ignition interlock device has been installed on each vehicle owned, each vehicle leased and each vehicle operated by that person as a precondition to the issuance of a new license or right to operate or the restoration of such person's license or right to operate.
Interlock Subject to Inspection	A certified ignition interlock device shall **be installed on all vehicles owned, leased and operated by the licensee for a period of 2 years** and person restricted by a certified ignition interlock device shall have such device inspected, maintained and monitored in accordance with such regulations as the registrar shall promulgate.
Non-compliance may result in lifetime revocation	The registrar may, after hearing, revoke for an extended period or for life, the license of whoever removes such device or fails to have it inspected, maintained or monitored on at least 2 occasions during the period of the restricted license or right to operate if the licensee has operated or attempted to operate a vehicle with a blood alcohol level that caused the certified ignition interlock device to prohibit a vehicle from starting on at least 2 occasions or that recorded a blood alcohol level in excess of.02 on at least 2 occasions. A person aggrieved by a decision of the registrar pursuant to this section may file an appeal in the superior court of the trial court department. If the court determines that the registrar abused his discretion, the court may vacate the suspension or revocation of a license or right to operate or reduce the period of suspension or revocation as ordered by the registrar.

OPERATION IN VIOLATION OF IGNITION INTERLOCK DEVICE LICENSE RESTRICTION
Chapter 90 § 24S

1.	Operation of a Motor Vehicle
2.	Upon any way or any place to which the public has a right of access, or upon any way or place to which members of the public have access as invitees or licensees,
3.	That is **not equipped with a certified functioning ignition interlock device**
4.	While his license or right to operate has been restricted to operating only motor vehicles equipped with such device.

Arrest Power, Penalties & Notes

IGNITION LOCK REQUIREMENTS & VIOLATIONS	
Arrest Powers	**Felony** – a police officer may effect an arrest for this offense committed in his/her presence or for an offense in the past, on probable cause.
Penalty	A fine of not less than $1,000 nor more than $15,000 and by imprisonment for not less than 180 days nor more than 2½ years or by a fine of not less than $1,000 nor more than $15,000 and by imprisonment in the **state prison (F)** for not less than 2½ years nor more than 5 years. **Minimum Mandatory**: the **sentence** imposed upon such person **shall not be reduced to less than 150 days**, nor suspended, nor shall any such person be eligible for probation, parole or furlough or receive any deduction from his sentence for good conduct until he shall have served 150 days of such sentence. The defendant may serve all or part of such 150-day sentence, to the extent such resources are available, in a correctional facility specifically designated by the department of correction for the incarceration and rehabilitation of drinking drivers.
Definition	For the purposes of this section the term "certified ignition interlock device" shall mean an alcohol breath screening device that prevents a vehicle from starting if it detects a blood alcohol concentration over a preset limit of.02 or 20 mg of alcohol per 100 ml of blood.

TAMPERING WITH IGNITION INTERLOCK DEVICE Chapter 90 § 24T	
1.	Interfere or Tamper
2.	With a certified ignition interlock device
3.	With the intent to disable the device
Arrest Power, Penalties & Notes	
Penalty	HOC for not less than 6 months nor more than 2½ years or by imprisonment in the **state prison (F)** for not less than 3 years nor more than 5 years
Powers of Arrest	**Felony** – a police officer may effect an arrest for this offense committed in his/her presence or for an offense in the past, on probable cause.

STARTING MOTOR VEHICLE EQUIPPED WITH IGNITION INTERLOCK DEVICE FOR ANOTHER PERSON UNDER A RESTRICTED LICENSE Chapter 90 § 24U	
1.	Knowingly
2.	• Breathes into a certified ignition interlock device or • Starts a motor vehicle equipped with such a device
3.	For the purpose of providing an operable motor vehicle to a person whose license or right to operate a vehicle is restricted to the operation of vehicles equipped with a certified ignition interlock device
Arrest Power, Penalties & Notes	
Penalty	**1st Offense**: a fine not less than $1,000 nor more than $5,000 or imprisonment in a HOC for not less than 6 months nor more than 2½ years in the HOC. **2nd Offense**: imprisonment in a **state prison (F)** for not less than 3 nor more than 5 years.

IGNITION LOCK REQUIREMENTS & VIOLATIONS	
Power of Arrest	**1st Offense: Misdemeanor** – there is no statutory authority granting powers of arrest for this offense. However, if the offense is committed in public, in the officer's presence, and is creating a **breach of the peace** an arrest would be lawful. **2nd Offense**: **Felony** – a police officer may effect an arrest for this offense committed in his/her presence or for an offense in the past, on probable cause.
Attorney Hanrahan's Note:	This statute does not require that the person required to utilize an interlocking device be intoxicated in order for this device to be violated.

PERMITTING PERSON WITH IGNITION INTERLOCK DEVISE LICENSE RESTRICTION TO OPERATE MOTOR VEHICLE WITHOUT DEVISE Chapter 90 § 12	
1.	Knowingly
2.	Permit a motor vehicle owned by him or under his control
3.	Which is not equipped with a functioning ignition interlock device
4.	To be operated by a person who has an ignition interlock restricted license
Arrest Power, Penalties & Notes	
Penalty	**Misdemeanor** - 1 year in the HOC and a fine of not more than $500 for a first offense or, for a second or subsequent offense by a fine of not more than $1,000 or imprisonment in a HOC for not more than 2½ years, or both.
RMV Action	The registrar may suspend for not more than **1 year** the motor vehicle registration of a vehicle used in the commission of a violation of this section or the license or right to operate of the person who commits a violation of this section, or both.
Power of Arrest	**Misdemeanor** – there is no statutory authority granting powers of arrest for this offense. However, if the offense is committed in public, in the officer's presence, and is creating a **breach of the peace** an arrest would be lawful.
Definition	For the purposes of this section the term "certified ignition interlock device" shall mean an alcohol breath screening device that prevents a vehicle from starting if it detects a blood alcohol concentration over a preset limit of.02 or 20 mg of alcohol per 100 ml of blood.

C. 90 § 24I POSSESSION OF ALCOHOLIC BEVERAGES IN MOTOR VEHICLES

Elements	
1.	Possession of an open container of alcoholic beverage
2.	Upon any way or in any place to which the public has a right of access, or upon any way or in any place to which members of the public have access as invitees or licensees
3.	In the passenger area of any motor vehicle
Exceptions	This shall not apply to: 1) the passengers of a motor vehicle designed, maintained and used for the **transportation of persons for compensation**, or 2) the **living quarters of a house coach or house trailer**. However, the driver of any motor vehicle, including but not limited to a house coach or house trailer, shall not possess an open container of alcoholic beverage.
ARREST POWER, PENALTIES & NOTES	
Power of Arrest	**CMVI** – there is no statutory authority granting powers of arrest for this offense. However, if the City/Town has an ordinance against public consumption of alcohol and the offense takes place in public arrest powers via 272 §59 may apply.
Penalty	$500 fine
RMV Action:	If operator was under the age of 18 he/she shall have his/her license or permit suspended for a period of **180 days** for a first offense and for a period of **one year for a second or subsequent offense.**
DEFINITIONS	
Open Container	A bottle, can or other receptacle used to contain a liquid that has been opened or has a broken seal or the contents of which have been partially removed or consumed; provided, however, that a bottle resealed pursuant to chapter 138 § 2 shall not be considered an open container; provided further, that **a resealed bottle shall not be transported in the passenger area.**
Passenger Area	The area designed to seat the driver and passengers while the motor vehicle is in operation and any area that is readily accessible to the driver or a passenger while in a seated position including, but not limited to, the glove compartment; provided, however, that the passenger area **shall not include a motor vehicle's trunk or a locked glove compartment** or, if a motor vehicle is not equipped with a trunk, **the area behind the last upright seat or an area not normally occupied by the driver or passenger**.

REGISTRATION, INSURANCE & TITLES

C. 90 § 9	UNREGISTERED MOTOR VEHICLE
	Elements
1.	No person shall, nor the owner or custodian permit,
2.	A motor vehicle or trailer
3.	to be operated, pushed, drawn or towed, or remain,
4.	upon any way
5.	unless it is duly registered and displays its number plate.
	Penalties & Notes
Power of Arrest	**NONE – Civil Infraction only**
Penalty	Missing Number Plate or Unregistered MV: 1st Offense: $100. Subsequent Offense: $1,000. Plus $5 for public safety training surcharge.
	Related Laws, Case Law & Other Important Information
Plate Confiscation	Plates on wrong vehicle, revoked or suspended plates displayed on a vehicle subject those plates to immediate confiscation by a police officer - 540 CMR 2.05(5)(c).
License, ID, SS card or Exemption required to register a vehicle 90 § 2	No registration shall be issued to a natural person for a motor vehicle or trailer unless such person holds a license, identification card issued under section 8E, social security number issued by Social Security Administration or other proof of legal residence; provided, however, that the registrar shall provide by regulation for exemptions for out-of-state students, military personnel, senior citizens and disabled persons.
Towing Exception	A motor vehicle which is being towed or drawn by a motor vehicle designed to draw or tow such vehicles need not be so registered if: a. the towing vehicle is properly registered and displays a valid repair plate, b. the towing vehicle maintains insurance which also provides coverage for the motor vehicle being towed, **and** c. the towing vehicle has been issued a certificate by the department of telecommunications and energy
Agricultural Exception	A tractor, trailer or truck may be operated without proper registration upon any way for a distance not exceeding **one-half mile**, if used exclusively for agricultural purposes, or **between one-half mile and 10 miles** if used exclusively for agricultural purposes and the owner maintains a proper policy of liability insurance.
New Vehicle Delivery Exception	A new automobile being delivered to a dealer by means of a tractor and trailer may be unloaded on a public way and driven by the person so delivering or his agents or servants without proper registration to a dealer's premises over a public way for a distance **not exceeding 300 feet** provided that the person so delivering, with respect to such new automobile, shall have filed with the registrar a motor vehicle liability policy or bond in compliance with the provisions of this chapter.

C. 90 § 9	UNREGISTERED MOTOR VEHICLE
Golf Cart Exception	A motor **vehicle designed for the carrying of golf clubs** and **not more than four persons** may be operated without such registration upon any way if such motor vehicle is **being used solely for the purpose of going from one part of the property of a golf course to another part of the property of the golf course**, provided that the owner of such motor vehicle shall have filed with the registrar a public liability policy or bond providing for the payment of damages to any person to the amount provided by section thirty-four A due to injuries sustained as a result of the operation of such vehicle.
Cemetery Vehicle Exception	A motor vehicle owned by a cemetery may be operated without such registration upon any way if such motor vehicle is being **used solely for the purpose of going from one part of the property of a cemetery to another part of the property of the cemetery**, provided that such vehicle **shall not travel more than one mile on any public way** and the owner of such motor vehicle shall have filed with the registrar a public liability policy or bond providing for the payment of damages to any person to the amount provided by section thirty-four A due to injuries sustained as a result of the operation of such vehicle.
Oversized Earth Moving Vehicle Exception	An earth-moving vehicle used exclusively for the building, repair and maintenance of highways which exceed the dimensions or weight limits imposed by section nineteen and the weight limits imposed by c. 85 § 30 may be operated without proper registration for a distance **not exceeding 300 yards** on any way adjacent to any highway or toll road being constructed, relocated or improved under contract with the commonwealth or any agency or political subdivision thereof or by a public instrumentality, Provided that a permit authorizing the operation of such a vehicle in excess of the stated weight or dimension limits has been issued by the commissioner of highways or the board or officer having charge of such way, and provided that such earth-moving vehicle shall be operated under such permit **only when directed by an officer authorized to direct traffic at the location where such earth-moving vehicle is being operated**. The operation of such an earth-moving vehicle shall conform to any terms or conditions set forth in such permit, and any person to whom any such permit is issued shall provide indemnity for his operation by means of a motor vehicle liability policy or bond conforming to the requirements of this chapter and shall furnish a certificate conforming to the requirements of section thirty-four A with each such application for a permit.
Military Personnel returning vehicle to Massachusetts from foreign country **90 § 9B**	The provisions of this chapter relative to the registration of motor vehicles and the display of number plates shall not apply to motor vehicles having registrations and displaying plates issued by the armed forces of the United States in foreign countries for vehicles owned by military personnel, but said exemption shall be in effect for a period of only **30 days** after the owner thereof has entered the commonwealth for the purpose of traveling either to his place of residence or to a point of military duty.
Police/Fire of Neighboring States **90 § 9B**	This chapter shall not apply to registration and display of number plates on fire apparatus or marked police vehicles from any one of the states of Maine, New Hampshire, Vermont, Rhode Island, Connecticut and New York providing that the state from which such fire apparatus or marked police vehicle comes does not require the registration of and the display of number plates on such apparatus or vehicle.
Registration Expires Noon on the Following Day **90 § 6**	Any motor vehicle or trailer may, if duly registered, be operated, pushed, drawn or towed or remain upon any way between the hours of noon on the date on which its registration expires and noon on the following day, if the following day is the first day of the new registration period, and if such vehicle or trailer displays its register number for either registration period.

C. 90 § 23	OPERATING/PERMITTING TO OPERATE WITH A SUSPENDED/REVOKED REGISTRATION
Elements	
1.	The defendant operates, or causes or permits another to operate
2.	a motor vehicle
3.	after the certificate of registration for such vehicle has been suspended or revoked
Arrest Power, Penalties & Notes	
Power of Arrest	**Misdemeanor** – there is no statutory authority granting warrantless powers of arrest for this offense.
Penalty	**Penalty 1st offense:** by a fine of not less than $500 nor more than $1,000 or by imprisonment for not more than 10 days, or both. **Penalty Subsequent offense:** by imprisonment for not less than 60 days nor more than 1year.
Attorney Hanrahan's Comment	This offense is not restricted to a public way. The way the statute is constructed is that the operator could be punished for operating the vehicle anywhere and he/she would be in violation.
Related Statutes, Case Law & Other Important Information	
License	See the license section of this manual for offenses dealing with suspended/revoked licenses.
Plate Confiscation	Plates on wrong vehicle, revoked or suspended plates displayed on a vehicle subject those plates to immediate confiscation by a police officer - 540 CMR 2.05(5)(c).

C. 90 § 2	7 DAY TRANSFER RULE
Requirements	The owner of a motor vehicle may transfer the registration to a newly acquired motor vehicle (new or used) if the following criteria is met: • The owner must be 18 years of age or older; • The owner must transfer ownership of the registered motor vehicle or trailer owned by him to another or lose possession of the vehicle; • The newly acquired vehicle must be the same type and have the same number of wheels. **Note**: The RMV Driver's manual states "the phrase *lose possession* means an involuntary circumstance, like theft or repossession."
Plates affixed	The Plates shall be attached to the newly acquired vehicle.
Timeframe	A period beginning from the date of transfer until 5:00 PM of the seventh calendar day following the date of transfer. The RMV Driver Manual states "you must transfer your registration to your new vehicle by 5:00 p.m. of the seventh day after transferring ownership of your former vehicle. The day of transfer counts as the first day."[1]

[1] RMV Driver's Manual, page 125

C. 90 § 2	7 DAY TRANSFER RULE
Documents that must be Carried	During this period any operator of the newly acquired vehicle shall carry: • an original copy of the bill of sale reciting the registration number to be transferred from the former vehicle to the newly acquired vehicle, or • the certificate of transfer issued by the dealer on a form approved by the registrar in place of the certificate of registration.

REGISTRATION TRANSFER RULES

Law/ Rule	Violation/Offense	Penalty
REMOVAL OF REGISTRATION UPON TRANSFER OF OWNERSHIP 90 § 2B	The owner of a motor vehicle who transfers the ownership of the vehicle to another or who terminates the registration shall remove from the vehicle any visible evidence furnished to him by the RMV regarding registration.	1ST OFF: \$35 +5 2ND OFF: \$75 +5 3RD OFF: \$150 +5
REGISTRATION; TRANSFER OF VEHICLE OWNERSHIP 90 § 2	Upon the transfer of ownership of any motor vehicle or trailer **its registration shall expire,** and the person in whose name such motor vehicle or trailer is registered **shall forthwith return the certificate of registration** to the registrar with a written notice containing the date of the transfer of ownership and the name, place of residence and address of the new owner.	1ST OFF: \$35 +5 2ND OFF: \$75 +5 3RD OFF: \$150 +5
RETURN OF NUMBER PLATES BY REPOSSESSOR 90 § 6C	Any person who takes possession of a motor vehicle by foreclosure or subrogation of title shall return the number plates issued for such vehicle to the person in whose name such plates had been issued as owner by the end of the second day following the day on which such possession was taken.	A fine of not less than \$10 nor more than \$100* Offense not listed on scheduled assessment
DEATH OR BANKRUPTCY OF OWNER 90 § 2	On the death, insolvency or bankruptcy of any owner of a motor vehicle or trailer, its registration shall be deemed to continue in force as a valid registration until the expiration date appearing on the certificate of registration or until the ownership of such motor vehicle or trailer is transferred by the legal representative of the estate of such owner, whichever occurs first, subject otherwise to all provisions of law applicable generally to registrations of motor vehicles or trailers; and provided, further, that if the owner of a motor vehicle or trailer for which a certificate of registration has been issued dies prior to the effective date appearing on the certificate of registration, such motor vehicle or trailer shall be deemed to be validly registered and said registration shall continue in force until the expiration date appearing on the certificate of registration, or until the ownership of such vehicle or trailer is transferred by the legal representative of the estate of such owner, whichever occurs first, subject, however, to all provisions of law applicable generally to registrations of motor vehicles or trailers.	

C. 90 § 23	ATTACHING PLATES/CONCEALING A MOTOR VEHICLE
	Attaching Plates
1.	The defendant attached, or permitted to be attached,
2.	To a motor vehicle or a motor vehicle trailer
3.	A number plate assigned to another motor vehicle or trailer.
	Concealing a Motor Vehicle
1.	The defendant : • obscures or permits to be obscured the figures on any number plate attached to any motor vehicle or trailer, or • fails to display on a motor vehicle or trailer the number plate and the register number duly issued,
2.	with intent to conceal the identity of such motor vehicle or trailer.
	Arrest Power, Penalties & Notes
Power of Arrest	**Misdemeanor** – there is no statutory authority granting warrantless powers of arrest for this offense.
Penalty	A fine of not more than $100 or by imprisonment for not more than 10 days, or both
Public Way	There is no requirement in the statute that this offense takes place on a public way.
	Related Statutes, Case Law & Other Important Information
Plate Confiscation	Plates on wrong vehicle, revoked or suspended plates displayed on a vehicle subject those plates to immediate confiscation by a police officer - 540 CMR 2.05(5)(c).

NEW/NON-RESIDENT REGISTRATION & REQUIREMENTS		
Law/Rule	**Violation/Offense**	**Penalty**
No grace period	The RMV Driver's Manual states "You must register your vehicle in Massachusetts as soon as you become a Massachusetts resident. The law does not provide a grace period."	See 90 § 9 unregistered
Non-Resident (Non-Student) May Operate Vehicle Registered In Foreign State Or Country In MA If They Have Insurance; otherwise only 30 days 90 § 3	A motor vehicle or trailer owned by a non-resident who has **complied with the laws relative to motor vehicles** and trailers (i.e. has proper insurance) and who has complied with the registration and operation of the state or country of registration, may be operated on the ways of this commonwealth without a Massachusetts registration, to the extent, as long as the state or country of registration grants substantially similar privileges to residents of Massachusetts. The RMV Driver's Manual states "nonresidents whose primary residences are in other states may not operate motor vehicles or trailers in Massachusetts for more than 30 total days in one year unless they have liability insurance."	See 90 § 9 unregistered and 90 § 34J uninsured MV
Non-residents who use their vehicle for business in MA **90 § 3**	Nonresidents must register in Massachusetts the motor vehicles or trailers they use for their Massachusetts businesses. If nonresidents use their vehicles in Massachusetts and one or more other states, they must register the average number of vehicles they use in Massachusetts. Other rules apply to vehicles owned by nonresidents who have "apportioned" license plates from other states.[1]	See 90 § 9 unregistered and 90 § 34J uninsured MV
MA Residents driving car registered in foreign state or country – 30 day limit **90 § 3**	Nonresidents who own motor vehicles or trailers that are registered in other states or countries must register those vehicles and trailers in Massachusetts if Massachusetts residents have or control those vehicles or trailers for more than 30 total days in one calendar year.[2] **Note:** 3 or more convictions for a violation of this entire section within any 24 month period, may subject the violator to a suspension of the right to operate, or the right to have any motor vehicle or trailer owned by such person or corporation operated in Massachusetts for a period not to exceed 6 months.	$250 for MA resident operating foreign registered car for more than 30 days within a year. Plus $5 Public Safety Surcharge.
FALSIFYING RESIDENCY FOR REGISTRATION PURPOSES **90 § 3½**	The defendant improperly registers a motor vehicle or trailer in another state or misrepresents the place of garaging of the motor vehicle or trailer within Massachusetts, for purposes of evading the payment of motor vehicle excise, sales and use taxes or insurance premiums, or to reduce the amount of one of these payments. **Note**: For purposes of this section, each taxable year that a motor vehicle or trailer is improperly registered shall be considered a separate offense, but **no more than 3 years** shall be the subject of prosecution.	**Criminal Penalty** **An alternative to criminal prosecution**: A violation of this section may be disposed of as a civil motor vehicle infraction in the amount of $500 under chapter 90C.

[1] RMV Driver Manual and c. 90 § 3
[2] RMV Driver Manual and c. 90 § 3

NEW/NON-RESIDENT REGISTRATION & REQUIREMENTS

FACTORS UTILIZED TO DETERMINE MASSACHUSETTS RESIDENCY FOR REGISTRATION PURPOSES 90 § 3½	Any person claiming to be a nonresident for purposes of section 3, shall be deemed to be a resident of the commonwealth during any period in which such person: • Obtained a Real Estate exemption pursuant to chapter 59; • Filed a Massachusetts resident income tax return pursuant to chapter 62; • Obtained a rental deduction claiming Massachusetts as his primary residence; • Declared in a home mortgage settlement document that the mortgaged property located in the commonwealth would be occupied as his principal residence; • Obtained homeowner's liability insurance coverage on property that was declared to be occupied as a principal residence; • Filed a certificate of residency and identified his place of residence in a city or town in Massachusetts in order to comply with a residency ordinance as a prerequisite for employment with a governmental entity; • Paid on his own behalf, or on behalf of a child or dependent for whom the person has custody, resident in-state tuition rates to attend a state-sponsored college, community college or university; • Applied for and received public assistance from the commonwealth for himself or his child or dependent of whom he has custody; • Has a child or dependent of whom he has custody who is enrolled in a public school in a city or town in the commonwealth, unless the cost of such education is paid for by him, such child or dependent, or by another education jurisdiction; • Is registered to vote in the Massachusetts; • Obtained any benefit, exemption, deduction, entitlement, license, permit or privilege by claiming principal residence in the commonwealth; or • Is a resident under any other written criteria under which the commissioner of revenue may determine residency in the commonwealth. Note: The custodian of the above records shall turn over these records to a police officer, certain local and RMV officials, for the purpose of investigating a violation of the a CHAPTER 90 registration violation.

SPECIAL RULES FOR STUDENTS IN MASSACHUSETTS

NONRESIDENT *STUDENT* REGISTRATION REQUIREMENTS 90 § 3

Criteria for Student Exemption	Every nonresident enrolled as a student at a school or college in Massachusetts who operates a motor vehicle registered in another state or country during any period beginning on September 1st of any year and ending on August 31st of the following year shall file in quadruplicate with the police department of the city or town in which such school or college is located, a statement signed by him under the penalties of perjury providing the following information: a. the registration number and make of the motor vehicle and the state or country of registration, b. the name and local and out-of-state address of the owner, c. the names and addresses of all insurers providing liability insurance covering operation of the motor vehicle, d. the legal residence of such nonresident and his residence while attending such school or college and the name and address of the school or college which he is attending.
Insurance Required	The nonresident student shall also maintain a proper policy of liability insurance.

NEW/NON-RESIDENT REGISTRATION & REQUIREMENTS	
Penalty	Any nonresident student who fails to comply with these provisions shall be punished by a fine of $200.
Police Department Requirement	The police department with whom any such statement is filed in quadruplicate shall send: ▪ 1 copy to the registrar of motor vehicles, ▪ 1 copy to the local assessor's office, and ▪ 1 copy to such school or college.
College or University Requirements	**Maintain a Register:** from the copies of the statements received from the police department, each school or college shall compile and maintain a register of all such nonresidents enrolled as students which shall be available for inspection at all reasonable times by the registrar, his agents, and police officers. Each school or college shall provide to all nonresident students the following warning in bold type not less than ½ inch in height: "IT IS UNLAWFUL FOR A NONRESIDENT STUDENT TO FAIL TO FILE A NONRESIDENT DRIVER STATEMENT WITH THE POLICE DEPARTMENT LOCATED IN THE SAME CITY OR TOWN AS THE SCHOOL OR COLLEGE ATTENDED, IN ACCORDANCE WITH SECTION 3 OF CHAPTER 90 OF THE MASSACHUSETTS GENERAL LAWS. FAILURE TO FILE SUCH STATEMENT IS PUNISHABLE BY A FINE NOT TO EXCEED $200." A written acknowledgment of receipt of this warning shall be required.
Decal Issued	Each school or college shall issue to each nonresident student a serially numbered or lettered decal as may be prescribed by the registrar, which decal **shall be affixed to the uppermost center portion of the windshield**.
School Penalty	Any such school or college which fails to compile and maintain a register, to issue a decal as required by this paragraph or to forward register data to the assessor's office of a municipality in which a nonresident student resides shall be punished by a fine of not more than $100 for each such offense.

ADDITIONAL REGISTRATION RULES & REQUIREMENTS

Law/ Rule	Violation/Offense	Penalty
CARRYING CERTIFICATE OF REGISTRATION 90 § 11	Every person **operating** a motor vehicle shall have the certificate of **registration** for the vehicle and for the trailer in some easily accessible place. **Exceptions:** the following are not required to carry their certificates of registration: dealers, • manufacturers, • repairmen, • owner-repairmen, • farmers • dealers in both boats and boat trailers **Rental Vehicle:** in the case of a rental vehicle, a Photostat copy of the certificate of registration, accompanied by the rental agreement, shall be sufficient. **Receipt in Lieu of Registration:** If the RMV is unable to issue promptly the certificate of registration applied for, they may issue a receipt for the fee paid, and said receipt shall be carried in lieu of the certificate, and for a period of 60 days from the date of its issue said receipt shall have the same force and effect given to the certificate by this chapter.	1ST OFF: $35 Plus $5 Public Safety Surcharge. 2ND OFF: $75 Plus $5 Public Safety Surcharge. 3RD OFF: $150 Plus $5 Public Safety Surcharge.
PROPER DISPLAY OF NUMBER PLATES 90 § 6	Every motor vehicle or trailer registered in Massachusetts when operated in or on any way in Massachusetts shall have its license plate displayed as follows: • one number plate to be attached at the front and one at the rear of the motor vehicle, and • one number plate to be attached at the rear of the trailer, **Note:** if the registrar issues only one number plate it shall be attached to the rear of the vehicle so that it shall always be plainly visible.	1ST OFF: $35 Plus $5 Public Safety Surcharge. 2ND OFF: $75 Plus $5 Public Safety Surcharge. 3RD OFF: $150 Plus $5 Public Safety Surcharge.
Multiple State Plates 90 § 6	A motor vehicle or trailer which by reason of its interstate operation is registered in Massachusetts and elsewhere may display the register number plates of this and any other state or country in which it is registered, if, while being operated on the ways of Massachusetts, the number plates furnished by the registrar, or temporary number plates authorized by him as hereinafter provided, are displayed as required hereby.	
RMV May Issue One Number Plate 90 § 9B	The RMV may issue one number plate, instead of two, for certain motor vehicles or for all motor vehicles. Such plate shall be displayed at the rear of the vehicle for which it is issued, and all consistent provisions of law or of rules and regulations relating to number plates shall apply to such plate.	

ADDITIONAL REGISTRATION RULES & REQUIREMENTS

<table>
<tr><td>VISIBILITY OF LICENSE PLATES
90 § 6</td><td>Visibility Requirements
• License plates shall be kept clean with the numbers legible
• License plates shall not be obscured in any manner by the installation of any device
• When headlights are required the rear register number shall be illuminated so as to be plainly visible at a distance of 60 feet.
540 CMR 2.23 Further Regulates the visibility of license plates:
<u>Display of Reflectorized License Plates</u>
1) On or after August 1, 1969, no reflectorized number plate issued by the Registrar of Motor Vehicles and mounted on any motor vehicle or trailer shall be covered with any glass, plastic or similar material if such material reduces the legibility or substantially diminishes the reflective qualities of such plate.
2) Any such number plate covered with any glass, plastic or similar material which reduces the legibility or substantially diminished the reflective qualities of such plate shall be deemed not to be maintained in good order, and in violation of the provision of said M.G.L. c. 90.
3) Nothing contained in 540 CMR 2.00 shall be construed to prohibit the use of any metal or other frame covering, the border of any such reflectorized number plate so long as such frame does not cover or obscure in any manner the register number or any other words, symbols or numbers lawfully imprinted on or affixed to such number plate.
Case Law Note: In the 2011 case of Com. v. Miller, a trooper stopped a motorist because he had a black piece of tape covering the words “Spirit of America” on his license plate. The motorist was subsequently arrested for OUI. The Trooper made the stop based on a violation of 540 CMR 2.23. 540 CMR 2.23 states in part "Nothing contained in 540 CMR 2.00 shall be construed to prohibit the use of any metal or other frame covering, the border of any such reflectorized number plate so long as <u>such frame does not cover or obscure in any manner the register number or any other words, symbols or numbers</u> lawfully imprinted on or affixed to such number plate" Because the wording specifically speaks to a plate frame from covering the plate and not specifically black tape, the stop was ruled invalid.
In the 2014 case of Commonwealth v. Bernard, the Appeals Court ruled that simply having a license plate cover, even one with a bluish tint, did not by itself violate c. 90 §6. There must be some proof that the cover obscured the registration numbers or otherwise affected the legibility of the numbers.</td><td>1ST OFF: $35
Plus $5 Public Safety Surcharge.
2ND OFF: $75
Plus $5 Public Safety Surcharge.
3RD OFF: $150
Plus $5 Public Safety Surcharge.</td></tr>
<tr><td>MILITARY SERVICE; VEHICLES PURCHASED IN ANOTHER STATE
90 § 5B</td><td colspan="2">A motor vehicle owned by a resident serving in the military service of the United States which was purchased by the resident in another state and registered in the other state, may be operated in Massachusetts without being registered in Massachusetts for a period of 30 days. At the expiration of said thirty day period, said motor vehicle shall be registered in accordance with the provisions of chapter 90.</td></tr>
<tr><td>TEMPORARY REGISTRATION PLATES
90 § 2D</td><td colspan="2">The RMV may issue to dealers temporary registration plates which shall be valid for not more than 20 days. Proper insurance shall be in effect prior to the issuance of temporary plates.</td></tr>
</table>

ADDITIONAL REGISTRATION RULES & REQUIREMENTS

Report address change	Chapter 90 § 26A requires that the holder of a Massachusetts vehicle registration must report a change of name or address to the RMV, in writing, within 30 days after the date on which the change was made.	1ST OFF: $35 +5 2ND OFF: $75 +5 3RD OFF: $150 +5
Registration Decal Not Displayed 540 CMR 2.05	The Registrar may issue a sticker or decal to validate a registration plate issued under M.G.L. c. 90, § 2. The owner of the vehicle shall attach such sticker or decal to the upper right hand corner of the rear registration plate, so as to cover any previously attached sticker. Government vehicles are exempt.	1ST OFF: $35 +5 2ND OFF: $75 +5 3RD OFF: $150 +5

C. 90 § 5 GENERAL REGISTRATIONS AND GENERAL REGISTRATION PLATES

ATTORNEY HANRAHAN'S NOTE: This chapter refers to general registration plates, such as Dealer and Repair plates. Most of the actual rules on the use of these plates come from the Code of Massachusetts Regulations (CMR).

General registrations and General registration number plates may be issued to any person engaged in the following occupations who meet the eligibility requirements stated in this chapter and the rules and regulations of the registry of motor vehicles

a. manufacturer;
b. dealer;
c. repairman;
d. recreational vehicle and recreational trailer dealer;
e. boat and boat trailer dealer;
f. farmer;
g. owner-contractor;
h. transporter;
i. person involved in the harvesting of forest products as defined by the regulations of the RMV

Vehicles with general registration plates shall be regarded as registered; provided however, that no motor vehicle or trailer so registered shall be <u>loaned or let for hire</u> for **more than 5 consecutive days**

False Statements	Whoever makes a false statement in an application for a general registration and number plate shall be punished by a fine of not less than $100 nor more than $500 or by imprisonment for not less than 30 days nor more than 2 years.

The below definitions are from the Massachusetts Department of Transportation

Dealer	A ***"Dealer"*** is defined as any person who is engaged principally and substantially in the business of buying, selling, or exchanging motor vehicles, trailers, or motor vehicle bodies and maintains a facility dedicated to carrying out said business and except for a person who exchanges such vehicles on a wholesale basis, is open to the public.
Dealer Plate Use	A **Dealer plate** may be issued by the Registrar to a person who is a licensed motor vehicle dealer and who qualifies under C. 90, Section 5 and under the RMV's regulations. (Licensed motor vehicle dealers who do not maintain the required facility dedicated to carrying out said business will not qualify.) Recreational Vehicle Dealers, Recreational Trailer Dealers, Boat Dealers and Boat Trailer Dealers may qualify for a Dealer plate under separate standards.
Repairman	***Repairman***, any person who is principally and substantially engaged in the business of repairing, altering, reconditioning, equipping or towing motor vehicles or trailers for the public and who maintains an established place of business, as defined in this section.
Repair Plate Use	A **Repair plate** is issued to a repair shop to allow the repairer to drive unregistered vehicles on the road for testing.
Transporter plate use	A **Transporter Plate** is issued to allow a transporter the ability to transport self propelling vehicles on the road.

REGISTRATION & PLATES

C. 90 § 5	GENERAL REGISTRATIONS AND GENERAL REGISTRATION PLATES
Transporter	***Transporter,*** any person principally and substantially engaged in the business of transporting or delivering motor vehicles under their own power not owned by him and who possesses a valid license for said business issued by the Department of Public Utilities, or any person or agent thereof, licensed to engage in the business of financing the purchase of or insuring motor vehicles who is required to take into possession such motor vehicles by foreclosure or subrogation of title.

HANDICAP PARKING PLATES & PLACARD

C. 90 § 2	MISUSE OF HANDICAP PARKING PLATE/PLACARD
Elements	
1.	The defendant wrongfully displays a handicapped plate on or a placard
2.	in a motor vehicle parked in a designated handicapped parking space or in a regular metered space or in a commercial parking space.
Arrest Power, Penalties & Notes	
Power of Arrest	**NONE**
Penalty	1st offense $500. Subsequent offense $1,000 (plus the additional $5 public safety training surcharge).
RMV ACTION	The registrar shall suspend the operator's license or right to operate of any person found to have violated the provisions of this section relative to the wrongful use or display of a special handicapped plate or parking identification placard for a period of 30 days for a first offense, for a period of 90 days for a second offense and for a period of one year for a third or subsequent offense. Such suspension shall be in addition to any other penalty, fine, suspension, revocation or requirement that may be imposed for such violation including, but not limited to, those applicable under section 37E of c. 266. The registrar may revoke the plate or placard as issued to a person upon a finding that the person to whom the plate or placard was issued willingly and without coercion or duress authorized, permitted or allowed it to be used by another person.
Related Statutes, Case Law & Other Important Information	
Handicap Placard theft and fraud	Chapter 90 § 24B makes it a felony to falsely make, steal, alter, forge or counterfeit or procure or to assist another to falsely make, steal, alter, forge or counterfeit a special parking ID disability placard.
Plate or Placard not both	The RMV does not permit a person to obtain both a disability placard and a disability plate.
Criteria	A physician, chiropractor or nurse practitioner may authorize a disability placard or plate. The user must be incapable of walking for more than 200 feet without resting or need a prosthetic aid or device, or require the use of portable oxygen.
540 CMR 17 Disability Plates and Placards	**Choice of Plate or Placard.** A person who satisfies the qualifications of 540 CMR 17.03(2) shall be entitled to either a plate or a placard. A person may choose to have a placard; but a plate shall be available only to a person who is a registered owner of the motor vehicle to which the plate is to be attached. The rights, privileges and obligations associated with a plate and a placard are the same. The Registrar may issue both a plate and a placard upon application and for good cause shown by the applicant.

C. 90 § 34J	UNINSURED MOTOR VEHICLE
Elements	
1.	The defendant: a. Operates b. Permits someone else to operate, or c. Permits to Remain
2.	A motor vehicle or trailer without adequate insurance
3.	a. on a public highway, b. on a private way laid out by statutory authority, c. on a way dedicated to public use, d. on a way under the control of park commissioners or a body with similar powers, or e. in a place to which the public has a right of access.
Arrest Power, Penalties & Notes	
Power of Arrest	**Misdemeanor** – there is no statutory authority granting warrantless powers of arrest for this offense. However, if the offense is committed in public, in the officer's presence, and is creating a **breach of the peace** an arrest would be lawful.
Penalty	A fine of not less than $500 nor more than $5,000 or by imprisonment for not more than 1 year in a HOC, or both such fine and imprisonment. **Note:** Any municipality that enforces the provisions of this section shall retain the fine.
RMV Action	Any person who is convicted of, or enters a plea of guilty shall have his or her **license** or right to operate a motor vehicle suspended for **60 days** by the RMV upon the registrar's receipt of notification from the clerk of any court which enters any conviction hereunder or which accepts such plea of guilty. For any subsequent conviction or plea of guilty within a 6 year period the offender's license or right to operate a motor vehicle shall be suspended for 1 year
Attorney Hanrahan's Comment	The actual reading of the statute uses the language "on a public or private way" and some officers have mistakenly interpreted this to mean that you are required to insure a motor vehicle that is being stored in your garage. The term private way refers to roadways which are "private" yet open to public use. See notes below.
Related Statutes, Case Law & Other Important Information	
Locations Regulated	Compulsory insurance is required only "upon the ways of the commonwealth or in any place therein to which the public has a right of access." G.L. c. 90, § 34A. "Way" is defined as "any public highway, private way laid out under authority of statute, way dedicated to public use, or way under the control of park commissioners or body having like powers." G.L. c. 90, § 1.[1]
Nonresident motorist	Nonresident motorists whose vehicles are validly registered in their home state may be operated in Massachusetts without being registered here, if their state grants reciprocal privileges. Nor are they required to comply with the Commonwealth's compulsory insurance requirements unless the vehicle is operated here for more than 30 days in the aggregate in any year or the owner acquires a regular home or business here. G.L. c.90, § 3; *Commonwealth v. Brann*, 23 Mass. App. Ct. 980, 504 N.E.2d 356 (1987).
Burden of proof	If the violator is a Massachusetts resident the police must prove lack of insurance. If the violator is licensed/registered out-of-state the violator must prove that he/she has proper insurance.

[1] 2009 Model Jury Instructions.

TITLE LAWS	
CREATION OF FALSE TITLE **90D § 32**	The defendant falsely makes, alters, forges, or counterfeits a certificate of title or salvage title. **Penalty:** by a fine of not more than $1,000 or by imprisonment in the **state prison (F)** for not more than 5 years, or in a jail or HOC for not more than 2 years, or both. **Arrest Powers**: **Felony** – a police officer may effect an arrest for this offense committed in his/her presence or for an offense in the past, on probable cause.
FALSIFICATION OF TITLE DOCUMENTS **90D § 32**	The defendant alters or forges an assignment of a certificate of title or salvage title, or supporting documents, or an assignment or release of a security interest on a certificate of title or a form the registrar prescribes. **Penalty:** a fine of not more than $1,000 or by imprisonment in the **state prison (F)** for not more than 5 years, or in a jail or HOC for not more than 2 years, or both. **Arrest Powers**: **Felony** – a police officer may effect an arrest for this offense committed in his/her presence or for an offense in the past, on probable cause.
POSSESSION OF FALSE TITLE **90D § 32**	The defendant has possession of or uses a certificate of title or salvage title, knowing it to have been altered, forged, or counterfeited. **Penalty:** a fine of not more than $1,000 or by imprisonment in the **state prison (F)** for not more than 5 years, or in a jail or HOC for not more than 2 years, or both. **Arrest Powers**: **Felony** – a police officer may effect an arrest for this offense committed in his/her presence or for an offense in the past, on probable cause.
FALSE TITLE APPLICATION **90D § 32**	The defendant uses a false or fictitious name or address, or makes a material false statement or fails to disclose a security interest, or conceals any other material fact, in an application for a certificate of title or salvage title; or supporting documents. **Penalty:** a fine of not more than $1,000 or by imprisonment in the **state prison (F)** for not more than 5 years, or in a jail or HOC for not more than 2 years, or both. **Arrest Powers**: **Felony** – a police officer may effect an arrest for this offense committed in his/her presence or for an offense in the past, on probable cause
DUPLICATE CERTIFICATE OF TITLE **90D §14**	If a certificate of title is lost, stolen, mutilated or destroyed or becomes illegible, the first lienholder or, if none, the owner or legal representative of the owner named in the certificate, or any other transferee who has sufficient proof of ownership as determined by the registrar, shall promptly make application for and may obtain a duplicate upon furnishing information satisfactory to the registrar. **The duplicate certificate of title shall contain the legend:** "This is a duplicate certificate and may be subject to the rights of a person under the original certificate". It shall be mailed to the first lienholder named in it or, if none, to the owner. The registrar shall not issue a new certificate of title to a transferee upon application made on a duplicate until **15 days** after receipt of the application. A person recovering an original certificate of title for which a duplicate has been issued shall promptly surrender the original to the registrar.
APPLY FOR TITLE WITIN 10 DAYS 90D § 2 & 4	An application for a new title must be made within 10 days of vehicle acquisition.

LICENSES, ID's and RIGHT TO OPERATE (suspensions and revocations)

C. 90 § 10	OPERATING WITHOUT A LICENSE	
Elements		
1.	Operation of a motor vehicle	
2.	On a way	
3.	Without having a valid license.	
Arrest Power, Penalties & Notes		
Power of Arrest	**Misdemeanor** – a person observed, by a police officer, operating a motor vehicle without a valid license may be arrested without a warrant pursuant to c. 90 § 21.	
Penalty	**1st offense:** a fine of not less than $500 nor more than $1,000 or by imprisonment for not more than 10 days, or both. **Subsequent Offense:** and for any subsequent offence by imprisonment for not less than 60 days nor more than 1 year.	
Related Statutes, Case Law & Other Important Information		
Report address change	Chapter 90 § 26A requires that the holder of a Massachusetts Driver's License must report a change of name or address to the RMV, in writing, within 30 days after the date on which the change was made.	1st Off: $35 +5 2nd Off: $75 +5 3rd Off: $150 +5
License must accessible	An operator of a motor vehicle must have his/her registration certificate "upon his person or in the vehicle, in some easily accessible place."	1st Off: $35 +5 2nd Off: $75 +5 3rd Off: $150 +5
Temporary License	In 2015 the RMV implemented self-service kiosks. Customers who use these kiosks to renew a driver's license will receive a printed receipt. This receipt is considered a temporary license and is valid for driving purposes for 30 days from the date of the transaction.	
No Grace Period	According to the RMV, operators licensed in other states who move into Massachusetts must obtain a Massachusetts driver's license once they establish residence in Massachusetts. There is no grace period. *See exemptions listed later in this section.	
Proper Class Required	The operator must also be licensed under the proper class and endorsement (e.g. a class D licensee would be unlicensed if operating a motorcycle – without at least a MC learner's permit). The Trial Court's assessment schedule lists these violations as criminal offenses. Also, 540 CMR 2.06(5)(b)(1) indicates that operating outside of class or endorsement is operating without being properly licensed. *Commonwealth v. Magarosian,* 261 Mass.228, 158 N.E. 771 (1927) (defendant licensed to operate one category of vehicle is unlicensed with respect to other categories of vehicles).	

C. 90 § 10	OPERATING WITHOUT A LICENSE	
License Classes	Class A	Any combination of vehicles with a gross combination weight rating (GCWR) of 26,001 or more pounds, provided the GVWR of the vehicle(s) being towed is in excess of 10,000 pounds. (Holders of a Class A license may, with any appropriate endorsements, operate all vehicles within Class B, C, and D.)
	Class B	Any single vehicle with a gross vehicle weight rating (GVWR) of 26,001 or more pounds, or any such vehicle towing a vehicle not in excess of 10,000 pounds GVWR. (Holders of a Class B license may, with appropriate endorsements, operate all vehicles within Class C and D.)
	Class C	Any single vehicle or combination of vehicles that does not meet the definition of Class A or Class B, but is either designed to transport 16 or more passengers including the driver, or is required to be placarded for hazardous materials under 49 CFR 172.500 or any other federal regulation. (Holders of a Class C license may operate all vehicles within Class D.)
	Class D	Any single vehicle or combination of vehicles that does not meet the definition of Class A, Class B, Class C, or Class M. (Typically passenger vehicles such as cars, SUVs, or family vans).
License Restrictions	**B** Corrective Lenses **C** Mechanical Aid (Adaptive Devices) **D** Prosthetic Aid **E** Automatic Transmission **F** Outside Mirror **G** Daylight Only **H** Restricted Hours **I** Junior Operator **J** Other **P** Use with Certified Driving Instructors Only **R** Bioptic telescopic lens **S** Proof of Current Blood Sugar Levels **Y** Restrict to 14 passenger capacity **Z** Ignition Interlock Required **Note**: an operator is considered **unlicensed** if driving contrary to an RMV restriction.	
Operator must be at least 16	No person **under sixteen years** of age shall operate a motor vehicle upon any way. Attorney Hanrahan's note: This age restriction will apply to out-of-state operators who are licensed in a state that permits persons under the age of 16 to operate.	
RMV Notification	*Watson v. Forbes,* 307 Mass. 383, 384-385, 30 N.E.2d 228, 229 (1940) (not a defense that defendant was never notified of expiration of license);	
Way	A license is required only for operation on "way."[1] This is generally understood to mean a way dedicated for public use.	
7 Statutory exceptions	General Laws c. 90, § 10 contains seven exceptions to the requirement of a Massachusetts license: 1. A person who is licensed in another state or country, has applied for a Massachusetts license but has not yet been given a driver's test, and has been issued a 60-day temporary permit by the Registry of Motor Vehicles; 2. A person who possesses a valid Massachusetts learner's permit (and complies with the provisions of the learner's permit); 3. A person who is licensed in another state and who is accompanying a spouse who is a member of the armed forces on assignment to Massachusetts; 4. A member of the armed forces on active duty who has a license issued by the state of his or her domicile; 5. A member of the armed forces within 45 days of returning from active duty outside the United States who has a license issued by the armed forces in a foreign country; **Attorney Hanrahan's Note**: According to the RMV's driver's manual if a Massachusetts license expires, or will expire, during active service in the US Armed Forces, the license is considered valid for 60 days following the holder's honorable discharge from the military. The operator must have in his possession is expired license and proof of discharge from the military. 6. A nonresident who is licensed in the state or country where the vehicle is registered, but for not more than 30 days in the aggregate annually or beyond 30 days after acquiring a regular abode or	

[1] *Santa Maria v. Trotto,* 297 Mass. 442, 446, 9 N.E.2d 540,543 (1937).

<table>
<tr><th>C. 90 § 10</th><th>OPERATING WITHOUT A LICENSE</th></tr>
<tr><td></td><td>place of business within Massachusetts unless Massachusetts liability insurance requirements are met; and
7. A nonresident who is licensed in the state or country of his or her domicile, if it grants reciprocal privileges to Massachusetts residents, but for not more than 30 days in the aggregate annually or beyond 30 days after acquiring a regular abode or place of business within Massachusetts unless Massachusetts liability insurance requirements are met. Note: the operator has his/her license on his/her person or in the vehicle in some easily accessible place</td></tr>
<tr><td>Out-of-State & Foreign Operators

90 § 10</td><td>A nonresident who holds a license under the laws of the state or country in which he resides may operate any motor vehicle of a type which he is licensed to operate under said license, duly registered in this commonwealth or in any state or country; provided, that he has the license on his person or in the vehicle in some easily accessible place, and that, as finally determined by the registrar, his state or country grants substantially similar privileges to residents of this commonwealth and prescribes and enforces standards of fitness for operations of motor vehicles substantially as high as those prescribed and enforced by this commonwealth.

Arrest Power: chapter 90 § 21 states in part "any officer authorized to make arrests may arrest without a warrant and keep in custody for not more than 24 hours, unless a Saturday, Sunday or a legal holiday intervenes, any person who, while operating a motor vehicle on any way, as defined in section one, violates the provisions of the first paragraph of c. 90 § 10..." The requirement of a non-resident to have his/her license readily available is in paragraph 1 of c. 90 § 10. However, discretion should be used.

Attorney Hanrahan's note: Operators from U.S. Territories are considered non-resident, foreign operators. Also, students residing in Massachusetts while attending school are not required to obtain a Massachusetts license provided that they are licensed in their state of residence.

See International Driver section for more on foreign operators.</td></tr>
<tr><td>Military Personnel and their spouses

90 § 10</td><td>The following are exempt from the requirements of obtaining a Massachusetts license while residing in Massachusetts:

Active Military personnel: a person on active duty in the armed forces of the United States and who has his possession a license to operate motor vehicles issued by the state where he is domiciled is exempt.

Spouse of Active Duty member: the spouse of a member of the armed forces of the United States who is accompanying such member on military or naval assignment to this commonwealth and who has a valid operator's license issued by another state is exempt from the requirements of obtaining a MA license.

Returning Military Personnel: a member of the armed forces of the United States returning from active duty outside the United States, and has in his possession a license to operate motor vehicles issued by said armed forces in a foreign country, is exempt for a period of not more than 45 days after his return.</td></tr>
<tr><th colspan="2">INTERNATIONAL DRIVERS</th></tr>
<tr><td>Foreign Nationals Operator

Summary</td><td>The foreign operator, duly licensed in his country of origin, can operate in Massachusetts. In order for a visitor from a foreign country to operate in Massachusetts they must be duly licensed from their home country. The burden is on the operator to show that he is properly licensed. If the country issues a license the operator must have it in his/her possession and present it on demand. Often times, the officer may not be able to read or understand the foreign license. The operator may also have either a passport or a so-called international driving permit. The international driving permit is not an actual</td></tr>
</table>

C. 90 § 10	OPERATING WITHOUT A LICENSE
	license but is designed to help interpret the driving privileges of the operator's home country. It is issued by AAA, a private corporation, and does not grant any actual driving privileges (although other states require an operator licensed in a foreign country to possess the AAA international driving permit, Massachusetts does not). The passport is also often helpful to help verify the operator's country of origin and to at least see if the document presented to be a license matches the information in the passport. The American Association of Motor Vehicle Administration, in conjunction with NHTSA, created a Resource Card to utilize when dealing with foreign operators. The two-sided card is available for your review and use in the Appendix of this manual.
1 Year Limit	A foreign visitor from one of the approved countries or territories may legally drive on the roads of the Commonwealth on his or her own country's valid license (limited to a licensed driver who is at least 18 years old and limited to a vehicle of the type covered by the license) for up to one (1) year from the date of arrival.[1] **Note**: According to the RMV, the year of eligibility to drive in Massachusetts begins again each time the foreign visitor lawfully re-enters the US ("up to one year from the date you entered the country as a visitor"). Also, the RMV Driver's manual states that although a foreign visitor may operator with a foreign license for up to 1 year "you must still apply for a Massachusetts license when you establish residency in the Commonwealth". [2]
International "Driver's License"	**The RMV does not recognize as valid any document purporting to be an *International Driver's License***, or any other document that confers driving privileges, **unless issued by the government agency that issues such licenses in the driver's country of residence and the driver is validly licensed in that country.** The governments of some countries issue an international version of their own domestic driver license to their validly licensed drivers who indicate a need for a driver's license that will be recognized in other countries. The international version of the domestic driver license includes translations (usually including into English).
"International Driving Permit"	An **International Driving Permit** serves primarily as a translation of a person's foreign driver's license into ten (10) major languages recognized by the United Nations. The Permit itself is a small (4" X 6"), gray covered, multi-page booklet with white pages, containing the driver's first and last name, the date and place of birth and the person's permanent address in the country of issuance. A Permit also contains a photograph of the driver and his/her signature. Other than the page containing the personal information and photograph, each page conveys the same information but in a separate language. It does ***not*** confer any driving privileges. The Permit is ***not*** a substitute for the person's valid driver license. A driver who is licensed in another country ***must*** carry his/her valid foreign driver license when driving in Massachusetts. The operator should also carry an INS document which shows the date that the operator last entered the U.S. The valid I-94 containing the date of admission to the U.S. should be sufficient.
RMV opinion	In the opinion of the Registry of Motor Vehicles, in instances where the operator is otherwise unlicensed or under suspension or revocation, or where his or her right to operate in the Commonwealth has been suspended or revoked, the possession of an International Driving Permit or International Driver's License has no legal effect.
Com. v. Chown	In the 2011 case of ***Com. v. Chown,*** the SJC ruled that when dealing with an non-resident operator who is licensed, or potentially licensed, in another state or country, but is suspected of having established residency in Massachusetts to the point that he is required to obtain a Massachusetts license the officer must investigate the specific elements determining residency in c. 90 § 3 ½ (which the court acknowledges cannot be performed in the field) before charging the operator under c. 90

[1] RMV Driver's Manual – although not specifically covered under MGL or referenced in the RMV driver's manual the 1 year limit presumably comes from the various international treaties of which the US is a signatory.
[2] RMV Driver's Manual, page 38.

C. 90 § 10	OPERATING WITHOUT A LICENSE
	§10 (unlicensed operation). **Case Facts:** On January 20, 2006, the defendant, Kristian A. Chown, was stopped for speeding and then arrested for operating a motor vehicle without a license in violation of G.L. c. 90, § 10. During the subsequent inventory search of his motor vehicle, police recovered drugs, cash, and other items. As a result, the defendant was indicted for trafficking in cocaine, in violation of and possession of marijuana with intent to distribute. During the stop the defendant had handed the officer, Sgt. Tynan, a recently issued Canadian driver's license. However, the sergeant was familiar with the defendant. The defendant's family owned a restaurant in the town and the Sgt. Tynan had stopped the defendant in the past, who at the time had a Massachusetts driver's license. The defendant also had a Massachusetts driving history dating back to 1989. The status of the defendant's Massachusetts driver's license was expired. The sergeant placed him under arrest for operating without a license under the premise that he was a Massachusetts resident operating without a license. The SJC ruled that in order to show that Chown was a Massachusetts resident and not a Canadian resident one of the factors in c. 90 § 3 ½, wherein the legislature listed elements that establish that someone if a Massachusetts resident, must be met. The SJC also acknowledged that these elements typically cannot be determined in the field. See c. 90 § 3 ½ for more.
Attorney Hanrahan's comments on *Com. v. Chown*	There are a few important variations that you should be familiar with: 1. **What if the defendant did not produce a Canadian license but only claimed to have one?** In this case the defendant could have been arrested for violating c. 90 § 10 (arrest powers via 90 §21) because a non-resident is required to have their non-resident license in *some easily accessible place*. 2. **What if the defendant's Canadian License came back suspended, revoked or expired?** In this case the defendant would have been operating without a license via c. 90 § 10 and could have been arrested. 3. **What is the defendant's Massachusetts license/right to operate was not expired but suspended or revoked?** In this case the defendant could have been arrested (via c. 90 § 23) even though he had a valid Canadian license because his right to operate had been suspended/revoked for some action, or inaction, on his part. The Canadian license would not trump his lack of right to operate in Massachusetts because that right would have been taken away.
You are a MA resident for licensing purposes when: **c. 90 § 3½**	Any person claiming to be a nonresident for purposes of section 3, shall be deemed to be a resident of the commonwealth during any period in which such person (note below are <u>summarized</u> see Registration section for detailed list): 1. claimed a **MA real estate tax exemption** (c. 59 § 5 and . 59 § 5C); 2. filed a Massachusetts **resident income tax** return pursuant to chapter 62; 3. obtained a **rental deduction** (c. 62 § 3); 4. declared in a home **mortgage settlement** document that the mortgaged property located in the commonwealth would be occupied as his **principal residence**; 5. obtained **homeowner's liability insurance** coverage on property that was declared to be occupied as a **principal residence**; 6. claimed **MA residency for employment** with a governmental entity; 7. paid **in-state tuition** rates to attend a state-sponsored college, community college or university; 8. applied for and received **public assistance** from the commonwealth for himself or a dependent; 9. has a child or dependent of whom he has custody who is **enrolled in a public school** in a city or

C. 90 § 10	OPERATING WITHOUT A LICENSE
	town in the commonwealth, unless the cost of such education is paid for by him, such child or dependent, or by another education jurisdiction; 10. is **registered to vote** in the commonwealth; 11. obtained any benefit, exemption, deduction, entitlement, license, permit or privilege by claiming principal residence in the commonwealth; or 12. is a resident under any other written criteria under which the commissioner of revenue may determine residency in the commonwealth.
	LICENSE REQUIREMENTS FOR OTHER VEHICLE TYPES
Moped operation unlicensed is a CMVI unless JV operator **c. 90 § 1B**	The operation of a motorized bicycle is regulated by chapter 90 § 1B. Chapter 90 § 1B states that "a motorized bicycle shall not be operated on any way by any person not possessing a valid driver's license or learner's permit." The scheduled assessment for violations of chapter 90 § 1B indicates that a violation of 90 § 1B is a civil fine unless committed by a juvenile then it would be handled under delinquency proceedings (a CMVI is "an automobile law violation for which the maximum penalty does not provide for imprisonment" except for... violations "committed by a juvenile under the age of seventeen who does not hold a valid operator's license." See G.L. c. 90C § 1). 90 § 10 requires that the operator a "motor vehicle". Under chapter 90 § 1 motorized bicycles are specifically exempt under the definition of a "motor vehicle."
Scooter operation **c. 90 § 1E**	Chapter 90 § 1E regulates the operation of motor scooters. Like mopeds (discussed above) a scooter can be operated with either a license or a learner's permit. The scheduled assessment lists a violation of c. 90 § 1E as a civil fine. However, unlicensed juvenile civil motor vehicle violations are handled as delinquency matters under G.L. c.90C, §1.

FAQs about International Driving Permits, International Driver Licenses & Driving Privileges for Foreign Licensed Drivers

The Massachusetts Registry of Motor Vehicles (RMV)

Appendix C

Massachusetts will honor valid Driver's Licenses and Registrations issued by the following countries*

Albania
Algeria
Argentina
Australia
Austria
The Bahamas
Bangladesh
Barbados
Belgium
Belize
Benin
Botswana
Brazil
Bulgaria
Cambodia
Canada
Central African Republic
Chile
Colombia
Congo
Dem. Rep of Congo
Costa Rica
Cote d'Ivoire
Cuba
Cyprus
Czech Rep.
Denmark
Dominican Republic
Ecuador
Egypt
El Salvador
Fiji
Finland
France (inc. Overseas Territories)
The Gambia
Georgia (Republic of)
Germany (by reciprocity)
Ghana
Greece
Grenada
Guatemala
Guyana
Haiti
Honduras
Hong Kong (China is not a party to this treaty but has made it applicable to Hong Kong and Macao)
Hungary
Iceland
India
Ireland
Israel
Italy
Jamaica
Japan
Jordan
Korea
Kyrgyz Rep.
Laos
Lebanon
Lesotho
Luxembourg
Macao (same as Hong Kong)
Madagascar
Malawi
Malaysia
Mali
Malta
Mauritius
Mexico
Monaco
Morocco
Namibia
Netherlands & Antilles and Aruba
New Zealand
Nicaragua
Niger
Norway
Panama
Papua New Guinea
Paraguay
Peru
Phillippines
Poland
Portugal (inc. Portuguese Territories)
Romania
Russian Fed.
Rwanda
St. Lucia
St. Vincent & Grenadines
San Marino
Senegal
Seychelles
Sierra Leone
Singapore
Slovak Rep.
South Africa (incl. Namibia)
Spain (incl. African localities and provinces)
Sri Lanka
Suriname
Swaziland
Sweden
Switzerland (by reciprocity)
Syrian Arab Republic
Taiwan
Tanzania
Thailand
Togo
Trinidad & Tobago
Tunisia
Turkey
Uganda
United Kingdom (Great Britain & Northern Ireland) & Cayman Islands, Gibraltar, Baliwick of Guernsey, Isle of Man, & States of Jersey
Uruguay
Vatican City
Venezuela
Vietnam Rep.
Western Samoa
Zambia
Zimbabwe

(Former Republics of the USSR)
Armenia
Azerbaijan
Belarus
Kazakstan
Moldova
Tajikistan
Turkmenistan
Ukraine
Uzbekistan
Latvia
Lithuania
Estonia

* From a List of Treaties and other International Agreements of the United States in Force on January 1, 2003. The RMV reserves the right to amend this list at any time based on additional information received from the U.S. Department of State or other sources.

4

Foreign National Drivers Roadside Documents

⊘International Drivers License
(Novelty Item – NEVER VALID AVAILABLE ONLINE TO ANYONE) Many versions available. This is a Fake Drivers License. ⊘

Foreign National Drivers License issued by country of origin. (May not be written in English)

International Driving Permit (IDP) Translates Foreign National Driver License (Issued in Foreign Country/Will have a foreign address)

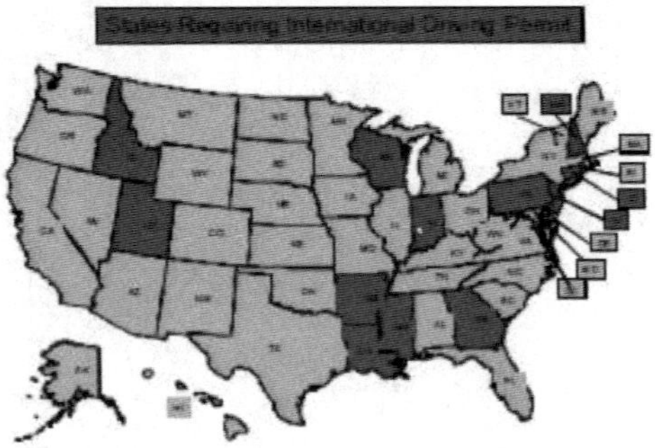

Permanent Resident Card permits an alien to reside and work in the USA. It has an expiration date, it must be renewed, but it does not indicate the alien's status has expired. Aliens with permanent residence must carry evidence of their status.

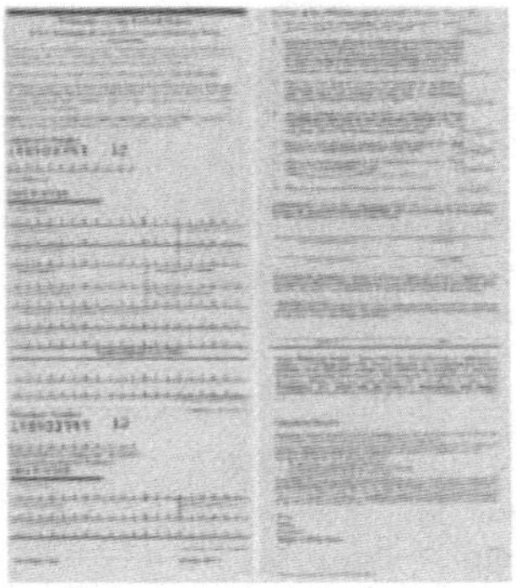

Form I-94W (green): Is issued to visitors who enter the U.S. under the Visa Waiver Program. The "W" stands for "Waiver".

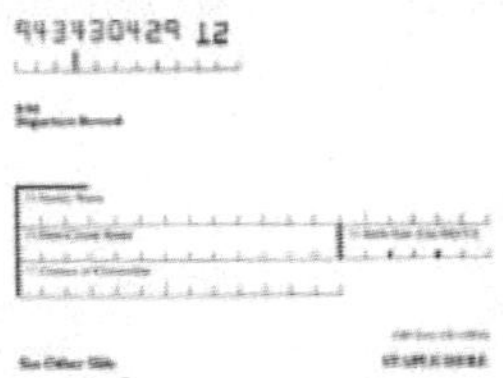

Form I-94 (white): It is issued to visitors who hold a valid U.S. visa, such as tourists, students, workers, etc.

Form I-94 Arrival/Departure Record The bottom portion is stapled to a page in the alien's passport. This document shows how long the bearer may remain in the U.S. and the terms of admission. The I-94 (NOT THE IMMIGRANT VISA), serves as evidence of legal status.

Foreign National Passport's primary purpose is to permit aliens to travel in the U.S. establishing their citizenship and to display any visas, entry stamps that may be necessary.

The Employment Authorization Document is issued to aliens who are permitted to work in the U.S. for a specific period of time.

Non Immigrant Visas are used for entry purposes and must be valid on the date of entry into the U.S. Non immigrants are admitted in the U.S. for a temporary period of time for a specific purpose, most often as tourists.

- **Not all inclusive of all documents that may be encountered** **September 2011**

C. 90 § 23	OPERATION AFTER SUSPENSION/REVOCATION
Elements	
1.	Operation of a motor vehicle
2.	While the defendant's license or right to operate in Massachusetts is suspended or revoked
3.	The defendant, or an agent (i.e. a household member or employer), had received notice from the RMV of the suspension/revocation.
Arrest Power, Penalties & Notes	
Power of Arrest	**Misdemeanor** – a person observed, by a police officer, operating a motor vehicle in public without a valid license may be arrested without a warrant pursuant to c. 90 § 21. Note: 90 § 21 authorizes an arrest "in public." However, the statute does not require public operation for a violation, thus a person violating this statute on private property should be summoned.
Penalty	**1st offense:** a fine of not less than $500 nor more than $1,000 or by imprisonment for not more than 10 days, or both. **Subsequent Offense:** and for any subsequent offence by imprisonment for not less than 60 days nor more than 1 year. **OUI or CDL Suspension/Revocation:** If the suspension was the result of an OUI conviction or involves a CDL violation the penalty carries a minimum mandatory sentence of **60 days.** However, this **only applies for Massachusetts OUI convictions**, not out of state convictions.[1]
Related Statutes, Case Law & Other Important Information	
RMV must send notice	Upon the suspension or revocation of a license or right to operate, the Registrar is required to send written notice to the driver's last address as appearing on Registry records, or to his last and usual residence. G.L. c. 90, § 22(d).
Defendant must have received notice	"Receipt" includes receipt by a household member, employer or other agent of the defendant; the Commonwealth is not required to prove actual personal knowledge on the defendant's part. The Registrar's proper mailing of a letter is prima facie evidence of receipt by the addressee.
Evasion of Notice	One who willfully evades notice may be deemed to have received constructive notice.[2] However, the fact that a certified letter was unclaimed, absent evidence of awareness and ability to claim it or evidence of wilful disregard of it, does not warrant conclusion that defendant received constructive notice of license revocation.[3]
Out of State Suspensions	Out-of-state suspensions apply in Massachusetts.[4]
Can you assume owner is operating?	Absent evidence to the contrary, a police officer has reasonable suspicion that a vehicle is being operated by the registered owner.[5]
Public way not an element	This offense does not require that the violation occur on a public way.[6]

[1] Commonwealth v. Lee, (2013)
[2] *Commonwealth v. Hampton,* 26 Mass. App. Ct. 938, 525 N.E.2d 1341 (1988).
[3] see *Police Commissioner of Boston v. Robinson*, 47 Mass. App. Ct. 767, 774, 716 N.E.2d 652, 658 (1999).
[4] G.L. c. 90 § 30B, also see 90 § 22(c)
[5] *Commonwealth v. Deramo*, 436 Mass. 40 (2002).
[6] *Commonwealth v. Murphy*, 409 Mass. 665, 568 N.E.2d 1143 (1991).

C. 90 § 23	OPERATION AFTER SUSPENSION/REVOCATION
A license cannot be Restricted and Revoked	In the 2013 case of ***Commonwealth v. Pettit***, the Appeals Court ruled that a person's license cannot be both revoked and restricted. The Court overturned the defendant's conviction for operating a vehicle without an ignition interlock device because the RMV revoked his license when he removed the device from his car.
Hardship license	An operator who is issued a hardship license for OUI and who operates beyond his permitted timeframe is not considered operating after suspension/revocation under c. 90 § 23.[1] The proper charge would be operating without a license under c. 90 § 10.
RMV Legal Counsel	Law enforcement can contact the RMV Legal Counsel for Suspensions at (857) 368-8207 (Law Enforcement Only).
Confiscate plate	Although not specifically delineated in the statute or a CMR, the RMV requests that a vehicle owner with a suspended or revoked license have his/her registration plates confiscated if discovered operating his/her own vehicle.

C. 90 § 12	PERMITTING/HIRING IMPROPER PERSON	
Law/Rule	**Violation/Offense**	**Penalty**
EMPLOYING IMPROPER PERSON	The knowingly employs for hire as a motor vehicle operator any person not properly licensed. **Registration Suspension**: The registrar may suspend for not more than **1 year** the motor vehicle registration of a vehicle used in the commission of a violation of this section (permitting/employing an improper person) or the license or right to operate of the person who commits a violation of this section, or both.	**1st Off: $1,000** Plus $5 Public Safety Surcharge. **Subsequent Off: Criminal** Plus $5 Public Safety Surcharge.
PERMITTING IMPROPER PERSON	The defendant knowingly permits a motor vehicle owned by him or under his control to be operated by a person who is unlicensed or whose license has been suspended or revoked. **Registration Suspension**: The registrar may suspend for not more than **1 year** the motor vehicle registration of a vehicle used in the commission of a violation of this section (permitting/employing an improper person) or the license or right to operate of the person who commits a violation of this section, or both.	**Criminal**
Leasing vehicle to improper person **c. 90 § 32C**	G.L. c. 90 § 32 states in part "no lessor shall lease any motor vehicle or trailer until the lessee shows that he or his authorized operator is the holder of a duly issued license to operate the type of motor vehicle or trailer which is being leased." This statute also prohibits the leasing of a vehicle to an intoxicated person.	**Criminal**
Power of Arrest	**Misdemeanor** – there is no statutory authority granting warrantless powers of arrest for this offense. However, if the offense is committed in public, in the officer's presence, and is creating a **breach of the peace** an arrest would be lawful.	

[1] *Commonwealth v. Murphy*, 68 Mass. App. Ct. 152 (2007).

C. 90 § 22I IMMEDIATE THREAT: MEDICAL

If a **health care provider** acting in his professional capacity or **law enforcement officer:**

a. has reasonable cause to believe that an operator is **not physically or medically capable of safely operating a motor vehicle,** or

b. has a cognitive or functional impairment that will affect that person's ability to safely operate a motor vehicle,

The health care provider or officer may make a report to the registrar, requesting medical evaluation of the operator's ability to safely operate a motor vehicle.

Important Information

Age	The report shall not be made solely on the basis of age.
Report Contents	The report shall state the health care provider's or officer's good faith belief that the operator cannot safely operate a motor vehicle and shall disclose the medical information underlying his good faith belief in his report to the registrar. The good faith belief shall be based upon personal observation, physical evidence, or, in the case of a law enforcement officer, an investigation which shall be described in the report. A report regarding an operator's ability to safely operate a motor vehicle shall not be based solely on the diagnosis of a medical condition or cognitive or functional impairment, but shall be based on observations or evidence of the actual affect of that condition or impairment on the operator's ability to safely operate a motor vehicle.
Health Care Provider	For the purposes of this section, **"health care provider"** shall mean a registered nurse, licensed practical nurse, physician, physician assistant, psychologist, occupational therapist, physical therapist, optometrist, ophthalmologist, osteopath or podiatrist who is a licensed health care provider under chapter 112.
Immunity from Civil Liability	A health care provider or law enforcement officer who reports, in good faith, pursuant to this section shall be immune from civil liability that might otherwise result from making the report. A health care provider or law enforcement officer who does not report shall be immune from civil liability that might otherwise result from not making the report.
RMV 30 Days to Evaluate	Not later than 30 days after receipt of the report, the registrar shall conduct a review to determine the operator's capacity for continued licensure to operate a motor vehicle. The commissioner of public health shall, in consultation with the registrar and with medical experts on cognitive or functional impairments, and with the medical advisory board established in section 8C, promulgate regulations designating the cognitive or functional impairments that are likely to affect a person's ability to safely operate a motor vehicle. The registrar shall consider information contained in a report under subsection (b) in determining whether to issue or suspend a license to operate a motor vehicle.
Reports are Confidential Records	A report to the registry pursuant to this section shall be confidential and shall be used by the registrar only to determine a person's qualifications to operate a motor vehicle. All reports made and all medical records reviewed and maintained by the registry under this section shall be confidential, or upon written request of the respondent to examine any medical records or reports made about the respondent under this section. A report made under this section shall not be a public record as defined in chapter 4 §7.
RMV Medical Affairs	The RMV Medical Affairs division can be reached at (857) 368-8020

C. 90 § 22	IMMEDIATE THREAT: DRIVING BEHAVIOR
The registrar may suspend or revoke **without a hearing** any certificate of registration or any license whenever the holder thereof has committed a violation of the motor vehicle laws of a nature which would give the registrar reason to believe that continuing operation by such holder is and will be so seriously improper as to constitute an immediate threat to the public safety.	
IMPORTANT INFORMATION	
14 Day Notice	**At least 14 days prior** to any such suspension or revocation, the registrar shall notify the operator in writing of his intention to suspend or revoke his license as of a specified date. The notice shall specify the reasons for the intended suspension or revocation and shall inform the operator of his right to request in writing a hearing within 14 days after the date of such notice on the question of whether there is just cause for such suspension or revocation.
Waiver of Right	Failure on the part of the operator to request a hearing as aforesaid shall constitute a waiver of his right to a hearing and the registrar may thereafter suspend or revoke the license or certificate on the date originally specified.
Subsequent Hearing	The operator shall be entitled to a hearing within 30 days of the suspension or revocation
After a Hearing	The registrar may, after due hearing, suspend or revoke any certificate of registration or any license, when he has reason to believe the holder thereof **is an incompetent person to operate motor vehicles**, or **is operating a motor vehicle improperly**. The registrar may also, after due hearing, suspend or revoke any certificate of registration.
30 Day max unless Physical or Mental Impairment	No suspension under this subsection shall be for a period in excess of 30 days unless the registrar finds that the operator is physically or mentally incapable of operating a motor vehicle.
Appeal	The motorist may appeal to the Board of Appeals on Motor Vehicle Liability Bonds.
RECIPROCITY	If the registrar receives official notice that a resident of Massachusetts or any person licensed to operate a motor vehicle in Massachusetts has been convicted in another state, country or jurisdiction of a motor vehicle violation, the registrar shall give the same effect to said conviction for the purposes of suspension, revocation, limitation or reinstatement of the right to operate a motor vehicle, as if said violation had occurred in the commonwealth. **Note:** if the suspension in Massachusetts would been longer than in the foreign state than the longer suspension will prevail. However, if the suspension in Massachusetts would have been less than the foreign state the longer Massachusetts suspension will still be imposed.

C. 90 § 22A	HABITUAL TRAFFIC OFFENDER; REVOCATION OF LICENSE
	A person shall be deemed an **habitual traffic offender** when the person has accumulated the following convictions within a 5 year period:
3 or more convictions, singularly or in combination, of these offenses	• OUI; • Operating a motor vehicle recklessly or negligently • Making a false statement in an application for a learner's permit or motor vehicle operator's license or in an application for registration of a motor vehicle • Leaving the scene of an MVA • Operating a motor vehicle after suspension or revocation; • Operating a motor vehicle without a license; • Using a motor vehicle during the commission of a felony
	or
Any 12 or more offenses which carry a 30 day suspension	**12 or more convictions** of offenses which are required by any provision of law to be reported to the registrar and for which the registrar is authorized or required to suspend or revoke the person's license or right to operate motor vehicles for a period of 30 days or more, including convictions of the offenses listed above.
	Important Information
6 Hour Period Exception	When a person who has **no prior record** of an automobile law violation, is convicted of more than one of the violations referred to in this section, if such offenses all occurred within a 6 hour period, such convictions shall for the purposes of this section be treated as a **single conviction**.
RMV hearing	When the records of the registrar on any person contain reports of such convictions as will constitute such person an habitual traffic offender, the registrar shall hold a hearing within six months from such third conviction, and shall give notice to such person that such hearing will be held to show cause why such person should not be designated as an habitual traffic offender. Such notice shall be sent not less than twenty-one days prior to the date for such hearing, shall contain a list of the person's convictions, and shall otherwise be in such form as the registrar shall prescribe.
Penalty	A person deemed a habitual traffic offender shall lose his/her license for a period of 4 years.

ADDITIONAL REQUIREMENTS OF LICENSE HOLDERS

Law/Rule	Violation/Offense	Penalty
License Must Be Accessible 90 § 11	Every person operating a motor vehicle shall have his **license** to operate, upon his person or in the vehicle, in some easily accessible place. **Receipt in Lieu of License:** If the RMV is unable to issue promptly the license applied for, they may issue a receipt for the fee paid, and said receipt shall be carried in lieu of the certificate or license as the case may be, and for a period of 60 days from the date of its issue said receipt shall have the same force and effect given to the certificate or license by this chapter. **Note:** see c. 90 § 10 (operating without a license), those operating on a non-Massachusetts license are required to carry their non-Massachusetts license. Failure to do so may violate c. 90 § 10 which is arrestable via 90 § 21.	**1ST OFF: $35** Plus $5 Public Safety Surcharge. **2ND OFF: $75** Plus $5 Public Safety Surcharge. **3RD OFF: $150** Plus $5 Public Safety Surcharge.

ADDITIONAL REQUIREMENTS OF LICENSE HOLDERS

REPORTING CHANGES OF NAME AND ADDRESS 90 § 26A	A Massachusetts licensed operator, or holder of a Massachusetts learner's permit, shall: • report a change of name, • report a change of residential or mailing address In writing to RMV **within 30 days** after the date on which any such change was made. **RMV action:** RMV may revoke or suspend the license or certificate of registration or learner's permit of a person violating this provision.	**1ST OFF: $35** Plus $5 Public Safety Surcharge. **2ND OFF: $75** Plus $5 Public Safety Surcharge. **3RD OFF: $150** Plus $5 Public Safety Surcharge.

C. 90 § 9F DISQUALIFICATION FROM OPERATING COMMERCIAL MOTOR VEHICLES

Any person, who holds a license to operate a motor vehicle, a license to operate a commercial motor vehicle or is unlicensed, is disqualified from operating a commercial motor vehicle and is prohibited from operating a commercial motor vehicle for a period of not less than 1 year if convicted of a first violation of:

a. Operating a commercial motor vehicle or a motor vehicle under the influence of alcohol or drugs;

b. Operating a commercial motor vehicle while the alcohol concentration in the person's blood or breath is 0.04 or more;

c. Leaving the scene of an accident involving a commercial motor vehicle or a motor vehicle driven by the person;

d. Refusing to submit to a chemical test or analysis of the persons breath or blood after operating a commercial motor vehicle or a motor vehicle; or

e. Using a commercial motor vehicle or a motor vehicle in the commission of a felony.

If any of the above violations occurred while transporting a hazardous material required to be placarded, the person shall be disqualified for a period of 3 years.

Any person shall be disqualified for life if convicted of 2 or more violations of any of the above offenses or for 2 or more refusals to submit to a chemical test or analysis of the persons breath or blood after operating a commercial motor vehicle or a motor vehicle, or any combination of those offenses, arising from 2 or more separate incidents.

C. 90 § 8	JUNIOR OPERATORS	
ELIGIBILITY	A junior operator's license may be issued to a minor under 18 years of age who has: • Held a valid Massachusetts learner's permit issued (or a similar law of another state) for a period of not less than 6months • Has maintained a driving record free of any surchargeable incidents • Has not had such permit suspended OUI related offense (including a BAC of .02% or higher) • Has not been convicted of violating any alcohol-related or drug-related law of the commonwealth or a similar alcohol-related or drug-related law of any other state. Note: for the purposes of this section, a CWOF or placed on file shall be deemed to be a conviction. • Attained the age of 16 and one-half years; • Successfully completed a driver education and training course approved by the registrar **And** • Presented a certified statement from a parent or guardian, (or designee 21 years of age or older if the applicant is an emancipated minor) that in addition to the requirements of the driver education and training course the applicant has completed not less than 40 hours of supervised driving, or 30 hours of supervised driving if the applicant has successfully completed a driver skills development program in a closed, off-road course. • Successfully completed such examination and driving test as the registrar may require; and • Submitted an application on a form furnished by the registrar, signed by both the applicant and a parent or guardian, along with the applicable fee.	
Law/Rule	**Violation/Offense**	**Penalty**
PASSENGER RESTRICTIONS FOR JUNIOR OPERATORS	**For the first 6 months no passengers under 18 years of age are permitted.** **Exceptions:** • An immediate family member of the operator, • Accompanied by another person, duly licensed by his state of residence, who is at least 21 years of age with at least 1 year of driving experience and who is occupying a seat beside the driver. • The operator is an "emancipated minor" and granted an exemption by the RMV. **RMV Action:** License suspension: 1st offense 60 days, 2nd 180 days, third or subsequent offense 1 year. Note: A junior operator whose license is suspended for a 2nd or subsequent violation of the 6 month passenger restriction shall not be eligible for license reinstatement until he also completes a program selected by the registrar that encourages attitudinal changes in young drivers . The suspension shall be imposed in addition to any other penalty, fine, suspension, revocation or requirement that may be imposed for such violation.	**1ST OFF: $35** Plus $5 Public Safety Surcharge. **2ND OFF: $75** Plus $5 Public Safety Surcharge. **3RD OFF: $150** Plus $5 Public Safety Surcharge.

C. 90 § 8	JUNIOR OPERATORS	
TIME RESTRICTION FOR JUNIOR OPERATORS	**Rule:** A junior operator may not operate a motor vehicle between the hours of **12:30 a.m. and 5:00 a.m.** unless accompanied by a parent or legal guardian. **Arrest powers** via c. 90 § 21 would be permissible if committed in the officer's presence. **RMV Action:** In addition to the penalty of operating without a license, the license of a junior operator deemed to be operating a motor vehicle without being duly licensed shall be suspended for 60 days for a first offense, for 180 days for a second offense and for 1 year for a third or subsequent offense; **Secondary enforcement:** between the hours of 12:30 a.m. and 1:00 a.m. and between 4:00 a.m. and 5:00 am (only when lawfully stopped for a violation of the motor vehicles laws or for some other offense). **Note:** The time restriction may be exempt for a firefighter or EMT in the performance of his/her duties.	**Criminal** Charges may be brought via C. 90 § 10 (Operating without a license).
ADDITIONAL PROVISIONS FOR JOL	The holder of a junior operator's license shall have the license in his possession at all times when operating a motor vehicle. No person holding a junior operator's license shall operate a vehicle requiring a commercial driver's license issued under c. 90F. **Parent Notification:** The RMV shall send notice of a suspension of a junior operator's license for a violation of c. 90 §8 to the junior operator, and to the junior operator's parent or guardian if the junior operator is not an emancipated minor.	
	Related Statutes, Case Law & Other Important Information	
MOTORCYCLE JUNIOR OPERATOR LICENSE	A minor under 18 years of age may be issued a motorcycle license or motorcycle endorsement if the minor: (i) Meets the requirements for a junior operator's license, and (ii) Successfully completes a motorcycle basic rider course approved by the registrar and presents proof of such completion in such form as the registrar may require. Note: The same penalties and restrictions apply for a junior operator motorcycle license.	

C. 90 § 8B	LEARNER'S PERMITS
Eligibility	Applicant must be **at least 16** years of age to obtain a learner's permit. **Documents for proof of age:** a birth, baptismal or school certificate or such other satisfactory evidence of his age as **the registrar may require.**
Duration	A learner's permit is valid for 2 years from the date of issue or until the holder shall have received a license to operate, whichever first occurs.
Road Tests	Each holder of a learner's permit, may take not more than 6 driving tests within a period of 12 months.
Scope of Use	A learner's permit allows the holder to operate a motor vehicle when be accompanied by an operator. The accompanying operator must: • be duly licensed by his state of residence (i.e. can be licensed out-of-state), • be 21 years of age or over, • have at least one year of driving experience, • occupy a seat beside the driver.
Violation Responsibility	The accompanying operator is liable for any motor vehicle infraction committed by the person operating on a learner's permit (except for a registry examiner during a road test).
Time Restriction	Permit holder who is **under 18** cannot operate between the hours of **12 a.m. and 5 a.m.**, unless: • accompanied by a parent or legal guardian who holds a valid license and has at least 1 year of driving experience. or, • in the case of an emancipated minor, unless accompanied by a person who is 21 years of age or older who holds a valid license and has at least 1 year of driving experience, and who occupies the seat beside the driver.

Arrest Power, Penalties & Notes

Penalty	1st offense $35.00. 2nd offense $75. 3rd offense $150
Attorney Hanrahan's Comment	According to the Trial Court's latest CMVI Assessment Schedule (2010) the Learner Permit violations are listed as **civil offenses** (non-criminal). However, most violations, such as driving without a duly licensed adult, would seemingly be a violation of 90 §10 (operating without a license). It is recommended that you consult with your local DA's office prior to taking criminal action as various districts may handle these types of offenses differently.

Related Statutes, Case Law & Other Important Information

RMV Action for Learner's Permit violation	1st offense: learner's permit suspended for 60 days, 2nd offense 180 days, 3rd or subsequent offense 1 year. The holder shall also required to complete a program selected by the registrar that encourages attitudinal changes in young drivers who have committed a violation of the motor vehicle laws.

C. 90 § 8B	LEARNER'S PERMITS
Motorized bicycle or motorized scooter:	Permit holders may operate a motorized bicycle and scooters with a learner's permit and no accompanying operator is required.
Motorcycle Learner's Permit	A holder of a motorcycle learner's permit cannot have any passengers and cannot operate after sunset or before sunrise.
Suspension Revocation	A person whose license or right to operate has been suspended or revoked is ineligible for a learner's permit.
Out of State Permit Holders	540 CMR 2.06 states in part "Learner's Permits and Licenses - Generally. (a) Unless prohibited by the state of issuance, an out-of-state operator with a learner's permit may operate in Massachusetts. Likewise, a Massachusetts learner's permit holder may operate in another state, unless otherwise prohibited."

ID CARDS	
Identification Cards For Persons Not Possessing Motor Vehicle Licenses 90 § 8E	Any person **14 years of age or older** who **does not have a valid license to operate motor vehicles** may make application to the RMV and be issued an identification card by the registrar and attested by the registrar as to true name, correct age, photograph and other identifying data as the registrar may require. Every application for an identification card shall be signed and verified by the applicant and shall contain such bona fide documentary evidence of the age and identity of such applicant as the registrar may require.
Identification change of address notification 90 § 8J	Whenever a person after applying for and receiving an identification card acquires an address different from the address shown on the identification card issued to him, he shall, within **30 days** thereafter, notify the registrar in writing of his old and new address

VIN ISSUES & OFFENSES

Law/ Rule	Violation/Offense	Penalty
VIN DISPLAY 90 § 7R	All motor vehicles, all trailer and semi-trailers manufactured for the model year **1978** and thereafter which are registered in Massachusetts, shall be equipped with and display a vehicle identification number VIN.	**1ST OFF: $35 +5** **2ND OFF: $75 +5** **3RD OFF: $150 +5**
REMOVING, ALTERING, DEFACING VEHICLE NUMBERS c. 266 § 139(a).	The defendant intentionally and maliciously removes, defaces, alters, changes, destroys, obliterates or mutilates or causes to be removed or destroyed or in any way defaced, altered, changed, obliterated or mutilated, the identifying number or numbers of a motor vehicle or trailer. **Arrest Powers**: **Felony** – a police officer may effect an arrest for this offense committed in his/her presence or for an offense in the past, on probable cause. **Note**: The possession of any motor vehicle or trailer by a person who knows, should know, or has reason to know that the identifying number or numbers of such vehicle has been removed, defaced, altered, changed, destroyed, obliterated or mutilated shall be a prima facie evidence of a violation of this paragraph.	A fine of not more than $1,000 or by imprisonment in the **state prison (F)** for not more than **3 years**, or both.
SELLING PARTS WITH ALTERED or MISSING NUMBERS c. 266 § 139(b)	The defendant sells, transfers, distributes, dispenses or otherwise disposes of or attempts to sell, transfer, distribute, dispense or otherwise dispose of any motor vehicle or trailer or motor vehicle part knowing or having reason to believe that the identifying number or numbers to said motor vehicle, trailer, or vehicle part have been so removed, defaced, altered, changed, destroyed, obliterated, or mutilated, unless authorized by law to do so. **Arrest Powers**: **Felony** – a police officer may effect an arrest for this offense committed in his/her presence or for an offense in the past, on probable cause.	A fine of not more than $1,000 or by imprisonment in the **state prison (F)** for not more than **3 years**, or both.
BUYING OR POSSESSING MOTOR VEHICLES OR PARTS WITH MISSING or ALTERED NUMBERS c. 266 § 139(c)	The defendant buys, receives, possesses, or obtains control of a motor vehicle, trailer, or motor vehicle part knowing or having reason to believe that an identifying number to said vehicle, trailer, or vehicle part has been removed, obliterated, tampered with, or altered, unless authorized by law to do so. **Arrest Powers**: **Misdemeanor** – statutory authority permits a police to effect an arrest for this offense committed in his/her presence, or for an offense in the past on probable cause.	A fine of not more than $500 or by imprisonment in a HOC for not more than 2 years, or both.

Related Statutes, Case Law & Other Important Information

Definition	The phrase "**identifying number or numbers**", as used in this section, shall mean the manufacturer's number or numbers identifying the motor vehicle, trailer or motor vehicle part as required to be contained in an application for registration by section two of c. ninety, including the identifying number or numbers as restored or substituted under authority of section thirty-two A of said c. ninety or similar law of another state
RMV Action for the above c. 266 § 139 offenses	The RMV shall revoke immediately the license or the right to operate motor vehicles of the person convicted or adjudged for any of the above offenses in § 139. No appeal, motion for new trial or exceptions shall operate to stay the revocation of such license or right to operate. The registrar of motor vehicles after having revoked the license or right to operate of any such person so convicted or adjudged shall issue a new license or reinstate such right to operate, if the prosecution of such person is finally terminated in his favor; otherwise, no new license shall be issued nor shall such right to operate be reinstated until **60 days** after the date of revocation following his original conviction or adjudication if for a first offense, or until **one year** after the date of revocation following any subsequent conviction or adjudication.

SEAT BELTS & OCCUPANT PROTECTION

Law/ Rule	Violation/Offense	Penalty
Child Safety Seat (under 8) **90 § 7AA**	A passenger in a motor vehicle on any way who is **under the age of 8** shall be fastened and secured by a child passenger restraint, **unless such passenger measures more than 57 inches in height** (4'9"). The child passenger restraint shall be properly fastened and secured according to the manufacturer's instructions.	**$25** Plus $5 Public Safety Surcharge.
Child Seat Belt Law (under 13) **90 § 7AA**	A passenger in a motor vehicle on any way that is under the age of 13 (and not required to be in a child safety seat) shall wear a safety belt which is properly adjusted and fastened according to the manufacturer's instructions.	**$25** Plus $5 Public Safety Surcharge.
Exceptions to Child Safety Seat and Seat Belt	The provisions of c. 90 § 7AA shall not apply to any such child who is: a. riding as a passenger in a school bus; b. riding as a passenger in a motor vehicle made before July 1st, 1966, that is not equipped with safety belts; c. physically unable to use either a conventional child passenger restraint or a child restraint specifically designed for children with special needs (must be duly certified in writing by a physician).	
Additional Provisions of 90 § 7AA	**Penalty Note**: The fine goes to the operator unless the operator is a taxi cab driver. Cab drivers are not responsible for this violation. **Not a moving violation:** A violation of this section shall not be deemed to be a conviction of a moving violation of the motor vehicle laws for the purpose of determining surcharges on motor vehicle premiums. **Primary Enforcement note**: Unlike an adult seat belt violation, a police officer can stop a motor vehicle solely for violating this statute.	
Adult Seat Belt Requirements (age 13 plus) **c. 90 § 13A**	No person shall operate a private passenger motor vehicle or ride in a private passenger motor vehicle, a vanpool vehicle or truck under 18,000 lbs. on any way unless such person is wearing a safety belt which is properly adjusted and fastened. **Exceptions:** • Any person riding in a motor vehicle manufactured **before July 1st, 1966** that is not equipped with belts • The side facing seat on which the factory did not install a seat belt in any car owned for the purpose of antique collection. • Any person who is physically unable to use safety belts (condition must be certified by a physician) • Any rural carrier of the United States Postal Service operating a motor vehicle while in the performance of his duties (however, the mail carrier shall be subject to department regulations regarding the use of safety belts or occupant crash protection devices) • Anyone involved in the <u>operation</u> of **taxis**, **liveries**, **tractors**, **trucks with gross weight of 18,000 or over**, **buses**, and **passengers of authorized emergency vehicles**. **Note**: although this statute exempts bus driver's c. 90 § 7B requires that school bus drivers wear seat belts.	**$25** Plus $5 Public Safety Surcharge. **If violator is 16 years or older the fine goes to the violator (unless taxi driver).** **Operator received additional fine for every child under 16.**

SEAT BELTS & OCCUPANT PROTECTION

Additional Provisions of c. 90 § 13A	**Secondary enforcement only:** The provisions of this section shall be enforced by law enforcement agencies only when an operator of a motor vehicle has been stopped for a violation of the motor vehicle laws or some other offense. **No Insurance Surcharge:** A violation of this section shall not be considered a conviction of a moving violation of the motor vehicle laws for the purpose of determining surcharges on motor vehicle premiums.	
Children In Bed Of Pick-Up Truck 90 § 7	No person shall operate (or permit to be operated) a motor vehicle, commonly known as a pick-up truck, with a child under the age of 12 years in the body of the truck • for a distance more than 5 miles, or • in excess of 5 mph, **Exception:** permitted if the truck is part of an official parade, or has affixed to it a legal "Owner Repair" or "Farm" license plate or a pick-up truck engaged in farming activities.	**1ST OFF: $35** Plus $5 Public Safety Surcharge. **2ND OFF: $75** Plus $5 Public Safety Surcharge. **3RD OFF: $150** Plus $5 Public Safety Surcharge.
Riding on The Exterior of the Vehicle 90 § 13	No person shall hang onto the outside of, or the rear-end of any vehicle, no operator shall knowingly permit someone to hang on the outside of his/her vehicle. **Exceptions:** a firefighter, garbage collector, or employees of public utility companies, acting pursuant to and during the course of their duties.	**1ST OFF: $35** **2ND OFF: $75** Plus $5 Public Safety Surcharge. **3RD OFF: $150** Plus $5 Public Safety Surcharge.
Being Pulled By A Motor Vehicle 90 § 13	No person on a pedacycle, motorcycle, roller skates, sled, or any similar device, shall hold fast or attach the device to any moving vehicle, (and no operator of a motor vehicle shall knowingly permit this), while the vehicle being operated on a "high way."	**1ST OFF: $35** Plus $5 Public Safety Surcharge. **2ND OFF: $75** Plus $5 Public Safety Surcharge. **3RD OFF: $150** Plus $5 Public Safety Surcharge.
Occupying a Trailer 90 § 13	No person or persons, except firefighters acting pursuant to their official duties, shall occupy a trailer or semi-trailer while such trailer or semi-trailer is being towed, pushed or drawn or is otherwise in motion upon any way.	**1ST OFF: $35** plus $5 **2ND OFF: $75** plus $5 **3RD OFF: $150** plus $5

Related Statutes, Case Law & Other Important Information

Child Passenger restraint **90 § 1**	"Child Passenger restraint", a specifically designed seating system which meets the United States Department of Transportation Federal Motor Vehicle Safety Standards, as established in 49 C.F.R. 571.213, which is either permanently affixed to a motor vehicle or is affixed to such vehicle by a safety belt or a universal attachment system.
Probable Cause	In the 2011 case of ***Com. v. Washington***, the SJC ruled that the standard to issue a seatbelt violation is **probable cause** that the defendant was not wearing his/her seatbelt and **observing an occupant without a seatbelt shortly after the vehicle has come to a stop** (i.e. when the officer approaches the vehicle) absent evidence to the contrary, **is probable cause** that the defendant was not wearing his/her seatbelt.
Police Exemption	Although not specifically exempt by statute, Attorney General Opinion 94/95-1 Police Officers are exempt from wearing seatbelts *when operating an emergency vehicle*. However, most agencies regulate this by way of policy.

PEDESTRIANS & CROSSWALKS		
Law/ Rule	**Violation/Offense**	**Penalty**
Approach of Pedestrian **90 § 14**	Upon **approaching a pedestrian** who is upon the traveled part of any way and not upon a sidewalk, every person operating a motor vehicle shall slow down.	**1ST OFF: $35** plus $5 **2ND OFF: $75** plus $5 **3RD OFF: $150** plus $5
Pedestrian in Crosswalk **89 § 11**	When traffic control signals are not in place or not in operation the driver of a vehicle shall yield the right of way, slowing down or stopping if need be so to yield, to a pedestrian crossing the roadway within a crosswalk marked in accordance with standards established by the department of highways: • if the **pedestrian is on that half of the traveled part of the way on which the vehicle is traveling**, or • if the pedestrian approaches from the **opposite half** of the traveled part of the way to **within 10 feet** of that half of the traveled part of the way on which said vehicle is traveling.	**$200** Plus $5 Public Safety Surcharge.
Passing a Vehicle Stopped at a Crosswalk **89 § 11**	No driver of a vehicle shall pass any other vehicle which has stopped at a marked crosswalk to permit a pedestrian to cross, nor shall any such operator enter a marked crosswalk while a pedestrian is crossing or until there is a sufficient space beyond the crosswalk to accommodate the vehicle he is operating, notwithstanding that a traffic control signal may indicate that vehicles may proceed.	**$200** Plus $5 Public Safety Surcharge.
Blind Pedestrian Crossing **90 § 14A**	Whenever a totally or partially blind pedestrian, **guided by a guide dog or carrying in a raised or extended position a cane or walking stick** which is white in color or white tipped with red, crosses or attempts to cross a way, the driver of every vehicle approaching the place where such pedestrian is **crossing or attempting to cross shall bring his vehicle to a full stop**, and before proceeding shall take such precautions as may be necessary to avoid injuring such pedestrian. **Control animal near Guide Dog:** A person who owns an animal shall restrain and control such animal on a leash when in proximity to a guide dog that is on a public or private way.	**$500** Plus $5 Public Safety Surcharge.
Pedestrian Injury Investigation **89 § 11**	Whenever a pedestrian is injured by a motor vehicle in a marked crosswalk, the department of state police or the municipal police department with jurisdiction of the street, in consultation with department of state police if deemed appropriate, shall conduct an investigation into the cause of the injury and any violation of this section or other law or ordinance and shall issue the appropriate civil or criminal citation or file an application for the appropriate criminal complaint, if any. This section shall not limit the ability of a district attorney or the attorney general to seek an indictment in connection with the operation of a motor vehicle which causes injury or death and which violates this section.	

MOTORCYCLE LAWS

Law/Rule	Violation/Offense	Penalty
Motorcycle Equipment Requirements **90 § 13**	**Permanent Fixed Seat Only** Whoever operates a motorcycle on the ways of the commonwealth shall ride only upon the permanent and regular seat attached to the motorcycle. **Passengers only when Motorcycle is Properly Equipped** A motorcycle operator, operating on the ways of the Commonwealth, shall not carry any other person, nor allow any other person to ride, on such motorcycle unless: • it is designed to carry more than one person, (in which case a passenger may ride upon the permanent and regular seat if the seat is designed for two persons, or upon another seat which is intended for a passenger and is firmly attached to the motorcycle to the rear of the operator if proper foot rests are provided for the passenger's use), or • upon a seat which is intended for a passenger and is firmly attached to the motorcycle in a side car.	**1ST OFF: $35** Plus $5 Public Safety Surcharge. **2ND OFF: $75** Plus $5 Public Safety Surcharge. **3RD OFF: $150** Plus $5 Public Safety Surcharge.
Motorcycle Passenger Restrictions **90 § 7**	• No person operating a motorcycle shall permit any person to ride as a passenger, unless such motorcycle is designed to carry more than one person; • No person operating a motorcycle shall permit a passenger to ride in front of the operator.	**1ST OFF: $35** plus $5 **2ND OFF: $75** plus $5 **3RD OFF: $150** plus $5
Motorcycles Passing And Riding In Tandem **89 § 4A**	The operators of motorcycles • shall not ride abreast of more than one other motorcycle, • shall ride single file when passing, • shall not pass any other motor vehicle within the same lane, except another motorcycle.	**$100** Plus $5 Public Safety Surcharge.
Headgear For Motorcycle **90 § 7**	Every person ○ operating a motorcycle, or ○ riding as a passenger on a motorcycle, or ○ in a sidecar attached to a motorcycle Shall wear protective head gear conforming with such minimum standards of construction and performance as the registrar may prescribe. No person operating a motorcycle **shall permit** any other person to ride as a passenger on such motorcycle or in a sidecar attached to such motorcycle unless such passenger is wearing such protective head gear. **Exception:** protective head gear not required if the motorcyclist is participating in a properly permitted public parade and is 18 years of age or older.	**1ST OFF: $35** Plus $5 Public Safety Surcharge. **2ND OFF: $75** Plus $5 Public Safety Surcharge. **3RD OFF: $150** Plus $5 Public Safety Surcharge.
Eye Protection for Motorcycle **90 § 7**	If a motorcycle is not equipped with a windshield or screen, the operator shall wear eye glasses, goggles or a protective face shield when operating such vehicle.	**1ST OFF: $35 +5** **2ND OFF: $75 +5** **3RD OFF: $150 +5**

MOTORCYCLE LAWS

MOTORCYCLE LAWS

Motorcycle Maximum Sound Levels 90 § 7U	**Public Way** No person shall operate a motorcycle intended for use on the highways of the commonwealth and registered under the provisions of 90 § 2 at any time or under any condition of grade, load, acceleration or deceleration in such a manner as to o exceed **82 decibels** when operated within a speed zone of **45 MPH or less**, or o exceed **86 decibels** when operated within a speed zone of **over 45 MPH** • measured at fifty feet using the prescribed highway vehicle sound level measurement procedure. **Off –Road (Recreation Vehicle)** No person shall operate a motorcycle intended for use off the highways of the commonwealth and registered under the provisions of 90B § 22 at any time that **exceeds 103 decibels** measured at twenty inches or one-half meter, using the prescribed stationary vehicle sound level measurement procedure. **Note:** For enforcement purposes a tolerance of plus two decibels shall be applied to all measured sound levels of in-use vehicles to provide for variances in equipment calibration, measurement site characteristics and measurement techniques.	**1ST OFF: $35** Plus $5 Public Safety Surcharge. **2ND OFF: $75** Plus $5 Public Safety Surcharge. **3RD OFF: $150** Plus $5 Public Safety Surcharge.

BICYCLE LAWS

SUMMARY: Bicyclists must now comply with all traffic laws and regulations (rules of the road type violations, not registration and inspection type violations). Police officers can now issue a civil citation to a bicyclist observed violating a traffic law or regulation. If the bicyclists refused to provide his/her name and address (or provides false info) the police officer can place him/her under arrest (this is the only scenario wherein a bicyclist can be arrested for his/her bicycle activities).

Although the civil motor vehicle citation can be used to fine the bicyclists the citation does not affect the person's insurance rates or his/her motor vehicle license status. The violations of the traffic laws/rules will result in a $20 fine and should be written under c. 85 § 11B (not the statute disobeyed, i.e. 89 § 9).

The following statute breakdowns include the specific provisions of the law:

Bicyclist Must Identify Self To Police **85 § 11E**	A police officer who observes a traffic law violation committed by a bicyclist may request the offender to state his true name and address. If the bicycle operator **refuses** to state his name and address or states a **false** name and address or a name and address which is not his name and address in ordinary use shall be punished by a fine of not less than $20 nor more than $50.
No other Arrests **85 § 11E**	No person shall be arrested without a warrant for any traffic law violation committed while operating a bicycle (other than refusing to identify self or falsely identifying self).
Police May Issue Civil Citation To Bicyclists **85 § 11E**	A police officer shall use the ticketing procedure described in chapter 90C to cite a bicyclist for a traffic law violation. **NOTE:** Bicyclists must comply with nearly all traffic laws. Failure to do so can result in a citation (nearly all fines are $20). See C. 85 § 11B for more.
Citations to Bicyclists Are Non-Surchargable **85 § 11E**	The citation shall not affect the status of the bicyclist's license to operate a motor vehicle nor shall it affect the bicyclist's status in the safe driver insurance plan. NOTE: When a citation is issued to a bicyclist, it shall be clearly indicated on the ticket that the violator is a bicyclist, and failure to do so shall be a defense to the violation.
Parental Responsibility **85 § 11E**	The officer may give the notice (citation) to the parent or guardian of the offender if offender is under 16 years of age.
Fines Collected by Municipality **85 § 11E**	All fines collected by a city or town pursuant to this section shall be used by the city or town for the development and implementation of bicycle safety programs.

BICYCLE LAWS

Bicycle Laws of the Road **85 § 11B**	**Bicycle Operators Subject to Traffic Laws and Regulations** Every person operating a bicycle upon a way shall be subject to the **traffic laws and regulations** of the commonwealth and the special regulations contained in Chapter 85 § 11B. **Attorney Hanrahan's Note:** This means that bicyclists must comply with the traffic laws and rules of the road or be subject to a citation. When writing a citation to bicyclist for a violation of a traffic law or regulation the fine amount is $20 and the rights of arrest do not apply (other than refusing to identify self or for providing false identification). If the operator commits any traffic movement violation issue them a $20 fine and cite under chapter 85 § 11B. **Exceptions:** **PASS ON RIGHT:** the bicycle operator may keep to the right when passing a motor vehicle which is moving in the travel lane of the way, **HAND SIGNALS:** the bicycle operator shall signal by either hand his intention to stop or turn; provided, however, that signals need not be made continuously and shall not be made when the use of both hands is necessary for the safe operation of the bicycle, and **SIDEWALKS:** bicycles may be ridden on sidewalks outside business districts when necessary in the interest of safety, unless otherwise directed by local ordinance. NOTE: A person operating a bicycle on the sidewalk shall yield the right of way to pedestrians and give an audible signal before overtaking and passing any pedestrian.
Right to Travel on Roadways 85 § 11B	Every person operating a bicycle upon a way shall have the right to use all public ways in the commonwealth except limited access or express state highways where signs specifically prohibiting bicycles have been posted.
Parental Responsibility 85 § 11B	The parent or guardian of any person under age eighteen shall not authorize or knowingly permit any such person to violate any of the provisions of this section. If the child is **under 16** the officer may issue the citation to the child's parent or guardian.
Impoundment 85 § 11B	A bicycle operated by a person under the age of 18 in violation of this section may be impounded by the police department, or in a town which has no police department, by the selectmen, for a period not to exceed 15 days.
Under 18 85 § 11B	A violation by a minor under the age of 18 shall not affect any civil right or liability nor shall such violation be considered a criminal offense.

Law/Rule	Violation/Offense	Penalty
Any Moving Violation	Any moving violation (stop signs, failure to yield, etc.) that an operator of a motor vehicle can be cited for, other than the specific exceptions noted above, a bicyclist can be cited for.	$20
Bicycle Travel within Lane 85 § 11B(1)	Bicyclists riding together shall not ride more than 2 abreast but, on a roadway with more than 1 lane in the direction of travel, bicyclists shall ride within a single lane. Bicyclist still have a duty to facilitate overtaking as required by c. 89 § 2.	$20
Bicycle Seat Requirements 85 § 11B(2)(i)	**OPERATOR:** The operator shall ride only upon or astride a permanent and regular seat attached to the bicycle. **PASSENGERS:** a passenger shall ride only upon or astride a permanent and regular seat attached to the bicycle or to a trailer towed by the bicycle.	$20

BICYCLE LAWS		
Bicycle Child Passengers 85 § 11B(2)(ii)	The operator shall not transport another person on a bicycle: • between the ages of 1 to 4 years, or • weighing 40 pounds or less Exceptions to this age/size restriction: • in a "baby seat", so-called, attached to the bicycle, in which such other person shall be able to sit upright; provided, however, that such seat is equipped with a harness to hold the passenger securely in the seat and that protection is provided against the feet or hands of such person hitting the spokes of the wheel of the bicycle; or • upon or astride a seat of a tandem bicycle equipped so that the other person can comfortably reach the handlebars and pedals. The operator shall not transport any person under the age of 1 year on a bicycle (even in a baby-seat or on a tandem bicycle as described above).	$20
Bicycle Helmet Requirements 85 § 11B(2)(iii):	Any person 16 years of age or younger **operating** a bicycle or being carried as a **passenger** on a bicycle on a public way, bicycle path or on any other public right-of-way shall wear a helmet. **Exceptions:** These requirements shall not apply to a passenger if the passenger is in an enclosed trailer or other device which adequately holds the passenger in place and protects the passenger's head from impact in an accident. **Helmet Specifications:** The helmet shall fit the person's head, shall be secured to the person's head by straps while the bicycle is being operated, and shall meet the standards for helmets established by the United States Consumer Product Safety Commission. NOTE: No penalty provided by law for a violation of this section.	NONE
Bicycle Audible Warning 85 § 11B(3)	The operator of a bicycle shall give an audible warning whenever necessary to insure safe operation of the bicycle. However, the use of a siren or whistle is prohibited.	$20
Bicycle Parking 85 § 11B(4)	The operator of a bicycle shall park his bicycle upon a way or a sidewalk in such a manner as not to obstruct vehicular or pedestrian traffic.	$20
Bicycle Towing 85 § 11B(5)	The operator shall not permit the bicycle to be drawn by any other moving vehicle. The operator shall not tow any other vehicle or person, except that bicycle trailers properly attached to the bicycle which allow for firm control and braking may be used.	$20
Bicycle Carrying Packages 85 § 11B(6)	The operator shall not carry any package, bundle or article. **Exception**: except in or on a basket, rack, trailer or other device designed for such purposes.	$20
No Hands 85 § 11B(6)	The operator shall keep at least one hand upon the handlebars at all times.	$20

BICYCLE LAWS		
Bicycle Brake Requirements 85 § 11B(7)	Every bicycle operated upon a way shall be equipped with a braking system to enable the operator to bring the bicycle traveling at a speed of 15 MPH to a smooth, safe stop within 30 feet on a dry, clean, hard, level surface. Note: Any federal product safety standards relating to bicycles which are more stringent than this requirement shall supersede this requirement.	$20
Bicycle Light Requirements 85 § 11B(8)	During the period from one-half hour after sunset to one-half hour before sunrise ▪ FRONT WHITE LIGHT: The operator shall display to the front of his bicycle a lamp emitting a white light visible from a distance of at least **500 feet**, and ▪ REAR RED LIGHT/REFLECTOR: To the rear of said bicycle either a lamp emitting a red light, or a red reflector visible for not less than **600 feet** when directly in front of lawful lower beams of headlamps on a motor vehicle. NOTES: A generator powered lamp which emits light only when the bicycle is moving shall meet the requirements of this clause. Any federal product safety standards relating to bicycles which are more stringent than this requirement shall supersede this requirement.	$20
Pedal Light Requirements 85 § 11B(9)	During the period from one-half hour after sunset to one-half hour before sunrise the operator shall display: • on each pedal of his bicycle a reflector, or • around each of his ankles reflective Material visible from the front and rear for a distance of **600 feet**, and reflectors or reflective material, either on said bicycle or on the person of the operator, **Side View:** The reflectors must be visible on each side for a distance of **600 feet**, when directly in front of lawful lower beams of headlamps of a motor vehicle.	$20
Bicycle Alterations 85 § 11B(10)	**Handlebars:** No bicycle shall be operated upon a way with handlebars so raised that the operator's hands are above his shoulders while gripping them. **Fork Alterations:** Any alteration to extend the fork of a bicycle from the original design and construction of the bicycle manufacturer is prohibited. Note: Any federal product safety standards relating to bicycles which are more stringent than this requirement shall supersede this requirement.	$20
Bicycle Accident Reporting 85 § 11B(11)	The operator of a bicycle shall report any accident involving either: • personal injury, or • property damage in excess of $100, To the police department in the city or town in which the accident occurred.	$20
Bicycle Racing 85 § 11B	Competitive bicycle races may be held on public ways, provided that such races are: ○ sponsored by or in cooperation with recognized bicycle organizations, and ○ the sponsoring organization shall have obtained the approval of the appropriate police department or departments. **Note:** Special regulations regarding the movement of bicycles during such races, or in training for races, including, but not limited to, permission to ride abreast, may be established by agreement between the police department and the sponsoring organization.	

SPECIALTY VEHICLES

MOPEDS & SCOOTERS		
Law/Rule	**Violation/Offense**	**Penalty**
Motorized Bicycle Definition 90 § 1	• A pedal bicycle which has a helper motor, or • A non-pedal bicycle which has a motor with a cylinder capacity not exceeding 50 cubic centimeters, an automatic transmission, and capable of a maximum speed of no more than 30 MPH.	
Moped Restrictions	A motorized bicycle (moped) shall **not** be operated upon any way: • by any person under 16 years of age, • at a speed in excess of 25 MPH. • by any person not possessing a valid driver's license or learner's permit Note: If person under 18 is operating a moped without a license/permit delinquency proceedings should be sought in lieu of a citation.	**1st Off: $25** Plus $5 Public Safety Surcharge. **2nd Off: $50** Plus $5 Public Safety Surcharge. **3rd Off: $100** Plus $5 Public Safety Surcharge.
Moped Rules of the Road	Every person operating a moped upon a way shall have the right to use all public ways in the Commonwealth except **limited access or express state highways where signs specifically prohibiting bicycles have been posted**, and **Shall be subject to the traffic laws and regulations** of the Commonwealth and the regulations contained in this section, **except** that: 1) the motorized bicycle operator **may keep to the right when passing** a motor vehicle which is moving in the travel lane of the way, and 2) the motorized bicycle operator **shall signal by either hand his intention to stop or turn**. Motorized bicycles **may be operated on bicycle lanes** adjacent to the various ways, but shall be **excluded from off-street recreational bicycle paths**.	**1st Off: $25** Plus $5 Public Safety Surcharge. **2nd Off: $50** Plus $5 Public Safety Surcharge. **3rd Off: $100** Plus $5 Public Safety Surcharge.
Moped Protective Headgear Required	Every person **operating** a motorized bicycle or **riding as a passenger** on a motorized bicycle shall wear protective headgear conforming with such minimum standards of construction and performance as the registrar may prescribe, and no person operating a motorized bicycle shall permit any other person to ride a passenger on such motorized bicycle unless such passenger is wearing such protective headgear.	**1st Off: $25** Plus $5 Public Safety Surcharge. **2nd Off: $50** Plus $5 Public Safety Surcharge. **3rd Off: $100** Plus $5 Public Safety Surcharge.
Moped Sale Requirements 90 § 1D	Any person who is engaged in the business of buying or selling bicycles or motorized bicycles shall, upon the sale of such motorized bicycle, affix a sticker or plate which shall bear a distinctive number, as prescribed by the registrar, to said bicycle upon a fee to be determined annually by the commissioner of administration under the provision of section three B of chapter seven. Said fee shall be forwarded to the registry of motor vehicles by such person. Said sticker shall be renewed biannually in the manner prescribed by the registrar.	

MOPEDS & SCOOTERS

Motorized Scooter Definition 90 § 1	**"Motorized scooter"**, any 2 wheeled tandem or 3 wheeled device, that has handlebars, designed to be stood or sat upon by the operator, powered by an electric or gas powered motor that is capable of propelling the device with or without human propulsion. The definition of "motorized scooter" shall not include: • a motorcycle, or • motorized bicycle, or • a 3 wheeled motorized wheelchair.	
Motorized Scooter Restrictions 90 § 1E	A motorized scooter shall **not** be operated on any way: • by a person not possessing a valid driver's license or learner's permit, • at a speed in excess of 20 miles per hour • at any time after sunset or before sunrise. • with a passenger, other than the operator (cite operator)	**1ST OFF: $25** Plus $5 Public Safety Surcharge **2ND OFF: $50** Plus $5 Public Safety Surcharge **3RD OFF: $100** Plus $5 Public Safety Surcharge
Motorized Scooter Rules of the Road 90 § 1E	A person operating a motorized scooter upon a way shall have the right to use all public ways in the commonwealth except limited access or express state highways where signs specifically prohibiting scooters or bicycles have been posted, and **shall be subject to all traffic laws and regulations** of the commonwealth and the regulations contained in this section**, except** that: (1) a scooter operator **shall keep to the right side of the road at all times**, including when passing a motor vehicle which is moving in the travel lane of the way; and (2) the scooter **shall be equipped with operational stop and turn signals** so that the operator can keep both hands on the handlebars at all times.	**1ST OFF: $25** Plus $5 Public Safety Surcharge **2ND OFF: $50** Plus $5 Public Safety Surcharge **3RD OFF: $100** Plus $5 Public Safety Surcharge
Protective Headgear Required 90 § 1E	A person operating a motorized scooter shall wear protective headgear conforming with such minimum standards of construction and performance as the registrar may prescribe.	**1ST OFF: $25 +5** **2ND OFF: $50 +5** **3RD OFF: $100** Plus $5 Public Safety Surcharge

LOW SPEED VEHICLES

LOW SPEED & LIMITED USE VEHICLES	
Low Speed Motor Vehicle Definition	 **Low-speed motor vehicle" or "low-speed vehicle"**, a motor vehicle which is: a. 4-wheeled, b. whose speed attainable in 1 mile is more than 20 miles per hour and not more than 25 MPH on a paved level surface, and c. whose gross vehicle weight rating is less than 3,000 pounds.
Low Speed Vehicle Equipment	All low-speed motor vehicles shall comply with the standards established in 49 C.F.R. § 571.500, as amended, and pursuant thereto, **shall be equipped with**: • Headlamps • front and rear turn signal lamps, • tail lamps, • stop lamps, • an exterior mirror mounted on the driver's side of the vehicle and • either an exterior mirror mounted on the passenger's side of the vehicle or an interior mirror, • a parking brake, • a windshield that conforms to the federal standards on glazing materials, • a vehicle identification number that conforms to the requirements of 49 C.F.R. pt 565 for such numbers, • a Type 1 or Type 2 seat belt assembly conforming to 49 C.F.R. § 571.209, installed at each designated seating position and • reflex reflectors; provided, that 1 reflector is red on each side as far to the rear as practicable and 1 reflector is red on the rear.
License required **90 § 1F**	A low-speed vehicle shall not be operated by a person under 16 years of age nor by any person not possessing a valid driver's license, except that a person who is at least 16 years of age who possesses a valid learner's permit may operate a low-speed vehicle on those ways, or portions of ways, where such operation is lawful, if accompanied by an operator duly licensed by his state of residence who is 21 years of age or over, who has had at least 1 year of driving experience and who is occupying a seat beside the driver. The holder of a junior operator's license shall be subject to the same license restrictions applicable to that license classification in the operation of a low-speed vehicle as if the license holder were operating any other motor vehicle
Low Speed Vehicles Registration &, Insurance Required	A low speed motor vehicle that meets the requirements of 49 C.F.R. § 571.500, as amended, and is equipped as herein provided, **may be registered in the commonwealth, subject to inspection and insurance requirements.** A low-speed vehicle shall not be operated upon any public way unless: • the **vehicle is registered** in accordance with the provisions of this chapter, • **displays the registration number** as provided in section 6, • **displays a slow moving vehicle emblem** on the rear of the vehicle as required by section 7 and by 540 C.M.R. § 22.11, • is equipped as required by 49 C.F.R. § 571.500, as amended, and as required by this chapter, • **meets the insurance certificate requirements** of section 34B and is titled under chapter 90D.

LOW SPEED & LIMITED USE VEHICLES	
Low Speed Vehicle Inspection Requirements 90 § 1F	Low-speed vehicles shall be subject to annual inspection as required by section 7A, except that low-speed vehicles whose sole source of power is generated electrically shall not be subject to the test for emissions. NOTE: The registrar may issue registration plates displaying the International Symbol of Access for a low-speed vehicle upon the same terms and conditions applicable to registrants of other motor vehicles and may issue a special parking identification placard bearing the same designation upon the same terms and conditions applicable to persons seeking a placard for a motor vehicle.
Operation of Low-Speed Motor Vehicles on Public Ways 90 § 1F	Every person lawfully operating a low-speed motor vehicle shall have the right to use all public ways in the commonwealth except limited access or express state highways or any public way with a speed limit of more than 30 miles per hour, and shall be subject to the traffic laws and regulations of the commonwealth and the provisions of this section.
Crossing a Public Way with Higher Speeds 90 § 1F	The above provision shall not prohibit a low-speed motor vehicle from crossing a public way at an intersection where the public way to be crossed has a posted speed limit between 30 and 45 miles per hour, provided the public way the low-speed vehicle is traveling on and the public way the low-speed vehicle is crossing the intersection to both have a speed limit no higher than 30 miles per hour and the intersection is controlled by traffic signals or stop signs.
Municipality May Impose Restrictions 90 §1F	A municipality may, by ordinance, prohibit the operation of low-speed vehicles on a way or a portion of a way within its jurisdiction and under its control, **regardless of posted speeds**, where it finds that use of the way or a particular portion of the way by low-speed motor vehicles would represent **an unreasonable risk of death or serious injury** to occupants of low-speed vehicles because of general traffic conditions which shall include, but not be limited to: excessive speeds of other vehicles, traffic volumes, use of the way by heavy trucks or other large vehicles or if the established speed limit on the way increases above 30 miles per hour beyond the point where a low-speed vehicle could safely exit the way. The municipality shall post signs where necessary to provide notice to the public of such prohibited access.
Penalty 90 § 1F	Violation of Low Speed Vehicle Requirement/Rule: 1st Offense - $75 2nd Offense - $150
Limited Use Vehicle 90 § 1H	A limited use vehicle can have two or more wheels. It can go faster than 30 mph, but not more than 40 mph. A limited use vehicle can either be a motorcycle or a passenger vehicle; it depends on how many wheels it has. A valid driver's license or learner's permit is required to drive a limited use vehicle. If the limited use vehicle is a motorcycle, the license or permit must be Class M. If the limited use vehicle is a passenger vehicle, the license or permit must be Class D. An operator cannot drive a limited use vehicle on a limited-access or express state highway or any road with a speed limit faster than 40 mph. Note: The Scheduled Assessment does not have a fine schedule (yet) for limited use vehicles.

School Buses

See fine chart at the end of this section for bus violations

Boats & Recreation Vehicles

See fine chart at the end of this section for bus violations.

EMERGENCY VEHICLE RELATED LAWS		
Law/Rule	**Violation/Offense**	**Penalty**
Obstruction of Emergency Vehicles 89 § 7	The defendant **willfully obstructs or retards** the members and apparatus of a **fire department** while going to a fire or responding to an alarm, **police patrol vehicles** and ambulances, and **ambulances** on a call for the purpose of hospitalizing a sick or injured. **Arrest**: No right of arrest unless breach of the peace and in presence of the officer.	**Criminal** **1st offense**: fine of $50.00 or by imprisonment 3 months.
Yield to Emergency Vehicles Responding to Emergency 89 § 7A	Upon the approach of **any fire apparatus, police vehicle, ambulance or disaster vehicle** which is going to a fire or responding to call, alarm or emergency situation, every person driving a vehicle on a way shall **immediatel**y drive said vehicle as **far as possible toward the right-hand curb or side of said way** and shall keep the same at a **standstill** until such fire apparatus, police vehicle, ambulance or disaster vehicle has passed. Note: pedestrians must also yield to emergency vehicle or face a whopping $1.00 fine.	$100 Plus $5 Public Safety Surcharge
Interfering With Fire Apparatus 89 § 7A	No person shall drive: • A **vehicle over a hose of a fire department** without the consent of a member of such department. • A vehicle **within 300 feet** of any **fire apparatus going to a fire or responding to an alarm**, • A vehicle, or park or leave a vehicle unattended, within **800 feet of a fire or within the fire lanes established by the fire department**, or upon or beside any traveled way, whether public or private, leading to the scene of a fire, in such a manner as to obstruct the approach to the fire of any fire apparatus or any ambulance, safety or police vehicle, or of any vehicle bearing an official fire or police department designation. **Tow vehicle for Obstructing:** Authorized police or fire department personnel may tow a vehicle found to be in violation of the provisions of this section or which is illegally parked or standing in a fire lane as established by the fire department, whether or not a fire is in progress.	$100 Plus $5 Public Safety Surcharge
Following Emergency Vehicle Too Closely 89 § 7A	No person shall operate a motor vehicle behind any: ○ fire apparatus, ○ ambulance, ○ safety or police vehicle ○ any vehicle bearing an official fire or police department designation which is operating with emergency systems on for a distance of 300 feet.	$100 Plus $5 Public Safety Surcharge

EMERGENCY VEHICLE RELATED LAWS

"MOVE OVER LAW" 89 § 7C	**Rule:** Upon approaching a stationary emergency vehicle, highway maintenance vehicle or recovery vehicle with flashing lights an operator shall: • proceed with due caution, • reduce the speed of the vehicle to that of a reasonable and safe speed for road conditions, and, • if practicable and on a highway having at least 4 lanes with not less than 2 lanes proceeding in the same direction as the operator's vehicle, yield the right-of-way by making a lane change into a lane not adjacent to that of the emergency response vehicle, highway maintenance vehicle or recovery vehicle; or • if changing lanes is impracticable, proceed with due caution and reduce the speed of the vehicle to that of a reasonable and safe speed for road conditions. Definitions for this law: **"Emergency response vehicle",** a **fire** apparatus**, police** vehicle**, ambulance,** or **disaster vehicle**. **"Highway maintenance vehicle",** a vehicle used for the maintenance of highways and roadways: (1) that is owned or operated by the executive office of transportation and public works, a county, a municipality or any political subdivision thereof; or (2) that is owned or operated by a person under contract with the executive office of transportation and public works, a county, a municipality or any political subdivision thereof. **"Recovery vehicle",** a vehicle that is specifically designed to assist a disabled vehicle or to tow a disabled vehicle.	$100 Plus $5 Public Safety Surcharge
Sirens Prohibited 90 § 16	No siren shall be mounted upon any motor vehicle except fire apparatus, ambulances, vehicles used in official line of duty by any member of the police or fire fighting forces of the commonwealth or any agency or political subdivision thereof, and vehicles owned by call fire fighters or by persons with police powers and operated in official line of duty, unless authorized by the registrar.	$50 Plus $5 Public Safety Surcharge.
Flashing Red Lights **90 § 7E**	No motor vehicle operated shall mount or display a flashing, rotating or oscillating red light in any direction. **Exceptions - The following vehicles may have flashing red lights:** • fire apparatus • ambulances • school buses • vehicles used for transporting school children • vehicle owned and operated by a forest warden • vehicle owned and operated by deputy forest warden • vehicle owned and operated by a chief or deputy chief of a municipal fire department vehicle, • vehicle owned and operated by a chaplain of a municipal fire department vehicle,	$300 Plus $5 Public Safety Surcharge.

EMERGENCY VEHICLE RELATED LAWS		
	• vehicle owned and operated by a member of a fire department of a town or • vehicle owned and operated by a call member of a fire department or • vehicle owned and operated by a member or a call member of an emergency medical service **Restrictions:** Such lights shall only be displayed when such owner or operator is proceeding to a fire or in response to an alarm and when the official duty of such owner or operator requires him to proceed to said fire or to respond to said alarm, and at no other time. **Permit Required**: No such red light shall be mounted or displayed on (a privately owned) vehicle until proper application has been made to the registrar by the head of the fire department and a written permit has been issued and delivered to the owner and operator. In the event that the operator is not the registered owner of the vehicle, no permit shall be issued until said owner forwards to the registrar a written statement certifying that he has knowledge that such red light will be mounted and displayed on said vehicle. **Permit Accessibility:** Any person operating a vehicle upon which flashing, rotating or oscillating red lights herein authorized are mounted shall have the permit for said lights upon his person or in the vehicle in some easily accessible place.	
Flashing Blue Lights c. 90 § 7E	No motor vehicle or trailer shall mount or display a blue light on such vehicle **Exceptions - The following vehicles may have flashing blue lights:** • a vehicle used solely for official business by any police department • railroad police department • college or university police department whose officers are appointed as special state police officers by the colonel of state police • a **privately owned vehicle owned and operated** by a police officer of any town or any agency of the commonwealth **while on official duty** and **when authorized by the officer's police chief** or agency head **and only by authority of a permit issued by the registrar**, • a vehicle operated by a duly appointed **medical examiner or a physician or surgeon** attached to a police department of any city or town only while on official duty and only by authority of a permit issued by the registrar • a vehicle operated by a police commissioner of a police department of any city only while on official duty and only by authority of a permit issued by the registrar • a vehicle actually being **used for the transportation of persons who are under** arrest, or in lawful custody under authority of any court, or committed to penal or mental institutions, and only by authority of a permit issued by the registrar, • a vehicle operated by a **chaplain of a municipal police department** while on official duty and only by authority of a permit issued by the registrar shall mount or display a flashing, rotating or oscillating blue light in any direction. **Privately owned vehicle requires registry permit:** No motor vehicle, as hereinbefore provided, requiring a permit from the registrar, until proper application has been made to the registrar by the head of the police department and such written permit has been issued and delivered to the owner and operator. Such notice shall include the place of residence and address of the owner and operator of the vehicle for which	$300 Plus $5 Public Safety Surcharge.

EMERGENCY VEHICLE RELATED LAWS

EMERGENCY VEHICLE RELATED LAWS		
	such permit is issued and the name of the make, vehicle identification number and the registration number of the vehicle for which such permit authorizes the display of blue lights. **Permit accessibility:** Any person operating a vehicle upon which blue lights have been authorized to be mounted or displayed, by permit, shall carry such permit for said lights upon his person or in the vehicle in some easily accessible place. **RMV notification:** Upon termination of the duties of such person which warranted the issuance of the permit, the chief of police shall immediately notify the registrar. **NOTE:** also see c. 90 § 71 - certain charitable organizations are permitted to use lights and sirens and c. 90 § 16 for restrictions on the use of sirens (below).	
EMERGENCY DISASTER SERVICE VEHICLES OF CHARITABLE CORPORATIONS; IDENTIFICATION AND EQUIPMENT c. 90 § 7E	Emergency disaster service vehicles (i.e. Samaritan vehicle – American Red Cross, etc.) may be equipped with sirens or other audible warning devices and with visible warning devices as provided in §7E. Such audible and visible warning devices may be used by the vehicle operator only when responding to an official alarm of fire or disaster and at no other time. Every such emergency disaster service motor vehicle shall be marked, on a part of the vehicle not readily removable, and in a conspicuous place, with the insignia of the corporation and with words identifying the vehicle as an emergency disaster service unit.	1ST OFF: $35 Plus $5 Public Safety Surcharge. 2ND OFF: $75 Plus $5 Public Safety Surcharge. 3RD OFF: $150 Plus $5 Public Safety Surcharge.

Operation of Emergency Vehicles 89 § 7B	**Rule:** The driver of a vehicle of a fire, police or recognized protective department and the driver of an ambulance **shall be subject to the provisions of any statute, rule, regulation, ordinance or by-law relating to the operation or parking** of vehicles:
	
	Exceptions: except that a driver of:
	• **fire apparatus** while going to a fire or responding to an alarm, or
	• a vehicle of a **police or recognized protective department** or
	• an **ambulance**,
	
	May in an **emergency** and **while in performance of a public duty** or while **transporting a sick or injured person** to a hospital or other destination where professional medical services are available, may:
	• drive such vehicle at a speed in excess of the applicable speed limit if he exercises caution and due regard under the circumstances for the safety of persons and property, and
	• may drive such vehicle through an intersection of ways contrary to any traffic signs or signals regulating traffic at such intersection **if** he::
	    ➢ first brings such vehicle to a **full stop** and then **proceeds with caution** and due regard for the safety of persons and property
	    ➢ is otherwise directed by a police officer regulating traffic at such intersection.
	
	Approaching School Bus - Must STOP: The driver of any such approaching emergency vehicle **shall comply** with the provisions of section fourteen of chapter ninety **<u>when approaching a school bus which has stopped to allow passengers to alight or board from the same, and whose red lamps are flashing.</u>**	

MV LAWS RELATED TO ANIMALS		
Law/Rule	**Violation/Offense**	**Penalty**
Striking, Injuring Or Killing Dogs Or Cats 272 § 80H	The operator of a motor vehicle that strikes and injures or kills a dog or cat shall forthwith report such an accident to the owner or custodian of the dog or cat or to a police officer in the town wherein such accident has occurred.	$50
Safe Transportation of Animals 90 §22H	No person shall transport an animal in the back of a motor vehicle in a space intended for a load on the vehicle on a public way unless • such space is enclosed, or • has side and tail racks to a height of at least 46 inches extending vertically from the floor, or • the animal is cross tethered to the vehicle, or • the animal is protected by a secured container or cage, or • the animal is otherwise protected in a manner which will prevent the animal from being thrown, falling or jumping out.	$50 Plus $5 Public Safety Surcharge.
Operation Near an Animal 90 §14	Every person operating a motor vehicle shall bring the vehicle and the motor propelling it **immediately to a stop** when approaching a **cow, horse or other draft animal** being led, ridden or driven, if such animal **appears to be frightened** and if the person in **charge thereof shall signal so to do** and if traveling in the opposite direction to that in which such animal is proceeding, said vehicle shall remain stationary so long as may be reasonable to allow such animal to pass; or, if traveling in the same direction, the person operating shall use reasonable caution in thereafter passing such animal.	**1ST OFF: $35** Plus $5 Public Safety Surcharge. **2ND OFF: $75** Plus $5 Public Safety Surcharge. **3RD OFF: $150** Plus $5 Public Safety Surcharge.
Leading, Driving... Dangerous Wild Animals on Public Ways 85 § 19	Whoever leads or drives a bear or other dangerous wild animal or causes it to travel upon or be conveyed over a public way unless properly secured in some covered vehicle or cage shall be punished by a fine of not less than 5.00 or more than $20.00. Any such animal which is found upon a public way not so secured or caged may be killed by a sheriff, constable or police officer	$20

PARKING & TOWING OF MOTOR VEHICLES		
Law/Rule	**Violation/Offense**	**Penalty**
Tampering or Destruction of Parking Tags 90 §2OD	The defendant unlawfully does any of the following: • tampers with or removes • unlawfully changes • mutilates or destroys • any (parking ticket) affixed to motor vehicle	Criminal a fine of not more than $50.00, or by imprisonment in jail for not more than one month, or by both such fine and imprisonment
Parking Fee exemption For Disabled Persons **c. 40 § 22A**	**No fee or penalty** (for parking meters) shall be imposed for the parking of any vehicle owned and driven by a **disabled veteran or by a handicapped person** and **bearing the distinctive number plates**...., or for any vehicle transporting a handicapped person and displaying the special authorized **parking identification plate** or for any vehicle bearing the official identification of a handicapped person issued by any other state or any Canadian Province.	
Vehicles Parked in Violation of Law; Removal **40 § 22D**	**Summary:** Local governments may impose parking rules and restrictions and may authorize the "chief officer of the police department or such sergeants or other officers of higher rank" to remove, to some convenient place any vehicle parked or standing on any part of any way under the control of the municipality in such a manner as to: • obstruct any curb ramp designed for use by handicapped persons as means of egress to a street or public way, • to occupy or obstruct any parking space reserved for a vehicle used by a disabled veteran or handicapped person (with proper credentials) • to impede in any way the removal or plowing of snow or ice or in violation of any rule or regulation which prohibits the parking or standing of all vehicles on such ways or portions thereof at such time and recites that **Violator pays removal fee**: whoever violates it shall be liable to charges for the removal and storage of the vehicles as well as subject to punishment by fine. **The following vehicles shall not removed**: • Vehicles owned by: 1. the Commonwealth 2. a political subdivision (City or Town) or 3. the United States , or • Any foreign diplomatic corps or by a foreign consular officer who is not a citizen of the United States and bearing a distinctive number plate or otherwise conspicuously marked as so owned or registered. The provisions of this section shall not apply to the city of Boston.	
MV Repossession c. 255B § 20C	Any creditor obtaining possession of a motor vehicle under the provisions of this chapter shall, within one hour after obtaining such possession, notify the police department of the city or town in which such possession occurred, giving such police department a description of the vehicle involved.	
Removal of Motor Vehicles from Private Ways or Property **266 § 120D**	**TOWING A MOTOR VEHICLE FROM PRIVATE PROPERTY** • No person shall remove a motor vehicle • Which is parked or standing on a private way or upon improved or enclosed property • Unless the operator of such vehicle has been forbidden so to park or stand, either directly or by posted notice, • By the person who has lawful control of such way or property. **Must Notify Police:** No vehicle shall be removed from such way or property without the consent of the owner of such vehicle unless the person who has lawful control of such way or property shall have	

PARKING & TOWING OF MOTOR VEHICLES

notified the chief of police or his designee that such vehicle is to be removed.

Police notification shall be made before any such vehicle shall be removed, and shall be in writing unless otherwise specified by such chief of police or police commissioner and shall include the address from which the vehicle is to be removed, the address to which the vehicle is to be removed, the registration number of the vehicle, the name of the person in lawful control of the way or property from which such vehicle is being removed, and the name of the person or company or other business entity removing the vehicle.

Vehicles so removed shall be stored in a convenient location.

Liability: Neither the city or town, nor its chief of police or police commissioner or his designee, shall be liable for any damages incurred during the removal or storage of any such vehicle removed under this section.

Penalty: Any person who, without notifying the chief of police or his designee, or the police commissioner or his designee, or without obtaining the consent of the owner, removes a vehicle from a private way or from improved or enclosed property as aforesaid, shall, in addition to any other penalty of law, be punished by a fine of not more than **$100**. The employer of such person if any, shall also be punished by a fine of not more than $100.

Note: Any person who purports to authorize the removal of a vehicle from a way or property as aforesaid without having fully complied with the provision of this section shall be punished by a fine of not more than $100.

In addition to any other penalty provided by law, the registered owner of a vehicle illegally parked or standing on a private way or upon improved or enclosed property shall be liable for charges for the removal and storage of such vehicle; provided, however, that the liability so imposed shall not exceed the following, and provided, further, that the vehicle has been removed after compliance with the provisions of this section:

(1) the maximum amount for towing or transportation of motor vehicles established by the department of telecommunications and energy for motor vehicles towed away when such towing is ordered by the police or other public authority under the provisions of section six B of c. one hundred and fifty-nine B; and

(2) the maximum charge for storage of non-commercial passenger motor vehicles with a maximum capacity of nine persons, shall be not more than the maximum storage charge allowed under the provisions of said section six B of said c. one hundred and fifty-nine B.

A person lawfully holding a vehicle removed under the provisions of this section may hold such vehicle until the registered owner pays the removal and storage charges.

Any person who is called to remove by towing a vehicle illegally parked or standing on a private way or upon improved or enclosed property may, at his discretion, if the owner appears to remove said vehicle before the towing is completed, charge said owner one half of the fee usually charged for such towing.

Any person who removes a vehicle illegally parked or standing on a private way or upon improved or enclosed property, or holds such a vehicle after its removal, and who has not complied in full with the provisions of this section, shall release such vehicle to its owner without assessing any charges for its removal or storage.

ABANDONED MOTOR VEHICLES

Removal of Abandoned or Stolen Vehicles from Public Places 90 § 24H	**No person shall remove an abandoned or stolen motor vehicle** on a public way or any place to which the public has right of access **without the express consent of the owne**r of such vehicle **or** without the **written permission of the police department**. The owner or operator of a motor vehicle that is designed to carry or tow another vehicle shall be licensed for that specific purpose or as a towing service. **Penalty**: **misdemeano**r - Any person convicted of violation of any provision of this section shall forfeit any license issued which is related to such violation and shall be punished by a fine of not less than $1,000 or by imprisonment for not less than 2 years, or both.
Abandoned Motor Vehicles; Removal and Disposal **90 § 22C**	**Summary**: If a vehicle is apparently abandoned on and has been left on a public or private way it can be towed and stored without the permission of the owner. Cities & Towns have the option of handling these matters as civil offenses or criminal offenses. Actual statutory language below: If the superintendent of streets or other officer having charge of the public ways in a city or town (or if a captain or lieutenant of the state police) reasonably deems that any motor **vehicle apparently abandoned** by its owner **and standing for more than 72 hours** upon a public or private way therein or on any property therein without the permission of the owner or lessee of said property is **worth less than the cost of removal and storage** and expenses incident to disposition...he may, without incurring liability on his part or on the part of the city, town or the commonwealth, **take possession of such motor vehicle and dispose thereof as refuse**. Any such superintendent or other officer of a city or town may, likewise, without liability, take possession of any such motor vehicle deemed worth more than the cost and expense as aforesaid, and deliver the same to the officer or member of the police department of the city or town, designated by the rules of said department as custodian of lost property, wherein said motor vehicle was found, who may dispose thereof pursuant to said sections seven to eleven, inclusive. Any such officer of said state police may, likewise, without liability, take possession of any such motor vehicle deemed worth more than the cost and expenses as aforesaid, and dispose thereof pursuant to said sections eighty-nine to ninety-four, inclusive, or said sections forty-five to forty-eight, inclusive.

ABANDONMENT OF MOTOR VEHICLES; PENALTIES; NON-CRIMINAL PROCEEDINGS 90 § 22B

NOTE: This statute has both a civil and a criminal provision for abandoning vehicles. The jurisdiction can decide which method it wants to take regarding abandoned vehicles.

CRIMINAL ACTION

ABANDONED MOTOR VEHICLE: Whoever abandons a motor vehicle registered or unregistered, upon any public or private way or upon any property other than his own without the permission of the owner or lessee of said property shall be fined (see below)

PENALTY: 1st offense: $250 Subsequent offense: $500

RMV ACTION: The registrar may revoke driver's license for a period not exceeding 3 months. Also, prohibited from registering another motor vehicle for 1 year, and no appeal, motion for new trial or exceptions shall operate to stay the revocation of the license or the prohibition of registration.

CIVIL ACTION

There shall be in any city or town which accepts the (civil remedy), a parking clerk designated or appointed. Said parking clerk, in addition to other duties provided by law, shall supervise and coordinate the processing of abandoned motor vehicles.

Said parking clerk shall have the authority to hire personnel, or may contract by competitive bid for services necessary to implement the provisions of this section.

ABANDONED MOTOR VEHICLES

FINE AND COSTS: (d) A person who abandons a motor vehicle, registered or unregistered, upon any public or private way, or upon the property of another, without the permission of the owner or lessee of said property, shall pay a civil penalty of two hundred and fifty dollars for the first such abandonment and five hundred dollars for each such abandonment thereafter and, in addition thereto shall be liable for costs incurred by a city or town in removing or disposing of such motor vehicle, including, but not limited to, towing, storage, processing and disposal charges.

AFFIX A TAG: (e) A police officer, or a person assigned responsibility for abandoned motor vehicles by the parking clerk, who determines that a motor vehicle has been abandoned shall attach a tag to said vehicle containing, but not limited to, the following information: the current date, the location of said vehicle, its make, color, registration number, if any, and its vehicle identification number; a telephone number or address at which the owner may obtain information regarding the status of the motor vehicle; the hearing procedure regarding abandoned motor vehicles, as provided herein; and, a statement that after a specified period of time, the vehicle may be towed and disposed of.

HEARING NOTICE: (f) After said tag has been affixed to such vehicle, if the owner's identity is ascertained and the motor vehicle is still deemed to be abandoned, the parking clerk or his designee shall send a written notice in a form approved by the registrar of motor vehicles by first class mail to the owner's last known address as contained in records of said registrar of motor vehicles. Such notice shall be deemed sufficient, whether or not actually received by the addressee, if mailed to the address furnished by said registrar. Such notice shall contain, but not be limited to, the following information regarding the abandoned vehicle: the current date, the location of said vehicle, make, color, registration number, if any, and its vehicle identification number; the amount of the fine and costs assessed for the offense and the scheduled date, time and place of the hearing before a hearing officer. Notwithstanding the hearing scheduled by the parking clerk, the owner shall be granted a hearing prior to the scheduled hearing date by appearing at the office of the parking clerk during its regular business hours and requesting an immediate hearing regarding the apparently abandoned motor vehicle. Notwithstanding the hearing scheduled by the parking clerk, the owner may elect to have the matter adjudicated in accordance with the provisions of subsection (h) (Hearing by Mail).

HEARING PROCESS (g) All such hearings shall be held before a person hereinafter referred to as a hearing officer who shall be the parking clerk or a designee of said parking clerk. Such hearings shall be informal, the rules of evidence shall not apply and decisions of the hearing officer shall be subject to judicial review as provided by section fourteen of c. thirty A. No appeal or exception shall operate to stay the imposition of the fine and costs, the revocation or nonrenewal of the license or the prohibition of registration as provided for herein.

HEARING BY MAIL (h) A person so notified to appear before the hearing officer may appear and contest or confess the alleged violation, either personally or through an agent duly authorized in writing or in the alternative, may confess the alleged violation by mailing to the parking clerk the notice accompanied by the fine and any costs assessed; provided, however, that such payment shall be made only by postal note, money order or registered check made payable to the city or town in which the violation occurred.

FAILS TO APPEAR/FAILS TO PAY: (i) If the owner fails to appear at a hearing, or fails to pay the fine and costs, the parking clerk shall, in the case of a person, notify the registrar of motor vehicles who shall place the matter on record and not renew the license of such person to operate a motor vehicle, and in the case of an entity, notify the appropriate person to revoke or not renew the owner's license or permit to operate a business pertaining to the towing, storing, servicing or dismantling of motor vehicles including, without limitation, automobile graveyards and junkyards. If the abandoned motor vehicle is registered in such owner's name or was last registered in his name, the registrar shall prohibit the registration and renewal of registration of any such motor vehicle under such owner's name. Such notice shall be in a form approved by the registrar of motor vehicles. Upon notification to the registrar of the owner's name, an additional ten dollar charge shall be assessed against such owner of the abandoned vehicle. Said ten dollar charge shall be collected by the city or town and notification of such collection shall be made to the registrar of motor vehicles each month. On or before September first of each year, the registrar shall certify the total number of ten dollar charges to be assessed against the city or town. This number shall equal the total number of notifications of actual collections by said city or town. The registrar shall transmit such certified assessments to the treasurer of the commonwealth who shall include such assessments in the warrants prepared in accordance with section twenty of c. fifty-nine. All such actions taken by the registrar shall remain in effect until said registrar receives notice from the parking clerk that the matter has been disposed of in accordance with the law.

ABANDONED MOTOR VEHICLES

MULTIPLE OFFENSES (j) Notwithstanding any other general or special law, ordinance or regulation to the contrary, if an owner has abandoned a motor vehicle on three occasions and has incurred a fine therefor, each subsequent abandonment, in addition to the fines and costs assessed herein, shall result, in the case of a person, in the revocation for one year of the owner's license to operate a motor vehicle, and in the case of an entity, in the revocation for one year of the owner's license or permit to operate a business pertaining to the towing, storing, servicing or dismantling of motor vehicles including, without limitation, automobile graveyards and junkyards. Such one year time period shall commence on the date on which the parking clerk's records indicate that a hearing was held and a fourth or subsequent abandonment was found or that a fine was received in the mail confessing a fourth or subsequent abandonment.

DISPOSE OF VEHICLE (k) Notwithstanding any other provisions of this section, whenever the clerk or a person designated or appointed by said clerk, shall deem that an abandoned motor vehicle is worth less than the cost of its removal, transportation and three days storage and expenses incidental to its disposal, said clerk or designee shall direct a carrier to take possession of such motor vehicle and dispose of it as refuse. A record of such disposal shall be made and kept in the office of said clerk for a period of two years. Neither said clerk, carrier nor the city or town shall be liable for such disposal. The owner of such vehicle shall be notified as hereinbefore provided and shall pay to said carrier all charges for removal, transportation, storage and disposal of such vehicle within fourteen days after the mailing of said notice or shall be subject to the fine herein provided as well as nonrenewal of such owner's license to operate and registration of a motor vehicle.

Abandoned Vehicles; Removal Of Parts **90 § 22E**	The defendant takes any part or accessory from an abandoned motor vehicle standing upon a public or private way or standing upon any property without the permission of the owner or lessee thereof. **Penalty:** a fine of not less than $50 nor more than $300. **Attorney Hanrahan's Note:** A larceny charge would probably be more appropriate, in most circumstances.

Vehicle Accidents

C. 90 § 24	LEAVING THE SCENE OF AN ACCIDENT
	Causing PROPERTY DAMAGE **Elements**
1.	The defendant operated a motor vehicle
2.	On a way, or in a place where the public has a right of access, or in a place where members of the public have access as invitees or licensees
3.	While the defendant was operating he/she caused damage to another vehicle or property by colliding with it or in some other way
4.	The defendant *knew* that he/she collided with another's property or in some way caused damage to another's property
5.	The defendant did not stop and make his/her name, home address and registration number of his/her vehicle.
	Causing PERSONAL INJURY **Elements**
1.	The defendant operated a motor vehicle
2.	On a way, or in a place where the public has a right of access, or in a place where members of the public have access as invitees or licensees
3.	Knowingly collides with or otherwise injures any person
4.	Goes away without stopping and making known one's name, residence, and motor vehicle registration number
5.	Where the collision caused injury to the person (but did not cause death)
	Causing DEATH **Elements**
1.	The defendant operated a motor vehicle
2.	On a way, or in a place where the public has a right of access, or in a place where members of the public have access as invitees or licensees
3.	Knowingly collides with or otherwise injures any person
4.	Goes away without stopping and making known one's name, residence, and motor vehicle registration number
5.	In order to avoid prosecution or evade apprehension.
6.	Where the death of victim was the result of the injuries sustained in the collision.

C. 90 § 24	LEAVING THE SCENE OF AN ACCIDENT
	Arrest Power, Penalties & Notes
Power of Arrest	**Property Damage only – misdemeanor:** there is no statutory authority granting warrantless powers of arrest for this offense. However, if the offense is committed in public, in the officer's presence, and is creating a **breach of the peace** an arrest would be lawful. **Physical Injury – misdemeanor**: c. 90 § 21 permits an arrest for this offense if the offense is committed in the officer's presence. **Death results – felony:** a police officer may effect a warrantless arrest for this offense provided he/she has probable cause that the suspect committed the offense.
Penalty	**Property Damage only - misdemeanor** - a fine of not less than $20 nor more than $200 or by imprisonment for not less than two weeks nor more than two years, or both. **Physical Injury - misdemeanor**: imprisonment for not less than 6 months nor more than 2 years and by a fine of not less than $500 nor more than $1,000. **Death results – felony:** imprisonment in the **state prison (F)** for not less than 2½ years nor more than 10 years and by a fine of not less than $1,000 nor more than $5,000 or by imprisonment in a jail or HOC for **not less than 1 year** nor more than 2½ years and by a fine of not less than $1,000 nor more than $5,000.
Attorney Hanrahan's Comment	When it comes to property damage, there must actually be property damaged, other than the defendant's property, in order to secure a conviction. It is important to note that there is an additional element for the offense that results in death. It must be proven that the defendant left in order to avoid prosecution or evade apprehension. This element is not required for the other two forms of this offense (see the 2013 case of *Commonwealth v. Muir*). Additionally, there are different schools of thought in relation to the "in-presence" requirement for the misdemeanor arrest power. Does this mean that the officer has to witness the collision? Or does it apply to the officer witnessing the suspect driving away? There is no definitive answer as it has not been decided by the Court (yet). The safest course of action would be to summons. If the person refuses to identify themselves, to the investigating officer, arrest powers via. 90§ 25 would apply.
	Related Statutes, Case Law & Other Important Information
Knowledge required	In the 2012 case of ***Commonwealth v. Daley***, the SJC ruled that leaving the scene of an accident causing injury to a person, resulting in that person's death, [G.L. c. 90 § 24(2) (a1/2) (2)] requires the Commonwealth to prove that the defendant **knew** he collided with a person "or otherwise" caused injury to a person, not just that he was involved in a collision. In this case, the operator knew he hit *something* on a dark snowy evening but it was not proved that he knew he hit a person.
Must provide information, not just offer it	In the 2015 case of ***Commonwealth v. Martinez***, G.L. c. 90 § 24(2)(a) requires an operator of a motor vehicle to properly identify himself after being involved in a motor vehicle accident. The *offer* of information is not enough. The statute requires that the operator *provide* the required information.
Collision	"Collide" means to strike together. The statute applies whenever the defendant is in some way an actor, a partial cause in the collision, but not where the defendant is merely a passive participant (e.g. where a pedestrian falls or walks into the defendant's stopped vehicle). *Commonwealth v. Bleakney,* 278 Mass. 198, 179 N.E. 400 (1932). An owner-passenger can be found guilty if he or she retained control over his chauffeur's operation of the vehicle. *Saltman, petitioner,* 289 Mass. 554, 194 N.E. 703 (1935).

C. 90 § 24	LEAVING THE SCENE OF AN ACCIDENT
Fault doesn't matter	The statute applies whether or not the defendant was at fault, since the statute "focuses on causation, not fault." *Commonwealth v. Robbins*, 414 Mass. 444, 446-448, 608 N.E.2d 735, 737-738 (1993).
Not a continuing offense	For purposes of the **statute of limitations**, the crime of leaving the scene of an accident is not a continuing offense. *Commonwealth v. Valchuis*, 40 Mass. App. Ct. 556, 561-562, 665 N.E.2d 1030, 1034 (1996) (offense involving personal injury).
Lesser included offense	The crime of leaving the scene causing physical injury is a lesser included offense of leaving the scene resulting in death. [1]

MOTOR VEHICLE ACCIDENT RELATED LAWS

Law/Rule	Violation/Offense	Penalty
Must Produce License & Registration at MVA 90 § 11	Any operator who knowingly collides with or causes injury or damage tony person or damage to any property shall, upon the request of the person injured or the person owning or in charge of the property damaged, plainly exhibit to such person his license and registration (if required to carry registration)	**1st Off: $35** Plus $5 Public Safety Surcharge. **2nd Off: $75** Plus $5 Public Safety Surcharge. **3rd Off: $150** Plus $5 Public Safety Surcharge.
Accident Reports; Supplemental Report 90 § 26	Every person operating a motor vehicle which is involved in an accident in which any person is killed or injured or in which there is damage in excess of $1,000 to any one vehicle or other property shall, within **5 days** after such accident, complete and RMV crash report and send a copy of the report to the police department having jurisdiction on the way where such accident occurred; **Exception:** the report shall not be required during the period of incapacity of any person who is physically incapable of making a report. If the operator is not the owner of the vehicle and is physically incapable of making such written report, the owner shall within 5 days after the accident make such report based on such knowledge as he may have and such information as he can obtain regarding the accident. **Case Law Note:** The SJC has ruled that a person may not forced to file an accident report if the report may incriminate the person (protection against self-incrimination).[2] **RMV Action:** The registrar may revoke or suspend the license of any person violating any provision of this section.	**1st Off: $35** Plus $5 Public Safety Surcharge. **2nd Off: $75** Plus $5 Public Safety Surcharge.
Investigation of Serious Motor Vehicle Accidents Requirements 90 § 29	The police department having jurisdiction over the place or the way where an accident occurred **shall notify the RMV forthwith** of any: 1. **Fatal accident, or** 2. **Accident involving serious injury**. **Accident Report Required:** The chief officer of the police department shall **notify the registrar within fifteen days, in a form prescribed by him, of the particulars of every accident (with injury, death or**	

[1] Com. v. Everton MUIR (2013)
[2] *Comm. v. Sasu*, 404 Mass. 596 (1989)

MOTOR VEHICLE ACCIDENT RELATED LAWS	
	property damage over $1,000) happens within the limits of his jurisdiction, together with such further information relative to such accident as the registrar may require, and shall also, if possible ascertain the name of the person operating such vehicle and notify the registrar of the same. **Police Shall Seize Suspended/Revoked License/Registration** Every such officer, upon the request of the RMV, shall demand forthwith the license of any operator and the certificate of registration and may take into his possession the number plates of any motor vehicle situated in a city or town within such officer's jurisdiction when said license or certificate has been suspended or revoked by the registrar and shall forward the said license, certificate and plates to the RMV. **License Suspension/Revocation for Fatal Accidents** Whenever the death of any person results from any such accident, the registrar shall suspend forthwith the license or right to operate of the person operating the motor vehicle in the accident, and shall order the license to be delivered to the RMV, **unless a preliminary investigation indicates that the operator may not have been at fault**; and the registrar shall revoke the same unless, upon investigation and after a hearing, he determines that the accident occurred without serious fault upon the part of the operator of such motor vehicle, and shall order the said license to be delivered to him if not already delivered as aforesaid.
Motor Boat Accidents; Duty of Operator to Report **90B § 9**	**Boat Operator must Render Assist if Able:** The operator of any motorboat involved in a collision, accident or other casualty shall, so far as he is able without serious danger to his own or other vessels or to any persons, render to other persons affected by the boating accident such assistance as may be practicable and as may be necessary in order to save them from any danger caused by the boating accident. **Must Provide Information:** The operator shall also give his name, address and identification of his vessel to any person injured and to the owner of any property damaged in the boating accident. **Definition:** Department of Fisheries, Wildlife and Environmental Law Enforcement (Environmental Police) In cases where **death, personal injury or property damage over $500 occurs**, the operator, shall **immediately** notify the Environmental Police. **Boat Accident Report:** • The operator of any motorboat involved in a boating accident, • shall file with Environmental Police • a full description of such boating accident (the report shall conform to the requirements of a boating accident report under the laws of the United States). **Time Limits:** Whenever death results from a boating accident, a **written report** shall be submitted within **48 hours**. For every other boating accident a written report shall be submitted within **5 days**. **Penalty:** $50 fine
Recreation Vehicle Accident Reports 90B § 27	The operator or owner of a snow vehicle or a recreation vehicle involved in a collision, accident or other such casualty resulting in death or injury to a person or damage to property in excess of 50 dollars shall notify a law enforcement officer immediately and file a report of the incident with the division within 48, on forms prescribed by the director. Penalty: $50 fine

MOTOR VEHICLE RELATED FRAUD	
Presenting a License of Someone Else to Police 90 § 23	The defendant exhibits to an officer authorized to make arrests, when requested by the officer to show his license, a license issued to another person with intent to conceal his identity. **Penalty 1st offense:** by a fine of not less than $500 nor more than $1,000 or by imprisonment for not more than 10 days, or both. **Penalty Subsequent offense:** by imprisonment for not less than 60 days nor more than 1 year. **Arrest Powers** – there is no statutorily empowered right of arrest, however if the suspect was operating or in charge of a motor vehicle he/she could be arrested v1a c. 90 § 25 (failure to submit).
Loaning a Driver's License 90 §24	The defendant loans or knowingly permits his license or learner's permit to operate motor vehicles to be used by any person. **Penalty:** a fine of not less than $20 nor more than $200 or by imprisonment for not less than 2 weeks nor more than 2 years, or both. **Arrest Powers**: **Misdemeanor** –no statutory authority granting powers of arrest for this offense.
False Statements in an RMV Application	The defendant makes false statements in an application for a license or learner's permit, or knowingly makes any false statement in an application for registration of a motor vehicle, **Penalty:** a fine of not less than $20 nor more than $200 or by imprisonment for not less than 2 weeks nor more than 2 years, or both. **Arrest Powers**: **Misdemeanor** – there is no statutory authority granting powers of arrest for this offense.
Fraudulent Registry documents 90 § 24B	The defendant falsely makes, steals, alters, forges or counterfeits or procures or assists another to falsely make, steal, alter, forge or counterfeit: • a learner's permit, • a license to operate, • a Massachusetts identification card, • a special parking identification disability placard, • a certificate of registration of a motor vehicle or trailer, • an inspection sticker **Penalty:** by a fine of not more than $500 or by imprisonment in the **state prison (F)** for not more than 5 years or in jail or HOC for not more than 2 years. **Arrest Powers**: **Felony** – a police officer may effect an arrest for this offense committed in his/her presence or for an offense in the past, on probable cause.
Registrar Signature Fraud 90 § 24B	The defendant forges or without authority uses the signature, facsimile of the signature, or validating signature stamp of the registrar or deputy registrar upon a genuine, stolen or falsely made, altered, forged or counterfeited • learner's permit, • license to operate motor vehicles, • certificate of registration of a motor vehicle or trailer • inspection sticker **Penalty:** by a fine of not more than $500 or by imprisonment in the state **prison (F)** for not more than 5 years or in jail or HOC for not more than 2 years.

MOTOR VEHICLE RELATED FRAUD

	Arrest Powers: Felony –on probable cause.
Possessing, Uttering, or Using a Fraudulent Registry Document **90 § 24B**	The defendant has in his possession, or utters publishes as true or in any way makes use of a falsely made, stolen, altered, forged or counterfeited: ▪ learner's permit ▪ license to operate motor vehicles ▪ a Massachusetts identification card ▪ a special parking identification disability placard ▪ certificate of registration of a motor vehicle or trailer ▪ inspection sticker **Penalty:** a fine of not more than $500 or by imprisonment in the **state prison (F)** for not more than 5 years or in jail or HOC for not more than 2 years. **Arrest Powers**: **Felony** – a police officer may effect an arrest for this offense committed in his/her presence or for an offense in the past, on probable cause.
Impersonation to Obtain Registry Document **90 § 24B**	The defendant falsely impersonates or procures or assists another to falsely impersonate the person named in an application for a license or learner's permit, or uses a name other than his own to falsely obtain such a license or whoever has in his possession, or utters, publishes as true, or in any way makes use of a license or learner's permit to operate motor vehicles that was obtained in such a manner. **Penalty**: a fine of not more than $500 or by imprisonment in the **state prison (F)** for not more than 5 years or in a jail or HOC for not more than 2 years. **Arrest Powers**: **Felony** – a police officer may effect an arrest for this offense committed in his/her presence or for an offense in the past, on probable cause. **RMV action:** Upon conviction the registrar who shall suspend immediately the license or right to operate of the person convicted, and no appeal, motion for new trial or exceptions shall operate to stay the suspension of the license or right to operate. The suspension shall continue 1 year from the date of conviction.
Using a MV without Authority	See the Theft Section of Statutory Law part of this manual for details on using a motor vehicle without authority (G.L. c. 90 § 94).
Related Statutes, Case Law & Other Important Information	
Other Fraud	For fraud related to insurance claims and motor vehicle theft see the general fraud in the statutory law section of this manual. For fraud related to the VIN number see the VIN ISSUES section of this manual.

Governor's Ban on Driving[1587]

The Governor of the Commonwealth of Massachusetts is authorized under chapter 639 of the Acts of 1950, as amended, to declare a Gubernatorial State of Emergency upon the occurrence of a natural or man-made disaster. This law gives the Governor broad authorities to implement emergency measures to ensure the safety and health of the residents of the Commonwealth, take appropriate steps to mobilize state assets and conduct other emergency business for the protection of the Commonwealth.

The Governor is authorized to exercise certain emergency powers when a Gubernatorial State of Emergency has been declared. These powers include the ability to exercise any and all authority over persons and property necessary for meeting the State of Emergency, including the taking and using of property for the protection of the Commonwealth. Actions such as ordering evacuations, restricting access, implementing curfews, **driving bans**, etc. can be stated in the declaration to protect the health and welfare of the citizens of the Commonwealth if determined to be warranted to meet the State of Emergency.

Attorney Hanrahan's note: the law does not specifically delineate a penalty for someone who disobeys a Governor's ban on driving. However, there are a wide variety of options that could be used dependant on the circumstances, from disorderly conduct (creating a hazardous condition) to operating negligently.

C. 85 § 17A. Soliciting from vehicles on public ways

Whoever, for the purpose of soliciting any alms, contribution or subscription or of selling any merchandise, except newspapers, or ticket of admission to any game, show, exhibition, fair, ball, entertainment or public gathering, signals a moving vehicle on any public way or causes the stopping of a vehicle thereon, or accosts any occupant of a vehicle stopped thereon at the direction of a police officer or signal man, or of a signal or device for regulating traffic,

Penalty: shall be punished by a fine of not more than $50.00.

- Whoever sells or offers for sale
- any item except newspapers
- within the limits of a state highway boundary without a permit issued by the department
- shall be punished as follows:

Penalty: 1st Offense: a fine of $50 and for each subsequent offense shall be punished by a fine of $100.

Note: Notwithstanding the provisions of the first sentence of this section, on any city or town way which is not under jurisdiction of the department, the chief of police of a city or town may issue a permit to nonprofit organizations to solicit on said ways in conformity with the rules and regulations established by the police department of said city or town.

C. 90 § 7. *Slow Moving Vehicle Must Display Emblem:*

- Every horse-drawn vehicle
- every other vehicle designed to operate at twenty-five miles an hour or less,
- every implement of husbandry,
- every farm tractor,
- each piece of special mobile equipment and other machinery (including all road construction and maintenance machinery)
- every low-speed motor vehicle
- traveling on a public way
- during day or night
- shall display on the rear of the vehicle an emblem designed by the RMV.

Note: The use of such emblem shall be **in addition to any lighting devices, flags or other equipment required by law**. Use of such emblem as a clearance marker or on wide machinery or on stationary objects on the highways is prohibited.
Penalty: 1st Offense $35 – 2nd Offense $75 – 3rd Offense $150

[1587] www.mass.gov

C. 89 § 3. Sleigh or sled; bells

No person shall travel on a way with a sleigh or sled drawn by a horse, unless there are at least three bells attached to some part of the harness.

C. 90 § 7R½. *Dealers insignias, logos or plates; placement on motor vehicles; consent*

No seller, or an agent or employee of a seller, of motor vehicles shall place on a motor vehicle an insignia, logo or other plate that advertises the name of the seller without first having obtained the written consent of the buyer of such motor vehicle. Such seller must provide a buyer with a written consent form at the time of the purchase of the motor vehicle. The original of such written consent form shall be retained by the seller and a copy retained by the buyer. Any such seller's failure to obtain written consent from the buyer shall enable the buyer to request that the seller remove any insignia, logo or plate and make all repairs necessary to restore the motor vehicle to its original condition. Each seller shall post in a conspicuous place, a notice explaining the buyer's rights under this section. **Penalty**: $200 fine

266 § 92A *Failing to remove police markings*

- Whoever,
- other than the commonwealth or any political subdivision thereof,
- sells any former police car to an ultimate user for other than police purposes without first having obliterated all evidence of distinctive police insignias or markings thereon, and painting the exterior of every marked state police vehicle thereof one solid color,
- shall be punished by a fine of not less than ten nor more than $500.

ARREST POWERS: **Misdemeanor** – there is no statutory authority granting powers of arrest for this offense.

C. 266 § 92A. *Motor vehicles; sale in certain condition; written disclosure on bill of sale*

- Whoever sells a motor vehicle
    - knowing that its engine or electrical parts have been submerged in water,

    or

    - knowing that it has been used as a **police car, a taxicab, a rental vehicle by a motor vehicle rental agency, a leased vehicle** which has been leased to any corporation, individual or entity, other than a motor vehicle rental company,
- without indicating such fact in writing on the bill of sale,
- shall be punished by a fine of not less than ten nor more than $500.

ARREST POWERS: **Misdemeanor** – there is no statutory authority granting powers of arrest for this offense.

C. 90 § 24A. *Use of motor vehicles in commission of felony, larceny or other crimes*

If a motor vehicle is used in connection with the commission of a felony, of any larceny, or of any offence punishable under any provision of sections twenty-two, one hundred and thirteen to one hundred and seventeen, inclusive, and one hundred and twenty of chapter two hundred and sixty-six, or section thirteen of chapter two hundred and sixty-nine, of which a person is convicted, the material facts relative to such use, including the registration number of the vehicle, so far as disclosed in the proceedings, shall be reported forthwith to the registrar by the clerk of the court in which the conviction occurs.

C. 255 § 13J Repossession of motor vehicles

Creditor's who repossesses a motor vehicle are required to notify the local police within 1 hour of recovering the vehicle. They are also responsible for returning the license plate.

C. 85 § 14A. Funeral processions

A funeral procession of not more than 10 vehicles shall have the right, except on Sundays and legal holidays, to use any parkway, boulevard or other public way to the same extent and subject to the same regulations and restrictions as vehicles commonly known as pleasure vehicles.

C. 85 § 16. Duty of driver at night to give name to officer on request

Every person shall while driving or in charge of or occupying a vehicle during the period from one hour after sunset to one hour before sunrise, when requested by a police officer, give his true name and address.

Penalty: punished by a fine of not more than $5.00

C. 266 § 120A.

In any prosecution for committing the crime of trespass by parking a motor vehicle upon a private way or upon improved or enclosed land, proof that the defendant named in the complaint was at the time of such parking the registered owner of such vehicle shall be prima facie evidence that the defendant was the person who parked such vehicle upon such way or land at such time.

Lighted cigarettes: throwing from vehicles or placing on forest/lands/ fields	Chapter 148 § 54 states "whoever drops or throws from any vehicle while the same is upon a public or private way running along or near forest land or open fields, or, except as permitted by law, drops, throws, deposits or otherwise places in or upon forest land, any lighted cigarette, cigar, match, live ashes or other flaming or glowing substance, or any substance or thing which in and of itself is likely to cause a fire, shall be punished by a fine of not more than $100 or by imprisonment for not more than 30 days."

C. 90 § 16. OPERATING ON AREAS NOT INTENDED FOR MOTOR VEHICLES

- No person shall **operate a motor vehicle**,
- nor shall any owner of such **vehicle permit it to be operated**,
- in or over **any way, public or private**,
- which **motor vehicles are prohibited from using**, provided notice of such (notice) is conspicuously posted at the entrance to such way.

Penalty: $50 fine

MISCELLANEOUS MOTOR VEHICLE LAWS

MV FINE CHART

OFFENSE	CHAPTER/SEC	PENALTY
A		
ACCIDENT REPORT, FAIL FILE	90 § 26	1st Off $35 2nd Off $75 3rd Off $150 Plus $5 Public Safety Training Surcharge
AFTERMARKET LIGHTING	540 CMR § 22.07	1st Off $35 2nd Off $75 3rd Off $150
ALCOHOL IN MV, POSSESS OPEN CONTAINER OF	90 § 24I	$500 Plus $5 Public Safety Training Surcharge
ALL TERRAIN/REC UTILITY VEH, UNDERAGE OP	90B § 26	Delinquency
ALLOW TO OPERATE YOUR VEHICLE - IMPROPER PERSON	90 § 12	Criminal
ANIMAL, TRANSPORT DANGEROUS WILD .	85 § 19	$20
ANIMAL, TRANSPORT UNPROTECTED	90 § 22H	$50 Plus $5 Public Safety Training Surcharge
AUDIBLE ALARM ON DUMP TRUCK, NO	90 § 7	1st Off $35 2nd Off $75 3rd Off $150 Plus $5 Public Safety Training Surcharge
AUDIBLE ALARM ON FLAMMABLES TANKER, NO	90 § 7	1st Off $35 2nd Off $35 3rd Off $150 Plus $5 Public Safety Training Surcharge
ANIMAL, VIOL BY-LAW ON TRANSPORT	85 § 10	$100
B		
BICYCLIST, FAIL YIELD ON TURN TO	90 § 14	1st Off $35 2nd Off $75 3rd $150 Plus $5 Public Safety Training Surcharge
BLIND PEDESTRIAN, FAIL STOP FOR	90 § 14A	$500 Plus $5 Public Safety Training Surcharge
BRAKE NOT SET	90 § 13	Not listed on Scheduled Assessment
BRAKES VIOLATION, MV	90 § 7	1st Off $35 2nd Off $75 3rd Off $150 Plus $5 Public Safety Training Surcharge
BREAKDOWN LANE VIOLATION	89 § 4B	$100 Plus $5 Public Safety Training Surcharge
C		
CARSEAT, CHILD UNDER 8 & UNDER 58 INCHES WITHOUT	90 § 7AA	$25 Plus $5 Public Safety Training Surcharge
CHILD 8-12 OR OVER 57 INCHES WITHOUT **SEAT BELT**	90 § 7AA	$25 Plus $5 Public Safety Training Surcharge
CHILD ENDANGERMENT WHILE **OUI**	90 § 24V	Criminal
CHILD UNDER 8 & UNDER 58 INCHES WITHOUT **CARSEAT**	90 § 7AA	$25 Plus $5 Public Safety Training Surcharge
CHILD UNDER 12 IN BODY OF **PICKUP TRUCK**	90 § 13	1st Off $35 2nd Off $75 3rd Off $150 Plus $5 Public Safety Training Surcharge
CHOCK BLOCKS NOT USED	90 § 13	1st Off $35 2nd Off $75 3rd Off $150 Plus $5 Public Safety Training Surcharge
CLOSED TO TRAVEL	90 § 16	$50 Plus $5 Public Safety Training Surcharge
CROSSWALK VIOLATION	89 § 11	$200 Plus $5 Public Safety Training Surcharge
CROSSWALK, BLOCKING	89 § 11	$200 Plus $5 Public Safety Training Surcharge
CROSSWALK, PASS MV STOPPED AT	89 § 11	$200 Plus $5 Public Safety Training Surcharge

CROSSWALK, PEDESTRIAN IN	89 § 11	$200 Plus $5 Public Safety Training Surcharge
D		
DOG/CAT, MOTORIST FL REPORT INJURY TO	272 § 80H	$50
DOOR, NEGLIGENTLY OPEN MV	90 § 14	$100 Plus $5 Public Safety Training Surcharge
DRIVING SCHOOL EQUIPMENT VIOLATION	90 § 32G	1st Off $35 2nd Off $75 3rd Off $150 Plus $5 Public Safety Training Surcharge
DRIVING SCHOOL NONCOMPLYING MV/SEMI	90 § 32G	1st Off $35 2nd Off $75 3rd Off $150 Plus $5 Public Safety Training Surcharge
DRIVING SCHOOL NO SEAT BELTS	90 § 32G	1st Off $35 2nd Off $75 3rd Off $150 Plus $5 Public Safety Training Surcharge
DRIVING SCHOOL STUDENT NO SEAT BELT	90 § 32G	1st Off $35 2nd Off $75 3rd Off $150 Plus $5 Public Safety Training Surcharge
E		
ELECTRONIC MESSAGE, OPERATOR SEND/READ	90 § 13B	1st Off $100 2nd Off $250 3rd Off $500 Plus $5 Public Safety Training Surcharge
EMERGENCY VEH, FAIL PULL OVER FOR	89 § 7A	$100 Plus $5 Public Safety Training Surcharge
EMERGENCY VEH, WITHIN 300 FT BEHIND	89 § 7A	$100 Plus $5 Public Safety Training Surcharge
EMERGENCY VEH, OBSTRUCT	89 § 7A	$100 Plus $5 Public Safety Training Surcharge
EMERGENCY VEH, OBSTRUCT STATIONARY	89 § 7C	$100 Plus $5 Public Safety Training Surcharge
EMERGENCY VEH, WILFULLY OBSTRUCT	89 § 7	Criminal
EQUIPMENT VIOLATION, MISCELLANEOUS MV	90 § 7	1st Off $35 2nd Off $75 3rd Off $150 Plus $5 Public Safety Training Surcharge
EXHAUST, ALTERED	90 § 16	$50 Plus $5 Public Safety Training Surcharge
F		
FIRE HOSE, DRIVE OVER	89 § 7A	$100 Plus $5 Public Safety Training Surcharge
FLARES VIOLATION BY COMMERCIAL VEHICLE	85 § 14B	$50
FLARES, COMMERCIAL VEH FAIL DEPLOY	85 § 14B	$50
FLARES, COMMERCIAL VEH OPERATE WITHOUT	85 § 14B	$50
FLASHING RED LIGHT VIOLATION	89 § 9	1st Off $100 Sub. Off: $150 Plus $5 Public Safety Training Surcharge
FLASHING/ROTATING/OSCILLATING LIGHT VIOLATION	90 § 7	1st Off $35 2nd Off $75 3rd Off $150 Plus $5 Public Safety Training Surcharge
G		
GIVE WAY TO PASSING VEH, FAIL TO	89 § 2	$100 Plus $5 Public Safety Training Surcharge
GVW CERTIFICATE, FAIL PRODUCE	90 § 19D	1st Off $35 2nd Off $75 3rd Off $150 Plus $5 Public Safety Training Surcharge
H		
HANDICAP PARKING PLATE MISUSE	90 § 2	1st Off $500 Sub. Off: $1000 Plus $5 Public Safety Training Surcharge
HAZARD LIGHTS VIOLATION	90 §7	1st Off $35 2nd Off $75 3rd Off $150 Plus $5 Public Safety Training Surcharge

HAZARDOUS MATERIALS TRANSPORT VIOL	540 CMR § 14.03	$500
HEADLIGHTS, ALTERNATING FLASHING	540 CMR § 22.05	1st Off $35 2nd Off $75 3rd Off $150
HEADLIGHTS, FAIL DIM	540 CMR § 22.05	1st Off $35 2nd Off $75 3rd Off $150
HEADPHONES ON OPERATOR	90 § 13	1st off $35 2nd off $75 3rd Off $150 Plus $5 Public Safety Training Surcharge
HEIGHT NO MARKINGS	90 § 19	$100 Plus $5 Public Safety Training Surcharge
HEIGHT VIOLATION	90 § 19	$100 Plus $5 Public Safety Training Surcharge
HEIGHT, OPERATE MV WITH MODIFIED	90 § 7P	1st Off $35 2nd Off $75 3rd Off $150 Plus $5 Public Safety Training Surcharge
HORN VIOLATION, MV	90 § 7	1st Off $35 2nd Off $75 3rd Off $150 Plus $5 Public Safety Training Surcharge
	I	
IDENTIFY SELF, MV OPERATOR REFUSE	90 § 25	Criminal
IDLE ENGINE OF STOPPED MV OVER 5 MINS	90 § 16A	1st Off: $100 2nd Off: $250 Plus $5 Public Safety Training Surcharge
IDLE ENGINE OF STOPPED MV ON SCHOOL PROPERTY	90 § 16B	1st Off $100 2nd Off $500 Plus $5 Public Safety Training Surcharge
IGNITION INTERLOCK, OPERATE WITHOUT	90 § 24S	Criminal
IMPEDED OPERATION	90 § 13	1st Off $35 2nd Off $75 3rd Off $150 Plus $5 Public Safety Training Surcharge
INJURE SURFACE OF WAY	85 § 30	$100
INSPECTION STICKER NOT DISPLAYED	90 § 20	$50 Plus $5 Public Safety Training Surcharge
INSPECTION/STICKER, NO	90 § 20	$50 Plus $5 Public Safety Training Surcharge
INTERSECTION, BLOCK	89 § 9	1st Off $100 Sub. Off: $150 Plus $5 Public Safety Training Surcharge
	J	
JUNIOR OPERATOR **TIME RESTRICTION** OPERATING 12:30–5 AM W/O PARENT	90 § 10	Delinquency, or Criminal
JUNIOR OPERATOR WITH PASSENGER UNDER 18	90 § 8	1st Off $35 2nd Off $75 3rd Off $150 Plus $5 Public Safety Training Surcharge
	K	
KEEP RIGHT FOR ONCOMING MV, FAIL TO	89 § 1	$100 Plus $5 Public Safety Training Surcharge
KEEP RIGHT ON HILL/OBSTRUCTED VIEW, FL	89 § 4	$100 Plus $5 Public Safety Training Surcharge
KEY NOT REMOVED FROM MV	90 § 13	1st Off $35 2nd Off $75 3rd Off $150 Plus $5 Public Safety Training Surcharge
	L	
LEARNERS PERMIT VIOLATION	90 § 8B	1st Off $35 2nd Off $75 3rd Off $150 Plus $5 Public Safety Training Surcharge
LEARNERS PERMIT—OP MCYCLE AT NIGHT	90 § 8B	1st Off $35 2nd Off $75 3rd Off $150 Plus $5 Public Safety Training Surcharge
LEARNERS PERMIT—OP MCYCLE W/PASSENGER	90 § 8B	1st Off $35 2nd $75 3rd $150 Plus $5 Public Safety Training Surcharge

LEARNERS PERMIT—OP NITE W/O PARENT	90 § 8B	1st Off $35 2nd Off $75 3rd Off $150 Plus $5 Public Safety Training Surcharge
LEASE MV LESSOR FAIL MAINTAIN INSURANCE	90 § 32E	Criminal
LEASE MV TO INTOXICATED DRIVER	90 § 32C	Criminal
LEASE MV WITHOUT SEEING DRIVERS LICENSE	90 § 32C	Criminal
LEAVE SCENE OF PERSONAL INJURY	90 § 24	Criminal
LEAVE SCENE OF PERSONAL INJURY & DEATH	90 § 24	Criminal
LEAVE SCENE OF PROPERTY DAMAG	90 § 24	Criminal
LEFT LANE RESTRICTION VIOLATION	89 § 4C	$100 Plus $5 Public Safety Training Surcharge
LEFT TURN, FAIL YIELD ON	90 § 14	1st Off $35 2nd Off $75 3rd Off $150 Plus $5 Public Safety Training Surcharge
LEFT TURN, IMPROPER	90 § 14	1st Off $35 2nd Off $75 3rd Off $150 Plus $5 Public Safety Training Surcharge
LENGTH VIOLATION	90 § 19	$100 Plus $5 Public Safety Training Surcharge
LICENSE CLASS, OPERATE MV IN VIOLATION	90 § 10	Criminal
LICENSE **NOT IN POSSESSION**	90 § 11	1st Off $35 2nd Off $75 3rd Off $150 Plus $5 Public Safety Training Surcharge
LICENSE **RESTRICTION**, OPERATE MV IN VIOL	90 § 10	Criminal
LICENSE REVOKED AS HTO, OPERATE MV WITH	90 § 23	Criminal
LICENSE **SUSPENDED FOR OUI**, OPER MV WITH	90 § 23	Criminal
LICENSE SUSPENDED FOR OUI-RELATED OFFENSE, OUI-RELATED OFFENSE WHILE	90 § 23	Criminal
LICENSE **SUSPENDED**, OPERATE MV WITH	90 § 23	Criminal
LICENSE, ALLOW ANOTHER TO USE	90 § 24	Criminal
LICENSE, EXHIBIT ANOTHER'S	90 § 23	Criminal
LICENSE, FAIL SHOW AFTER ACCIDENT	90 § 11	1st Off $35 2nd Off $75 3rd Off $150 Plus $5 Public Safety Training Surcharge
LICENSE, REFUSE PRODUCE	90 § 25	Criminal
LICENSE/REGIS/PLATES, REFUSE PRODUCE	90 § 25	Criminal
LIGHTS VIOLATION, MV (i.e. not working properly)	90 § 7	1st Off $35 2nd Off $75 3rd Off $150 Plus $5 Public Safety Training Surcharge
LIGHTING, **AFTERMARKET**	540 CMR § 22.07	1st Off $35 2nd Off $75 3rd Off $150 Plus $5 Public Safety Training Surcharge
LOW-SPEED VEHICLE VIOLATION	90 § 1F	1st Off $75 Subsq. Off $150 Plus $5 Public Safety Training Surcharge
	M	
MANSLAUGHTER WHILE OUI	265 § 13½	Criminal
MARKED LANES VIOLATION Motorcycle lane violation Passing violation	89 § 4A	$100 Plus $5 Public Safety Training Surcharge
METAL TIRES +4 MPH	85 § 31	$100

MIRROR VIOLATION	90 § 7	1st Off $35 2nd Off $75 3rd Off $150 Plus $5 Public Safety Training Surcharge
MISCELLANEOUS MUNIC MV ORDINANCE/BY-LAW VIOL	85 § 10	$20
MOBILE PHONE, OPERATOR UNDER 18 USE	90 § 8M	1st Off $100 2nd Off $250 3rd Off $500 Plus $5 Public Safety Training Surcharge
MOBILE PHONE, OPERATOR USE IMPROPERLY	90 § 13	1st Off $35 2nd Off $75 3rd Off $150 Plus $5 Public Safety Training Surcharge
MOBILE PHONE, PUB TRANSPORT MV OPERATOR USE	90 § 12A	$500 Plus $5 Public Safety Training Surcharge
MOPED HELMET VIOLATION	90 § 1B	1st Off $25 2nd Off $50 3rd Off $100 Plus $5 Public Safety Training Surcharge
MOPED MISCELLANEOUS TRAFFIC VIOL	90 § 1B	1st Off $25 2nd Off $50 3rd Off $100 Plus $5 Public Safety Training Surcharge
MOPED ON RESTRICTED HWAY	90 § 1B	1st Off $25 2nd Off $50 3rd Off $100 Plus $5 Public Safety Training Surcharge
MOPED OPERATION +17 WITHOUT LIC	90 § 1B	1st Off $25 2nd Off $50 3rd Off $100 Plus $5 Public Safety Training Surcharge
MOPED OPERATION BY UNLIC -17	90 § 1B	1st Off $25 2nd Off $50 3rd Off $100 Plus $5 Public Safety Training Surcharge
MOPED SPEED VIOLATION	90 § 1B	1st Off $25 2nd Off $50 3rd Off $100 Plus $5 Public Safety Training Surcharge
MOPED VIOLATION	90 § 1B	1st Off $25 2nd Off $50 3rd Off $100 Plus $5 Public Safety Training Surcharge
MOTOR CARRIER SAFETY VIOLATION	540 CMR § 14.03	1st Off $35 2nd Off $75 3rd Off $150
MOTOR VEH ORDINANCE/BY-LAW VIOLATION	85 § 10	$20
MOTOR VEH DOOR, NEGLIGENTLY OPEN	90 § 14	$100 Plus $5 Public Safety Training Surcharge
MOTOR VEH IN AREA CLOSED TO TRAVEL	90 § 18	1st Off $35 2nd Off $75 3rd Off $150 Plus $5 Public Safety Training Surcharge
MOTOR VEH HOMICIDE BY NEGLIGENT OP	90 § 24G	Criminal
MOTOR VEH HOMICIDE BY RECKLESS OP	90 § 24G	Criminal
MOTOR VEH HOMICIDE OUI—DRUGS	90 § 24G	Criminal
MOTOR VEH HOMICIDE OUI—DRUGS & NEGLIG	90 § 24G	Criminal
MOTOR VEH HOMICIDE OUI—DRUGS & RECKLESS	90 § 24G	Criminal
MOTOR VEH HOMICIDE OUI—LIQUOR	90 § 24G	Criminal
MOTOR VEH HOMICIDE OUI—LIQUOR & NEGLIG	90 § 24G	Criminal
MOTOR VEH HOMICIDE OUI—LIQUOR & RECKL	90 § 24G	Criminal
MOTOR VEH IN FELONY/LARCENY	90 § 24A	Criminal
MOTOR VEH HOMICIDE OUI—LIQUOR	90 § 24G	Criminal
MOTORCYCLE CARRY PASSENGER, SOLO	90 § 7	1st Off $35 2nd Off $75 3rd Off $150 Plus $5 Public Safety Training Surcharge

MOTORCYCLE DRIVER BEHIND PASSENGER	90 § 7	1st Off $35 2nd Off $75 3rd Off $150 Plus $5 Public Safety Training Surcharge
MOTORCYCLE EQUIPMENT VIOLATION	90 § 7	1st Off $35 2nd Off $75 3rd Off $150 Plus $5 Public Safety Training Surcharge
MOTORCYCLE EQUIP/OPERATION VIOLATION	90 § 7	1st Off $35 2nd Off $75 3rd Off $150 Plus $5 Public Safety Training Surcharge
MOTORCYCLE **GOGGLES/FACESHIELD** VIOLATION	90 § 7	1st Off $35 2nd Off $75 3rd Off $150 Plus $5 Public Safety Training Surcharge
MOTORCYCLE **HANDLEBAR** VIOLATION	540 CMR § 4.06	$25
MOTORCYCLE **HELMET** VIOLATION	90 § 7	1st Off $35 2nd Off $75 3rd Off $150 Plus $5 Public Safety Training Surcharge
MOTORCYCLE LANES VIOLATION	89 § 4A	$100
MOTORCYCLE, NOISY	90 § 7U	1st Off $35 2nd Off $75 3rd Off $150 Plus $5 Public Safety Training Surcharge
MOTORCYCLE PASSENGER VIOLATION	90 § 7	1st Off $35 2nd Off $75 3rd Off $150 Plus $5 Public Safety Training Surcharge
MOTORIZED **SCOOTER** VIOLATION	90 § 1E	1st Off $25 2nd Off $50 3rd Off $100 Plus $5 Public Safety Training Surcharge
MUD GUARDS VIOLATION ON COMMERCIAL MV	90 § 7	1st Off $35 2nd Off $75 3rd Off $150 Plus $5 Public Safety Training Surcharge
MUFFLER MISSING/NOISY	90 § 16	$50
MUFFLER VIOLATION	90 § 7	1st Off $35 2nd Off $75 3rd Off $150 Plus $5 Public Safety Training Surcharge
MUNICIPAL **MV ORDINANCE/BY-LAW VIOL**	85 § 10	$20
NAME/ADDRESS CHANGE, FAIL NOTIFY RMV OF	90 § 26A	1st Off $35 2nd Off $75 3rd Off $150 Plus $5 Public Safety Training Surcharge
NAME/ADDRESS, GIVE POLICE FALSE	90 §25	Criminal
NAME/ADDRESS, MV OP REFUSE GIVE AT NT	85 § 16	$5.00
NAME/ADDRESS, **REFUSE** GIVE POLICE	90 § 25	Criminal
NEGLIGENT OPERATION OF MOTOR VEH	90 § 24	Criminal
NEGLIGENT OPERATION & INJURY FROM MOBILE PHONE USE	90 § 24	Criminal
NOISE, HARSH & OBJECTIONABLE	90 § 16	$50 Plus $5 Public Safety Training Surcharge
NONRESIDENT STUDENT DECAL, FAIL DISPLAY	90 § 3	$200 Plus $5 Public Safety Training Surcharge
NONRESIDENT STUDENT FAIL REGISTER MV	90 § 3	$200 Plus $5 Public Safety Training Surcharge
NUMBER PLATE COVERED WITH GLASS/PLASTIC	90 § 6	1st Off $35 2nd Off $75 3rd Off $150 Plus $5 Public Safety Training Surcharge
NUMBER PLATE MISSING	90 § 6	1st Off $35 2nd Off $75 3rd Off $150 Plus $5 Public Safety Training Surcharge
NUMBER PLATE MISSING	90 § 9	1st Off $35 2nd Off $75 3rd Off $150

NUMBER PLATE OBSCURED	90 § 6	1st Off $35 2nd Off $75 3rd Off $150 Plus $5 Public Safety Training Surcharge
NUMBER PLATE UNLIT	90 § 6	1st Off $35 2nd Off $75 3rd Off $150 Plus $5 Public Safety Training Surcharge
NUMBER PLATE VIOLATION	90 § 6	1st Off $35 2nd Off $75 3rd Off $150 Plus $5 Public Safety Training Surcharge
NUMBER PLATE VIOLATION TO CONCEAL ID	90 § 23	Criminal
NUMBER PLATE, MISUSE MILITARY	90 § 5A	$50 Plus $5 Public Safety Training Surcharge
NUMBER PLATE, MISUSE OF DEALER/REPAIR	540 CMR § 18.04	Criminal
NUMBER PLATE, MISUSE OFFICIAL	90 § 2	$25 Plus $5 Public Safety Training Surcharge
NUMBER PLATE, REFUSE PRODUCE	90 § 25	Criminal Plus $5 Public Safety Training Surcharge
O		
ONE WAY STREET VIOLATION	85 § 10	$20
OPERATION OF MV, IMPROPER	90 § 16	$50 Plus $5 Public Safety Training Surcharge
OUI—DRUGS	90 § 24	Criminal
OUI—DRUGS & SERIOUS INJURY	90 § 24L	Criminal
OUI—DRUGS & SERIOUS INJURY & NEGLIGENT	90 § 24L	Criminal
OUI—DRUGS & SERIOUS INJURY & RECKLESS	90 § 24L	Criminal
OUI-RELATED OFFENSE WHILE LICENSE SUSPENDED FOR OUI-RELATED OFFENSE	90 § 23	Criminal
OUT-OF-SVCE ORDER VIOLATION	90F § 9	$1,000 Plus $5 Public Safety Training Surcharge
OUT-OF-SVCE ORDER VIOL, EMPLOYER PERMIT	90F § 4	$2,500 Plus $5 Public Safety Training Surcharge
OUTSIDE OF MV, PERMIT PERSON HANG ON	90 § 13	1st Off $35 2nd Off $75 3rd Off $150 Plus $5 Public Safety Training Surcharge
OVERHANG +4 FT WITHOUT FLAG/LIGHT	90 § 7	1st Off $35 2nd Off $75 3rd Off $150 Plus $5 Public Safety Training Surcharge
OVERHANG +4 FT WITHOUT FLAG/LIGHT	90 § 19	$100 Plus $5 Public Safety Training Surcharge
OVERHANG +15 FT WITHOUT FOLLOW CAR	90 § 19	$100 Plus $5 Public Safety Training Surcharge
OVERSIZE MV	90 § 19	$100 Plus $5 Public Safety Training Surcharge
P		
PASSING ON RIGHT	89 § 2	$100 Plus $5 Public Safety Training Surcharge
PASSING VIOLATION	89 § 2	$100 Plus $5 Public Safety Training Surcharge
PASSING VIOLATION	89 § 4A	$100 Plus $5 Public Safety Training Surcharge
PUPIL TRANSPORT VEHICLE OVERCROWDED	90 § 7D	Criminal
PUPIL TRANSPORT VEHICLE VIOLATION	90 § 7D	1st Off $35 2nd Off $75 3rd Off $150 Plus $5 Public Safety Training Surcharge
PUPILS, TRANSPORT WITHOUT LICENSE	90 § 8A½	1st Off $35 2nd Off $75 3rd Off $150 Plus $5 Public Safety Training Surcharge

R		
RACING MOTOR VEHICLE	90 § 17B	Criminal
RACING MOTOR VEHICLE	90 § 24	Criminal
RAILROAD CROSSING—INFLAMMABLE LOAD FAIL STOP	90 § 15	$200 Plus $5 Public Safety Training Surcharge
RAILROAD CROSSING—SCHL BUS/EXPLOSIVES-FLAMMABLES	90 § 15	$500 Plus $5 Public Safety Training Surcharge
RAILROAD CROSSING—SLOW, FAIL	90 § 15	$200 Plus $5 Public Safety Training Surcharge
RAILROAD CROSSING—STOP FOR LIGHT/GATE, FAIL	90 § 15	$200 Plus $5 Public Safety Training Surcharge
RAILROAD CROSSING VIOLATION REC VEH—OPERATOR UNDER 18 WITHOUT SAFETY COURSE	90B § 21	$500 Plus $5 Public Safety Training Surcharge
RECKLESS OPERATION OF MOTOR VEHICLE	90 § 24	Criminal
RED LIGHT – FAIL TO STOP	89 § 9	$100 Plus $5 Public Safety Training Surcharge
RED/BLUE LIGHT VIOLATION, MV	90 § 7E	$300 Plus $5 Public Safety Training Surcharge
RED/BLUE LIGHT WITHOUT AUTHORITY	90 § 7E	$300 Plus $5 Public Safety Training Surcharge
RED/BLUE LIGHT WITHOUT PERMIT IN POSSESSION	90 § 7E	$300 Plus $5 Public Safety Training Surcharge
REFLECTOR VIOLATION ON COMMERCIAL MV	90 § 7	1st Off $35 2nd Off $75 3rd Off $150 Plus $5 Public Safety Training Surcharge
REGISTER MV IMPROPERLY TO AVOID TAXES/PREMIUMS	90 § 3½	Criminal/$500 Plus $5 Public Safety Training Surcharge
REGISTER MV OPERATED +30 DAYS YEAR, FL .	90 § 3	$250 Plus $5 Public Safety Training Surcharge
REGISTRATION LEFT IN TRANSFERRED MV	90 § 2B	1st Off $35 2nd Off $75 3rd Off $150 Plus $5 Public Safety Training Surcharge
REGISTRATION NOT IN POSSESSION	90 § 11	1st Off $35 2nd Off $75 3rd Off $150 Plus $5 Public Safety Training Surcharge
REGISTRATION STICKER MISSING	540 CMR § 2.05	1st Off $35 2nd Off $75 3rd Off $150 Plus $5 Public Safety Training Surcharge
REGISTRATION, REFUSE PRODUCE	90 § 25	Criminal
REVOKED PERMIT STICKER, FAIL REMOVE	90 § 19D	1st Off $35 2nd $75 3rd $150 Plus $5 Public Safety Training Surcharge
RIGHT LANE, FAIL DRIVE IN	89 § 4B	$100 Plus $5 Public Safety Training Surcharge
RIGHT LANE, HEAVY COMM VEH FAIL DRIVE IN	89 § 4B	$100 Plus $5 Public Safety Training Surcharge
RIGHT TURN, IMPROPER	90 § 14	1st Off $35 2nd Off $75 3rd Off $150 Plus $5 Public Safety Training Surcharge
RIGHT-ON-RED VIOLATION	89 § 8	$35 Plus $5 Public Safety Training Surcharge
REGISTRATION SUSPENDED, OP MV WITH	90 § 23	Criminal
REGISTRATION, FAIL SHOW AFTER ACCIDENT	90 § 11	1st Off $35 2nd Off $75 3rd Off $150 Plus $5 Public Safety Training Surcharge
REGISTRATION, FL SURRENDER ON TRANSFER	90 § 2	1st Off $35 2nd Off $75 3rd Off $150 Plus $5 Public Safety Training Surcharge
REGISTRATION, REFUSE PRODUCE	90 § 25	Criminal

REVOKED PERMIT STICKER, FAIL REMOVE	90 § 19D	1st Off $35 2nd Off $75 3rd Off $150 Plus $5 Public Safety Training Surcharge
RIGHT LANE, FAIL DRIVE IN	89 § 4B	$100 Plus $5 Public Safety Training Surcharge
RIGHT TURN, IMPROPER	90 § 14	1st Off $35 2nd Off $75 3rd Off $150 Plus $5 Public Safety Training Surcharge
RIGHT-ON-RED VIOLATION	89 § 8	$100 Plus $5 Public Safety Training Surcharge
S		
SAFETY CHAINS VIOL ON TRAILER	90 § 7	1st Off $35 2nd Off $75 3rd Off $150 Plus $5 Public Safety Training Surcharge
SAFETY GLASS VIOLATION	90 § 9A	1st Off $35 2nd Off $75 3rd Off $150
SAFETY STANDARDS, MV NOT MEETING RMV	90 § 20	$25
SAMARITAN VEHICLE MISUSE SIREN/LIGHT	90 § 7I	1st Off $35 2nd Off $75 3rd Off $150
SCHOOL BUS +40 MPH	90 § 17	$50, plus $10 for each M.P.H over limit, plus $50 head injury sur-charge
SCHOOL BUS INSPECTION VIOLATION	90 § 20	$50 Plus $5 Public Safety Training Surcharge
SCHOOL BUS INSPECTION, FAIL PERFORM POST-TRIP	90 § 7B	$100 Plus $5 Public Safety Training Surcharge
SCHOOL BUS OPERATE WITH STANDEES	90 § 7L	$500 Plus $5 Public Safety Training Surcharge
SCHOOL BUS OPERATION/EQUIPMENT VIOL	90 § 7B	1st Off $35 2nd Off $75 3rd Off $150 Plus $5 Public Safety Training Surcharge
SCHOOL BUS OVERCROWDED	90 § 7B	Criminal
SCHOOL BUS—ALCOHOL CONSUMED ON	90 § 7B	1st Off $35 2nd Off $75 3rd Off $150 Plus $5 Public Safety Training Surcharge
SCHOOL BUS—BOARD/DISCHARGE IMPROPERLY	90 § 7B	1st Off $35 2nd Off $75 3rd Off $150 Plus $5 Public Safety Training Surcharge
SCHOOL BUS—DOORS OPEN WHILE MOVING	90 § 7B	1st Off $35 2nd Off $75 3rd Off $150 Plus $5 Public Safety Training Surcharge
SCHOOL BUS—DRIVER WITHOUT SEATBELT ON	90 § 7B	1st Off $35 2nd Off $75 3rd Off $150 Plus $5 Public Safety Training Surcharge
SCHOOL BUS—EQUIPMENT NOT REMOVED	90 § 7B	1st Off $35 2nd Off $75 3rd Off $150 Plus $5 Public Safety Training Surcharge
SCHOOL Bus- EQUIPMENT VIOLATION	90 § 7B	1st Off $35 2nd Off $75 3rd Off $150 Plus $5 Public Safety Training Surcharge
SCHOOL BUS—FLASHERS MISUSED/UNUSED	90 § 7B	1st Off $35 2nd Off $75 3rd Off $150 Plus $5 Public Safety Training Surcharge
SCHOOL BUS—FUEL WHILE OCCUPIED	90 § 7B	1st Off $35 2nd Off $75 3rd $150 Plus $5 Public Safety Training Surcharge
SCHOOL BUS—OPERATE WITHIN 100 FT of	90 § 14	1st Off $35 2nd Off $75 3rd Off$150 Plus $5 Public Safety Training Surcharge
SCHOOL BUS—PRETRIP INSPECTION, NO	90 § 7B	1st Off $35 2nd Off $75 3rd Off $150 Plus $5 Public Safety Training Surcharge

SCHOOL BUS—SMOKE ON	90 § 7B	1st Off $35 2nd $75 3rd $150 Plus $5 Public Safety Training Surcharge
SCHOOL BUS—UNLICENSED OPERATION	90 § 7B	1st Off $35 2nd Off $75 3rd Off $150 Plus $5 Public Safety Training Surcharge
SCHOOL BUS, FAIL STOP FOR	90 § 14	1st Off $250 2nd:Off $1,000 3rd Off $2,000 Plus $5 Public Safety Training Surcharge
SCHOOL BUS, OPERATE WITHIN 100 FT OF	90 § 14	1st Off $35 2nd Off $75 3rd Off $150 Plus $5 Public Safety Training Surcharge
SCHOOL BUS, USE MOBILE PHONE WHILE OPERATING	90 § 7B	1st Off $35 2nd Off $75 3rd Off $150 Plus $5 Public Safety Training Surcharge
SEAT BELT MISSING	90 § 7	1st Off $35 2nd Off $75 3rd Off $150 Plus $5 Public Safety Training Surcharge
SEAT BELT, **CHILD 8-12 OR OVER 57 INCHES WITHOUT**	90 § 7AA	$25 Plus $5 Public Safety Training Surcharge
SEAT BELT, FAIL WEAR	90 § 13A	$25; operator subject to $25 assessment for each passenger in violation Plus $5 Public Safety Training Surcharge
SIGN NAME, MV OPERATOR REFUSE	90 § 25	Criminal
SIGNAL, FAIL TO	90 § 14B	$25 Plus $5 Public Safety Training Surcharge
SIREN, IMPROPER	90 § 16	$50 Plus $5 Public Safety Training Surcharge
SLOW AT INTERSECTION, FAIL	90 § 14	1st Off $35 2nd Off $75 3rd Off $150 Plus $5 Public Safety Training Surcharge
SLOW FOR BICYCLIST, FAIL	90 § 14	1st Off $35 2nd Off $75 3rd Off $150 Plus $5 Public Safety Training Surcharge
SLOW FOR PEDESTRIAN, FAIL	90 § 14	1st Off $35 2nd Off $75 3rd Off $150 Plus $5 Public Safety Training Surcharge
SLOW FOR STOPPED STREET RAILWAY, FAIL	90 § 14	1st Off $35 2nd Off $75 3rd Off $150 Plus $5 Public Safety Training Surcharge
SLOW MOVING EMBLEM VIOL	90 § 7	1st Off $35 2nd Off $75 3rd Off $150
SLOW WHEN VIEW OBSTRUCTED, FAIL	90 § 14	1st Off $35 2nd Off $75 3rd Off $150 Plus $5 Public Safety Training Surcharge
SLOW, FAIL TO	90 § 14	1st Off $35 2nd Off $75 3rd Off $150 Plus $5 Public Safety Training Surcharge
SMOKE/POLLUTANTS, UNNECESSARY	90 § 16	$50 Plus $5 Public Safety Training Surcharge
SNOW PLOW/HITCH, FAIL REMOVE	90 § 19K	1st Off Warning 2nd Off $250 3rd Off $500 Plus $5 Public Safety Training Surcharge
SNOW/REC VEH—300 FT OF RESIDENCE	323 CMR § 3.03	Not listed on Scheduled Assessment
SNOW/REC VEH—ADDRESS CHANGE, FAIL REPORT	90B § 22	$250 Plus $5 Public Safety Training Surcharge
SNOW/REC VEH—ALLOW UNDER 18 OPERATE IMPROP	90B § 26	1st Off $250 Sub. Off $1,000 Plus $5 Public Safety Training Surcharge
SNOW/REC VEH—ANIMAL, MOLEST	323 CMR § 3.03	$100
SNOW/REC VEH—BEACH DUNE, DAMAGE	323 CMR § 3.03	$100
SNOW/REC VEH—BRAKES VIOLATION .	323 CMR § 3.07	$100

SNOW/REC VEH—DAMAGE LANDOWNER'S PROP	323 CMR § 3.03	$100
SNOW/REC VEH—DAMAGE PROPERTY, ON	90B § 26	$500 Plus $5 Public Safety Training Surcharge
SNOW/REC VEH—EQUIPMENT VIOLATION	90B § 24	$250 Plus $5 Public Safety Training Surcharge
SNOW/REC VEH—EQUIPMENT VIOLATION	323 CMR § 3.07	$100
SNOW/REC VEH—FIREARM, OP WHILE CARRY	90B § 26	$1,000 Plus $5 Public Safety Training Surcharge
SNOW/REC VEH—FUMES, EXCESS	90B § 24	$250 Plus $5 Public Safety Training Surcharge
SNOW/REC VEH—GROWING STOCK, DAMAGE	90B § 26	$250 Plus $5 Public Safety Training Surcharge
SNOW/REC VEH—HELMET VIOLATION .	90B § 26	1st Off $250 Sub Off $1,000 Plus $5 Public Safety Training Surcharge
SNOW/REC VEH—KEEP RIGHT, FAIL	323 CMR § 3.03	$100
SNOW/REC VEH—LEAVE SCENE OF PERSONAL INJURY	90B § 26B	Criminal
SNOW/REC VEH—LEAVE SCENE OF PROPERTY DAMAGE	90B § 26B	Criminal
SNOW/REC VEH—LIGHTS VIOLATION	323 CMR § 3.07	$100
SNOW/REC VEH—MUFFLER VIOLATION	323 CMR § 3.07	$100
SNOW/REC VEH—NEGLIGENT/RECKLESS OP	90B § 26B	Criminal
SNOW/REC VEH—NEGLIGENT/RECKLESS OP & DEATH	90B § 26B	Criminal
SNOW/REC VEH—NEGLIGENT/RECKLESS OP & SERIOUS INJURY	90B § 26B	Criminal
NO SNOW COVER	323 CMR § 3.03	$100
SNOW/REC VEH—NOISE VIOLATION	90B § 24	$250
SNOW/REC VEH—NUMBER PLATE OBSCURED	323 CMR § 3.05	$100
SNOW/REC VEH—NUMBER PLATE VIOLATION	323 CMR § 3.05	$100
SNOW/REC VEH—OPERATE 11PM—6AM	323 CMR § 3.03	Not listed on Scheduled Assessment
SNOW/REC VEH—OPERATE ON PUBLIC LAND	323 CMR § 3.03	$250#
SNOW/REC VEH—OPERATE UNDERAGE	323 CMR § 3.03	$100
SNOW/REC VEH—OUI BY −21—DRUGS	90B § 26A	Criminal
SNOW/REC VEH—OUI BY +21—DRUGS	90B § 26A	Criminal
SNOW/REC VEH—OUI BY −21—LIQUOR OR .02%	90B § 26A	Criminal
SNOW/REC VEH—OUI BY +21—LIQUOR OR .08%	90B § 26A	Criminal
SNOW/REC VEH—PASSING VIOLATION	323 CMR § 3.03	$100
SNOW/REC VEH—PUBLIC PROPERTY, ON	90B § 26	$250
SNOW/REC VEH—PUBLIC WAY VIOL	90B § 25	1st Off $250 Sub Off $1000
SNOW/REC VEH—RACE/RALLY	323 CMR § 3.03	Not listed on Scheduled Assessment
SNOW/REC VEH—REFUSE STOP FOR POLICE	90B § 26	1st Off $250 Sub Off $1000#
SNOW/REC VEH—REGIS NUMBER NOT DISPLAYED	323 CMR § 3.05	$100
SNOW/REC VEH—REGISTRATION REVOKED, OP WITH	90B § 26	$250#

SNOW/REC VEH—SPARK ARRESTOR VIOLATION	323 CMR § 3.07	$100
SNOW/REC VEH—SPEEDING	323 CMR § 3.03	$100
SNOW/REC VEH—STICKER/NUMBER PLATE,UNAUTH	323 CMR § 3.05	$100
SNOW/REC VEH—TRANSFER UNREPORTED	90B § 23	$250#
SNOW/REC VEH—UNREGISTERED	90B § 22	$500
SNOW/REC VEH—WETLAND	323 CMR § 3.03	$100
SNOW/REC VEH—WILDLIFE, HARASS	90B § 26	$250
SNOW/REC VEH—WITHOUT LANDOWNER'S OK	323 CMR § 3.03	$100
SNOW/REC VEHICLE VIOLATION	323 CMR § 3.03	$100
SPECIAL FUELS, USE WITHOUT LICENSE	64E § 2	$100
SPECIAL NEEDS STUDENTS VEH FAIL ID OWNER	90 § 7CC	$100 Plus $5 Public Safety Training Surcharge
SPEEDING (NOT POSTED)	90 § 17	$50, plus $10 for each M.P.H over limit, plus $50 head injury surcharge. Plus $5 Public Safety Training Surcharge
SPEEDING IN CONSTRUCTION ZONE	90 § 17	$100, plus $20 for each M.P.H over limit, plus $50 head injury surcharge. Plus $5 Public Safety Training Surcharge
SPEEDING IN VIOL SPECIAL REGULATION **(POSTED LIMIT)**	90 § 18	$50, plus $10 for each M.P.H over limit, plus $50 head injury surcharge. Plus $5 Public Safety Training Surcharge
SPEEDING ON COUNTY BRIDGE VIOL BY-LAW	85 § 20	$2
SPEEDING WHILE OVERWEIGHT VIOL PERMIT	90 § 17	1st Off $100 plus $50 head injury surcharge 2nd Off $150 plus $50 head injury surcharge 3rd Off $300 plus $50 head injury surcharge Plus $5 Public Safety Training Surcharge
SPOT LIGHT, IMPROPER	90 § 16	$50 Plus $5 Public Safety Training Surcharge
STOP FOR FRIGHTENED COW/HORSE, FAIL	90 § 14	1st Off $35 2nd Off $75 3rd Off $150 Plus $5 Public Safety Training Surcharge
STOP FOR POLICE, FAIL	90 § 25	Criminal
STOP SIGN VIOLATION	89 § 9	1st Off $100 Subsq Off $150 Plus $5 Public Safety Training Surcharge
STOP, FAIL SIGNAL BEFORE	90 § 14B	$25 Plus $5 Public Safety Training Surcharge
STOP/YIELD, FAIL TO	89 § 9	1st Off $100# Subsq Off $150 Plus $5 Public Safety Training Surcharge
STUDENT MOTOR VEH REGISTRATION VIOL	90 § 3	$200 Plus $5 Public Safety Training Surcharge
T		
TELEVISION VISIBLE TO MV OPERATOR	90 § 3	1st Off $35 2nd Off $75 3rd Off $150 Plus $5 Public Safety Training Surcharge
TIRE OUTSIDE FENDER	90 § 19	$100 Plus $5 Public Safety Training Surcharge
TIRE TREAD DEPTH VIOLATION	90 § 7Q	1st Off $35 2nd Off $75 3rd Off $150 Plus $5 Public Safety Training Surcharge
TIRE WIDTH BY-LAW VIOLATION	40 § 21	$300
TIRES, STUDDED	90 § 16	$50 Plus $5 Public Safety Training Surcharge
TOW MORE THAN ONE MV/TRAILER	90 § 19	$100 Plus $5 Public Safety Training Surcharge
TRESPASS WITH MOTOR VEHICLE	266 § 121A	$250

TRUCK FAIL DISPLAY OWNER'S NAME	540 CMR § 2.22	1st Off $35 2nd Off $75 3rd Off $150
TURN, FAIL **SIGNAL** BEFORE	90 § 14B	$25 Plus $5 Public Safety Training Surcharge
TURN, IMPROPER	90 § 14	1st Off $35 2nd Off $75 3rd Off $150
U		
UNATTENDED RUNNING MOTOR VEH	90 § 13	1st Off $35 2nd Off $75 3rd Off $150 Plus $5 Public Safety Training Surcharge
UNINSURED MOTOR VEHICLE	90 § 32J	Criminal
UNLICENSED OPERATION OF MV	90 § 10	Criminal
UNLICENSED OPERATOR, **EMPLOYING**	90 § 12	$1,000 Plus $5 Public Safety Training Surcharge
UNLICENSED/SUSPENDED OPERATION OF MV, ALLOW TO OPERATE YOUR VEHICLE	90 § 12	Criminal
UNREGISTERED MOTOR VEHICLE	90 § 9	1st Off $100 Subsq Off $1,000 Plus $5 Public Safety Training Surcharge
UNSAFE OPERATION OF MV	90 § 13	1st Off $35 2nd Off $75 3rd Off $150 Plus $5 Public Safety Training Surcharge
V		
VEHICLE ID NUMBER (VIN) NOT DISPLAYED	90 § 7R	1st Off $35 2nd Off $75 3rd Off $150 Plus $5 Public Safety Training Surcharge
VOC STUDENT TRANSPORT VIOLATION	90 § 7D½	1st Off $35 2nd Off $75 3rd Off$150 Plus $5 Public Safety Training Surcharge
W		
WEIGHED, REFUSE TO BE	90 § 19A	$500 Plus $5 Public Safety Training Surcharge
WEIGHT CERTIFICATE VIOLATION	90 § 19D	1st Off $35 2nd Off $75 3rd Off $150 Plus $5 Public Safety Training Surcharge
WEIGHT VIOL & NO STICKER	85 § 30A	$100
WEIGHT VIOLATION	85 § 30	$100
WEIGHT VIOLATION	90 § 19A	$40 per 1000 lbs or fraction there-of overweight up to 10,000 lbs; $80 per 1000lbs or fraction over-weight over 10,000 lbs Plus $5 Public Safety Training Surcharge
WEIGHT VIOLATION IN VIOL FEDERAL LAW	90 § 19E	1st Off $35 2nd Off $75 3rd Off $150
WEIGHT VIOLATION ON BRIDGE	85 § 34, 35	$200
WEIGHT VIOLATION WITH IRREDUCIBLE LOAD	90 § 19A	$10 per 1000lbs or fraction thereof over-weight, but not more than $500 Plus $5 Public Safety Training Surcharge
WEIGHT VIOLATION, TRAILER	90 § 19	$100 Plus $5 Public Safety Training Surcharge
WIDTH VIOLATION	90 § 19	$100 Plus $5 Public Safety Training Surcharge
WINDOW OBSTRUCTED/NONTRANSPARENT	90 § 9D	$250 Plus $5 Public Safety Training Surcharge
Y		
YIELD AT INTERSECTION, FAIL	89 § 8	$35 Plus $5 Public Safety Training Surcharge
YIELD ON LEFT TURN, FAIL	89 § 8	$35 Plus $5 Public Safety Training Surcharge
YIELD SIGN VIOLATION	89 § 9	1st Off $100 Subsq Off $150 Plus $5 Public Safety Training Surcharge